AIRFRAME AND POWERPLANT MECHANICS POWERPLANT HANDBOOK

DEPARTMENT OF TRANSPORTATION

FEDERAL AVIATION ADMINISTRATION

Flight Standards Service

First Edition 1971
First Revision 1976

For sale by the Superintendent of Documents, U.S. Government Printing Office
Washington, D.C- 20402 - Price $6.50

Stock No. 050-007-00373-1

PREFACE

This advisory circular is printed for persons preparing for a mechanics certificate with a powerplant rating. It is intended to provide basic information on principles, fundamentals, and technical procedures in the areas relating to the powerplant rating. This is designed to serve as a guide for students enrolled in a formal course of instruction, as well as the individual who is studying on his own.

This volume is devoted to an explanation of the units which make up each of the systems that bring fuel, air, and ignition together in an aircraft engine for combustion. It also contains information on engine construction features, lubrication systems, exhaust systems, cooling systems, cylinder removal and replacement, compression checks, and valve adjustments.

Because there are so many different types of aircraft engines in use today, it is reasonable to expect minor differences to exist in like system components. To avoid undue repetition, the practice of using representative systems and units is carried out throughout the advisory circular. Subject-matter treatment throughout the text is from a generalized point of view and its use can be supplemented by reference to manufacturer's manuals and other textbooks if more detail is desired. This advisory circular is not intended to replace, substitute for, or supersede official regulations or manufacturer's instructions which should be consulted for final authority.

Grateful acknowledgement is extended to the manufacturers of engine, propellers, and powerplant accessories for their cooperation in making material available for inclusion in this handbook.

The advancements in aeronautical technology dictate that this advisory circular be brought up-to-date periodically. It has been updated, errors have been corrected, new material has been added, and some material has been rearranged to improve the usefulness of the handbook. We would appreciate, however, having errors brought to our attention, as well as suggestions for improving its usefulness. Your comments and suggestions will be retained in our files until such time as the next revision is completed.

Address all correspondence relating to this handbook to:

Department of Transportation
Federal Aviation Administration
Flight Standards National Field Office
P.O. Box 25082
Oklahoma City, Oklahoma 73125

The companion advisory circulars to AC 65–12A are the Airframe and Powerplant Mechanics General Handbook, AC 65–9A, and the Airframe and Powerplant Mechanics Airframe Handbook, AC 65–15A.

CONTENTS

CHAPTER 2.—(Cont.)

CHAPTER 3.—ENGINE FUEL AND FUEL METERING SYSTEMS

CHAPTER 4.—ENGINE IGNITION AND ELECTRICAL SYSTEMS

CHAPTER 4.—(Cont.)

CHAPTER 5.–ENGINE STARTING SYSTEMS

CHAPTER 6.—LUBRICATION AND COOLING SYSTEMS

CHAPTER 7.—PROPELLERS

CHAPTER 7.—(Cont.)

CHAPTER 10.—ENGINE MAINTENANCE AND OPERATION

CHAPTER 1

THEORY AND CONSTRUCTION OF AIRCRAFT ENGINES

GENERAL

For an aircraft to remain in level unaccelerated flight, a thrust must be provided that is equal to and opposite in direction to the aircraft drag. This thrust, or propulsive force, is provided by a suitable type of heat engine.

All heat engines have in common the ability to convert heat energy into mechanical energy, by the flow of some fluid mass through the engine. In all cases, the heat energy is released at a point in the cycle where the pressure is high, relative to atmospheric.

These engines are customarily divided into groups or types depending upon:

(1) The working fluid used in the engine cycle,

(2) the means by which the mechanical energy is transmitted into a propulsive force, and

(3) the method of compressing the engine working fluid.

The types of engines are illustrated in figure 1–1.

Engine Type	*Major Means of Compression*	*Engine Working Fluid*	*Propulsive Working Fluid*
Turbojet.	Turbine-driven compressor.	Fuel/air mixture.	Same as engine working fluid.
Turboprop.	Turbine-driven compressor.	Fuel/air mixture.	Ambient air.
Ramjet.	Ram compression due to high flight speed.	Fuel/air mixture.	Same as engine working fluid.
Pulse-jet.	Compression due to combustion.	Fuel/air mixture.	Same as engine working fluid.
Reciprocating.	Reciprocating action of pistons.	Fuel/air mixture.	Ambient air.
Rocket.	Compression due to combustion.	Oxidizer/fuel mixture.	Same as engine working fluid.

FIGURE 1–1. Types of engines.

The propulsive force is obtained by the displacement of a working fluid (not necessarily the same fluid used within the engine) in a direction opposite to that in which the airplane is propelled. This is an application of Newton's third law of motion. Air is the principal fluid used for propulsion in every type of powerplant except the rocket, in which only the byproducts of combustion are accelerated and displaced.

The propellers of aircraft powered by reciprocating or turboprop engines accelerate a large mass of air through a small velocity change. The fluid (air) used for the propulsive force is a different quantity than that used within the engine to produce the mechanical energy. Turbojets, ramjets, and pulse-jets accelerate a smaller quantity of air through a large velocity change. They use the same working fluid for propulsive force that is used within the engine. A rocket carries its own oxidizer rather than using ambient air for combustion. It discharges the gaseous byproducts of combustion through the exhaust nozzle at an extremely high velocity.

Engines are further characterized by the means of compressing the working fluid before the addition of heat. The basic methods of compression are:

(1) The turbine-driven compressor (turbine engine).

(2) The positive displacement, piston-type com-

pressor (reciprocating engine).

(3) Ram compression due to forward flight speed (ramjet).

(4) Pressure rise due to combustion (pulse-jet and rocket).

A more specific description of the major engine types used in commercial aviation is given later in this chapter.

COMPARISON OF AIRCRAFT POWERPLANTS

In addition to the differences in the methods employed by the various types of powerplants for producing thrust, there are differences in their suitability for different types of aircraft. The following discussion points out some of the important characteristics which determine their suitability.

General Requirements

All engines must meet certain general requirements of efficiency, economy, and reliability. Besides being economical in fuel consumption, an aircraft engine must be economical (the cost of original procurement and the cost of maintenance) and it must meet exacting requirements of efficiency and low weight per horsepower ratio. It must be capable of sustained high-power output with no sacrifice in reliability; it must also have the durability to operate for long periods of time between overhauls. It needs to be as compact as possible, yet have easy accessibility for maintenance. It is required to be as vibration free as possible and be able to cover a wide range of power output at various speeds and altitudes.

These requirements dictate the use of ignition systems that will deliver the firing impulse to the spark plugs or igniter plugs at the proper time in all kinds of weather and under other adverse conditions. Fuel-metering devices are needed that will deliver fuel in the correct proportion to the air ingested by the engine regardless of the attitude, altitude, or type of weather in which the engine is operated. The engine needs a type of oil system that delivers oil under the proper pressure to all of the operating parts of the engine when it is running. Also, it must have a system of damping units to damp out the vibrations of the engine when it is operating.

Power and Weight

The useful output of all aircraft powerplants is thrust, the force which propels the aircraft. Since the reciprocating engine is rated in b.hp. (brake horsepower) and the gas turbine engine is rated in pounds of thrust, no direct comparison can be made. However, since the reciprocating engine/propeller combination receives its thrust from the propeller, a comparison can be made by converting the horsepower developed by the reciprocating engine to thrust.

If desired, the thrust of a gas turbine engine can be converted into t.hp. (thrust horsepower). But it is necessary to consider the speed of the aircraft. This conversion can be accomplished by using the formula:

$$\text{t.hp.} = \frac{\text{thrust x aircraft speed (m.p.h.)}}{\text{375 mile-pounds per hour}}.$$

The value 375 mile-pounds per hour is derived from the basic horsepower formula as follows:

$$1 \text{ hp.} = 33{,}000 \text{ ft.-lb. per minute.}$$
$$33{,}000 \times 60 = 1{,}980{,}000 \text{ ft.-lb. per hour.}$$
$$\frac{1{,}980{,}000}{5{,}280} = 375 \text{ mile-pounds per hour.}$$

One horsepower equals 33,000 ft.-lb. per minute or 375 mile-pounds per hour. Under static conditions, thrust is figured as equivalent to approximately 2.6 pounds per hour.

If a gas turbine is producing 4,000 pounds of thrust and the aircraft in which the engine is installed is traveling at 500 m.p.h., the t.hp. will be:

$$\frac{4000 \times 500}{375} = 5{,}333.33 \text{ t.hp.}$$

It is necessary to calculate the horsepower for each speed of an aircraft, since the horsepower varies with speed. Therefore, it is not practical to try to rate or compare the output of a turbine engine on a horsepower basis.

The aircraft engine operates at a relatively high percentage of its maximum power output throughout its service life. The aircraft engine is at full power output whenever a takeoff is made. It may hold this power for a period of time up to the limits set by the manufacturer. The engine is seldom held at a maximum power for more than 2 minutes, and usually not that long. Within a few seconds after lift-off, the power is reduced to a power that is used for climbing and that can be maintained for longer periods of time. After the aircraft has climbed to cruising altitude, the power of the engine(s) is further reduced to a cruise power which can be maintained for the duration of the flight.

If the weight of an engine per brake horsepower (called the specific weight of the engine) is decreased, the useful load that an aircraft can carry and the performance of the aircraft obviously are increased. Every excess pound of weight carried by an aircraft engine reduces its performance. Tremendous gains in reducing the weight of the aircraft engine through improvement in design and metallurgy have resulted in reciprocating engines now producing approximately 1 hp. for each pound of weight.

Fuel Economy

The basic parameter for describing the fuel economy of aircraft engines is usually specific fuel consumption. Specific fuel consumption for turbojets and ramjets is the fuel flow (lbs./hr.) divided by thrust (lbs.), and for reciprocating engines the fuel flow (lbs./hr.) divided by brake horsepower. These are called "thrust specific fuel consumption" and "brake specific fuel consumption," respectively. Equivalent specific fuel consumption is used for the turboprop engine and is the fuel flow in pounds per hour divided by a turboprop's equivalent shaft horsepower. Comparisons can be made between the various engines on a specific fuel consumption basis.

At low speed, the reciprocating and turbopropeller engines have better economy than the turbojet engines. However, at high speed, because of losses in propeller efficiency, the reciprocating or turbopropeller engine's efficiency becomes less than that of the turbojet. Figure 1–2 shows a comparison of average thrust specific fuel consumption of three types of engines at rated power at sea level.

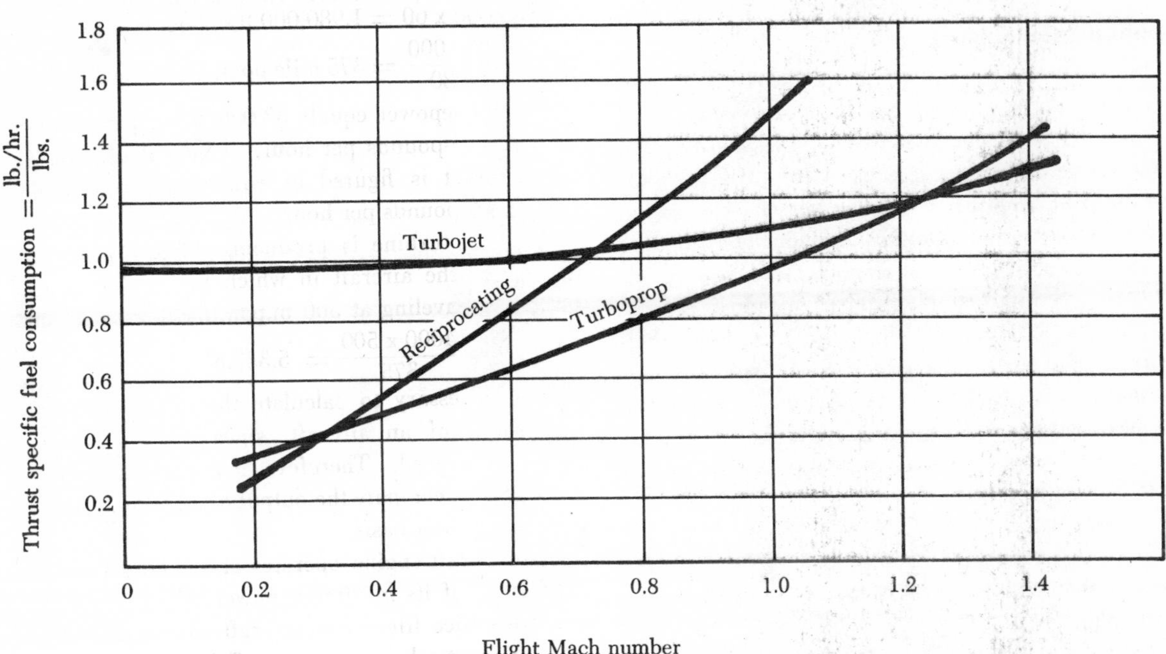

FIGURE 1–2. Comparison of fuel consumption for three types of engines at rated power at sea level.

Durability and Reliability

Durability and reliability are usually considered identical factors since it is difficult to mention one without including the other. An aircraft engine is reliable when it can perform at the specified ratings in widely varying flight attitudes and in extreme weather conditions. Standards of powerplant reliability are agreed upon by the FAA, the engine manufacturer, and the airframe manufacturer. The engine manufacturer ensures the reliability of his product by design, research, and testing. Close control of manufacturing and assembly procedures is maintained, and each engine is tested before it leaves the factory.

Durability is the amount of engine life obtained while maintaining the desired reliability. The fact that an engine has successfully completed its type or proof test indicates that it can be operated in a normal manner over a long period before requiring overhaul. However, no definite time interval between overhauls is specified or implied in the engine rating. The TBO (time between overhauls) varies with the operating conditions such as engine temperatures, amount of time the engine is operated at high-power settings, and the maintenance received.

Reliability and durability are thus built into the

engine by the manufacturer, but the continued reliability of the engine is determined by the maintenance, overhaul, and operating personnel. Careful maintenance and overhaul methods, thorough periodical and preflight inspections, and strict observance of the operating limits established by the engine manufacturer will make engine failure a rare occurrence.

Operating Flexibility

Operating flexibility is the ability of an engine to run smoothly and give desired performance at all speeds from idling to full-power output. The aircraft engine must also function efficiently through all the variations in atmospheric conditions encountered in widespread operations.

Compactness

To effect proper streamlining and balancing of an aircraft, the shape and size of the engine must be as compact as possible. In single-engine aircraft, the shape and size of the engine also affect the view of the pilot, making a smaller engine better from this standpoint, in addition to reducing the drag created by a large frontal area.

Weight limitations, naturally, are closely related to the compactness requirement. The more elongated and spreadout an engine is, the more difficult it becomes to keep the specific weight within the allowable limits.

Powerplant Selection

Engine specific weight and specific fuel consumption were discussed in the previous paragraphs, but for certain design requirements, the final powerplant selection may be based on factors other than those which can be discussed from an analytical point of view. For that reason, a general discussion of powerplant selection is included here.

For aircraft whose cruising speeds will not exceed 250 m.p.h. the reciprocating engine is the usual choice. When economy is required in the low-speed range, the conventional reciprocating engine is chosen because of its excellent efficiency. When high-altitude performance is required, the turbosupercharged reciprocating engine may be chosen because it is capable of maintaining rated power to a high altitude (above 30,000 feet).

In the range of cruising speeds from 180 to 350 m.p.h. the turbopropeller engine performs better than other types of engines. It develops more power per pound of weight than does the reciprocating engine, thus allowing a greater fuel load or payload for engines of a given power. The maximum overall efficiency of a turboprop powerplant is less than that of a reciprocating engine at low speed. Turboprop engines operate most economically at high altitudes, but they have a slightly lower service ceiling than do turbosupercharged reciprocating engines. Economy of operation of turboprop engines, in terms of cargo-ton-miles per pound of fuel, will usually be poorer than that of reciprocating engines because cargo-type aircraft are usually designed for low-speed operation. On the other hand, cost of operation of the turboprop may approach that of the reciprocating engine because it burns cheaper fuel.

Aircraft intended to cruise from high subsonic speeds up to Mach 2.0 are powered by turbojet engines. Like the turboprop, the turbojet operates most efficiently at high altitudes. High-speed, turbojet-propelled aircraft fuel economy, in terms of miles per pound of fuel, is poorer than that attained at low speeds with reciprocating engines.

However, reciprocating engines are more complex in operation than other engines. Correct operation of reciprocating engines requires about twice the instrumentation required by turbojets or turboprops, and it requires several more controls. A change in power setting on some reciprocating engine installations may require the adjustment of five controls, but a change in power on a turbojet requires only a change in throttle setting. Furthermore, there are a greater number of critical temperatures and pressures to be watched on reciprocating engine installations than on turbojet or turboprop installations.

TYPES OF RECIPROCATING ENGINES

Many types of reciprocating engines have been designed. However, manufacturers have developed some designs that are used more commonly than others and are therefore recognized as conventional. Reciprocating engines may be classified according to cylinder arrangement with respect to the crankshaft (in-line, V-type, radial, and opposed) or according to the method of cooling (liquid cooled or air cooled). Actually, all engines are cooled by transferring excess heat to the surrounding air. In air-cooled engines, this heat transfer is direct from the cylinders to the air. In liquid-cooled engines, the heat is transferred from the cylinders to the coolant, which is then sent through tubing and cooled within a radiator placed in the airstream. The radiator must be large enough to cool the liquid efficiently. Heat is transferred to air more slowly than it is to a liquid. Therefore, it is necessary to provide thin metal fins on the cylinders of an air-cooled engine in order to have increased surface for sufficient heat transfer. Most aircraft engines are air cooled.

In-line Engines

An in-line engine generally has an even number of cylinders, although some three-cylinder engines have been constructed. This engine may be either liquid cooled or air cooled and has only one crankshaft, which is located either above or below the cylinders. If the engine is designed to operate with the cylinders below the crankshaft, it is called an inverted engine.

The in-line engine has a small frontal area and is better adapted to streamlining. When mounted with the cylinders in an inverted position, it offers the added advantages of a shorter landing gear and greater pilot visibility. The in-line engine has a higher weight-to-horsepower ratio than most other engines. With increase in engine size, the air cooled, in-line type offers additional handicaps to proper cooling; therefore, this type of engine is, to a large degree, confined to low- and medium-horsepower engines used in light aircraft.

Opposed or O-type Engines

The opposed-type engine, shown in figure 1–3, has two banks of cylinders directly opposite each other with a crankshaft in the center. The pistons of both cylinder banks are connected to the single crankshaft. Although the engine can be either liquid cooled or air cooled, the air-cooled version is used predominantly in aviation. It can be mounted with the cylinders in either a vertical or horizontal position.

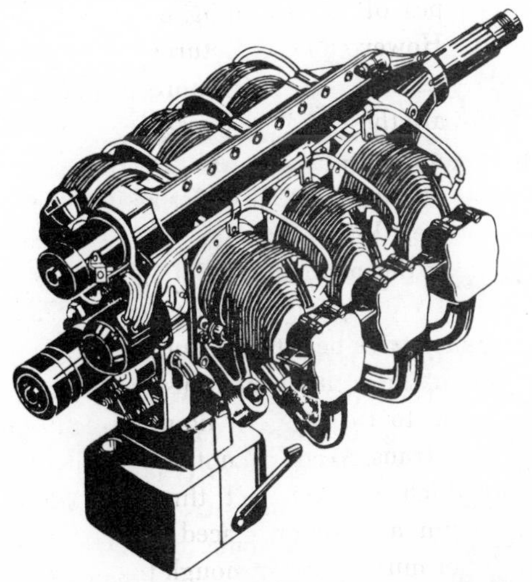

FIGURE 1–3. Opposed engine.

The opposed-type engine has a low weight-to-horsepower ratio, and its narrow silhouette makes it ideal for horizontal installation on the aircraft wings. Another advantage is its comparative freedom from vibration.

V-type Engines

In the V-type engines, the cylinders are arranged in two in-line banks generally set 60° apart. Most of the engines have 12 cylinders, which are either liquid cooled or air cooled. The engines are designated by a V, followed by a dash and the piston displacement in cubic inches, for example, V-1710.

Radial Engines

The radial engine consists of a row, or rows, of cylinders arranged radially about a central crankcase (see figure 1–4). This type of engine has proven to be very rugged and dependable. The number of cylinders composing a row may be either three, five, seven, or nine. Some radial engines have two rows of seven or nine cylinders arranged radially about the crankcase. One type has four rows of cylinders with seven cylinders in each row.

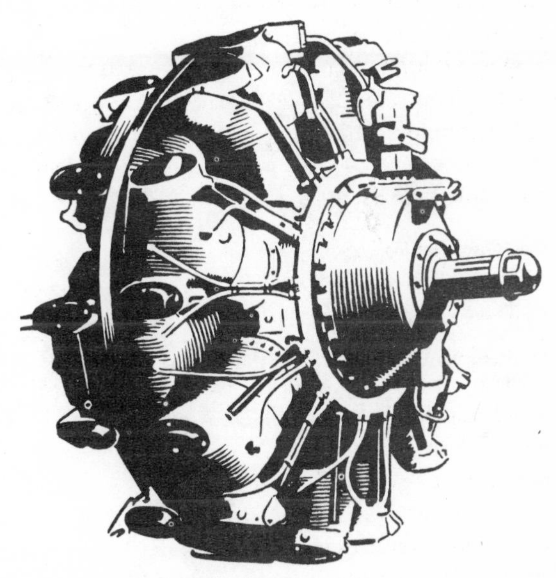

FIGURE 1–4. Radial engine.

The power output from the different sizes of radial engines varies from 100 to 3,800 horsepower.

RECIPROCATING ENGINE DESIGN AND CONSTRUCTION

The basic parts of a reciprocating engine are the crankcase, cylinders, pistons, connecting rods, valves, valve-operating mechanism, and crankshaft. In the head of each cylinder are the valves and spark plugs. One of the valves is in a passage leading from the induction system; the other is in a passage leading to the exhaust system. Inside each cylinder is a movable piston connected to a crankshaft by a connecting rod. Figure 1–5 illustrates the basic parts of a reciprocating engine.

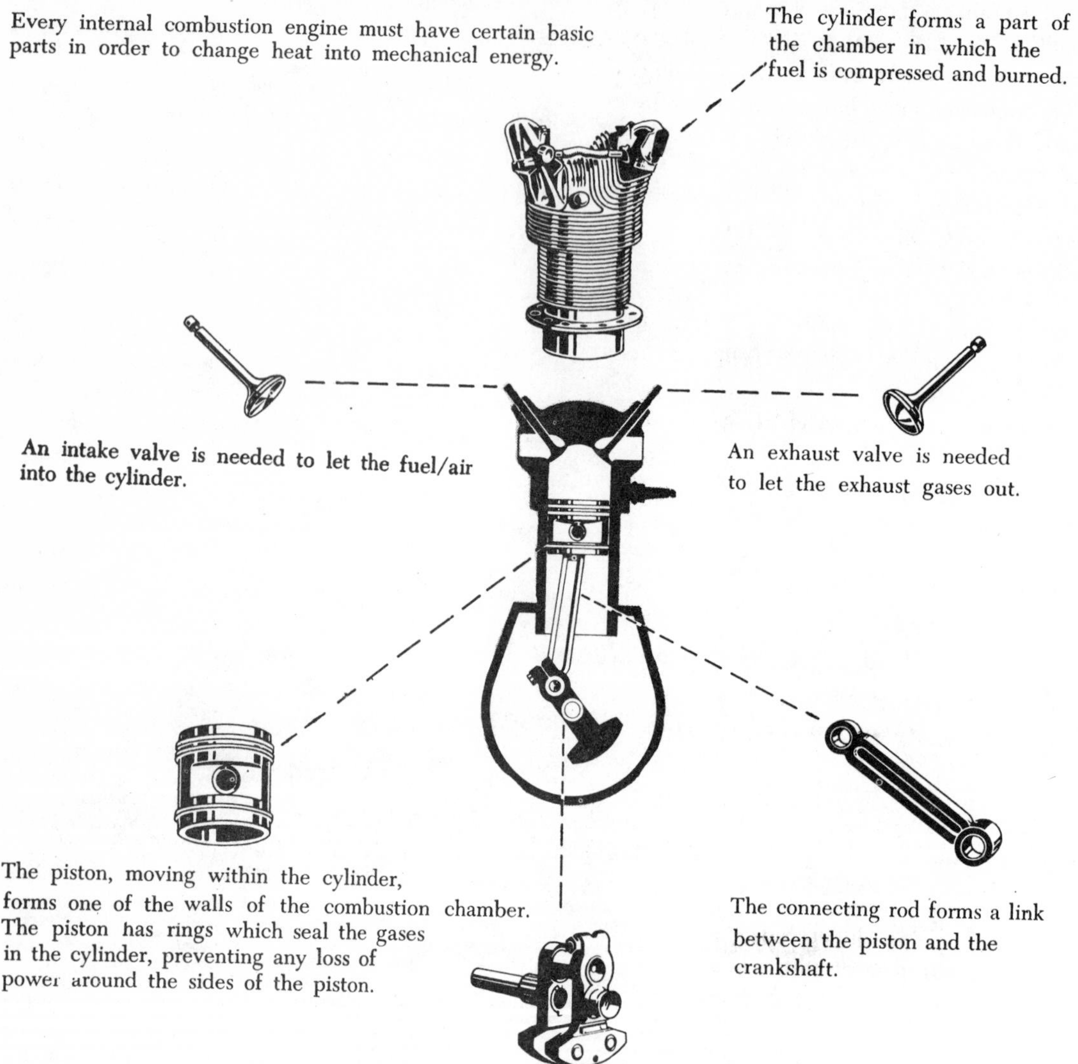

Every internal combustion engine must have certain basic parts in order to change heat into mechanical energy.
The cylinder forms a part of the chamber in which the fuel is compressed and burned.
An intake valve is needed to let the fuel/air into the cylinder.
An exhaust valve is needed to let the exhaust gases out.
The piston, moving within the cylinder, forms one of the walls of the combustion chamber. The piston has rings which seal the gases in the cylinder, preventing any loss of power around the sides of the piston.
The connecting rod forms a link between the piston and the crankshaft.
The crankshaft and connecting rod change the straight line motion of the piston to a rotary turning motion. The crankshaft in an aircraft engine also absorbs the power or work from all the cylinders and transfers it to the propeller.

FIGURE 1–5. Basic parts of a reciprocating engine.

Crankcase Sections

The foundation of an engine is the crankcase. It contains the bearings in which the crankshaft revolves. Besides supporting itself, the crankcase must provide a tight enclosure for the lubricating oil and must support various external and internal mechanisms of the engine. It also provides support for attachment of the cylinder assemblies, and the powerplant to the aircraft. It must be sufficiently rigid and strong to prevent misalignment of the crankshaft and its bearings. Cast or forged aluminum alloy is generally used for crankcase construction because it is light and strong. Forged steel crankcases are used on some of the high-power output engines.

The crankcase is subjected to many variations of

vibrational and other forces. Since the cylinders are fastened to the crankcase, the tremendous expansion forces tend to pull the cylinder off the crankcase. The unbalanced centrifugal and inertia forces of the crankshaft acting through the main bearing subject the crankcase to bending moments which change continuously in direction and magnitude. The crankcase must have sufficient stiffness to withstand these bending moments without objectional deflections. If the engine is equipped with a propeller reduction gear, the front or drive end will be subjected to additional forces.

In addition to the thrust forces developed by the propeller under high-power output, there are severe centrifugal and gyroscopic forces applied to the crankcase due to sudden changes in the direction of flight, such as those occurring during maneuvers of the airplane. Gyroscopic forces are, of course, particularly severe when a heavy propeller is installed.

Radial Engines

The engine shown in figure 1–6 is a single-row, nine-cylinder radial engine of relatively simple construction, having a one-piece nose and a two-section main crankcase.

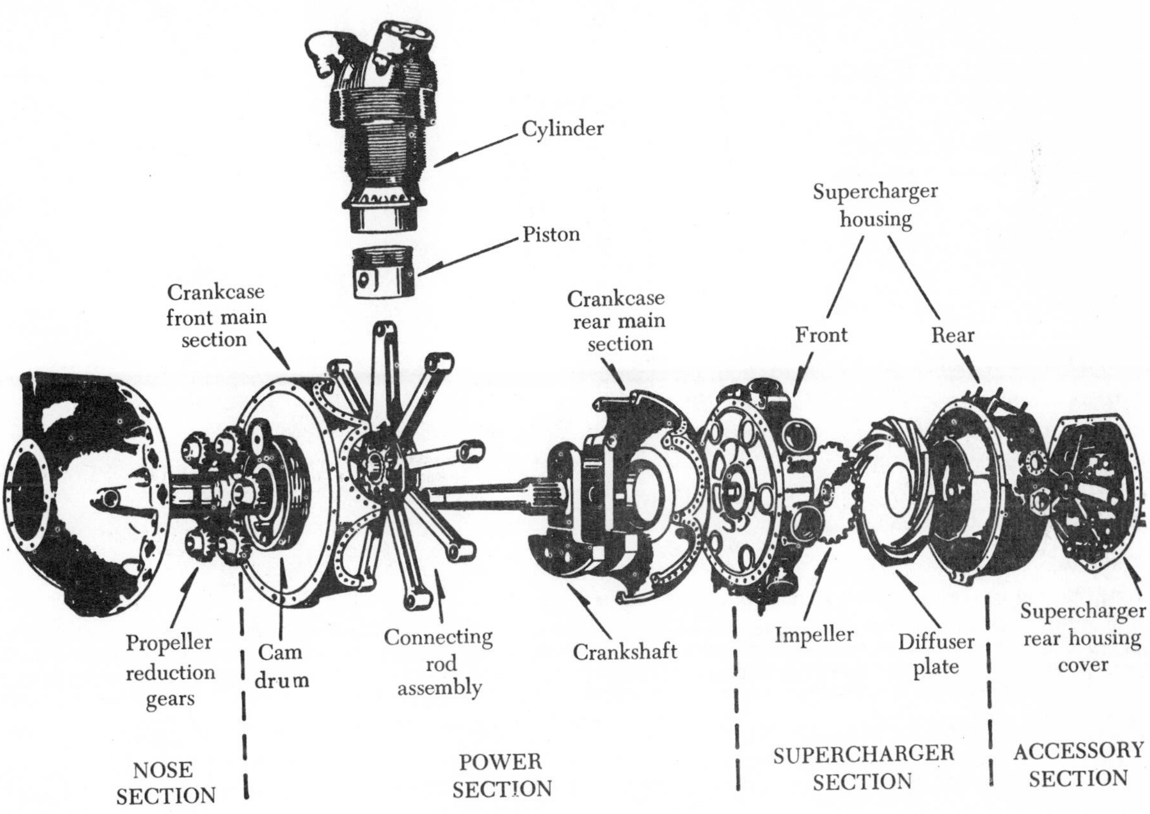

FIGURE 1–6. Engine sections.

The larger twin-row engines are of slightly more complex construction than the single-row engines. For example, the crankcase of the Wright R-3350 engine is composed of the crankcase front section, four crankcase main sections (the front main, the front center, the rear center, and the rear main sections), the rear cam and tappet housing, the supercharger front housing, the supercharger rear housing, and the supercharger rear housing cover. Pratt and Whitney engines of comparable size incorporate the same basic sections, although the construction and the nomenclature differ considerably.

Nose Section

The shape of nose sections varies considerably. In general, it is either tapered or round in order to place the metal under tension or compression instead of shear stresses. A tapered nose section is used quite frequently on direct-drive, low-powered engines, because extra space is not required to house the propeller reduction gear. It is usually cast of either aluminum alloy or magnesium since the low power developed and the use of a lightweight propeller do not require a more expensive forged nose section.

The nose section on engines which develop from 1,000 to 2,500 hp. is usually rounded and sometimes ribbed to get as much strength as possible. Aluminum alloy is the most widely used material because of its adaptability to forging processes and its vibration-absorbing characteristics.

The design and construction of the nose section is an important factor since it is subjected to a wide variation of forces and vibration. For instance, if the valve mechanism is located in front of the cylinders, the vibration and forces occurring at the tappet and guide assembly are applied near the flanged portion of the case. The forces created by the propeller reduction gear are applied to the case as a whole. Careful vibration surveys are conducted during the experimental testing of newly designed engines to see that these conditions will not become detrimental throughout the operating range of the engine.

The mounting of the propeller governor varies. On some engines it is located on the rear section, although this complicates the installation, especially if the propeller is operated or controlled by oil pressure, because of the distance between the governor and propeller. Where hydraulically operated propellers are used, it is good practice to mount the governor on the nose section as close to the propeller as possible to reduce the length of the oil passages. The governor is then driven either from gear teeth on the periphery of the bell gear or by some other suitable means.

Since the nose section transmits many varied forces to the main or power section, it must be properly secured to transmit the loads efficiently. It also must have intimate contact to give rapid and uniform heat conduction, and be oiltight to prevent leakage. This is usually accomplished by an offset or ground joint, secured by studs or capscrews.

On some of the larger engines, a small chamber is located on the bottom of the nose section to collect the oil. This is called the nose section oil sump.

Power Section

On engines equipped with a two-piece master rod and a solid-type crankshaft, the main or power crankcase section may be solid, usually of aluminum alloy. The front end of this section is open when the diaphragm plate in which the front main bearing is mounted is removed. The knuckle pins may be removed through this opening by a suitable knuckle-pin puller. The master rod is then removed by disassembling the split end and pulling the shank out through the master rod cylinder hole. There is also an engine equipped with this crankshaft and master rod arrangement which uses a split case crankcase held together by through bolts.

The split main section (aluminum or magnesium alloy) may be slightly more expensive, but permits better control over the quality of the casting or forging. The split main section is generally necessary when a solid master rod and a split-type crankshaft are used.

This portion of the engine is often called the power section, because it is here that the reciprocating motion of the piston is converted to rotary motion of the crankshaft.

Because of the tremendous loads and forces from the crankshaft assembly and the tendency of the cylinders to pull the crankcase apart, especially in extreme conditions when a high-powered engine is detonated, the main crankcase section must be very well designed and constructed. It is good practice to forge this section from aluminum alloy to obtain uniformity in the density of the metal and maximum strength. One large engine uses a forged alloy steel main section, which is slightly heavier but has very great strength. The design of the forged sections is usually such that both halves can be made in the same die in order to reduce manufacturing costs. Any variations can be taken care of during the machining operation. The two halves are joined on the center line of the cylinders and held together by suitable high-strength bolts.

The machined surfaces on which the cylinders are mounted are called cylinder pads. They are provided with a suitable means of retaining or fastening the cylinders to the crankcase. The general practice in securing the cylinder flange to the pad is to mount studs in threaded holes in the crankcase.

On engines equipped with the steel main section, capscrews are being utilized because the threads may be tapped in the stronger material and are not as likely to be stripped or stretched by installing and removing threaded members.

The inner portion of the cylinder pads are sometimes chamfered or tapered to permit the installation of a large rubber O-ring around the cylinder skirt, which effectively seals the joint between the cylinder and the crankcase pads against oil leakage.

Because oil is thrown about the crankcase,

especially on inverted in-line and radial-type engines, the cylinder skirts extend a considerable distance into the crankcase sections to reduce the flow of oil into the inverted cylinders. The piston and ring assemblies, of course, have to be arranged so that they will throw out the oil splashed directly into them.

As mentioned previously, the nose section is secured to one side of the main section unit, and the diffuser or blower section is attached to the other side.

Diffuser Section

The diffuser or supercharger section generally is cast of aluminum alloy, although, in a few cases, the lighter magnesium alloy is used.

Mounting lugs are spaced about the periphery of this section to attach the engine assembly to the engine mount or framework provided for attaching the powerplant to the fuselage of single-engine aircraft or to the wing nacelle structure of multiengine aircraft. The mounting lugs may be either integral with the diffuser section or detachable, as in the case of flexible or dynamic engine mounts.

The mounting arrangement supports the entire powerplant including the propeller, and therefore is designed to provide ample strength for rapid maneuvers or other loadings.

Because of the elongation and contraction of the cylinders, the intake pipes which carry the mixture from the diffuser chamber through the intake valve ports are arranged to provide a slip joint which must be leakproof. The atmospheric pressure on the outside of the case of an unsupercharged engine will be higher than on the inside, especially when the engine is operating at idling speed. If the engine is equipped with a supercharger and operated at full throttle, the pressure will be considerably higher on the inside than on the outside of the case.

If the slip joint connection has a slight leakage, the engine may idle fast due to a slight leaning of the mixture. If the leak is quite large, it may not idle at all. At open throttle, a small leak probably would not be noticeable in operation of the engine, but the slight leaning of the fuel/air mixture might cause detonation or damage to the valves and valve seats.

On some radial engines, the intake pipe has considerable length and on some in-line engines, the intake pipe is at right angles to the cylinders. In these cases, flexibility of the intake pipe or its arrangement eliminates the need for a slip joint. In any case, the engine induction system must be arranged so that it will not leak air and change the desired fuel/air ratio.

Accessory Section

The accessory (rear) section usually is of cast construction, and the material may be either aluminum alloy, which is used most widely, or magnesium, which has been used to some extent. On some engines, it is cast in one piece and provided with means for mounting the accessories, such as magnetos, carburetors, and fuel, oil, and vacuum pumps, and starter, generator, etc., in the various locations required to facilitate accessibility. Other adaptations consist of an aluminum alloy casting and a separate cast magnesium cover plate on which the accessory mounts are arranged.

Recent design practice has been toward standardizing the mounting arrangement for the various accessories so that they will be interchangeable on different makes of engines. For example, the increased demands for electric current on large aircraft and the requirements of higher starting torque on powerful engines have resulted in an increase in the size of starters and generators. This means that a greater number of mounting bolts must be provided and, in some cases, the entire rear section strengthened.

Accessory drive shafts are mounted in suitable bronze bushings located in the diffuser and rear sections. These shafts extend into the rear section and are fitted with suitable gears from which power takeoffs or drive arrangements are carried out to the accessory mounting pads. In this manner the various gear ratios can be arranged to give the proper drive speed to magneto, pump, and other accessories to obtain correct timing or functioning.

In some cases there is a duplication of drives, such as the tachometer drive, to connect instruments located at separate stations.

The accessory section provides a mounting place for the carburetor, or master control, fuel injection pumps, engine-driven fuel pump, tachometer generator, synchronizing generator for the engine analyzer, oil filter, and oil pressure relief valve.

Accessory Gear Trains

Gear trains, containing both spur- and bevel-type gears, are used in the different types of engines for driving engine components and accessories. Spur-type gears are generally used to drive the heavier loaded accessories or those requiring the least play or backlash in the gear train. Bevel gears permit angular location of short stub shafts leading to the various accessory mounting pads.

Practically all high-powered engines are equipped with a supercharger. From 75 to 125 hp. may be required to drive the supercharger. The acceleration and deceleration forces imposed on the supercharger gear train when opening and closing the throttle make some kind of antishock device necessary to relieve excessive loads. The current practice on large radial engines is to use a main accessory drive gear which is fitted with several springs between the rim of the gear and drive shaft. This device, called the spring-loaded accessory drive gear, permits absorption of forces of high magnitude, preventing damage to the accessory gear trains. When an engine is equipped with a two-speed supercharger, the oil-pressure operated clutches act as shock absorbers to protect the supercharger gear train.

On the low-powered, opposed, and in-line engines, the accessory gear trains are usually simple arrangements. Many of these engines use synthetic rubber or spring couplings to protect the magneto and generator gear trains from excessive loads.

Opposed and In-line Types

The crankcases used on engines having opposed or in-line cylinder arrangements vary in form for the different types of engines, but in general they are approximately cylindrical. One or more sides are surfaced to serve as a base to which the cylinders are attached by means of capscrews, bolts, or studs. These accurately machined surfaces are frequently referred to as cylinder pads.

The crankshaft is carried in a position parallel to the longitudinal axis of the crankcase and is generally supported by a main bearing between each throw. The crankshaft main bearings must be supported rigidly in the crankcase. This usually is accomplished by means of transverse webs in the crankcase, one for each main bearing. The webs form an integral part of the structure and, in addition to supporting the main bearings, add to the strength of the entire case.

The crankcase is divided into two sections in a

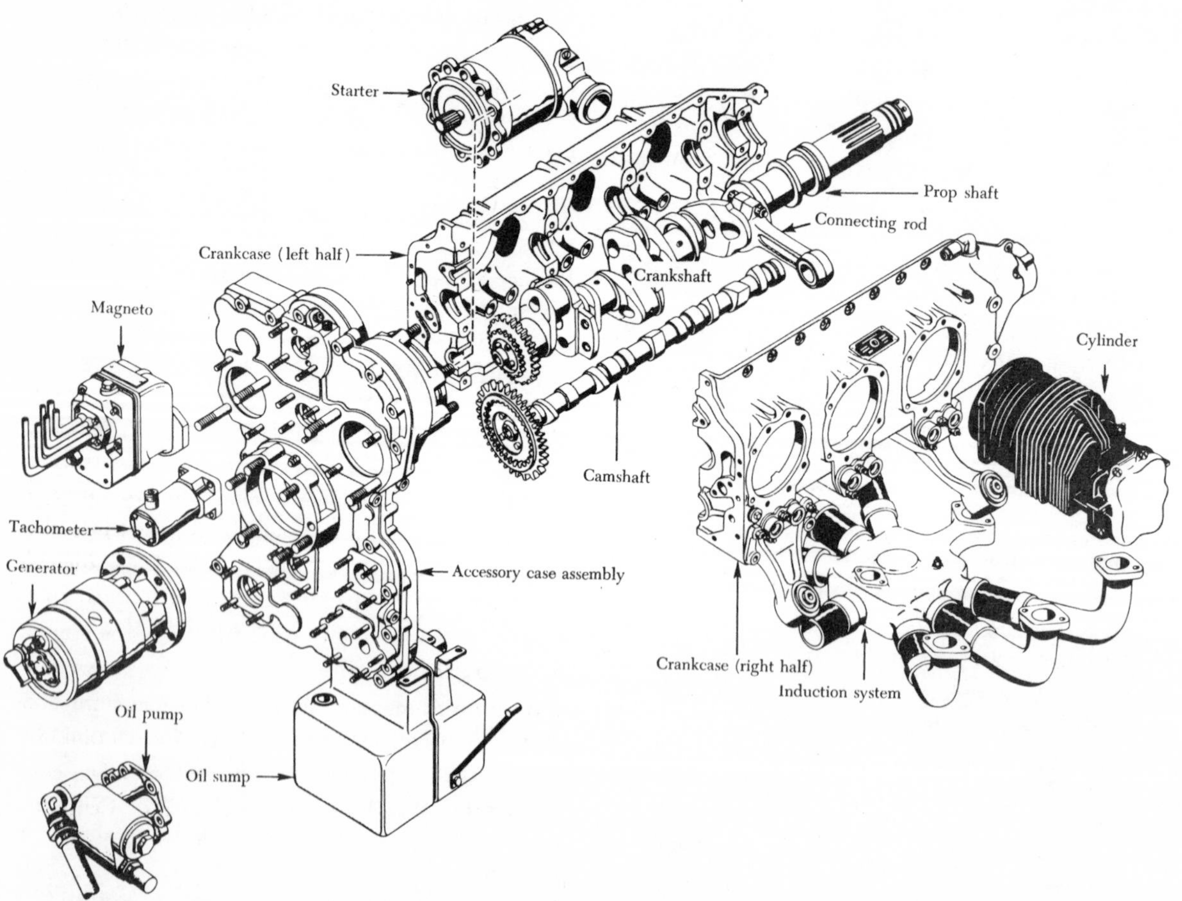

FIGURE 1–7. Typical opposed engine exploded into component assemblies.

longitudinal plane. This division may be in the plane of the crankshaft so that one-half of the main bearing (and sometimes camshaft bearings) are carried in one section of the case and the other half in the opposite section. (See figure 1–7.) Another method is to divide the case in such a manner that the main bearings are secured to only one section of the case on which the cylinders are attached, thereby providing means of removing a section of the crankcase for inspection without disturbing the bearing adjustment.

CRANKSHAFTS

The crankshaft is the backbone of the reciprocating engine. It is subjected to most of the forces developed by the engine. Its main purpose is to transform the reciprocating motion of the piston and connecting rod into rotary motion for rotation of the propeller. The crankshaft, as the name implies, is a shaft composed of one or more cranks located at specified points along its length. The cranks, or throws, are formed by forging offsets into a shaft before it is machined. Since crankshafts must be very strong, they generally are forged from a very strong alloy, such as chromium-nickel-molybdenum steel.

A crankshaft may be of single-piece or multipiece construction. Figure 1–8 shows two representative types of solid crankshafts used in aircraft engines. The four-throw construction may be used either on four-cylinder horizontal opposed or four-cylinder in-line engines.

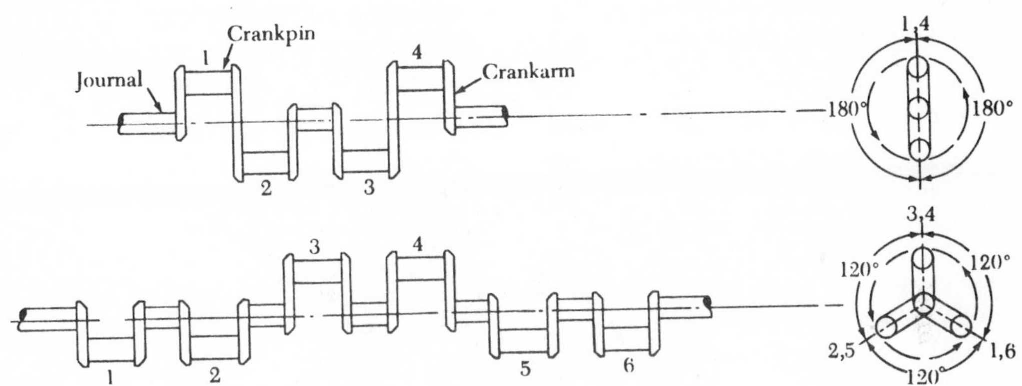

FIGURE 1–8. Solid types of crankshafts.

The six-throw shaft is used on six-cylinder in-line engines, 12-cylinder V-type engines, and six-cylinder opposed engines.

Crankshafts of radial engines may be the single-throw, two-throw, or four-throw type, depending on whether the engine is the single-row, twin-row, or four-row type. A single-throw radial engine crankshaft is shown in figure 1–9.

No matter how many throws it may have, each crankshaft has three main parts—a journal, crankpin, and crank cheek. Counterweights and dampers, although not a true part of a crankshaft, are usually attached to it to reduce engine vibration.

The journal is supported by, and rotates in, a main bearing. It serves as the center of rotation of the crankshaft. It is surface-hardened to reduce wear.

The crankpin is the section to which the connecting rod is attached. It is off-center from the main journals and is often called the throw. Two crank cheeks and a crankpin make a throw. When a force is applied to the crankpin in any direction other than parallel or perpendicular to and through the center line of the crankshaft, it will cause the crankshaft to rotate. The outer surface is hardened by nitriding to increase its resistance to wear and to provide the required bearing surface. The crankpin is usually hollow. This reduces the total weight of the crankshaft and provides a passage for the transfer of lubricating oil. The hollow crankpin also serves as a chamber for collecting sludge, carbon deposits, and other foreign material. Centrifugal force throws these substances to the outside of the chamber and thus keeps them from reaching the connecting-rod bearing surface. On some engines a passage is drilled in the crank cheek to allow oil

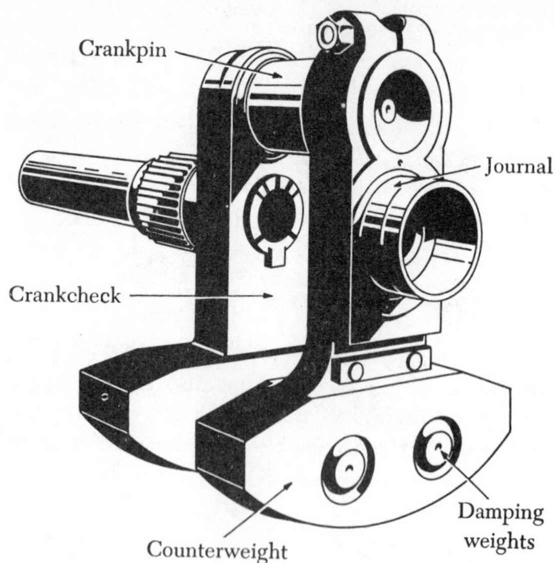

FIGURE 1–9. A single-throw radial engine crankshaft.

from the hollow crankshaft to be sprayed on the cylinder walls.

The crank cheek connects the crankpin to the main journal. In some designs, the cheek extends beyond the journal and carries a counterweight to balance the crankshaft. The crank cheek must be of sturdy construction to obtain the required rigidity between the crankpin and the journal.

In all cases, the type of crankshaft and the number of crankpins must correspond with the cylinder arrangement of the engine. The position of the cranks on the crankshaft in relation to the other cranks of the same shaft is expressed in degrees.

The simplest crankshaft is the single-throw or 360° type. This type is used in a single-row radial engine. It can be constructed in one or two pieces. Two main bearings (one on each end) are provided when this type of crankshaft is used.

The double-throw or 180° crankshaft is used on double-row radial engines. In the radial-type engine, one throw is provided for each row of cylinders.

Crankshaft Balance

Excessive vibration in an engine not only results in fatigue failure of the metal structures, but also causes the moving parts to wear rapidly. In some instances, excessive vibration is caused by a crankshaft which is not balanced. Crankshafts are balanced for static balance and dynamic balance.

A crankshaft is statically balanced when the weight of the entire assembly of crankpins, crank cheeks, and counterweights is balanced around the axis of rotation. When testing the crankshaft for static balance, it is placed on two knife edges. If the shaft tends to turn toward any one position during the test, it is out of static balance.

A crankshaft is dynamically balanced when all the forces created by crankshaft rotation and power impulses are balanced within themselves so that little or no vibration is produced when the engine is operating. To reduce vibration to a minimum during engine operation, dynamic dampers are incorporated on the crankshaft. A dynamic damper is merely a pendulum which is so fastened to the crankshaft that it is free to move in a small arc. It is incorporated in the counterweight assembly. Some crankshafts incorporate two or more of these assemblies, each being attached to a different crank cheek. The distance the pendulum moves and its vibrating frequency correspond to the frequency of the power impulses of the engine. When the vibration frequency of the crankshaft occurs, the pendulum oscillates out of time with the crankshaft vibration, thus reducing vibration to a minimum.

Dynamic Dampers

The construction of the dynamic damper used in one engine consists of a movable slotted-steel counterweight attached to the crank cheek. Two spool-shaped steel pins extend into the slot and pass through oversized holes in the counterweight and crank cheek. The difference in the diameter between the pins and the holes provides a pendulum effect. An analogy of the functioning of a dynamic damper is shown in figure 1–10.

CONNECTING RODS

The connecting rod is the link which transmits forces between the piston and the crankshaft. Connecting rods must be strong enough to remain rigid under load and yet be light enough to reduce the inertia forces which are produced when the rod and piston stop, change direction, and start again at the end of each stroke.

There are three types of connecting-rod assemblies: (1) The plain-type connecting rod, (2) the fork-and-blade connecting rod, and (3) the master-and-articulated-rod assembly. (See figure 1–11.)

Master-and-Articulated Rod Assembly

The master-and-articulated rod assembly is commonly used in radial engines. In a radial engine the piston in one cylinder in each row is connected to the crankshaft by a master rod. All other pistons in the row are connected to the master rod by an

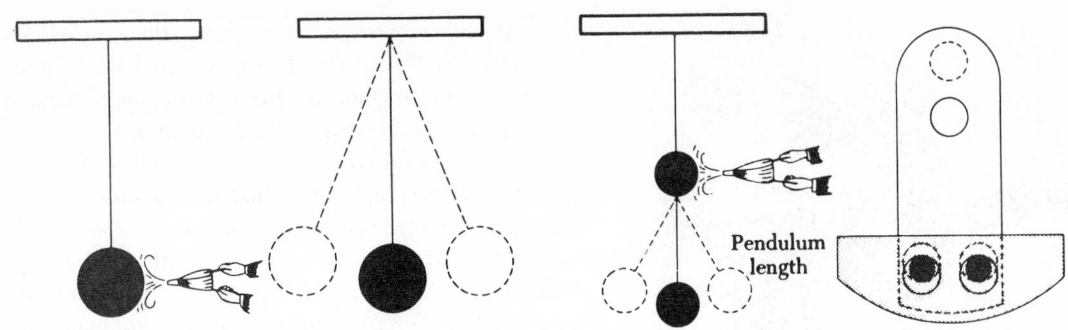

If a simple pendulum is given a series of regular impulses at a speed corresponding to its natural frequency (using a bellows to simulate a power impulse in an engine) it will commence swinging, or vibrating, back and forth from the impulses. Another pendulum, suspended from the first, would absorb the impulses and swing itself, leaving the first stationary. The dynamic damper is a short pendulum hung on the crankshaft and tuned to the frequency of the power impulses to absorb vibration in the same manner.

FIGURE 1–10. Principles of a dynamic damper.

articulated rod. In an 18-cylinder engine which has two rows of cylinders, there are two master rods and 16 articulated rods. The articulated rods are constructed of forged steel alloy in either the I- or H-shape, denoting the cross-sectional shape. Bronze bushings are pressed into the bores in each end of the articulated rod to provide knuckle-pin and piston-pin bearings.

The master rod serves as the connecting link between the piston pin and the crankpin. The crankpin end, or the "big end," contains the crankpin or master rod bearing. Flanges around the big end provide for the attachment of the articulated rods. The articulated rods are attached to the master rod by knuckle pins, which are pressed into holes in the master rod flanges during assembly. A plain bearing, usually called a piston-pin bushing, is installed in the piston end of the master rod to receive the piston pin.

When a crankshaft of the split-spline or split-clamp type is employed, a one-piece master rod is used. The master and articulated rods are assembled and then installed on the crankpin; the crankshaft sections are then joined together. In engines that use the one-piece type of crankshaft, the big end of the master rod is split, as is the master rod bearing. The main part of the master rod is installed on the crankpin; then the bearing cap is set in place and bolted to the master rod.

The centers of the knuckle pins do not coincide with the center of the crankpin. Thus, while the crankpin center describes a true circle for each revolution of the crankshaft, the centers of the knuckle pins describe an elliptical path (see figure 1–12).

The elliptical paths are symmetrical about a center line through the master rod cylinder. It can be seen that the major diameters of the ellipses are not the same. Thus, the link rods will have varying degrees of angularity relative to the center of the crank throw.

Because of the varying angularity of the link rods and the elliptical motion of the knuckle pins, all pistons do not move an equal amount in each cylinder for a given number of degrees of crank throw movement. This variation in piston position between cylinders can have considerable effect on engine operation. To minimize the effect of these factors on valve and ignition timing, the knuckle-pin holes in the master rod flange are not equidistant from the center of the crankpin, thereby offsetting to an extent the effect of the link rod angularity.

Another method of minimizing the adverse effects on engine operation is to use a compensated magneto. In this magneto the breaker cam has a number of lobes equal to the number of cylinders on the engine. To compensate for the variation in piston position due to link rod angularity, the breaker cam lobes are ground with uneven spacing. This allows the breaker contacts to open when the piston is in the correct firing position. This will be further outlined during the discussion on ignition timing in Chapter 4.

Knuckle Pins

The knuckle pins are of solid construction except for the oil passages drilled in the pins, which lubri-

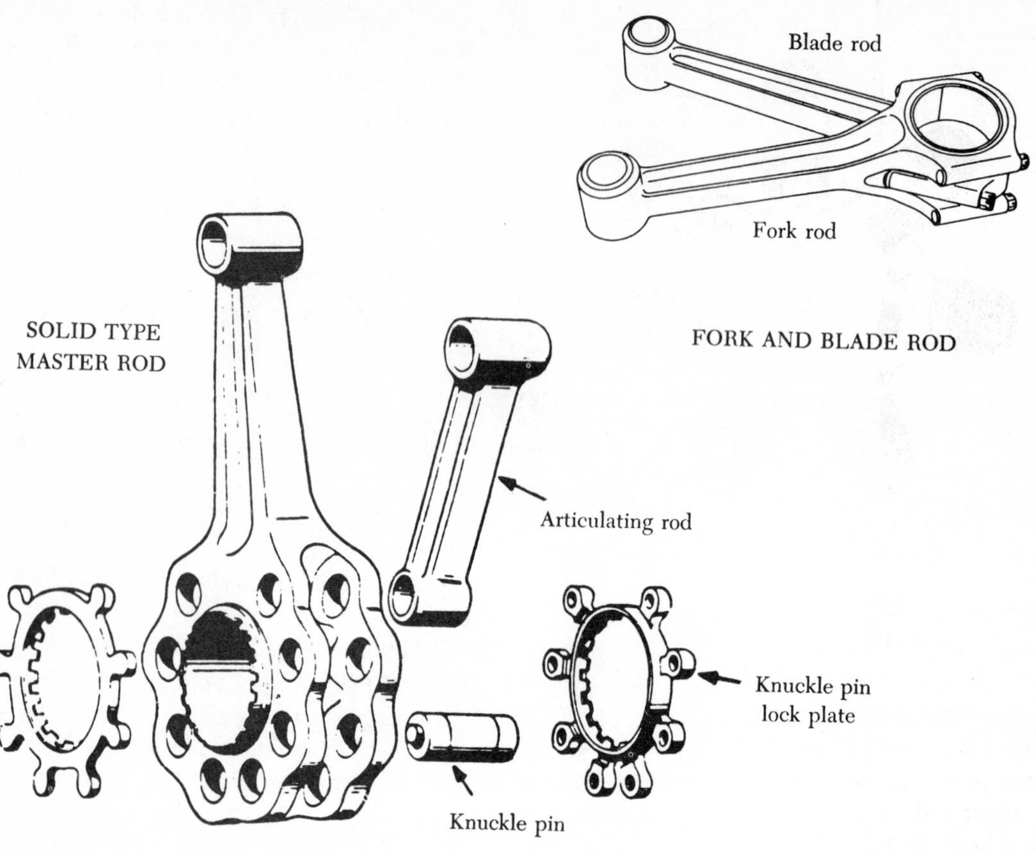

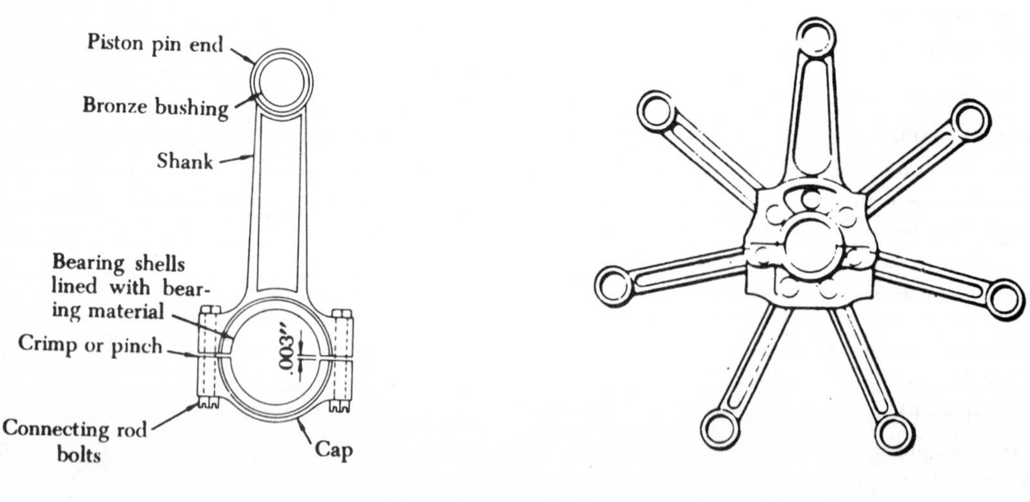

FIGURE 1–11. **Connecting rod assemblies.**

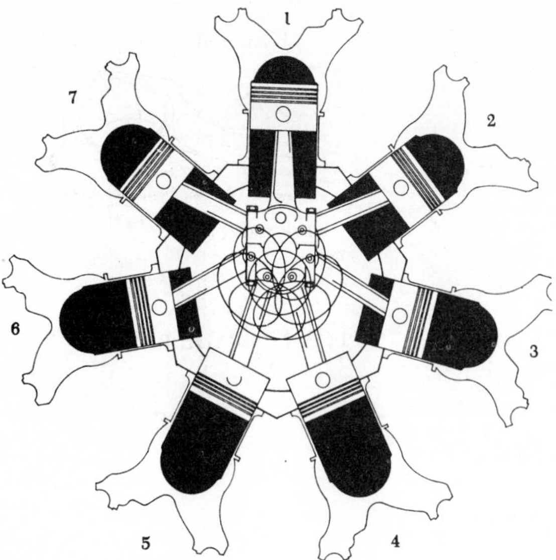

FIGURE 1–12. Elliptical travel path of knuckle pins in an articulated rod assembly.

cate the knuckle-pin bushings. These pins may be installed by pressing into holes in the master rod flanges so that they are prevented from turning in the master rod. Knuckle pins may also be installed with a loose fit so that they can turn in the master rod flange holes, and also turn in the articulating rod bushings. These are called "full-floating" knuckle pins. In either type of installation a lock plate on each side retains the knuckle pin and prevents a lateral movement of it.

Plain-Type Connecting Rods

Plain-type connecting rods are used in in-line and opposed engines. The end of the rod attached to the crankpin is fitted with a cap and a two-piece bearing. The bearing cap is held on the end of the rod by bolts or studs. To maintain proper fit and balance, connecting rods should always be replaced in the same cylinder and in the same relative position.

Fork-and-Blade Rod Assembly

The fork-and-blade rod assembly is used primarily in V-type engines. The forked rod is split at the crankpin end to allow space for the blade rod to fit between the prongs. A single two-piece bearing is used on the crankshaft end of the rod.

PISTONS

The piston of a reciprocating engine is a cylindrical member which moves back and forth within a steel cylinder. The piston acts as a moving wall within the combustion chamber. As the piston moves down in the cylinder, it draws in the fuel/air mixture. As it moves upward, it compresses the charge, ignition occurs, and the expanding gases force the piston downward. This force is transmitted to the crankshaft through the connecting rod. On the return upward stroke, the piston forces the exhaust gases from the cylinder.

Piston Construction

The majority of aircraft engine pistons are machined from aluminum alloy forgings. Grooves are machined in the outside surface of the piston to receive the piston rings, and cooling fins are provided on the inside of the piston for greater heat transfer to the engine oil.

Pistons may be either the trunk type or the slipper type; both are shown in figure 1–13. Slipper-type pistons are not used in modern, high-powered engines because they do not provide adequate strength or wear resistance. The top face of the piston, or head, may be either flat, convex, or concave. Recesses may be machined in the piston head to prevent interference with the valves.

As many as six grooves may be machined around the piston to accommodate the compression rings and oil rings. (See figure 1–13.) The compression rings are installed in the three uppermost grooves; the oil control rings are installed immediately above the piston pin. The piston is usually drilled at the oil control ring grooves to allow surplus oil scraped from the cylinder walls by the oil control rings to pass back into the crankcase. An oil scraper ring is installed at the base of the piston wall or skirt to prevent excessive oil consumption. The portions of the piston walls that lie between each pair of ring grooves are called the ring lands.

In addition to acting as a guide for the piston head, the piston skirt incorporates the piston-pin bosses. The piston-pin bosses are of heavy construction to enable the heavy load on the piston head to be transferred to the piston pin.

Piston Pin

The piston pin joins the piston to the connecting rod. It is machined in the form of a tube from a nickel steel alloy forging, casehardened and ground. The piston pin is sometimes called a wristpin because of the similarity between the relative motions of the piston and the articulated rod and that of the human arm.

The piston pin used in modern aircraft engines is the full-floating type, so called because the pin is

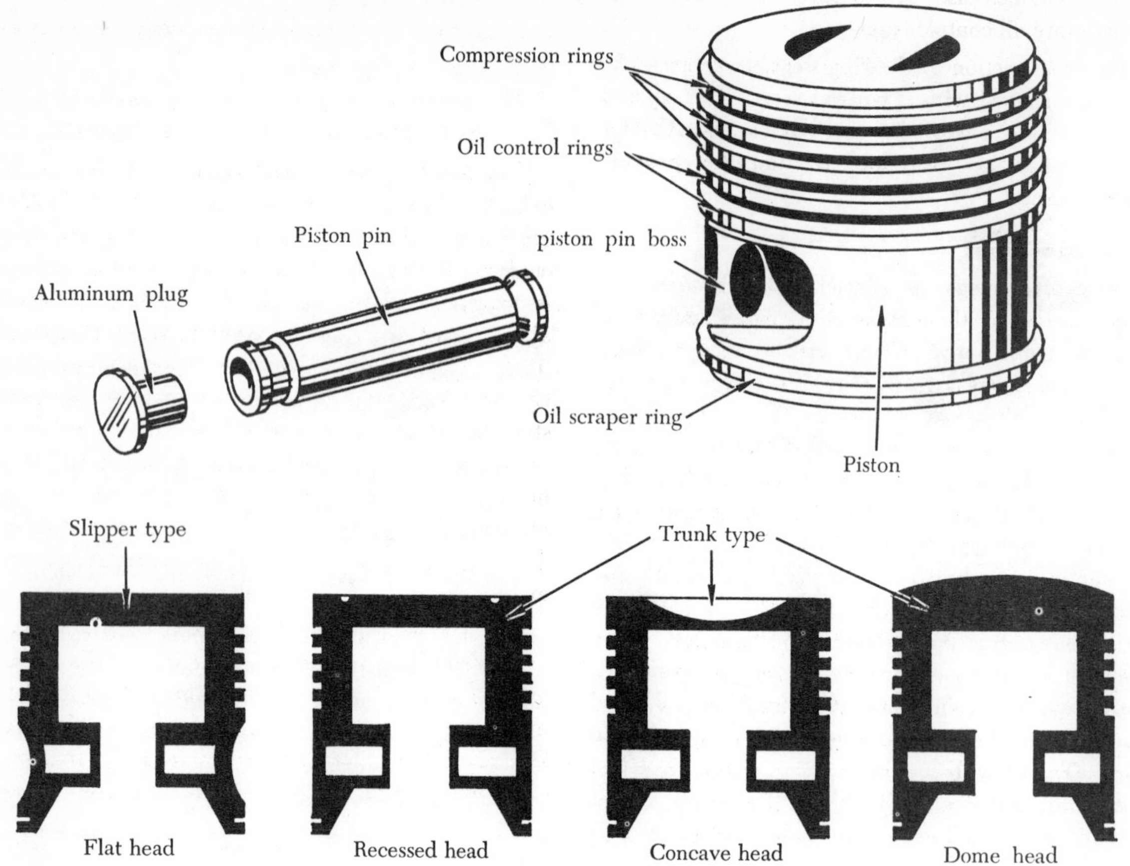

FIGURE 1–13. Piston assembly and types of pistons.

free to rotate in both the piston and in the connecting rod piston-pin bearing.

The piston pin must be held in place to prevent the pin ends from scoring the cylinder walls. In earlier engines, spring coils were installed in grooves in the piston-pin bores at either end of the pin. The current practice is to install a plug of relatively soft aluminum in the pin ends to provide a good bearing surface against the cylinder wall.

PISTON RINGS

The piston rings prevent leakage of gas pressure from the combustion chamber and reduce to a minimum the seepage of oil into the combustion chamber. The rings fit into the piston grooves but spring out to press against the cylinder walls; when properly lubricated, the rings form an effective gas seal.

Piston Ring Construction

Most piston rings are made of high-grade cast iron. After the rings are made, they are ground to the cross section desired. They are then split so that they can be slipped over the outside of the piston and into the ring grooves which are machined in the piston wall. Since their purpose is to seal the clearance between the piston and the cylinder wall, they must fit the cylinder wall snugly enough to provide a gastight fit; they must exert equal pressure at all points on the cylinder wall; and they must make a gastight fit against the sides of the ring grooves.

Gray cast iron is most often used in making piston rings. However, many other materials have been tried. In some engines, chrome-plated mild steel piston rings are used in the top compression ring groove because these rings can better withstand the high temperatures present at this point.

Compression Ring

The purpose of the compression rings is to prevent the escape of gas past the piston during engine operation. They are placed in the ring grooves immediately below the piston head. The number of compression rings used on each piston is determined by the type of engine and its design, although most aircraft engines use two compression rings plus one or more oil control rings.

The cross section of the ring is either rectangular or wedge shaped with a tapered face. The tapered face presents a narrow bearing edge to the cylinder wall which helps to reduce friction and provide better sealing.

Oil Control Rings

Oil control rings are placed in the grooves immediately below the compression rings and above the piston pin bores. There may be one or more oil control rings per piston; two rings may be installed in the same groove, or they may be installed in separate grooves. Oil control rings regulate the thickness of the oil film on the cylinder wall. If too much oil enters the combustion chamber, it will burn and leave a thick coating of carbon on the combustion chamber walls, the piston head, the spark plugs, and the valve heads. This carbon can cause the valves and piston rings to stick if it enters the ring grooves or valve guides. In addition, the carbon can cause spark plug misfiring as well as detonation, preignition, or excessive oil consumption. To allow the surplus oil to return to the crankcase, holes are drilled in the piston ring grooves or in the lands next to these grooves.

Oil Scraper Ring

The oil scraper ring usually has a beveled face and is installed in the groove at the bottom of the piston skirt. The ring is installed with the scraping edge away from the piston head or in the reverse position, depending upon cylinder position and the engine series. In the reverse position, the scraper ring retains the surplus oil above the ring on the upward piston stroke, and this oil is returned to the crankcase by the oil control rings on the downward stroke.

CYLINDERS

The portion of the engine in which the power is developed is called the cylinder. The cylinder provides a combustion chamber where the burning and expansion of gases take place, and it houses the piston and the connecting rod.

There are four major factors that need to be considered in the design and construction of the cylinder assembly. These are:

(1) It must be strong enough to withstand the internal pressures developed during engine operation.

(2) It must be constructed of a lightweight metal to keep down engine weight.

(3) It must have good heat-conducting properties for efficient cooling.

(4) It must be comparatively easy and inexpensive to manufacture, inspect, and maintain.

The head is either produced singly for each cylinder in air-cooled engines, or is cast "in-block" (all cylinder heads in one block) for liquid-cooled engines. The cylinder head of an air-cooled engine is generally made of aluminum alloy, because aluminum alloy is a good conductor of heat and its light weight reduces the overall engine weight. Cylinder heads are forged or die-cast for greater strength. The inner shape of a cylinder head may be flat, semispherical, or peaked, in the form of a house roof. The semispherical type has proved most satisfactory because it is stronger and aids in a more rapid and thorough scavenging of the exhaust gases.

The cylinder used in the air-cooled engine is the overhead valve type shown in figure 1–14. Each cylinder is an assembly of two major parts: (1) The cylinder head, and (2) the cylinder barrel. At assembly, the cylinder head is expanded by heating and then screwed down on the cylinder barrel which

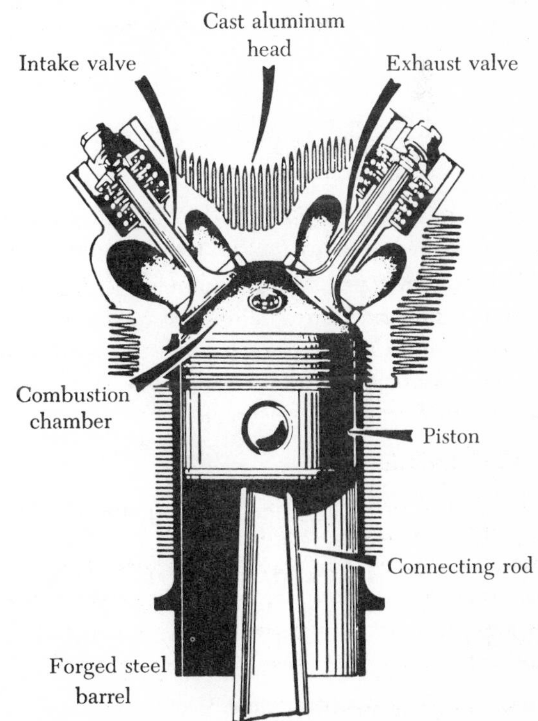

FIGURE 1–14. Cutaway view of the cylinder assembly.

has been chilled; thus, when the head cools and contracts, and the barrel warms up and expands, a gastight joint results. While the majority of the cylinders used are constructed in this manner, some are one-piece aluminum alloy sand castings. The piston bore of a sand cast cylinder is fitted with a steel liner which extends the full length of the cylinder barrel section and projects below the cylinder flange of the casting. This liner is easily removed, and a new one can be installed in the field.

Cylinder Heads

The purpose of the cylinder head is to provide a place for combustion of the fuel/air mixture and to give the cylinder more heat conductivity for adequate cooling. The fuel/air mixture is ignited by the spark in the combustion chamber and commences burning as the piston travels toward top dead center on the compression stroke. The ignited charge is rapidly expanding at this time, and pressure is increasing so that as the piston travels through the top dead center position, it is driven downward on the power stroke. The intake and exhaust valve ports are located in the cylinder head along with the spark plugs and the intake and exhaust valve actuating mechanisms.

After casting, the spark plug bushings, valve guides, rocker arm bushings, and valve seats are installed in the cylinder head. Spark plug openings may be fitted with bronze or steel bushings that are shrunk and screwed into the openings. Stainless steel Heli-Coil spark plug inserts are used in many engines currently manufactured. Bronze or steel valve guides are usually shrunk or screwed into drilled openings in the cylinder head to provide guides for the valve stems. These are generally located at an angle to the center line of the cylinder. The valve seats are circular rings of hardened metal which protect the relatively soft metal of the cylinder head from the hammering action of the valves and from the exhaust gases.

The cylinder heads of air-cooled engines are subjected to extreme temperatures; it is therefore necessary to provide adequate fin area, and to use metals which conduct heat rapidly. Cylinder heads of air-cooled engines are usually cast or forged singly. Aluminum alloy is used in the construction for a number of reasons. It is well adapted for casting or for the machining of deep, closely spaced fins, and it is more resistant than most metals to the corrosive attack of tetraethyl lead in gasoline. The greatest improvement in air cooling has resulted from reducing the thickness of the fins and increasing their depth. In this way the fin area has been increased from approximately 1,200 sq. in. to more than 7,500 sq. in. per cylinder in modern engines. Cooling fins taper from 0.090 in. at the base to 0.060 in. at the tip end. Because of the difference in temperature in the various sections of the cylinder head, it is necessary to provide more cooling-fin area on some sections than on others. The exhaust valve region is the hottest part of the internal surface; therefore, more fin area is provided around the outside of the cylinder in this section.

Cylinder Barrels

In general, the cylinder barrel in which the piston operates must be made of a high-strength material, usually steel. It must be as light as possible, yet have the proper characteristics for operating under high temperatures. It must be made of a good bearing material and have high tensile strength.

The cylinder barrel is made of a steel alloy forging with the inner surface hardened to resist wear of the piston and the piston rings which bear against it. This hardening is usually done by exposing the steel to ammonia or cyanide gas while the steel is very hot. The steel soaks up nitrogen from the gas which forms iron nitrides on the exposed surface. As a result of this process, the metal is said to be nitrided.

In some instances the barrel will have threads on the outside surface at one end so that it can be screwed into the cylinder head. Some air-cooled cylinder barrels have replaceable aluminum cooling fins attached to them, while others have the cooling fins machined as an integral part of the barrel.

CYLINDER NUMBERING

Occasionally it is necessary to refer to the left or right side of the engine or to a particular cylinder. Therefore, it is necessary to know the engine directions and how cylinders of an engine are numbered.

The propeller shaft end of the engine is always the front end, and the accessory end is the rear end, regardless of how the engine is mounted in an aircraft. When referring to the right side or left side of an engine, always assume you are viewing it from the rear or accessory end. As seen from this position, crankshaft rotation is referred to as either clockwise or counterclockwise.

Radial engine cylinders are numbered clockwise as viewed from the accessory end. In-line and V-type engine cylinders are usually numbered from the rear. In V-engines, the cylinder banks are known as the right bank and the left bank, as viewed from the accessory end.

The numbering of engine cylinders is shown in figure 1–15. Note that the cylinder numbering of the opposed engine shown begins with the right rear as No. 1, and the left rear as No. 2. The one forward of No. 1 is No. 3; the one forward of No. 2, is No. 4, and so on. The numbering of opposed engine cylinders is by no means standard. Some manufacturers number their cylinders from the rear and others from the front of the engine. Always refer to the appropriate engine manual to determine the correct numbering system used by the manufacturer.

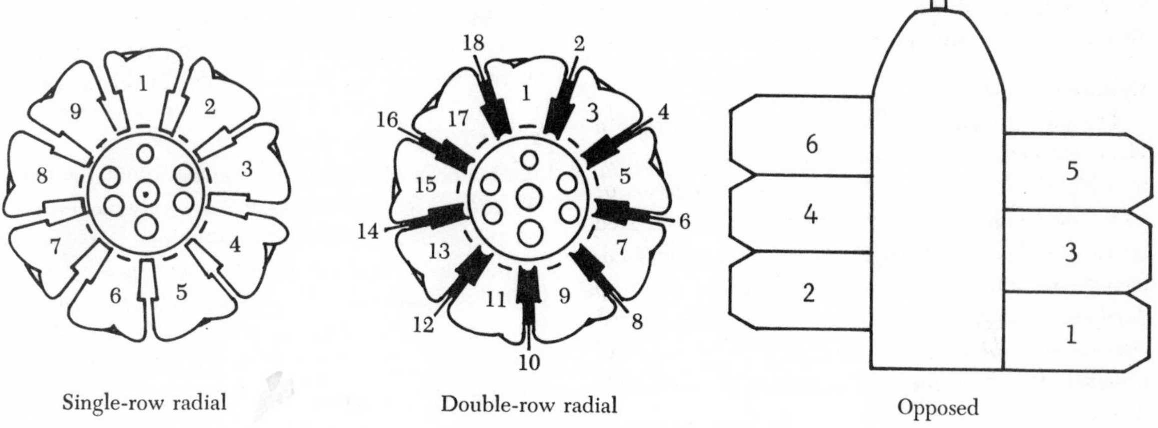

FIGURE 1–15. Numbering of engine cylinders.

Single-row radial engine cylinders are numbered clockwise when viewed from the rear end. Cylinder No. 1 is the top cylinder. In double-row engines, the same system is used, in that the No. 1 cylinder is the top one in the rear row. No. 2 cylinder is the first one clockwise from No. 1, but No. 2 is in the front row. No. 3 cylinder is the next one clockwise to No. 2, but is in the rear row. Thus, all odd-numbered cylinders are in the rear row, and all even-numbered cylinders are in the front row.

FIRING ORDER

The firing order of an engine is the sequence in which the power event occurs in the different cylinders. The firing order is designed to provide for balance and to eliminate vibration to the greatest extent possible. In radial engines the firing order must follow a special pattern, since the firing impulses must follow the motion of the crankthrow during its rotation. In in-line engines the firing orders may vary somewhat, yet most orders are arranged so that the firing of cylinders is evenly distributed along the crankshaft. Six-cylinder in-line engines generally have a firing order of 1–5–3–6–2–4. Cylinder firing order in opposed engines can usually be listed in pairs of cylinders, as each pair fires across the center main bearing. The firing order of six-cylinder opposed engines is 1–4–5–2–3–6. The firing order of one model four-cylinder opposed engine is 1–4–2–3, but on another model it is 1–3–2–4.

Single-Row Radial Engines

On a single-row radial engine, first, all the odd-numbered cylinders fire in numerical succession; then the even-numbered cylinders fire in numerical succession. On a five-cylinder radial engine, for example, the firing order is 1–3–5–2–4, and on a seven-cylinder radial engine it is 1–3–5–7–2–4–6. The firing order of a nine-cylinder radial engine is 1–3–5–7–9–2–4–6–8.

Double-Row Radial Engines

On a double-row radial engine, the firing order is somewhat complicated. The firing order is arranged with the firing impulse occurring in a cylinder in one row and then in a cylinder in the other row; therefore, two cylinders in the same row never fire in succession.

An easy method for computing the firing order of a 14-cylinder, double-row radial engine is to start with any number from 1 to 14, and ***add 9 or subtract 5*** (these are called the firing order numbers), whichever will give an answer between 1 and 14, inclusive. For example, starting with 8, 9 cannot be added since the answer would then be more than 14; therefore, subtract 5 from 8 to get 3, add 9 to 3 to get 12, subtract 5 from 12 to get 7, subtract 5 from 7 to get 2, and so on.

The firing order numbers of an 18-cylinder, double-row radial engine are 11 and 7; that is, begin with any number from 1 to 18 and ***add 11 or subtract 7***. For example, beginning with 1, add 11 to get 12; 11 cannot be added to 12 because the total would be more than 18, so subtract 7 to get 5, add 11 to 5 to get 16, subtract 7 from 16 to get 9, subtract 7 from 9 to get 2, add 11 to 2 to get 13, and continue this process for 18 cylinders.

VALVES

The fuel/air mixture enters the cylinders through the intake valve ports, and burned gases are expelled through the exhaust valve ports. The head of each valve opens and closes these cylinder ports. The valves used in aircraft engines are the conventional poppet type. The valves are also typed by their shape and are called either mushroom or tulip because of their resemblance to the shape of these plants. Figure 1–16 illustrates various shapes and types of these valves.

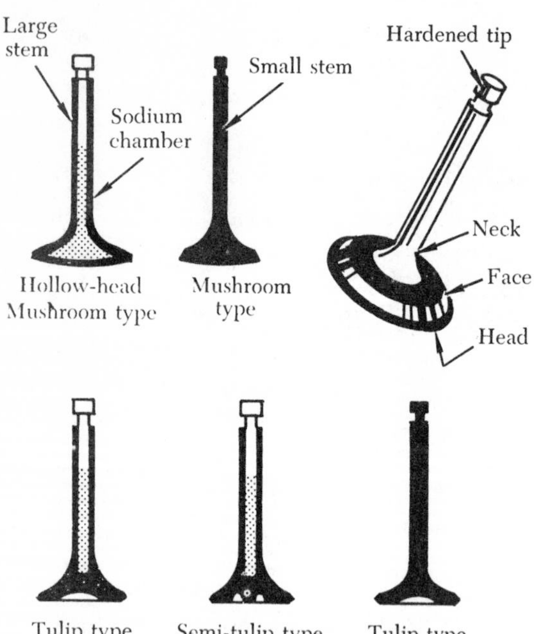

FIGURE 1–16. Valve types.

Valve Construction

The valves in the cylinders of an aircraft engine are subjected to high temperatures, corrosion, and operating stresses; thus, the metal alloy in the valves must be able to resist all these factors.

Because intake valves operate at lower temperatures than exhaust valves, they can be made of chrome-nickel steel. Exhaust valves are usually made of nichrome, silchrome, or cobalt-chromium steel.

The valve head has a ground face which forms a seal against the ground valve seat in the cylinder head when the valve is closed. The face of the valve is usually ground to an angle of either 30° or 45°. In some engines, the intake-valve face is ground to an angle of 30°, and the exhaust valve face is ground to a 45° angle.

Valve faces are often made more durable by the application of a material called stellite. About 1/16 inch of this alloy is welded to the valve face and ground to the correct angle. Stellite is resistant to high-temperature corrosion and also withstands the shock and wear associated with valve operation. Some engine manufacturers use a nichrome facing on the valves. This serves the same purpose as the stellite material.

The valve stem acts as a pilot for the valve head and rides in the valve guide installed in the cylinder head for this purpose. The valve stem is surface-hardened to resist wear. The neck is the part that forms the junction between the head and the stem. The tip of the valve is hardened to withstand the hammering of the valve rocker arm as it opens the valve. A machined groove on the stem near the tip receives the split-ring stem keys. These stem keys form a lock ring to hold the valve spring retaining washer in place.

Some intake and exhaust valve stems are hollow and partially filled with metallic sodium. This material is used because it is an excellent heat conductor. The sodium will melt at approximately 208° F., and the reciprocating motion of the valve circulates the liquid sodium and enables it to carry away heat from the valve head to the valve stem, where it is dissipated through the valve guide to the cylinder head and the cooling fins. Thus, the operating temperature of the valve may be reduced as much as 300° to 400° F. Under no circumstances should a sodium-filled valve be cut open or subjected to treatment which may cause it to rupture. Exposure of the sodium in these valves to the outside air will result in fire or explosion with possible personal injury.

The most commonly used intake valves have solid stems, and the head is either flat or tulip shaped. Intake valves for low-power engines are usually flat headed.

In some engines, the intake valve may be the tulip type and have a smaller stem than the exhaust valve, or it may be similar to the exhaust valve but have a solid stem and head. Although these valves are similar, they are not interchangeable since the faces of the valves are constructed of different material. The intake valve will usually have a flat milled on the tip to identify it.

VALVE-OPERATING MECHANISM

For a reciprocating engine to operate properly, each valve must open at the proper time, stay open for the required length of time, and close at the proper time. Intake valves are opened just before the piston reaches top dead center, and exhaust valves remain open after top dead center. At a particular instant, therefore, both valves are open at the same time (end of the exhaust stroke and beginning of the intake stroke). This valve-overlap permits better volumetric efficiency and lowers the cylinder operating temperature. This timing of the valves is controlled by the valve-operating mechanism.

The valve lift (distance that the valve is lifted off its seat) and the valve duration (length of time the valve is held open) are both determined by the shape of the cam lobes.

Typical cam lobes are illustrated in figure 1–17. The portion of the lobe that gently starts the valve-operating mechanism moving is called a ramp, or step. The ramp is machined on each side of the cam lobe to permit the rocker arm to be eased into contact with the valve tip and thus reduce the shock load which would otherwise occur.

The valve-operating mechanism consists of a cam ring or camshaft equipped with lobes, which work against a cam roller or a cam follower. (See figs. 1–18 and 1–19.) The cam follower, in turn, pushes a push rod and ball socket, which, in turn, actuates a rocker arm which opens the valve. Springs, which slip over the stem of the valves and which are held in place by the valve-spring retaining washer and stem key, close each valve and push the valve mechanism in the opposite direction when the cam roller or follower rolls along a low section of the cam ring.

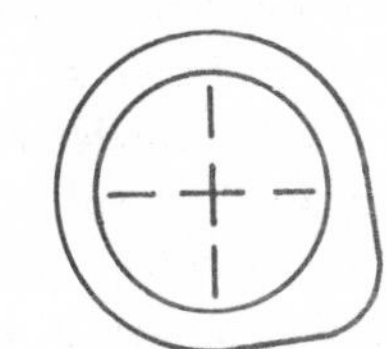

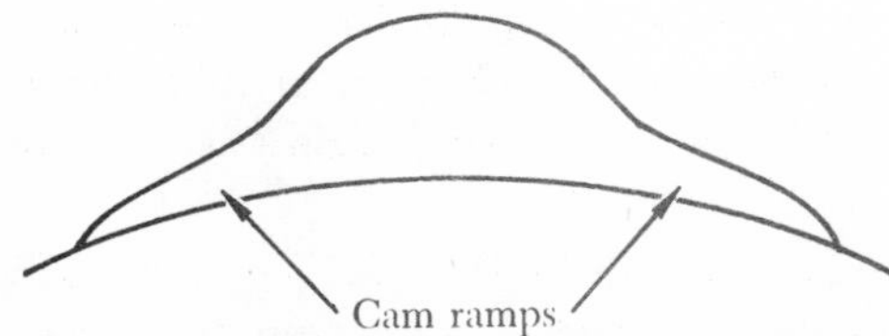

FIGURE 1–17. Typical cam lobes.

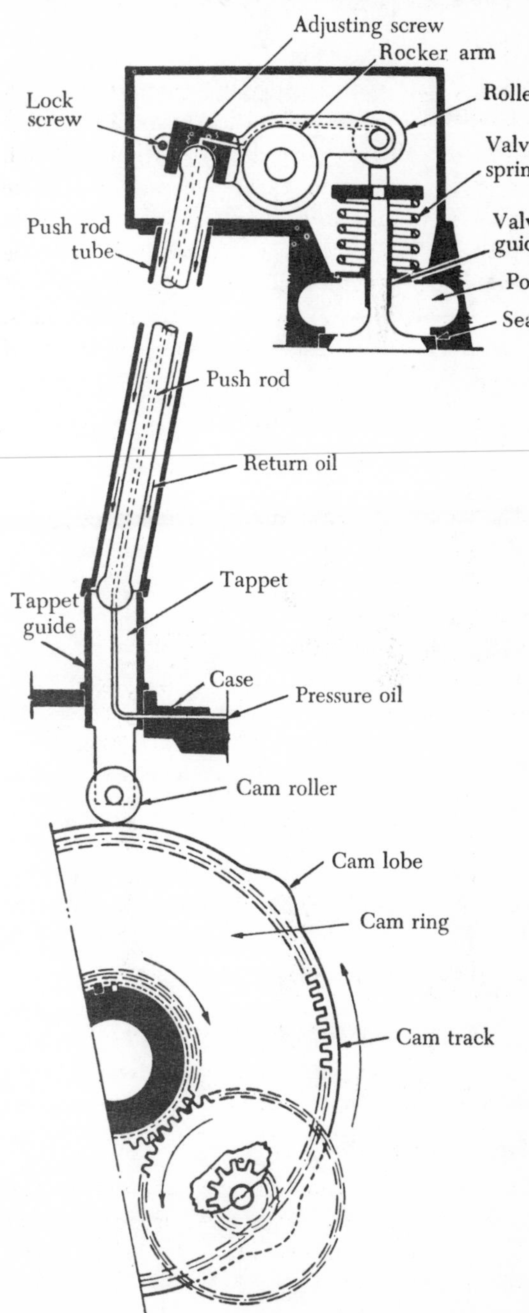

FIGURE 1–18. Valve-operating mechanism (radial engine).

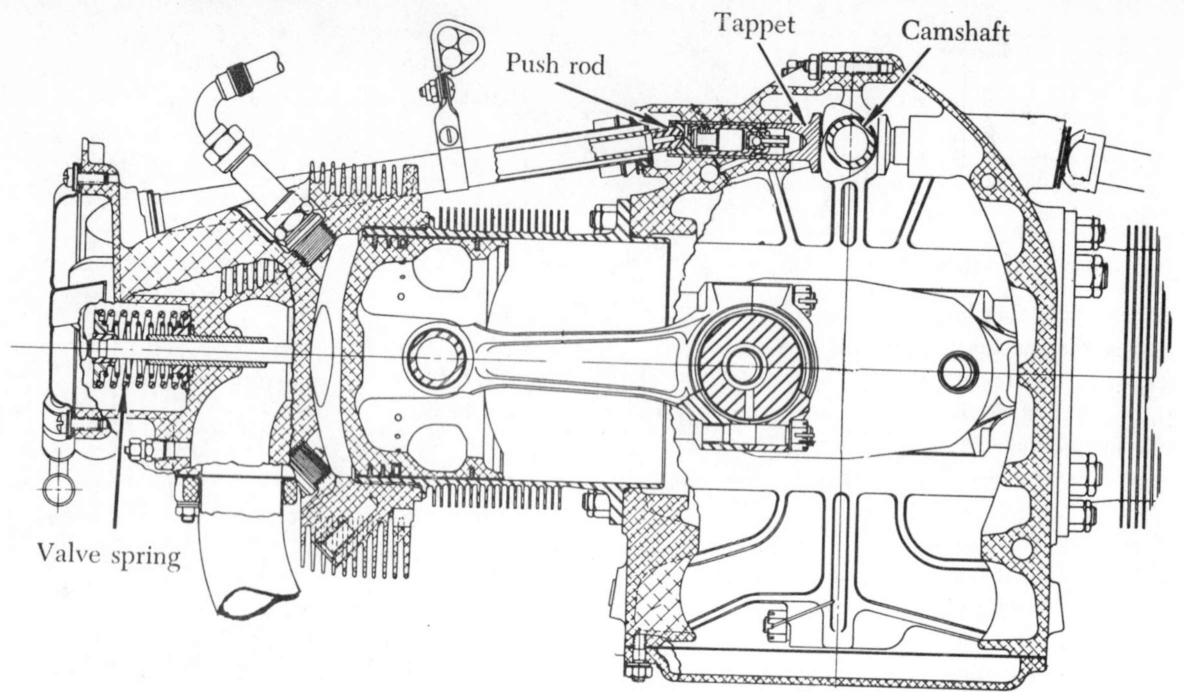

FIGURE 1–19. Valve-operating mechanism (opposed engine).

Cam Ring

The valve mechanism of a radial engine is operated by one or two cam rings, depending upon the number of rows of cylinders. In a single-row radial engine one ring with a double cam track is used. One track operates the intake valves; the other, the exhaust valves. The cam ring is a circular piece of steel with a series of cams or lobes on the outer surface. The surface of these lobes and the space between them (on which the cam rollers ride) is known as the cam track. As the cam ring revolves, the lobes cause the cam roller to raise the tappet in the tappet guide, thereby transmitting the force through the push rod and rocker arm to open the valve.

In a single-row radial engine, the cam ring is usually located between the propeller reduction gearing and the front end of the power section. In a twin-row radial engine, a second cam for the operation of the valves in the rear row is installed between the rear end of the power section and the supercharger section.

The cam ring is mounted concentrically with the crankshaft and is driven by the crankshaft at a reduced rate of speed through the cam intermediate drive gear assembly. The cam ring has two parallel sets of lobes spaced around the outer periphery, one set (cam track) for the intake valves and the other for the exhaust valves. The cam rings used may have four or five lobes on both the intake and the exhaust tracks. The timing of the valve events is determined by the spacing of these lobes and the speed and direction at which the cam rings are driven in relation to the speed and direction of the crankshaft.

The method of driving the cam varies on different makes of engines. The cam ring can be designed with teeth on either the inside or outside periphery. If the reduction gear meshes with the teeth on the outside of the ring, the cam will turn in the direction of rotation of the crankshaft. If the ring is driven from the inside, the cam will turn in the opposite direction from the crankshaft. This method is illustrated in figure 1–18.

A study of figure 1–20 will show that a four-lobe cam may be used on either a seven-cylinder or nine-cylinder engine. On the seven-cylinder it will rotate in the same direction as the crankshaft, and on the nine-cylinder, opposite the crankshaft rotation. On the nine-cylinder engine the spacing between cylinders is 40°, and the firing order is 1–3–5–7–9–2–4–6–8. This means that there is a space of 80° between firing impulses. The spacing on the four lobes of the cam ring is 90°, which is greater than the spacing between impulses. Therefore, to obtain proper relation of valve operations and firing order, it is necessary to drive the cam opposite the crankshaft rotation.

5 cylinders		7 cylinders		9 cylinders		
Number of lobes	Speed	Number of lobes	Speed	Number of lobes	Speed	Direction of rotation
3	1/6	4	1/8	5	1/10	**With crankshaft.**
2	1/4	3	1/6	4	1/8	**Opposite crankshaft.**

FIGURE 1–20. Radial engines, cam ring table.

Using the four-lobe cam on the seven-cylinder engine, the spacing between the firing of the cylinders will be greater than the spacing of the cam lobes. Therefore, it will be necessary for the cam to rotate in the same direction as the crankshaft.

A formula that sometimes is used in figuring cam speed is: Cam ring speed = 1/2 ÷ by the number of lobes on either cam track.

One-half is the speed at which the cam would operate if it were equipped with a single lobe for each valve. It is divided by the number of lobes, which will determine how much the speed will have to be reduced.

In a twin-row, 14-cylinder radial engine which has seven cylinders in each row or bank, the valve mechanism may consist of two separate assemblies, one for each row. It could be considered as two seven-cylinder engines in tandem having the firing impulses properly spaced or lapped. For instance, in a twin-row engine, two four-lobe cam rings may be used. The cams are driven by gears attached to the crankshaft through gear teeth on the periphery of each cam.

Camshaft

The valve mechanism of an opposed engine is operated by a camshaft. The camshaft is driven by a gear that mates with another gear attached to the crankshaft (see figure 1–21). The camshaft always rotates at one-half the crankshaft speed. As the camshaft revolves, the lobes cause the tappet assembly to rise in the tappet guide, transmitting the force through the push rod and rocker arm to open the valve.

Tappet Assembly

The tappet assembly consists of:

(1) A cylindrical tappet, which slides in and out in a tappet guide installed in one of the crankcase sections around the cam ring.

(2) A cam follower or tappet roller, which follows the contour of the cam ring and lobes.

(3) A tappet ball socket or push rod socket.

(4) A tappet spring.

The function of the tappet assembly is to convert

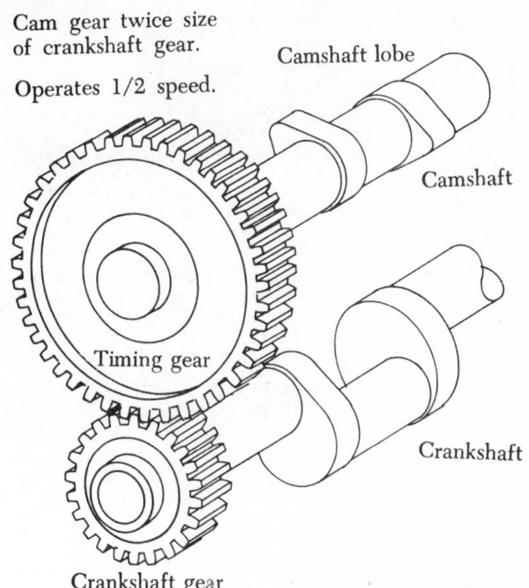

FIGURE 1–21. Cam drive mechanism opposed-type aircraft engine.

the rotational movement of the cam lobe into reciprocating motion and to transmit this motion to the push rod, rocker arm, and then to the valve tip, opening the valve at the proper time. The purpose of the tappet spring is to take up the clearance between the rocker arm and the valve tip to reduce the shock load when the valve is opened. A hole is drilled through the tappet to allow engine oil to flow to the hollow push rods to lubricate the rocker assemblies.

Hydraulic Valve Tappets

Some aircraft engines incorporate hydraulic tappets which automatically keep the valve clearance at zero, eliminating the necessity for any valve clearance adjustment mechanism. A typical hydraulic tappet (zero-lash valve lifter) is shown in figure 1–22.

When the engine valve is closed, the face of the tappet body (cam follower) is on the base circle or back of the cam, as shown in figure 1–22. The light plunger spring lifts the hydraulic plunger so that its outer end contacts the push rod socket, exerting a light pressure against it, thus eliminating any clearance in the valve linkage. As the plunger moves outward, the ball check valve moves off its seat. Oil from the supply chamber, which is directly connected with the engine lubrication system, flows in and fills the pressure chamber. As the camshaft rotates, the cam pushes the tappet body and the hydraulic lifter cylinder outward. This

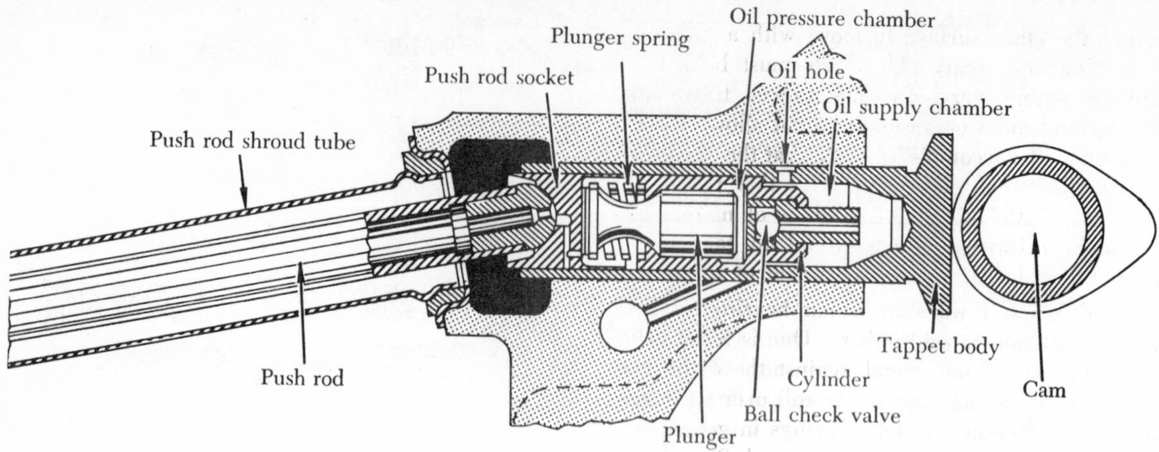

FIGURE 1–22. Hydraulic valve tappets.

action forces the ball check valve onto its seat; thus, the body of oil trapped in the pressure chamber acts as a cushion. During the interval when the engine valve is off its seat, a predetermined leakage occurs between plunger and cylinder bore which compensates for any expansion or contraction in the valve train. Immediately after the engine valve closes, the amount of oil required to fill the pressure chamber flows in from the supply chamber, preparing for another cycle of operation.

Push Rod

The push rod, tubular in form, transmits the lifting force from the valve tappet to the rocker arm. A hardened-steel ball is pressed over or into each end of the tube. One ball end fits into the socket of the rocker arm. In some instances the balls are on the tappet and rocker arm, and the sockets are on the push rod. The tubular form is employed because of its lightness and strength. It permits the engine lubricating oil under pressure to pass through the hollow rod and the drilled ball ends to lubricate the ball ends, rocker-arm bearing, and valve-stem guide. The push rod is enclosed in a tubular housing that extends from the crankcase to the cylinder head.

Rocker Arms

The rocker arms transmit the lifting force from the cams to the valves. Rocker arm assemblies are supported by a plain, roller, or ball bearing, or a combination of these, which serves as a pivot. Generally one end of the arm bears against the push rod and the other bears on the valve stem. One end of the rocker arm is sometimes slotted to accommodate a steel roller. The opposite end is constructed with either a threaded split clamp and locking bolt or a tapped hole.

The arm may have an adjusting screw for adjusting the clearance between the rocker arm and the valve stem tip. The screw is adjusted to the specified clearance to make certain that the valve closes fully.

Valve Springs

Each valve is closed by two or three helical-coiled springs. If a single spring were used, it would vibrate or surge at certain speeds. To eliminate this difficulty, two or more springs (one inside the other) are installed on each valve. Each spring will therefore vibrate at a different engine speed, and rapid damping out of all spring-surge vibrations during engine operation will result. Two or more springs also reduce danger of weakness and possible failure by breakage due to heat and metal fatigue.

The springs are held in place by split locks installed in the recess of the valve spring upper retainer or washer, and engage a groove machined into the valve stem. The functions of the valve springs are to close the valve and to hold the valve securely on the valve seat.

Hydraulic Valve Lifters

Hydraulic valve lifters are normally adjusted at the time of overhaul. They are assembled dry (no lubrication), clearances checked, and adjustments are usually made by use of pushrods having different lengths. A minimum and maximum valve clearance is established. Any measurement between these extremes is acceptable but approximately half way between the extremes is desired. Hydraulic valve lifters require less maintenance, are better lubricated, and operate more quietly than the screw adjustment type.

BEARINGS

A bearing is any surface which supports, or is supported by, another surface. A good bearing must be composed of material that is strong enough to withstand the pressure imposed on it and should permit the other surface to move with a minimum of friction and wear. The parts must be held in position within very close tolerances to provide efficient and quiet operation, and yet allow freedom of motion. To accomplish this, and at the same time reduce friction of moving parts so that power loss is not excessive, lubricated bearings of many types are used. Bearings are required to take radial loads, thrust loads, or a combination of the two.

There are two ways in which bearing surfaces move in relation to each other. One is by the sliding movement of one metal against the other, and the second is for one surface to roll over the other. The three different types of bearings in general use are plain, roller, and ball (see figure 1–23).

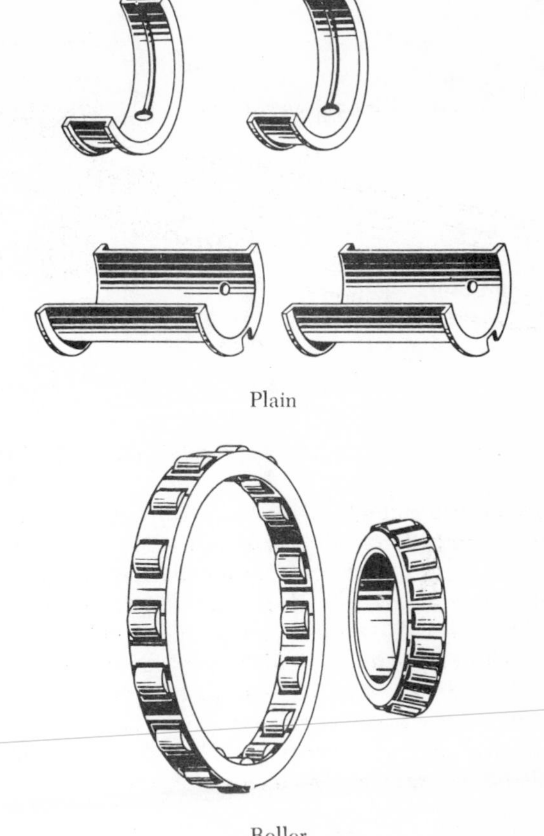

Plain

Roller

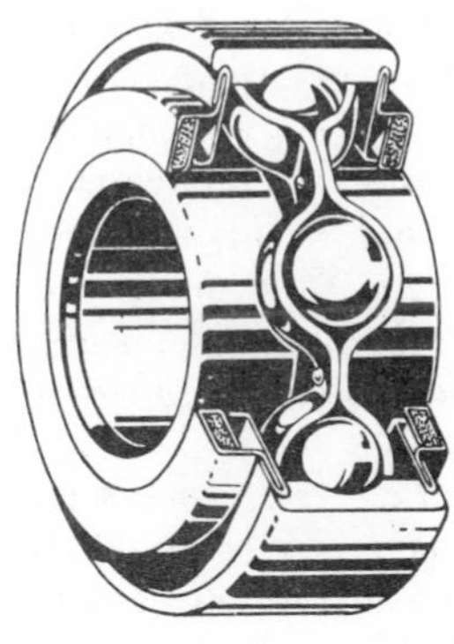

Ball

FIGURE 1–23. Bearings.

Plain Bearings

Plain bearings are generally used for the crankshaft, cam ring, camshaft, connecting rods, and the accessory drive shaft bearings. Such bearings are usually subjected to radial loads only, although some have been designed to take thrust loads.

Plain bearings are usually made of nonferrous (having no iron) metals, such as silver, bronze, aluminum, and various alloys of copper, tin, or lead. Master rod or crankpin bearings in some engines are thin shells of steel, plated with silver on both the inside and the outside surfaces and with lead-tin plated over the silver on the inside surface only. Smaller bearings, such as those used to support various shafts in the accessory section, are called bushings. Porous Oilite bushings are widely used in this instance. They are impregnated with oil so that the heat of friction brings the oil to the bearing surface during engine operation.

Ball Bearings

A ball bearing assembly consists of grooved inner and outer races, one or more sets of balls, and, in bearings designed for disassembly, a bearing retainer. They are used for supercharger impeller shaft bearings and rocker arm bearings in some engines. Special deep-groove ball bearings are used in aircraft engines to transmit propeller thrust to the engine nose section.

Roller Bearings

Roller bearings are made in many types and shapes, but the two types generally used in the aircraft engine are the straight roller and the tapered roller bearings. Straight roller bearings are used where the bearing is subjected to radial loads only. In tapered roller bearings, the inner- and outer-race bearing surfaces are cone shaped. Such bearings will withstand both radial and thrust loads. Straight roller bearings are used in high-power aircraft engines for the crankshaft main bearings. They are also used in other applications where radial loads are high.

PROPELLER REDUCTION GEARING

The increased brake horsepower delivered by a high-horsepower engine results partly from increased crankshaft r.p.m. It is therefore necessary to provide reduction gears to limit the propeller rotation speed to a value at which efficient operation is obtained. Whenever the speed of the blade tips approaches the speed of sound, the efficiency of the propeller decreases rapidly. The general practice has been to provide reduction gearing for propellers of engines whose speeds are above 2,000 r.p.m., because propeller efficiency decreases rapidly above this speed.

Since reduction gearing must withstand extremely high stresses, the gears are machined from steel forgings. Many types of reduction gearing systems are in use. The three types (fig. 1–24) most commonly used are:

(1) Spur planetary.
(2) Bevel planetary.
(3) Spur and pinion.

The planetary reduction gear systems are used with radial and opposed engines, and the spur and pinion system is used with in-line and V-type engines. Two of these types, the spur planetary and the bevel planetary, are discussed here.

The spur planetary reduction gearing consists of a large driving gear or sun gear splined (and sometimes shrunk) to the crankshaft, a large stationary gear, called a bell gear, and a set of small spur planetary pinion gears mounted on a carrier ring. The ring is fastened to the propeller shaft, and the planetary gears mesh with both the sun gear and the stationary bell or ring gear. The stationary gear is bolted or splined to the front-section housing. When the engine is operating, the sun gear rotates. Because the planetary gears are meshed with this ring, they also must rotate. Since they also mesh with the stationary gear, they will walk or roll around it as they rotate, and the ring in which they are mounted will rotate the propeller shaft in the same direction as the crankshaft but at a reduced speed.

In some engines, the bell gear is mounted on the propeller shaft, and the planetary pinion gear cage is held stationary. The sun gear is splined to the crankshaft and thus acts as a driving gear. In such an arrangement, the propeller travels at a reduced speed, but in opposite direction to the crankshaft.

In the bevel planetary reduction gearing system, the driving gear is machined with beveled external teeth and is attached to the crankshaft. A set of mating bevel pinion gears is mounted in a cage attached to the end of the propeller shaft. The pinion gears are driven by the drive gear and walk around the stationary gear, which is bolted or splined to the front-section housing. The thrust of the bevel pinion gears is absorbed by a thrust ball bearing of special design. The drive and the fixed gears are generally supported by heavy-duty ball bearings. This type of planetary reduction assembly is more compact than the other one described and can therefore be used where a smaller propeller gear step-down is desired.

PROPELLER SHAFTS

Propeller shafts may be three major types; tapered, splined, or flanged. Tapered shafts are identified by taper numbers. Splined and flanged shafts are identified by SAE numbers.

The propeller shaft of most low-power output engines is forged as part of the crankshaft. It is tapered and a milled slot is provided so that the propeller hub can be keyed to the shaft. The keyway and key index of the propeller are in relation to the #1 cylinder top dead center. The end of the shaft is threaded to receive the propeller retaining nut. Tapered propeller shafts are common on older and in-line engines.

The propeller shaft of a high-output engine generally is splined. It is threaded on one end for a propeller hub nut. The thrust bearing, which absorbs propeller thrust, is located around the shaft and transmits the thrust to the nose-section housing. The shaft is threaded for attaching the thrust-bearing retaining nut. On the portion protruding from the housing (between the two sets of threads), splines are located to receive the splined propeller hub. The shaft is generally machined from a steel-alloy forging throughout its length. The propeller shaft may be connected by reduction gearing to the engine crankshaft, but in smaller engines the propeller shaft is simply an extension of the engine crankshaft. To turn the propeller shaft, the engine crankshaft must revolve.

Flanged propeller shafts are used on medium or low powered reciprocating and turbojet engines. One end of the shaft is flanged with drilled holes to accept the propeller mounting bolts. The installation may be a short shaft with internal threading to accept the distributor valve to be used with a controllable propeller. The flanged propeller shaft is a normal installation on most approved reciprocating engines.

RECIPROCATING ENGINE OPERATING PRINCIPLES

A study of this section will help in understanding the basic operating principles of reciprocating engines. The principles which govern the relationship between the pressure, volume, and temperature of gases are the basic principles of engine operation.

An internal-combustion engine is a device for converting heat energy into mechanical energy. Gasoline is vaporized and mixed with air, forced or drawn into a cylinder, compressed by a piston, and then ignited by an electric spark. The conversion of the resultant heat energy into mechancial energy and then into work is accomplished in the cylinder. Figure 1–25 illustrates the various engine compo-

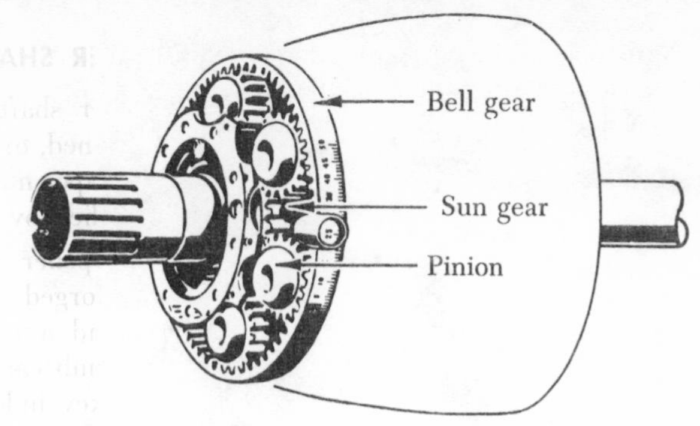

Spur-planetary

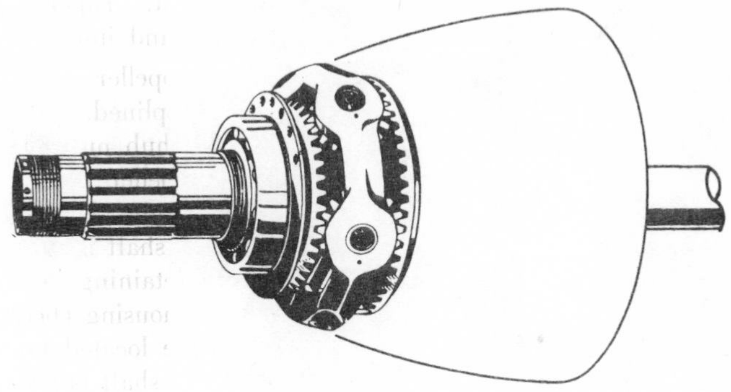

Bevel planetary

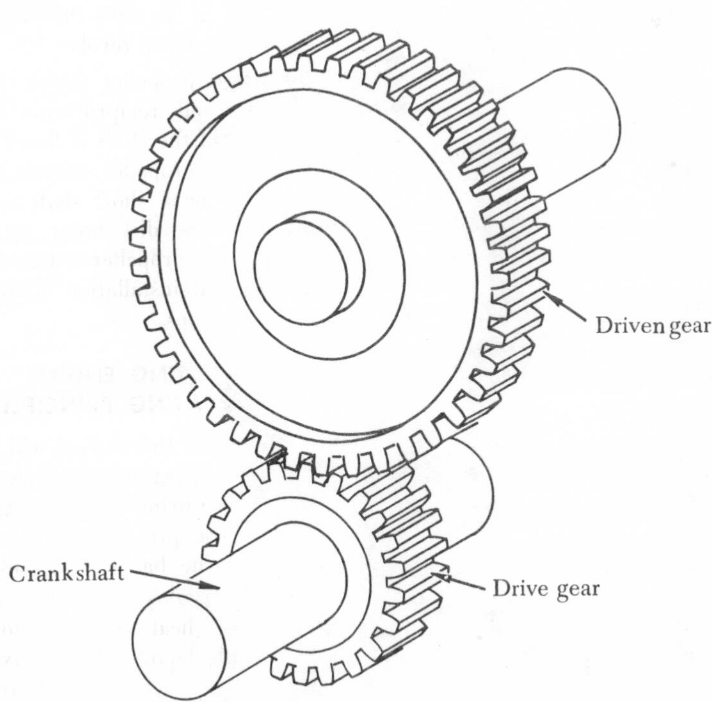

Spur and pinion

FIGURE 1–24. Reduction gears.

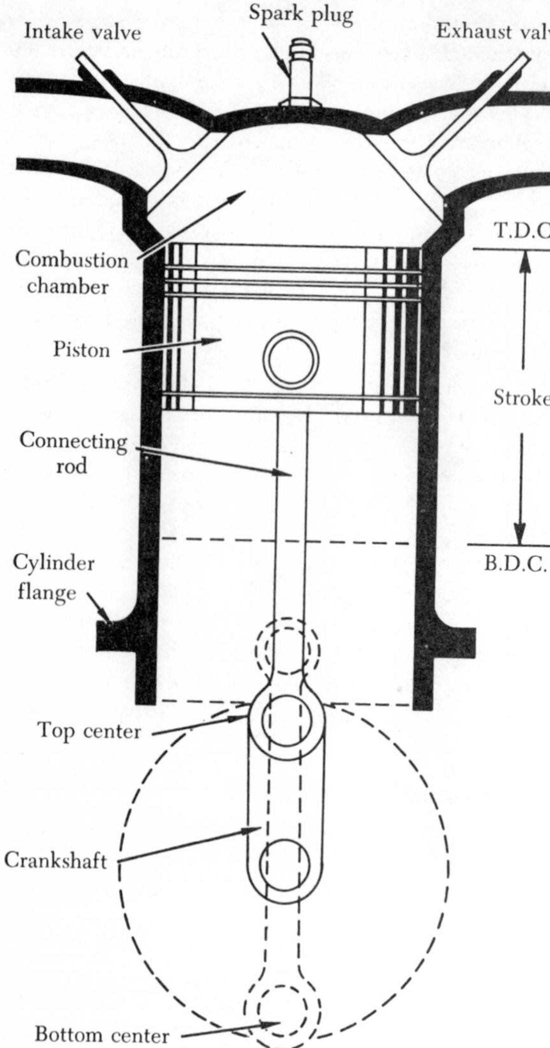

FIGURE 1–25. Components and terminology of engine operation.

nents necessary to accomplish this conversion and also presents the principal terms used to indicate engine operation.

The operating cycle of an internal combustion reciprocating engine includes the series of events required to induct, compress, ignite, burn, and expand the fuel/air charge in the cylinder, and to scavenge or exhaust the byproducts of the combustion process.

When the compressed mixture is ignited, the resultant gases of combustion expand very rapidly and force the piston to move away from the cylinder head. This downward motion of the piston, acting on the crankshaft through the connecting rod, is converted to a circular or rotary motion by the crankshaft.

A valve in the top or head of the cylinder opens to allow the burned gases to escape, and the momentum of the crankshaft and the propeller forces the piston back up in the cylinder where it is ready for the next event in the cycle. Another valve in the cylinder head then opens to let in a fresh charge of the fuel/air mixture.

The valve allowing for the escape of the burning exhaust gases is called the exhaust valve, and the valve which lets in the fresh charge of the fuel/air mixture is called the intake valve. These valves are opened and closed mechanically at the proper times by the valve-operating mechanism.

The bore of a cylinder is its inside diameter. The stroke is the distance the piston moves from one end of the cylinder to the other, specifically, from T.D.C. (top dead center) to B.D.C. (bottom dead center), or vice versa (see figure 1–25).

OPERATING CYCLES

There are two operating cycles in general use: (1) The two-stroke cycle, and (2) the four-stroke cycle. At the present time, the two-stroke-cycle engine is fast disappearing from the aviation scene and will not be discussed. As the name implies, two-stroke-cycle engines require only one upstroke and one downstroke of the piston to complete the required series of events in the cylinder. Thus the engine completes the operating cycle in one revolution of the crankshaft.

Most aircraft reciprocating engines operate on the four-stroke cycle, sometimes called the Otto cycle after its originator, a German physicist. The four-stroke-cycle engine has many advantages for use in aircraft. One advantage is that it lends itself readily to high performance through supercharging.

In this type of engine, four strokes are required to complete the required series of events or operating cycle of each cylinder, as shown in figure 1–26. Two complete revolutions of the crankshaft (720°) are required for the four strokes; thus, each cylinder in an engine of this type fires once in every two revolutions of the crankshaft.

FOUR-STROKE CYCLE

In the following discussion of the four-stroke-cycle engine operation, it should be realized that the timing of the ignition and the valve events will vary considerably in different engines. Many factors influence the timing of a specific engine, and it is most important that the engine manufacturer's recommendations in this respect be followed in maintenance and overhaul. The timing of the valve and ignition events is always specified in degrees of crankshaft travel.

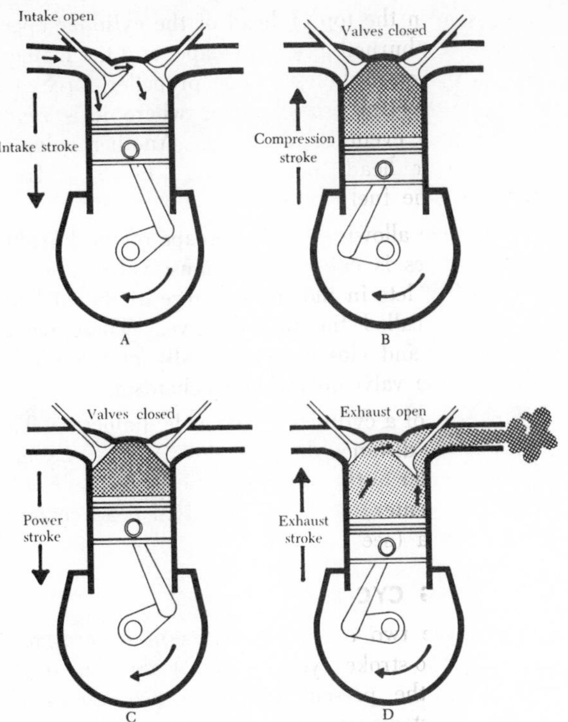

FIGURE 1–26. Four-stroke cycle.

In the following paragraphs, the timing of each event is specified in terms of degrees of crankshaft travel on the stroke during which the event occurs. It should be remembered that a certain amount of crankshaft travel is required to open a valve fully; therefore, the specified timing represents the start of opening rather than the full-open position of the valve.

Intake Stroke

During the intake stroke, the piston is pulled downward in the cylinder by the rotation of the crankshaft. This reduces the pressure in the cylinder and causes air under atmospheric pressure to flow through the carburetor, which meters the correct amount of fuel. The fuel/air mixture passes through the intake pipes and intake valves into the cylinders. The quantity or weight of the fuel/air charge depends upon the degree of throttle opening.

The intake valve is opened considerably before the piston reaches top dead center on the exhaust stroke, in order to induce a greater quantity of the fuel/air charge into the cylinder and thus increase the horsepower. The distance the valve may be opened before top dead center, however, is limited by several factors, such as the possibility that hot gases remaining in the cylinder from the previous cycle may flash back into the intake pipe and the induction system.

In all high-power aircraft engines, both the intake and the exhaust valves are off the valve seats at top dead center at the start of the intake stroke. As mentioned above, the intake valve opens before top dead center on the exhaust stroke (valve lead), and the closing of the exhaust valve is delayed considerably after the piston has passed top dead center and has started the intake stroke (valve lag). This timing is called valve overlap and is designed to aid in cooling the cylinder internally by circulating the cool incoming fuel/air mixture, to increase the amount of the fuel/air mixture induced into the cylinder, and to aid in scavenging the byproducts of combustion.

The intake valve is timed to close about 50° to 75° past bottom dead center on the compression stroke depending upon the specific engine, to allow the momentum of the incoming gases to charge the cylinder more completely. Because of the comparatively large volume of the cylinder above the piston when the piston is near bottom dead center, the slight upward travel of the piston during this time does not have a great effect on the incoming flow of gases. This late timing can be carried too far because the gases may be forced back through the intake valve and defeat the purpose of the late closing.

Compression Stroke

After the intake valve is closed, the continued upward travel of the piston compresses the fuel/air mixture to obtain the desired burning and expansion characteristics.

The charge is fired by means of an electric spark as the piston approaches top dead center. The time of ignition will vary from 20° to 35° before top dead center, depending upon the requirements of the specific engine, to ensure complete combustion of the charge by the time the piston is slightly past the top dead center position.

Many factors affect ignition timing, and the engine manufacturer has expended considerable time in research and testing to determine the best setting. All engines incorporate devices for adjusting the ignition timing, and it is most important that the ignition system be timed according to the engine manufacturer's recommendations.

Power Stroke

As the piston moves through the top dead center position at the end of the compression stroke and starts down on the power stroke, it is pushed downward by the rapid expansion of the burning gases within the cylinder head with a force that can be greater than 15 tons (30,000 p.s.i.) at maximum power output of the engine. The temperature of these burnning gases may be between 3,000° and 4,000°F.

As the piston is forced downward during the power stroke by the pressure of the burning gases exerted upon it, the downward movement of the connecting rod is changed to rotary movement by the crankshaft. Then the rotary movement is transmitted to the propeller shaft to drive the propeller. As the burning gases are expanded, the temperature drops to within safe limits before the exhaust gases flow out through the exhaust port.

The timing of the exhaust valve opening is determined by, among other considerations, the desirability of using as much of the expansive force as possible and of scavenging the cylinder as completely and rapidly as possible. The valve is opened considerably before bottom dead center on the power stroke (on some engines at 50° and 75° before B.D.C.) while there is still some pressure in the cylinder. This timing is used so that the pressure can force the gases out of the exhaust port as soon as possible. This process frees the cylinder of waste heat after the desired expansion has been obtained and avoids overheating the cylinder and the piston. Thorough scavenging is very important, because any exhaust products remaining in the cylinder will dilute the incoming fuel/air charge at the start of the next cycle.

Exhaust Stroke

As the piston travels through bottom dead center at the completion of the power stroke and starts upward on the exhaust stroke, it will begin to push the burned exhaust gases out the exhaust port. The speed of the exhaust gases leaving the cylinder creates a low pressure in the cylinder. This low or reduced pressure speeds the flow of the fresh fuel/air charge into the cylinder as the intake valve is beginning to open. The intake valve opening is timed to occur at 8° to 55° before top dead center on the exhaust stroke on various engines.

RECIPROCATING ENGINE POWER AND EFFICIENCIES

All aircraft engines are rated according to their ability to do work and produce power. This section presents an explanation of work and power and how they are calculated. Also discussed are the various efficiencies that govern the power output of a reciprocating engine.

Work

The physicist defines work as "Work is force times distance. Work done by a force acting on a body is equal to the magnitude of the force multiplied by the distance through which the force acts."

Work (W) = Force (F) x Distance (D).

Work is measured by several standards, the most common unit is called foot-pound. If a 1-pound mass is raised 1 foot, 1 ft.-lb. (foot-pound) of work has been performed. The greater the mass and the greater the distance, the greater the work.

Horsepower

The common unit of mechanical power is the hp. (horsepower). Late in the 18th century, James Watt, the inventor of the steam engine, found that an English workhorse could work at the rate of 550 ft.-lb. per second, or 33,000 ft.-lb. per minute, for a reasonable length of time. From his observations came the hp., which is the standard unit of power in the English system of measurement. To calculate the hp. rating of an engine, divide the power developed in ft.-lb. per minute by 33,000, or the power in ft.-lb. per second by 550.

$$\text{hp.} = \frac{\text{ft.-lb. per min.}}{33{,}000}, \text{ or}$$

$$= \frac{\text{ft.-lb. per sec.}}{550}.$$

As stated above, work is the product of force and ditsance, and power is work per unit of time. Consequently, if a 33,000-lb. weight is lifted through a vertical distance of 1 ft. in 1min., the power expended is 33,000 ft.-lb. per min., or exactly 1 hp.

Work is performed not only when a force is applied for lifting; force may be applied in any direction. If a 100-lb. weight is dragged along the ground, a force is still being applied to perform work, although the direction of the resulting motion is approximately horizontal. The amount of this force would depend upon the roughness of the ground.

If the weight were attached to a spring scale graduated in pounds, then dragged by pulling on the scale handle, the amount of force required could be measured. Assume that the force required is 90 lbs., and the 100-lb. weight is dragged 660 ft. in 2 min. The amount of work performed in the 2 min. will be 59,400 ft.-lb., or 29,700 ft.-lb. per min. Since 1 hp. is 33,000 ft.-lb. per min., the hp. expended in this case will be 29,700 divided by 33,000, or 0.9 hp.

Piston Displacement

When other factors remain equal, the greater the piston displacement the greater the maximum horsepower an engine will be capable of developing. When a piston moves from bottom dead center to top dead center, it displaces a specific volume. The volume displaced by the piston is known as piston displacement and is expressed in cubic inches for most American-made engines and cubic centimeters for others.

The piston displacement of one cylinder may be obtained by multiplying the area of the cross section of the cylinder by the total distance the piston moves in the cylinder in one stroke. For multi-cylinder engines this product is multiplied by the number of cylinders to get the total piston displacement of the engine.

Since the volume (V) of a geometric cylinder equals the area (A) of the base multiplied by the altitude (H), it is expressed mathematically as:

$$V = A \times H.$$

For our purposes, the area of the base is the area of the cross section of the cylinder or of the piston top.

Area Of A Circle

To find the area of a circle it is necessary to use a number called pi. This number represents the ratio of the circumference to the diameter of any circle. Pi cannot be found exactly because it is a never-ending decimal, but expressed to four decimal places it is 3.1416, which is accurate enough for most computations.

The area of a circle, as in a rectangle or triangle, must be expressed in square units. The distance that is one-half the diameter of a circle is known as the radius. The area of any circle is found by squaring the radius and multiplying by pi. (π). The formula is expressed thus:

$$A = \pi R^2.$$

Where A is the area of a circle; pi is the given constant; and r is the radius of the circle, which is equal to ½ the diameter or $R = \frac{D}{2}$

Example

Compute the piston displacement of the PWA 14 cylinder engine having a cylinder with a 5.5 inch diameter and a 5.5 inch stroke. Formulas required are:

$$R = \frac{D}{2}$$

$$A = \pi R^2$$

$$V = A \times H$$

Total V=V x N (number of cylinders)

Substitute values into these formulas and complete the calculation.

$$R = \frac{D}{2} \quad R = 5.5/2 = 2.75$$

$$A = \pi R^2 \quad A = 3.1416\ (2.75 \times 2.75)$$

$$A = 3.1416 \times 7.5625 = 23.7584 \text{ sq. inches}$$

$$V = A \times H \quad V = 23.7584 \times 5.5 \quad V = 130.6712$$

Total V=V x N Total V=130.6712 x 14 Total V=1829.3968

Rounded off to the next whole number total piston displacement equals 1830 cu. in.

Another method of calculating the piston displacement uses the diameter of the piston instead of the radius in the formula for the area of the base.

$$A = \tfrac{1}{4}\ (\pi)\ (D)^2$$

Substituting $A = \tfrac{1}{4} \times 3.1416 \times 5.5 \times 5.5$

$A = .7854 \times 30.25$ $A = 23.758$ square inches.

From this point on the calculations are identical to the preceding example.

Compression Ratio

All internal-combustion engines must compress the fuel/air mixture to receive a reasonable amount of work from each power stroke. The fuel/air charge in the cylinder can be compared to a coil spring, in that the more it is compressed the more work it is potentially capable of doing.

The compression ratio of an engine (see figure 1–27) is a comparison of the volume of space in a cylinder when the piston is at the bottom of the stroke to the volume of space when the piston is at the top of the stroke. This comparison is expressed as a ratio, hence the term "compresion ratio." Compression ratio is a controlling factor in the maximum horsepower developed by an engine, but it is limited by present-day fuel grades and the high engine speeds and manifold pressures required for takeoff. For example, if there are 140 cu. in. of space in the cylinder when the piston is at the bottom and there are 20 cu. in. of space when the piston is at the top of the stroke, the compression ratio would be 140 to 20. If this ratio is expressed in fraction form, it would be 140/20, or 7 to 1, usually represented as 7:1.

To grasp more thoroughly the limitation placed on compression ratios, manifold pressure and its effect on compression pressures should be understood. Manifold pressure is the average absolute pressure of the air or fuel/air charge in the intake manifold and is measured in units of inches of mercury (Hg). Manifold pressure is dependent on engine speed (throttle setting) and supercharging. The engine-driven internal supercharger (blower) and the external exhaust-driven supercharger (turbo) are actually centrifugal-type air compressors. The operation of these superchargers increases the weight of the charge entering the cylinder. When either one or both are used with the aircraft engine, the manifold pressure may be considerably higher than the pressure of the outside atmosphere. The advantage of this condition is that a greater amount of charge is forced into a given cylinder volume, and a greater power results.

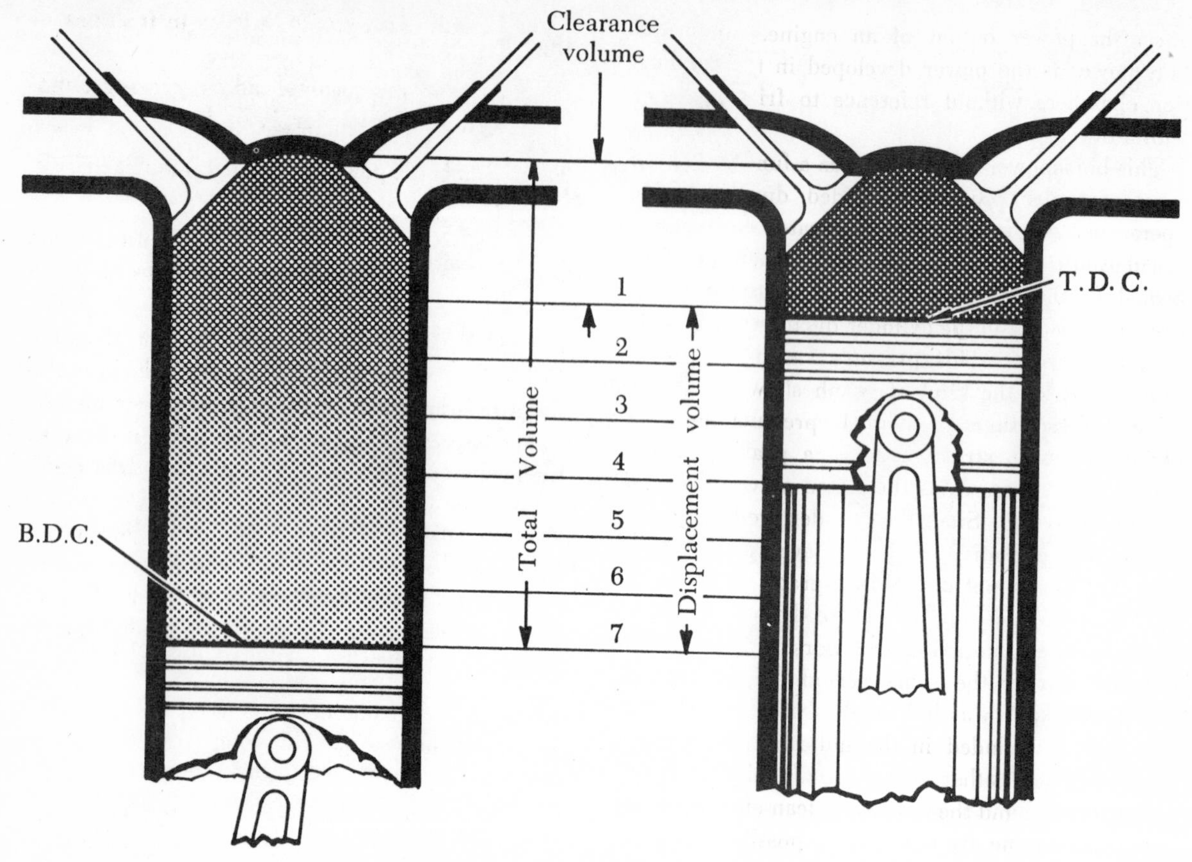

FIGURE 1–27. Compression ratio.

Compression ratio and manifold pressure determine the pressure in the cylinder in that portion of the operating cycle when both valves are closed. The pressure of the charge before compression is determined by manifold pressure, while the pressure at the height of compression (just prior to ignition) is determined by manifold pressure times the compression ratio. For example, if an engine were operating at a manifold pressure of 30″ Hg with a compression ratio of 7:1, the pressure at the instant before ignition would be approximately 210″ Hg. However, at a manifold pressure of 60″ Hg the pressure would be 420″ Hg.

Without going into great detail, it has been shown that the compression event magnifies the effect of varying the manifold pressure, and the magnitude of both affects the pressure of the fuel charge just before the instant of ignition. If the pressure at this time becomes too high, premature ignition or knock will occur and produce overheating.

One of the reasons for using engines with high compression ratios is to obtain long-range fuel economy, that is, to convert more heat energy into useful work than is done in engines of low compression ratio. Since more heat of the charge is converted into useful work, less heat is absorbed by the cylinder walls. This factor promotes cooler engine operation, which in turn increases the thermal efficiency.

Here, again, a compromise is needed between the demand for fuel economy and the demand for maximum horsepower without knocking. Some manufacturers of high-compression engines suppress knock at high manifold pressures by injecting an antiknock fluid into the fuel/air mixture. The fluid acts primarily as a coolant so that more power can be delivered by the engine for short periods, such as at takeoff and during emergencies, when power is critical. This high power should be used for short periods only.

Indicated Horsepower

The indicated horsepower produced by an engine is the horsepower calculated from the indicated mean effective pressure and the other factors which affect the power output of an engine. Indicated horsepower is the power developed in the combustion chambers without reference to friction losses within the engine.

This horsepower is calculated as a function of the actual cylinder pressure recorded during engine operation. To facilitate the indicated horsepower calculations, a mechanical indicating device, attached to the engine cylinder, scribes the actual pressure existing in the cylinder during the complete operating cycle. This pressure variation can be represented by the kind of graph shown in figure 1–28. Notice that the cylinder pressure rises on the compression stroke, reaches a peak after top center, then decreases as the piston moves down on the power stroke. Since the cylinder pressure varies during the operating cycle, an average pressure, line AB, is computed. This average pressure, if applied steadily during the time of the power stroke, would do the same amount of work as the varying pressure during the same period. This average pressure is known as indicated mean effective pressure and is included in the indicated horsepower calculation with other engine specifications. If the characteristics and the indicated mean effective pressure of an engine are known, it is possible to calculate the indicated horsepower rating.

The indicated horsepower for a four-stroke-cycle engine can be calculated from the following formula, in which the letter symbols in the numerator are arranged to spell the word "plank" to assist in memorizing the formula:

$$\text{Indicated horsepower} = \frac{PLANK}{33{,}000}.$$

Where:

P = Indicated mean effective pressure in p.s.i.

L = Length of the stroke in ft. or in fractions of a foot.

A = Area of the piston head or cross-sectional area of the cylinder, in sq. in.

N = Number of power strokes per minute; $\frac{\text{r.p.m.}}{2}$.

K = Number of cylinders.

In the formula above, the area of the piston times the indicated mean effective pressure gives the force acting on the piston in pounds. This force multiplied by the length of the stroke in feet gives the work performed in one power stroke, which, multiplied by the number of power strokes per minute, gives the number of ft.-lb. per minute of work produced by one cylinder. Multiplying this result by the number of cylinders in the engine gives the amount of work performed, in ft.-lb., by the engine. Since hp. is defined as work done at the rate of 33,000 ft.-lb. per min., the total number of ft.-lb. of work performed by the engine is divided by 33,000 to find the indicated horsepower.

Example

Given:

Indicated mean effective pressure (P)	= 165 lbs./sq. in.
Stroke (L)	= 6 in. or .5 ft.
Bore	= 5.5 in.
r.p.m.	= 3,000
No. of cylinders (K)	= 12

$$\text{Indicated hp.} = \frac{PLANK}{33{,}000 \text{ ft.-lbs./min.}}.$$

Find indicated hp.:

A is found by using the equation

$A = 1/4\pi D^2$

$A = 1/4 \times 3.1416 \times 5.5 \times 5.5$

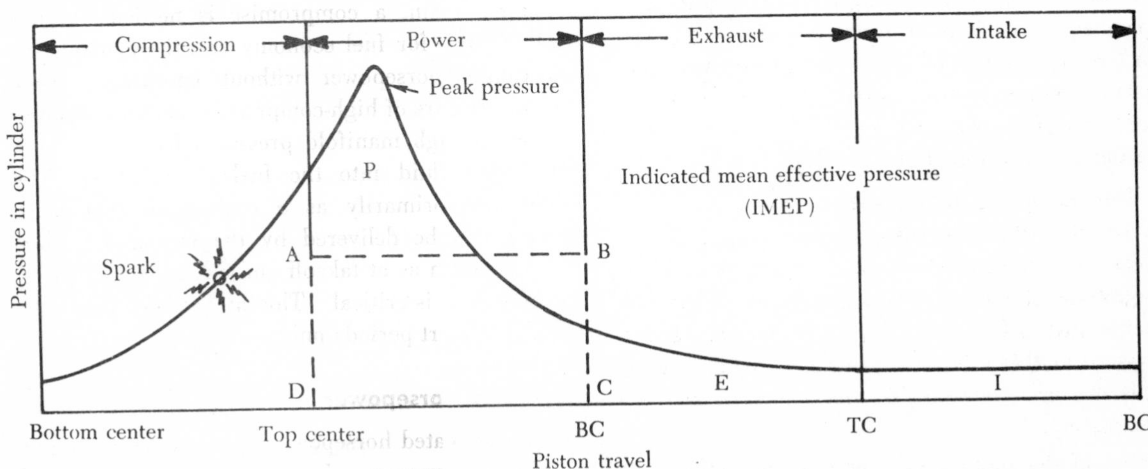

FIGURE 1–28. Cylinder pressure during power cycle.

$= 23.76$ sq. in.

N is found by multiplying the r.p.m. by 1/2:

$N = 1/2 \times 3{,}000$

$= 1{,}500$ r.p.m.

Now, substituting in the formula:

$$\text{Indicated hp.} = \frac{165 \times .5 \times 23.76 \times 1{,}500 \times 12}{33{,}000 \text{ ft.-lbs./min.}}$$

$$= 1069.20.$$

Brake Horsepower

The indicated horsepower calculation discussed in the preceding paragraph is the theoretical power of a frictionless engine. The total horsepower lost in overcoming friction must be subtracted from the indicated horsepower to arrive at the actual horsepower delivered to the propeller. The power delivered to the propeller for useful work is known as b.hp. (brake horsepower). The difference between indicated and brake horsepower is known as friction horsepower, which is the horsepower required to overcome mechanical losses such as the pumping action of the pistons and the friction of the pistons and the friction of all moving parts.

In practice, the measurement of an engine's b.hp. involves the measurement of a quantity known as torque, or twisting moment. Torque is the product of a force and the distance of the force from the axis about which it acts, or

Torque = Force x Distance
(at right angles to the force).

Torque is a measure of load and is properly expressed in pound-inches (lb.-in.) or pound-feet (lb.-ft.) and should not be confused with work, which is expressed in inch-pounds (in.-lbs.) or foot-pounds (ft.-lbs.).

There are a number of devices for measuring torque, of which the Prony brake, dynamometer, and torquemeter are examples. Typical of these devices is the Prony brake (figure 1–29), which measures the usable power output of an engine on a test stand. It consists essentially of a hinged collar, or brake, which can be clamped to a drum splined to the propeller shaft. The collar and drum form a friction brake which can be adjusted by a wheel. An arm of a known length is rigidly attached to or is a part of the hinged collar and terminates at a point which bears on a set of scales. As the propeller shaft rotates, it tends to carry the hinged collar of the brake with it and is prevented from doing so only by the arm that bears on the scale. The scale reads the force necessary to arrest the motion of the arm. If the resulting force registered on the scale is multiplied by the length of the arm, the resulting product is the torque exerted by the rotating shaft. Example: If the scale registers 200 lbs. and the length of the arm is

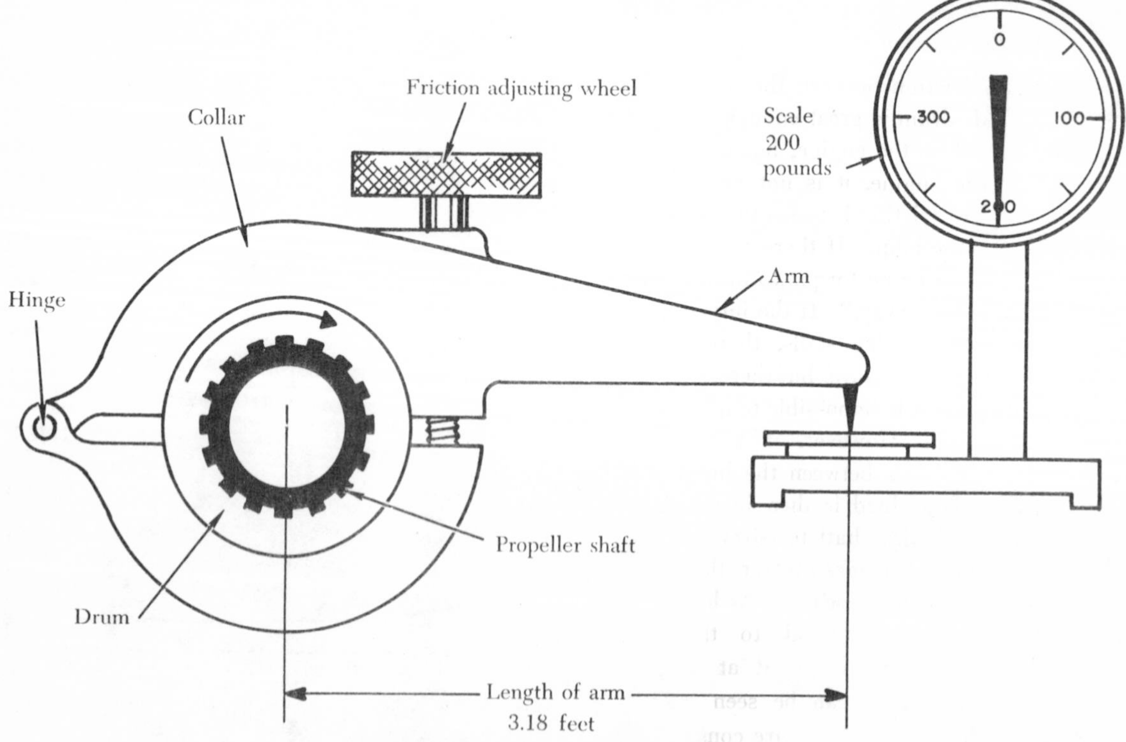

FIGURE 1–29. Typical Prony brake.

3.18 ft., the torque exerted by the shaft is:

$$200 \text{ lb.} \times 3.18 \text{ ft.} = 636 \text{ lb.-ft.}$$

Once the torque is known, the work done per revolution of the propeller shaft can be computed without difficulty by the equation:

$$\text{Work per revolution} = 2\pi \times \text{torque.}$$

If work per revolution is multiplied by the r.p.m., the result is work per minute, or power. If the work is expressed in ft.-lbs. per min., this quantity is divided by 33,000; the result is the brake horsepower of the shaft. In other words:

$$\text{Power} = \text{Work per revolution} \times \text{r.p.m.}$$

$$\text{and b.hp.} = \frac{\text{Work per revolution} \times \text{r.p.m.}}{33{,}000},$$

$$\text{or b.hp.} = \frac{2\pi \times \text{force on the scales (lbs.)} \times \text{length of arm (ft.)} \times \text{r.p.m.}}{33{,}000}.$$

Example

Given:

Force on scales = 200 lbs.
Length of arm = 3.18 ft.
r.p.m. = 3,000
π = 3.1416.

Find b.hp.:

Substituting in equation—

$$\text{b.hp.} = \frac{6.2832 \times 200 \times 3.18 \times 3{,}000}{33{,}000}$$

$$= 363.2$$

$$= 363.$$

As long as the friction between the brake collar and propeller shaft drum is great enough to impose an appreciable load on the engine, but is not great enough to stop the engine, it is not necessary to know the amount of friction between the collar and drum to compute the b.hp. If there were no load imposed, there would be no torque to measure, and the engine would "run away." If the imposed load is so great that the engine stalls, there may be considerable torque to measure, but there will be no r.p.m. In either case it is impossible to measure the b.hp. of the engine. However, if a reasonable amount of friction exists between the brake drum and the collar and the load is then increased, the tendency of the propeller shaft to carry the collar and arm about with it becomes greater, thus imposing a greater force upon the scales. As long as the torque increase is proportional to the r.p.m. decrease, the horsepower delivered at the shaft remains unchanged. This can be seen from the equation in which 2π and 33,000 are constants and torque and r.p.m. are variables. If the change in r.p.m. is inversely proportional to the change in torque, their product will remain unchanged. Therefore, b.hp. remains unchanged. This is important. It shows that horsepower is the function of both torque and r.p.m., and can be changed by changing either torque or r.p.m., or both.

Friction Horsepower

Friction horsepower is the indicated horsepower minus brake horsepower. It is the horsepower used by an engine in overcoming the friction of moving parts, drawing in fuel, expelling exhaust, driving oil and fuel pumps, and the like. On modern aircraft engines, this power loss through friction may be as high as 10 to 15% of the indicated horsepower.

Friction and Brake Mean Effective Pressures

The IMEP (indicated mean effective pressure), discussed previously, is the average pressure produced in the combustion chamber during the operating cycle and is an expression of the theoretical, frictionless power known as indicated horsepower. In addition to completely disregarding power lost to friction, indicated horsepower gives no indication as to how much actual power is delivered to the propeller shaft for doing useful work. However, it is related to actual pressures which occur in the cylinder and can be used as a measure of these pressures.

To compute the friction loss and net power output, the indicated horsepower of a cylinder may be thought of as two separate powers, each producing a different effect. The first power overcomes internal friction, and the horsepower thus consumed is known as friction horsepower. The second power, known as brake horsepower, produces useful work at the propeller. Logically, therefore, that portion of IMEP that produces brake horsepower is called BMEP (brake mean effective pressure). The remaining pressure used to overcome internal friction is called FMEP (friction mean effective pressure). This is illustrated in figure 1–30. IMEP is a useful expression of total cylinder power output, but is not a real physical quantity; likewise, FMEP and BMEP are theoretical but useful expressions of friction losses and net power output.

Although BMEP and FMEP have no real existence in the cylinder, they provide a convenient means of representing pressure limits, or rating engine performance throughout its entire operating range. This is true since there is a relationship between IMEP, BMEP, and FMEP.

One of the basic limitations placed on engine operation is the pressure developed in the cylinder during combustion. In the discussion of compression ratios and indicated mean effective pressure, it was found that, within limits, the increased pressure resulted in increased power. It was also noted that if the cylinder pressure was not controlled

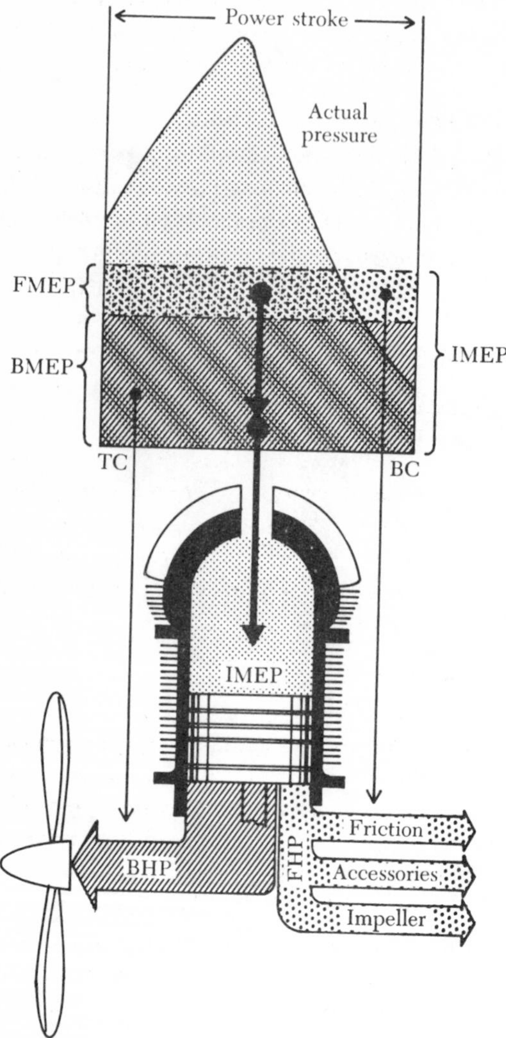

FIGURE 1–30. Powers and pressures.

within close limits, it would impose dangerous internal loads that might result in engine failure. It is therefore important to have a means of determining these cylinder pressures as a protective measure and for efficient application of power.

If the b.hp. is known, the BMEP can be computed by means of the following equation:

$$\text{BMEP} = \frac{\text{b.hp. x } 33{,}000}{\text{LANK}}.$$

Example

Given:

b.hp. $= 1{,}000$
Stroke $= 6$ in.
Bore $= 5.5$ in.
r.p.m. $= 3{,}000$
No. of cyls. $= 12$.

Find BMEP:

Find length of stroke (in ft.):
$L = 0.5$.

Find area of cylinder bore:
$A = 1/4\pi D^2$
$= 0.7854 \text{ x } 5.5 \text{ x } 5.5$
$= 23.76$ sq. in.

Find No. of power strokes per min.:
$N = 1/2 \text{ x r.p.m.}$
$= 1/2 \text{ x } 3{,}000$
$= 1{,}500.$

Then substituting in the equation:

$$\text{BMEP} = \frac{1{,}000 \text{ x } 33{,}000}{.5 \text{ x } 23.76 \text{ x } 1{,}500 \text{ x } 12}$$

$= 154.32$ lbs. per sq. in.

Thrust Horsepower

Thrust horsepower can be considered as the result of the engine and the propeller working together. If a propeller could be designed to be 100% efficient, the thrust- and the brake-horsepower would be the same. However, the efficiency of the propeller varies with the engine speed, attitude, altitude, temperature, and airspeed, thus the ratio of the thrust horsepower and the brake horsepower delivered to the propeller shaft will never be equal. For example, if an engine develops 1,000 b.hp., and it is used with a propeller having 85 percent efficiency, the thrust horsepower of that engine-propeller combination is 85 percent of 1,000 or 850 thrust hp. Of the four types of horsepower discussed, it is the thrust horsepower that determines the performance of the engine-propeller combination.

EFFICIENCIES

Thermal Efficiency

Any study of engines and power involves consideration of heat as the source of power. The heat produced by the burning of gasoline in the cylinders causes a rapid expansion of the gases in the cylinder, and this, in turn, moves the pistons and creates mechanical energy.

It has long been known that mechanical work can be converted into heat and that a given amount of heat contains the energy equivalent of a certain amount of mechanical work. Heat and work are theoretically interchangeable and bear a fixed relation to each other. Heat can therefore be measured in work units (for example, ft.-lbs.) as well as in heat units. The B.t.u. (British thermal unit) of heat is the quantity of heat required to raise the temperature of 1 lb. of water 1° F. It is equivalent to 778 ft.-lbs. of mechanical work. A pound of petroleum fuel, when burned with enough air to consume it completely, gives up about 20,000 B.t.u., the equivalent of 15,560,000 ft.-lbs. of mechanical work. These quantities express the heat energy of the fuel in heat and work units, respectively.

The ratio of useful work done by an engine to the heat energy of the fuel it uses, expressed in work or heat units, is called the thermal efficiency of the engine. If two similar engines use equal amounts of fuel, obviously the engine which converts into work the greater part of the energy in the fuel (higher thermal efficiency) will deliver the greater amount of power. Furthermore, the engine which has the higher thermal efficiency will have less waste heat to dispose of to the valves, cylinders, pistons, and cooling system of the engine. A high thermal efficiency also means a low specific fuel consumption and, therefore, less fuel for a flight of a given distance at a given power. Thus, the practical importance of a high thermal efficiency is threefold, and it constitutes one of the most desirable features in the performance of an aircraft engine.

Of the total heat produced, 25 to 30% is utilized for power output; 15 to 20% is lost in cooling (heat radiated from cylinder head fins); 5 to 10% is lost in overcoming friction of moving parts; and 40 to 45% is lost through the exhaust. Anything which increases the heat content that goes into mechanical work on the piston, which reduces the friction and pumping losses, or which reduces the quantity of unburned fuel or the heat lost to the engine parts, increases the thermal efficiency.

The portion of the total heat of combustion which is turned into mechanical work depends to a great extent upon the compression ratio. Compression ratio is the ratio of the piston displacement plus combustion chamber space to the combustion chamber space. Other things being equal, the higher the compression ratio, the larger is the proportion of the heat energy of combustion turned into useful work at the crankshaft. On the other hand, increasing the compression ratio increases the cylinder head temperature. This is a limiting factor, for the extremely high temperature created by high compression ratios causes the material in the cylinder to deterioriate rapidly and the fuel to detonate.

The thermal efficiency of an engine may be based on either b.hp. or i.hp. and is represented by the formula:

$$\text{Indicated thermal efficiency} = \frac{\text{i.hp. x } 33{,}000}{\text{weight of fuel burned/min. x heat value x } 778}.$$

The formula for brake thermal efficiency is the same as shown above, except the value for b.hp. is inserted instead of the value for i.hp.

Example

An engine delivers 85 b.hp. for a period of 1 hr. and during that time consumes 50 lbs. of fuel. Assuming the fuel has a heat content of 18,800 B.t.u. per lb., find the thermal efficiency of the engine:

$$\frac{85 \text{ x } 33{,}000}{.833 \text{ x } 18{,}800 \text{ x } 778} = \frac{2{,}805{,}000}{12{,}184{,}569}.$$

Brake thermal efficiency = 0.23 or 23%.

Reciprocating engines are only about 34% thermally efficient; that is, they transform only about 34% of the total heat produced by the burning fuel into mechanical energy. The remainder of the heat is lost through the exhaust gases, the cooling system, and the friction within the engine. Thermal distribution in a reciprocating engine is illustrated in figure 1–31.

Mechanical Efficiency

Mechanical efficiency is the ratio that shows how much of the power developed by the expanding gases in the cylinder is actually delivered to the output shaft. It is a comparison between the b.hp. and the i.hp. It can be expressed by the formula:

$$\text{Mechanical efficiency} = \frac{\text{b.hp.}}{\text{i.hp.}}.$$

Brake horsepower is the useful power delivered to the propeller shaft. Indicated horsepower is the total hp. developed in the cylinders. The difference between the two is f.hp. (friction horsepower), the power lost in overcoming friction.

The factor that has the greatest effect on mechanical efficiency is the friction within the engine itself. The friction between moving parts in an engine remains practically constant throughout an engine's speed range. Therefore, the mechanical efficiency of an engine will be highest when the engine is running at the r.p.m. at which maximum b.hp. is developed. Mechanical efficiency of the average aircraft reciprocating engine approaches 90%.

Heat released
by combustion.

25-30% is converted
into useful power.

40-45% is carried
out with exhaust.

5-10% is removed
by the oil.

15-20% is removed
by fins.

FIGURE 1–31. Thermal distribution in an engine.

Volumetric Efficiency

Volumetric efficiency, another engine efficiency, is a ratio expressed in terms of percentages. It is a comparison of the volume of fuel/air charge (corrected for temperature and pressure) inducted into the cylinders to the total piston displacement of the engine. Various factors cause departure from a 100% volumetric efficiency.

The pistons of an unsupercharged engine displace the same volume each time they sweep the cylinders from top center to bottom center. The amount of charge that fills this volume on the intake stroke depends on the existing pressure and temperature of the surrounding atmosphere. Therefore, to find the volumetric efficiency of an engine, standards for atmospheric pressure and temperature had to be established. The U.S. standard atmosphere was established in 1958 and provides the necessary pressure and temperature values to calculate volumetric efficiency.

The standard sea-level temperature is 59° F. or 15° C. At this temperature the pressure of one atmosphere is 14.69 lbs./sq. in., and this pressure will support a column of mercury 29.92 in. high. These standard sea-level conditions determine a standard density, and if the engine draws in a volume of charge of this density exactly equal to its piston displacement, it is said to be operating at 100% volumetric efficiency. An engine drawing in less volume than this has a volumetric efficiency lower than 100%. An engine equipped with a high-speed internal or external blower may have a volumetric efficiency greater than 100%. The equation for volumetric efficiency is:

$$\text{Volumetric efficiency} = \frac{\text{Volume of charge (corrected for temperature and pressure)}}{\text{Piston displacement}}.$$

Many factors decrease volumetric efficiency; some of these are:

(1) Part-throttle operation.
(2) Long intake pipes of small diameter.
(3) Sharp bends in the induction system.
(4) Carburetor air temperature too high.
(5) Cylinder-head temperature too high.
(6) Incomplete scavenging.
(7) Improper valve timing.

Propulsive Efficiency

A propeller is used with an engine to provide thrust. The engine supplies b.hp. through a rotating shaft, and the propeller absorbs the b.hp. and converts it into thrust hp. In this conversion, some power is wasted. Since the efficiency of any machine is the ratio of useful power output to the power input, propulsive efficiency (in this case, propeller efficiency) is the ratio of thrust hp. to b.hp. On the average, thrust hp. constitutes approximately 80% of the b.hp. The other 20% is lost in friction and slippage. Controlling the blade angle of the propeller is the best method of obtaining maximum propulsive efficiency for all conditions encountered in flight.

During takeoff, when the aircraft is moving at low speeds and when maximum power and thrust are required, a low propeller blade angle will give maximum thrust. For high-speed flying or diving, the blade angle is increased to obtain maximum thrust and efficiency. The constant-speed propeller is used to give required thrust at maximum efficiency for all flight conditions.

TURBINE ENGINE CONSTRUCTION

In a reciprocating engine the functions of intake, compression, combustion, and exhaust all take place in the same combustion chamber; consequently, each must have exclusive occupancy of the chamber during its respective part of the combustion cycle. A significant feature of the gas turbine engine, however, is that a separate section is devoted to each function, and all functions are performed simultaneously without interruption.

A typical gas turbine engine consists of:

(1) An air inlet.
(2) Compressor section.
(3) Combustion section.
(4) Turbine section.
(5) Exhaust section.
(6) Accessory section.
(7) The systems necessary for starting, lubrication, fuel supply, and auxiliary purposes, such as anti-icing, cooling, and pressurization.

The major components of all turbine engines are basically the same; however, the nomenclature of the component parts of various engines currently in use will vary slightly due to the difference in each manufacturer's terminology. These differences are reflected in the applicable maintenance manuals.

The greatest single factor influencing the construction features of any gas turbine engine is the type compressor (axial flow or centrifugal flow) for which the engine is designed. Later in the chapter a detailed description of compressors is given, but for the time being examine figures 1–32 and 1–33. Notice the physical effect the two types of compressors have on engine construction features. It is obvious that there is a difference in their length and diameter.

Note that in the axial-flow engine the air inlet

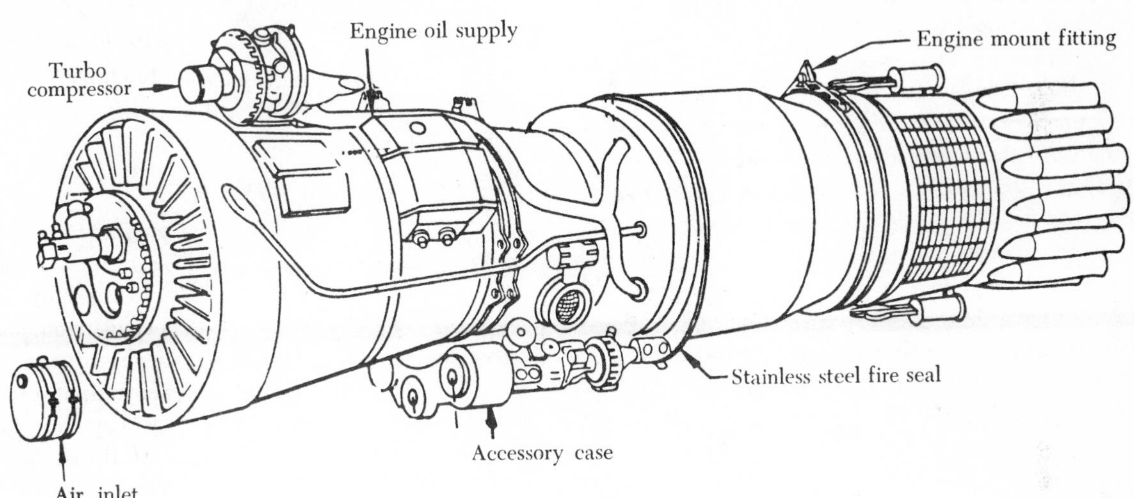

FIGURE 1–32. Axial-flow engine.

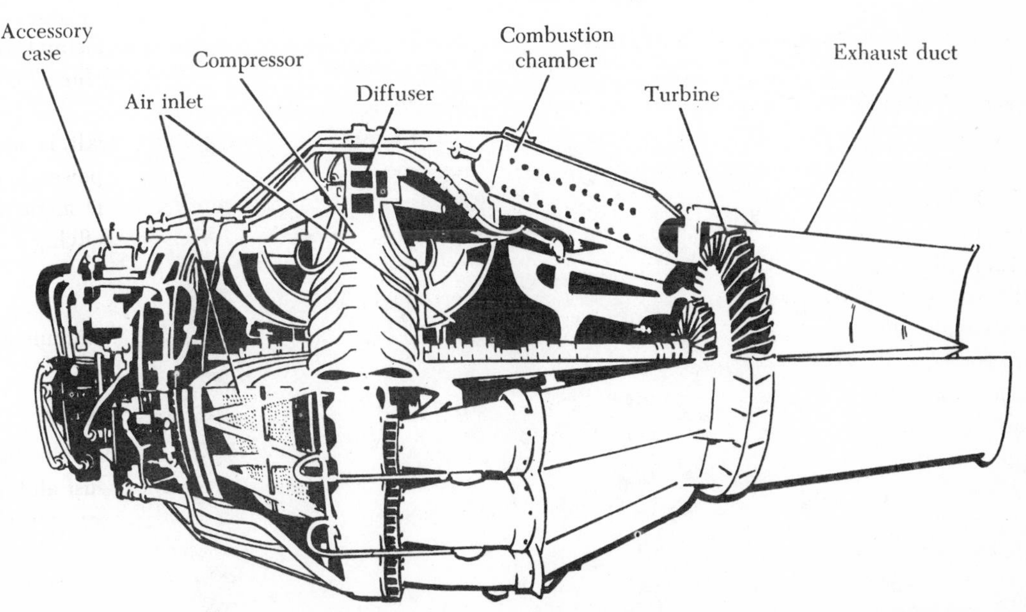

FIGURE 1–33. Centrifugal-flow engine.

duct is one of the major engine components; on the other hand, in the centrifugal-flow engine, air enters the air inlet and is directed to the compressor inducer vanes through circumferential inlets located in front and back of the impeller. The inlets are screened to prevent entry of foreign objects that could cause serious damage to the metal components if allowed to enter the compressor.

The accessories of the two types of engines are located at different points on the engines. This is necessary because of engine construction. The front of the axial-flow engine is utilized for air entrance; consequently, the accessories must be located elsewhere.

Other than the features previously mentioned, there is little visual dissimilarity between the remaining major components of the two engines.

AIR ENTRANCE

The air entrance is designed to conduct incoming air to the compressor with a minimum energy loss resulting from drag or ram pressure loss; that is, the flow of air into the compressor should be free of turbulence to achieve maximum operating efficiency. Proper design contributes materially to aircraft performance by increasing the ratio of compressor discharge pressure to duct inlet pressure.

The amount of air passing through the engine is dependent upon three factors:

(1) The compressor speed (r.p.m.).
(2) The forward speed of the aircraft.
(3) The density of the ambient (surrounding) air.

Inlets may be classified as:

(1) *Nose* inlets, located in the nose of the fuselage, or powerplant pod or nacelle.
(2) *Wing* inlets, located along the leading edge of the wing, usually at the root for single-engine installations.
(3) *Annular* inlets, encircling, in whole or in part, the fuselage or powerplant pod or nacelle.
(4) *Scoop* inlets, which project beyond the immediate surface of the fuselage or nacelle.
(5) *Flush* inlets, which are recessed in the side of the fuselage, powerplant pod, or nacelle.

There are two basic types of air entrances in use: the single entrance and the divided entrance. Generally, it is advantageous to use a single entrance with an axial-flow engine to obtain maximum ram pressure through straight flow. It is used almost exclusively on wing or external installations where the unobstructed entrance lends itself readily to a single, short, straight duct.

A divided entrance offers greater opportunity to diffuse the incoming air and enter the plenum chamber with the low velocity required to utilize efficiently a double-entry compressor. (The plenum chamber is a storage place for ram air, usually asso-

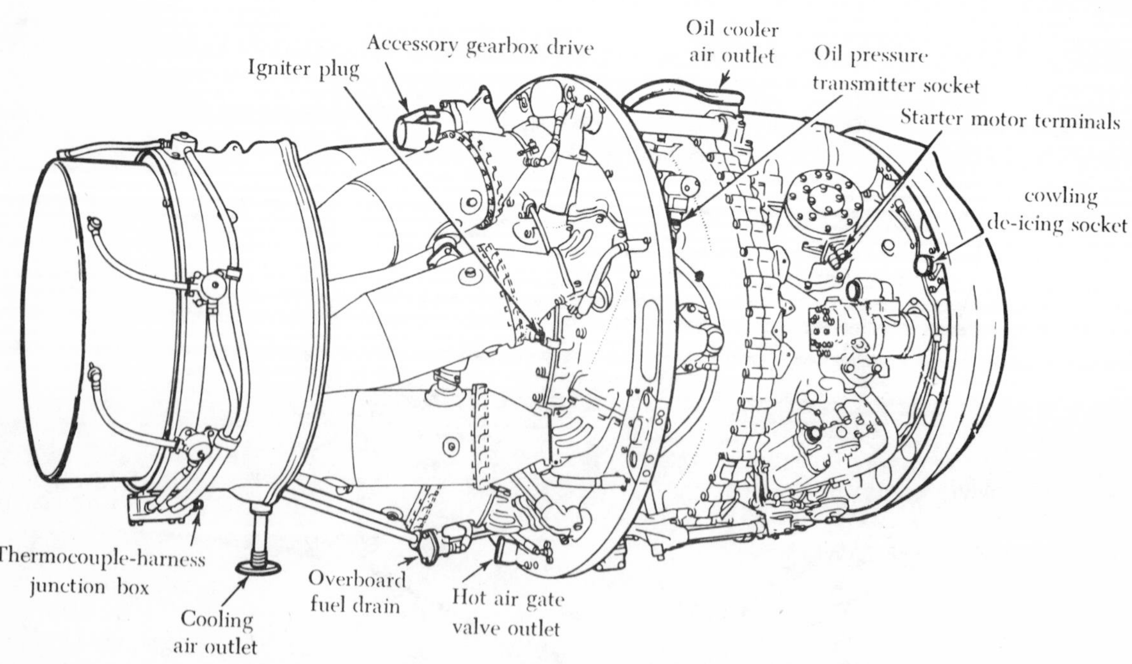

FIGURE 1–34. Accessory location on a centrifugal-flow engine.

ciated with fuselage installations.) It is also advantageous when the equipment installation or pilot location makes the use of a single or straight duct impractical. In most cases the divided entrance permits the use of very short ducts with a resultant small pressure drop through skin friction.

ACCESSORY SECTION

The accessory section of the turbojet engine has various functions. The primary function is to provide space for the mounting of accessories necessary for operation and control of the engine. Generally, it also includes accessories concerned with the aircraft, such as electric generators and fluid power-pumps. Secondary functions include acting as an oil reservoir and/or oil sump, and housing the accessory drive gears and reduction gears.

The arrangement and driving of accessories have always been major problems on gas turbine engines. Driven accessories are usually mounted on common pads either ahead of or adjacent to the compressor section, depending on whether the engine is centrifugal flow or axial flow. Figures 1–34 and 1–35 illustrate the accessory arrangement of a centrifugal-flow engine and an axial-flow engine, respectively.

The components of the accessory section of all centrifugal- and axial-flow engines have essentially the same purpose even though they often differ quite extensively in construction details and nomenclature.

The basic elements of the centrifugal-flow engine accessory section are (1) the accessory case, which has machined mounting pads for the engine-driven accessories, and (2) the gear train, which is housed within the accessory case.

The accessory case may be designed to act as an oil reservoir. If an oil tank is utilized, a sump is usually provided below the front bearing support for the drainage and scavenging of oil used to lubricate bearings and drive gears.

The accessory case is also provided with adequate tubing or cored passages for spraying lubricating oil on the gear train and supporting bearings.

The gear train is driven by the engine rotor through an accessory drive shaft gear coupling, which splines with a shaft gear and the rotor assembly compressor hub. The reduction gearing within the case provides suitable drive speeds for each engine accessory or component. Because the rotor

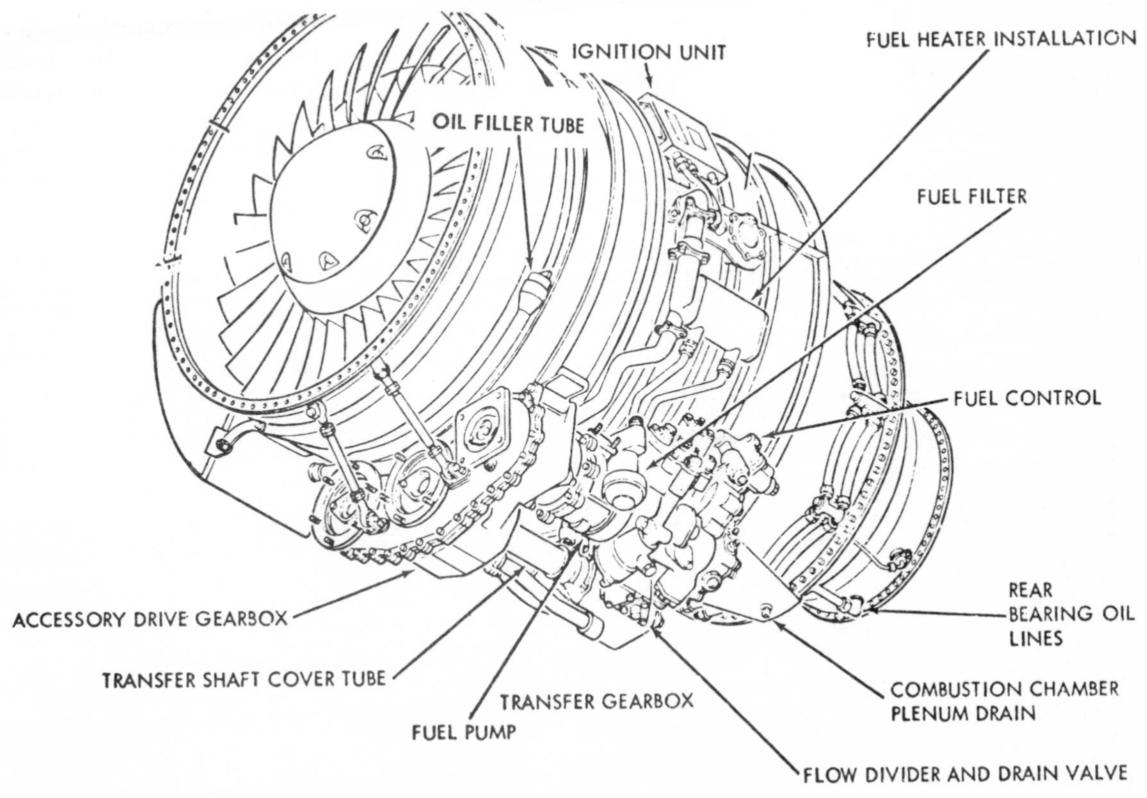

FIGURE 1–35. Accessory arrangement on an axial-flow engine.

operating r.p.m. is so high, the accessory reduction gear ratios are relatively high. The accessory drives are supported by ball bearings assembled in the mounting pad bores of the accessory case.

The components of an axial-flow engine accessory section are an accessory gearbox and a power takeoff assembly, housing the necessary drive shafts and reduction gears. Figure 1–36 shows the location of the accessory gearbox.

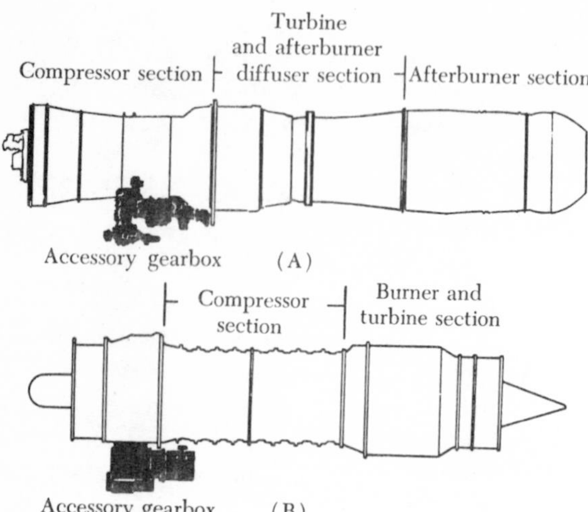

FIGURE 1–36. (A) Accessory gearbox mounted beneath the compressor; (B) Accessory gearbox mounted beneath the front bearing support.

Although the close relationship of the accessory gearbox and the power takeoff necessitates their being located near each other, two factors affect the location of gearboxes. They are engine diameter and engine installation.

Designers are forever striving to reduce engine diameter to make the engine more streamlined, thereby increasing aircraft performance by reducing drag. Also, engine installation in a particular aircraft may dictate the location or re-arrangement of the accessory gearboxes.

The accessory gearbox has basically the same functions as the accessory case of the centrifugal-flow engine. It has the usual machined mounting pads for the engine accessories, and it houses and supports the accessory drive gear trains. Also included are adequate tubing and cored passages for lubricating the gear trains and their supporting bearings.

The accessories usually provided on engines are the fuel control with its governing device; the high-pressure fuel pump(s); oil pressure pump and scavenge pump(s); auxiliary fuel pump and sometimes a starting fuel pump; and several engine accessories including starter, generator, and tachometer. Although these accessories are for the most part essential, the particular combination of engine-driven accessories depends upon the use for which the engine is designed.

The accessories mentioned above (except starters) are the engine-driven type. Also associated with the engine systems are the nondriven accessories, such as ignition exciters, fuel or oil filters, barometric units, drip valves, compressor bleed valves, and relief valves.

COMPRESSOR SECTION

The compressor section of the turbojet engine has many functions. Its primary function is to supply air in sufficient quantity to satisfy the requirements of the combustion burners. Specifically, to fulfill its purpose, the compressor must increase the pressure of the mass of air received from the air inlet duct and then discharge it to the burners in the quantity and at the pressures required.

A secondary function of the compressor is to supply bleed-air for various purposes in the engine and aircraft.

The bleed-air is taken from any of the various pressure stages of the compressor. The exact location of the bleed ports is, of course, dependent on the pressure or temperature required for a particular job. The ports are small openings in the compressor case adjacent to the particular stage from which the air is to be bled; thus, varying degrees of pressure or heat are available simply by tapping into the appropriate stage. Air is often bled from the final or highest pressure stage, since at this point, pressure and air temperature are at a maximum. At times it may be necessary to cool this high-pressure air. If it is used for cabin pressurization or other purposes where excess heat would be uncomfortable or detrimental, the air is sent through a refrigeration unit.

Bleed air is utilized in a wide variety of ways, including driving the previously mentioned remote-driven accessories. Some of the current applications of bleed air are:

(1) Cabin pressurization, heating, and cooling.
(2) Deicing and anti-icing equipment.
(3) Pneumatic starting of engines.
(4) Auxiliary drive units (ADU).

(5) Control-booster servosystems.

(6) Power for running instruments.

The compressor section's location depends on the type of compressor. Figures 1–32 and 1–33 have already illustrated how the arrangement of engine components varies with compressor type. In the centrifugal-flow engine, the compressor is located between the accessory section and the combustion section; in the axial-flow engine the compressor is located between the air inlet duct and the combustion section.

Compressor Types

The two principal types of compressors currently being used in turbojet aircraft engines are centrifugal flow and axial flow. The compressor type is a means of engine classification.

Much use has been made of the terms "centrifugal flow" and "axial flow" to describe the engine and compressor. However, the terms are applicable to the flow of air through the compressor.

In the centrifugal-flow engine, the compressor achieves its purpose by picking up the entering air and accelerating it outwardly by centrifugal action. In the axial-flow engine, the air is compressed while continuing in its original direction of flow, thus avoiding the energy loss caused by turns. From inlet to exit the air flows along an axial path and is compressed at a ratio of approximately 1.25:1 per stage. The components of each of these two types of compressors have their individual functions in the compression of air for the combustion section.

Centrifugal-flow Compressors

The centrifugal-flow compressor consists basically of an impeller (rotor), a diffuser (stator), and a compressor manifold, illustrated in figure 1–37. The two main functional elements are the impeller and the diffuser. Although the diffuser is a separate unit and is placed inside and bolted to the manifold; the entire assembly (diffuser and manifold) is often referred to as the diffuser. For clarification during compressor familiarization, the units are treated individually.

The impeller is usually made from forged aluminum alloy, heat-treated, machined, and smoothed for minimum flow restriction and turbulence.

In some types the impeller is fabricated from a single forging. This type impeller is shown in figure 1–37 (A). In other types the curved inducer vanes are separate pieces as illustrated in figure 1–38.

The impeller, whose function is to pick up and accelerate the air outwardly to the diffuser, may be either of two types—single entry or double entry. Both are similar in construction to the reciprocating engine supercharger impeller, the double-entry type being similar to two impellers back to back. However, because of the much greater combustion air requirements in turbojet engines, the impellers are larger than supercharger impellers.

The principal differences between the two types of impellers are the size and the ducting arrangement. The double-entry type has a smaller diameter, but is usually operated at a higher rotational speed to assure sufficient airflow. The single-entry impeller permits convenient ducting directly to the impeller eye (inducer vanes) as opposed to the more complicated ducting necessary to reach the rear side of the double-entry type. Although slightly more efficient in receiving air, the single-entry impeller must be large in diameter to deliver the same quantity of air as the double-entry type. This, of course, increases the overall diameter of the engine.

Included in the ducting for double-entry compressor engines is the plenum chamber. This chamber is necessary for a double-entry compressor because the air must enter the engine at almost right angles to the engine axis. Therefore, the air must, in order to give a positive flow, surround the engine compressor at a positive pressure before entering the compressor.

Included in some installations, as a necessary part of the plenum chamber, are the auxiliary air-intake doors (blow-in doors). These blow-in doors admit air to the engine compartment during ground operation, when air requirements for the engine are in excess of the airflow through the inlet ducts. The doors are held closed by spring action when the engine is not operating. During operation, however, the doors open automatically whenever engine compartment pressure drops below atmospheric pressure. During takeoff and flight, ram air pressure in the engine compartment aids the springs in holding the doors closed.

The diffuser is an annular chamber provided with a number of vanes forming a series of divergent passages into the manifold. The diffuser vanes direct the flow of air from the impeller to the manifold at an angle designed to retain the maximum amount of energy imparted by the impeller. They also deliver the air to the manifold at a velocity and pressure satisfactory for use in the combustion

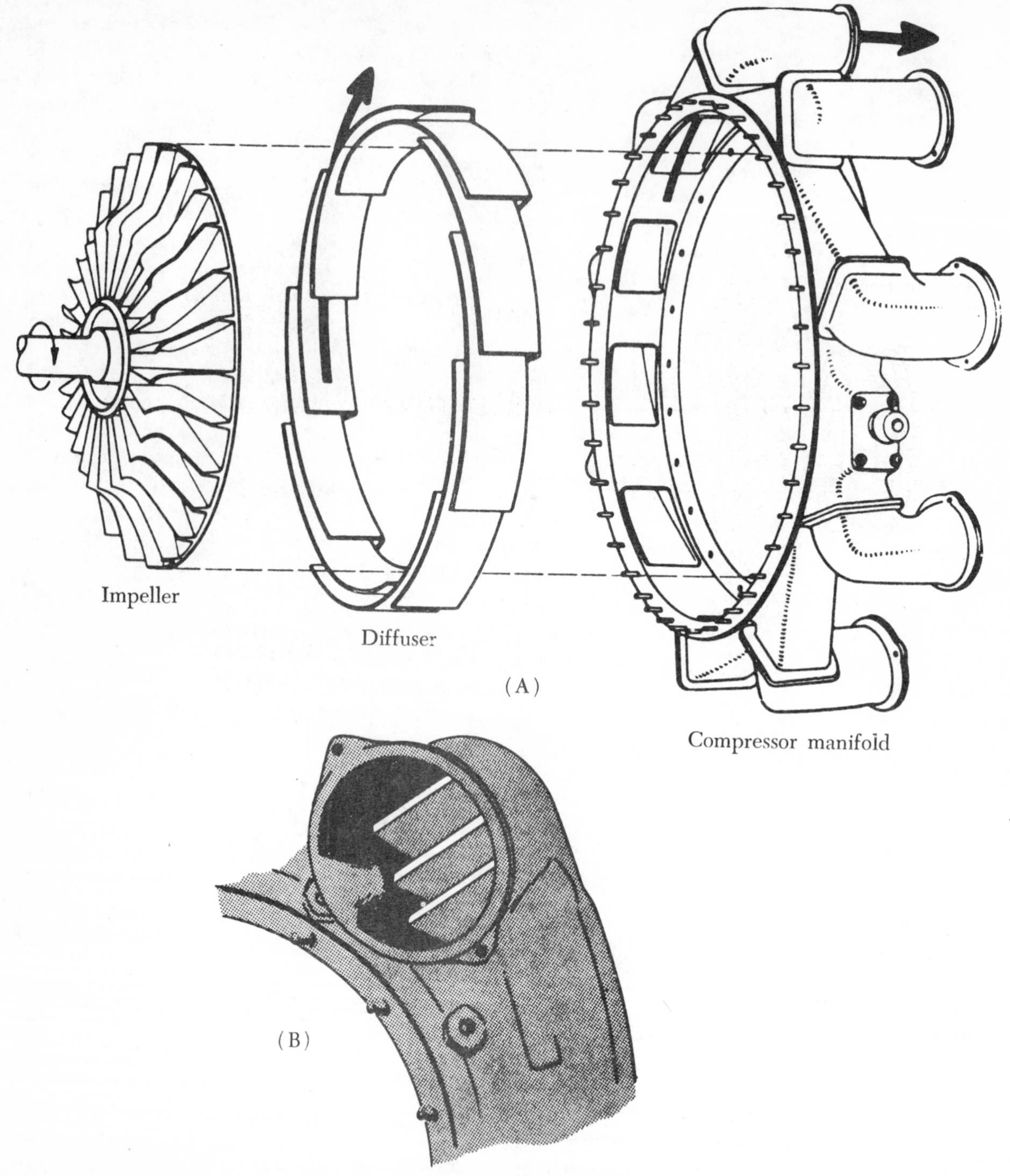

FIGURE 1–37. (A) Components of a centrifugal compressor; (B) Air outlet elbow with turning vanes for reducing air pressure losses.

chambers. Refer to figure 1–37 (A) and notice the arrow indicating the path of airflow through the diffuser, then through the manifold.

The compressor manifold shown in figure 1–37 (A) diverts the flow of air from the diffuser, which is an integral part of the manifold, into the combustion chambers. The manifold will have one outlet port for each chamber so that the air is evenly divided. A compressor outlet elbow is bolted to each of the outlet ports. These air outlets are constructed in the form of ducts and are known by a variety of names, such as air outlet ducts, outlet elbows, or

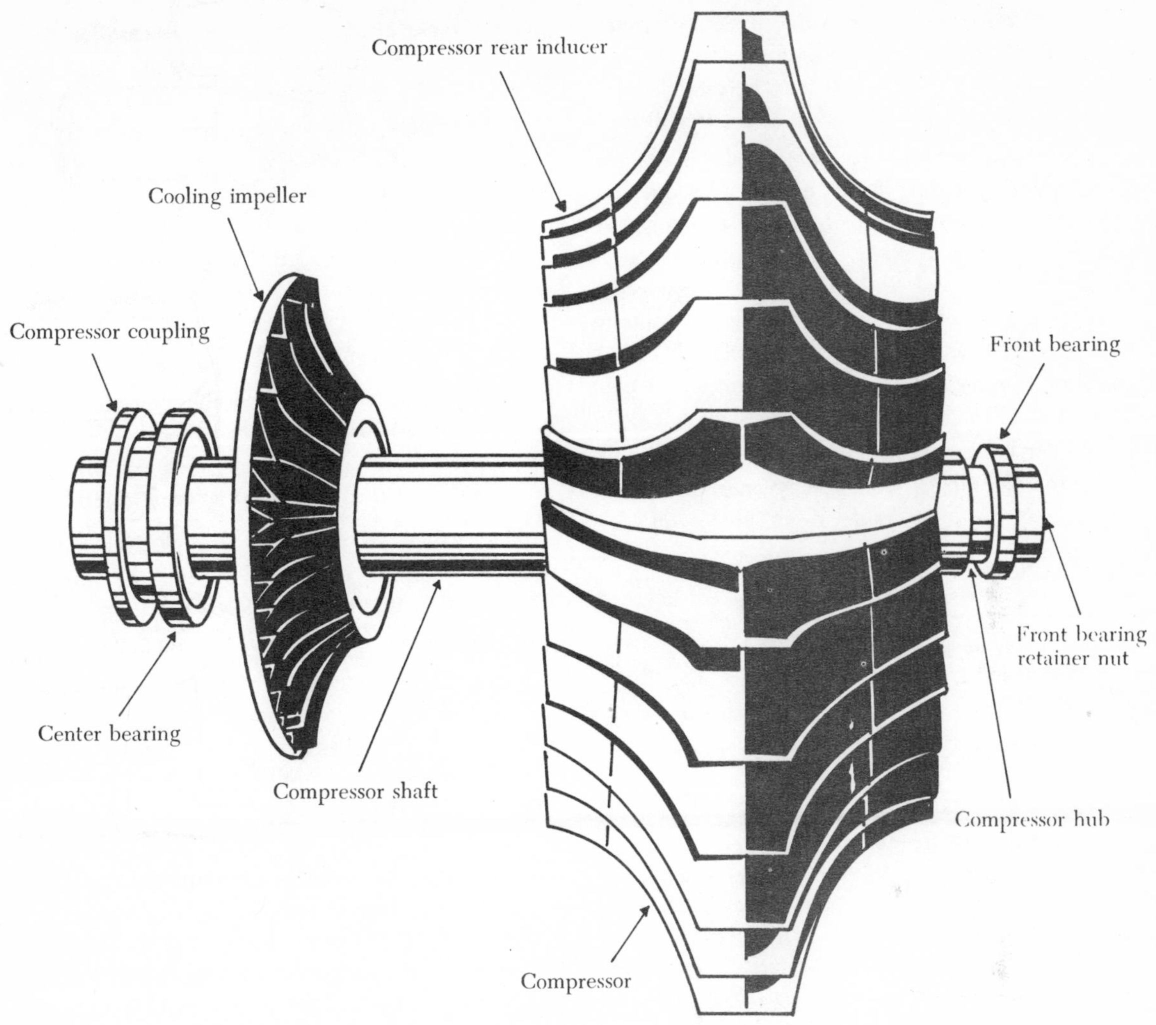

FIGURE 1–38. Double entry impeller with inducer vanes as separate pieces.

combustion chamber inlet ducts. Regardless of the terminology used, these outlet ducts perform a very important part of the diffusion process; that is, they change the radial direction of the airflow to an axial direction, where the diffusion process is completed after the turn. To help the elbows perform this function in an efficient manner, turning vanes (cascade vanes) are sometimes fitted inside the elbows. These vanes reduce air pressure losses by presenting a smooth, turning surface. (See figure 1–37 (B).)

Axial-flow Compressor

The axial-flow compressor has two main elements, a rotor and a stator. The rotor has blades fixed on a spindle. These blades impel air rearward in the same manner as a propeller because of their angle and airfoil contour. The rotor, turning at high speed, takes in air at the compressor inlet and impels it through a series of stages. The action of the rotor increases the compression of the air at each stage and accelerates it rearward through several stages. With this increased velocity, energy is transferred from the compressor to the air in the form of velocity energy. The stator blades act as diffusers at each stage, partially converting high velocity to pressure. Each consecutive pair of rotor and stator blades constitutes a pressure stage. The number of rows of blades (stages) is determined by the amount of air and total pressure rise required. The greater the number of stages, the higher the compression ratio. Most present-day engines utilize from 10 to 16 stages.

The stator has rows of blades, or vanes, dovetailed into split rings, which are in turn attached inside an enclosing case. The stator vanes project radially toward the rotor axis and fit closely on either side of each stage of the rotor.

The compressor case, into which the stator vanes are fitted, is horizontally divided into halves. Either the upper or lower half may be removed for inspection or maintenance of rotor and stator blades.

The function of the vanes is twofold. They are designed to receive air from the air inlet duct or from each preceding stage of the compressor and deliver it to the next stage or to the burners at a workable velocity and pressure. They also control the direction of air to each rotor stage to obtain the maximum possible compressor blade efficiency. Shown in figure 1–39 are the rotor and stator elements of a typical axial-flow compressor.

The rotor blades are usually preceded by an inlet guide vane assembly. The guide vanes direct the airflow into the first stage rotor blades at the proper angle and impart a swirling motion to the air entering the compressor. This pre-swirl, in the direction of engine rotation, improves the aerodynamic characteristics of the compressor by reducing the drag on the first-stage rotor blades. The inlet guide vanes are curved steel vanes usually welded to steel inner and outer shrouds. The inlet guide vanes may be preceded by a protective inlet screen. This screen reduces the chance of accidental entry of foreign bodies, such as stones, dirt, clothing, or other debris, into the compressor.

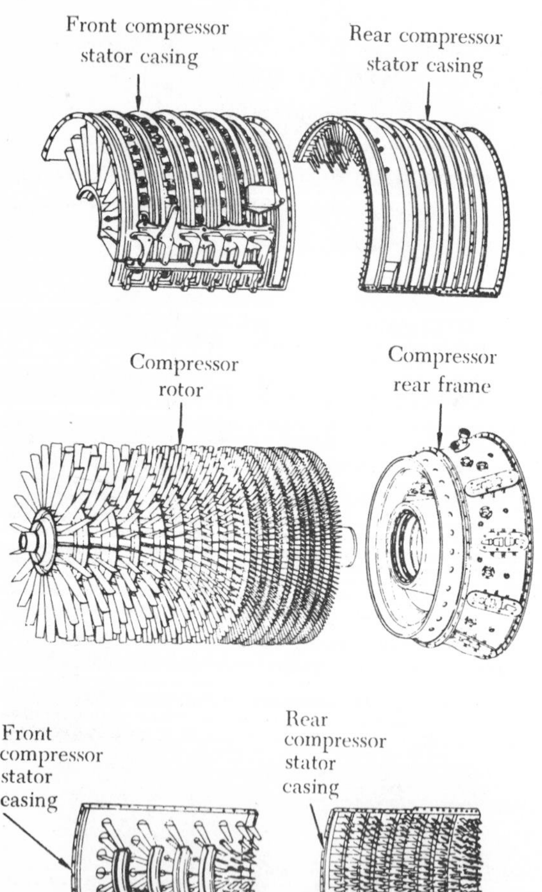

FIGURE 1–39. Rotor and stator components of an axial-flow compressor.

At the discharge end of the compressor, the stator vanes are constructed to straighten the airflow to eliminate turbulence. These vanes are called straightening vanes or the outlet vane assembly.

The casings of axial-flow compressors not only support the stator vanes and provide the outer wall of the axial path the air follows, but they also provide the means for extracting compressor air for various purposes.

The stator vanes are usually made of steel with corrosion- and erosion-resistant qualities. Quite frequently they are shrouded (or enclosed) by a band of suitable material to simplify the fastening problem. The vanes are welded into the shrouds, and the outer shroud is secured to the compressor housing inner wall by radial retaining screws.

The rotor blades are usually made of stainless steel. Methods of attaching the blades in the rotor disk rims vary in different designs, but they are commonly fitted into disks by either bulb-type or fir-tree-type roots. (See figure 1–40.) The blades are then locked by means of screws, peening, locking wires, pins, or keys.

Compressor blade tips are reduced in thickness by cutouts, referred to as blade "profiles." These profiles prevent serious damage to the blade or housing should the blades contact the compressor housing. This condition can occur if rotor blades become excessively loose or if rotor support is reduced by a malfunctioning bearing. Even though blade profiles greatly reduce such possibilities, occasionally a blade may break under stress of rubbing and cause considerable damage to compressor blades and stator vane assemblies.

The blades vary in length from entry to discharge because the annular working space (drum to casing) is reduced progressively toward the rear by the decrease in the casing diameter (see figure 1–41).

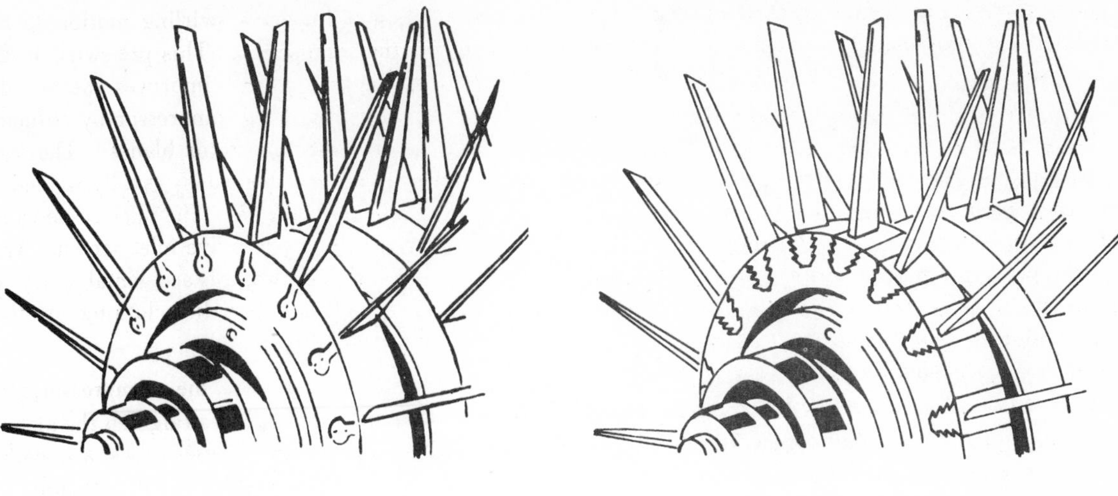

FIGURE 1–40. Common retention methods used on compressor rotor blades.

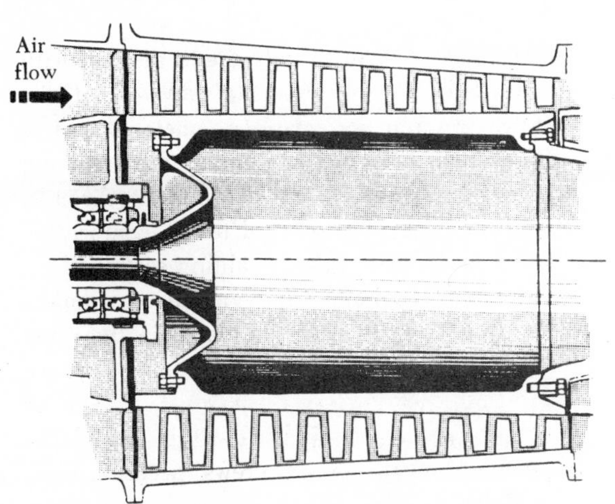

FIGURE 1–41. Drum-type compressor rotor.

Before leaving the subject of rotor familiarization, it may be well to mention that the rotor features either drum-type or disk-type construction.

The drum-type rotor consists of rings that are flanged to fit one against the other, wherein the entire assembly can then be held together by through bolts. This type of construction is satisfactory for low-speed compressors where centrifugal stresses are low.

The disk-type rotor consists of a series of disks machined from aluminum forgings, shrunk over a steel shaft, with rotor blades dovetailed into the disk rims. Another method of rotor construction is to machine the disks and shaft from a single aluminum forging, and then to bolt steel stub shafts on the front and rear of the assembly to provide bearing support surfaces and splines for joining the turbine shaft. The disk-type rotors are used almost exclusively in all present-day, high-speed engines and are the type referred to in this text. The drum-type and disk-type rotors are illustrated in figures 1–41 and 1–42, respectively.

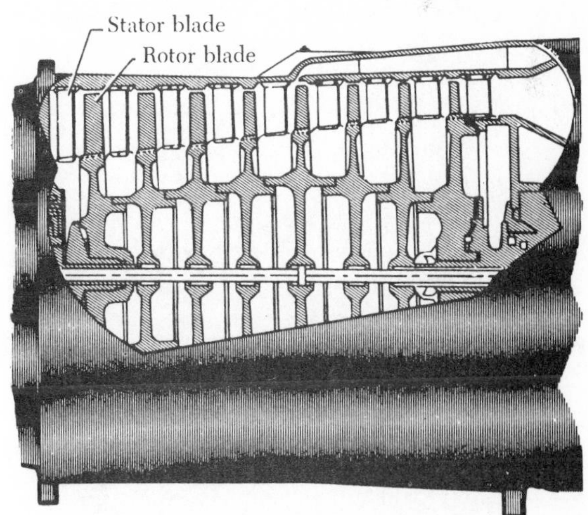

FIGURE 1–42. Disk-type compressor rotor.

The coverage of axial-flow compressors up to this point has dealt solely with the conventional single-rotor type. Actually, there are two configurations of the axial compressor currently in use, the single rotor and the dual rotor, sometimes referred to as solid spool and split spool, respectively.

One version of the solid-spool compressor uses

variable inlet guide vanes. Also, the first few rows of stator vanes are variable. This is the arrangement on the General Electric CJ805 engine. It incorporates a 17-stage compressor, and the angles of the inlet guide vanes and the first six stages of the stator vanes are variable. During operation, air enters the front of the engine and is directed into the compressor at the proper angle by the variable inlet guide and variable stator vanes. The air is compressed and forced into the combustion section. A fuel nozzle which extends into each combustion liner atomizes the fuel for combustion.

These variables are controlled in direct relation to the amount of power the engine is required to produce by the pilot's power lever position.

One version of the split-spool compressor is found in Pratt and Whitney's JT3C engine. It incorporates two compressors with their respective turbines and interconnecting shafts, which form two physically independent rotor systems.

As previously mentioned, centrifugal- and axial-flow engines dominate the gas-turbine field. There are, however, several possible configurations of these engine types, some of which have been tried experimentally, while others are still in the design or laboratory stage of development.

From an analysis of the centrifugal- and axial-flow engine compressors at their present stage of development, the axial-flow type appears to have definite advantages. The advent of the split-spool axial compressor made these advantages even more positive by offering greater starting flexibility and improved high-altitude performance.

The advantages and disadvantages of both types of compressors are included in the following list. Bear in mind that even though each compressor type has merits and limitations, the performance potential is the key to further development and use.

The centrifugal-flow compressor's advantages are:

(1) High pressure rise per stage.
(2) Good efficiencies over wide rotational speed range.
(3) Simplicity of manufacture, thus low cost.
(4) Low weight.
(5) Low starting power requirements.

The centrifugal-flow compressor's disadvantages are:

(1) Large frontal area for given airflow.
(2) More than two stages are not practical because of losses in turns between stages.

The axial-flow compressor's advantages are:

(1) High peak efficiencies.
(2) Small frontal area for given airflow.
(3) Straight-through flow, allowing high ram efficiency.
(4) Increased pressure rise by increasing number of stages with negligible losses.

The axial-flow compressor's disadvantages are:

(1) Good efficiencies over only narrow rotational speed range.
(2) Difficulty of manufacture and high cost.
(3) Relatively high weight.
(4) High starting power requirements. (This has been partially overcome by split compressors.)

COMBUSTION SECTION

The combustion section houses the combustion process, which raises the temperature of the air passing through the engine. This process releases energy contained in the air/fuel mixture. The major part of this energy is required at the turbine to drive the compressor. The remaining energy creates the reaction or propulsion and passes out the rear of the engine in the form of a high-velocity jet.

The primary function of the combustion section is, of course, to burn the fuel/air mixture, thereby adding heat energy to the air. To do this efficiently the combustion chamber must:

(1) Provide the means for proper mixing of the fuel and air to assure good combustion.
(2) Burn this mixture efficiently.
(3) Cool the hot combustion products to a temperature which the turbine blades can withstand under operating conditions.
(4) Deliver the hot gases to the turbine section.

The location of the combustion section is directly between the compressor and the turbine sections. The combustion chambers are always arranged coaxially with the compressor and turbine regardless of type, since the chambers must be in a through-flow position to function efficiently.

All combustion chambers contain the same basic elements:

(1) A casing.
(2) A perforated inner liner.
(3) A fuel injection system.
(4) Some means for initial ignition.
(5) A fuel drainage system to drain off unburned fuel after engine shutdown.

There are currently three basic types of combustion chambers, variations within these types being in detail only. These types are:

(1) The multiple-chamber or can type.

(2) The annular or basket type.

(3) The can-annular type.

The can-type combustion chamber is typical of the type used on both centrifugal- and axial-flow engines. It is particularly well suited for the centrifugal compressor engine, since the air leaving the compressor is already divided into equal portions as it leaves the diffuser vanes. It is then a simple matter to duct the air from the diffuser into the respective combustion chambers, arranged radially around the axis of the engine. The number of chambers will vary, since in the past (or development years) as few as two and as many as 16 chambers have been used. The present trend indicates the use of about eight or 10 combustion chambers. Figure 1–43 illustrates the arrangement for can-type combustion chambers. On American-built engines these chambers are numbered in a clockwise direction facing the rear of the engine with the No. 1 chamber at the top.

Each of the can-type combustion chambers consists of an outer case or housing, within which there is a perforated stainless steel (highly heat-resistant) combustion chamber liner or inner liner. (See figure 1–44.) The outer case is divided to facilitate liner replacement. The larger section or chamber body encases the liner at the exit end, and the smaller chamber cover encases the front or inlet end of the liner.

The interconnector (flame propagation) tubes are a necessary part of the can-type combustion chambers. Since each can is a separate burner operating independently of the other cans, there must be some way to spread combustion during the initial starting operation. This is accomplished by interconnecting all the chambers so that as the flame is started by the spark igniter plugs in two of the lower chambers, it will pass through the tubes and ignite the combustible mixture in the adjacent chamber, and continue on until all the chambers are burning.

The flame tubes will vary in construction details from one engine to another, although the basic components are almost identical.

The interconnector tubes are shown in figure 1–45. Bear in mind that not only must the chambers be interconnected by an outer tube (in this case a ferrule), but there must also be a slightly longer tube inside the outer one to interconnect the chamber liners where the flame is located. The outer tubes or jackets around the interconnecting flame tubes not only afford airflow between the chambers, but they also fulfill an insulating function around the hot flame tubes.

The spark igniters previously mentioned are normally two in number, and are located in two

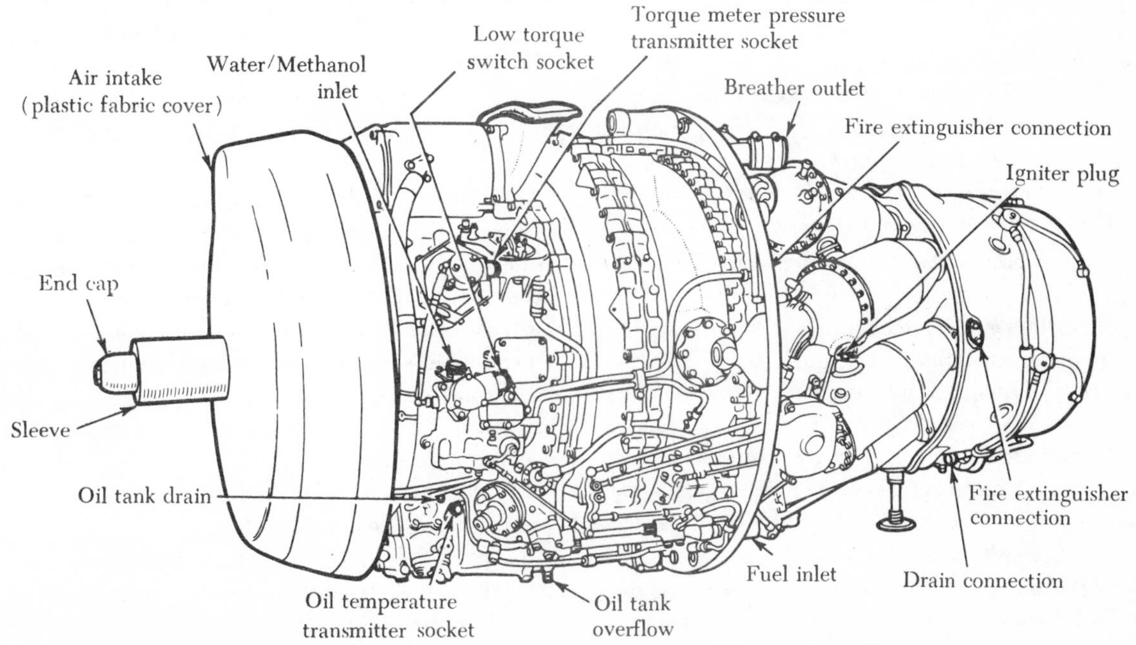

FIGURE 1–43. Can-type combustion chamber arrangement.

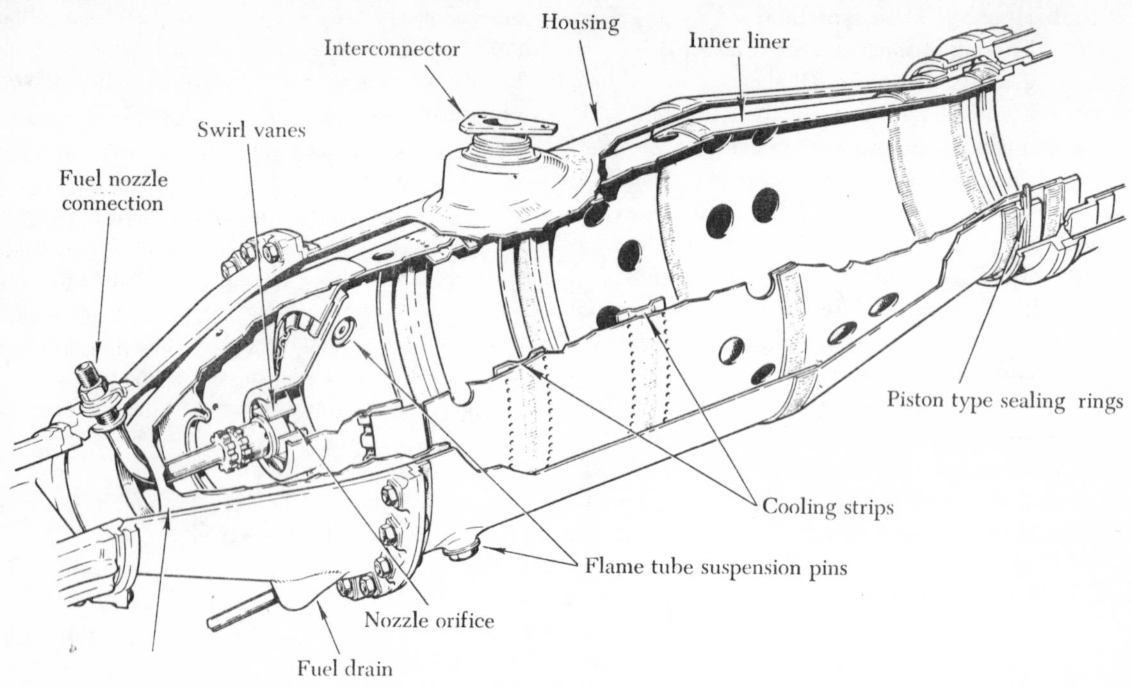

FIGURE 1–44. Can-type combustion chamber.

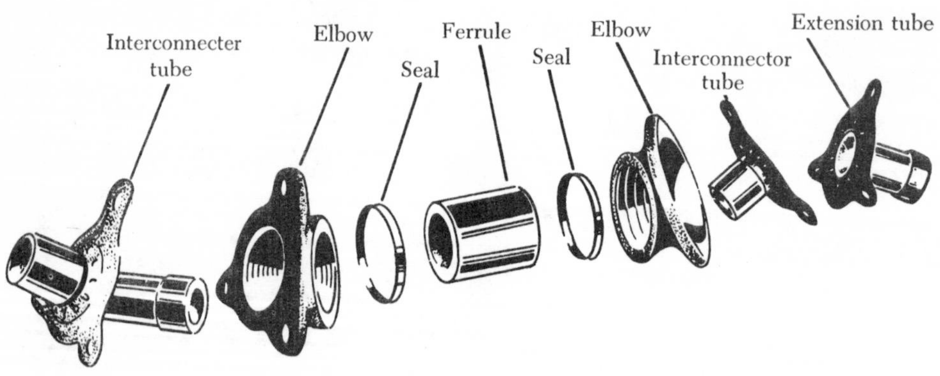

FIGURE 1–45. Interconnecting flame tubes for can-type combustion chambers.

of the can-type combustion chambers.

Another very important requirement in the construction of combustion chambers is providing the means for draining unburned fuel. This drainage prevents gum deposits in the fuel manifold, nozzles, and combustion chambers. These deposits are caused by the residue left when the fuel evaporates. Probably most important is the danger of afterfire if the fuel is allowed to accumulate after shutdown. If the fuel is not drained, a great possibility exists, that at the next starting attempt, the excess fuel in the combustion chamber will ignite, and tailpipe temperature will go beyond safe operating limits.

The liners of the can-type combustors (figure 1–44) have perforations of various sizes and shapes, each hole having a specific purpose and effect on the flame propagation within the liner. The air entering the combustion chamber is divided by the proper holes, louvers, and slots into two main streams—primary and secondary air. The primary or combustion air is directed inside the liner at the front end, where it mixes with the fuel and is burned. Secondary or cooling air passes between the outer casing and the liner and joins the combustion gases through larger holes toward the rear of the liner, cooling the combustion gases from about 3,500° F. to near 1,500° F. To aid in atomization of the fuel, holes are provided around the fuel nozzle in the dome or inlet end of the can-type combustor liner. Louvers are also provided along the axial length of the liners to direct a cooling layer of air along the inside wall of the liner. This layer of air also tends to control the flame pattern by keeping it centered in the liner, thereby preventing burning of the liner walls.

Figure 1–46 illustrates the flow of air through the louvers in the double-annular combustion chamber.

Some provision is always made in the combustion chamber case, or in the compressor air outlet elbow, for installation of a fuel nozzle. The fuel nozzle delivers the fuel into the liner in a finely atomized spray. The finer the spray, the more rapid and efficient the burning process.

Two types of fuel nozzles currently being used in the various types of combustion chambers are the simplex nozzle and the duplex nozzle. The construction features of these nozzles are covered in greater detail in Chapter 3, "Engine Fuel and Fuel Metering Systems."

The annular combustion chamber consists basically of a housing and a liner, as does the can type. The liner consists of an undivided circular shroud extending all the way around the outside of the turbine shaft housing. The chamber may be constructed of one or more baskets; that is, if two or more chambers are used, they are placed one outside the other in the same radial plane, hence, the double-annular chamber. The double-annular chamber is illustrated in figure 1–47.

The spark igniter plugs of the annular combustion chamber are the same basic type used in the can combustion chambers, although construction details may vary. There are usually two plugs mounted on the boss provided on each of the chamber housings. The plugs must be long enough to protrude from the housing into the outer annulus of the double-annular combustion chamber.

The can-annular type combustion chamber is a development by Pratt and Whitney for use in their JT3 axial-flow turbojet engine. Since this engine was to feature the split-spool compressor, it required a combustion chamber capable of meeting the stringent requirements of maximum strength and limited length with a high overall efficiency. These requirements were necessary because of the high air pressures and velocities present in a split-spool compressor, along with the shaft length limitations explained in the following two paragraphs.

The split compressor requires two concentric shafts joining the turbine stages to their respective compressors. The front compressor joined to the rear turbine stages requires the longest shaft. Because this shaft is inside the other, a limitation of diameter is imposed, with the result that the distance between the front compressor and the rear

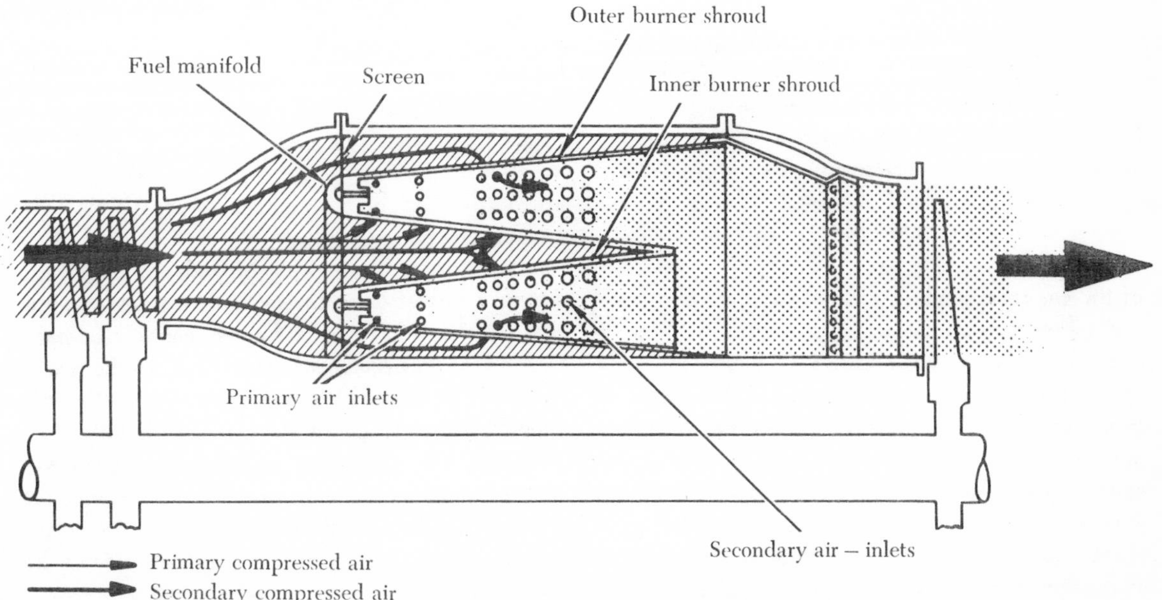

FIGURE 1–46. Components and airflow of a double-annular chamber.

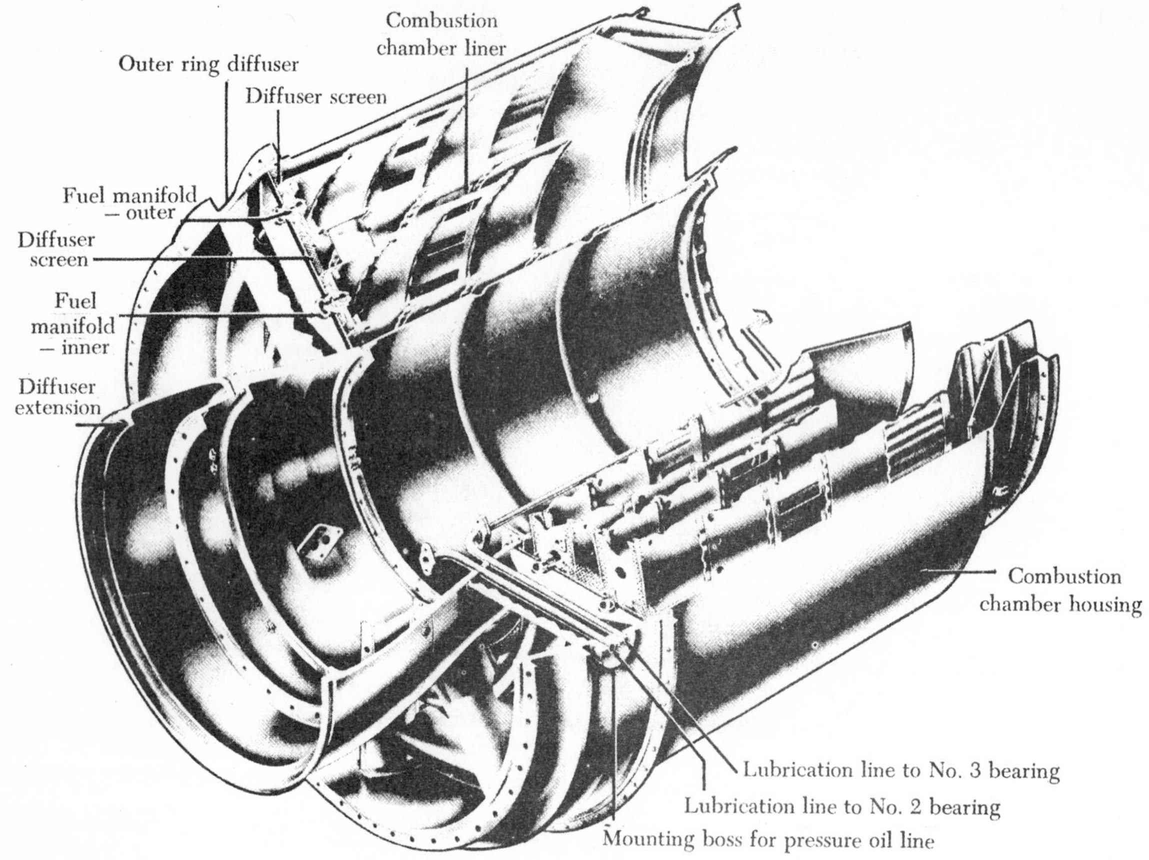

FIGURE 1–47. Double-annular combustion chamber.

turbine must be limited if critical shaft lengths are to be avoided.

Since the compressor and turbine are not susceptible to appreciable shortening, the necessary shaft length limitation had to be absorbed by developing a new type of burner. The designers had to develop a design that would give the desired performance in much less relative distance than had been previously assigned for this purpose.

The can-annular combustion chambers are arranged radially around the axis of the engine, the axis in this instance being the rotor shaft housing. Figure 1–48 shows this arrangement to advantage.

The combustion chambers are enclosed in a removable steel shroud, which covers the entire burner section. This feature makes the burners readily available for any required maintenance.

The burners are interconnected by projecting flame tubes which facilitate the engine-starting process as mentioned previously in the can-type combustion chamber familiarization. These flame tubes function identically with those previously discussed, but they differ in construction details.

Figure 1–48 also shows that each combustion chamber contains a central bullet-shaped perforated liner. The size and shape of the holes are designed to admit the correct quantity of air at the proper velocity and angle required. Cutouts are provided in two of the bottom chambers for installation of the spark igniters. Notice also in figure 1–48 how the combustion chambers are supported at the aft end by outlet duct clamps which secure them to the turbine nozzle assembly.

Again refer to figure 1–48 and notice how the forward face of each chamber presents six apertures which align with the six fuel nozzles of the corresponding fuel nozzle cluster. These nozzles are the dual-orifice (duplex) type requiring the use of a flow-divider (pressurizing valve), as mentioned in the can-type combustion chamber discussion. Around each nozzle are pre-swirl vanes for imparting a swirling motion to the fuel spray, which results in better atomization of the fuel, better burning and efficiency.

The swirl vanes perform two important functions imperative to proper flame propagation:

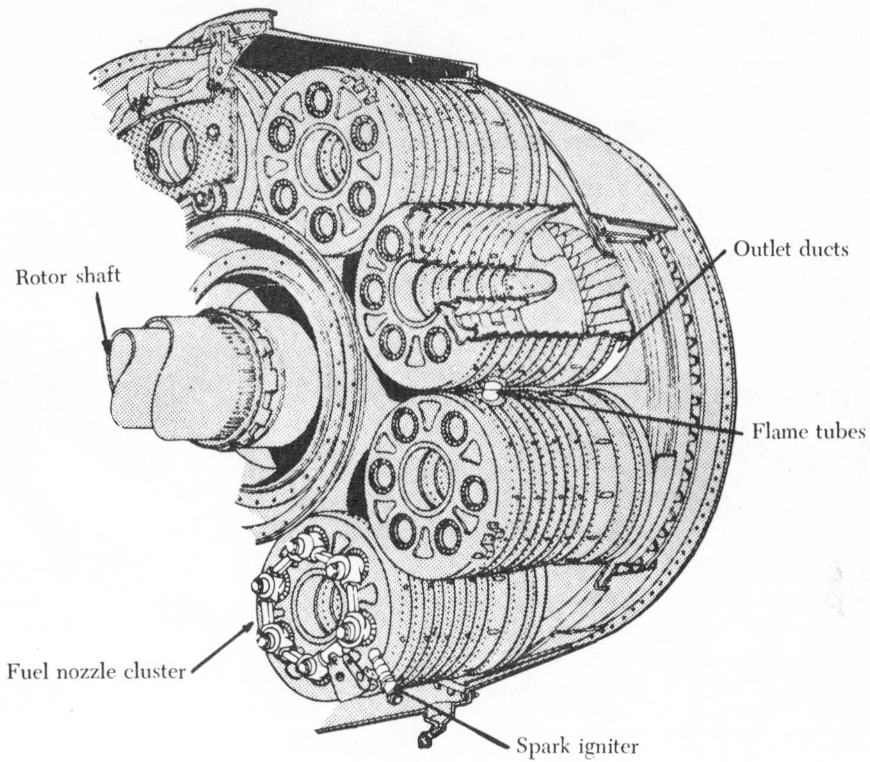

FIGURE 1–48. Can-annular combustion chamber components and arrangement.

(1) High flame speed: Better mixing of air and fuel, ensuring spontaneous burning.

(2) Low air velocity axially: Swirling eliminates flame moving axially too rapidly.

The swirl vanes greatly aid flame propagation, since a high degree of turbulence in the early combustion and cooling stages is desirable. The vigorous mechanical mixing of the fuel vapor with the primary air is necessary, since mixing by diffusion alone is too slow. This same mechanical mixing is also established by other means, such as placing coarse screens in the diffuser outlet, as is the case in most axial-flow engines.

The can-annular combustion chambers also must have the required fuel drain valves located in two or more of the bottom chambers, assuring proper drainage and elimination of residual fuel burning at the next start.

The flow of air through the holes and louvers of the can-annular chambers is almost identical with the flow through other types of burners. Special baffling is used to swirl the combustion airflow and to give it turbulence. Figure 1–49 shows the flow of combustion air, metal cooling air, and the diluent or gas cooling air. Pay particular attention to the direction of airflow indicated by the arrows.

Turbine Section

The turbine transforms a portion of the kinetic (velocity) energy of the exhaust gases into mechanical energy to drive the compressor and accessories. This is the sole purpose of the turbine and this function absorbs approximately 60 to 80% of the total pressure energy from the exhaust gases. The exact amount of energy absorption at the turbine is determined by the load the turbine is driving; that is, the compressor size and type, number of accessories, and a propeller and its reduction gears if the engine is a turbo-propeller type.

The turbine section of a turbojet engine is located aft, or downstream of the combustion chamber section. Specifically, it is directly behind the combustion chamber outlet.

The turbine assembly consists of two basic elements, the stator and the rotor, as does the compressor unit. These two elements are shown in figures 1–50 and 1–51, respectively.

The stator element is known by a variety of names, of which turbine nozzle vanes, turbine guide vanes, and nozzle diaphragm are three of the most commonly used. The turbine nozzle vanes are located directly aft of the combustion chambers and immediately forward of the turbine wheel.

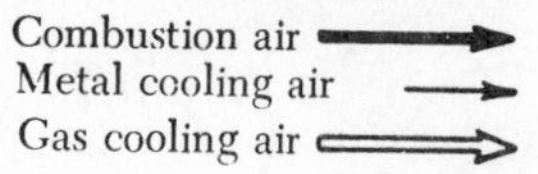

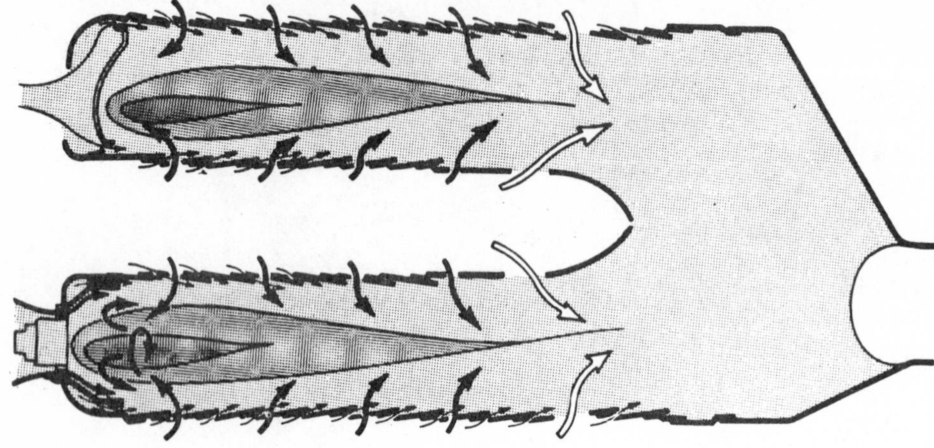

FIGURE 1–49. Airflow through a can-annular chamber.

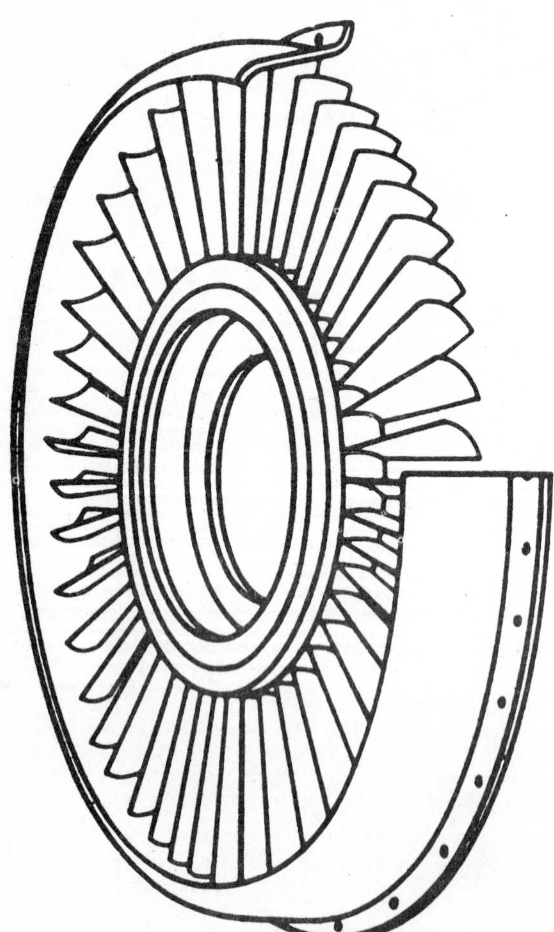

FIGURE 1–50. Stator element of the turbine assembly.

The function of the turbine nozzles is twofold. First, after the combustion chamber has introduced the heat energy into the mass airflow and delivered it evenly to the turbine nozzles, it becomes the job of the nozzles to prepare the mass air flow for driving the turbine rotor. The stationary blades or vanes of the turbine nozzles are contoured and set at such an angle that they form a number of small nozzles discharging the gas at extremely high speed; thus, the nozzle converts a varying portion of the heat and pressure energy to velocity energy which

FIGURE 1–51. Rotor element of the turbine assembly.

can then be converted to mechanical energy through the rotor blades.

The second purpose of the turbine nozzle is to deflect the gases to a specific angle in the direction of turbine wheel rotation. Since the gas flow from the nozzle must enter the turbine blade passageway while it is still rotating, it is essential to aim the gas in the general direction of turbine rotation.

The turbine nozzle assembly consists of an inner shroud and an outer shroud between which are fixed the nozzle vanes. The number of vanes employed vary with different types and sizes of engines. Figure 1–52 illustrates typical turbine nozzles featuring loose and welded vanes.

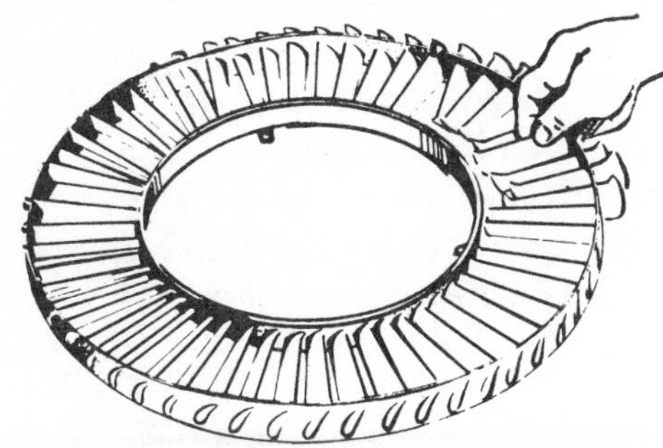

(A) Turbine nozzle vane assembly with loose fitting vanes;

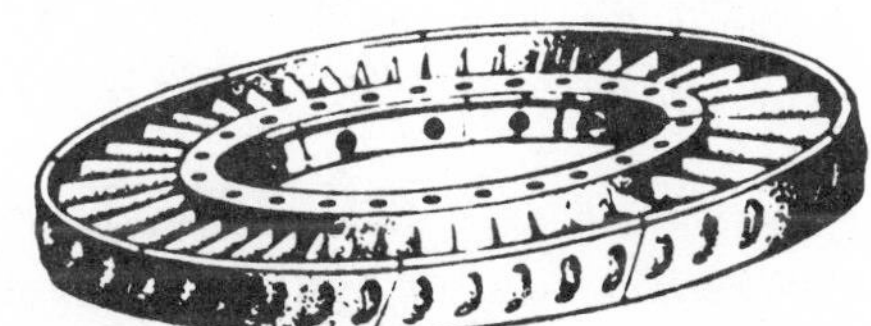

(B) Turbine nozzle vane assembly with welded vanes.

FIGURE 1–52. Typical turbine nozzles.

The blades or vanes of the turbine nozzle may be assembled between the outer and inner shrouds or rings in a variety of ways. Although the actual elements may vary slightly in their configuration and construction features, there is one characteristic peculiar to all turbine nozzles; that is, the nozzle vanes must be constructed to allow for thermal expansion. Otherwise, there would be severe distortion or warping of the metal components because of rapid temperature changes.

The thermal expansion of turbine nozzles is accomplished by one of several methods. One method necessitates the vanes being assembled loosely in the supporting inner and outer shrouds. (See figure 1–52(A).)

Each vane fits into a contoured slot in the shrouds, which conforms with the airfoil shape of the vane. These slots are slightly larger than the vanes to give a loose fit. For further support the inner and outer shrouds are encased by an inner and an outer support ring, which give increased strength and rigidity. These support rings also facilitate removal of the nozzle vanes as a unit; otherwise, the vanes could fall out as the shrouds were removed.

Another method of thermal expansion construction is to fit the vanes into inner and outer shrouds; however, in this method the vanes are welded or riveted into position. (See figure 1–52(B).) Some means must be provided to allow for thermal expansion; therefore, either the inner or the outer shroud ring is cut into segments. These saw cuts dividing the segments will allow sufficient expansion to prevent stress and warping of the vanes.

The rotor element of the turbine section consists essentially of a shaft and a wheel. (See figure 1–51.)

The turbine wheel is a dynamically balanced unit consisting of blades attached to a rotating disk. The disk, in turn, is attached to the main power-transmitting shaft of the engine. The jet gases leaving the turbine nozzle vanes act on the blades of the turbine wheel, causing the assembly to rotate at a very high rate of speed. The high rotational speed imposes severe centrifugal loads on the turbine wheel, and at the same time the elevated temperatures result in a lowering of the strength of the material. Consequently, the engine speed and temperature must be controlled to keep turbine operation within safe limits.

The turbine disk is referred to as such when in an unbladed form. When the turbine blades are installed, the disk then becomes the turbine wheel. The disk acts as an anchoring component for the turbine blades. Since the disk is bolted or welded to the shaft, the blades can transmit to the rotor shaft the energy they extract from the exhaust gases.

The disk rim is exposed to the hot gases passing through the blades and absorbs considerable heat from these gases. In addition, the rim also absorbs heat from the turbine buckets (blades) by conduction. Hence, disk rim temperatures normally are high and well above the temperatures of the more remote inner portion of the disk. As a result of these temperature gradients, thermal stresses are added to the rotational stresses.

There are various means to relieve, at least partially, the aforementioned stresses. One such means is to bleed cooling air back onto the face of the disk.

Another method of relieving the thermal stresses of the disk is incidental to blade installation. A series of grooves or notches, conforming to the blade root design, are broached in the rim of the disk. These grooves attach the turbine blades to the disk, and at the same time space is provided by the notches for thermal expansion of the disk. Sufficient clearance exists between the blade root and the notch to permit movement of the turbine blade when the disk is cold. During engine operation, expansion of the disk decreases the clearance. This causes the bucket root to fit tightly in the disk rim.

The turbine shaft, illustrated in figure 1–51, is usually fabricated from alloy steel. It must be capable of absorbing the high torque loads that are exerted when a heavy axial-flow compressor is started.

The methods of connecting the shaft to the turbine disk vary. In one method, the shaft is welded to the disk, which has a butt or protrusion provided for the joint. Another method is by bolting. This method requires that the shaft have a hub which matches a machined surface on the disk face. The bolts then are inserted through holes in the shaft hub and anchored in tapped holes in the disk. Of the two methods, the latter is more common.

The turbine shaft must have some means for attachment to the compressor rotor hub. This is usually accomplished by a spline cut on the forward end of the shaft. The spline fits into a coupling device between the compressor and turbine shafts. If a coupling is not used, the splined end of the turbine shaft may fit into a splined recess in the compressor rotor hub. This splined coupling arrangement is used almost exclusively with centrifugal compressor engines, while the axial compressor engine may use either of these described methods.

There are various ways of attaching turbine blades or buckets, some similar to compressor blade attachment. The most satisfactory method used is the fir-tree design shown in figure 1–53.

The blades are retained in their respective grooves by a variety of methods; some of the more common ones are peening, welding, locktabs, and riveting. Figure 1–54 shows a typical turbine wheel using rivets for blade retention.

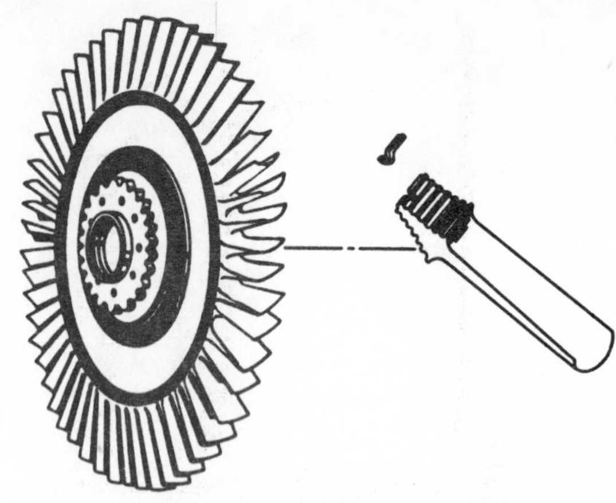

FIGURE 1–53. Turbine blade with fir-tree design and lock-tab method of blade retention.

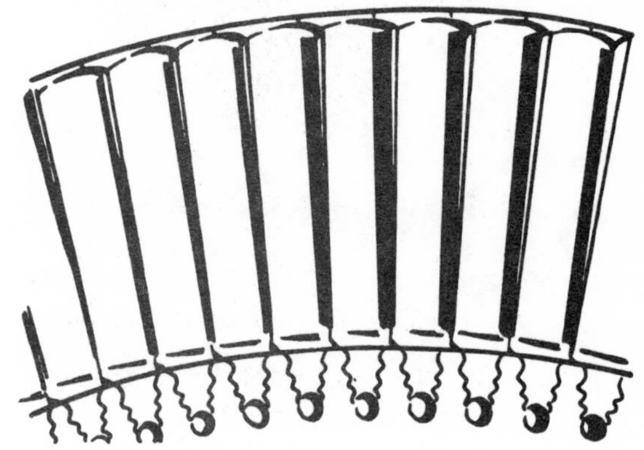

FIGURE 1–54. Riveting method of turbine blade retention.

The peening method of blade retention is used frequently in various ways. One of the most common applications of peening requires a small notch to be ground in the edge of the blade fir-tree root prior to the blade installation. After the blade is inserted into the disk, the notch is filled by the disk metal, which is "flowed" into it by a small punchmark made in the disk adjacent to the notch. The tool used for this job is similar to a center punch.

Another method of blade retention is to construct the root of the blade so that it will contain all the elements necessary for its retention. This method, illustrated in figure 1–55, shows that the blade root has a stop made on one end of the root so that the blade can be inserted and removed in one direction only, while on the opposite end is a tang. This tang is bent to secure the blade in the disk.

Turbine blades may be either forged or cast, depending on the composition of the alloys. Most

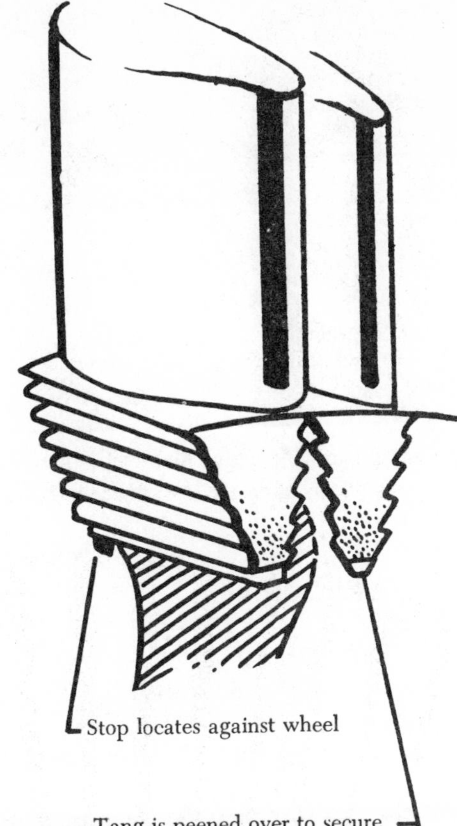

FIGURE 1–55. Turbine bucket, featuring tang method of blade retention.

blades are precision-cast and finish-ground to the desired shape.

Most turbines are open at the outer perimeter of the blades; however, a second type called the shrouded turbine is sometimes used. The shrouded turbine blades, in effect, form a band around the outer perimeter of the turbine wheel. This improves efficiency and vibration characteristics, and permits lighter stage weights; on the other hand, it limits turbine speed and requires more blades (see figure 1–56).

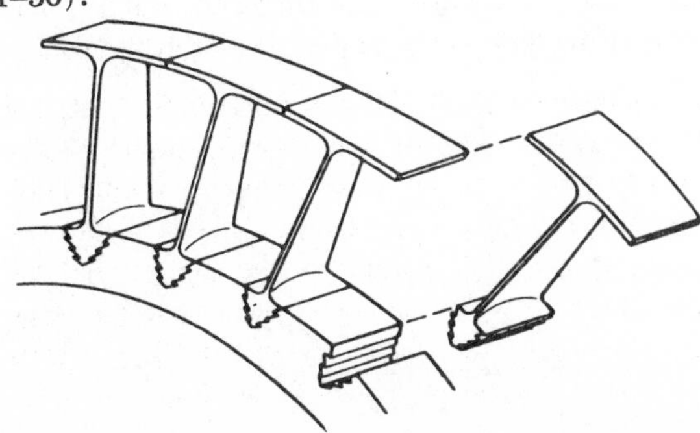

FIGURE 1–56. Shrouded turbine blades.

In turbine rotor construction, it occasionally becomes necessary to utilize turbines of more than one stage. A single turbine wheel often cannot absorb enough power from the exhaust gases to drive the components dependent on the turbine for rotative power, and thus, it is necessary to add additional turbine stages.

A turbine stage consists of a row of stationary vanes or nozzles, followed by a row of rotating blades. In some models of turboprop engine, as many as five turbine stages have been utilized successfully. It should be remembered that, regardless of the number of wheels necessary for driving engine components, there is always a turbine nozzle preceding each wheel.

As was brought out in the preceding discussion of turbine stages, the occasional use of more than one turbine wheel is warranted in cases of heavy rotational loads. It should also be pointed out that the same loads that necessitate multiple-stage turbines often make it advantageous to incorporate multiple compressor rotors.

In the single-stage rotor turbine (figure 1–57), the power is developed by one rotor, and all engine-driven parts are driven by this single wheel. This arrangement is used on engines where the need for low weight and compactness predominates.

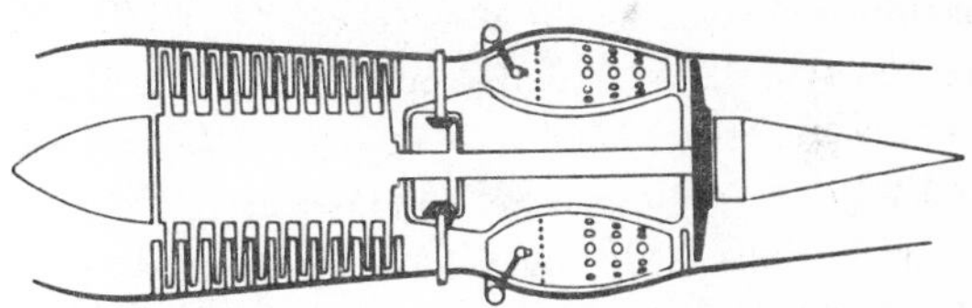

FIGURE 1–57. Single-stage rotor turbine.

In the multiple-rotor turbine the power is developed by two or more rotors. It is possible for each turbine rotor to drive a separate part of the engine. For example, a triple-rotor turbine can be so arranged that the first turbine drives the rear half of the compressor and the accessories, the second turbine drives the front half of the compressor, and the third turbine furnishes power to a propeller. (See figure 1–58.)

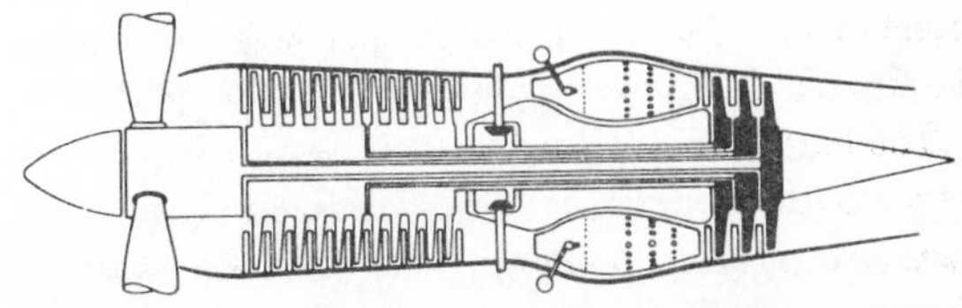

FIGURE 1–58. Multiple-rotor turbine.

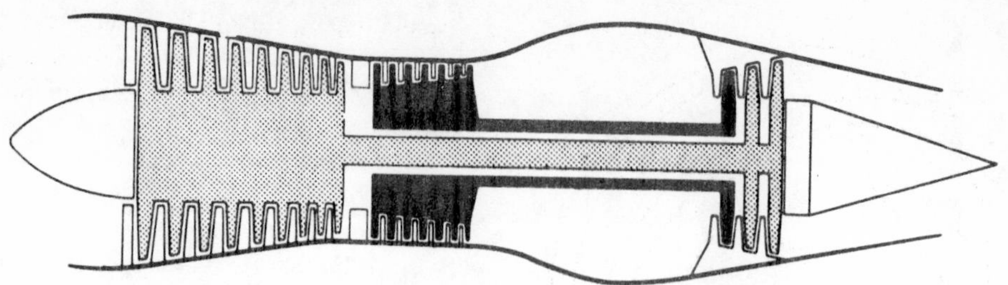

FIGURE 1–59. Dual-rotor turbine for split-spool compressor.

The turbine rotor arrangement for a dual-rotor turbine, such as required for a split-spool compressor, is similar to the arrangement in figure 1–58. The difference is that where the third turbine is used for a propeller in figure 1–58, it would be joined with the second turbine to make a two-stage turbine for driving the front compressor. This arrangement is shown in figure 1–59.

The remaining element to be discussed concerning turbine familiarization is the turbine casing or housing. The turbine casing encloses the turbine wheel and the nozzle vane assembly, and at the same time gives either direct or indirect support to the stator elements of the turbine section. It always has flanges provided front and rear for bolting the assembly to the combustion chamber housing and the exhaust cone assembly, respectively. A turbine casing is illustrated in figure 1–60.

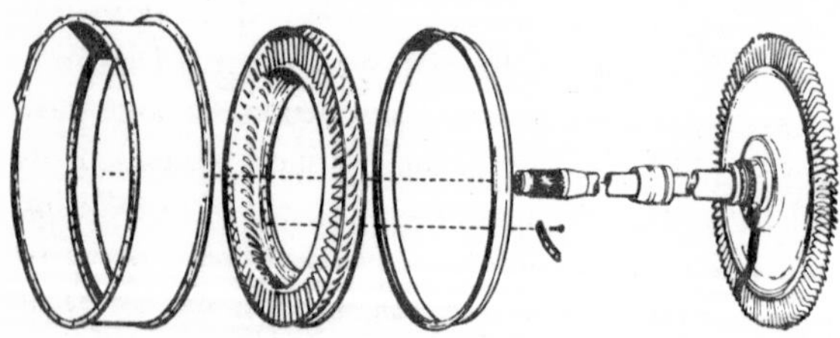

FIGURE 1–60. Turbine casing assembly.

Exhaust Section

The exhaust section of the turbojet engine is made up of several components, each of which has its individual functions. Although the components have individual purposes, they also have one common function: They must direct the flow of hot gases rearward in such a manner as to prevent turbulence and at the same time impart a high final or exit velocity to the gases.

In performing the various functions, each of the components affects the flow of gases in different ways as described in the following paragraphs.

The exhaust section is located directly behind the turbine section and ends when the gases are ejected at the rear in the form of a high-velocity jet. The components of the exhaust section include the exhaust cone, tailpipe (if required), and the exhaust or jet nozzle. Each component is discussed individually.

The exhaust cone collects the exhaust gases discharged from the turbine buckets and gradually converts them into a solid jet. In performing this, the velocity of the gases is decreased slightly and the pressure increased. This is due to the diverging passage between the outer duct and the inner cone; that is, the annular area between the two units increases rearward.

The exhaust cone assembly consists of an outer shell or duct, an inner cone, three or four radial hollow struts or fins, and the necessary number of tie rods to aid the struts in supporting the inner cone from the outer duct.

The outer shell or duct is usually made of stainless steel and is attached to the rear flange of the turbine case. This element collects the exhaust gases and delivers them either directly or via a tailpipe to the jet nozzle, depending, of course, on whether or not a tailpipe is required. In some engine installations a tailpipe is not needed. For instance, when the engine is installed in nacelles or pods, a short tailpipe is all that is required, in which case the exhaust duct and exhaust nozzle will suffice. The duct must be constructed to include such features as a predetermined number of thermocouple bosses for installing tailpipe temperature thermocouples, and there must also be the insertion holes for the supporting tie rods. In some cases, tie rods are not used for supporting the inner cone. If such is the case, the hollow struts provide the sole support of the inner cone, the struts being spot-welded in position to the inside surface of the duct and to the inner cone, respectively (see figure 1–61).

The radial struts actually have a twofold function. They not only support the inner cone in the exhaust

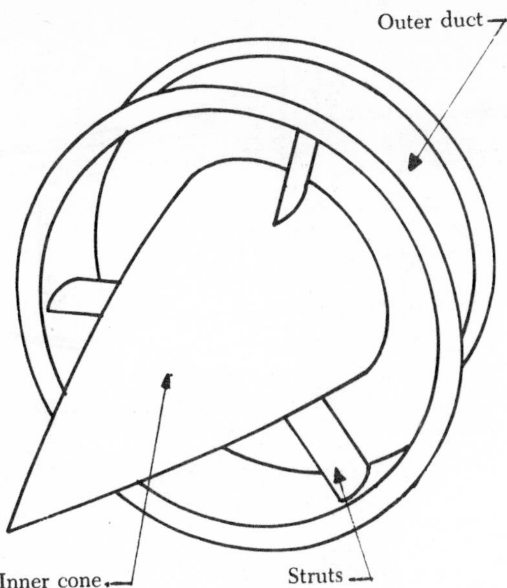

FIGURE 1–61. Exhaust collector with welded support struts.

duct, but they also perform the important function of straightening the swirling exhaust gases that would otherwise leave the turbine at an angle of approximately 45°.

The centrally located inner cone fits rather closely against the rear face of the turbine disk, preventing turbulence of the gases as they leave the turbine wheel. The cone is supported by the radial struts. In some configurations a small hole is located in the exit tip of the cone. This hole allows cooling air to be circulated from the aft end of the cone, where the pressure of the gases is relatively high, into the interior of the cone and consequently against the face of the turbine wheel. The flow of air is positive, since the air pressure at the turbine wheel is relatively low due to rotation of the wheel; thus air circulation is assured. The gases used for cooling the turbine wheel will return to the main path of flow by passing through the clearance between the turbine disk and the inner cone.

The exhaust cone assembly is the terminating component of the basic engine. The remaining components (the tailpipe and jet nozzle) are usually considered airframe components.

The tailpipe is used primarily to pipe the exhaust gases out of the airframe. The use of a tailpipe imposes a penalty on the operating efficiency of the engine in the form of heat and duct (friction) losses. These losses materially affect the final velocity of the exhaust gases and, hence, the thrust.

The tailpipe terminates in a jet nozzle located just forward of the end of the fuselage. Most installations use a single direct exhaust as opposed to a dual exit exhaust to obtain the advantages of low-weight, simplicity, and minimum duct losses (see figure 1–62).

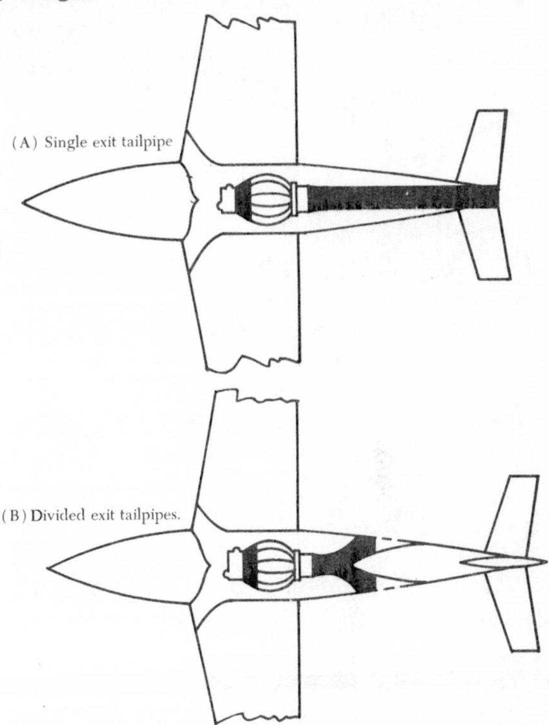

FIGURE 1–62. (A) Single exit tailpipe, (B) Divided exit tailpipes.

The tailpipe is usually constructed so that it is semiflexible. Again the necessity for this feature is dependent on its length. On extremely long tailpipes, a bellows arrangement is incorporated in its construction, allowing movement both in installation and maintenance, and in thermal expansion. This eliminates stress and warping which would otherwise be present.

The heat radiation from the exhaust cone and tailpipe could damage the airframe components surrounding these units. For this reason, some means of insulation had to be devised. There are several suitable methods of protecting the fuselage structure; two of the most common are insulation blankets and shrouds.

The insulation blanket, illustrated in figures 1–63 and 1–64, consists of several layers of aluminum foil, each separated by a layer of fiber glass or some other suitable material. Although these blankets protect the fuselage from heat radiation, they are primarily used to reduce heat losses from the exhaust system. The reduction of heat losses improves engine performance. A typical insulation blanket

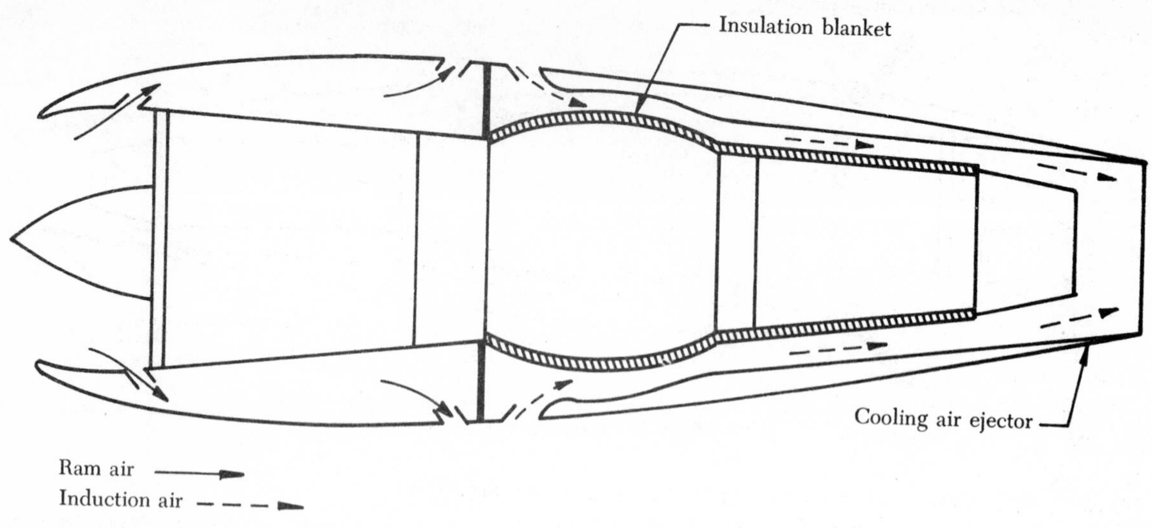

FIGURE 1–63. Exhaust system insulation blanket.

and the temperatures in the exhaust section are shown in figure 1–64. This blanket contains fiber glass as the low conductance material and aluminum foil as the radiation shield. The blanket should be suitably covered to prevent its becoming soaked with oil.

The heat shroud consists of a stainless steel envelope enclosing the exhaust system (see figure 1–65).

The exhaust or jet nozzle imparts to the exhaust gases the all-important final boost in velocity. The jet nozzle, like the tailpipe, is not included as part of the basic powerplant, but is supplied as a component of the airframe. The nozzle is attached to the rear of the tailpipe, if a tailpipe is required, or to the rear flange of the exhaust duct if a tailpipe is not necessary.

There are two types of jet nozzle design. They

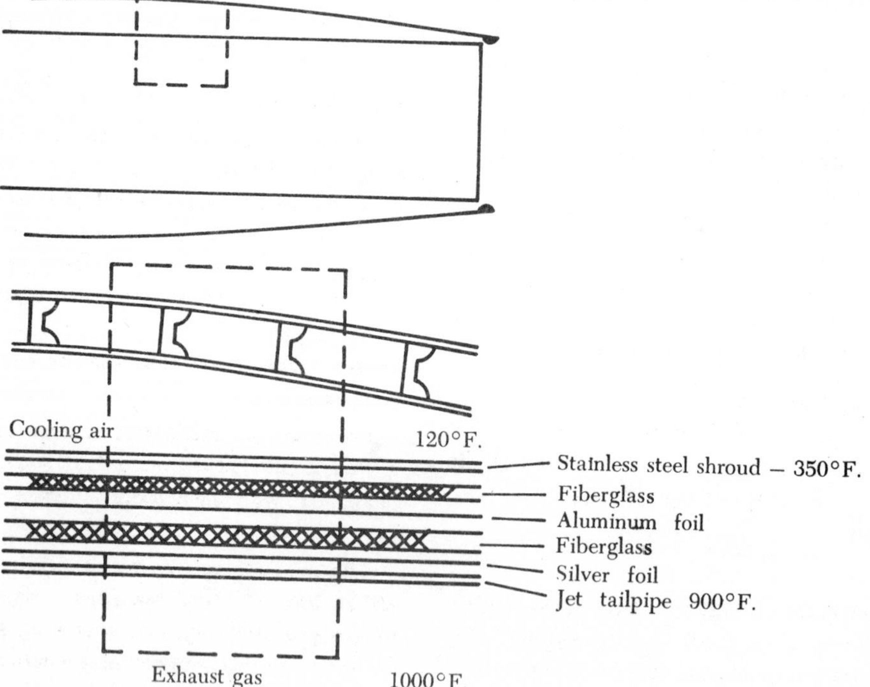

FIGURE 1–64. Insulation blanket with the temperatures which would be obtained at the various locations shown.

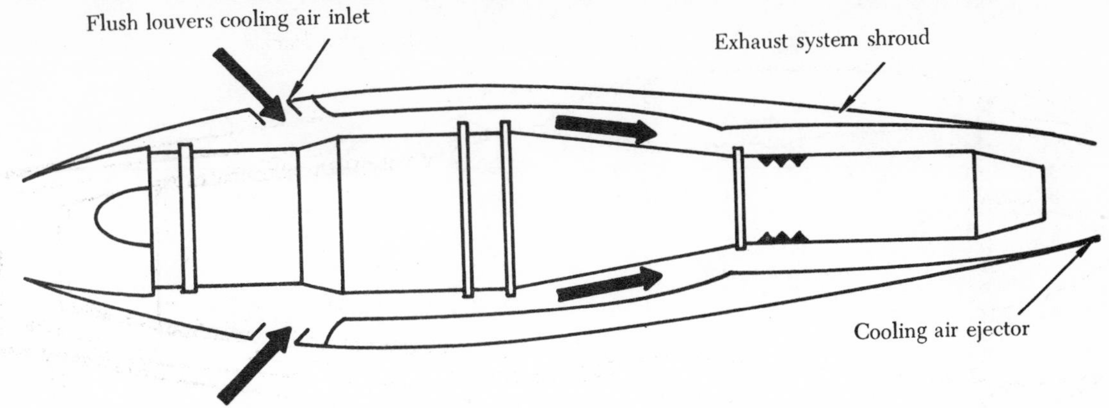

FIGURE 1–65. Exhaust system shroud.

are the converging design, for subsonic gas velocities, and the converging-diverging design for supersonic gas velocities. These are discussed in greater detail in Chapter 2, "Induction and Exhaust Systems."

The jet nozzle opening may be either fixed-area or variable-area. The fixed-area is the simpler of the two jet nozzles. Since there are no moving parts, any adjustment in nozzle area must be made mechanically.

Adjustments in nozzle area are sometimes necessary because the size of the exit orifice will directly affect the operating temperature of the engine. When necessary, a fixed-area nozzle can be adjusted in one of several ways. One method of changing nozzle area is to use inserts, which fit inside the nozzle and are held in place by screws.

The inserts are of varying curvatures and sizes. The different size inserts allow a change in nozzle area to be made in varying increments. Thus, through experience a mechanic can run the engine at maximum speed with one combination of inserts, check the temperature, and substitute another combination to make up a temperature deficiency or remedy an excess temperature situation.

MAJOR SUBASSEMBLIES

The assemblies included in the discussion that follows are integral parts of, or a combination of, the components which comprise the major sections of a turbojet engine.

Diffuser

The diffuser is the divergent section of the engine. It has the all-important function of changing high-velocity compressor discharge air to static pressure. This prepares the air for entry into the burner cans at low velocity so that it will burn with a flame that will not blow out.

Air Adapters

The air adapters of the centrifugal compressor are illustrated in figure 1–37 along with the diffuser. The purpose of the air outlet ducts is to deliver air from the diffuser to the individual can-type combustion chambers. In some instances, fuel nozzles or igniter plugs are also mounted in the air outlet duct.

Engine Rotor

The engine rotor is a combination of the compressor and turbine rotors on a common shaft. The common shaft is provided by joining the turbine and compressor shafts by a suitable method. The engine rotor is supported by bearings, which are seated in suitable bearing housings.

Main Bearings

The main bearings have the critical function of supporting the main engine rotor. The number of bearings necessary for proper engine support will, for the most part, be decided by the length and weight of the engine rotor. The length and weight are directly affected by the type of compressor used in the engine. Naturally, a split-spool axial compressor will require more support than a centrifugal compressor.

Probably the minimum number of bearings required would be three, while some of the later models of split-spool axial compressor engines require six or more.

The gas turbine rotors are usually supported by either ball or roller bearings. Hydrodynamic or slipper-type bearings are receiving some attention for use on turbine powerplants where operating rotor speeds approach 45,000 r.p.m. and where excessive bearing loads during flight are anticipated. (See figure 1–66.) In general, the ball or roller anti-

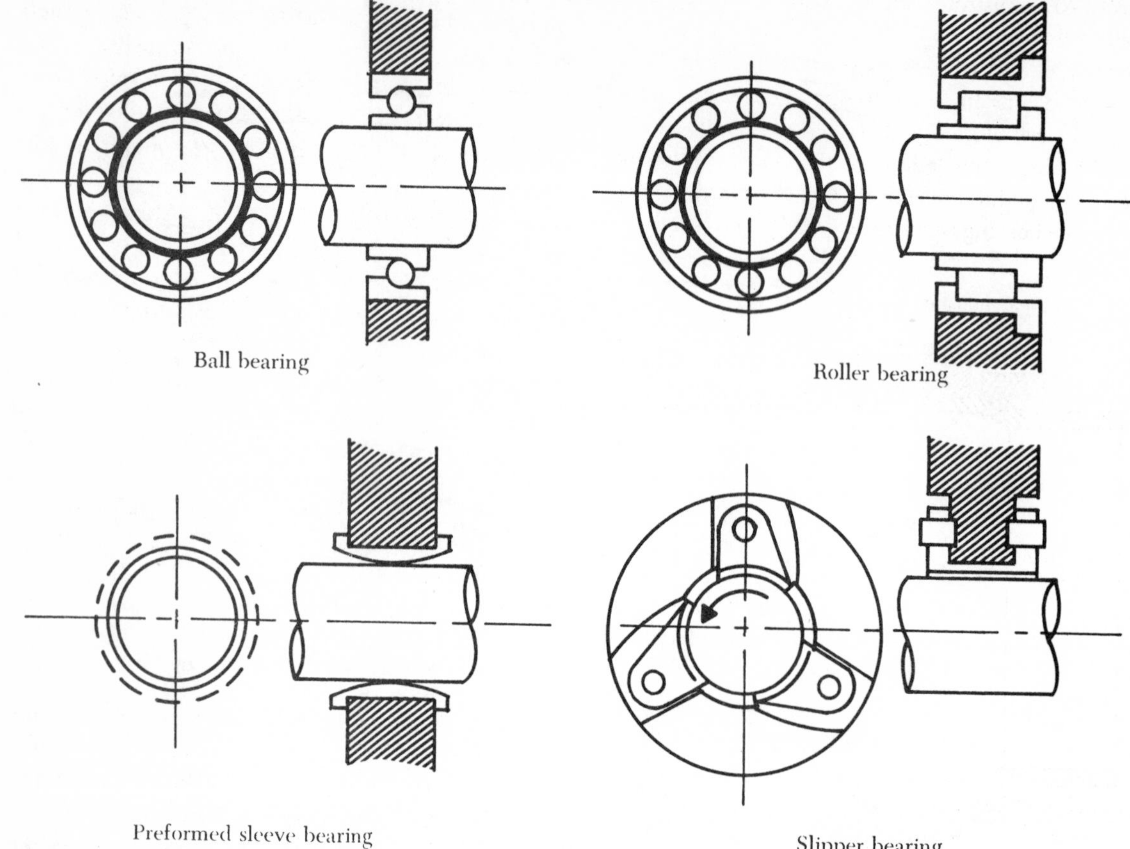

FIGURE 1–66. Type of main bearings used for gas turbine rotor support.

friction bearings are preferred largely on the basis that they:

(1) Offer little rotational resistance.
(2) Facilitate precision alignment of rotating elements.
(3) Are relatively inexpensive.
(4) Are easily replaced.
(5) Withstand high momentary overloads.
(6) Are simple to cool, lubricate, and maintain.
(7) Accommodate both radial and axial lods.
(8) Are relatively resistant to elevated temperatures.

The main disadvantages are their vulnerability to foreign matter and tendency to fail without appreciable warning.

Usually the ball bearings are positioned on the compressor or turbine shaft so that they can absorb any axial (thrust) loads or radial loads. Because the roller bearings present a larger working surface, they are better equipped to support radial loads than thrust loads. Therefore, they are used primarily for this purpose.

A typical ball or roller bearing assembly includes a bearing support housing, which must be strongly constructed and supported in order to carry the radial and axial loads of the rapidly rotating rotor. The bearing housing usually contains oil seals to prevent the oil leaking from its normal path of flow. It also delivers the oil to the bearing for its lubrication, usually through spray nozzles.

The oil seals may be the labyrinth or thread (helical) type. These seals also may be pressurized to minimize oil leaking along the compressor shaft. The labyrinth seal is usually pressurized, but the helical seal depends solely on reverse threading to stop oil leakage. These two types of seals are very similar, differing only in thread size and the fact that the labyrinth seal is pressurized.

Another type of oil seal used on some of the later engines is the carbon seal. These seals are usually spring loaded and are similar in material and application to the carbon brushes used in electrical motors. Carbon seals rest against a surface provided to create a sealed bearing cavity or void; thus, the oil is prevented from leaking out along the shaft into the compressor airflow or the turbine section.

Figure 1–67 illustrates an oil seal of the spring-loaded carbon type.

The ball or roller bearing is fitted into the bearing housing and may have a self-aligning feature. If a bearing is self-aligning, it is usually seated in a spherical ring, thus allowing the shaft a certain amount of radial movement without transmitting stress to the bearing inner race.

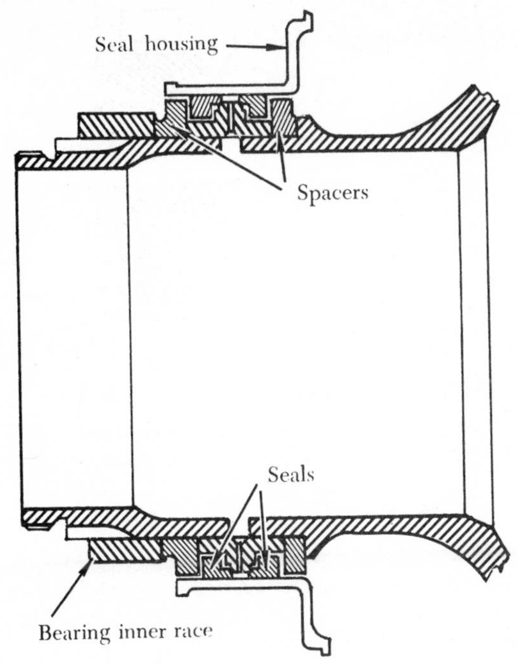

FIGURE 1–67. Carbon oil seal.

The bearing surface is usually provided by a machined journal on the appropriate shaft. The bearing is usually locked in position by a steel snapring, or other suitable locking device.

The rotor shaft also provides the matching surface for the oil seals in the bearing housing. These machined surfaces are called lands and fit in rather close to the oil seal, although not actually touching. If rubbing occurs, eventual wear and leakage will result.

TURBOPROP ENGINES

The turboprop (turbo-propeller) engine is a combination of a gas turbine and a propeller. Turboprops are basically similar to turbojet engines in that both have a compressor, combustion chamber(s), turbine, and a jet nozzle, all of which operate in the same manner on both engines. However, the difference is that the turbine in the turboprop engine usually has more stages than that in the turbojet engine. In addition to operating the compressor and accessories, the turboprop turbine transmits increased power forward, through a shaft and a gear train, to drive the propeller. The increased power is generated by the exhaust gases passing through additional stages of the turbine.

Refer to figure 1–58, which shows a multiple-rotor turbine with coaxial shafts for independent driving of the compressor and propeller. Although there are three turbines utilized in this illustration, as many as five turbine stages have been used for driving the two rotor elements, propeller, and accessories.

The exhaust gases also contribute to engine power output through jet reaction, although the amount of energy available for jet thrust is considerably reduced.

Since the basic components of the turbojet and the turboprop engines differ only slightly in design features, it should be fairly simple to apply acquired knowledge of the turbojet to the turboprop.

The typical turboprop engine can be broken down into assemblies as follows:

(1) The power section assembly, which contains the usual major components of gas turbine engines (compressor, combustion chamber, turbine, and exhaust sections).

(2) The reduction gear or gearbox assembly which contains those sections peculiar to turboprop configurations.

(3) The torquemeter assembly, which transmits the torque from the engine to the gearbox of the reduction section.

(4) The accessory drive housing assembly.

These assemblies are illustrated in figure 1–68.

The turboprop engine can be used in many different configurations. It is often used in transport aircraft, but can be adapted for use in single-engine aircraft.

TURBOSHAFT ENGINES

A gas turbine engine that delivers power through a shaft to operate something other than a propeller is referred to as a turboshaft engine. Turboshaft engines are similar to turboprop engines. The power takeoff may be coupled directly to the engine turbine, or the shaft may be driven by a turbine of its own (free turbine) located in the exhaust stream. The free turbine rotates independently. This principle is used extensively in current production turboshaft engines. The turboshaft engine is currently being used to power helicopters.

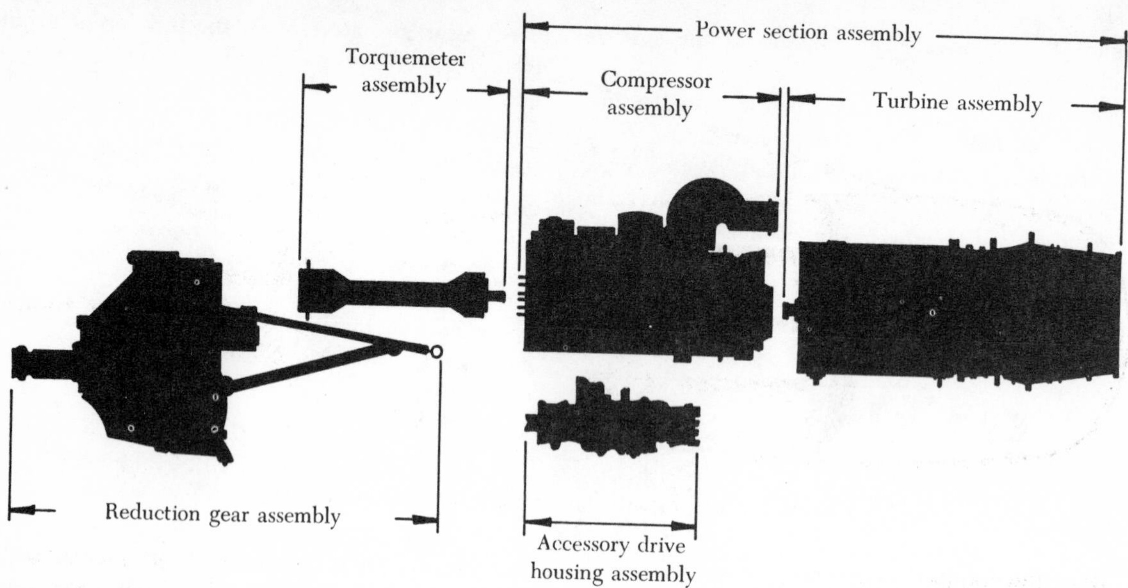

FIGURE 1–68. Turboprop engine major components.

TURBOFAN ENGINES

The turbofan gas turbine engine (figure 1–69) is, in principle, the same as a turboprop, except that the propeller is replaced by a duct-enclosed axial-flow fan. The fan can be a part of the first-stage compressor blades or can be mounted as a separate set of fan blades. The blades can be mounted forward of the compressor, or aft of the turbine wheel.

The general principle of the fan engine is to convert more of the fuel energy into pressure. With more of the energy converted to pressure, a greater product of pressure times area can be achieved. One of the big advantages is that the turbofan produces this additional thrust without increasing fuel flow. The end result is savings in fuel with the consequent increase in range.

Because more of the fuel energy is turned into pressure in the turbofan engine, another stage must be added in the turbine to provide the power to drive the fan, and thus increase the expansion through the turbine. This means that there will be less energy left over and less pressure in back of the turbine. Also, the jet nozzle has to be larger in area. The end result is that the main engine does not develop as much jet nozzle thrust as a straight turbojet engine.

The fan more than makes up for the dropoff in thrust of the main engine. Depending on the fan design, it will produce somewhere around 50% of the turbofan engine's total thrust. In an 18,000 lb. thrust engine about 9,000 lbs. will be developed by the fan and the remaining 9,000 lbs. by the main engine. The same basic turbojet engine without a fan will develop about 12,000 lbs. of thrust.

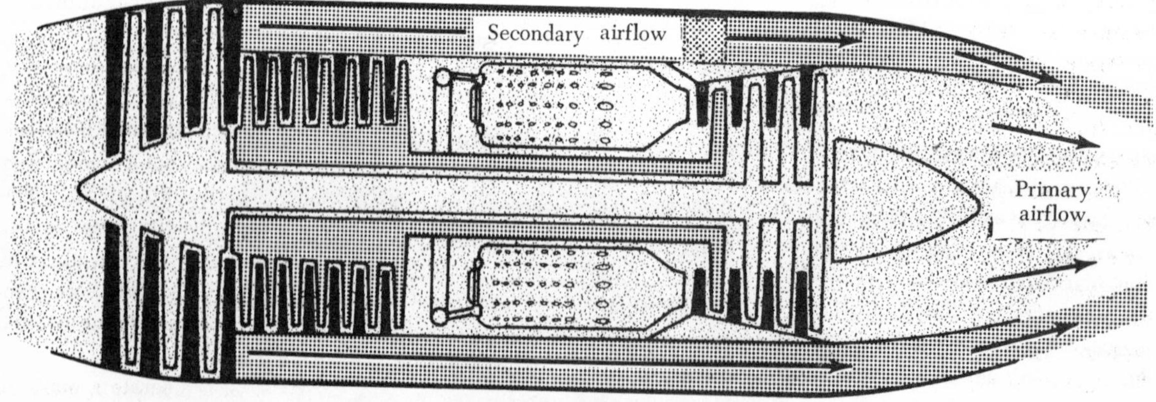

FIGURE 1–69. Forward turbofan engine.

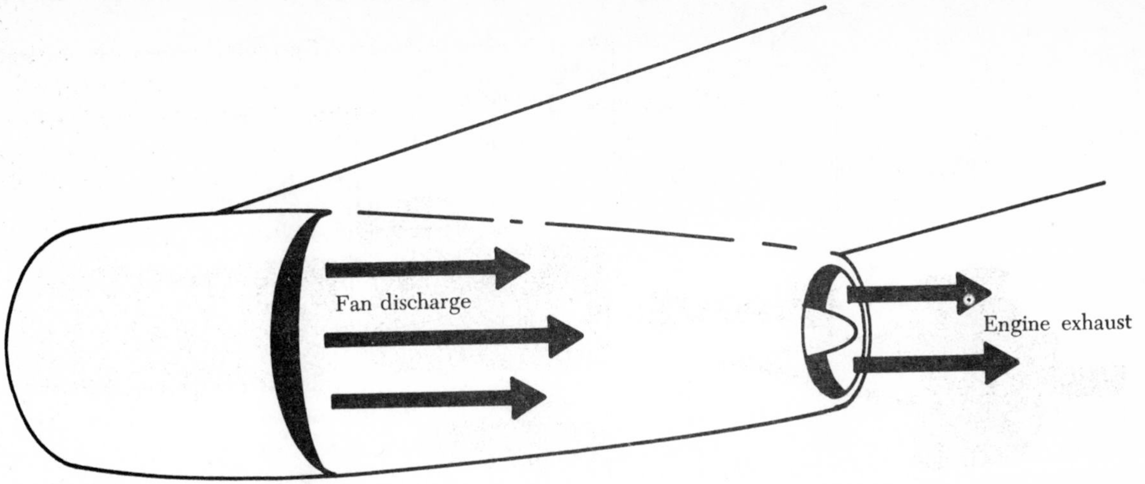

FIGURE 1–70. Forward-fan turbofan engine installation.

Two different duct designs are used with forward-fan engines. The air leaving the fan can be ducted overboard (figure 1–70), or it can be ducted along the outer case of the basic engine to be discharged through the jet nozzle. The fan air is either mixed with the exhaust gases before it is discharged or it passes directly to the atmosphere without prior mixing.

Turbofans, sometimes called fanjets, are becoming the most widely used gas turbine engine. The turbofan is a compromise between the good operating efficiency and high-thrust capability of a turboprop and the high-speed, high-altitude capability of a turbojet.

TURBINE ENGINE OPERATING PRINCIPLES

The principle used by a turbojet engine as it provides force to move an airplane is based on Newton's law of momentum. This law shows that a force is required to accelerate a mass; therefore, if the engine accelerates a mass of air, it will apply a force on the aircraft. The propeller and turbojet engines are very closely related. The propeller generates thrust by giving a relatively small acceleration to a large quantity of air. The turbojet engine achieves thrust by imparting greater acceleration to a smaller quantity of air.

The mass of air is accelerated within the engine by the use of a continuous-flow cycle. Ambient air enters the inlet diffuser where it is subjected to changes in temperature, pressure, and velocity due to ram effect. The compressor then increases pressure and temperature of the air mechanically. The air continues at constant pressure to the burner section where its temperature is increased by combustion of fuel. The energy is taken from the hot gas by expanding through a turbine which drives the compressor, and by expanding through a tailpipe designed to discharge the exhaust gas at high velocity to produce thrust.

The high-velocity jet from a turbojet engine may be considered a continuous recoil, imparting force against the aircraft in which it is installed, thereby producing thrust. The formula for thrust can be derived from Newton's second law, which states that force is proportional to the product of mass and acceleration. This law is expressed in the formula:

$$F = M \times A$$

where;

F = Force in pounds.
M = Mass in slugs.
A = Acceleration in ft. per sec. per sec.

In the above formula "mass" is similar to "weight," but it is actually a different quantity. Mass refers to the quantity of matter, while weight refers to the pull of gravity on that quantity of matter. At sea level under standard conditions, 1 lb. of mass will have a weight of 1 lb.

To calculate the acceleration of a given mass, the gravitational constant is used as a unit of comparison. The force of gravity is 32.2 ft./sec.^{2} (or feet per second squared). This means that a free-falling 1-lb. object will accelerate at the rate of 32.2 feet per second each second that gravity acts on it. Since the object mass weighs 1 lb., which is also the actual force imparted to it by gravity, we can assume that a force of 1 lb. will accelerate a 1-lb. object at the rate of 32.2 ft./sec.^{2}.

Also, a force of 10 lbs. will accelerate a mass of 10 lbs. at the rate of 32.2 ft./sec.^{2}. This is assuming there is no friction or other resistance to overcome. It is now apparent that the ratio of the force (in pounds) is to the mass (in pounds) as the acceleration in ft./sec.^{2} is to 32.2. Using M to represent the mass in pounds, the formula may be expressed thus:

$$\frac{F}{M} = \frac{A}{g}$$

or,

$$F = \frac{MA}{g}$$

where;

F = Force.
M = Mass.
A = Acceleration.
g = gravity.

In any formula involving work, the time factor must be considered. It is convenient to have all time factors in equivalent units; i.e., seconds, minutes, or hours. In calculating jet thrust, the term "pounds of air per second" is convenient, since the time factor is the same as the time in the force of gravity, namely, seconds.

THRUST

Using the foregoing formula, compute the force necessary to accelerate a mass of 50 lbs., 100 ft./sec.^{2}, as follows:

$$F = \frac{50 \text{ lb. x } 100 \text{ ft./sec.}^2}{32.2 \text{ ft./sec.}^2}$$

$$F = \frac{50 \text{ x } 100}{32.2}$$

$$F = 155 \text{ lb.}$$

This illustrates that if the velocity of 50 lbs. of mass per sec. is increased by 100 ft./sec.^{2}, the resulting thrust is 155 lbs.

Since the turbojet engine accelerates a mass of air, the following formula can be used to determine jet **thrust:**

$$F = \frac{M_s (V_2 - V_1)}{g}$$

where;

F = Force in lbs.
M_s = Mass flow in lbs./sec.
V_1 = Inlet velocity.
V_2 = Jet velocity (exhaust).
$V_2 - V_1$ = Change in velocity; difference between inlet velocity and jet velocity.
g = Acceleration of gravity, or 32.2 ft./sec.^{2}.

As an example, to use the formula for changing the velocity of 100 lbs. of mass airflow per sec. from 600 ft./sec. to 800 ft./sec., the formula can be applied as follows:

$$F = \frac{100 \ (800 - 600)}{32.2}$$

$$F = \frac{20{,}000}{32.2}$$

$$F = 621 \text{ pounds.}$$

As shown by the formula, if the mass airflow per second and the difference in the velocity of the air from the intake to the exhaust is known, it is easy to compute the force necessary to produce the change in the velocity. Therefore, the jet thrust of the engine must be equal to the force required to accelerate the airmass through the engine. Then, by using the symbol "T" for thrust pounds, the formula becomes:

$$T = \frac{M_s (V_2 - V_1)}{g}.$$

It is easy to see from this formula that the thrust of a gas turbine engine can be increased by two methods: first, by increasing the mass flow of air through the engine, and second, by increasing the jet velocity.

If the velocity of the turbojet engine remains constant with respect to the aircraft, the jet thrust will decrease if the speed of the aircraft is increased. This is because V_1 will increase in value. This does not present a serious problem, however, because as the aircraft speed increases, more air enters the engine, and jet velocity increases. The resultant net thrust is almost constant with increased airspeed.

The Brayton cycle is the name given to the thermodynamic cycle of a gas turbine engine to produce thrust. This is a varying volume constant-pressure cycle of events and is commonly called the constant-pressure cycle. A more recent term is continuous combustion cycle.

The four continuous and constant events are the intake, compression, expansion (includes power), and exhaust. These cycles will be discussed as they apply to a gas turbine engine.

In the intake cycle, air enters at ambient pressure and a constant volume. It leaves the intake at an increased pressure and a decrease in volume. At the compressor section, air is received from the intake at an increased pressure, slightly above ambient, and a slight decrease in volume. Air enters the compressor where it is compressed. It leaves the compressor with a large increase in pressure and decrease in volume. This is caused by the mechanical action of the compressor. The next step, the expansion, takes place in the combustion chamber by burning fuel which expands the air by heat. The pressure remains relatively constant, but a marked increase in volume takes place. The expanding gases move rearward through the turbine assembly and are converted from velocity energy to mechanical energy by the turbine.

The exhaust section, which is a convergent duct, converts the expanding volume and decreasing pressure of the gases to a final high velocity. The force created inside the jet engine to keep this cycle continuous has an equal and opposite reaction (thrust) to move the aircraft forward.

Bernoulli's principle (whenever a stream of any fluid has its velocity increased at a given point, the pressure of the stream at that point is less than the rest of the stream) is applied to the jet engine through the design of the air ducts. The two types of ducts are the convergent and the divergent.

The convergent duct increases velocity and decreases pressure. The divergent duct decreases velocity and increases pressure. The convergent principle is usually used for the tailpipe and exhaust nozzle. The divergent principle is used in the compressor where the air is slowing and pressurizing.

GAS TURBINE ENGINE PERFORMANCE

Thermal efficiency is a prime factor in gas turbine performance. It is the ratio of net work produced by the engine to the chemical energy supplied in the form of fuel.

The three most important factors affecting the thermal efficiency are turbine inlet temperature, compression ratio, and the component efficiencies of the compressor and turbine. Other factors that affect thermal efficiency are compressor inlet temperature and burner efficiency.

Figure 1–71 shows the effect that changing compression ratio has on thermal efficiency when compressor inlet temperature and the component efficiencies of the compressor and turbine remain constant.

The effect that compressor and turbine component efficiencies have on thermal efficiency when turbine and compressor inlet temperatures remain constant is shown in figure 1–72. In actual operation, the turbine engine tailpipe temperature varies directly with turbine inlet temperature at a constant

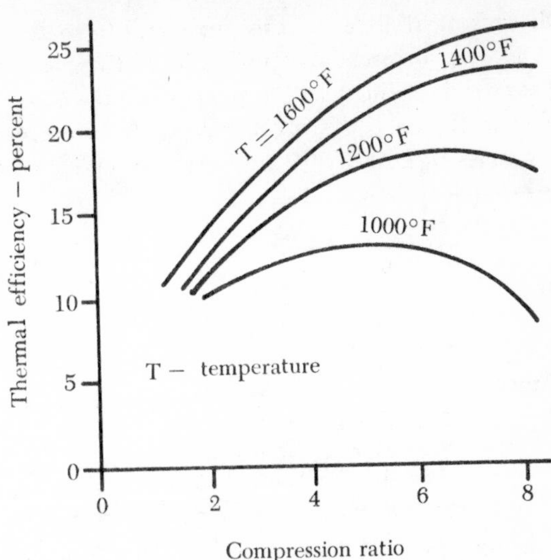

FIGURE 1–71. The effect of compression ratio on thermal efficiency.

compression ratio. R.P.M. is a direct measure of compression ratio; therefore, at constant r.p.m. maximum thermal efficiency can be obtained by maintaining the highest possible tailpipe temperature. Since engine life is greatly reduced at a high turbine inlet temperature, the operator should not exceed the tailpipe temperatures specified for continuous operation. Figure 1–73 illustrates the effect of turbine inlet temperature on turbine bucket life.

In the previous discussion, it has been assumed that the state of the air at the inlet to the com-

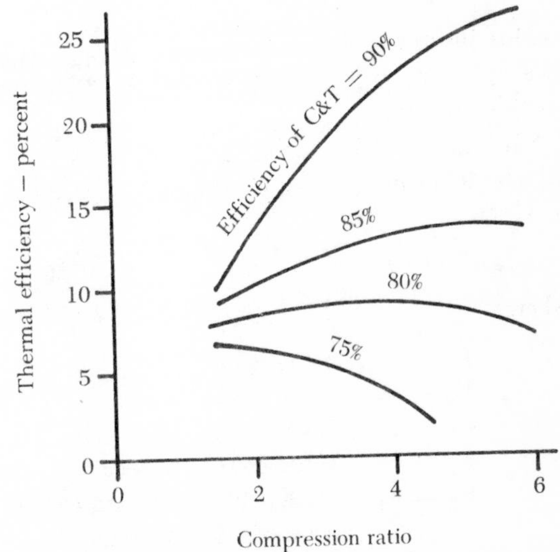

FIGURE 1–72. Turbine and compressor efficiency vs. thermal efficiency.

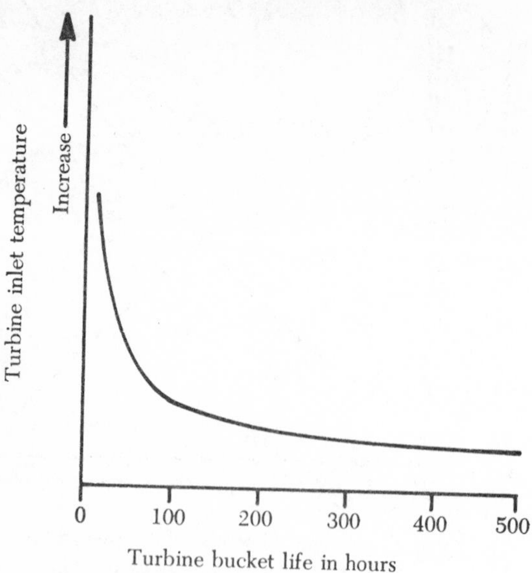

FIGURE 1–73. Effect of turbine inlet temperature on turbine bucket life.

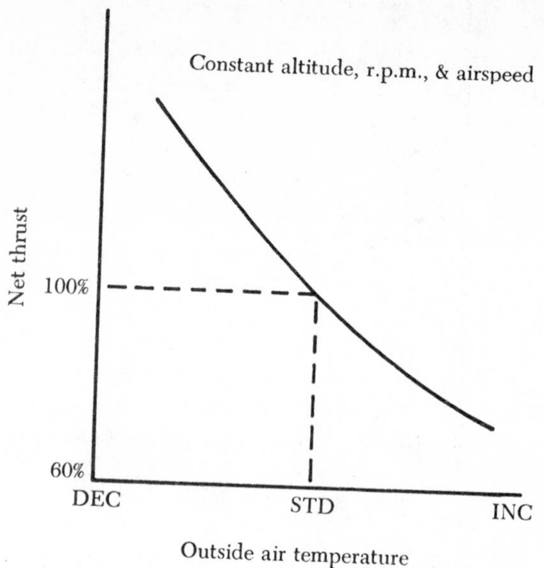

FIGURE 1–74. Effect of OAT on thrust output.

pressor remained constant. Since the turbojet engine is a practical application of a turbine engine, it becomes necessary to analyze the effect of varying inlet conditions on the power produced. The three principal variables that affect inlet conditions are the speed of the aircraft, the altitude of the aircraft, and the ambient temperature. To make the analysis simpler, the combination of these three variables can be represented by a single variable, called "stagnation density."

The power produced by a turbine engine is proportional to the stagnation density at the inlet. The next three illustrations show how changing the density by varying altitudes, airspeed, and outside air temperature affects the power level of the engine.

Figure 1–74 shows that the thrust output improves rapidly with a reduction in OAT (outside air temperature) at constant altitude, r.p.m., and airspeed. This increase occurs partly because the energy required per pound of airflow to drive the compressor varies directly with the temperature, thus leaving more energy to develop thrust. In addition, the thrust output will increase since the air at reduced temperature has an increased density. The increase in density causes the mass flow through the engine to increase.

The altitude effect on thrust, as shown in figure 1–75, can also be discussed as a density and temperature effect. In this case, an increase in altitude causes a decrease in pressure and temperature. Since the temperature lapse rate is less than the pressure lapse rate as altitude is increased, the density is decreased. Although the decreased temperature increases thrust, the effect of decreased density more than offsets the effect of the colder temperature. The net result of increased altitude is a reduction in the thrust output.

The effect of airspeed on the thrust of a turbojet engine is shown in figure 1–76. To explain the airspeed effect, it is first necessary to understand the effect of airspeed on the factors which combine to produce net thrust. These factors are specific thrust and engine airflow. Specific thrust is the pounds of net thrust developed per pound of airflow

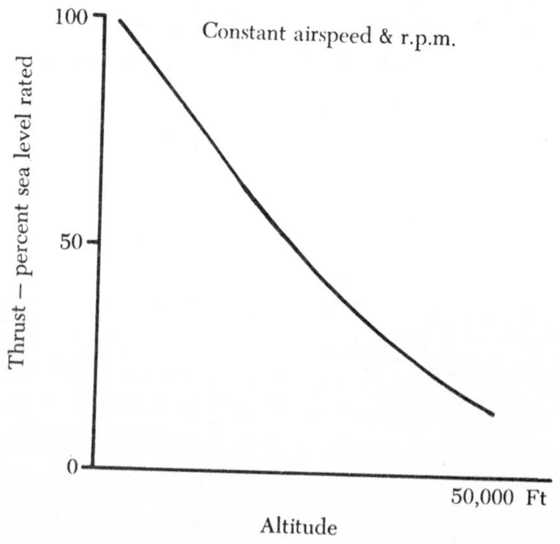

FIGURE 1–75. Effect of altitude on thrust output.

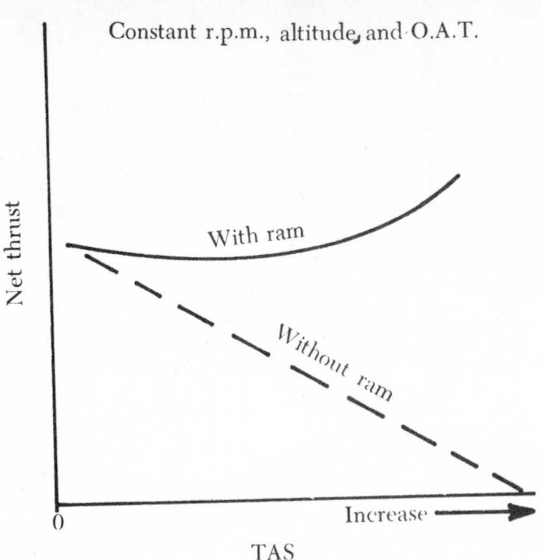

FIGURE 1–76. Effect of airspeed on net thrust.

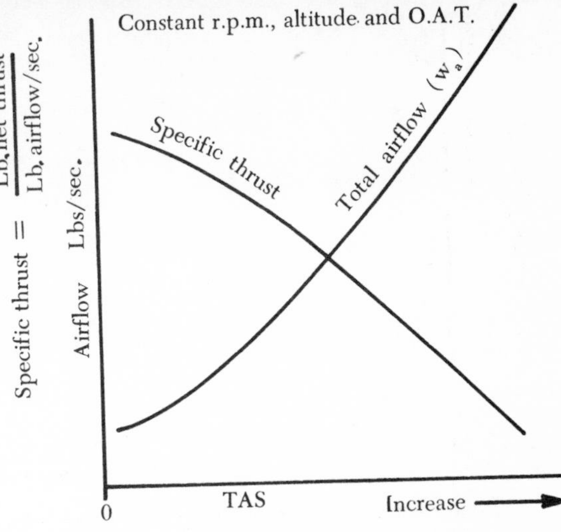

FIGURE 1–77. Effect of airspeed on specific thrust and total engine airflow.

per second. It is the remainder of specific gross thrust minus specific ram drag.

As airspeed is increased, the ram drag increases rapidly. The exhaust jet velocity remains relatively constant; thus the effect of the increase in airspeed results in decreased specific thrust as shown in figure 1–76. In the low-speed range, the specific thrust decreases faster than the airflow increases and causes a decrease in net thrust. As the airspeed increases into the higher range, the airflow increases faster than the specific thrust decreases and causes the net thrust to increase until sonic velocity is reached. The effect of the combination on net thrust is illustrated in figure 1–77.

Ram Recovery

A rise in pressure above existing outside atmospheric pressure at the engine inlet, as a result of the forward velocity of an aircraft, is referred to as ram. Since any ram effect will cause an increase in compressor entrance pressure over atmospheric, the resulting pressure rise will cause an increase in the mass airflow and jet velocity, both of which tend to increase thrust.

Although ram effect increases the engine thrust, the thrust being produced by the engine decreases for a given throttle setting as an aircraft gains airspeed. Therefore, two opposing trends occur when an aircraft's speed is increased. What actually takes place is the net result of these two different effects.

An engine's thrust output temporarily decreases as aircraft speed increases from static, but soon ceases to decrease; towards the high speeds, thrust output begins to increase again.

CHAPTER 2

INDUCTION AND EXHAUST SYSTEMS

RECIPROCATING ENGINE INDUCTION SYSTEMS

The induction system of an aircraft reciprocating engine consists of a carburetor, an airscoop or ducting that conducts air to the carburetor, and an intake manifold. These units form a long curved channel which conducts air and the fuel/air mixture to the cylinders.

These three units of a typical induction system are usually supplemented by a temperature-indicating system and temperature-controlling unit in some form of alternate air valve and a carburetor heat source. Additionally, a system for compressing the fuel/air mixture may be included.

Since many engines installed in light aircraft do not use any type of compressor or supercharging device, induction systems for reciprocating engines can be broadly classified as supercharged or naturally aspirated (nonsupercharged).

Nonsupercharged Induction Systems

The nonsupercharged engine is commonly used in light aircraft. The induction systems of these engines may be equipped with either a carburetor or a fuel-injection system. If a carburetor is used, it may be a float-type or a pressure-type carburetor. If fuel injection is used, it will normally be either a constant flow or a pulsed system.

Figure 2–1 is a diagram of an induction system used in a nonsupercharged engine equipped with a carburetor. In this induction system, carburetor cold air is admitted at the leading edge of the nose cowling below the propeller spinner, and is passed through an air filter into air ducts leading to the carburetor. An air valve is located at the carburetor for selecting an alternate warm air source to prevent carburetor icing.

The cold-air valve admits air from the outside air scoop for normal operation and is controlled by a control knob in the cockpit. The warm-air valve admits warm air from the engine compartment for operation during icing conditions and is spring loaded to the "closed" position. When the cold air door is closed, engine suction opens the spring-loaded warm-air valve. If the engine should backfire with the warm-air valve open, spring tension automatically closes the warm-air valve to keep flames out of the engine compartment.

The carburetor air filter is installed in the air scoop in front of the carburetor air duct. Its purpose is to stop dust and other foreign matter from entering the engine through the carburetor. The screen consists of an aluminum alloy frame and a deeply crimped screen, arranged to present maximum screen area to the airstream.

The carburetor air ducts consist of a fixed duct riveted to the nose cowling and a flexible duct between the fixed duct and the carburetor air valve. The carburetor air ducts provide a passage for cold, outside air to the carburetor.

Air enters the system through the ram-air intake. The intake opening is located in the slipstream so the air is forced into the induction system, giving a ram effect.

The air passes through the ducts to the carburetor. The carburetor meters the fuel in proportion to the air and mixes the air with the correct amount of fuel. The carburetor can be controlled from the cockpit to regulate the flow of air and, in this way, power output of the engine can be controlled.

The carburetor air temperature indicating system shows the temperature of the air at the carburetor inlet. If the bulb is located at the engine side of the carburetor, the system measures the temperature of the fuel/air mixture.

Additional Units of the Induction System

The units of a typical induction system previously discussed satisfy the needs of the engine insofar as its ability to produce power is concerned. There are two additional units that add nothing to help the engine do its work but are vital to efficient engine operation. One unit is the preheater; the other is the fluid deicing unit.

Induction system ice can be prevented or eliminated by raising the temperature of the air that passes through the system, using a preheater lo-

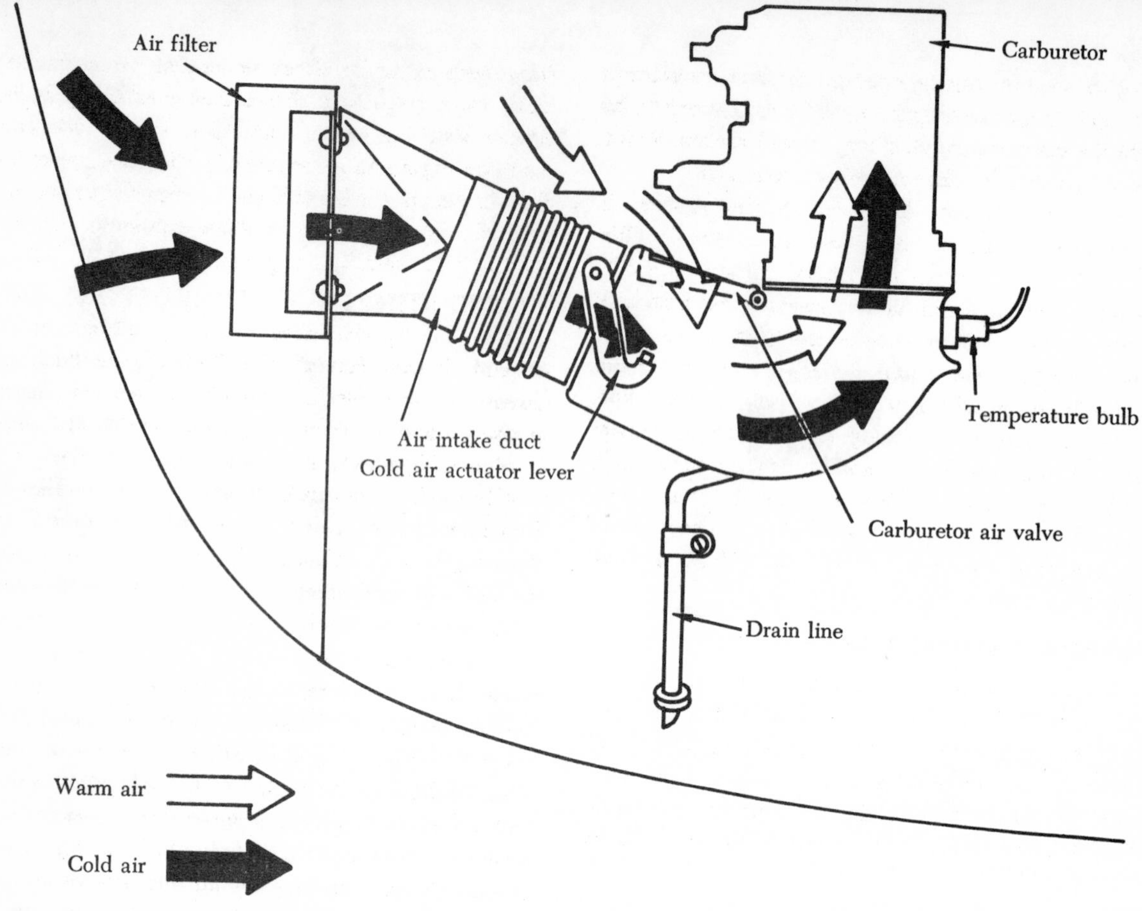

FIGURE 2–1. Nonsupercharged induction system using a carburetor.

cated upstream near the induction system inlet and well ahead of the dangerous icing zones. Heat is usually obtained through a control valve that opens the induction system to the warm air circulating in the engine compartment. When there is danger of induction system icing, move the cockpit control toward the "hot" position until a carburetor air temperature is obtained that will provide the necessary protection.

Throttle ice or any ice that restricts airflow or reduces manifold pressure can best be removed by using full carburetor heat. If the heat from the engine compartment is sufficient and the application has not been delayed, it is only a matter of a few minutes until the ice is cleared. If the air temperature in the engine compartment is not high enough to be effective against icing, the preheat capacity can be increased by closing the cowl flaps and increasing engine power. However, this may prove ineffective if the ice formation has progressed so far that the loss of power makes it impossible to generate sufficient heat to clear the ice.

Improper or careless use of carburetor heat can be just as dangerous as the most advanced stage of induction system ice. Increasing the temperature of the air causes it to expand and decrease in density. This action reduces the weight of the charge delivered to the cylinder and causes a noticeable loss in power because of decreased volumetric efficiency. In addition, high intake air temperature may cause detonation and engine failure, especially during takeoff and high-power operation. Therefore, during all phases of engine operation, the carburetor temperature must afford the greatest protection against icing and detonation. When there is no danger of icing, the heat control is normally kept in the "cold" position. It is best to leave the control in this position if there are particles of dry snow or ice in the air. The use of heat may melt the ice or snow, and the resulting moisture may collect and freeze on the walls of the induction system.

To prevent damage to the heater valves in the case of backfire, carburetor heaters should not be used while starting the engine. Also, during ground operation only enough carburetor heat should be used to give smooth engine operation. The carburetor air inlet temperature gage must be monitored to be sure the temperature does not exceed the maximum value specified by the engine manufacturer.

On some aircraft the basic deicing system is supplemented by a fluid deicing system. This auxiliary system consists of a tank, a pump, suitable spray nozzles in the induction system, and a cockpit control unit. This system is intended to clear ice whenever the heat from the engine compartment is not high enough to prevent or remove ice. The use of alcohol as a deicing agent tends to enrich the fuel mixture, but at a high-power output such slight enrichment is desired. At low throttle settings, however, the use of alcohol may over-enrich the mixture; therefore, alcohol should be applied with great care.

INDUCTION SYSTEM ICING

A short discussion concerning the formation and the place of formation of induction system ice (fig. 2–2) is helpful to the mechanic, even though he is not normally concerned with operations that occur only when the aircraft is in flight. But the mechanic should know something about induction system icing because of its effect on engine performance. Even when inspection shows that everything is in proper working order, induction system ice can cause an engine to act erratically and lose power in the air, yet the engine will perform perfectly on the ground. Many engine troubles commonly attributed to other sources are actually caused by induction system icing.

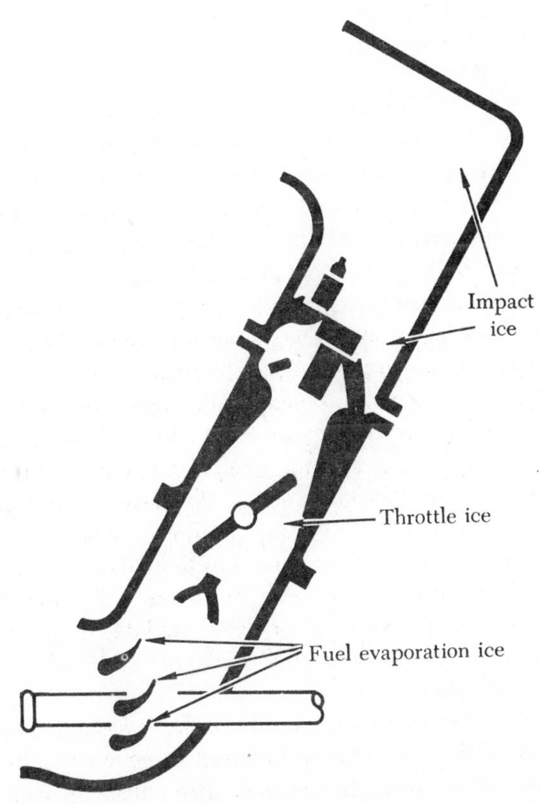

FIGURE 2–2. Types of induction system ice.

Induction system icing is an operating hazard because it can cut off the flow of the fuel/air charge or vary the fuel/air ratio. Ice can form in the induction system while an aircraft is flying in clouds, fog, rain, sleet, snow, or even clear air that has a high moisture content (high humidity). Induction system icing is generally classified in three types: (1) Impact ice, (2) fuel evaporation ice, and (3) throttle ice. Chapter 3 discusses types of icing in more detail.

To understand why part-throttle operation can lead to icing, the throttle area during this operation must be examined. When the throttle is placed in a partly closed position, it, in effect, limits the amount of air available to the engine. The glide which windmills a fixed-pitch propeller causes the engine to consume more air than it normally would at this same throttle setting, thus aggravating the lack of air behind the throttle. The partly closed throttle, under these circumstances, establishes a much higher than normal air velocity past the throttle, and an extremely low pressure area is produced. The low-pressure area lowers the temperature of the air surrounding the throttle valves by the same physical law that raises the temperature of air as it is compressed. If the temperature in this air falls below freezing and moisure is present, ice will form on the throttles and nearby units in much the same manner that impact ice forms on units exposed to below freezing temperatures.

Throttle ice may be minimized on engines equipped with controllable-pitch propellers by the use of a higher than normal BMEP (brake mean effective pressure) at this low power. The high BMEP decreases the icing tendency because a large throttle opening at low engine r.p.m. partially removes the temperature-reducing obstruction that part-throttle operation offers.

Induction System Filtering

While dust is merely an annoyance to most individuals, it is a serious source of trouble to an aircraft engine. Dust consists of small particles of hard, abrasive material that can be carried into the engine cylinders by the very air the engine breathes. It can also collect on the fuel-metering elements of the carburetor, upsetting the proper relation between airflow and fuel flow at all powers. It acts on the cylinder walls by grinding down these surfaces and the piston rings. It then contaminates the oil and is carried through the engine, causing further wear on the bearings and gears. In extreme cases an accumulation may clog an oil passage and cause oil starvation.

Although dust conditions are most critical at ground level, dust of sufficient quantity to obscure a pilot's vision has been reported in flight. In some parts of the world, dust can be carried to extremely high altitudes. Continued operation under such conditions without engine protection will result in extreme engine wear and produce excessive oil consumption.

When operation in dusty atmosphere is necessary, the engine can be protected by an alternate induction system air inlet which incorporates a dust filter. This type of air filter system normally consists of a filter element, a door, and an electrically operated actuator. When the filter system is operating, air is drawn through a louvered access panel that does not face directly into the airstream. With this entrance location, considerable dust is removed as the air is forced to turn and enter the duct. Since the dust particles are solid, they tend to continue in a straight line, and most of them are separated at this point. Those that are drawn into the louvers are easily removed by the filter.

In flight, with air filters operating, consideration must be given to possible icing conditions which may occur from actual surface icing or from freezing of the filter element after it becomes rainsoaked. Some installations have a spring-loaded filter door which automatically opens when the filter is excessively restricted. This prevents the airflow from being cut off when the filter is clogged with ice or dirt. Other systems use an ice guard in the filtered-air entrance.

The ice guard consists of a coarse-mesh screen located a short distance from the filtered-air entrance. In this location the screen is directly in the path of incoming air so that the air must pass through or around the screen. When ice forms on the screen, the air, which has lost its heavy moisture particles, will pass around the iced screen and into the filter element.

The efficiency of any filter system depends upon proper maintenance and servicing. Periodic removal and cleaning of the filter element is essential to satisfactory engine protection.

Induction System Inspection and Maintenance

The induction system should be checked for cracks and leaks during all regularly scheduled engine inspections. The units of the system should be checked for security of mounting. The system should be kept clean at all times, since pieces of rags or paper can restrict the airflow if allowed to enter the air intakes or ducts, and loose bolts and nuts can cause serious damage if they pass into the engine.

On systems equipped with a carburetor air filter, the filter should be checked regularly. If it is dirty or does not have the proper oil film, the filter element should be removed and cleaned. After it has dried, it is usually immersed in a mixture of oil and rust-preventive compound. The excess fluid should be allowed to drain off before the filter element is reinstalled.

Induction System Troubleshooting

The following chart provides a general guide to the most common induction system troubles.

PROBABLE CAUSE	ISOLATION PROCEDURE	CORRECTION
1. Engine fails to start—		
(a) Induction system obstructed.	(a) Inspect airscoop and air ducts.	(a) Remove obstructions.
(b) Air leaks.	(b) Inspect carburetor mounting and intake pipes.	(b) Tighten carburetor and repair or replace intake pipe.
2. Engine runs rough—		
(a) Loose air ducts.	(a) Inspect air ducts.	(a) Tighten air ducts.
(b) Leaking intake pipes.	(b) Inspect intake pipe packing nuts.	(b) Tighten nuts.

PROBABLE CAUSE	ISOLATION PROCEDURE	CORRECTION
(c) Engine valves sticking.	(c) Remove rocker arm cover and check valve action.	(c) Lubricate and free sticking valves.
(d) Bent or worn valve push rods.	(d) Inspect push rods.	(d) Replace worn or damaged push rods.
3. Low power—		
(a) Restricted intake duct.	(a) Examine intake duct.	(a) Remove restrictions.
(b) Broken door in carburetor air valve.	(b) Inspect air valve.	(b) Replace air valve.
(c) Dirty air filter.	(c) Inspect air filter.	(c) Clean air filter.
4. Engine idles improperly—		
(a) Shrunken intake packing.	(a) Inspect packing for proper fit.	(a) Replace packing.
(b) Hole in intake pipe.	(b) Inspect intake pipes.	(b) Replace defective intake pipes.
(c) Loose carburetor mounting.	(c) Inspect mount bolts.	(c) Tighten mount bolts.

Supercharged Induction Systems

Supercharging systems used in reciprocating engine induction systems are normally classified as either internally driven or externally driven (turbosupercharged).

Internally driven superchargers compress the fuel/air mixture after it leaves the carburetor, while externally driven superchargers (turbochargers) compress the air before it is mixed with the metered fuel from the carburetor. Each increase in the pressure of the air or fuel/air mixture in an induction system is called a stage. Superchargers can be classified as single-stage, two-stage, or multi-stage, depending on the number of times compression occurs. Superchargers may also operate at different speeds. Thus, they can be referred to as single-speed, two-speed, or variable-speed superchargers.

Combining the methods of classification provides the nomenclature normally used to describe supercharger systems. Thus, from a simple single-stage system that operates at one fixed speed ratio, it is possible to progress to a single-stage, two-speed, mechanically clutched system or a single-stage, hydraulically clutched supercharger. Even though two-speed or multi-speed systems permit varying the output pressure, the system is still classified as a single-stage of compression if only a single impeller is used, since only one increase (or decrease) in compression can be obtained at a time.

INTERNALLY DRIVEN SUPERCHARGERS

Internally driven superchargers are used almost exclusively in high-horsepower reciprocating engines. Except for the construction and arrangement of the various types of superchargers, all induction systems with internally driven superchargers are almost identical. The reason for this similarity is that all modern aircraft engines require the same air temperature control to produce good combustion in the engine cylinders. For example, the temperature of the charge must be warm enough to ensure complete fuel vaporization and, thus, even distribution; but at the same time it must not be so hot that it reduces volumetric efficiency or causes detonation. With these requirements, all induction systems that use internal-driven superchargers must include pressure and temperature-sensing devices and the necessary units required to warm or cool the air.

Single-Stage, Single-Speed Supercharger Systems

The simple induction system shown in figure 2–3 is used to explain the location of units and the path of the air and fuel/air mixture.

Air enters the system through the ram air intake. The intake opening is located so that the air is forced into the induction system, giving a ram effect.

The air passes through ducts to the carburetor. The carburetor meters the fuel in proportion to the

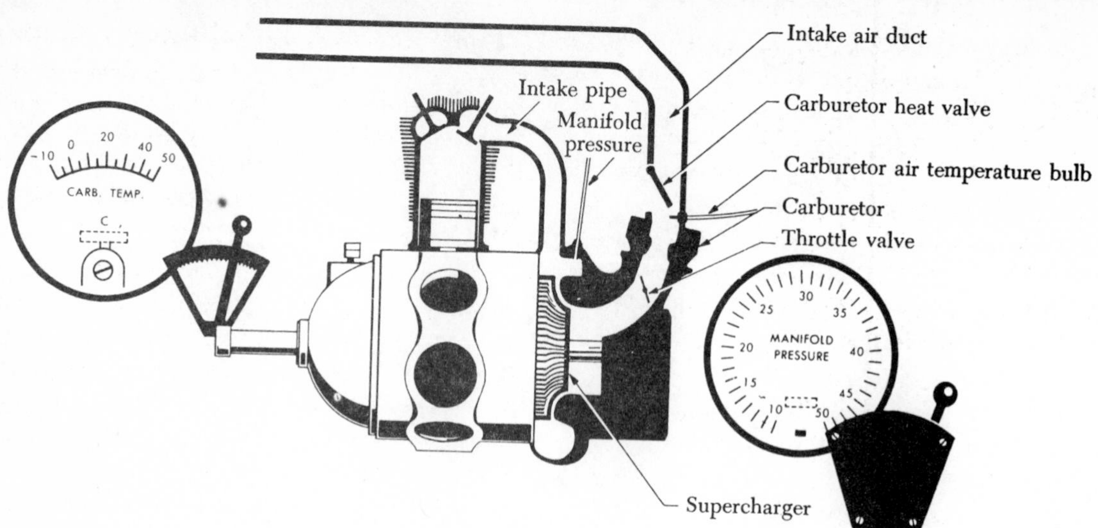

FIGURE 2–3. Simple induction system.

air and mixes the air with the correct amount of fuel. The carburetor can be controlled from the cockpit to regulate the flow of air. In this way, the power output of the engine can be controlled.

The manifold pressure gage measures the pressure of the fuel/air mixture before it enters the cylinders. It is an indication of the performance that can be expected of the engine.

The carburetor air temperature indicator measures either the temperature of the inlet air or of the fuel/air mixture. Either the air inlet or the mixture temperature indicator serves as a guide so that the temperature of the incoming charge may be kept within safe limits.

If the temperature of the incoming air at the entrance to the carburetor scoop is 100° F., there will be approximately a 50° F. drop in temperature because of the partial vaporization of the fuel at the carburetor discharge nozzle. Partial vaporization takes place and the air temperature falls due to absorption of the heat by vaporization. The final vaporization takes place as the mixture enters the cylinders where higher temperatures exist.

The fuel, as atomized into the airstream which flows in the induction system, is in a globular form. The problem, then, becomes one of uniformly breaking up and distributing the fuel remaining in globular form to the various cylinders. On engines equipped with a large number of cylinders, the uniform distribution of the mixture becomes a greater problem, especially at high engine speeds when full advantage is taken of large air capacity.

One method of improving fuel distribution is shown in figure 2–4. This device is known as a distribution impeller. The impeller is attached directly to the end of the rear shank of the crankshaft by bolts or studs. Since the impeller is attached to

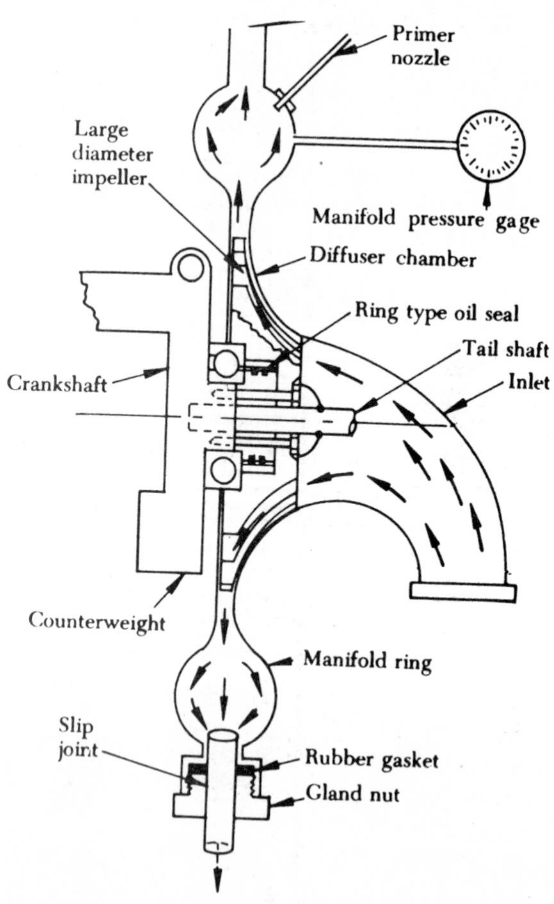

FIGURE 2–4. Distribution impeller arrangement used on a radial engine.

the end of the crankshaft and operates at the same speed, it does not materially boost or increase the pressure on the mixture flowing into the cylinders. But the fuel remaining in the globular form will be broken up into finer particles as it strikes the impeller, thereby coming in contact with more air. This will create a more homogeneous mixture with a consequent improvement in distribution to the various cylinders, especially on acceleration of the engine or when low temperatures prevail.

When greater pressure is desired on the fuel/air mixture in the induction system to charge the cylinders more fully, the diffuser or blower section contains a high-speed impeller. Unlike the distribution impeller, which is connected directly to the crankshaft, the supercharger, or blower impeller, is driven through a gear train from the crankshaft.

The impeller is located centrally within the diffuser chamber. The diffuser chamber surface may be any one of three general designs: (1) Venturi type (figure 2–4), (2) vaned type (A of figure 2–5), or (3) airfoil type (B of figure 2–5).

The venturi-type diffuser is equipped with plain surfaces, sometimes more or less restricted sectionally to form the general shape of a venturi between the impeller tips and the manifold ring. This type has been most widely used on medium-powered, supercharged engines or those in which lower volumes of mixtures are to be handled and where turbulence of the mixture between the impeller tips and the manifold chamber is not critical.

On large-volume engines ranging from 450 hp. upwards, in which the volume of mixture is to be handled at higher velocities and turbulence is a more important factor, either a vane or airfoil type diffuser is widely used. The vanes or airfoil section straightens the airflow within the diffuser chamber to obtain an efficient flow of gases.

The intake pipes on early model engines extended in a direct path from the manifold ring to the intake port on the cylinder. In the more recent designs, however, the intake pipes extend from the manifold ring on a tangent and the pipe is curved as it extends toward the intake port, which has also been streamlined or shaped to promote efficient flow of gases into the cylinder. This reduces turbulence to a minimum. This has been one of the important methods of increasing the breathing capacity or volume of air which a given design of engine might handle. Increases in supercharger efficiency have been one of the major factors in increasing the power output of modern engines.

The gear ratio of the impeller gear train varies from approximately 6:1 to 12:1. Impeller speed on an engine equipped with a 10:1 impeller gear ratio operating at 2,600 r.p.m. would be 26,000 r.p.m. This requires that the impeller unit be a high-grade forging, usually of aluminum alloy, carefully designed and constructed. Because of the high ratio of all supercharger gear trains, considerable acceleration and deceleration forces are created when the engine speed is increased or decreased rapidly. This

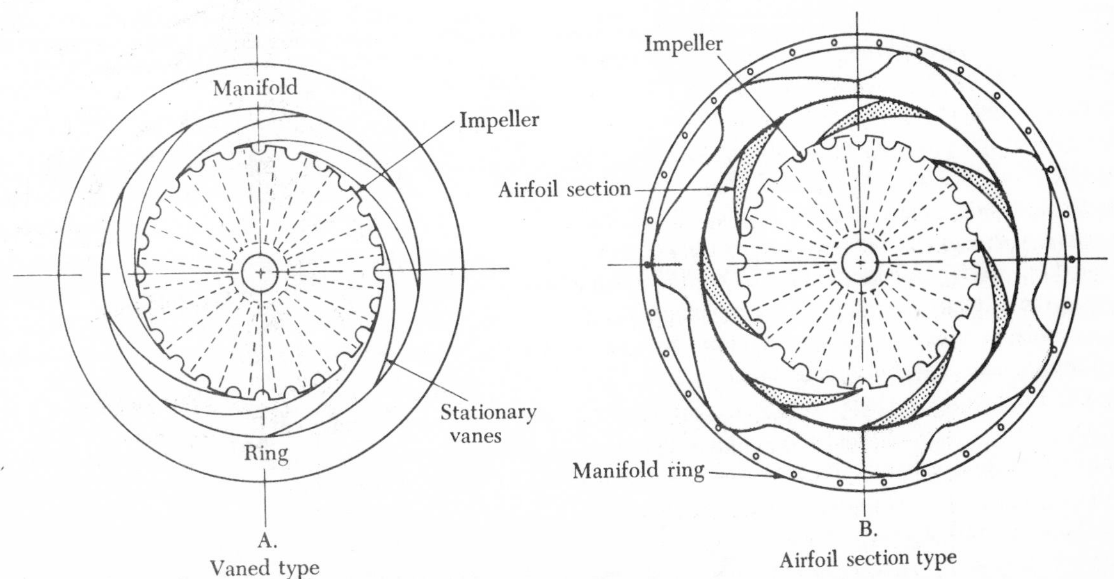

FIGURE 2–5. Supercharger diffuser design (vaned and airfoil section types).

necessitates that the impeller be splined on the shaft. In addition, some sort of spring-loaded or antishock device must be incorporated in the gear train between the crankshaft and impeller.

An oil seal is usually provided around the impeller shaft just forward of the impeller unit. The functions of the seal on this unit are to minimize the passage of lubricating oil and vapors from the crankcase into the diffuser chamber when the engine is idling and to minimize the leakage of the fuel/air mixture into the crankcase when the pressure on the mixture is high at open throttle.

The clearance between the diffuser section and the impeller is obtained by varying the length of the oil seal or the thickness of spacers commonly called shims. Close clearance is necessary to give the greatest possible compression of the mixture and to eliminate, insofar as possible, leakage around the fore and aft surfaces of the impeller. The impeller shaft and intermediate drive shaft assemblies may be mounted on antifriction ball or roller bearings or on friction-type bushings.

The impeller shaft and gear are usually forged integrally of very high grade steel. The impeller end of the shaft is splined to give as much driving surface as possible. The intermediate shaft and large and small gears also are one piece. Both of these units are held within very close running balance or dynamic limits due to the high speeds and stresses involved.

Single-Stage, Two-Speed Supercharger Systems

Some aircraft engines are equipped with internally driven superchargers which are single-stage, two-speed systems. The impeller in such systems can be driven at two different speeds by means of clutches. A schematic of such a supercharger is shown in figure 2–6.

This unit is equipped with a means of driving the impeller directly from the crankshaft at a ratio of 10:1, which is accomplished by moving the control in the cockpit, thereby applying oil pressure through the high-speed clutch and thus locking the entire intermediate gear assembly. This is called "high blower" and is used above a specified altitude ranging from 7,000 to 12,000 ft. Below these levels, the control is positioned to release the pressure on the high-speed clutch and apply it to the low-speed clutch. This locks the sun pinion of the small planetary gear. The impeller then is driven through the spider and shaft assembly on which the planetary pinions are caused to rotate by the large bell gear. In this case, the impeller is driven at a ratio of approximately 7:1 relative to crankshaft speed. (See figure 2–7.) This condition is called "low blower" and is used during takeoff and for all altitudes below those at which best efficiency can be obtained in "high blower."

In effect, this gives two engines in one. It improves the power output characteristics over a range of operating conditions varying from sea level to approximately 20,000 ft. Naturally, a device of this kind complicates and increases considerably the initial and maintenance costs of the engine. A higher grade fuel is also required to withstand the additional pressures and, in some cases, higher temperatures created within the combustion chamber due to more complete fuel charging of the cylinder. The addition of this unit also complicates the operation of the powerplant because it requires more attention and adds to the variables which must be controlled.

Another example of a two-stage, two-speed supercharger system is shown in figure 2–8, where the blower and intermediate rear sections are opened to show their internal construction. In this example, the blower case supports the engine in the aircraft. It has eight pads on the outer circumference for the engine mounting brackets. A liner in the center of the case accommodates the oil seal rings in the impeller shaft front ring carrier. The blower case houses the impeller, which is driven by clutches at either 7.15 or 8.47 times crankshaft speed. An annulus around the case delivers the fuel and air mixture from the impeller to 14 ports in the case. Attached to each of these ports is an intake pipe through which the fuel and air mixture proceeds to the inlet valve of its cylinder.

Intermediate Rear Case

The intermediate rear case houses the impeller drive gear train and supports a vaned diffuser (see figure 2–9). The impeller ratio selector valve is mounted on a pad on the top left of the case. From the carburetor mounting flange on the top of the case, a large duct leads down to carry the intake air to the impeller. The fuel transfer pipe from the carburetor connects with a passage in the case behind the carburetor mounting flange. This passage leads to the fuel feed valve. The fuel feed valve delivers fuel to the fuel slinger, which mixes the fuel with the intake air. The cover and diaphragm assembly of the fuel feed valve are mounted on the forward side of the carburetor flange. An accelerating pump is fastened to a pad on the right side of the case just below the carburetor flange. At the lowest point in

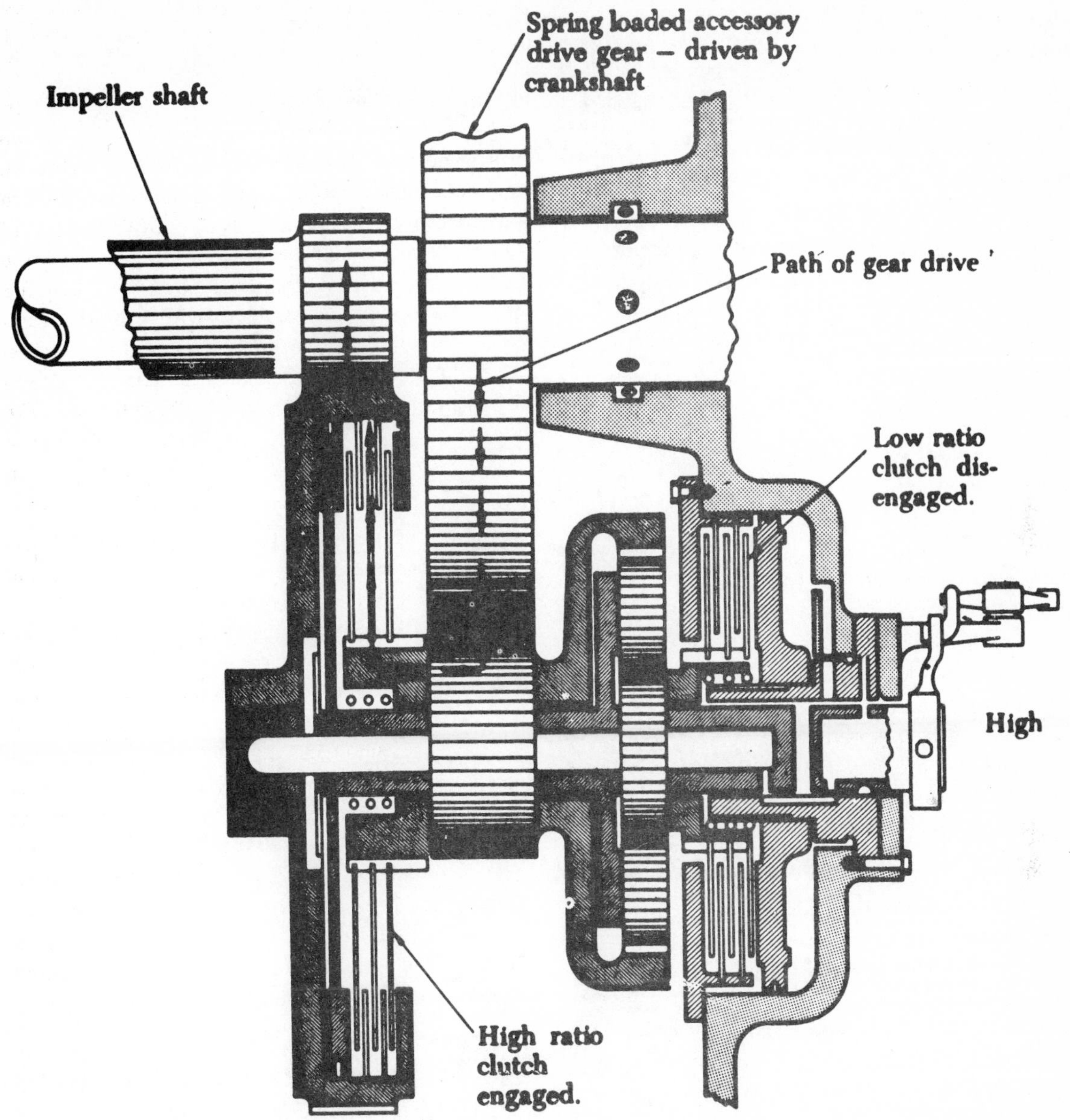

FIGURE 2–6. Schematic diagram of two-speed supercharger in high ratio.

the carburetor air duct, drilled passages lead down to the automatic fuel drain valve in the bottom of the case, which discharges any fuel that may accumulate while the engine is being started.

The intermediate rear case also houses the dual-ratio clutches and the impeller ratio selector valve. Both a high(8.47:1)—and a low(7.15:1)—ratio clutch are mounted on each of two shafts, one on each side of the impeller shaft. These shafts are supported at the front end by bushings in the rear case. The shafts are driven by the accessory drive gear through pinions splined to the shafts. The clutch cones are splined to the clutch shafts and, when engaged, drive the clutch gears, which, in turn, drive the spur gears on the impeller shaft. The selector valve directs pressure oil to oil chambers between the cones and the gears of either the two low or the two high clutches. The oil pressure causes the cones to engage the segments that, in turn, engage the gears of whichever pair of clutches are selected to drive the impeller. Drain oil from the disengaged pair of clutches is forced back through the selector valve and discharged into the intermediate rear case.

To assist in cleaning sludge out of the clutches,

each clutch gear is equipped with a creeper gear having one more tooth than the clutch gear. A bleed hole in the creeper gear itself alines momentarily with each of the bleed holes in the corresponding clutch gear. The pressure oil within the engaged clutch spurts out, carrying the sludge with it.

EXTERNALLY DRIVEN SUPERCHARGERS

Externally driven superchargers are designed to deliver compressed air to the inlet of the carburetor or fuel/air control unit of an engine. Externally driven superchargers derive their power from the energy of engine exhaust gases directed against some form of turbine. For this reason, they are commonly called turbosuperchargers or turbochargers.

TURBOSUPERCHARGER SYSTEM FOR LARGE RECIPROCATING ENGINES

In some high-altitude aircraft the internal supercharger is supplemented by an external turbosupercharger driven by a portion of the exhaust gas from the aircraft engine. This type of supercharger is mounted ahead of the carburetor as shown in figure 2–10 to pressurize the air at the carburetor

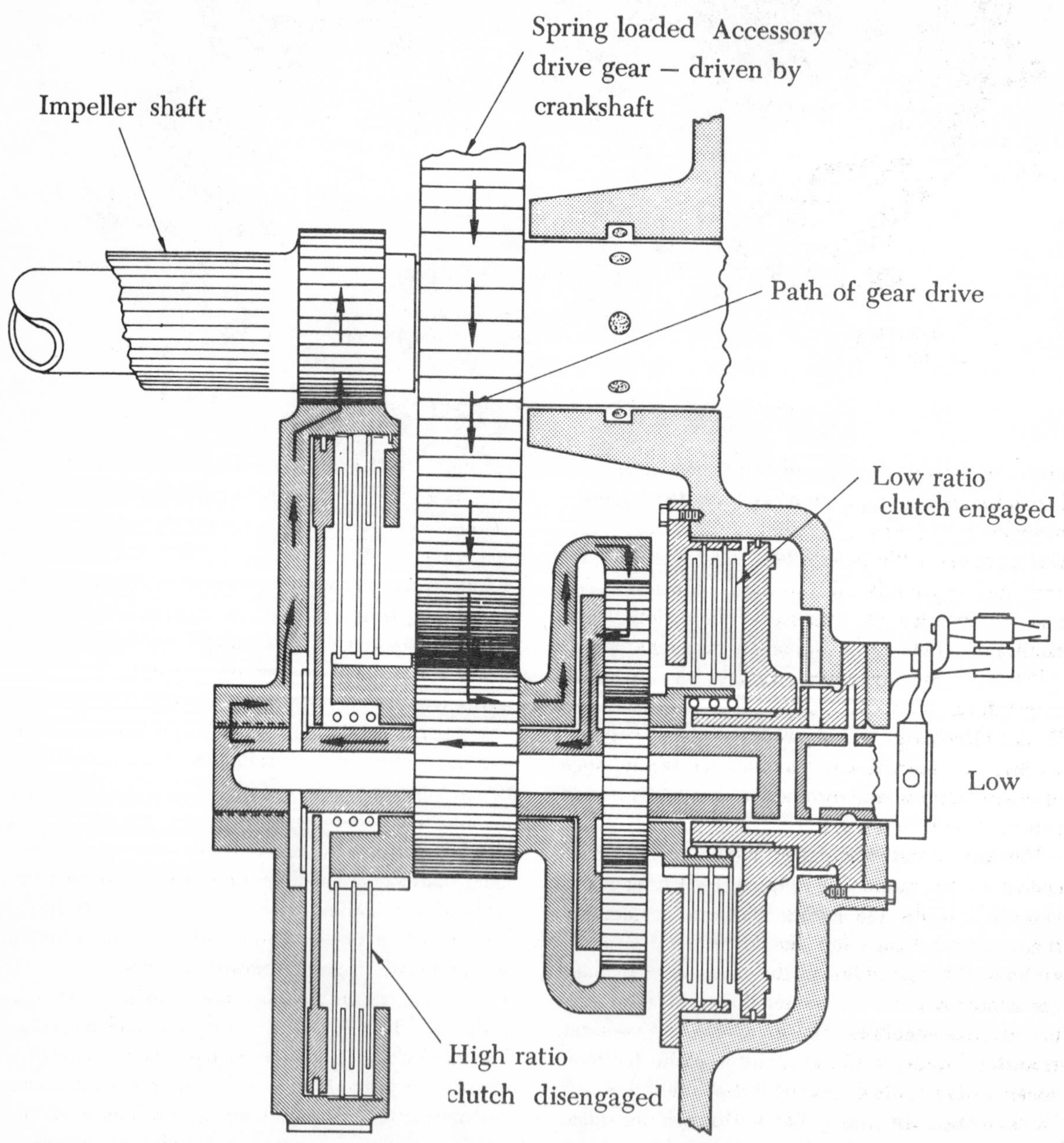

FIGURE 2–7. Schematic diagram of two-speed supercharger in low ratio.

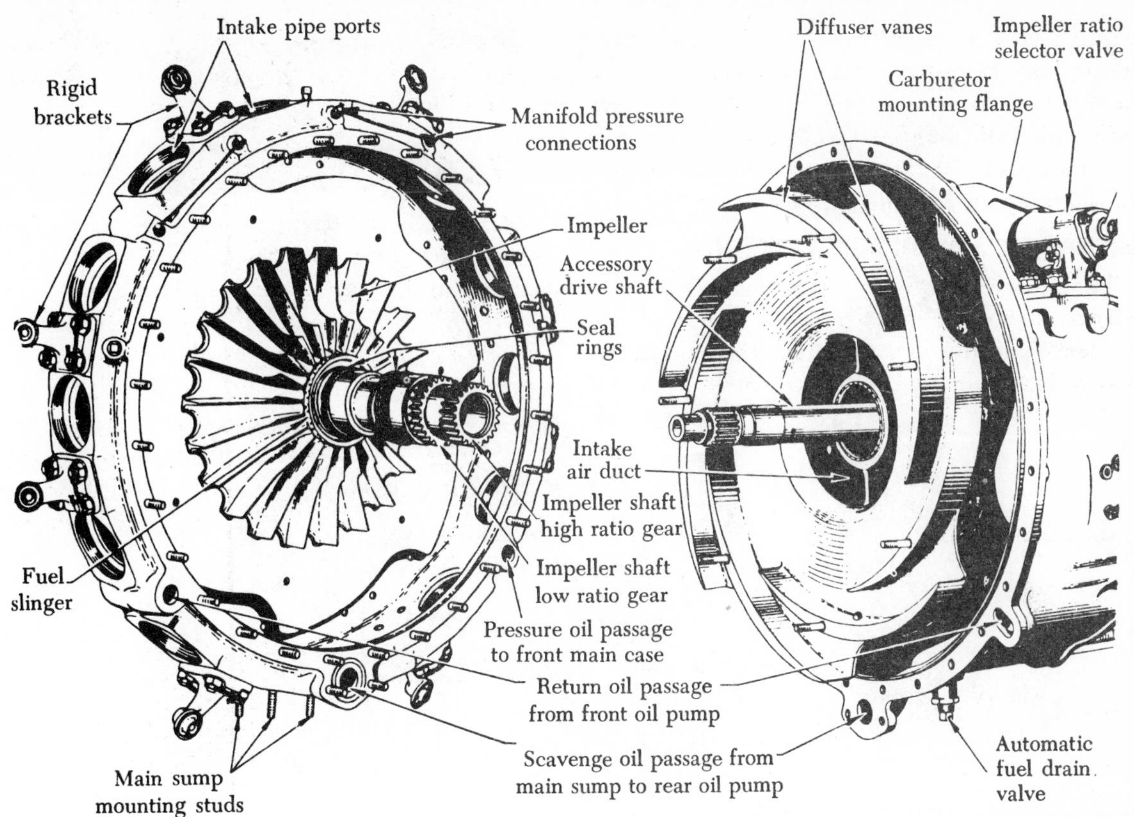

FIGURE 2–8. Blower and intermediate rear sections.

inlet. If the air pressure entering the carburetor is maintained at approximately sea level density throughout the aircraft's climb to altitude, there will be none of the power loss experienced in aircraft not equipped with turbos. However, this type of supercharger imposes an induction system requirement not needed in other supercharger installations. As air moves through the turbo, its temperature is raised because of compression. If the hot air charge is not properly cooled before it reaches the internal supercharger, the second stage of supercharging will produce a final charge temperature that is too great.

The air in turbo-equipped induction systems is cooled by an intercooler (figure 2–10), so called because it cools the charge between compression stages rather than after the last stage. The hot air flows through tubes in the intercooler in much the same manner that water flows in the radiator of an automobile. Fresh outside air, separate from the charge, is collected and piped to the intercooler so that it flows over and cools the tubes. As the induction air charge flows through the tubes, heat is removed and the charge is cooled to a degree that the engine can tolerate without detonation occurring. Control for the cooling air is provided by intercooler shutters which regulate the amount of air that passes over and around the tubes of the intercooler.

The typical turbosupercharger is composed of three main parts:

(1) The compressor assembly.

(2) The exhaust gas turbine assembly.

(3) The pump and bearing casing.

These major sections are shown in figure 2–11. In addition to the major assemblies, there is a baffle between the compressor casing and the exhaust-gas turbine that directs cooling air to the pump and bearing casing, and also shields the compressor from the heat radiated by the turbine. In installations where cooling air is limited, the baffle is replaced by a regular cooling shroud that receives its air directly from the induction system.

The compressor assembly (A of figure 2–11) is made up of an impeller, a diffuser, and a casing. The air for the induction system enters through a circular opening in the center of the compressor casing, where it is picked up by the blades of the impeller, which gives it high velocity as it travels outward toward the diffuser. The diffuser vanes

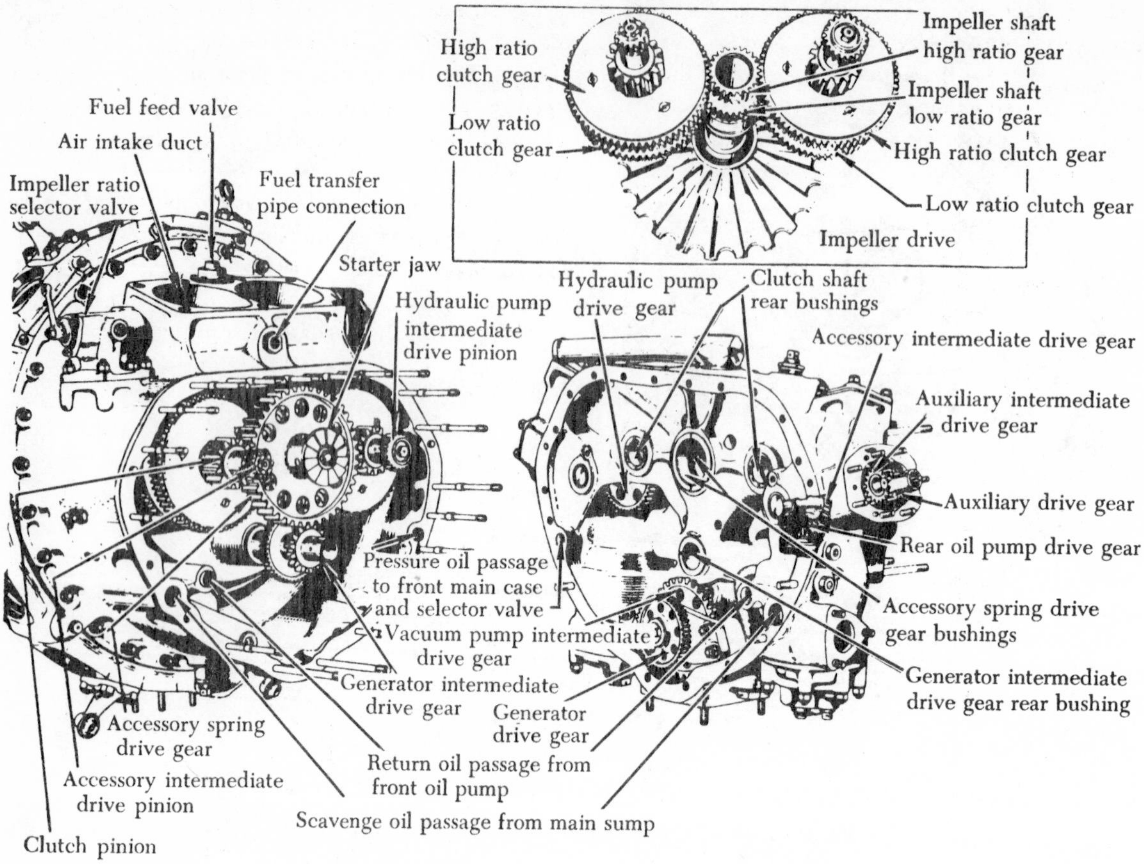

High ratio clutch gear
Low ratio clutch gear
Impeller shaft high ratio gear
Impeller shaft low ratio gear
High ratio clutch gear
Low ratio clutch gear
Impeller drive
Fuel feed valve
Air intake duct
Impeller ratio selector valve
Fuel transfer pipe connection
Starter jaw
Hydraulic pump intermediate drive pinion
Hydraulic pump drive gear
Clutch shaft rear bushings
Accessory intermediate drive gear
Auxiliary intermediate drive gear
Auxiliary drive gear
Rear oil pump drive gear
Pressure oil passage to front main case and selector valve
Vacuum pump intermediate drive gear
Accessory spring drive gear bushings
Generator intermediate drive gear rear bushing
Generator intermediate drive gear
Generator drive gear
Accessory spring drive gear
Accessory intermediate drive pinion
Return oil passage from front oil pump
Scavenge oil passage from main sump
Clutch pinion

FIGURE 2–9. Intermediate rear and rear case sections.

Intercooler
Internally driven supercharger.
Turbosupercharger

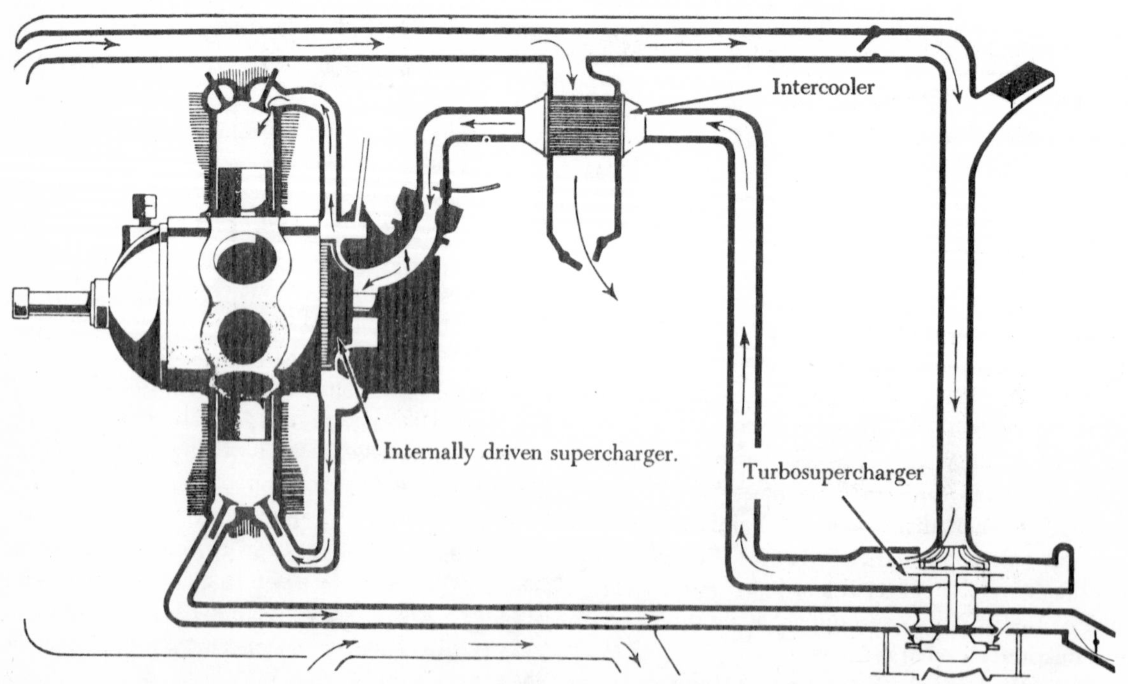

FIGURE 2–10. Induction system with turbosupercharger.

direct the airflow as it leaves the impeller and also converts the high velocity of the air to high pressure.

Motive power for the impeller is furnished through the impeller's attachment to the turbine wheel shaft of the exhaust-gas turbine. This complete assembly is referred to as the rotor. The rotor revolves on the ball bearings at the rear end of the pump and bearing casing and the roller bearing at the turbine end. The roller bearing carries the radial (centrifugal) load of the rotor, and the ball bearing supports the rotor at the impeller end and bears the entire thrust (axial) load and part of the radial load.

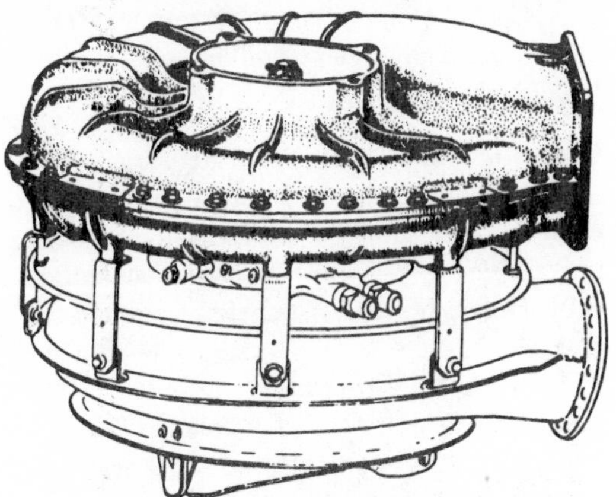

A. Compressor assembly

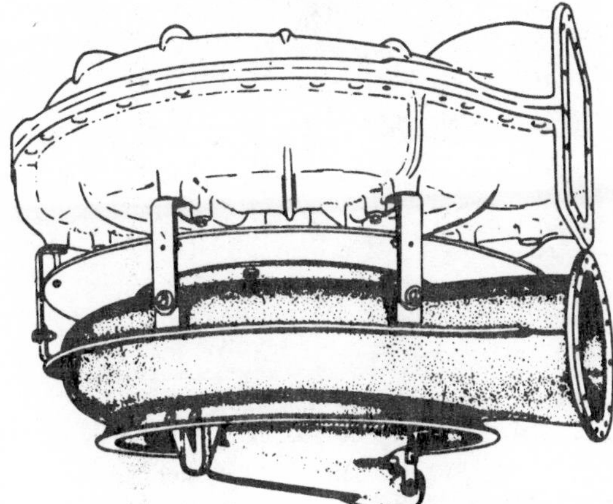

B. Exhaust gas turbine assembly

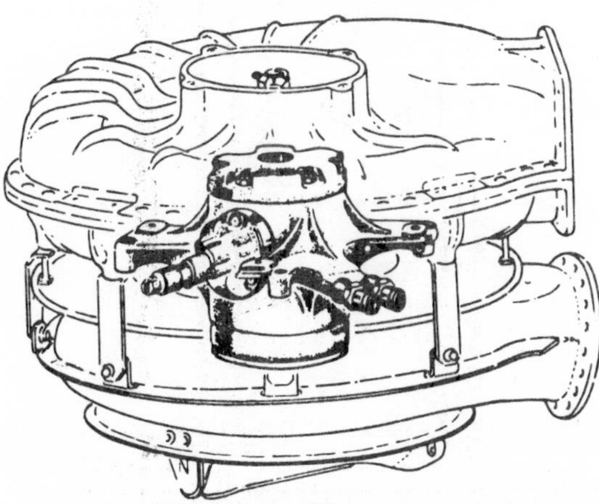

C. Pump and bearing casing

FIGURE 2–11. Main sections of a typical turbosupercharger.

The exhaust gas turbine assembly (B of figure 2–11) consists of the turbine wheel (bucket wheel), nozzle box, butterfly valve (waste gate), and cooling cap. The turbine wheel, driven by exhaust gases, drives the impeller. The nozzle box collects and directs the exhaust gases onto the turbine wheel, and the waste gate regulates the amount of exhaust gases directed to the turbine by the nozzle box. The cooling cap controls a flow of air for turbine cooling.

The waste gate (figure 2–12) controls the volume of the exhaust gas that is directed onto the turbine and thereby regulates the speed of the rotor (turbine and impeller).

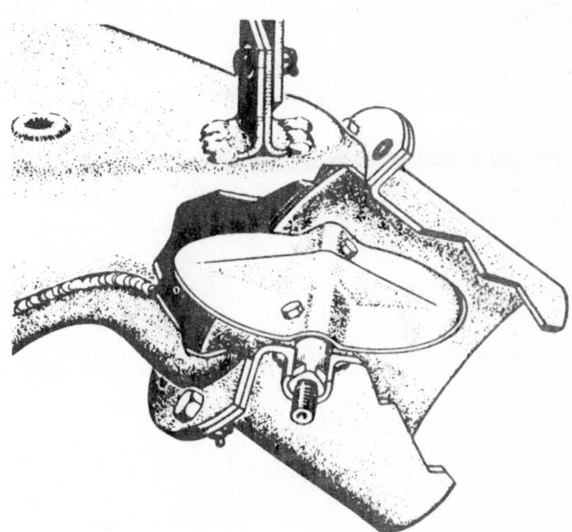

FIGURE 2–12. Waste gate assembly.

If the waste gate is completely closed, all the exhaust gases are "backed up" and forced through the nozzle box and turbine wheel. If the waste gate is partially closed, a corresponding amount of exhaust gas is directed to the turbine. The nozzles of the nozzle box allow the gases to expand and reach high velocity before they contact the turbine wheel. The exhaust gases, thus directed, strike the cuplike buckets, arranged radially around the outer edge of the turbine, and cause the rotor (turbine and impeller) to rotate. The gases are then exhausted overboard through the spaces between the buckets. When the waste gate is fully open, nearly all of the exhaust gases pass overboard through the tailpipe.

TURBOCHARGER

An increasing number of engines used in light aircraft are equipped with externally driven supercharger systems. These superchargers are powered by the energy of exhaust gases and are usually referred to as "turbocharger" systems rather than "turbosuperchargers."

On many small aircraft engines, the turbocharger system is designed to be operated only above a certain altitude; for example, 5,000 ft., since maximum power without supercharging is available below that altitude.

The location of the air induction and exhaust systems of a typical turbocharger system for a small aircraft is shown in figure 2–13.

Induction Air System

The induction air system shown in figure 2–14 consists of a filtered ram-air intake located on the side of the nacelle. An alternate air door within the nacelle permits compressor suction to automatically admit alternate air (heated engine compartment air) if the induction filter becomes clogged. The alternate air door can be operated manually in the event of filter clogging. A separately mounted exhaust-driven turbocharger is included in each air induction system. The turbocharger is automatically controlled by a pressure controller, to maintain manifold pressure at approximately 34.5 in. Hg from sea level to the critical altitude (typically 16,000 ft.) regardless of temperature. The turbocharger is completely automatic, requiring no pilot action up to the critical altitude.

Controllers and Waste-Gate Actuator

The waste-gate actuator and controllers use engine oil for power supply. (Refer to turbocharger system schematic in figure 2–15.) The turbocharger is controlled by the waste gate and waste-gate actuator, an absolute pressure and a rate-of-change controller. A pressure ratio controller controls the waste-gate actuator above critical altitude (16,000 ft.). The waste-gate bypasses the engine exhaust gases around the turbocharger turbine inlet. The waste-gate actuator, which is physically connected to the waste gate by mechanical linkage, controls the position of the waste-gate butterfly valve. The absolute pressure controller and the rate-of-change

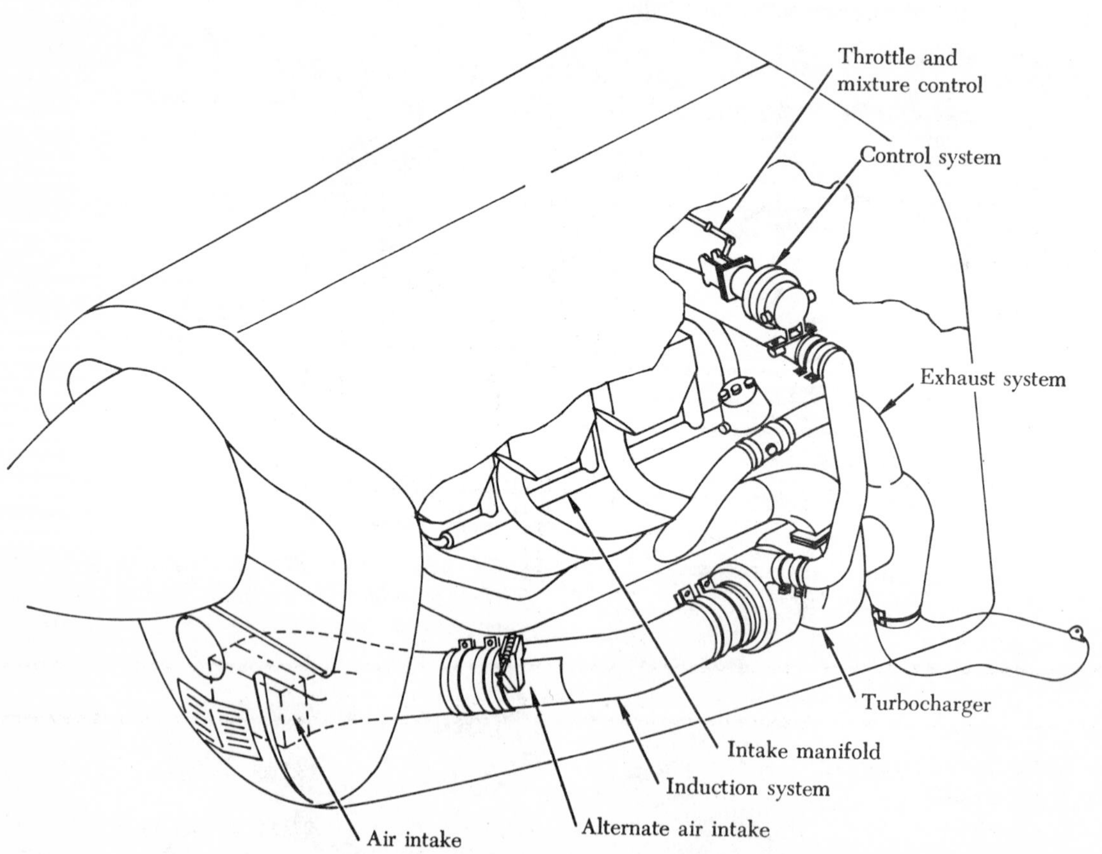

FIGURE 2–13. Turbocharger induction and exhaust systems.

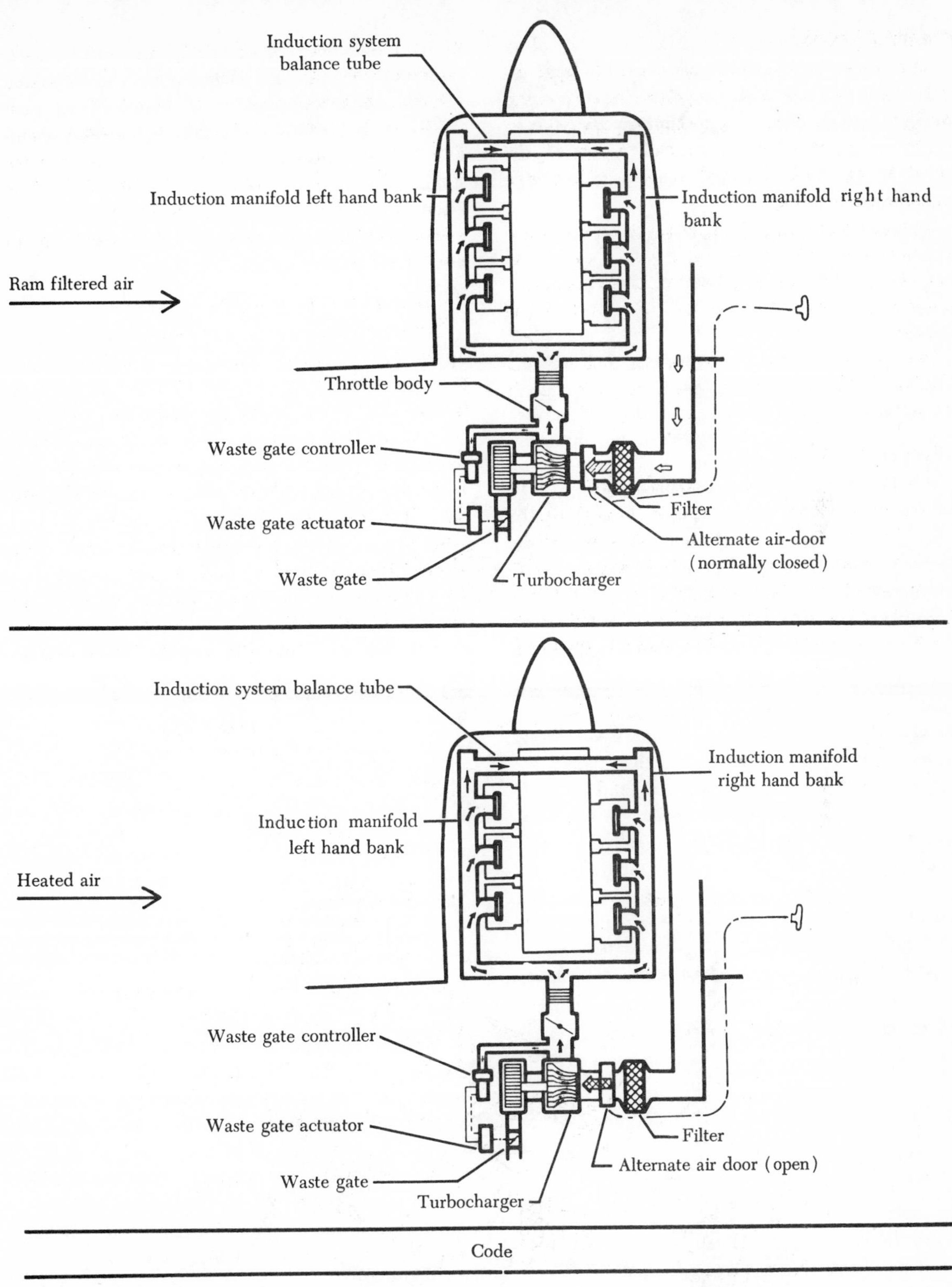

FIGURE 2–14. Induction air system schematic.

controller have a two-fold function: (1) The absolute pressure controller controls the maximum turbocharger compressor discharge pressure (34 ±.5 in. Hg to critical altitude, approximately 16,000 ft.); and (2) the rate-of-change controller controls the rate at which the turbocharger compressor discharge pressure will increase.

SEA-LEVEL BOOSTED TURBOCHARGER SYSTEM

Some turbocharger systems are designed to operate from sea level up to their critical altitude. These engines, sometimes referred to as sea-level boosted engines, can develop more power at sea level than an engine without turbocharging.

Figure 2–16 is a schematic of a sea level booster turbocharger system. This system is automatically regulated by three components shown in the schematic: (1) The exhaust bypass valve assembly, (2) the density controller, and (3) the differential pressure controller. It should be noted that some turbocharger systems are not equipped with automatic control devices. They are similar in design and operation to the system shown in figure 2–16, except that the turbocharger output is manually controlled.

By regulating the waste gate position and the "fully open" and "closed" positions (figure 2–16), a constant power output can be maintained. When the waste gate is fully open, all the exhaust gases are directed overboard to the atmosphere, and no air is compressed and delivered to the engine air inlet. Conversely, when the waste gate is fully closed, a maximum volume of exhaust gases flows into the turbocharger turbine, and maximum supercharging is accomplished. Between these two extremes of waste gate position, constant power output can be achieved below the maximum altitude at which the system is designed to operate.

A critical altitude exists for every possible power setting below the maximum operating ceiling, and if the aircraft is flown above this altitude without a corresponding change in the power setting, the waste gate will be automatically driven to the "fully closed" position in an effort to maintain a constant power output. Thus, the waste gate will be almost fully open at sea level and will continue to move toward the "closed" position as the aircraft climbs, in order to maintain the preselected manifold pressure setting.

When the waste gate is fully closed (leaving only a small clearance to prevent sticking) the manifold pressure will begin to drop if the aircraft continues to climb. If a higher power setting cannot be selected, the turbocharger's critical altitude has been reached. Beyond this altitude, the power output will continue to decrease.

The position of the waste gate valve, which determines power output, is controlled by oil pressure. Engine oil pressure acts on a piston in the waste gate assembly which is connected by linkage to the waste gate valve. When oil pressure is increased on the piston, the waste gate valve moves toward the "closed" position, and engine output power increases. Conversely, when the oil pressure is decreased, the waste gate valve moves toward the "open" position, and output power is decreased.

The position of the piston attached to the waste gate valve is dependent on bleed oil which controls the engine oil pressure applied to the top of the piston. Oil is returned to the engine crankcase through two control devices, the density controller and the differential pressure controller. These two controllers, acting independently, determine how much oil is bled back to the crankcase, and thus establishes the oil pressure on the piston.

The density controller is designed to limit the manifold pressure below the turbocharger's critical altitude, and regulates bleed oil only at the "full throttle" position. The pressure- and temperature-sensing bellows of the density controller react to pressure and temperature changes between the fuel injector inlet and the turbocharger compressor. The bellows, filled with dry nitrogen, maintains a constant density by allowing the pressure to increase as the temperature increases. Movement of the bellows re-positions the bleed valve, causing a change in the quantity of bleed oil, which changes the oil pressure on top of the waste gate piston. (See figure 2–16.)

The differential pressure controller functions during all positions of the waste gate valve other than the "fully open" position, which is controlled by the density controller. One side of the diaphragm in the differential pressure controller senses air pressure upstream from the throttle; the other side samples pressure on the cylinder side of the throttle valve (figure 2–16). At the "wide open" throttle position when the density controller controls the waste gate, the pressure across the differential pressure controller diaphragm is at a minimum and the controller spring holds the bleed valve closed. At "part throttle" position, the air differential is increased, opening the bleed valve to bleed oil to the engine crankcase and re-position the waste gate piston.

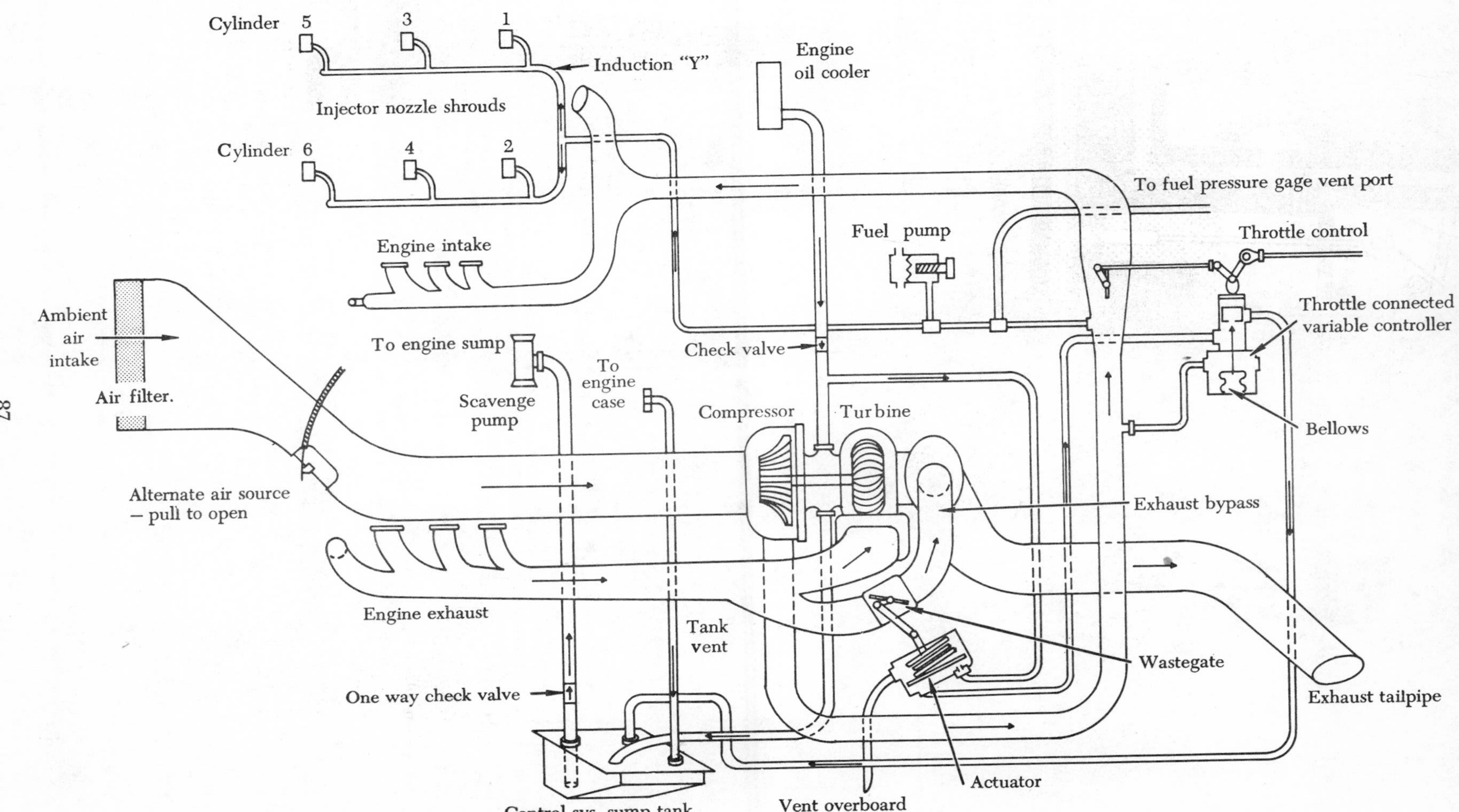

FIGURE 2–15. Schematic of a typical turbocharger system.

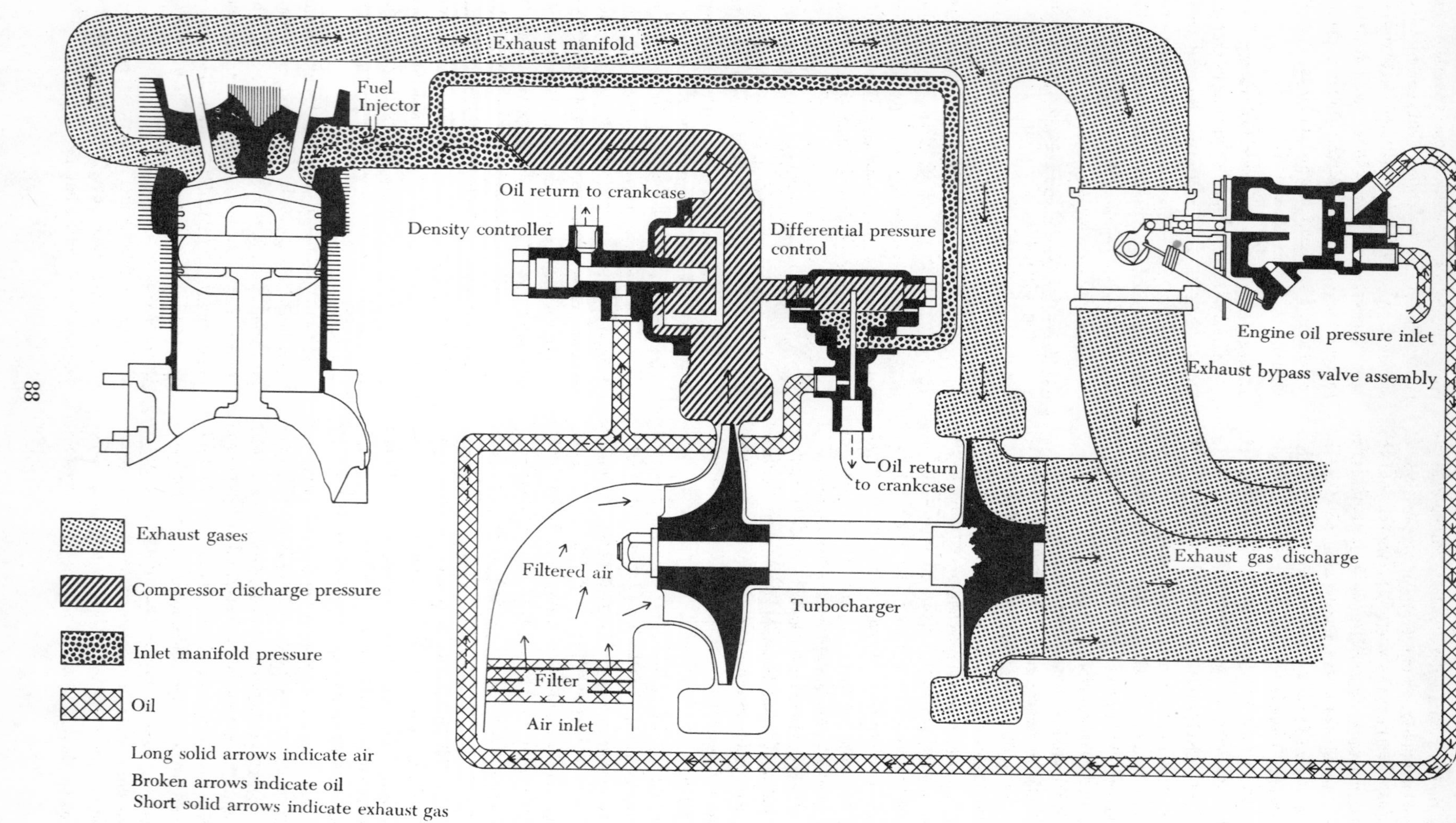

FIGURE 2–16. Turbocharger controllers and waste-gate actuater system schematic.

Thus, the two controllers operate independently to control turbocharger operation at all positions of the throttle. Without the overriding function of the differential pressure controller during part-throttle operation, the density controller would position the waste gate valve for maximum power. The differential pressure controller reduces injector entrance pressure and continually re-positions the valve over the whole operating range of the engine.

The differential pressure controller reduces the unstable condition known as "bootstrapping" during part-throttle operation. Bootstrapping is an indication of unregulated power change that results in the continual drift of manifold pressure. This condition can be illustrated by considering the operation of a system when the waste gate is fully closed. During this time, the differential pressure controller is not modulating the waste gate valve position. Any slight change in power caused by a change in temperature or r.p.m. fluctuation will be magnified and will result in manifold pressure change since the slight change will cause a change in the amount of exhaust gas flowing to the turbine. Any change in exhaust gas flow to the turbine will cause a change in power output and will be reflected in manifold pressure indications. Bootstrapping, then, is an undesirable cycle of turbocharging events causing the manifold pressure to drift in an attempt to reach a state of equilibrium.

Bootstrapping is sometimes confused with the condition known as "overboost," but bootstrapping is not a condition which is detrimental to engine life. An overboost condition is one in which manifold pressure exceeeds the limits prescribed for a particular engine and can cause serious damage.

Thus, the differential pressure controller is essential to smooth functioning of the automatically controlled turbocharger, since it reduces bootstrapping by reducing the time required to bring a system into equilibrium. There is still a great deal more throttle sensitivity with a turbocharged engine than with a naturally aspirated engine. Rapid movement of the throttle can cause a certain amount of manifold pressure drift in a turbocharged engine. This condition, less severe than bootstrapping, is called "overshoot." While overshoot is not a dangerous condition, it can be a source of concern to the pilot or operator who selects a particular manifold pressure setting only to find it has changed in a few seconds and must be reset. Since the automatic controls cannot respond rapidly enough to abrupt changes in throttle settings to eliminate the inertia of turbocharger speed changes, overshoot must be controlled by the operator. This can best be accomplished by slowly making changes in throttle setting, accompanied by a few seconds' wait for the system to reach a new equilibrium. Such a procedure is effective with turbocharged engines, regardless of the degree of throttle sensitivity.

Turbocharger System Troubleshooting

Table 1 includes some of the most common turbocharger system malfunctions, together with their cause and repair. These troubleshooting procedures are presented as a guide only and should not be substituted for applicable manufacturer's instructions or troubleshooting procedures.

TURBOCOMPOUND SYSTEMS FOR RECIPROCATING ENGINES

The turbocompound engine consists of a conventional, reciprocating engine in which exhaust-driven turbines are coupled to the engine crankshaft. This system of obtaining additional power is sometimes called a PRT (power recovery turbine) system. It is not a supercharging system, and it is not connected in any manner to the air induction system of the aircraft.

The PRT system enables the engine to recover power from the exhaust gases that would be otherwise directed overboard. Depending on the type of engine, the amount of horsepower recovered varies with the amount of input power. An average of 130 horsepower from each of three turbines in a system is typical for large reciprocating engines.

A power recovery turbine's geared connection to the engine crankshaft is shown in figure 2–17.

Typically there are three power-recovery turbines on each engine, located 120° apart. They are numbered, viewed from the rear of the engine, in a clockwise direction. Number 1 turbine is located in the 3-o'clock position, and number 3 turbine in the 11-o'clock position. Turbine position in relationship to the exhaust system of the various cylinders on an 18-cylinder engine is shown in the schematic of figure 2–18.

The exhaust collector nozzle for each segment of cylinders (figure 2–18) directs the exhaust gases onto the turbine wheel. The turbine wheel shaft transmits the power to the engine crankshaft through gears and a fluid coupling. The fluid coupling prevents torsional vibration from being transmitted to the crankshaft.

Power recovery turbine systems, because of weight and cost considerations, are used exclusively on very large reciprocating engines.

TABLE 1. Troubleshooting turbocharger system.

Trouble	*Probable Cause*	*Remedy*
Aircraft fails to reach critical altitude.	Damaged compressor or turbine wheel.	Replace turbocharger.
	Exhaust system leaks.	Repair leaks.
	Faulty turbocharger bearings.	Replace turbocharger.
	Waste gate will not close fully.	Refer to "waste gate" in the trouble column.
	Malfunctioning controller.	Refer to "differential controller" in the trouble column.
Engine surges.	Bootstrapping.	Ensure engine is operated in proper range.
	Waste gate malfunction.	Refer to "waste gate" in the trouble column.
	Controller malfunction.	Refer to "differential controller" in the trouble column.
Waste gate will not close fully.	Waste gate bypass valve bearings tight.	Replace bypass valve.
	Oil inlet orifice blocked.	Clean orifice.
	Controller malfunction.	Refer to "controller" in the trouble column.
	Broken waste gate linkage.	Replace linkage and adjust waste gate for proper opening and closing.
Waste gate will not open.	Oil outlet obstructed.	Clean and reconnect oil return line.
	Broken waste gate linkage.	Replace linkage and adjust waste gate opening and closing.
	Controller malfunction.	Refer to "controller" in the trouble column.
Differential controller malfunctions.	Seals leaking.	Replace controller.
	Diaphragm broken.	Replace controller.
	Controller valve stuck.	Replace controller.
Density controller malfunctions.	Seals leaking.	Replace controller.
	Bellows damaged.	Replace controller.
	Valve stuck.	Replace controller.

TURBOJET ENGINE INLET DUCT SYSTEMS

Although no direct parallel can be drawn, the turbine engine air-inlet duct is somewhat analogous to the air induction system of reciprocating engines.

The engine inlet and the inlet ducting of a turbine engine furnish a relatively distortion-free, high-energy supply of air, in the required quantity, to the face of the compressor. A uniform and steady airflow is necessary to avoid compressor stall and excessive internal engine temperatures at the turbine. The high energy enables the engine to produce an optimum amount of thrust. Normally, the air-inlet duct is considered an airframe part, and not a part of the engine. However, the duct is so important to engine performance that it must be considered in any discussion of the complete engine.

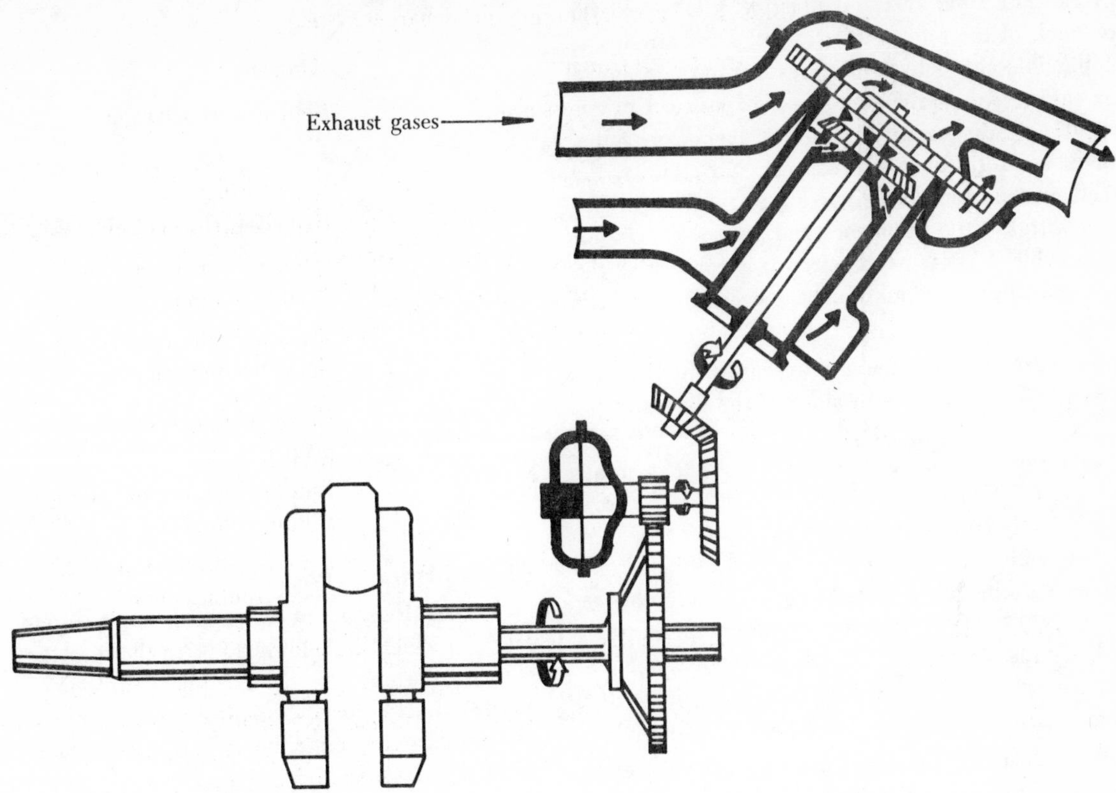

FIGURE 2–17. Transmission of turbine power to crankshaft.

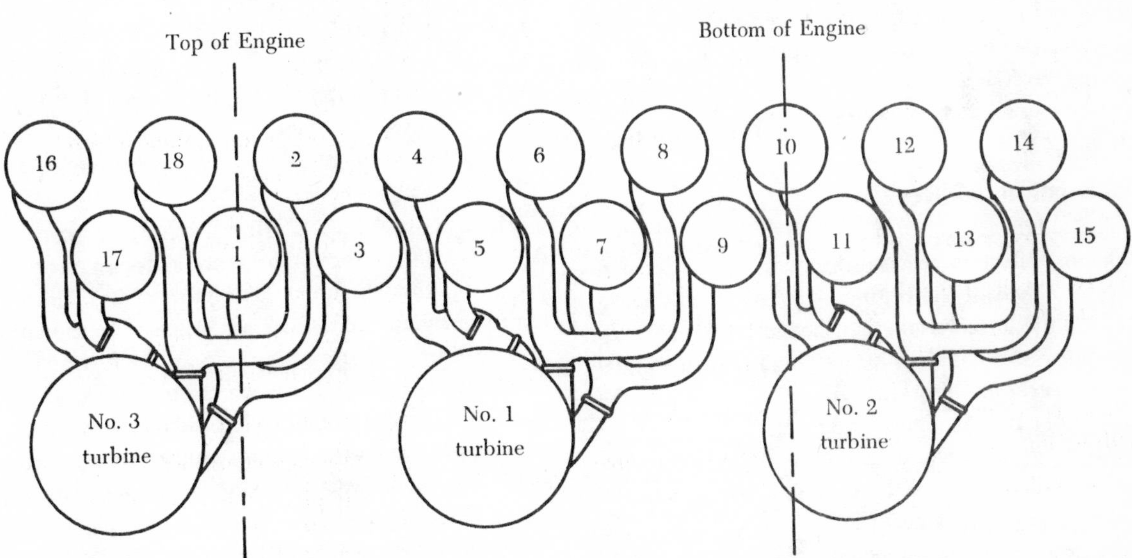

FIGURE 2–18. Schematic diagram of a PRT system.

A gas turbine engine consumes six to 10 times as much air per hour as a reciprocating engine of equivalent size. The air-entrance passage is correspondingly larger. Furthermore, it is more critical than a reciprocating engine airscoop in determining engine and aircraft performance, especially at high airspeeds. Inefficiencies of the duct result in successively magnified losses through other components of the engine.

The inlet duct has two engine functions and one

aircraft function. First, it must be able to recover as much of the total pressure of the free airstream as possible and deliver this pressure to the front of the engine with a minimum loss of pressure or differential. This is known as "ram recovery" or, sometimes, as "total pressure recovery." Secondly, the duct must uniformly deliver air to the compressor inlet with as little turbulence and pressure variation as possible. As far as the aircraft is concerned, the duct must hold to a minimum the drag effect, which it creates.

Pressure drop or differential is caused by the friction of the air along both sides of the duct and by the bends in the duct system. Smooth flow depends upon keeping the amount of turbulence to a minimum as the air enters the duct. The duct must have a sufficiently straight section to ensure smooth, even airflow within. The choice of configuration of the entrance to the duct is dictated by the location of the engine within the aircraft and the airspeed, altitude, and attitude at which the aircraft is designed to operate. There are two basic types of inlet ducts, the single-entrance duct and the divided-entrance duct.

With ducts of any type, careful construction is very essential. Good workmanship is also needed when an inlet duct is repaired. Surprisingly small amounts of airflow distortion can result in appreciable loss in engine efficiency or can be responsible for otherwise unexplainable compressor stalls. Protruding rivet heads or poor sheet metal work can play havoc with an otherwise acceptable duct installation.

Single-Entrance Duct

The single-entrance type of duct is the simplest and most effective because the duct inlet is located directly ahead of the engine and aircraft in such a position that it scoops undisturbed air. Figure 2–19 illustrates the single-entrance duct on a single-engine, turbojet aircraft. Also, the duct can be built either in a straight configuration or with only relatively gentle curvatures. In a single-engine aircraft installation where the engine is mounted in the fuselage, the duct is necessarily long. While some pressure drop is occasioned by the long duct, the condition is offset by smooth airflow characteristics. In multi-engine installations, a short, straight duct, or one that is nearly straight, is a necessity. Although this short, straight duct results in minimum pressure drop, the engine is apt to suffer from inlet turbulence, especially at slow airspeeds or high angles of attack.

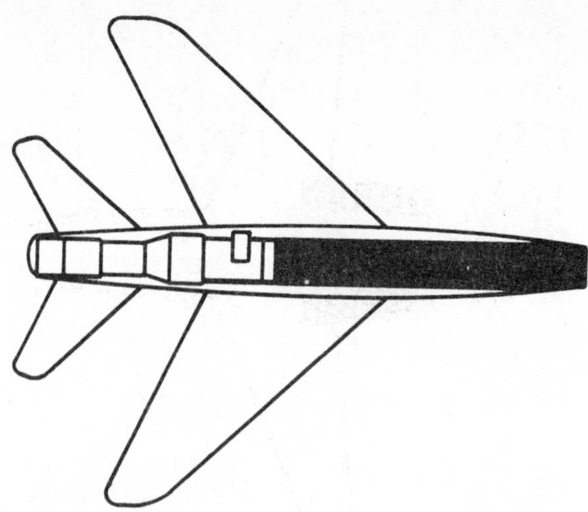

FIGURE 2–19. Aircraft with single-entrance duct.

Divided-Entrance Duct

The requirements of high-speed, single-engine aircraft, in which the pilot sits low in the fuselage and close to the nose, render it difficult to employ the single-entrance duct. Some form of a divided duct which takes air from either side of the fuselage may be required. This divided duct can be either a wing-root inlet or a scoop at each side of the fuselage, as shown in figure 2–20. Either type of duct presents more problems to the aircraft designer than a single-entrance duct because of the difficulty of obtaining sufficient airscoop area without imposing prohibitive amounts of drag. Internally, the problem is the same as that encountered with the single-entrance duct; that is, to construct a duct of reasonable length, yet with as few bends as possible.

The wing-root inlet on aircraft on which the wing is located fairly far aft presents a design problem because, although short, the duct must have considerable curvature to deliver air properly to the compressor inlet. Scoops at the sides of the fuselage are often used. These side scoops are placed as far forward as possible to permit a gradual bend toward the compressor inlet, making the airflow characteristics approach those of a single-entrance duct. A series of small rods is sometimes placed in the side-scoop inlet to assist in straightening the incoming airflow and to prevent turbulence.

Variable-Geometry Duct

The main function of an inlet duct is to furnish the proper amount of air to the engine inlet. In a typical turbojet engine, the maximum airflow requirements are such that the Mach number of the airflow directly ahead of the face of the engine is

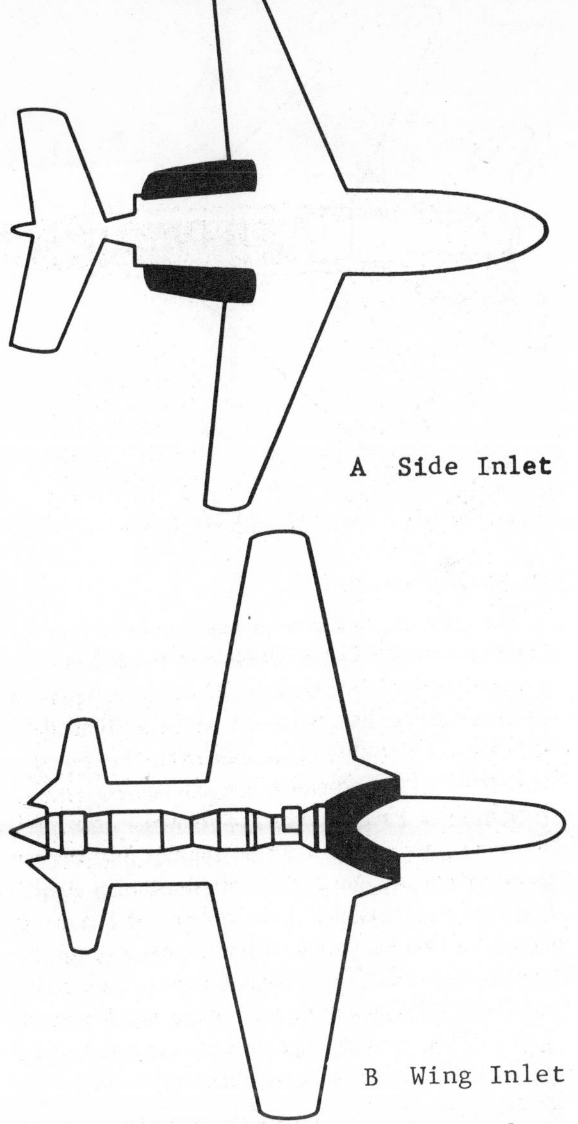

FIGURE 2–20. Two types of divided-entrance ducts.

about 0.5, or a little less. Therefore, under practically all flight conditions except takeoff or landing, the velocity of the airflow as it enters the air-inlet duct must be reduced through the duct before the same air is ready to enter the compressor. To accomplish this, inlet ducts are designed to function as diffusers, and thus decrease the velocity and increase the static pressure of the air passing through them. For subsonic multi-engine aircraft, a normal inlet duct, therefore, increases in size, front to rear, along the length of the duct, as illustrated in figure 2–21.

A supersonic diffuser progressively decreases in area in the downstream direction. Therefore, a supersonic inlet duct will follow this general config-

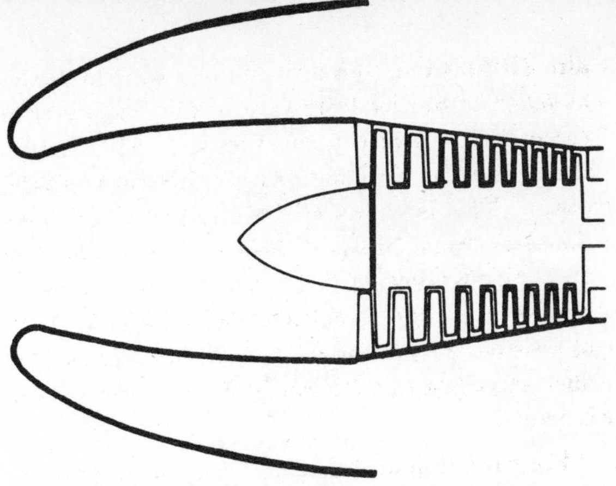

FIGURE 2–21. Divergent subsonic inlet duct.

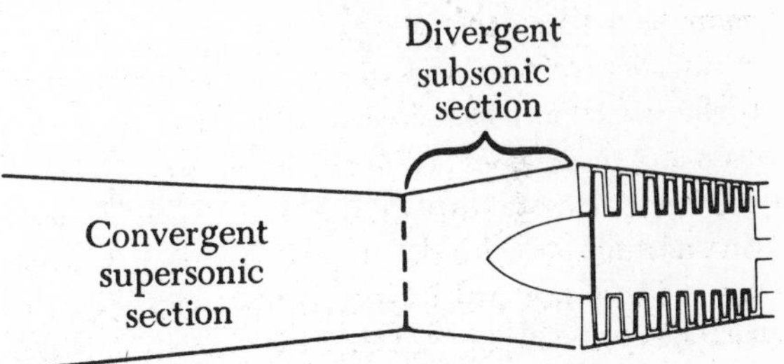

FIGURE 2–22. Supersonic inlet duct.

uration until the velocity of the incoming air is reduced to Mach 1.0. The aft section of the duct will then commence to increase in area, since this part must act as a subsonic diffuser. (See figure 2–22.) In practice, inlet ducts for supersonic aircraft will only follow this general design insofar as practical, depending upon the design features of the aircraft. For very high speed aircraft, the inside area of configuration of the duct will be changed by a mechanical device as the speed of the aircraft increases or decreases. A duct of this type is usually known as a variable-geometry inlet duct.

Two methods are used to diffuse the inlet air and slow the inlet airflow at supersonic flight speeds. One is to vary the area, or geometry, of the inlet duct either by using a movable restriction, such as a ramp or wedge, inside the duct. Still another system is some sort of a variable airflow bypass arrangement which extracts part of the inlet airflow from the duct ahead of the engine. In some cases, a combination of both systems is used.

The other method is the use of a shock wave in the airstream. A shock wave is a thin region of discontinuity in a flow of air or gas, during which the speed, pressure, density, and temperature of the air or gas undergo a sudden change. Stronger shock waves produce larger changes in the properties of the air or gas. A shock wave is willfully set up in the supersonic flow of the air entering the duct, by means of some restriction or small obstruction which automatically protrudes into the duct at high flight Mach numbers. The shock wave results in diffusion of the airflow, which, in turn, slows down the velocity of the airflow. In at least one aircraft installation, both the shock method and the variable-geometry method of causing diffusion are used in combination. The same device which changes the area of the duct also sets up a shock wave that further reduces the speed of the incoming air within the duct. The amount of change in duct area and the magnitude of the shock are varied automatically with the airspeed of the aircraft.

With a variable-geometry inlet, the so-called inlet "buzz" which sometimes occurs during flight at high Mach numbers can often be prevented by changing the amount of inlet-area variation that takes place when the variable-geometry inlet system is in operation. The "buzz" is an airflow instability which occurs when a shock wave is alternately swallowed and regurgitated by the inlet. At its worst, the condition can cause violent fluctuations in pressure through the inlet, which may result in damage to the inlet structure or, possibly, to the engine itself. A suitable variable-geometry duct will eliminate the "buzz" by increasing the stability of the airflow within the inlet duct.

Bellmouth Compressor Inlets

Although not a duct in the true sense of the word, a bellmouth inlet is usually installed on an engine being calibrated in a ground test stand, to lead the outside static air to the inlet guide vanes of the compressor. This type of inlet is easily attached and removed. It is designed with the single objective of obtaining very high aerodynamic efficiency. Essentially, the inlet is a bell-shaped funnel having carefully rounded shoulders which offer practically no air resistance (see figure 2–23). Duct loss is so slight that it is considered zero. The engine can, therefore, be operated without the complications resulting from losses common to an installed aircraft duct. Engine performance data, such as rated thrust and thrust specific fuel consumption, are obtained while using a bellmouth compressor inlet. Usually, the inlets are fitted with protective screening. In this case, the efficiency which is lost as the air passes through the screen must be taken into account when very accurate engine data are necessary.

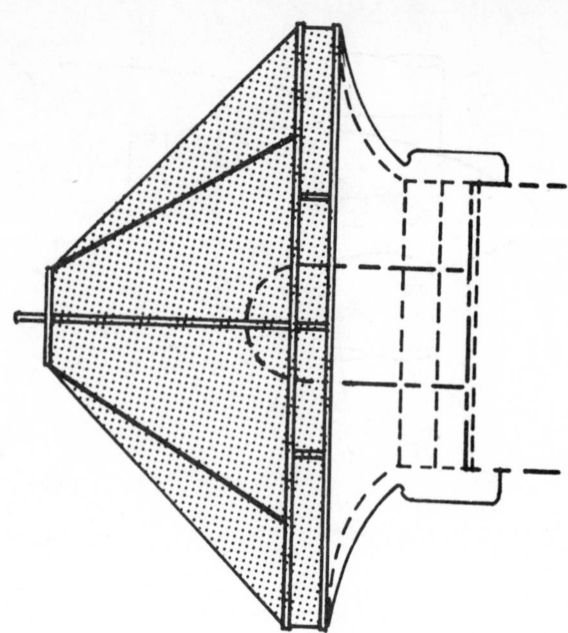

FIGURE 2–23. Bellmouth compressor inlet.

TURBOPROP COMPRESSOR INLETS

The air inlet on a turboprop is more of a problem than that on a turbojet because the propeller drive shaft, the hub, and the spinner must be considered in addition to the usual other inlet design factors. The ducted spinner arrangement (figure 2–24A) is generally considered the best inlet design of the turboprop engine as far as airflow and aerodynamic characteristics are concerned. However, the ducted spinner is heavier, and is more difficult to maintain and to anti-ice than the conventional streamline spinner arrangement which is frequently used. A conical spinner, which is a modified version of the streamline spinner, is sometimes employed. In either event, the arrangement of the spinner and the inlet duct is similar to that shown in figure 2–24B. When the nose section of the turboprop engine is offset from the main axis of the engine, an arrangement similar to that in figure 2–24C may be employed.

Compressor-Inlet Screens

The appetite of a gas turbine for nuts, small bolts, rags, small hand tools, and the like, is well known. To prevent the engine from readily ingesting such items, a compressor-inlet screen is sometimes placed across the engine air inlet at some location along the inlet duct.

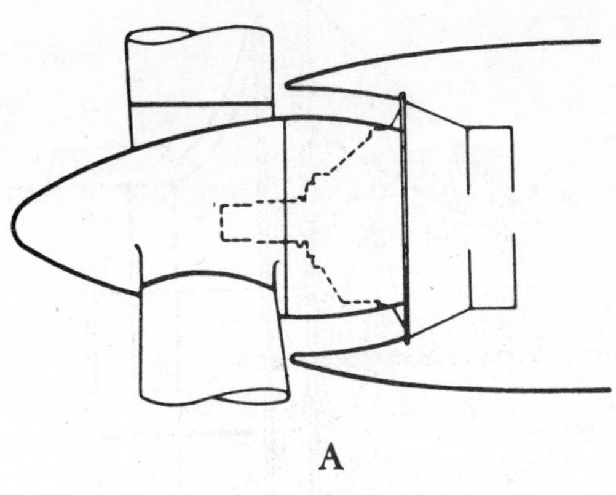

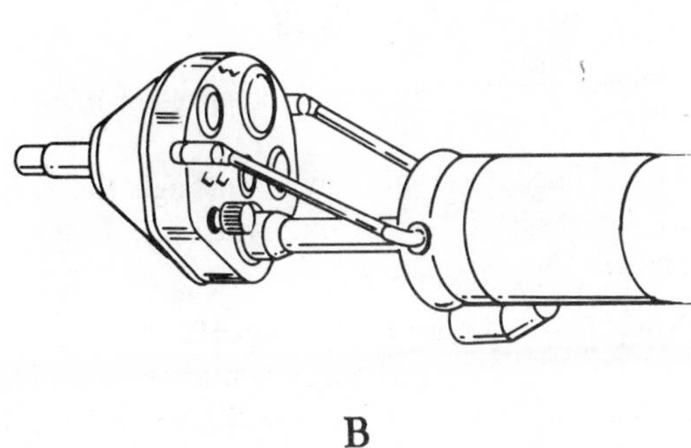

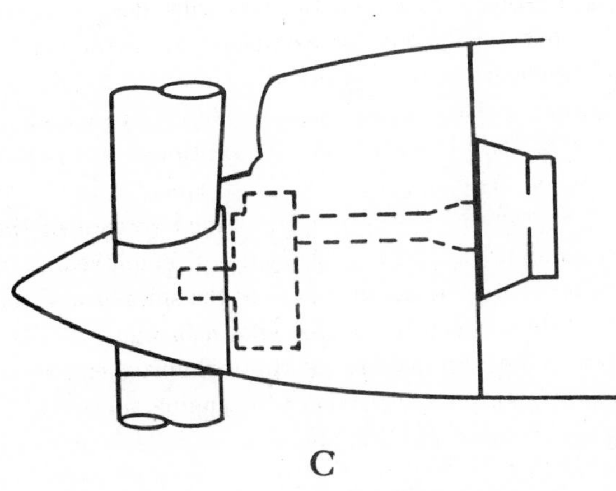

FIGURE 2–24. Turboprop compressor inlets.

The advantages and disadvantages of a screen of this type vary. If the engine is readily subject to internal damage, as would be the case for instance, of an engine having an axial compressor fitted with aluminum compressor blades, an inlet screen is almost a necessity. Screens, however, add appreciably to inlet-duct pressure loss, and are very susceptible to icing. Failures due to fatigue are also a problem. A failed screen can sometimes cause more damage than no screen at all. In some instances, inlet screens are made retractable and may be withdrawn from the airstream after takeoff or whenever icing conditions prevail. Such screens are subject to mechanical failure, and add both weight and bulk to the installation. In large engines having steel or titanium compressor blades which do not damage easily, the disadvantages of compressor screens outweigh the advantages, so they are not generally used.

Turbofan Engine Fan Sections

Although some turbofan engines have their fan section, or blades, integral with the turbine, aft of the combustion chamber, other versions are usually constructed with the fan at the forward end of the compresser. In dual-compressor engines, the fan is integral with the relatively slow-turning, low-pressure compressor, which allows the fan blades to rotate at low tip speed for best fan efficiency. The forward fan permits the use of a conventional air-inlet duct, resulting in low inlet-duct loss. The forward fan reduces engine damage from ingested foreign material because much of any material that may be ingested will be thrown radially outward, and will pass through the fan discharge rather than through the main part of the engine.

The fan consists of one or more stages of rotating blades and stationary vanes that are somewhat larger than the forward stages of the compressor to which they are attached. The air accelerated by the fan tips forms a secondary airstream which is ducted overboard without passing through the main engine. The air which passes through the center of the fan becomes the primary airstream through the engine itself (see figure 2–25).

The air from the fan exhaust, which is ducted overboard, may be discharged in either of two ways: (1) To the outside air through short ducts, directly behind the fan, as shown in figure 2–26 and in the sketch of a bifurcated duct configuration, figure 2–27, or (2) ducted all the way to the rear of the engine, where it is exhausted to the outside air in the vicinity of the engine tailpipe.

RECIPROCATING ENGINE EXHAUST SYSTEMS

The reciprocating engine exhaust system is fundamentally a scavenging system that collects and disposes of the high-temperature, noxious

FIGURE 2–25. Airflow through a forward-fan engine.

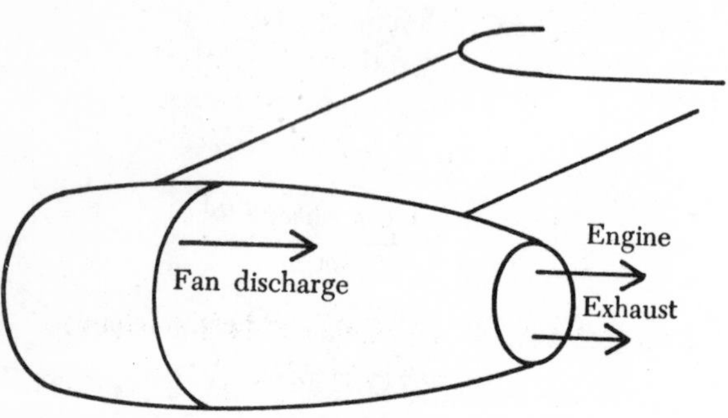

FIGURE 2–26. Typical forward-fan turbofan engine installation.

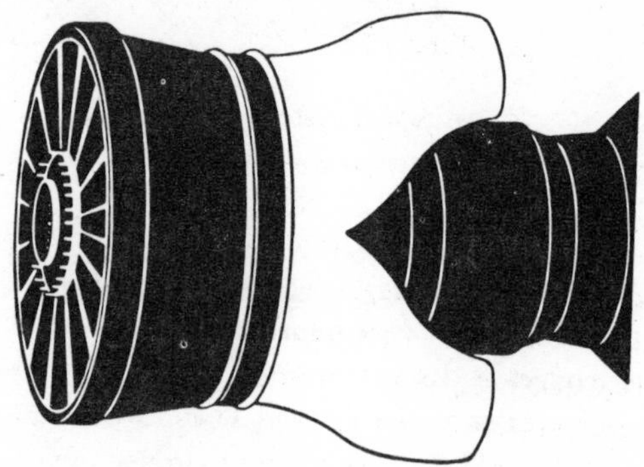

FIGURE 2–27. Bifurcated duct configuration.

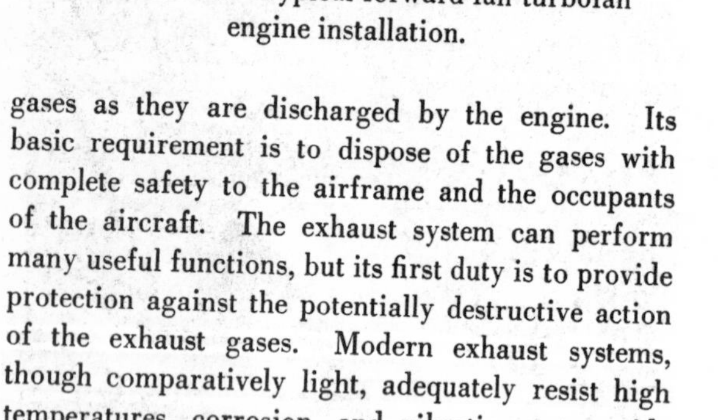

gases as they are discharged by the engine. Its basic requirement is to dispose of the gases with complete safety to the airframe and the occupants of the aircraft. The exhaust system can perform many useful functions, but its first duty is to provide protection against the potentially destructive action of the exhaust gases. Modern exhaust systems, though comparatively light, adequately resist high temperatures, corrosion, and vibration to provide long, trouble-free operation with a minimum of maintenance.

There are two general types of exhaust systems in use on reciprocating aircraft engines: the short stack (open) system and the collector system. The short stack system is generally used on nonsupercharged engines and low-powered engines where noise level is not too objectionable. The collector system is used on most large nonsupercharged engines and on all turbosupercharged engines and installations where it would improve nacelle streamlining or provide easier maintenance in the nacelle area. On turbosupercharged engines the exhaust gases must be collected to drive the turbine compressor of the supercharger. Such systems have individual exhaust headers which empty into a common collector ring with only one outlet. From this outlet, the hot exhaust gas is routed via a tailpipe to the nozzle box of the turbosupercharger to drive the turbine. Although the collector system raises the back pressure of the exhaust system, the gain in horsepower from turbosupercharging more than offsets the loss in horsepower that results from increased back pressure.

The short stack system is relatively simple, and its removal and installation consists essentially of removing and installing the holddown nuts and clamps.

In figure 2–28, the location of the exhaust system components of a horizontally opposed engine is shown in a side view. The exhaust system in this installation consists of a down-stack from each cylinder, an exhaust collector tube on each side of the engine, and an exhaust ejector assembly protruding aft and down from each side of the firewall. The down-stacks are connected to the cylinders with high-temperature locknuts and

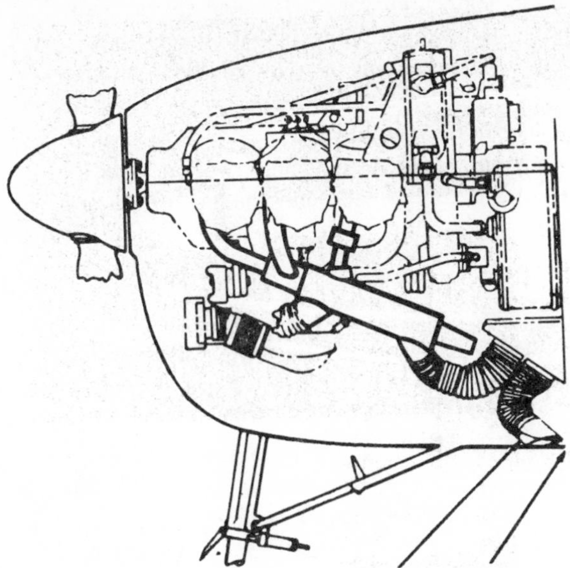

FIGURE 2–28. Exhaust system of a horizontally opposed engine.

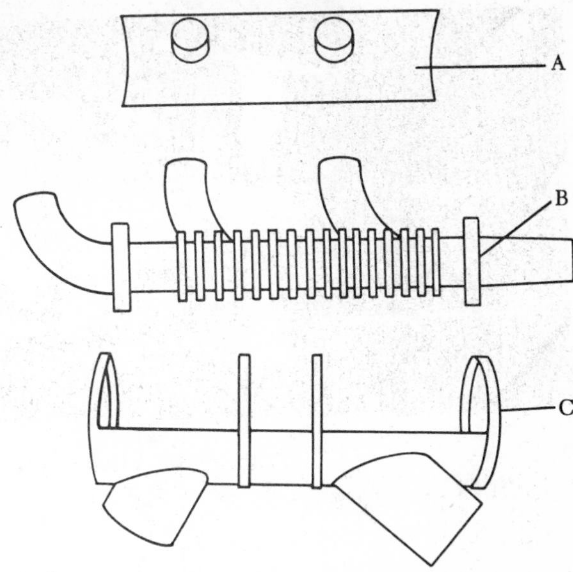

A. Upper sheet jacket.

B. Heat exchanger collector tube.

C. Lower sheet jacket.

FIGURE 2–29. Exploded view of heater exhaust shroud assembly.

secured to the exhaust collector tube by ring clamps.

A cabin heater exhaust shroud is installed around each collector tube. (See figure 2–29.)

The collector tubes terminate at the exhaust ejector openings at the firewall and are tapered to deliver the exhaust gases at the proper velocity to induce an airflow through the exhaust ejectors. The exhaust ejectors consist of a throat and duct assembly which utilizes the pumping action of the exhaust gases to induce a flow of cooling air through all parts of the engine compartment.

Radial Engine Exhaust Collector Ring System

Figure 2–30 shows the exhaust collector ring installed on a 14-cylinder radial engine. The collector ring is a welded corrosion-resistant steel assembly manufactured in seven sections, with each section collecting the exhaust from two cylinders. The sections are graduated in size (figure 2–31). The small sections are on the inboard side, and the largest sections are on the outboard side at the point where the tailpipe connects to the collector ring. Each section of the collector ring is bolted to a bracket on the blower section of the engine, and is partly supported by a sleeve connection between the collector ring ports and the short stack on the engine exhaust ports. The exhaust tailpipe is joined to the collector ring by a telescoping expansion joint, which allows enough slack for the removal of segments of the collector ring without removing the tailpipe.

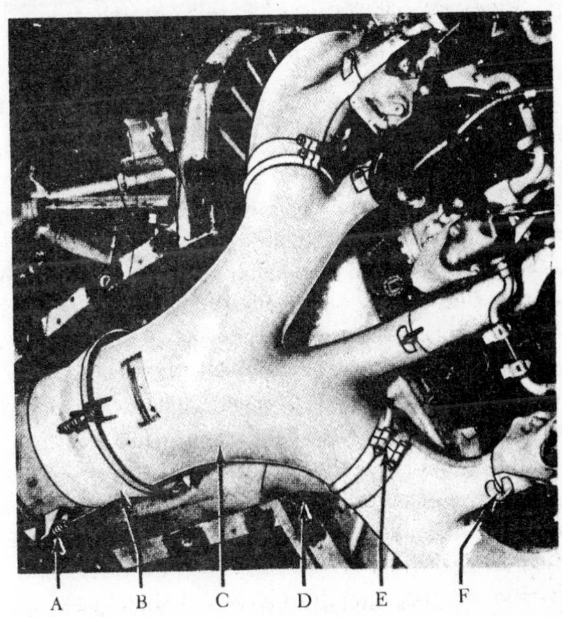

A. Clamp assembly

B. Telescoping flange

C. Main exhaust segment

D. Engine diaphragm

E. Clamp assembly

F. Clevis pin & washer

FIGURE 2–30. Installed exhaust collector ring.

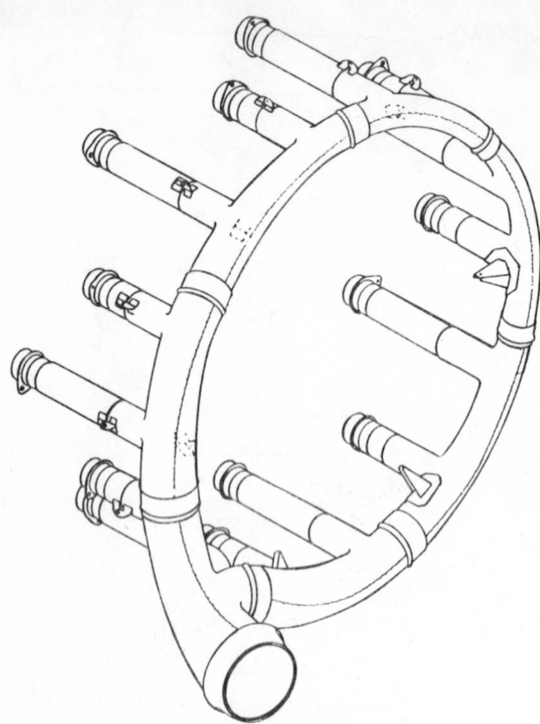

FIGURE 2–31. Exhaust collector ring.

The exhaust tailpipe is a welded, corrosion-resistant steel assembly consisting of the exhaust tailpipe and, on some aircraft, a muff-type heat exchanger.

Manifold and Augmentor Exhaust Assembly

Some radial engines are equipped with a combination exhaust manifold and augmentor assembly. On a typical 18-cylinder engine, two exhaust assemblies and two augmentor assemblies are used. Each manifold assembly collects exhaust gases from nine cylinders and discharges the gases into the forward end of an augmentor assembly.

Four stacks of each manifold assembly are siamese exhaust stacks, each receiving the exhaust from two cylinders (see figure 2–32). The firing order of the two cylinders exhausting into each exhaust stack is as widely separated as possible. Front row cylinders are connected to stacks by port extensions.

This type of exhaust manifold is manufactured from corrosion-resistant steel, and has either a plain sandblast or a ceramic-coated finish.

The exhaust gases are directed into the augmentor bellmouths. The augmentors are designed to produce a venturi effect to draw an increased airflow over the engine to augment engine cooling.

An augmentor vane is located in each tailpipe. When the vane is fully closed, the cross-sectional area of the tailpipe is reduced by approximately 45%. The augmentor vanes are operated by an electrical actuator, and indicators adjacent to the augmentor vane switches in the cockpit show vane positions. The vanes may be moved toward the "closed" position to decrease the velocity of flow through the augmentor to raise the engine temperature.

RECIPROCATING ENGINE EXHAUST SYSTEM MAINTENANCE PRACTICES

Any exhaust system failure should be regarded as a severe hazard. Depending on the location and type of failure, an exhaust system failure can result in carbon monoxide poisoning of crew and passengers, partial or complete loss of engine power, or an aircraft fire. Exhaust system failures generally reach a maximum rate of occurrence at 100 to 200 hours of aircraft operating time. More than 50% of all exhaust system failures occur within 400 hours.

Exhaust System Inspection

While the type and location of exhaust system components vary somewhat with the type of aircraft, the inspection requirements for most reciprocating engine exhaust systems are very similar. The following paragraphs include a discussion of the most common exhaust system inspection items and procedures for all reciprocating engines. Figure 2–33 shows the primary inspection areas of three types of exhaust systems.

Before the removal and installation of representative exhaust systems are discussed, a precaution to be observed when performing maintenance on any exhaust system should be mentioned. Galvanized or zinc-plated tools should never be used on the exhaust system, and exhaust system parts should never be marked with a lead pencil. The lead, zinc, or galvanized mark is absorbed by the metal of the exhaust system when heated, creating a distinct change in its molecular structure. This change softens the metal in the area of the mark, causing cracks and eventual failure.

After a complete exhaust system has been installed, the air induction scoop or duct, the fuel drain lines, the cowl flaps, and all pieces of engine cowl are installed and secured. When these items have been inspected for security, the engine is operated to allow the exhaust system to heat up to

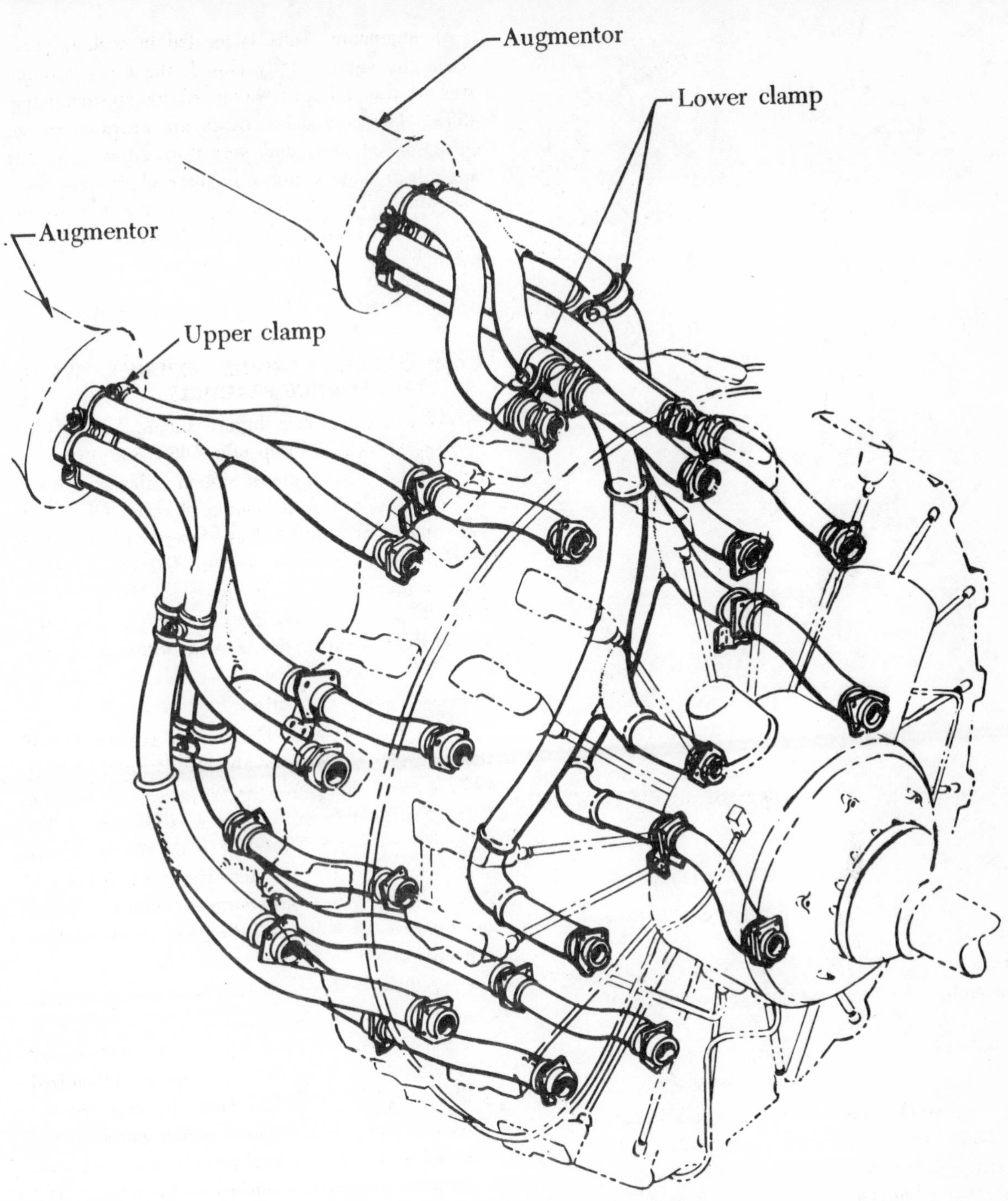

FIGURE 2–32. Exhaust manifold installation.

normal operating temperatures. The engine is then shut down and the cowling removed to expose the exhaust system.

Each clamped connection and each exhaust port connection should be inspected for evidence of exhaust gas leakage. An exhaust leak is indicated by a flat gray or a sooty black streak on the pipes in the area of the leak. An exhaust leak is usually the result of poor alignment of two mating exhaust system members. When a leaking exhaust connection is discovered, the clamps should be loosened and the leaking units repositioned to ensure a gas-

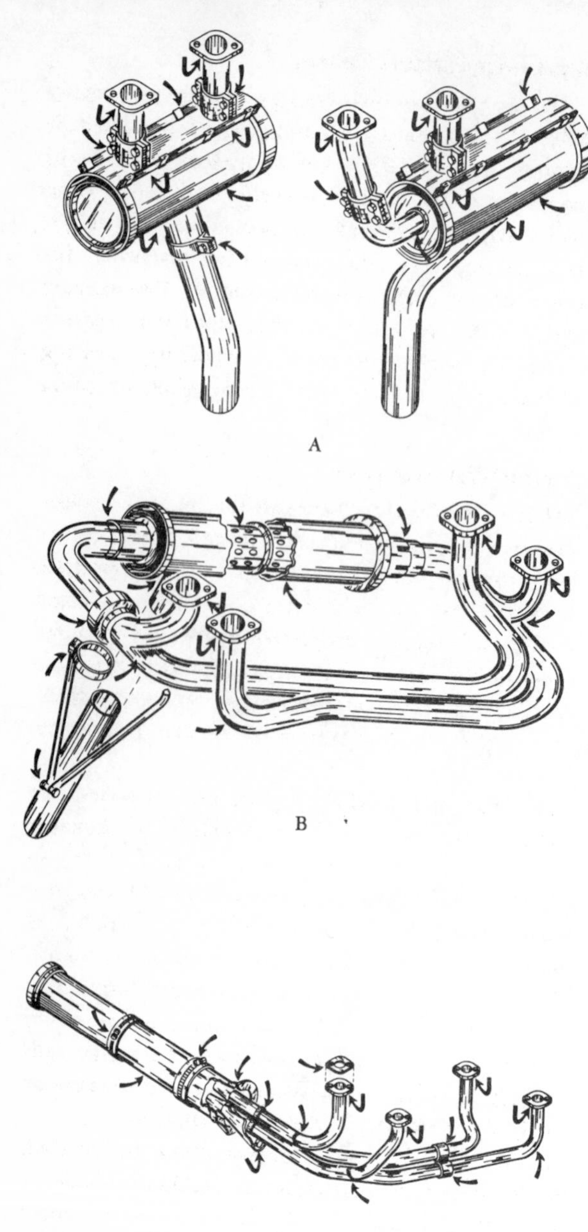

FIGURE 2–33. Primary inspection areas (A. Separate system; B. Crossover-type system; C. Exhaust/augmentor system.)

tight fit. After repositioning, the system nuts should be re-tightened enough to eliminate any looseness without exceeding the specified torque. If tightening to the specified torque does not eliminate looseness, the bolts and nuts should be replaced, since they have probably stretched. After tightening to the specified torque, all nuts should be safetied.

With the cowling removed, all necessary cleaning operations can be performed. Some exhaust units are manufactured with a plain sandblast finish. Others may have a ceramic-coated finish. Ceramic-coated stacks should be cleaned by degreasing only. They should never be cleaned with sandblast or alkali cleaners.

During the inspection of an exhaust system, close attention should be given to all external surfaces of the exhaust system for cracks, dents, or missing parts. This also applies to welds, clamps, supports, and support attachment lugs, bracing, slip joints, stack flanges, gaskets, and flexible couplings. Each bend should be examined, as well as areas adjacent to welds; and any dented areas or low spots in the system should be inspected for thinning and pitting due to internal erosion by combustion products or accumulated moisture. An ice pick or similar pointed instrument is useful in probing suspected areas. The system should be disassembled as necessary to inspect internal baffles or diffusers.

If a component of the exhaust system is inaccessible for a thorough visual inspection or is hidden by nonremovable parts, it should be removed and checked for possible leaks. This can often best be accomplished by plugging the openings of the component, applying a suitable internal pressure (approximately 2 p.s.i.), and submerging it in water. Any leaks will cause bubbles that can be readily detected.

The procedures required for an installation inspection are also performed during most regular inspections. Daily inspection of the exhaust system usually consists of checking the exposed exhaust system for cracks, scaling, excessive leakage, and loose clamps.

Muffler and Heat Exchanger Failures

Approximately half of all muffler and heat exchanger failures can be traced to cracks or ruptures in the heat exchanger surfaces used for cabin and carburetor heat sources. Failures in the heat exchanger surface (usually in the outer wall) allow exhaust gases to escape directly into the cabin heat system. These failures, in most cases, are caused by thermal and vibration fatigue cracking in areas of stress concentration.

Failure of the spot-welds which attach the heat transfer pins can result in exhaust gas leakage. In addition to a carbon monoxide hazard, failure of heat exchanger surfaces can permit exhaust gases to be drawn into the engine induction system, causing engine overheating and power loss.

Exhaust Manifold and Stack Failures

Exhaust manifold and stack failures are usually fatigue failures at welded or clamped points; for example, stack-to-flange, stack-to-manifold, and crossover pipe or muffler connections. Although these failures are primarily fire hazards, they also present carbon monoxide problems. Exhaust gases can enter the cabin via defective or inadequate seals at firewall openings, wing strut fittings, doors, and wing root openings.

Internal Muffler Failures

Internal failures (baffles, diffusers, etc.) can cause partial or complete engine power loss by restricting the flow of the exhaust gases. As opposed to other failures, erosion and carburization caused by the extreme thermal conditions are the primary causes of internal failures. Engine backfiring and combustion of unburned fuel within the exhaust system are probable contributing factors. In addition, local hot-spot areas caused by uneven exhaust gas flow can result in burning, bulging, or rupture of the outer muffler wall.

Exhaust Systems with Turbocharger

When a turbocharger or a turbosupercharger system is included, the engine exhaust system operates under greatly increased pressure and temperature conditions. Extra precautions should be taken in exhaust system care and maintenance. During high-pressure altitude operation, the exhaust system pressure is maintained at or near sea level values. Due to the pressure differential, any leaks in the system will allow the exhaust gases to escape with torch-like intensity that can severely damage adjacent structures.

A common cause of malfunction is coke deposits (carbon buildup) in the waste gate unit causing erratic system operation. Excessive deposit buildups may cause the waste gate valve to stick in the "closed" position, causing an overboost condition. Coke deposit buildup in the turbo itself will cause a gradual loss of power in flight and low manifold pressure reading prior to takeoff. Experience has shown that periodic de-coking, or removal of carbon deposits, is necessary to maintain peak efficiency. Clean, repair, overhaul, and adjust the system components and controls in accordance with the applicable manufacturer's instructions.

Augmentor Exhaust System

On exhaust systems equipped with augmentor tubes, the augmentor tubes should be inspected at regular intervals for proper alignment, security of attachment, and general overall condition. Even where augmentor tubes do not contain heat exchanger surfaces, they should be inspected for cracks along with the remainder of the exhaust system. Cracks in augmentor tubes can present a fire or carbon monoxide hazard by allowing exhaust gases to enter the nacelle, wing, or cabin areas.

Exhaust System Repairs

It is generally recommended that exhaust stacks, mufflers, tailpipes, etc., be replaced with new or reconditioned components rather than repaired. Welded repairs to exhaust systems are complicated by the difficulty of accurately identifying the base metal so thet the proper repair materials can be selected. Changes in composition and grain structure of the original base metal further complicate the repair.

However, when welded repairs are necessary, the original contours should be retained; the exhaust system alignment must not be warped or otherwise affected. Repairs or sloppy weld beads which protrude internally are not acceptable as they cause local hot-spots and may restrict exhaust gas flow. When repairing or replacing exhaust system components, the proper hardware and clamps should always be used. Steel or low-temperature, self-locking nuts should not be substituted for brass or special high-temperature locknuts used by the manufacturer. Old gaskets should never be re-used. When disassembly is necessary, gaskets should be replaced with new ones of the same type provided by the manufacturer.

TURBINE ENGINE EXHAUST DUCTS

The term "exhaust duct" is applied to the engine exhaust pipe, or tailpipe, which connects the turbine outlet to the jet nozzle of a non-afterburning engine. Although an afterburner might also be considered a type of exhaust duct, afterburning is a subject in itself which is discussed later in this chapter.

If the engine exhaust gases could be discharged directly to the outside air in an exact axial direction at the turbine exit, an exhaust duct might not be necessary. This, however, is not practical. A larger total thrust can be obtained from the engine if the gases are discharged from the aircraft at a higher velocity than is permissible at the turbine outlet. An exhaust duct is therefore added, both to collect and straighten the gas flow as it comes from the turbine and to increase the velocity of the gases before they are discharged from the exhaust nozzle at the rear of the duct. Increasing the velocity of the gases increases their momentum and increases the thrust produced.

An engine exhaust duct is often referred to as the engine tailpipe; although the duct, itself, is essentially a simple, stainless steel, conical or cylindrical pipe. The assembly also includes an engine tailcone and the struts inside the duct. The tailcone and the struts add strength to the duct, impart an axial direction to the gas flow, and smooth the gas flow.

Immediately aft of the turbine outlet, and usually just forward of the flange to which the exhaust duct is attached, the engine is instrumented for turbine discharge pressure. One or more pressure probes are inserted into the exhaust duct to provide adequate sampling of the exhaust gases. In large engines, it is not practical to measure the internal temperature at the turbine inlet, so the engine is often also instrumented for exhaust gas temperature at the turbine outlet.

Conventional Convergent Exhaust Nozzle

The rear opening of a turbine engine exhaust duct is called the exhaust nozzle (figure 2–34). The nozzle acts as an orifice, the size of which determines the density and velocity of the gases as they emerge from the engine.

In most non-afterburning engines the exhaust nozzle area is quite critical. Adjusting the area of the exhaust nozzle will change both the engine performance and the exhaust gas temperature. Some engines are trimmed to their correct exhaust gas temperature by altering the exhaust nozzle area. When this is the case, small tabs, which may be bent as required, are provided on the exhaust duct at the nozzle opening; or small, adjustable pieces called "mice" are fastened, as needed, around the perimeter of the nozzle to change the area.

Convergent-Divergent Exhaust Nozzle

Whenever the engine pressure ratio is high enough to produce exhaust gas velocities which might exceed Mach 1 at the engine exhaust nozzle, more thrust can be gained by using a convergent-divergent type of nozzle (figure 2–5). The advantage of a convergent-divergent nozzle is greatest at high Mach numbers because of the resulting higher pressure ratio across the engine exhaust nozzle.

To ensure that a constant weight or volume of a gas will flow past any given point after sonic velocity is reached, the rear part of a supersonic exhaust duct is enlarged to accommodate the additional weight or volume of a gas that will flow at supersonic rates. If this is not done, the nozzle will not operate efficiently. This section of the exhaust duct is known as divergent.

When a divergent duct is used in combination with a conventional exhaust duct, it is called a convergent-divergent exhaust duct. In the convergent-divergent, or C-D nozzle, the convergent section is designed to handle the gases while they remain subsonic, and to deliver the gases to the throat of the nozzle just as they attain sonic velocity. The divergent section handles the gases, further increasing their velocity, after they emerge from the throat and become supersonic.

TURBOPROP EXHAUST SYSTEM

In a typical turboprop exhaust system, the exhaust gases are directed from the turbine section

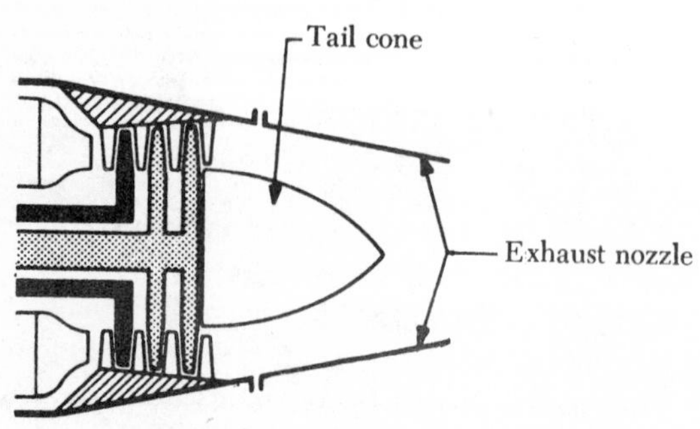

FIGURE 2–34. Conventional convergent exhaust duct.

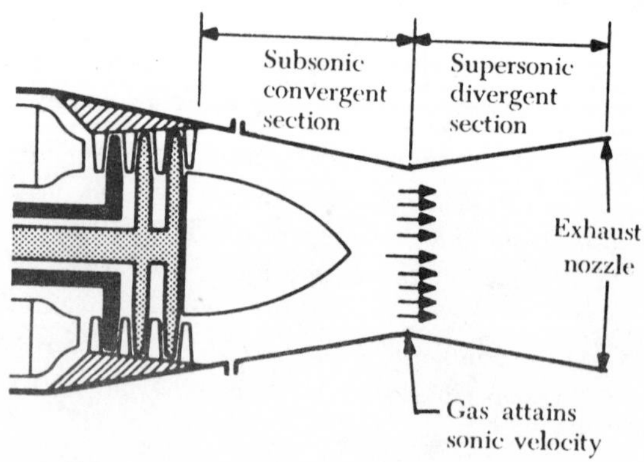

FIGURE 2–35. Convergent-divergent exhaust duct (nozzle).

of the engine to the atmosphere through a tailpipe assembly.

In a typical installation the tailpipe assembly is mounted in the nacelle and is attached at its forward end to the firewall. The forward section of the tailpipe is funnel shaped and surrounds but does not contact the turbine exhaust section. This arrangement forms an annular gap which serves as an air ejector for the air surrounding the engine hot section. As the high-velocity exhaust gases enter the tailpipe, a low pressure effect is produced which causes the air around the engine hot section to flow through the annular gap into the tailpipe.

An exhaust tailpipe of this type is usually manufactured in two sections (see figure 2–36). Both the forward funnel-shaped section and the rear section are made of corrosion-resistant steel, and a corrosion-resistant, high-temperature clamp secures the two sections together in a gastight joint.

The mounting flange welded to the forward edge of the forward tailpipe section mates to the engine side of the firewall and is secured to it with screws. An integral bellows section permits expansion between the firewall and two fixed bearing fittings, which can be adjusted to move the tailpipe in a vertical plane.

The rear section of the tailpipe is secured to the airframe by two support arms, one on each side of the tailpipe. The support arms are attached to the upper surface of the wing in such a way that free movement fore and aft is permitted to compensate for expansion.

The tailpipe assembly is wrapped in an insulating blanket to shield the surrounding area from the high heat produced by the exhaust gases. Such blankets may be made of stainless steel laminated sheet on the outside and fiber glass on the inside.

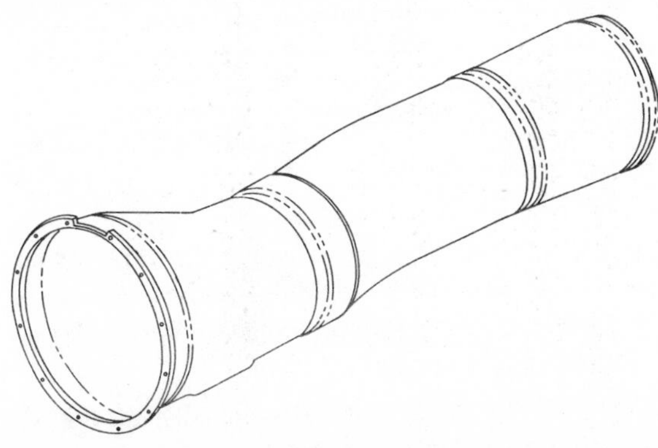

FIGURE 2–36. Two-section turboprop exhaust tailpipe.

THRUST REVERSERS

The difficult problem of stopping an aircraft after landing greatly increases with the higher airspeeds and greater gross weights, common to most of the larger, modern aircraft, which result in higher wing loadings and increased landing speeds. In many instances, wheel brakes can no longer be entirely relied upon to slow the aircraft within a reasonable distance, immediately after touchdown. The reversible pitch propeller has solved the problem for reciprocating-engine and turboprop-powered airplanes. Commercial turbojet aircraft, however, must rely upon reversing the thrust produced by their engines.

An engine thrust reverser (see figure 2–37) not only provides a ground-speed braking force, but, if suitable, is desirable for in-flight use prior to landing. Some means of slowing the airspeed and increasing the rate of sink during descent, such as a dive brake, some form of wing spoiler, or a thrust reverser that can be used while airborne, is almost a necessity for turbojet aircraft.

Many forms of thrust reversers have been proposed, and quite a number have been tested with a considerable degree of success. The most successful thrust reversers can be divided into two categories, the mechanical-blockage type and the aerodynamic-blockage type. Mechanical blockage is accomplished by placing a removable obstruction in the exhaust gas stream, usually somewhat to the rear of the nozzle. The engine exhaust gases are mechanically blocked and diverted at a suitable angle in the reverse direction by an inverted cone, half-sphere, or other means of obstruction, which is placed in position to reverse the flow of exhaust gases. In the aerodynamic-blockage type of thrust reverser, thin airfoils or obstructions are placed in the gas stream, either along the length of the exhaust duct or immediately aft of the exhaust nozzle. In one adaptation of the aerodynamic reverser, vanes inside the duct create swirling of the gases in a manner which centrifuges them into a cascade of turning vanes. At least one current-model, commercial turbojet aircraft uses a combination of the mechanical-blockage and

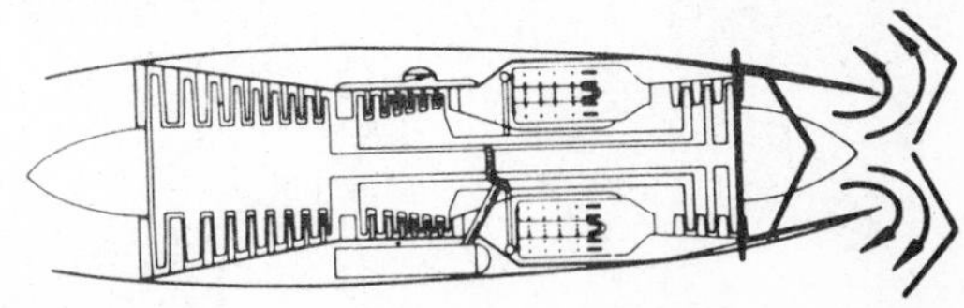

FIGURE 2–37. Operation of the thrust reverser.

aerodynamic-blockage type reversers.

A thrust reverser must not affect engine operation either when the reverser is operating or when it is not. It must be able to withstand high temperatures, and must be mechanically strong, relatively light in weight, reliable, and "fail-safe." When not in use, it should not add appreciably to the engine frontal area, and must be streamlined into the configuration of the engine nacelle. To satisfy the minimum braking requirements after landing, a thrust reverser should be able to produce in reverse at least 50% of the full forward thrust of which the engine is capable.

The clamshell-type of mechanical-blockage reverser (figure 2–38) adequately satisfies most of these requirements and, in one form or another, has been adopted for use on non-afterburning engines. At throttle positions below idle, the reverser operates to form a turning barrier in the path of escaping exhaust gases, which, in turn, nullifies and reverses the forward thrust of the engine. Throttle positions below idle cause the engine to accelerate in controllable amounts up to full r.p.m. so that either partial or full reverse thrust may be used at will. When the reverser is not in use, the clamshell doors retract and nest neatly around the engine exhaust duct, usually forming the rear section of the engine nacelle. Most thrust reversers in use at this time are combined with an engine exhaust silencer.

Engine Noise Suppressors

Aircraft powered by large turbojet engines require some sort of silencing device or noise suppressor for the engine exhaust gases when operating from airports located in or near thickly populated areas. Two types of noise suppressors are used, one being a portable device, separate from the aircraft, for use on the ground by maintenance activities; it is positioned at the rear of an engine whenever prolonged engine operation is anticipated. The other type of noise suppressor is an integral, airborne part of the aircraft engine installation or engine tailpipe. Only this latter form of suppressor, which primarily suppresses engine noise during takeoff, climb, approach, and landing, will be discussed here.

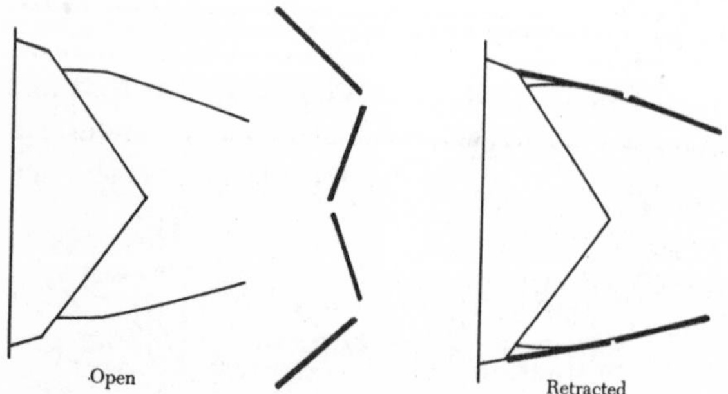

FIGURE 2–38. Mechanical blockage thrust reverser.

It is generally accepted that the amount of sound attenuation required for turbojet aircraft will be the amount necessary to moderate the engine noise to a level which will be no more objectionable than the noise produced by a reciprocating engine and propeller combination, operating under similar conditions. Although the amount of attenuation necessary is usually about 12 decibels, the manner in which the noise of a turbojet aircraft can be reduced to a level that is as acceptable as that of a reciprocating-engine aircraft is not simple to determine. The propeller, which is a major source of noise in reciprocating-engine aircraft, has a noise pattern which rises sharply to a maximum level as the plane of the propeller passes an individual on the ground, and then drops off almost as sharply after the propeller has gone by. The turbojet aircraft produces a sharp rise in noise, which reaches a peak after the aircraft has passed an individual on the ground, and is at an angle of approximately 45° to him. The noise then persists at a high level for a considerable period of time as compared with that of a reciprocating engine with a propeller (see figure 2–39).

There are three sources of noise involved in the operation of a gas turbine engine. The engine air intake and vibration from engine housing are sources of some noise, but the noise thus generated does not compare in magnitude with that produced by the engine exhaust as illustrated in figure 2–40. The noise produced by the engine exhaust is caused by the high degree of turbulence of a high-velocity jet stream moving through a relatively quiet atmosphere.

For a distance of a few nozzle diameters downstream behind the engine, the velocity of the jet stream is high, and there is little mixing of the atmosphere with the jet stream. In this region, the turbulence within the high-speed jet stream is a very fine grain turbulence, and produces relatively high-frequency noise.

Farther downstream, as the velocity of the jet stream slows down, the jet stream mixes with the atmosphere, and turbulence of a coarser type begins. Compared with noise from other portions of

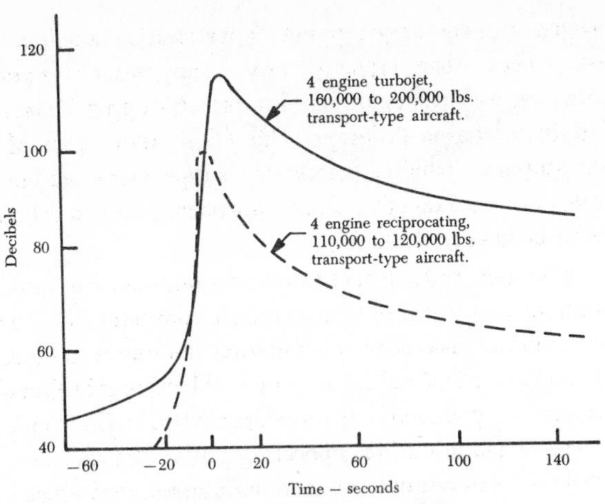

FIGURE 2–39. Noise levels.

the jet stream, noise from this portion has a much lower frequency. As the energy of the jet stream finally is dissipated in large turbulent swirls, a greater portion of the energy is converted into noise. The noise generated as the exhaust gases dissipate is at a frequency near the low end of the audible range. The lower the frequency of the noise, the greater the distance that it will travel. This means that the low-frequency noises will reach an individual on the ground in greater volume than the high-frequency noises, and hence will be more objectionable. High-frequency noise is weakened more rapidly than low-frequency noise, both by distance and the interference of buildings, terrain, and atmospheric disturbances. A deep-voiced, low-frequency foghorn, for example, may be heard much farther than a shrill, high-frequency whistle, even though both may have the same overall volume (decibels) at their source.

Noise levels vary with engine thrust and are proportional to the amount of work done by the engine on the air which passes through it. An engine having relatively low airflow but high thrust due to high turbine discharge (exhaust gas) temperature, pressure, and/or afterburning will produce a gas stream of high velocity and therefore high noise levels. A larger engine, handling more air, will be quieter at the same thrust. Thus, the noise level can be considerably reduced by operating the engine at lower power settings, and large engines operating at partial thrust will be less noisy than smaller engines operating at full thrust.

Compared with a turbojet, a turbofan version of the same engine will be quieter during takeoff. The noise level produced by a fan-type engine is less, principally because the exhaust gas velocities ejected at the engine tailpipe are slower than those for a turbojet of comparative size.

Fan engines require a larger turbine to provide additional power to drive the fan. The large turbine, which usually has an additional turbine stage, reduces the velocity of the gas and therefore reduces the noise produced, because exhaust gas noise is proportional to exhaust gas velocity. The exhaust from the fan, itself, is at a relatively low velocity, and therefore does not create a noise problem.

Because of the characteristic of low-frequency noise to linger at a relatively high volume, effective noise reduction for a turbojet aircraft must be

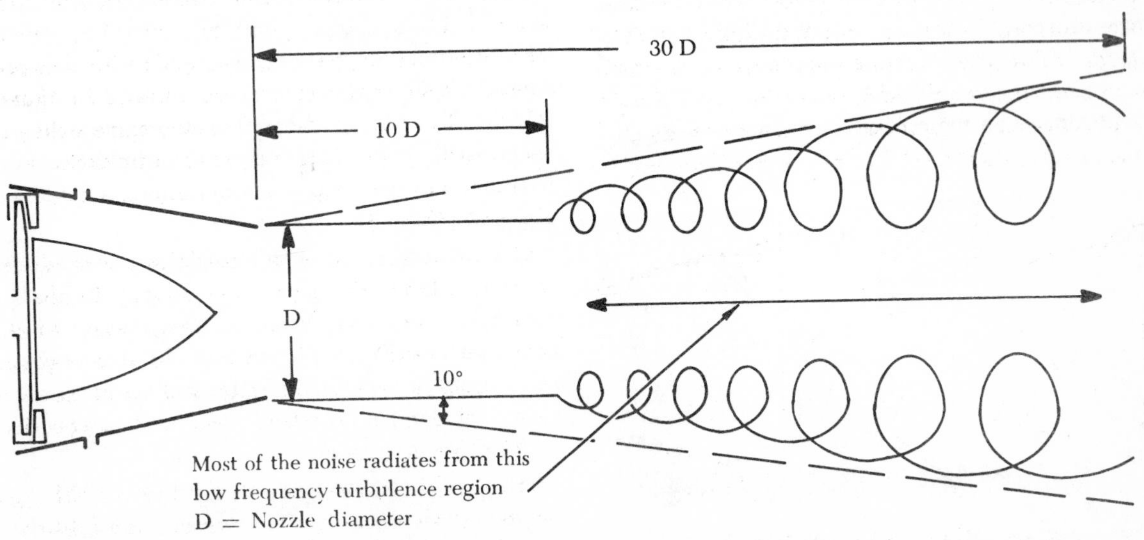

FIGURE 2–40. Turbojet exhaust noise pattern.

achieved by revising the noise pattern or by changing the frequency of the noise emitted by the jet nozzle.

The noise suppressors in current use are either of the corrugated-perimeter type, shown in figure 2–41, or the multi-tube type, shown in figure 2–42. Both types of suppressors break up the single, main jet exhaust stream into a number of smaller jet streams. This increases the total perimeter of the nozzle area and reduces the size of the eddies created as the gases are discharged into the open air. Although the total noise-energy remains unchanged, the frequency is raised considerably. The size of the eddies scales down, at a linear rate, with the size of the exhaust stream. This has two effects. First, the change in frequency may put some of the noise above the audibility range of the human ear, and, secondly, high frequencies within the audible range, while perhaps more annoying, are more highly attenuated by atmospheric absorption than are low frequencies. Thus, the falloff in intensity is greater and the noise level is less at any given distance from the aircraft.

ENGINE AIR-INLET VORTEX DESTROYER

When turbojet engines are operating on the ground, an engine air-inlet vortex can sometimes

FIGURE 2–41. Rear view of corrugated-perimeter noise suppressor.

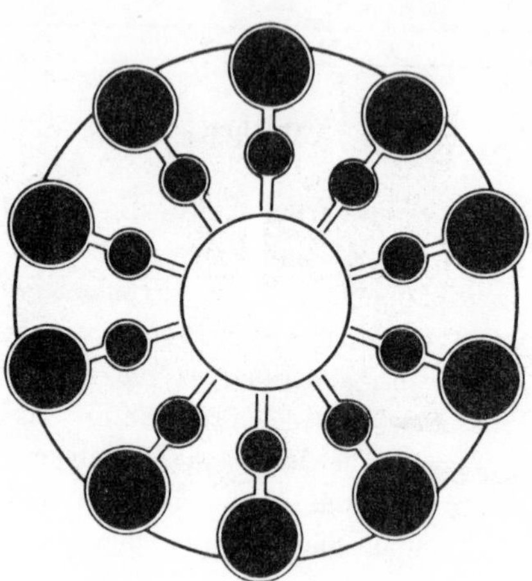

FIGURE 2–42. Rear view of multi-tube noise suppressor.

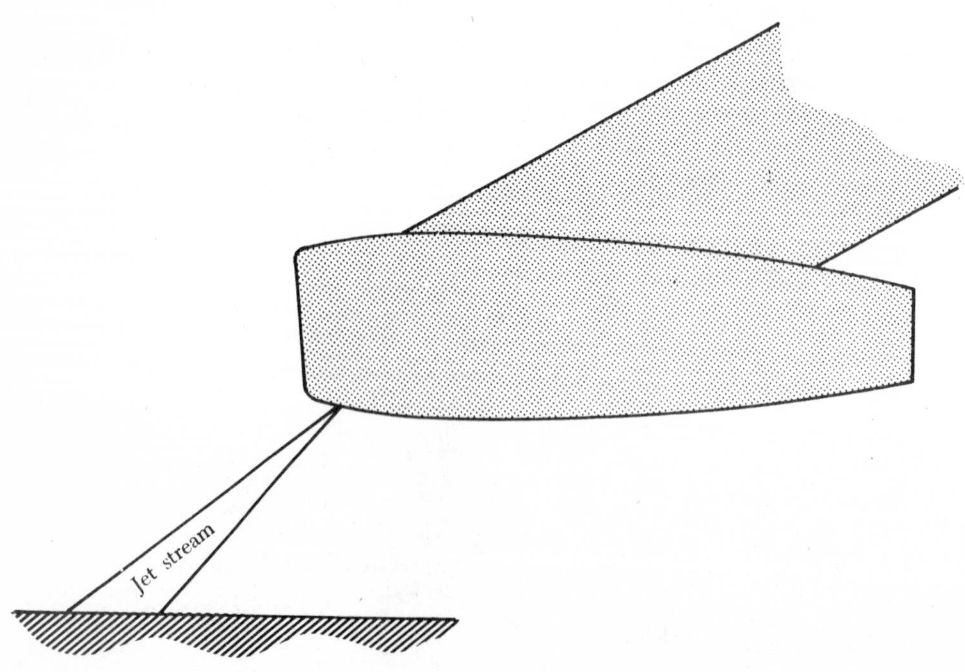

FIGURE 2–43. Inlet vortex destroyer jet stream.

form between the engine air inlet and the ground. This vortex can cause a strong suction force capable of lifting small foreign objects from the ground into the engine inlet. The ingestion of such debris can cause engine damage or even failure.

To minimize the ingestion of runway debris, some turbojet engines are equipped with an engine air-inlet vortex destroyer. This destroyer is a small jet stream directed downward from the lower leading edge of the noise cowl to the ground to destroy the swirling vortex base. Figure 2–43 illustrates the general direction and size of the vortex-destroying jet blast.

Figure 2–44 is a diagram showing the location of the jet stream nozzle and the control valve. Bleed air from the engine is used as the vortex-destroying air stream. It is controlled by a valve located in the nose cowl. The control valve is usually a two-position valve that is opened by a landing gear safety switch. The valve closes when the aircraft leaves the runway and the weight of the aircraft is removed from the landing gear.

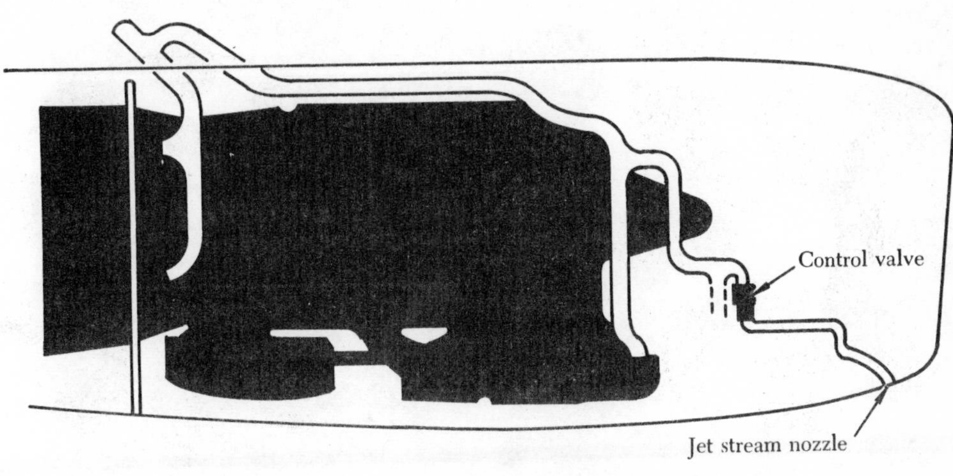

FIGURE 2–44. Location of vortex destroyer components.

CHAPTER 3

ENGINE FUEL AND FUEL METERING SYSTEMS

FUEL SYSTEM REQUIREMENTS

Improvements in aircraft and engines have increased the demands on the fuel system, making it more complicated and increasing the installation, adjustment, and maintenance problems. The fuel system must supply fuel to the carburetor or other metering device under all conditions of ground and air operation. It must function properly at constantly changing altitudes and in any climate. The system should be free of tendency to vapor lock, which can result from changes in ground and in-flight climatic conditions.

On small aircraft a simple gravity-feed fuel system consisting of a tank to supply fuel to the engine is often installed. On multi-engine aircraft, complex systems are necessary so that fuel can be pumped from any combination of tanks to any combination of engines. Provisions for transferring fuel from one tank to another may also be included on large aircraft.

Vapor Lock

Normally the fuel remains in a liquid state until it is discharged into the air stream and then instantly changes to a vapor. Under certain conditions, however, the fuel may vaporize in the lines, pumps, or other units. The vapor pockets formed by this premature vaporization restrict the fuel flow through units which are designed to handle liquids rather than gases. The resulting partial or complete interruption of the fuel flow is called vapor lock. The three general causes of vapor lock are the lowering of the pressure on the fuel, high fuel temperatures, and excessive fuel turbulence.

At high altitudes, the pressure on the fuel in the tank is low. This lowers the boiling point of the fuel and causes vapor bubbles to form. This vapor trapped in the fuel may cause vapor lock in the fuel system.

Transfer of heat from the engine tends to cause boiling of the fuel in the lines and the pump. This tendency is increased if the fuel in the tank is warm. High fuel temperatures often combine with low pressure to increase vapor formation. This is most apt to occur during a rapid climb on a hot day. As the aircraft climbs, the outside temperature drops, but the fuel does not lose temperature rapidly. If the fuel is warm enough at takeoff, it retains enough heat to boil easily at high altitude.

The chief causes of fuel turbulence are sloshing of the fuel in the tanks, the mechanical action of the engine-driven pump, and sharp bends or rises in the fuel lines. Sloshing in the tank tends to mix air with the fuel. As this mixture passes through the lines, the trapped air separates from the fuel and forms vapor pockets at any point where there are abrupt changes in direction or steep rises. Turbulence in the fuel pump often combines with the low pressure at the pump inlet to form a vapor lock at this point.

Vapor lock can become serious enough to block the fuel flow completely and stop the engine. Even small amounts of vapor in the inlet line restrict the flow to the engine-driven pump and reduce its output pressure.

To reduce the possibility of vapor lock, fuel lines are kept away from sources of heat; also, sharp bends and steep rises are avoided. In addition, the volatility of the fuel is controlled in manufacture so that it does not vaporize too readily. The major improvement in reducing vapor lock, however, is the incorporation of booster pumps in the fuel system. These pumps keep the fuel in the lines to the engine-driven pump under pressure. The slight pressure on the fuel reduces vapor formation and aids in moving a vapor pocket along. The booster pump also releases vapor from the fuel as it passes through the pump. The vapor moves upward through the fuel in the tank and out the tank vents.

To prevent the small amount of vapor which remains in the fuel from upsetting its metering action, vapor eliminators are installed in some fuel systems ahead of the metering device or are built into this unit.

BASIC FUEL SYSTEM

The basic parts of a fuel system include tanks, booster pumps, lines, selector valves, strainers, engine-driven pumps, and pressure gages. A review of Chapter 4 in the General Handbook will provide some information concerning these components. Additional information is presented later in this chapter.

Generally, there are several tanks, even in a simple system, to store the required amount of fuel. The location of these tanks depends on both the fuel system design and the structural design of the aircraft. From each tank, a line leads to the selector valve. This valve is set from the cockpit to select the tank from which fuel is to be delivered to the engine. The booster pump forces fuel through the selector valve to the main line strainer. This filtering unit, located in the lowest part of the system, removes water and dirt from the fuel. During starting, the booster pump forces fuel through a bypass in the engine-driven pump to the metering device. Once the engine-driven pump is rotating at sufficient speed, it takes over and delivers fuel to the metering device at the specified pressure.

The airframe fuel system begins with the fuel tank and ends at the engine fuel system. The engine fuel system usually includes the engine-driven pumps and the fuel metering systems. In aircraft powered with a reciprocating engine, the fuel metering system consists of the air- and fuel-control devices from the point where the fuel enters the first control unit until the fuel is injected into the supercharger section, intake pipe, or cylinder. For example, the fuel metering system of the Continental IO-470L engine consists of the fuel/air control unit, the injector pump, the fuel manifold valve, and the fuel discharge nozzles. On the Pratt and Whitney R-1830-94 engine, the fuel metering system consists of the carburetor, the fuel feed valve, and the carburetor accelerating pump. In the latter case, the fuel feed valve and the accelerating pump are mounted on the engine and are engine manufacturer's parts. However, they still constitute a part of the basic fuel metering system.

The fuel metering system on current reciprocating engines meters the fuel at a predetermined ratio to airflow. The airflow to the engine is controlled by the carburetor or fuel/air control unit.

The fuel metering system of the gas turbine engine consists of a jet fuel control and may extend to and include the fuel nozzles. On some turboprop engines a temperature datum valve is a part of the engine fuel system. The rate of fuel delivery is a function of air mass flow, compressor inlet temperature, compressor discharge pressure, r.p.m., and combustion chamber pressure.

The fuel metering system must operate satisfactorily to ensure efficient engine operation as measured by power output, operating temperatures, and range of the aircraft. Because of variations in design of different fuel metering systems, the expected performance of any one piece of equipment, as well as the difficulties it can cause, will vary.

FUEL METERING DEVICES FOR RECIPROCATING ENGINES

This section explains the systems which deliver the correct mixture of fuel and air to the engine combustion chambers. In the discussion of each system, the general purpose and operating principles are stressed, with particular emphasis on the basic principles of operation. No attempt is made to give detailed operating and maintenance instructions for specific types and makes of equipment. For the specific information needed to inspect or maintain a particular installation or unit, consult the manufacturer's instructions.

The basic requirement of a fuel metering system

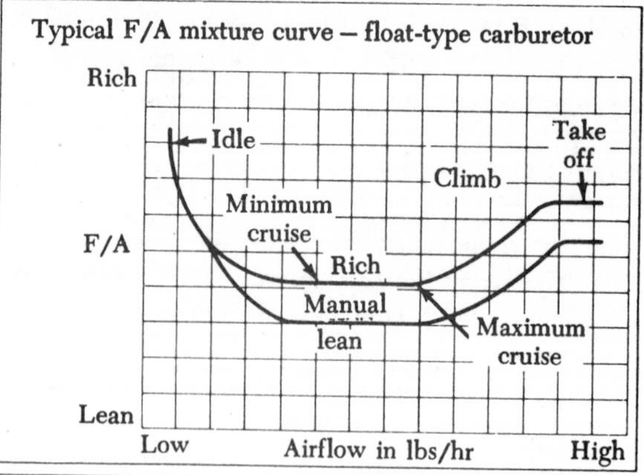

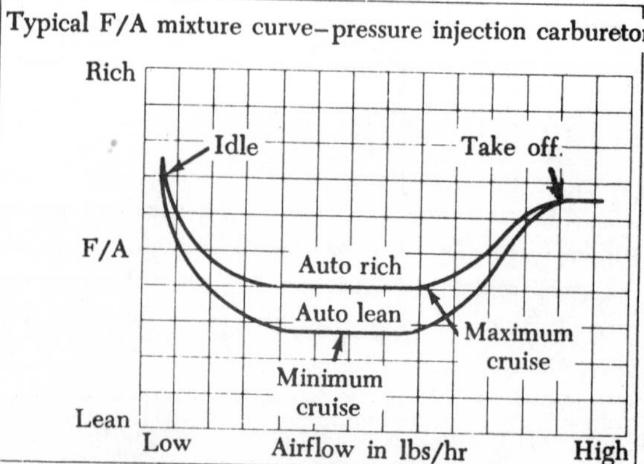

FIGURE 3–1. Fuel/air mixture curves.

is the same, regardless of the type of system used or the model engine on which the equipment is installed. It must meter fuel proportionately to air to establish the proper fuel/air mixture ratio for the engine at all speeds and altitudes at which the engine may be operated. In the fuel/air mixture curves shown in figure 3–1, note that the basic best power and best economy fuel/air mixture requirements for all reciprocating engines are approximately the same.

A second requirement of the fuel metering system is to atomize and distribute the fuel from the carburetor into the mass airflow in such a manner that the air charges going to all cylinders will hold similar amounts of fuel so that the fuel/air mixture reaching each cylinder is of the same ratio.

Carburetors tend to run richer at altitude than at ground level, because of the decreased density of the airflow through the carburetor throat for a given volume of air per hour to the engine. Thus, it is necessary that a mixture control be provided to lean the mixture and compensate for this natural enrichment. Some aircraft use carburetors in which the mixture control is operated manually. Other aircraft employ carburetors which automatically lean the carburetor mixture at altitude to maintain the proper fuel/air mixture.

The rich mixture requirements for an aircraft engine are established by running a power curve to determine the fuel/air mixture for obtaining maximum usable power. This curve (figure 3–2) is plotted at 100-r.p.m. intervals from idle speed to takeoff speed.

Since it is necessary in the power range to add fuel to the basic fuel/air mixture requirements to keep cylinder-head temperatures in a safe range, the fuel mixture must become gradually richer as powers above cruise are used. (See figure 3–1.) In the power range, the engine will run on a much leaner mixture, as indicated in the curves. However, on the leaner mixture, cylinder-head temperature would exceed the maximum permissible temperatures and detonation would occur.

The best economy setting is established by running a series of curves through the cruise range, as shown in the graph in figure 3–3, the low point (auto-lean) in the curve being the fuel/air mixture where the minimum fuel per horsepower is used. In this range the engine will operate normally on slightly leaner mixtures and will obviously operate on richer mixtures than the low-point mixture. If a mixture leaner than that specified for the engine is used, the leanest cylinder of the engine is apt to backfire, because the slower burning rate of the lean mixture results in a continued burning in the cylinder when the next intake stroke starts.

Fuel/Air Mixtures

Gasoline and other liquid fuels will not burn at all unless they are mixed with air. If the mixture is to burn properly within the engine cylinder, the ratio of air to fuel must be kept within a certain range.

It would be more accurate to state that the fuel is burned with the oxygen in the air. Seventy-eight percent of air by volume is nitrogen, which is inert and does not participate in the combustion process, and 21% is oxygen. Heat is generated by burning the mixture of gasoline and oxygen. Nitrogen and gaseous byproducts of combustion absorb this heat energy and turn it into power by expansion. The mixture proportion of fuel and air by weight is of extreme importance to engine performance. The

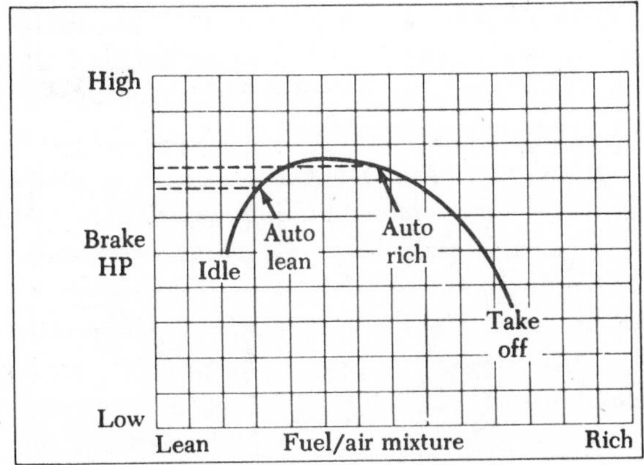

FIGURE 3–2. Power versus fuel/air mixture curve.

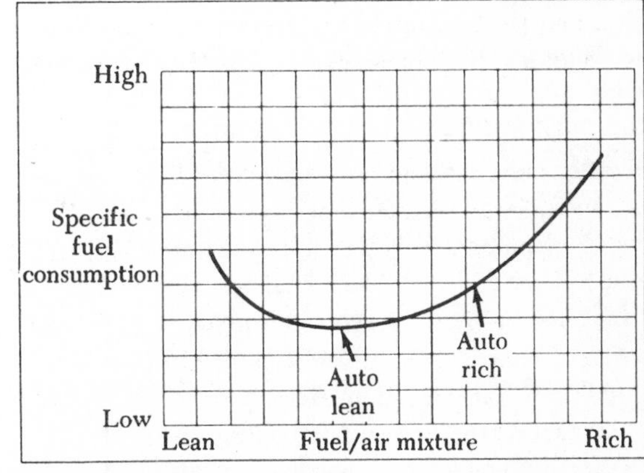

FIGURE 3–3. Specific fuel consumption curve.

characteristics of a given mixture can be measured in terms of flame speed and combustion temperature.

The composition of the fuel/air mixture is described by the mixture ratio. For example, a mixture with a ratio of 12 to 1 (12:1) is made up of 12 lbs. of air and 1 lb. of fuel. The ratio is expressed in weight because the volume of air varies greatly with temperature and pressure. The mixture ratio can also be expressed as a decimal. Thus, a fuel/air ratio of 12:1 and a fuel/air ratio of 0.083 describe the same mixture ratio. Air and gasoline mixtures as rich as 8:1 and as lean as 16:1 will burn in an engine cylinder. The engine develops maximum power with a mixture of approximately 12 parts of air and 1 part of gasoline.

From the chemist's point of view the perfect mixture for combustion of fuel and air would be 0.067 lb. of fuel to 1 lb. of air (mixture ratio of 15:1). The scientist calls this chemically correct combination a stoichiometric mixture (pronounced stoy-key-o-metric). With this mixture (given sufficient time and turbulence), all the fuel and all the oxygen in the air will be completely used in the combustion process. The stoichiometric mixture produces the highest combustion temperatures because the proportion of heat released to a mass of charge (fuel and air) is the greatest. However, the mixture is seldom used because it does not result in either the greatest economy or the greatest power for the airflow or manifold pressure.

If more fuel is added to the same quantity of air charge than the amount giving a chemically perfect mixture, changes of power and temperature will occur. The combustion gas temperature will be lowered as the mixture is enriched, and the power will increase until the fuel/air ratio is approximately 0.0725. From 0.0725 fuel/air ratio to 0.080 fuel/air ratio the power will remain essentially constant even though the combustion temperature continues downward. Mixtures from 0.0725 fuel/air ratio to 0.080 fuel/air ratio are called best power mixtures, since their use results in the greatest power for a given airflow or manifold pressure. In this fuel/air ratio range, there is no increase in the total heat released, but the weight of nitrogen and combustion products is augmented by the vapor formed with the excess fuel; thus, the working mass of the charge is increased. In addition, the extra fuel in the charge (over the stoichiometric mixture) speeds up the combustion process, which provides a favorable time factor in converting fuel energy into power.

Enriching a fuel/air ratio above 0.080 results in the loss of power besides reduction of temperature, as the cooling effects of excess fuel overtake the favorable factor of increased mass. The reduced temperature and slower rate of burning lead to an increasing loss of combustion efficiency.

If, with constant airflow, the mixture is leaned below 0.067 fuel/air ratio, power and temperature will decrease together. This time, the loss of power is not a liability but an asset. The purpose in leaning is to save fuel. Air is free and available in limitless quantities. The object is to obtain the required power with the least fuel flow and to let the air consumption take care of itself.

A measure of the economical use of fuel is called SFC (specific fuel consumption), which is the lbs. of fuel per hr. per hp. Thus, SFC = lbs. fuel/hr./hp. By using this ratio, the engine's use of fuel at various power settings can be compared. When leaning below 0.067 fuel/air ratio with constant airflow, even though the power diminishes, the cost in fuel to support each horsepower hour (SFC) also is lowered for a while. While the mixture charge is becoming weaker, this loss of strength occurs at a rate slower than that of the reduction of fuel flow. This favorable tendency continues until a mixture strength known as best economy is reached. With this fuel/air ratio, the required hp. is developed with the least fuel flow, or, to put it another way, a given fuel flow produces the most power.

The best economy fuel/air ratio varies somewhat with r.p.m. and other conditions, but, for cruise powers on most reciprocating engines, it is sufficiently accurate to define this range of operation as being from 0.060 to 0.065 fuel/air ratios with retard spark, and from 0.055 to 0.061 fuel/air ratios with advance spark. These are the most commonly used fuel/air ratios on aircraft where manual leaning is practiced.

Below the best economical mixture strength, power and temperature continue to fall with constant airflow while the SFC increases. As the fuel/air ratio is reduced further, combustion becomes so cool and slow that power for a given manifold pressure becomes so low as to be uneconomical. The cooling effect of rich or lean mixtures results from the excess fuel or air over that needed for combustion. Internal cylinder cooling is obtained from unused fuel when fuel/air ratios above 0.067 are used. The same function is performed by excess air when fuel/air ratios below 0.067 are used.

Varying the mixture strength of the charge produces changes in the engine operating condiition affecting power, temperature, and spark-timing requirements. The best power fuel/air ratio is desirable when the greatest power from a given airflow is required. The best economy mixture results from obtaining the given power output with the least fuel flow. The fuel/air ratio which gives most efficient operation varies with engine speed and power output.

In the graph showing this variation in fuel/air ratio (figure 3–1), note that the mixture is rich at both idling and high-speed operation and is lean through the cruising range. At idling speed, some air or exhaust gas is drawn into the cylinder through the exhaust port during valve overlap. The mixture which enters the cylinder through the intake port must be rich enough to compensate for this gas or additional air. At cruising power, lean mixtures save fuel and increase the range of the airplane. An engine running near full power requires a rich mixture to prevent overheating and detonation. Since the engine is operated at full power for only short periods, the high fuel consumption is not a serious matter. If an engine is operating on too lean a mixture and adjustments are made to increase the amount of fuel, the power output of the engine increases rapidly at first, then gradually until maximum power is reached. With a further increase in the amount of fuel, the power output drops gradually at first, then more rapidly as the mixture is further enriched.

There are specific instructions concerning mixture ratios for each type of engine under various operating conditions. Failure to follow these instructions will result in poor performance and often in damage to the engine. Excessively rich mixtures result in loss of power and waste of fuel. With the engine operating near its maximum output, very lean mixtures will cause a loss of power and under certain conditions, serious overheating. When the engine is operated on a lean mixture, the cylinder head temperature gage should be watched closely. If the mixture is excessively lean, the engine may backfire through the induction system or stop completely. Backfire results from slow burning of the lean mixture. If the charge is still burning when the intake valve opens, it ignites the fresh mixture and the flame travels back through the combustible mixture in the induction system.

CARBURETION PRINCIPLES

Venturi Principles

The carburetor must measure the airflow through the induction system and use this measurement to regulate the amount of fuel discharged into the airstream. The air measuring unit is the venturi, which makes use of a basic law of physics: ***as the velocity of a gas or liquid increases, the pressure decreases.*** As shown in the diagram of the simple venturi (figure 3–4), it is a passageway or tube in which there is a narrow portion called the throat. As the air speeds up to get through the narrow portion, its pressure drops. Note that the pressure in the throat is lower than that in any other part of the venturi. This pressure drop is proportional to the velocity and is, therefore, a measure of the airflow. The basic operating principle of most carburetors depends on the differential pressure between the inlet and the venturi throat.

Application of Venturi Principle to Carburetor

The carburetor is mounted on the engine so that air to the cylinders passes through the barrel, the part of the carburetor which contains the venturi. The size and shape of the venturi depends on the requirements of the engine for which the carburetor is designed. A carburetor for a high-powered engine may have one large venturi or several small ones. The air may flow either up or down the venturi, depending on the design of the engine and the carburetor. Those in which the air passes downward are known as downdraft carburetors, and those in which the air passes upward are called updraft carburetors.

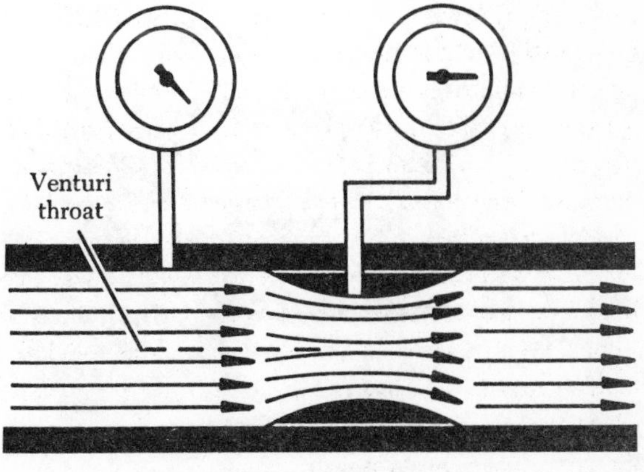

As air passes through the throat of the venturi, there is an increase in velocity and a drop in pressure
Venturi throat

FIGURE 3–4. Simple venturi.

Air can be drawn through a rubber tube by placing one end in the mouth and exerting a sucking action. Actually, the pressure inside the tube is lowered and atmospheric pressure pushes air into the open end. Air flows through the induction system in the same manner. When a piston moves toward the crankshaft on the intake stroke, the pressure in the cylinder is lowered. Air rushes through the carburetor and intake manifold to the cylinder due to the higher pressure at the carburetor intake. Even in a supercharged engine operating at high manifold pressure, there is still a low pressure at the engine side of the carburetor. Atmospheric pressure at the air intake pushes air through the carburetor to the supercharger inlet.

The throttle valve is located between the venturi and the engine. Mechanical linkage connects this valve with the throttle lever in the cockpit. By means of the throttle, airflow to the cylinders is regulated and controls the power output of the engine. It is the throttle valve in your automobile carburetor which opens when you "step on the gas." Actually, more air is admitted to the engine, and the carburetor automatically supplies enough additional gasoline to maintain the correct fuel/air ratio. The throttle valve obstructs the passage of air very little when it is parallel with the flow. This is the wide-open position. Throttle action is illustrated in figure 3–5. Note how it restricts the airflow more and more as it rotates toward the closed position.

Metering and Discharge of Fuel

In the illustration showing the discharge of fuel into the airstream (figure 3–6), locate the inlet through which fuel enters the carburetor from the engine-driven pump. The float-operated needle valve regulates the flow through the inlet and, in this way, maintains the correct level in the fuel chamber. This level must be slightly below the

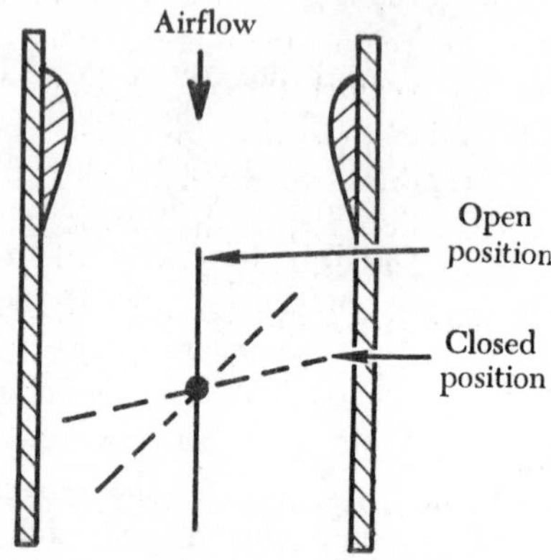

FIGURE 3–5. Throttle action.

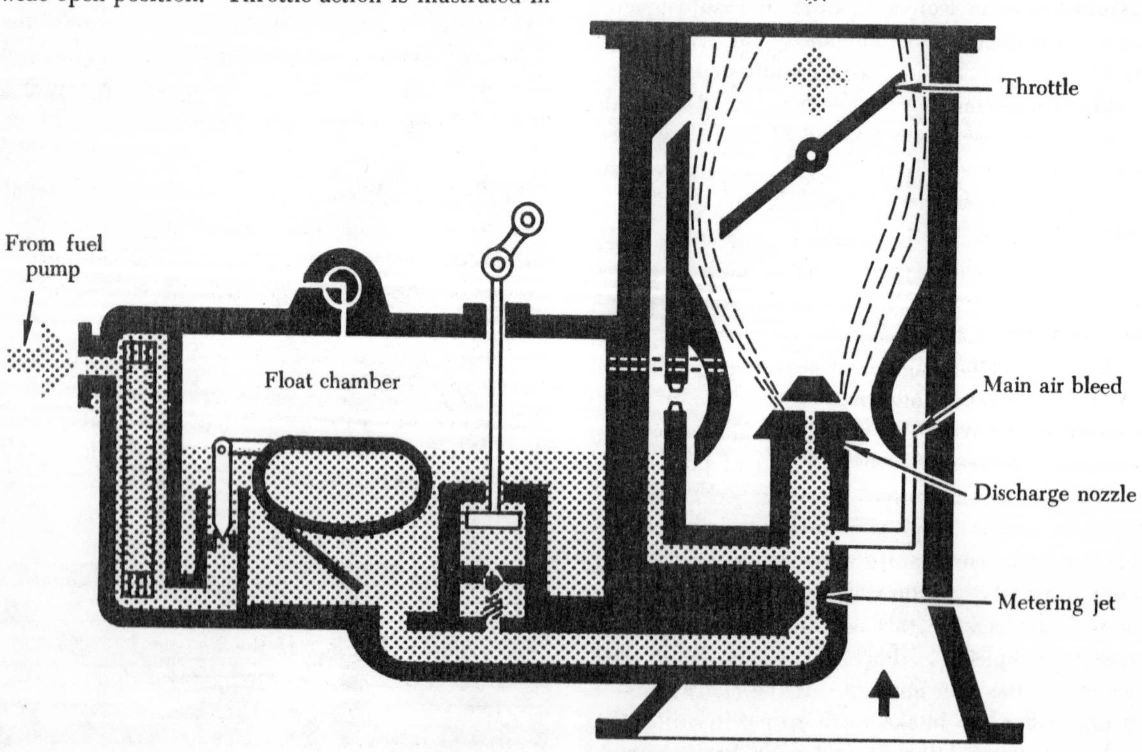

FIGURE 3–6. Fuel discharge.

outlet of the discharge nozzle to prevent overflow when the engine is not running.

The discharge nozzle is located in the throat of the venturi at the point where the lowest drop in pressure occurs as air passes through the carburetor to the engine cylinders. Thus, there are two different pressures acting on the fuel in the carburetor—a low pressure at the discharge nozzle and a higher (atmospheric) pressure in the float chamber. The higher pressure in the float chamber forces the fuel through the discharge nozzle into the airstream. If the throttle is opened wider to increase the airflow to the engine, there is a greater drop in pressure at the venturi throat. Because of the higher differential pressure, the fuel discharge increases in proportion to the increase in airflow. If the throttle is moved toward the "closed" position, the airflow and fuel flow decrease.

The fuel must pass through the metering jet (figure 3–6) to reach the discharge nozzle. The size of this jet determines the rate of fuel discharge at each differential pressure. If the jet is replaced with a larger one, the fuel flow will increase, resulting in a richer mixture. If a smaller jet is installed, there will be a decrease in fuel flow and a leaner mixture.

CARBURETOR SYSTEMS

To provide for engine operation under various loads and at different engine speeds, each carburetor has six systems:

(1) Main metering.
(2) Idling.
(3) Accelerating.
(4) Mixture control.
(5) Idle cutoff.
(6) Power enrichment or economizer.

Each of these systems has a definite function. It may act alone or with one or more of the others.

The main metering system supplies fuel to the engine at all speeds above idling. The fuel discharged by this system is determined by the drop in pressure in the venturi throat.

A separate system is necessary for idling because the main metering system is unreliable at very low engine speeds. At low speeds the throttle is nearly closed. As a result, the velocity of the air through the venturi is low and there is little drop in pressure. Consequently, the differential pressure is not sufficient to operate the main metering system, and no fuel is discharged from this system. Therefore, most carburetors have an idling system to supply fuel to the engine at low engine speeds.

The accelerating system supplies extra fuel during increases in engine power. When the throttle is opened to obtain more power from the engine, the airflow through the carburetor increases. The main metering system then increases the fuel discharge. During sudden acceleration, however, the increase in airflow is so rapid that there is a slight time lag before the increase in fuel discharge is sufficient to provide the correct mixture ratio with the new airflow. By supplying extra fuel during this period, the accelerating system prevents a temporary leaning out of the mixture and gives smooth acceleration.

The mixture control system determines the ratio of fuel to air in the mixture. By means of a cockpit control, the mechanic, pilot, or engineer can select the mixture ratio to suit operating conditions. In addition to these manual controls, many carburetors have automatic mixture controls so that the fuel/air ratio, once it is selected, does not change with variations in air density. This is necessary because, as the airplane climbs and the atmospheric pressure decreases, there is a corresponding decrease in the weight of air passing through the induction system. The volume, however, remains constant, and, since it is the volume of airflow which determines the pressure drop at the throat of the venturi, the carburetor tends to meter the same amount of fuel to this thin air as to the dense air at sea level. Thus, the natural tendency is for the mixture to become richer as the airplane gains altitude. The automatic mixture control prevents this by decreasing the rate of fuel discharge to compensate for the decrease in air density.

The carburetor has an idle cutoff system so that the fuel can be shut off to stop the engine. This system, incorporated in the manual mixture control, stops the fuel discharge from the carburetor completely when the mixture control lever is set to the "idle cutoff" position. In any discussion of the idle cutoff system, this question usually comes up: Why is an aircraft engine stopped by shutting off the fuel rather than by turning off the ignition? To answer this question, it is necessary to examine the results of both methods. If the ignition is turned off with the carburetor still supplying fuel, fresh fuel/air mixture continues to pass through the induction system to the cylinders while the engine is coasting to a stop. If the engine is excessively hot, this combustible mixture may be ignited by local hot spots within the combustion chambers, and the engine may keep on running or kick backward. Again, the mixture may pass out of the cylinders unburned but be ignited in the hot exhaust manifold. More often, however, the engine will come to an apparently normal stop but have a combustible mixture in the induction passages, the cylinders, and the exhaust system. This is an unsafe condition since the engine may kick over after it has been stopped and seriously injure anyone near the propeller. On the other hand, when the engine is shut down by means of the idle cutoff system, the spark plugs continue to ignite the fuel/air mixture until the fuel discharge from the carburetor ceases. This alone should prevent the engine from coming to a stop with a combustible mixture in the cylinders.

Some engine manufacturers suggest that just before the propeller stops turning, the throttle be opened wide so that the pistons can pump fresh air through the induction system, the cylinders, and the exhaust system as an added precaution against accidental kick-over. After the engine has come to a complete stop, the ignition switch is turned to the "off" position.

The power enrichment system automatically increases the richness of the mixture during high-power operation. In this way, it makes possible the variation in fuel/air ratio necessary to fit different operating conditions. Remember that at cruising speeds a lean mixture is desirable for economy reasons, while at high-power output the mixture must be rich to obtain maximum power and to aid in cooling the engine. The power enrichment system automatically brings about the necessary change in the fuel/air ratio. Essentially, it is a valve which is closed at cruising speeds and opens to supply extra fuel to the mixture during high-power operation. Although it increases the fuel flow at high power, the power enrichment system is actually a fuel saving device. Without this system, it would be necessary to operate the engine on a rich mixture over the complete power range. The mixture would then be richer than necessary at cruising speed to ensure safe operation at maximum power. The power enrichment system is sometimes called an "economizer" or a "power compensator."

Although the various systems have been discussed separately, the carburetor functions as a unit. The fact that one system is in operation does not necessarily prevent another from functioning. At the same time that the main metering system is discharging fuel in proportion to the airflow, the mixture control system determines whether the resultant mixture will be rich or lean. If the throttle is suddenly opened wide, the accelerating and power enrichment systems act to add fuel to that already being discharged by the main metering system.

CARBURETOR TYPES

In the discussion of the basic carburetor principles, the fuel was shown stored in a float chamber and discharged from a nozzle located in the venturi throat. With a few added features to make it workable, this becomes the main metering system of the float-type carburetor. This type of carburetor, complete with idling, accelerating, mixture control, idle cutoff, and power enrichment systems, is probably the most common of all carburetor types.

However, the float-type carburetor has several distinct disadvantages. In the first place, imagine the effect that abrupt maneuvers have on the float action. In the second place, the fact that its fuel must be discharged at low pressure leads to incomplete vaporization and difficulty in discharging fuel into some types of supercharged systems. The chief disadvantage of the float carburetor, however, is its icing tendency. Since the float carburetor must discharge fuel at a point of low pressure, the discharge nozzle must be located at the venturi throat, and the throttle valve must be on the engine side of the discharge nozzle. This means that the drop in temperature due to fuel vaporization takes place within the venturi. As a result, ice readily forms in the venturi and on the throttle valve.

A pressure-type carburetor discharges fuel into the airstream at a pressure well above atmospheric. This results in better vaporization and permits the discharge of fuel into the airstream on the engine side of the throttle valve. With the discharge nozzle located at this point, the drop in temperature due to fuel vaporization takes place after the air has passed the throttle valve and at a point where engine heat tends to offset it. Thus, the danger of fuel vaporization icing is practically eliminated. The effects of rapid maneuvers and rough air on the pressure-type carburetors are negligible since its fuel chambers remain filled under all operating conditions.

CARBURETOR ICING

There are three general classifications of carburetor icing that are common for all aircraft:

(1) Fuel evaporation ice.

(2) Throttle ice.

(3) Impact ice.

Fuel evaporation ice or refrigeration ice is formed because of the decrease in air temperature resulting from the evaporation of fuel after it is introduced into the airstream. It frequently occurs in those systems where the fuel is injected into the air upstream from the carburetor throttle, as in the case of float-type carburetors. It occurs less frequently in the systems in which the fuel is injected into the air downstream from the carburetor. Engines employing spinner or impeller injection of fuel are free of this type of ice, except those that have turning vanes (to change the direction of flow) at the entrance to the impeller. In this type, ice can be deposited on the turning vanes. Refrigeration ice can be formed at carburetor air temperatures as high as 100° F. over a wide range of atmospheric humidity conditions, even at relative humidities well below 100%. Generally, fuel evaporation ice will tend to accumulate on the fuel distribution nozzle, the turning vanes, and any protuberances in the carburetor. This type of ice can lower manifold pressure, interfere with fuel flow, and affect mixture distribution.

Throttle ice is formed on the rear side of the throttle, usually when the throttle is in a partially "closed" position. The rush of air across and around the throttle valve causes a low pressure on the rear side; this sets up a pressure differential across the throttle, which has a cooling effect on the fuel/air charge. Moisture freezes in this low-pressure area and collects as ice on the low-pressure side. Throttle ice tends to accumulate in a restricted passage. The occurrence of a small amount of ice may cause a relatively large reduction in airflow and manifold pressure. A large accumulation of ice may jam the throttles and cause them to become inoperable. Throttle ice seldom occurs at temperatures above 38° F.

Impact ice is formed either from water present in the atmosphere as snow, sleet, or subcooled liquid water, or from liquid water which impinges on surfaces that are at temperatures below 30° F. Because of inertia effects, impact ice collects on or near a surface that changes the direction of the airflow. This type of ice may build up on the carburetor elbow, as well as the carburetor screen and metering elements. The most dangerous impact ice is that which collects on the carburetor screen and causes a very rapid throttling of airflow and power. In general, danger from impact ice exists only when ice forms on the leading edges of the aircraft structure.

Under some conditions ice may enter the carburetor in a comparatively dry state and will not adhere to the screen or walls; therefore, it will not affect engine airflow or manifold pressure. This ice may enter the carburetor and gradually build up internally in the carburetor air metering passages and affect carburetor metering characteristics.

FLOAT-TYPE CARBURETORS

A float-type carburetor consists essentially of a main air passage through which the engine draws its supply of air, a mechanism to control the quantity of fuel discharged in relation to the flow of air, and a means of regulating the quantity of fuel/air mixture delivered to the engine cylinders.

The essential parts of a float-type carburetor are illustrated in figure 3–7. These parts are:

(1) The float mechanism and its chamber.
(2) The main metering system.
(3) The idling system.
(4) The mixture control system.
(5) The accelerating system.
(6) The economizer system.

Float Mechanism

A float chamber is provided between the fuel supply and the metering system of the carburetor. The float chamber provides a nearly constant level of fuel to the main discharge nozzle. This level is usually about 1/8 in. below the holes in the main discharge nozzle. The fuel level must be maintained slightly below the discharge nozzle outlet holes to provide the correct amount of fuel flow and to prevent fuel leakage from the nozzle when the engine is not operating.

The level of fuel in the float chamber is kept nearly constant by means of a float-operated needle valve and a seat. The needle seat is usually made of bronze. The needle valve is constructed of hardened steel, or it may have a synthetic rubber section which fits the seat. With no fuel in the float chamber, the float drops toward the bottom of the chamber and allows the needle valve to open wide. As fuel is admitted from the supply line, the float rises and closes the valve when the fuel reaches a predetermined level. When the engine is running and fuel is being drawn out of the float chamber, the valve assumes an intermediate position so that the valve opening is just sufficient to supply the required amount of fuel and keep the level constant.

With the fuel at the correct level, the discharge rate is controlled accurately by the air velocity through the carburetor and the atmospheric pressure on top of the fuel in the float chamber. A vent or small opening in the top of the float chamber allows air to enter or leave the chamber as the level

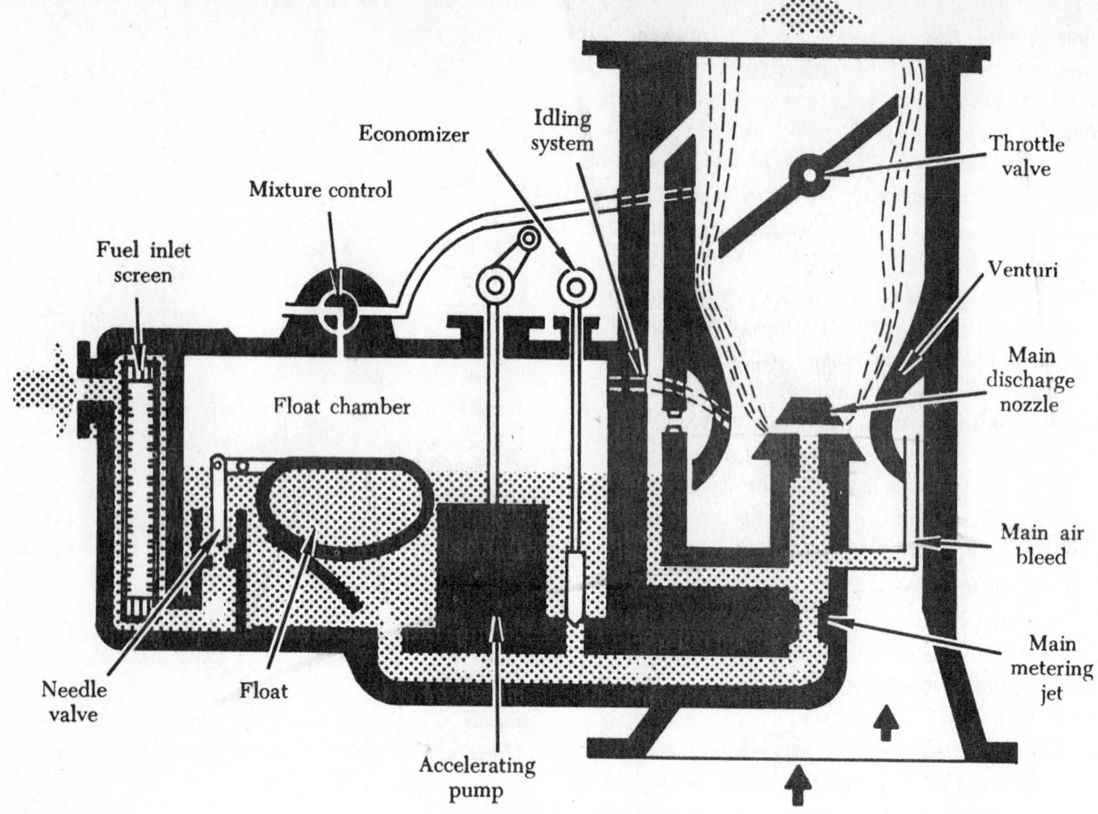

FIGURE 3–7. A float-type carburetor.

of fuel rises or falls. This vent passage is open into the engine air intake; thus, the air pressure in the chamber is always the same as that existing in the air intake.

Main Metering System

The main metering system supplies fuel to the engine at all speeds above idling and consists of:

(1) A venturi.
(2) A main metering jet.
(3) A main discharge nozzle.
(4) A passage leading to the idling system.
(5) The throttle valve.

Since the throttle valve controls the mass airflow through the carburetor venturi it must be considered a major unit in the main metering system as well as in other carburetor systems. A typical main metering system is illustrated in figure 3–8.

The venturi performs three functions: (1) Proportions the fuel/air mixture, (2) decreases the pressure at the discharge nozzle, and (3) limits the airflow at full throttle.

The fuel discharge nozzle is located in the carburetor barrel so that its open end is in the throat or narrowest part of the venturi.

A main metering orifice, or jet, is placed in the

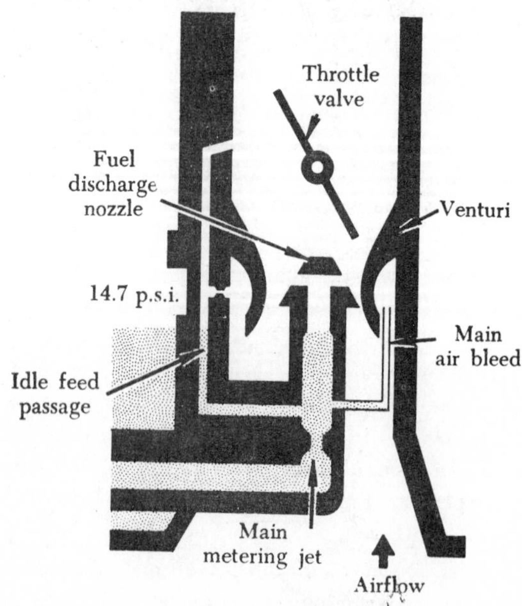

FIGURE 3–8. Main metering system.

fuel passage between the float chamber and the discharge nozzle to limit the fuel flow when the throttle valve is wide open.

When the engine crankshaft is revolved with the carburetor throttle open, the low pressure created in the intake manifold acts on the air passing through the carburetor barrel. Due to the difference in pressure between the atmosphere and the intake manifold, air will flow from the air intake through the carburetor barrel into the intake manifold. The volume of airflow depends upon the degree of throttle opening.

As the air flows through the venturi, its velocity increases. This velocity increase creates a low pressure area in the venturi throat. The fuel discharge nozzle is exposed to this low pressure. Since the float chamber is vented to atmospheric pressure, a pressure drop across the discharge nozzle is created. It is this pressure difference, or metering force, that causes fuel to flow from the discharge nozzle. The fuel comes out of the nozzle in a fine spray, and the tiny particles of fuel in the spray quickly vaporize in the air.

The metering force in most carburetors increases as the throttle opening is increased. A pressure drop of at least 0.5 in. Hg is required to raise the fuel in the discharge nozzle to a level where it will discharge into the airstream. At low engine speeds where the metering force is considerably reduced, the fuel delivery from the discharge nozzle would decrease if an air bleed (air metering jet) were not incorporated in the carburetor.

The decrease in fuel flow in relation to airflow is due to two factors: (1) The fuel tends to adhere to the walls of the discharge nozzle and break off intermittently in large drops instead of forming a fine spray, and (2) a part of the metering force is required to raise the fuel level from the float chamber level to the discharge nozzle outlet.

The basic principle of the air bleed can be explained by simple diagrams as shown in figure 3–9. In each case, the same degree of suction is applied to a vertical tube placed in the container of liquid. As shown in A, the suction applied on the upper end of the tube is sufficient to lift the liquid a distance of about 1 in. above the surface. If a small hole is made in the side of the tube above the surface of the liquid, as in B, and suction is applied, bubbles of air will enter the tube and the liquid will be drawn up in a continuous series of small slugs or drops. Thus, air "bleeds" into the tube and partially reduces the forces tending to retard the flow of liquid through the tube. However, the large opening at the bottom of the tube effectively prevents any great amount of suction from being exerted on the air bleed hole or vent. Similarly, an air bleed hole which is too large in proportion to the size of the tube would reduce the suction available to lift the liquid. If the system is modified by placing a metering orifice in the bottom of the tube and air is taken in below the fuel level by means of an air bleed tube, a finely divided emulsion of air and liquid is formed in the tube, as shown in C.

In a carburetor, a small air bleed is led into the fuel nozzle slightly below the fuel level. The open end of the air bleed is in the space behind the venturi wall, where the air is relatively motionless and approximately at atmospheric pressure. The

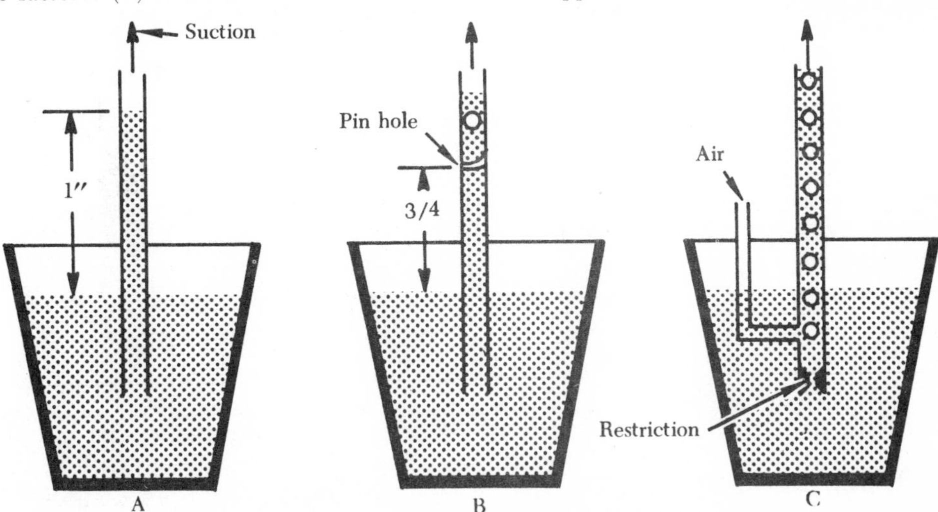

FIGURE 3–9. Air bleed principle.

low pressure at the tip of the nozzle not only draws fuel from the float chamber but also draws air from behind the venturi. Air bled into the main metering fuel system decreases the fuel density and destroys surface tension. This results in better vaporization and control of fuel discharge, especially at lower engine speeds.

The throttle, or butterfly valve, is located in the carburetor barrel near one end of the venturi. It provides a means of controlling engine speed or power output by regulating the airflow to the engine. This valve is a disk which can rotate on an axis, so that it can be turned to open or close the carburetor air passage. Where more than one throttle valve is necessary, they may be attached to the same throttle shaft or to separate shafts. In the latter case, it is necessary to check the uniformity of opening or synchronization.

Idling System

With the throttle valve closed at idling speeds, air velocity through the venturi is so low that it cannot draw enough fuel from the main discharge nozzle; in fact, the spray of fuel may stop altogether. However, low pressure (piston suction) exists on the engine side of the throttle valve. In order to allow the engine to idle, a fuel passageway is incorporated to discharge fuel from an opening in the low pressure area near the edge of the throttle valve. This opening is called the idling jet. With the throttle open enough so that the main discharge nozzle is operating, fuel does not flow out of the idling jet. As soon as the throttle is closed far enough to stop the spray from the main discharge nozzle, fuel flows out the idling jet. A separate air bleed, known as the idle air bleed, is included as part of the idling system. It functions the same as the main air bleed. An idle mixture adjusting device is also incorporated. A typical idling system is illustrated in figure 3–10.

Mixture Control System

As altitude increases, the air becomes less dense. At an altitude of 18,000 ft. the air is only half as dense as it is at sea level. This means that a cubic foot of space contains only half as much air at 18,000 ft. as at sea level. An engine cylinder full of air at 18,000 ft. contains only half as much oxygen compared to a cylinder full of air at sea level.

The low pressure area created by the venturi is dependent upon air velocity rather than air density. The action of the venturi draws the same volume of fuel through the discharge nozzle at a high altitude as it does at a low altitude. Therefore, the fuel mixture becomes richer as altitude increases. This can be overcome either by a manual or an automatic mixture control.

On float-type carburetors two types of purely manual or cockpit controllable devices are in general use for controlling fuel/air mixtures, the needle type and the back-suction type. The two types are illustrated in figures 3–11 and 3–12.

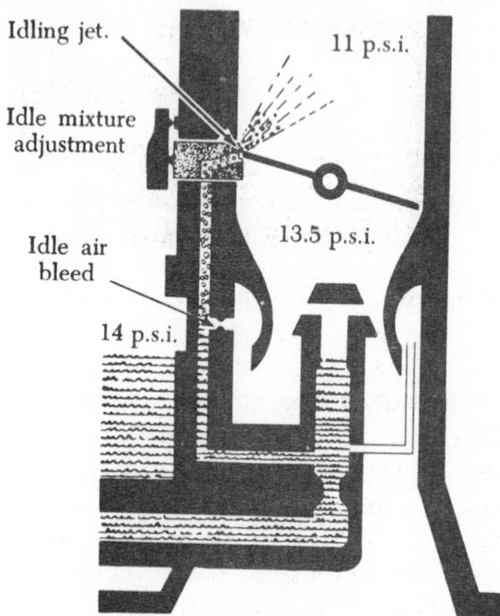

FIGURE 3–10. Idling system.

FIGURE 3–11. Needle-type mixture control system.

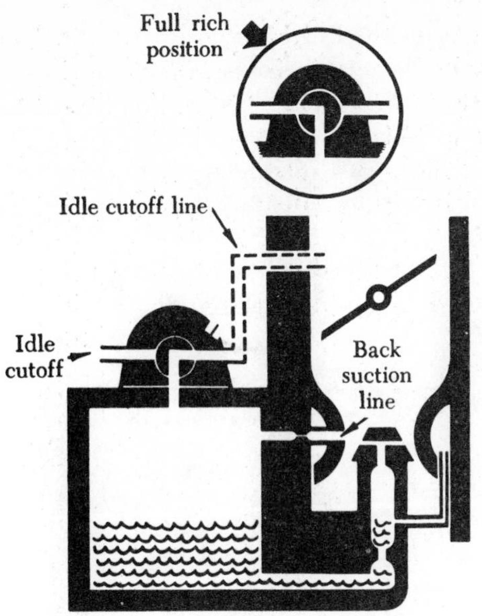

FIGURE 3–12. Back-suction type mixture control system.

With the needle-type system, manual control is provided by a needle valve in the base of the float chamber (figure 3–11). This can be raised or lowered by adjusting a control in the cockpit. Moving the control to "rich" opens the needle valve wide, which permits the fuel to flow unrestricted to the nozzle. Moving the control to "lean" closes the valve part way and restricts the flow of fuel to the nozzle.

The back-suction type mixture control system is the most widely used. In this system (figure 3–12) a certain amount of venturi low pressure acts upon the fuel in the float chamber so that it opposes the low pressure existing at the main discharge nozzle. An atmospheric line, incorporating an adjustable valve, opens into the float chamber. When the valve is completely closed, pressures on the fuel in the float chamber and at the discharge nozzle are almost equal and fuel flow is reduced to maximum lean. With the valve wide open, pressure on the fuel in the float chamber is greatest and fuel mixture is richest. Adjusting the valve to positions between these two extremes controls the mixture.

The quadrant in the cockpit is usually marked "lean" near the back end and "rich" at the forward end. The extreme back position is marked "idle cutoff" and is used when stopping the engine.

On float carburetors equipped with needle-type mixture control, placing the mixture control in idle cutoff seats the needle valve, thus shutting off fuel flow completely. On carburetors equipped with back-suction mixture controls, a separate idle cutoff line, leading to the extreme low pressure on the engine side of the throttle valve, is incorporated. (See the dotted line in figure 3–12.) The mixture control is so linked that when it is placed in the "idle cutoff" position, it opens another passage which leads to piston suction; when placed in other positions, the valve opens a passage leading to the atmosphere. To stop the engine with such a system, close the throttle and place the mixture in the "idle cutoff" position. Leave the throttle closed until the engine has stopped turning over and then open the throttle completely.

Accelerating System

When the throttle valve is opened quickly, a large volume of air rushes through the air passage of the carburetor. However, the amount of fuel that is mixed with the air is less than normal. This is because of the slow response rate of the main metering system. As a result, after a quick opening of the throttle, the fuel/air mixture leans out momentarily.

To overcome this tendency, the carburetor is equipped with a small fuel pump called an accelerating pump. A common type of accelerating system used in float carburetors is illustrated in figure 3–13. It consists of a simple piston pump operated through linkage, by the throttle control, and a line opening into the main metering system or the carburetor barrel near the venturi. When the throttle is closed, the piston moves back and fuel fills the cylinder. If the piston is pushed forward slowly, the fuel seeps past it back into the float chamber, but if pushed rapidly, it will emit a charge of fuel and enrich the mixture in the venturi.

Economizer System

For an engine to develop maximum power at full throttle, the fuel mixture must be richer than for cruise. The additional fuel is used for cooling the engine to prevent detonation. An economizer is essentially a valve which is closed at throttle settings below approximately 60 to 70% of rated power. This system, like the accelerating system, is operated by the throttle control.

A typical economizer system, as shown in figure 3–14, consists of a needle valve which begins to open when the throttle valve reaches a predetermined point near the wide-open position. As the throttle continues to open, the needle valve is opened further and additional fuel flows through it. This additional fuel supplements the flow from the main metering jet direct to the main discharge nozzle.

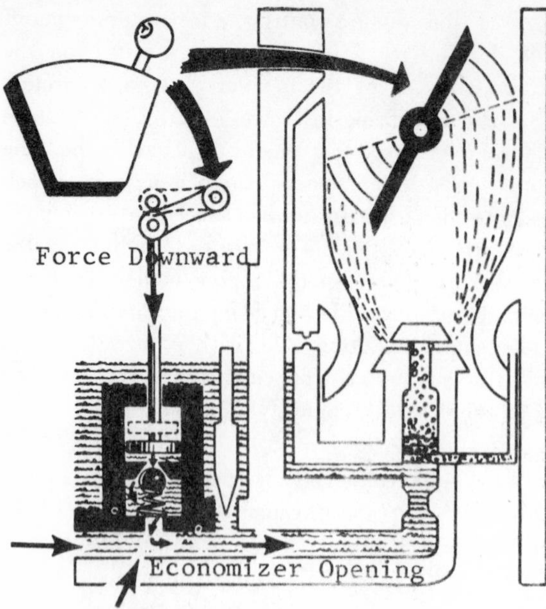

FIGURE 3–13. Accelerating system.

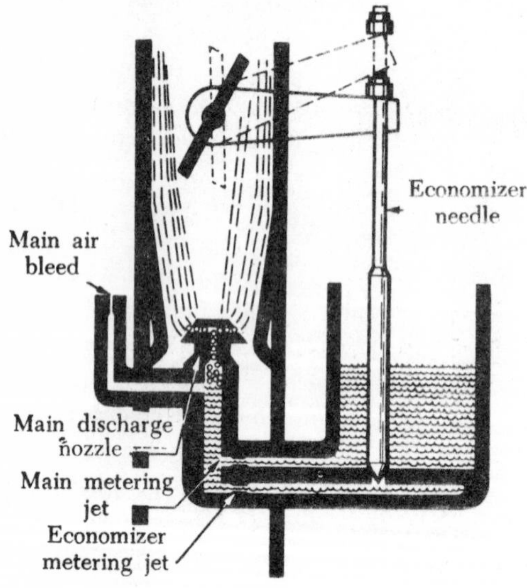

FIGURE 3–14. A needle-valve type economizer system.

A pressure-operated economizer system is shown in figure 3–15. This type has a sealed bellows located in an enclosed compartment. The compartment is vented to engine manifold pressure. When the manifold pressure reaches a certain value, the bellows is compressed and opens a valve in a carburetor fuel passage, supplementing the normal quantity of fuel being discharged through the main nozzle.

Another type of economizer is the back-suction system shown in figure 3–16. Fuel economy in

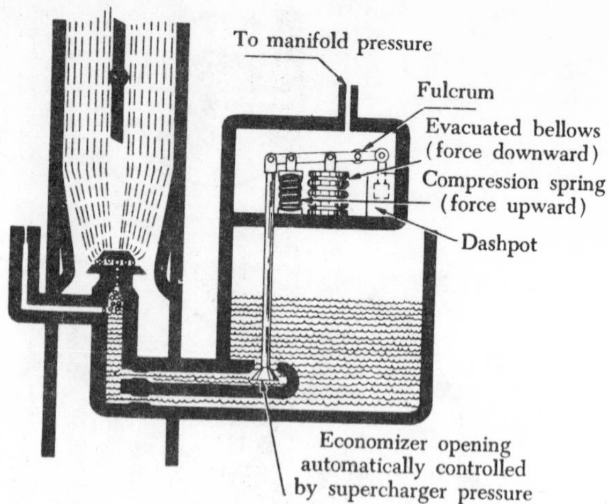

FIGURE 3–15. A pressure-operated economizer system.

cruising is provided by reducing the effective pressure acting on the fuel level in the float compartment. With the throttle valve in cruising position, suction is applied to the float chamber through an economizer hole and back-suction economizer channel and jet. The suction thus applied to the float chamber opposes the nozzle suction applied by the venturi. Fuel flow is reduced, thus leaning the mixture for cruising economy.

Another type mixture control system uses a metering valve which is free to rotate in a stationary metering sleeve. Fuel enters the main and idling systems through a slot cut in the mixture sleeve. Fuel metering is accomplished by the relative position between one edge of the slot in the hollow metering valve and one edge of the slot in the metering sleeve. Moving the mixture control to reduce the size of the slot provides a leaner mixture for altitude compensation.

PRESSURE INJECTION CARBURETORS

Pressure injection carburetors are distinctly different from float-type carburetors, as they do not incorporate a vented float chamber or suction pickup from a discharge nozzle located in the venturi tube. Instead, they provide a pressurized fuel system that is closed from the engine fuel pump to the discharge nozzle. The venturi serves only to create pressure differentials for controlling the quantity of fuel to the metering jet in proportion to airflow to the engine.

Typical Injection Carburetor

The injection carburetor is a hydromechanical device employing a closed feed system from the fuel

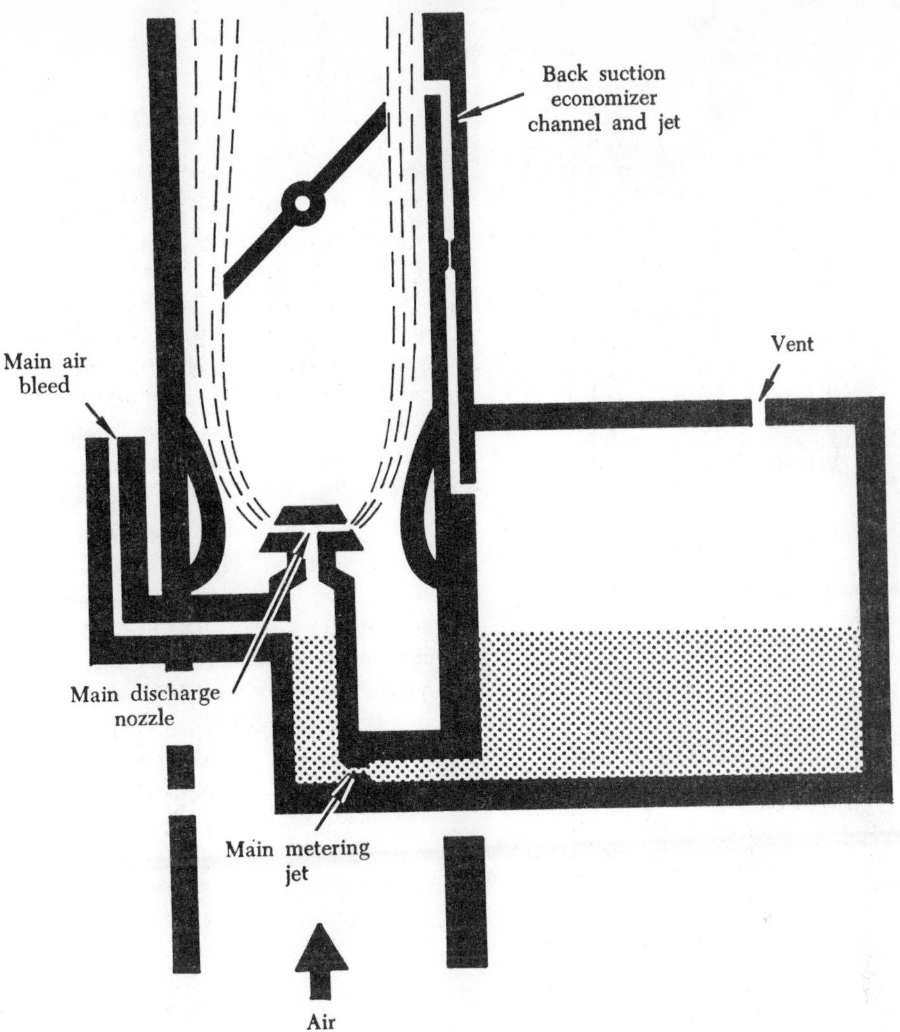

FIGURE 3–16. Back-suction economizer system.

pump to the discharge nozzle. It meters fuel through fixed jets according to the mass airflow through the throttle body and discharges it under a positive pressure.

The illustration in figure 3–17 represents a pressure-type carburetor simplified to the extent that only the basic parts are shown. Note the two small passages, one leading from the carburetor air inlet to the left side of the flexible diaphragm and the other from the venturi throat to the right side of the diaphragm.

When air passes through the carburetor to the engine, the pressure on the right of the diaphragm is lowered because of the drop in pressure at the venturi throat. As a result, the diaphragm moves to the right, opening the fuel valve. Pressure from the engine-driven pump then forces fuel through the open valve to the discharge nozzle, where it sprays into the airstream. The distance the fuel valve opens is determined by the difference between the two pressures acting on the diaphragm. This difference in pressure is proportional to the airflow through the carburetor. Thus, the volume of airflow determines the rate of fuel discharge.

The pressure injection carburetor is an assembly of the following units:

(1) Throttle body.
(2) Automatic mixture control.
(3) Regulator unit.
(4) Fuel control unit; some are equipped with an adapter.

Throttle Body

The throttle body contains the throttle valves, main venturi, boost venturi, and the impact tubes. All air entering the cylinders must flow through the

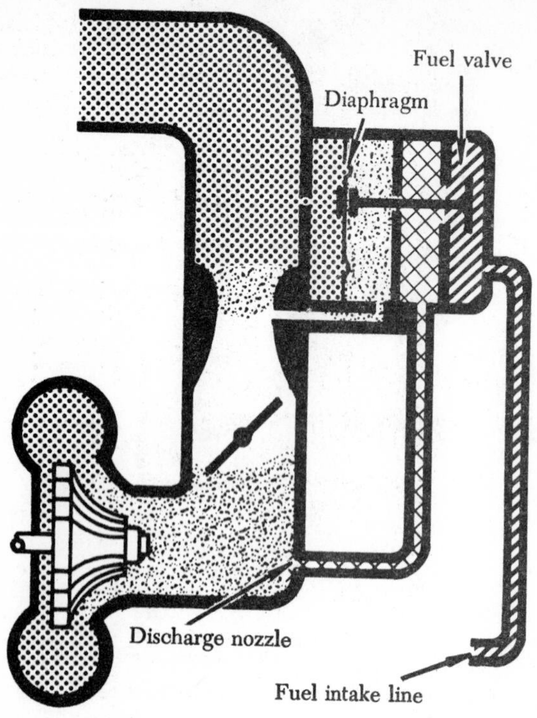

FIGURE 3–17. Pressure-type carburetor.

throttle body; therefore, it is the air control and measuring device. The airflow is measured by volume and by weight so that the proper amount of fuel can be added to meet the engine demands under all conditions.

As air flows through the venturis, its velocity is increased and its pressure is decreased (Bernoulli's principle). This low pressure is vented to the low-pressure side of the air diaphragm (chamber B, figure 3–18), in the regulator assembly. The impact tubes sense carburetor inlet air pressure and direct it to the automatic mixture control, which measures the air density. From the automatic mixture control the air is directed to the high-pressure side of the air diaphragm (chamber A). The pressure differential of the two chambers acting upon the air diaphragm is known as the air metering force which opens the fuel poppet valve.

The throttle body controls the airflow with the throttle valves. The throttle valves may be either rectangular or disk shaped, depending on the design of the carburetor. The valves are mounted on a shaft which is connected by linkage to the idle valve and to the throttle control in the cockpit. A throttle stop limits the travel of the throttle valve and has an adjustment which sets engine idle speed.

Regulator Unit

The regulator (figure 3–18) is a diaphragm-controlled unit which is divided into five chambers and

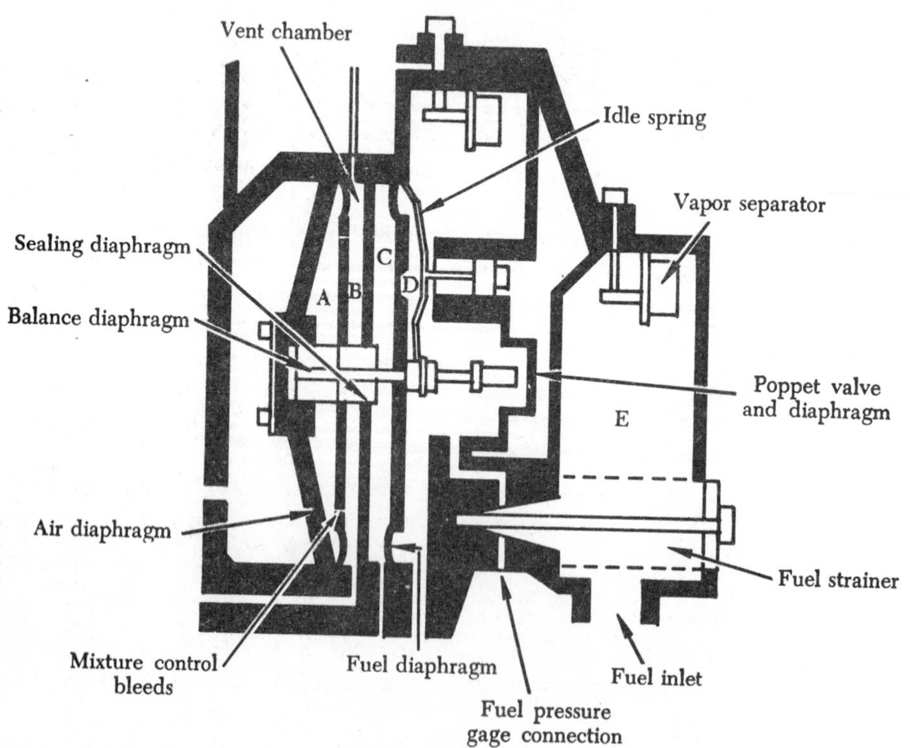

FIGURE 3–18. Regulator unit.

contains two regulating diaphragms and a poppet valve assembly. Chamber A is regulated air-inlet pressure from the air intake. Chamber B is boost venturi pressure. Chamber C contains metered fuel pressure controlled by the discharge nozzle or fuel feed valve. Chamber D contains unmetered fuel pressure controlled by the opening of the poppet valve. Chamber E is fuel pump pressure, controlled by the fuel pump pressure relief valve. The poppet valve assembly is connected by a stem to the two main control diaphragms.

The carburetor fuel strainer, located in the inlet to chamber E, is a fine mesh screen through which all the fuel must pass as it enters chamber D. The strainer must be removed and cleaned at scheduled intervals.

The purpose of the regulator unit is to regulate the fuel pressure to the inlet side of the metering jets in the fuel control unit. This pressure is automatically regulated according to the mass airflow to the engine.

Referring to figure 3–18, assume that for a given airflow in lbs./hr. through the throttle body and venturi, a negative pressure of one-fourth p.s.i. is established in chamber B. This tends to move the diaphragm assembly and the poppet valve in a direction to open the poppet valve, permitting more fuel to enter chamber D. The pressure in chamber C is held constant at 5 p.s.i. (10 p.s.i. on some installations) by the discharge nozzle or impeller fuel feed valve. Therefore, the diaphragm assembly and poppet valve will move in the open direction until the pressure in chamber D is 5-1/4 p.s.i. Under these pressures, there is a balanced condition of the diaphragm assembly with a pressure drop of one-fourth p.s.i. across the jets in the fuel control unit (auto-rich or auto-lean).

Fuel Control Unit

The fuel control unit (figure 3–19) is attached to the regulator assembly and contains all metering jets and valves. The idle and power enrichment valves, together with the mixture control plates, select the jet combinations for the various settings, i.e., auto-rich, auto-lean, and idle cutoff.

If nozzle pressure (chamber C pressure) rises to 5-1/2 p.s.i., the diaphragm assembly balance will be upset, and the diaphragm assembly will move to open the poppet valve to establish the necessary 5-3/4 p.s.i. pressure in chamber D. Thus, the one-fourth p.s.i. differential between chamber C and chamber D is re-established, and the pressure drop across the metering jets will remain the same.

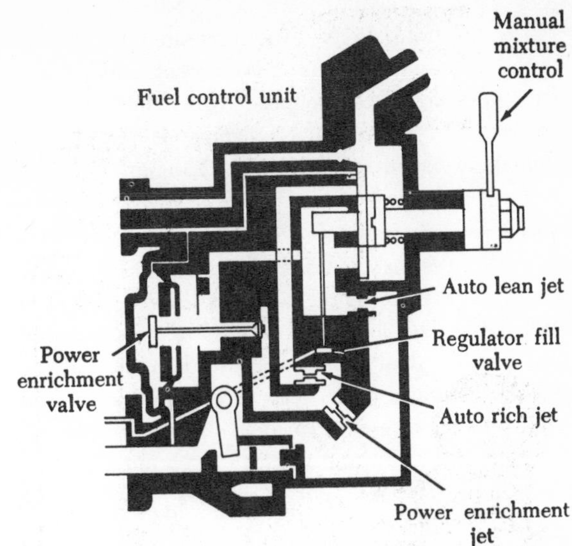

FIGURE 3–19. Fuel control unit.

If the fuel inlet pressure is increased or decreased, the fuel flow into chamber D will tend to increase or decrease with the pressure change, causing the chamber D pressure to do likewise. This will upset the balanced condition previously established, and the poppet valve and diaphragm assembly will respond by moving to increase or decrease the flow to re-establish the pressure at the one-fourth p.s.i. differential.

When the mixture control plates are moved from auto-lean to auto-rich or vice versa, thereby selecting a different set of jets or cutting one or two in or out of the system, the fuel flow changes. However, when the mixture position is altered, the diaphragm and poppet valve assembly will reposition to maintain the established pressure differential of one-fourth p.s.i. between chambers C and D, maintaining the established differential across the jets.

Under low-power settings (low airflows), the difference in pressure created by the boost venturi is not sufficient to accomplish consistent regulation of the fuel. Therefore, an idle spring, shown in figure 3–18, is incorporated in the regulator. As the poppet valve moves toward the closed position, it contacts the idle spring. The spring holds the poppet valve off its seat far enough to provide more fuel than is needed for idling. This potentially over-rich mixture is regulated by the idle valve. At idling speed the idle valve restricts the fuel flow to the proper amount. At higher speeds it is withdrawn from the fuel passage and has no metering effect.

Vapor vent systems are provided in these carburetors to eliminate fuel vapor created by the fuel pump, heat in the engine compartment, and the pressure drop across the poppet valve. The vapor vent is located in the fuel inlet (chamber E) or, on some models of carburetors, in both chambers D and E.

The vapor vent system operates in the following way. When air enters the chamber in which the vapor vent is installed, the air rises to the top of the chamber, displacing the fuel and lowering its level. When the fuel level has reached a predetermined position, the float (which floats in the fuel) pulls the vapor vent valve off its seat, permitting the vapor in the chamber to escape through the vapor vent seat, its connecting line, and back to the fuel tank.

If the vapor vent valve sticks in a closed position or the vent line from the vapor vent to the fuel tank becomes clogged, the vapor-eliminating action will be stopped. This will cause the vapor to build up within the carburetor to the extent that vapor will pass through the metering jets with the fuel. With a given-size carburetor metering jet, the metering of vapor will reduce the quantity of fuel metered. This will cause the fuel/air mixture to lean out, usually intermittently.

If the vapor vent valve sticks open or the vapor vent float becomes filled with fuel and sinks, a continuous flow of fuel and vapor occurs through the vent line. It is important to detect this condition, as the fuel flow from the carburetor to the fuel supply tank may cause an overflowing tank with resultant increased fuel consumption.

To check the vent system, disconnect the vapor vent line where it attaches to the carburetor, and turn the fuel booster pump on while observing the vapor vent connection at the carburetor. Move the carburetor mixture control to auto-rich; then return it to idle cutoff. When the fuel booster pump is turned on, there should be an initial ejection of fuel and air followed by a cutoff with not more than a steady drip from the vent connection. On installations where a fixed bleed from the D chamber is connected to the vapor vent in the fuel inlet by a short external line, there should be an initial ejection of fuel and air followed by a continuing small stream of fuel. If there is no flow, the valve is sticking closed; if there is a steady flow, it is sticking open.

The purpose of the fuel control unit is to meter and control the fuel flow to the discharge nozzle. The basic unit consists of three jets and four valves arranged in series, parallel, and series-parallel hookups. (See figure 3–19.) These jets and valves receive fuel under pressure from the regulator unit and then meter the fuel as it goes to the discharge nozzle. The manual mixture control valve controls the fuel flow. By using proper size jets and regulating the pressure differential across the jets, the right amount of fuel is delivered to the discharge nozzle, giving the desired fuel/air ratio in the various power settings. It should be remembered that the inlet pressure to the jets is regulated by the regulator unit and the outlet pressure is controlled by the discharge nozzle.

The jets in the basic fuel control unit are the auto-lean jet, the auto-rich jet, and power enrichment jet. The basic fuel flow is the fuel required to run the engine with a lean mixture and is metered by the auto-lean jet. The auto-rich jet adds enough fuel to the basic flow to give a slightly richer mixture than best power mixture when the manual mixture control is in the "auto-rich" position.

The four valves in the basic fuel control unit are:

(1) The idle needle valve.

(2) The power enrichment valve.

(3) The regulator fill valve.

(4) The manual mixture control.

The functions of these valves are as follows:

(1) The idle needle valve meters the fuel in the idle range only. It is a round, contoured needle valve or a cylinder valve placed in series with all other metering devices of the basic fuel control unit. The idle needle valve is connected by linkage to the throttle shaft so that it will restrict the fuel flowing at low-power settings (idle range).

(2) The manual mixture control is a rotary disk valve consisting of a round stationary disk with ports leading from the auto-lean jet, the auto-rich jet, and two smaller ventholes. Another rotating part, resembling a cloverleaf, is held against the stationary disk by spring tension and rotated over the ports in that disk by the manual mixture control lever. All ports and vents are closed in the "idle cutoff" position. In the "auto-lean" position, the ports from the auto-lean jet and the two ventholes are open. The port from the auto-rich jet remains closed in this position. In the "auto-rich" position, all ports are open. The valve plate positions are illustrated in figure 3–20. The three positions of the manual mixture control lever make it possible to select a lean mixture or a rich mixture, or to stop fuel flow

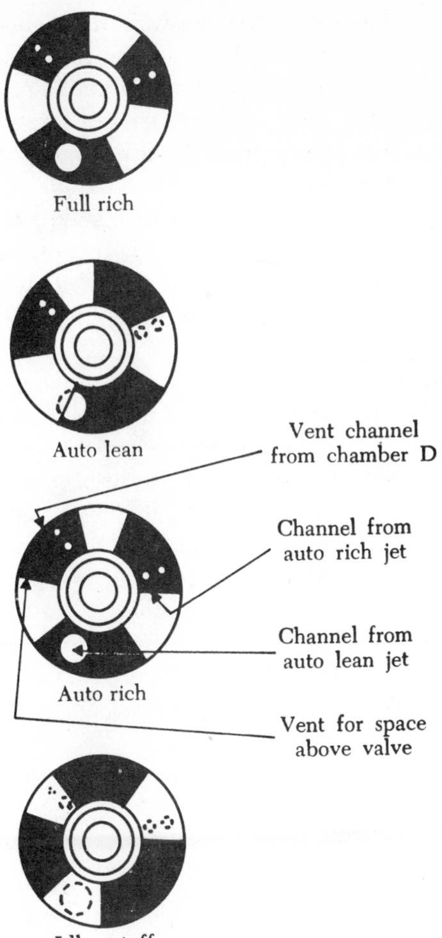

FIGURE 3–20. Manual mixture control valve plate positions.

entirely. The "idle cutoff" position is used for starting or stopping the engine. During starting, fuel is supplied by the primer.

(3) The regulator fill valve is a small poppet-type valve located in a fuel passage which supplies chamber C of the regulator unit with metered fuel pressure. In idle cutoff, the flat portion of the cam lines up with the valve stem, and a spring closes the valve. This provides a means of shutting off the fuel flow to chamber C and thus provides for a positive idle cutoff.

(4) The power enrichment valve is another poppet-type valve. It is in parallel with the auto-lean and auto-rich jets, but it is in series with the power enrichment jet. This valve starts to open at the beginning of the power range. It is opened by the unmetered fuel pressure overcoming metered fuel pressure and spring tension. The power enrichment valve continues to open wider and wider during the power range until the combined flow through the valve and the auto-rich jet exceeds that of the power enrichment jet. At this point the power enrichment jet takes over the metering and meters fuel throughout the power range.

(5) Carburetors equipped for water injection are modified by the addition of a derichment valve and a derichment jet. The derichment valve and derichment jet are in series with each other and parallel with the power enrichment jet.

The carburetor controls fuel flow by varying two basic factors. The fuel control unit, acting as a pressure-reducing valve, determines the metering pressure in response to the metering forces. The regulator unit, in effect, varies the size of the orifice through which the metering pressure forces the fuel. It is a basic law of hydraulics that the amount of fluid that passes through an orifice varies with the size of the orifice and the pressure drop across it. The internal automatic devices and mixture control act together to determine the effective size of the metering passage through which the fuel passes. The internal devices, fixed jets, and variable power enrichment valve are not subject to direct external control.

Automatic Mixture Control (AMC)

The automatic mixture control unit (figure 3–21)

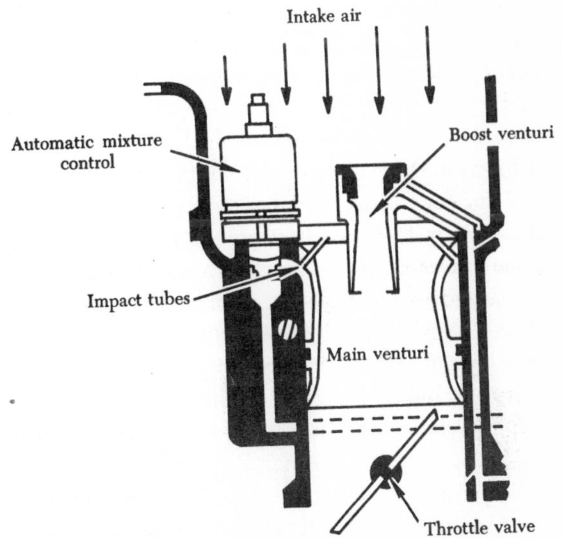

FIGURE 3–21. Automatic mixture control and throttle body.

consists of a bellows assembly, calibrated needle, and seat. The purpose of the automatic mixture control is to compensate for changes in air density due to temperature and altitude changes.

The automatic mixture control contains a metallic bellows, sealed at 28 in. Hg, absolute pressure, which responds to changes in pressure and temperature. In the illustration, note that the automatic mixture control is located at the carburetor air inlet. As the density of the air changes, the expansion and contraction of the bellows moves the tapered needle in the atmospheric line. At sea level, the bellows is contracted and the needle is not in the atmospheric passage. As the aircraft climbs and the atmospheric pressure decreases, the bellows expands, inserting the tapered needle farther and farther into the atmospheric passage and restricting the flow of air to chamber A of the regulator unit (figure 3–18). At the same time, air leaks slowly from chamber A to chamber B through the small bleed (often referred to as the back-suction bleed, or mixture control bleed). The rate at which air leaks through this bleed is about the same at high altitude as it is at sea level. Thus, as the tapered needle restricts the flow of air into chamber A, the pressure on the left side of the air diaphragm decreases; as a result, the poppet valve moves toward its seat, reducing the fuel flow to compensate for the decrease in air density. The automatic mixture control can be removed and cleaned, provided the lead seal at the point of adjustment is not disturbed.

Adapter Unit

The purpose of the adapter is to adapt the carburetor to the engine. This unit may also contain the discharge nozzle and the accelerating pump (see figure 3–22). On engines using fuel feed valves, however, the discharge nozzle is eliminated, since the fuel feed valve serves the same purpose and is built into the engine. Where a spinner injection discharge valve is used in place of the discharge nozzle, the accelerating pump is usually housed on the side of the throttle body, and the adapter is then nothing more than a spacer and has no working parts.

The discharge nozzle is a spring-loaded valve which maintains metered fuel pressure. Before fuel can pass through the discharge nozzle, enough pressure must be built up against the diaphragm to overcome the tension of the spring which is on the air side of the diaphragm. The diaphragm then rises, lifting the attached valve, and the fuel is sprayed out the nozzle. Secured to the nozzle is a diffuser which

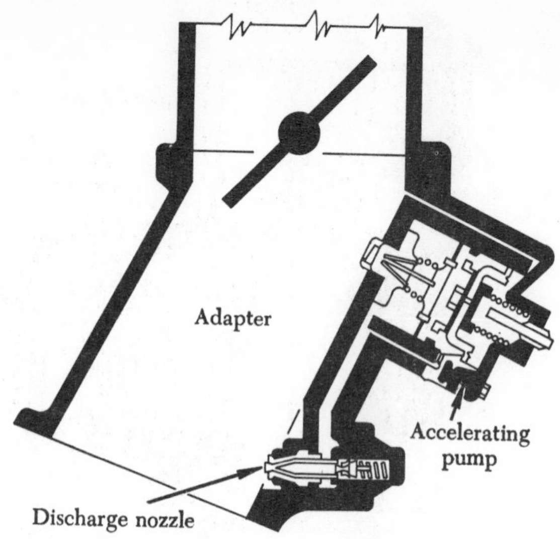

FIGURE 3–22. Adapter.

is designed to improve distribution and atomization of the fuel into the airstream. There are three types of diffusers used in adapter-mounted discharge nozzles—the rake, the bar, and the bow tie. Two other diffusers built into some engines are the slinger ring used with the fuel feed valve and the spinner ring used with the spinner injection discharge valve.

The acceleration pump is used to compensate for the inherent lag in fuel flow during rapid acceleration of the engine.

Pressure Injection Carburetor Systems

The pressure-type carburetor, like the float-type carburetor, contains a main metering system, an idling system, an accelerating system, a mixture control system (both manual and automatic), an idle cutoff system, and a power enrichment system. A schematic representation of a pressure injection carburetor, PD series, is illustrated in figure 3–23.

Main Metering System

Perhaps the most noticeable feature of the main metering system is the double venturi. In figure 3–23, note that the lower opening of the boost venturi is near the throat of the main one. Thus, the drop in pressure within the main venturi causes an acceleration in airflow through the boost venturi and, consequently, a still greater pressure drop at its throat. As a result, a greater differential in pressure and a greater air metering force are obtained.

To make use of this metering force, the throat of the boost venturi and the inlet to the main venturi are connected to the air chambers of the carburetor. There are two of these air chambers, A and B.

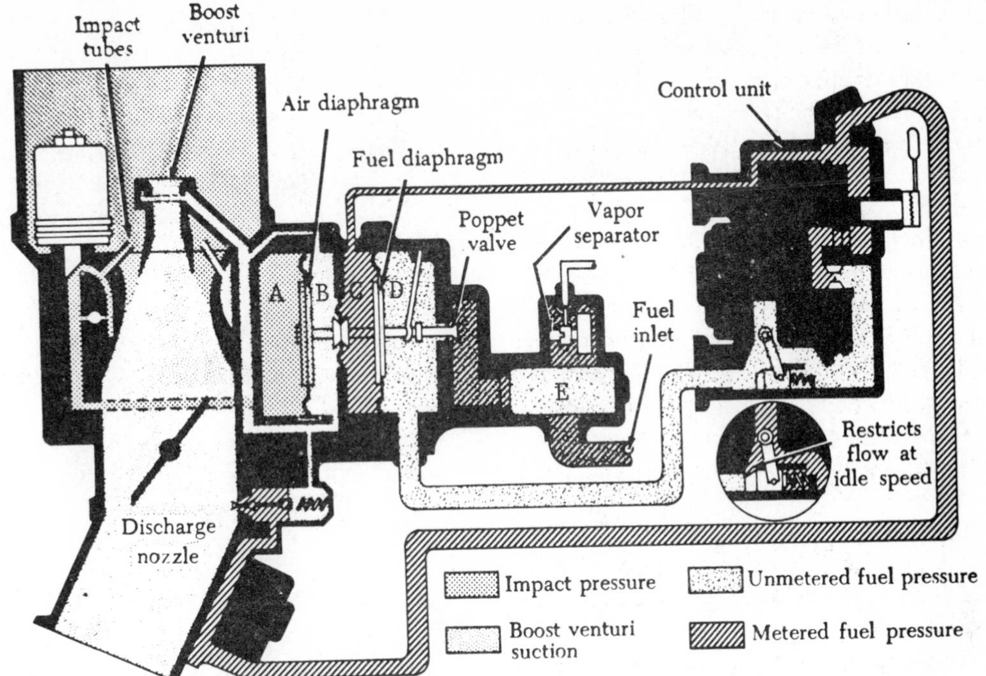

FIGURE 3–23. Schematic representation of a pressure injection carburetor, PD series.

Chambers C and D are fuel chambers. The passages from chamber B to the throat of the boost venturi can be easily traced. The other passage is less direct. It leads from chamber A to the space behind the main venturi. The impact tubes vent this space to the pressure at the carburetor air inlet. In some induction systems, the pressure at the carburetor air inlet is slightly above atmospheric because of ram effect. If there is a turbo or other supercharger ahead of the carburetor, the inlet pressure is considerably higher than atmospheric under certain operating conditions.

In all systems, the drop in pressure at the throat of the boost venturi is proportional to the airflow. This causes a lowering of the pressure in chamber B. Thus the pressures in the two air chambers differ, impact pressure in chamber A and boost venturi suction in chamber B. This pressure difference is a measure of airflow. The air-chamber diaphragm moves in the direction of the lower pressure (to the right), opening the poppet valve. This allows fuel, delivered to the carburetor inlet under pressure from the engine-driven pump, to enter chamber D. This fuel passes through the control unit to the discharge nozzle, where it forces the valve off its seat and sprays into the airstream. The pressure in the fuel discharge line is determined by setting of the nozzle. The pressure at which the engine-driven pump delivers fuel to the carburetor varies with different models. However, it is always well above the discharge nozzle setting.

Chamber C is filled with fuel at the same pressure as that in the discharge line. The function of chamber C is to allow fuel to be discharged under pressure and to compensate for variations of pressures in the discharge line. The discharge nozzle acts as a relief valve to hold this pressure relatively constant regardless of the volume of fuel being discharged. This metered fuel pressure acts on the left side of the fuel diaphragm. The fuel admitted to chamber D through the poppet valve exerts pressure against the opposite side of the diaphragm. The unmetered fuel pressure in chamber D varies with the position of the poppet valve and the rate of fuel discharge. During engine operation, it is higher than that in chamber C. Thus, there are two forces acting on the poppet valve: (1) A force on the air diaphragm (difference in pressure between chambers A and B) tending to open the valve, and (2) a force on the fuel diaphragm (difference in pressures between chambers D and C) tending to close the valve. The poppet valve moves toward the open position until the fuel pressure in chamber D is high enough to make these forces balance. This balance is reached when the fuel discharge and the airflow are in the correct proportion.

To prevent air in the fuel from upsetting the metering of the carburetor, there is a vapor separator at the fuel inlet. A small float and needle valve are positioned in the vapor separator chamber. When there are no vapors in the chamber, the float is raised and holds the needle valve closed. As vapors gather, the fuel level in the chamber drops, lowering the float until the needle valve opens. The vapors then escape through the vent line to one of the fuel tanks. This action is not an opening and closing process, but one in which the needle takes an intermediate position which allows vapors to escape as fast as they gather.

Idling System

In the pressure-type carburetor, the fuel follows the same path at idling as it does when the main metering system is in operation. Because of the low velocity of the air through the venturi, however, the differential pressure on the air diaphragm is not sufficient to regulate the fuel flow. Instead, the idle spring in chamber D holds the poppet valve off its seat to admit fuel from the carburetor inlet during operation at idling speeds. The inset in figure 3–23 shows how the idle valve meters this fuel from chamber D to the discharge nozzle. This valve is connected to the throttle linkage in such a manner that it regulates the fuel flow only during the first few degrees of throttle opening. At higher speeds, it is withdrawn from the fuel passage and has no metering effect.

Accelerating System

The accelerating pump is entirely automatic in operation. In the illustration in figure 3–24, note that the vacuum passage connects the pump vacuum chamber with the air passage at the engine side of the throttle valve. The air pressure at the engine side of the throttle valve varies with the throttle position. When the throttle is nearly closed and is restricting the airflow to the engine, the pressure is low because of piston suction. In the left-hand drawing, the throttle is nearly closed, and, as a result, the low pressure in the vacuum chamber has caused the diaphragm to move to the right. This compresses the spring and stores fuel on the left side of the diaphragm. When the throttle is opened, the pressure on the engine side of the throttle valve increases. As a result, the low pressure in the vacuum chamber is lost, and the spring moves the diaphragm to the left, discharging the fuel stored during the lower throttle setting. This fuel, added to that from the main metering system, compensates for the sudden increase in airflow and gives smooth acceleration.

Mixture Control System

The mixture control system contains both automatic and manually operated units. The automatic mixture control varies the air pressure in chamber A to compensate for changes in air density. The manual mixture control provides for selecting the fuel/air ratio to fit engine operating conditions.

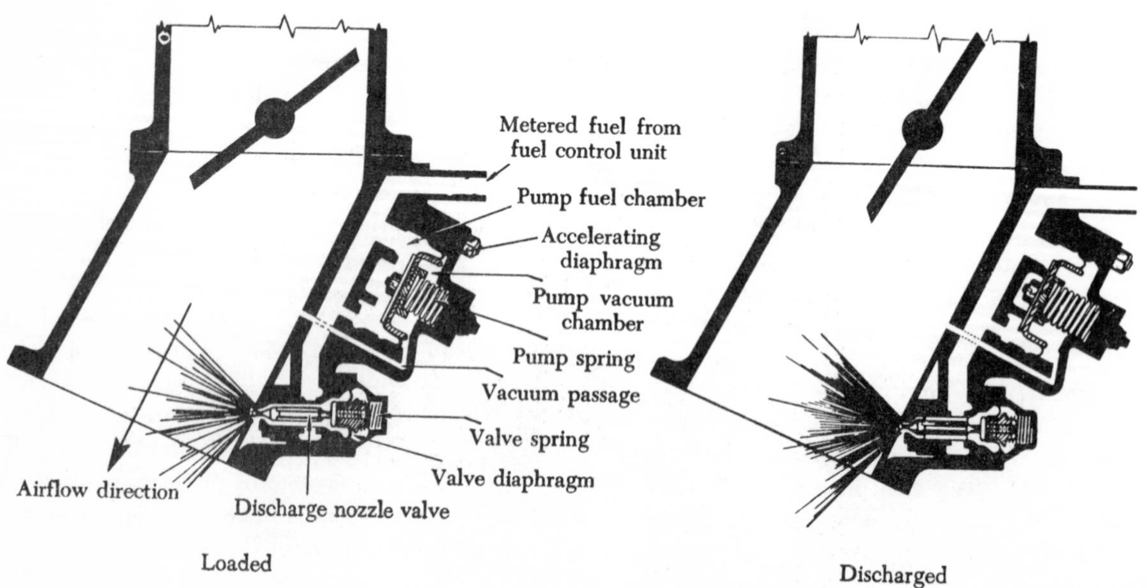

FIGURE 3–24. A single-diaphragm accelerating pump.

The automatic mixture control contains a sealed, metallic bellows, which responds to changes in pressure and temperature. As the density of the air changes, the expansion and contraction of the bellows moves the tapered needle in the atmospheric line. At sea level, the bellows is contracted and the needle is withdrawn from the atmospheric passage. Refer to the illustration showing the sea level condition in figure 3–25. As the aircraft climbs and the atmospheric pressure decreases, the bellows expands, inserting the tapered needle farther and farther into the atmospheric passage and restricting the flow of air to chamber A. At the same time, air leaks slowly from chamber A to chamber B through the small bleed. Thus, as the tapered needle restricts the flow of air into chamber A, the pressure on the left side of the air diaphragm decreases; as a result, the poppet valve moves toward its seat, reducing the fuel flow to compensate for the decrease in air density.

In the illustration of the manual mixture control, figure 3–23, note that fuel enters the control unit from chamber D, passes through it, and out to the discharge nozzle. The path of the fuel through the control unit is determined by the cloverleaf valve. The movable disk of this valve is rotated from the cockpit by means of a mixture control lever, which is linked to the lever on the carburetor.

The position that the movable disk takes when the cockpit control is set to auto-lean is shown in figure 3–26. Note that the large opening in the fixed disk is partially uncovered. This allows the fuel delivered to the control unit from chamber D to pass through the auto-lean metering jet, the auto-lean

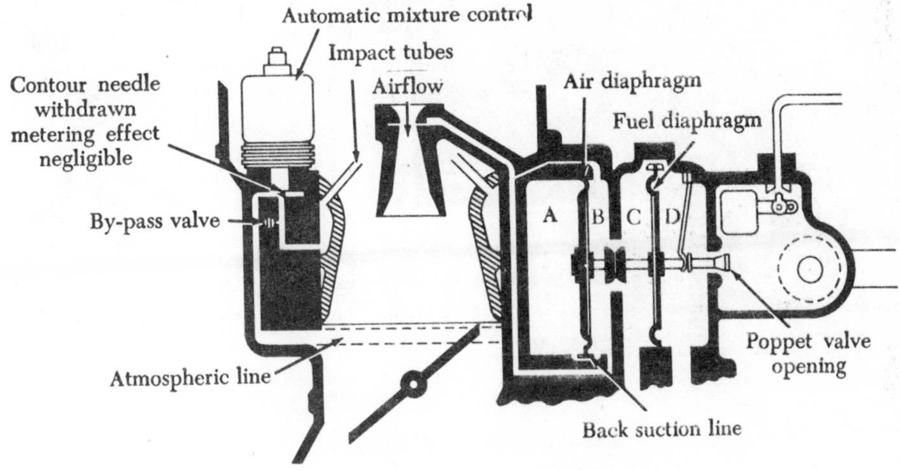

At sea level

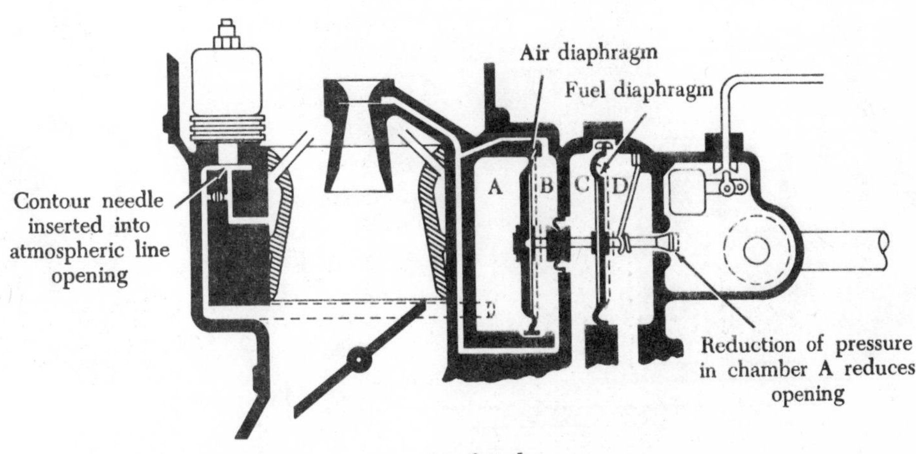

At altitude

FIGURE 3–25. Automatic mixture control system.

channel, and the opening in the fixed disk into the discharge line. The rate of flow depends on the size of the jet and the fuel pressure from chamber D. The cloverleaf valve has no metering effect since the opening in the fixed disk is larger than the metering jet.

In figure 3–27 note that, in the "auto-rich" setting, the movable disk uncovers two additional openings in the fixed disk. Fuel then flows into the discharge line through both the automatic lean and the automatic rich metering jets. Thus, for each pressure, the fuel flow increases and a richer mixture is supplied to the engine.

In all mixture settings, the position of the movable disk determines which jets will meter the fuel. The fuel discharge then depends on the size and number of jets through which fuel can pass and on the fuel pressure as determined by the pressure drop in the carburetor venturi. In the "auto-lean" and "auto-rich" settings of the manual mixture control, the automatic mixture control varies the fuel pressure with changes in air density. Thus, during "auto-lean" and "auto-rich" operation, the rate of fuel discharge depends on three factors: (1) The volume of airflow through the venturi, (2) the air density, and (3) the setting of the manual mixture control.

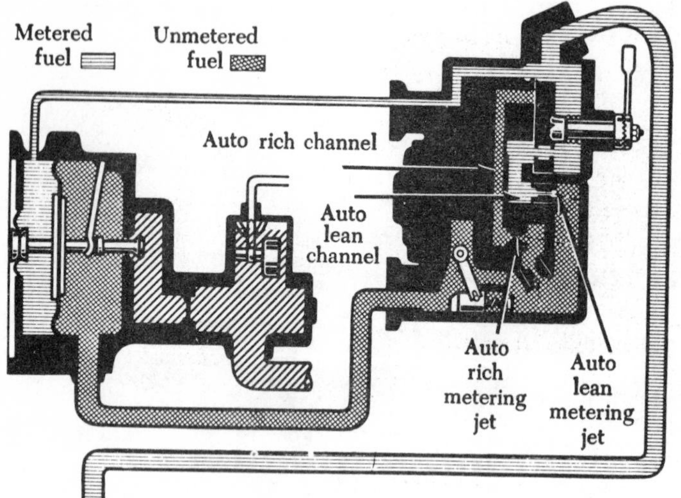

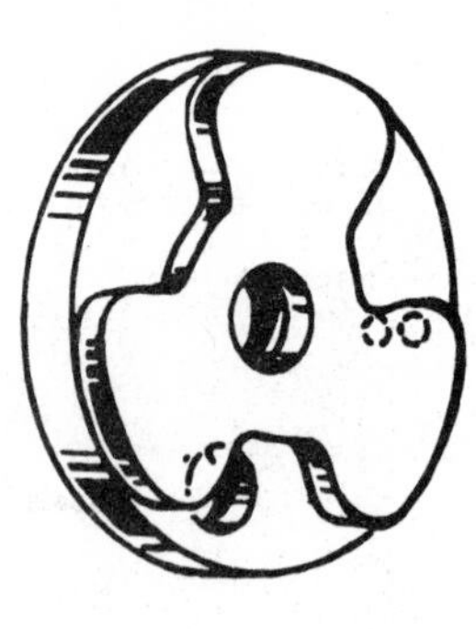

FIGURE 3–26. Manual mixture control, auto-lean setting.

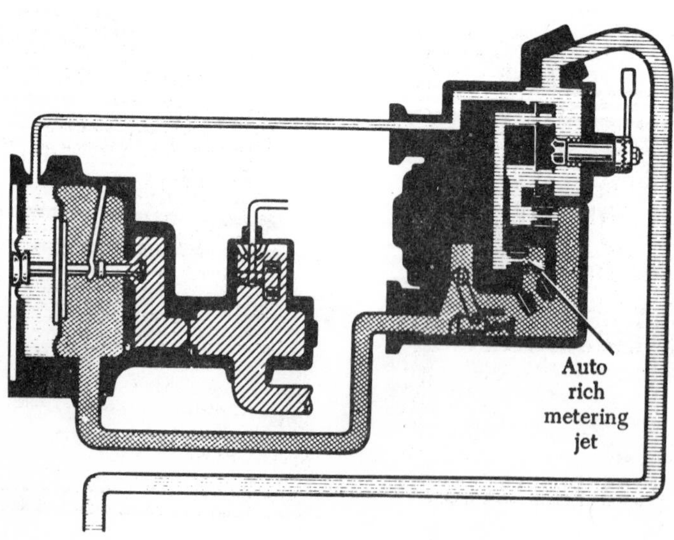

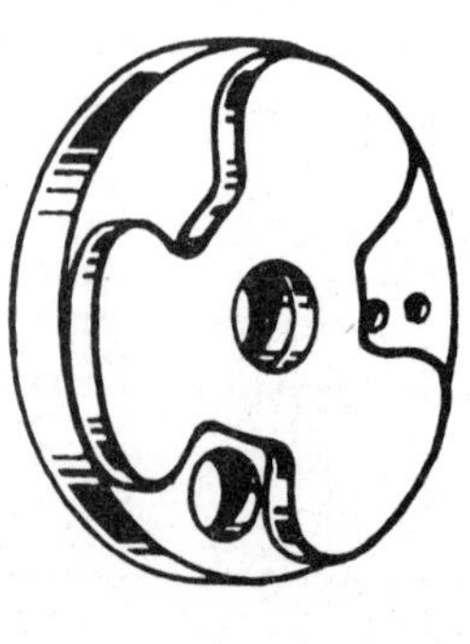

FIGURE 3–27. Manual mixture control, auto-rich setting.

Idle Cutoff System

To stop the engine, the manual mixture control lever in the cockpit is set to idle cutoff. This rotates the cloverleaf valve to the corresponding position. As shown in figure 3–28, the movable disk then covers all the openings and completely stops the fuel discharge.

Power Enrichment System

The power enrichment system is illustrated in figure 3–29. Note that the power enrichment valve is diaphragm operated. The chamber to the left of the diaphragm is connected to chamber D. A passage connects the chamber to the right of the diaphragm with the automatic lean channel. Thus, metered fuel pressure (the pressure at the discharge nozzle and in chamber C), acts on the right side of the diaphragm. At low engine speeds, the metered fuel pressure plus the force of the spring holds the valve on its seat. As the poppet valve opens farther at higher engine speeds, the pressure in chamber D increases. When this pressure, acting on the left side of the diaphragm, is high enough to overcome the combined forces of the spring and the metered fuel pressure, the power enrichment valve opens. Note how this increases the fuel flow to the discharge nozzle to provide a richer mixture for operation at high power output.

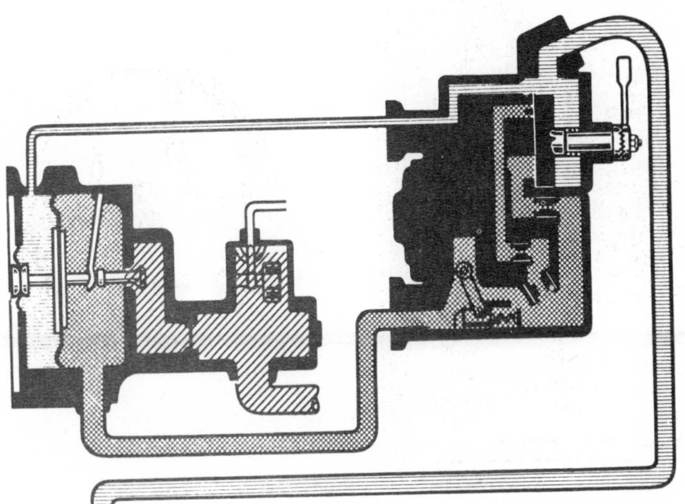

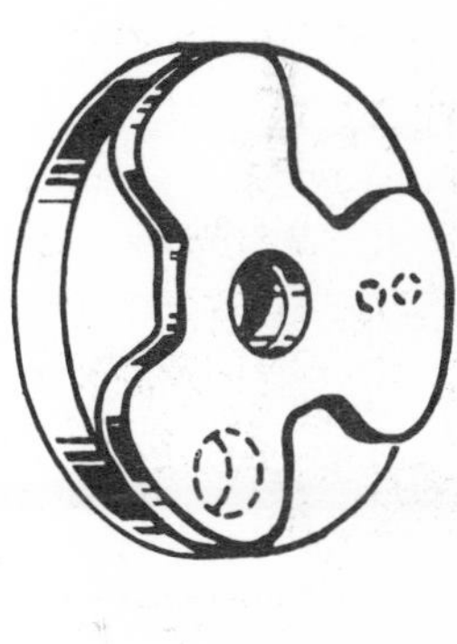

FIGURE 3–28. Manual mixture control in idle cutoff.

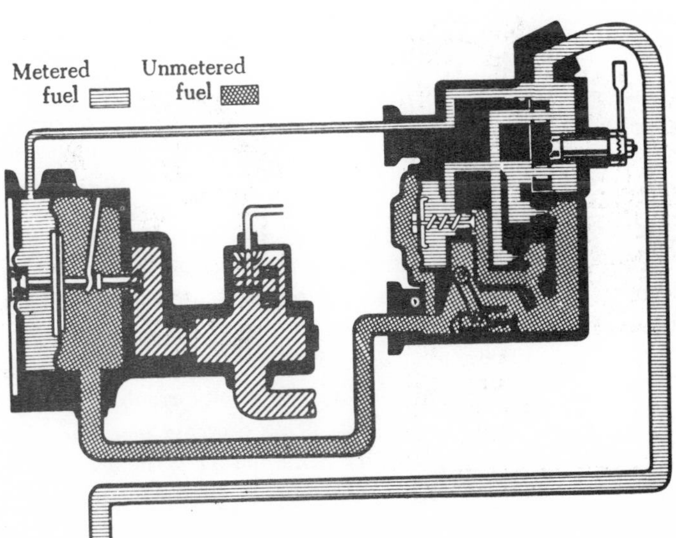

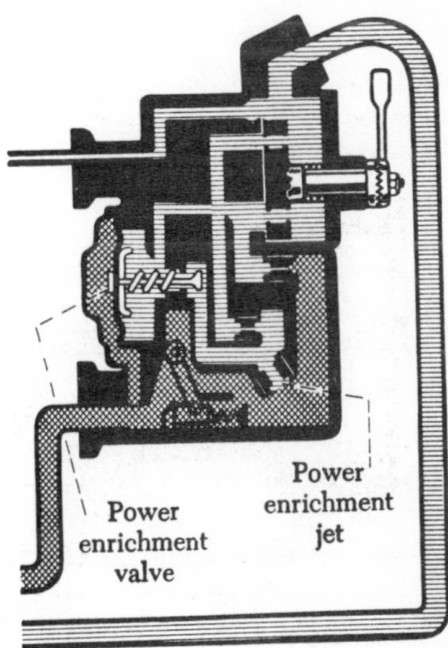

FIGURE 3–29. Power enrichment system.

STROMBERG PS SERIES CARBURETOR

The PS series carburetor is a low-pressure, single-barrel, injection-type carburetor. The carburetor consists basically of the air section, the fuel section, and the discharge nozzle, all mounted together to form a complete fuel metering system. This carburetor is similar to the pressure-injection carburetor; therefore, its operating principles are the same.

In this type carburetor (figure 3–30), metering is accomplished on a mass airflow basis. Air flowing through the main venturi creates a suction at the throat of the venturi which is transmitted to the B chamber in the main regulating part of the carburetor and to the vent side of the fuel discharge nozzle diaphragm. The incoming air pressure is transmitted to A chamber of the regulating part of the carburetor and to the main discharge bleed in the main fuel discharge jet. The discharge nozzle consists of a spring-loaded diaphragm connected to the discharge nozzle valve, which controls the flow of fuel injected into the main discharge jet. Here it is mixed with air to accomplish distribution and atomization into the airstream entering the engine.

In the PS series carburetor, as in the pressure-injection carburetor, the regulator spring has a fixed tension, which will tend to hold the poppet valve open during idling speeds, or until the D chamber pressure equals approximately 4 p.s.i. The discharge nozzle spring has a variable adjustment which, when tailored to maintain 4 p.s.i., will result in a balanced pressure condition of 4 p.s.i. in chamber C of the discharge nozzle assembly, and 4 p.s.i. in chamber D. This produces a zero drop across the main jets at zero fuel flow.

At a given airflow, if the suction created by the venturi is equivalent to one-fourth pound, this pressure decrease is transmitted to chamber B and to the vent side of the discharge nozzle. Since the area of the air diaphragm between chambers A and B is twice as great as that between chambers B and D, the one-fourth-pound decrease in pressure in chamber B will move the diaphragm assembly to the right to open the poppet valve. Meanwhile the decreased pressure on the vent side of the discharge nozzle assembly will cause a lowering of the total pressure from 4 lbs. to 3-3/4 lbs. The greater pressure of the metered fuel (4-1/4 lbs.) results in a differential across the metering head of one-fourth pound (for the one-fourth pound pressure differential created by the venturi).

The same ratio of pressure drop across the jet to venturi suction will apply throughout the range. Any increase or decrease in fuel inlet pressure will tend to upset the balance in the various chambers in the manner already described. When this occurs, the main fuel regulator diaphragm assembly repositions to restore the balance.

The mixture control, whether operated manually or automatically, compensates for enrichment at altitude by bleeding impact air pressure into B chamber, thereby increasing the pressure (decreasing the suction) in B chamber. Increasing the pressure in chamber B tends to move the diaphragm and poppet valve more toward the closed position, thus restricting fuel flow to correspond proportionately to the decrease in air density at altitude.

The idle valve and economizer jet can be combined in one assembly. The unit is controlled manually by the movement of the valve assembly. At low airflow positions, the tapered section of the valve becomes the predominant jet in the system, controlling the fuel flow for the idle range. As the valve moves to the cruise position, a straight section on the valve establishes a fixed orifice effect which controls the cruise mixture. When the valve is pulled full-open by the throttle valve, the jet is pulled completely out of the seat, and the seat size becomes the controlling jet. This jet is calibrated for takeoff power mixtures.

An airflow-controlled power enrichment valve can also be used with this carburetor. It consists of a spring-loaded, diaphragm-operated metering valve. Refer to figure 3–31 for a schematic view of an airflow power enrichment valve. One side of the diaphragm is exposed to unmetered fuel pressure, and the other side to venturi suction plus spring tension. When the pressure differential across the diaphragm establishes a force strong enough to compress the spring, the valve will open and supply an additional amount of fuel to the metered fuel circuit in addition to the fuel supplied by the main metering jet.

Accelerating Pump

The accelerating pump is a spring-loaded diaphragm assembly located in the metered fuel channel with the opposite side of the diaphragm vented to the engine side of the throttle valve. With this arrangement, opening the throttle results in a rapid decrease in suction. This decrease in suction permits the spring to extend and move the accelerating pump diaphragm. The diaphragm and spring action displace the fuel in the accelerating pump and force it out the discharge nozzle.

Vapor is eliminated from the top of the main fuel

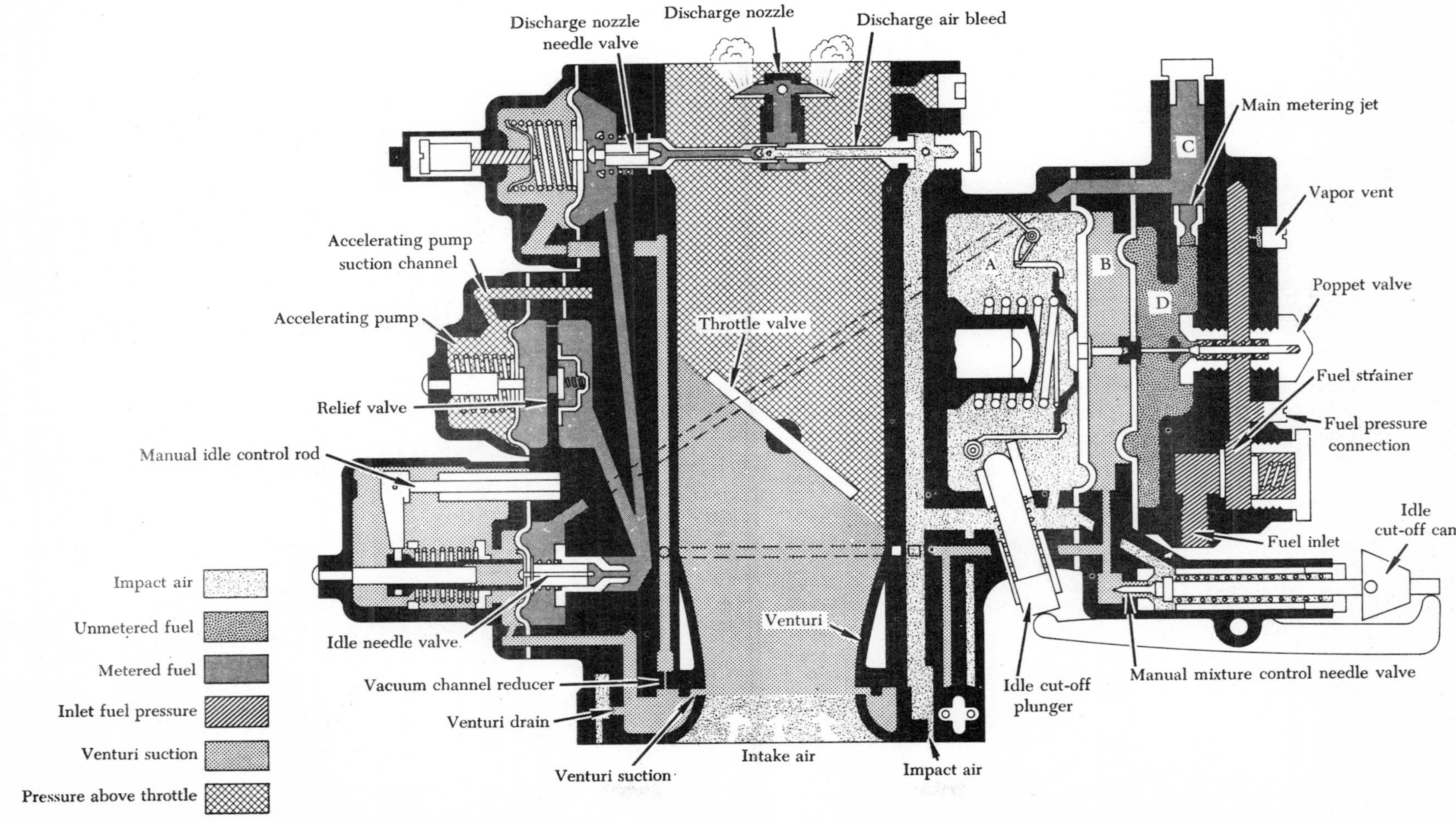
Discharge nozzle needle valve
Discharge nozzle
Discharge air bleed
Main metering jet
C
Vapor vent
A
B
D
Poppet valve
Accelerating pump suction channel
Accelerating pump
Throttle valve
Fuel strainer
Relief valve
Fuel pressure connection
Manual idle control rod
Idle cut-off cam
Fuel inlet
Impact air
Unmetered fuel
Metered fuel
Inlet fuel pressure
Venturi suction
Pressure above throttle
Idle needle valve
Venturi
Vacuum channel reducer
Venturi drain
Idle cut-off plunger
Manual mixture control needle valve
Intake air
Impact air
Venturi suction

FIGURE 3–30. Schematic diagram of the PS series carburetor.

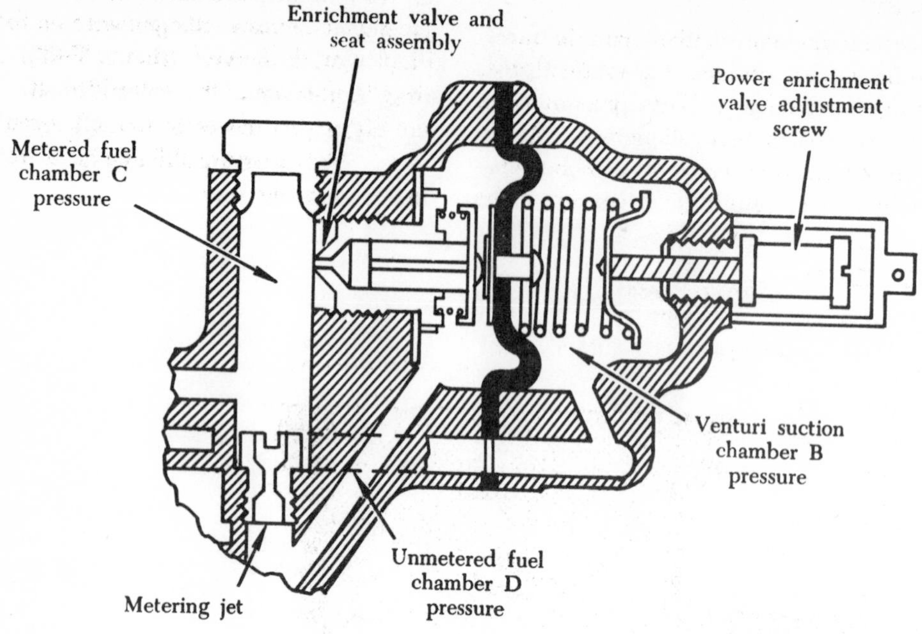

FIGURE 3–31. Airflow power enrichment valve.

chamber D through a bleed hole, then through a vent line back to the main fuel tank in the aircraft.

Manual Mixture Control

A manual mixture control provides a means of correcting for enrichment at altitude. It consists of a needle valve and seat that form an adjustable bleed between chamber A and chamber B. The valve can be adjusted to bleed off the venturi suction to maintain the correct fuel/air ratio as the aircraft gains altitude.

When the mixture control lever is moved to the "idle cutoff" position, a cam on the linkage actuates a rocker arm which moves the idle cutoff plunger inward against the release lever in chamber A. The lever compresses the regulator diaphragm spring to relieve all tension on the diaphragm between A and B chambers. This permits fuel pressure plus poppet valve spring force to close the poppet valve, stopping the fuel flow. Placing the mixture control lever in idle cutoff also positions the mixture control needle valve off its seat and allows metering suction within the carburetor to bleed off.

DIRECT FUEL-INJECTION SYSTEMS

The direct fuel-injection system has many advantages over a conventional carburetor system. There is less danger of induction system icing, since the drop in temperature due to fuel vaporization takes place in or near the cylinder. Acceleration is also improved because of the positive action of the injection system. In addition, direct fuel injection improves fuel distribution. This reduces the overheating of individual cylinders often caused by variation in mixture due to uneven distribution. The fuel-injection system also gives better fuel economy than a system in which the mixture to most cylinders must be richer than necessary so that the cylinder with the leanest mixture will operate properly.

Fuel-injection systems vary in their details of construction, arrangement, and operation. The Bendix and Continental fuel-injection systems will be discussed in this section. They are described to provide an understanding of the operating principles involved. For the specific details of any one system, consult the manufacturer's instructions for the equipment involved.

Bendix Fuel-Injection System

The Bendix RSA series fuel-injection system consists of an injector, flow divider, and fuel discharge nozzle. It is a continuous-flow system which measures engine air consumption and uses airflow forces to control fuel flow to the engine.

Fuel Injector

The fuel injector assembly consists of (1) an airflow section, (2) a regulator section, and (3) a fuel metering section. Some fuel injectors are equipped with an automatic mixture control unit.

Airflow Section

The airflow consumption of the engine is measured by sensing impact pressure and venturi throat pressure in the throttle body. These pressures are vented to the two sides of an air diaphragm. Movement of the throttle valve causes a change in engine air consumption. This results in a change in the air velocity in the venturi. When airflow through the engine increases, the pressure on the left of the diaphragm is lowered (figure 3–32) due to the drop in pressure at the venturi throat. As a result, the diaphragm moves to the left, opening the ball valve. This pressure differential is referred to as the air metering force.

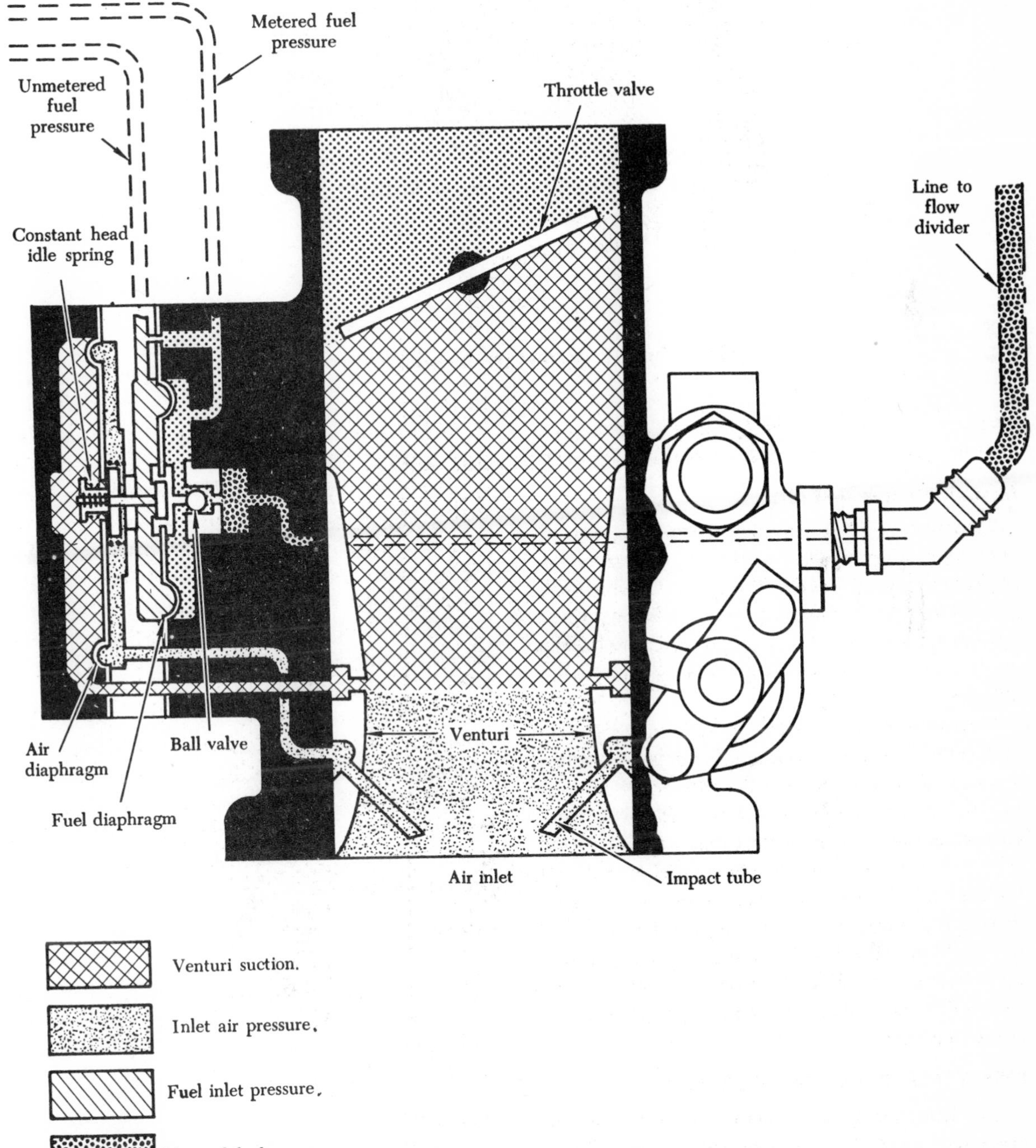

FIGURE 3–32. Airflow section of a fuel injector.

Regulator Section

The regulator section consists of a fuel diaphragm which opposes the air metering force. Fuel inlet pressure is applied to one side of the fuel diaphragm and metered fuel pressure is applied to the other side. The differential pressure across the fuel diaphragm is called the fuel metering force.

The distance the ball valve opens is determined by the difference between the pressures acting on the diaphragms. This difference in pressure is proportional to the airflow through the injector. Thus, the volume of airflow determines the rate of fuel flow.

Under low power settings the difference in pressure created by the venturi is insufficient to accomplish consistent regulation of the fuel. A constant-head idle spring is incorporated to provide a constant fuel differential pressure. This allows an adequate final flow in the idle range.

Fuel Metering Section

The fuel metering section, shown in figure 3–33, is attached to the air metering section and contains an inlet fuel strainer, a manual mixture control valve, an idle valve, and the main metering jet. In some models of injectors, a power enrichment jet is also located in this section. The purpose of the fuel metering section is to meter and control the fuel flow to the flow divider.

Flow Divider

The metered fuel is delivered from the fuel control unit to a pressurized flow divider. This unit keeps metered fuel under pressure, divides fuel to the various cylinders at all engine speeds, and shuts off the individual nozzle lines when the control is placed in idle cutoff.

Referring to the schematic diagram in figure 3–34, metered fuel pressure enters the flow divider

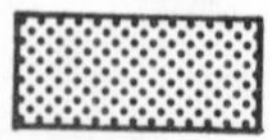

Fuel inlet pressure.

Metered fuel pressure.

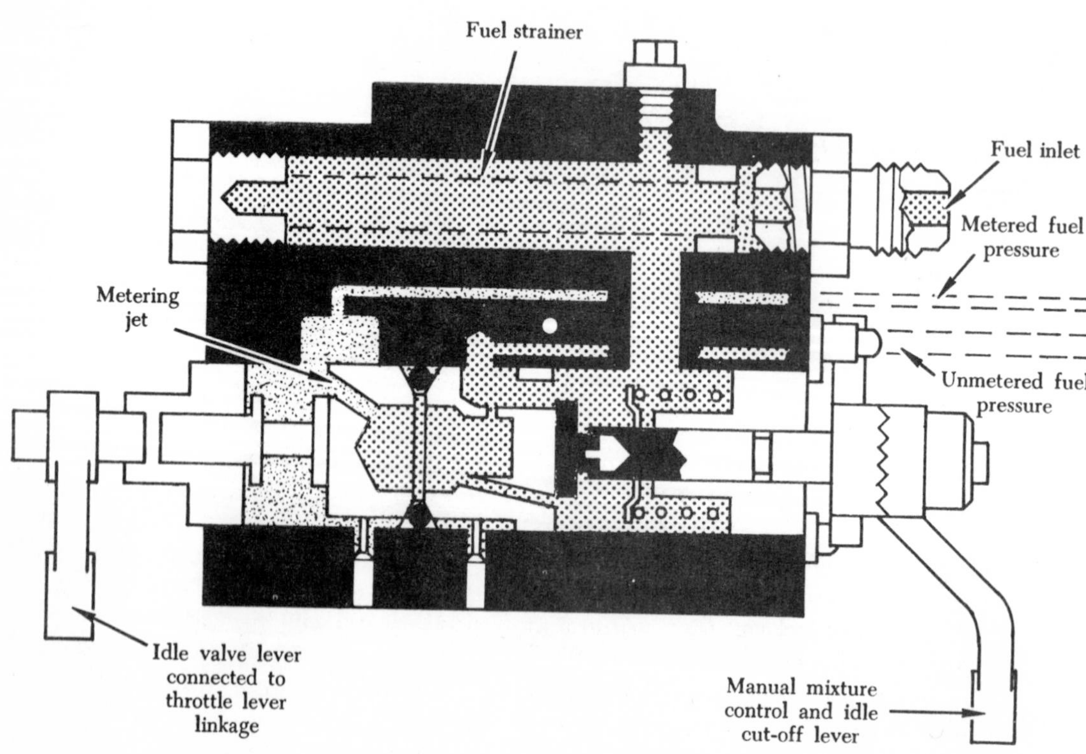

FIGURE 3–33. Fuel metering section of the injector.

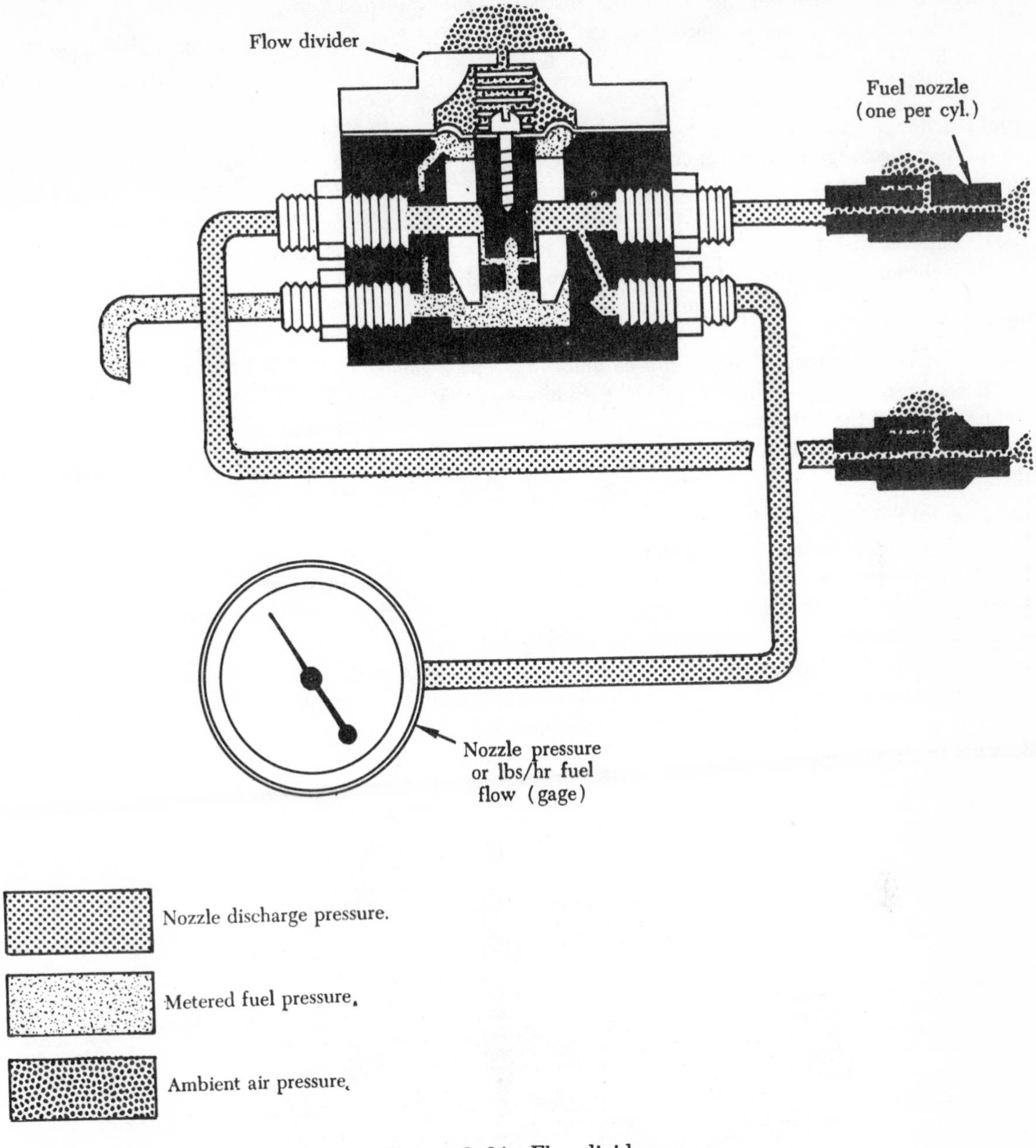

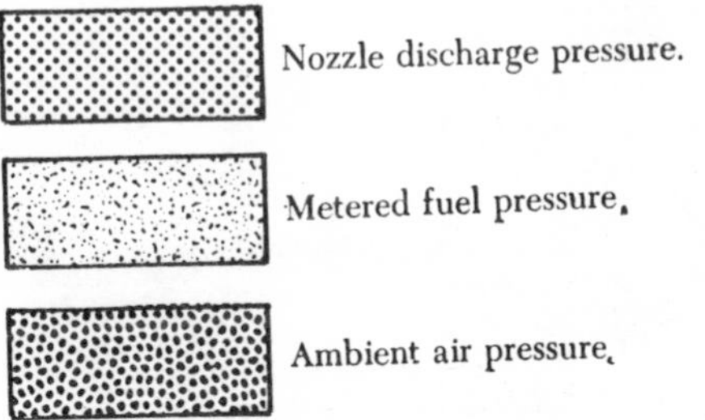

FIGURE 3–34. Flow divider.

through a channel that permits fuel to pass through the inside diameter of the flow divider needle. At idle speed, the fuel pressure from the regulator must build up to overcome the spring force applied to the diaphragm and valve assembly. This moves the valve upward until fuel can pass out through the annulus of the valve to the fuel nozzle. Since the regulator meters and delivers a fixed amount of fuel to the flow divider, the valve will open only as far as necessary to pass this amount to the nozzles. At idle the opening required is very small; thus the fuel for the individual cylinders is divided at idle by the flow divider.

As fuel flow through the regulator is increased above idle requirements, fuel pressure builds up in the nozzle lines. This pressure fully opens the flow divider valve, and fuel distribution to the engine becomes a function of the discharge nozzles.

A fuel pressure gage, calibrated in pounds-per-hour fuel flow can be used as a fuel flow meter with the Bendix RSA injection system. This gage is connected to the flow divider and senses the pressure being applied to the discharge nozzle. This pressure is in direct proportion to fuel flow and indicates the engine power output and fuel consumption.

Fuel Discharge Nozzles

The fuel discharge nozzles (figure 3–34) are of the air bleed configuration. There is one nozzle for each cylinder located in the cylinder head. The nozzle outlet is directed into the intake port. Each nozzle incorporates a calibrated jet. The jet size is determined by the available fuel inlet pressure and the maximum fuel flow required by the engine. The fuel is discharged through this jet into an ambient air pressure chamber within the nozzle assembly. Before entering the individual intake valve chambers, the fuel is mixed with air to aid in atomizing the fuel.

Continental Fuel-Injection System

The Continental fuel-injection system injects fuel into the intake valve port in each cylinder head. The system consists of a fuel injector pump, a control unit, a fuel manifold, and a fuel discharge nozzle. It is a continuous-flow type which controls fuel flow to match engine airflow. The continuous-flow system permits the use of a rotary vane pump which does not require timing to the engine.

Fuel-Injection Pump

The fuel pump is a positive-displacement, rotary-vane type, with a splined shaft for connection to the accessory drive system of the engine. A spring-loaded, diaphragm-type relief valve is provided. The relief valve diaphragm chamber is vented to atmospheric pressure. A sectional view of a fuel-injection pump is shown in figure 3–35.

Fuel enters at the swirl well of the vapor separator. Here, vapor is separated by a swirling motion so that only liquid fuel is delivered to the pump. The vapor is drawn from the top center of the swirl well by a small pressure-jet of fuel and is directed into the vapor return line. This line carries the vapor back to the fuel tank.

Ignoring the effect of altitude or ambient air conditions, the use of a positive-displacement, engine-driven pump means that changes in engine speed affect total pump flow proportionally. Since the pump provides greater capacity than is required by the engine, a recirculation path is required. By arranging a calibrated orifice and relief valve in this path, the pump delivery pressure is also maintained in proportion to engine speed. These provisions assure proper pump pressure and fuel delivery for all engine operating speeds.

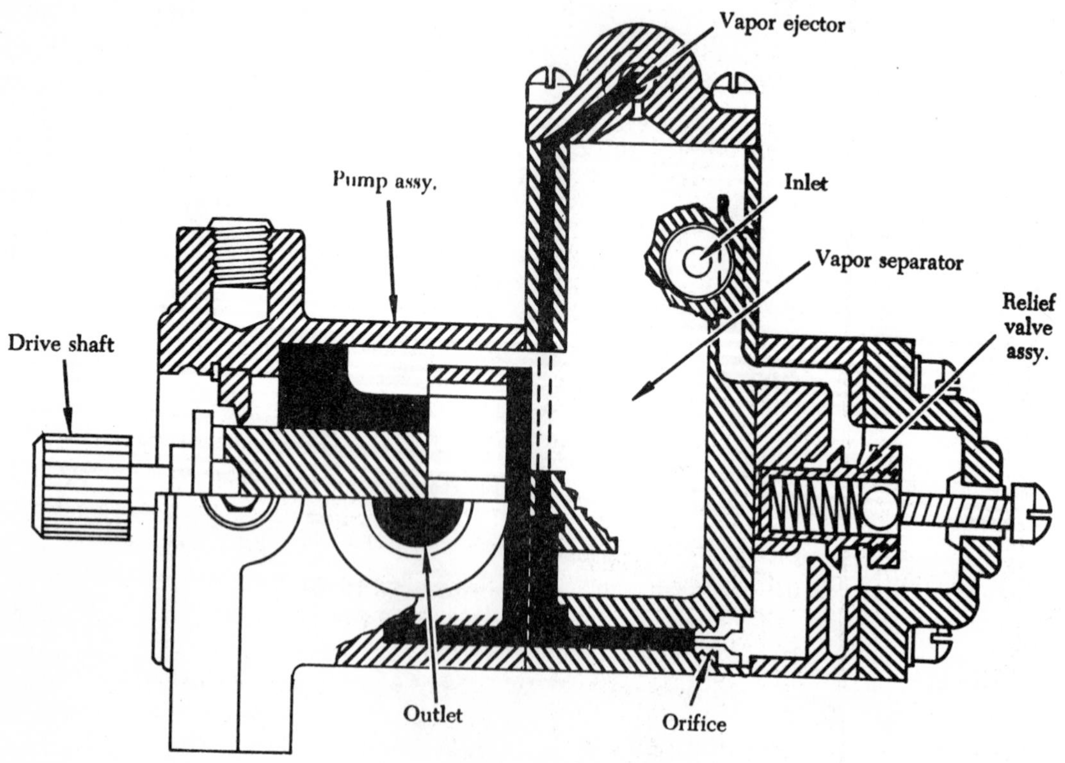

FIGURE 3–35. Fuel-injection pump.

A check valve is provided so that boost pump pressure to the system can bypass the engine-driven pump for starting. This feature also suppresses vapor formation under high ambient temperatures of the fuel. Further, this permits use of the auxiliary pump as a source of fuel pressure in the event of engine-driven pump failure.

Fuel/Air Control Unit

The function of the fuel/air control assembly is to control engine air intake and to set the metered fuel pressure for proper fuel/air ratio. The air throttle is mounted at the manifold inlet, and its butterfly valve, positioned by the throttle control in the aircraft, controls the flow of air to the engine (see figure 3–36).

The air throttle assembly is an aluminum casting which contains the shaft and butterfly-valve assembly. The casting bore size is tailored to the engine size, and no venturi or other restriction is used.

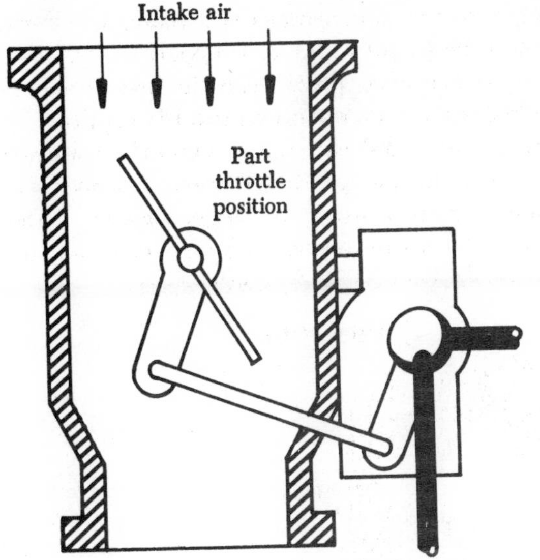

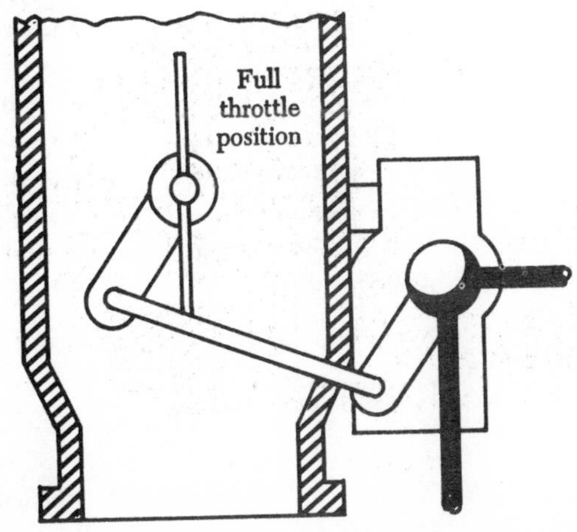

FIGURE 3–36. Fuel/air control unit.

Fuel Control Assembly

The fuel control body is made of bronze for best bearing action with the stainless steel valves. Its central bore contains a metering valve at one end and a mixture control valve at the other end. Each stainless steel rotary valve includes a groove which forms a fuel chamber.

Fuel enters the control unit through a strainer and passes to the metering valve (figure 3–37). This rotary valve has a cam-shaped edge on the outer part of the end face. The position of the cam at the fuel delivery port controls the fuel passed to the manifold valve and the nozzles. The fuel return port connects to the return passage of the center metering plug. The alignment of the mixture control valve with this passage determines the amount of fuel returned to the fuel pump.

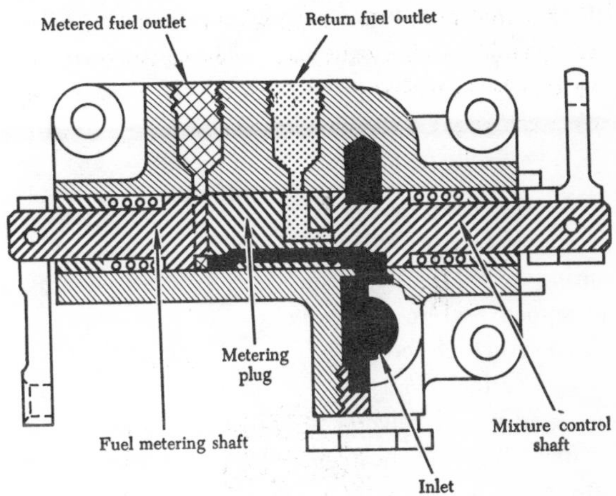

FIGURE 3–37. Fuel control assembly.

By connecting the metering valve to the air throttle, the fuel flow is properly proportioned to airflow for the correct fuel/air ratio. A control level is mounted on the mixture control valve shaft and connected to the cockpit mixture control.

Fuel Manifold Valve

The fuel manifold valve (figure 3–38) contains a fuel inlet, a diaphragm chamber, and outlet ports for the lines to the individual nozzles. The spring-loaded diaphragm operates a valve in the central bore of the body. Fuel pressure provides the force for moving the diaphragm. The diaphragm is enclosed by a cover that retains the diaphragm

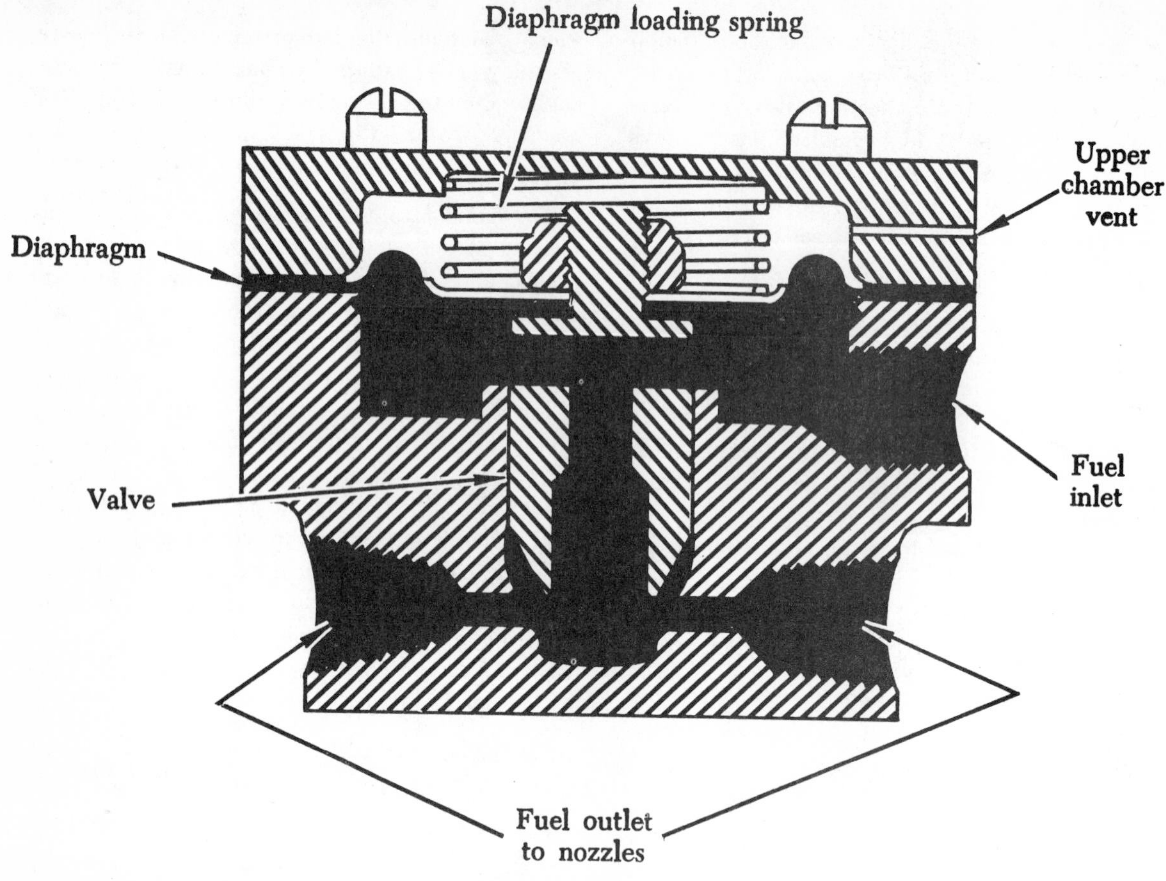

FIGURE 3–38. Fuel manifold valve assembly.

loading spring. When the valve is down against the lapped seat in the body, the fuel lines to the cylinders are closed off. The valve is drilled for passage of fuel from the diaphragm chamber to its base, and a ball valve is installed within the valve. All incoming fuel must pass through a fine screen installed in the diaphragm chamber.

From the fuel-injection control valve, fuel is delivered to the fuel manifold valve, which provides a central point for dividing fuel flow to the individual cylinders. In the fuel manifold valve a diaphragm raises or lowers a plunger valve to open or close the individual cylinder fuel supply ports simultaneously.

Fuel Discharge Nozzle

The fuel discharge nozzle is located in the cylinder head with its outlet directed into the intake port. The nozzle body, illustrated in figure 3–39, contains a drilled central passage with a counterbore at each end. The lower end is used as a chamber for fuel/air mixing before the spray leaves the nozzle. The upper bore contains a removable orifice for calibrating the nozzles. Nozzles are calibrated in several ranges, and all nozzles furnished for one engine are of the same range and are identified by a letter stamped on the hex of the nozzle body.

Drilled radial holes connect the upper counterbore with the outside of the nozzle body. These holes enter the counterbore above the orifice and draw air through a cylindrical screen fitted over the nozzle body. A shield is press-fitted on the nozzle body and extends over the greater part of the filter screen, leaving an opening near the bottom. This provides both mechanical protection and an abrupt change in the direction of airflow which keeps dirt and foreign material out of the nozzle interior.

CARBURETOR MAINTENANCE

The removal procedures will vary with both the type of carburetor concerned and the type of engine on which it is used. Always refer to the applicable manufacturer's technical instructions for a particular installation. Generally the procedures will be much the same, regardless of the type of carburetor con-

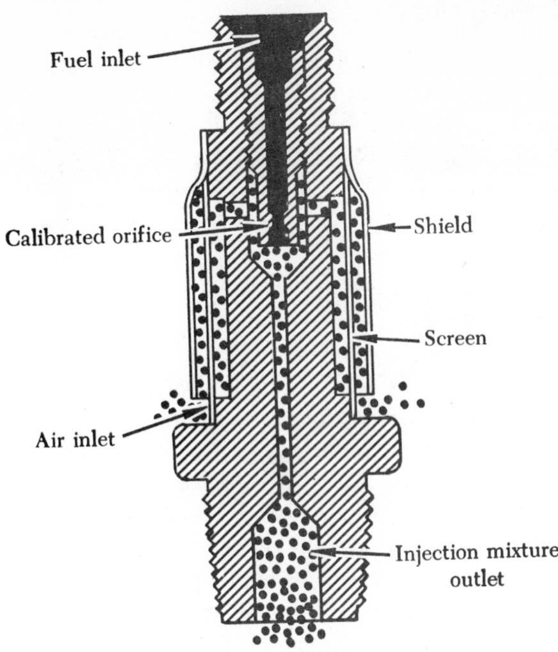

FIGURE 3–39. Fuel discharge nozzle.

cerned. Some general precautions are discussed below.

Before removing a carburetor, make sure the fuel shutoff (or selector) valve is closed. Disconnect the throttle and mixture control linkages, and lockwire the throttle valve in the closed position. Disconnect the fuel inlet line and all vapor return, gage, and primer lines. Figure 3–40 illustrates the installation connection points on a typical carburetor.

If the same carburetor is to be re-installed, do not alter the rigging of the throttle and mixture controls. Remove the airscoop or airscoop adapter. Remove the air screens and gaskets from the carburetor. Remove the nuts and washers securing the carburetor to the engine. When removing a

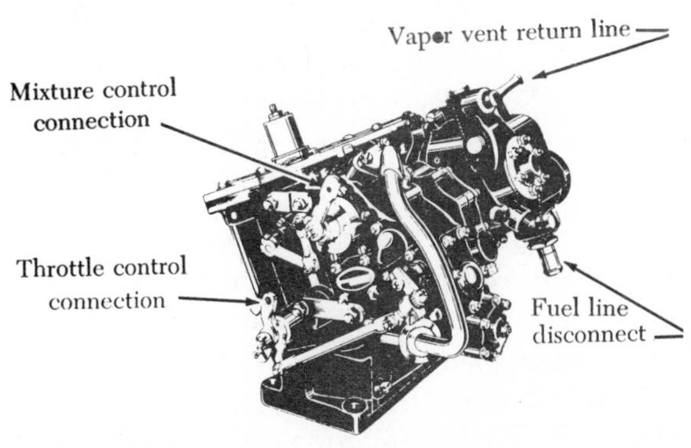

FIGURE 3–40. Carburetor installation connecting points.

downdraft carburetor, use extreme care to ensure that nothing is dropped into the engine. Remove the carburetor. Immediately install a protective cover on the carburetor mounting flange of the engine to prevent small parts or foreign material from falling into the engine. When there is danger of foreign material entering open fuel lines during removal or installation of the carburetor, plug or cover them with tape.

Installation of Carburetor

Check the carburetor for proper lockwiring before installation on an engine. Be sure that all shipping plugs have been removed from the carburetor openings.

Remove the protective cover from the carburetor mounting flange on the engine. Place the carburetor mounting flange gasket in position. On some engines, bleed passages are incorporated in the mounting pad. The gasket must be installed so that the bleed hole in the gasket is aligned with the passage in the mounting flange.

Inspect the induction passages for the presence of any foreign material before installing the carburetor.

As soon as the carburetor is placed in position on the engine, close and lockwire the throttle valves in the "closed" position until the remainder of the installation is completed.

Where it is feasible, place the carburetor deck screen in position to further eliminate the possibility of foreign objects entering the induction system.

When installing a carburetor that uses diaphragms for controlling fuel flow, connect the fuel lines and fill the carburetor with fuel. To do this, turn on the fuel booster pump and move the mixture control from the "idle cutoff" position. Continue the flow until oil-free fuel flows from the supercharger drain valve. This indicates that the preservative oil has been flushed from the carburetor.

Turn off the fuel flow, plug the fuel inlet and vapor vent outlet, and then allow the carburetor, filled with fuel, to stand for a minimum of 8 hours. This is necessary in order to soak the diaphragms and render them pliable to the degree they were when the unit was originally calibrated.

Tighten the carburetor mounting bolts to the value specified in the table of torque limits in the applicable maintenance manual. Tighten and safety any other nuts and bolts incidental to the installation of the carburetor before connecting the throttle and mixture-control levers. After the carburetor has been bolted to the engine, check the throttle and mixture-control lever on the unit for freedom of movement before connecting the control cables or linkage. Check the vapor vent lines from the carburetor to the aircraft fuel tank for restriction by blowing through the line.

Rigging Carburetor Controls

Connect and adjust carburetor or fuel metering equipment throttle controls so that full movement of the throttle is obtained with corresponding full movement of the control in the cockpit. In addition, check and adjust the throttle-control linkages so that springback on the throttle quadrant in the aircraft is equal in both the "full open" and "full closed" positions. Correct any excess play or looseness of control linkage or cables.

When installing carburetors or fuel metering equipment incorporating manual-type mixture controls that do not have marked positions, adjust the mixture control mechanism to provide an equal amount of springback at both the rich and lean end of the control quadrant in the cockpit when the mixture control on the carburetor or fuel metering equipment is moved through the full range. Where mixture controls with detents are used, rig the control mechanism so that the designated positions on the control quadrant in the aircraft will agree with the corresponding positions on the carburetor or fuel metering equipment.

In all cases check the controls for proper positioning in both the "advance" and "retard" positions. Correct excess play or looseness of control linkage or cables. Safety all controls properly to eliminate the possibility of loosening from vibration during operation.

Adjusting Idle Mixtures

Excessively rich or lean idle mixtures result in incomplete combustion within the engine cylinder, with resultant formation of carbon deposits on the spark plugs and subsequent spark plug fouling. In addition, excessively rich or lean idle mixtures make it necessary to taxi at high idle speeds with resultant fast taxi speeds and excessive brake wear. Each engine must have the carburetor idle mixture tailored for the particular engine and installation, if best operation is to be obtained.

Engines which are properly adjusted, insofar as valve operation, cylinder compression, ignition, and carburetor idle mixture are concerned, will idle at the prescribed r.p.m. for indefinite periods without loading up, overheating, or spark plug fouling. If an engine will not respond to idle mixture adjustment with the resultant stable idling characteristics previously outlined, it is an indication that some other phase of engine operation is not correct. In such cases, determine and correct the cause of the difficulty. On all aircraft installations where manifold pressure gages are used, the manifold pressure gage will give a more consistent and larger indication of power change at idle speed than will the tachometer. Therefore, utilize the manifold pressure gage when adjusting the idle fuel/air mixture. Check and adjust the idle mixture and speed on all type reciprocating engines as discussed in the following paragraphs.

Always make idle mixture adjustments with cylinder head temperatures at normal values (about 150° to 170° C.) and never with temperatures approaching the maximum allowable.

The idle mixture adjustment is made on the idle fuel control valve. It should not be confused with the adjustment of the idle speed stop. The importance of idle mixture adjustment cannot be overstressed. Optimum engine operation at low speeds can be obtained only when proper fuel/air mixtures are delivered to every cylinder of the engine. Excessively rich idle mixtures and the resultant incomplete combustion are responsible for more spark plug fouling than any other single cause. Excessively lean idle mixtures result in faulty acceleration. Furthermore, the idle mixture adjustment affects the fuel/air mixture and engine operation well up into the cruise range.

On an engine having a conventional carburetor, the idle mixture is checked by manually leaning the mixture with the cockpit mixture control. Move the carburetor mixture control slowly and smoothly toward the "idle cutoff" position. At the same time, watch the manifold pressure gage to determine whether the manifold pressure decreases prior to increasing as the engine ceases firing. The optimum mixture is obtained when a manifold pressure decrease immediately precedes the manifold pressure increase as the engine ceases firing. The amount of decrease will vary with the make and model engine and the installation. As a general rule, the amount of manifold pressure decrease will be approximately one-fourth inch.

On installations that do not use a manifold pressure gage, it will be necessary to observe the tachometer for an indication of an r.p.m. change. With most installations, the idle mixture should be adjusted to provide an r.p.m. rise prior to decreasing as the engine ceases to fire. This r.p.m. increase will vary from 10 to 50 r.p.m., depending on the installation.

Following the momentary increase in r.p.m., the engine speed will start to drop. Immediately move the mixture control back to auto-rich to prevent the engine from cutting out completely.

On direct fuel-injection engines, the mixture change during manual leaning with the mixture control is usually so rapid that it is impossible to note any momentary increase in r.p.m. or decrease in manifold pressure. Therefore, on these engines, the idle mixture is set slightly leaner than best power and is checked by enriching the mixture with the primer. To check the idle mixture on a fuel-injection installation, first set the throttle to obtain the proper idle speed. Then momentarily depress the primer switch while observing the tachometer and manifold pressure gage. If the idle mixture is correct, the fuel added by the primer will cause a momentary increase in engine speed and a momentary drop in manifold pressure. If the increase in engine speed or the decrease in manifold pressure exceeds the limits specified for the particular installation, the idle mixture is too lean (too far on the lean side of best power). If the r.p.m. drops off when the mixture is enriched with the primer, the idle mixture setting is too rich.

Before checking the idle mixture on any engine, warm up the engine until oil and cylinder head temperatures are normal. Keep the propeller control in the increase r.p.m. setting throughout the entire process of warming up the engine, checking the idle mixture, and making the idle adjustment. Keep the mixture control in auto-rich except for the manual leaning required in checking the idle mixture on carburetor-equipped engines. When using the primer to check the idle mixture on fuel-injection engines, merely flick the primer switch; otherwise, too much additional fuel will be introduced and a satisfactory indication will be obtained even though the idle mixture is set too lean.

If the check of the idle mixture reveals it to be too lean or too rich, increase or decrease the idle fuel flow as required. Then repeat the check. Continue checking and adjusting the idle mixture until it checks out properly. During this process, it may be desirable to move the idle speed stop completely out of the way and to hold the engine speed at the desired r.p.m. by means of the throttle. This will eliminate the need for frequent readjustments of the idle stop as the idle mixture is improved and the idle speed picks up. After each adjustment, "clear" the engine by briefly running it at higher r.p.m. This prevents fouling of the plugs which might otherwise be caused by incorrect idle mixture.

After adjusting the idle mixture, recheck it several times to determine definitely that the mixture is correct and remains constant on repeated changes from high power back to idle. Correct any inconsistency in engine idling before releasing the aircraft for service.

On Stromberg injection-type carburetors and direct fuel-injection master control units, the idle control link located between the idle valve stem in the fuel control unit and the idle control lever on the throttle shaft incorporates a bushing arrangement at each end (see figure 3–41). Be sure that the bolt is tight and has the washers, wave washers, and bushings assembled. In addition, there must be no play between the link and the lever. If there is any play at either end of the link, erratic mixtures will result.

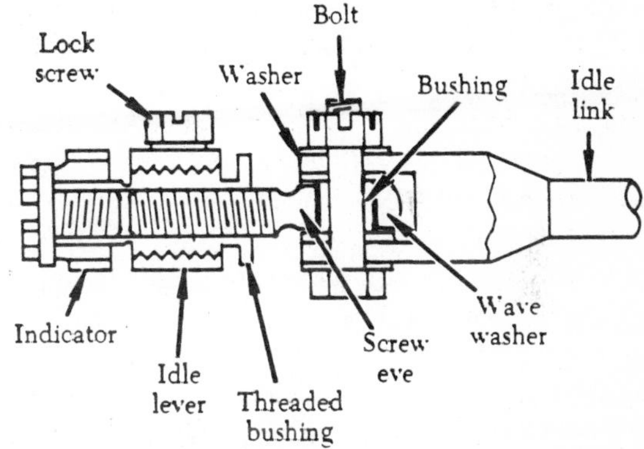

FIGURE 3–41. Idle mixture adjusting mechanism for Stromberg injection carburetors.

If sufficient mixture change cannot be accomplished by the normal idle mixture adjustment on the Stromberg injection carburetor, disconnect the link at the idle valve end by removing the bolt, washers, and wave washers. Then, to further alter the mixture, turn out or in (out to enrich, in to lean). One turn of the screw eye is equivalent to 13 notches or clicks on the normal idle adjustment.

Idle Speed Adjustment

After adjusting the idle mixture, reset the idle stop to the idle r.p.m. specified in the aircraft maintenance manual. The engine must be warmed up thoroughly and checked for ignition system malfunctioning. Throughout any carburetor adjustment procedure, run the engine up periodically to approximately half of normal rated speed to clear the engine.

Some carburetors are equipped with an eccentric screw to adjust idle r.p.m. Others use a spring-loaded screw to limit the throttle valve closing. In either case, adjust the screw as required to increase or decrease r.p.m. with the throttle retarded against the stop. Open the throttle to clear the engine; close the throttle and allow the r.p.m. to stabilize. Repeat this operation until the desired idling speed is obtained.

FUEL SYSTEM INSPECTION AND MAINTENANCE

The inspection of a fuel system installation consists basically of an examination of the system for conformity to design requirements together with functional tests to prove correct operation.

Since there are considerable variations in the fuel systems used on different aircraft, no attempt has been made to describe any particular system in detail. It is important that the manufacturer's instructions for the aircraft concerned be followed when performing inspection or maintenance functions.

Complete System

Inspect the entire system for wear, damage, or leaks. Make sure that all units are securely attached and properly safetied.

The drain plugs or valves in the fuel system should be opened to check for the presence of sediment or water. The filter and sump should also be checked for sediment, water, or slime. The filters or screens, including those provided for flowmeters and auxiliary pumps, must be clean and free from corrosion.

The controls should be checked for freedom of movement, security of locking, and freedom from damage due to chafing.

The fuel vents should be checked for correct positioning and freedom from obstruction; otherwise, fuel flow or pressure fueling may be affected. Filler neck drains should be checked for freedom from obstruction.

If booster pumps are installed, the system should be checked for leaks by operating the pumps. During this check, the ammeter or loadmeter should be read and the readings of all the pumps, where applicable, should be approximately the same.

Fuel Tanks

All applicable panels in the aircraft skin or structure should be removed and the tanks inspected for corrosion on the external surfaces, for security of attachment, and for correct adjustment of straps and slings. Check the fittings and connections for leaks or failures.

Some fuel tanks manufactured of light alloy materials are provided with inhibitor cartridges to reduce the corrosive effects of combined leaded fuel and water. Where applicable, the cartridge should be inspected and renewed at the specified periods.

Lines and Fittings

Be sure that the lines are properly supported and that the nuts and clamps are securely tightened. To tighten hose clamps to the proper torque, use a hose-clamp torque wrench. If this wrench is not available, tighten the clamp finger-tight plus the number of turns specified for the hose and clamp. (Refer to Airframe and Powerplant Mechanics General Handbook, AC 65–9, Chapter 5.) If the clamps do not seal at the specified torque, replace the clamps, the hose, or both. After installing new hose, check the clamps daily and tighten if necessary. When this daily check indicates that cold flow has ceased, inspect the clamps at less frequent intervals.

Replace the hose if the plys have separated, if there is excessive cold flow, or if the hose is hard and inflexible. Permanent impressions from the clamp and cracks in the tube or cover stock indicate excessive cold flow. Replace hose which has collapsed at the bends or as a result of misaligned fittings or lines. Some hose tends to flare at the ends beyond the clamps. This is not an unsatisfactory condition unless leakage is present.

Blisters may form on the outer synthetic rubber cover of hose. These blisters do not necessarily affect the serviceability of the hose. When a blister is discovered on a hose, remove the hose from the aircraft and puncture the blister with a pin. The blister should then collapse. If fluid (oil, fuel, or hydraulic) emerges from the pinhole in the blister, reject the hose. If only air emerges, pressure test the hose at 1-1/2 times the working pressure. If no fluid leakage occurs, the hose can be regarded as serviceable.

Puncturing the outer cover of the hose may permit the entry of corrosive elements, such as water, which could attack the wire braiding and ultimately result in failure. For this reason, puncturing the outer covering of hoses exposed to the elements should be avoided.

The external surface of hose may develop fine cracks, usually short in length, which are caused by surface aging. The hose assembly may be regarded as serviceable, provided these cracks do not penetrate to the first braid.

Selector Valves

Rotate selector valves and check for free operation, excessive backlash, and accurate pointer indication. If the backlash is excessive, check the entire operating mechanism for worn joints, loose pins, and broken drive lugs. Replace any defective parts. Inspect cable control systems for worn or frayed cables, damaged pulleys, or worn pulley bearings.

Pumps

During an inspection of booster pumps, check for the following conditions: (1) Proper operation, (2) leaks and condition of fuel and electrical connections, and (3) wear of motor brushes. Be sure the drain lines are free of traps, bends, or restrictions.

Check the engine-driven pump for leaks and security of mounting. Check the vent and drain lines for obstructions.

Main Line Strainers

Drain water and sediment from the main line strainer at each preflight inspection. Remove and clean the screen at the periods specified in the airplane maintenance manual. Examine the sediment removed from the housing. Particles of rubber are often early warnings of hose deterioration. Check for leaks and damaged gaskets.

Fuel Quantity Gages

If a sight gage is used, be sure that the glass is clear and that there are no leaks at the connections. Check the lines leading to it for leaks and security of attachment.

Check the mechanical gages for free movement of the float arm and for proper synchronization of the pointer with the position of the float.

On the electrical and electronic gages, be sure that both the indicator and the tank units are securely mounted and that their electrical connections are tight.

Fuel Pressure Gage

Check the pointer for zero tolerance and excessive oscillation. Check the cover glass for looseness and for proper range markings. Check the lines and connections for leaks. Be sure that there is no obstruction in the vent. Replace the instrument if it is defective.

Pressure Warning Signal

Inspect the entire installation for security of mounting and condition of the electrical, fuel, and air connections. Check the lamp by pressing the test switch to see that it lights. Check the operation by turning the battery switch on, building up pressure with the booster pump, and observing the pressure at which the light goes out. If necessary, adjust the contact mechanism.

WATER INJECTION SYSTEM FOR RECIPROCATING ENGINES

There are a few of these now being used, but the water injection system enables more power to be obtained from the engine at takeoff than is possible without water injection. The carburetor (operating at high-power settings) delivers more fuel to the engine than it actually needs. A leaner mixture would produce more power; however, the additional fuel is necessary to prevent overheating and detonation. With the injection of the antidetonant fluid, the mixture can be leaned out to that which produces maximum power, and the vaporization of the water-alcohol mixture then provides the cooling formerly supplied by the excess fuel, see fig. 3–42.

Operating on this best power mixture, the engine develops more power even though the manifold pressure and r.p.m. settings remain unchanged. In addition though, the manifold pressure can be increased to a point which would cause detonation without injection of the water-alcohol mixture. Thus, the increase in power with the antidetonant injection is two-fold: the engine can be operated on the best power mixture, and the maximum manifold pressure can be increased.

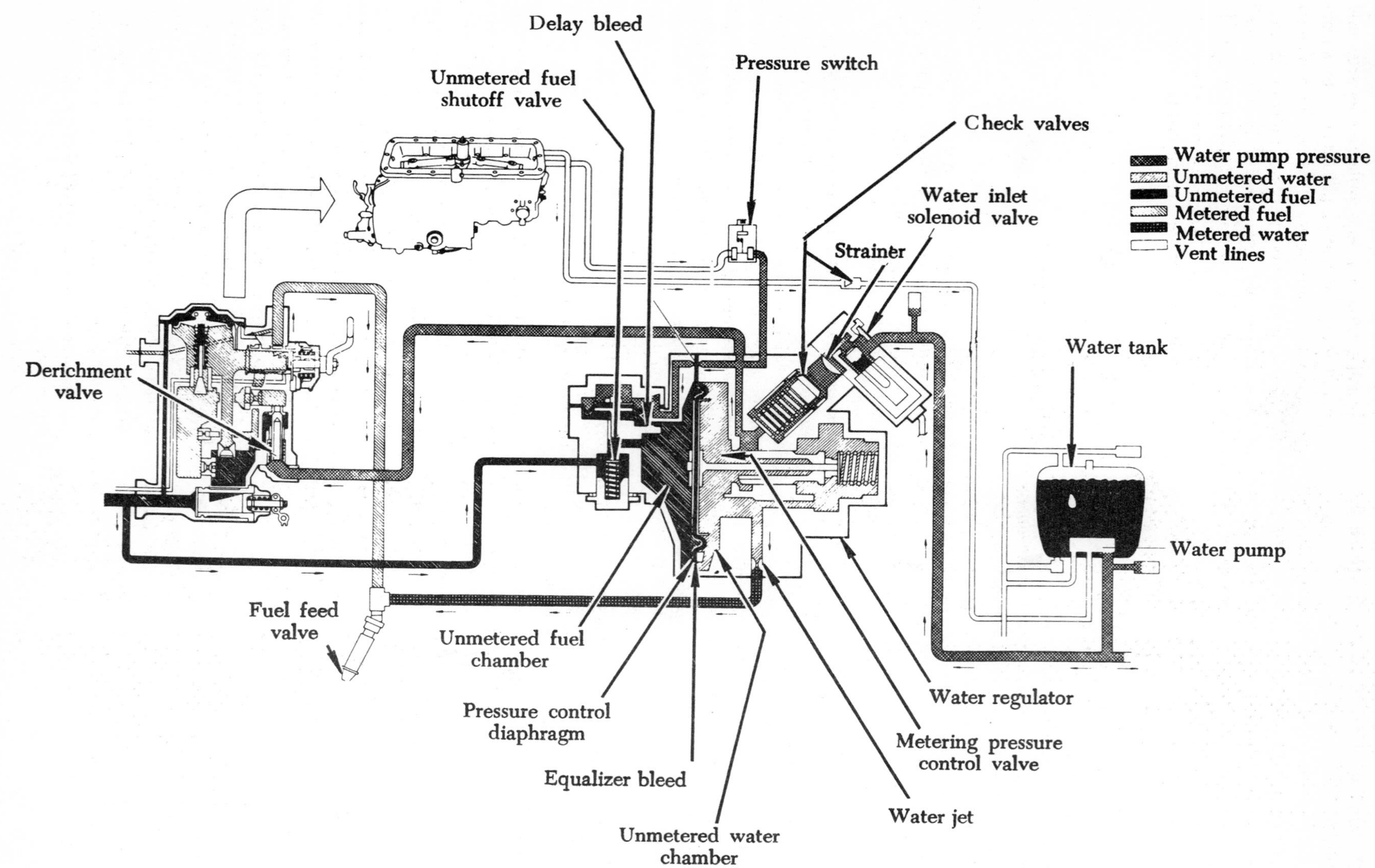

FIGURE 3–42. Schematic diagram of a typical ADI system.

TURBINE ENGINE FUEL SYSTEM—GENERAL REQUIREMENTS

The fuel system is one of the more complex aspects of the gas turbine engine. The variety of methods used to meet turbine engine fuel requirements makes reciprocating engine carburetion seem a simple study by comparison.

It must be possible to increase or decrease the power at will to obtain the thrust required for any operating condition. In turbine-powered aircraft this control is provided by varying the flow of fuel to the combustion chambers. However, turboprop aircraft also use variable-pitch propellers; thus, the selection of thrust is shared by two controllable variables, fuel flow and propeller blade angle.

The quantity of fuel supplied must be adjusted automatically to correct for changes in ambient temperature or pressure. If the quantity of fuel becomes excessive in relation to mass airflow through the engine, the limiting temperature of the turbine blades can be exceeded, or it will produce compressor stall and a condition referred to as "rich blowout." Rich blowout occurs when the amount of oxygen in the air supply is insufficient to support combustion and when the mixture is cooled below the combustion temperature by the excess fuel. The other extreme, "lean die-out," occurs if the fuel quantity is reduced proportionally below the air quantity.

The fuel system must deliver fuel to the combustion chambers not only in the right quantity, but also in the right condition for satisfactory combustion. The fuel nozzles form part of the fuel system and atomize or vaporize the fuel so that it will ignite and burn efficiently. The fuel system must also supply fuel so that the engine can be easily started on the ground and in the air. This means that the fuel must be injected into the combustion chambers in a combustible condition when the engine is being turned over slowly by the starting system, and that combustion must be sustained while the engine is accelerating to its normal running speed.

Another critical condition to which the fuel system must respond occurs during a slam acceleration. When the engine is accelerated, energy must be furnished to the turbine in excess of that necessary to maintain a constant r.p.m. However, if the fuel flow increases too rapidly, an overrich mixture can be produced, with the possibility of a rich blowout.

Turbojet, turbofan, and turboprop engines are equipped with a fuel control unit which automatically satisfies the requirements of the engine. Although the basic requirements apply generally to all gas turbine engines, the way in which individual fuel controls meet these needs cannot be conveniently generalized. Each fuel control manufacturer has his own peculiar way of meeting the engine demands.

JET FUEL CONTROLS

Fuel controls can be divided into two basic groups: (1) Hydromechanical and (2) electronic. The electronic fuel control is a combination of the two basic groups. Most fuel controls in use today are the completely hydromechanical type.

Regardless of the type, all fuel controls accomplish essentially the same functions, but some sense more engine variables than others. The fuel control senses power lever position, engine r.p.m., either compressor inlet pressure or temperature, and burner pressure or compressor discharge pressure. These variables affect the amount of thrust that an engine will produce for a given fuel flow.

Hydromechanical

Jet fuel controls are extremely complicated devices. The hydromechanical types are composed of speed governors, servo systems, sleeve and pilot valves, feedback or followup devices, and metering systems. In addition, electronic fuel controls incorporate amplifiers, thermocouples, relays, electrical servo systems, switches, and solenoids. Each fuel control must be studied if it is to be understood. However, it is not within the scope of this handbook to discuss each type. Instead, one type of electronic fuel control system and a typical hydromechanical fuel control will be discussed. In the discussion of each, the general purpose and operating principles are stressed. No attempt is made to give detailed operating and maintenance instructions for specific types and makes of equipment. For the specific information needed to inspect or maintain a particular installation or unit, consult the manufacturer's instructions.

Electronic

The principal components of the turboprop temperature datum system (Allison 501–D13 engine) are the temperature datum valve, coordinator, fuel control, speed sensitive control, fuel manifold drain valve, and electronic temperature datum control (see figure 3–43).

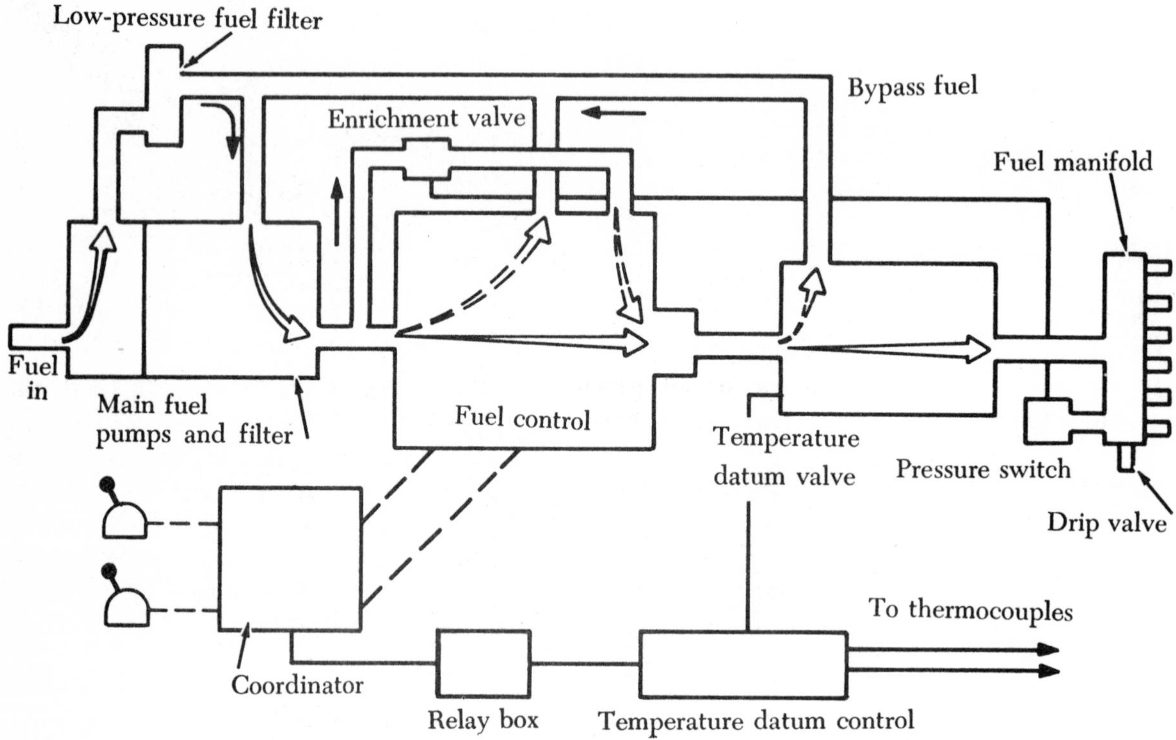

FIGURE 3–43. Allison 501–D13 engine fuel system schematic.

Temperature Datum Valve

The temperature datum valve (figure 3–44) is a fuel flow trimming device in the engine fuel system between the main fuel control and the engine fuel manifold. The datum valve, operating in conjunction with an associated electronic temperature datum control, trims metered fuel supplied from the main fuel control to maintain a preselected turbine inlet temperature.

The valve consists of a venturi, a regulator valve, a metering valve and sleeve assembly, and a pressurizing valve. The datum valve features a variable-take stop screw, actuated by a solenoid valve and a drive piston. This limits the total amount that engine fuel flow can be reduced.

The regulator valve maintains a pressure head across the metering valve orifice proportional to the amount of fuel being supplied to the datum valve.

The metering valve is positioned in its sleeve and orifice by the datum valve motor in response to signals from the associated electronic control. Motor rotation is applied through reduction gearing to the metering valve drive pinion. The metering valve determines the percentage of fuel to be trimmed from the metered engine fuel supply and bypassed to the engine pumps.

The pressurizing valve is located immediately ahead of the datum valve fuel outlet. The valve is spring loaded to maintain a back pressure on the fuel system. The low-pressure side of the pressurizing valve is vented, through a damping bleed, to bypass pressure and the boost pump outlet. The

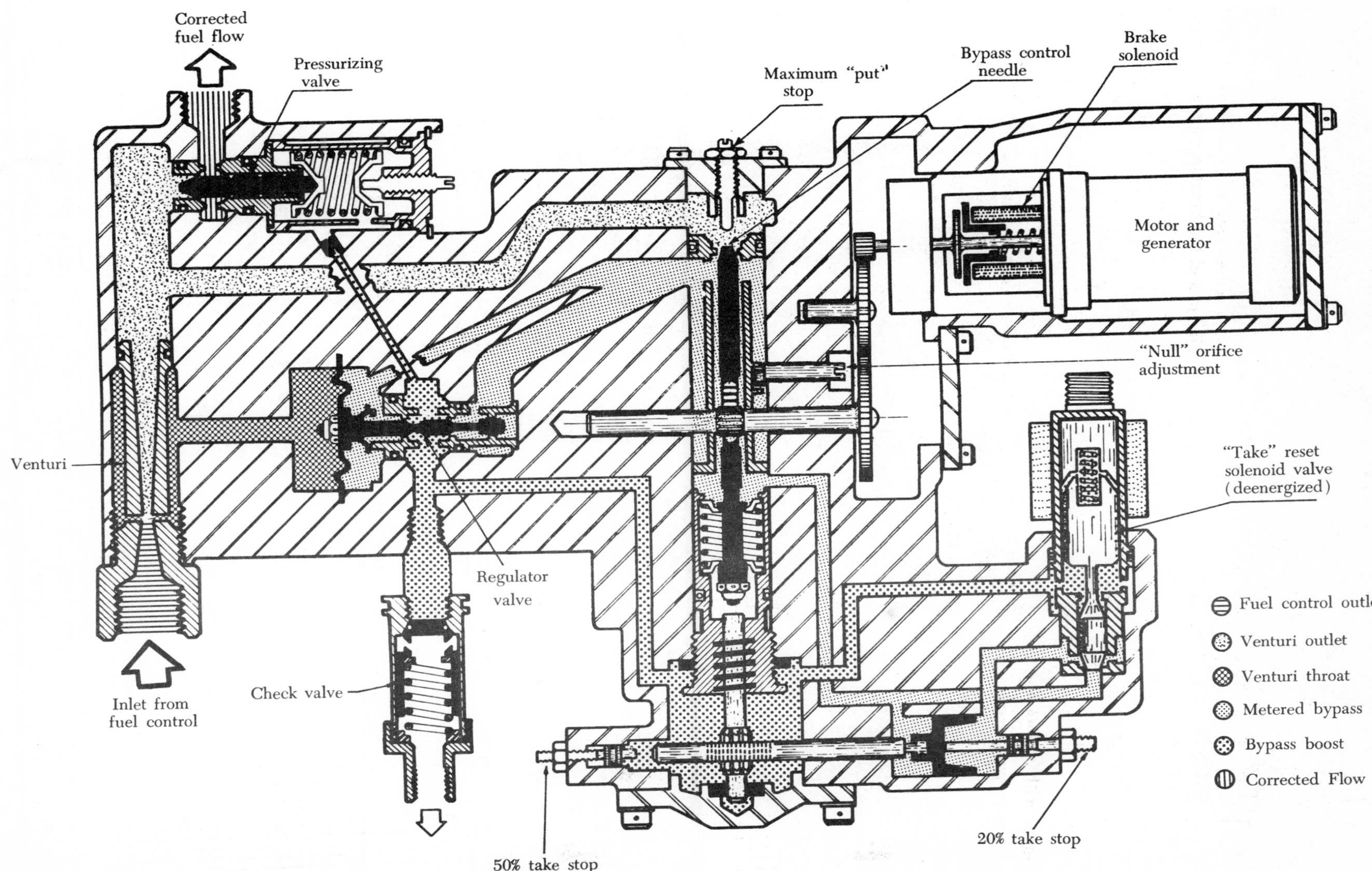

FIGURE 3–44. Temperature datum valve schematic.

damping bleed minimizes effects of fuel pressure surges on pressurizing valve operation.

The variable-take stop screw permits reduction in nominal fuel flow to the engine. The stop is positioned by a drive piston. A two-position solenoid valve directs fluid pressure to the drive piston, to establish the take position of the stop screw.

Venturi and Regulator Valve

Metered fuel under main fuel control outlet pressure enters the datum valve through a venturi. Fuel pressure at the venturi throat is sampled to provide a pressure signal inversely proportional to the amount of fuel entering the datum valve.

Fuel under venturi throat pressure is applied to one side of the regulator valve diaphragm to provide a valve-positioning force inversely proportional to fuel flow through the inlet venturi.

Fuel from the venturi outlet is channeled directly to the pressurizing valve at the datum outlet. The metering valve trims fuel in excess of engine requirements from this fuel flow and directs this excess fuel to the regulator valve. Fuel under venturi outlet pressure flows past the metering valve and through the metering valve orifice to the regulator valve. This fuel is bypassed through the opened valve to the bypass outlet and engine pump inlets. Simultaneously, metered bypass pressure is reduced until it becomes equal to venturi throat pressure on the opposite side of the diaphragm.

When metered bypass pressure equals venturi throat pressure on the opposite side of the regulator valve diaphragm, a regulated orifice bypassing excess engine fuel is established by the regulator valve. Simultaneously, the proper pressure drop for trimming from the venturi throat fuel supply is established across the metering valve orifice. At this balanced condition, the pressure rise from the inlet venturi throat to the venturi exit equals the pressure drop across the metering valve orifice.

When the metering valve is at the "null" position, approximately 20% of the total metered fuel supplied the datum valve is returned to the engine pumps.

Metering Valve

The metering valve is repositioned in its orifice from the "null" position to vary the percentage of fuel trimmed from venturi fuel in the datum valve, thus adjusting the amount of fuel delivered to engine burners. The metering valve is driven in either a "put" or "take" direction from the "null" position, according to engine temperature requirements. Metering valve positioning signals are supplied from an associated electronic control that senses the engine temperatures.

When the metering valve is driven towards its orifice, it moves in a put direction to reduce flow from the venturi throat to metered bypass. This causes fuel flow to the engine burners to be increased above the nominal 100% supplied when the metering valve is at the "null" position. Simultaneously, metered bypass pressure is reduced, permitting venturi throat pressure to reduce the regulator valve opening through which fuel is bypassed to the engine pumps. Metering valve orifice closing can continue until the metering valve contacts the maximum put stop. The maximum put stop is adjusted during datum valve calibration.

When the metering valve is driven away from its orifice, it moves in a take direction to increase the flow from the venturi throat to metered bypass. This causes fuel flow to engine burners to be reduced below that normally supplied when the metering valve is at the "null" position. Simultaneously, metered bypass pressure is increased to move the regulator valve diaphragm against venturi throat pressure, thus increasing the regulator valve opening through which fuel is bypassed to the engine pumps. Metering valve orifice opening can continue until the metering valve contacts the variable take stop. The variable take stop permits take action by the datum valve. Engine fuel flow can be reduced, providing maximum engine temperature protection during starting. When engine speed reaches and exceeds a preselected value, the solenoid valve on the datum valve is de-energized. Solenoid valve action repositions the variable take stop. Fuel flow can then be reduced sufficiently to reduce any normal over-temperature conditions during engine operation.

Motor Operation

The metering valve is positioned in its orifice by a two-phase motor within the datum valve. Motor operating voltage is supplied from the electronic control operating in association with the datum valve. The phase of voltage supplied to the motor determines the direction of motor rotation and subsequent metering valve movement. Voltage phase, in turn, is determined by the type of temperature correction required, *i.e.*, if engine fuel flow should be increased to increase temperature, or reduced to lower temperature. Motor rotation is transmitted through reduction gears to the metering valve drive gear on one end of the pinion shaft. The opposite end of the pinion shaft is welded to a tube carrying the metering valve drive pinion. This type of pinion shaft construction provides a torsion shaft that reduces shock on the reduction gear train and motor if the metering valve is driven against either stop.

Generator Operation

The datum valve motor has a generator coupled on the motor shaft. While the motor is driving the metering valve to change valve position, this coupled generator produces an a.c. voltage proportional to motor rotational speed. The a.c. voltage is fed back to the associated electronic control.

The phase of this a.c. voltage is determined by the direction of motor-generator rotation. Magnitude of the a.c. voltage is proportional to rotational speed. Thus, the feedback voltage provides a rate signal telling the electronic control the rate at which the metering valve is moving.

Within the electronic control, this voltage damps, or reduces, the temperature error signal that initiated motor rotation. The rate of error signal reduction is proportional to the rate at which the motor-generator is rotating. Error signal reduction causes a corresponding reduction of variable phase voltage supplied to the datum valve motor.

The error signal damping approximates dashpot action in achieving datum valve stability by reducing inertia force without loss of torque under stall conditions. Thus, as turbine inlet temperature approaches a corrected value, voltage to the motor is reduced and the motor stalls. When the motor stalls, the metering valve has been properly repositioned to provide a temperature-corrected fuel flow.

Motor Brake

A solenoid-operated brake is incorporated on the motor output shaft between the motor and the reduction gearbox. The brake is disengaged when the solenoid is energized, and engaged when the solenoid is de-energized. Brake operating voltage is controlled by engine, aircraft, and electronic control circuitry.

When the brake solenoid is de-energized and the brake engaged, spring loading holds the brake shoe against a disk on the power transmission shaft through the brake. This action prevents the motor from rotating even though variable-phase voltage is supplied to the motor.

When the solenoid is energized and the brake released, the brake armature, on which the brake shoe is located, is lifted against spring force into the core of the solenoid. This releases the power transmission shaft and permits motor rotation to be applied to the reduction gearbox.

COORDINATOR

The coordinator bolts to the rear face of the fuel control and houses the power lever shaft, mechanical discriminator, manual fuel cutoff shaft, switches and actuating cams, temperature selector potentiometer, potentiometer drive gears, and the necessary electrical wiring.

The unit coordinates the propeller, electronic temperature datum control, and fuel control. It receives signals through linkage from the cockpit power lever and the cockpit emergency handle and transmits these signals to the fuel control and propeller regulator through a system of levers and links.

The potentiometer in the coordinator is driven from the power lever shaft through a gear set. Above a certain nominal coordinator position, the potentiometer schedules the turbine inlet temperature by sending an electrical signal for the desired temperature to the electronic temperature datum control.

The switch in the coordinator is actuated by a cam on the power lever shaft to transfer the function of the temperature datum control from temperature limiting to temperature controlling at a certain nominal coordinator position.

FUEL CONTROL

The fuel control is mounted on the accessories drive housing and is mechanically linked to the coordinator. The fuel control is designed to perform the following functions:

(1) Provide a means of varying fuel flow to permit a selection of power that is coordinated with propeller blade angle and engine speed.

(2) Regulate the rate of fuel metering during acceleration to prevent excessive turbine inlet temperature.

(3) Control the rate of decrease of fuel metering during deceleration to prevent flameout.

(4) Control engine and propeller speed outside the limits of operation of the propeller governor. This includes reverse thrust, low-speed ground idle, flight idle, and high-speed ground idle.

(5) Provide a measure of engine protection during overspeed conditions by reducing fuel flow and turbine inlet temperature.

(6) Provide a starting fuel flow schedule which, in conjunction with the temperature datum valve, avoids over-temperature and compressor surge.

(7) Compensate for changes in air density caused by variations in compressor inlet air temperature and pressure.

(8) Provide a means of cutting off fuel flow electrically and manually.

The fuel control senses compressor inlet pressure, compressor inlet temperature, and engine speed. Using these three factors and the setting of the power lever, the fuel control meters the proper amount of fuel throughout the range of engine operation. Pressure and temperature compensating systems are designed to maintain constant turbine inlet temperature as the compressor inlet conditions vary.

The fuel control is scheduled richer than the nominal engine requirements to accommodate the temperature datum valve which bypasses part of the control output when in the "null" position. This excess flow to the temperature datum valve gives it the capacity to add as well as subtract fuel to maintain the temperature scheduled by the coordinator potentiometer and the temperature datum control.

The control includes a cutoff valve for stopping fuel flow to the engine. The cutoff valve, which can be manually or electrically controlled, is actuated by mechanical linkage and an electrical actuator. The mechanical cutoff is tied in with the emergency control input linkage. Both must be in the "open" position to permit fuel flow. During an engine start, the motor-operated valve remains closed until the engine reaches a speed where the speed-sensitive control actuates and opens the motor-operated valve, permitting fuel flow to the engine.

SPEED-SENSITIVE CONTROL

The speed-sensitive control (figure 3–45) is mounted on the tachometer pad of the accessories housing. It contains three switches which are actuated at certain speeds by a flyweight system. During a start one switch turns on the fuel and ignition, parallels fuel pump elements, energizes the starting fuel enrichment system when fuel enrichment switch is on, and closes the drip valve; another switch shuts off the ignition, de-energizes the drip valve which is then held closed by fuel pressure, and shifts the fuel pumps from parallel to series operation; and still another switch shifts the temperature datum control from start limiting and limits the temperature datum valve to a certain reduction of engine fuel flow.

FUEL MANIFOLD DRAIN VALVE

The fuel output from the temperature datum valve is connected to the fuel manifold. The manifold consists of sections of flexible steel braided hose which connect at the bottom of the engine to a drain valve. These sections connect directly to the fuel nozzles.

A spring-loaded, solenoid-operated drain valve is located at the bottom of the fuel manifold. It is designed to drain the manifold when the fuel pressure drops below a certain amount while the engine is being stopped to prevent fuel from dripping into the combustion chambers.

During the starting cycle, the valve is closed by energizing the solenoid. It is held closed by fuel pressure within the manifold when the engine is running.

SYSTEM OPERATION

The temperature datum control system is essentially a servo system. Thus, system operation is based on any error, or variation from desired engine temperature conditions. The electronic temperature datum control senses any temperature error and supplies an error-correcting signal to the two-phase servomotor in the associated temperature datum valve.

The reference to which engine temperatures are compared is established within the electronic control. This reference is a millivoltage equivalent to engine thermocouple-generated millivoltage for a desired temperature. Any variation between the reference and thermocouple-generated millivoltages causes an error-correcting signal to be supplied to the temperature datum valve servomotor.

Three different reference temperature conditions are used during temperature datum control system operation. These conditions are normal limiting, start limiting, and controlling. Temperature value of the controlling reference temperature is scheduled as a function of power lever angle.

The normal limiting reference temperature is available throughout the entire operating range of the engine. It is the maximum safe engine-operating temperature. During limiting operation, engine temperature is prevented from exceeding this value by the temperature datum control system. The normal limiting temperature is effective throughout the power lever travel range below the angle at which

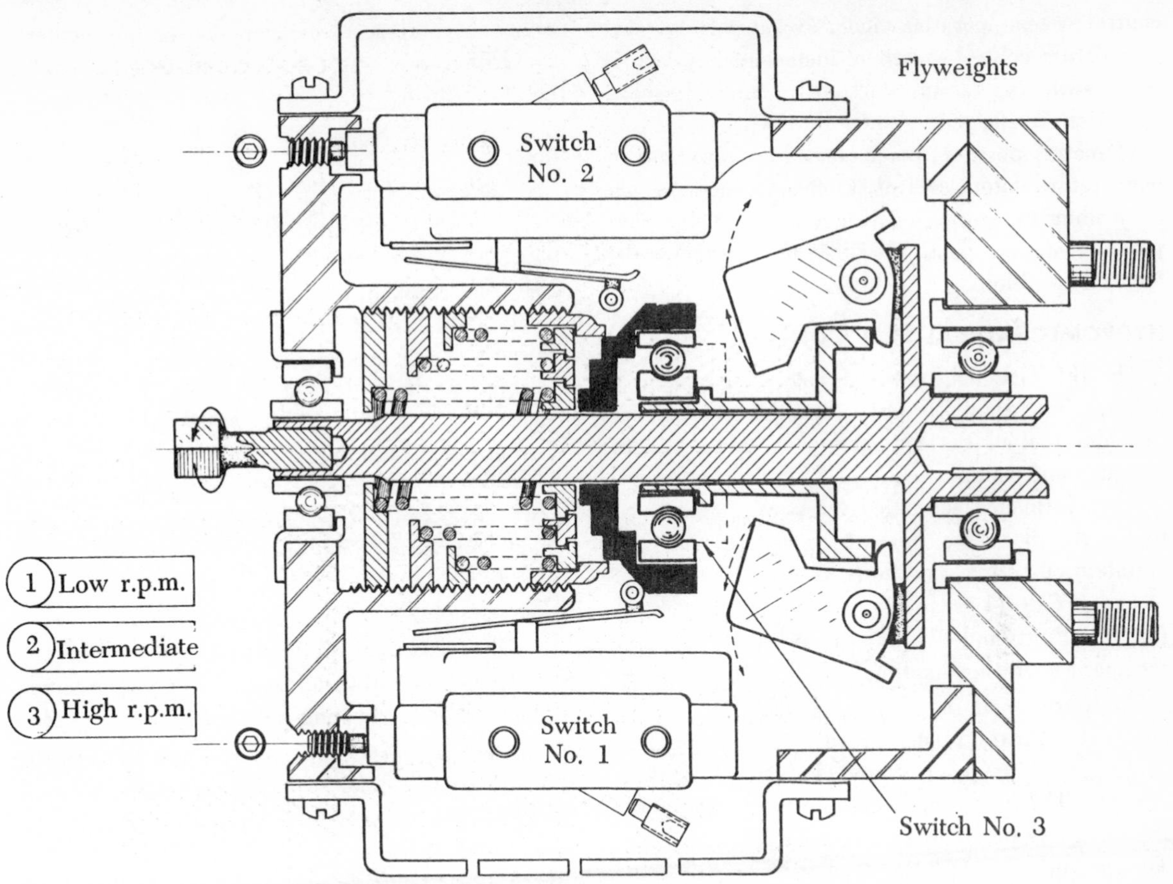

FIGURE 3–45. Speed-sensitive control.

crossover to controlling operation occurs, and whenever the aircraft temperature datum control switch is moved to the "locked" position, as during aircraft landing.

The start limiting temperature is effective only during engine starting and operation up to a preselected speed. Temperature value of the start limiting temperature is less than the normal limiting temperature. The start limiting temperature protects the engine from excessive temperature transients during engine starting.

Reference temperature is scheduled according to power lever angle in the controlling range of engine operation. Temperature value of the reference is scheduled according to desired engine power.

Either temperature limiting or temperature controlling operation is selected by engine and aircraft switches. The engine switches include a speed-sensitive switch and two power-lever-actuated switches in the engine coordinator. The aircraft switch is the pilot-actuated temperature datum control switch.

Engine switches select which limiting temperature value, normal or start, is effective, and switch the temperature datum control system from limiting to controlling operations.

The speed-sensitive switch selects the desired reference for start limiting operation during initial engine starting. The electronic control remains in the start limiting condition until the speed switch opens. When the speed switch opens, the electronic control is switched to normal limiting temperature operation.

The power-lever-actuated switches establish the power lever angle at which crossover from temperature limiting to temperature controlling operation occurs. At power lever angles less than the crossover point, these switches hold the temperature datum control system in limiting operation. After the crossover angle is reached and passed, these switches re-align the temperature datum control system for temperature controlling operation.

The temperature datum control switch provides for manually selecting a desired temperature datum control system operating mode. When the temperature datum control switch is in the "locked" position, switching from start to normal limiting operation is effected. When the switch is in the "automatic" position, other conditions occur. The temperature datum control system is switched from controlling to limiting operation whenever the temperature datum control switch is moved to the "locked" position.

HYDROMECHANICAL FUEL CONTROL

The JFC (jet fuel control) schedules the quantity of fuel flow required by a turbojet engine. It provides fuel to the combustion chambers at the pressure and volume required to maintain the engine performance scheduled by power lever position. At the same time it limits fuel flow to maintain operating conditions within safe limits.

The JFC12–11 is an all-mechanical fuel control for the Pratt and Whitney turbojet engine. A schematic operating diagram is shown in figure 3–46.

The purpose of the JFC is to meter fuel to the engine to control r.p.m., prevent overheating and surging, and prevent either rich blowout or lean die-out. This is accomplished by supplying signals from engine r.p.m. (N_2) and burner pressure (P_B). The control then schedules fuel flow (W_f) in lbs./hr. to keep the engine running at the desired setting selected by the power lever and within the engine's operating limits.

Two control levers are provided. The power lever controls engine r.p.m. during all forward and reverse thrust operations. A fuel shutoff lever controls engine starting and shutdown by operating the fuel shutoff, windmill bypass feature, and manifold dump valve signal in the proper sequence.

When the power lever is moved to a selected setting, a certain percentage of available thrust is expected from the engine. Thrust results from the acceleration imparted to the mass of air flowing through the engine. Consequently, any variation in air density through changes in pressure or temperature will affect the thrust due to the change in mass airflow. In the range of engine operation from sea level to altitude, atmospheric pressure variations have a greater effect on air density than the changes in ambient temperature. For any steady state condition of engine operation (mass airflow through the engine constant), a definite amount of fuel is needed, and, therefore, the fuel/air ratio (W_f/P_B) will be constant.

A measure of airflow through the engine is given by burner pressure. Burner pressure alone is a rough measure of airflow and is used to schedule fuel flow during deceleration to prevent lean die-out. During acceleration, fuel flow is scheduled as a function of r.p.m. and burner pressure to prevent rich blowout, surging, or overheating.

The equilibrium curve of an engine, illustrated in figure 3–47, indicates the job the fuel control must do. Fuel flow during starting is limited by the acceleration line and will drop off to the value required for idle operation as the engine r.p.m. increases to idle. This decrease in the fuel flow occurs along a droop line, which is a governing characteristic built into the fuel control for better control of r.p.m. without surging or hunting. The power lever position varies compression of a speeder spring to select the proper droop line setting.

To accelerate from idle to maximum, the power lever is moved forward. Fuel flow increases rapidly at first and then more gradually according to a schedule for acceleration that will avoid surge conditions and overheating the engine. Just before maximum is reached, fuel flow begins to decrease along a droop line so that the r.p.m. will level off at maximum without hunting.

For deceleration from maximum, the fuel flow drops abruptly to the minimum flow schedule and follows that back to idle. Although the minimum fuel flow ratio is shown as a straight line in figure 3–47, fuel flow varies with burner pressure and, thus, is higher at maximum r.p.m. than at idle r.p.m.

FUEL CONTROL DESCRIPTION

Metering System Operation

Fuel is supplied to the inlet of the fuel control unit from the aircraft tanks through a series of boost pumps. The fuel is passed through the screens and filters of the aircraft fuel system before it is directed to the fuel control. Fuel entering the inlet port of the fuel control unit passes through a coarse 200-mesh screen filter (see figure 3–48). If the filter becomes clogged, it will allow unfiltered fuel to bypass because it is spring loaded and will be lifted off its seat if the differential pressure across the screen becomes greater than 25 to 30 p.s.i. Some of the fuel that has passed through the coarse filter is directed to the fine filter. All high-pressure fuel used in the valves and servos of the fuel control passes through the fine filter. This filter is a 35-micron screen and is also spring loaded. If it becomes clogged, unfiltered fuel will bypass the filter when the differential pressure is 10 to 17 p.s.i.

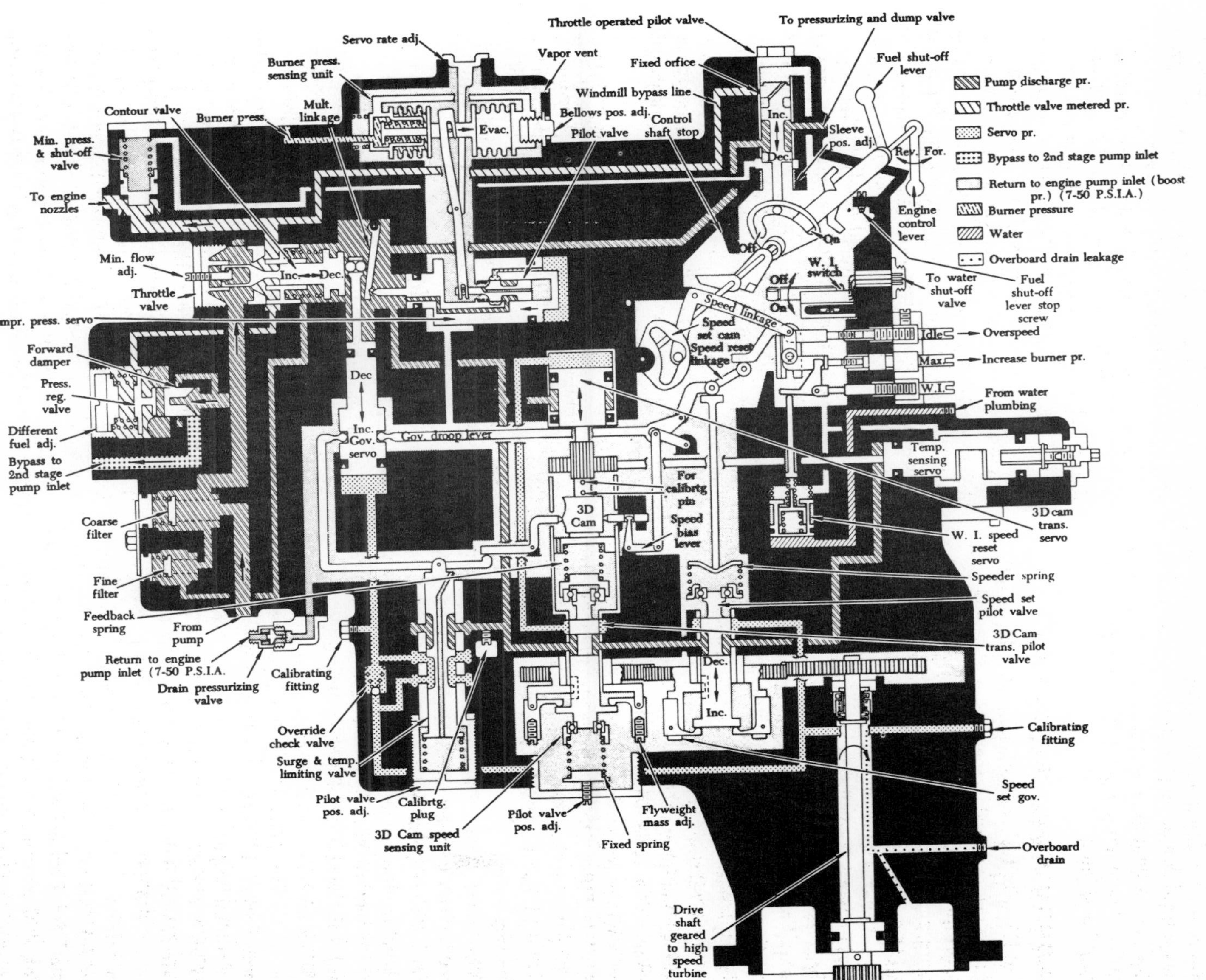

Throttle operated pilot valve
To pressurizing and dump valve
Servo rate adj.
Vapor vent
Fixed orfice
Fuel shut-off lever
Burner press. sensing unit
Windmill bypass line
Contour valve
Burner press.
Mult. linkage
Evac.
Bellows pos. adj.
Control shaft stop
Pilot valve
Sleeve pos. adj.
Inc.
Dec.
Rev.
For.
Min. press. & shut-off valve
To engine nozzles
Engine control lever
Pump discharge pr.
Throttle valve metered pr.
Servo pr.
Bypass to 2nd stage pump inlet
Return to engine pump inlet (boost pr.) (7-50 P.S.I.A.)
Burner pressure
Water
Overboard drain leakage
Off
On
Min. flow adj.
Throttle valve
W. I. switch
To water shut-off valve
Fuel shut-off lever stop screw
Speed linkage
Compr. press. servo
Speed set cam
Speed reset linkage
Idle
Overspeed
Forward damper
Max
Increase burner pr.
Press. reg. valve
W.I.
From water plumbing
Different fuel adj.
Gov. droop lever
Temp. sensing servo
Bypass to 2nd stage pump inlet
Gov. servo
For calibrtg pin
3D cam trans. servo
Coarse filter
3D Cam
Speed bias lever
W. I. speed reset servo
Speeder spring
Fine filter
Speed set pilot valve
Feedback spring
From pump
3D Cam trans. pilot valve
Return to engine pump inlet (7-50 P.S.I.A.
Calibrating fitting
Drain pressurizing valve
Calibrating fitting
Override check valve
Surge & temp. limiting valve
Speed set gov.
Pilot valve pos. adj.
Calibrtg. plug
Pilot valve pos. adj.
Flyweight mass adj.
3D Cam speed sensing unit
Fixed spring
Overboard drain
Drive shaft geared to high speed turbine

FIGURE 3–46. JFC12–11 schematic operating diagram.

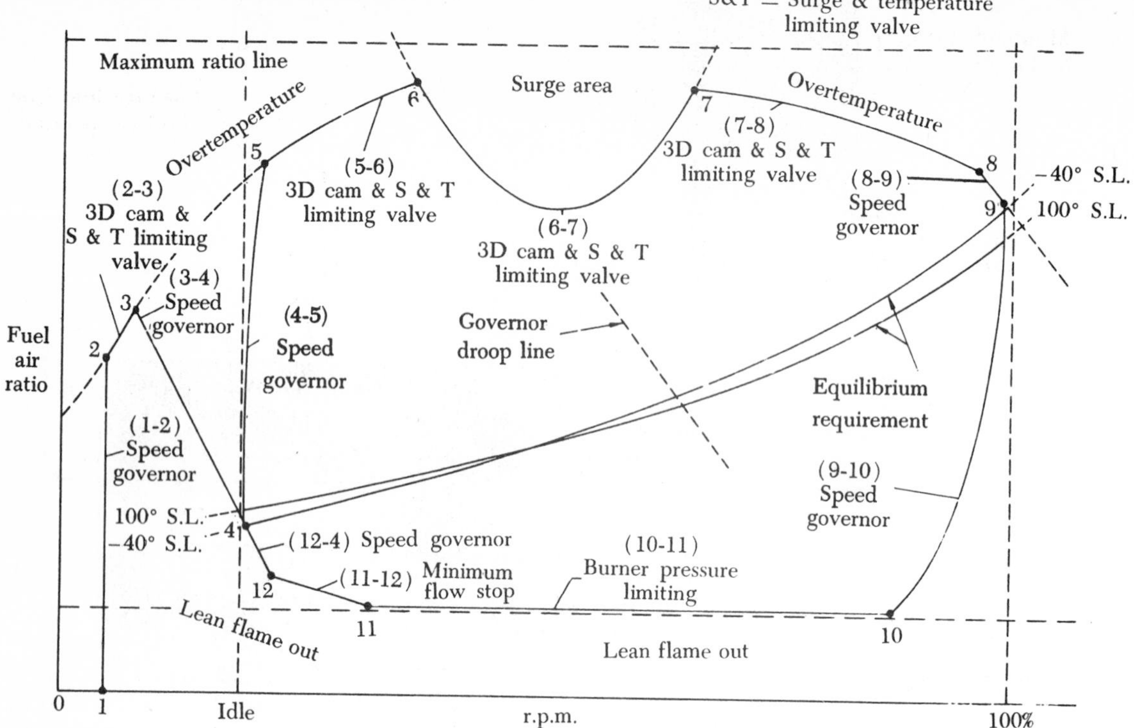

FIGURE 3–47. Engine operating conditions (equilibrium curve).

Pressure-Regulating Valve

The pressure-regulating valve diaphragm, shown in figure 3–48, is exposed on one side to pump output pressure and on the other side to the combined effect of throttle valve discharge pressure and a spring force preset to maintain the desired pressure drop across the throttle valve. The spring force is adjustable to allow compensation for use of various fuels. With a constant pressure drop across the throttle valve, flow through the throttle valve will be proportional to its orifice area. Any excess fuel above that required to maintain the set pressure differential is bypassed back to the interstage section of the supply pump. The damping orifice in the passage to the pressure-regulating valve minimizes valve chatter.

Throttle Valve

The throttle valve, figure 3–48, is the main metering valve. It consists of a spring-loaded, cylindrical contoured valve which moves within a sharp-edged orifice. This valve controls the main fuel flow from the engine pump to the fuel nozzles. Since a constant pressure differential is maintained across the throttle valve by the pressure regulating valve, each position of the valve represents a definite fuel flow regardless of throttle valve discharge pressure. A positive minimum flow adjustment is provided on the throttle valve. The valve is spring loaded to its minimum flow position, but never closes completely. The throttle valve spring moves the valve in the decrease-flow direction, and the combined action of the compressor pressure servo and the governor servo moves the valve in the increase-flow direction. The throttle valve outlet directs the metered fuel to the minimum pressure and shutoff valve. The metered fuel also acts on the spring side of the pressure-regulating valve and is delivered to the throttle-operated pilot valve, where it can bypass to drain when the fuel shutoff lever is placed in the "off" position.

Shutoff and Minimum Pressure Valve

The shutoff and minimum pressure valve is a shuttle-type valve acted upon on one side by throttle valve discharge pressure and on the other by a combination of spring force and either high-pressure fuel during shutoff or JFC body drain pressure during normal operation. The spring also holds the valve closed following engine shutdown. During normal operation, when the spring side of the valve is backed up by body drain pressure, if the throttle valve discharge pressure falls below a preset value, the valve will move toward the "closed" position,

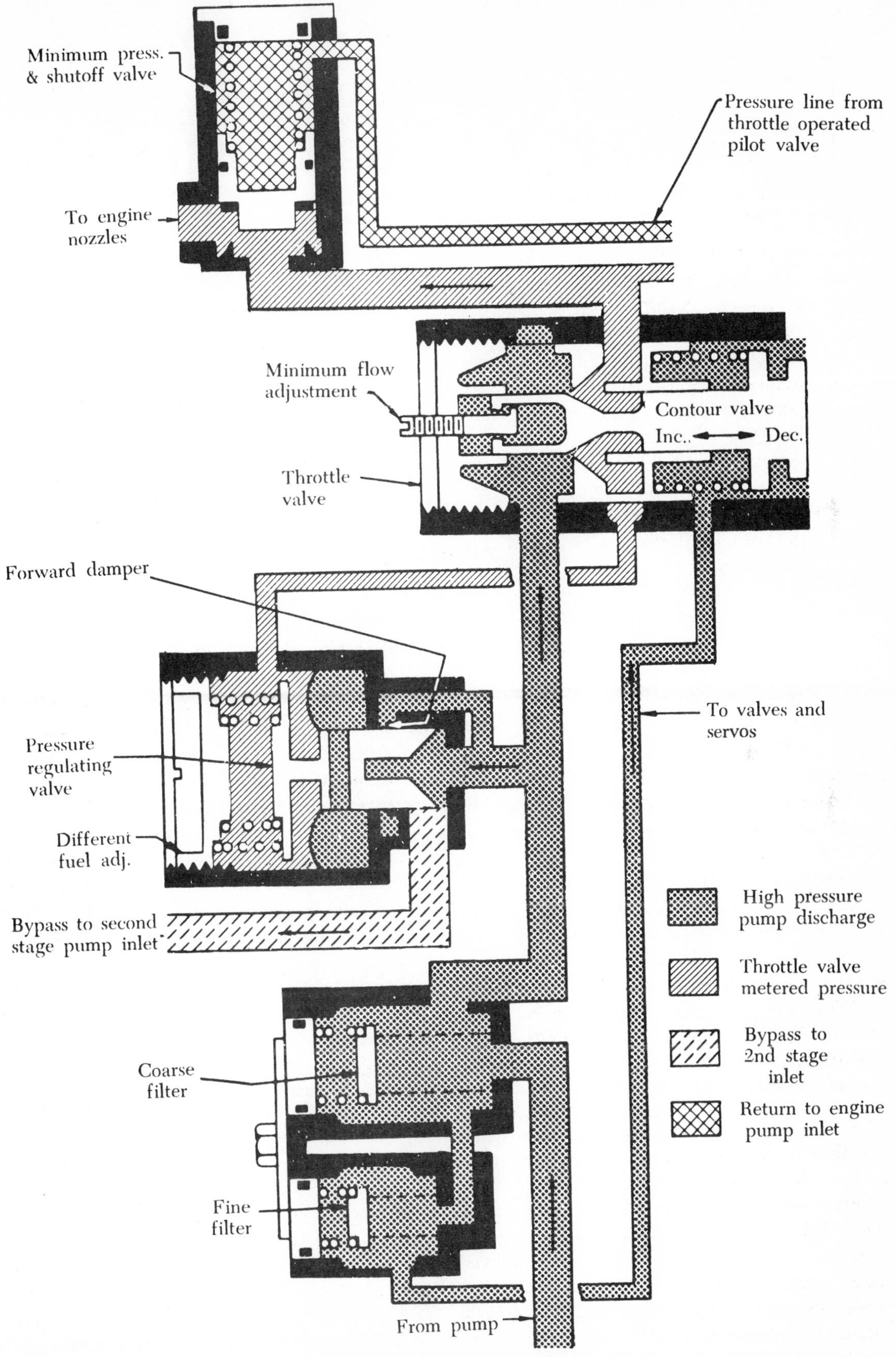
Minimum press.
& shutoff valve
Pressure line from
throttle operated
pilot valve
To engine
nozzles
Minimum flow
adjustment
Contour valve
Inc.
Dec.
Throttle
valve
Forward damper
To valves and
servos
Pressure
regulating
valve
Different
fuel adj.
High pressure
pump discharge
Bypass to second
stage pump inlet
Throttle valve
metered pressure
Bypass to
2nd stage
inlet
Coarse
filter
Return to engine
pump inlet
Fine
filter
From pump

FIGURE 3–48. Metering system.

restricting flow from the fuel control until the throttle valve discharge pressure increases again to the preset value. This ensures that sufficient pressure is always available for operation of the servos and valves. The metered fuel flows from the minimum pressure and shutoff valve to the fuel outlet of the control and then to the manifold drain valve and the engine manifolds.

Throttle-Operated Pilot Valve

The pressure signal which actuates the shutoff and minimum pressure valve originates from the throttle-operated pilot valve (figure 3–49). In addition to this pressure signal, the throttle-operated pilot valve performs two other functions. The porting of this valve determines the sequence of these functions. This pilot valve is positioned by a cam mounted on a shaft rotated by the shutoff lever in the cockpit.

In the operating or "on" position, the pilot valve directs high-pressure fuel to the engine-pressurizing and dump valve, where it works against a spring to hold the dump valve closed. As previously mentioned, the spring side of the minimum pressure and shutoff valve is exposed to the body cavity drain, allowing the downstream pressure from the throttle valve to force the valve open. The third function of the throttle-operated pilot valve is to block the windmill bypass line.

When the fuel shutoff lever is moved to the "off" position, the pilot valve is repositioned by the cam. First, the windmill bypass line is opened. The pilot-operated throttle valve also directs high-pressure fuel to the spring side of the minimum pressure and shutoff valve, ensuring closing of the valve. The valve now allows the pressure line to the engine pressurizing and dump valve to drain into the body cavity, permitting the spring to open the valve, and any fuel in the engine manifold is drained.

During shutdown in flight, the engine windmills, and the engine-driven fuel pump continues to operate. Since the outflow from the fuel control is shut off, the pump output must be relieved. This may be done by the pump relief valve (1,000 p.s.i.) or by the fuel control. To avoid the conditions of high pump load and high temperature which accompany relief valve operation, the bypass function is performed within the fuel control at a minimum pressure.

The windmill bypass line brings metered fuel pressure (metered by the throttle valve) to a port in the throttle-operated pilot valve housing. If the pilot valve is positioned to shut off fuel flow to the engine, metered fuel pressure is bled through the bypass line and pilot valve housing to the low pressure of the body cavity. Decreased metered fuel pressure also reduces the force on the spring side of the pressure regulator diaphragm. This allows the regulator valve to open more fully and bypass the pump output.

If a shutdown is made during a high-pressure operating condition (maximum power lever position), an orifice in the windmill bypass line is so designed that pressure in the body cavity cannot increase to a value that could damage the fuel control.

Computing System Operation

By positioning the main metering valve, the computing system selects a fuel flow for each condition of engine operation. This fuel flow is established by the position of the contour valve. Figure 3–50 is a schematic representation of the computing system. The units that comprise this system and their operation are described in the following paragraphs.

Burner Pressure Servo Assembly

The burner pressure servo assembly controls the position of the compressor pressure servo. The position of the compressor pressure servo provides the input to the multiplying linkage which acts upon the throttle valve. The burner pressure servo assembly consists of two bellows, one of which is vented to burner pressure and the other is evacuated. The two bellows are installed, diametrically opposed, on a rigid frame with their movable ends connected to a common link.

If burner pressure increases during operation, the left bellows extends. This motion is transmitted through a lever connected to the bellows link and moves the pilot valve in the compressor pressure servo. Motion of the pilot valve directs high-pressure fuel to the governor servo chamber. The cross-sectional area of the governor servo valve is larger at the servo chamber end than at the opposite end, which is acted upon by high-pressure fuel. Therefore, the increased pressure in the servo chamber causes the governor servo valve to move, thus changing the input to the multiplying linkage of the throttle valve. Assuming that the governor servo is stationary, an increase in burner pressure will cause an increase in fuel flow. As the compressor pressure servo moves, the fuel passage opened by the movement of the pilot valve is gradually closed so that the servo, by following the pilot valve, assumes a new equilibrium position.

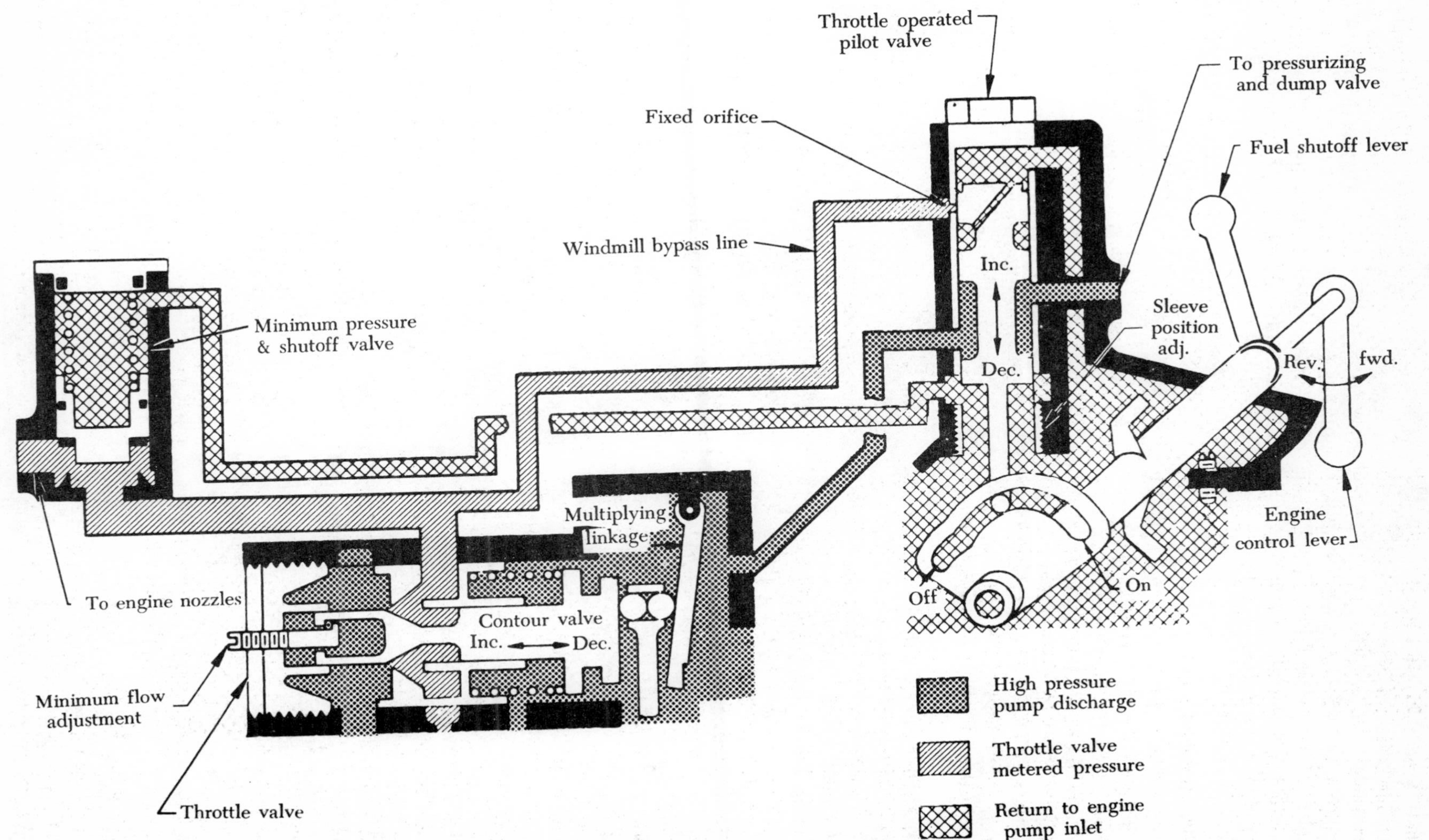
Throttle operated pilot valve
To pressurizing and dump valve
Fixed orifice
Fuel shutoff lever
Windmill bypass line
Inc.
Dec.
Sleeve position adj.
Rev.
fwd.
Minimum pressure & shutoff valve
Multiplying linkage
Engine control lever
To engine nozzles
Off
On
Contour valve
Inc.
Dec.
Minimum flow adjustment
Throttle valve
High pressure pump discharge
Throttle valve metered pressure
Return to engine pump inlet

FIGURE 3–49. Throttle-operated pilot valve.

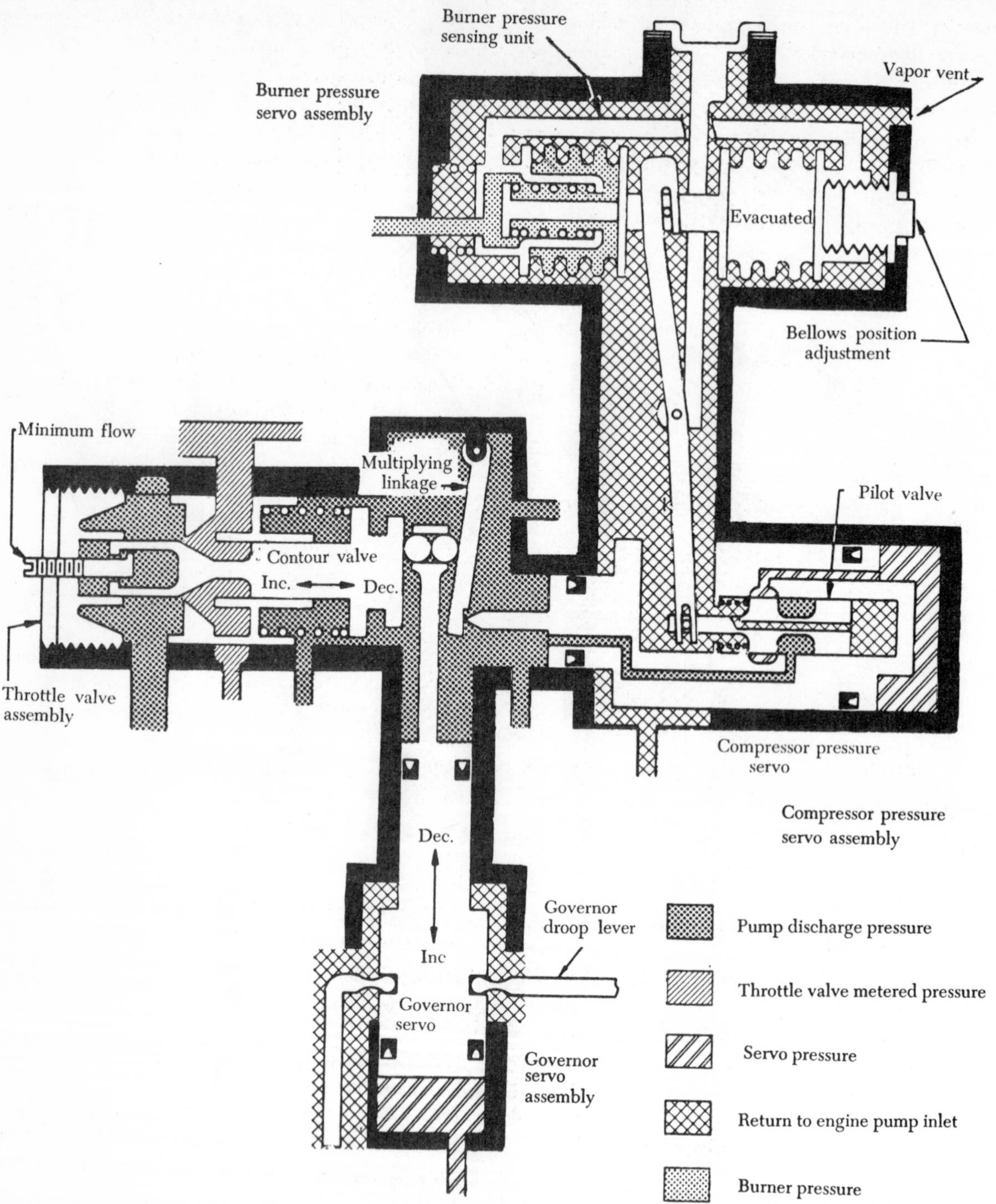

FIGURE 3–50. Computing system.

If burner pressure decreases, the bellows contracts, moving the pilot valve so that the governor servo chamber is drained to body pressure. High fuel pressure acting on the small area end of the governor valve servo moves the governor servo, thus changing the input to the multiplying linkage of the throttle valve. Assuming that the governor servo is stationary, a decrease in burner pressure causes a decrease in fuel flow. The compressor pressure servo valve moves to a new equilibrium position as it again follows the pilot valve.

Governor Servo

The governor servo controls fuel flow as a function of set speed and engine speed, taking into account the effects of CIT (compressor inlet temperature) and engine operating limitations. The governor servo (figure 3–50) acts upon the throttle valve through the multiplying linkage and in conjunction with the compressor pressure servo. For a discussion of the governor servo operation, it will be assumed that the compressor pressure servo valve is stationary.

The governor servo is a shuttle valve with high-pressure fuel acting on a small area at one end and servo pressure from the pilot valve of the speed governor acting on the other end. If, because of a change in servo pressure, the force exerted by this pressure on the large area end of the governor servo is greater than that exerted by the high pressure on the opposite end, the governor servo moves and, through the multiplying linkage, allows the throttle valve to travel in the decrease-flow direction. Conversely, if the force exerted by the servo pressure is less than that exerted by the high pressure, the governor servo moves and drives the throttle valve in the increase-flow direction. The flow of servo fuel to the governor servo is controlled by (1) the speed governor and (2) the surge and temperature limiting pilot valve.

FUEL SCHEDULING SYSTEM

Speed-Set Governor

The speed-set governor (figure 3–51) controls the position of the governor servo. It is a centrifugal, permanent-droop type governor driven by the engine high-speed rotor (N_2) through a gear train. As engine speed increases, the flyweights tend to move outward, lifting the speed set pilot valve. Conversely, when engine speed decreases, the flyweights move inward and the pilot valve is lowered. The power lever in the cockpit positions the speed-setting cam in the fuel control unit to manipulate a system of levers and thus control the compression of the speeder spring. The speeder spring exerts force on the speed-set pilot valve. The condition of "on-speed" indicates the speeder spring force and the flyweight force are equal.

When the r.p.m. exceeds that for which the power lever is set, the flyweights of the speed-set governor move out, lifting the pilot valve. This meters high-pressure fuel to the governor servo through the override check valve. The servo moves upward, causing a decrease in fuel/air ratio. As the governor servo position is altered, the droop lever moves about a pivot point. Movement of the droop lever alters the speeder spring compression. The speeder spring force on the pilot valve and the r.p.m. centrifugal force on the flyweights balance, resulting in an "on-speed" equilibrium condition.

Conversely, if the high compressor r.p.m. is lower than the power lever setting demands, the flyweights move in, allowing governor servo pressure to drain to boost pressure. This permits the high-pressure fuel on the opposite end of the servo to shift it downward to increase fuel/air ratio. Repositioning the droop lever alters speeder spring force. The flyweight and speeder spring forces will again balance to an "on-speed" condition.

Operating conditions are not constant; thus, the position of the equilibrium curve may change. This curve is illustrated in figure 3—47. Speed-set governor droop characteristics are utilized to provide new on-speed settings. For example, dense air may load the engine compressor, causing speed to decrease. In this case the flyweight force is less than the speeder spring force, and the pilot valve moves down to increase fuel flow. This corrects the drop in r.p.m. The droop lever decreases speeder spring force on the pilot valve. The droop lever sets the slightly lower final r.p.m. as the system comes "on-speed" for the new equilibrium condition.

The operating conditions may cause the engine speed to increase. Fuel flow is decreased to correct the condition, but the droop lever resets the speed-set governor to an "on-speed" condition at slightly higher r.p.m. The droop characteristics indirectly control maximum turbine temperature by limiting turbine r.p.m.

Starting

During start, a proper amount of fuel must be supplied to ensure rapid starts while maintaining turbine inlet temperatures within specified limits.

When starting an engine, the fuel shutoff lever is not moved until approximately 12 to 16% r.p.m. is indicated on the tachometer. At this speed the shutoff lever is moved to the "on" position. The light-up speed has now been attained, but cranking must continue until the engine can accelerate beyond its self-sustaining speed. When the shutoff lever has been advanced to the "on" position, acceleration proceeds as follows: (1) the power lever calls for maximum increase of fuel flow, and (2) the speed-set cam positions the speed linkage so that the speed-set governor speeder spring is compressed beyond the force required to counterbalance the forces of the centrifugal flyweights.

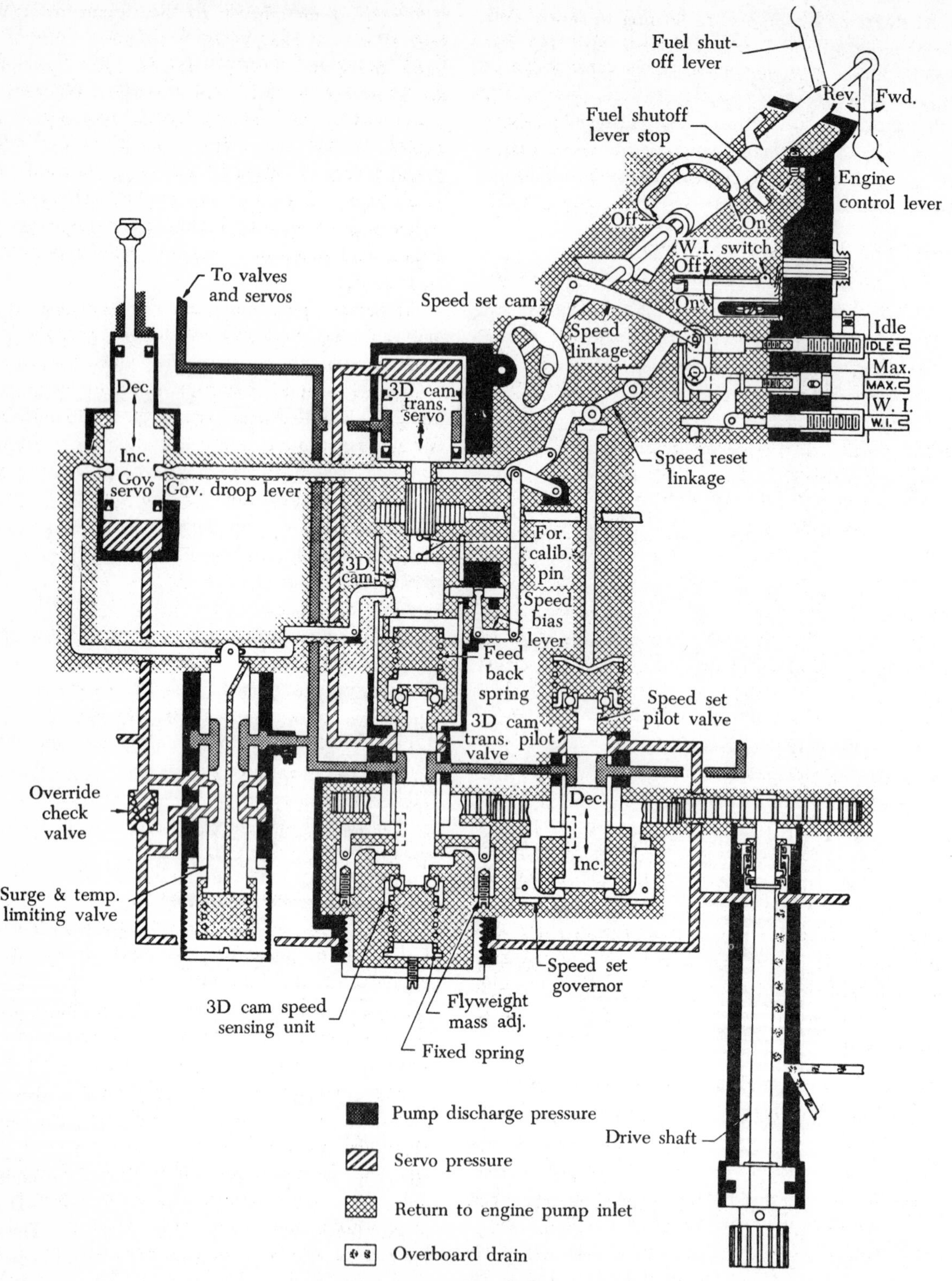
Fuel shut-off lever
Rev.
Fwd.
Fuel shutoff lever stop
Engine control lever
Off
On
W.I. switch
Off
On
Speed set cam
Speed linkage
Idle
IDLE
Max.
MAX.
W. I.
W.I.
To valves and servos
Dec.
Inc.
Gov. servo
Gov. droop lever
3D cam trans. servo
Speed reset linkage
For. calib. pin
3D cam
Speed bias lever
Feed back spring
Speed set pilot valve
3D cam trans. pilot valve
Override check valve
Dec.
Inc.
Surge & temp. limiting valve
Speed set governor
3D cam speed sensing unit
Flyweight mass adj.
Fixed spring
Pump discharge pressure
Servo pressure
Return to engine pump inlet
Overboard drain
Drive shaft

FIGURE 3–51. Scheduling system.

At start, the flyweights are turning so slowly that the speeder spring force is greater than the flyweight force, and the speed-setting pilot valve is moved down. This exposes the governor servo pressure line to body drain, and the high pressure at the opposite end of the governor servo drives the servo downward to increase fuel flow. This action is represented by points 1 and 2 in figure 3–47.

Surge and Temperature Limiting Valve

This limiting valve (figure 3–51) overrides the action of the speed governor during rapid accelerations to ensure that surge and temperature operational limits of the engine are not exceeded. The position of the limiting pilot valve is controlled by a linkage. The linkage is actuated by the governor servo position and by engine r.p.m. and compressor inlet temperature.

During steady state operation, a passage through the limiting valve is open between the speed governor and the governor servo, allowing a flow of fuel so that the governor servo will be controlled by the speed governor. During rapid accelerations, however, the limiting pilot valve is moved to restrict or block this passage. Pressure is thus metered across the land of the limiting pilot valve, which will move the governor servo to control the fuel flow to the engine at the maximum safe rate.

As the engine reaches the set r.p.m., the speed governor will direct high-pressure fuel to the governor servo to decrease fuel flow. Since the passage through the limiting pilot valve may still be blocked, an override check valve is provided so that the high-pressure fuel can bypass the blocked passage, reach the governor servo, and decrease the fuel flow to avoid speed overshoot. As the governor servo moves to decrease fuel flow, the limiting pilot valve will be returned to the "steady state" operating position.

Three-Dimensional Cam and Translating Unit

The three-dimensional cam operates through linkages to provide a speed surge limit input to the surge and temperature limiting valve and a force input to the speed governor speeder spring. The 3–D cam is actually two cams on a common shaft. Two separate contours (cams) have been machined on its surface. One contoured surface biases the surge and temperature limiting valve position. The other cam surface is ineffective in the JFC12–11 fuel control. The 3–D cam and translating unit are shown in figure 3–52.

Engine r.p.m. is sensed by a centrifugal flyweight speed-sensing unit driven by the engine through a gear train. A pilot valve is balanced between a fixed spring and flyweight forces. The flyweights do not move the 3–D cam directly. The cam is positioned by the 3–D cam translational servo connected to the cam. The cam servo has high-pressure fuel (7–50 p.s.i.) acting on its small area at all times. The large area of the 3–D cam servo either is acted upon by high-pressure fuel from the engine fuel pump or is vented to the fuel control body drain.

As engine speed increases, the flyweights move outward. The force of the flyweights plus the feedback spring moves the pilot valve downward, compressing the fixed spring. The pilot valve opens the port from the large area of the 3–D cam servo. When the servo pressure in the chamber is directed to the body drain cavity, the high-pressure fuel acting on the small area lifts the cam servo piston and cam upward. As the cam translates (moves vertically), the force on the feedback spring is decreased. This increases the net force opposing the flyweight force. The result is that the pilot valve re-centers itself and the cam servo stops moving.

When engine speed is reduced, the fixed spring forces the flyweights inward, allowing the fixed spring to displace the pilot valve upward. This directs high-pressure fuel to the cam servo chamber. The servo and the cam move downward. As the cam translates, the increased force on the feedback spring re-centers the pilot valve.

Engine Overspeed Protection

If the r.p.m. signal to the fuel control is disrupted, the speed-set governor will react as though an engine underspeed condition exists. The speeder spring forces the pilot valve down and dumps governor servo pressure. The governor servo calls for more fuel, which tends to overspeed the engine.

The 3–D cam translating pilot valve is also positioned by an r.p.m. signal. With the r.p.m. signal disrupted, the fixed spring pushes the pilot valve upward. High-pressure fuel is directed through the pilot valve and forces the cam servo and 3–D cam downward to the zero % r.p.m. position. The cam contour at zero % r.p.m. provides a known, constant fuel flow. This action prevents the scheduling of excess fuel and protects the engine against overspeed if the fuel control drive fails.

Engine Acceleration

The acceleration schedule is shown as points 4, 5,

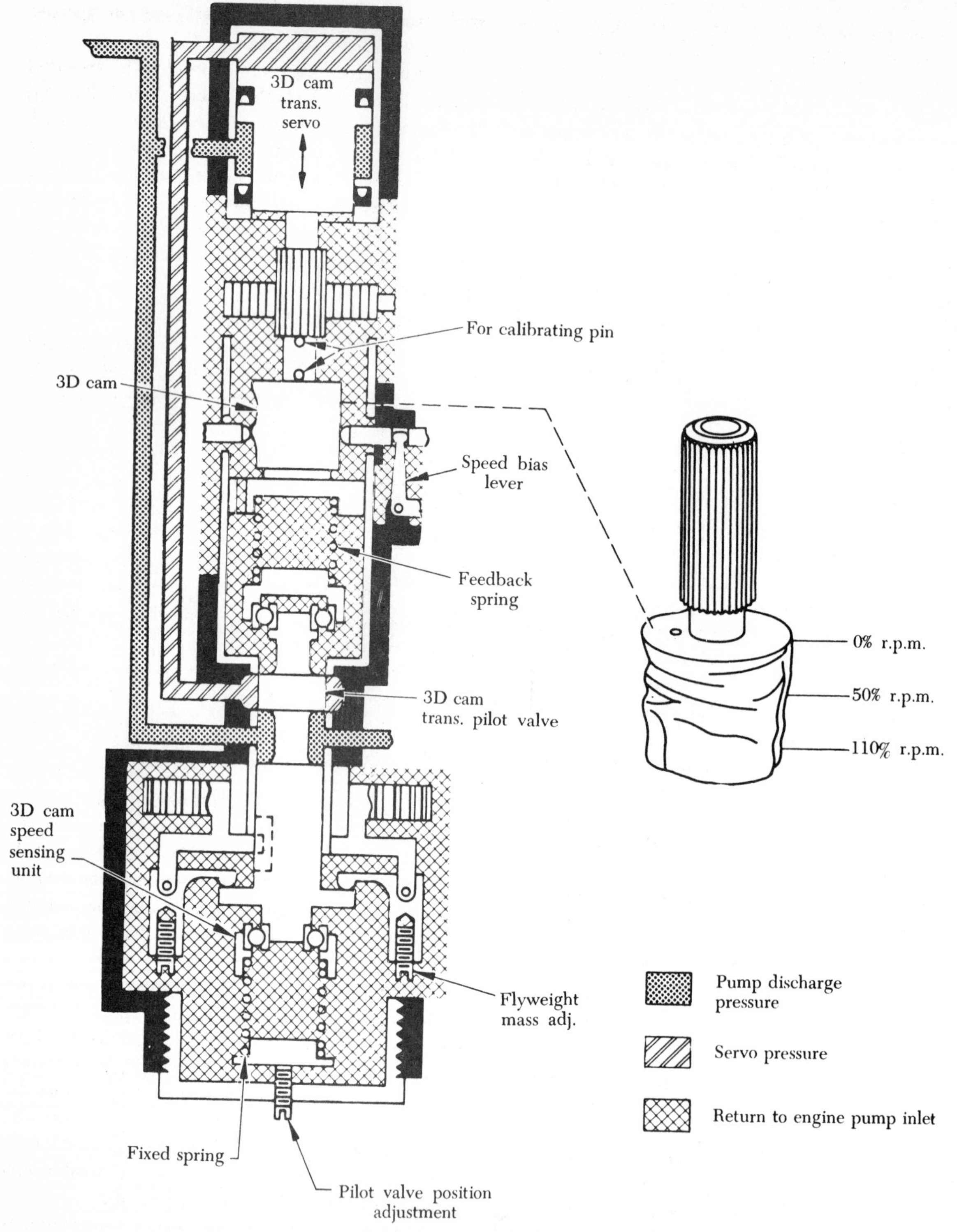

FIGURE 3–52. Three-dimensional cam and translating unit.

6, 7, 8, and 9 in figure 3–47. Governor servo positioning is similar to that of the starting schedule.

At "idle," the engine is operating at the left end of the equilibrium curve at point 4. To initiate acceleration, the power lever in the cockpit is moved toward "takeoff," causing an immediate jump in fuel flow.

As the power lever is moved, the speed-set cam

increases the load on the speeder spring. This increase of speeder spring force causes the speed governor pilot valve to move down, allowing servo pressure to drain from the large area end of the governor servo. High pressure at the opposite end forces the governor servo down to increase fuel/air ratio. This action is represented between points 4 and 5.

Fuel scheduling during acceleration from points 5 and 8 is similar to the operation discussed under starting with the power lever set at idle.

Beyond point 8, governor-droop characteristics reduce the fuel/air ratio as compressor speed increases until equilibrium operation is achieved at point 9.

Engine Deceleration

When deceleration is desired, the power lever in the cockpit is retarded, reducing the speeder spring compression. The speed governor pilot valve moves up (from centrifugal forces), and high-pressure fuel is directed to the underside of the governor servo through the override check valve. This moves the governor servo up to minimum ratio, represented as point 10 in figure 3–47. The fuel flow from point 10 – 11 is determined by the position of the compressor pressure servo. The burner pressure schedules the fuel flow as the engine drops in r.p.m. This continues until the throttle valve itself comes against its minimum flow stop, where it can close no further. This is point 11 – 12 on the curve. The minimum flow limit represents the minimum self-sustaining ability of the engine. The minimum fuel/air ratio is scheduled to avoid the lean flameout areas.

WATER INJECTION RE-SET SYSTEM

On warm days, thrust is reduced because of the decrease in air density. This can be compensated for by injecting water at the compressor inlet or diffuser case. This lowers the air temperature and increases air density. A microswitch in the fuel control is actuated by the control shaft when the power lever is moved toward the maximum power position.

A water injection speed re-set servo, figure 3–53, re-sets the speed adjustment to a higher value during water injection. Without this adjustment, the fuel control would decrease r.p.m. so that no additional thrust would be realized during water injection.

The servo is a shuttle valve which is acted upon by water pressure during water injection. Movement of the servo displaces a lever on the cam-operated lever linkage to the speed governor speeder spring, increasing the force of the speeder spring and increasing the set speed. Because the resulting r.p.m. will usually be higher while water is flowing, increased thrust during water injection is ensured.

If the water injection system is not armed in the cockpit or if there is no water available, nothing happens when the water injection switch in the fuel control unit is actuated. When water is available, a portion of it is directed to the water injection speed re-set servo.

JET FUEL CONTROL MAINTENANCE

The repair of the jet fuel control is very limited. The only repairs permitted in the field are the replacement of the control and adjustments afterwards. These adjustments are limited to the idle r.p.m. and the maximum speed adjustment, commonly called trimming the engine. Both adjustments are made in the normal range of operation.

During engine trimming the fuel control is checked for idle r.p.m., maximum r.p.m., acceleration, and deceleration. The procedures used to check the fuel control vary depending on the aircraft and engine installation.

The engine is trimmed in accordance with the procedures in the maintenance or overhaul manual for a particular engine. In general, the procedure consists of obtaining the ambient air temperature and the field barometric pressure (not sea level) immediately preceding the trimming of the engine. Care must be taken to obtain a true temperature reading comparable to that of the air which will enter the engine. Using these readings, the desired turbine discharge pressure or EPR (engine pressure ratio) reading is computed from charts published in the maintenance manual.

The engine is operated at full throttle (or at the fuel control trim stop) for a sufficient period of time to ensure that it has completely stabilized. Five minutes is the usual recommended stabilization period. A check should be made to ensure that the compressor air-bleed valves have fully closed and that all accessory drive air bleed for which the trim curve has not been corrected (such as a cabin air-conditioning unit) has been turned off.

When the engine has stabilized, a comparison is made of the observed and the computed turbine discharge pressure (or EPR) to determine the approximate amount of trimming required. If a trim is necessary, the engine fuel control is then adjusted to obtain the target turbine discharge pressure or EPR on the gage. Immediately following

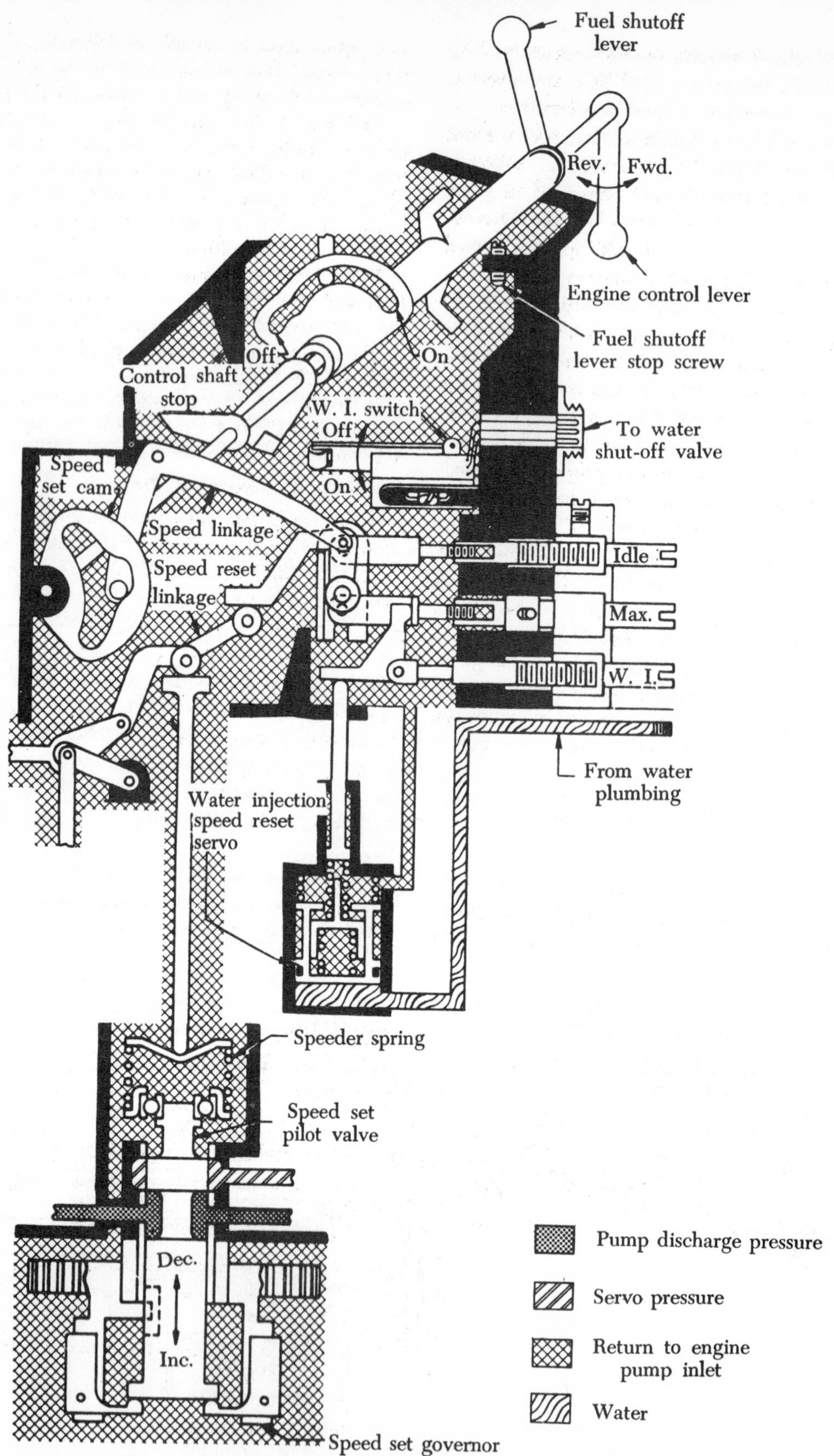
Fuel shutoff lever
Rev.
Fwd.
Engine control lever
Fuel shutoff lever stop screw
Off
On
Control shaft stop
W. I. switch
Off
On
To water shut-off valve
Speed set cam
Speed linkage
Speed reset linkage
Idle
Max.
W. I.
From water plumbing
Water injection speed reset servo
Speeder spring
Speed set pilot valve
Dec.
Inc.
Speed set governor
Pump discharge pressure
Servo pressure
Return to engine pump inlet
Water

FIGURE 3–53. **Water injection re-set system.**

the fuel control adjustment, the tachometer reading is observed and recorded. Fuel flow and exhaust gas temperature readings should also be taken.

On Pratt and Whitney engines, using a dual-spool compressor, the observed N_2 tachometer reading is next corrected for speed bias by means of temperature/r.p.m. curve. The observed tachometer reading is divided by the percent trim speed obtained from the curve. The result is the new engine trim speed in percent, corrected to standard day (59° F. or 15° C.) temperature. The new trim speed in r.p.m. may be calculated when the r.p.m. at which the tachometer reads 100% is known. This value may be obtained from the appropriate engine manual. If all these procedures have been performed satisfactorily, the engine has been properly trimmed.

Engine trimming should always be carried out under precisely controlled conditions with the aircraft headed into the wind. Precise control is necessary to ensure maintenance of a minimum thrust level upon which the aircraft performance is based. In addition, precise control of engine trimming contributes to better engine life in terms of both maximum time between overhaul and minimum out-of-commission time due to engine maintenance requirements. Engines should never be trimmed if icing conditions exist.

ENGINE FUEL SYSTEM COMPONENTS

Main Fuel Pumps (Engine-Driven)

Main fuel pumps deliver a continuous supply of fuel at the proper pressure and at all times during operation of the aircraft engine. The engine-driven fuel pumps must be capable of delivering the maximum needed flow at high pressure to obtain satisfactory nozzle spray and accurate fuel regulation.

Fuel pumps for turbojet engines are generally positive displacement gear or piston types. The term "positive displacement" means that the gear or piston will supply a fixed quantity of fuel to the engine for every revolution of the pump gears or for each stroke of the piston.

These fuel pumps may be divided into two distinct system categories: (1) Constant displacement and (2) variable displacement. Their use depends on the system used to regulate the flow of fuel to the fuel controls. This may be a pressure relief valve (barometric unit) for constant displacement (gear) pumps, or a method for regulating pump output in the variable displacement (piston) pumps.

Constant Displacement Pump

Gear-type pumps have approximately straight line flow characteristics, whereas fuel requirements fluctuate with flight or ambient air conditions. Hence, a pump of adequate capacity at all engine operating conditions will have excess capacity over most of the range of operation. This is the characteristic which requires the use of a pressure relief valve for disposing of excess fuel. A typical constant displacement gear-type pump is illustrated in figure 3–54. The impeller, which is driven at a greater speed than the high-pressure elements, increases the fuel pressure from 15 to 45 p.s.i., depending upon engine speed.

The fuel is discharged from the boost element (impeller) to the two high-pressure gear elements. Each of these elements discharges fuel through a

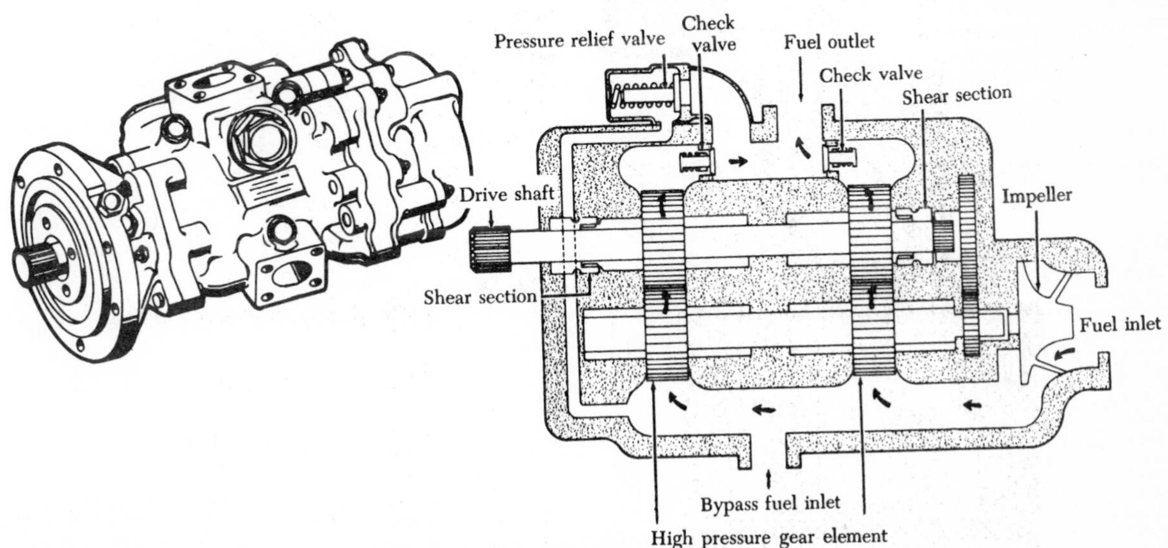

FIGURE 3–54. Engine-driven fuel pump.

check valve to a common discharge port. The high-pressure elements deliver approximately 51 gallons per minute at a discharge pressure of 850 p.s.i.g.

Shear sections are incorporated in the drive systems of each element. Thus, if one element fails, the other element continues to operate. The check valves prevent circulation through the inoperative element. One element can supply enough fuel to maintain moderate aircraft speeds.

A relief valve is incorporated in the discharge port of the pump. This valve opens at approximately 900 p.s.i. and is capable of bypassing the total flow at 960 p.s.i. This allows fuel in excess of that required for engine operation to be recirculated. The bypass fuel is routed to the inlet side of the two high-pressure elements.

Variable Displacement Pump

The variable displacement pump system differs from the constant displacement pump system. Pump displacement is changed to meet varying fuel flow requirements; that is, the amount of fuel discharged from the pump can be made to vary at any one speed. With a pump of variable flow, the applicable fuel control unit can automatically and accurately regulate the pump pressure and delivery to the engine.

Where variable displacement pumps are installed, two similar pumps are provided, connected in parallel. Either pump can carry the load if the other fails during normal parallel operations. At times one pump may be insufficient to meet power requirements. Pump duplication increases safety in operation, especially during takeoffs and landings.

The positive displacement, variable-stroke type pump incorporates a rotor, a piston, a maximum speed governor, and a relief valve mechanism.

Fuel Heater

Gas turbine engine fuel systems are very susceptible to the formation of ice in the fuel filters. When the fuel in the aircraft fuel tanks cools to 32° F., or below, residual water in the fuel tends to freeze when it contacts the filter screen.

A fuel heater operates as a heat exchanger to warm the fuel. The heater can use engine bleed air or engine lubricating oil as a source of heat. The former type is called an air-to-liquid exchanger, and the latter type is known as a liquid-to-liquid exchanger.

The function of a fuel heater is to protect the engine fuel system from ice formation. However, should ice form, the heater can also be used to thaw ice on the fuel screen.

In some installations the fuel filter is fitted with a pressure-drop warning switch, which illuminates a warning light on the cockpit instrument panel. If ice begins to collect on the filter surface, the pressure across the filter will slowly decrease. When the pressure reaches a predetermined value, the warning light flashes on.

Fuel deicing systems are designed to be used intermittently. The control of the system may be manual, by a switch in the cockpit, or automatic, using a thermostatic sensing element in the fuel heater to open or close the air or oil shutoff valve. A fuel heater that is automatic in operation is illustrated in figure 3–55.

Fuel Filters

A low-pressure filter is installed between the supply tanks and the engine fuel system to protect the engine-driven fuel pump and various control devices. An additional high-pressure fuel filter is installed between the fuel pump and the fuel control to protect the fuel control from contaminants.

The three most common types of filters in use are the micron filter, the wafer screen filter, and the plain screen mesh filter. The individual use of each of these filters is dictated by the filtering treatment required at a particular location.

The micron filter (figure 3–56) has the greatest filtering action of any present-day filter type and, as the name implies, is rated in microns. (A micron is the thousandth part of 1 millimeter.) The porous cellulose material frequently used in construction of the filter cartridges is capable of removing foreign matter measuring from 10 to 25 microns. The minute openings make this type of filter susceptible to clogging; therefore, a bypass valve is a necessary safety factor.

Since the micron filter does such a thorough job of removing foreign matter, it is especially valuable between the fuel tank and engine. The cellulose material also absorbs water, preventing it from passing through the pumps. If water does seep through the filter, which happens occasionally when filter elements become saturated with water, the water can and does quickly damage the working elements of the fuel pump and control units, since these elements depend solely on the fuel for their lubrication. To reduce water damage to pumps and control units, periodic servicing and replacement of filter elements is imperative! Daily draining of fuel tank sumps and low-pressure filters will eliminate much filter trouble and prevent undue maintenance of pumps and fuel control units.

The most widely used filter is the 200-mesh and

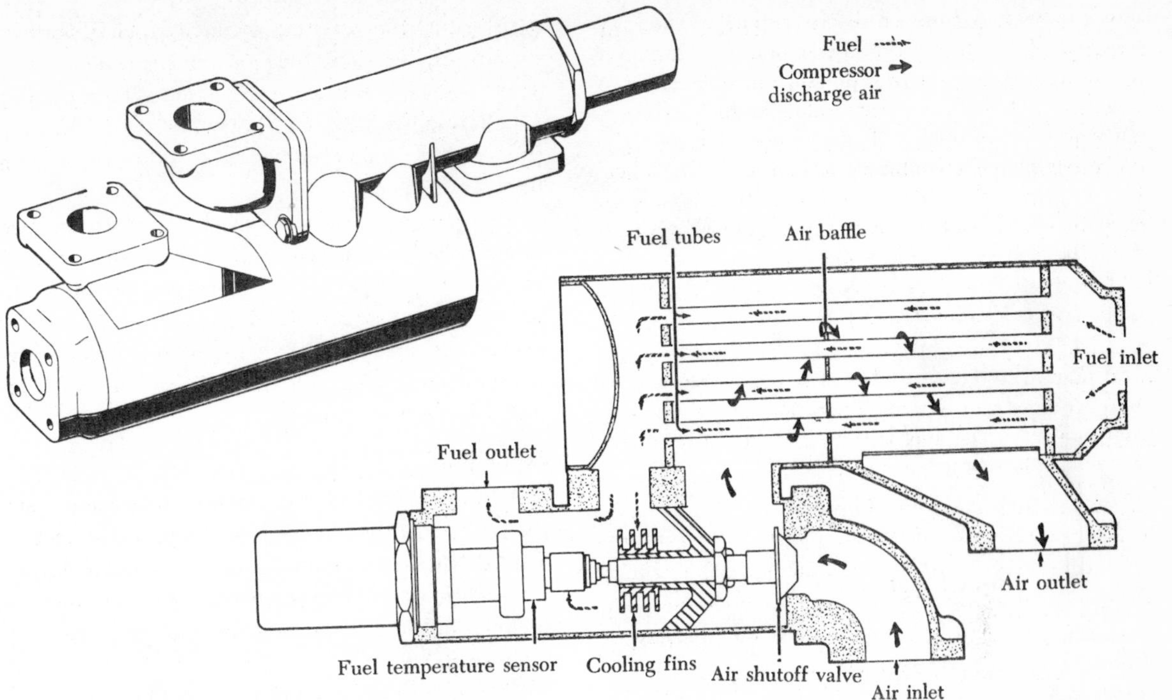

FIGURE 3–55. Fuel heater.

the 35-mesh micron filters. They are used in fuel pumps, fuel controls, and between the fuel pump and fuel control where removal of micronic-size particles is needed. These filters, usually made of fine-mesh steel wire, are a series of layers of wire.

The wafer screen type of filter (figure 3–57) has a replaceable element, which is made of layers of screen disks of bronze, brass, steel, or similar material. This type of filter is capable of removing micronic-size particles. It also has the strength to withstand high pressure.

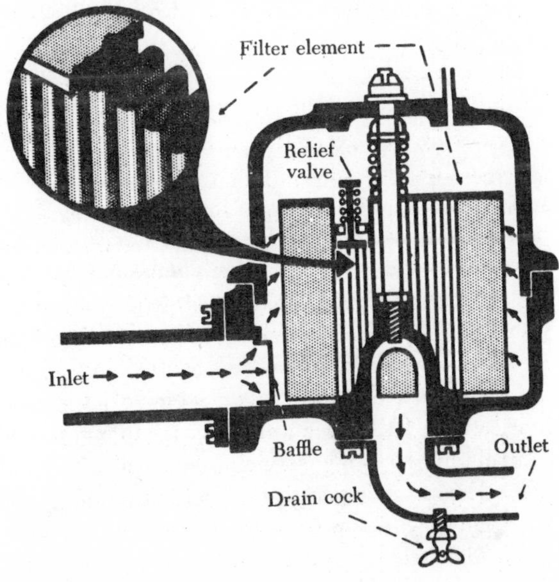

FIGURE 3–56. Aircraft fuel filter.

The plain screen mesh filter is the most common type. It has long been used in internal-combustion engines of all types for fuel and oil strainers. In present-day turbojet engines it is used in units where filtering action is not so critical, such as in fuel lines before the high-pressure pump filters. The mesh size of this type of filter varies greatly according to the purpose for which it is used.

Fuel Spray Nozzles and Fuel Manifolds

Although fuel spray nozzles are an integral part of the fuel system, their design is closely related to the type of combustion chamber in which they are installed. The fuel nozzles inject fuel into the combustion area in a highly atomized, precisely patterned spray so that burning is completed evenly and in the shortest possible time and in the smallest possible space. It is very important that the fuel be evenly distributed and well centered in the flame area within the liners. This is to preclude the formation of any hot spots in the combustion chambers and to prevent the flame burning through the liner.

Fuel nozzle types vary considerably between engines, although for the most part fuel is sprayed into the combustion area under pressure through small orifices in the nozzles. The two types of fuel nozzles

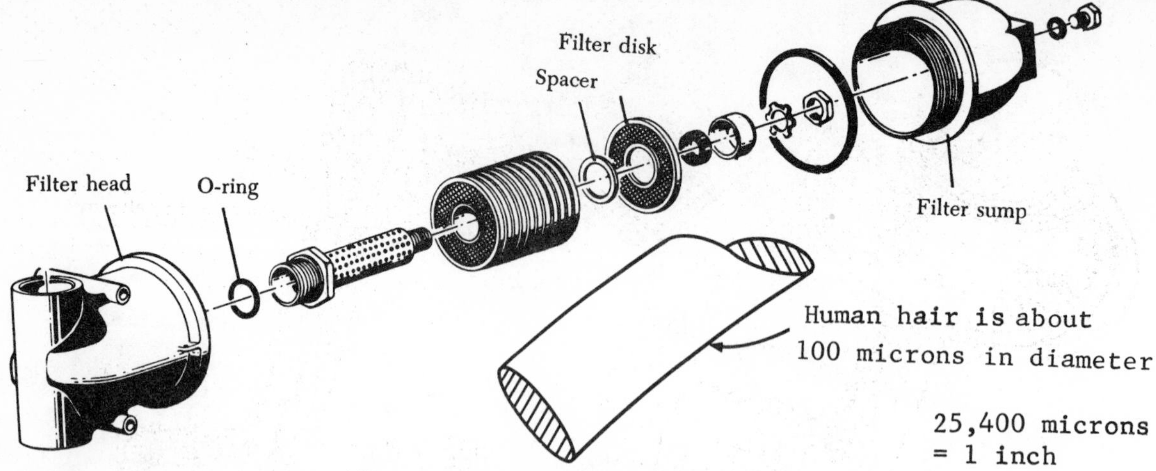

FIGURE 3–57. Wafer screen filter.

generally used are the simplex and the duplex configurations. The duplex nozzle usually requires a dual manifold and a pressurizing valve or flow divider for dividing primary and main fuel flow, but the simplex nozzle requires only a single manifold for proper fuel delivery.

The fuel nozzles can be constructed to be installed in various ways. The two methods used quite frequently are: (1) External mounting wherein a mounting pad is provided for attachment of the nozzles to the case or the inlet air elbow, with the nozzle near the dome; or (2) internal mounting at the liner dome, in which case the chamber cover must be removed for replacement or maintenance of the nozzle.

Simplex Fuel Nozzle

The simplex fuel nozzle was the first type nozzle used in turbojet engines and was replaced in most installations with the duplex nozzle, which gave better atomization at starting and idling speeds. The simplex nozzle (figure 3–58) is still being used to a limited degree. Each of the simplex nozzles consists of a nozzle tip, an insert, and a strainer made up of fine-mesh screen and a support.

Duplex Fuel Nozzle

The duplex fuel nozzle is the nozzle most widely used in present-day gas turbine engines. As mentioned previously, its use requires a flow divider, but at the same time it offers a desirable spray pattern for combustion over a wide range of operating pressures. A nozzle typical of this type is illustrated in figure 3–59.

Flow Divider

A flow divider in each nozzle creates primary and secondary fuel supplies which are discharged through separate, concentric spray tips, thus providing the proper spray angle at all fuel flows. Fuel enters the inlet of the nozzle and passes through a screen. A drilled passage in the nozzle stem directs the fuel through a second screen and into the primary spin chamber. The entry ports to the spin chamber are drilled to cause an abrupt change in direction of the fuel as it enters the chamber, thus, imparting a spinning motion to the fuel. The spinning motion of the fuel establishes the spray angle and aids in atomization of the fuel for better combustion. Fuel from the spin chamber is discharged through the primary spray tip into the combustion liner.

Operating Principle

When fuel pressure reaches approximately 90 p.s.i.g., the pressure opens the flow divider and fuel is directed into a second drilled passage in the stem. Fuel from the secondary passage is directed into the secondary spin chamber. Spinning fuel from the secondary spin chamber is discharged through the secondary spray tip into the combustion liners. Figure 3–60 illustrates the spray pattern of a typical duplex nozzle.

A small quantity of air is scooped out of the main airstream by the shroud around the nozzle tip, to cool the nozzle tip. In addition, the cooling airflow improves combustion by retarding the accumulation of carbon deposits on the face of the nozzle, and by providing some of the air for combustion, which

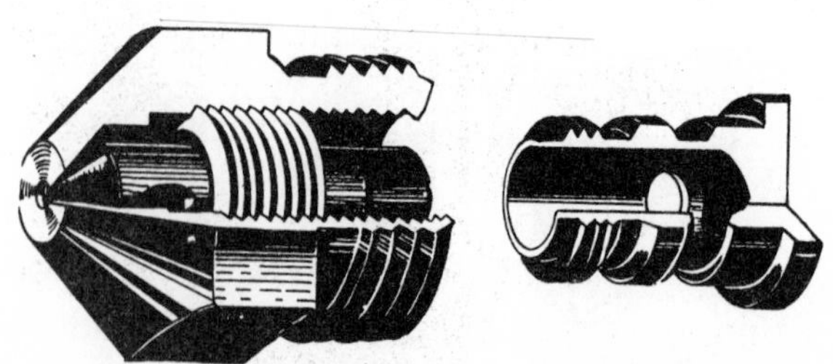

FIGURE 3–58. A typical simplex fuel nozzle.

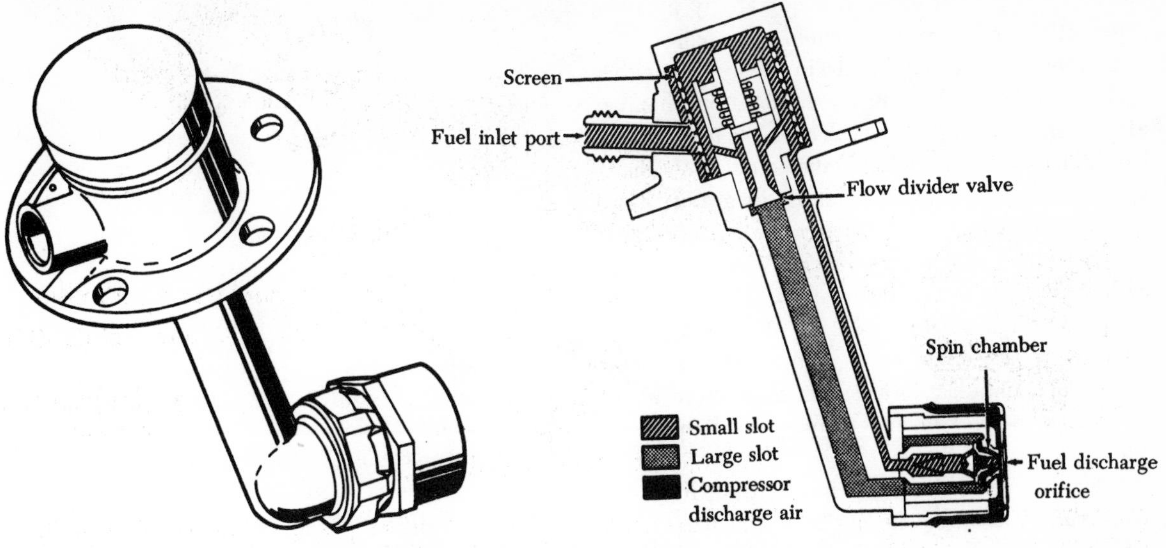

FIGURE 3–59. Duplex fuel nozzle.

helps contain the fire in the center of the liner.

Fuel Pressurizing and Dump Valves

The fuel pressurizing valve is usually required on engines incorporating duplex fuel nozzles to divide the flow into primary and main manifolds. At the fuel flows required for starting and altitude idling, all the fuel passes through the primary line. As the fuel flow increases, the valve begins to open the main line until at maximum flow the main line is passing approximately 90% of the fuel.

Fuel pressurizing valves will usually trap fuel forward of the manifold, giving a positive cutoff. This cutoff prevents fuel from dribbling into the manifold and through the fuel nozzles, eliminating to a major degree after-fires and carbonization of the fuel nozzles. Carbonization occurs because combustion chamber temperatures are lowered and the fuel is not completely burned.

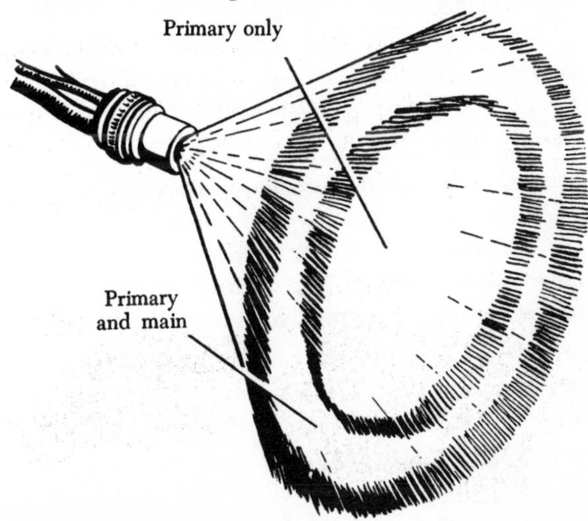

FIGURE 3–60. Duplex nozzle spray pattern.

A typical example of this arrangement is the fuel pressurizing and dump valve used on the Pratt and Whitney JT3 engine. This valve performs two major functions as indicated by its name: (1) During engine operation it divides metered fuel flow into two portions, primary and secondary, as required for atomization at the fuel nozzles; and (2) at engine shutdown it provides a dump system which connects the fuel manifolds to an overboard drain.

A flow divider performs essentially the same function as a pressurizing valve. It is used, as the name implies, to divide flow to the duplex fuel nozzles. It is not unusual for units performing identical functions to have different nomenclature between engines.

Drain Valves

The drain valves are units used for draining fuel from the various components of the engine where accumulated fuel is most likely to present operating problems. The possibility of combustion chamber accumulation with the resultant fire hazard is one problem. A residual problem is leaving lead and/or gum deposits, after evaporation, in such places as fuel manifolds and fuel nozzles.

In some instances the fuel manifolds are drained by an individual unit known as a drip or dump valve. This type of valve may operate by pressure differential, or it may be solenoid operated.

The combustion chamber drain valve drains either fuel which accumulates in the combustion chamber after each shutdown or fuel that may have accumulated during a false start. If the combustion chambers are the can type, fuel will drain by gravity down through the flame tubes or interconnecter tubes until it gathers in the lower chambers, which are fitted with drain lines to the drain valve. If the combustion chamber is of the basket or annular type, the fuel will merely drain through the airholes in the liner and accumulate in a trap in the bottom of the chamber housing, which is connected to the drain line.

After the fuel accumulates in the drain lines, the drain valve allows the fuel to be drained whenever pressure within the manifold or the burner(s) has been reduced to near atmospheric pressure. It is imperative that this valve be in good working condition to drain accumulated fuel after each shutdown. Otherwise, a hot start during the next starting attempt or an after-fire after shutdown is likely to occur.

FUEL QUANTITY INDICATING UNITS

Fuel quantity units vary from one installation to the next. A fuel counter or indicator, mounted on the instrument panel, is electrically connected to a flowmeter installed in the fuel line to the engine.

The fuel counter, or totalizer, is similar in appearance to an automobile odometer. When the aircraft is serviced with fuel, the counter is manually set to the total number of pounds of fuel in all tanks. As fuel passes through the measuring element of the flowmeter, it sends electrical impulses to the fuel counter. These impulses actuate the fuel counter mechanism so that the number of pounds passing to the engine is subtracted from the original reading. Thus, the fuel counter continually shows the total quantity of fuel, in pounds, remaining in the aircraft. However, there are certain conditions which will cause the fuel counter indication to be inaccurate. Any jettisoned fuel is indicated on the fuel counter as fuel still available for use. Any fuel which leaks from a tank or a fuel line upstream of the flowmeter is not counted.

WATER OR COOLANT INJECTION

The sensitivity of turbine engines to compressor inlet temperature results in an appreciable loss of available thrust, or power in the case of a turboprop engine, on a hot day. It is sometimes necessary to augment the thrust output. Water injection is a means of increasing engine thrust. It reduces hot section temperatures, fuel flow can be increased and greater thrust thereby obtained.

Thrust increase is particularly desirable at takeoff when an aircraft engine is called upon for the greatest output of power, therefore the water injection system is designed to function only at high engine power.

The effect upon engine thrust depends upon the type of coolant used, the proportion of the ingredients, and the quantity of the coolant flow. For effective cooling, a liquid with a high heat of vaporization is required. Water, is the most desirable coolant. Alcohol is added occasionally in varying proportions, either to lower the freezing point of the coolant or to eliminate the need for separate enrichment of the fuel mixture, which might be necessary if only pure water were used. When alcohol is added, some small amount of additional thrust may be produced as the alcohol is burned. However, the efficiency of the combustion of the alcohol is usually quite low. The heating value of methyl or ethyl alcohol is only about half that of kerosene or gasoline. Most of the flow of the alcohol/air mixture will not pass through that part of the combustion zone where temperatures are high enough to support efficient combustion of the weak alcohol/air mixture.

Very few powerplants using water injection are in use today.

Water Injection System Operation

A typical dual water injection system is illustrated in figure 3–61. The dual system is actually two independent systems. One system injects water at the compressor inlet section of the engine. Thrust is augmented largely through the effect of increasing mass airflow. The other system injects water into the engine diffuser case. This system increases thrust largely through the cooling principle which permits higher fuel flows.

The water injection system is designed for dual operation at ambient temperatures above 40° F. (5° C.). At temperatures up to 40° F., compressor inlet injection should not be used because of the hazardous inlet icing that could occur.

Water from the aircraft tank system is routed to two shutoff valves which govern flow to the two water injection controls. The shutoff valves are armed by the actuation of a cockpit switch. The selected valve(s) open or close upon receipt of an electrical signal from the fuel control water injection switch. With the power lever advanced to takeoff, this switch supplies an "open" signal to the selected shutoff valve(s). Conversely, when the power lever is retarded below the water turn-on point, the switch supplies a "close" signal to the shutoff valve(s).

Water from the open shutoff valve flows to the water injection controls. Since the water injection system is used only when power settings are at, or near, their maximum, the controls do not vary or meter water flow. Instead, they maintain a constant pressure head across a fixed orifice, thereby maintaining a constant water flow to the engine.

Water from the compressor inlet water injection control is directed to a manifold and is sprayed directly into the compressor at this point. Water from the diffuser case control passes through a check valve and is then directed to a split manifold from which it is sprayed into the diffuser case. When the water injection system is not in use, the check valve prevents high-temperature compressor discharge air from backing up into the water injection system plumbing, where it might damage the controls or valves.

Drain valves located downstream of the water shutoff valves drain the engine water lines when the injection system is turned off, thus preventing water from freezing in these lines.

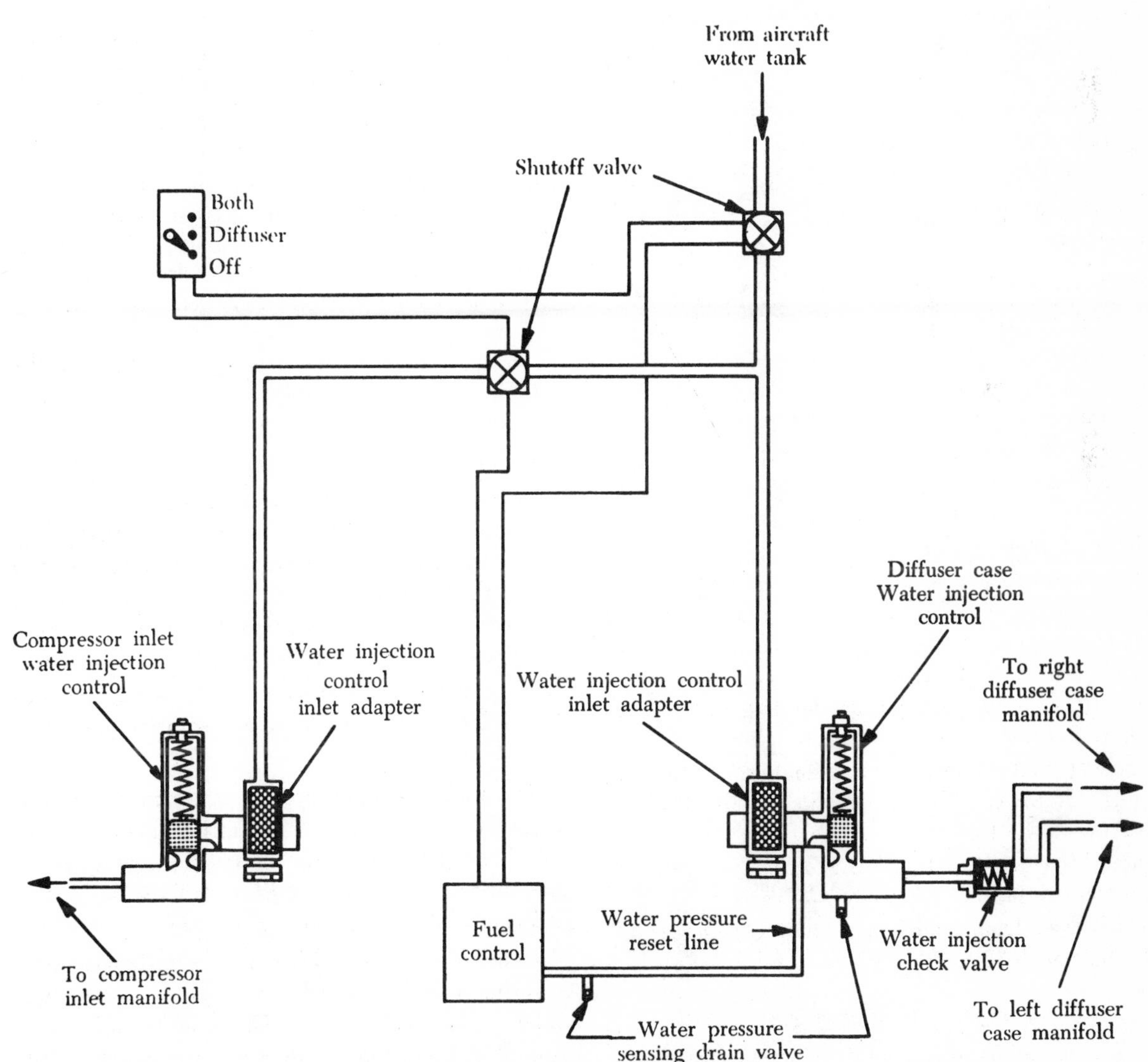

FIGURE 3–61. A typical water injection system.

CHAPTER 4

ENGINE IGNITION AND ELECTRICAL SYSTEMS

RECIPROCATING ENGINE IGNITION SYSTEMS

The basic requirements for reciprocating engine ignition systems are the same, regardless of the type of engine involved or the make of the components of the ignition system. All ignition systems must deliver a high-tension spark to each cylinder of the engine in firing order at a predetermined number of degrees ahead of the top dead center position of the piston. The voltage output of the system must be such that the spark will jump the gap in the spark plug under all operating conditions.

Ignition systems can be divided into two classifications: battery-ignition or magneto-ignition systems.

Ignition systems are also classified as either single- or dual-ignition systems. The single-ignition system, usually consisting of one magneto and the necessary wiring, was used on most small-volume, slow-speed engines. The single-ignition system is still in use on a few small, opposed-type light aircraft engines.

BATTERY IGNITION SYSTEM

A few aircraft still use a battery ignition system. In this system, the source of energy is a battery or generator, rather than a magneto. This system is similar to that used in most automobiles. A cam driven by the engine opens a set of points to interrupt the flow of current in a primary circuit. The resulting collapsing magnetic field induces a high voltage in the secondary of the ignition coil, which is directed by a distributor to the proper cylinder. Figure 4–1 shows a simplified schematic of a battery ignition system.

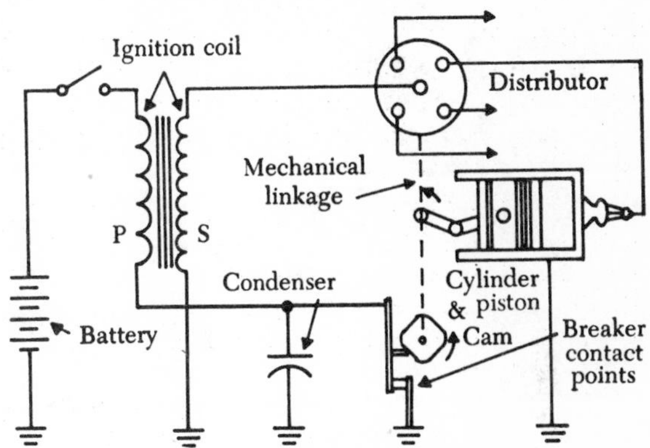

FIGURE 4–1. Battery ignition system.

MAGNETO IGNITION SYSTEM OPERATING PRINCIPLES

The magneto, a special type of engine-driven a.c. generator, uses a permanent magnet as a source of energy. The magneto develops the high voltage which forces a spark to jump across the spark plug gap in each cylinder. Magneto operation is timed to the engine so that a spark occurs only when the piston is on the proper stroke at a specified number of crankshaft degrees before the top-dead-center piston position.

Aircraft magneto ignition systems can be classified as either high tension or low tension. The low-tension magneto system, covered in a later section of this chapter, generates a low voltage, which is distributed to a transformer coil near each spark plug. This system eliminates some problems inherent in the high-tension system.

The high-tension magneto system is the older of the two systems and, despite some disadvantages, is still the most widely used aircraft ignition system.

High-Tension Magneto System

The high-tension magneto system can be divided, for purposes of discussion, into three distinct circuits. These are: (1) The magnetic, (2) the primary electrical, and (3) the secondary electrical circuits.

The magnetic circuit consists of a permanent multipole rotating magnet, a soft iron core, and pole shoes. The magnet is geared to the aircraft engine and rotates in the gap between two pole shoes to furnish the magnetic lines of force (flux) necessary to produce an electrical voltage. The poles of the magnet are arranged in alternate polarity so that the flux can pass out of the north pole

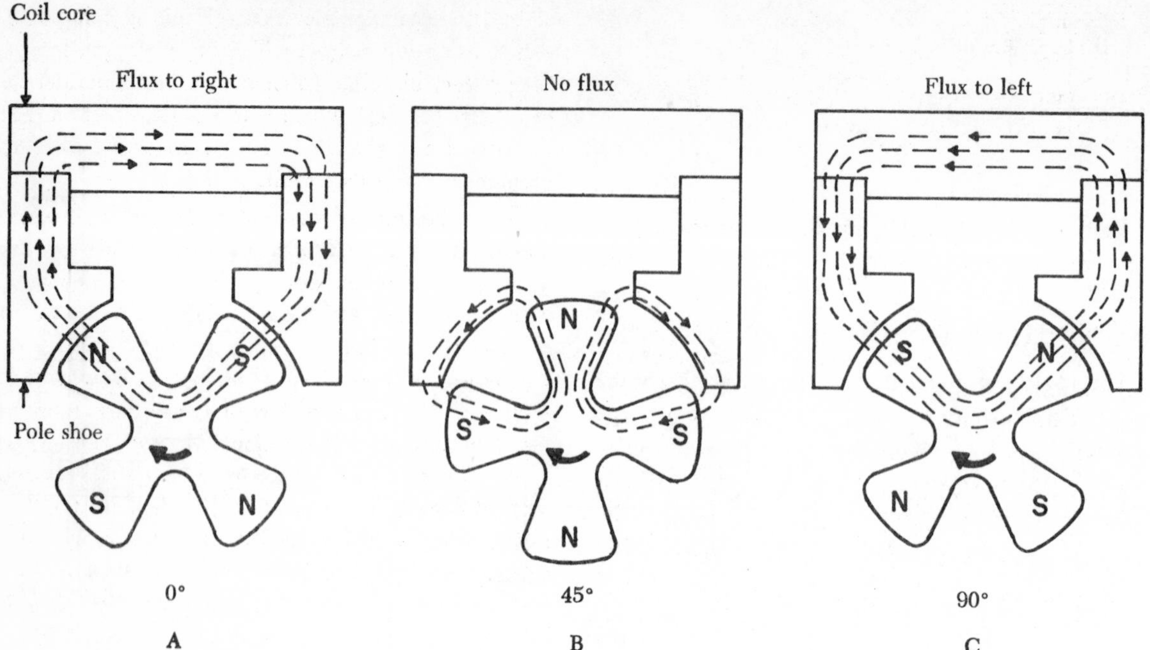

FIGURE 4–2. Magnetic flux at three positions of the rotating magnet.

through the coil core and back to the south pole of the magnet. When the magnet is in the position shown in A of figure 4–2, the number of magnetic lines of force through the coil core is maximum because two magnetically opposite poles are perfectly aligned with the pole shoes.

This position of the rotating magnet is called the "full-register" position and produces a maximum number of magnetic lines of force (flux flow) clockwise through the magnetic circuit and from left to right through the coil core. When the magnet is moved away from the full register position, the amount of flux passing through the coil core begins to decrease. This results because the magnet's poles are moving away from the pole shoes, allowing some lines of flux to take a shorter path through the ends of the pole shoes.

As the magnet moves farther and farther from the full-register position, more and more lines of flux are short-circuited through the pole-shoe ends. Finally, at the neutral position (45° from the full-register position) all flux lines are short-circuited, and no flux flows through the coil core (B of figure 4–2). As the magnet moves from full register to the neutral position, the number of flux lines through the coil core decreases in the same manner as the gradual collapse of flux in the magnetic field of an ordinary electromagnet.

The neutral position of the magnet is that position where one of the poles of the magnet is centered between the pole shoes of the magnetic circuit. As the magnet is moved clockwise from this position, the lines of flux that had been short-circuited through the pole-shoe ends begin to flow through the coil core again. But this time the flux lines flow through the coil core in the opposite direction, as shown in C of figure 4–2. The flux flow reverses as the magnet moves out of the neutral position because the north pole of the rotating permanent magnet is opposite the right pole shoe instead of the left, as illustrated in A of figure 4–2.

When the magnet is again moved a total of 90°, another full-register position is reached, with a maximum flux flow in the opposite direction. The 90° of magnet travel is illustrated graphically in figure 4–3, where a curve shows how the flux density in the coil core (without a primary coil around the core) changes as the magnet is rotated.

Figure 4–3 shows that as the magnet moves from the full-register position (0°), flux flow decreases and reaches a zero value as it moves into the neutral position (45°). While the magnet moves through the neutral position, flux flow reverses and begins to increase as indicated by the curve below the horizontal line. At the 90° position another position of maximum flux is reached. Thus, for one revolution (360°) of the four-pole magnet, there will be four positions of maximum flux, four positions of zero flux, and four flux reversals.

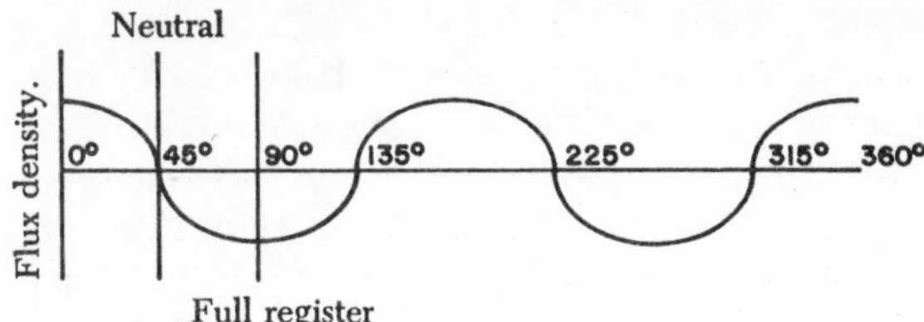

FIGURE 4–3. Change in flux density as magnet rotates.

This discussion of the magnetic circuit demonstrates how the coil core is affected by the rotating magnet. It is subjected to an increasing and decreasing magnetic field, and a change in polarity each 90° of magnet travel.

When a coil of wire as part of the magneto's primary electrical circuit is wound around the coil core, it is also affected by the varying magnetic field.

The primary electrical circuit (figure 4–4) consists of a set of breaker contact points, a condenser, and an insulated coil.

The coil is made up of a few turns of heavy copper wire, one end of which is grounded to the coil core, and the other end to the ungrounded side of the breaker points. (See figure 4–4.) The primary circuit is complete only when the ungrounded breaker point contacts the grounded breaker point. The third unit in the circuit, the condenser (capacitor), is wired in parallel with the breaker points. The condenser prevents arcing at the points when the circuit is opened, and hastens the collapse of the magnetic field about the primary coil.

The primary breaker closes at approximately full-register position. When the breaker points are closed, the primary electrical circuit is completed, and the rotating magnet will induce current flow in the primary circuit. This current flow generates its own magnetic field, which is in such a direction that it opposes any change in the magnetic flux of the permanent magnet's circuit.

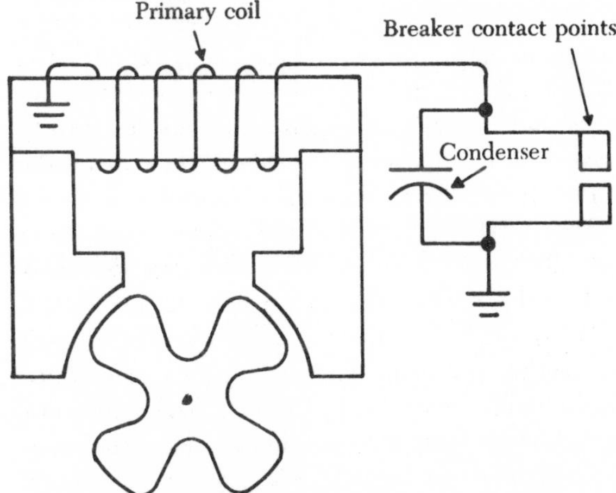

FIGURE 4–4. Primary electrical circuit of a high-tension magneto.

While the induced current is flowing in the primary circuit, it will oppose any decrease in the magnetic flux in the core. This is in accordance with Lenz's law, stated as follows: "An induced current always flows in such a direction that its magnetism opposes the motion or the change that induced it." (For a review of Lenz's law, refer to the Airframe and Powerplant Mechanics General Handbook, AC 65–9, Chapter 8.) Thus, the current flowing in the primary circuit holds the flux in the core at a high value in one direction until the rotating magnet has time to rotate through the neutral position, to a point a few degrees beyond neutral. This position is called the E-gap position (E stands for "efficiency").

With the magnetic rotor in E-gap position and the primary coil holding the magnetic field of the magnetic circuit in the opposite polarity, a very high rate of flux change can be obtained by opening the primary breaker points. Opening the breaker points stops the flow of current in the primary circuit, and allows the magnetic rotor to quickly reverse the field through the coil core. This sudden flux reversal produces a high rate of flux change in the core, which cuts across the secondary coil of the magneto (wound over and insulated from the primary coil), inducing the pulse of high-voltage current in the secondary needed to fire a spark plug. As the rotor continues to rotate to approximately full-register position, the primary breaker points close again and the cycle is repeated to fire the next spark plug in firing order.

The sequence of events can now be reviewed in greater detail to explain how the state of extreme magnetic stress occurs.

With the breaker points, cam, and condenser connected in the circuit as shown in figure 4–5, the action that takes place as the magnetic rotor turns is depicted by the graph curve in figure 4–6. At the top (A) of figure 4–6 the original static flux curve of the magnets is shown. Shown below the static flux curve is the sequence of opening and closing the magneto breaker points. Note that opening and closing the breaker points is timed by the breaker cam. The points close when a maximum amount of flux is passing through the coil core and open at a

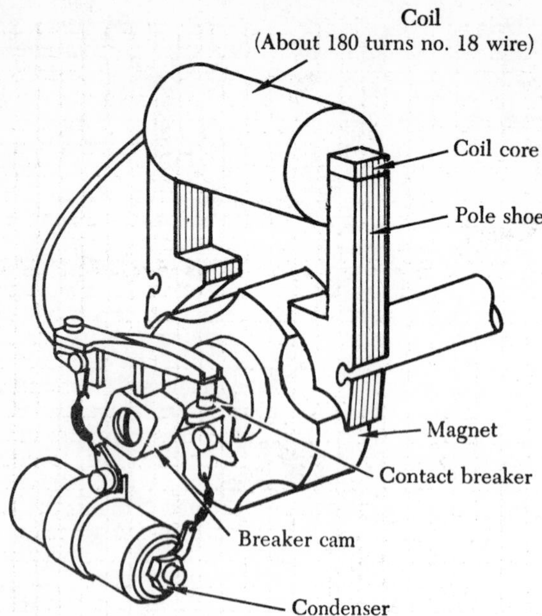

FIGURE 4–5. Components of a high-tension magneto circuit.

position after neutral. Since there are four lobes on the cam, the breaker points will close and open in the same relation to each of the four neutral positions of the rotor magnet. Also, the point opening and point closing intervals are approximately equal.

Starting at the maximum flux position (marked "0°" at the top of figure 4–6), the sequence of events in the following paragraphs occurs.

As the magnet rotor is turned toward the neutral position, the amount of flux through the core starts to decrease (D of figure 4–6). This change in flux linkages induces a current in the primary winding (C of figure 4–6). This induced current creates a magnetic field of its own. This magnetic field opposes the change of flux linkages inducing the current. Without current flowing in the primary coil, the flux in the coil core decreases to zero as the magnet rotor turns to neutral, and starts to increase in the opposite direction (dotted static flux curve in D of figure 4–6). But the electromagnetic action of the primary current prevents the flux from changing and temporarily holds the field instead of allowing it to change (resultant flux line in D of figure 4–6).

As a result of the holding process, there is a very high stress in the magnetic circuit by the time the magnet rotor has reached the position where the breaker points are about to open.

The breaker points, when opened, function with the condenser to interrupt the flow of current in the primary coil, causing an extremely rapid change in flux linkages. The high voltage in the secondary winding discharges across the gap in the spark plug to ignite the fuel/air mixture in the engine cylinder Each spark actually consists of one peak discharge, after which a series of small oscillations takes place. They continue to occur until the voltage becomes too low to maintain the discharge. Current flows in the secondary winding during the time that it takes for the spark to completely discharge. The energy or stress in the magnetic circuit is completely dissipated by the time the contacts close for the production of the next spark.

Breaker Assembly

Breaker assemblies, used in high-tension magneto ignition systems, automatically open and close the primary circuit at the proper time in relation to piston position in the cylinder to which an ignition spark is being furnished. The interruption of the primary current flow is accomplished through a pair of breaker contact points, made of an alloy which resists pitting and burning.

Most breaker points used in aircraft ignition systems are of the pivotless type, in which one of the breaker points is movable and the other stationary (see figure 4–7). The movable breaker point attached to the leaf spring is insulated from the magneto housing and is connected to the primary coil (figure 4–7). The stationary breaker point is grounded to the magneto housing to complete the primary circuit when the points are closed, and can be adjusted so that the points can open at the proper time.

Another part of the breaker assembly is the cam follower which is spring-loaded against the cam by the metal leaf spring. The cam follower is a Micarta block (or similar material) which rides the cam and moves upward to force the movable breaker contact away from the stationary breaker contact each time a lobe of the cam passes beneath the follower. A felt oiler pad is located on the underside of the metal spring leaf to lubricate and prevent corrosion of the cam.

A simpler type of breaker assembly may still be found on some aircraft engines in the lower power range. This type, called the pivot type, has one hinged or pivoted arm with a contact point on the end opposite to the pivot or hinge point. The other contact point is secured to a stationary plate. A rubbing block, usually made of fibrous material, is located near the middle point of the movable breaker arm. When the engine rotates the cam, the lobes exert pressure against the rubbing block, causing the movable breaker arm to swing on its pivot point, opening the contact points.

The breaker-actuating cam may be directly driven by the magneto rotor shaft or through a gear train from the rotor shaft. Most large radial engines use

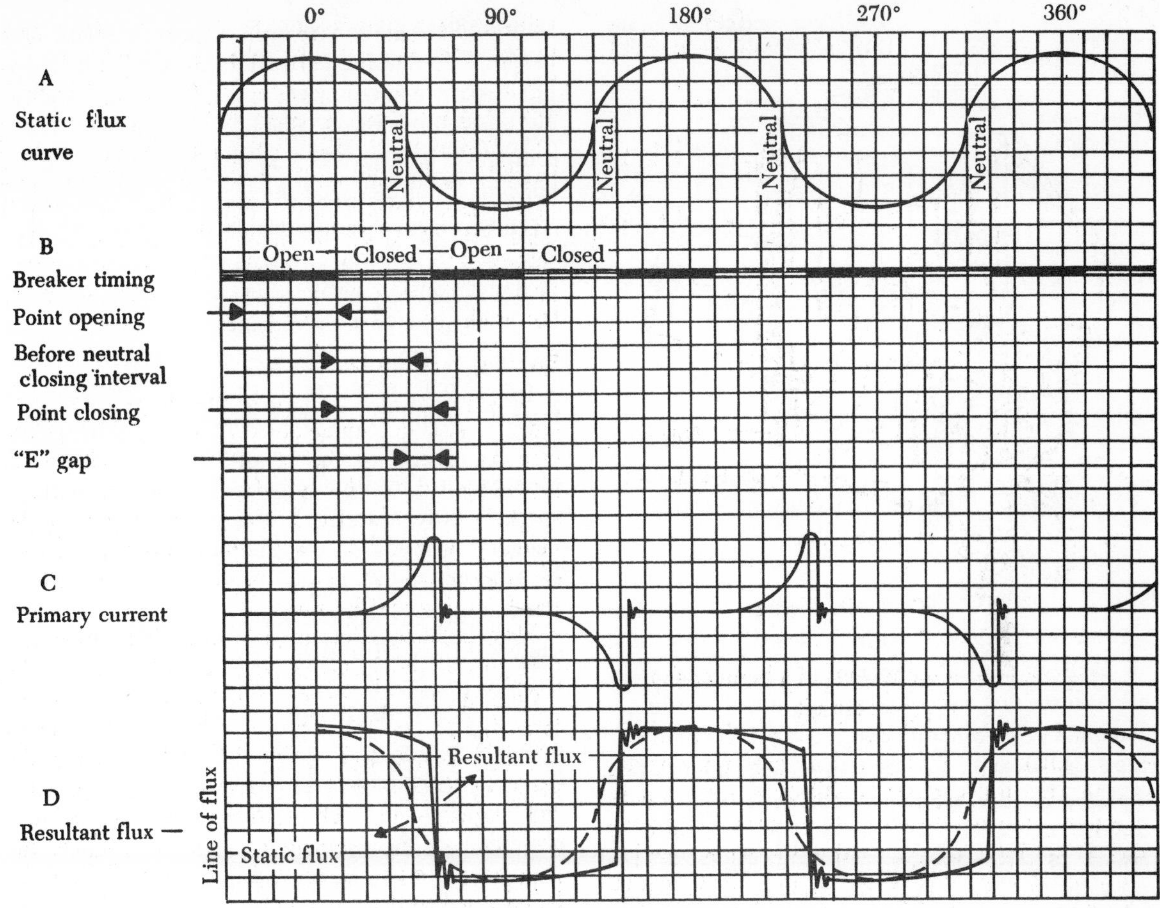

FIGURE 4–6. Magneto flux curves.

a compensated cam, which is designed to operate with a specific engine and has one lobe for each cylinder to be fired by the magneto. The cam lobes are machine ground at unequal intervals to compensate for the top-dead-center variations of each position. A compensated 14-lobe cam, together with a two-, four-, and eight-lobe uncompensated cam, is shown in figure 4–8.

The unequal spacing of the compensated cam lobes, although it provides the same relative piston position for ignition to occur, causes a slight variation of the E-gap position of the rotating magnet and thus a slight variation in the high-voltage impulses generated by the magneto. Since the spacing between each lobe is tailored to a particular cylinder of a particular engine, compensated cams are marked to show the series of the engine, the location of the master rod or rods, the lobe used for magneto timing, the direction of cam rotation, and the E-gap specification in degrees past neutral of magnet rotation. In addition to these markings, a step is cut across the face of the cam, which, when aligned with scribed marks on the magneto housing, places the rotating magnet in the E-gap position for the timing cylinder. Since the breaker points should begin to open when the rotating magnet moves into the E-gap position, alignment of the step on the cam with marks in the housing provides a quick and easy method of establishing the exact E-gap position to check and adjust the breaker points.

Coil Assembly

The magneto coil assembly consists of the soft iron core around which is wound the primary coil and the secondary coil, with the secondary coil wound on top of the primary coil.

The secondary coil is made up of a winding containing approximately 13,000 turns of fine, insulated wire, one end of which is electrically grounded to the primary coil or to the coil core and the other end connected to the distributor rotor. The primary and secondary coils are encased in a nonconducting material of bakelite, hard rubber, or varnished cambric. The whole assembly is then fastened to

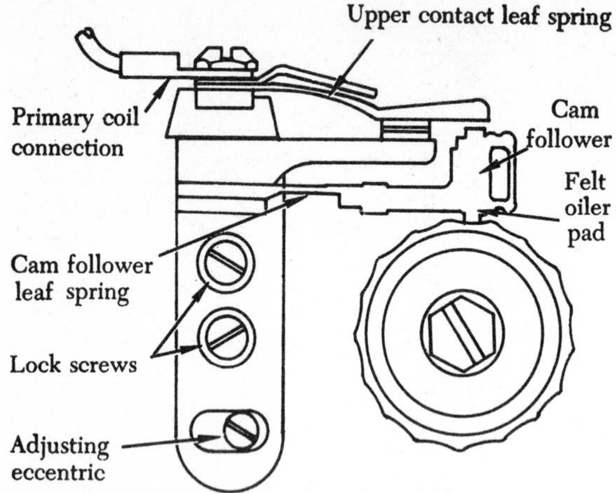

FIGURE 4–7. Pivotless type breaker assembly and cam.

the pole shoes with screws and clamps.

When the primary circuit is closed, the current flow through the primary coil produces magnetic lines of force that cut across the secondary windings, inducing an electromotive force. When the primary circuit is broken, the magnetic field about the primary windings collapses, causing the secondary windings to be cut by the lines of force. The strength of the voltage induced in the secondary windings, when all other factors are constant, is determined by the number of turns of wire. Since most high-tension magnetos have many thousands of turns of wire in the secondary, a very high voltage, often as high as 20,000 volts, is generated in the secondary circuit to jump the air gap of the spark plug in the cylinder.

Distributor

The high voltage induced in the secondary coil is directed to the distributor, which consists of two parts. The revolving part is called a distributor rotor and the stationary part is called a distributor block. The rotating part, which may take the shape of a disk, drum, or finger, is made of a nonconducting material with an embedded conductor. The stationary part consists of a block also made of nonconducting material that contains terminals and terminal receptacles into which the wiring that connects the distributor to the spark plug is attached. In some ignition systems, the distributor assembly is an integral part of the magneto assembly, but others are remotely located and separately driven.

As the magnet moves into the E-gap position for the No. 1 cylinder and the breaker points just separate, the distributor rotor aligns itself with the No. 1 electrode in the distributor block. The secondary voltage induced as the breaker points open enters the rotor where it arcs a small air gap to the No. 1 electrode in the block.

Since the distributor rotates at one-half crankshaft speed on all four-stroke-cycle engines, the distributor block will have as many electrodes as there are engine cylinders, or as many electrodes as cylinders served by the magneto. The electrodes are located circumferentially around the distributor block so that, as the rotor turns, a circuit is completed to a different cylinder and spark plug each time there is alignment between the rotor finger and an electrode in the distributor block. The electrodes of the distributor block are numbered consecutively in the direction of distributor rotor travel (see figure 4–9).

The distributor numbers represent the magneto sparking order rather than the engine cylinder numbers. The distributor electrode marked "1" is connected to the spark plug in the No. 1 cylinder; distributor electrode marked "2" to the second cylinder to be fired; distributor electrode marked "3" to the third cylinder to be fired, and so forth.

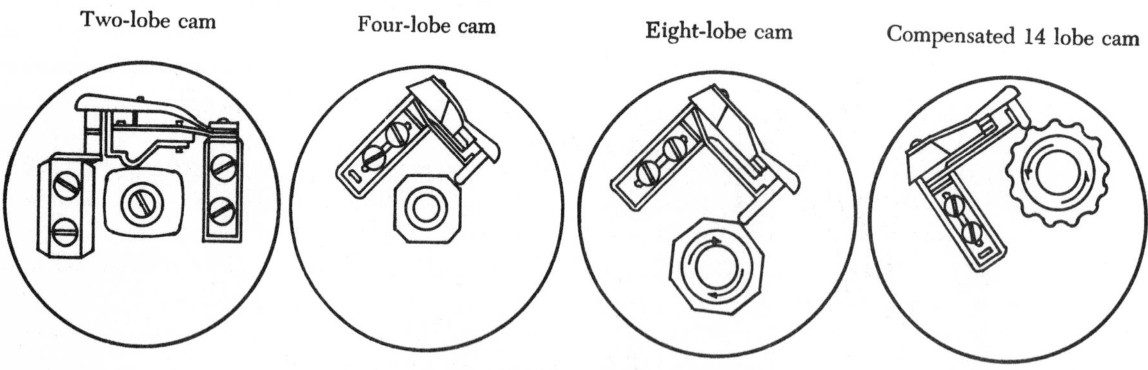

FIGURE 4–8. Typical breaker assemblies.

In figure 4–9 the distributor rotor finger is aligned with the distributor electrode marked "3," which fires the No. 5 cylinder of a 9-cylinder radial engine. Since the firing order of a 9-cylinder radial engine is 1–3–5–7–9–2–4–6–8, the third electrode in the magneto sparking order serves the No. 5 cylinder.

In installations where the magneto and distributor rotors are combined in one assembly, the distributor finger will have been timed at the time of overhaul or manufacture. On engines where the distributor is separate from the magneto, the distributor, as well as the magneto, must be manually adjusted to the timing cylinder to effect proper distribution of the high-voltage impulses.

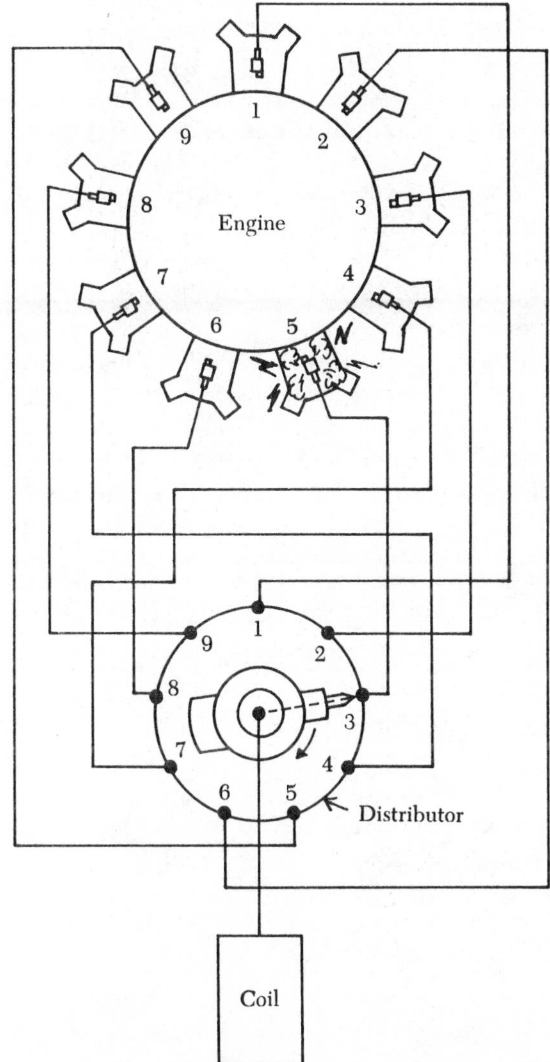

FIGURE 4–9. Relation between distributor terminal numbers and cylinder numbers.

Magneto and Distributor Venting

Since magneto and distributor assemblies are subjected to sudden changes in temperature, the problems of condensation and moisture are considered in the design of these units. Moisture in any form is a good conductor of electricity; and if absorbed by the nonconducting material in the magneto, such as distributor blocks, distributor fingers, and coil cases, it can create a stray electrical conducting path. The high-voltage current that normally arcs across the air gaps of the distributor can flash across a wet insulating surface to ground, or the high-voltage current can be misdirected to some spark plug other than the one that should be fired. This condition is called "flashover" and usually results in cylinder misfiring. For this reason coils, condensers, distributors and distributor rotors are waxed so that moisture on such units will stand in separate beads and not form a complete circuit for flashover.

Flashover can lead to carbon tracking, which appears as a fine pencil-like line on the unit across which flashover occurs. The carbon trail results from the electric spark burning dirt particles which contain hydrocarbon materials. The water in the hydrocarbon material is evaporated during flashover, leaving carbon to form a conducting path for current. And when moisture is no longer present, the spark will continue to follow the track to the ground.

Magnetos cannot be hermetically sealed to prevent moisture from entering a unit because the magneto is subject to pressure and temperature changes in altitude. Thus, adequate drains and proper ventilation reduce the tendency of flashover and carbon tracking. Good magneto circulation also ensures that corrosive gases produced by normal arcing across the distributor air gap are carried away. In some installations, pressurization of various parts of the ignition system is essential to maintain a higher absolute pressure and to eliminate flashover.

Regardless of the method of venting employed, the vent bleeds or valves must be kept free of obstructions. Further, the air circulating through the components of the ignition system must be free of oil, since even minute amounts of oil on ignition parts will result in flashover and carbon tracking.

Ignition Harness

The ignition harness contains an insulated wire for each cylinder that the magneto serves in the engine. One end of each wire is connected to the distributor block and the other end is connected to the proper spark plug. The ignition harness serves a dual purpose. It supports the wires and protects them from damage by engine heat, vibration, or weather. It also serves as a conductor for stray magnetic fields that surround the wires as they momentarily carry high-voltage current. By conducting these magnetic lines of force to the ground, the ignition harness cuts down electrical interference with the aircraft radio and other electrically sensitive equipment. When the radio and other electrical equipment are protected in this manner, the ignition harness wiring is said to be a shield. Without this shielding, radio communication would become virtually impossible.

A common type of ignition harness is a manifold formed to fit around the crankcase of the engine with flexible extensions terminating at each spark plug. A typical high-tension ignition harness is shown in figure 4–10.

Another type is known as the sealed or filled type. A harness of this type has the ignition wires placed in a ring manifold so that the spark plug end of each wire terminates at the manifold outlets. This assembly is then filled with an insulating gelatin which eliminates chafing and moisture condensation. Separate spark plug leads are attached to the manifold outlets. In this manner, it is possible to renew the spark plug end of a lead without replacing the entire length of cable between the spark plug and the distributor.

In installations where the magnetos are mounted on the accessory section of the engine, two large flexible conduits, each containing one-half of the ignition wires, lead aft from the harness to the point where they are connected to the magneto. (See figure 4–11.) In this type of ignition harness, the ignition wires are continuous from the distributor block to the spark plug. If trouble develops, the entire lead must be replaced.

Ignition Switches

All units in an aircraft ignition system are controlled by an ignition switch in the cockpit. The type of switch used varies with the number of engines on the aircraft and the type of magnetos used. All switches, however, turn the system off and on in much the same manner. The ignition switch is different in at least one respect from all other types of switches in that when the ignition switch is in the "off" position, a circuit is completed through the switch to ground. In other electrical switches, the "off" position normally breaks or opens the circuit.

The ignition switch has one terminal connected to the primary electrical circuit between the coil and the breaker contact points. The other terminal of the switch is connected to the aircraft ground (structure). As shown in figure 4–12, two ways to complete the primary circuit are: (1) Through the closed breaker points to ground, or (2) through the closed ignition switch to ground.

In figure 4–12, it can be seen that the primary current will not be interrupted when the breaker contacts open, since there is still a path to ground through the closed (off) ignition switch. Since primary current is not stopped when the contact

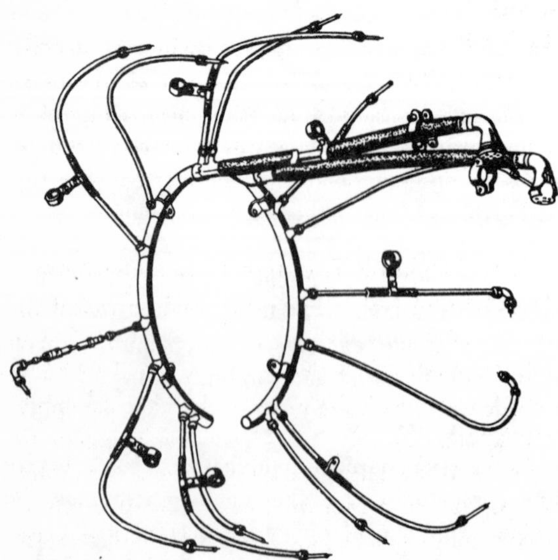

FIGURE 4–10. A high-tension ignition harness.

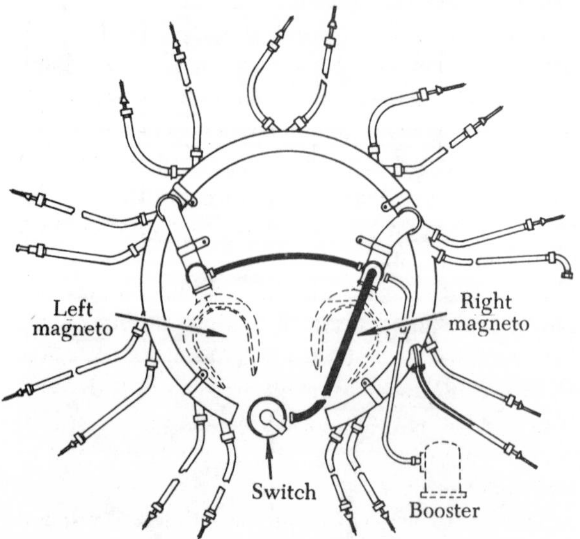

FIGURE 4–11. Accessory-mounted, nine-cylinder engine ignition harness.

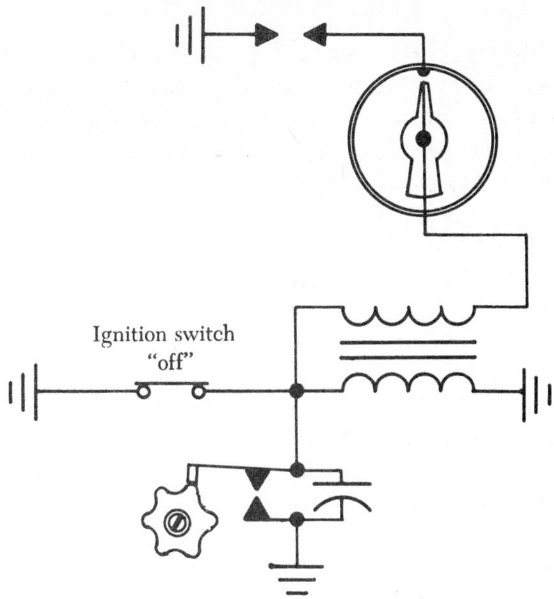

FIGURE 4–12. Typical ignition switch in "off" position.

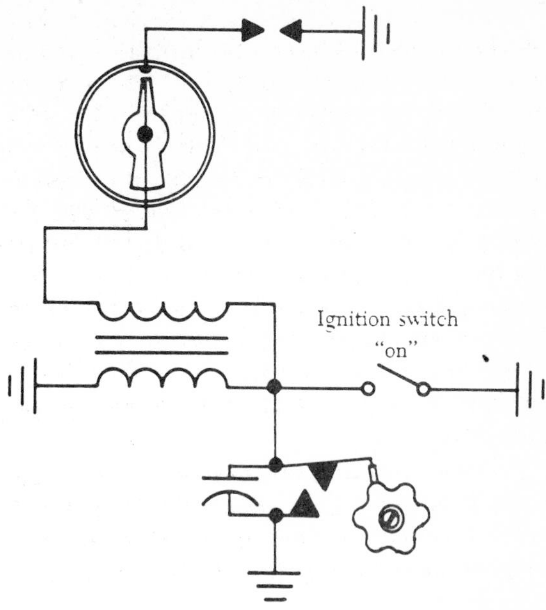

FIGURE 4–13. Typical ignition switch in the "on" position.

points open (figure 4–12), there can be no sudden collapse of the primary coil flux field and no high voltage induced in the secondary coil to fire the spark plug.

As the magnet rotates past the E-gap position, a gradual breakdown of the primary flux field occurs. But that breakdown occurs so slowly that the induced voltage is too low to fire the spark plug. Thus, when the ignition switch is in the "off" position (switch closed), the contact points are as completely short-circuited as if they were removed from the circuit, and the magneto is inoperative.

When the ignition switch is placed in the "on" position (switch open), as shown in figure 4–13, the interruption of primary current and the rapid collapse of the primary coil flux field is once again controlled or triggered by the opening of the breaker contact points. When the ignition switch is in the "on" position, the switch has absolutely no effect on the primary circuit.

Many single-engine aircraft ignition systems employ a dual-magneto system, in which the right magneto supplies the electric spark for the front plugs in each cylinder, and the left magneto fires the rear plugs. One ignition switch is normally used to control both magnetos. An example of this type of switch is shown in figure 4–14.

This switch has four positions: off, left, right, and both. In the "off" position, both magnetos are grounded and thus are inoperative. When the switch is placed in the "left" position, only the left magneto operates; in the "right" position, only the right magneto operates. In the "both" position, both magnetos operate. The "right" and "left" positions are used to check dual-ignition systems, allowing one system to be turned off at a time. Figure 4–14 also refers to the ignition system battery circuit which is discussed with auxiliary ignition units in a following section.

Most twin-engine switches provide the operator with independent control of each magneto in an engine by rotary switches on each side of the ignition switch.

In addition, a toggle master switch is usually incorporated in the switch to ground all the magneto primaries. Thus, in an emergency, all ignition for both engines (four magneto primaries) can be cut off by one movement of this switch. (See figure 4–15.)

Single and Dual High-Tension System Magnetos

High-tension system magnetos used on radial engines are either single- or dual-type magnetos. The single magneto design incorporates the distributor in the housing with the magneto breaker assembly, rotating magnet, and coil. The dual magneto incorporates two magnetos in one housing. One rotating magnet and a cam are common to two sets of breaker points and coils. Two separate distributor units are mounted on the engine apart from the magneto.

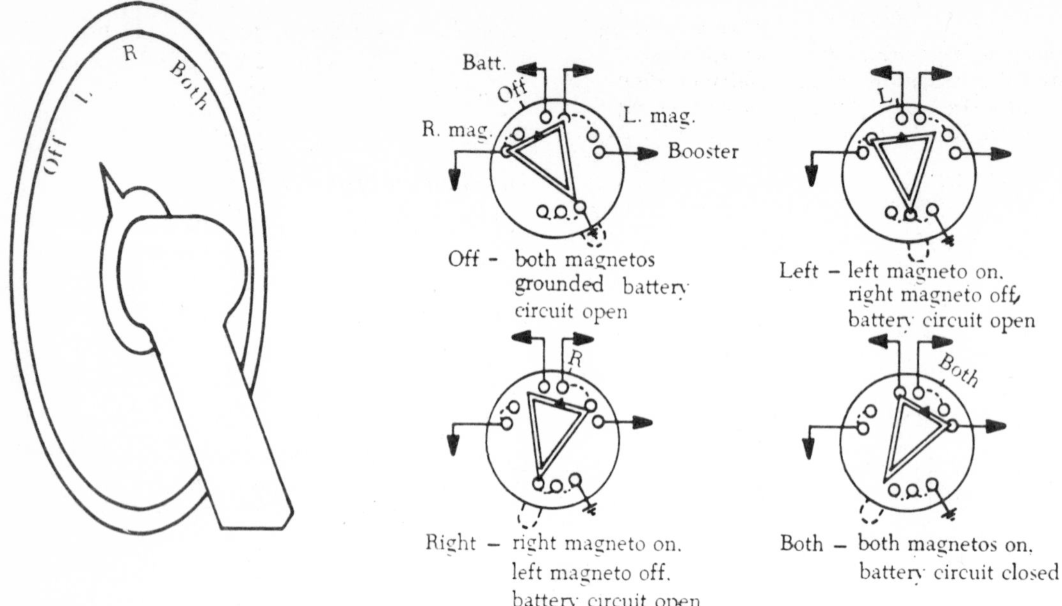

FIGURE 4–14. Switch positions for one ignition switch that controls two magnetos.

Magneto Mounting Systems

Single-type magnetos may be designed for either base-mounting or flange-mounting. Dual-type magnetos are all flange mounted.

Base-mounted magnetos are secured to a mounting bracket on the engine. Flange-mounted magnetos are attached to the engine by a flange around the driven end of the rotating shaft of the magneto. Elongated slots in the mounting flange permit adjustment through a limited range to aid in timing the magneto to the engine.

Low-Tension Magneto System

High tension ignition systems have been in use for more than half a century. Many refinements in the design have been made, but certain underlying problems have remained and others have intensified; such as:

(1) The increase in the number of cylinders per engine.

(2) The requirement that all radio-equipped aircraft have their ignition wires enclosed in metal conduits.

(3) The trend toward all-weather flying.

(4) The increased operation at high altitudes.

To meet these problems, low tension ignition systems were developed.

Electronically, the low-tension system is different from the high-tension system. In the low-tension system, low-voltage is genertaed in the magneto and flows to the primary winding of a transformer coil located near the spark plug. There the voltage is increased to a high voltage by transformer action and conducted to the spark plug by very short high-tension leads. Figure 4–16 is a simplified schematic of a typical low-tension system.

The low-tension system virtually eliminates flashover in both the distributor and the harness because the air gaps within the distributor have been eliminated by the use of a brush-type distributor, and high voltage is present only in short leads between the transformer and spark plug.

Although a certain amount of electrical leakage is characteristic of all ignition systems, it is more pronounced on radio-shielded installations because the metal conduit is at ground potential and close to the ignition wires throughout their entire length. In low-tension systems, however, this leakage is reduced considerably because the current throughout most of the system is transmitted at a low voltage potential. Although the leads between the transformer coils and the spark plugs of a low-tension ignition system are short, they are high-tension (high voltage) conductors, and are subject to the same failures that occur in high-tension systems.

Operation of Low-Tension Ignition System

The magnetic circuit of a typical low-tension magneto system consists of a rotating permanent magnet, the pole shoes, and the coil core (see figure 4–17). The cylindrical magnet is constructed with seven

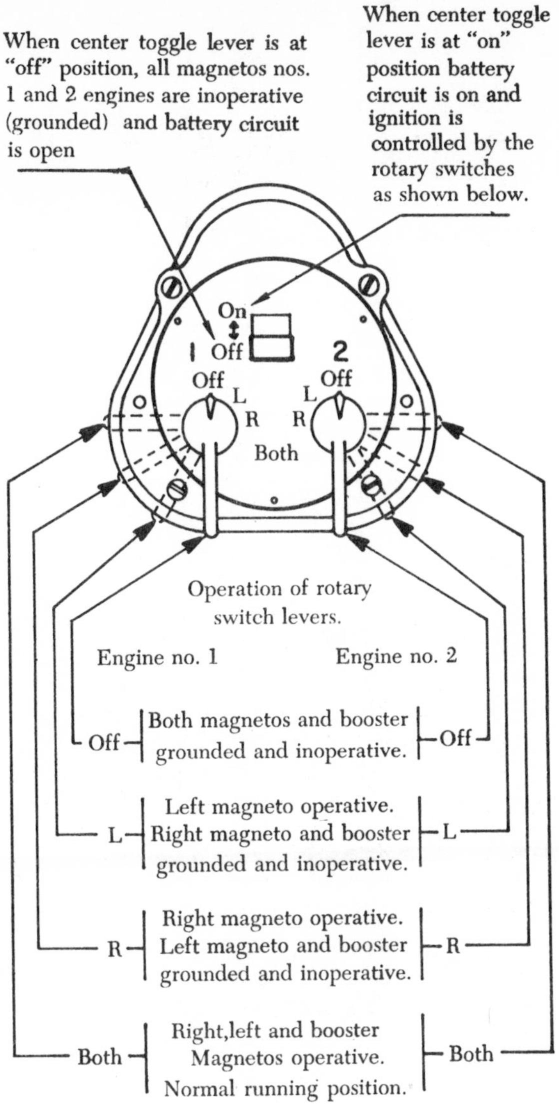

When center toggle lever is at "off" position, all magnetos nos. 1 and 2 engines are inoperative (grounded) and battery circuit is open

When center toggle lever is at "on" position battery circuit is on and ignition is controlled by the rotary switches as shown below.

On
Off
1
2
Off
L
R
Off
L
R
Both

Operation of rotary switch levers.

Engine no. 1		Engine no. 2
Off	Both magnetos and booster grounded and inoperative.	Off
L	Left magneto operative. Right magneto and booster grounded and inoperative.	L
R	Right magneto operative. Left magneto and booster grounded and inoperative.	R
Both	Right, left and booster Magnetos operative. Normal running position.	Both

FIGURE 4–15. Magneto switch for a twin-engine aircraft.

pole pieces of one polarity, staggered between seven pole pieces of the opposite polarity.

When the magnet is inserted in the magnetic circuit of figure 4–17 with three of the magnet's north poles perfectly alined with the pole shoes, a maximum static flux flow is produced from right to left in the coil core. When the magnet is rotated clockwise until the adjacent poles align with the pole shoes, flux flow in the coil core will have decreased from a maximum to zero in one direction, and then increased to a maximum in the opposite direction. This constitutes one flux reversal. Fourteen such flux reversals occur during each revolution of the magnet, or seven for each revolution of the engine crankshaft. Voltage production in the magneto coil of a low-tension magneto occurs in the same manner as in the primary magnetic circuit of a high-tension magneto.

Low-Tension System Distributor

Each current pulse produced by the low-tension magneto is directed to the various transformer coils in proper firing order by the brush-type distributor (see figure 4–18).

The distributor assembly consists of a rotating part, called a distributor brush, and a stationary part, called a distributor block. The rotor (A of figure 4–18) has two separate sets of distributor brushes which ride on the three concentric tracks of the distributor block (B of figure 4–18). These tracks are divided into seven segments, each of which is electrically insulated from the other. The outer track consists of a series of alternate long and short electrode sections. The seven long electrode sections of the outer track are electrically dead and serve only to provide a nearly continuous path for distributor brushes to ride. The low-voltage current from the magneto enters the distributor through a wire connected to one of the short electrode sections of the outside track.

Since all the short electrode sections, though separated by electrically dead sections, are connected together internally, each one has magneto coil voltage impressed upon it.

The distributor rotor has two pickup brushes (A of figure 4–18), one at each end of the rotor. The lower pickup brush is electrically connected to the D or C row brush that rides the middle tracks of the distributor block. (Refer to A, B, and C of figure 4–18.)

As the breaker points open, magneto coil current is available to the short electrode sections of the outside track. (See figure 4–19.) At that instant only one of the distributor rotor pickup brushes is on a short electrode section. The other pickup brush is on an electrically insulated (dead) section of the same track. The pickup brush on a short electrode section picks up the magneto coil current and directs it to an electrode section of the middle track. If the magneto is a No. 1 magneto (R-1 or L-1), the middle track will serve the seven cylinders in the "D" row; if it is a No. 2 magneto (R-2 or L-2), this track will serve the seven cylinders of the "C" row (figure 4–18). Similarly, the inside track serves the seven cylinders of the "B" row if it is a No. 1 magneto, or the seven cylinders of the "A"

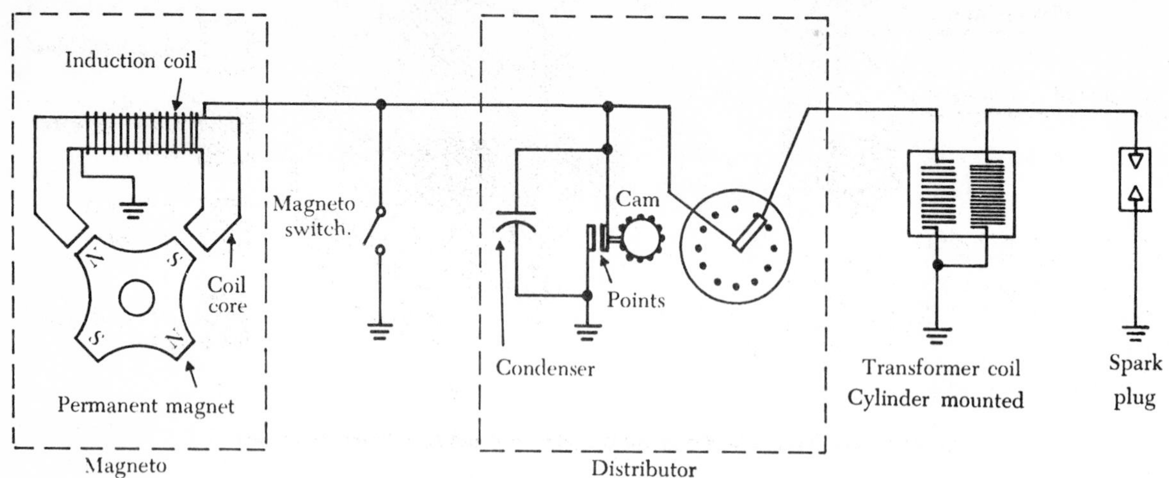

FIGURE 4–16. Simplified low-tension ignition system schematic.

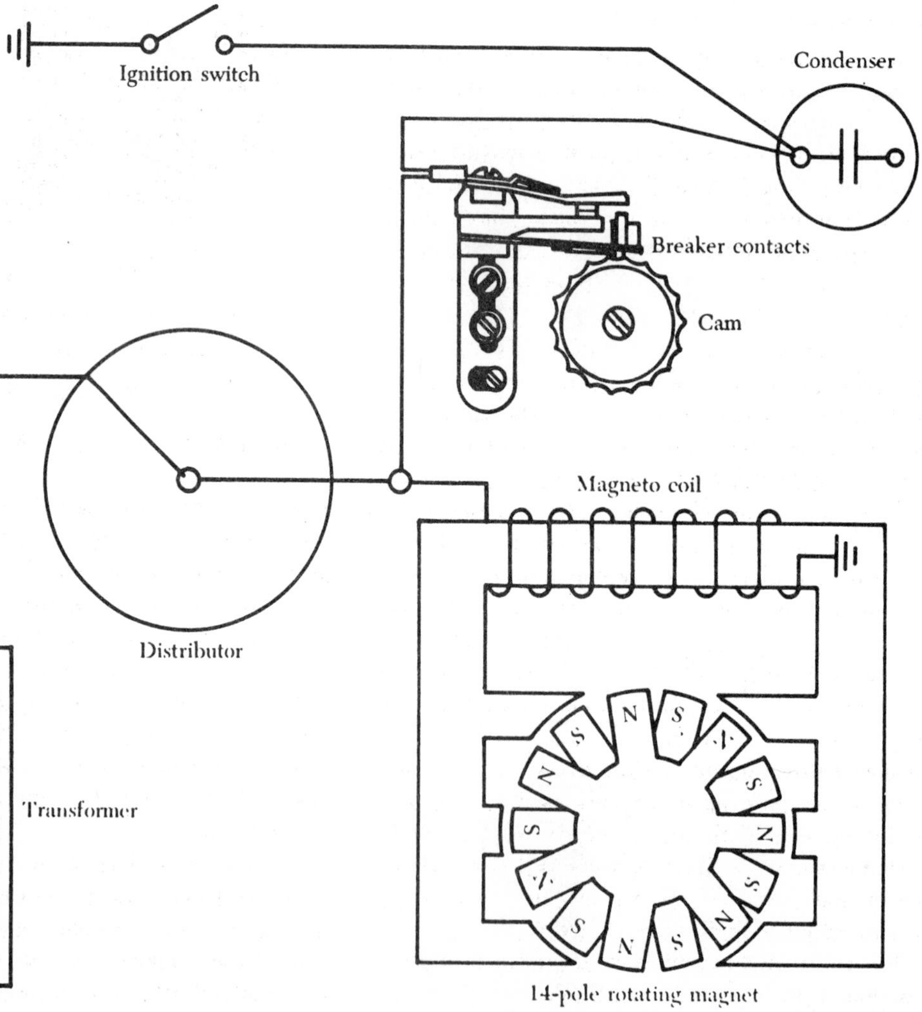

FIGURE 4–17. Low-tension system using a 14-pole rotating magnet.

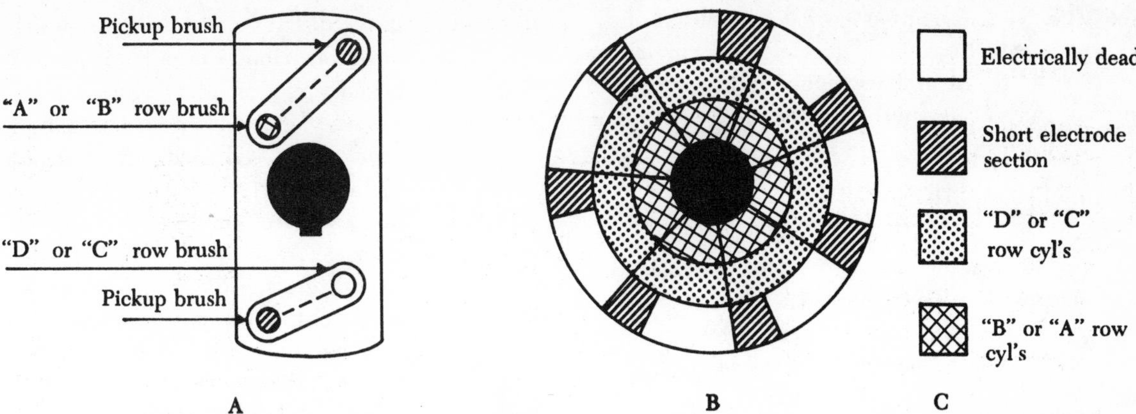

FIGURE 4–18. Brush-type distributor for a low-tension magneto system.

row if it is a No. 2 magneto. Since each electrode section of the middle and inside tracks is connected to a separate transformer coil, the rotating distributor brush determines which transformer coil receives the self-induced current surge.

In operation, any one magneto will serve first a cylinder in one row and then a cylinder in the other row. For example, in figure 4–19, the transformer of the fifth cylinder in the magneto sparking order is receiving the self-induced current surge. The next transformer to receive a surge of current in the magneto's sparking order will be the sixth cylinder, which is served by an electrode section on the inside tracks.

The sixth transformer coil in the magneto's sparking order is energized as the pickup brush for the inside track moves clockwise off an electrically insulated section and onto the next short electrode section. Current is then picked off the outside track and directed to the electrode section of the inside track that serves the transformer for the sixth cylinder in sparking order. While the transformer coil for the sixth cylinder is receiving its current surge, the pickup brush for the middle track is on an insulated section of the outside track and does not interfere with the flow of the self-induced current surge. As the distributor brush continues in a clockwise direction, the pickup brush for the inside track moves onto an electrically insulated section. At the same time, the pickup brush for the middle track moves onto a short electrode section to deliver the current surge to the transformer serving the seventh cylinder in the magneto sparking order.

The relatively low self-induced current leaves the distributor through the wires leading to the transformers. The wires are connected to the circular ignition manifold by a plug connector. For this

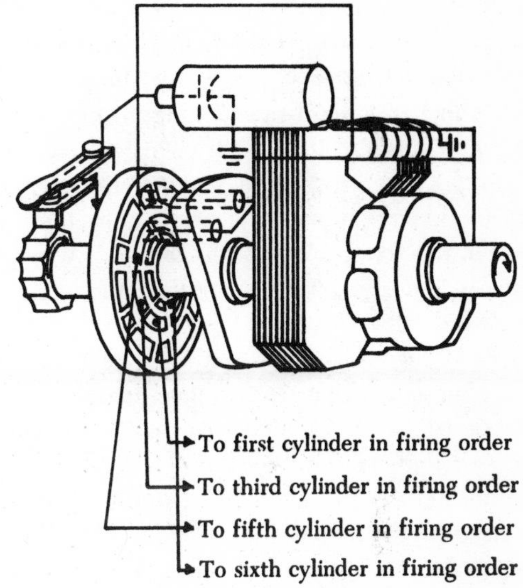

FIGURE 4–19. Brush-type distributor operation.

magneto system there are 60 cables within the circular ignition manifold. Four cables (one for each of the four magnetos) run from the ignition switch to the terminal in the cannon plug connected to the ignition switch wire. The remaining 56 cables connect the distributor electrode sections of the inside and middle tracks of four magnetos to the primary coils of the spark plug transformers. The current from the secondary coil of the transformer is conducted to the spark plug by a short, high-tension shielded cable.

Low-tension magnetos are turned off and on in the same manner that high-tension systems are controlled, i.e., by a switch connected to the ground wire of the magneto coil circuit. When the switch is closed (off position), a direct low-resistance path to ground is made available to the magneto coil whether the breaker points are open or closed.

Since the closed ignition switch provides a low-resistance path to ground, magneto coil current is not directed to the primary coil of the transformer. Instead, current is short-circuited by way of the closed ignition switch.

AUXILIARY IGNITION UNITS

During engine starting, the output of either a high- or low-tension magneto is low because the cranking speed of the engine is low. This is understandable when the factors that determine the amount of voltage induced in a circuit are considered.

To increase the value of an induced voltage, the strength of the magnetic field must be increased by using a stronger magnet, by increasing the number of turns in the coil, or by increasing the rate of relative motion between the magnet and the conductor.

Since the strength of the rotating magnet and the number of turns in the coil are constant factors in both high- and low-tension magneto ignition systems, the voltage produced depends upon the speed at which the rotating magnet is turned. When the engine is being cranked for starting, the magnet is rotated at about 80 r.p.m. Since the value of the induced voltage is so low, a spark may not jump the spark plug gap. Thus, to facilitate engine starting, an auxiliary device is connected to the magneto to provide a high ignition voltage.

Ordinarily, such auxiliary ignition units are energized by the battery and connected to the right magneto or distributor. Reciprocating engine starting systems normally include one of the following types of auxiliary starting systems: booster coil, induction vibrator (sometimes called starting vibrator), impulse coupling, or other specialized retard breaker and vibrator starting systems.

Booster Coil

The booster coil assembly (figure 4–20) consists of two coils wound on a soft iron core, a set of contact points, and a condenser. The primary winding has one end grounded at the internal grounding strip and its other end connected to the moving contact point. The stationary contact is fitted with a terminal to which battery voltage is applied when the magneto switch is placed in the "start" position, or automatically applied when the starter is engaged. The secondary winding, which contains several times as many turns as the primary coil, has one end grounded at the internal grounding strip and the other terminated at a high-tension terminal. The high-tension terminal is connected to an electrode in the distributor by an ignition cable.

Since the regular distributor terminal is grounded through the primary or secondary coil of a high-tension magneto, the high voltage furnished by the booster coil must be distributed by a separate circuit in the distributor rotor. This is accomplished by using two electrodes in one distributor rotor. The main electrode or "finger" carries the magneto output voltage, and the auxiliary electrode distributes only the output of the booster coil. The auxiliary electrode is always located so that it trails the main electrode, thus retarding the spark during the starting period.

Figure 4–21 illustrates, in schematic form, the booster coil components shown in figure 4–20. In operation, battery voltage is applied to the positive (+) terminal of the booster coil through the start switch. This causes current to flow through the closed contact points (figure 4–21) to the primary coil and ground. Current flow through the primary coil sets up a magnetic field about the coil which magnetizes the coil core. As the core is magnetized, it attracts the movable contact point, which is normally held against the stationary contact point by a spring.

As the movable contact point is pulled toward the iron core, the primary circuit is broken, collapsing the magnetic field that extended about the coil core. Since the coil core acts as an electromagnet only when current flows in the primary coil, it loses its magnetism as soon as the primary coil circuit is broken. This permits the action of the spring to close the contact points and again complete the primary coil circuit. This, in turn, re-magnetizes the coil core, and again attracts the movable contact point, which again opens the primary coil circuit. This action causes the movable contact point to vibrate rapidly, as long as the start switch is held in the closed (on) position. The result of this action is a continuously expanding and collapsing magnetic field that links the secondary coil of the booster coil. With several times as many turns in the secondary as in the primary, the induced voltage that results from lines of force linking the secondary is high enough to furnish ignition for the engine.

The condenser (figure 4–21), which is connected across the contact points, has an important function in this circuit. As current flow in the primary coil is interrupted by the opening of the contact points, the high self-induced voltage that accompanies each collapse of the primary magnetic field surges into the condenser. Without a condenser, an arc would

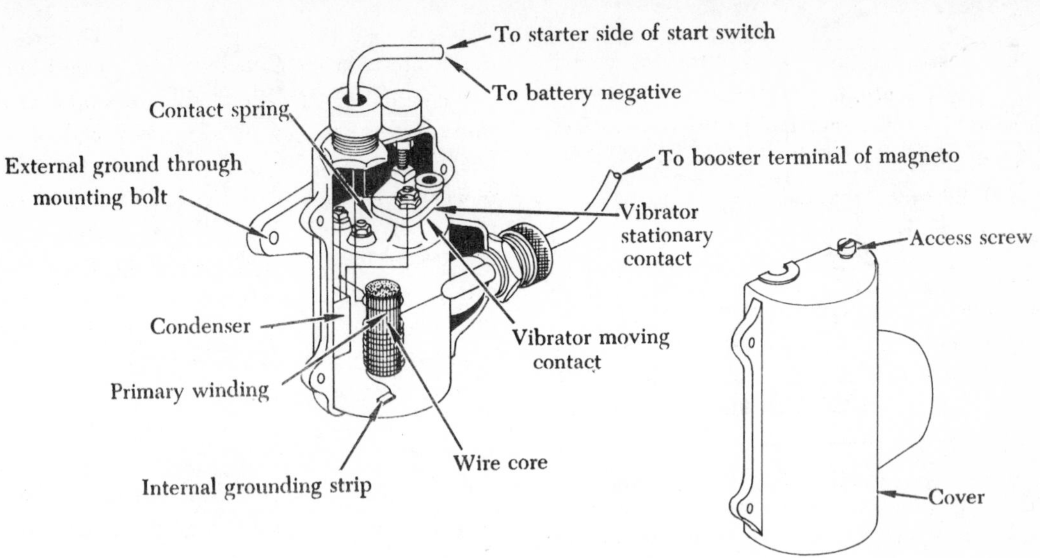

FIGURE 4–20. Booster coil.

jump across the points with each collapse of the magnetic field. This would burn and pit the contact points and greatly reduce the voltage output of the booster coil.

Induction Vibrator

The induction vibrator (or starting vibrator) shown in figure 4–22 consists essentially of an electrically operated vibrator, a condenser, and a relay. These units are mounted on a base plate and enclosed in a metal case.

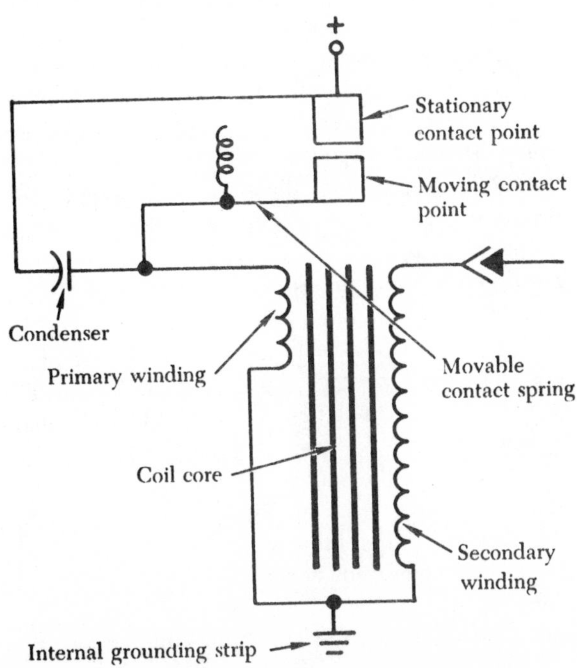

FIGURE 4–21. Booster coil schematic.

The starting vibrator, unlike the booster coil, does not produce the high ignition voltage within itself. The function of this starting vibrator is to change the direct current of the battery into a pulsating direct current and deliver it to the primary coil of the magneto. It also serves as a relay for disconnecting the auxiliary circuit when it is not in use.

As shown in figure 4–22, the positive terminal of the starting vibrator is connected into the starter meshing solenoid circuit. Closing this switch energizes the meshing solenoid and causes current to flow through the relay coil to ground. At the same time, current also flows through the vibrator coil and its contact points. Since current flow through the relay coil establishes a magnetic field that attracts and closes the relay points, the vibrator circuit is now complete to the magneto. The electrical path that battery current takes in the magneto is determined by the position of the primary breaker contact points; if the points are closed, current flows through them to ground; if the points are open, current flows through the primary coil to ground.

Current flow in the vibrator coil sets up a magnetic field that attracts and opens the vibrator points. When the vibrator points open, current flow in the coil stops, and the magnetic field that attracted the movable vibrator contact point disappears. This allows the vibrator points to close and again permits battery current to flow in the vibrator coil. This completes a cycle of operation. The cycle, however, occurs many times per second, so rapidly, in fact, that the vibrator points produce an audible buzz.

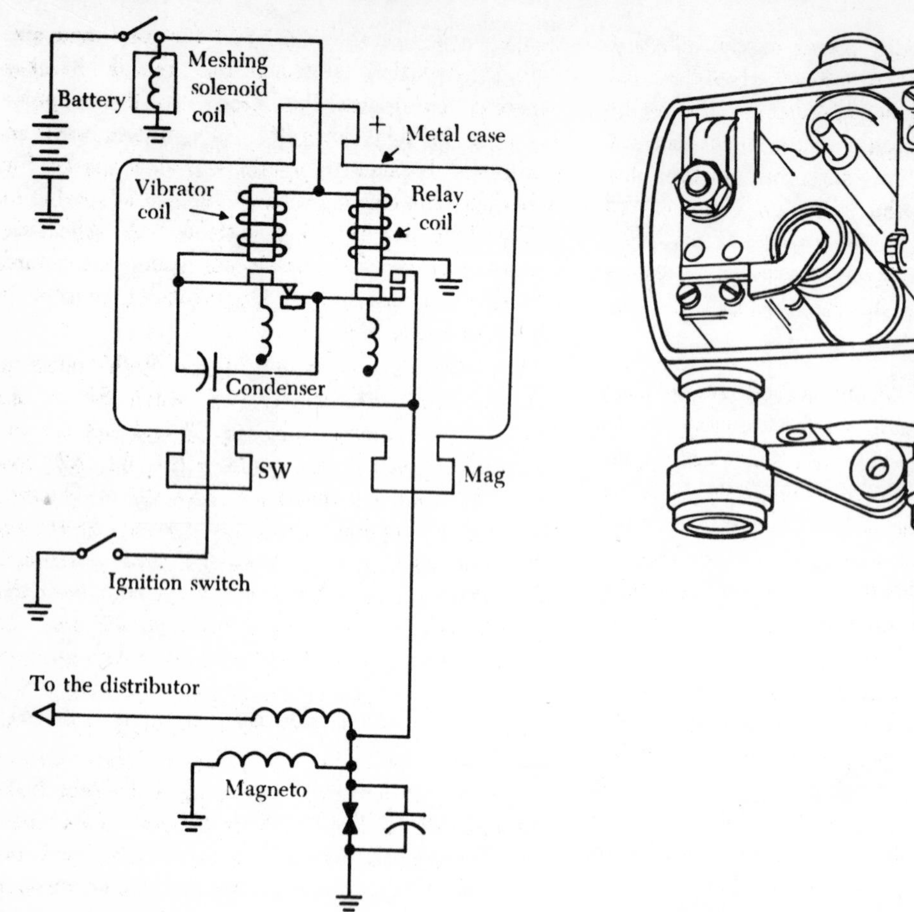

FIGURE 4–22. Induction vibrator.

Each time the vibrator points close, current flows to the magneto. If the primary breaker contact points are closed, almost all the battery current passes to ground through them, and very little passes through the primary coil. Thus, no appreciable change in flux in the primary coil occurs. When the magneto breaker contact points open, current that had been flowing through the breaker points is now directed through the primary coil to ground. Since this current is being interrupted many times per second, the resulting magnetic field is building and collapsing across the primary and secondary coils of the magneto many times per second.

The rapid successions of separate voltages induced in the secondary coil will produce a "shower" of sparks across the selected spark plug air gap. The succession of separate voltages is distributed through the main distributor finger to the various spark plugs because the breaker contact points trigger the sparks just as they do when the magneto is generating its own voltage. Ignition systems that use an induction vibrator have no provision for retarding the spark; hence they will not have a trailing auxiliary distributor electrode.

When starting an engine equipped with an induction vibrator, the ignition switch must be kept in the "off" position until the starter has cranked the propeller through one revolution. Then, while the propeller is still turning, the ignition switch should be turned to the "on" (or both) position. If this precaution is not observed, engine kickback will probably result from ignition before top center and low cranking r.p.m. After the propeller has completed at least one revolution, it will have gained sufficient momentum to prevent kickback.

As soon as the engine begins firing and the starter switch is released, the electric circuit from the battery to the induction vibrator is opened. When battery current is cut off from the induction vibrator, the relay points open and break the connection between the induction vibrator and the magneto. This connection must be broken to prevent the magneto from being grounded out at the relay coil. If the relay points of the induction vibrator did not open when battery current was cut off, primary current in the magneto would not be interrupted when the breaker points open; instead, primary current would flow back through the relay and vibrator points of the induction vibrator and then to ground through the relay coil. In this event, the magneto would be just as inoperative as though the ignition switch were placed in the "off" position.

Impulse Coupling

Engines having a small number of cylinders are sometimes equipped with what is known as an impulse coupling. This is a unit which will, at the time of spark production, give one of the magnetos attached to the engine a brief acceleration and produce a hot spark for starting. This device consists of small flyweights and spring assemblies located within the housing which attaches the magneto to the accessory shaft.

The magneto is flexibly connected through the impulse coupling by means of the spring so that at low speed the magneto is temporarily held while the accessory shaft is rotated until the pistons reach approximately a top center position. At this point the magneto is released and the spring kicks back to its original position, resulting in a quick twist of the rotating magnet. This, being equivalent to high-speed magneto rotation, produces a hot spark.

After the engine is started and the magneto reaches a speed at which it furnishes sufficient current, the flyweights in the coupling fly outward due to centrifugal force and lock the two coupling members together. That makes it a solid unit, returning the magneto to a normal timing position relative to the engine. The presence of an impulse coupling is identified by a sharp clicking noise as the crankshaft is turned at cranking speed past top center on each cylinder.

Use of the impulse coupling produces impact forces on the magneto, the engine drive parts, and various parts of the coupling unit. Often the flyweights become magnetized and do not engage the stop pins; congealed oil on the flyweights during cold weather may produce the same results. Another disadvantage of the impulse coupling is that it can produce only one spark for each firing cycle of the cylinder. This is a disadvantage especially during adverse starting conditions.

High-Tension Retard Breaker Vibrator

The retard breaker magneto and starting vibrator system is used as part of the high-tension system on many small aircraft. Designed for four- and six-cylinder ignition systems, the retard breaker magneto eliminates the need for the impulse coupling in light aircraft. This system uses an additional breaker to obtain retarded sparks for starting. The starting vibrator is also adaptable to many helicopter ignition systems. A schematic diagram of an ignition system using the retard breaker magneto and starting vibrator concept is shown in figure 4–23.

With the magneto switch in the "both" position (figure 4–23) and the starter switch S1 in the "on" position, starter solenoid L3 and coil L1 are energized, closing relay contacts R4, R1, R2, and R3. R3 connects the right magneto to ground, keeping it inoperative during starting operation. Electrical current flows from the battery through R1, vibrator points V1, coil L2, through both the retard breaker points, and through R2 and the main breaker points of the left magneto to ground.

The energized coil L2 opens vibrator points V1, interrupting the current flow through L2. The magnetic field about L2 collapses, and vibrator points V1 close again. Once more current flows through L2, and again V1 vibrator points open. This process is repeated continuously, and the interrupted battery current flows to ground through the main and retard breaker points of the left magneto.

Since relay R4 is closed, the starter is energized and the engine crankshaft is rotated. When the engine reaches its normal advance firing position, the main breaker points of the left magneto open. The interrupted surges of current from the vibrator can still find a path to ground through the retard breaker points, which do not open until the retarded firing position of the engine is reached. At this point in crankshaft travel, the retard points open. Since the main breaker points are still open, the magneto primary coil is no longer shorted, and current produces a magnetic field around T1.

Each time the vibrator points V1 open, current flow through V1 is interrupted. The collapsing field about T1 cuts through the magneto coil secondary and induces a high-voltage surge of energy used to fire the spark plug. Since the V1 points are opening and closing rapidly and continuously, a shower of sparks is furnished to the cylinders when both the main and retard breaker points are open.

After the engine begins to accelerate, the manual starter switch is released, causing L1 and L3 to

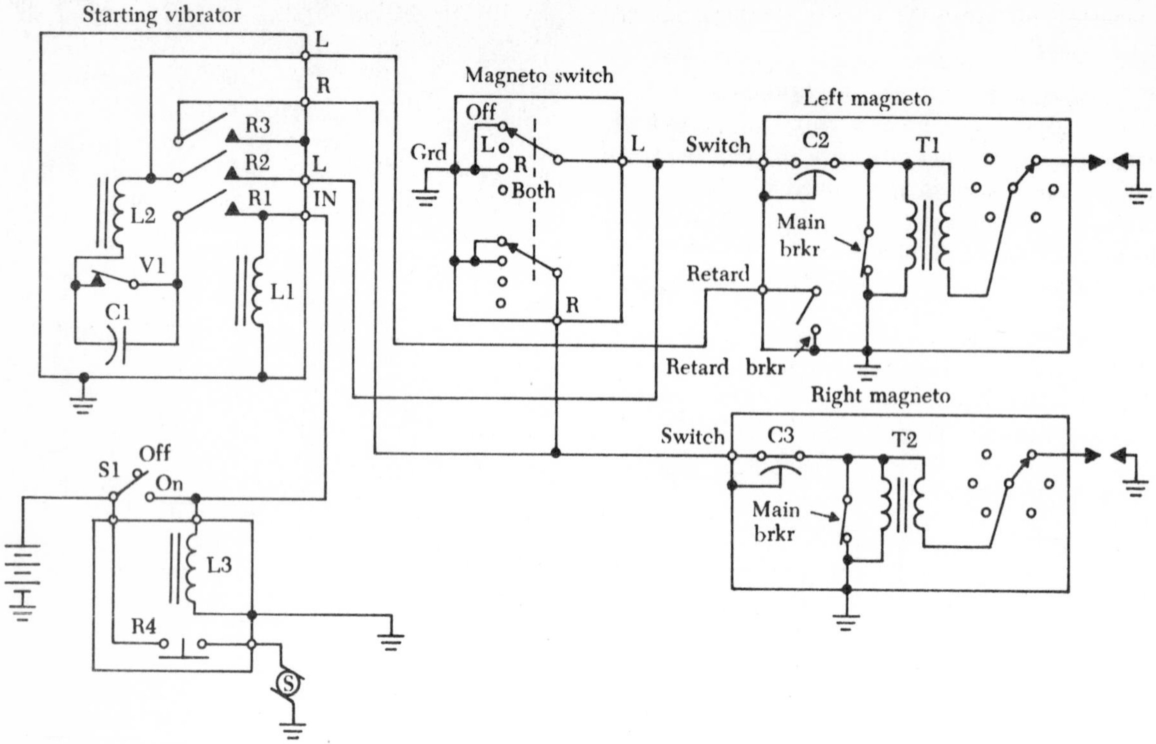

FIGURE 4–23. High-tension, retard breaker magneto and starting vibrator circuit.

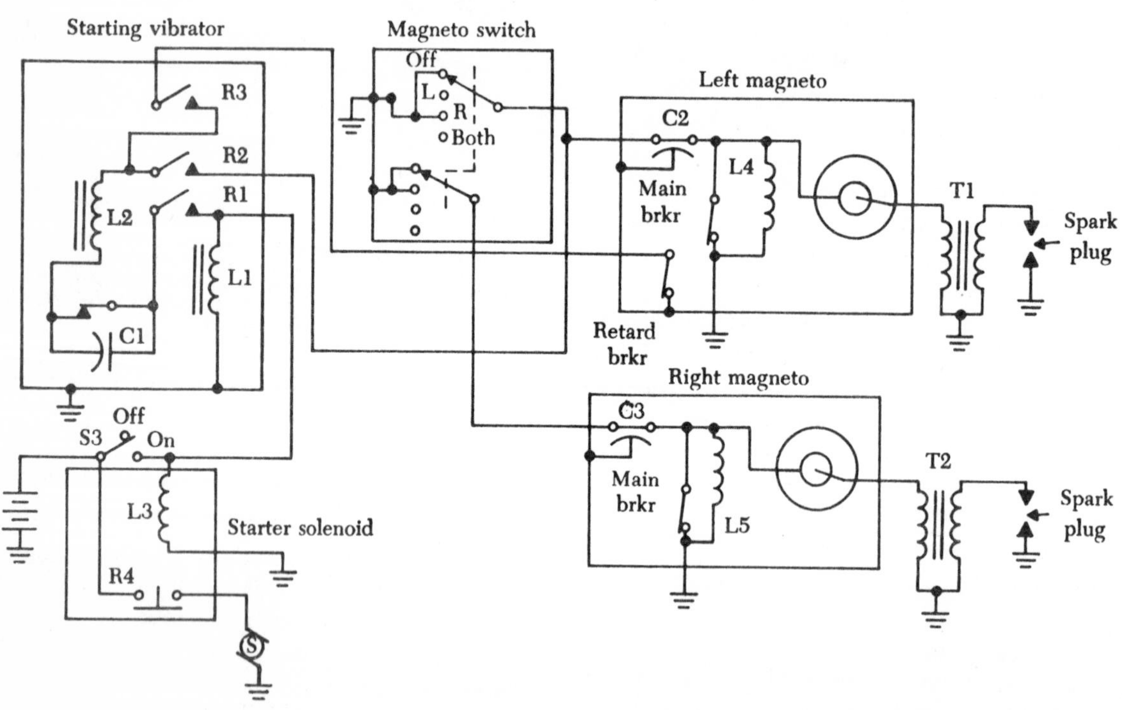

FIGURE 4–24. Low-tension retard breaker magneto and starting vibrator circuit.

become de-energized. This action causes both the vibrator and retard breaker circuits to become inoperative. It also opens relay contact R3, which removes the ground from the right magneto. Both magnetos now fire at the advance (normal running) piston position.

Low-Tension Retard Breaker Vibrator

The system, designed for four- and six-cylinder light aircraft eliminates the disadvantages of both impulse coupling and high-tension ignition systems. A typical system, shown in figure 4–24, consists of a retard breaker magneto, a single breaker magneto, a starting vibrator, transformer coils, and a starter and ignition switch.

To operate the system shown in figure 4–24, place the starter switch S3 in the "on" position. This energizes starter solenoid L3 and coil L1, closing relay contacts R1, R2, R3, and R4. With the magneto switch in the "L" position, current flows through R1, the vibrator points, L2, R2, and through the main breaker points to ground. Current also flows through R3 and the retard breaker points to ground. Current through L2 builds up a magnetic field which opens the vibrator points. Then the current stops flowing through L2, reclosing the points. These surges of current flow through both the retard and main breaker points to ground.

Since the starter switch is closed, the engine crankshaft is turning. When it has turned to the normal advance (running) ignition position, the main breaker points of the magneto open. But current still flows to ground through the closed retard breaker points. As the engine continues to turn, the retard ignition position is reached, and the retard breaker points open. Since the main breaker points are still open, current must flow to ground through coil L4, producing a magnetic field around the coil L4.

As the engine continues to turn, the vibrator breaker points open, collapsing the L4 magnetic field through T1 primary, inducing a high voltage in the secondary of T1 to fire the spark plug.

When the engine fires, the starter switch is released, deenergizing L1 and L3. This opens the vibrator circuit and retard breaker points circuit. The ignition switch is then turned to the "both" position, permitting the right magneto to operate in time with the left magneto.

SPARK PLUGS

The function of the spark plug in an ignition system is to conduct a short impulse of high voltage current through the wall of the combustion chamber. Inside the combustion chamber it provides an air gap across which this impulse can produce an electric spark to ignite the fuel/air charge. While the aircraft spark plug is simple in construction and operation, it is nevertheless the direct or indirect cause of a great many malfunctions in aircraft engines. But spark plugs provide a great deal of trouble-free operation, considering the adverse conditions under which they operate.

In each cylinder of an engine operating at 2,100 r.p.m., approximately 17 separate and distinct high-voltage sparks bridge the air gap of a single spark plug each second. This appears to the naked eye as a continuous fire searing the spark plug electrodes at temperatures of over 3,000° F. At the same time the spark plug is subjected to gas pressures as high as 2,000 p.s.i. and electrical pressure as high as 15,000 volts.

The three main components of a spark plug (figure 4–25) are the electrode, insulator, and outer shell. The outer shell, threaded to fit into the cylinder, is usually made of finely machined steel and is often plated to prevent corrosion from engine gases and possible thread seizure. Close-tolerance screw threads and a copper gasket prevent cylinder gas pressure from escaping around the plug. Pressure that might escape through the plug is retained by inner seals between the outer metal shell and the insulator, and between the insulator and the center electrode assembly.

The insulator provides a protective core around the electrode. In addition to affording electrical insulation, the ceramic insulator core also transfers heat from the ceramic tip, or nose, to the cylinder.

The types of spark plugs used in different engines

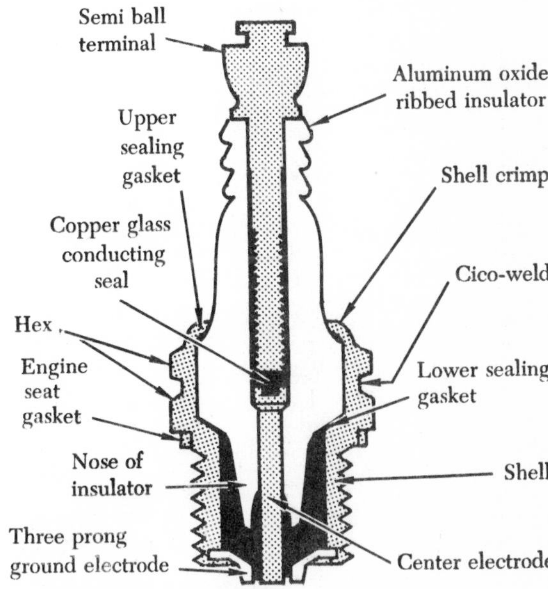

FIGURE 4–25. A typical spark plug.

vary in respect to heat, range, reach, thread size, or other characteristics of the installation requirements of different engines.

The heat range of a spark plug is a measure of its ability to transfer heat to the cylinder head. The plug must operate hot enough to burn off deposits which can cause fouling, yet remain cool enough to prevent a preignition condition. The length of the nose core is the principal factor in establishing the plug's heat range. "Hot" plugs have a long insulator nose that creates a long heat transfer path, whereas "cold" plugs have a relatively short insulator to provide a rapid transfer of heat to the cylinder head (figure 4–26).

If an engine were operated at only one speed, spark plug design would be greatly simplified. Because flight demands impose different loads on the engine, spark plugs must be designed to operate as hot as possible at slow speeds and light loads, and as cool as possible at cruise and takeoff power.

The choice of spark plugs to be used in a specific aircraft engine is determined by the engine manufacturer after extensive tests. When an engine is certificated to use hot or cold spark plugs, the plug used is determined by how the engine is to be operated.

A spark plug with the proper reach (figure 4–27) will ensure that the electrode end inside the cylinder is in the best position to achieve ignition. The spark plug reach is the threaded portion inserted in the spark plug bushing of the cylinder. Spark plug seizure and/or improper combustion within the cylinder will probably occur if a plug with the wrong reach is used.

RECIPROCATING ENGINE IGNITION SYSTEM MAINTENANCE AND INSPECTION

An aircraft's ignition system is the result of careful design and thorough testing. In all probability the ignition system will provide good, dependable service, provided it is maintained properly. However, difficulties can occur which will affect ignition system performance. The most common of these maintenance difficulties, together with the most generally accepted methods of ignition inspection, are discussed in this section.

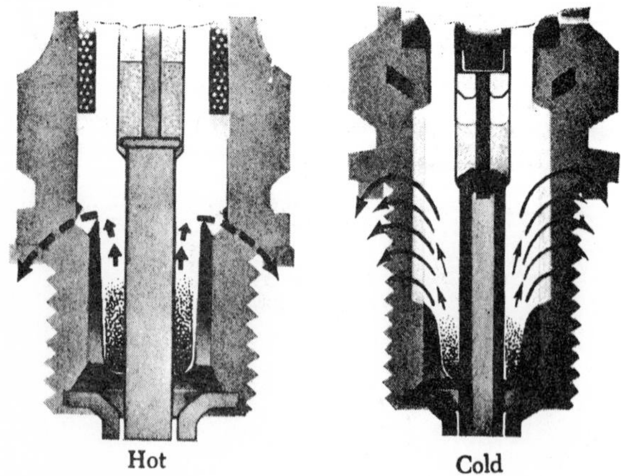

FIGURE 4–26. Hot and cold spark plugs.

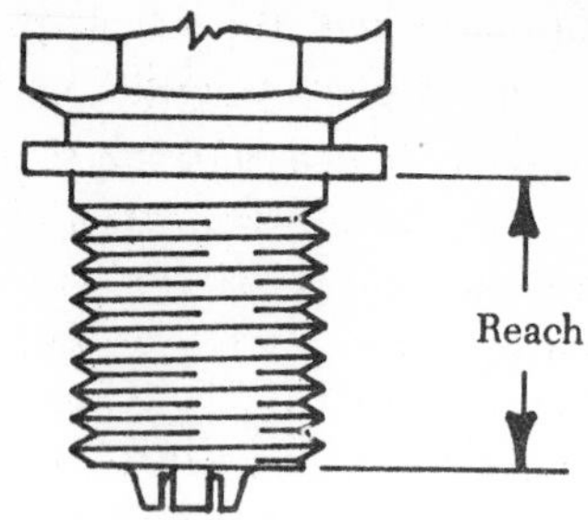

FIGURE 4–27. Spark plug reach.

Breakdown of insulating materials, burning and pitting of breaker points, and short circuits or broken electrical connections are not uncommon. These defects must be found and corrected.

Less common are the irregularities that involve human error. For example, ignition timing requires precise adjustment and painstaking care so that the following four conditions occur at the same instant:

(1) The piston in the No. 1 cylinder must be in a position a prescribed number of degrees before top dead center on the compression stroke.

(2) The rotating magnet of the magneto must be in the E-gap position.

(3) The breaker points must be just opening on the No. 1 cam lobe.

(4) The distributor finger must be aligned with the electrode serving the No. 1 cylinder.

If one of these conditions is out of synchronization with any of the others, the ignition system is said to be "out of time."

When ignition in the cylinder occurs before the optimum crankshaft position is reached, the timing is said to be "early." If ignition occurs too early, the piston rising in the cylinder will be opposed by the full force of combustion. This condition results in a loss of engine power, overheating, and possible detonation and preignition. If ignition occurs at a time after the optimum crankshaft position is reached, the ignition timing is said to be "late." If it occurs too late, not enough time will be allowed to consume the fuel/air charge, and combustion will be incomplete. As a result, the engine loses power, and a greater throttle opening will be required to carry a given propeller load.

More common irregularities are those caused by moisture forming on different parts of the ignition system. Moisture can enter ignition system units through cracks or loose covers, or it can result from condensation. "Breathing," a situation which occurs during the readjustment of the system from low to high atmospheric pressure, can result in drawing in moisture-laden air. Ordinarily the heat of the engine is sufficient to evaporate this moisture, but occasionally the moist air condenses as the engine cools. The result is an appreciable moisture accumulation, which causes the insulation materials to lose their electrical resistance. A slight amount of moisture contamination may cause reduction in magneto output by short-circuiting to ground a part of the high-voltage current intended for the spark plug. If the moisture accumulation is appreciable, the entire magneto output may be dissipated to ground by way of flashover and carbon tracking. Moisture accumulation during flight is extremely rare, because the high operating temperature of the system is effective in preventing condensation; hence difficulties from this cause will probably be more evident during ground operation.

Aircraft spark plugs take the blame unjustly for many ignition system malfunctions. Spark plugs are often diagnosed as being faulty when the real malfunction exists in some other system. Malfunctioning of the carburetor, poor fuel distribution, too much valve overlap, leaking primer system, or poor idle speed and mixture settings will show symptoms that are the same as those for faulty ignition. Unfortunately, many of these conditions can be temporarily improved by a spark plug change, but the trouble will recur in a short time because the real cause of the malfunction has not been eliminated. A thorough understanding of the various engine systems, along with meticulous inspection and good maintenance methods, can substantially reduce such errors.

MAGNETO IGNITION TIMING DEVICES

When the many opportunities for errors in timing the ignition system to the engine are considered, the emphasis placed on the correct use of timing devices that follows is easily justified. Errors can easily occur in positioning the piston in the timing cylinder. It can be placed at the wrong crankshaft degree, or at the correct crankshaft degree but on the wrong stroke. When positioning the magneto's rotating magnet, an error can be made by not removing the backlash in the gear train. The breaker point assemblies may not be perfectly synchronized, or they may be synchronized but not opening at E-gap. Any other errors will alter the final spark timing. Because of the many chances for error, timing devices have been developed to ensure more consistent and accurate timing methods.

Built-in Engine Timing Reference Marks

Most reciprocating engines have timing reference marks built into the engine. On an engine which has no propeller reduction gear, the timing mark will normally be on the propeller flange edge (figure 4–28). The TC (top center) mark stamped on the edge will align with the crankcase split line below the crankshaft when the No. 1 piston is at top dead center. Other flange marks indicate degrees before top center. On some engines there are degree markings on the propeller reduction drive gear. To time these engines, the plug provided on the exterior of the reduction gear housing must be removed to view the timing marks. On other engines, the timing marks are on a crankshaft flange and can be viewed by removing a plug from the crankcase. In every case, the engine manufac-

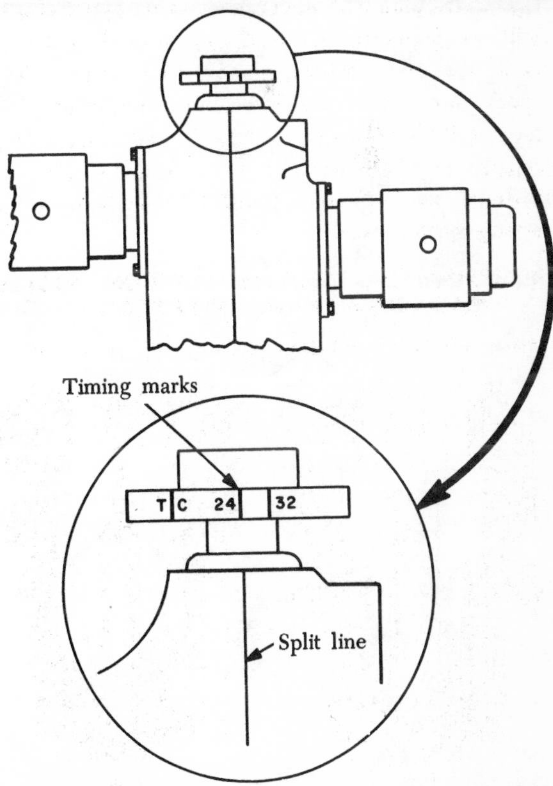

FIGURE 4–28. Propeller flange timing marks.

turer's instructions will give the location of built-in timing reference marks.

In using built-in timing marks (figure 4–29) to position the crankshaft, be sure to sight straight across the stationary pointer or mark on the nose section, the propeller shaft, crankshaft flange, or bell gear. Sighting at an angle will result in an error in positioning the crankshaft.

While many engines have timing reference marks, they leave something to be desired. The main drawback is the backlash factor. The amount of backlash in any system of gears will vary between installations and will even vary between two separate checks on the same piece of equipment. This results because there is no way of imposing a load on the gear train in a direction opposite the direction of crankshaft rotation. Another unfavorable aspect in the use of timing marks on the reduction gear is the small error that exists when sighting down the reference mark to the timing mark inside the housing on the reduction gear. Because there is depth between the two reference marks, each mechanic must have his eye in exactly the same plane. If not, each man will select a different crankshaft position for ignition timing.

Timing Disks

The timing disk is a more accurate crankshaft positioning device than the timing reference marks. This device consists of a disk and a pointer mechanism mounted on an engine-driven accessory or its mounting pad. The pointer, which is indirectly connected to the accessory drive, indicates the number of degrees of crankshaft travel on the disk. The disk is marked off in degrees of crankshaft travel. By applying a slight torque to the accessory drive gear in a direction opposite that of the normal rotation, the backlash in the accessory gear train can be removed to the extent that a specific crankshaft position can be obtained with accuracy time after time.

Not all timing disks are marked off in the same number of degrees. For example, the disk designed for use on one type of engine is mounted on the fuel pump drive pad. Since the fuel pump is driven at the same speed as the crankshaft, the pointer will describe a complete circle when the crankshaft completes one revolution. Hence, the disk is laid out in one-degree increments throughout a total of 360°. However, the timing disk used on another engine is mounted on top of the magneto, which is driven at one-half crankshaft speed. With this arrangement the crankshaft will move one degree while the pointer moves only one-half a degree. Therefore, the disk is marked off in 720 one-half-degree increments, each one-half degree indicating one full degree of crankshaft travel.

A modification of the timing disk is the timing plate Figure 4–30. The markings will vary according to the specifications of the engine. This plate is installed on the thrust nut corner plate bolts and the pointer attached to the propeller shaft.

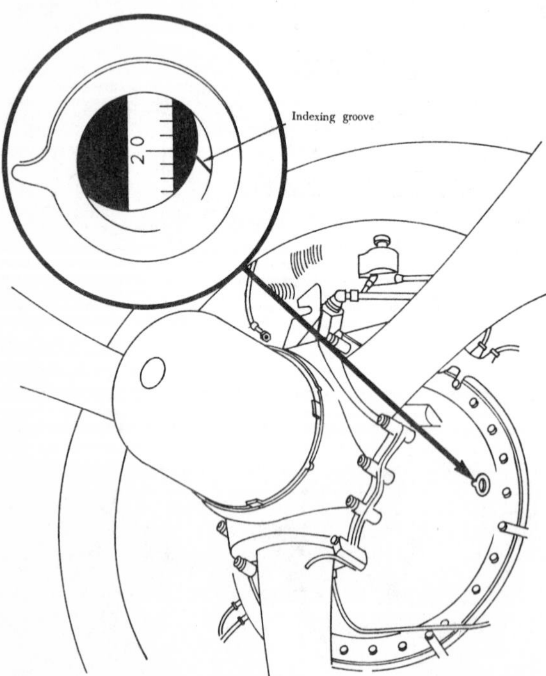

FIGURE 4–29. Typical built-in timing mark on propeller reduction gear.

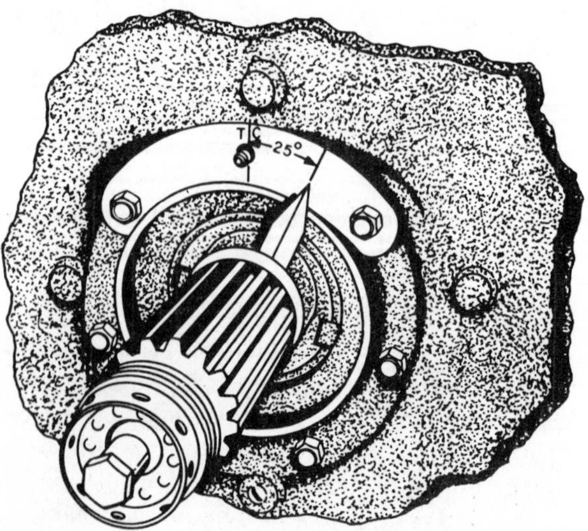

FIGURE 4-30. A timing plate and pointer

Piston Position Indicators

Any given piston position, whether it is to be used for ignition, valve, or injection pump timing, is referenced to a piston position called top dead center. This piston position is not to be confused with a rather hazily defined piston position called top center.

A piston in top center has little value from a timing standpoint because the corresponding crankshaft position may vary from 1° to 5° for this piston position. This is illustrated in figure 4–31 which is exaggerated to emphasize the "no travel" zone of the piston. Notice that the piston does not move while the crankshaft describes the small arc from position A to position B. This "no travel" zone occurs between the time the crankshaft and connecting rod stop pushing the piston upward, and continues until the crankshaft has swung the lower end of the connecting rod into a position where the crankshaft can start pulling the piston downward.

Top dead center is a piston and crankshaft position from which all other piston and crankshaft locations are referenced. When a piston is in the top-dead-center position, it will be a maximum distance from the center of the crankshaft and also in the center of the "no travel" zone. This places the piston in a position where a straight line can be drawn through the center of the crankshaft journal, the crankpin, and the piston pin, as shown in the right-hand diagram of figure 4–31. With such an alignment, a force applied to the piston could not move the crankshaft.

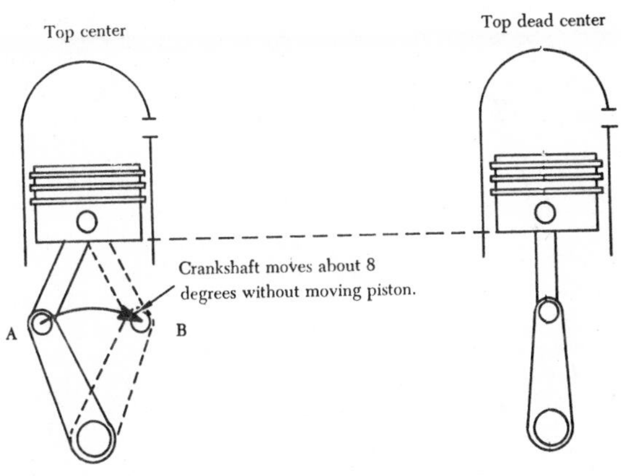

FIGURE 4–31. Illustrating the difference between top center and top dead center.

Perhaps the earliest piston position indicator was a wooden rod or pencil. One end of this simple device was inserted at an angle through the spark plug hole of the timing cylinder until it came to rest on the top far edge of the piston, as shown in figure 4–32. Then the crankshaft was rotated until the piston stopped moving the end of the rod outward. At this point the mechanic would grasp the rod with his thumbnail resting at a point where the rod contacted the top edge of the spark plug hole. With his thumbnail still in this position he would then extract the rod and cut a notch about 1 in. above the thumbnail location. This notch provided the mechanic with an arbitrary reference point somewhere before top dead center.

Such an inexact procedure cannot be relied on to find the same piston position each time. All piston position indicators in use today screw into the spark plug hole so that the indicator always enters the cylinder in exactly the same plane and its indicating rod always contacts the same part of the piston head.

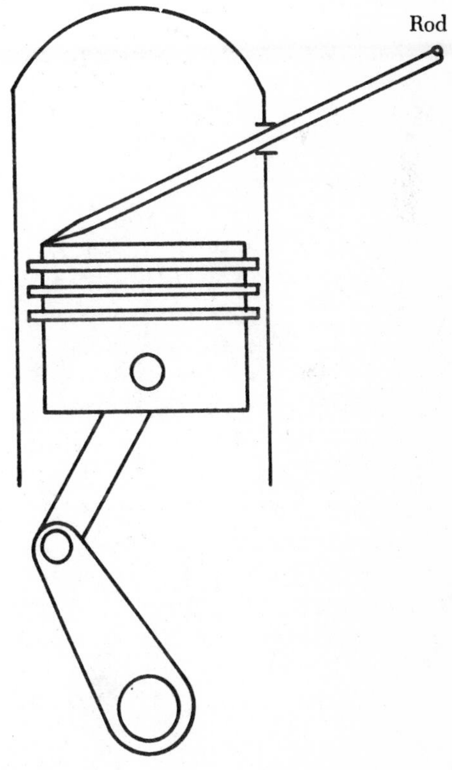

FIGURE 4–32. Simple piston position indicator.

One of the various piston position indicators in use today is a Time-Rite indicator (figure 4–33). It serves the purpose of a piston position indicator and, in a limited degree, as a timing disk. The device consists of two parts, a body shell and a face. The shell is essentially an adapter which screws into the spark plug hole and supports the face. The face snaps into the adapter and contains a spring-loaded compensated indicator arm, a slide pointer, a removable scale calibrated in degrees, an indicator light, and a frame which extends behind the face to form a hinge point for the compensated indicator arm. One end of the compensated arm extends into the cylinder through the spark plug hole and is actuated by piston movement. The other end of the arm extends through a slot in the face and actuates the slide pointer over the scale.

Furnished with the Time-Rite is a variety of different arms and graduated scales. Both arms and scales are compensated for the particular engine for which they are marked. Compensation is necessary because of variations in piston stroke and spark plug hole locations in different cylinders. The arms are compensated by varying their shapes and lengths, and the scales are compensated by the spacing of the degree markings. In this way a particular arm and scale combination will indicate true piston position if used correctly.

To ensure even greater accuracy with the Time-Rite, a small light, powered by a miniature dry cell battery, is mounted in its face. When the compensated arm contacts the slide pointer, an electrical circuit is completed and the light comes on. This light provides greater accuracy because the slide pointer can be positioned at the desired degree setting on the scale and the crankshaft slowly rotated by bumping the propeller shaft until the light just flashes on. The propeller shaft must be moved slowly and carefully so that the arm will not overshoot and move the slide pointer beyond the desired degree setting after the light flashes on.

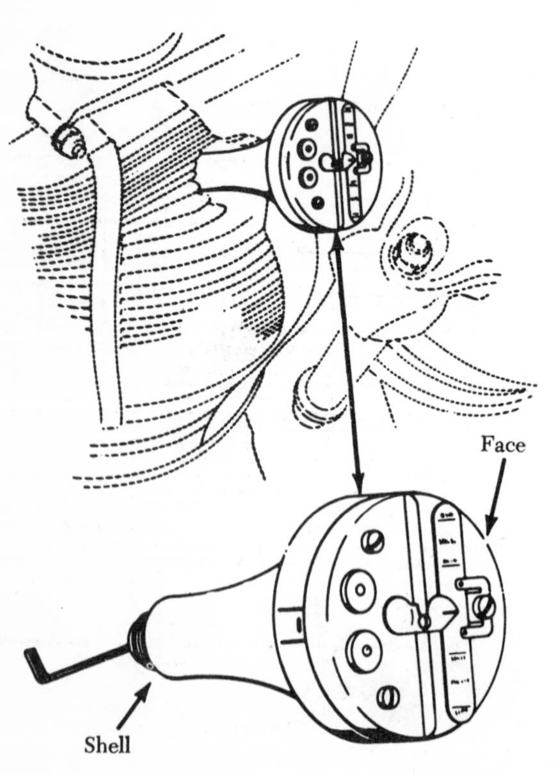

FIGURE 4–33. Time-Rite indicator.

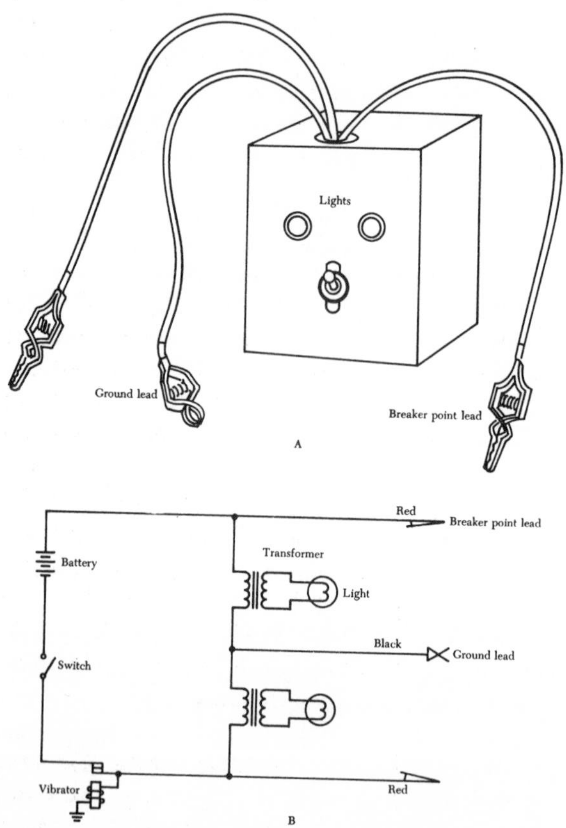

FIGURE 4–34. Timing light and wiring diagram.

There are two other common types of piston position indicators in use, both of which operate on the piston-positioning principle. One features a scale of reference points. The other is simply a light which comes on when the piston touches the actuating arm and goes out when the piston moves below the reach of the arm.

Timing Lights

Timing lights are used to help determine the exact instant that the magneto points open. There are two general types of timing lights in common use. Both have two lights and three external wire connections. Although both have internal circuits that are somewhat different, their function is very much the same. One type of light and its internal circuit are shown in figure 4–34.

Three wires plug into the top of the light box (A of figure 4–34). There are also two lights on the front face of the unit, and a switch to turn the unit on and off. The wiring diagram (B of figure 4–34) shows that the unit contains a battery, a vibrator coil, and two transformers. To use the timing light, the center lead, marked "ground lead," is connected to the case of the magneto being tested. The other leads are connected to the primary leads of the breaker point assembly of the magnetos being timed.

With the leads connected in this manner, it can be easily determined whether the points are open or closed by turning on the switch and observing the two lights. If the points are closed, most of the current will flow through the breaker points and not through the transformers, and the lights will not come on. If the points are open, the current will flow through the transformer and the lights will glow. Some models of timing lights operate in the reverse manner, *i.e.*, the light goes out when the points open. Each of the two lights is operated separately by the set of breaker points to which it is connected. This makes it possible to observe the time, or point in reference to magneto rotor rotation, that each set of points opens.

Most timing lights use dry cell batteries that must be replaced after long use. Attempts to use a timing light with weak batteries may result in erroneous readings because of low current flow in the circuits.

CHECKING THE INTERNAL TIMING OF A MAGNETO

When replacing a magneto or preparing a magneto for installation, the first concern is with the internal timing of the magneto. For each magneto model, the manufacturer determines how many degrees beyond the neutral position a pole of the rotor magnet should be to obtain the strongest spark at the instant of breaker point separation. This angular displacement from the neutral position, known as the E-gap angle, will vary with different magneto models. On one model a "step" is cut on the end of the breaker cam for checking internal timing of the magneto. When a straightedge is laid along this step and it coincides with the timing marks on the rim of the breaker housing, the magneto rotor is then in the E-gap position, and the breaker contact points should just begin to open.

Another method for checking E-gap is to align a timing mark with a pointed chamfered tooth (figure 4–35). The breaker points should be just starting to open when these marks line up.

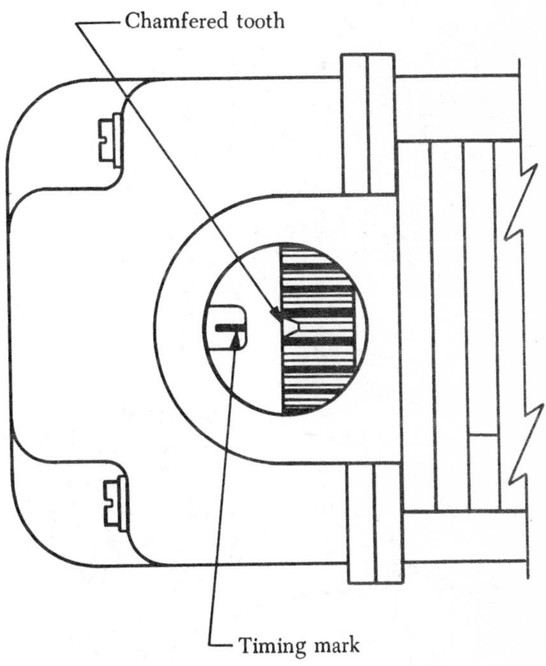

FIGURE 4–35. Timing marks which indicate No. 1 firing position of magneto.

In a third method the E-gap is correct when a timing pin is in place and red marks, visible through a vent hole in the side of the magneto case, are aligned (figure 4–36). The contact points should be just opening when the rotor is in the position just described.

Bench timing the magneto involves positioning the magneto rotor at the E-gap position and setting the breaker points to open when the timing lines or marks provided for that purpose are perfectl aligned.

The magneto breaker points are protected by a cover. Removal of this cover exposes the magneto rotor cam and breaker points, as shown in figure 4–37.

To begin bench timing the magneto, connect the two red leads of the timing light to the two primary leads retaining screw. Connect the remaining black lead to the case of the magneto to provide an electrical ground.

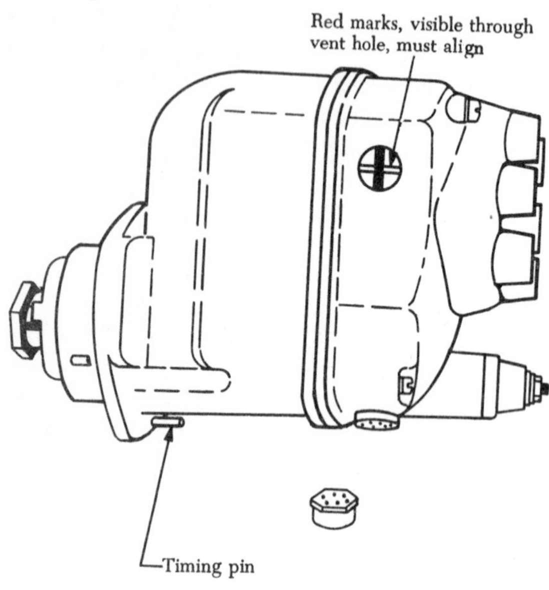

FIGURE 4–36. Checking magneto E-gap.

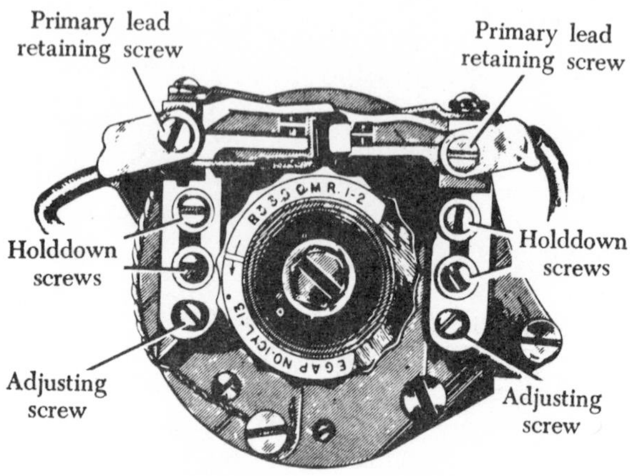

FIGURE 4–37. Magneto breaker points and compensated cam.

With most magnetos of this type, a special tool is used to receive the splined drive shaft of the magneto. This tool holds the magneto with the breaker points in the upright position, and it holds the magneto rotor stationary during the bench timing process. Rotor motion can still be simulated by rotating the magneto around the rotor. Some types of magneto rotor-holding tools are designed with a clamp to lock the rotor to the magneto case to establish the desired relationship between the two.

With the magneto installed on the holding tool and the timing light installed, the position where the timing marks on the magneto rotor and on the magneto align perfectly can be located. Lock the holding tool in this position. With the rotor positioned and locked, both holddown screws (figure 4–37) can be loosened. Then tighten these two screws enough that some drag (friction) is felt when the adjusting screw shifts the grounded breaker point.

High-Tension Magneto Bench Timing

In the following discussion, the procedures for bench timing a twin-row radial engine magneto are outlined for an example only. Consult the manufacturer's instructions in every case before bench timing any magneto.

To bench time a magneto certain items of equipment are necessary. Normally included are a timing light, a tool for holding the magneto, a common screwdriver to loosen the point assembly screws, and a straightedge for checking the rotor for E-gap position.

Turn on the timing light. Move the adjusting screw back and forth until the timing light for the set of points being adjusted just comes on. Lock this set of breaker points by tightening the two holddown screws without changing the setting of the breaker points.

The magneto rotor lock should be unlocked, and the adjusted set of points should be checked with the straightedge and timing lights to determine that the points open exactly at the E-gap position. This is accomplished by holding the straightedge on the rotor cam step and turning the magneto case around the rotor shaft still supported in the magneto holding device. First, rotate the magneto case in the direction indicated by the arrow on the cam rotor until the light goes out. This indicates that the breaker points have completely closed. Then rotate the magneto case in the opposite direction. This will cause the magneto rotor to again come back to the E-gap position in the normal direction of rotation. If the setting is correct, the magneto rotor cam will line up in the E-gap position, as indicated by the straightedge, at the exact instant that the timing light comes on to indicate that the points are open. The correct internal timing of one set of breaker points has been accomplished.

There are several ways to set the remaining set of breaker points to open at the E-gap position. Perhaps the easiest method is to use the already adjusted set of breaker points as a check point. By using the light indication of the adjusted points as a true reference point for E-gap position, the second set can be synchronized to open at exactly the same time.

When the two holddown screws on the second set of points (figure 4–37) are loosened enough to permit the adjustment screw to move the grounded part of the points, the breaker points can be adjusted until the light for this set of points comes on at exactly the same time as the first set. Then the lockscrews should be tightened without changing the position of the breaker points before rotating the magneto case to see that both lights come on simultaneously. The magneto is now ready to be installed on the engine. This requires timing the magneto to the engine.

Timing the High-Tension Magneto to the Engine

When replacing magnetos on aircraft engines, two factors must be considered: (1) The internal timing of the magneto, including breaker point adjustment, which must be correct to obtain maximum potential voltage from the magneto, and (2) the crankshaft position at which the spark occurs.

A breaker point gap should never be compared with another, since it would not be known if either set of breaker points were opening at the proper number of degrees before top dead center of the timing position of the engine. The magneto must be timed by first adjusting the internal timing of the magneto and then by checking and adjusting the ignition points to open at this position. If the reference timing mark for the magneto lines up when the timing piston is at a prescribed number of degrees ahead of true top dead center and both the right and left set of breaker points open at that instant and remain open for the prescribed number of degrees, the internal magneto timing is correct, proper magneto-to-engine timing exists, and all phases of magneto operation are synchronized. In no case should the breaker points be adjusted when the internal timing of the magneto, as designated by internal timing reference marks, is off in relation to the prescribed piston position.

For timing the magneto to the engine in the following example, a timing light is used. The timing light is designed in such a way that one of two lights will come on when the points open. The timing light incorporates two lights; hence, when connecting the timing light to the magneto, the leads should be connected so that the light on the right-hand side of the box represents the breaker points on the right side of the magneto, and the light on the left-hand side represents the left breaker points. The proper connection of wires can be established by turning the timing light on and then touching one of the red wires against the black wire. If the right light goes out, the red lead used should be connected to the magneto housing or the engine to effect a ground. When using the timing light to check a magneto in a complete ignition system installed on the aircraft, the master ignition switch for the aircraft must be turned on and the ignition switch for the engine turned to "both." Otherwise, the lights will not indicate breaker point opening. With the ignition switch on and the timing light connected, the magneto is rendered inoperative; hence, no firing impulses can occur when the propeller is turned.

After determining that the magneto internal timing is correct, turn the engine crankshaft until the piston of the No. 1 cylinder is in the firing position on the compression stroke. The firing position can be determined by referring to the engine manufacturer's service manual. Locate the firing position by using a piston position indicator.

To establish crankshaft position with the piston position indicator:

(1) Remove the most accessible spark plug from the No. 1 cylinder.

(2) Install the correct contact arm and calibrated scale for the engine involved. (Consult applicable manufacturer's instructions for correct contact arm and calibrated scale.)

(3) Pull the propeller through in the direction of rotation until the No. 1 piston is coming up on the compression stroke. This can be determined by holding the thumb over the spark plug hole until the compression blows the thumb off the hole.

(4) Separate the piston position indicator assembly and screw the housing into the spark plug bushing until it is seated firmly. Insert the indicator assembly into the body with the hook-end up or down as indicated on the scale.

(5) Push the slide pointer upward in the slot until it reaches the end of the slot and is stopped by the indicator arm (figure 4–38).

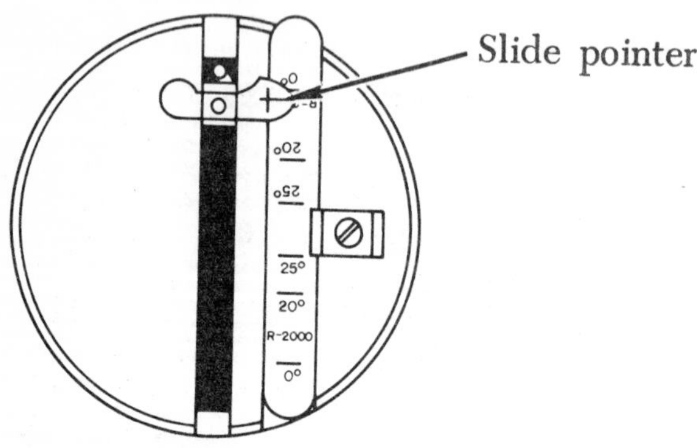

FIGURE 4–38. Positioning the slide pointer.

(6) Pull the propeller through slowly in the direction of rotation until the indicating arm has moved the slide pointer the maximum distance, and the indicating arm starts to move back upward in the slot (figure 4–39).

(7) Move the calibrated scale so that the zero mark on the scale aligns with the scribe mark on the slide pointer.

(8) Move the slide pointer back to the top of the slot, or until it contacts the indicating arm.

(9) Turn the propeller in the direction opposite to which it normally rotates until the indicating arm has returned to the top of the slot.

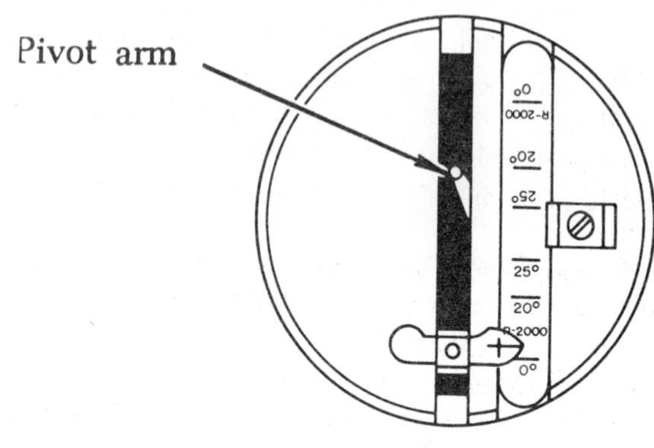

FIGURE 4–39. Slide pointer at maximum position.

(10) Recheck the zero mark of the calibrated scale against the reference mark on the slide pointer (figure 4–40).

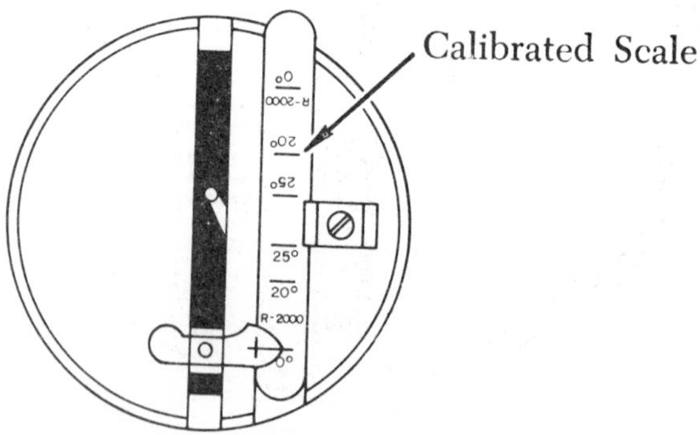

FIGURE 4–40. Rechecking the zero mark against reference mark on slide pointer.

(11) Again move the slide pointer to the top of the slot, or until it contacts the indicating arm.

(12) Pull the propeller through in the direction of rotation. Movement of the slide pointer by the indicating arm will indicate crankshaft position in relation to true top dead center on the calibrated scale (figure 4–41).

(13) Set the engine crankshaft at the prescribed number of degrees ahead of true top dead center (ignition timing) as specified in the applicable manufacturer's instruction.

While holding the magneto cam in the firing position for the No. 1 cylinder, as indicated by the alignment of the reference marks for the magneto, install the magneto splined drive into the engine drive.

Connect the timing light to the magneto and breaker points, and with the light and ignition switch turned on, rotate the magneto assembly, first in the direction of rotation and then in the opposite direction. Accomplish this procedure to determine that the timing light goes off and then on when the cam lobe for the No. 1 cylinder, usually marked by a white dot, lifts the breaker points as the magneto is rotated on its mount.

If the slots in the mounting flange of the magneto do not permit sufficient movement to effect breaker point opening for the No. 1 cylinder, move the magneto out of position far enough to permit turning the magneto drive shaft one spline in the advance or retard direction. Then install the magneto in position again and repeat the previous check for point opening.

After the magneto spline-to-engine female spline relationship has been established (permitting point opening and closing with slight rocking of the magneto), install the magneto attaching nuts on the studs and tighten slightly. The nuts must not be so tight as to prevent the movement of the magneto assembly when the magneto mounting flange is tapped with a mallet.

While holding the backlash out of the magneto gears and drive coupling, tap the magneto to advance or retard it until the timing marks align (figure 4–42). This times the internal timing of the magneto to the prescribed number of degrees before top center. After completing this adjustment, tighten the mounting nuts. Then move the propeller opposite the direction of rotation one blade, and then pull it slowly in the direction of rotation until the crankshaft position is again at the prescribed

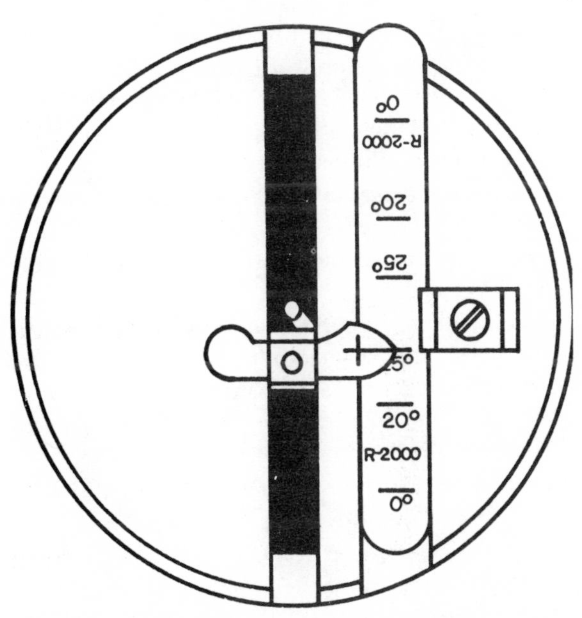

FIGURE 4–41. Moving crankshaft to piston firing position.

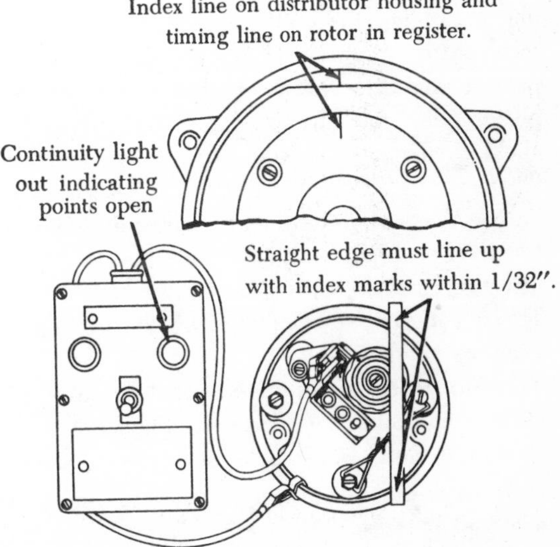

FIGURE 4–42. Scale in position for checking E-gap.

number of degrees ahead of top dead center. (The purpose of this check is to eliminate the possibility of error because of backlash in the engine gear-train assembly and magneto gears.) If the timing mark does not line up, loosen the mounting nuts and shift the magneto until the scale or straightedge will line up with the timing mark when the propeller is pulled through to the prescribed number of degrees.

Reconnect the timing light. Move the propeller one blade opposite the direction of rotation and then, while observing the timing light, move the propeller in the direction of rotation until the prescribed number of degrees ahead of top dead center is reached. Be sure that the lights for both sets of points come on within one-half-degree crankshaft movement of the prescribed crankshaft position.

After the points have been adjusted as necessary, recheck the point-adjusting lockscrew for tightness. Always check the point opening after tightening the lockscrew.

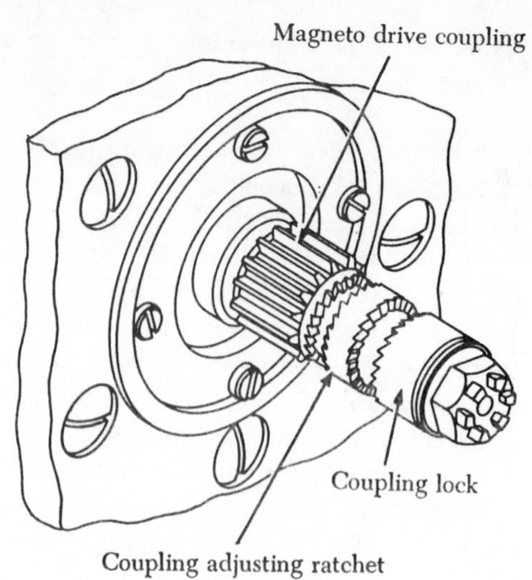

FIGURE 4–43. Magneto ratchet arrangement.

Timing Magneto Using Magneto Drive Ratchet

Because of the ignition harness design on some engines, it is not possible to rotate the magneto on its mount to accomplish minute changes in magneto timing. Provisions for accomplishing magneto-to-engine timing are provided by a ratchet arrangement on the end of the magneto drive shaft (figure 4–43). When the drive shaft nut has been loosened about 1/8 in., the clamping action of the ratchet mechanism is eliminated and the drive coupling is held against the ratchets only by a spring. In this position the coupling can be turned, producing a clicking effect between the ratchets, which are held by the spring. A typical timing ratchet has 24 teeth on one side and 23 teeth on the other side. Turning the drive coupling one click or tooth in the clockwise direction moves it 15° in a clockwise direction. Turning the drive coupling counterclockwise one click or tooth moves it counterclockwise 15.65°. Therefore, turning the drive coupling clockwise one click, then counterclockwise one click, gives a net change of 0.65° in a counterclockwise direction.

To time this type of magneto, special timing tools are usually prescribed by the applicable manufacturer's instruction. Otherwise, the instructions follow generally those discussed previously, except that fine timing adjustments are made to the magneto drive coupling ratchet.

Timing Rigid-Mounted Magneto Without Special Tools

Some types of high-tension magnetos can be timed to the engine without special tools by using procedures similar to the following example:

(1) Install the proper equipment for establishing crankshaft position.

(2) Set the crankshaft to the prescribed number of degrees ahead of top center for the ignition to fire as specified in the applicable manufacturer's instruction.

(3) Remove the magneto cover and place a straightedge or scale along the cam step (A of figure 4–44). Align the straightedge with the timing mark on the rim of the casting.

(4) While holding the cam in the firing position, place the magneto in position on the engine, allowing the cam to move as necessary so that the splined drive gear of the magneto will slip into place in the engine drive.

(5) Hold the cam opposite the direction of rotation to remove slack from the magneto and the engine gear train. Then, while holding the slack out of the gear drive train, place a straightedge across the step in the magneto cam and put a pencil mark on the housing (B of figure 4–44).

(6) Remove the magneto from the engine, and using a straightedge on the cam step, align

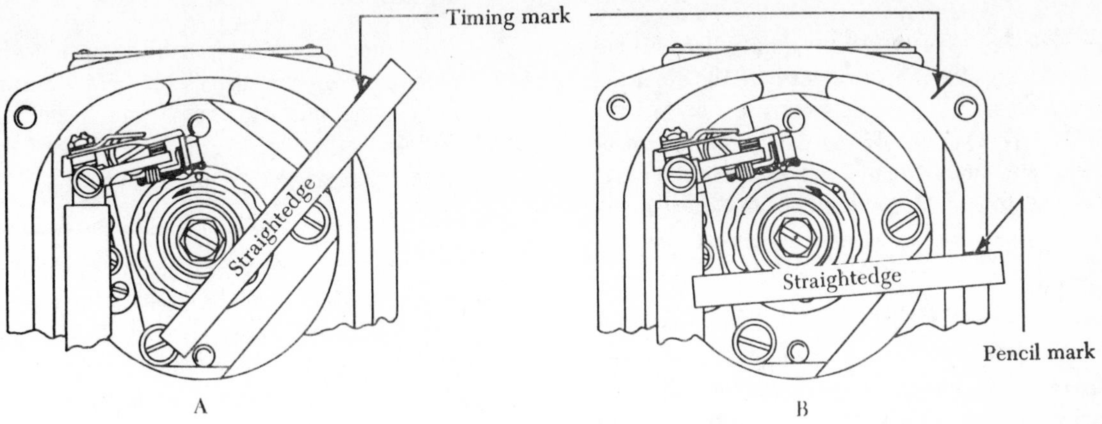

FIGURE 4–44. Aligning straightedge.

the cam step with the pencil mark on the housing. While holding the cam in this position, apply force to the magneto drive in the direction of rotation to remove the slack from the gears in the magneto. With the slack removed and the step on the cam aligned with the pencil mark, make another pencil mark on one spline of the drive shaft and a corresponding mark on the casting (A of figure 4–45).

(7) Turn the magneto cam to the No. 1 firing position where the straightedge lines up with the timing mark (as in A of figure 4–44). The result is a drive coupling alignment similar to that shown in view B of figure 4–45).

(8) While holding the cam in its correct timing position, ratchet the drive coupling until the marked tooth of the spline lines up with the pencil mark on the casting (A of figure 4–45).

(9) Tighten the drive shaft nut of the magneto and secure it with a cotter pin. Now install the magneto while holding the cam in the No. 1 firing position.

(10) After the magneto is installed and before tightening the attaching nuts, recheck the alignment of the cam step with the timing mark. When making this check, rotate the cam opposite the direction of rotation to remove the slack from the magneto and engine gears.

(11) Move the propeller one blade in the opposite direction of rotation. Then move the propeller slowly in the direction of rotation until the crankshaft is at the designated number of degrees ahead of top dead center (firing position). Recheck the alignment of the straightedge with the reference mark. If correct alignment is not obtained, remove the magneto and change the ratchet mechanism on the magneto drive shaft as necessary.

(12) Ground the black lead of the timing light to the engine, and connect one of the red leads to the magneto breaker points. Turn the propeller in the opposite direction of

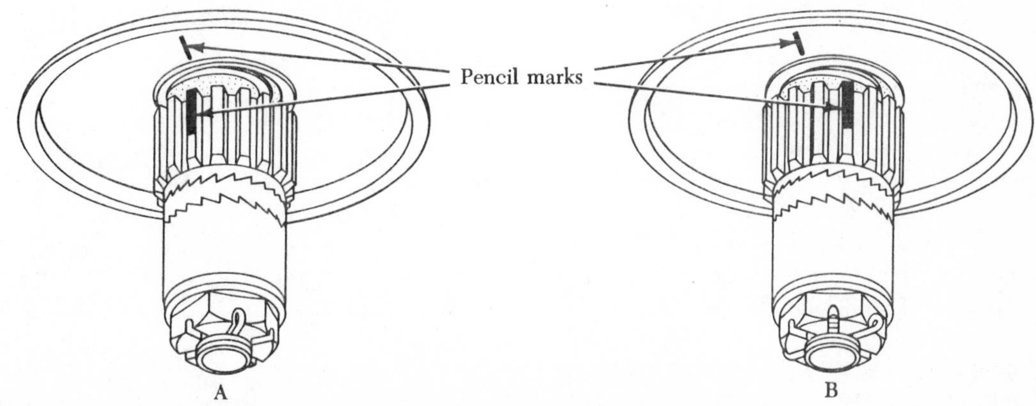

FIGURE 4–45. Marking drive spline.

rotation. Then, with the timing light turned on, move the propeller slowly in the direction of rotation until the points break for the No. 1 cylinder. If the points do not break within plus or minus one-half-degree crankshaft travel of the position specified in the manufacturer's instructions, repeat the timing procedure.

TIMING HIGH-TENSION SYSTEM DISTRIBUTOR FINGERS

Distributor fingers are basic parts for right and left magnetos on many models of engines. When the distributors are separate, a vernier adjustment is provided for proper distributor-finger timing. Distributor fingers on some engines are timed by shifting the distributor finger drive flange and selecting the proper mounting boltholes for the distributor finger. On any engine incorporating separate distributors, be sure that the distributor finger aligns with the electrode for No. 1 cylinder when the crankshaft is the prescribed number of degrees ahead of top center for the magneto to fire.

On engines, proper distributor finger timing is obtained by first establishing true top-dead-center position. Then the crankshaft is set at the prescribed number of degrees ahead of top center for the ignition to fire. Finally, the distributor finger is adjusted to align with the No. 1 electrode when all backlash has been removed from the distributor finger drive gears.

Since there are several different types of high-tension system distributors, always consult applicable manufacturer's instructions before timing a distributor to an engine. A summary of the procedures used in timing one type of distributor is included as an example of typical procedures.

To time the distributor to the engine, loosen the housing and remove some of the spark plug leads attached to the distributor. The housing is loosened by removing the base clamp ring and loosening the manifold clamp rings. Then the distributor housing is pushed back to expose the distributor finger.

The next step in the distributor timing procedure is to remove the distributor finger to expose the nut which locks the drive coupling. Then loosen the coupling nut and install the proper distributor timing tool. Rotate the coupling unit against the normal line with the scribed line on the parting surface. Tighten the coupling nut in this position after all backlash has been removed from the distributor drive gears. The timing tool can now be removed and the distributor finger installed.

The distributor housing assembly can now be placed in position on the distributor base. Secure all clamp rings on the distributor and install the spark plug leads that were removed. Safety the distributor as necessary.

Low-Tension Magneto System Timing Procedures

In timing the magneto to the engine, a number of different indicators may be used to locate the piston's top-dead-center position. In this example, a top center indicator light (figure 4–46) will be used with a disk attached to the starter pad on the engine accessory section.

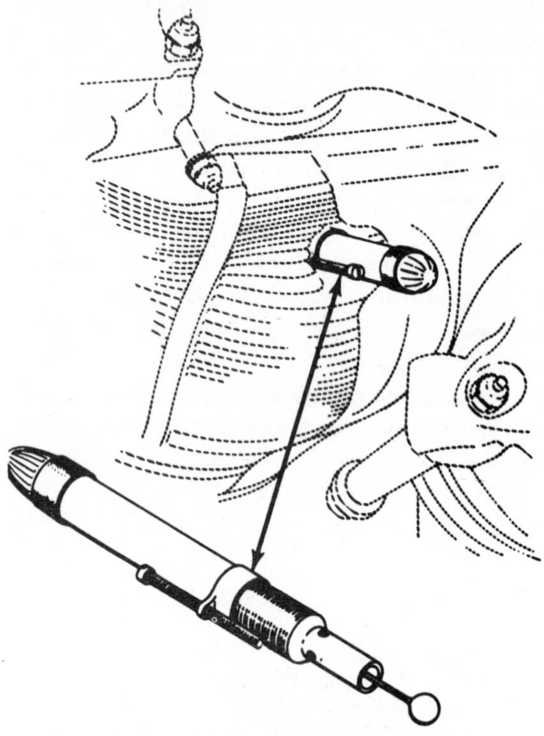

FIGURE 4–46. Top center indicator light.

To use the top center indicator light for finding top dead center, turn the propeller in the normal direction of rotation until the compression stroke is found. Install the top center indicator light in the spark plug hole. Turn the propeller in the normal direction of rotation until the light comes on, which indicates that the piston has moved the indicator arm. When the light comes on, stop and record the timing disk degree reading. Move the propeller in the direction of normal rotation until the light goes out. At this time, record the degree reading appearing on the timing disk. Compute the number of degrees of travel from the time the light came on until it went out. Halfway between the light-on and the light-out indications is top dead center.

Before installing any part of the ignition system, always make sure that the unit being installed has been properly checked and inspected for correct operation. Examine all exterior screws for tightness, and see that all safety wire is installed where necessary. Use a new gasket on the mounting pad.

After locating top dead center, back the propeller approximately three-fourths of a turn in the opposite direction of rotation. Then turn the propeller in the direction of rotation until the piston is in the normal firing position.

Make sure the magneto drive shaft has been tightened and a cotter pin installed. Remove the spring clip from the timing plunger, which holds the plunger in the "out" position. There are four notches in the magneto shaft; the plunger fits into these notches during the timing operation to hold the magneto shaft in the correct E-gap position. Press down the plunger and turn the magneto drive shaft until the plunger falls into one of the notches. Then set the magneto on the engine mounting pad (figure 4–47), holding the plunger in position so that it does not slip.

If the spline on the drive member will not mesh when the magneto is properly positioned on the mounting flange, move the magneto away from the mounting pad and rotate the magneto shaft 90° so that the plunger bottoms in the next slot on the magneto shaft. Put the magneto back on the mounting pad again and see if the splines and the mounting flange slots will match. If they do not match, repeat this procedure until the splines will mesh and the magneto is positioned properly on the mounting flange. After the correct position has been found, hold the magneto in this position and tighten the stud nuts which secure the magneto to the engine mounting flange.

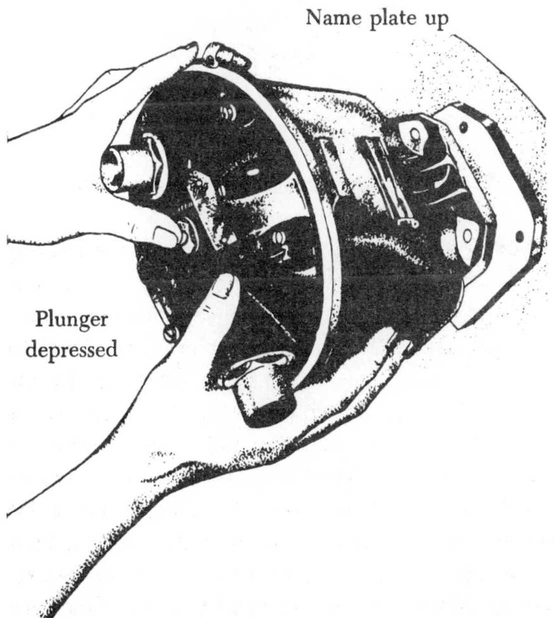

FIGURE 4–47. Installing a magneto.

To determine that the magneto is mounted in the E-gap position, slowly turn the propeller. As it nears the normal firing position for No. 1 cylinder, push the plunger in. It should fall in a notch when the firing position is reached.

Installing Low-Tension System Distributor

The distributor in a low-tension system, such as that discussed in the foregoing low-tension system, is installed as a separate unit. It is flange-mounted, with elongated slots used for adjustments.

Before installing the distributor, always check the master rod designation on the distributor plate against the engine data plate to see that the distributor has the correct breaker, corresponding to the master rod location in the engine.

Leave the piston at the specified number of degrees before top dead center used for timing the magneto. To prevent foreign particles from entering the unit, do not remove the protective covering until just before installing the distributor. At that time, remove the clamping ring and take off the distributor's protective cover. Rotate the distributor drive shaft until the line marked "1" on the finger is lined up with the line marked "Time-Open" on the collector plate, as shown in figure 4–48.

Keeping the distributor in this position, install it on the mounting flange, making sure the studs are aligned approximately in the center of the elongated slots in the distributor mounting flange as shown in figure 4–48.

If they do not align themselves in the middle of the flange slots, remove the distributor and shift the drive gear one tooth on its spline. Then reinstall the magneto, making sure the finger is still lined up with "1" position. When the right setting has been found for the drive gear, take the distributor off the mounting pad, tighten the end nut, and install a new cotter pin in the castellated nut. Reinstall the distributor and screw the holddown nuts finger-tight on the mounting bolts.

Connect the timing light red lead to the insulated side of the "1" main breaker and the black lead to the housing, as shown in figure 4–49. Then rotate

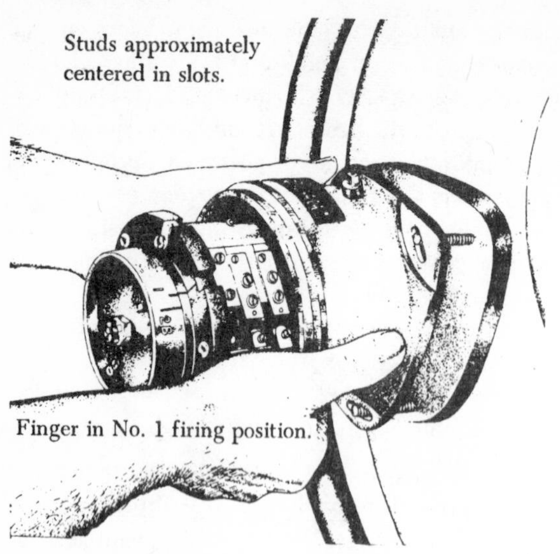
Studs approximately
centered in slots.
Finger in No. 1 firing position.

FIGURE 4–48. Distributor installation.

the distributor clockwise on its mounting pad until the timing light comes on, indicating that the points are just beginning to open. Tighten the flange hold-down nut with the distributor in this position. Mount the other distributor on the engine, using the same procedure.

After both distributors have been installed, their operation must be synchronized. Connect a red lead of the timing light to each main breaker and the black lead to ground. Back the propeller at least a fourth of a turn, and then turn it slowly in the direction of normal rotation through the No. 1 firing position to see if both main breaker points are opening at the same instant. If both timing lights come on at the same time, the distributors are synchronized.

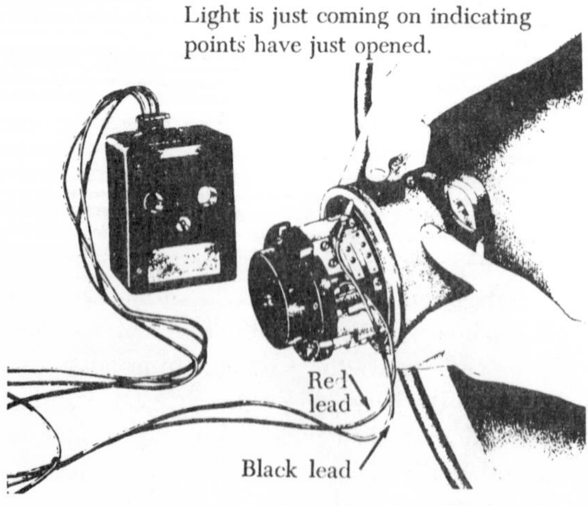
Light is just coming on indicating
points have just opened.
Red
lead
Black lead

FIGURE 4–49. Timing the low-tension distributor to the engine.

If the lights do not come on at the same time, the distributors must be re-synchronized. To do this, turn the second distributor slightly on its mounting pad until both sets of points (one on each distributor) open at the same instant, which must also be at the instant No. 1 cylinder reaches its firing point.

Replace the distributor heads and secure the clamping rings on the distributors. The ignition system is now ready for an operational check.

Performing Ignition System Checks

There are normally three ignition checks performed on aircraft during engine runup. The first is performed during engine warmup. The second is performed at field barometric manifold pressure. The third is performed prior to engine shutdown.

The first ignition check is normally made during warmup. Most manufacturers' instructions recommend this check during the warmup period. Actually, this check is a combination of the ignition system check and ignition switch check and is used to check the ignition system for proper functioning before other checks are made. The second check is performed as the ignition system check and is used to check the individual magnetos, harnesses, and spark plugs. The third check is performed as the ignition switch check and is used to check the switch for proper grounding for ground safety purposes.

The ignition system check is usually performed with the power check. The ignition check is sometimes referred to as the field barometric check, because on large engines it is performed with the engine operating at a manifold pressure equal to the field barometric pressure. The power check is also performed at the same manifold pressure setting. The ignition check should not be confused with the full throttle check. The exact r.p.m. and manifold pressure for making this check can be found in the applicable manufacturer's instructions.

The barometric pressure used as a reference will be the reading obtained from the manifold pressure gage for the engine involved prior to starting the engine and after engine shutdown. After reaching the engine r.p.m. specified for the ignition system check, allow the r.p.m. to stabilize. Place the ignition switch in the "right" position and note the r.p.m. drop on the tachometer. Return the switch to the "both" position. Allow the switch to remain in the "both" position for a few seconds so that the r.p.m. will again stabilize. Place the ignition switch in the "left" position and again note the r.p.m. drop. Return the ignition switch to the "both" position.

In performing this check, lightly tap the rim of the tachometer to ensure that the tachometer indicator pointer moves freely. A sticking tachometer pointer can conceal ignition malfunctions. There is also a tendency to perform this check too rapidly, which will result in wrong indications. Single ignition operation for as long as 1 minute is not considered excessive, but this time interval generally should not be exceeded.

Record the amount of the total r.p.m. drop which occurs immediately and also the amount which occurs slowly for each switch position. This breakdown in r.p.m. drop provides useful information. This ignition system check is usually performed at the beginning of the engine run-up, because if the r.p.m. drops were not within the prescribed limits, it would affect all other later checks.

Ignition Switch Check

The ignition switch check is usually made at 700 r.p.m. On those aircraft engine installations that will not idle at this low r.p.m., set the engine speed to the minimum possible to perform this check. When the speed to perform this check is obtained, momentarily turn the ignition switch to the "off" position. The engine should completely quit firing. After a drop of 200 to 300 r.p.m. is observed, return the switch to the "both" position as rapidly as possible. Do this quickly to eliminate the possibility of afterfire and backfire when the ignition switch is returned to "both."

If the ignition switch is not returned quickly enough, the engine r.p.m. will drop off completely and the engine will stop. In this case, leave the ignition switch in the "off" position and place the mixture control in "idle-cutoff" position to avoid overloading the cylinders and exhaust system with raw fuel. When the engine has completely stopped, allow it to remain inoperative for a short time before restarting.

The ignition switch check is performed to see that all magneto ground leads are electrically grounded. If the engine does not cease firing in the "off" position, the magneto ground lead, more commonly referred to as the "P" lead, is open; and the trouble must be corrected.

Replacement of Ignition Leads

When defective leads are revealed by an ignition harness test, continue the test to determine whether the leads or distributor block are defective. If the difficulty is in an individual ignition lead, determine whether the electrical leak is at the spark plug elbow or elsewhere. Remove the elbow, pull the ignition lead out of the manifold a slight amount, and repeat the harness test on the defective lead. If this stops the leakage, cut away the defective portion of the lead, and re-install the elbow assembly, integral seal, and cigarette (figure 4–50).

If the lead is too short to repair in the manner just described, or the electrical leak is inside the harness, replace the defective lead. If the harness is not the re-wirable type, the entire harness must be replaced. Ignition lead replacement procedures are as follows:

(1) Disassemble the magneto or distributor so that the distributor block is accessible.

(2) Loosen the piercing screw in the distributor block for the lead to be replaced, and remove the lead from the distributor block.

(3) Remove approximately 1 in. of insulation from the distributor-block end of the defective lead and approximately 1 in. of insulation from the end of the replacement cable. Splice this end to the end of the lead to be replaced and solder the splice.

(4) Remove the elbow adapter from the spark-plug end of the defective lead, and then pull the old lead out and the new lead into the harness. While pulling the leads through the harness, have someone push the replacement lead into the ignition manifold at the distributor end to reduce the force required to pull the lead through the ignition manifold.

(5) When the replacement lead has been pulled completely through the manifold, force the ignition lead up into the manifold from the distributor-block end to provide extra length for future repairs which may be necessary because of chafing at the spark plug elbow.

(6) Remove approximately 3/8 inch of insulation from the distributor-block end. Bend the ends of the wire back and prepare the ends of the cable for installation into the distributor-block well as illustrated in figure 4–49. Insert the lead in the distributor and tighten the piercing screw.

(7) Remove approximately 1/4 inch of insulation from the spark plug end of the lead and install the elbow, integral seal, and cigarette as illustrated in figure 4–50.

(8) Install a marker on the distributor end of the cable to identify its cylinder number. If a new marker is not available, use the marker removed from the defective cable.

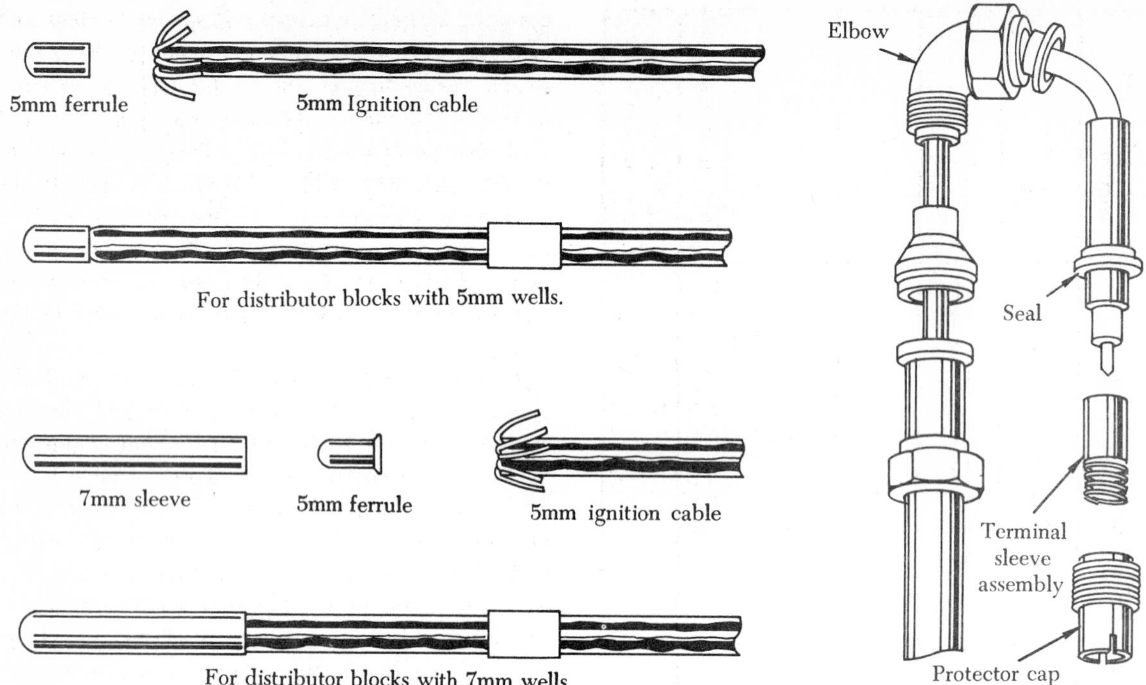

FIGURE 4–50. Replacement procedure for ignition lead terminals.

Replacement of Ignition Harness

Replace a complete rewirable ignition harness only when the shielding of the manifold is damaged or when the number of defective leads makes it more practical to replace the harness than to replace the individual leads. Replace a cast-filled harness only when leakage in the cast-filled portion is indicated. Before replacing any harness to correct engine malfunctioning, make extensive ignition harness tests. Typical procedures for installing an ignition harness are:

(1) Install the ignition harness on the engine. Tighten and safety the holddown nuts and bolts, and install and tighten the individual lead brackets according to instructions. The ignition harness is then ready for connection of the individual leads to the distributor block. A band is attached to each lead at the distributor end of the harness to identify the cylinder for the lead. However, each lead should be checked individually with a continuity or timing light prior to connecting it.

(2) Check for continuity by grounding the lead at the cylinder and then checking at the distributor-block end to establish that the lead grounded is as designated on the band for the lead.

(3) After checking all leads for proper identification, cut them to the proper length for installation into the distributor block. Before cutting the leads, however, force them back into the manifold as far as possible to provide surplus wire in the ignition manifold. This extra wire may be needed at a later date in the event that chafing of a lead at the spark plug elbow necessitates cutting a short section of wire from the spark-plug end of the harness. After cutting each lead to length, remove approximately 3/8 inch of insulation from the end and prepare the lead for insertion into the distributor block. Before installing the lead, back out the set screw in the distributor block far enough to permit slipping the end of the wire into the hole without force. Insert the lead into the block and tighten the set screw. Connect the wires in firing order, i.e., the first cylinder to fire No. 1 location on the block, the second in the firing order to No. 2 location, etc. Distributor block-to-cylinder connections for various engines are shown in the chart in figure 4–51.

After connecting each lead, check continuity between the lead and its distributor-block electrode with a continuity light or timing light. To perform

Distributor Block Number	18-Cylinder Radial	14-Cylinder Radial	9-Cylinder Radial	7-Cylinder Radial	6-Cylinder Horizontally Opposed	4-Cylinder Horizontally Opposed
1	1	1	1	1	1	1
2	12	10	3	3	4	3
3	5	5	5	5	5	2
4	16	14	7	7	2	4
5	9	9	9	2	3	
6	2	4	2	4	6	
7	13	13	4	6		
8	6	8	6			
9	17	3	8			
10	10	12				
11	3	7				
12	14	2				
13	7	11				
14	18	6				
15	11					
16	4					
17	15					
18	8					

FIGURE 4–51. Chart for connecting leads of distributor blocks of various engines.

this check, ground the ignition lead (to the engine) at the spark-plug end, ground one test lead, and touch the other test lead to the proper distributor-block electrode. If the light does not indicate a complete circuit, the set screw is not making contact with the ignition wire, or the lead is connected to the wrong block location. Correct any faulty connections before installing the distributor block.

Checking Ignition Booster Systems

To check the booster coil for proper operation, remove the high-tension lead from the booster coil. Install one end of a length of 7-mm. test ignition cable in the booster coil and hold the other end 3/8 inch from a suitable ground. Have an assistant make sure the manual mixture control is in the "idle cutoff" position, the fuel shutoff valve and booster pump for that engine are in the "off" position, and the battery switch is on. If the engine is equipped with an inertia or combination starter, the assistant should close the engage or mesh switch. Do not energize the starter prior to engaging it. If the engine is equipped with a direct-cranking starter, be sure the propeller is clear and close the start switch. As the engage, mesh, or start switch (depending on the engine starting system) is closed, continuous sparking should be observed from the end of the test lead. These sparks should be fat and snap with a bright blue arc to be considered satisfactory. If the booster coil is operating satisfactorily, signal the assistant to release the starter switch. Then remove the test lead and re-install the regular high-tension lead in the booster coil.

To check the induction vibrator, make sure the manual mixture control is in "idle cutoff," the fuel shutoff valve and booster pump for that engine are in the "off" position, and the battery switch is on. Since the induction vibrator will buzz whether the ignition switch is "on" or "off," leave the switch "off" during the check. If the engine is equipped with an inertia or combination starter, make the check by closing the engage or mesh switch; if the engine is equipped with a direct-cranking starter, see that the propeller is clear and close the start switch. An assistant, stationed close to the induction vibrator, should listen for an audible buzzing sound. If the unit buzzes when the starter is engaged or cranked, the induction vibrator is operating properly.

SPARK PLUG INSPECTION AND MAINTENANCE

Spark plug operation can often be a major source of engine malfunctions because of lead, graphite, or carbon fouling and because of spark plug gap erosion. Most of these failures, which usually accompany normal spark plug operation, can be minimized by good operational and maintenance practices.

Carbon Fouling of Spark Plugs

Carbon fouling (figure 4–52) from fuel is associated with mixtures that are too rich to burn or mixtures that are so lean they cause intermittent firing. Each time a spark plug does not fire, raw fuel and oil collect on the nonfiring electrodes and nose insulator. These difficulties are almost invariably associated with an improper idle mixture adjustment, a leaking primer, or carburetor malfunctions that cause too rich a mixture in the idle range. A rich fuel/air mixture is detected by soot or black smoke coming from the exhaust and by an increase in r.p.m. when the idling fuel/air mixture is leaned to "best power." The soot that forms as a result of overly rich, idle fuel/air mixtures settles on the inside of the combustion chamber because the heat

FIGURE 4–52. Carbon-fouled spark plug.

of the engine and the turbulence in the combustion chamber are slight. At higher engine speeds and powers, however, the soot is swept out and does not condense out of the charge in the combustion chamber.

Even though the idling fuel/air mixture is correct, there is a tendency for oil to be drawn into the cylinder past the piston rings, valve guides, and impeller shaft oil seal rings. At low engine speeds, the oil combines with the soot in the cylinder to form a solid which is capable of shorting out the spark plug.

Spark plugs that are wet or covered with lubricating oil are usually grounded out during the engine start. In some cases these plugs may clear up and operate properly after a short period of engine operation.

Engine oil that has been in service for any length of time will hold in suspension minute carbon particles that are capable of conducting an electric current. Thus, a spark plug will not arc the gap between the electrodes when the plug is full of oil. Instead, the high-voltage impulse flows through the oil from one electrode to the other without a spark just as surely as though a wire conductor were placed between the two electrodes. Combustion in the affected cylinder does not occur until, at a higher r.p.m., increased airflow has carried away the excess oil. Then, when intermittent firing starts, combustion assists in emitting the remaining oil. In a few seconds the engine is running clean with white fumes of evaporating and burning oil coming from the exhaust.

Lead Fouling of Spark Plugs

Lead fouling of aviation spark plugs is a condition likely to occur in any engine using "leaded fuels." Lead is added to aviation fuel to improve its antiknock qualities. The lead, however, has the undesirable effect of forming lead oxide during combustion. This lead oxide forms as a solid with varying degrees of hardness and consistency. Lead deposits on combustion chamber surfaces are good electrical conductors at high temperatures and cause misfiring. At low temperatures the same deposits may be good insulators. In either case, lead formations on aircraft spark plugs, such as shown in figure 4–53, prevent their normal operation. To minimize the formation of lead deposits, ethylene dibromide is added to the fuel as a scavenging agent which combines with the lead during combustion.

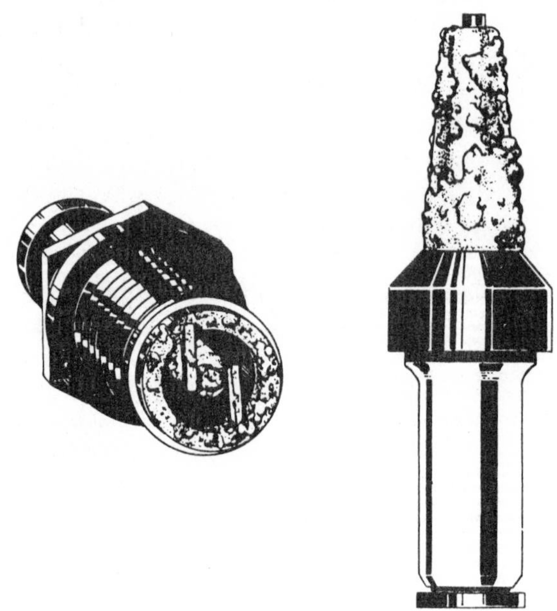

FIGURE 4–53. Lead-fouled spark plug.

Lead fouling may occur at any power setting, but perhaps the power setting most conducive to lead fouling is cruising with lean mixtures. At this power, the cylinder head temperature is relatively low and there is an excess of oxygen over that needed to consume all the fuel in the fuel/air mixture. Oxygen, when hot, is very active and aggressive; and when all the fuel has been consumed, some of the excess oxygen unites with some of the lead and some of the scavenger agent to form oxygen compounds of lead or bromine or both. Some of these undesirable lead compounds solidify and build up in layers as they contact the relatively cool cylinder walls and spark plugs.

Although lead fouling may occur at any power setting, experience indicates that the lead buildup is generally confined to a specific combustion temperature range, and combustion temperatures higher or lower than this specific range minimize the lead-fouling tendency. If lead fouling is detected before the spark plugs become completely fouled, the lead can normally be eliminated or reduced by either a sharp rise or a sharp decrease in combustion temperature. This imposes a thermal shock on cylinder parts, causing them to expand or contract. Since there is a different rate of expansion between deposits and metal parts on which they form, the deposits chip off or are loosened and then scavenged from the combustion chamber by the exhaust or are burned in the combustion process.

Several methods of producing thermal shock to cylinder parts are used. The method used, of course, depends on the accessory equipment installed on the engine. A sharp rise in combustion temperatures can be obtained on all engines by operating them at full takeoff power for approximately 1 minute. When using this method to eliminate fouling, the propeller control must be placed in low pitch (high r.p.m.) and the throttle advanced slowly to produce takeoff r.p.m. and manifold pressure. Slow movement of the throttle control provides reasonable freedom from backfiring in the affected cylinders during the application of power.

Another method of producing thermal shock is the use of excessively rich fuel/air mixtures. This method suddenly cools the combustion chamber because the excess fuel does not contribute to combustion; instead, it absorbs heat from the combustion area. Some carburetor installations use two-position manual mixture controls, which provide a lean mixture setting for cruising economy and a richer mixture setting for all powers above cruising. Neither manual mixture control setting in this type of configuration is capable of producing an excessively rich fuel/air mixture. Even when the engine is operated in auto-rich at powers where an auto-lean setting would be entirely satisfactory, the mixture is not rich enough.

Therefore, to obtain a richer fuel/air mixture than the carburetor is capable of delivering, the primer system is used to supplement the normal fuel flow. Enrichment and thermal shock can be effected by the primer at all engine speeds, but its effectiveness in removing lead decreases as fuel metering through normal channels increases. The reason for this is that all electric primers deliver a nearly constant fuel flow at all engine speeds and powers in a like period of time. Therefore, comparatively speaking, the primer will enrich the lean mixtures of low engine speeds far more than it would the richer mixtures accompanying higher engine speeds.

Regardless of the power setting at which primer purging is used, the primer should be used continuously for a 2-minute interval. If normal engine operation is not restored after a 2-minute interval, it may be necessary to repeat the process several times. Some priming systems prime only the cylinders above the horizontal centerline of the engine; in which case, only those cylinders receiving the priming charge can be purged.

On engines equipped with water injection, combustion temperature can be sharply decreased by manual operation of the water injection system. Water injection is normally reserved for high-power operation; but when it is used for purging purposes, the system is most effective when activated in the cruising range, it is accompanied by a momentary power loss. This power loss can be traced to the following factors. First of all, the derichment jet is not metering the fuel in the cruising range. Hence, when the derichment valve is closed by the water injection system, there is no decrease in fuel flow from the carburetor. Secondly, when the water regulator first starts to meter, it meters fuel that was backed up into the water transfer line during normal "dry" operation. This fuel, plus the unchanged fuel flow from the carburetor, produces an overrich mixture, temporarily flooding the engine. As soon as this fuel is consumed by the engine, engine power returns, but to a value slightly less than was obtained before water injection. When water injection is used to lower combustion temperatures, it should be limited to a short (approximately 1-minute) interval, even though several intervals may be necessary to free the cylinders of the lead deposit.

Some water injection system installations are considered automatic; that is, the operator has no control over the power at which the system will "cut in." These systems start injecting water automatically at some predetermined manifold pressure if the water pump has been turned on. When these systems are used for lead purging, the full benefit of water injection cannot be obtained because at high-power settings where the automatic system starts to operate, more heat is generated by the engine, the fuel/air ratio is leaned, and the combustion temperature cannot be lowered as much. Regardless of how lead is removed from cylinder parts, whether it is by high-power operation, by use of the primer, or by use of the water injection system, the corrective action must be initiated before the spark plugs are completely shorted or fouled out.

Graphite Fouling of Spark Plugs

As a result of careless and excessive application of thread lubricant to the spark plug, the lubricant will flow over the electrodes and cause shorting. Shorting occurs because graphite is a good electrical conductor. The elimination of service difficulties caused by graphite is up to the aviation mechanics. Use care when applying the lubricant to make certain that smeared fingers, rags, or brushes do not contact the electrodes or any part of the ignition system except the spark plug threads. Practically no success has been experienced in trying to burn off or dislodge the thread lubricant.

Gap Erosion of Spark Plugs

Erosion of the electrodes takes place in all aircraft spark plugs as the spark jumps the airgap between the electrodes. (See figure 4–54.)

The spark carries with it a portion of the electrode, part of which is deposited on the other electrode, and the remainder is blown off in the combustion chamber. As the airgap is enlarged by erosion, the resistance that the spark must overcome in jumping the airgap also increases. This means that the magneto must produce a higher voltage to overcome the higher resistance. With higher voltages in the ignition system, a greater tendency exists for the spark to discharge at some weak insulation point in the ignition harness. Since the resistance of an airgap also increases as the pressure in the engine cylinder increases, a double danger exists at takeoff and during sudden acceleration with enlarged airgaps. Insulation breakdown, premature flash-over, and carbon tracking result in misfiring of the spark plug, and go hand in hand with excessive spark plug gap. Wide gap settings also raise the "coming in speed" of a magneto and therefore cause hard starting.

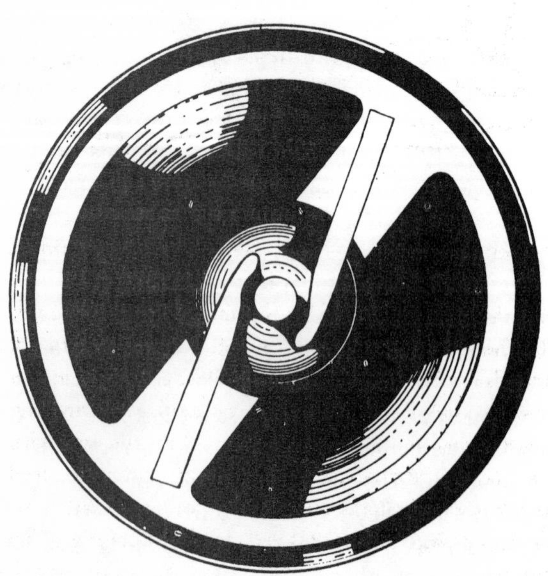

FIGURE 4–54. Spark plug gap erosion.

Spark plug manufacturers have partially overcome the problem of gap erosion by using a hermetically sealed resistor in the center electrode of some spark plugs. This added resistance in the high-tension circuit reduces the peak current at the instant of firing. This reduced current flow aids in preventing metal disintegration in the electrodes. Also, due to the high erosion rate of steel or any of its known alloys, spark plug manufacturers are using tungsten or an alloy of nickel for their massive electrode plugs and platinum plating for their fine wire electrode plugs.

Spark Plug Removal

Spark plugs should be removed for inspection and servicing at the intervals recommended by the manufacturer. Since the rate of gap erosion varies with different operating conditions, engine models, and type of spark plug, engine malfunction traceable to faulty spark plugs may occur before the regular servicing interval is reached. Normally, in such cases, only the faulty plugs are replaced.

Careful handling of the used and replacement plugs during installation and removal of spark plugs from an engine cannot be overemphasized, since spark plugs can be easily damaged. To prevent damage, spark plugs should always be handled individually, and new and reconditioned plugs should be stored in separate cartons. A common method of storage is illustrated in figure 4–55. This is a drilled tray, which prevents the plugs from bumping against one another and damaging the fragile insulators and threads. If a plug is dropped on the floor or other hard surface, it should not be installed in an engine, since the shock of impact usually causes small, invisible cracks in the insulators. The plug should be tested under controlled

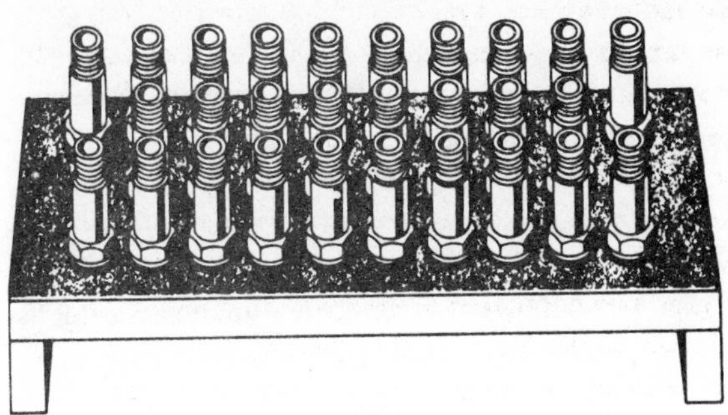

FIGURE 4–55. Spark plug tray.

pressure conditions before use.

Before a spark plug can be removed, the ignition harness lead must be disconnected. Using the special spark plug coupling elbow wrench, loosen and remove the spark plug to elbow coupling nut from the spark plug. Take care to pull the lead straight out and in line with the centerline of the plug barrel. If a side load is applied, as shown in figure 4–56, damage to the barrel insulator and the ceramic lead terminal may result. If the lead cannot be removed easily in this manner, the neoprene collar may be stuck to the shielding barrel. Break loose the neoprene collar by twisting the collar as though it were a nut being unscrewed from a bolt.

After the lead has been disconnected, select the proper size deep socket for spark plug removal. Apply a steady pressure with one hand on the hinge handle holding the socket in alignment with the other hand. Failure to hold the socket in correct alignment, as shown in figure 4–57, will cause the socket to cock to one side and damage the spark plug.

In the course of engine operation, carbon and other products of combustion will be deposited across the spark plug and cylinder, and some carbon may even penetrate the lower threads of the shell. As a result, a high torque is generally required to break the spark plug loose. This factor imposes a shearing load on the shell section of the plug; and if the load is great enough, the plug may break off, leaving the shell section in the cylinder spark plug hole.

Inspection and Maintenance Prior to Installation

Before installing new or reconditioned spark plugs in the engine cylinders, clean the spark plug bushings or Heli-Coil inserts.

Brass or stainless steel spark plug bushings are usually cleaned with a spark plug bushing cleanout tap. Before inserting the cleanout tap in the spark plug hole, fill the flutes of the tap (channels between threads) with clean grease to prevent hard carbon or other material removed by the tap from dropping into the inside of the cylinder. Align the tap with the bushing threads by sight where possible, and start the tap by hand until there is no possibility of the tap being cross-threaded in the bushing. To start the tap on some installations where the spark plug hole is located deeper than can be reached by a clenched hand, it may be necessary to use a short

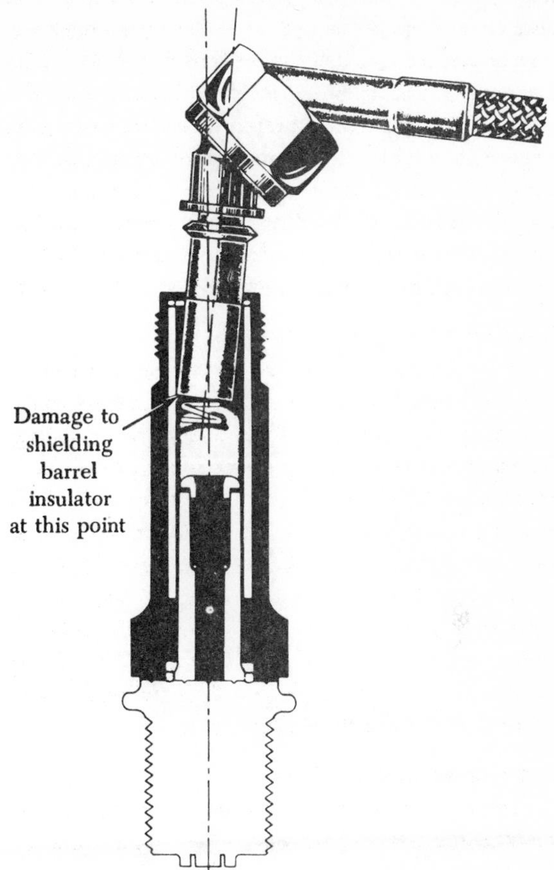

FIGURE 4–56. Improper lead removal technique.

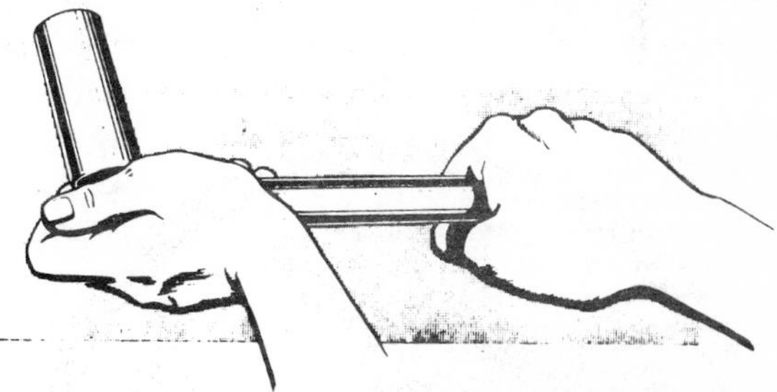

FIGURE 4–57. Proper spark plug removal technique.

length of hose slipped over the square end of the tap to act as an extension. When screwing the tap into the bushing, be sure that the full tap cutting thread reaches the bottom thread of the bushing. This will remove carbon deposits from the bushing threads without removing bushing metal, unless the pitch diameter of the threads has contracted as the result of shrinkage or some other unusual condition. If, during the thread-cleaning process, the bushing is found to be loose or is loosened in the cylinder or the threads are cross-threaded or otherwise seriously damaged, replace the cylinder.

Spark plug Heli-Coil inserts are cleaned with a round wire brush, preferably one having a diameter slightly larger than the diameter of the spark plug hole. A brush considerably larger than the hole may cause removal of material from the Heli-Coil proper or from the cylinder head surrounding the insert. Also, the brush should not disintegrate with use, allowing wire bristles to fall into the cylinder. Clean the insert by carefully rotating the wire brush with a power tool. When using the power brush, be careful that no material is removed from the spark plug gasket seating surface, since this may cause a change in the spark plug's heat range, combustion leakage, and eventual cylinder damage. Never clean the Heli-Coil inserts with a cleaning tap, since permanent damage to the insert will result. If a Heli-Coil insert is damaged as a result of normal operation or while cleaning it, replace it according to the applicable manufacturer's instructions.

Using a lint-free rag and cleaning solvent, wipe the spark plug gasket seating surface of the cylinder to eliminate the possibility of dirt or grease being accidentally deposited on the spark plug electrodes at the time of installation.

Before the new or reconditioned plugs are installed, they must be inspected for each of the following conditions:

(1) Be sure the plug is of the approved type, as indicated by the applicable manufacturer's instructions.

(2) Check for evidence of rust-preventive compound on the spark plug exterior and core insulator and on the inside of the shielding barrel. Rust-preventive compound accumulations are removed by washing the plug with a brush and cleaning solvent. It must then be dried with a dry air blast.

(3) Check both ends of the plug for nicked or cracked threads and any indication of cracks in the nose insulator.

(4) Inspect the inside of the shielding barrel for cracks in the barrel insulator, and the center electrode contact for rust and foreign material which might cause poor electrical contact.

(5) Inspect the spark plug gasket. A gasket that has been excessively flattened, scarred, dented, or distorted by previous use must not be used. When the thermocouple gasket is used, do not use an additional gasket.

The gap setting should be checked with a round wire thickness gage, as shown in figure 4–58. A flat type gage will give an incorrect clearance indication because the massive ground electrodes are contoured to the shape of the round center electrode. When using the wire thickness gage, insert the gage in each gap parallel to the centerline of the center electrode. If the gage is tilted slightly, the indication will be incorrect. Do not install a plug that does not have an airgap within the specified clearance range.

Spark Plug Installation

Prior to spark plug installation, carefully coat the first two or three threads from the electrode end of the shell with a graphite base antiseize compound. Prior to application, stir the antiseize compound to ensure thorough mixing. When applying the antiseize compound to the threads, be extremely careful

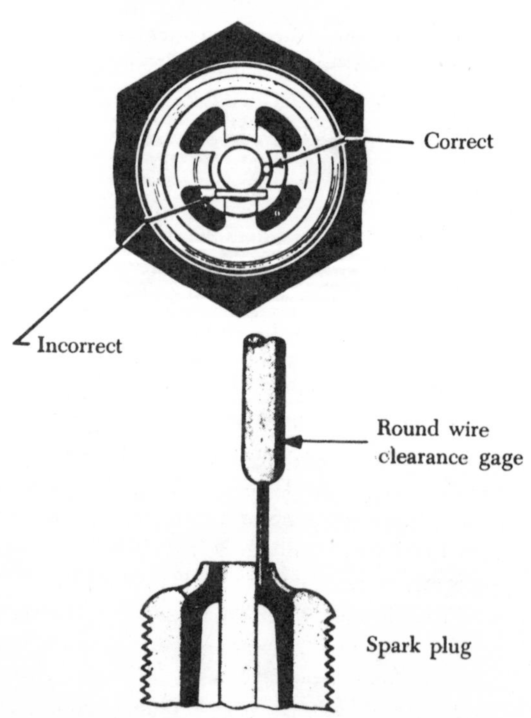

FIGURE 4–58. Use of a gap-measuring gage.

that none of the compound gets on the ground or center electrodes or on the nose of the plug, where it can spread to the ground or center electrode during installation. This precaution is mentioned because the graphite in the compound is an excellent electrical conductor and could cause permanent fouling.

To install a spark plug, start it into the cylinder without using a wrench of any kind, and turn it until the spark plug is seated on the gasket. If the plug can be screwed into the cylinder with comparative ease, using the fingers, this indicates good, clean threads. In this case, only a small additional tightening torque will be needed to compress the gasket to form a gastight seal. If, on the other hand, a high torque is needed to install the plug, dirty or damaged threads on either the plug or plug bushing are indicated. The use of excessive torque might compress the gasket out of shape and distort and stretch the plug shell to a point where breakage would result during the next removal or installation. Shell stretching occurs as excessive torque continues to screw the lower end of the shell into the cylinder after the upper end has been stopped by the gasket shoulder. As the shell stretches (figure 4–59), the seal between the shell and core insulator is opened, creating a loss of gas tightness or damage to the core insulator. After a spark plug has been seated with the fingers, use a torque wrench and tighten to the specified torque.

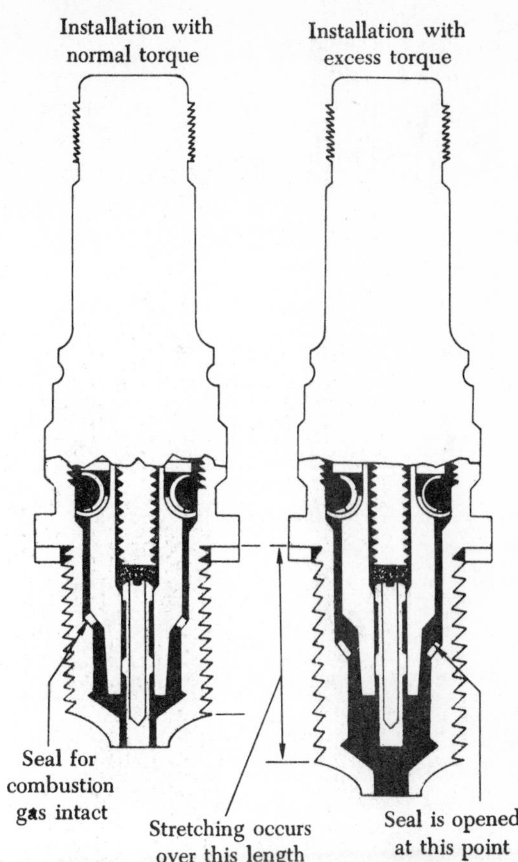

FIGURE 4–59. Effect of excessive torque in installing a spark plug.

Spark Plug Lead Installation

Before installing the spark plug lead, carefully wipe the terminal sleeve (sometimes referred to as "cigarette") and the integral seal with a cloth moistened with acetone, MEK, or an approved solvent. After the plug lead is cleaned, inspect it for cracks and scratches. If the terminal sleeve is damaged or heavily stained, replace it.

Application of a light coating of an insulating material to the outer surface of the terminal sleeve and also filling the space occupied by the contact spring is sometimes recommended. Such insulating material, by occupying the space in the electrical contact area of the shielding barrel, prevents moisture from entering the contact area and shorting the spark plug. Some manufacturers recommend the use of such insulating compounds only when moisture in the ignition system becomes a problem, and others have discontinued entirely the use of such materials.

After inspection of the spark plug lead, slip the lead into the shielding barrel of the plug with care. Then tighten the spark plug coupling elbow nut with the proper tool. Most manufacturers' instructions specify the use of a tool designed to help prevent an overtorque condition. After the coupling nut is tightened, avoid checking for tightness by twisting the body of the elbow.

After all plugs have been installed, torqued, and the leads properly installed, start the engine and perform a complete ignition system operational check.

Breaker Point Inspection

Inspection of the magneto consists essentially of a periodic breaker point and dielectric inspection. After the magneto has been inspected for security of mounting, remove the magneto cover, or breaker cover, and check the cam for proper lubrication. Under normal conditions there is usually ample oil in the felt oiler pad of the cam follower to keep the cam lubricated between overhaul periods. However, during the regular routine inspection, examine the felt pad on the cam follower to be sure it contains sufficient oil for cam lubrication. Make this check by pressing the thumbnail against the oiler pad. If oil appears on the thumbnail, the pad contains sufficient oil for cam lubrication. If there is no evidence of oil on the fingernail, apply one drop of a light aircraft engine oil to the bottom felt pad and one drop to the upper felt pad of the follower assembly, as shown in figure 4–60.

After application, allow at least 15 minutes for the felt to absorb the oil. At the end of 15 minutes, blot off any excess oil with a clean, lint-free cloth. During this operation, or any time the magneto cover is off, use extreme care to keep the breaker compartment free of oil, grease, or engine cleaning solvents, since each of these has an adhesiveness which collects dirt and grime that could foul an otherwise good set of breaker contact points.

After the felt oiler pad has been inspected, serviced, and found to be satisfactory, visually inspect the breaker contacts for any condition that may interfere with proper operation of the magneto. If the inspection reveals an oily or gummy substance on the sides of the contacts, swab the contacts with a flexible wiper, such as a pipe cleaner dipped in acetone or some other approved solvent. By forming a hook on the end of the wiper, ready access can be gained to the back side of the contacts.

To clean the contact mating surfaces, force open the breaker points enough to admit a small swab. Whether spreading the points for purposes of cleaning or checking the surfaces for condition, always apply the opening force at the outer end of the mainspring and never spread the contacts more than one-sixteenth (0.0625) in. If the contacts are spread wider than recommended, the mainspring (the spring carrying the movable contact point) is likely to take a permanent set. If the mainspring takes a permanent set, the movable contact point loses some of its closing tension and the points will then either "bounce" or "float," preventing the normal induction buildup of the magneto.

A swab can be made by wrapping a piece of linen tape or a small piece of lint-free cloth over one of the leaves of a clearance gage and dipping the swab in an approved solvent. Then pass the swab between the carefully separated contact surfaces until the surfaces are clean. During this entire operation take care that drops of solvent do not fall on lubricated parts, such as the cam, follower block, or felt oiler pad.

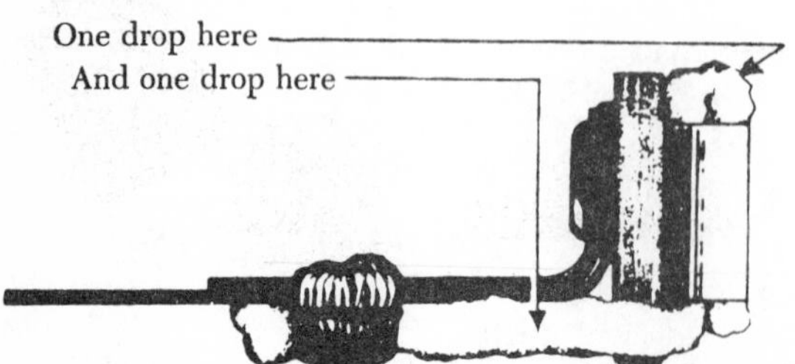

FIGURE 4–60. Oiling the cam follower.

To inspect the breaker contact surfaces, it is necessary to know what a normal operating set of contacts looks like, what surface condition is considered as permissible wear, and what surface condition is cause for dressing or replacement. The probable cause of an abnormal surface condition can also be determined from the contact appearance. The normal contact surface (figure 4–61) has a dull gray, sandblasted (almost rough) appearance over the area where electrical contact is made. This gray, sandblasted appearance indicates that the points have worn in and have mated to each other and are providing the best possible electrical contact.

This is not meant to imply that this is the only acceptable contact surface condition. Slight, smooth-surfaced irregularities, without deep pits or high peaks, such as shown in figure 4–62, are considered normal wear and are not cause for dressing or replacement.

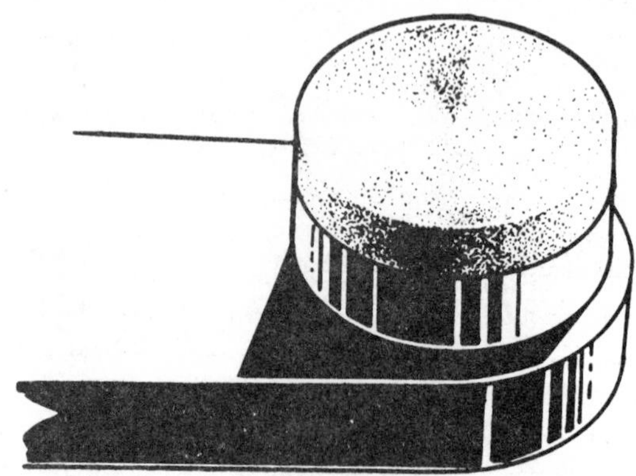

FIGURE 4–61. Normal contact surface.

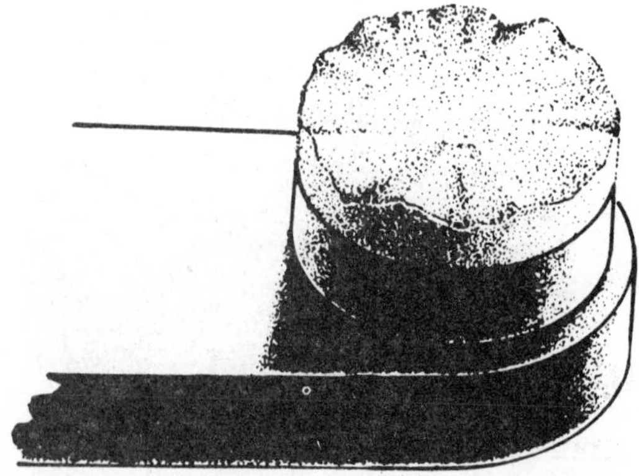

FIGURE 4–62. Points with normal irregularities.

However, when wear advances to a point where the slight, smooth irregularities develop into well-defined peaks extending noticeably above the surrounding surface, as illustrated in figure 4–63, the breaker contacts must be dressed or replaced.

Unfortunately, when a peak forms on one contact, the mating contact will have a corresponding pit or hole. This pit is more troublesome than the peak because it penetrates the platinum pad of the contact surface. It is sometimes difficult to judge whether a contact surface is pitted deeply enough to require dressing, because in the final analysis this depends on how much of the original platinum is left on the contact surface. The danger arises from the possibility that the platinum pad may already be thin as a result of long service life and previous dressings. At overhaul facilities, a gage is used to measure the remaining thickness of the pad, and no difficulty in determining the condition of the pad exists. But at line maintenance activities, this gage is generally unavailable. Therefore, if the peak is quite high or the pit quite deep, do not dress these contacts; instead, remove and replace them with a new or reconditioned assembly. A comparison between figures 4–62 and 4–63 will help to draw the line between "minor irregularities" and "well-defined peaks."

Some examples of possible breaker contact surface conditions are illustrated in figure 4–64. Item A illustrates an example of erosion or wear called "frosting." This condition results from an open-circuited condenser and is easily recognized by the coarse, crystalline surface and the black "sooty" appearance of the sides of the points. The lack of effective condenser action results in an arc of intense heat being formed each time the points open. This, together with the oxygen in the air, rapidly oxidizes and erodes the platinum surface of the points, producing the coarse, crystalline, or frosted appearance. Properly operating points have a fine-grained, frosted, or silvery appearance and should not be confused with the coarse-grained and sooty point caused by faulty condenser action.

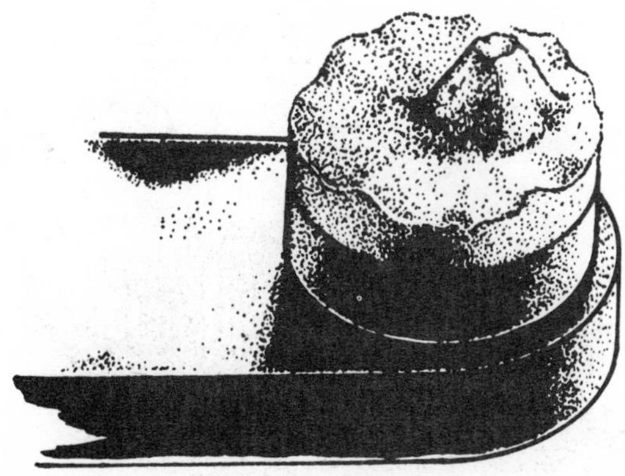

FIGURE 4–63. Points with well-defined peaks.

Items B and C of figure 4–64 illustrate badly pitted points. These points are identified by a fairly even contact edge (in the early stage) and minute pits or pocks in or near the center of the contact surface with a general overall smoky appearance. In more advanced stages, the pit may develop into a large, jagged crater, and eventually the entire contact surface will take on a burned, black, and crumpled appearance. Pitted points, as a general rule, are caused by dirt and impurities on the contact surfaces. If points are excessively pitted, a new or reconditioned breaker assembly must be installed.

Item D of figure 4–64 illustrates a "crowned" point and can be readily identified by the concave center and a convex rim on the contact surface. This condition results from improper dressing, as may be the case when an attempt is made to dress points while they are still installed in the magneto. In addition to an uneven or unsquare surface, the tiny particles of foreign material and metal that

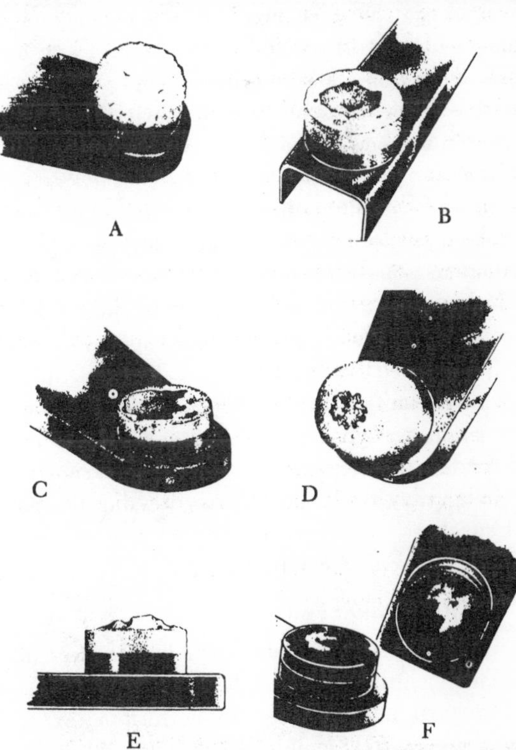

FIGURE 4–64. Examples of contact surface condition.

remain between the points after the dressing operation fuse and cause uneven burning of the inner contact surface. This burning differs from "frosting" in that a smaller arc produces less heat and less oxidation. In this instance the rate of burning is more gradual. "Crowned" points, if not too far gone, may be cleaned and returned to service. If excessive crowning has taken place, the points must be removed and replaced with a new or reconditioned set.

Item E of figure 4–64 illustrates a "built-up point that can be recognized by the mound of metal which has been transferred from one point to another. "Buildup," like the other conditions mentioned, results primarily from the transfer of contact material by means of the arc as the points separate. But, unlike the others, there is no burning or oxidation in the process because of the closeness of the pit of one point and the buildup of the other. This condition may result from excessive breaker point spring tension, which retards the opening of the points or causes a slow, lazy break. It can also be caused by a poor primary condenser or a loose connection at the primary coil. If excessive buildup has occurred, a new or reconditioned breaker assembly must be installed.

Item F of figure 4–64 illustrates "oily points," which can be recognized by their smoked and smudged appearance and by the lack of any of the above-mentioned irregularities. This condition may be the result of excessive cam lubrication or of oil vapors which may come from within or outside the magneto. A smoking or fuming engine, for example, could produce the oil vapors. These vapors then enter the magneto through the magneto ventilator and pass between and around the points. These conductive vapors produce arcing and burning on the contact surfaces. The vapors also adhere to the other surfaces of the breaker assembly and form the sooty deposit. Oily points can ordinarily be made serviceable by using a suitable cleaning procedure. However, the removal of smoke and smudge may reveal a need for dressing the points. If so, dress the points or install a new or reconditioned breaker assembly.

Dressing Breaker Points

Generally speaking, disassembly and dressing of breaker points should not be a regular routine step of magneto maintenance. By performing expensive and unnecessary maintenance on the point assemblies, many sets of points reach the scrap bin prematurely, with perhaps two-thirds to three-fourths of the platinum contact surface material filed away by repeated dressing operations. In a majority of the cases, breaker points will remain in satisfactory condition between overhaul periods with only routine inspection, cleaning, and lubrication.

If the breaker contacts have deep pits, mounds, or burnt surfaces, they should be dressed or replaced according to the maintenance practice recommended by the manufacturer. If dressing of breaker contacts is approved, a special contact point dressing kit will normally be available. The kit includes a contact point dressing block and adapters to hold the contacts during the dressing operation, a special file to remove the peaks and mounds, and a very fine whetstone to be used in the final dressing operation to remove any ridges or burrs left by the file.

While dressing a set of contacts that have pits and peaks, do not try to remove the pit completely. File only enough material to smooth and flatten the surface around the pit. This will usually leave plenty of contact area around the hole (figure 4–65) and the assembly will perform in the same manner as a new set of points. It is obvious that if the pit were deep, most of the platinum pad might be removed if an attempt were made to entirely eliminate the pit by filing.

In dressing off the peaked side of the set of contacts, the peak should be entirely filed off. The surface of this contact should be perfectly smooth and flat to provide the largest possible contact area against the other contact, which now will have a slightly decreased area due to the remaining pit. In completing the dressing operation, it is not necessary to obtain a mirror finish on the contact area; only a few strokes of the stone (figure 4–66) will

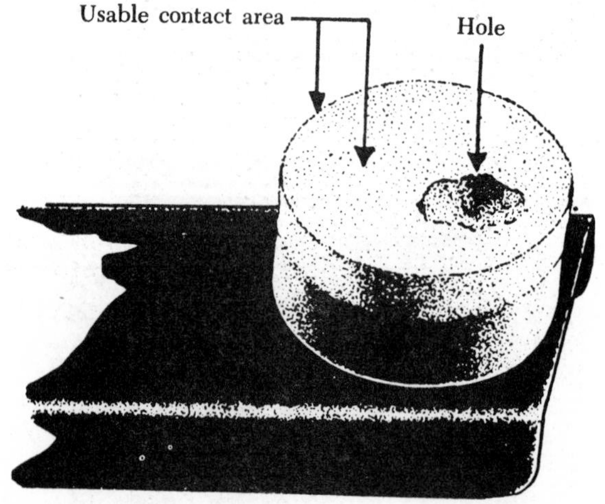

FIGURE 4–65. Pitted point after dressing.

be required to remove any ridges left by the file.

The primary objective is to have the contact surfaces flat so that they will provide a satisfactory contact area when assembled. A full contact area for the two reconditioned surfaces is often difficult to obtain, since it requires perfect flatness of the surfaces. This difficulty is somewhat compromised by an approach which permits about a two-thirds full contact area (figure 4–67), if the usable area is on the side away from the cam follower block. The actual contact surface can be checked by holding the assembled breaker in front of a light and observing whether light can be seen between the contact surfaces.

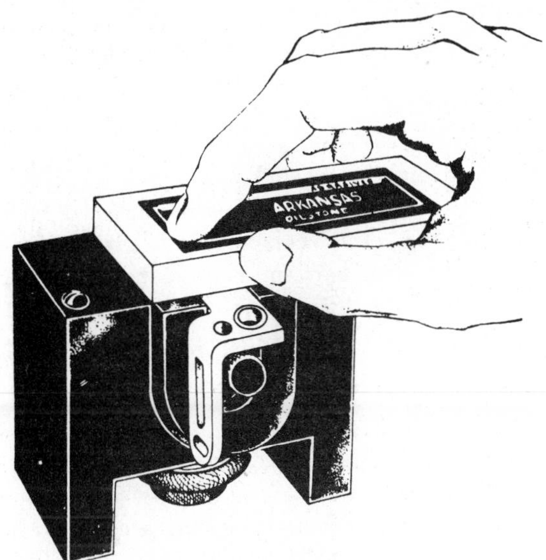

FIGURE 4–66. Using the contact point dressing stone.

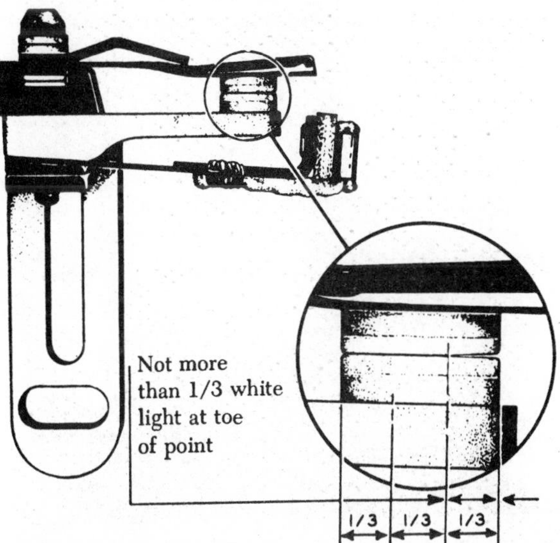

FIGURE 4–67. Checking breaker contact area.

If the breaker contact points have been removed for any reason, the replacement or reconditioned points must be installed and precisely timed to open just as the rotating magnet of the magneto moves into the E-gap position for the No. 1 cylinder.

Dielectric Inspection

Another phase of magneto inspection is the dielectric inspection. This inspection is a visual check for cleanliness and cracks. If inspection reveals that the coil cases, condensers, distributor rotor, or blocks are oily or dirty or have any trace of carbon tracking, they will require cleaning and possibly waxing to restore their dielectric qualities.

Clean all accessible condensers and coil cases which contain condensers by wiping them with a lint-free cloth moistened with acetone. Many parts of this type have a protective coating. This protective coating is not affected by acetone, but it may be damaged by scraping or by the use of other cleaning fluids. Never use unapproved cleaning solvents or improper cleaning methods. Also, when cleaning condensers or parts which contain condensers, do not dip, submerge, or saturate the parts in any solution because the solution used may seep inside the condenser and short out the plates.

Coil cases, distributor blocks, distributor rotors, and other dielectric parts of the ignition system are treated with a wax coating when they are new and again at overhaul. The waxing of dielectrics aids their resistance to moisture absorption, carbon tracking, and acid deposits. When these parts become dirty or oily, some of the original protection is lost, and carbon tracking may result.

If any hairline carbon tracks or acid deposits are present on the surface of the dielectric, immerse the part in approved cleaning solvent and scrub it vigorously with a stiff bristle brush. When the carbon track or acid deposits have been removed, wipe the part with a clean, dry cloth to remove all traces of the solvent used for cleaning. Then coat the part with a special ignition-treating wax. After wax treating the part, remove excess wax deposits and re-install the part in the magneto.

Ignition Harness Maintenance

Although the ignition harness is simple, it is a vital link between the magneto and spark plug. Because the harness is mounted on the engine and exposed to the atmosphere, it is vulnerable to heat, moisture, and the effects of changing altitude. These factors, plus aging insulation and normal gap erosion, work against efficient engine operation. The insulation may break down on a wire inside the harness and allow the high voltage to leak through the insulation to the harness shielding instead of going to the spark plug. Open circuits may result from broken wires or poor connections. A bare wire may be in physical contact with the shielding, or two wires may be shorted together.

Any serious defect in an individual lead prevents the high-tension impulse from reaching the spark plug to which the lead is connected. As a result this plug will not fire. When only one spark plug is firing in a cylinder, the charge is not consumed as quickly as it would be if both plugs were firing. This factor causes the peak pressure of combustion to occur later on the power stroke. If the peak pressure occurs later than normal, a loss of power in that cylinder results. However, the power loss from a single cylinder becomes a minor factor when the effect of a longer burning time is considered. A longer burning time overheats the affected cylinder, causing detonation, possible pre-ignition, and perhaps permanent damage to the cylinder.

The insulated wire that carries the electrical impulse is a special type of cable designed to prevent excessive losses of electrical energy. This wire is known as high-tension ignition cable and is manufactured in three diameters. The outside diameters of cables in current use are 5, 7, or 9 mm. (millimeters). The reason for different cable diameters is that the amount and kind of insulation around the conducting core determines the amount of electrical loss during transmission of the high voltage. Since the conducting core carries only a weak current, the conductor is of a small diameter.

The 9-mm. cable has only a limited application now because it is of early design and has a relatively thick layer of insulation. For the most part, present-day engines use the 7-mm. size, but there are a few systems which are designed to use 5-mm. cable. The increased use of the smaller size cable is largely due to improvements in the insulation material, which permits a thinner insulating sheath. Adapter sleeves have been designed for the ends of the smaller improved cable so that it can be used in re-wirable harnesses where the distributor wells were originally designed for larger cable.

One type of cable construction uses a core consisting of 19 strands of fine copper wire covered with a rubber sheath. This, in turn, is covered by a reinforcing braid and an outside coat of lacquer (A of figure 4–68). A newer type of construction (B of figure 4–68) has a core of seven strands of stainless steel wire covered with a rubber sheath. Over this is woven a reinforcing braid, and a layer of neoprene is added to complete the assembly. This type of construction is superior to the older type primarily because the neoprene has improved resistance to heat, oil, and abrasion.

High-Tension Ignition Harness Faults

Perhaps the most common and most difficult high-tension ignition system faults to detect are high-voltage leaks. This is leakage from the core conductor through insulation to the ground of the shielded manifold. A certain small amount of leakage exists even in brand new ignition cable during normal operation. Various factors then combine to produce first a high rate of leakage and then complete breakdown. Of these factors, moisture in any form is probably the worst. Under high-voltage

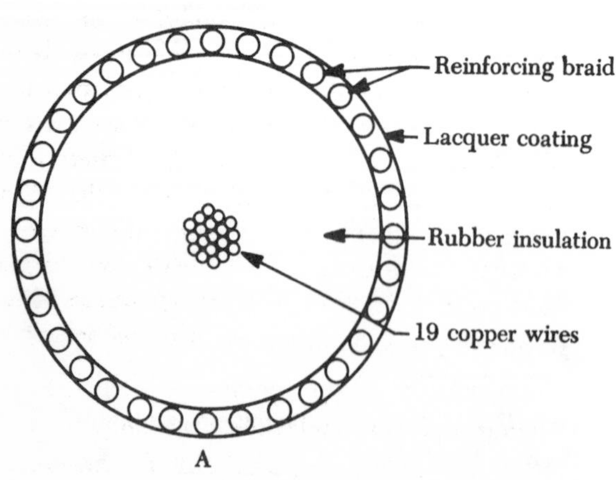

A. Older types of construction

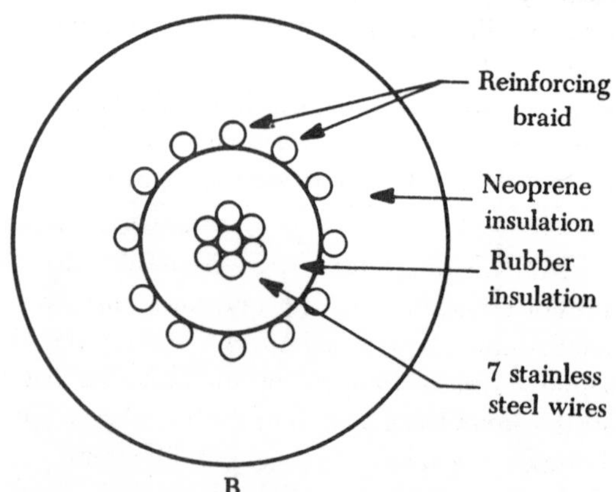

B. Newer types of construction

FIGURE 4–68. Cross-sectional view of typical high-tension ignition cable.

stress, an arc forms and burns a path across the insulator where the moisture exists. If there is gasoline or oil or grease present, it will break down and form carbon. The burned path is called a carbon track, since it is actually a path of carbon particles. With some types of insulation, it may be possible to remove the carbon track and restore the insulator to its former useful condition. This is generally true of porcelain, ceramics, and some of the plastics because these materials are not hydrocarbons, and any carbon track forming on them is the result of a dirt film that can be wiped away.

Differences in location and amount of leakage will produce different indications of malfunction during engine operation. Indications are generally misfiring or crossfiring. The indication may be intermittent, changing with manifold pressure or with climate conditions. An increase in manifold pressure increases the compression pressure and the resistance of the air across the airgap of the spark plugs. An increase in the resistance at the airgap opposes the spark discharge and produces a tendency for the spark to discharge at some weak point in the insulation. A weak spot in the harness may be aggravated by moisture collecting in the harness manifold. With moisture present, continued engine operation will cause the intermittent faults to become permanent carbon tracks. Thus, the first indication of ignition harness unserviceability may be engine misfiring or roughness caused by partial leakage of the ignition voltage.

Figure 4–69, showing a cross section of a harness, demonstrates four faults that may occur. Fault A shows a short from one cable conductor to another. This fault usually causes misfiring, since the spark is short circuited to a plug in a cylinder where the cylinder pressure is low. Fault B illustrates a cable with a portion of its insulation scuffed away. Although the insulation is not completely broken down, more than normal leakage exists, and the spark plug to which this cable is connected may be lost during takeoff when the manifold pressure is quite high.

Fault C is the result of condensation collecting in the lowest portion of the ignition manifold. This condensation may completely evaporate during engine operation, but the carbon track that is formed by the initial flashover remains to allow continued flashover whenever high manifold pressure exists. Fault D may be caused by a flaw in the insulation or the result of a weak spot in the insulation which is aggravated by the presence of moisture. However, since the carbon track is in direct contact with the metal shielding, it will probably result in flashover under all operating conditions.

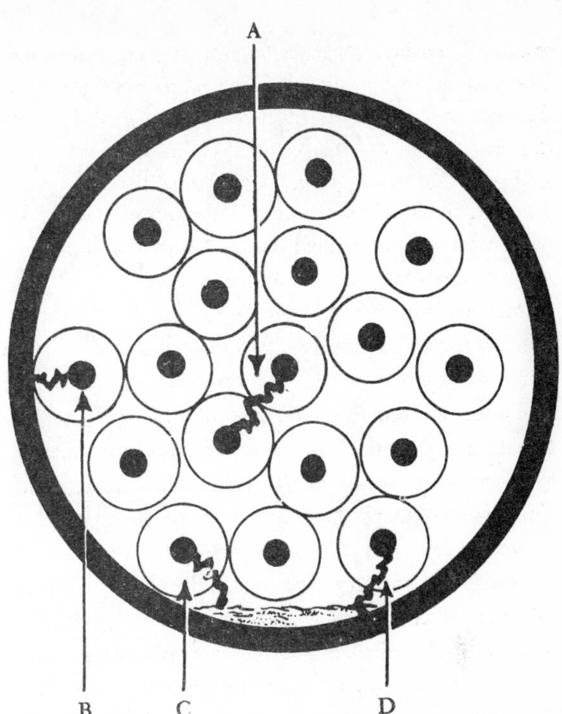

FIGURE 4–69. Cross section of an ignition harness.

Harness Testing

The electrical test of the ignition harness checks the condition or effectiveness of the insulation around each cable in the harness. The principle of this test involves application of a definite voltage to each lead and then measurement with a very sensitive meter of the amount of current leakage between the lead and the grounded harness manifold. This reading, when compared with known specifications, becomes a guide to the condition or serviceability of the cable. As mentioned earlier, there is a gradual deterioration of flexible insulating material. When new, the insulation will have a low rate of conductivity, so low, in fact, that under several thousand volts of electrical pressure the current leakage will be only a very few millionths of an ampere. Natural aging will cause an extremely slow, but certain, change in the resistance of insulating material, allowing an ever-increasing rate of current leakage.

Testing High-Tension Ignition Harness

Several different types of test devices are used for determining the serviceability of high-tension ignition harness. One common type of tester, illustrated in figure 4–70, is capable of applying a direct current in any desired voltage from zero to 15,000 volts with a 110-volt, 60-cycle input. The current leakage between ignition cable and ignition manifold is measured on two scales of a microammeter that is graduated to read from zero to 100 μa. (microampere) and from zero to 1,000 μa. Since 1,000 μa. are equal to 1 ma. (milliampere), the zero to 1,000 scale is called the ma. scale and the other a μa. scale. Readings may be obtained on either scale by the use of a high- or low-resistance range switch located on the right of the ammeter. Current-limiting resistors are used in both ranges to prevent damage to the test circuit through accidental application of excessive voltages.

The voltage impressed on the cable being tested is indicated on a voltmeter calibrated to read from zero to 15,000 volts. A control knob at the left of the voltmeter permits a voltage adjustment to the recommended test voltage. In addition to the ammeter and voltmeter, a neon light is provided to indicate flashover, which may be too rapid to cause noticeable needle deflection on the microammeter.

The control switches for the tester (figure 4–70) include a filament switch, plate switch, and remote switch. The filament switch completes a circuit

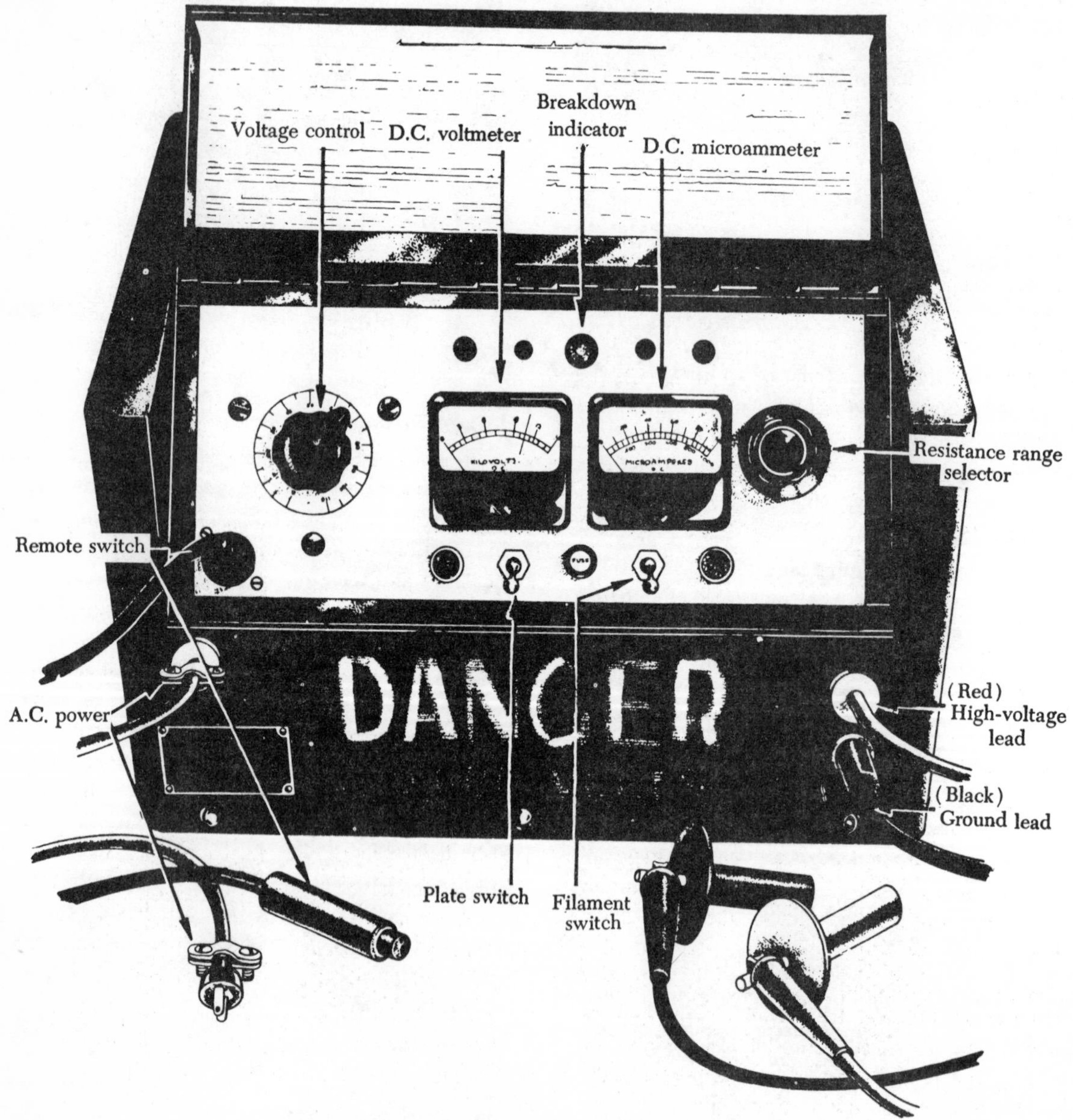

FIGURE 4–70. High-tension ignition harness tester.

between the a.c. input circuit and the filament element of the rectifier tube. Current flow to the filament heats the filament and prepares the tube for operation. The tube function, however, is not complete until the plate of the same tube is energized. The plate voltage of the rectifier is dependent on two switches, the plate control switch and the remote switch. The plate control switch arms or readies the plate circuit for operation. With the plate and filament switches on, depressing the remote switch will place the tube in operation and impress the test voltage to an ignition cable if the test leads are connected. The pushbutton remote switch must be plugged into a socket in the lower left-hand corner of the instrument panel. This switch arrangement permits operation of the tester at distances up to 5 ft.

The following paragraphs illustrate the use of this type of test unit. These instructions are presented as a general guide only. Consult the applicable manufacturer's instructions before performing an ignition harness test.

The ignition harness need not be removed from the engine to perform the harness test. If the test is performed with the harness on the engine, all spark plug leads must be disconnected from the plugs because the voltage applied during the test is high enough to cause an arc across the unpressurized airgap. After each lead is disconnected, each lead contact, except the lead to be tested, should be positioned against the cylinder so that it will be well grounded. The reason for grounding all spark plug leads during the test is to check and detect excessive leakage or breakdown resulting from short circuiting between two ignition leads. If the spark plug leads were ungrounded during the test, short circuiting could not be detected because all spark plug leads would have open circuits and only the insulation leakage to the ground potential of the harness manifold could be indicated. However, when all leads are grounded except the lead receiving the test voltage, a complete circuit is formed through short-circuited leads, and any leakage or excessive current flow to ground is indicated by the microammeter or the flashing of the neon light breakdown indicator.

When all the spark plug leads have been detached from the spark plugs and grounded to the engine, prepare the harness tester for the test. Begin by connecting the earth-ground binding post on the back of the tester to a rod driven into the earth or to a well-grounded object. Connect the red high-voltage lead (figure 4–70) to the high-voltage terminal on the tester. Connect the other end of the high-voltage test lead to the ignition harness lead being tested. Plug one end of the black ground lead into the ground receptacle on the front of the tester and the other end to the engine or some other common ground. Plug the remote switch lead into the ignition tester panel. Make sure all switches are turned off and the high-voltage control knob is set at zero; then connect the power supply lead to a 110-volt, 60-cycle a.c. power supply line. Turn the filament switch on and allow about 10 seconds for the filament in the tube to heat. After a 10-second interval, turn the plate switch on. With the plate and filament switches on, adjust the voltage that will be applied to each ignition cable during the test.

Adjustment is made by depressing the remote switch and rotating the high-voltage control knob clockwise until the voltmeter registers 10,000 volts. Just as soon as the recommended voltage is reached, release the remote switch. Releasing the remote switch automatically turns off the high-voltage supply. Once the voltage is adjusted to the recommended value, no further voltage adjustment is necessary throughout the test. The final step in setting up the tester is positioning the resistance range selector to the "high" position so that the current leakage can be easily read on the microammeter.

The test is usually started with the No. 1 cylinder. Since all spark plug leads are already grounded and the red high-voltage lead is connected to the No. 1 cylinder lead, test this lead by simply depressing the remote switch and observing the microammeter. When the test indication is known, release the remote switch, remove the high-voltage test lead, ground the ignition lead just tested, and proceed to the next lead in the cylinder numbering order. It is important that each lead, whether it tests good or bad, be re-grounded before conducting a further lead test. As the testing progresses around the engine, note only those leads by number which give an indication of excessive leakage (more than 50 μa.) or of breakdown indicated by flashing breakdown indicator.

At the completion of the test, at least two leads in any harness will probably show faults. This can be explained by referring to figure 4–71 and noting the position of the distributor rotor. When the test voltage is applied to the bottom lead of the illustration, a flashover may occur across the small distributor airgap and through the magneto primary coil to ground or through the ignition switch to ground. With synchronized firing, this apparent fault will

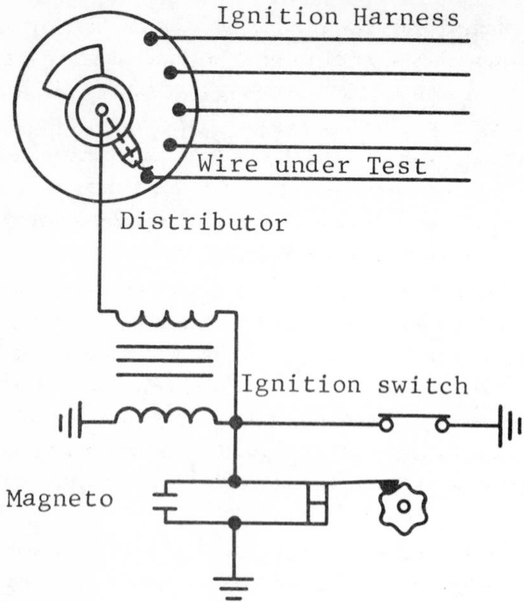

FIGURE 4–71. Breakdown not attributed to insulation failure.

show up in both front and rear spark plug leads for a particular cylinder. To determine whether or not a real breakdown exists in these cables, turn the propeller about one-fourth to one-half revolution and repeat the test on these leads. This will move the distributor rotor away from the lead terminal being tested and give an accurate indication of lead condition. Do not turn the propeller immediately after an apparently bad lead is located, since the distributor rotor may stop opposite another lead which has not been tested, making it necessary to turn the propeller again.

Anytime a majority of the leads show excessive leakage, the fault may be dirty or improperly treated distributor blocks. If this is the case, clean or wax the distributor block according to the procedures outlined in the applicable manufacturer's instructions.

D.C. Insulation Tester

There are several types of small, lightweight, portable testers that can operate from a regular 115-volt, 60-cycle a.c. power input or from an aircraft's 28-volt d.c. power supply.

These testers use essentially the same meters and switches as the high-tension ignition harness tester already discussed. Further, the indications of leakage and breakdown are practically the same. This type of tester is a portable instrument and can be hand-carried to any location.

THE ENGINE ANALYZER

The engine analyzer is an adaptation of the laboratory oscilloscope. It is a portable or permanently installed instrument, whose function is to detect, locate, and identify engine operating abnormalities such as those caused by a faulty ignition system, detonation, sticking valves, poor fuel injection, or the like. The need for a more positive means of detecting and locating operational troubles became evident with the introduction of the larger, more complex aircraft engines.

The majority of aircraft operational troubles are due to a faulty ignition system and are the type which usually show up at low altitude or during ground operation. However, many engine difficulties, especially those of the ignition system, occur during flight at high altitudes. Since high-altitude conditions cannot be simulated on the ground, it is desirable to have a unit which can, at all times, indicate engine operation abnormalities.

Engine analyzers are generally classified into two types. One type produces evidence of the condition of the ignition system only. The other type reveals abnormal vibrations during operation such as those caused by detonation, valve sticking, and poor fuel distribution, as well as ignition malfunctions.

Analyzers are designed to be used as portable analyzers or as permanently installed equipment in an aircraft. Most standard models contain the ignition voltage control feature and selector switches, which permit the use of either the induction pickup, the breaker assembly, or the three-phase generator for synchronization.

The weight of airborne and portable-airborne installations will vary with the particular installation involved. On a typical twin-engine transport aircraft equipped with low-tension ignition, the portable/airborne installation weighs about 22.0 lbs. (including wire, connectors, and equipment). The airborne installation weighs approximately 45.5 lbs.

An airborne installation is one in which the ignition analyzer unit and its associated equipment are permanently installed in the aircraft. No storage locker for the leads is used. A portable/airborne installation is one in which the associated equipment is permanently installed in the aircraft, but the analyzer is eliminated. A storage locker for the leads is used. In the latter instance, the analyzer is carried from aircraft to aircraft to make ignition checks, or it is flown with the aircraft for those ignition checks to be made at altitude.

The airborne analyzer installation has one major

advantage: the analyzer is always with the aircraft. To make such an installation involves the added cost of the analyzer. Obviously, it demands that the aircraft have personnel on board able to operate the instrument in flight. It permits flight personnel to check the ignition system before landing and, thus, makes it possible to have the difficulties promptly attended to after landing.

The diagram in figure 4–72 illustrates an airborne ignition analyzer installation in a typical aircraft. It shows that one breaker and filter assembly is required per engine. Only one relay/resistor box is required per aircraft. An exception to this rule is those aircraft having certain types of high-tension ignition installations. These installations require one relay/resistor box per engine.

The synchronizing breaker assembly "triggers" the horizontal sweep circuit of the cathode-ray tube. It operates at one-half engine crankshaft speed and is timed 3° to 4° before the firing of the No. 1 cylinder.

The radio interference filter is mounted on the firewall and in the ignition primary circuit. The number of units per filter depends on the number of ground wires carried in each ignition primary circuit. A unit normally consists of a choke coil and one or two condensers wired in parallel with the magneto primary condenser. The filter is required because the associated analyzer equipment is not radio shielded. It also permits the analyzer primary circuit wiring to be unshielded.

The relay/resistor box contains an isolating resistor for each engine. It also contains hermetically sealed relays, which will permit the selective and individual bypassing of the resistors for any engine. The isolating resistors are to prevent any short-to-ground in the analyzer circuit from grounding an engine magneto. The bypass relays permit the ignition voltage control to be used.

The panel assembly contains an engine and condition selector switch, individual relay operation toggle switches for each engine (guards are installed to prevent accidental operation of the switch), and a power switch complete with fuse and pilot light. It is the control center for the analyzer.

A block diagram of an ignition analyzer is shown

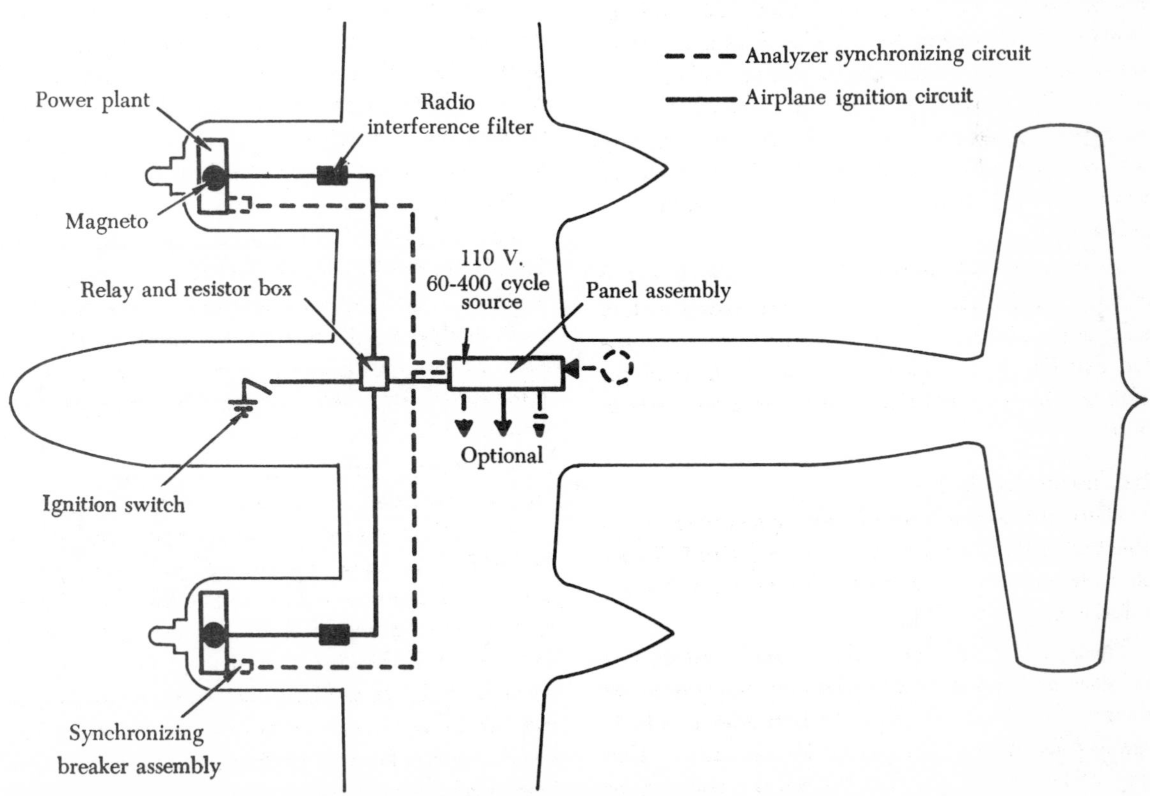

FIGURE 4–72. Twin-engine analyzer installation.

in figure 4–73. Signals can be traced from any of the three possible types of signal pickup devices to the display on the face of the cathode-ray tube.

Figure 4–74 illustrates six typical engine analyzer patterns. Although additional training is required before one can accurately interpret the meaning of each signal, the configuration of the signals in figure 4–74 shows that every malfunction presents a distinctive and recognizable picture.

TURBINE ENGINE IGNITION SYSTEMS

Since turbine ignition systems are operated for a brief period during the engine-starting cycle, they are, as a rule, more trouble-free than the typical reciprocating engine ignition system. Most turbojet engines are equipped with a high-energy, capacitor-type ignition system. Both turbojet and turboprop engines may be equipped with an electronic-type ignition system, which is a variation of the simpler capacitor-type system.

Turbojet Engine Ignition System

The typical turbojet engine is equipped with a capacitor-type (capacitor discharge) ignition system consisting of two identical independent ignition units operating from a common low-voltage d.c. electrical power source, the aircraft battery. Turbojet engines can be ignited readily in ideal atmospheric conditions, but since they often operate in the low temperatures of high altitudes, it is imperative that the system be capable of supplying a high-heat-intensity spark. Thus, a high voltage is supplied to arc across a wide igniter spark gap, providing the ignition system with a high degree of reliability under widely varying conditions of altitude, atmospheric pressure, temperature, fuel vaporization, and input voltage.

A typical ignition system includes two exciter units, two transformers, two intermediate ignition leads, and two high-tension leads. Thus, as a safety factor, the ignition system is actually a dual system, designed to fire two igniter plugs. Figure 4–75 shows one side of a typical ignition system.

Figure 4–76 is a functional schematic diagram of a typical capacitor-type turbojet ignition system. A 24-volt d.c. input voltage is supplied to the input receptacle of the exciter unit.

Before the electrical energy reaches the exciter

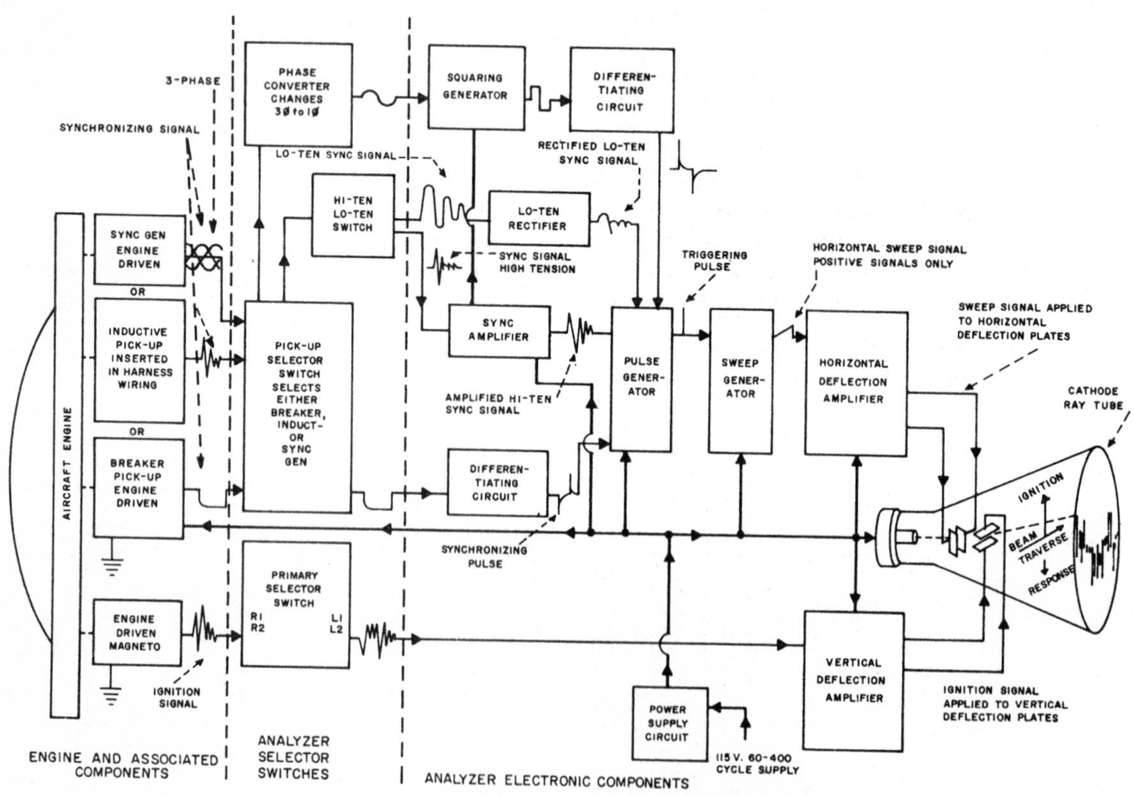

FIGURE 4–73. Diagram of ignition analyzer.

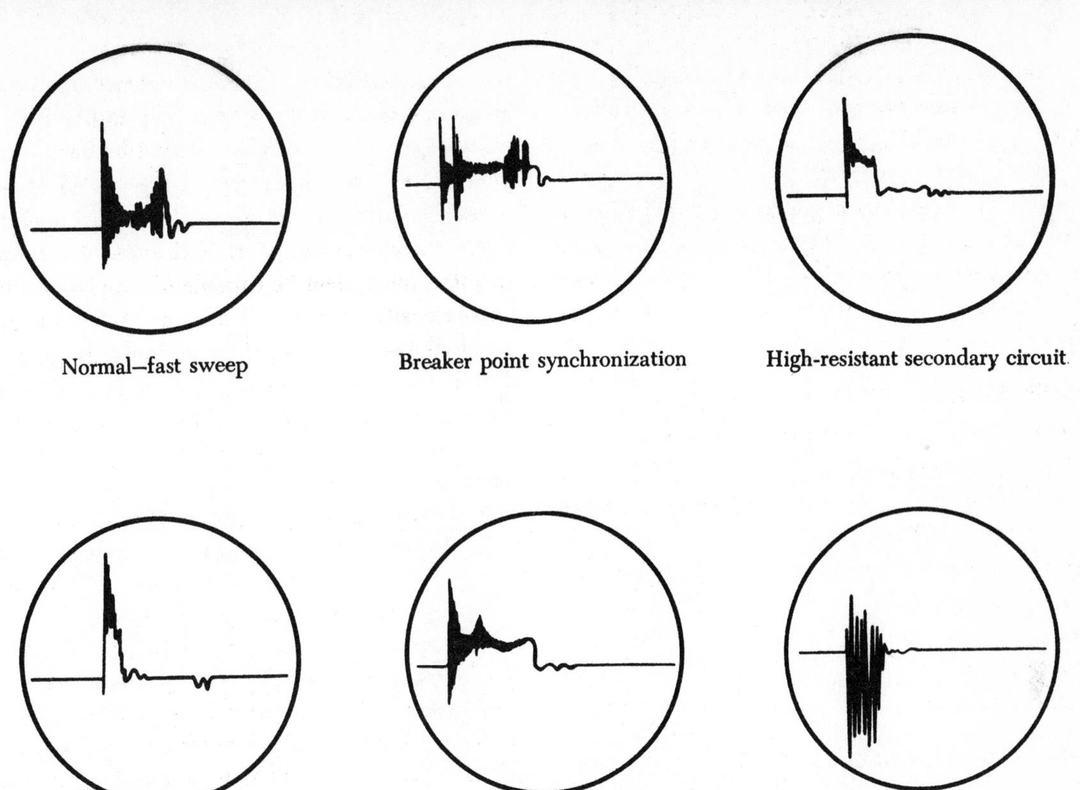

FIGURE 4–74. Typical engine analyzer patterns.

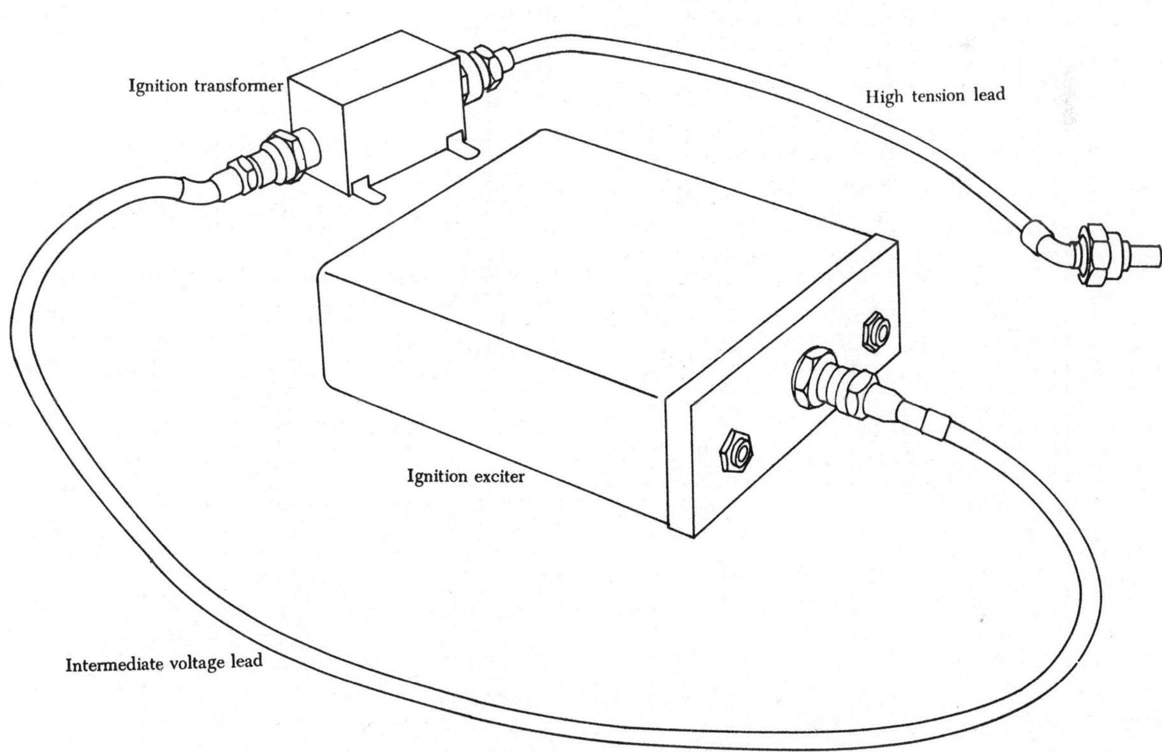

FIGURE 4–75. One side of a typical ignition system.

unit, it passes through a filter which prevents noise voltage from being induced into the aircraft electrical system. The low-voltage input power operates a d.c. motor, which drives one multi-lobe cam and one single-lobe cam. At the same time, input power is supplied to a set of breaker points that are actuated by the multi-lobe cam.

From the breaker points, a rapidly interrupted current is delivered to an auto transformer. When the breaker closes, the flow of current through the primary winding of the transformer establishes a magnetic field. When the breaker opens, the flow of current stops, and the collapse of the field induces a voltage in the secondary of the transformer. This voltage causes a pulse of current to flow into the storage capacitor through the rectifier, which limits the flow to a single direction. With repeated pulses the storage capacitor thus assumes a charge, up to a maximum of approximately 4 joules. (One joule per second equals 1 watt.)

The storage capacitor is connected to the spark igniter through the triggering transformer and a contactor, normally open. When the charge on the capacitor has built up, the contactor is closed by the mechanical action of the single-lobe cam. A portion of the charge flows through the primary of the triggering transformer and the capacitor connected in series with it.

This current induces a high voltage in the secondary which ionizes the gap at the spark igniter.

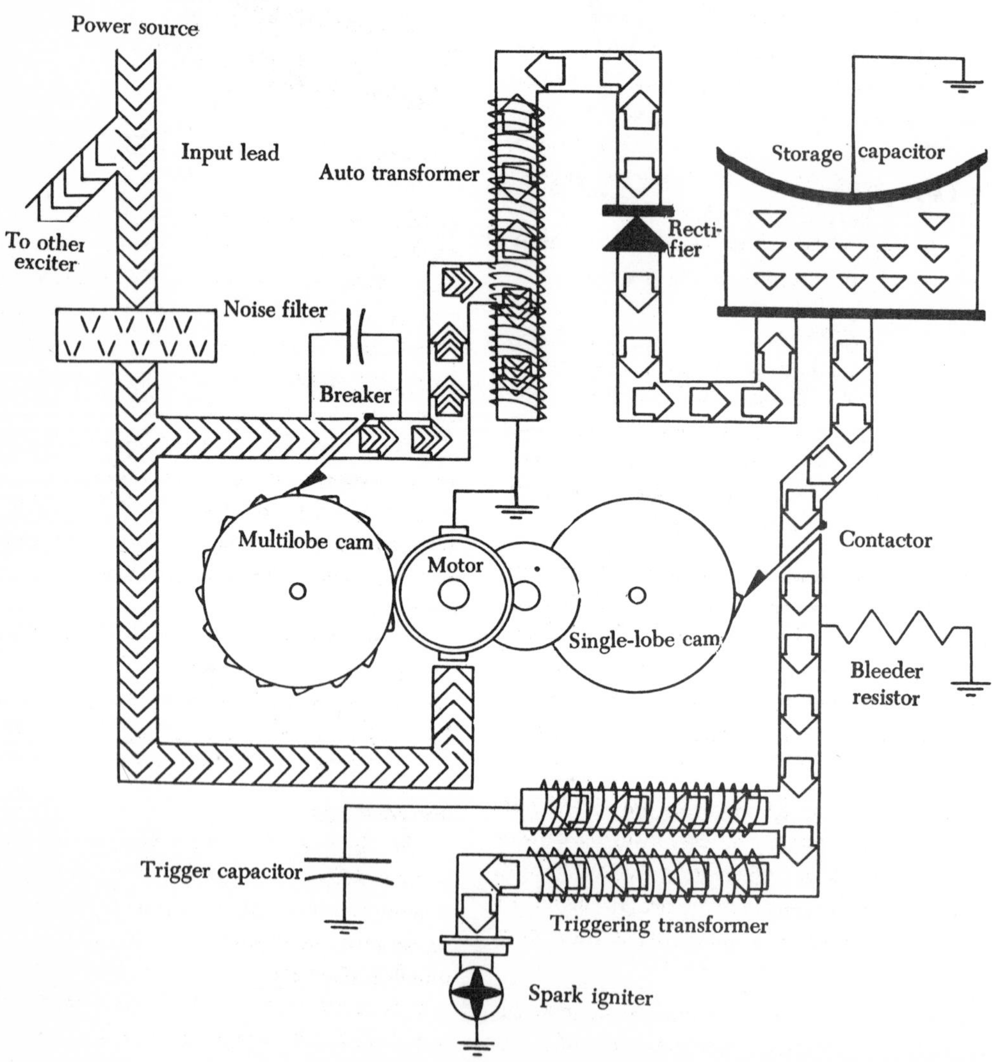

FIGURE 4–76. Capacitor-type ignition system schematic.

When the spark igniter is made conductive, the storage capacitor discharges the remainder of its accumulated energy together with the charge from the capacitor in series with the primary of the triggering transformer.

The spark rate at the spark igniter will vary in proportion to the voltage of the d.c. power supply which affects the r.p.m. of the motor. However, since both cams are geared to the same shaft, the storage capacitor will always accumulate its store of energy from the same number of pulses before discharge.

The employment of the high-frequency triggering transformer, with a low reactance secondary winding, holds the time duration of the discharge to a minimum. This concentration of maximum energy in minimum time achieves an optimum spark for ignition purposes, capable of blasting carbon deposits and vaporizing globules of fuel.

All high voltage in the triggering circuits is completely isolated from the primary circuits. The complete exciter is hermetically sealed, protecting all components from adverse operating conditions, eliminating the possibility of flashover at altitude due to pressure change. This also ensures shielding against leakage of high-frequency voltage interfering with the radio reception of the aircraft.

Electronic Ignition System

This modified capacity-type system provides ignition for turbojet and turboprop engines. Like other turbine ignition systems, it is required only for starting the engine; once combustion has begun, the flame is continuous. Figure 4–77 shows the components of a typical electronic ignition system.

The system consists of a dynamotor/regulator/filter assembly, an exciter unit, two high-tension transformer units, two high-tension leads, and two igniter plugs. Used with these components are the necessary interconnecting cables, leads, control switches, and associated equipment for operation in an aircraft.

The dynamotor is used to step up the direct current of the aircraft battery or the external power supply to the operating voltage of the exciter unit. This voltage is used to charge two storage capacitors which store the energy to be used for ignition purposes.

In this system, the energy required to fire the igniter plug in the engine burner is not stored in an inductor coil as in conventional types of igniters.

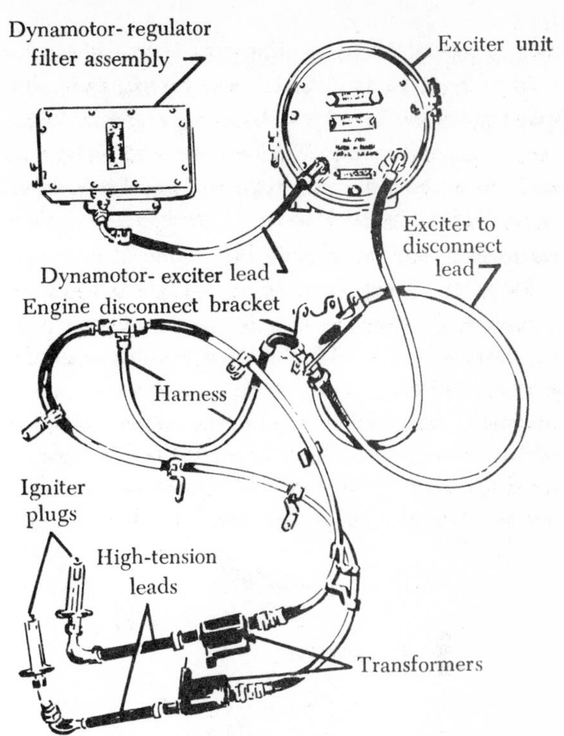

FIGURE 4–77. Typical electronic ignition system.

Instead, the energy is stored in capacitors. Each discharge circuit incorporates two storage capacitors. Both are located in the exciter unit. The voltage across these capacitors is stepped up by transformer units. At the instant of igniter plug firing, the resistance of the gap is lowered sufficiently to permit the larger capacitor to discharge across the gap. The discharge of the second capacitor is of low voltage but of very high energy. The result is a spark of great heat intensity, capable not only of igniting abnormal fuel mixtures but also of burning away any foreign deposits on the plug electrodes.

The exciter is a dual unit, and it produces sparks at each of the two igniter plugs. A continuous series of sparks is produced until the engine starts. The battery current is then cut off, and the plugs do not fire while the engine is operating.

Igniter Plugs

The igniter plug of a turbine engine ignition system differs considerably from the spark plug of a reciprocating engine ignition system. Its electrode must be capable of withstanding a current of much higher energy than the electrode of a conventional spark plug. This high-energy current can quickly cause electrode erosion, but the short periods of operation minimize this aspect of igniter maintenance. The electrode gap of the typical igniter plug is designed much larger than that of a spark plug, since the operating pressures are much lower and the spark can arc more easily than is the case for a spark plug. Finally, electrode fouling, so common to the spark plug, is minimized by the heat of the high-intensity spark.

Figure 4–78 is a cutaway illustration of a typical annular-gap igniter plug, sometimes referred to as a "long reach" igniter because it projects slightly into the combustion-chamber liner to produce a more effective spark.

Another type of igniter plug, the constrained-gap plug (figure 4–79) is used in some types of turbine engines. It operates at a much cooler temperature because it does not project into the combustion-chamber liner. This is possible because the spark does not remain close to the plug, but arcs beyond the face of the combustion-chamber liner.

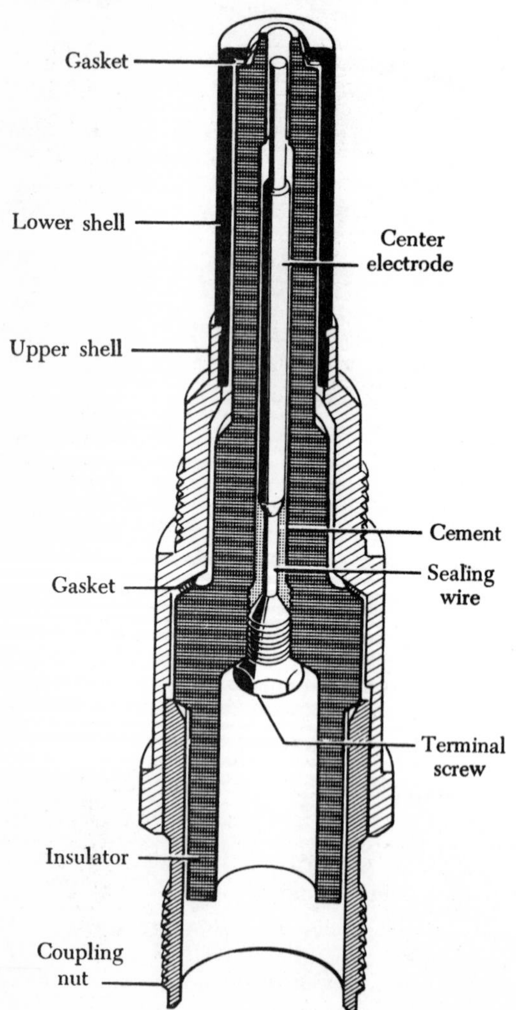

FIGURE 4–78. Typical annular-gap igniter plug.

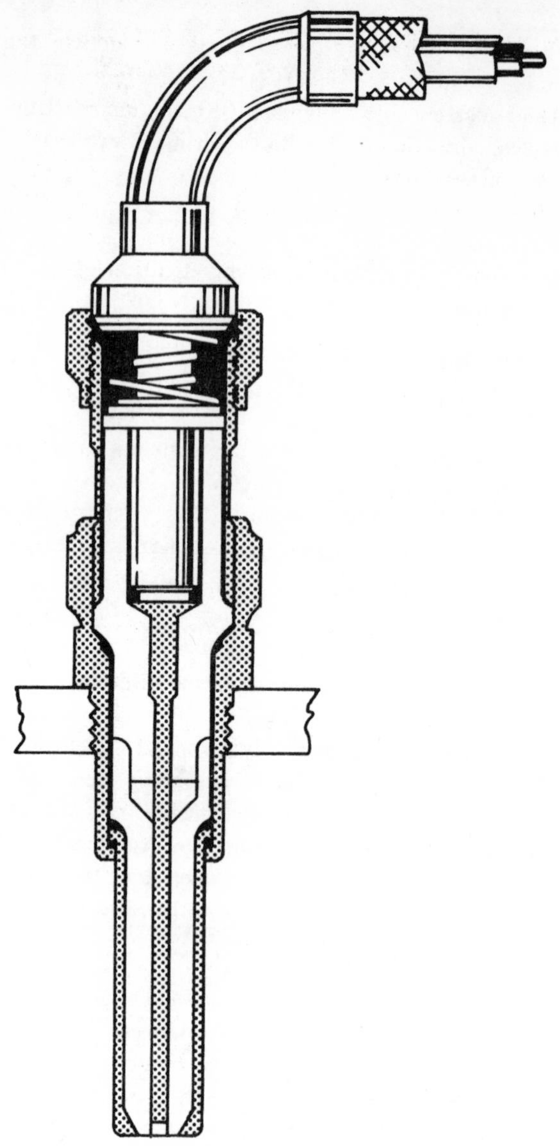

FIGURE 4–79. Constrained-gap igniter plug.

IGNITION SYSTEM INSPECTION AND MAINTENANCE

Maintenance of the typical turbine engine ignition system consists primarily of inspection, test, troubleshooting, removal, and installation.

Inspection

Inspection of the ignition system normally includes the following:

Inspection/Check	*Repair*
Security of components, bolts, and brackets.	Tighten and secure as required.
Shorts or high-voltage arcing.	Replace faulty components and wiring.
Loose connections.	Secure, tighten, and safety as required.

REMOVAL, MAINTENANCE, AND INSTALLATION OF IGNITION SYSTEM COMPONENTS

The following instructions are typical procedures suggested by many gas turbine manufacturers. These instructions are applicable to the engine ignition components illustrated in figure 4–77. Always consult the applicable manufacturer's instructions before performing any ignition system maintenance.

Ignition System Leads

(1) Remove clamps securing ignition leads to engine.
(2) Remove safety wire and disconnect electrical connectors from exciter units.
(3) Remove safety wire and disconnect lead from igniter plug.
(4) Discharge any electrical charge stored in the system by grounding, and remove ignition leads from engine.
(5) Clean leads with approved drycleaning solvent.
(6) Inspect connectors for damaged threads, corrosion, cracked insulators, and bent or broken connector pins.
(7) Inspect leads for worn or burned areas, deep cuts, fraying, and general deterioration.
(8) Perform continuity check of ignition leads.
(9) Re-install leads, reversing the removal procedure.

Igniter Plugs

(1) Disconnect ignition leads from igniter plugs.
(2) Remove igniter plugs from mounts.
(3) Inspect igniter plug gap surface material.
(4) Inspect for fretting of igniter plug shank.
(5) Replace an igniter plug whose surface is granular, chipped, or otherwise damaged.
(6) Replace dirty or carbonized igniter plugs.
(7) Install igniter plugs in mounting pads.
(8) Check for proper clearance between chamber liner and igniter plug.
(9) Tighten igniter plugs to manufacturer's specified torque.
(10) Safety-wire igniter plugs.

POWERPLANT ELECTRICAL SYSTEMS

The satisfactory performance of any modern aircraft depends to a very great degree on the continuing reliability of electrical systems and subsystems. Improperly or carelessly installed or maintained wiring can be a source of both immediate and potential danger. The continued proper performance of electrical systems depends upon the knowledge and technique of the mechanic who installs, inspects, and maintains the electrical wire and cable of the electrical systems.

The procedures and practices outlined in this section are general recommendations and are not intended to replace the manufacturer's instructions in approved practices.

For the purpose of this discussion, a wire is described as a single solid conductor, or a stranded conductor covered with an insulating material. Figure 4–80 illustrates these two definitions of a wire.

The term cable as used in aircraft electrical installations includes the following:

(1) Two or more separately insulated conductors in the same jacket (multi-conductor cable).
(2) Two or more separately insulated conductors twisted together (twisted pair).
(3) One or more insulated conductors, covered with a metallic braided shield (shielded cable).
(4) A single insulated center conductor with a metallic braided outer conductor (radio frequency cable). The concentricity of the center conductor and the outer conductor is carefully controlled during manufacture to ensure that they are coaxial.

Wire Size

Wire is manufactured in sizes according to a standard known as the AWG (American wire gage). As shown in the chart in figure 4–81, the wire diameters become smaller as the gage numbers become larger. The largest wire size shown in figure 4–81 is number 0000, and the smallest is

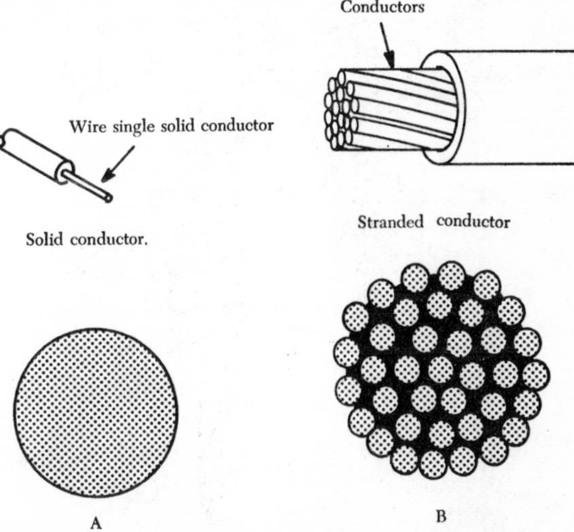

FIGURE 4–80. Two types of aircraft wire.

Gage number	Diameter (mils)	Cross section: Circular mils	Cross section: Square inches	Ohms per 1,000 ft.: 25°C. (=77°F.)	Ohms per 1,000 ft.: 65°C. (=149°F.)
0000	460.0	212,000.0	0.166	0.0500	0.0577
000	410.0	168,000.0	.132	.0630	.0727
00	365.0	133,000.0	.105	.0795	.0917
0	325.0	106,000.0	.0829	.100	.116
1	289.0	83,700.0	.0657	.126	.146
2	258.0	66,400.0	.0521	.159	.184
3	229.0	52,600.0	.0413	.201	.232
4	204.0	41,700.0	.0328	.253	.292
5	182.0	33,100.0	.0260	.319	.369
6	162.0	26,300.0	.0206	.403	.465
7	144.0	20,800.0	.0164	.508	.586
8	128.0	16,500.0	.0130	.641	.739
9	114.0	13,100.0	.0103	.808	.932
10	102.0	10,400.0	.00815	1.02	1.18
11	91.0	8,230.0	.00647	1.28	1.48
12	81.0	6,530.0	.00513	1.62	1.87
13	72.0	5,180.0	.00407	2.04	2.36
14	64.0	4,110.0	.00323	2.58	2.97
15	57.0	3,260.0	.00256	3.25	3.75
16	51.0	2,580.0	.00203	4.09	4.73
17	45.0	2,050.0	.00161	5.16	5.96
18	40.0	1,620.0	.00128	6.51	7.51
19	36.0	1,290.0	.00101	8.21	9.48
20	32.0	1,020.0	.000802	10.4	11.9
21	28.5	810.0	.000636	13.1	15.1
22	25.3	642.0	.000505	16.5	19.0
23	22.6	509.0	.000400	20.8	24.0
24	20.1	404.0	.000317	26.2	30.2
25	17.9	320.0	.000252	33.0	38.1
26	15.9	254.0	.000200	41.6	48.0
27	14.2	202.0	.000158	52.5	60.6
28	12.6	160.0	.000126	66.2	76.4
29	11.3	127.0	.0000995	83.4	96.3
30	10.0	101.0	.0000789	105.0	121.0
31	8.9	79.7	.0000626	133.0	153.0
32	8.0	63.2	.0000496	167.0	193.0
33	7.1	50.1	.0000394	211.0	243.0
34	6.3	39.8	.0000312	266.0	307.0
35	5.6	31.5	.0000248	335.0	387.0
36	5.0	25.0	.0000196	423.0	488.0
37	4.5	19.8	.0000156	533.0	616.0
38	4.0	15.7	.0000123	673.0	776.0
39	3.5	12.5	.0000098	848.0	979.0
40	3.1	9.9	.0000078	1,070.0	1,230.0

FIGURE 4–81. American wire gage for standard annealed solid copper wire.

number 40. Larger and smaller sizes are manufactured but are not commonly used.

Wire size may be determined by using a wire gage (figure 4–82). This type of gage will measure wires ranging in size from number zero to number 36. The wire to be measured is inserted in the smallest slot that will just accommodate the bare wire. The gage number corresponding to that slot indicates the wire size. The slot has parallel sides and should not be confused with the semicircular opening at the end of the slot. The opening simply permits the free movement of the wire all the way through the slot.

Gage numbers are useful in comparing the diameter of wires, but not all types of wire or cable can be accurately measured with a gage. Large wires are usually stranded to increase their flexibility. In such cases, the total area can be determined by multiplying the area of one strand (usually computed in circular mils when diameter or gage number is known) by the number of strands in the wire or cable.

Factors Affecting the Selection of Wire Size

Several factors must be considered in selecting the size of wire for transmitting and distributing electric power.

One factor is the allowable power loss (I^2R loss) in the line. This loss represents electrical energy converted into heat. The use of large conductors will reduce the resistance and therefore the I^2R loss. However, large conductors are more expensive initially than small ones; they are heavier and require more substantial supports.

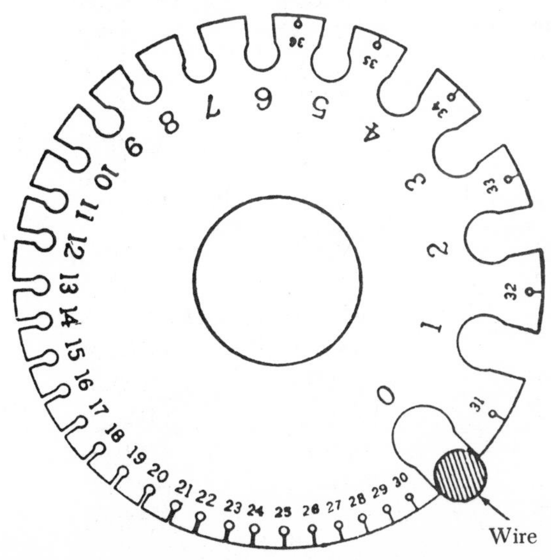

FIGURE 4–82. A wire gage.

A second factor is the permissible voltage drop (IR drop) in the line. If the source maintains a constant voltage at the input to the line, any variation in the load on the line will cause a variation in line current and a consequent variation in the IR drop in the line. A wide variation in the IR drop in the line causes poor voltage regulation at the load. The obvious remedy is to reduce either current or resistance. A reduction in load current lowers the amount of power being transmitted, whereas a reduction in line resistance increases the size and weight of conductors required. A compromise is generally reached whereby the voltage variation at the load is within tolerable limits and the weight of line conductors is not excessive.

A third factor is the current-carrying ability of the conductor. When current is drawn through the conductor, heat is generated. The temperature of the wire will rise until the heat radiated, or otherwise dissipated, is equal to the heat generated by the passage of current through the line. If the conductor is insulated, the heat generated in the conductor is not so readily removed as it would be if the conductor were not insulated. Thus, to protect the insulation from too much heat, the current through the conductor must be maintained below a certain value.

When electrical conductors are installed in locations where the ambient temperature is relatively high, the heat generated by external sources constitutes an appreciable part of the total conductor heating. Allowance must be made for the influence of external heating on the allowable conductor current, and each case has its own specific limitations. The maximum allowable operating temperature of insulated conductors varies with the type of conductor insulation being used.

Tables are available that list the safe current ratings for various sizes and types of conductors covered with various types of insulation. The chart in figure 4–83 shows the current-carrying capacity, in amperes, of single copper conductors at an ambient temperature of below 30° C. This example provides measurements for only a limited range of wire sizes.

Factors Affecting Selection of Conductor Material

Although silver is the best conductor, its cost limits its use to special circuits where a substance with high conductivity is needed.

The two most generally used conductors are copper and aluminum. Each has characteristics

Size	Rubber or thermo-plastic	Thermoplastic asbestos, var-cam, or asbestos var-cam	Impregnated asbestos	Asbestos	Slow-burning or weather-proof
0000	300	385	475	510	370
000	260	330	410	430	320
00	225	285	355	370	275
0	195	245	305	325	235
1	165	210	265	280	205
2	140	180	225	240	175
3	120	155	195	210	150
4	105	135	170	180	130
6	80	100	125	135	100
8	55	70	90	100	70
10	40	55	70	75	55
12	25	40	50	55	40
14	20	30	40	45	30

FIGURE 4–83. Current-carrying capacity of wire (in amperes).

that make its use advantageous under certain circumstances; also, each has certain disadvantages.

Copper has a higher conductivity; it is more ductile (can be drawn out), has relatively high tensile strength, and can be easily soldered. It is more expensive and heavier than aluminum.

Although aluminum has only about 60% of the conductivity of copper, it is used extensively. Its lightness makes possible long spans, and its relatively large diameter for a given conductivity reduces corona, the discharge of electricity from the wire when it has a high potential. The discharge is greater when smaller diameter wire is used than when larger diameter wire is used. Some bus bars are made of aluminum instead of copper, where there is a greater radiating surface for the same conductance. The characteristics of copper and aluminum are compared in table 2.

TABLE 2. Characteristics of copper and aluminum.

Characteristic	*Copper*	*Aluminum*
Tensile strength (lb./in.^{2})	55,000	25,000
Tensile strength for same conductivity (lb.)	55,000	40,000
Weight for same conductivity (lb.)	100	48
Cross section for same conductivity (C.M.)	100	160
Specific resistance (Ω/mil ft.)	10.6	17

Voltage Drop in Aircraft Wire and Cable

It is recommended that the voltage drop in the main power cables from the aircraft generation source or the battery to the bus should not exceed 2% of the regulated voltage when the generator is carrying rated current or the battery is being discharged at a 5-minute rate. Table 3 shows the recommended maximum voltage drop in the load circuits between the bus and the utilization equipment.

TABLE 3. Recommended maximum voltage drop in load circuits.

Nominal system voltage	*Allowable voltage drop*	
	Continuous operation	*Intermittent operation*
14	0.5	1
28	1	2
115	4	8
200	7	14

The resistance of the current return path through the aircraft structure is always considered negligible. However, this is based on the assumption that adequate bonding of the structure or a special electric current return path has been provided which is capable of carrying the required electric current with a negligible voltage drop. A resistance measurement of 0.005 ohms from ground point of the generator or battery to ground terminal of any electrical device is considered satisfactory. Another satisfactory method of determining circuit resistance is to check the voltage drop across the circuit. If the voltage drop does not exceed the limit established by the aircraft or product manufacturer, the resistance value for the circuit is considered satisfactory. When using the voltage drop method of checking a circuit, the input voltage must be maintained at a constant value.

The chart in figure 4–84 applies to copper conductors carrying direct current. Curves 1, 2, and 3 are plotted to show the maximum ampere rating for the specified conductor under the specified conditions shown. To select the correct size of conductor, two major requirements must be met. First, the size must be sufficient to prevent an excessive voltage drop while carrying the required current over the required distance. Secondly, the size must be sufficient to prevent overheating of the cable while carrying the required current. The charts in figures 4–84 and 85 can simplify these determinations. To use this chart to select the proper size of conductor, the following must be known:

(1) The conductor length in feet.

(2) The number of amperes of current to be carried.

(3) The amount of voltage drop permitted.

(4) Whether the current to be carried will be intermittent or continuous, and if continuous, whether it is a single conductor in free air, in a conduit, or in a bundle.

Assume that it is desired to install a 50-foot conductor from the aircraft bus to the equipment in a 28-volt system. For this length, a 1-volt drop is permissible for continuous operation. By referring to the chart in figure 4–84 the maximum number of feet a conductor may be run carrying a specified current with a 1-volt drop can be determined. In this example the number 50 is selected.

Assuming the current required by the equipment is 20 amperes, the line indicating the value of 20 amperes should be selected from the diagonal lines. Follow this diagonal line downward until it intersects the horizontal line number 50. From this point, drop straight down to the bottom of the chart to find that a conductor between size No. 8 and No. 10 is required to prevent a greater drop than 1 volt. Since the indicated value is between two numbers, the larger size, No. 8, should be selected. This is the smallest size which should be used to avoid an excessive voltage drop.

To determine that the conductor size is sufficient to preclude overheating, disregard both the numbers along the left side of the chart and the horizontal lines. Assume that the conductor is to be a single wire in free air carrying continuous current. Place a pointer at the top of the table on the diagonal line numbered 20 amperes. Follow this line until the pointer intersects the diagonal line marked "curve 2." Drop the pointer straight down to the bottom of the chart. This point is between numbers 16 and 18. The larger size, No. 16, should be selected. This is the smallest-size conductor acceptable for carrying 20-ampere current in a single wire in free air without overheating.

If the installation is for equipment having only an intermittent (Max. 2 min.) requirement for power, the chart in figure 4–84 is used in the same manner.

Conductor Insulation

Two fundamental properties of insulation materials (for example, rubber, glass, asbestos, and plastic) are insulation resistance and dielectric strength. These are entirely different and distinct properties.

Insulation resistance is the resistance to current leakage through and over the surface of insulation materials. Insulation resistance can be measured with a megger without damaging the insulation, and data so obtained serves as a useful guide in determining the general condition of insulation. However, the data obtained in this manner may not give a true picture of the condition of the insulation. Clean, dry insulation having cracks or other faults

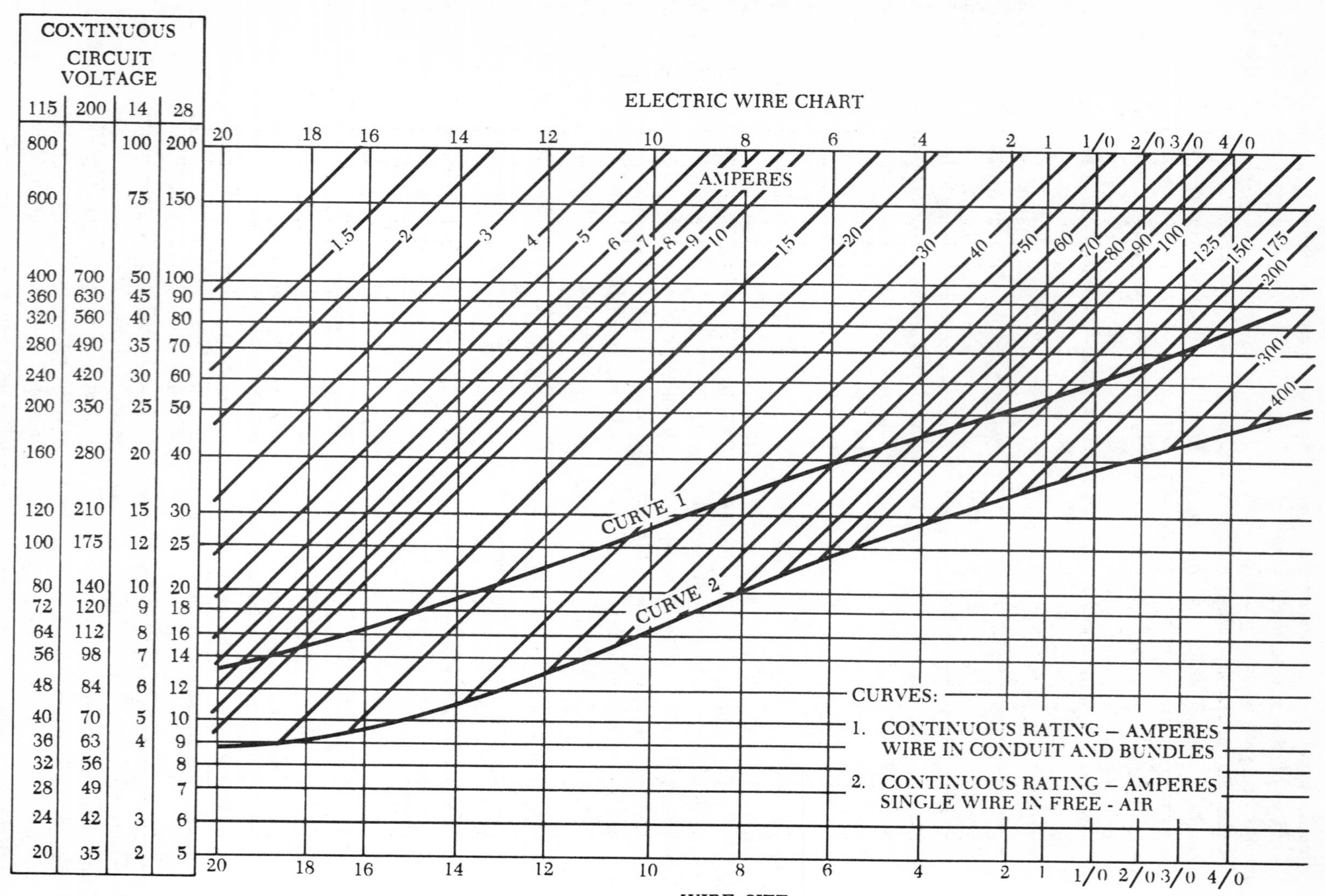

FIGURE 4–84. Conductor chart, continuous rating. (Applicable to copper conductors.)

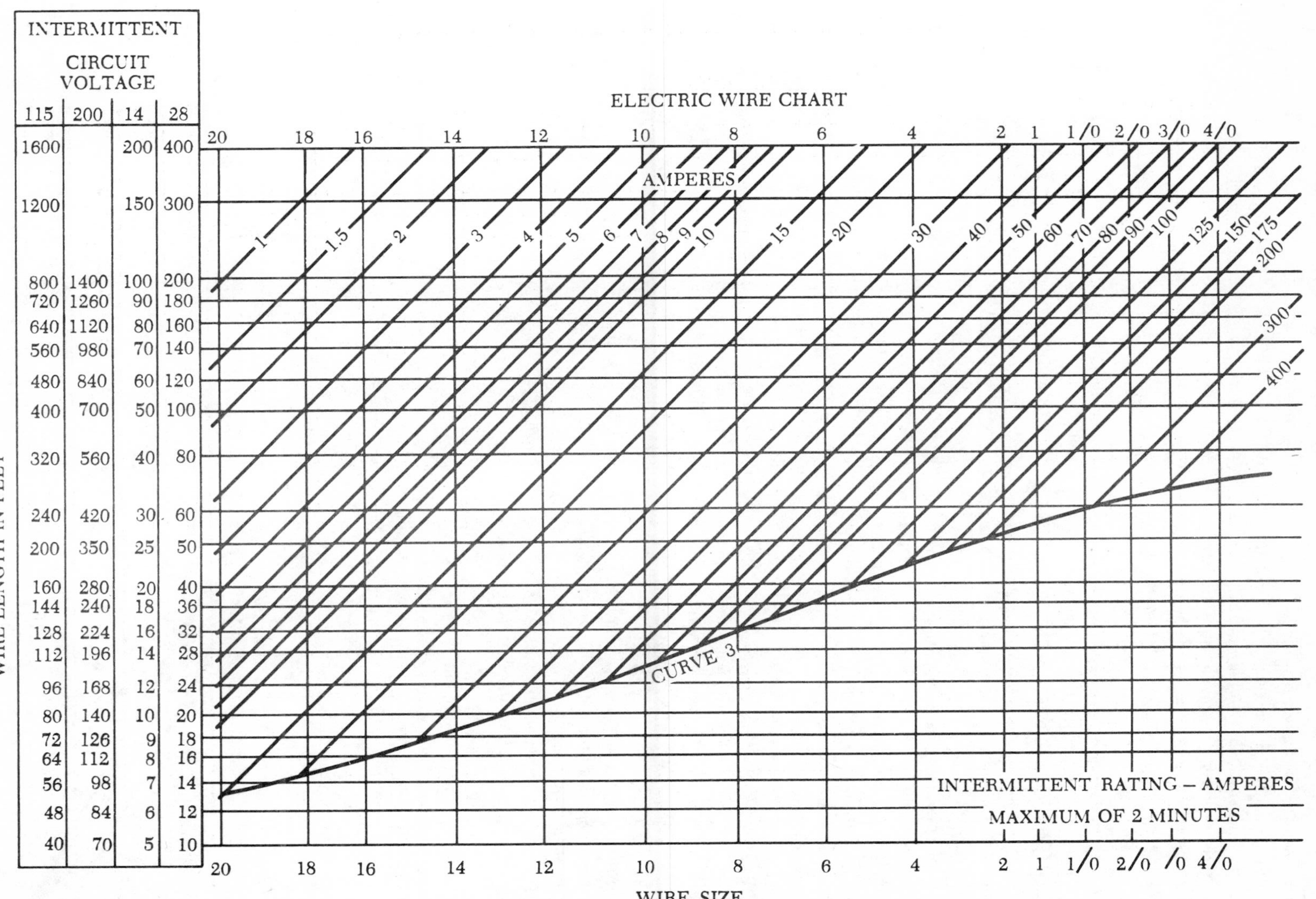

FIGURE 4–85. Conductor chart, intermittent rating. (Applicable to copper conductors.)

may show a high value of insulation resistance but would not be suitable for use.

Dielectric strength is the ability of the insulator to withstand potential difference and is usually expressed in terms of the voltage at which the insulation fails because of the electrostatic stress. Maximum dielectric strength values can be measured by raising the voltage of a test sample until the insulation breaks down.

Because of the expense of insulation and its stiffening effect, together with the great variety of physical and electrical conditions under which the conductors are operated, only the necessary minimum insulation is applied for any particular type of cable designed to do a specific job.

The type of conductor insulation material varies with the type of installation. Such types of insulation as rubber, silk, and paper are no longer used extensively in aircraft systems. More common today are such materials as vinyl, cotton, nylon, Teflon, and Rockbestos.

Identifying Wire and Cable

To aid in testing and repair operations, many maintenance activities mark wire or cable with a combination of letters and numbers which identify the wire, the circuit it belongs to, the gage number, and other information necessary to relate the wire or cable to a wiring diagram. Such markings are called the identification code.

There is no standard procedure for marking and identifying wiring, each manufacturer normally develops his own identification code. Figure 4–86 illustrates one identification system and shows the usual spacing in marking a wire. The number 22 in the code refers to the system in which the wire is installed, e.g., the VHF system. The next set of numbers, 013, is the wire number, and 18 indicates the wire size.

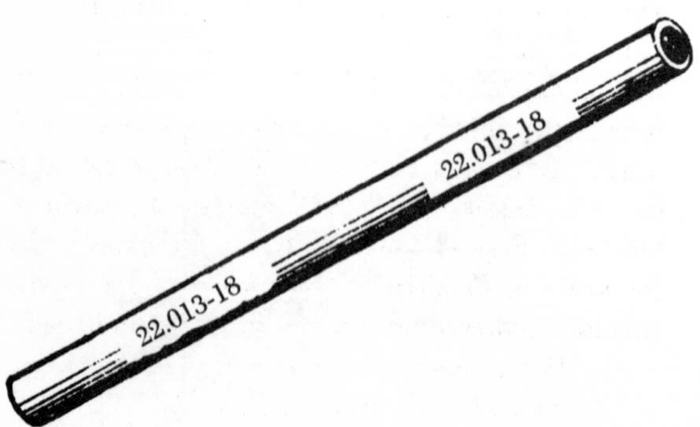

FIGURE 4–86. Wire identification code.

Some system components, especially plugs and jacks, are identified by a letter or group of letters and numbers added to the basic identification number. These letters and numbers may indicate the location of the component in the system. Interconnected cables are also marked in some systems to indicate location, proper termination, and use.

In any system, the marking should be legible, and the stamping color should contrast with the color of the wire insulation. For example, use black stamping with light-colored backgrounds, or white stamping on dark-colored backgrounds.

Most manufacturers mark the wires at intervals of not more than 15 in. lengthwise and within 3 in. of each junction or terminating point. Figure 4–87 shows wire identification at a terminal block.

Coaxial cable and wires at terminal blocks and junction boxes are often identified by marking or stamping a wiring sleeve rather than the wire itself. For general-purpose wiring, flexible vinyl sleeving, either clear or white opaque, is commonly used. For high-temperature applications, silicone rubber or silicone fiber glass sleeving is recommended. Where resistance to synthetic hydraulic fluids or other solvents is necessary, either clear or white opaque nylon sleeving can be used.

While the preferred method is to stamp the identification marking directly on the wire or on sleeving, other methods are often employed. Figure 4–88 shows two alternate methods. One method uses a marked sleeve tied in place. The other uses a pressure-sensitive tape.

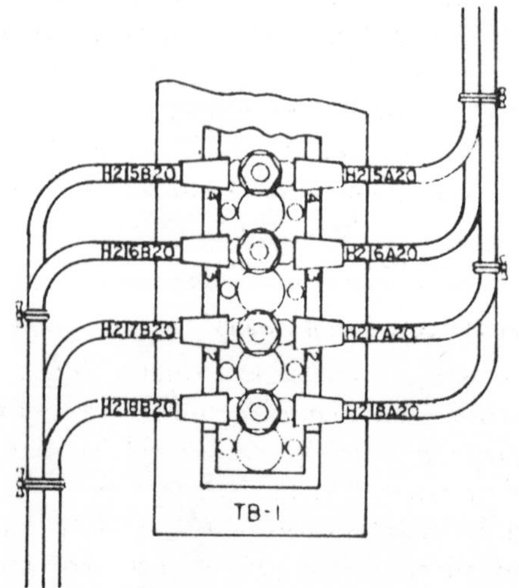

FIGURE 4–87. Wire identification at a terminal block.

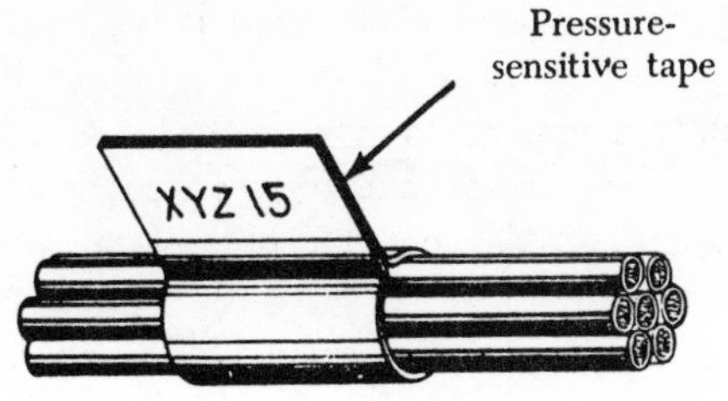

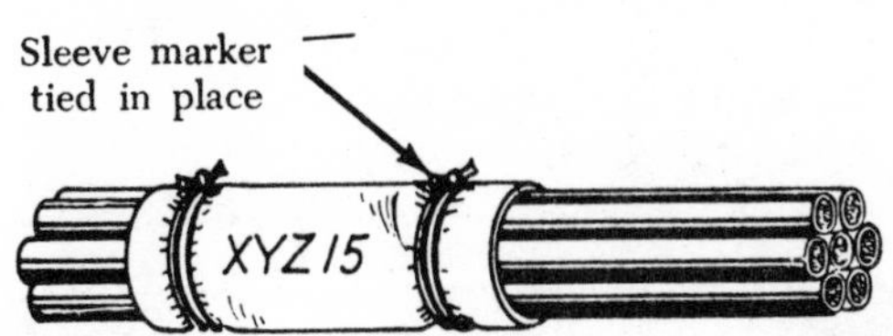

FIGURE 4–88. Alternate methods of identifying wire bundles.

Electrical Wiring Installation

The following recommended procedures for installing aircraft electrical wiring are typical of those used on most types of aircraft. For purposes of this discussion, the following definitions are applicable:

(1) Open wiring—any wire, wire group, or wire bundle not enclosed in conduit.

(2) Wire group—two or more wires going to the same location, tied together to retain identity of the group.

(3) Wire bundle—two or more wire groups tied together because they are going in the same direction at the point where the tie is located.

(4) Electrically protected wiring—wires which include (in the circuit) protections against overloading, such as fuses, circuit breakers, or other limiting devices.

(5) Electrically unprotected wiring—wires (generally from generators to main bus distribution points) which do not have protection, such as fuses, circuit breakers, or other current-limiting devices.

Wire Groups and Bundles

Grouping or bundling certain wires, such as electrically unprotected power wiring and wiring to duplicate vital equipment, should be avoided.

Wire bundles should generally be limited in size to a bundle of 75 wires, or 2 in. in diameter where practicable. When several wires are grouped at junction boxes, terminal blocks, panels, etc., identity of the group within a bundle can be retained as shown in figure 4–89.

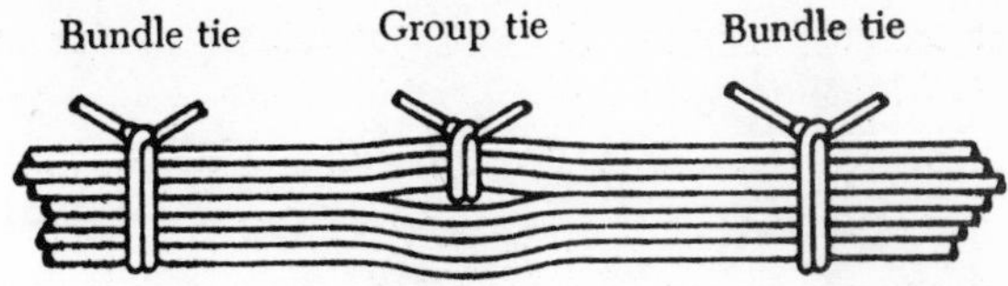

FIGURE 4–89. Group and bundle ties.

Twisting Wires

When specified on the engineering drawing, parallel wires must be twisted. The following are the most common examples:

(1) Wiring in the vicinity of magnetic compass or flux valve.

(2) Three-phase distribution wiring.

(3) Certain other wires (usually radio wiring).

Twist the wires so that they will lie snugly against each other, making approximately the number of twists per foot shown in table 4. Always check wire insulation for damage after twisting. If the insulation is torn or frayed, replace the wire.

TABLE 4. Recommended number of twists per foot.

	Wire Size									
	#22	#20	#18	#16	#14	#12	#10	#8	#6	#4
2 Wires	10	10	9	8	7½	7	6½	6	5	4
3 Wires	10	10	8½	7	6½	6	5½	5	4	3

Spliced Connections in Wire Bundles

Spliced connections in wire groups or bundles should be located so that they can be easily inspected. Splices should also be staggered (figure 4–90) so that the bundle does not become excessively enlarged. All noninsulated splices should be covered with plastic, securely tied at both ends.

Slack in Wiring Bundles

Single wires or wire bundles should not be installed with excessive slack. Slack between supports should normally not exceed 1/2 in. This is the maximum it should be possible to deflect the wire with normal hand force. However, this may be exceeded if the wire bundle is thin and the clamps are far apart. But the slack should never be so great that the wire bundle can abrade against any surface it touches. Figure 4–91 illustrates the proper slack for wires in bundles. A sufficient amount of slack should be allowed near each end of a bundle to:

(1) Permit easy maintenance.

(2) Allow replacement of terminals.

(3) Prevent mechanical strain on the wires, wire junctions, or supports.

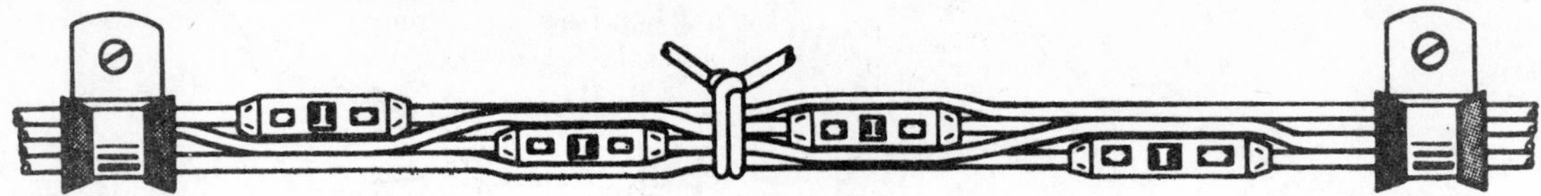

FIGURE 4–90. Staggered splices in wire bundle.

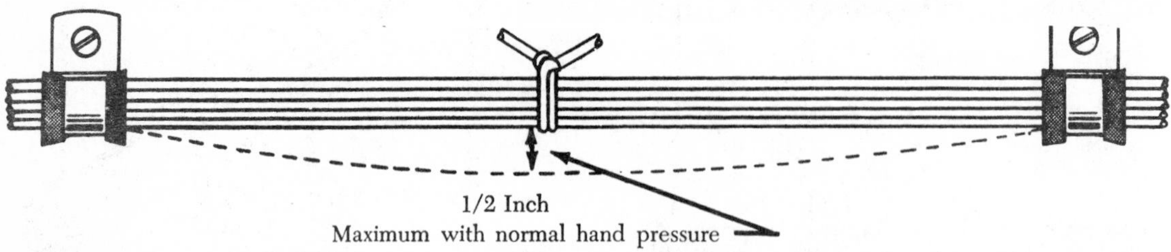

FIGURE 4–91. Slack in wire bundle between supports.

(4) Permit free movement of shock and vibration-mounted equipment.

(5) Permit shifting of equipment for purposes of maintenance.

Bend Radii

Bends in wire groups or bundles should not be less than 10 times the outside diameter of the wire group or bundle. However, at terminal strips, where wire is suitably supported at each end of the bend, a minimum radius of three times the outside diameter of the wire, or wire bundle, is normally acceptable. There are, of course, exceptions to these guidelines in the case of certain types of cable; for example, coaxial cable should never be bent to a smaller radius than six times the outside diameter.

Routing and Installation

All wiring should be installed so that it is mechanically and electrically sound and neat in appearance. Whenever practicable, wires and bundles should be routed parallel with, or at right angles to, the stringers or ribs of the area involved. An exception to this general rule is the coaxial cables, which are routed as directly as possible.

The wiring must be adequately supported throughout its length. A sufficient number of supports must be provided to prevent undue vibration of the unsupported lengths. All wires and wire groups should be routed and installed to protect them from:

(1) Chafing or abrasion.

(2) High temperature.

(3) Being used as handholds, or as support for personal belongings and equipment.

(4) Damage by personnel moving within the aircraft.

(5) Damage from cargo stowage or shifting.

(6) Damage from battery acid fumes, spray, or spillage.

(7) Damage from solvents and fluids.

Protection Against Chafing

Wires and wire groups should be installed so that they are protected against chafing or abrasion in those locations where contact with sharp surfaces or other wires would damage the insulation. Damage to the insulation can cause short circuits, malfunctions, or inadvertent operation of equipment. Cable clamps should be used to support wire bundles (figure 4–92 at each hole through a bulkhead. If wires come closer than 1/4 in. to the edge of the hole, a suitable grommet is used in the hole, as shown in figure 4–93.

Sometimes it is necessary to cut nylon or rubber grommets to facilitate installation. In these instances, after insertion, the grommet can be secured in place with general-purpose cement. The slot should be at the top of the hole, and the cut should be made at an angle of 45° to the axis of the wire bundle hole.

Protection Against High Temperature

To prevent insulation deterioration, wires should be kept separate from high-temperature equipment, such as resistors, exhaust stacks, heating ducts, etc. The amount of separation is normally specified by engineering drawings. Some wires must invariably be run through hot areas. These wires must be insulated with high-temperature material such as asbestos, fiber glass, or Teflon. Additional protection is also often required in the form of conduits. A low-temperature insulated wire should never be used to replace a high-temperature insulated wire.

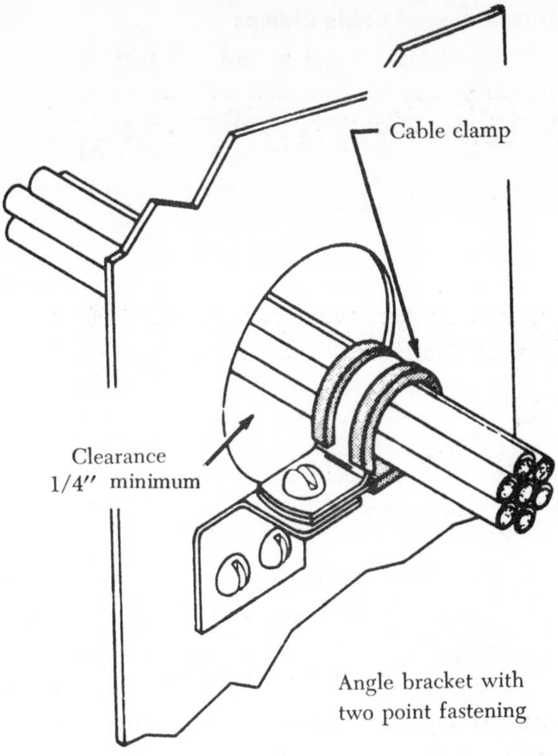

FIGURE 4–92. Cable clamp at bulkhead hole.

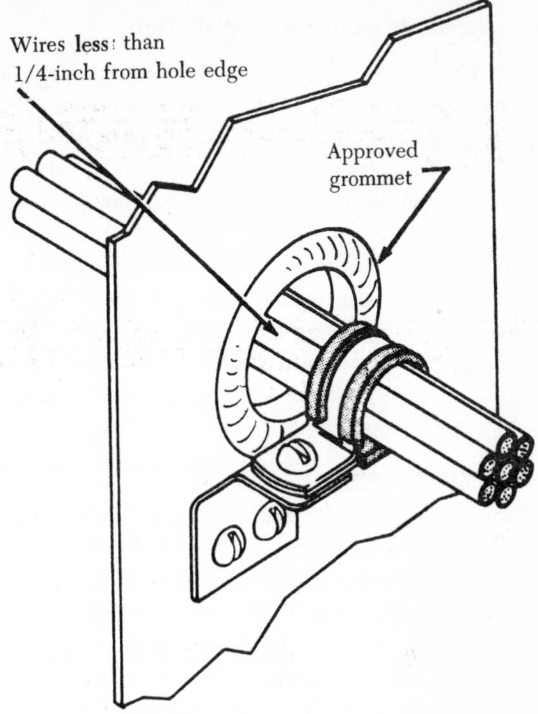

FIGURE 4–93. Cable clamp and grommet at bulkhead hole.

Many coaxial cables have soft plastic insulation, such as polyethylene, which is especially subject to deformation and deterioration at elevated temperatures. All high-temperature areas should be avoided when installing these cables.

Additional abrasion protection should be given to asbestos wires enclosed in conduit. Either conduit with a high-temperature rubber liner should be used, or asbestos wires can be enclosed individually in high-temperature plastic tubes before being installed in the conduit.

Protection Against Solvents and Fluids

Avoid installing wires in areas where they will be subjected to damage from fluids. Wires should not be placed in the lowest 4 inches of the aircraft fuselage, except those that must terminate in that area. If there is a possibility that wiring without a protective nylon outer jacket may be soaked with fluids, plastic tubing should be used to protect it. This tubing should extend past the exposure area in both directions and should be tied at each end. If the wire has a low point between the tubing ends, provide a 1/8 in. drainage hole, as shown in figure 4–94. This hole should be punched into the tubing after the installation is complete and the low point definitely established by using a hole punch to cut a half circle. Care should be taken not to damage any wires inside the tubing when using the punch.

Wire also should never be routed below a battery. All wires in the vicinity of a battery should be inspected frequently. Wires discolored by battery fumes should be replaced.

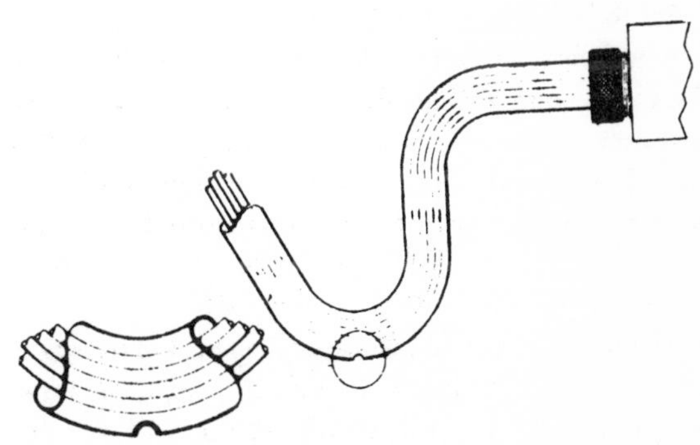

Drainage hole 1/8-inch diameter at lowest point in tubing. Make the hole after installation is complete and lowest point is firmly established

FIGURE 4–94. Drainage hole in low point of tubing.

Protection of Wires in Wheel Well Area

Wires located in wheel wells are subject to many additional hazards, such as exposure to fluids, pinching, and severe flexing in service. All wire bundles should be protected by sleeves of flexible tubing securely held at each end. There should be no relative movement at points where flexible tubing is secured. These wires and the insulating tubing should be inspected carefully at very frequent intervals, and wires or tubing should be replaced at the first sign of wear. There should be no strain on attachments when parts are fully extended, but slack should not be excessive.

Routing Precautions

When wiring must be routed parallel to combustible fluid or oxygen lines for short distances, as much separation as possible should be maintained. The wires should be on a level with, or above, the plumbing lines. Clamps should be spaced so that if a wire is broken at a clamp, it will not contact the line. Where a 6 in. separation is not possible, both the wire bundle and the plumbing line can be clamped to the same structure to prevent any relative motion. If the separation is less than 2 in. but more than 1/2 in., two cable clamps back-to-back (figure 4–95) can be used to maintain a rigid separation only, and not for support of the bundle. No wire should be routed so that it is located nearer than 1/2 in. to a plumbing line. Neither should a wire or wire bundle be supported from a plumbing line that carries flammable fluids or oxygen.

Wiring should be routed to maintain a minimum clearance of at least 3 in. from control cables. If this cannot be accomplished, mechanical guards should be installed to prevent contact between wiring and control cables.

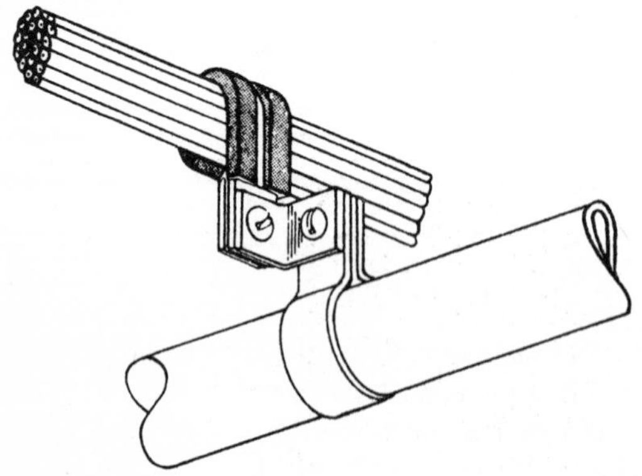

FIGURE 4–95. Separation of wires from plumbing lines.

Installation of Cable Clamps

Cable clamps should be installed with regard to the proper mounting angle (figure 4–96). The mounting screw should be above the wire bundle. It is also desirable that the back of the cable clamp rest against a structural member where practicable.

Figure 4–97 shows some typical mounting hardware used in installing cable clamps.

Be sure that wires are not pinched in cable clamps. Where possible, mount them directly to structural members, as shown in figure 4–98.

Clamps can be used with rubber cushions to secure wire bundles to tubular structures as shown in figure 4–99. Such clamps must fit tightly but should not be deformed when locked in place.

LACING AND TYING WIRE BUNDLES

Wire groups and bundles are laced or tied with cord to provide ease of installation, maintenance, and inspection. This section describes and illustrates recommended procedures for lacing and tying wires with knots which will hold tightly under all conditions. For the purposes of this discussion, the following terms are defined:

(1) Tying is the securing together of a group or bundle of wires by individual pieces of cord tied around the group or bundle at regular intervals.

(2) Lacing is the securing together of a group or bundle of wires by a continuous piece of cord forming loops at regular intervals around the group or bundle.

(3) A wire group is two or more wires tied or laced together to give identity to an individual system.

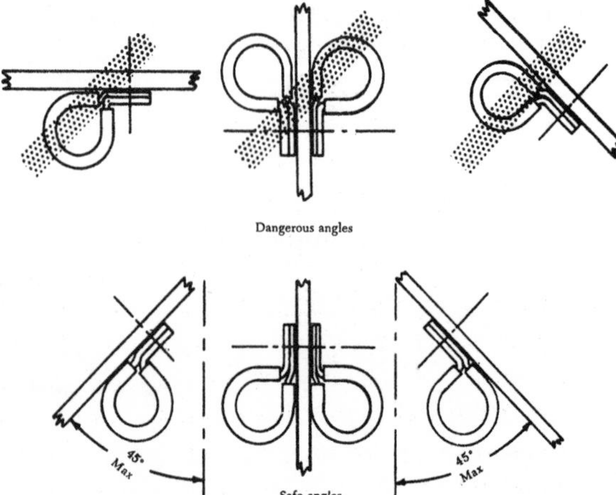

FIGURE 4–96. Proper mounting angle for cable clamps.

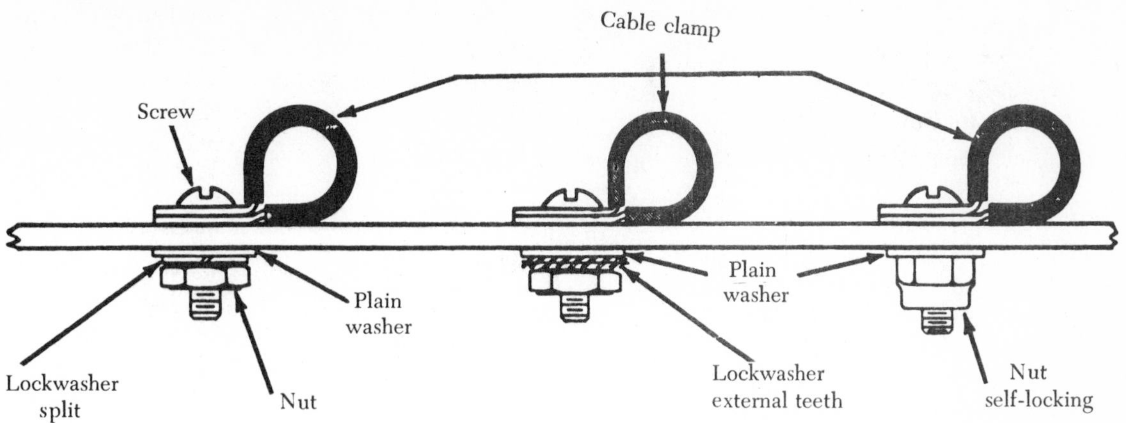

FIGURE 4–97. Typical mounting hardware for cable clamps.

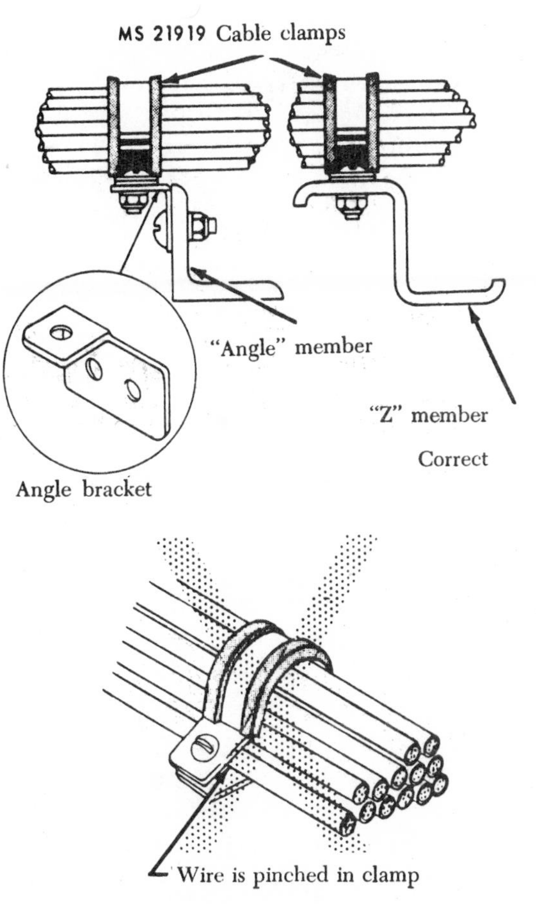

FIGURE 4–98. Mounting cable clamp to structure.

(4) A wire bundle is two or more wires or groups tied or laced together to facilitate maintenance.

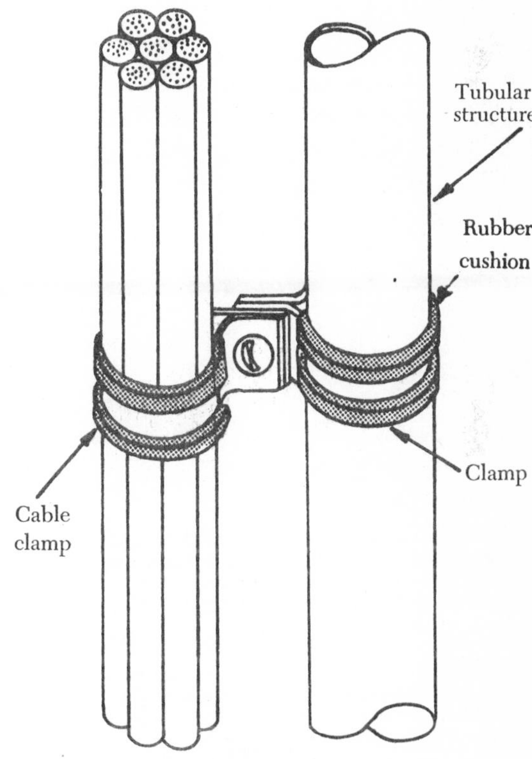

FIGURE 4–99. Installing cable clamp to tubular structure.

The material used for lacing and tying is either cotton or nylon cord. Nylon cord is moisture- and fungus-resistant, but cotton cord must be waxed before using to give it these necessary protective characteristics.

Single-Cord Lacing

Figure 4–100 shows the steps in lacing a wire

bundle with a single cord. The lacing procedure is started at the thick end of the wire group or bundle with a knot consisting of a clove hitch with an extra loop. The lacing is then continued at regular intervals with half hitches along the wire group or bundle and at each point where a wire or wire group branches off. The half hitches should be spaced so that the bundle is neat and secure. The lacing is ended by tying a knot consisting of a clove hitch with an extra loop. After the knot is tied, the free ends of the lacing cord should be trimmed to approximately 3/8 in.

Double-Cord Lacing

Figure 4–101 illustrates the procedure for double-cord lacing. The lacing is started at the thick end of the wire group or bundle with a bowline-on-a-bight knot (A of figure 4–101). At regular intervals along the wire group or bundle, and at each point where a wire branches off, the lacing is continued using half hitches, with both cords held firmly together. The half hitches should be spaced so that the group or bundle is neat and secure. The lacing is ended with a knot consisting of a half hitch, continuing one of the cords clockwise and the other counterclockwise and then tying the cord ends with a square knot. The free ends of the lacing cord should be trimmed to approximately 3/8 in.

Lacing Branch-Offs

Figure 4–102 illustrates a recommended procedure for lacing a wire group that branches off the main wire bundle. The branch-off lacing is started with a knot located on the main bundle just past the branch-off point. Continue the lacing along the branched-off wire group, using regularly spaced half hitches. If a double cord is used, both cords should be held snugly together. The half hitches should be spaced to lace the bundle neatly and securely. End the lacing with the regular terminal knot used in single- or double-cord lacing, as applicable, and trim the free ends of the lacing cord neatly.

Tying

All wire groups or bundles should be tied where supports are more than 12 in. apart. Ties are made using waxed cotton cord, nylon cord, or fiber glass cord. Some manufacturers permit the use of pressure-sensitive vinyl electrical tape. When permitted, the tape should be wrapped three turns around the bundle and the ends heat sealed to prevent unwinding of the tape. Figure 4–103

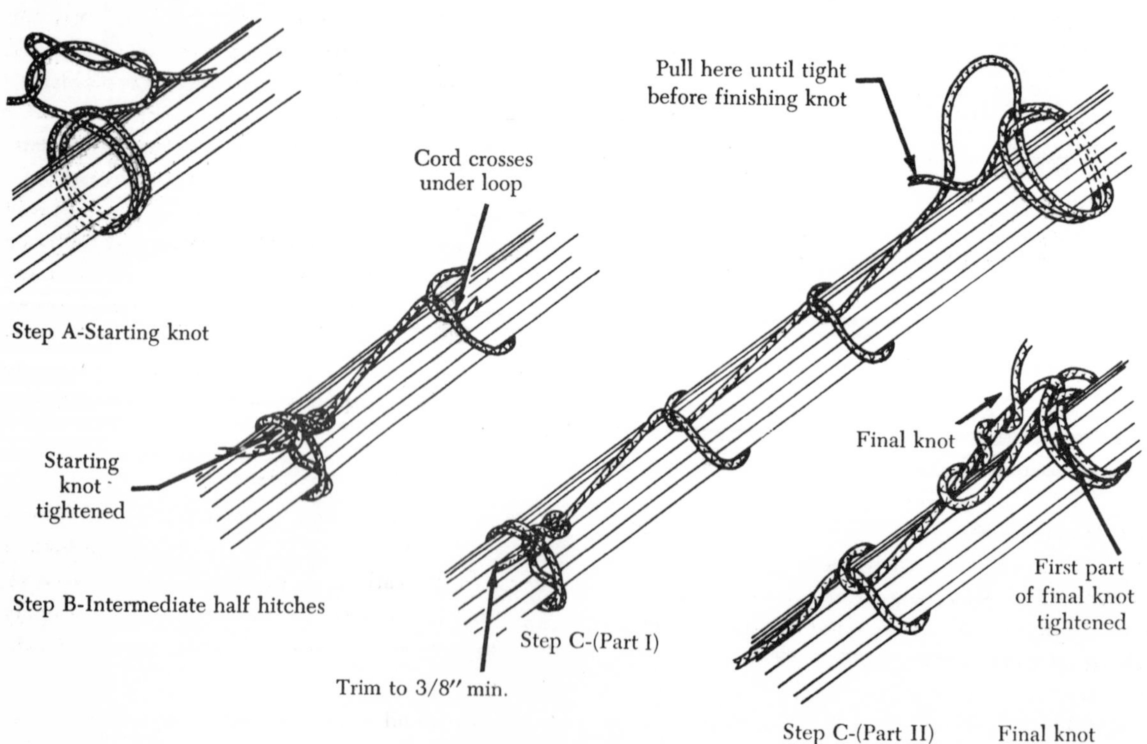

FIGURE 4–100. Single-cord lacing.

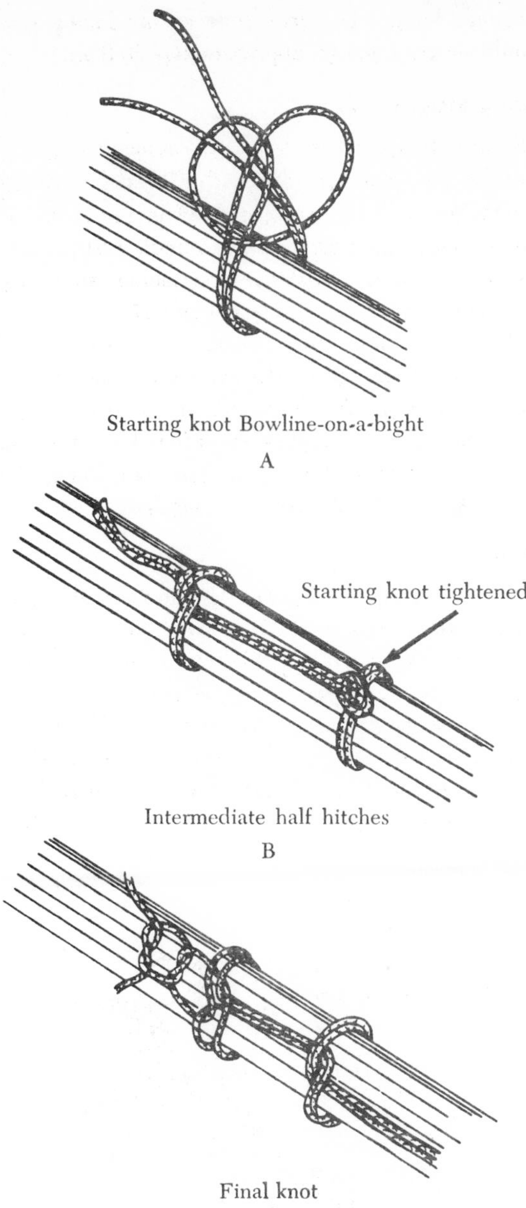

FIGURE 4–101. Double-cord lacing.

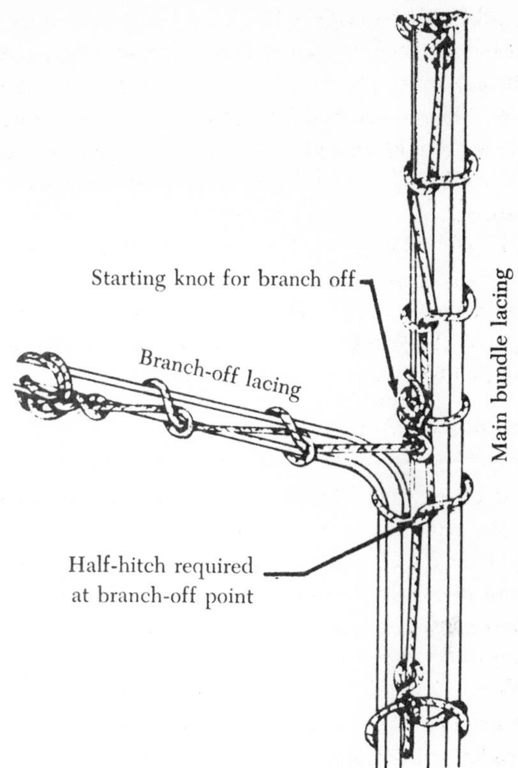

FIGURE 4–102. Lacing a branch-off.

illustrates a recommended procedure for tying a wire group or bundle. The tie is started by wrapping the cord around the wire group to tie a clove-hitch knot. Then a square knot with an extra loop is tied and the free ends of the cord trimmed.

Temporary ties are sometimes used in making up and installing wire groups and bundles. Colored cord is normally used to make temporary ties, since they are removed when the installation is complete.

Whether lacing or tying, bundles should be secured tightly enough to prevent slipping, but not so tightly that the cord cuts into or deforms the insulation. This applies especially to coaxial cable, which has a soft dielectric insulation between the inner and outer conductor. Coxial cables have been damaged by the use of lacing materials or by methods of lacing or tying wire bundles which cause a concentrated force on the cable insulation. Elastic lacing materials, small diameter lacing cord, and excessive tightening deform the interconductor insulation and result in short circuits or impedance changes. Flat nylon braided waxed lacing tape should be used for lacing or tying any wire bundles containing coaxial cables.

The part of a wire group or bundle located inside a conduit is not tied or laced, but wire groups or bundles inside enclosures, such as junction boxes, should be laced only.

CUTTING WIRE AND CABLE

To make installation, maintenance, and repair easier, runs of wire and cable in aircraft are broken at specified locations by junctions, such as connectors, terminal blocks, or buses. Before assembly to these junctions, wires and cables must be cut to length.

All wires and cables should be cut to the lengths specified on drawings and wiring diagrams. The cut should be made clean and square, and the wire or cable should not be deformed. If necessary, large-diameter wire should be re-shaped after cutting. Good cuts can be made only if the blades of cutting tools are sharp and free from nicks. A dull blade will deform and extrude wire ends.

STRIPPING WIRE AND CABLE

Nearly all wire and cable used as electrical conductors are covered with some type of insulation. In order to make electrical connections with the wire, a part of this insulation must be removed to expose the bare conductor.

Copper wire can be stripped in a number of ways depending on the size and insulation. Table 5 lists some types of stripping tools recommended for various wire sizes and types of insulation.

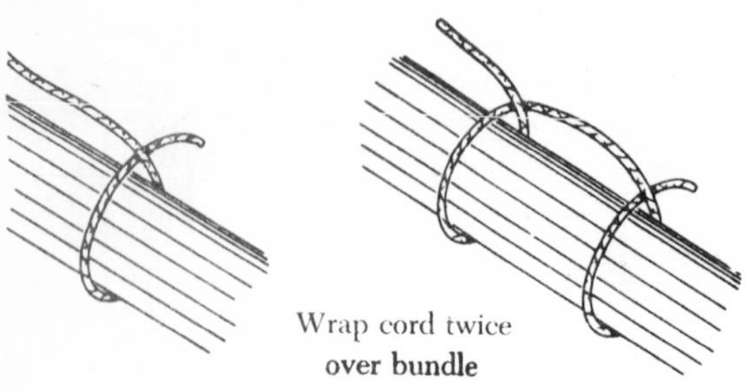

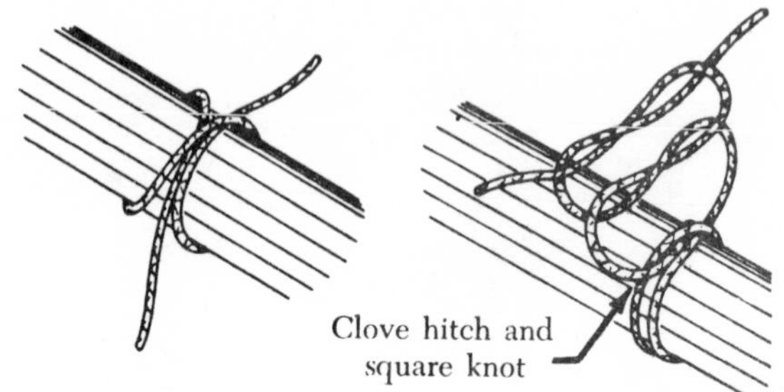

FIGURE 4–103. Tying a wire group or bundle.

TABLE 5. Wire strippers for copper wire.

Stripper	*Wire Size*	*Insulations*
Hot-blade	#26 — #4	All except asbestos
Rotary, electric	#26 — #4	All
Bench	#20 — #6	All
Hand pliers	#26 — #8	All
Knife	#2 — #0000	All

Aluminum wire must be stripped using extreme care, since individual strands will break very easily after being nicked.

The following general precautions are recommended when stripping any type of wire:

(1) When using any type of wire stripper, hold the wire so that it is perpendicular to the cutting blades.

(2) Adjust automatic stripping tools carefully; follow the manufacturer's instructions to avoid nicking, cutting, or otherwise damaging strands. This is especially important for aluminum wires and for copper wires smaller than No. 10. Examine stripped wires for damage. Cut off and re-strip (if length is sufficient), or reject and replace any wires with more than the allowable number of nicked or broken strands listed in the manufacturer's instructions.

(3) Make sure insulation is clean-cut with no frayed or ragged edges. Trim if necessary.

(4) Make sure all insulation is removed from stripped area. Some types of wires are supplied with a transparent layer of insulation between the conductor and the primary insulation. If this is present, remove it.

(5) When using hand-plier strippers to remove lengths of insulation longer than 3/4 in., it is easier to accomplish in two or more operations.

(6) Re-twist copper strands by hand or with pliers if necessary to restore natural lay and tightness of strands.

A pair of hand wire strippers is shown in figure 4–104. This tool is commonly used to strip most types of wire.

The following general procedures describe the steps for stripping wire with a hand stripper. (Refer to figure 4–105.)

FIGURE 4–104. Light-duty hand wire strippers.

(1) Insert wire into exact center of correct cutting slot for wire size to be stripped. Each slot is marked with wire size.

(2) Close handles together as far as they will go.

(3) Release handles, allowing wire holder to return to the "open" position.

(4) Remove stripped wire.

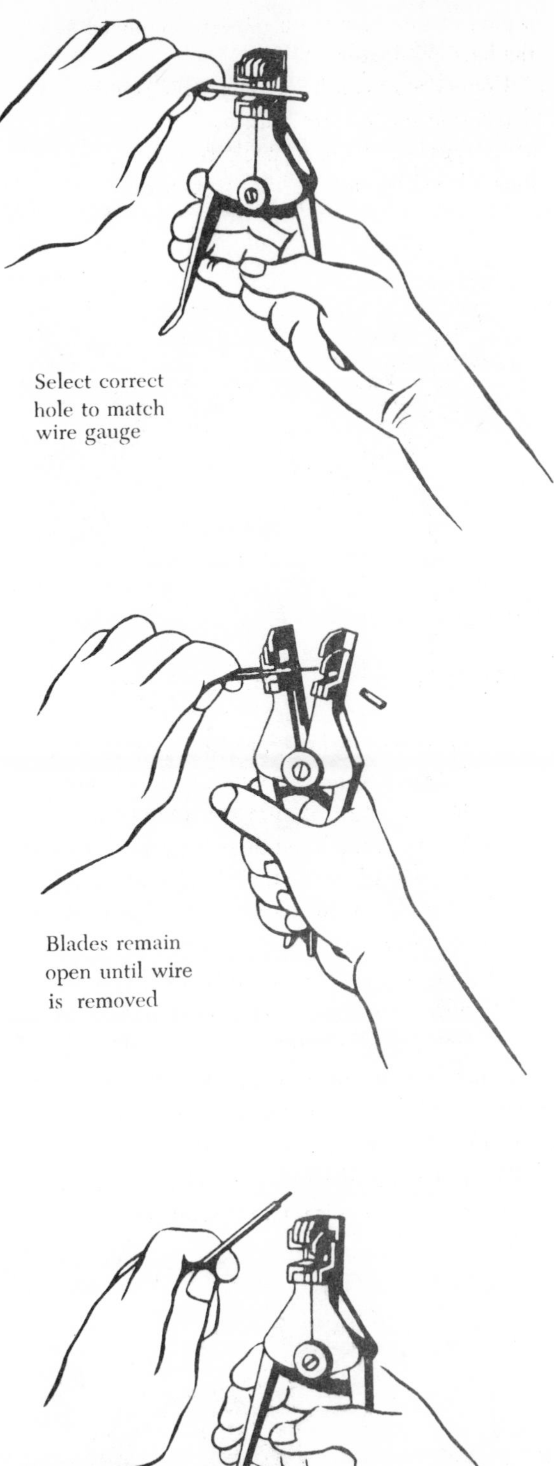
Select correct
hole to match
wire gauge
Blades remain
open until wire
is removed

FIGURE 4–105. Stripping wire with hand stripper.

Solderless Terminals and Splices

Splicing of electrical cable should be kept to a minimum and avoided entirely in locations subject to extreme vibrations. Individual wires in a group or bundle can usually be spliced, provided the completed splice is located so that it can be inspected periodically. The splices should be staggered so that the bundle does not become excessively enlarged. Many types of aircraft splice connectors are available for splicing individual wires. Self-insulated splice connectors are usually preferred; however, a noninsulated splice connector can be used if the splice is covered with plastic sleeving secured at both ends. Solder splices may be used, but they are particularly brittle and not recommended.

Electric wires are terminated with solderless terminal lugs to permit easy and efficient connection to and disconnection from terminal blocks, bus bars, or other electrical equipment. Solderless splices join electric wires to form permanent continuous runs. Solderless terminal lugs and splices are made of copper or aluminum and are preinsulated or uninsulated, depending on the desired application.

Terminal lugs are generally available in three types for use in different space conditions. These are the flag, straight, and right-angle lugs. Terminal lugs are "crimped" (sometimes called "staked" or "swaged") to the wires by means of hand or power crimping tools.

The following discussion describes recommended methods for terminating copper and aluminum wires using solderless terminal lugs. It also describes the method for splicing copper wires using solderless splices.

Copper Wire Terminals

Copper wires are terminated with solderless, preinsulated straight copper terminal lugs. The insulation is part of the terminal lug and extends beyond its barrel so that it will cover a portion of the wire insulation, making the use of an insulation sleeve unnecessary (figure 4–106).

In addition, preinsulated terminal lugs contain an insulation grip (a metal reinforcing sleeve) beneath the insulation for extra gripping strength on the wire insulation. Preinsulated terminals accommodate more than one size of wire; the insulation is usually

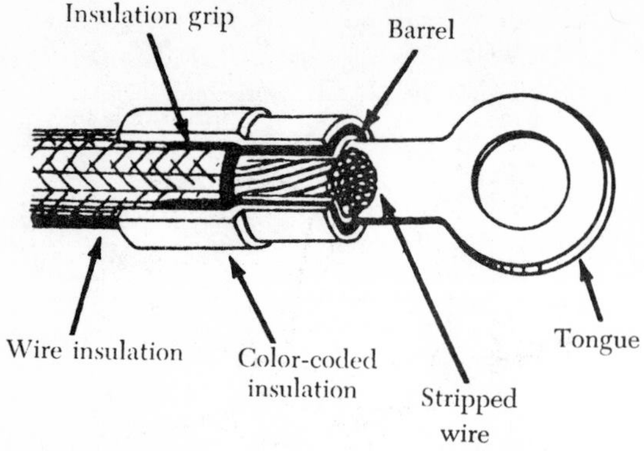

FIGURE 4–106. Preinsulated terminal lug.

color-coded to identify the wire sizes that can be terminated with each of the terminal lug sizes.

Crimping Tools

Hand, portable power, and stationary power tools are available for crimping terminal lugs. These tools crimp the barrel of the terminal lug to the conductor and simultaneously crimp the insulation grip to the wire insulation.

Hand crimping tools all have a self-locking ratchet that prevents opening the tool until the crimp is complete. Some hand crimping tools are equipped with a nest of various size inserts to fit different size terminal lugs. Others are used on one terminal lug size only. All types of hand crimping tools are checked by gages for proper adjustment of crimping jaws.

Figure 4–107 shows a terminal lug inserted into a hand tool. The following general guidelines outline the crimping procedure:

(1) Strip the wire insulation to proper length.

(2) Insert the terminal lug, tongue first, into the hand tool barrel crimping jaws until the terminal lug barrel butts flush against the tool stop.

(3) Insert the stripped wire into the terminal lug barrel until the wire insulation butts flush against the end of the barrel.

(4) Squeeze the tool handles until the ratchet releases.

(5) Remove the completed assembly and examine it for proper crimp.

Some types of uninsulated terminal lugs are insulated after assembly to a wire by means of pieces of transparent flexible tubing called "sleeves." The sleeve provides electrical and mechanical protection at the connection. When the size of the sleeving used is such that it will fit tightly over the terminal lug, the sleeving need not be tied; otherwise, it should be tied with lacing cord (figure 4–108).

Aluminum Wire Terminals

Aluminum wire is being used increasingly in aircraft systems because of its weight advantage over copper. However, bending aluminum will cause "work hardening" of the metal, making it brittle. This results in failure or breakage of strands much sooner than in a similar case with copper wire. Aluminum also forms a high-resistant oxide film immediately upon exposure to air. To compensate for these disadvantages, it is important to use the most reliable installation procedures.

Only aluminum terminal lugs are used to terminate aluminum wires. They are generally available in three types: (1) Straight, (2) right-angle, and (3) flag. All aluminum terminals incorporate an inspection hole (figure 4–108) which permits check-

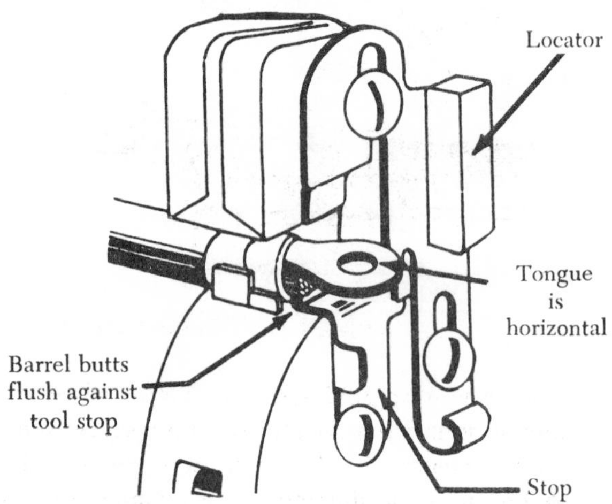

FIGURE 4–107. Inserting terminal lug into hand tool.

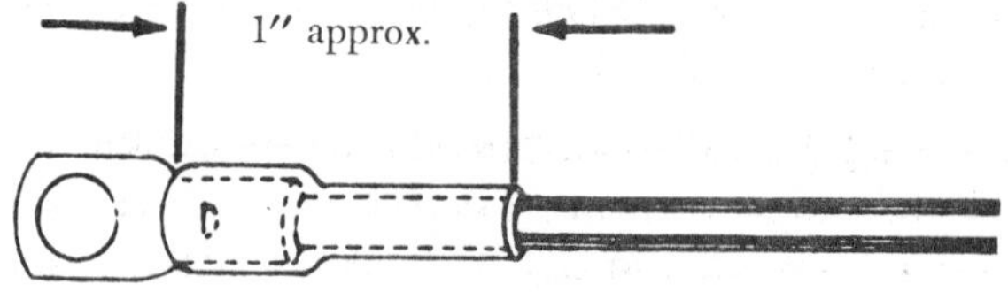

Tight or shrunk sleeve

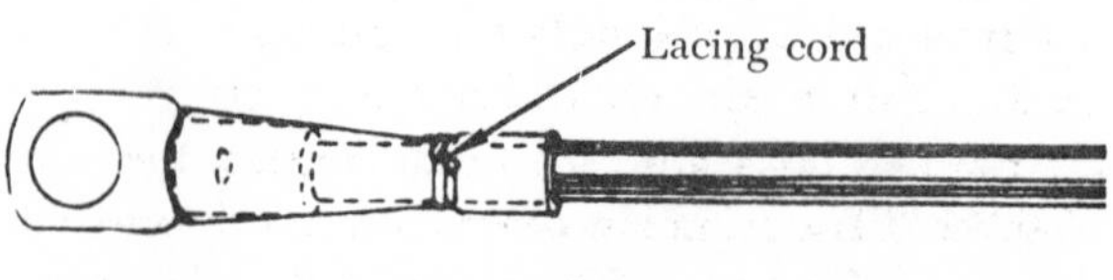

Loose sleeve

FIGURE 4–108. Insulating sleeves.

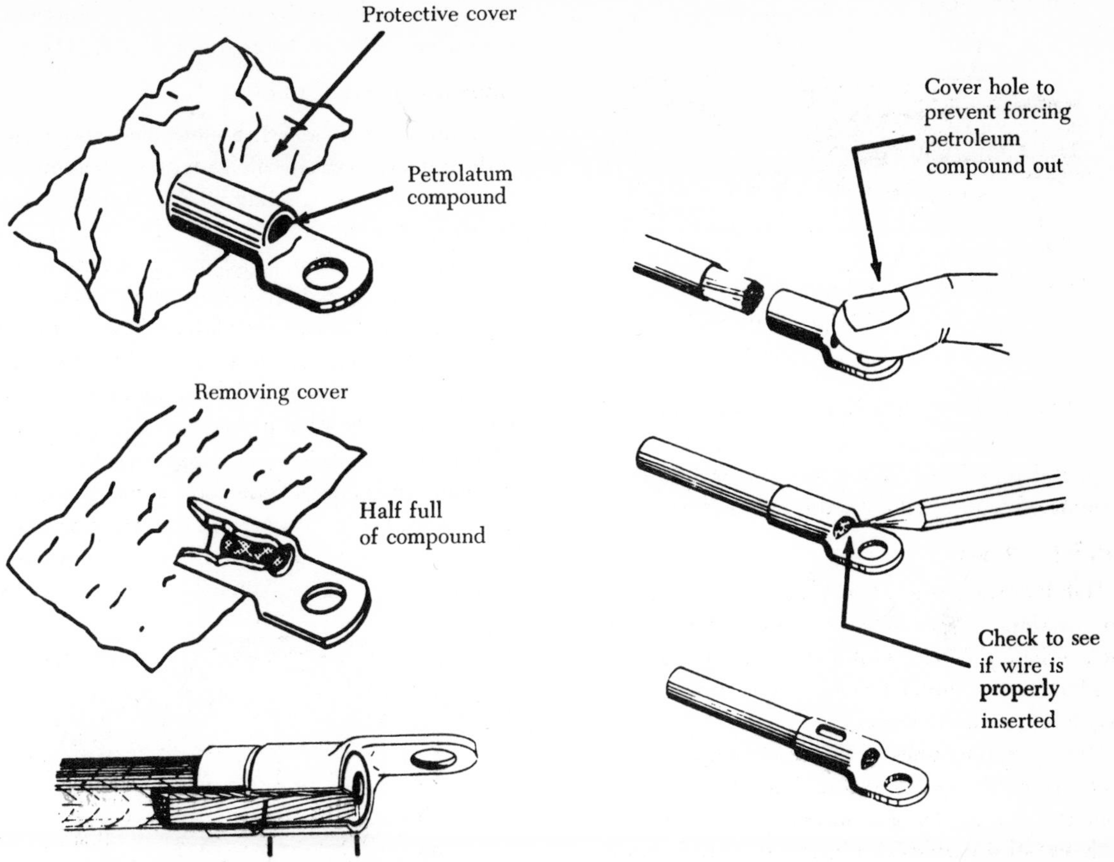

FIGURE 4–109. Inserting aluminum wire into aluminum terminal lugs.

ing the depth of wire insertion. The barrel of aluminum terminal lugs is filled with a petrolatum-zinc dust compound. This compound removes the oxide film from the aluminum by a grinding process during the crimping operation. The compound will also minimize later oxidation of the completed connection by excluding moisture and air. The compound is retained inside the terminal lug barrel by a plastic or foil seal at the end of the barrel.

Splicing Copper Wires Using Preinsulated Wires

Preinsulated permanent copper splices join small wires of sizes 22 through 10. Each splice size can be used for more than one wire size. Splices are usually color-coded in the same manner as preinsulated, small copper terminal lugs. Some splices are insulated with white plastic. Splices are also used to reduce wire sizes as shown in figure 4–110.

Crimping tools are used to accomplish this type of splice. The crimping procedures are the same as those used for terminal lugs, except that the crimping operation must be done twice, one for each end of the splice.

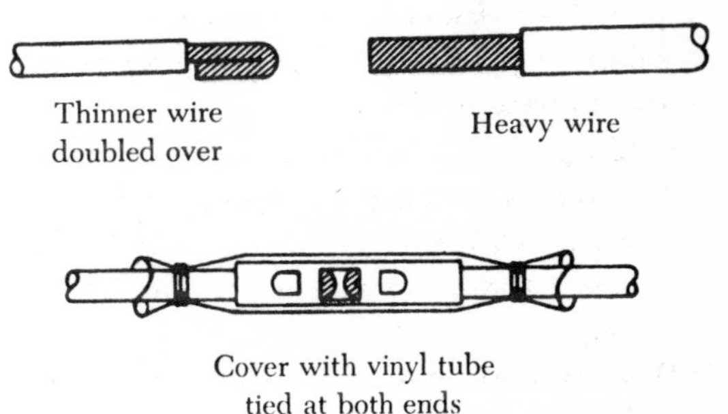

FIGURE 4–110. Reducing wire size with a permanent splice.

EMERGENCY SPLICING REPAIRS

Broken wires can be repaired by means of crimped splices, by using terminal lugs from which the tongue has been cut off, or by soldering together and potting broken strands. These repairs are applicable to copper wire. Damaged aluminum wire must not be temporarily spliced. These repairs are for temporary emergency use only and should be replaced as soon as possible with permanent repairs. Since some manufacturers prohibit splicing, the applicable manufacturer's instructions should always be consulted.

Splicing with Solder and Potting Compound

When neither a permanent splice nor a terminal lug is available, a broken wire can be repaired as follows (see figure 4–111):

(1) Install a piece of plastic sleeving about 3 in. long, and of the proper diameter to fit loosely over the insulation, on one piece of the broken wire.

(2) Strip approximately 1-1/2 in. from each broken end of the wire.

(3) Lay the stripped ends side by side and twist one wire around the other with approximately four turns.

(4) Twist the free end of the second wire around the first wire with approximately four turns. Solder the wire turns together, using 60/40 tin-lead resin-core solder.

(5) When solder is cool, draw the sleeve over the soldered wires and tie at one end. If potting compound is available, fill the sleeve with potting material and tie securely.

(6) Allow the potting compound to set without touching for 4 hrs. Full cure and electrical characteristics are achieved in 24 hrs.

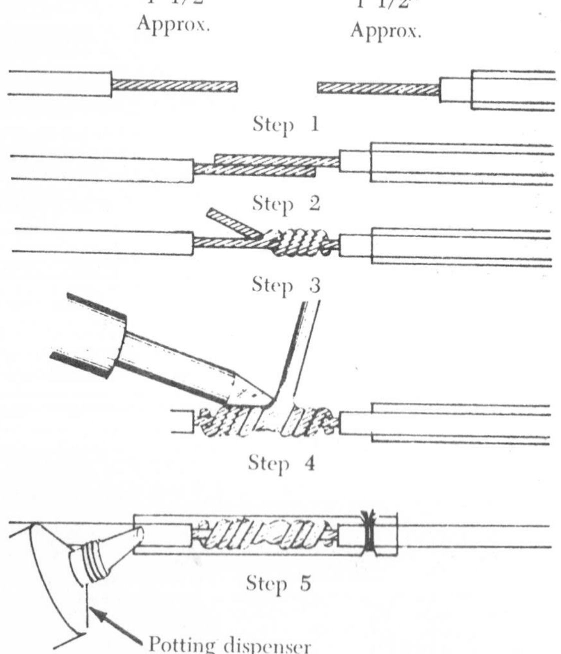

FIGURE 4–111. Repairing broken wire by soldering and potting.

CONNECTING TERMINAL LUGS TO TERMINAL BLOCKS

Terminal lugs should be installed on terminal blocks in such a manner that they are locked against movement in the direction of loosening (figure 4–112).

Terminal blocks are normally supplied with studs secured in place by a plain washer, an external tooth lockwasher, and a nut. In connecting terminals, a recommended practice is to place copper terminal lugs directly on top of the nut, followed with a plain washer and elastic stop nut, or with a plain washer, split steel lockwasher, and plain nut.

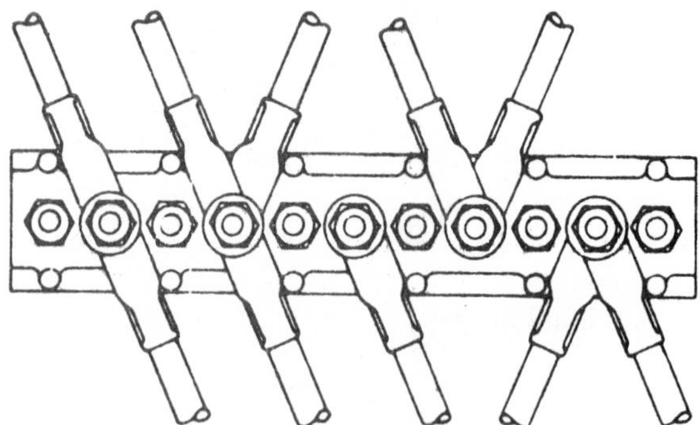

FIGURE 4–112. Connecting terminals to terminal block.

Aluminum terminal lugs should be placed over a plated brass plain washer, followed with another plated brass plain washer, split steel lockwasher, and plain nut or elastic stop nut. The plated brass washer should have a diameter equal to the tongue width of the aluminum terminal lug. Consult the manufacturer's instructions for recommended dimensions of these plated brass washers. Do not place any washer in the current path between two aluminum terminal lugs or between two copper terminal lugs. Also, do not place a lockwasher directly against the tongue or pad of the aluminum terminal.

To join a copper terminal lug to an aluminum terminal lug, place a plated brass plain washer over the nut which holds the stud in place; follow with the aluminum terminal lug, a plated brass plain washer, the copper terminal lug, plain washer, split steel lockwasher and plain nut or self-locking, all metal nut. As a general rule use a torque wrench to tighten nuts to ensure sufficient contact pressure. Manufacturer's instructions provide installation torques for all types of terminals.

BONDING AND GROUNDING

Bonding is the electrical connecting of two or more conducting objects not otherwise connected adequately. Grounding is the electrical connecting of a conducting object to the primary structure for return of current. Primary structure is the main frame, fuselage, or wing structure of the aircraft. Bonding and grounding connections are made in aircraft electrical systems to:

(1) Protect aircraft and personnel against hazards from lightning discharge.
(2) Provide current return paths.
(3) Prevent development of radio-frequency potentials.
(4) Protect personnel from shock hazard.
(5) Provide stability of radio transmission and reception.
(6) Prevent accumulation of static charge.

General Bonding and Grounding Procedures

The following general procedures and precautions are recommended when making bonding or grounding connections.

(1) Bond or ground parts to the primary aircraft structure where practicable.
(2) Make bonding or grounding connections in such a manner that no part of the aircraft structure is weakened.
(3) Bond parts individually if possible.
(4) Install bonding or grounding connections against smooth, clean surfaces.
(5) Install bonding or grounding connections so that vibration, expansion or contraction, or relative movement in normal service will not break or loosen the connection.
(6) Install bonding and grounding connections in protected areas whenever possible.

Bonding jumpers should be kept short as practicable, and installed in such a manner that the resistance of each connection does not exceed 0.003 ohm. The jumper should not interfere with the operation of movable aircraft elements, such as surface controls; normal movement of these elements should not result in damage to the bonding jumper.

To be sure a low-resistance connection has been made, nonconducting finishes, such as paint and anodizing films, should be removed from the surface to be contacted by the bonding terminal.

Electrolytic action can rapidly corrode a bonding connection if suitable precautions are not observed. Aluminum alloy jumpers are recommended for most cases; however, copper jumpers can be used to bond together parts made of stainless steel, cadmium-plated steel, copper, brass, or bronze. Where contact between dissimilar metals cannot be avoided, the choice of jumper and hardware should be such that corrosion is minimized, and the part most likely to corrode will be the jumper or associated hardware. Parts A and B of figure 4–113 illustrate some proper hardware combinations for making bonding connections. At locations where finishes are removed, a protective finish should be applied to the completed connection to prevent corrosion.

The use of solder to attach bonding jumpers should be avoided. Tubular members should be bonded by means of clamps to which the jumper is attached. The proper choice of clamp material minimizes the probability of corrosion. When bonding jumpers carry a substantial amount of ground return current, the current rating of the jumper should be adequate, and it should be determined that a negligible voltage drop is produced.

Bonding and grounding connections are normally made to flat surfaces by means of through-bolts or screws where there is easy access for installation. The three general types of bolted connections are:

(1) In making a stud connection (figure 4–114), a bolt or screw is locked securely to the structure, thus becoming a stud. Grounding or bonding jumpers can be removed or added to the shank of the stud without removing the stud from the structure.
(2) Nut-plates are used where access to the nut for repairs is difficult. Nut-plates (figure 4–115) are riveted or welded to a clean area of the structure.

Bonding and grounding connections are also made to a tab (figure 4–115) riveted to a structure. In such cases it is important to clean the bonding or grounding surface and make the connection as though the connection were being made to the structure. If it is necessary to remove the tab for any reason, the rivets should be replaced with rivets one size larger, and the mating surfaces of the structure and the tab should be clean and free of anodic film.

Bonding or grounding connections can be made to aluminum alloy, magnesium, or corrosion-resistant steel tubular structure as shown in figure 4–116, which shows the arrangement of hardware for bonding with an aluminum jumper. Because of the ease with which aluminum is deformed, it is necessary to distribute screw and nut pressure by means of plain washers.

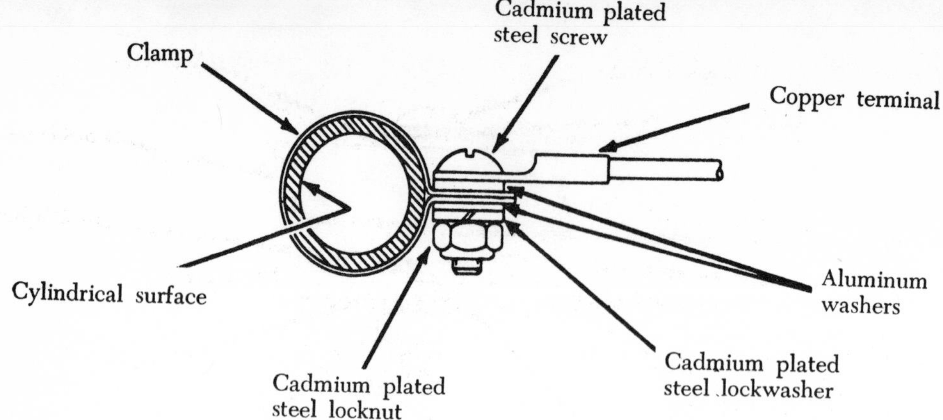

A. Copper jumper connection to tubular structure.

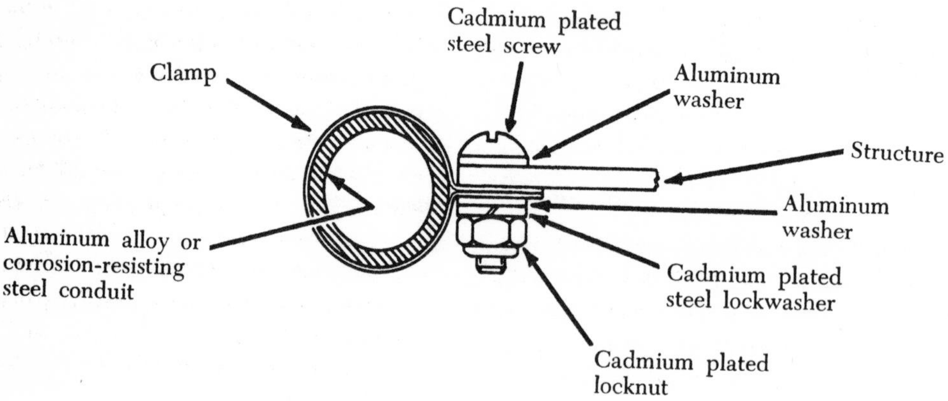

B. Bonding conduit to structure.

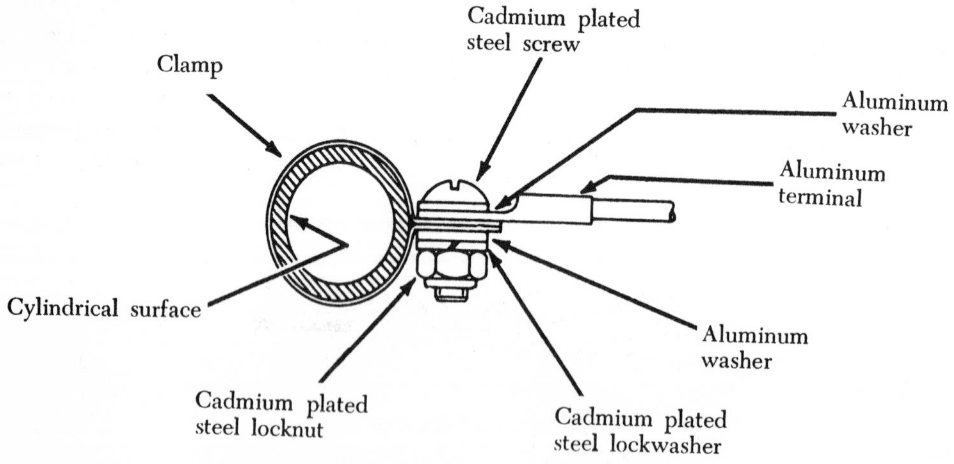

C. Aluminum jumper connection to tubular structure.

FIGURE 4–113. Hardware combinations used in making bonding connections.

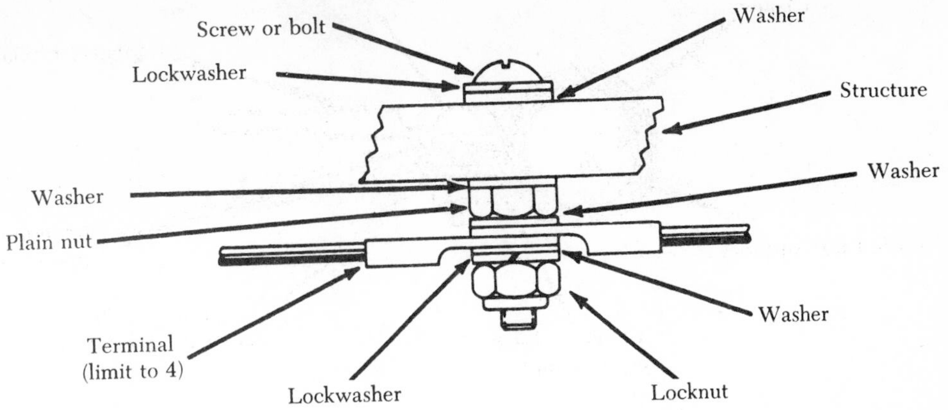

FIGURE 4–114. Stud bonding or grounding to a flat surface.

Hardware used to make bonding or grounding connections should be selected on the basis of mechanical strength, current to be carried, and ease of installation. If connection is made by aluminum or copper jumpers to the structure of a dissimilar material, a washer of suitable material should be installed between the dissimilar metals so that any corrosion will occur on the washer.

Hardware material and finish should be selected on the basis of the material of the structure to which attachment is made and on the material of the jumper and terminal specified for the bonding or grounding connection. Either a screw or bolt of the proper size for the specified jumper terminal should be used. When repairing or replacing existing bonding or grounding connections, the same type of hardware used in the original connection should always be used.

CONNECTORS

Connectors (plugs and receptacles) facilitate maintenance when frequent disconnection is required. Since the cable is soldered to the connector inserts, the joints should be individually installed and the cable bundle firmly supported to avoid damage by vibration. Connectors have been particularly vulnerable to corrosion in the past, due to condensation within the shell. Special connectors with waterproof features have been developed which may replace nonwaterproof plugs in areas where moisture causes a problem. A connector of the same basic type and design should be used when replacing a connector. Connectors that are susceptible to corrosion difficulties may be treated with a chemically inert waterproof jelly. When replacing connector assemblies, the socket-type insert should be used on the half which is "live" or "hot" after the connector is disconnected to prevent unintentional grounding.

Types of Connectors

Connectors are identified by AN numbers and are divided into classes with the manufacturer's variations in each class. The manufacturer's variations are differences in appearance and in the method of meeting a specification. Some commonly used connectors are shown in figure 4–118. There are five basic classes of AN connectors used in most aircraft. Each class of connector has slightly different construction characteristics. Classes A,

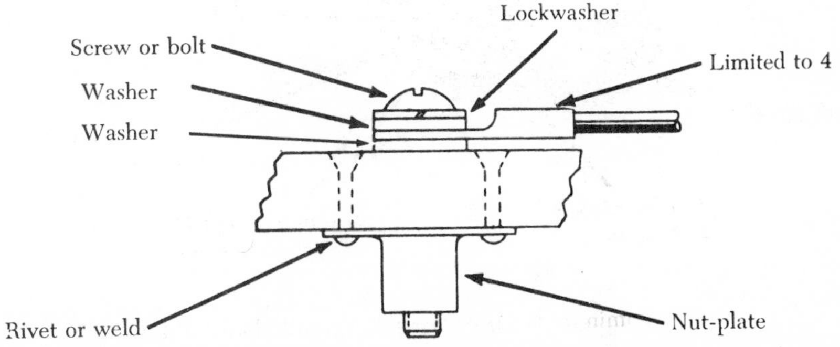

FIGURE 4–115. Nut-plate bonding or grounding to flat surface.

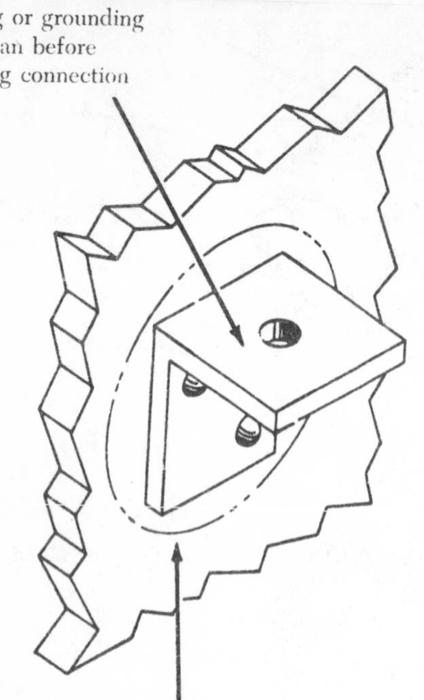

FIGURE 4–116. Bonding or grounding tab riveted to structure.

B, C, and D are made of aluminum, and class K is made of steel.

(1) Class A—Solid, one-piece back shell general-purpose connector.

(2) Class B—Connector back shell separates into two parts lengthwise. Used primarily where it is important that the soldered connectors are readily accessible. The back shell is held together by a threaded ring or by screws.

(3) Class C—A pressurized connector with inserts that are not removable. Similar to a class A connector in appearance, but the inside sealing arrangement is sometimes different. It is used on walls or bulkheads of pressurized equipment.

(4) Class D—Moisture- and vibration-resistant connector which has a sealing grommet in the back shell. Wires are threaded through tight-fitting holes in the grommet, thus sealing against moisture.

(5) Class K—A fireproof connector used in areas where it is vital that the electric current is not interrupted, even though the connector may be exposed to continuous open flame. Wires are crimped to the pin or socket contacts and the shells are made of steel. This class of connector is normally longer than other connectors.

Connector Identification

Code letters and numbers are marked on the coupling ring or shell to identify a connector. This code (figure 4–119) provides all the information necessary to obtain the correct replacement for a defective or damaged part.

Many special-purpose connectors have been designed for use in aircraft applications. These include subminiature and rectangular shell connectors, and connectors with short body shells, or of split-shell construction.

Installation of Connectors

The following procedures outline one recommended method of assembling connectors to receptacles:

(1) Locate the proper position of the plug in relation to the receptacle by aligning the key

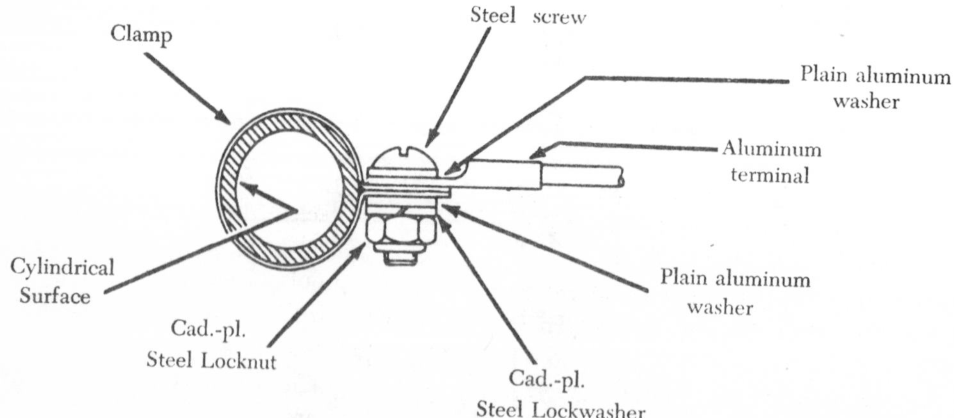

FIGURE 4–117. Bonding or grounding connections to a cylindrical surface.

FIGURE 4–118. AN connectors.

of one part with the groove or keyway of the other part.

(2) Start the plug into the receptacle with a slight forward pressure and engage the threads of the coupling ring and receptacle.

(3) Alternately push in the plug and tighten the coupling ring until the plug is completely seated.

(4) Use connector pliers to tighten coupling rings one-sixteenth to one-eighth of a turn beyond finger tight if space around the connector is too small to obtain a good finger grip.

(5) Never use force to mate connectors to receptacles. Do not hammer a plug into its receptacle, and never use a torque wrench or pliers to lock coupling rings.

A connector is generally disassembled from a receptacle in the following manner:

(1) Use connector pliers to loosen coupling rings which are too tight to be loosened by hand.

(2) Alternately pull on the plug body and unscrew

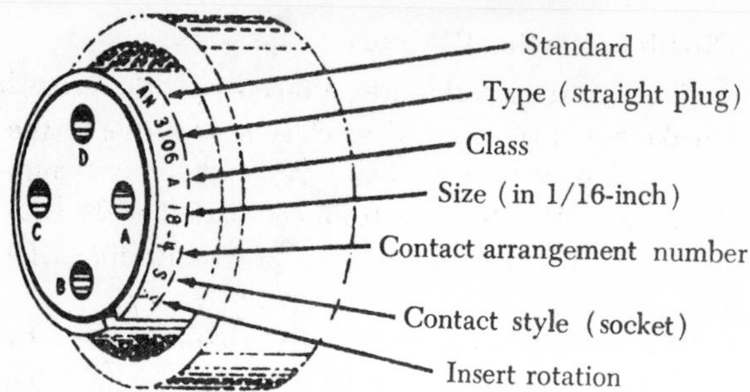

FIGURE 4–119. AN connector marking.

the coupling ring until the connector is separated.

(3) Protect disconnected plugs and receptacles with caps or plastic bags to keep debris from entering and causing faults.

(4) Do not use excessive force, and do not pull on attached wires.

CONDUIT

Conduit is used in aircraft installations for the mechanical protection of wires and cables. It is available in metallic and nonmetallic materials and in both rigid and flexible form.

When selecting conduit size for a specific cable bundle application, it is common practice to allow for ease in maintenance and possible future circuit expansion by specifying the conduit inner diameter about 25% larger than the maximum diameter of the conductor bundle. The nominal diameter of a rigid metallic conduit is the outside diameter. Therefore, to obtain the inside diameter, subtract twice the tube wall thickness.

From the abrasion standpoint, the conductor is vulnerable at the ends of the conduit. Suitable fittings are affixed to conduit ends in such a manner that a smooth surface comes in contact with the conductor within the conduit. When fittings are not used, the conduit end should be flared to prevent wire insulation damage. The conduit is supported by clamps along the conduit run.

Many of the common conduit installation problems can be avoided by proper attention to the following details:

(1) Do not locate conduit where it can be used as a handhold or footstep.

(2) Provide drain holes at the lowest point in a conduit run. Drilling burrs should be carefully removed from the drain holes.

(3) Support the conduit to prevent chafing against the structure and to avoid stressing its end fittings.

Damaged conduit sections should be repaired to prevent injury to the wires or wire bundle. The minimum acceptable tube bend radii for rigid conduit as prescribed by the manufacturer's instructions should be carefully followed. Kinked or wrinkled bends in a rigid conduit are normally not considered acceptable.

Flexible aluminum conduit is widely available in two types: (1) Bare flexible and (2) rubber-covered conduit. Flexible brass conduit is normally used instead of flexible aluminum where necessary to minimize radio interference. Flexible conduit may be used where it is impractical to use rigid conduit, such as areas that have motion between conduit ends or where complex bends are necessary. Transparent adhesive tape is recommended when cutting flexible conduit with a hacksaw to minimize fraying of the braid.

ELECTRICAL EQUIPMENT INSTALLATION

This section provides general procedures and safety precautions for installation of commonly used aircraft electrical equipment and components. Electrical load limits, acceptable means of controlling or monitoring electrical loads, and circuit protection devices are subjects with which mechanics must be familiar to properly install and maintain aircraft electrical systems.

Electrical Load Limits

When installing additional electrical equipment that consumes electrical power in an aircraft, the total electrical load must be safely controlled or managed within the rated limits of the affected components of the aircraft's power-supply system.

Before any aircraft electrical load is increased, the associated wires, cables, and circuit-protection devices (fuses or circuit breakers) should be checked to determine that the new electrical load (previous maximum load plus added load) does not exceed the rated limits of the existing wires, cables, or protection devices.

The generator or alternator output ratings prescribed by the manufacturer should be compared with the electrical loads which can be imposed on the affected generator or alternator by installed equipment. When the comparison shows that the probable total connected electrical load can exceed the output load limits of the generator(s) or alternator(s), the load should be reduced so that an overload cannot occur. When a storage battery is part of the electrical power system, ensure that the battery is continuously charged in flight, except when short intermittent loads are connected, such as a radio transmitter, a landing-gear motor, or other similar devices which may place short-time demand loads on the battery.

Controlling or Monitoring the Electrical Load

Placards are recommended to inform crewmembers of an aircraft about the combinations of loads that can safely be connected to the power source.

In installations where the ammeter is in the battery lead, and the regulator system limits the maximum current that the generator or alternator can deliver, a voltmeter can be installed on the system bus. As long as the ammeter does not read "discharge" (except for short intermittent loads such as operating the gear and flaps) and the voltmeter remains at "system voltage," the generator or alternator will not be overloaded.

In installations where the ammeter is in the generator or alternator lead, and the regulator system does not limit the maximum current that the generator or alternator can deliver, the ammeter can be redlined at 100% of the generator or alternator rating. If the ammeter reading is never allowed to exceed the red line, except for short, intermittent loads, the generator or alternator will not be overloaded.

Where the use of placards or monitoring devices is not practicable or desired, and where assurance is needed that the battery in a typical small aircraft generator/battery power source will be charged in flight, the total continuous connected electrical load may be held to approximately 80% of the total rated generator output capacity. (When more than one generator is used in parallel, the total rated output is the combined output of the installed generators.)

When two or more generators are operated in parallel and the total connected system load can exceed the rated output of one generator, means must be provided for quickly coping with the sudden overloads which can be caused by generator or engine failure. A quick load-reduction system can be employed or a specified procedure used whereby the total load can be reduced to a quantity which is within the rated capacity of the remaining operable generator or generators.

Electrical loads should be connected to inverters, alternators, or similar aircraft electrical power sources in such a manner that the rated limits of the power source are not exceeded, unless some type of effective monitoring means is provided to keep the load within prescribed limits.

Circuit Protection Devices

Conductors should be protected with circuit breakers or fuses located as close as possible to the electrical power-source bus. Normally, the manufacturer of the electrical equipment specifies the fuse or circuit breaker to be used when installing the equipment.

The circuit breaker or fuse should open the circuit before the conductor emits smoke. To accomplish this, the time/current characteristic of the protection device must fall below that of the associated conductor. Circuit-protector characteristics should be matched to obtain the maximum utilization of the connected equipment.

Figure 4–120 shows an example of the chart used in selecting the circuit breaker and fuse protection for copper conductors. This limited chart is applicable to a specific set of ambient temperatures and wire bundle sizes, and is presented as a typical example only. It is important to consult such guides before selecting a conductor for a specific purpose. For example, a wire run individually in the open air may be protected by the circuit breaker of the next higher rating to that shown on the chart.

All re-settable circuit breakers should open the circuit in which they are installed regardless of the position of the operating control when an overload or circuit fault exists. Such circuit breakers are referred to as "trip-free." Automatic re-set circuit breakers automatically re-set themselves periodically. They should not be used as circuit protection devices in aircraft.

Switches

A specifically designed switch should be used in all circuits where a switch malfunction would be

Wire AN gauge copper	Circuit breaker amperage	Fuse amp.
22	5	5
20	7.5	5
18	10	10
16	15	10
14	20	15
12	30	20
10	40	30
8	50	50
6	80	70
4	100	70
2	125	100
1		150
0		150

FIGURE 4–120. Wire and circuit protector chart.

hazardous. Such switches are of rugged construction and have sufficient contact capacity to break, make, and carry continuously the connected load current. Snap-action design is generally preferred to obtain rapid opening and closing of contacts regardless of the speed of the operating toggle or plunger, thereby minimizing contact arcing.

The nominal current rating of the conventional aircraft switch is usually stamped on the switch housing. This rating represents the continuous current rating with the contacts closed. Switches should be derated from their nominal current rating for the following types of circuits:

(1) High rush-in circuits—Circuits containing incandescent lamps can draw an initial current which is 15 times greater than the continuous current. Contact burning or welding may occur when the switch is closed.

(2) Inductive circuits—Magnetic energy stored in solenoid coils or relays is released and appears as an arc as the control switch is opened.

(3) Motors—Direct-current motors will draw several times their rated current during starting, and magnetic energy stored in their armature and field coils is released when the control switch is opened.

The chart in figure 4–121 is typical of those available for selecting the proper nominal switch rating when the continuous load current is known. This selection is essentially a derating to obtain reasonable switch efficiency and service life.

Nominal system Voltage	Type of load	Derating factor
24 V.D.C.	Lamp	8
24 V.D.C.	Inductive (Relay-Solenoid)	4
24 V.D.C.	Resistive (Heater)	2
24 V.D.C.	Motor	3
12 V.D.C.	Lamp	5
12 V.D.C.	Inductive (Relay-Solenoid)	2
12 V.D.C.	Resistive (Heater)	1
12 V.D.C.	Motor	2

FIGURE 4–121. Switch derating factors.

Hazardous errors in switch operation can be avoided by logical and consistent installation. Two position "on-off" switches should be mounted so that the "on" position is reached by an upward or forward movement of the toggle. When the switch controls movable aircraft elements, such as landing gear or flaps, the toggle should move in the same direction as the desired motion. Inadvertent operation of a switch can be prevented by mounting a suitable guard over the switch.

Relays

Relays are used as switching devices where a weight reduction can be achieved or electrical controls can be simplified. A relay is an electrically operated switch and is therefore subject to dropout under low system voltage conditions. The foregoing discussion of switch ratings is generally applicable to relay contact ratings.

CHAPTER 5

ENGINE STARTING SYSTEMS

GENERAL

Most aircraft engines are started by a device called a starter. A starter is a mechanism capable of developing large amounts of mechanical energy that can be applied to an engine, causing it to rotate.

In the early stages of aircraft development, relatively low-powered engines were started by pulling the propeller through a part of a revolution by hand. Some difficulty was often experienced in cold weather starting when lubricating oil temperatures were near the congealing point. In addition, the magneto systems delivered a weak starting spark at the very low cranking speeds. This was often compensated for by providing a hot spark, using such ignition system devices as the booster coil, induction vibrator, or impulse coupling.

Some small, low-powered aircraft which use hand-cranking of the propeller for starting are still being operated. For general instructions on starting this type of aircraft, refer to the Airframe and Powerplant Mechanics General Handbook, AC 65–9, Chapter 11.

RECIPROCATING ENGINE STARTING SYSTEMS

Throughout the development of the aircraft reciprocating engine from the earliest use of starting systems to the present, a number of different starter systems have been used. The most common of these are:

(1) Cartridge starter. (Not in common use.)

(2) Hand inertia starter. (Not in common use.)

(3) Electric inertia starter. (Not in common use.)

(4) Combination inertia starter. (Not in common use.)

(5) Direct-cranking electric starter.

Most reciprocating engine starters are of the direct-cranking electric type. A few older model aircraft are still equipped with one of the types of inertia starters, and in very rare instances an example of the hand cranking, hand inertia, or cartridge starter may be found. Thus, only a brief description of these starting systems is included in this section.

Inertia Starters

There are three general types of inertia starters: (1) Hand inertia starters, (2) electric inertia starters, and (3) combination hand and electric inertia starters.

The operation of all types of inertia starters depends on the kinetic energy stored in a rapidly rotating flywheel for cranking ability. (Kinetic energy is energy possessed by a body by virtue of its state of motion, which may be movement along a line or spinning action.) In the inertia starter, energy is stored slowly during an energizing process by a manual hand crank or electrically with a small motor. The flywheel and movable gears of a combination hand electric inertia starter are shown in figure 5–1. The electrical circuit for an electric inertia starter is shown in figure 5–2.

During the energizing of the starter, all movable parts within it, including the flywheel, are set in motion. After the starter has been fully energized, it is engaged to the crankshaft of the engine by a cable pulled manually or by a meshing solenoid which is energized electrically. When the starter is engaged or meshed, flywheel energy is transferred to the engine through sets of reduction gears and a torque overload release clutch (see figure 5–3).

Direct-Cranking Electric Starter

The most widely used starting system on all types of reciprocating engines utilizes the direct-cranking electric starter. This type of starter provides instant and continual cranking when ener-

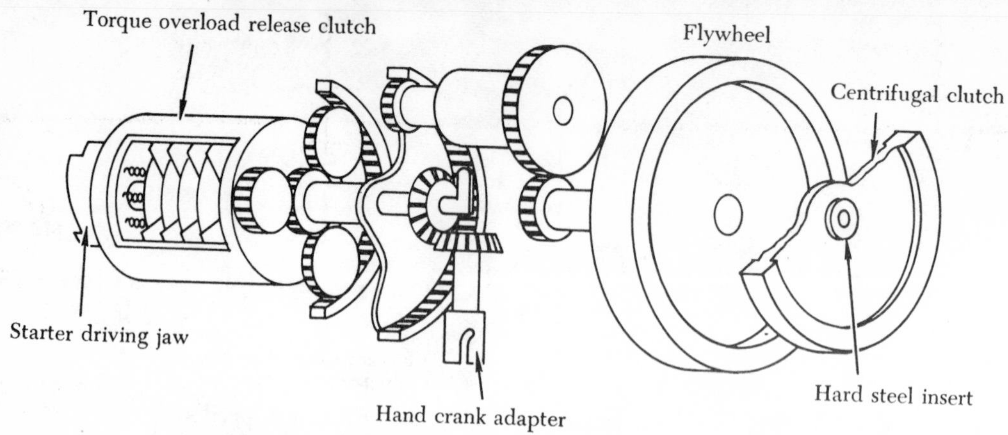

FIGURE 5–1. Combination hand and electric inertia starter.

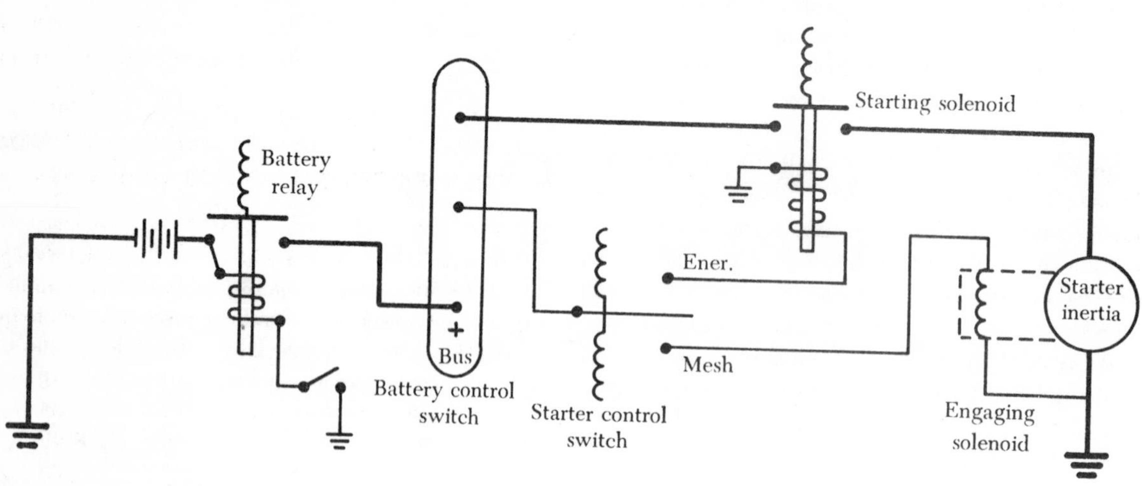

FIGURE 5–2. Electric inertia starting circuit.

gized. The direct-cranking electric starter consists basically of an electric motor, reduction gears, and an automatic engaging and disengaging mechanism which is operated through an adjustable torque overload release clutch. A typical circuit for a direct-cranking electric starter is shown in figure 5–4.

The engine is cranked directly when the starter solenoid is closed. Since no flywheel is used in the direct-cranking electric starter, there is no preliminary storing of energy as in the case of an inertia starter.

As shown in figure 5–4, the main cables leading from the starter to the battery are heavy-duty to carry the high-current flow which may be as high as 350 amperes, depending on the starting torque

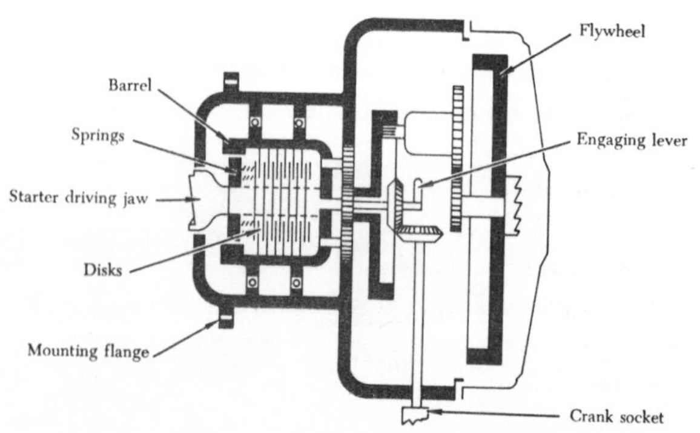

FIGURE 5–3. Torque overload release clutch.

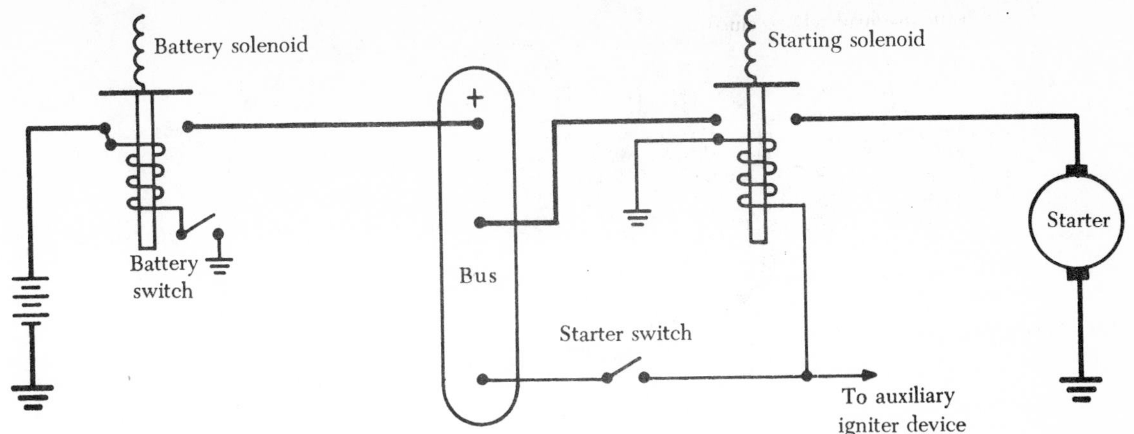

FIGURE 5–4. Typical starting circuit using a direct-cranking electric starter.

required. The use of solenoids and heavy wiring with a remote control switch reduces overall cable weight and total circuit voltage drop.

The typical starter motor is a 12- or 24-volt, series-wound motor, which develops high starting torque. The torque of the motor is transmitted through reduction gears to the overload release clutch. Typically, this action actuates a helically splined shaft, moving the starter jaw outward to engage the engine cranking jaw before the starter jaw begins to rotate. After the engine reaches a predetermined speed, the starter automatically disengages.

The schematic in figure 5–5 provides a pictorial arrangement of an entire starting system for a light twin-engine aircraft.

STARTING SYSTEM USING COMBINATION INERTIA STARTER

The following discussion covers one type of starting system used on a large reciprocating twin-engine aircraft. This system includes, for each engine, a combination inertia starter, a booster coil, a single-pole, double-throw switch in the cockpit, and the necessary solenoids and wiring. The combination inertia starter is shown in figure 5–6.

External hand-starting controls, incorporating a starter crank extension and a starting control cable, are provided for starting the engine by hand (figure 5–7).

Two starter switches are located on the cockpit electrical panel. Placing a switch in the "up" position operates the starter. The same switch, placed in the "down" position, operates the meshing (starter-engaging) solenoid and the ignition booster coil. The "off" position of the switch is midway between the two other positions.

A battery-operated booster coil, mounted in a shielded case, is installed on the engine mount of each engine. Flexible conduit shields the leads from the coil to one of the magnetos on each engine.

DIRECT-CRANKING ELECTRIC STARTING SYSTEM FOR LARGE RECIPROCATING ENGINES

In a typical high-horsepower reciprocating engine starting system, the direct-cranking electric starter consists of two basic components: a motor assembly and a gear section. The gear section is bolted to the drive end of the motor to form a complete unit.

The motor assembly consists of the armature and motor pinion assembly, the end bell assembly, and the motor housing assembly. The motor housing also acts as the magnetic yoke for the field structure.

The starter motor is a nonreversible, series interpole motor. Its speed varies directly with the applied voltage and inversely with the load.

The starter gear section, shown in figure 5–8, consists of a housing with an integral mounting flange, planetary gear reduction, a sun and integral gear assembly, a torque-limiting clutch, and a jaw and cone assembly.

When the starter circuit is closed, the torque developed in the starter motor is transmitted to the starter jaw through the reduction gear train and clutch. The starter gear train converts the high-speed low-torque of the motor to the low-speed high-torque required to crank the engine.

In the gear section the motor pinion engages the gear on the intermediate countershaft. (Refer to figure 5–8). The pinion of the countershaft engages the internal gear. The internal gear is an integral part of the sun gear assembly and is rigidly attached

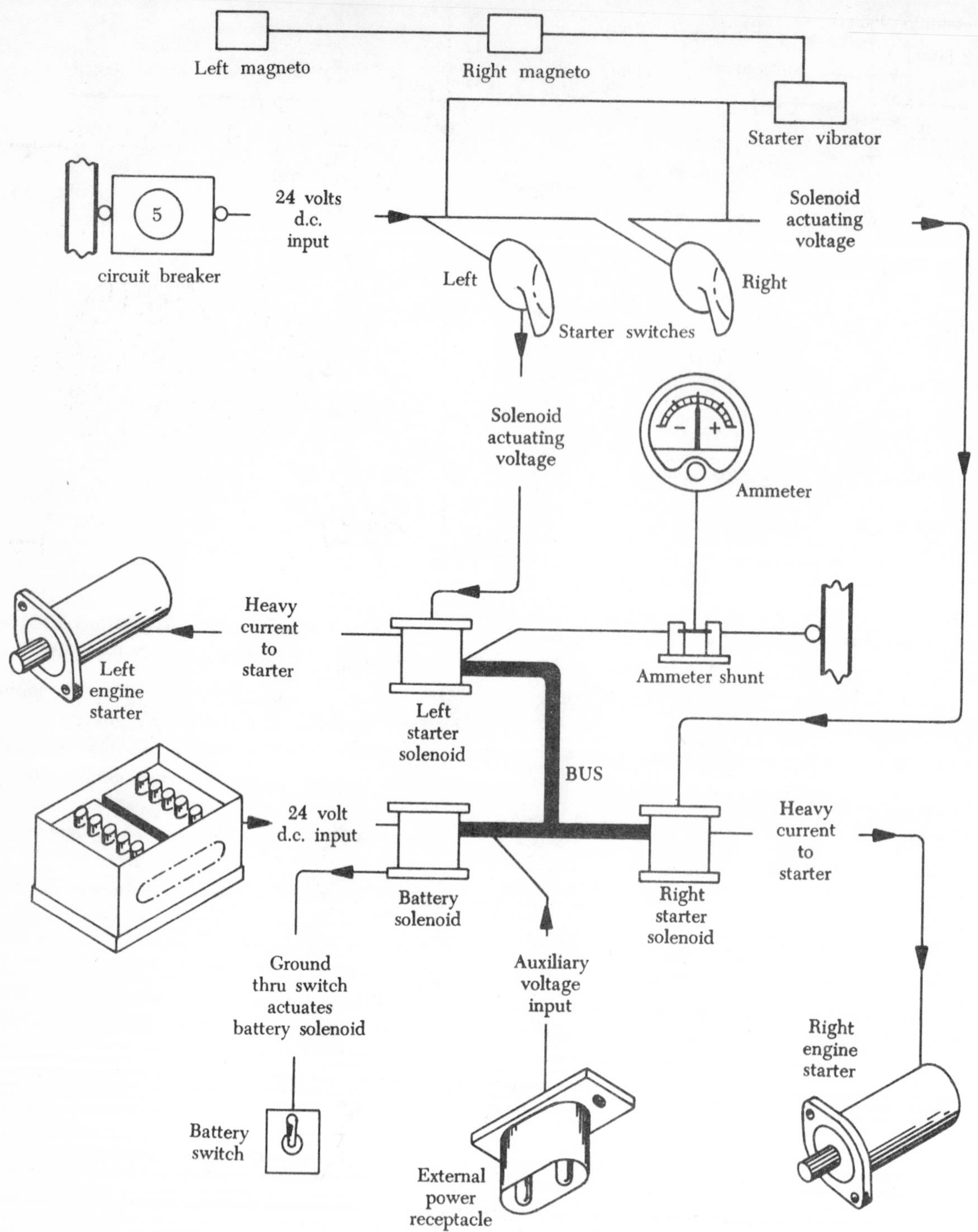

FIGURE 5–5. Engine starting schematic for a light twin-engine aircraft.

to the sun gear shaft. The sun gear drives three planet gears, which are part of the planetary gear assembly.

The individual planet gear shafts are supported by the planetary carrying arm, a barrel-like part shown in figure 5–8. The carrying arm transmits torque from the planet gears to the starter jaw as follows:

(1) The cylindrical portion of the carrying arm is splined longitudinally around the inner surface.

(2) Mating splines are cut on the exterior surface

Mounting flange
Brush cover band
Starter Jaw
Motor unit
Base unit
Hand crank
flexible cable
connection
Manual jaw meshing
cable and handle
Jaw meshing
cable spring
Electrical receptacle
Brush lifting and jaw
meshing lever
Jaw meshing
solenoid

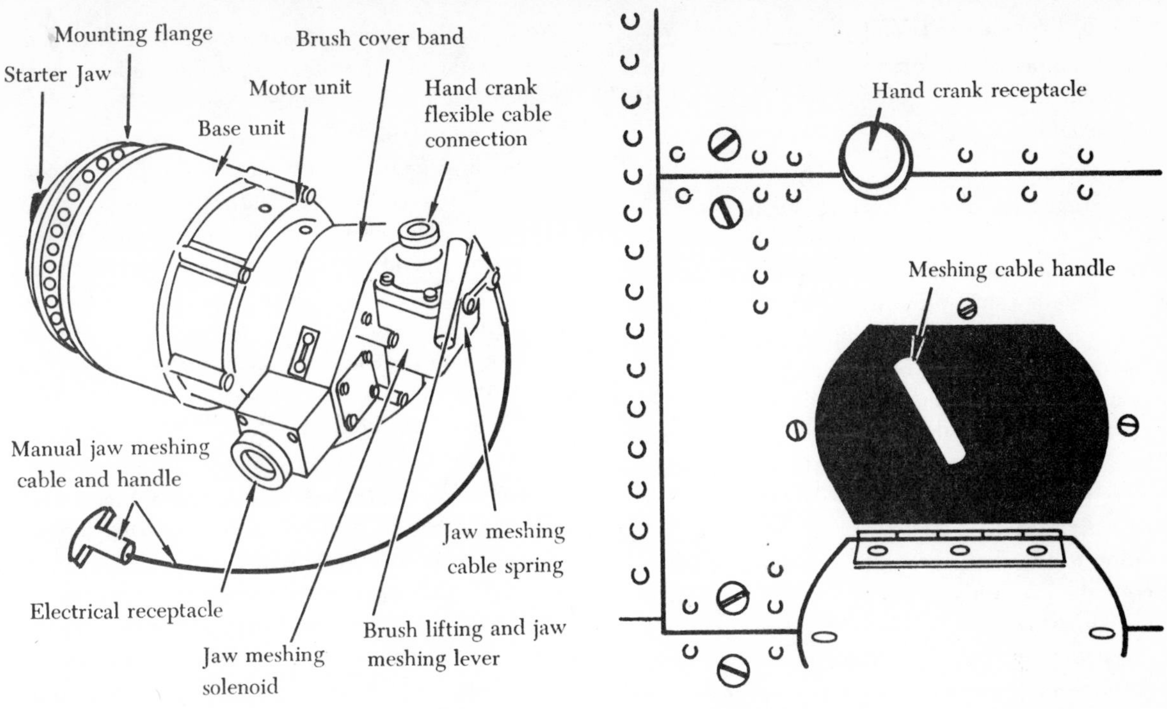

FIGURE 5–6. Combination inertia starter.

Hand crank receptacle
Meshing cable handle

FIGURE 5–7. Hand-starting controls.

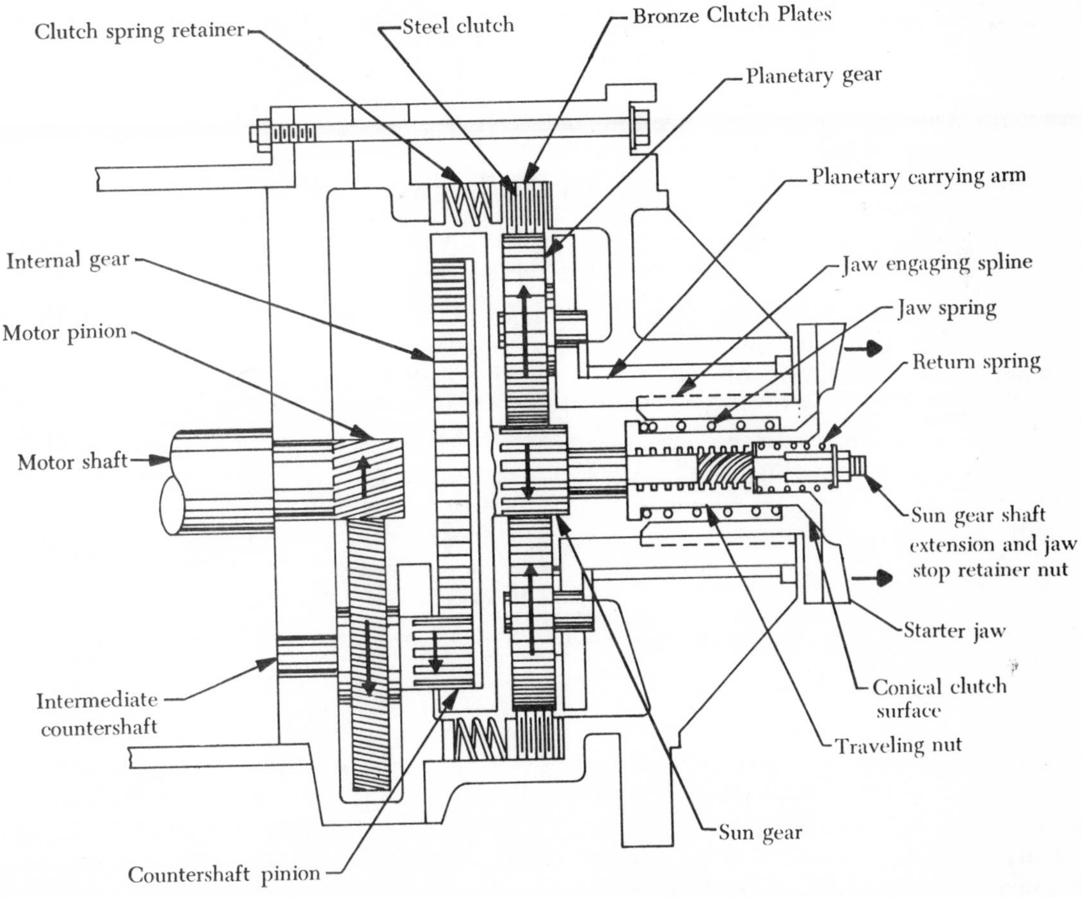

Clutch spring retainer
Steel clutch
Bronze Clutch Plates
Planetary gear
Planetary carrying arm
Internal gear
Jaw engaging spline
Jaw spring
Motor pinion
Return spring
Motor shaft
Sun gear shaft
extension and jaw
stop retainer nut
Starter jaw
Intermediate
countershaft
Conical clutch
surface
Traveling nut
Sun gear
Countershaft pinion

FIGURE 5–8. Starter gear section.

of the cylindrical part of the starter jaw.

(3) The jaw slides fore and aft inside the carrying arm to engage and disengage with the engine.

The three planet gears also engage the surrounding internal teeth on the six steel clutch plates (figure 5–8). These plates are interleaved with externally splined bronze clutch plates which engage the sides of the housing, preventing them from turning. The proper pressure is maintained upon the clutch pack by a clutch spring retainer assembly.

A cylindrical traveling nut inside the starter jaw extends and retracts the jaw. Spiral jaw-engaging splines around the inner wall of the nut mate with similar splines cut on an extension of the sun gear shaft (figure 5–8). Being splined in this fashion, rotation of the shaft forces the nut out and the nut carries the jaw with it. A jaw spring around the traveling nut carries the jaw with the nut and tends to keep a conical clutch surface around the inner wall of the jaw head seated against a similar surface around the under side of the nut head. A return spring is installed on the sun gear shaft extension between a shoulder formed by the splines around the inner wall of the traveling nut and a jaw stop retaining nut on the end of the shaft.

Because the conical clutch surfaces of the traveling nut and the starter jaw are engaged by jaw spring pressure, the two parts tend to rotate at the same speed. However, the sun gear shaft extension turns six times faster than the jaw. The spiral splines on it are cut left hand, and the sun gear shaft extension, turning to the right in relation to the jaw, forces the traveling nut and the jaw out from the starter its full travel (about 5/16 in.) in approximately 12° of rotation of the jaw. The jaw moves out until it is stopped either by engagement with the engine or by the jaw stop retaining nut. The travel nut continues to move slightly beyond the limit of jaw travel, just enough to relieve some of the spring pressure on the conical clutch surfaces.

As long as the starter continues to rotate, there is just enough pressure on the conical clutch surfaces to provide torque on the spiral splines which balances most of the pressure of the jaw spring. If the engine fails to start, the starter jaw will not retract, since the starter mechanism provides no retracting force. However, when the engine fires and the engine jaw overruns the starter jaw, the sloping ramps of the jaw teeth force the starter jaw into the starter against the jaw spring pressure. This disengages the conical clutch surfaces entirely, and the jaw spring pressure forces the traveling nut to slide in along the spiral splines until the conical clutch surfaces are again in contact.

With the starter and engine both running, there will be an engaging force keeping the jaws in contact, which will continue until the starter is de-energized. However, the rapidly moving engine jaw teeth, striking the slowly moving starter jaw teeth, hold the starter jaw disengaged. As soon as the starter comes to rest, the engaging force is removed, and the small return spring will throw the starter jaw into its fully retracted position, where it will remain until the next start.

When the starter jaw first engages the engine jaw, the motor armature has had time to reach considerable speed because of its high starting torque. The sudden engagement of the moving starter jaw with the stationary engine jaw would develop forces sufficiently high to severely damage the engine or the starter were it not for the plates in the clutch pack, which slip when the engine torque exceeds the clutch-slipping torque.

In normal direct-cranking action, the internal gear clutch plates (steel) are held stationary by the friction of the bronze plates, with which they are interleaved. When the torque imposed by the engine exceeds the clutch setting, however, the internal gear clutch plates rotate against the clutch friction, which allows the planet gears to rotate while the planetary carrying arm and the jaw remain stationary. When the engine comes up to the speed at which the starter is trying to drive it, the torque drops off to a value less than the clutch setting, the internal gear clutch plates are again held stationary, and the jaw rotates at the speed at which the motor is attempting to drive it.

The starter control switches are shown schematically in figure 5–9. The engine selector switch must be positioned, and both the starter switch and the safety switch (wired in series) must be closed before the starter can be energized.

Current is supplied to the starter control circuit through a circuit breaker, labeled "Starter, Primer, and Induction Vibrator" in figure 5–9. When the engine selector switch is in position for the engine start, closing the starter and safety switches energizes the starter relay located in the firewall junction box.

Energizing the starter relay completes the power circuit to the starter motor. The current necessary for this heavy load is taken directly from the master bus through the starter bus cable.

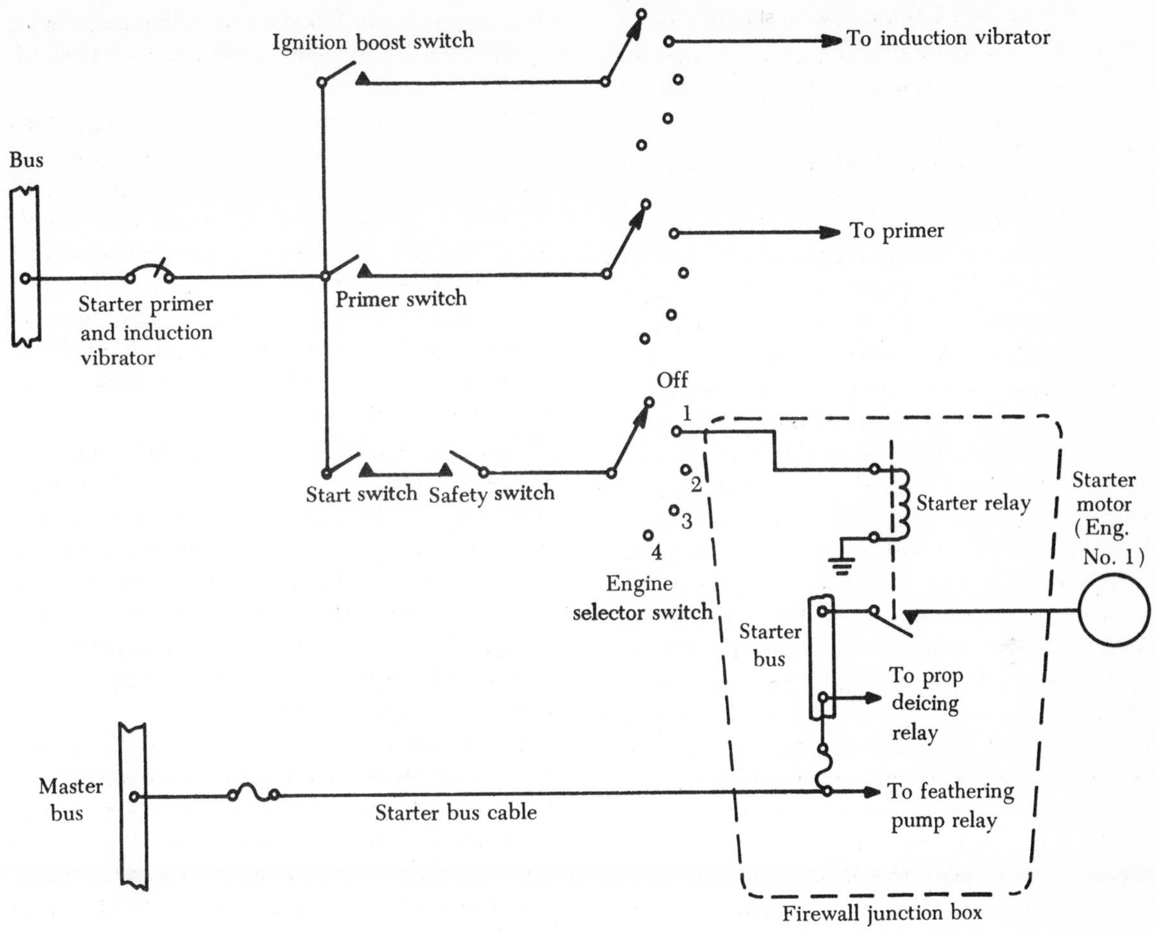

FIGURE 5–9. Starter control circuit.

After energizing the starter for 1 minute, it should be allowed to cool for at least 1 minute. After a second or subsequent cranking period of 1 minute, it should cool for 5 minutes.

DIRECT-CRANKING ELECTRIC STARTING SYSTEM FOR SMALL AIRCRAFT

Most small reciprocating-engine aircraft employ a direct-cranking electric starting system. Some of these systems are automatically engaged starting systems, while others are manually engaged.

The automatically engaged starting systems employ an electric starter mounted on an engine adapter. A starter solenoid is activated by either a push button or an ignition key on the instrument panel. When the solenoid is activated, its contacts close and electrical energy energizes the starter motor. Initial rotation of the starter motor engages the starter through an overrunning clutch in the starter adapter, which incorporates worm reduction gears.

Manually engaged starting systems on many small aircraft employ a manually operated overrunning-clutch drive pinion to transmit power from an electric starter motor to a crankshaft starter drive gear (see figure 5–10). A knob or handle on the instrument panel is connected by a flexible control to a lever on the starter. This lever shifts the starter drive pinion into the engaged position, and closes the starter switch contacts when the starter knob or handle is pulled. The starter lever is attached to a return spring which returns the lever and the flexible control to the "off" position. When the engine starts, the overrunning action of the clutch protects the starter drive pinion until the shift lever can be released to disengage the pinion.

As shown for the typical unit in figure 5–10, there is a specified length of travel for the starter gear pinion. It is important that the starter lever move the starter pinion gear this proper distance before the adjustable lever stud contacts the starter switch.

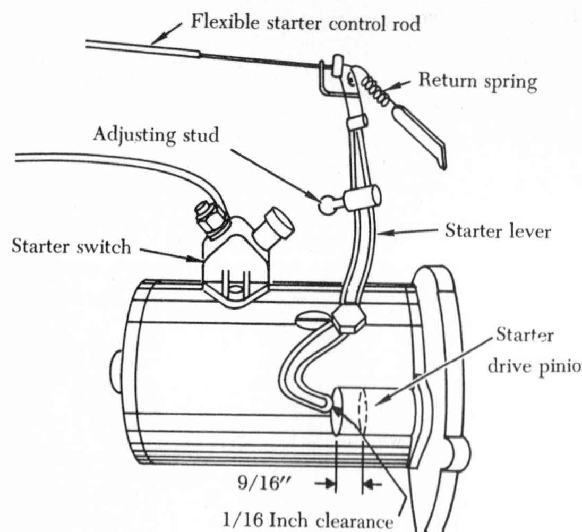

FIGURE 5–10. Starter lever controls and adjustment.

Starting System Maintenance Practices

Most starting system maintenance practices include replacing the starter brushes and brush springs, cleaning dirty commutators, and turning down burned or out-of-round starter commutators.

As a rule, starter brushes should be replaced when worn down to approximately one-half their original length. Brush spring tension should be sufficient to give brushes a good firm contact with the commutator. Brush leads should be unbroken and lead terminal screws tight.

A glazed or dirty starter commutator can be cleaned by holding a strip of double-0 sandpaper or a brush seating stone against the commutator as it is turned. The sandpaper or stone should be moved back and forth across the commutator to avoid wearing a groove. Emery paper or carborundum should never be used for this purpose because of their possible shorting action.

Roughness, out-of-roundness, or high-mica conditions are reasons for turning down the commutator. In the case of a high-mica condition, the mica should be undercut after the turning operation is accomplished. (Refer to the Airframe and Powerplant Mechanics General Handbook, AC 65–9 for a review of high-mica commutators in motors.)

Troubleshooting Small Aircraft Starting Systems

The troubleshooting procedures listed in table 6 are typical of those used to isolate malfunctions in small aircraft starting systems.

GAS TURBINE ENGINE STARTERS

Gas turbine engines are started by rotating the compressor. On dual-axial-compressor engines, the high-pressure compressor is the only one rotated by the starter. To start a gas turbine engine it is necessary to accelerate the compressor to provide sufficient air to support combustion in the burners. Once fuel has been introduced and the engine has fired, the starter must continue to assist the engine to reach a speed above the self-accelerating speed of the engine. The torque supplied by the starter must be in excess of the torque required to overcome compressor inertia and the friction loads of the engine.

The basic types of starters which have been developed for gas turbine engines are d.c. electric motor, air turbine, and combustion. An impingement starting system is sometimes used on small engines. An impingement starter consists of jets of compressed air piped to the inside of the compressor or turbine case so that the jet air-blast is directed onto the compressor or turbine rotor blades, causing them to rotate.

The graph in figure 5–11 illustrates a typical starting sequence for a gas turbine engine, regardless of the type of starter employed.

As soon as the starter has accelerated the compressor sufficiently to establish airflow through the engine, the ignition is turned on, and then the fuel. The exact sequence of the starting procedure is important since there must be sufficient airflow through the engine to support combustion before the fuel/air mixture is ignited. At low engine cranking speeds, the fuel flow rate is not sufficient

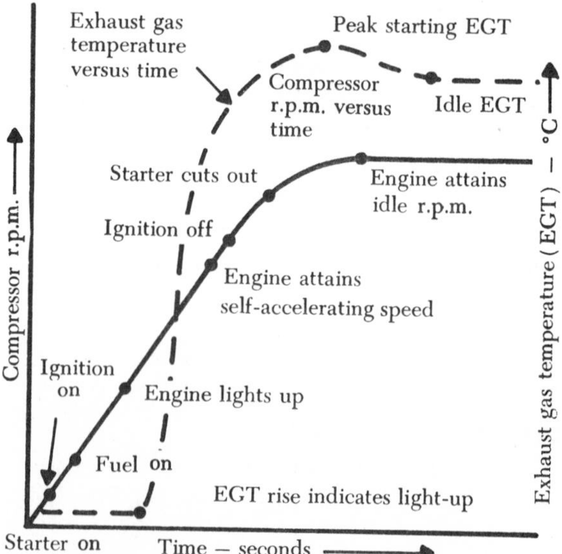

FIGURE 5–11. Typical gas turbine engine starting sequence.

TABLE 6. Small Aircraft Troubleshooting Procedures.

PROBABLE CAUSE	ISOLATION PROCEDURE	REMEDY
Starter Will Not Operate:		
Defective master switch or circuit.	Check master circuit.	Repair circuit.
Defective starter switch or switch circuit.	Check switch circuit continuity.	Replace switch or wires.
Starter lever does not activate switch.	Check starter lever adjustment.	Adjust starter lever in accordance with manufacturer's instructions.
Defective starter.	Check through items above. If another cause is not apparent, starter is defective.	Remove and repair or replace starter.
Starter Motor Runs, But Does Not Turn Crankshaft:		
Starter lever adjusted to activate switch without engaging pinion with crankshaft gear.	Check starter lever adjustment.	Adjust starter lever in accordance with manufacturer's instructions.
Defective overrunning clutch or drive.	Remove starter and check starter drive and overrunning clutch.	Replace defective parts.
Damaged starter pinion gear or crankshaft gear.	Remove and check pinion gear and crankshaft gear.	Replace defective parts.
Starter Drags:		
Low battery.	Check battery.	Charge or replace battery.
Starter switch or relay contacts burned or dirty.	Check contacts.	Replace with serviceable unit.
Defective starter.	Check starter brushes, brush spring tension for solder thrown on brush cover.	Repair or replace starter.
Dirty, worn commutator.	Clean, and check visually.	Turn down commutator.
Starter Excessively Noisy:		
Worn starter pinion.	Remove and examine pinion.	Replace starter drive.
Worn or broken teeth on crankshaft gears.	Remove starter and turn over engine by hand to examine crankshaft gear.	Replace crankshaft gear.

to enable the engine to accelerate, and for this reason the starter continues to crank the engine until after self-accelerating speed has been attained. If assistance from the starter were cut off below the self-accelerating speed, the engine would either fail to accelerate to idle speed, or might even decelerate because it could not produce sufficient energy to sustain rotation or to accelerate during the initial phase of the starting cycle. The starter must continue to assist the engine considerably above the self-accelerating speed to avoid a delay in the starting cycle, which would result in a hot or hung (false) start, or a combination of both. At the proper points in the sequence, the starter and usually the ignition will be automatically cut off.

Electric Starting Systems

Electric starting systems for gas turbine aircraft are of two general types: (1) Direct-cranking electrical systems and (2) starter-generator systems.

Direct-cranking electric starting systems are similar to those used on reciprocating engines. Starter-generator starting systems are also similar to direct-cranking electrical systems. Electrically, the two systems may be identical, but the starter-generator is permanently engaged with the engine shaft through the necessary drive gears, while the direct-cranking starter must employ some means of disengaging the starter from the shaft after the engine has started.

Direct-Cranking Gas Turbine Starters

On some direct-cranking starters used on gas turbine engines no overload release clutch or gear reduction mechanism is used. This is because of the low torque and high speed requirement for starting gas turbine engines. A reduced voltage mechanism is utilized, however, in the starting systems to prevent damage to the engaging assembly during starting.

Figure 5–12 shows the circuit of a reduced voltage control. The mechanism is mounted in an explosion-proof housing which contains five relays and a 0.042-ohm resistor. When the battery switch is closed, the time-delay relay coil is energized. The ground circuit for the coil of this relay is completed through the starter.

When the starter switch is moved to the start position, a circuit is completed to the coil of the acceleration relay. The closed relay contacts complete a circuit from the bus through the closed contacts, the 0.042-ohm resistor, the series relay coil, and finally through the starter motor to ground. Since the 0.042-ohm resistor causes a voltage drop, low voltage is applied to the starter motor and damage from an otherwise high torque is prevented. The time-delay relay returns to its normal "closed" position since no difference in potential exists between the time-delay relay coil terminals with the acceleration relay contacts closed.

The closed time-delay relay completes a circuit to the motor relay coil (figure 5–12). With the motor relay energized, a complete circuit exists through the relay and the series relay coil to the starter, bypassing the 0.042-ohm resistor.

When current of 200 amperes or more flows to the starter, the series relay coil is energized sufficiently to close the series relay contacts. The starter switch may then be allowed to return to its normal "off" position because the starter circuit is complete through the stop relay and the series relay contacts to the motor relay coil.

As the starter motor increases in r.p.m., a counter-electromotive force builds up enough to allow the series relay to open and break the circuit to the motor relay. Therefore, the starting period is controlled automatically by the speed of the starter motor.

Starter-Generator Starting System

Many gas turbine aircraft are equipped with starter-generator systems. These starting systems use a combination starter-generator which operates as a starter motor to drive the engine during starting; and, after the engine has reached a self-sustain-

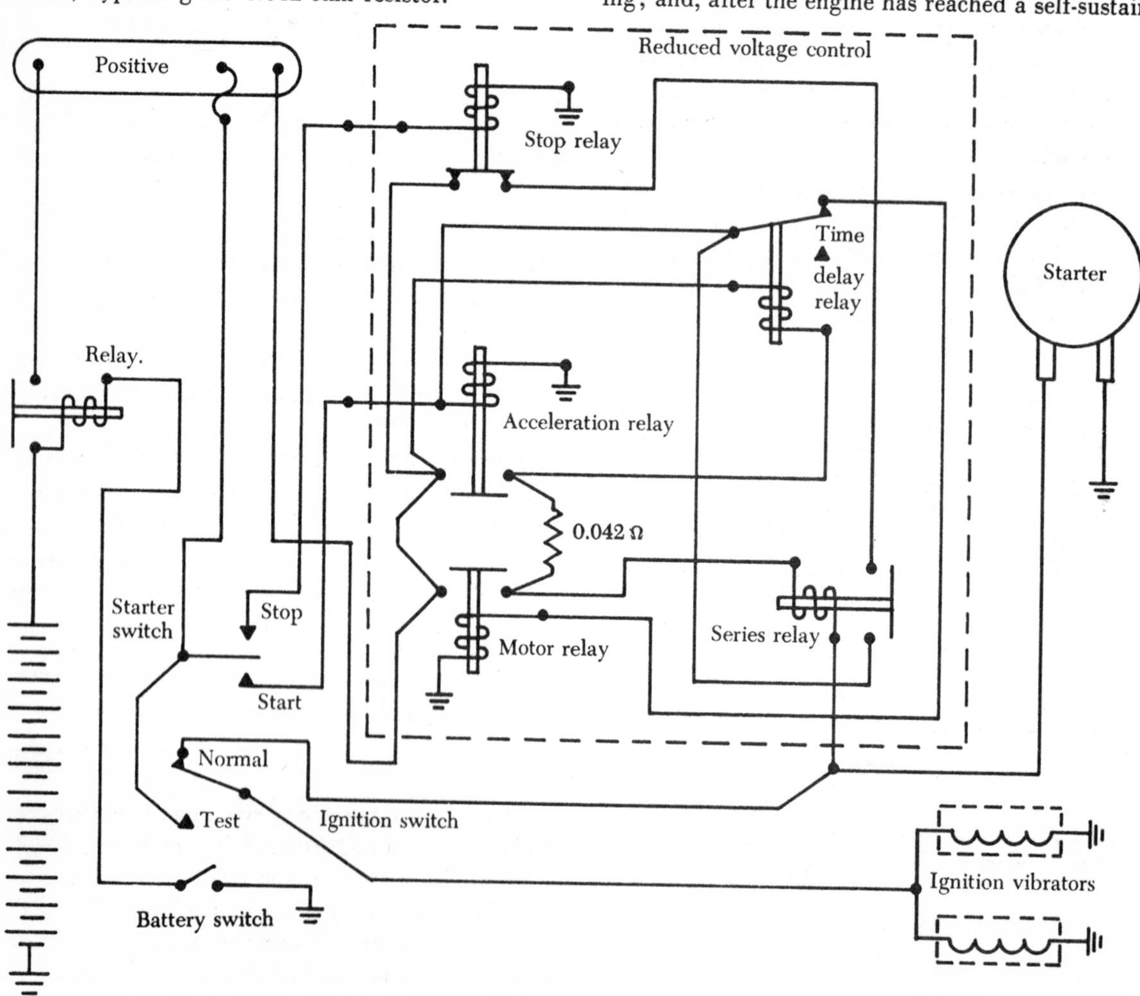

FIGURE 5–12. Reduced voltage control circuit for gas turbine, direct-cranking starting system.

ing speed, operates as a generator to supply the electrical system power.

The starter-generator unit, shown pictorially and schematically in figure 5–13, is basically a shunt generator with an additional heavy series winding. This series winding is electrically connected to produce a strong field and a resulting high torque for starting.

Starter-generator units are desirable from an economical standpoint, since one unit performs the functions of both starter and generator. Additionally, the total weight of starting system components is reduced, and fewer spare parts are required.

The starter-generator internal circuit shown in figure 5–14 has four field windings: (1) A series field ("C" field), (2) a shunt field, (3) a compensating field, and (4) an interpole or commutating winding. During starting, the series ("C" field), compensating, and commutating windings are used. The unit is similar to a direct-cranking starter since all of the windings used during starting are in series with the source. While acting as a starter, the unit makes no practical use of its shunt field. A source of 24 volts and 1,500 amperes is usually required for starting.

When operating as a generator, the shunt, compensating, and commutating windings are used. The "C" field is used only for starting purposes. The shunt field is connected in the conventional voltage control circuit for the generator. Compensating and commutating (interpoles) windings provide almost sparkless commutation from no load to full load.

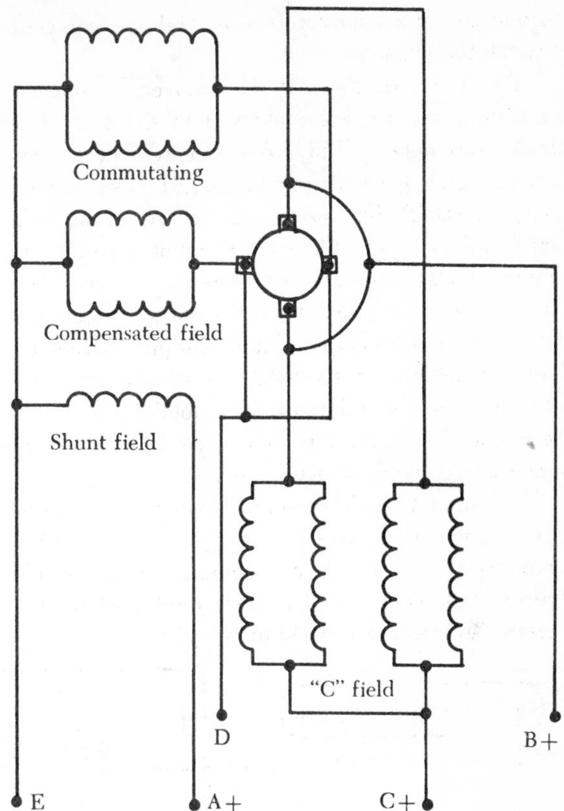

FIGURE 5–14. Starter-generator internal circuit.

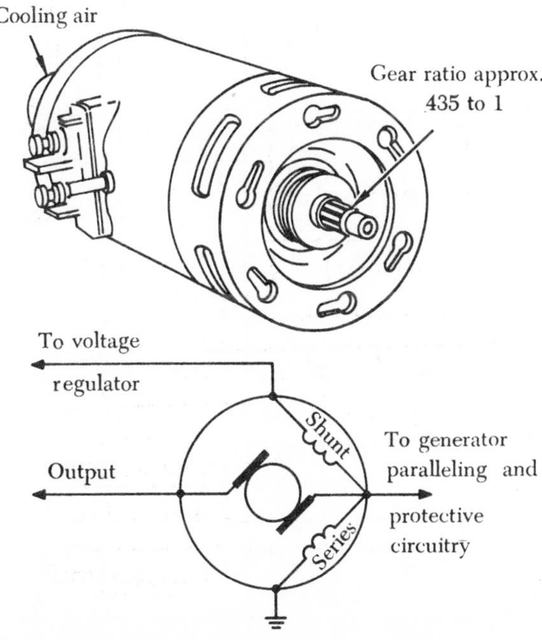

FIGURE 5–13. Typical starter-generator.

Figure 5–15 illustrates the external circuit of a starter-generator with an undercurrent controller. This unit controls the starter-generator when it is used as a starter. Its purpose is to assure positive action of the starter and to keep it operating until the engine is rotating fast enough to sustain combustion. The control block of the undercurrent controller contains two relays; one is the motor relay, which controls the input to the starter. The other, the undercurrent relay, controls the operation of the motor relay.

The sequence of operation for the starting system shown in figure 5–15 is discussed in the following paragraphs.

To start an engine equipped with an undercurrent relay, it is first necessary to close the engine master switch. This completes the circuit from the aircraft's bus to the start switch, to the fuel valves, and to the throttle relay. Energizing the throttle relay starts the fuel pumps, and completing the fuel valve circuit gives the necessary fuel pressure for starting the engine.

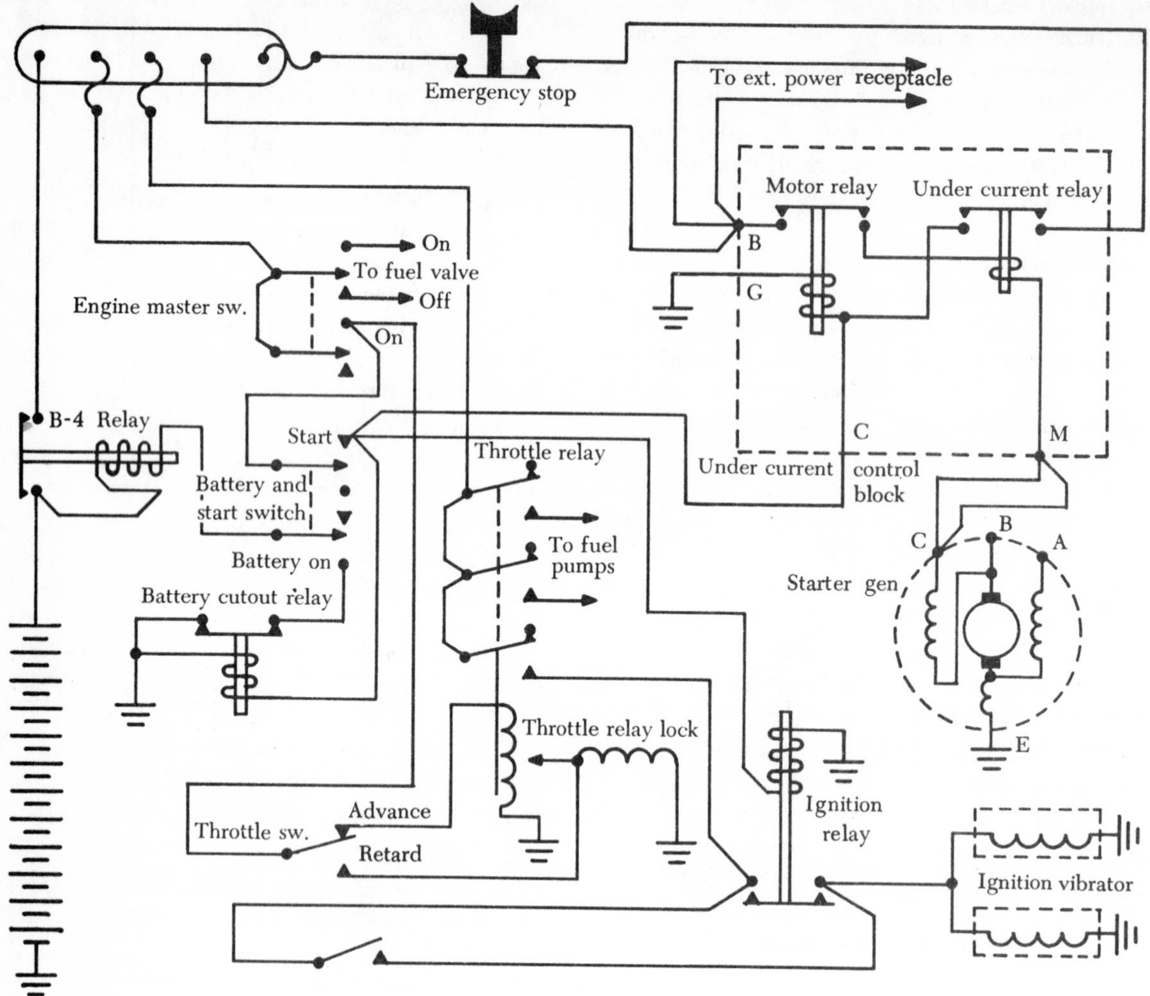

FIGURE 5–15. Starter-generator circuit.

As the battery and start switch is turned on, three relays close. They are the motor relay, the ignition relay, and the battery cutout relay. The motor relay closes the circuit from the power source to the starter motor; the ignition relay closes the circuit to the ignition units; and the battery cutout relay disconnects the battery. (Opening the battery circuit is necessary because the heavy drain of the starter motor would damage the battery.)

Closing the motor relay allows a very high current to flow to the motor. Since this current flows through the coil of the undercurrent relay, it closes. Closing the undercurrent relay completes a circuit from the positive bus to the motor relay coil, ignition relay coil, and battery cutout relay coil. The start switch is allowed to return to its normal "off" position, and all units continue to operate.

As the motor builds up speed, the current draw of the motor begins to decrease, and as it decreases to less than 200 amps, the undercurrent relay opens. This action breaks the circuit from the positive bus to the coils of the motor, ignition, and battery cutout relays. The de-energizing of these relay coils halts the start operation.

After the procedures described are completed, the engine should be operating efficiently and ignition should be self-sustaining. If, however, the engine fails to reach sufficient speed to halt the starter operation, the stop switch may be used to break the circuit from the positive bus to the main contacts of the undercurrent relay.

On a typical aircraft installation, one starter-generator is mounted on each engine gearbox. During starting, the starter-generator unit functions as a d.c. starter motor until the engine has reached a predetermined self-sustaining speed. Aircraft equipped with two 24-volt batteries can supply the electrical load required for starting by operating the batteries in a series configuration.

The following description of the starting procedure used on a four-engine turbojet aircraft equipped with starter-generator units is typical of most starter-generator starting systems.

Starting power, which can be applied to only one starter-generator at a time, is connected to a terminal of the selected starter-generator through a corresponding starter relay. Engine starting is controlled from an engine start panel. A typical start panel (figure 5–16) contains the following switches: an engine selector switch, a power selector switch, an air start switch, and a start switch.

The engine selector switch shown in figure 5–16 has five positions ("1," "2," "3," "4," and "OFF") and is turned to the position corresponding to the engine to be started. The power selector switch is used to select the electrical circuit applicable to the power source (ground power unit or battery) being used. The air-start switch, when placed in the "NORMAL" position, arms the ground starting circuit. When placed in the "AIR START" position, the igniters can be energized independently of the throttle ignition switch. The start switch when in the "START" position completes the circuit to the starter-generator of the engine selected to be started, and causes the engine to rotate. The engine start panel shown also includes a battery switch.

When an engine is selected with the engine selector switch, and the start switch is held in the "START" position, the starter relay corresponding to the selected engine is energized and connects that

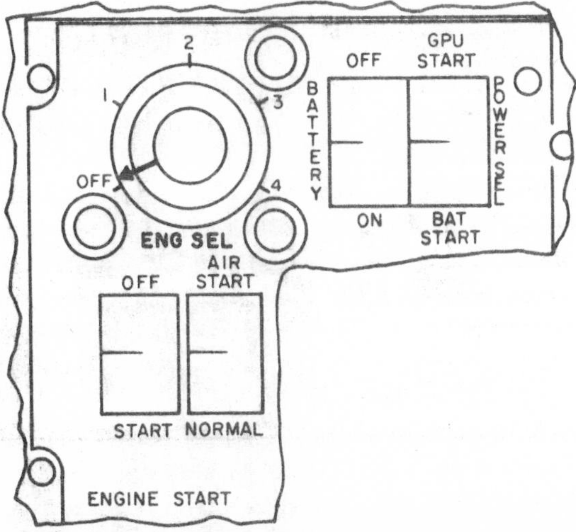

FIGURE 5–16. Engine start panel.

engine's starter-generator to the starter bus. When the start switch is placed in the "START" position, a start lock-in relay is also energized. Once energized, the start lock-in relay provides its own holding circuit and remains energized providing closed circuits for various start functions.

An overvoltage lockout relay is provided for each starter-generator. During ground starting, the overvoltage lockout relay for the selected starter-generator is energized through the starting control circuits. When an overvoltage lockout relay is energized, overvoltage protection for the selected starter-generator is suspended. A bypass of the voltage regulator for the selected starter-generator is also provided to remove undesirable control and resistance from the starting shunt field.

On some aircraft a battery lockout switch is installed in the external power receptacle compartment. When the door is closed, activating the switch, the ground starting control circuits function for battery starting only. When the door is open, only external power ground starts can be accomplished.

A battery series relay is also a necessary unit in this starting system. When energized, the battery series relay connects the two 24-volt batteries in series to the starter bus, providing an initial starting voltage of 48 volts. The large voltage drop which occurs in delivering the current needed for starting reduces the voltage to approximately 20 volts at the instant of starting. The voltage gradually increases as starter current decreases with engine acceleration and the voltage on the starter bus eventually approaches its original maximum of 48 volts.

Some multi-engine aircraft equipped with starter-generators include a parallel start relay in their starting system. After the first two engines of a four-engine aircraft are started, current flow for starting each of the last two engines passes through a parallel start relay which shifts the battery output from series to parallel. When starting the first two engines, the starting power requirement necessitates connecting the two batteries in series. After two or more engine generators are providing power, the combined power of the batteries in series is not required. Thus, the battery circuit is shifted from series to parallel when the parallel start relay is energized.

To start an engine with the aircraft batteries, the start switch is placed in the "START" position (figure 5–16). This completes a circuit through a circuit breaker, the throttle ignition switch, and the engine selector switch to energize the start lock-in relay. Power then has a path from the start switch through the "BAT START" position of the power selector switch to energize the battery series relay, which connects the aircraft batteries in series to the starter bus.

Energizing the No. 1 engine's starter relay directs power from the starter bus to the No. 1 starter-generator, which then cranks the engine.

At the time the batteries are connected to the starter bus, power is also routed to the appropriate bus for the throttle ignition switch. The ignition system is connected to the starter bus through an overvoltage relay which does not become energized until the engine begins accelerating and the starter bus voltage reaches about 30 volts.

As the engine is turned by the starter to approximately 10% r.p.m., the throttle is advanced to the "IDLE" position. This action actuates the throttle ignition switch, energizing the igniter relay. When the igniter relay is closed, power is provided to excite the igniters and fire the engine.

When the engine reaches about 25 to 30% r.p.m., the start switch is released to the "OFF" position. This removes the start and ignition circuits from the engine start cycle, and the engine accelerates under its own power.

Troubleshooting a Starter-Generator Starting System

The procedures listed in table 7 are typical of those used to repair malfunctions in a starter-generator starting system similar to the system described in this section. These procedures are presented as a guide only. The appropriate manufacturer's instructions and approved maintenance directives should always be consulted for the aircraft involved.

AIR TURBINE STARTERS

The air turbine starters are designed to provide high starting torque from a small, lightweight source. The typical air turbine starter weighs from one-fourth to one-half as much as an electric starter capable of starting the same engine. It is capable of developing twice as much torque as the electric starter.

The typical air turbine starter consists of an axial flow turbine which turns a drive coupling through

TABLE 7. Starter-Generator Starting System Troubleshooting Procedures.

PROBABLE CAUSE	ISOLATION PROCEDURE	REMEDY
Engine Does Not Rotate During Start Attempt:		
Low supply voltage to the starter.	Check voltage of the battery or external power source.	Adjust voltage of the external power source or charge batteries.
Power switch is defective.	Check switch for continuity.	Replace switch.
Ignition switch in throttle quadrant.	Check switch for continuity.	Replace switch.
Start-lockout relay energized.	Check position of generator control switch.	Place switch in "OFF" position.
Battery series relay is defective.	With start circuit energized, check for 48 volts d.c. across battery series relay coil.	Replace relay if no voltage is present.
Starter relay is defective.	With start circuit energized, check for 48 volts d.c. across starter relay coil.	Replace relay if no voltage is present.
Defective starter.	With start circuit energized, check for proper voltage at the starter.	If voltage is present, replace the starter.
Start lock-in relay defective.	With start circuit energized, check for 28 volts d.c. across the relay coil.	Replace relay if voltage is not present.
Starter drive shaft in component drive gearbox is sheared.	Listen for sounds of starter rotation during an attempted start. If the starter rotates but the engine does not, the drive shaft is sheared.	Replace the engine.
Engine Starts But Does Not Accelerate To Idle:		
Insufficient starter voltage.	Check starter terminal voltage.	Use larger capacity ground power unit or charge batteries.
Engine Fails To Start When Throttle Is Placed In Idle:		
Defective ignition system.	Turn on system and listen for spark-igniter operation.	Clean or replace spark igniters, or replace exciters, or leads to igniters.

a reduction gear train and a starter clutch mechanism.

The air to operate an air turbine starter is supplied from either a ground-operated compressor or the bleed air from another engine. Auxiliary compressed-air bottles are available on some aircraft for operating the air turbine starter.

Figure 5–17 is a cutaway view of an air turbine starter. The starter is operated by introducing air of sufficient volume and pressure into the starter inlet. The air passes into the starter turbine housing, where it is directed against the rotor blades by the nozzle vanes, causing the turbine rotor to turn. As the rotor turns, it drives the reduction gear train and clutch arrangement, which includes the rotor pinion, planet gears and carrier, sprag clutch assembly, output shaft assembly, and drive coupling.

The sprag clutch assembly engages automatically as soon as the rotor starts to turn, but disengages as soon as the drive coupling turns more rapidly than the rotor side. When the starter reaches this overrun speed, the action of the sprag clutch allows the gear train to coast to a halt. The output shaft assembly and drive coupling continue to turn as long as the engine is running.

A rotor switch actuator, mounted in the turbine rotor hub, is set to open the turbine switch when the starter reaches cutout speed. Opening the turbine switch interrupts an electrical signal to the pressure-regulating valve. This closes the valve and shuts off the air supply to the starter.

The turbine housing contains the turbine rotor, the rotor switch actuator, and the nozzle components which direct the inlet air against the rotor blades. The turbine housing incorporates a turbine rotor containment ring designed to dissipate the energy of blade fragments and direct their discharge at low energy through the exhaust duct in the event of rotor failure due to excessive turbine overspeed.

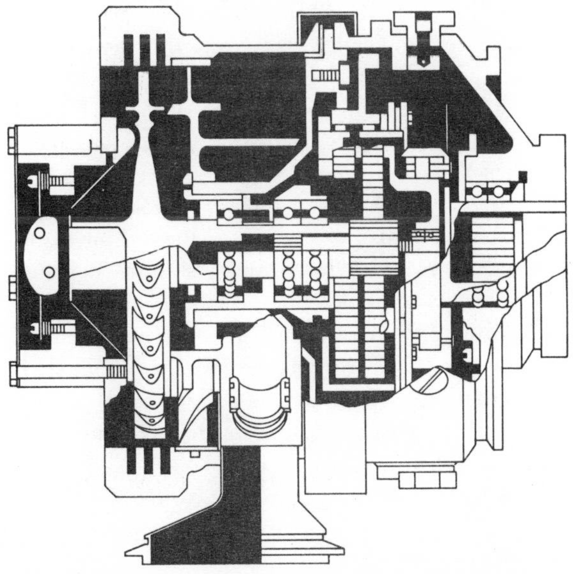

FIGURE 5–17. Cutaway of an air turbine starter.

The transmission housing contains the reduction gears, the clutch components, and the drive coupling. The transmission housing also provides a reservoir for the lubricating oil. Oil is added to the transmission housing sump through a port at the top of the starter. This port is closed by a vent plug containing a ball valve which allows the sump to be vented to the atmosphere during normal flight, but prevents loss of oil during inverted flight. The housing also incorporates two oil-level holes, which are used to check the oil quantity. A magnetic drain plug in the transmission drain opening attracts any ferrous particles which may be in the oil.

The ring gear housing, which is internal, contains the rotor assembly. The switch housing contains the turbine switch and bracket assembly.

To facilitate starter installation and removal, a mounting adapter is bolted to the mounting pad on the engine. Quick-detach clamps join the starter to the mounting adapter and inlet duct. Thus, the starter is easily removed for maintenance or overhaul by disconnecting the electrical line, loosening the clamps, and carefully disengaging the drive coupling from the engine starter drive as the starter is withdrawn.

The air turbine starter shown in figure 5–17 is used to start large gas turbine engines. The starter is mounted on an engine pad, and its drive shaft is splined by mechanical linkage to the engine compressor. Air from any suitable source, such as a ground-operated or airborne compressor unit, is used to operate the starter. The air is directed through a combination pressure-regulating and shutoff valve in the starter inlet ducting. This valve regulates the pressure of the starter operating air and shuts off the air supply when the maximum allowable starter speed has been reached.

The pressure-regulating and shutoff valve, shown in figure 5–18, consists of two subassemblies: (1) The pressure-regulating valve and (2) the pressure-regulating valve control.

The regulating valve assembly consists of a valve housing containing a butterfly-type valve (figure 5–18). The shaft of the butterfly valve is connected through a cam arrangement to a servo piston. When the piston is actuated, its motion on the cam causes

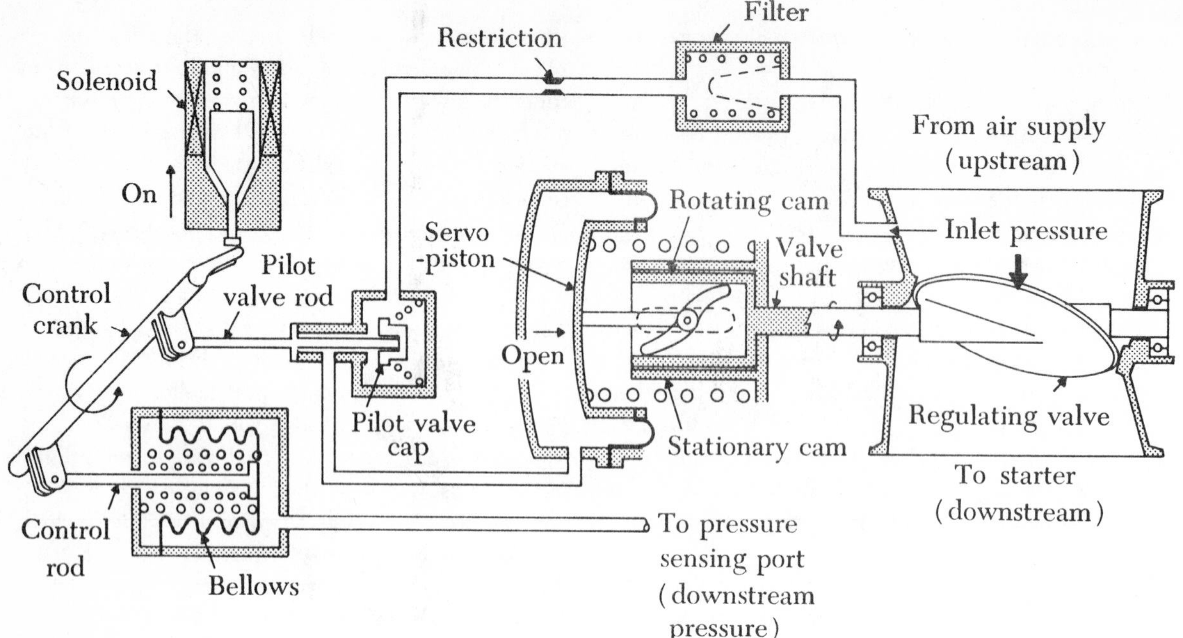

FIGURE 5–18. Pressure-regulating and shutoff valve in "on" position.

rotation of the butterfly valve. The slope of the cam track is designed to provide small initial travel and high initial torque when the starter is actuated. The cam track slope also provides more stable action by increasing the opening time of the valve.

The control assembly is mounted on the regulating valve housing and consists of a control housing in which a solenoid is used to stop the action of the control crank in the "off" position (figure 5–18). The control crank links a pilot valve, which meters pressure to the servo piston, with the bellows connected by an air line to the pressure-sensing port on the starter.

Turning on the starter switch energizes the regulating valve solenoid. The solenoid retracts and allows the control crank to rotate to the "open" position. The control crank is rotated by the control rod spring moving the control rod against the closed end of the bellows. Since the regulating valve is closed and downstream pressure is negligible, the bellows can be fully extended by the bellows spring.

As the control crank rotates to the open position, it causes the pilot valve rod to open the pilot valve allowing upstream air, which is supplied to the pilot valve through a suitable filter and a restriction in the housing, to flow into the servo piston chamber. The drain side of the pilot valve, which bleeds the servo chamber to the atmosphere, is now closed by the pilot valve rod and the servo piston moves inboard (figure 5–18). This linear motion of the servo piston is translated to rotary motion of the valve shaft by the rotating cam, thus opening the regulating valve. As the valve opens, downstream pressure increases. This pressure is bled back to the bellows through the pressure-sensing line and compresses the bellows. This action moves the control rod, thereby turning the control crank and moving the pilot valve rod gradually away from the servo chamber to vent to the atmosphere (figure 5–18). When downstream (regulated) pressure reaches a preset value, the amount of air flowing into the servo through the restriction equals the amount of air being bled to the atmosphere through the servo bleed and the system is in a state of equilibrium.

When the valve is open, the regulated air passing through the inlet housing of the starter impinges on the turbine, causing it to turn. As the turbine turns, the gear train is activated and the inboard clutch gear, which is threaded onto a helical screw, moves forward as it rotates and its jaw teeth engage those of the outboard clutch gear to drive the output shaft of the starter. The clutch is an overrunning type to facilitate positive engagement and minimize chatter. When starting speed is reached, a set of flyweights in a centrifugal cutout switch actuates a plunger which breaks the ground circuit of the solenoid.

When the ground circuit is broken, and the solenoid is de-energized, the pilot valve is forced back to the "off" position, opening the servo chamber to the atmosphere (see figure 5–19). This action allows the actuator spring to move the regulating valve to the "closed" position. To keep leakage to a minimum in the "off" position, the pilot valve incorporates an inner cap which seals off the upstream pressure to the servo and the servo chamber bleed passage.

When the air to the starter is terminated, the outboard clutch gear, driven by the engine, will begin to turn faster than the inboard clutch gear, and the inboard clutch gear, actuated by the return spring, will disengage the outboard clutch gear, allowing the rotor to coast to a halt. The outboard clutch shaft will continue to turn with the engine.

Air Turbine Starter Troubleshooting Guide

The troubleshooting procedures listed in table 8 are applicable to air turbine starting systems equipped with a combination pressure-regulating and shutoff valve. These procedures should be used as a guide only, and are not intended to supplant the manufacturer's instructions.

Turbine Engine Cartridge Starters

The turbine engine cartridge starter, sometimes called the solid-propellant starter, is used on some large turbine engines. It is similar in operation to the air turbine starter, but must be constructed to withstand the high temperatures resulting from burning a solid-propellant charge to supply the energy for starting. Protection is also provided against excessive torque pressures and overspeeding of the starter turbine.

Since cartridge starters are similar in operation to air turbine starters, some manufacturers make available a turbine engine starter that can be operated using gas generated by a cartridge, compressed air from a ground supply cart, or engine cross-bleed air. A typical cartridge/pneumatic starter is described in detail in the next section.

CARTRIDGE / PNEUMATIC TURBINE ENGINE STARTER

A typical cartridge/pneumatic turbine engine starter is shown in figure 5–20. This type of starter may be operated as an ordinary air turbine starter, from a ground-operated air supply or an engine cross-bleed source. It may also be operated as a cartridge starter.

The principal components of the cartridge starter are illustrated in the schematic diagram of figure 5–21. Reference to this diagram will facilitate understanding of the following discussion of a typical cartridge starter operation.

To accomplish a cartridge start, a cartridge is first placed in the breech cap. The breech is then closed on the breech chamber by means of the breech handle and rotated a part-turn to engage the lugs between the two breech sections. This rotation

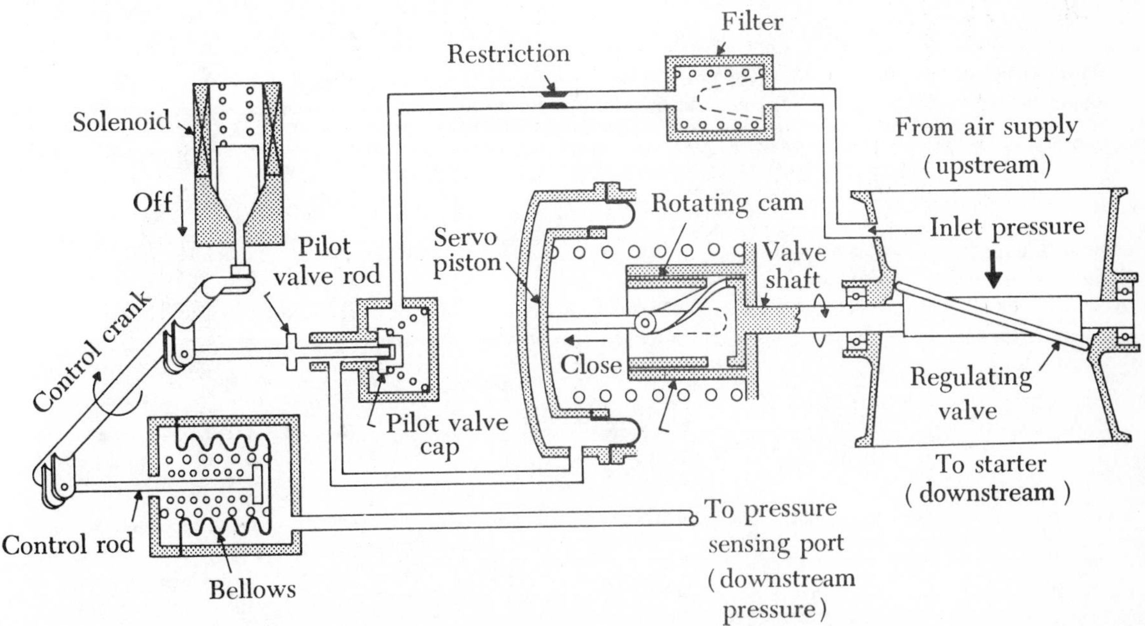

FIGURE 5–19. Pressure-regulating and shutoff valve in "off" position.

TABLE 8. Air Turbine Starter System Troubleshooting Procedures.

TROUBLE	PROBABLE CAUSE	REMEDY
Starter does not operate (no rotation).	No air supply.	Check air supply.
	Electrical open in cutout switch.	Check switch continuity. If no continuity, remove starter and adjust or replace switch.
	Sheared starter drive coupling.	Remove starter and replace drive coupling.
	Internal starter discrepancy.	Remove and replace starter.
Starter will not accelerate to normal cutoff speed.	Low starter air supply.	Check air source pressure.
	Starter cutout switch set improperly.	Adjust rotor switch actuator.
	Valve pressure regulated too low.	Replace valve.
	Internal starter malfunction.	Remove and replace starter.
Starter will not cut off.	Low air supply.	Check air supply.
	Rotor switch actuator set too high.	Adjust switch actuator assembly.
	Starter cutout switch shorted.	Replace switch and bracket assembly.
External oil leakage.	Oil level too high.	Drain oil and re-service properly.
	Loose vent, oil filler, or magnetic plugs.	Tighten magnetic plug to proper torque. Tighten vent and oil filler plugs as necessary and lockwire.
	Loose clamp band assembly.	Tighten clamp band assembly to higher torque.
Starter runs, but engine does not turn over.	Sheared drive coupling.	Remove starter and replace the drive coupling. If couplings persist in breaking in unusually short periods of time, remove and replace starter.
Starter inlet will not line up with supply ducting.	Improper installation of starter on engine, or improper indexing of turbine housing on starter.	Check installation and/or indexing for conformance with manufacturer's installation instructions and the proper index position of the turbine housing specified for the aircraft.
Metallic particles on magnetic drain plug.	Small fuzzy particles indicate normal wear.	No remedial action required.
	Particles coarser than fuzzy, such as chips, slivers, etc., indicate internal difficulty.	Remove and replace starter.
Broken nozzle vanes.	Large foreign particles in air supply.	Remove and replace starter and check air supply filter.
Oil leakage from vent plug assembly.	Improper starter installation position.	Check installed position for levelness of oil plugs and correct as required in accordance with manufacturer's installation instructions.
Oil leakage at drive coupling.	Leaking rear seal assembly.	Remove and replace starter.

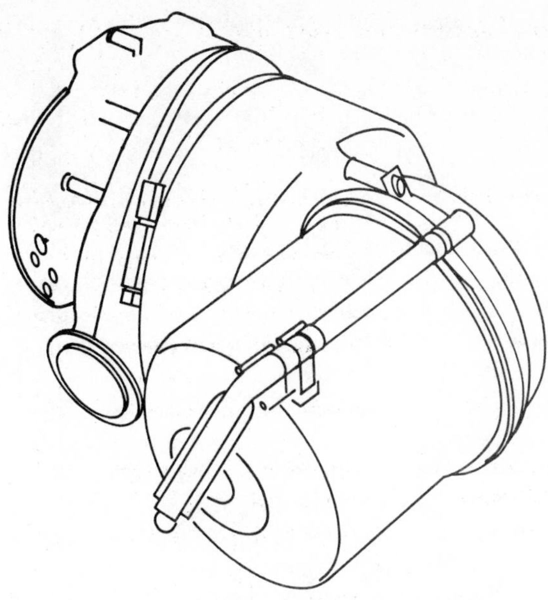

FIGURE 5–20. Cartridge/pneumatic starter.

allows the lower section of the breech handle to drop into a socket and completes the cartridge ignition circuit. Until the ignition circuit is completed, it is impossible to fire the cartridge.

The cartridge is ignited by applying voltage through the connector at the end of the breech handle. This energizes the insulated ignition contact at the entrance of the breech cap, which touches a point on the cartridge itself. The circuit is completed to ground by the ground clip, a part of the cartridge which contacts the inner wall of the breech cap. A schematic of a cartridge/pneumatic starter electrical system is shown in figure 5–22.

Upon ignition, the cartridge begins to generate gas. The gas is forced out of the breech to the hot gas nozzles which are directed toward the buckets on the turbine rotor, and rotation is produced. Gas emerging from the opposite side of the turbine wheel enters an exhaust ring in the exhaust duct, where it is collected and passed out of the starter

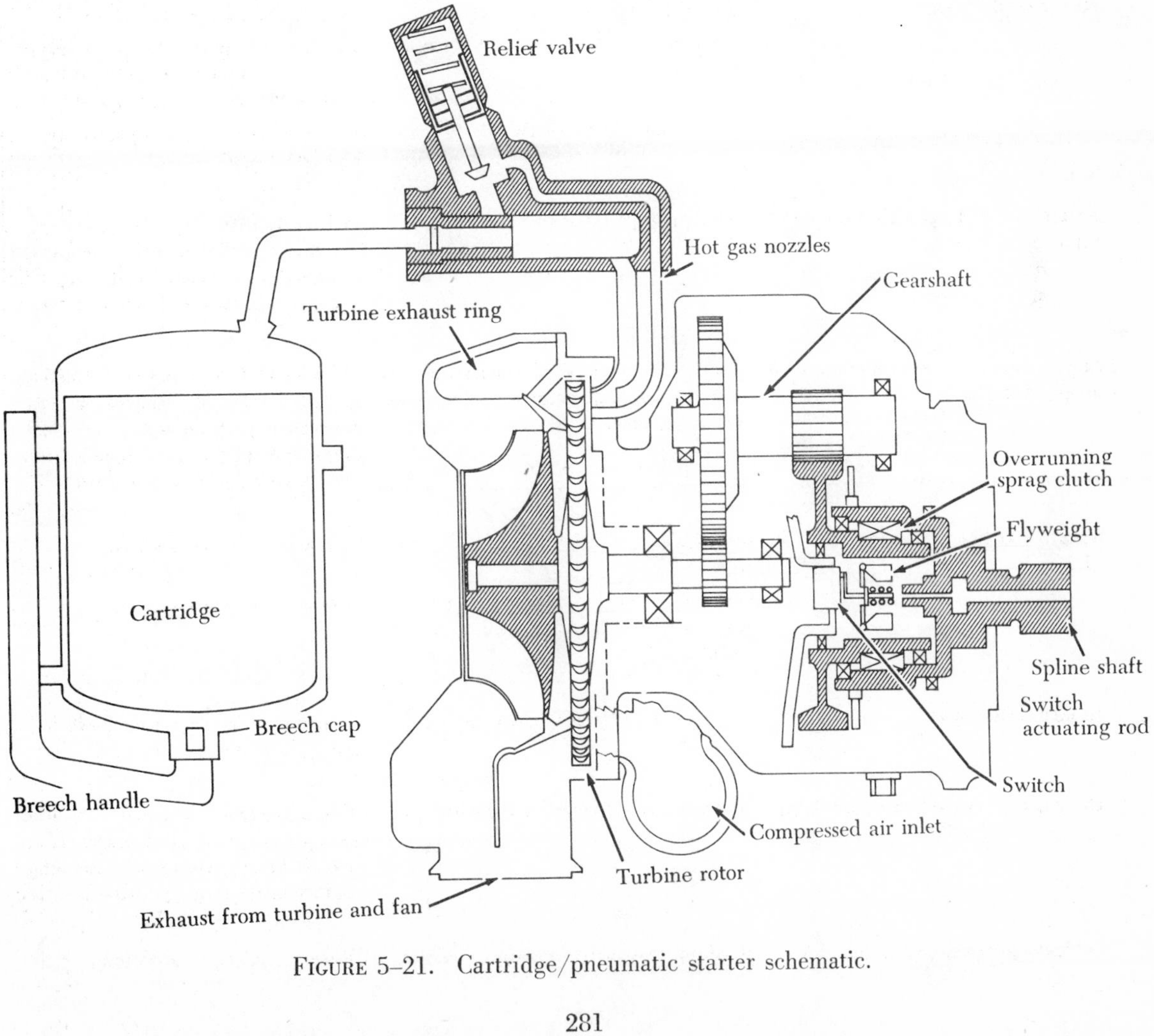

FIGURE 5–21. Cartridge/pneumatic starter schematic.

via the overboard exhaust collector. Before reaching the nozzle, the hot gas passes an outlet leading to the relief valve. This valve directs hot gas to the turbine, bypassing the hot gas nozzle, as the pressure rises above the preset maximum. Thus, the pressure of the gas within the hot gas circuit is maintained at the optimum level.

The cartridge/pneumatic starter can also be operated by compressed air from a ground cart, or by engine cross-bleed air led by ducting on the aircraft to the compressed air inlet. The air passes into the nozzle ring and is directed against the buckets of the turbine rotor by vanes placed around the ring. Rotation is thus produced in essentially the same manner as during a cartridge start. Compressed air leaving the turbine rotor collects in the same exhaust ring and is directed overboard via the exhaust collector.

Whether starting is accomplished by cartridge or compressed air, some opposing force is required to keep turbine speed within safe limits. This opposing force is provided by the aerodynamic braking fan. The fan is connected directly to the turbine shaft. It is supplied with air from the aircraft nacelle and its output is carried off by an exhaust ring concentric with, and located within, the turbine exhaust ring. Hot gas or compressed air exhaust and aerodynamic braking fan output are kept separate up to the overboard exhaust collector.

The gearshaft is part of a two-stage reduction which reduces the maximum turbine speed of approximately 60,000 r.p.m. to an output of approximately 4,000 r.p.m. The large gear of the final output turns the output spline shaft assembly through an overrunning clutch.

The overunning sprag clutch is situated in the output area between the gear shaft on which the final drive gear is located and the output spline shaft assembly. The clutch is a one-way overrunning type; its purpose is to prevent the engine from driving the starter after it begins to operate under its own power. The nature of the sprag clutch is such that it can transmit torque in only one direction. Thus, the driving member can operate through the clutch to deliver its full torque to the engine, but the driven member cannot become the driver, even though revolving in the same direction. Any tendency to do so will disengage the clutch. When the engine has been started and the starter has completed its cycle and stopped, only the output spline shaft assembly and the outer (driven) part of the clutch will be revolving. The other parts of the starter will be at rest.

In the event of a malfunction or lockup of the overrunning output clutch, the engine would, without other safety provision, drive the starter up to a speed above the design "burst r.p.m." of the turbine rotor. To prevent this, the starter is designed with a disengaging output spline shaft assembly. This assembly consists of two spring-loaded, splined sections held together by a tension bolt. A series of ratchet teeth interlock the mating sections of the spline. If internal failure causes the engine to exert excessive torque on the shaft, the ratchet teeth will tend to separate the two shaft sections. The separating force is sufficient to shear the

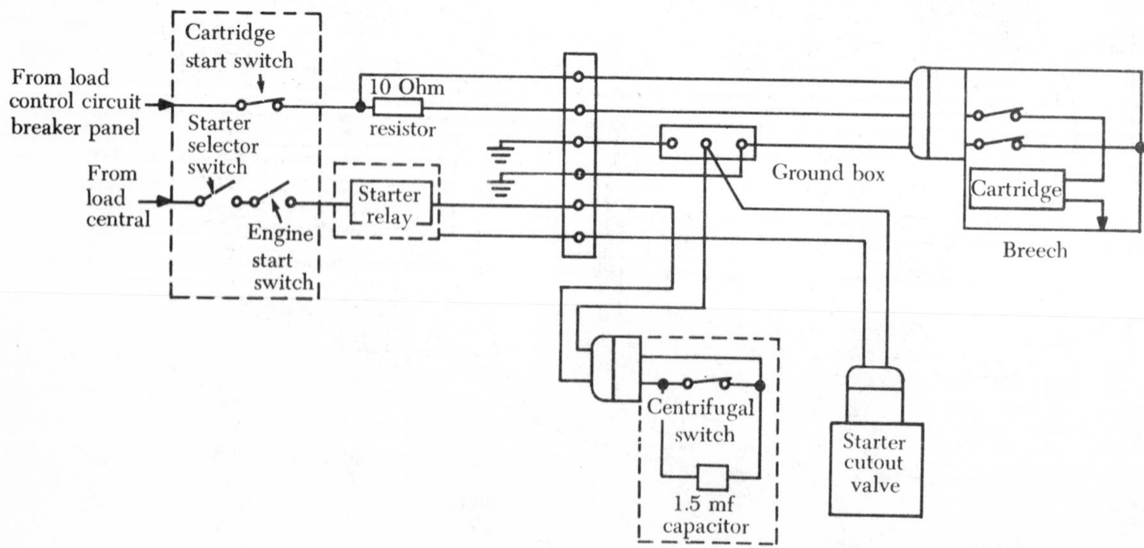

FIGURE 5–22. Cartridge/pneumatic starter electrical schematic.

tension bolt and completely disengage the starter. Both the tension bolt and shaft will shear and disengage the starter if startup torque exceeds the shaft shear section design limits.

During pneumatic starts, a relay shuts off the compressed air when the output has reached a predetermined speed. This is accomplished by an engine-speed sensor which monitors r.p.m. at the starter mounting pad. The sensor is actuated by a pair of flyweights. At speeds below starter cutoff speed, an actuator rod presses against a switch; as the starter approaches cutoff speed, a centrifugal force created by output shaft rotation causes the pair of flyweights to compress a spring, lift the actuator rod, and open the switch. The cutoff speed can be regulated by adjusting the screw that controls the pressure on the spring.

This cartridge/pneumatic starter is lubricated by a splash system. Oil slingers attached to the clutch output race pick up oil from the sump and distribute it throughout the interior of the starter as the output spline revolves. A catching cup construction in the housing, coupled with an oil tube arrangement, carries the oil into the overrunning clutch and other hard-to-reach areas. Since the part to which the slingers are attached is constantly spinning, even after the starter has completed its cycle, starter lubrication continues as long as the aircraft engine is operating. The oil sump contains a magnetic plug to collect contamination.

FUEL/AIR COMBUSTION TURBINE STARTER

The fuel/air combustion starter is used to start both turbojet and turboprop engines by using the combustion energy of conventional jet engine fuel and compressed air. The starter consists of a turbine-driven power unit and auxiliary fuel, air, and ignition systems. Operation of this type starter is, in most installations, fully automatic; actuation of a single switch causes the starter to fire and accelerate the engine from rest to starter cutoff speed.

The combustion starter (figure 5–23) is a gas turbine engine which delivers its power through a high-ratio reduction gear system. The compressed air is normally stored in a shatter-proof cylinder near the combustion gas turbine.

The fuel/air combustion starter was developed primarily for short-flight, air-carrier aircraft. The installed combustion starter provided quick starting at air terminals without ground starting equipment. The use of compressed air cylinders to directly drive a conventional air turbine starter is now replacing fuel/air combustion starters. This type of starting system provides several starts from a bottle of compressed air. Provisions are normally included to re-charge the compressed air cylinder from an installed auxiliary power unit.

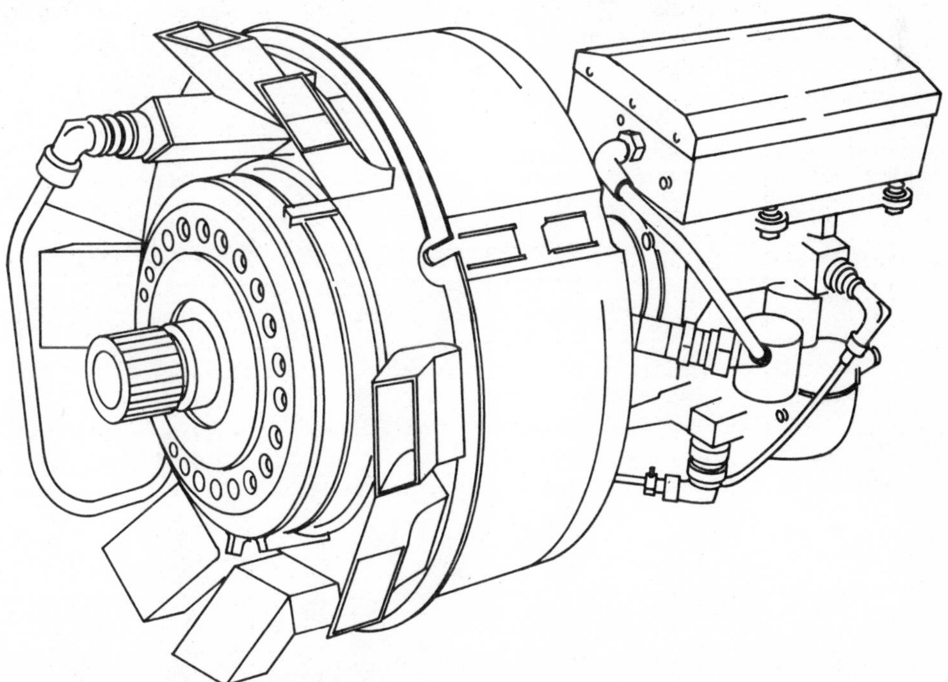

FIGURE 5–23. Fuel/air combustion starter.

CHAPTER 6

LUBRICATION AND COOLING SYSTEMS

PRINCIPLES OF ENGINE LUBRICATION

The primary purpose of a lubricant is to reduce friction between moving parts. Because liquid lubricants (oils) can be circulated readily, they are used universally in aircraft engines.

In theory, fluid lubrication is based on the actual separation of the surfaces so that no metal-to-metal contact occurs. As long as the oil film remains unbroken, metallic friction is replaced by the internal fluid friction of the lubricant. Under ideal conditions, friction and wear are held to a minimum.

In addition to reducing friction, the oil film acts as a cushion between metal parts. This cushioning effect is particularly important for such parts as reciprocating engine crankshaft and connecting rods, which are subject to shock-loading. As oil circulates through the engine, it absorbs heat from the parts. Pistons and cylinder walls in reciprocating engines are especially dependent on the oil for cooling. The oil also aids in forming a seal between the piston and the cylinder wall to prevent leakage of the gases from the combustion chamber. Oils also reduce abrasive wear by picking up foreign particles and carrying them to a filter, where they are removed.

REQUIREMENTS AND CHARACTERISTICS OF RECIPROCATING ENGINE LUBRICANTS

While there are several important properties which a satisfactory reciprocating engine oil must possess, its viscosity is most important in engine operation. The resistance of an oil to flow is known as its viscosity. An oil which flows slowly is viscous or has a high viscosity. If it flows freely, it has a low viscosity. Unfortunately, the viscosity of oil is affected by temperature. It is not uncommon for some grades of oil to become practically solid in cold weather. This increases drag and makes circulation almost impossible. Other oils may become so thin at high temperature that the oil film is broken, resulting in rapid wear of the moving parts. The oil selected for aircraft engine lubrication must be light enough to circulate freely, yet heavy enough to provide the proper oil film at engine operating temperatures. Since lubricants vary in properties and since no one oil is satisfactory for all engines and all operating conditions, it is extremely important that only the recommended grade be used.

Several factors must be considered in determining the proper grade of oil to use in a particular engine. The operating load, rotational speeds, and operating temperatures are the most important. The operating conditions to be met in the various types of engines will determine the grade of the lubricating oil to be used.

The oil used in reciprocating engines has a relatively high viscosity because of:

(1) Large engine operating clearances due to the relatively large size of the moving parts, the different materials used, and the different rates of expansion of the various materials.

(2) High operating temperatures.

(3) High bearing pressures.

The following characteristics of lubricating oils measure their grade and suitability:

(1) Flash point and fire point are determined by laboratory tests that show the temperature at which a liquid will begin to give off ignitable vapors (flash) and the temperature at which there are sufficient vapors to support a flame (fire). These points are established for engine oils to determine that they can withstand the high temperatures encountered in an engine.

(2) Cloud point and pour point also help to indicate suitability. The cloud point of an oil is the temperature at which its wax content, normally held in solution, begins to solidify and separate into tiny crystals, causing the oil to appear cloudy or hazy. The pour point of an oil is the lowest temperature at which it will flow or can be poured.

(3) Specific gravity is a comparison of the weight of the substance to the weight of an equal volume of distilled water at a specified

temperature. As an example, water weighs approximately 8 lbs. to the gallon; an oil with a specific gravity of 0.9 would weigh 7.2 lbs. to the gallon.

Generally, commercial aviation oils are classified numerically, such as 80, 100, 140, etc., which are an approximation of their viscosity as measured by a testing instrument called the Saybolt Universal Viscosimeter. In this instrument a tube holds a specific quantity of the oil to be tested. The oil is brought to an exact temperature by a liquid bath surrounding the tube. The time in seconds required for exactly 60 cubic centimeters of oil to flow through an accurately calibrated orifice is recorded as a measure of the oil's viscosity.

If actual Saybolt values were used to designate the viscosity of oil, there probably would be several hundred grades of oil. To simplify the selection of oils, they often are classified under an SAE (Society of Automotive Engineers) system, which divides all oils into seven groups (SAE 10 to 70) according to viscosity at either 130° or 210° F.

SAE ratings are purely arbitrary and bear no direct relationship to the Saybolt or other ratings. The letter "W" occasionally is included in the SAE number giving a designation such as SAE 20W. This letter "W" indicates that the oil, in addition to meeting the viscosity requirements at the testing temperature specifications, is a satisfactory oil for winter use in cold climates.

Although the SAE scale has eliminated some confusion in the designation of lubricating oils, it must not be assumed that this specification covers all the important viscosity requirements. An SAE number indicates only the viscosity (grade) or relative viscosity; it does not indicate quality or other essential characteristics. It is well known that there are good oils and inferior oils that have the same viscosities at a given temperature and, therefore, are subject to classification in the same grade. The SAE letters on an oil container are not an endorsement or recommendation of the oil by the Society of Automotive Engineers.

Although each grade of oil is rated by an SAE number, depending on its specific use, it may be rated with a commercial aviation grade number or an Army and Navy specification number. The correlation between these grade-numbering systems is shown in figure 6–1.

Commercial Aviation No.	Commercial SAE No.	Army and Navy Specification No.
65	30	1065
80	40	1080
100	50	1100
120	60	1120
140	70	

FIGURE 6–1. Grade designations for aviation oils.

RECIPROCATING ENGINE LUBRICATION SYSTEMS

Dry-Sump Systems

Many reciprocating aircraft engines have pressure dry-sump lubrication systems. The oil supply in this type of system is carried in a tank. A pressure pump circulates the oil through the engine; scavenger pumps then return it to the tank as quickly as it accumulates in the engine sumps. The need for a separate supply tank is apparent when considering the complications that would result if large quantities of oil were carried in the engine crankcase. On multi-engine aircraft, each engine is supplied with oil from its own complete and independent system.

Although the arrangement of the oil systems in different aircraft varies widely and the units of which they are composed differ in construction details, the functions of all such systems are the same. A study of one system will clarify the general operation and maintenance requirements of other systems.

The principal units in a typical reciprocating engine dry-sump oil system include an oil supply tank, an engine oil pump, an oil cooler, an oil control valve, an actuator for an oil-cooler air-exit control, a firewall shutoff valve, the necessary tubing, and quantity, pressure, and temperature indicators. Most of these units are shown in figure 6–2.

Oil Tanks

Oil tanks generally are constructed of aluminum alloy. The oil tank usually is placed close to the engine and high enough above the oil pump inlet to ensure gravity feed. Oil tank capacity varies with the different types of aircraft, but generally it is sufficient to ensure an adequate supply of oil for the total fuel supply. The tank filler neck is positioned to provide sufficient room for oil expansion and for foam to collect. The filler cap or cover is marked with the word "OIL" and the tank capacity. A drain in the filler cap well disposes of any overflow caused by the filling operation. Oil tank vent lines are provided to ensure proper tank

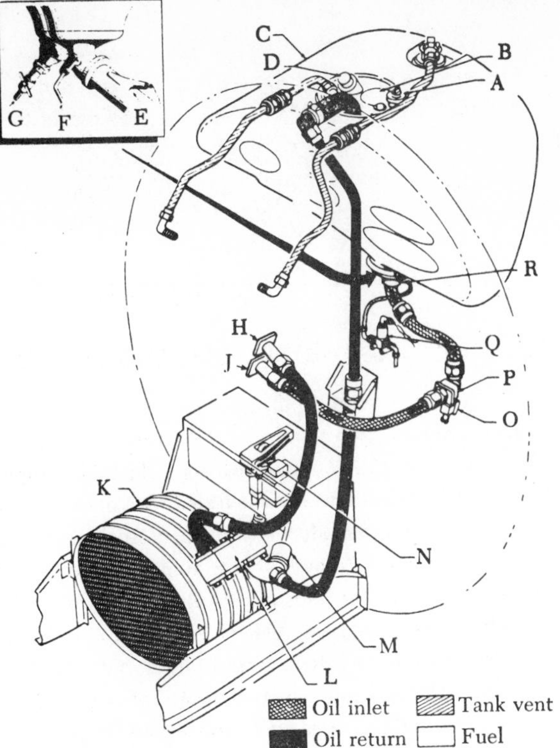

A. Dipstick screw plug
B. Filler neck
C. Oil tank
D. Oil quantity transmitter
E. Oil temperature bulb
F. Fuel connection for oil dilution
G. Sump drain valve
H. Oil outlet from engine
J. Oil inlet to engine
K. Oil cooler
L. Oil control valve
M. Floating control thermostat
N. Air exit flap actuator
O. Oil system drain valve
P. Firewall shutoff valve.
Q. Oil dilution valve
R. Oil tank sump

FIGURE 6–2. Typical lubrication system.

ventilation in all attitudes of flight. These lines usually are connected to the engine crankcase to prevent the loss of oil through the vents. This indirectly vents the tanks to the atmosphere through the crankcase breather.

Some oil tanks have a built-in hopper (figure 6–3), or temperature accelerating well, that extends from the oil return fitting on top of the oil tank to the outlet fitting in the sump in the bottom of the tank. In some systems, the hopper tank is open to the main oil supply at the lower end; other systems have flapper-type valves that separate the main oil supply from the oil in the hopper.

The opening at the bottom of the hopper in one type and the flapper-valve-controlled openings in the other allow oil from the main tank to enter the hopper and replace the oil consumed by the engine. Whenever the hopper tank includes the flapper-

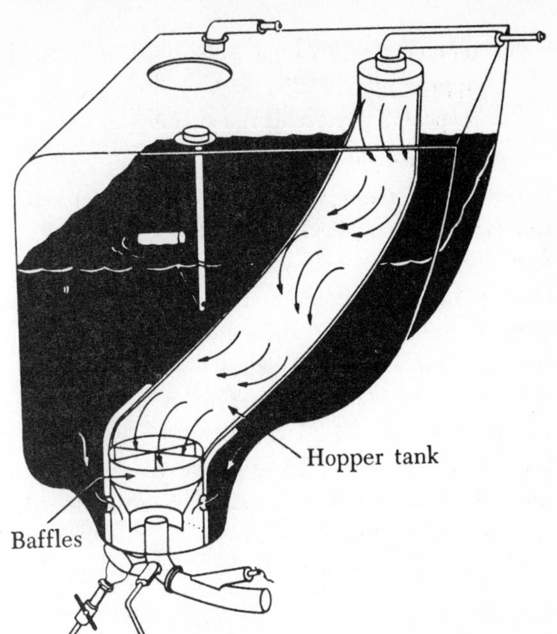

FIGURE 6–3. Oil tank with hopper.

valve-controlled openings, the valves are operated by differential oil pressure.

By separating the circulating oil from the surrounding oil in the tank, less oil is circulated. This hastens the warming of the oil when the engine is started. A hopper tank also makes oil dilution practical because only a relatively small volume of oil will have to be diluted. When it is necessary to dilute the oil, gasoline is added at some point in the inlet oil line to the engine, where it mixes with the circulating oil.

The return line in the top of the tank is positioned to discharge the returned oil against the wall of the hopper in a swirling motion. This method considerably reduces foaming. Baffles in the bottom of the hopper tank break up this swirling action to prevent air from being drawn into the line to the oil pressure pumps. In the case of oil-controlled propellers, the main outlet from the hopper tank may be in the form of a standpipe so that there will always be a reserve supply of oil for propeller feathering in case of engine failure. An oil tank sump, attached to the undersurface of the tank, acts as a trap for moisture and sediment (figure 6–2). The water and sludge can be drained by manually opening the drain valve in the bottom of the sump.

Most aircraft oil systems are equipped with the dipstick-type quantity gage, often called a bayonet gage. Some systems also have an oil-quantity-indicating system that shows the quantity of oil during flight. One type system consists essentially of an arm and float mechanism that rides the level of the oil and actuates an electric transmitter on top of the tank. The transmitter is connected to a cockpit gage, which indicates the quantity of oil in gallons.

Oil Pump

Oil entering the engine is pressurized, filtered, and regulated by units within the engine. They will be discussed, along with the external oil system, to provide a concept of the complete oil system.

As oil enters the engine (figure 6–4), it is pressurized by a gear-type pump. This pump is a positive displacement pump that consists of two meshed gears that revolve inside a housing. The clearance between the teeth and housing is small. The pump inlet is located on the left, and the discharge port is connected to the engine's system pressure line. One gear is attached to a splined drive shaft that extends from the pump housing to an accessory drive shaft on the engine. Seals are used to prevent leakage around the drive shaft. As the lower gear is rotated counterclockwise, the driven (idler) gear turns clockwise.

As oil enters the gear chamber, it is "picked up" by the gear teeth, trapped between them and the sides of the gear chamber, and is carried around the outside of the gears and discharged from the pressure port into the oil screen passage. The pressurized oil flows to the oil filter, where any solid particles suspended in the oil are separated from it, preventing possible damage to moving parts of the engine. Oil under pressure then opens the oil filter check valve mounted in the top of the filter. This valve is closed by a light spring loading of 1 to 3 pounds when the engine is not operating to prevent gravity-fed oil from entering the engine and settling in the lower cylinders of radial engines. If oil were permitted to lie in the lower cylinders, it would gradually seep by the rings of the piston and fill the combustion chamber, contributing to a possible liquid lock.

The bypass valve, located between the pressure side of the oil pump and the oil filter, permits unfiltered oil to bypass the filter and enter the engine when the oil filter is clogged or during a cold engine start. The spring loading on the bypass valve allows the valve to open before the oil pressure collapses the filter, or, in the case of cold, congealed oil, it provides a low-resistance path around the filter. It is felt that dirty oil in an engine is better than no lubrication at all.

Oil Filters

The oil filters used on aircraft engines are usually one of three types: (1) Screen, (2) Cuno, or (3) Air-Maze. A screen-type filter (figure 6–4) with its double-walled construction provides a large filtering area in a compact unit. As oil passes through the

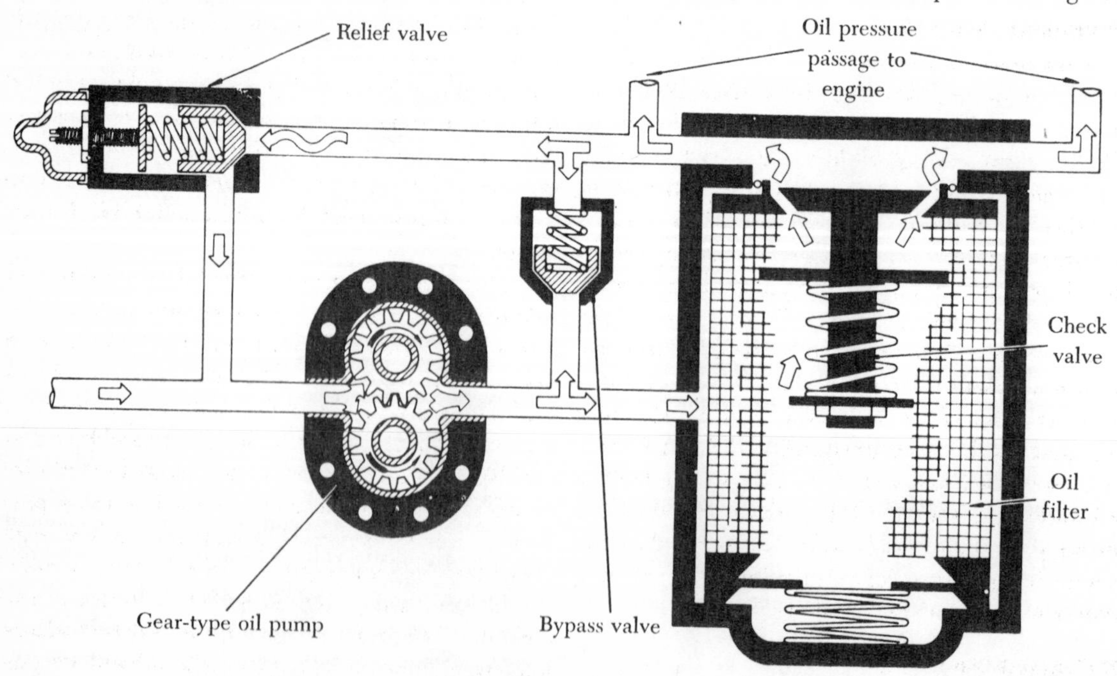

FIGURE 6–4. Engine oil pump and associated units.

fine-mesh screen, dirt, sediment, and other foreign matter are removed and settle to the bottom of the housing. At regular intervals the cover is removed and the screen and housing cleaned with a solvent.

The Cuno oil filter has a cartridge made of disks and spacers. A cleaner blade fits between each pair of disks. The cleaner blades are stationary, but the disks rotate when the shaft is turned. Oil from the pump enters the cartridge well that surrounds the cartridge and passes through the spaces between the closely spaced disks of the cartridge, then through the hollow center, and on to the engine. Any foreign particles in the oil are deposited on the outer surface of the cartridge. When the cartridge is rotated, the cleaner blades comb the foreign matter from the disks. The cartridge of the manually operated Cuno filter is turned by an external handle. Automatic Cuno filters have a hydraulic motor built into the filter head. This motor, operated by engine oil pressure, rotates the cartridge whenever the engine is running. There is a manual turning nut on the automatic Cuno filter for rotating the cartridge manually during inspections.

The Air-Maze filter contains a series of round, fine-meshed screens mounted on a hollow shaft. The oil from the pump enters the well, surrounds the screens, and then passes through them and the shaft before entering the engine. The carbon deposits that collect on the screens actually improve their filtering efficiency.

Oil Pressure Relief Valve

An oil pressure relief valve (figure 6–4), limits oil pressure to a predetermined value, depending on the installation. The oil pressure must be sufficiently high to ensure adequate lubrication of the engine and its accessories at high speeds and powers. On the other hand, the pressure must not be too high, as leakage and damage to the oil system may result. The oil pressure is adjusted by removing an acorn-shaped cap, loosening the locknut, and turning the adjusting screw. On most aircraft engines, turning the screw clockwise increases the tension of the spring that holds the relief valve on its seat and increases the oil pressure; turning the adjusting screw counterclockwise decreases the spring tension and lowers the pressure. The exact procedure for adjusting the oil pressure and the factors that will vary an oil pressure setting are included in applicable manufacturer's instructions.

Oil Pressure Gage

Usually the oil pressure gage indicates the pressure at which the oil enters the engine from the pump. This gage warns of possible engine failure caused by an exhausted oil supply, failure of the oil pump, burned-out bearings, ruptured oil lines, or other causes that may be indicated by a loss of oil pressure.

One type of oil pressure gage uses a Bourdon-tube mechanism that measures the difference between oil pressure and cabin (atmospheric) pressure. This gage is constructed the same as other Bourdon-type gages except that it has a small restriction built into the instrument case or into the nipple connection leading to the Bourdon tube. This restriction prevents the surging action of the oil pump from damaging the gage or causing the pointer to oscillate too violently with each pressure pulsation. The oil pressure gage has a scale ranging from zero to 200, or from zero to 300 p.s.i. Operation range markings are placed on the cover glass, or the face of the gage, to indicate the safe range of oil pressure for a given installation.

A dual-type oil pressure gage is available for use on multi-engine aircraft. The dual indicator contains two Bourdon tubes, housed in a standard instrument case, one tube being used for each engine. The connections extend from the back of the case to each engine. There is one common movement assembly, but the moving parts function independently. In some installations, the line leading from the engine to the pressure gage is filled with light oil. Since the viscosity of this oil will not vary much with changes in temperature, the gage will respond better to changes in oil pressure. In time, engine oil will mix with some of the light oil in the line to the transmitter, and during cold weather, the thicker mixture will cause sluggish instrument readings. To correct this condition, the gage line must be disconnected, drained, and refilled with light oil.

The trend is toward electrical transmitters and indicators for oil- and fuel-pressure-indicating systems in all aircraft. In this type of indicating system, the oil pressure being measured is applied to the inlet port of the electrical transmitter, where it is conducted to a diaphragm assembly by a capillary tube. The motion produced by the diaphragm's expansion and contraction is amplified through a lever and gear arrangement. The gear varies the electrical value of the indicating circuit, which, in turn, is reflected on the indicator in the cockpit. This type of indicating system replaces long fluid-filled tubing lines with an almost weightless piece of wire.

When the circulating oil has performed its function of lubricating and cooling the moving parts of the engine, it drains into the sumps in the lowest parts of the engine. Oil collected in these sumps is "picked up" by gear or gerotor-type scavenger pumps as quickly as it accumulates. These pumps have a greater capacity than the pressure pump. In dry sump engines, this oil leaves the engine, passes through the oil temperature regulator, and returns to the supply tank.

Oil Temperature Regulator

As discussed previously, the viscosity of the oil varies with its temperature. Since the viscosity affects its lubricating properties, the temperature at which the oil enters an engine must be held within close limits. Generally, the oil leaving an engine must be cooled before it is re-circulated. Obviously, the amount of cooling must be controlled if the oil is to return to the engine at the correct temperature. The oil temperature regulator, located in the return line to the tank, provides this controlled cooling. As the name implies, this unit regulates the temperature by either cooling the oil or passing it on to the tank without cooling, depending on the temperature at which it leaves the engine. The regulator consists of two main parts: (1) A cooler and (2) an oil control valve (see figure 6–2). The cooler transfers the heat from the oil to the air, while the control valve regulates the flow of oil through the cooler.

Indicating Oil Temperature

In dry-sump lubricating systems the oil temperature bulb may be anywhere in the oil inlet line between the supply tank and the engine. Oil systems for wet-sump engines have the temperature bulb located where it senses oil temperature after the oil passes through the oil cooler. In either system the bulb is located so that it measures the temperature of the oil before it enters the engine's hot sections.

An oil temperature gage in the cockpit is connected to the oil temperature bulb by electrical leads. The oil temperature will be indicated on the gage. Any malfunction of the oil cooling system will appear as an abnormal reading.

Oil flow in the system shown in figure 6–2 can be traced from the oil outlet fitting of the tank. The next units through which oil must flow to reach the engine are the drain valve and the firewall shutoff valve. The drain valve in this installation is a manual, two-position valve. It is located in the lowest part of the oil inlet line to the engine to permit complete drainage of the tank and its inlet supply line. The firewall shutoff valve is an electric motor-driven gate valve installed in the inlet oil line at the firewall of the nacelle. This valve shuts off the oil supply when there is a fire, when there is a break in the oil supply line, or when engine maintenance is performed that requires the oil to be shut off. In some aircraft the firewall shutoff valves for the oil system, fuel system, and hydraulic system are controlled by a single switch or mechanical linkage; other systems have separate control switches for each valve.

Oil Cooler

The cooler (figure 6–5), either cylindrical or elliptical shaped, consists of a core enclosed in a double-walled shell. The core is built of copper or aluminum tubes with the tube ends formed to a hexagonal shape and joined together in the honeycomb effect shown in figure 6–5. The ends of the copper tubes of the core are soldered, whereas aluminum tubes are brazed or mechanically joined. The tubes touch only at the ends so that a space exists between them along most of their lengths. This allows oil to flow through the spaces between the tubes while the cooling air passes through the tubes.

The space between the inner and outer shells is known as the annular or bypass jacket. Two paths are open to the flow of oil through a cooler. From the inlet it can flow halfway around the bypass jacket, enter the core from the bottom, and then

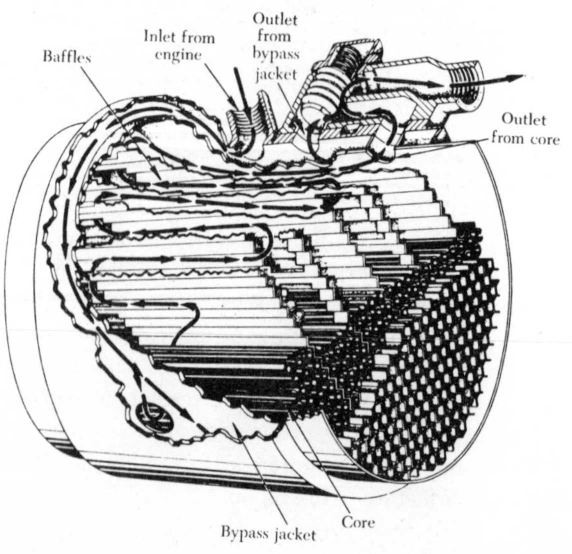

FIGURE 6–5. Oil cooler.

pass through the spaces between the tubes and out to the oil tank. This is the path the oil follows when it is hot enough to require cooling. As the oil flows through the core, it is guided by baffles, which force the oil to travel back and forth several times before it reaches the core outlet. The oil can also pass from the inlet completely around the bypass jacket to the outlet without passing through the core. Oil follows this bypass route when the oil is cold or when the core is blocked with thick, congealed oil.

Flow Control Valve

The flow control valve determines which of the two possible paths the oil will take through a cooler. There are two openings in a flow control valve which fit over the corresponding outlets at the top of the cooler. When the oil is cold, a bellows within the flow control contracts and lifts a valve from its seat. Under this condition, oil entering the cooler has a choice of two outlets and two paths. Following the path of least resistance, the oil flows around the jacket and out past the thermostatic valve to the tank. This allows the oil to warm up quickly and, at the same time, heats the oil in the core. As the oil warms up and reaches its operating temperature, the bellows of the thermostat expands and closes the outlet from the bypass jacket. The oil must now flow through the core into an opening in the base of the control valve, and out to the tank. No matter which path it takes through the cooler, the oil always flows over the bellows of the thermostatic valve.

Surge Protection Valves

When oil in the system is congealed, the scavenger pump may build up a very high pressure in the oil return line. To prevent this high pressure from bursting the oil cooler or blowing off the hose connections, some aircraft have surge, protection valves in the engine lubrication systems.

One type of surge valve (figure 6–6) is incorporated in the oil cooler flow control valve; another type is a separate unit in the oil return line.

The surge protection valve (figure 6–6) incorporated in a flow control valve is the more common type. Although this flow control valve differs from the one just described, it is essentially the same except for the surge protection feature. The high-pressure operation condition is shown in figure 6–6, where the high oil pressure at the control valve inlet has forced the surge valve (C) upward. Note how this movement has opened the surge valve and, at the same time, seated the poppet valve (E). The closed poppet valve prevents oil from entering the cooler proper; therefore, the scavenge oil passes directly to the tank through outlet (A) without passing through either the cooler bypass jacket or the core. When the pressure drops to a safe value, the spring forces the surge and poppet valves downward, closing the surge valve (C) and opening the poppet

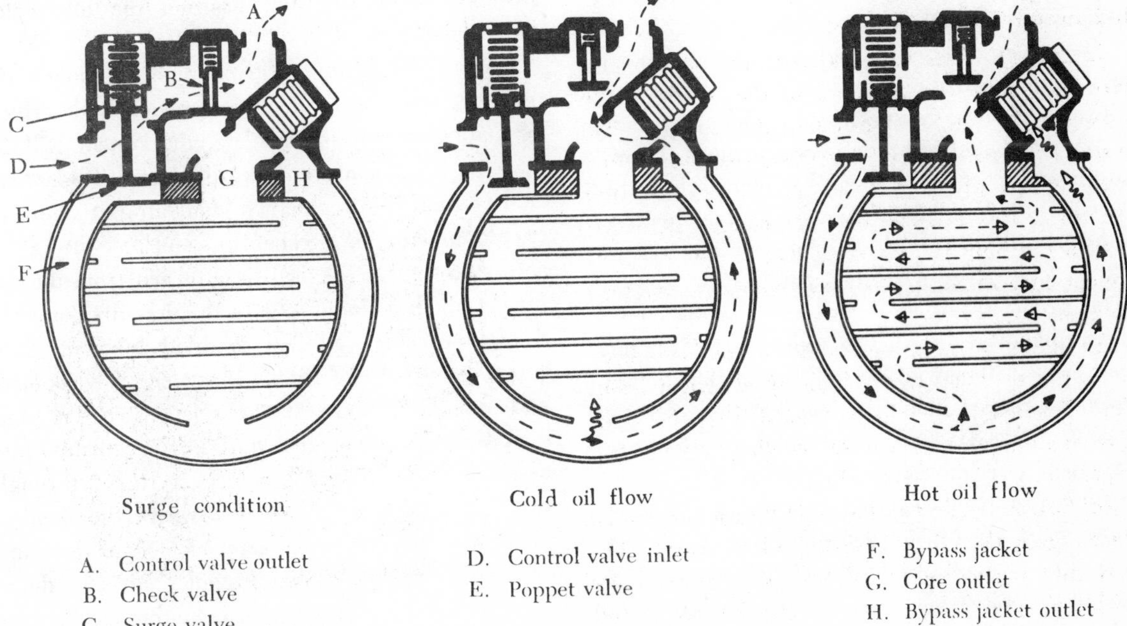

FIGURE 6–6. Control valve with surge protection.

valve (E). Oil then passes from the control valve inlet (D), through the open poppet valve, and into the bypass jacket (F). The thermostatic valve, according to oil temperature, then determines oil flow either through the bypass jacket to port (H) or through the core to port (G). The check valve (B) opens to allow the oil to reach the tank return line.

Airflow Controls

By regulating the airflow through the cooler, the temperature of the oil can be controlled to fit various operating conditions. For example, the oil will reach operating temperature more quickly if the airflow is cut off during engine warmup. There are two methods in general use: one method employs shutters installed on the rear of the oil cooler, and the other uses a flap on the air-exit duct.

In some cases, the oil cooler air-exit flap is opened manually and closed by linkage attached to a cockpit lever. More often, the flap is opened and closed by an electric motor.

One of the most widely used automatic oil temperature control devices is the floating control thermostat that provides manual and automatic control of the oil inlet temperatures. With this type of control the oil cooler air-exit door is opened and closed automatically by an electrically operated actuator. Automatic operation of the actuator is determined by electrical impulses received from a controlling thermostat inserted in the oil pipe leading from the oil cooler to the oil supply tank. The actuator may be operated manually by an oil cooler air-exit door control switch. Placing this switch in the "open" or "closed" position produces a corresponding movement of the cooler door. Placing the switch in the "auto" position puts the actuator under the automatic control of the floating control thermostat (figure 6–7). The thermostat shown in figure 6–7 is adjusted to maintain a normal oil temperature so that it will not vary more than approximately 5° to 8° C., depending on the installation.

During operation, the temperature of the engine oil flowing over the bimetal element (B of figure 6–7) causes it to wind or unwind slightly. This movement rotates shaft (A) and the grounded center contact arm (C). As the grounded contact arm is rotated, it is moved toward either the open or closed floating contact arm (G). The two floating contact arms are oscillated by the cam (F), which is continuously rotated by an electric motor (D) through a gear train (E). When the grounded center contact arm is positioned by the bimetal element so that it will touch one of the floating

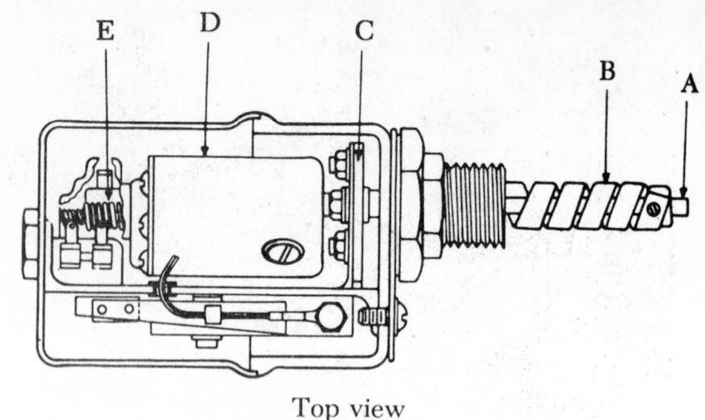

Top view

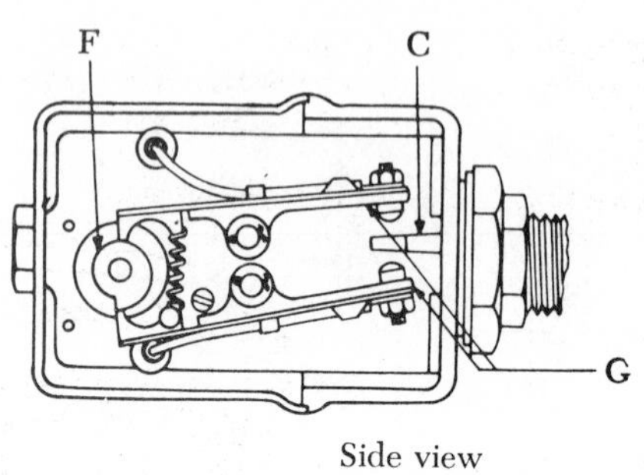

Side view

A. Shaft
B. Bimetal element
C. Grounded center contact arm
D. Electric motor
E. Gear train
F. Cam
G. Floating contact arm

FIGURE 6–7. Floating control thermostat.

contact arms, an electric circuit to the oil cooler exit-flap actuator motor is completed, causing the actuator to operate and position the oil cooler air-exit flap.

In some lubrication systems, dual oil coolers are used. If the typical oil system previously described is adapted to two oil coolers, the system will be modified to include a flow divider, two identical coolers and flow regulators, dual air-exit doors, a two-door actuating mechanism, and a Y-fitting, as shown in figure 6–8. Oil is returned from the engine through a single tube to the flow divider (E), where the return oil flow is divided equally into two tubes (C), one for each cooler. The coolers and regulators have the same construction and operation as the cooler and flow regulator just described. Oil from the coolers is routed through two tubes (D) to a Y-fitting, where the floating control thermostat (A) samples oil temperature and positions the two oil cooler air-exit doors through the use of a two-door actuating mechanism. From the Y-fitting the lubricating oil is returned to the tank, where it completes its circuit.

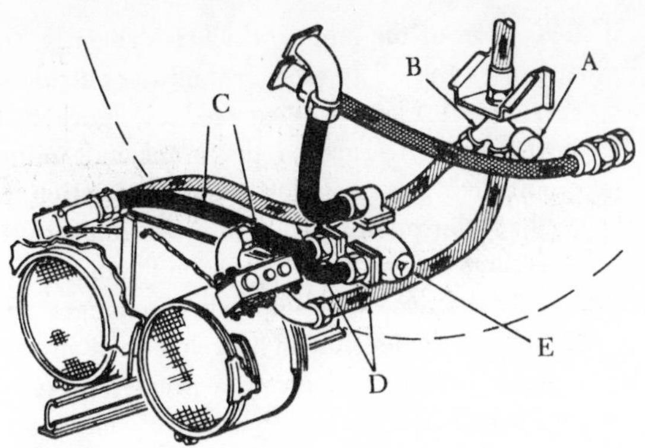

A. Floating control thermostat
B. Y-fitting
C. Inlet to cooler tubes
D. Outlet from cooler tubes
E. Flow divider

FIGURE 6–8. Dual oil cooler system.

INTERNAL LUBRICATION OF RECIPROCATING ENGINES

The lubricating oil is distributed to the various moving parts of a typical internal-combustion engine by one of the three following methods: (1) Pressure, (2) splash, or (3) a combination of pressure and splash.

Pressure Lubrication

In a typical pressure-lubrication system (figure 6–9), a mechanical pump supplies oil under pressure to the bearings throughout the engine. The oil flows into the inlet or suction side of the oil pump through a line connected to the tank at a point higher than the bottom of the oil sump. This prevents sediment which falls into the sump from being drawn into the pump. The pump forces the

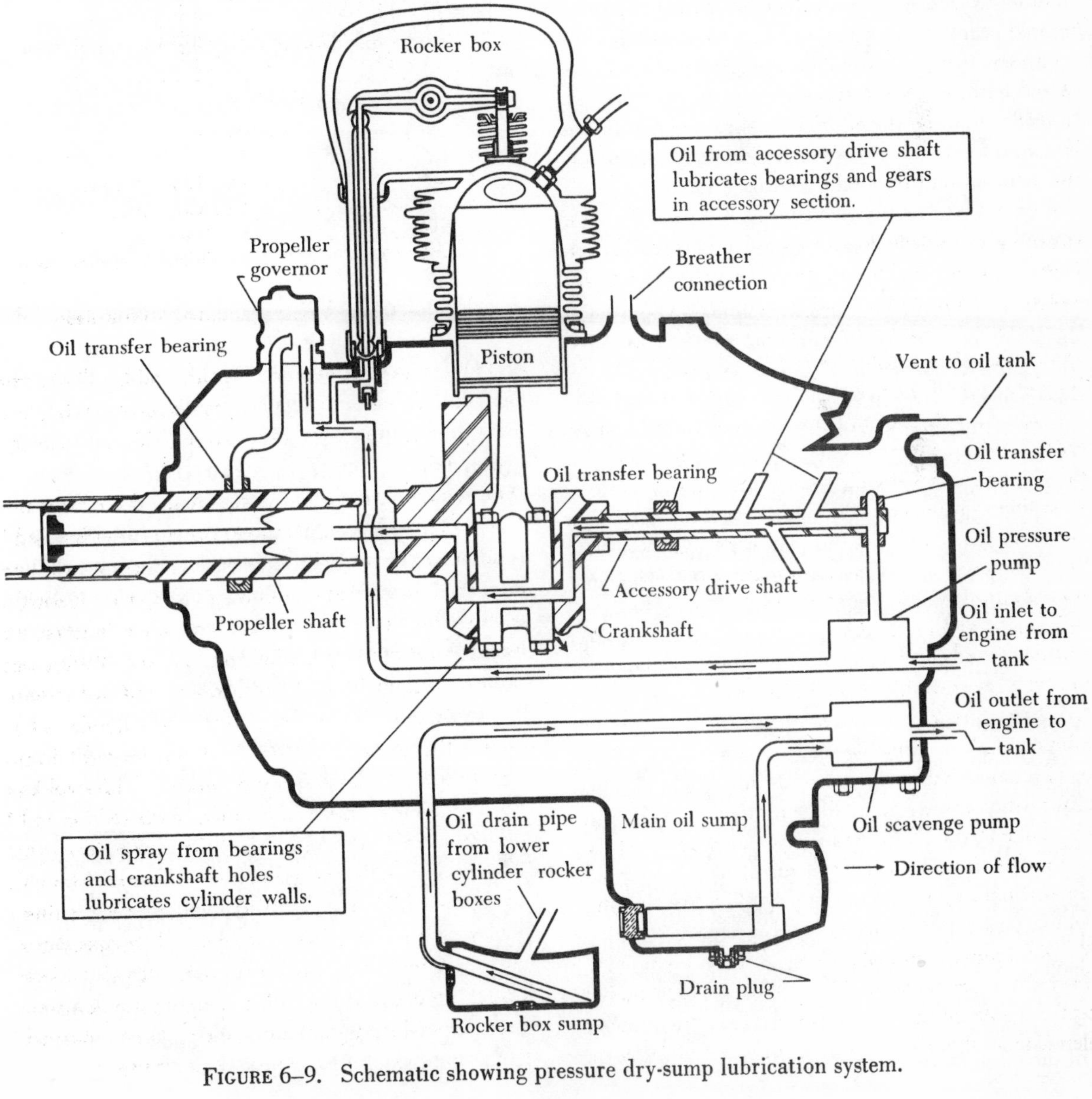

FIGURE 6–9. Schematic showing pressure dry-sump lubrication system.

oil into a manifold that distributes the oil through drilled passages to the crankshaft bearings and other bearings throughout the engine.

Oil flows from the main bearings through holes drilled in the crankshaft to the lower connecting rod bearings. Each of these holes through which the oil is fed is located so that the bearing pressure at the point will be as low as possible.

Oil reaches a hollow camshaft (in an in-line or opposed engine), or a camplate or camdrum (in a radial engine), through a connection with the end bearing, or the main oil manifold; it then flows out to the various camshaft, camdrum, or camplate bearings and the cams.

The engine cylinder surfaces receive oil sprayed from the crankshaft and also from the crankpin bearings. Since oil seeps slowly through the small crankpin clearances before it is sprayed on the cylinder walls, considerable time is required for enough oil to reach the cylinder walls, especially on a cold day when the oil flow is more sluggish. This is one of the chief reasons for diluting the engine oil with gasoline for cold weather starting.

Combination Splash-and-Pressure Lubrication

The pressure-lubrication system is the principal method of lubricating aircraft engines. Splash lubrication may be used in addition to pressure lubrition on aircraft engines, but it is never used by itself; hence, aircraft-engine lubrication systems are always either the pressure type or the combination pressure-and-splash type, usually the latter.

The advantages of pressure lubrication are:

(1) Positive introduction of oil to the bearings.

(2) Cooling effect caused by the large quantities of oil which can be (pumped) circulated through a bearing.

(3) Satisfactory lubrication in various attitudes of flight.

Wet-Sump Lubrication

A simple form of a wet-sump system is shown in figure 6–10. The system consists of a sump or pan in which the oil supply is contained. The level (quantity) of oil is indicated or measured by a vertical rod that protrudes into the oil from an elevated hole on top of the crankcase. In the bottom of the sump (oil pan) is a screen strainer having a suitable mesh or series of openings to strain undesirable particles from the oil and yet pass sufficient quantity to the inlet or (suction) side of the oil pressure pump.

The rotation of the pump, which is driven by the engine, causes the oil to pass around the outside of the gears in the manner illustrated in figure 6–4. This develops a pressure in the crankshaft oiling system (drilled passage-holes). The variation in the speed of the pump from idling to full-throttle operating range of the engine and the fluctuation of oil viscosity because of temperature changes are compensated by the tension on the relief valve spring. The pump is designed to create a greater pressure than probably will ever be required to compensate for wear of the bearings or thinning out of oil. The parts oiled by pressure throw a lubricating spray into the cylinder and piston assemblies. After lubricating the various units on which it sprays, the oil drains back into the sump and the cycle is repeated.

The main disadvantages of the wet-sump system are:

(1) The oil supply is limited by the sump (oil pan) capacity.

(2) Provisions for cooling the oil are difficult to arrange because the system is a self-contained unit.

(3) Oil temperatures are likely to be higher on large engines because the oil supply is so close to the engine and is continuously subjected to the operating temperatures.

(4) The system is not readily adaptable to inverted flying since the entire oil supply will flood the engine.

LUBRICATION SYSTEM MAINTENANCE PRACTICES

The following lubrication system practices are typical of those performed on small, single-engine aircraft. The oil system and components are those used to lubricate a 225 hp., six-cylinder, horizontally opposed, air-cooled engine.

The oil system is the dry-sump type, using a pressure lubrication system sustained by engine-driven, positive-displacement, gear-type pumps. The system (figure 6–11) consists of an oil cooler (radiator), a 3-gal. (U.S.) oil tank, oil pressure pump and scavenge pump, and the necessary interconnecting oil lines. Oil from the oil tank is pumped to the engine, where it circulates under pressure, then collects in the cooler, and is returned to the oil tank. A thermostat in the cooler controls oil temperature by allowing part of the oil to flow through the cooler and part to flow directly into the oil supply tank. This arrangement allows hot engine oil, with a temperature still below 65° C. (150° F.),

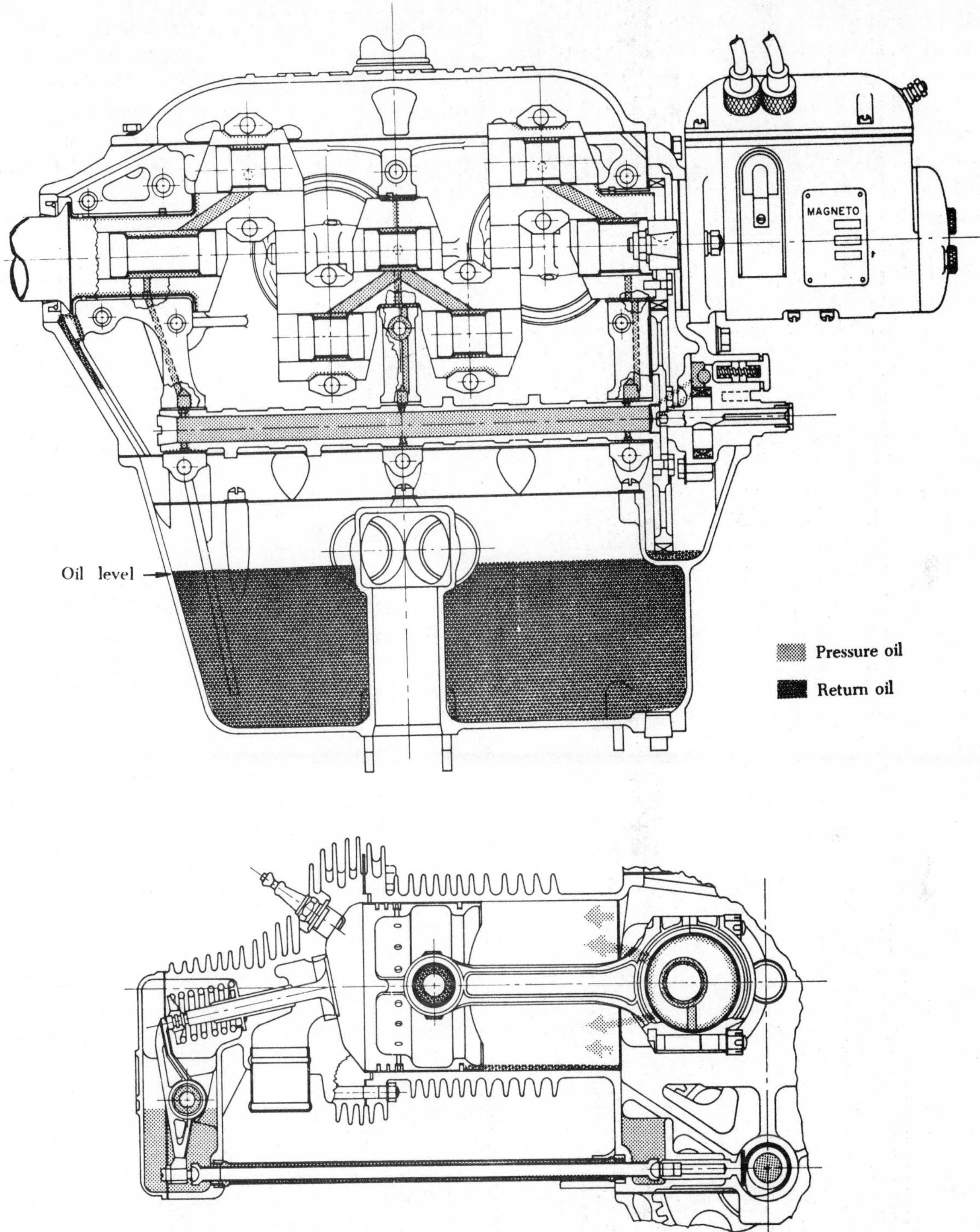

FIGURE 6–10. Schematic view of a typical wet-sump lubrication system.

to mix with the cold uncirculated oil in the tank. This raises the complete engine oil supply to operating temperature in a shorter period of time.

The oil tank, constructed of welded aluminum, is serviced through a filler neck located on the tank and equipped with a spring-loaded locking cap. Inside the tank a weighted, flexible rubber oil hose is mounted so that it is re-positioned automatically to ensure oil pickup during inverted maneuvers. A dipstick guard is welded inside the tank for the

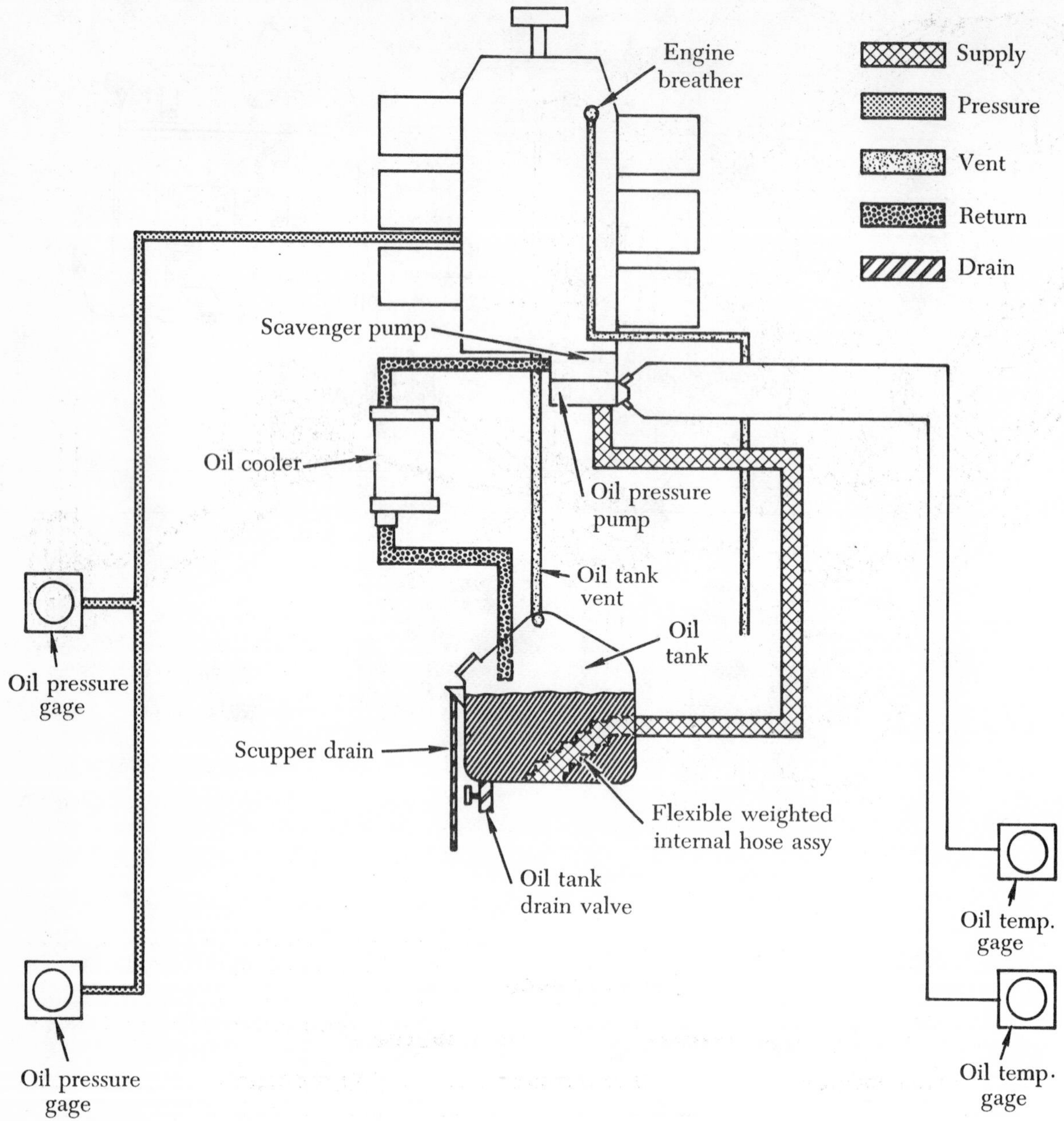

FIGURE 6–11. Oil system schematic.

protection of the flexible oil hose assembly. During normal flight, the oil tank is vented to the engine crankcase by a flexible line at the top of the tank. However, during inverted flight the normal vent is covered or submerged below the oil level within the tank. Therefore, a secondary vent and check-valve arrangement is incorporated in the tank for inverted operation. During an inversion, when air in the oil tank reaches a certain pressure, the check valve in the secondary vent line will unseat and allow air to escape from the tank. This assures an uninterrupted flow of oil to the engine.

The location of the oil system components in relation to each other and to the engine is shown in figure 6–12.

Oil Tank

Repair of an oil tank usually requires that the tank be removed. The removal and installation procedures normally remain the same regardless of whether the engine is removed or not.

First, the oil must be drained. Most light aircraft

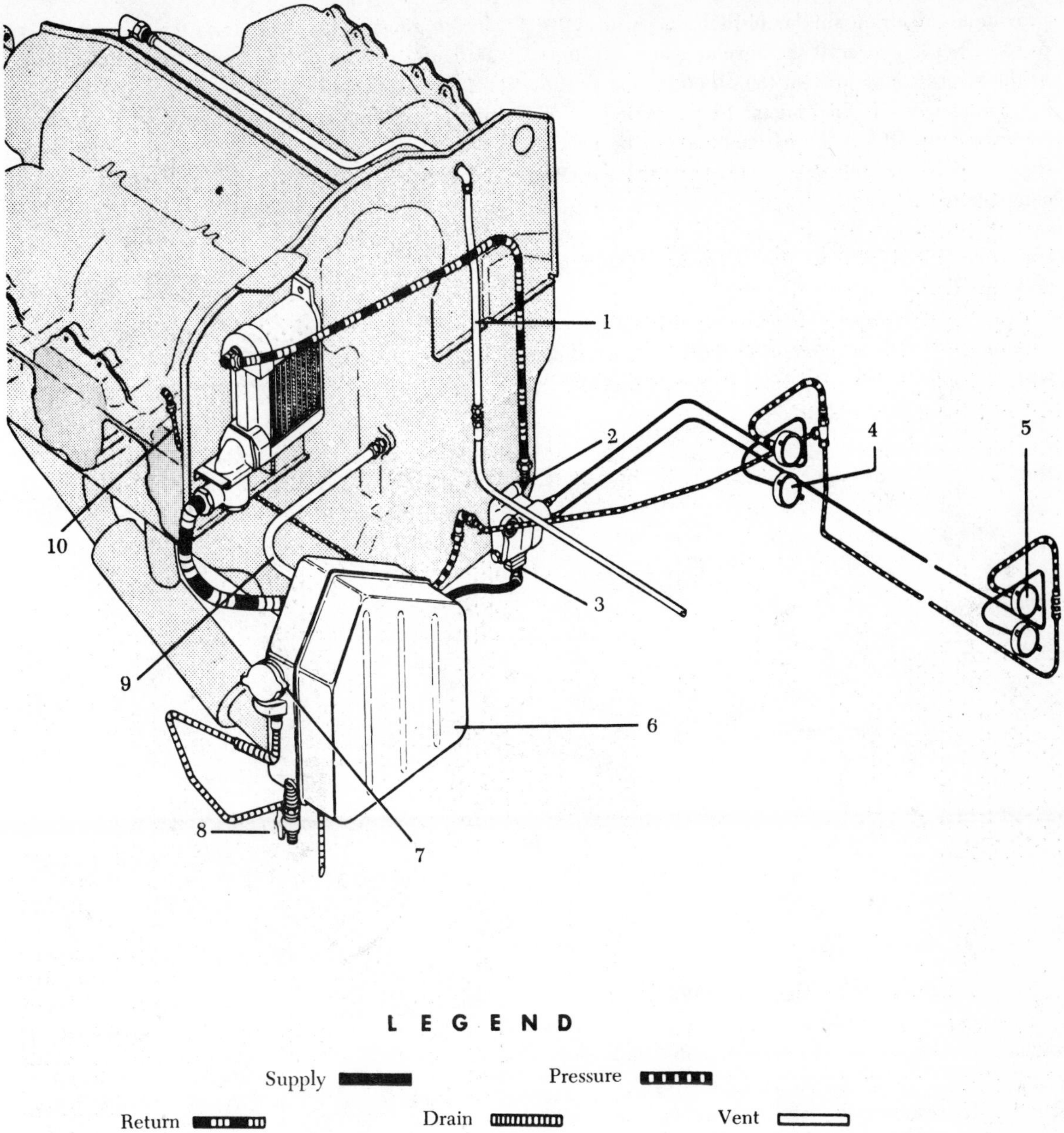

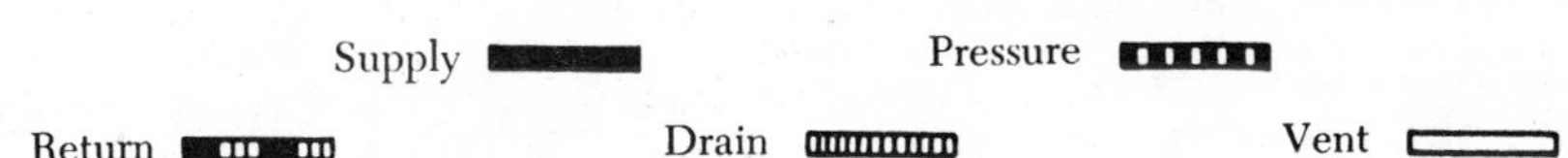

1. Engine breather
2. Oil outlet
3. Oil inlet
4. Oil temperature gage
5. Oil pressure gage
6. Oil tank
7. Oil filler
8. Oil tank drain
9. Oil tank vent line
10. Engine oil pressure line

FIGURE 6–12. Oil system perspective.

provide an oil drain similar to that shown in figure 6–13. On some aircraft the normal ground attitude of the aircraft may prevent the oil tank from draining completely. If the amount of undrained oil is excessive, the aft portion of the tank can be raised slightly after the tank straps have been loosened to complete the drainage.

After the oil tank has been drained, the cowl assembly is removed to provide access to the oil tank installation.

After disconnecting the oil inlet and vent lines (figure 6–14), the scupper drain hose and bonding wire can be removed.

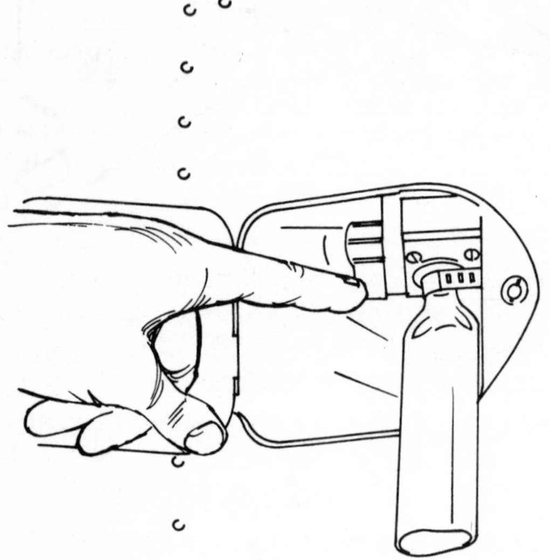

FIGURE 6–13. Oil tank drain.

The securing straps fitted around the tank can now be removed, as shown in figure 6–15. Any safety wire securing the clamp must be removed before the clamp can be loosened and the strap disconnected.

The tank can now be lifted out of the aircraft. The tank is re-installed by reversing the sequence used in the tank removal.

After installation, the oil tank should be filled to capacity (figure 6–16).

After the oil tank has been filled, the engine should be run for at least 2 minutes. Then the oil level should be checked, and, if necessary, sufficient oil should be added to bring the oil up to the proper level on the dipstick. (See figure 6–17.)

Oil Cooler

The oil cooler (figure 6–18) used with this aircraft's opposed-type engine is the honeycomb type. With the engine operating and an oil temperature below 65° C. (150° F.), an oil cooler bypass valve opens, allowing oil to bypass the core. This valve

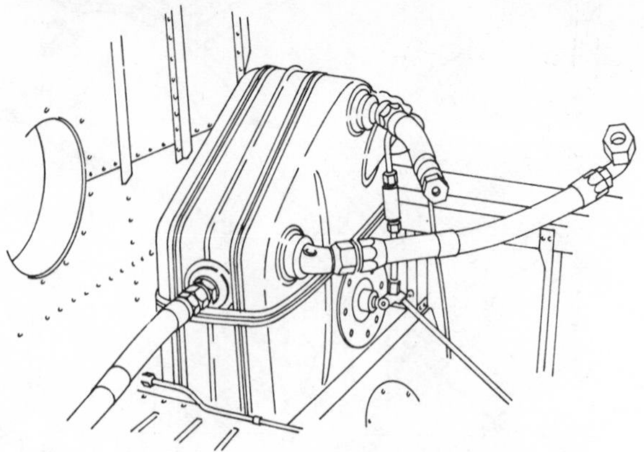

FIGURE 6–14. Disconnecting oil lines.

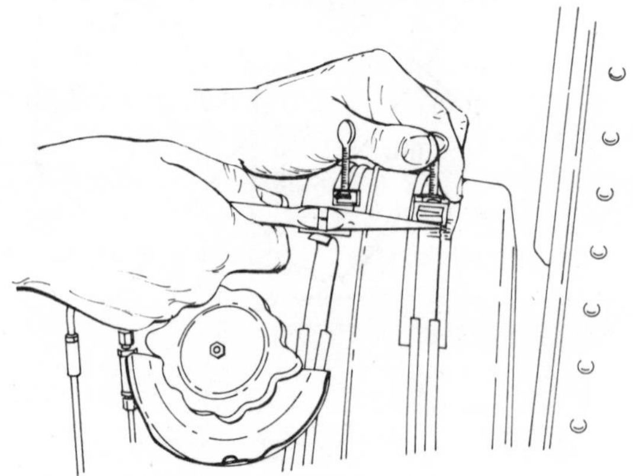

FIGURE 6–15. Removal of securing straps.

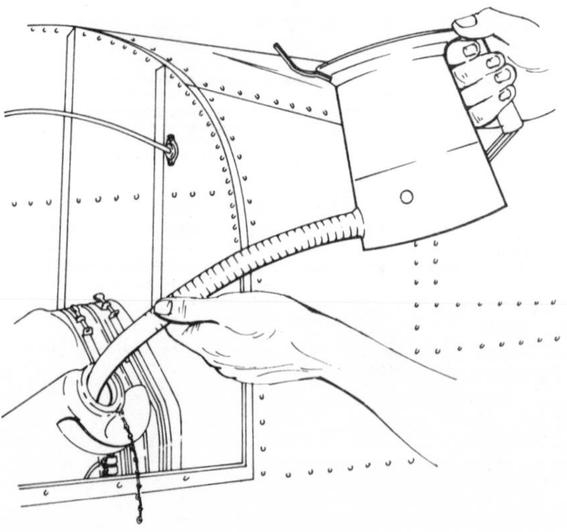

FIGURE 6–16. Filling an oil tank.

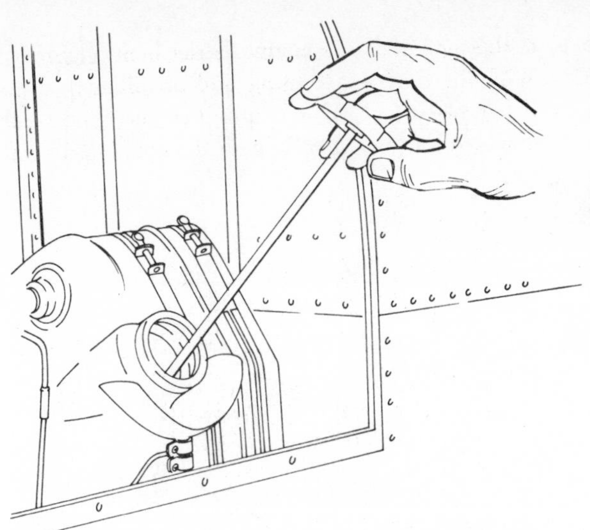

FIGURE 6–17. Checking oil level with dipstick.

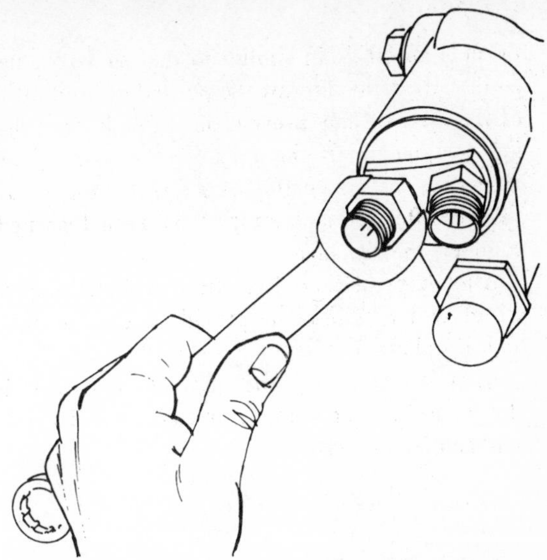

FIGURE 6–19. Removing oil temperature bulb.

begins to close when the oil temperature reaches approximately 65° C. (150° F.). When the oil temperature reaches 85° C. (185° F.), ±2° C., the valve is closed completely, diverting all oil flow through the cooler core.

Oil Temperature Bulbs

Most oil temperature bulbs are mounted in the pressure oil screen housing. They relay an indication of engine oil inlet temperature to the oil-temperature indicators mounted on the instrument panel. Temperature bulbs can be replaced by removing the safety wire and disconnecting the wire

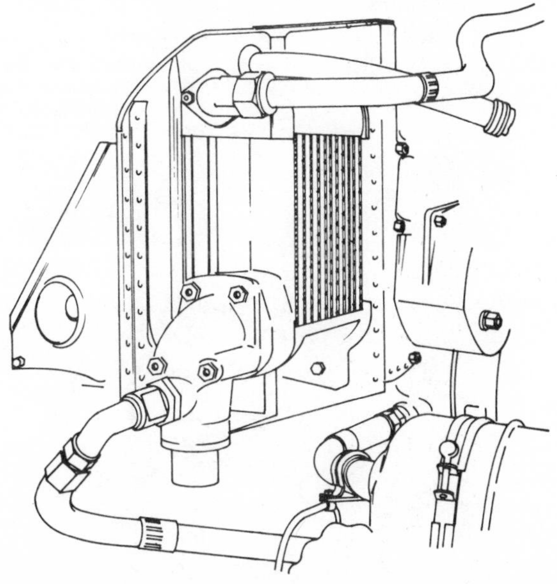

FIGURE 6–18. Oil cooler.

leads from the temperature bulbs; then remove the temperature bulbs, using the proper wrench, as shown in figure 6–19.

Pressure and Scavenge Oil Screens

Sludge will accumulate on the pressure and scavenge oil screens (figure 6–20) during engine operation. These screens must be removed, inspected, and cleaned at the intervals specified by the manufacturer.

Typical removal procedures include removing the safety devices and loosening the oil screen housing or cover plate. A suitable container should be provided to collect the oil that will drain from the filter housing or cavity. The container must be clean so that the oil collected in it can be examined for foreign particles. Any contamination already present in the container will give a false indication of the engine condition. This could result in a premature engine removal.

After the screens are removed, they should be inspected for contamination and for the presence of metal particles that may indicate engine internal failure. The screen must be cleaned prior to re-installing in the engine. In some cases it is necessary to disassemble the filter for inspection and cleaning. The manufacturer's procedures should be followed when disassembling and re-assembling an oil screen assembly.

When re-installing a filter, use new O-rings and gaskets, and tighten the filter housing or cover retaining nuts to the torque value specified in the

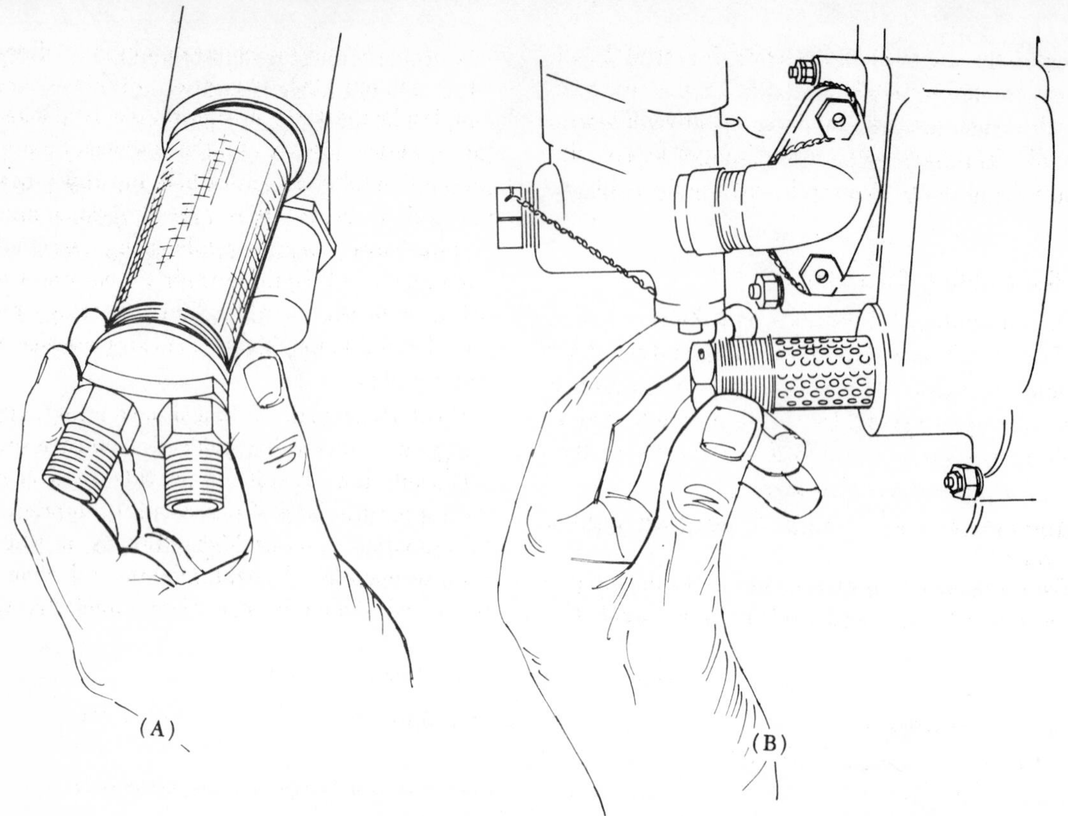

FIGURE 6–20. (A) Oil pressure screen and (B) Scavenge oil screen assembly.

applicable maintenance manual. Filters should be safetied as required.

Oil Pressure Relief Valve

An oil pressure relief valve limits oil pressure to the value specified by the engine manufacturer. Oil pressure settings vary from 35 p.s.i. to 90 p.s.i., depending on the installation. The oil pressure must be high enough to ensure adequate lubrication of the engine and accessories at high speeds and powers. On the other hand, the pressure must not be too high, since leakage and damage to the oil system may result. The oil pressure is adjusted by removing a cover nut, loosening a locknut, and turning the adjusting screw. (See figure 6–21.) Turn the adjusting screw clockwise to increase the pressure, or counterclockwise to decrease the pressure. Make the pressure adjustments while the engine is idling and tighten the adjustment screw locknut after each adjustment. Check the oil pressure reading while the engine is running at the r.p.m. specified in the manufacturer's maintenance manual. This may be from 1,900 r.p.m. to 2,300 r.p.m. The oil pressure reading should be between the limits prescribed by the manufacturer.

Draining Oil

Oil, in service, is constantly exposed to many harmful substances that reduce its ability to protect moving parts. The main contaminants are:

(1) Gasoline.
(2) Moisture.
(3) Acids.
(4) Dirt.
(5) Carbon.
(6) Metallic particles.

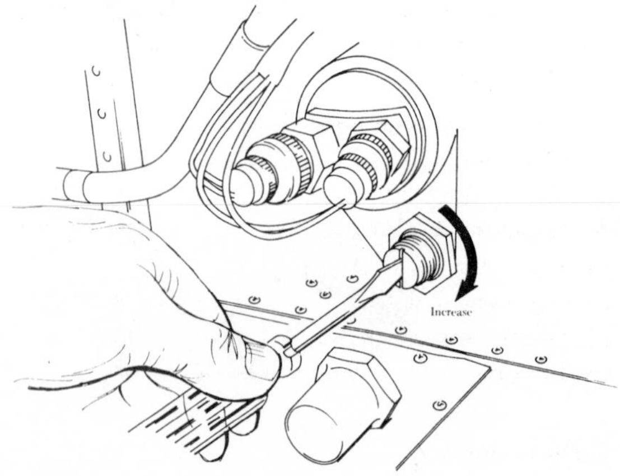

FIGURE 6–21. Oil pressure relief valve adjustment.

Because of the accumulation of these harmful substances, common practice is to drain the entire lubrication system at regular intervals and refill with new oil. The time between oil changes varies with each make and model aircraft and engine combination.

Troubleshooting Oil Systems

The outline of malfunctions and their remedies, listed in table 9, can expedite troubleshooting of the lubrication system. The purpose of this section is to present typical troubles. It is not intended to imply that any of the troubles are exactly as they may be in a particular airplane.

REQUIREMENTS FOR TURBINE ENGINE LUBRICANTS

There are many requirements for turbine engine lubricating oils, but because of the small number of moving parts and the complete absence of reciprocating motion, the lubrication problems are less complex in the turbine engine than in the reciprocating engine. Because of the absence of reciprocating motion, plus the use of ball and roller bearings, the turbine engine uses a less viscous lubricant. The turboprop engine, while using essentially the same type of oil as the turbojet, must use a higher viscosity oil because of the higher bearing pressures introduced by the highly loaded propeller reduction gearing.

Gas turbine engine oil must have a high viscosity for good load-carrying ability but must also be of sufficiently low viscosity to provide good flow ability. It must also be of low volatility to prevent loss by evaporation at the high altitudes at which the engines operate. In addition, the oil should not foam and should be essentially nondestructive to

TABLE 9. Oil System Troubleshooting Procedures.

TROUBLE	ISOLATION PROCEDURE	REMEDY
1. Excessive Oil Consumption.		
Oil line leakage.	Check external lines for evidence of oil leakage.	Replace or repair defective lines.
Accessory seal leakage.	Check for leak at accessories immediately after engine operation.	Replace accessory and/or defective accessory oil seal.
Low grade of oil.		Fill tank with proper grade oil.
Failing or failed bearing.	Check sump and oil pressure pump screen for metal particles.	Replace engine if metal particles are found.
2. High or Low Indicated Oil Pressure.		
Defective pressure gage.	Check indicator.	Replace indicator if defective.
Improper operation of oil pressure relief valve.	Erratic pressure indications either excessively high or low.	Remove, clean, and inspect relief valve.
Inadequate oil supply.	Check oil quantity.	Fill oil tank.
Diluted or contaminated oil.		Drain engine and tank; refill tank.
Clogged oil screen.		Remove and clean oil screen.
Oil viscosity incorrect.	Make sure correct oil is being used.	Drain engine and tank; refill tank.
Oil pump pressure relief valve adjustment incorrect.	Check pressure relief valve adjustment.	Make correct adjustment on oil pump pressure relief valve.
3. High or Low Indicated Oil Temperature.		
Defective temperature gage.	Check indicator.	Replace indicator if defective.
Inadequate oil supply.	Check oil quantity.	Fill oil tank.
Diluted or contaminated oil.		Drain engine and tank; refill tank.
Obstruction in oil tank.	Check tank.	Drain oil and remove obstruction.
Clogged oil screen.		Remove and clean oil screens.
Obstruction in oil cooler passages.	Check cooler for blocked or deformed passages.	Replace oil cooler if defective.
4. Oil Foaming.		
Diluted or contaminated oil.		Drain engine and tank; refill tank.
Oil level in tank too high.	Check oil quantity.	Drain excess oil from tank.

natural or synthetic rubber seals in the lubricating system. Also, with high-speed antifriction bearings, the formation of carbons or varnishes must be held to a minimum.

The many requirements for lubricating oils are met in the synthetic oils developed specifically for turbine engines. Synthetic oil has two principal advantages over petroleum oil. It has less tendency to deposit lacquer and coke and less tendency to evaporate at high temperature. Its principal disadvantage is that it tends to blister or remove paint wherever it is spilled. Painted surfaces should be wiped clean with a petroleum solvent after spillage.

Oil change intervals for turbine engines vary widely from model to model, depending on the severity of the oil temperature conditions imposed by the specific airframe installation and engine configuration. The applicable manufacturer's instructions should be followed.

Synthetic oil for turbine engines usually is supplied in sealed 1-quart or 1-gallon metal cans. Although this type of container was chosen to minimize contamination, it has often been found necessary to filter the oil to remove metal slivers, can sealants, etc., which may occur as a result of opening the can.

Some oil grades for use in turbojet engines may contain oxidation preventives, load-carrying additives, and substances that lower the pour point, in addition to synthetic chemical-base materials.

TURBINE ENGINE LUBRICATION SYSTEMS

Both wet- and dry-sump lubrication systems are used in gas turbine engines. Most turbojet engines are of the axial-flow configuration, and use a dry-sump lubrication system. However, some turbine engines are equipped with a combination dry- and wet-type of lubrication system.

Wet-sump engines store the lubricating oil in the engine proper, while dry-sump engines utilize an external tank mounted most generally on the engine or somewhere in the aircraft structure near the engine. To ensure proper temperature, oil is routed through either an air-cooled or a fuel-cooled oil cooler.

The exhaust turbine bearing is the most critical lubricating point in a gas turbine engine because of the high temperature normally present. In some engines air cooling is used in addition to oil cooling the bearing which supports the turbine. Air cooling, when used, is furnished by a cooling air impeller mounted on the compressor shaft just aft of the main compressor. Also, some turbine wheels may have a circle of air-pumping vanes on their front side to cause air to flow over the turbine disk, which reduces heat radiation to the bearing surface. Axial-flow engines sometimes use compressor air to aid in cooling the turbine or its supporting bearing. This bleed-air, as it is called, is usually bled off the fourth or fifth stage, since at this point air has enough pressure but has not yet become too warm (as the air is compressed, it becomes heated).

The use of cooling air on bearings and turbines eliminates the necessity of using oil coolers in the wet-sump lubrication systems, since a considerable amount of the heat normally present is dissipated by the cooling air rather than absorbed by the oil. Also, the use of cooling air substantially reduces the quantity of oil necessary to provide adequate cooling of the bearings. Engines that depend solely on lubricating oil for bearing cooling normally require oil coolers, although of a relatively small capacity. When an oil cooler is required, usually a greater quantity of oil is necessary to provide for circulation between the cooler and engine.

Turbojet Dry-Sump Lubrication

In a turbojet dry-sump lubrication system, the oil supply is carried in a tank mounted on the engine. With this type of system, a larger oil supply can be carried and the temperature of the oil can readily be controlled. An oil cooler usually is included in a dry-sump oil system (figure 6–22). This cooler may be air cooled or fuel cooled. The dry-sump oil system allows the axial-flow engines to retain their comparatively small diameter by designing the oil tank and the oil cooler to conform with the streamlined design of the engines.

The following component descriptions include most of those found in the various turbojet lubrication systems. However, since engine oil systems vary somewhat according to engine model and manufacturer, not all of these components will necessarily be found in any one system.

Although the dry-sump systems use an oil tank which contains most of the oil supply, a small sump usually is included on the engine to hold a small supply of oil. It usually contains the oil pump, the scavenge and pressure inlet strainers, scavenge return connection, pressure outlet ports, an oil filter, and mounting bosses for the oil pressure gage and temperature bulb connections.

A view of a typical oil tank is shown in figure 6–23. It is designed to furnish a constant supply of oil to the engine during any aircraft attitude. This is done by a swivel outlet assembly mounted inside the tank, a horizontal baffle mounted in the center

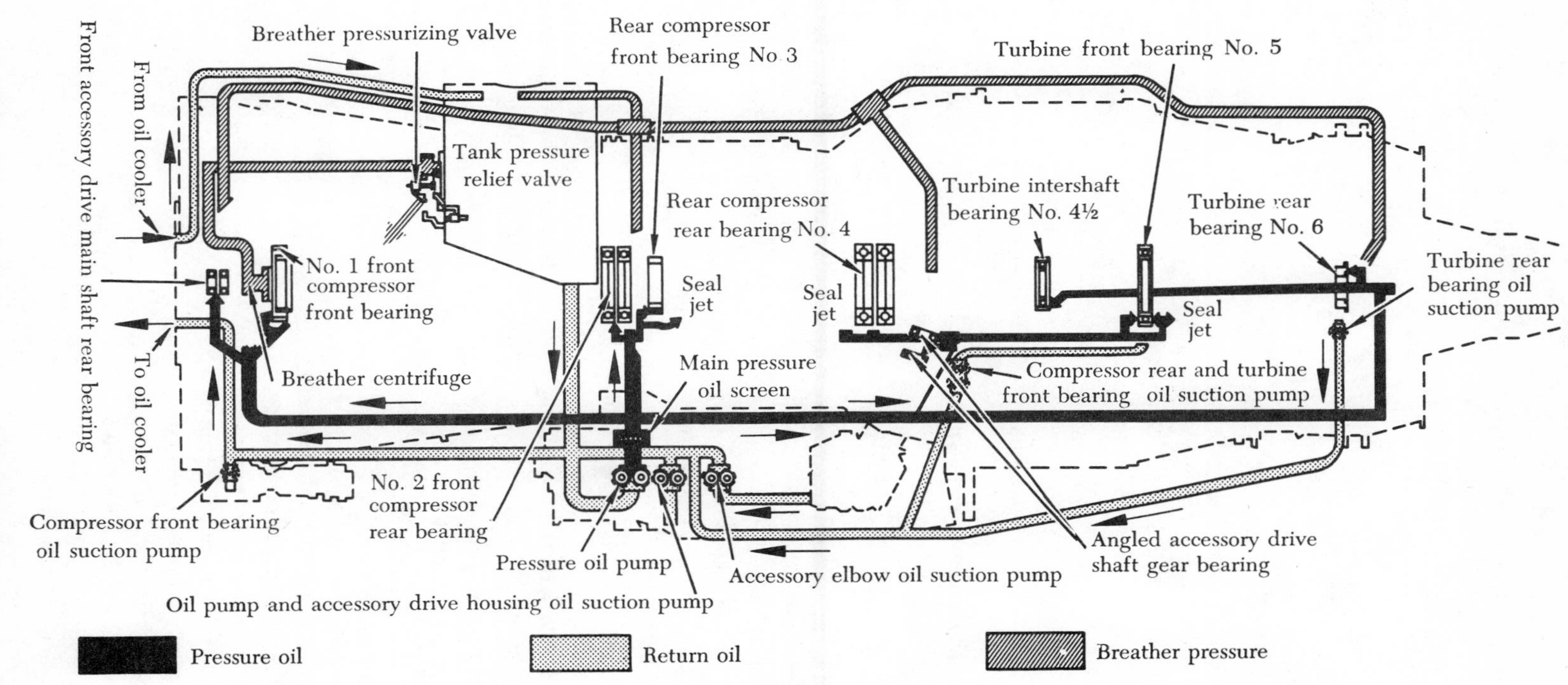
Breather pressurizing valve
Rear compressor front bearing No 3
Turbine front bearing No. 5
Tank pressure relief valve
Rear compressor rear bearing No. 4
Turbine intershaft bearing No. 4½
Turbine rear bearing No. 6
From oil cooler
No. 1 front compressor front bearing
Seal jet
Seal jet
Seal jet
Turbine rear bearing oil suction pump
Front accessory drive main shaft rear bearing
To oil cooler
Breather centrifuge
Main pressure oil screen
Compressor rear and turbine front bearing oil suction pump
No. 2 front compressor rear bearing
Compressor front bearing oil suction pump
Pressure oil pump
Accessory elbow oil suction pump
Angled accessory drive shaft gear bearing
Oil pump and accessory drive housing oil suction pump
Pressure oil
Return oil
Breather pressure

FIGURE 6–22. A turbojet dry-sump lubrication system.

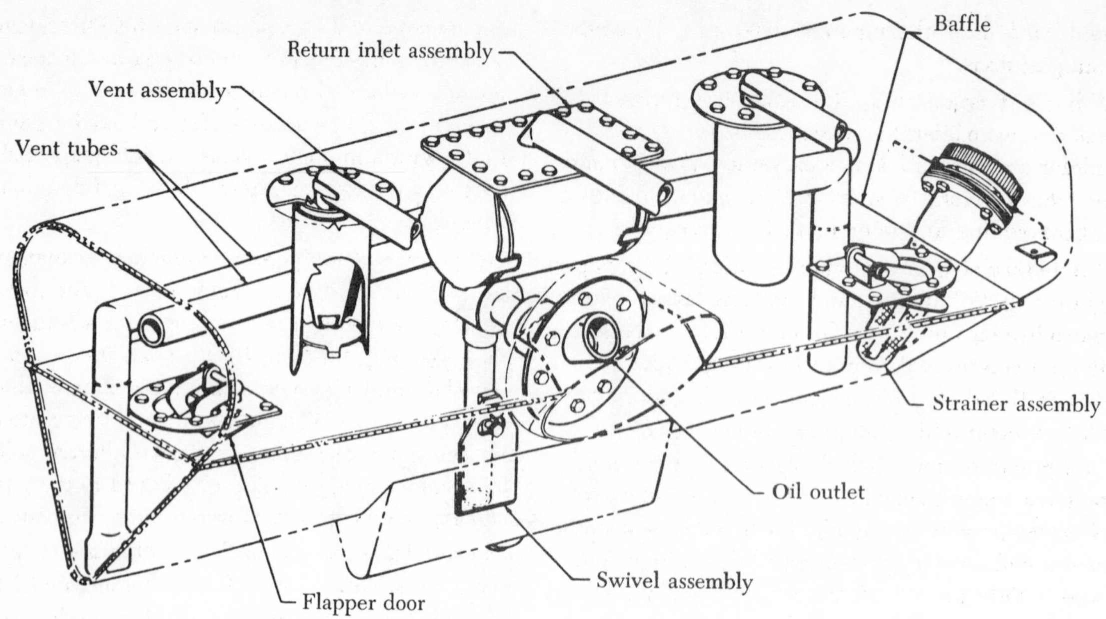

FIGURE 6–23. Oil tank.

of the tank, two flapper check valves mounted on the baffle, and a positive vent system.

The swivel outlet fitting is controlled by a weighted end, which is free to swing below the baffle. The flapper valves in the baffle are normally open; they close only when the oil in the bottom of the tank tends to rush to the top of the tank during decelerations. This traps the oil in the bottom of the tank where it is picked up by the swivel fitting. A sump drain is located in the bottom of the tank.

The vent system inside the tank (figure 6–23) is so arranged that the airspace is vented at all times even though oil may be forced to the top of the tank by deceleration of the aircraft.

All oil tanks are provided with expansion space. This allows for expansion of the oil after heat is absorbed from the bearings and gears and after the oil foams as a result of circulating through the system. Some tanks also incorporate a de-aerator tray for separating air from the oil returned to the top of the tank by the scavenger system. Usually these de-aerators are the "can" type in which oil enters at a tangent. The air released is carried out through the vent system in the top of the tank. In most oil tanks a pressure buildup is desired within the tank to assure a positive flow of oil to the oil pump inlet. This pressure buildup is made possible by running the vent line through an adjustable check relief valve. The check relief valve normally is set to relieve at about 4 p.s.i. pressure on the oil pump inlet.

Experience has shown there is little need for an oil dilution system. If the air temperature is abnormally low, the oil may be changed to a lighter grade. Some engines may provide for the installation of an immersion-type oil heater.

Oil Pump

The oil pump is designed to supply oil under pressure to the parts of the engine that require lubrication. Many oil pumps consist not only of a pressure supply element, but scavenge elements as well. However, there are some oil pumps which serve a single function; that is, they either supply or scavenge the oil. The number of pumping elements, both pressure and scavenge, will depend largely on the type and model of the engine. For instance, axial-flow engines have a long rotor shaft, which means that more bearings normally will be required for support than on a centrifugal-flow engine. Therefore, the oil pump elements for both supply and scavenge must be several in number or of larger capacity. In all types of pumps, the scavenge elements have a greater pumping capacity than the pressure element to prevent oil from collecting in the bearing sumps.

The pumps may be one of several types, each type having certain advantages and limitations. The three most common oil pumps are the gear, gerotor, and piston, the gear type being the most commonly used. Each of these pumps has several possible configurations.

The gear-type oil pump illustrated in figure 6–24 has only two elements, one for pressure oil and one for scavenging. However, some types of pumps may have several elements, two or more elements for scavenging and one or more for pressure.

A relief valve in the discharge side of the pump (figure 6–24) limits the output pressure of the pump by bypassing oil to the pump inlet when the outlet pressure exceeds a predetermined limit. Also shown is the shaft shear section, which causes the shaft to shear if the pump gears should seize.

The gerotor pump, like the gear pump, usually contains a single element for oil pressure and several elements for scavenging oil. Each of the elements, pressure and scavenge, is almost identical in shape; however, the capacity of the elements can be controlled by varying the size of the gerotor elements. For example, the pressure element may have a pumping capacity of 3.1 g.p.m. (gallon per minute) as compared to 4.25 g.p.m. capacity for the scavenge elements. Consequently, the pressure element is smaller, since the elements are all driven by a common shaft. The pressure is determined by engine r.p.m. with a minimum pressure at idling speed and maximum pressure at intermediate and maximum engine speeds.

A typical set of gerotor pumping elements is shown in figure 6–25. Each set of gerotors is separated by a steel plate, making each set an individual pumping unit consisting of an inner and an outer element. The small star-shaped inner element has external lobes that fit within and are matched with the outer element, which has internal lobes. The small element fits on and is keyed to the pump shaft and acts as a drive for the outer free-turning element. The outer element fits within a steel plate having an eccentric bore. In one engine model the oil pump has four elements, one for oil feed and three for scavenge. In some models, pumps have six elements, one for feed and five for scavenge. In

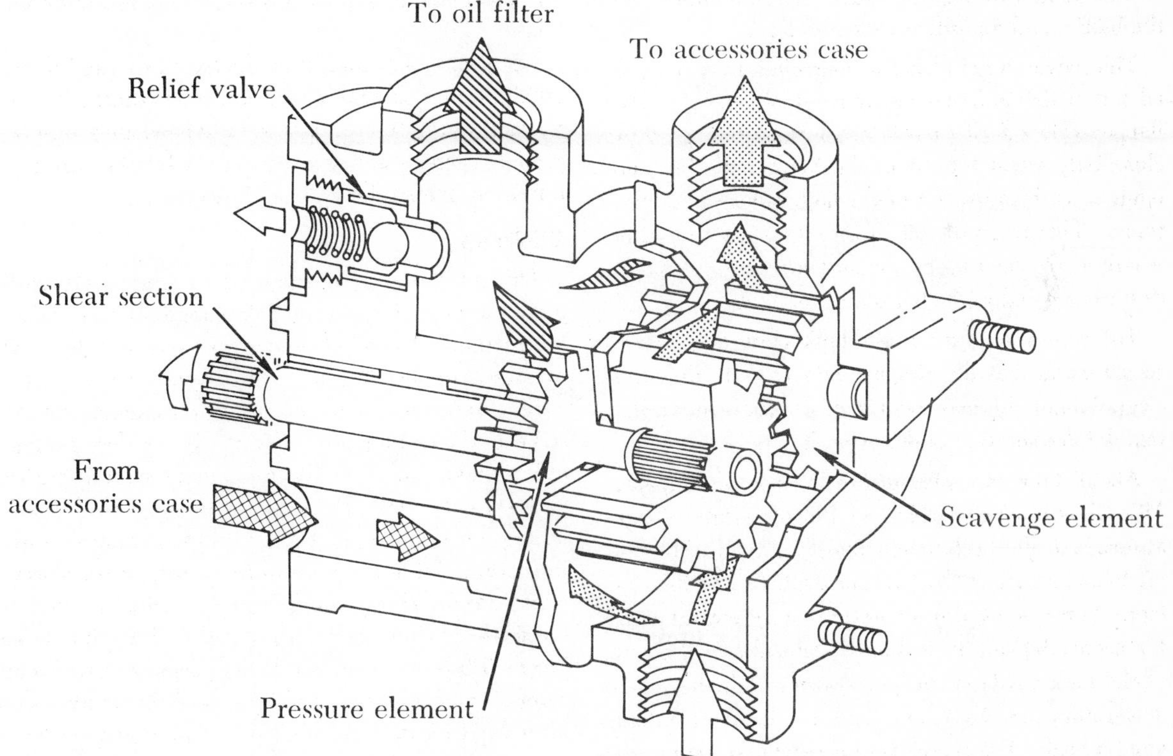

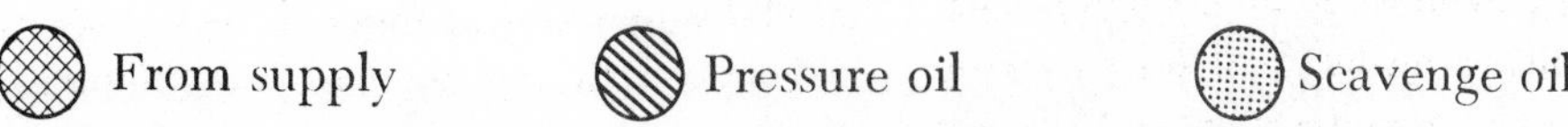

FIGURE 6–24. Cutaway view of gear oil pump.

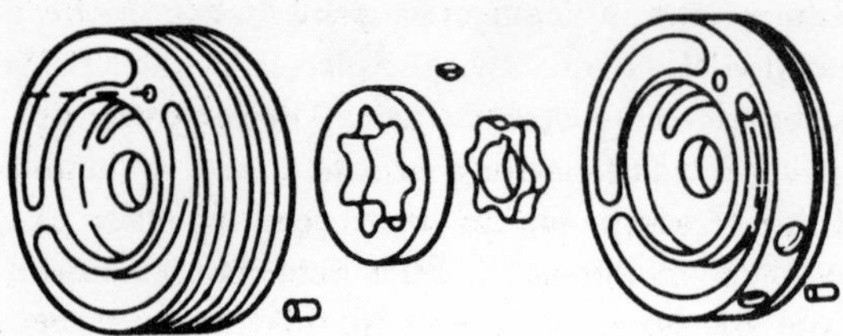

FIGURE 6–25. Typical gerotor pumping elements.

each case the oil flows as long as the engine shaft is turning.

The piston-type lubrication pump is a multi-plunger type. The output of each piston supplies a separate jet. Oil drained from the points of lubrication is scavenged by a separate pump element and returned to the reservoir. The piston-type pump is used to a lesser extent than either of the other types.

Filters

Filters are an important part of the lubrication system, since they remove foreign particles that may be in the oil. This is particularly important in gas turbines, as very high engine speeds are attained, and the antifriction types of ball and roller bearings would become damaged quite rapidly if lubricated with contaminated oil. Also, there are usually a number of drilled or core passages leading to various points of lubrication. Since these passages are usually rather small, they are easily clogged.

There are several types of filters used for filtering the lubricating oil. The filtering elements come in a variety of configurations. Since it would be impractical to include every type, only the more common filter types are discussed.

One common type of oil filter uses a replaceable laminated paper element, such as those used in hydraulic systems. In another type the filter element is made up of a series of spacers and screens, as shown in figure 6–26. This filter is made up of a stack of metal disks covered with a screen and separated by spacers so that the oil can flow through the screens and out the outlet port of the strainer body.

Another type of filter, used as a main oil strainer, is shown in figure 6–27. The filtering element interior is made of stainless steel.

Each of the oil filters mentioned has certain advantages. In each case the filter selected is the one that best meets the individual needs of a particular engine. The filters discussed generally are used as main oil filters; that is, they strain the oil as it leaves the pump before being piped to the

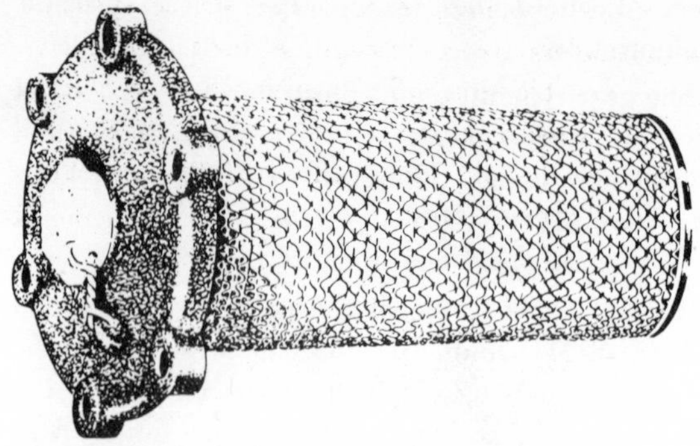

FIGURE 6–26. Spacers-and-screens oil filter.

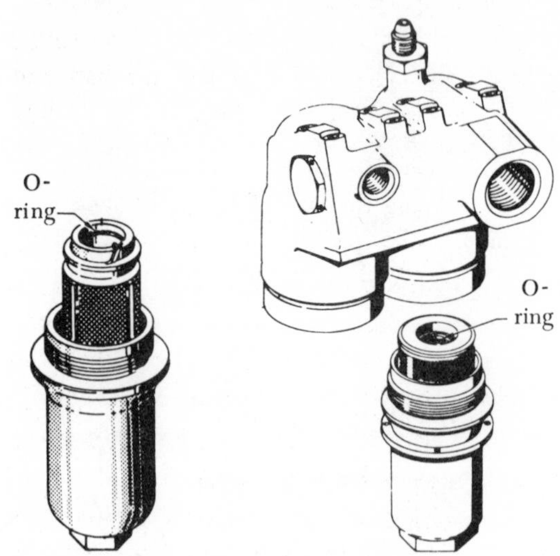

FIGURE 6–27. Filtering assembly.

various points of lubrication. In addition to the main oil filters, there are also secondary filters located throughout the system for various purposes. For instance, there may be a finger screen filter, which is sometimes used for straining scavenged oil. Also, there are fine-mesh screens, called "last chance" filters, for straining the oil just before it passes from the spray nozzles onto the bearing surfaces.

The components of a typical main oil filter include a housing, which has an integral relief (or bypass) valve and, of course, the filtering element.

The filter bypass valve prevents the oil flow from being stopped if the filter element becomes clogged. The bypass valve opens whenever a certain pressure is reached. If this occurs, the filtering action is lost, allowing unfiltered oil to be pumped to the bearings.

Oil Pressure Relief Valve

An oil pressure relief valve is included in the pressure oil line to limit the maximum pressure within the system. This valve is especially important if an oil cooler is incorporated in the system, since the coolers are easily ruptured because of their thin-wall construction. The relief valve is preset to relieve pressure and bypass the oil back to the inlet side of the oil pump whenever the pressure exceeds the preset limit.

Oil Jets

Oil jets (or nozzles) are located in the pressure lines adjacent to, or within, the bearing compartments and rotor shaft couplings. The oil from these nozzles is delivered in the form of an atomized spray. Some engines use an air-oil mist spray, which is produced by tapping high-pressure bleed-air from the compressor to the oil nozzle outlet. This method is considered adequate for ball and roller bearings; however, the solid oil spray method is considered the better of the two methods.

The oil jets are easily clogged because of the small orifice in their tips; consequently, the oil must be free of any foreign particles. If the last-chance filters in the oil jets should become clogged, bearing failure usually results, since nozzles are not accessible for cleaning except during engine overhaul. To prevent damage from clogged oil jets, main oil filters are checked frequently for contamination.

Lubrication System Gage Connections

Gage connection provisions are incorporated in the oil system for oil pressure and oil temperature. The oil pressure gage measures the pressure of the lubricant as it leaves the pump on its way to the oil jets.

Two of the most common methods of obtaining oil temperature indications are: (1) A thermocouple fitting in the oil line or (2) an oil temperature bulb inserted in the oil line.

The oil pressure gage connection is located in the pressure line between the pump and the various points of lubrication. The oil temperature gage connection usually is located in the pressure inlet to the engine.

Lubrication System Vents

Vents or breathers are lines or openings in the oil tanks or accessory cases of the various engines, depending on whether the engine has a dry- or wet-sump lubrication system.

The vent in an oil tank keeps the pressure within the tank from rising above or falling below that of the outside atmosphere. However, the vent may be routed through a check relief valve, which is preset to maintain a slight (approximately 4 p.s.i.) pressure on the oil to assure a positive flow to the oil pump inlet.

In the accessory case the vent (or breather) is a screen-protected opening, which allows accumulated air pressure within the accessory case to escape to the atmosphere. The scavenged oil carries air into the accessory case and this air must be vented; otherwise, the pressure buildup within the accessory case would stop the flow of oil draining from the bearing, thus forcing this oil past the rear bearing oil seal and into the compressor housing. Oil leakage could, of course, cause any of several results, the least of which would be the use of too much oil. A more serious result would occur if oil leakage were great enough to cause burning in the combustion area, which could cause turbine failure because of a hotspot.

The screened breathers usually are located in the front center of the accessory case to prevent oil leakage through the breather when the aircraft is in unusual flight attitudes. Some breathers may have a baffle to prevent oil leakage during flight maneuvers.

A vent which leads directly to the bearing compartment may be used in some engines. This vent equalizes pressure around the front bearing surface so that the lower pressure at the first compressor stage will not cause oil to be forced past the bearing rear oil seal into the compressor.

Lubrication System Check Valve

Check valves are sometimes installed in the oil supply lines of dry-sump oil systems to prevent reservoir oil from seeping (by gravity) through the oil pump elements and high-pressure lines into the engine after shutdown. Check valves, by stopping flow in an opposite direction, prevent accumulations of undue amounts of oil in the accessory gearbox, compressor rear housing, and combustion chamber. Such accumulations could cause excessive loading of the accessory drive gears during starts, contamination of the cabin pressurization air, or internal oil fires.

The check valves usually are the spring-loaded, ball-and-socket type, constructed for free flow of pressure oil. The pressure required to open these valves will vary, but the valves generally require from 2 to 5 p.s.i. to permit oil to flow to the bearings.

Lubrication System Thermostatic Bypass Valves

Thermostatic bypass valves are included in oil systems using an oil cooler. Although these valves may be called different names, their purpose is always to maintain proper oil temperature by varying the proportion of the total oil flow passing through the oil cooler. A cutaway view of a typical thermostatic bypass valve is shown in figure 6–28. This valve consists of a valve body, having two inlet ports and one outlet port, and a spring-loaded thermostatic element valve.

The valve is spring loaded because the pressure drop through the oil cooler could become too great because of denting or clogging of the cooler tubing. In such case, the valve will open, bypassing the oil around the cooler.

Oil Coolers

Oil coolers are used in the lubricating systems of some turbine engines to reduce the temperature of the oil to a degree suitable for recirculation through the system.

Previous discussion has disclosed that oil coolers are not required in wet-sump lubrication systems because of the use of cooling air, which is forced around the turbine wheel and turbine bearings. This cooling air, furnished by an auxiliary impeller on the rotor shaft or by bleeding off compressor air, reduces the heat that normally would be absorbed by the oil. Another factor that further reduces oil heat in wet-sump systems is that the air entering the engine first flows around the accessory case, thus cooling the oil by cooling the reservoir.

Dry-sump lubrication systems require coolers for several reasons. First, air cooling of bearings by using compressor bleed-air is not as good as forced air cooling from the auxiliary impeller because of the heat present in compressor bleed-air. Second, the axial-flow engine normally will require a greater number of bearings, which means that more heat will be transferred to the oil. Third, the air entering the axial-flow engine does not flow around the oil reservoir as it does on the wet-sump system. Consequently, the oil cooler is the only means of dissipating the oil heat.

Two basic types of oil coolers in general use are the air-cooled oil cooler and the fuel-cooled oil cooler. The fuel-cooled oil cooler acts as a fuel/oil heat exchanger in that the fuel cools the oil and the oil heats the fuel. The air-cooled oil cooler normally is installed at the forward end of the engine. It is similar in construction and operation to the air-cooled cooler used on reciprocating engines.

Fuel/Oil Heat Exchanger

The fuel/oil heat exchanger illustrated in figure 6–29 is designed to cool the hot oil and to preheat the fuel for combustion. Fuel flowing to the engine must pass through the heat exchanger; however, there is a thermostatic valve which controls the oil flow, and the oil may bypass the cooler if no cooling is needed. The fuel/oil heat exchanger consists of a series of joined tubes with an inlet and outlet port. The oil enters the inlet port, moves around the fuel tubes, and goes out the oil outlet port.

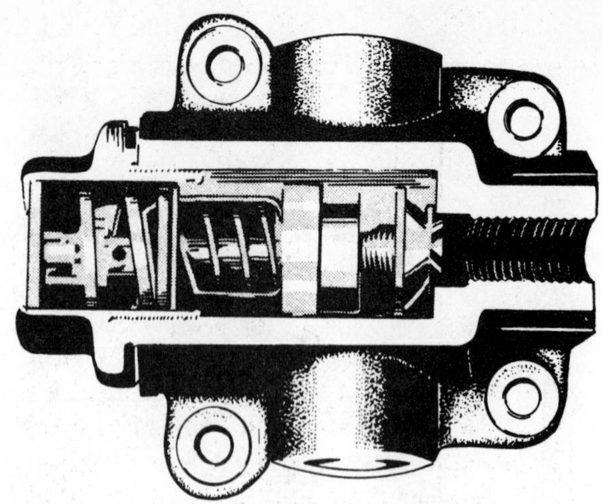

FIGURE 6–28. A typical thermostatic bypass valve.

The heat exchanger cooler has the advantage of allowing the engine to retain its small frontal area. Since the cooler is mounted on the engine, it offers little drag.

TYPICAL DRY-SUMP LUBRICATION SYSTEM

The turbojet lubrication system shown in figure 6–30 is representative of turbine engines using a dry-sump system. The lubrication system is of a self-contained, high-pressure design. It consists of the pressure, scavenge, and breather subsystems.

The pressure system supplies oil to the main engine bearings and to the accessory drives. The scavenger system returns the oil to the engine oil tank, which usually is mounted on the compressor case. It is connected to the inlet side of the pressure oil pump and completes the oil flow cycle. A breather system connecting the individual bearing compartments and the oil tank with the breather pressurizing valve completes the engine lubrication system.

Oil Pressure System Maintenance

The oil pressure branch of the engine lubrication system (figure 6–30) is pressurized by a gear-type pressure pump located in the left side of the oil pump and accessory drive housing. The pressure pump receives engine oil at its lower (inlet) side

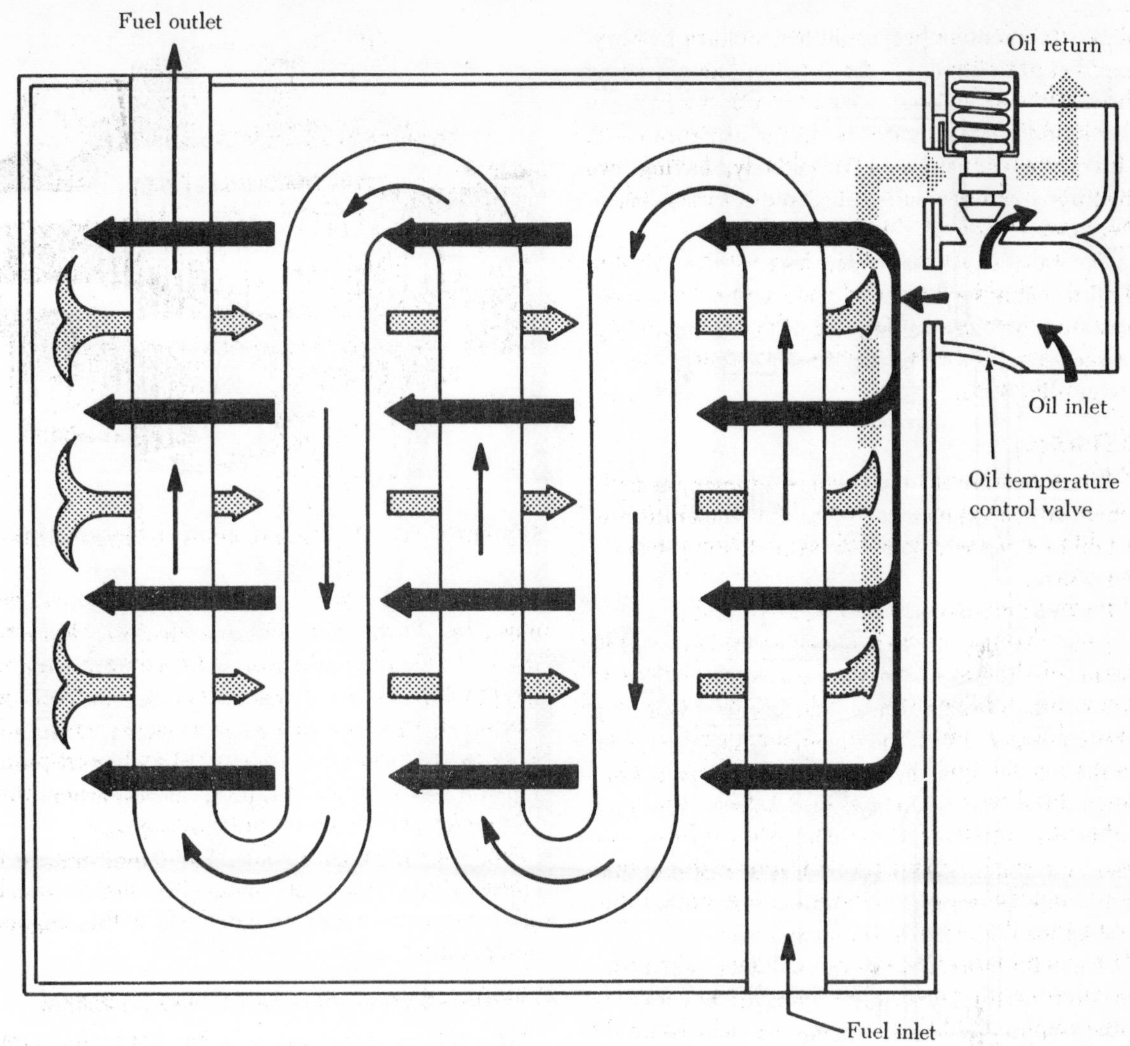

FIGURE 6–29. Fuel/oil heat exchanger cooler.

and discharges pressurized oil to an oil filter located on the housing.

From the oil filter, which is equipped with a bypass valve for operation in case the filter clogs, the pressurized oil is transmitted to a cored passage running through the bottom of the oil pump and accessory drive housing. Near the rear of the housing, this passage is intersected by two passages, one passage transmits pressurized oil to the engine rear bearings. The other passage carries pressurized oil to an axial passage leading to the compressor front bearing support for lubricating the front compressor front bearing and front accessory drive gears.

Intersecting the axial passage is another passage having a smaller bore, which carries pressure oil to the center of the oil pump and accessory drive housing. It is then transmitted into the compressor intermediate case to lubricate the front compressor rear bearing and the rear compressor front bearing. Also intersecting the upper axial passage are two passages conducting oil to the pressure oil gage and to the pressure relief valve. Pressurized oil distributed to the engine main bearings is sprayed on the bearings through fixed orifice nozzles, thus providing a relatively constant oil flow at all engine operating speeds.

The pressure relief valve is located downstream of the pump. It is adjusted to maintain a proper pressure to the oil metering jets in the engine. The pressure relief valve is easily accessible for adjustment.

Maintenance of gas turbine lubrication systems consists mainly of adjusting, removing, cleaning and replacing various components.

To adjust the oil pressure, first remove the adjust-

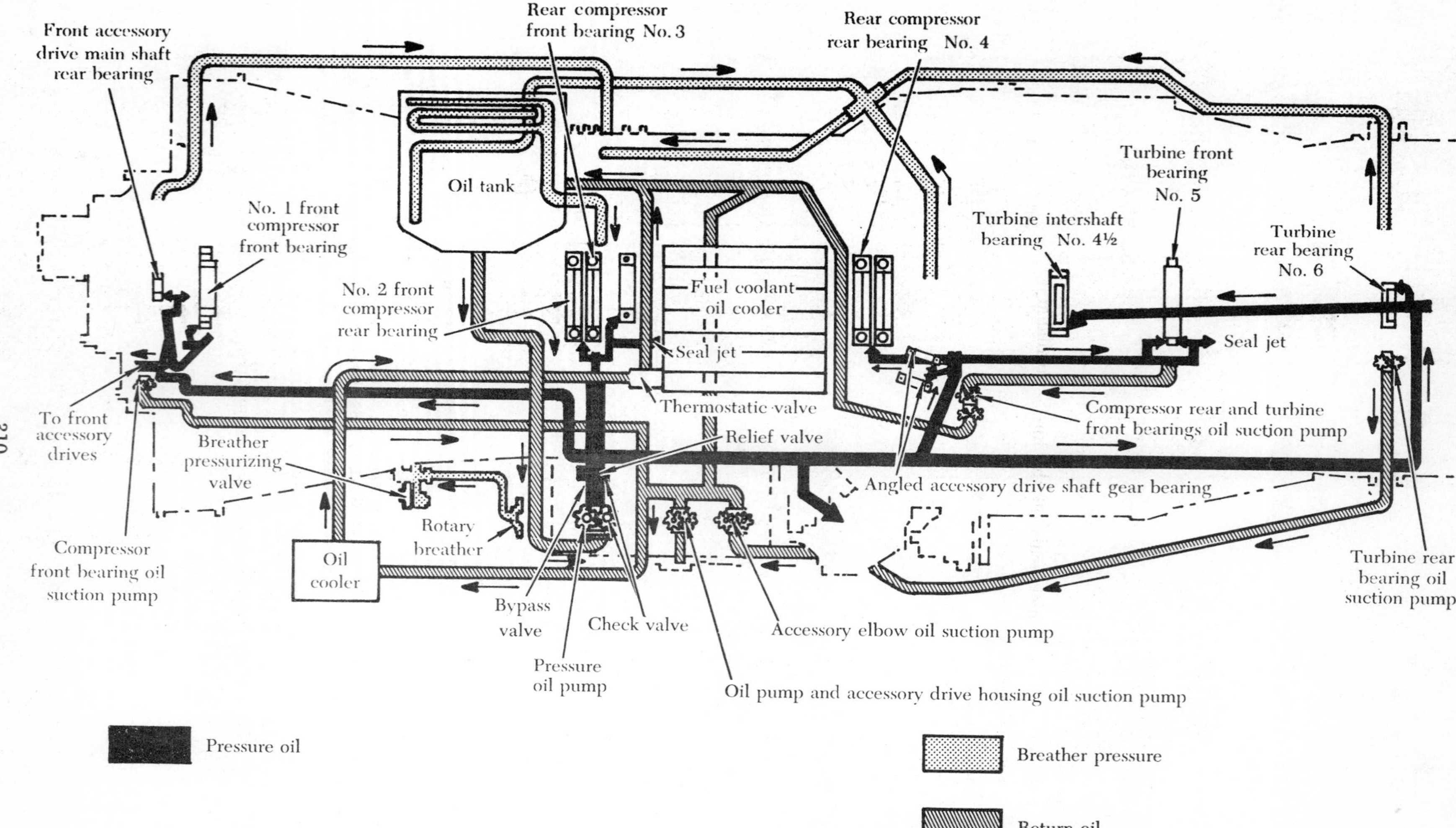
Front accessory drive main shaft rear bearing
Rear compressor front bearing No. 3
Rear compressor rear bearing No. 4
No. 1 front compressor front bearing
Oil tank
No. 2 front compressor rear bearing
Fuel coolant oil cooler
Seal jet
Turbine front bearing No. 5
Turbine intershaft bearing No. 4½
Turbine rear bearing No. 6
Seal jet
Thermostatic valve
Compressor rear and turbine front bearings oil suction pump
To front accessory drives
Relief valve
Breather pressurizing valve
Angled accessory drive shaft gear bearing
Rotary breather
Compressor front bearing oil suction pump
Oil cooler
Turbine rear bearing oil suction pump
Bypass valve
Check valve
Accessory elbow oil suction pump
Pressure oil pump
Oil pump and accessory drive housing oil suction pump
Pressure oil
Breather pressure
Return oil

FIGURE 6–30. **Typical turbine engine dry-sump lubricating system.**

ing screw acorn cap on the oil pressure relief valve. Then loosen the locknut and turn the adjusting screw clockwise to increase, or counterclockwise to decrease, the oil pressure. In a typical turbojet lubrication system, the adjusting screw is adjusted to provide an oil pressure of 45, ±5 p.s.i.g., at approximately 75% of normal rated thrust. The adjustment should be made while the engine is idling; thus, it may be necessary to perform several adjustments before the desired pressure is obtained. When the proper pressure setting is achieved, the adjusting screw locknut is tightened, and the acorn cap is installed with a new gasket, tightened, and secured with lockwire.

Oil Filter Maintenance

The oil filter should be removed at every regular inspection. It should be disassembled, cleaned, and any worn or damaged filter elements replaced. The following steps illustrate typical oil filter removal procedures:

(1) Provide a suitable container for collecting the drained oil.

(2) Remove the filter cover and withdraw the filter assembly (figure 6–31). Discard the old seal.

(3) Install the oil filter assembly in a holding fixture and remove the plug from the filter cover. The filter must be installed in a proper fixture before removing the cover plug to prevent the stacked screens and spacers from flying off under their spring tension.

(4) Carefully remove the filter cover from the fixture; then slide the screens and spacers onto a suitable cleaning rod, keeping them in their proper order. The parts should not be able to slide off the rod during the cleaning operation.

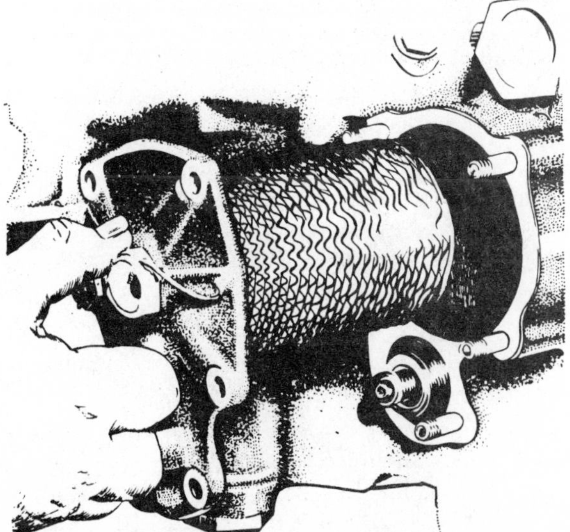

FIGURE 6–31. Removing the oil filter assembly.

(5) Separate the screens and spacers by sliding the parts along the rod. Examine the screens and spacers for foreign matter that would indicate an unsatisfactory condition in the engine.

(6) Immerse the screens and spacers in an approved carbon remover at room temperature for a few minutes. Rinse them in a degreaser fluid or cleaning solvent. Then blow them dry with an air jet.

(7) Assemble the filter spacers and screens on the baffle, using the holding fixture. Make certain that an outlet spacer will be at both ends. Also, make sure each screen is located between an outlet spacer and an inlet spacer. Install the outer end plate on the screen and spacer buildup; then install the cover on the end plate. Place a new seal on the cover plug and install the plug in the threaded end of the baffle. The plug must be tightened to the torque prescribed in the manufacturer's instructions so that the spacers and screens cannot be rotated by hand.

(8) Secure the cover plug with lockwire. Then remove the filter assembly from the holding fixture.

Scavenge System

The scavenge system scavenges the main bearing compartments and, under certain temperature conditions, circulates the scavenged oil through the oil cooler(s) and back to the tank. The scavenge oil system, illustrated in figure 6–30, includes six gear-type pumps. The compressor front bearing oil scavenge pump is driven by the front accessory drive coupling through an intermediate drive gear. It scavenges accumulated oil from the front accessory case. It directs the oil through an external line to a central collecting point in the main accessory case.

The accessory drive housing oil suction pump is driven by an intermediate drive gear. It scavenges oil accumulated from pump leakage and from the No. 2 oil compartment. The oil return from No. 2 and 3 bearings is through internal passages to a central collecting point in the main accessory case.

The accessory elbow oil suction pump, located in the main accessory case, scavenges oil from the angled accessory drive gear housing (accessory elbow housing) and returns it to the central collecting point in the main accessory case. Oil accumulates in the accessory elbow housing by gravity flow from its bushings and bearings and scavenged oil from No. 6 bearing.

The compressor rear bearing oil suction pump is located in the compartment formed by the diffuser inner duct weldment and the No. 5 bearing support, known as the No. 3 oil compartment. The pump is driven by the accessory drive shaft gear. It is secured to the inner duct weldment by an adapter. It scavenges oil from No. 4 and 4-1/2 bearings when the engine is in a level position. When the engine is in a nosedown position, the oil from No. 5 bearing will flow forward to be scavenged by the compressor rear bearing oil suction pump. This pump also directs the scavenged oil to a central collecting point in the main accessory case.

The turbine front bearing oil suction pump is located in the same housing and compartment as the compressor rear bearing oil suction pump. It is driven by the accessory drive shaft gear. It scavenges the oil from No. 5 bearing when the engine is in a level position. When the engine is in a noseup position, the oil from No. 4 and 4-1/2 bearings will flow aft to be scavenged by the turbine front bearing oil suction pump. The turbine front bearing oil suction pump also directs the scavenged oil to the central collecting point in the main accessory case.

The turbine rear bearing oil suction pump is located on the rear inner face of the turbine rear bearing sump, which is the No. 4 oil compartment. It is attached to the turbine rear bearing sump and is driven by a pinion gear. This pump scavenges the oil from the No. 6 bearing compartment and directs the scavenged oil through a passage in the turbine case strut. From there it is directed to the accessory housing where the accessory elbow oil suction pump returns it to the central collecting point in the main accessory case.

There are two controls in the scavenge system to help route the oil for proper cooling. The oil temperature regulator valve is located at the entrance to the fuel/oil heat exchanger (cooler). It operates within a range of 165° F. to full-open 185° F. It directs the flow of return oil around the fuel lines in the cooler (until the valve opens, oil will bypass the cooler). The fuel temperature sensing switch is located in the fuel outlet line of the fuel/oil heat exchanger. It operates within a range of 200° F. to 205° F. to actuate the doors in the air-cooled oil cooler, which will allow air to pass through to cool the oil that is flowing through the cooler at all times.

Maintenance at all regular inspections includes the check for oil leaks and security of mounting of scavenging system components.

Breather Pressurizing System

The breather pressurizing system ensures a proper oil spray pattern from the main bearing oil jets and furnishes a pressure head to the scavenge system. Breather tubes in the compressor inlet case, the oil tank, the diffuser case, and the turbine exhaust case are connected to external tubing at the top of the engine. By means of this tubing, the vapor-laden atmospheres of the various bearing compartments and the oil tank are brought together in the compressor intermediate case annulus. The bearing compartment shared by the front compressor rear bearing and the rear compressor front bearing is also vented (through hollow vanes) to the compressor intermediate case annulus. From the annulus the vapors enter the main accessory case, which is mounted at the bottom of the compressor intermediate case.

The breather pressurizing valve (figure 6–32) consists of an aneroid-operated (spring and bellows) valve and a spring-loaded blowoff valve. Pressurization is provided by compressor air which leaks by the seals and enters the oil system.

At sea level pressure the breather pressurizing valve is open. It closes gradually with increasing altitude and maintains an oil system pressure sufficient to assure jet oil flows similar to those at sea level. The spring-loaded blowoff valve acts as a pressure relief for the entire breather system. It will open only if pressure above a predetermined maximum value builds up in the system.

A pressure-equalizing valve limits the pressure supplied to the carbon air/oil seal. This aids in preventing overpressurizing in all compartments of the breather system. Air under pressure of up to 54 p.s.i.g. is directed to the pressure equalizing valve. All pressure greater than the 24, ±2 p.s.i.g., preset value of the pressure equalizing valve is spilled into the intermediate case.

The rotary breather (air/oil separator) removes oil from the air by centrifugal action. Its purpose is to reduce the air pressure across the carbon seal. The air from the ninth compressor stage, regardless of the pressure, is directed over the

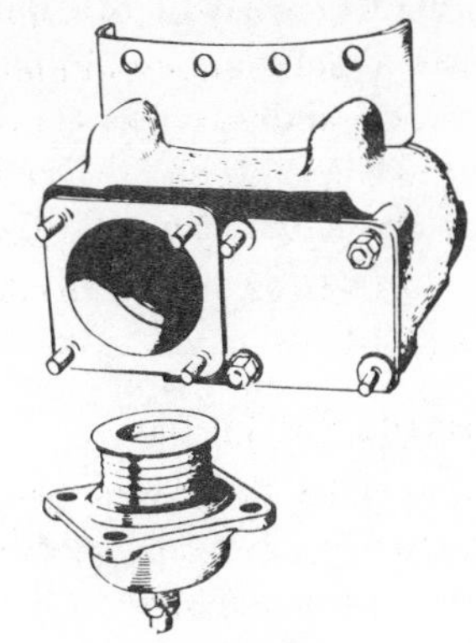

(A) Breather pressurizing valve

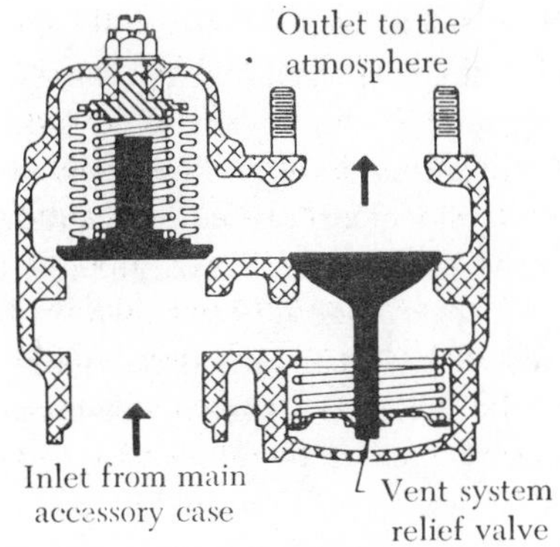

(B) Sectional view of breather pressurizing valve

FIGURE 6–32. Breather pressurizing valve.

forward segment of the carbon seal. The air across the rear carbon seal prevents oil from the No. 2 bearing from entering the airstream. This air is spilled into the intermediate case breather annulus. The air over 25 p.s.i.g. that is directed through the pressure-equalizing valve is also directed to the breather pressurizing valve.

Turbine Engine Wet-Sump Lubrication System

In some engines the lubrication system is of the wet-sump type. There are relatively few engines using a wet-sump type of oil system, because only a few models of centrifugal-flow engines are in operation. A schematic diagram of a wet-sump oil system is shown in figure 6–33.

The components of a wet-sump system are similar to many of those of a dry-sump system. The major difference between the two systems is the location of the oil reservoir.

The reservoir for the wet-sump oil system may be either the accessory gearcase, which consists of the accessory gear casing and the front compressor bearing support casing (figure 6–33), or it may be a sump mounted on the bottom of the accessory case. Regardless of configuration, reservoirs for wet-sump systems are an integral part of the engine and contain the bulk of the engine oil supply.

Included in the wet-sump reservoir shown in figure 6–33 are the following components:

(1) A bayonet-type gage indicates the oil level in the sump.

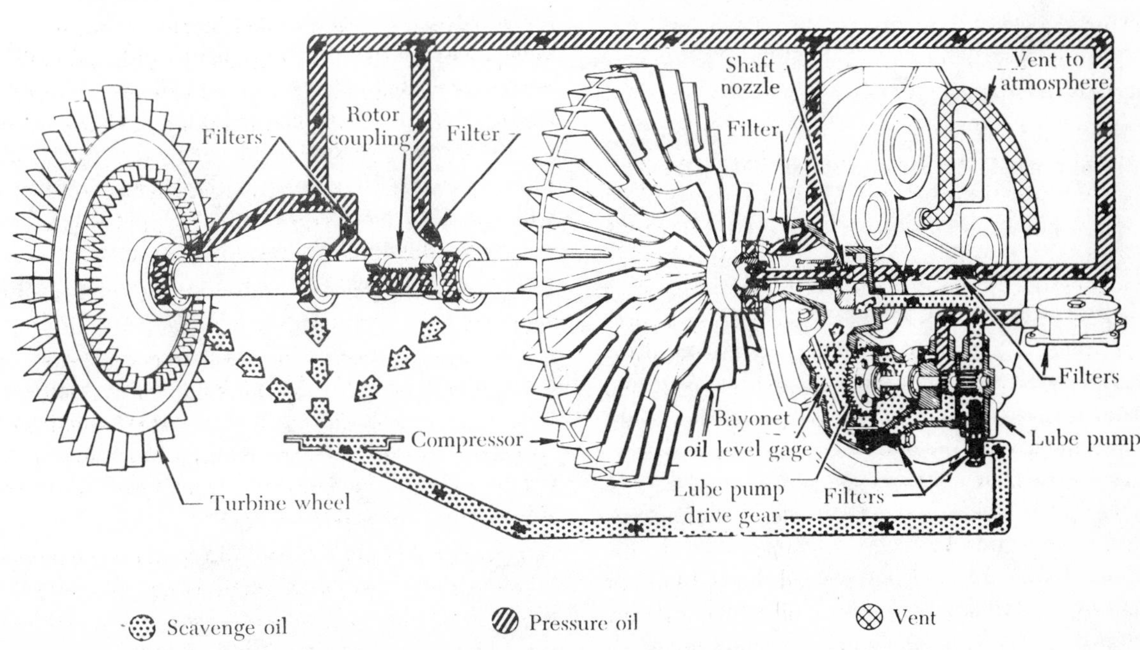

FIGURE 6–33. Turbojet engine wet-sump lubrication system.

(2) Two or more finger strainers (filters) are inserted in the accessory case for straining pressure and scavenged oil just before it leaves or enters the sump. These strainers aid the main oil strainer.

(3) A vent or breather equalizes pressure within the accessory casing.

(4) A magnetic drain plug may be provided to drain the oil and also to trap any ferrous metal particles in the oil. This plug should always be examined closely during inspections. The presence of metal particles may indicate gear or bearing failure.

(5) Provision may also be made for a temperature bulb and an oil pressure fitting.

This system is typical of all engines using a wet-sump lubrication system. The bearing and drive gears in the accessory drive casing are lubricated by a splash system. The oil for the remaining points of lubrication leaves the pump under pressure and passes through a filter to jet nozzles that direct the oil into the rotor bearings and couplings. Most wet-sump pressure systems are variable-pressure systems in which the pump outlet pressure depends on the engine r.p.m.

The scavenged oil is returned to the reservoir (sump) by gravity and by pump suction. Oil from the front compressor bearing and the accessories drive coupling shaft drains directly into the reservoir. Oil from the turbine coupling and the remaining rotor shaft bearings drains into a sump from which the oil is pumped by the scavenge element through a finger screen into the reservoir.

ENGINE COOLING SYSTEMS

Excessive heat is always undesirable in both reciprocating and turbine aircraft engines. If means were not available for its control or elimination, major damage or complete engine failure would occur.

Reciprocating Engine Cooling Systems

An internal-combustion engine is a heat machine that converts chemical energy in the fuel into mechanical energy at the crankshaft. It does not do this without some loss of energy, however, and even the most efficient aircraft engines may waste 60 to 70% of the original energy in the fuel. Unless most of this waste heat is rapidly removed, the cylinders may become hot enough to cause complete engine failure.

Excessive heat is undesirable in any internal-combustion engine for three principal reasons:

(1) It affects the behavior of the combustion of the fuel/air charge.

(2) It weakens and shortens the life of engine parts.

(3) It impairs lubrication. If the temperature inside the engine cylinder is too great, the fuel/air mixture will be preheated, and combustion will occur before the desired time. Since premature combustion causes detonation, knocking, and other undesirable conditions, there must be a way to eliminate heat before it causes damage.

One gallon of aviation gasoline has enough heat value to boil 75 gallons of water; thus, it is easy to see that an engine which burns 4 gallons of fuel per minute releases a tremendous amount of heat. About one-fourth of the heat released is changed into useful power. The remainder of the heat must be dissipated so that it will not be destructive to the engine. In a typical aircraft powerplant, half of the heat goes out with the exhaust, and the other is absorbed by the engine. Circulating oil picks up part of this soaked-in heat and transfers it to the airstream through the oil cooler. The engine cooling system takes care of the rest.

Cooling is a matter of transferring the excess heat from the cylinders to the air, but there is more to such a job than just placing the cylinders in the airstream.

A cylinder on a large engine is roughly the size of a gallon jug. Its outer surface, however, is increased by the use of cooling fins so that it presents a barrel-sized exterior to the cooling air. Such an arrangement increases the heat transfer by radiation. If too much of the cooling fin area is broken off, the cylinder cannot cool properly and a hotspot will develop. Therefore, cylinders are normally replaced when a specified number of square inches of fins are missing.

Cowling and baffles are designed to force air over the cylinder cooling fins (figure 6–34). The baffles

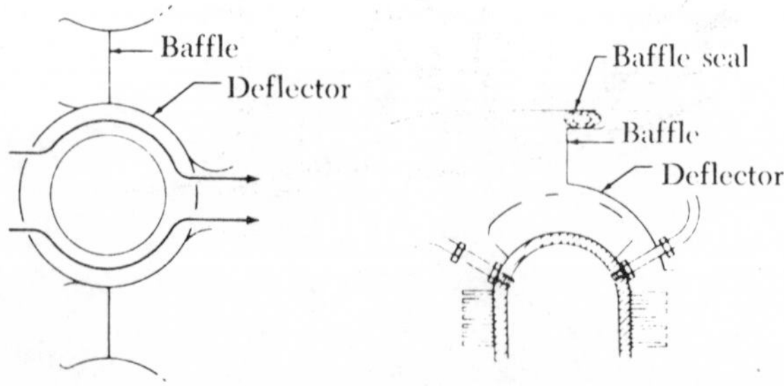

FIGURE 6–34. Heat dissipation.

direct the air close around the cylinders and prevent it from forming hot pools of stagnant air while the main streams rush by unused. Blast tubes are built into the baffles to direct jets of cooling air onto the rear spark plug elbows of each cylinder to prevent overheating of ignition leads.

An engine can have an operating temperature that is too low. For the same reasons that an engine is warmed up before takeoff, it is kept warm during flight. Fuel evaporation and distribution and oil circulation depend on an engine being kept warm. The automobile engine depends on a thermostatic valve in the water system to keep the engine in its most efficient temperature range. The aircraft engine, too, has temperature controls. These controls regulate air circulation over the engine. Unless some controls are provided, the engine will overheat on takeoff and get too cold in high-speed and low-power letdowns.

The most common means of controlling cooling is the use of cowl flaps, as illustrated in figure 6–35.

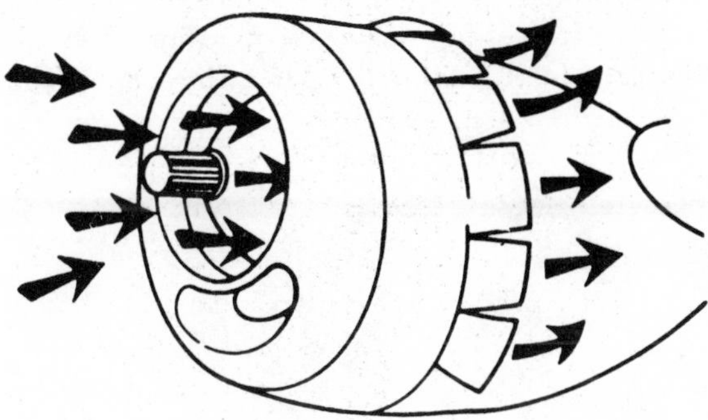

FIGURE 6–35. Regulating the cooling airflow.

These flaps are opened and closed by electric-motor-driven jackscrews, by hydraulic actuators, or manually in some light aircraft. When extended for increased cooling, the cowl flaps produce drag and sacrifice streamlining for the added cooling. On takeoff, the cowl flaps are opened only enough to keep the engine below the red-line temperature. Heating above the normal range is allowed so that drag will be as low as possible. During ground operations, the cowl flaps should be opened wide since drag does not matter.

Some aircraft use augmentors (figure 6–36) to provide additional cooling airflow. Each nacelle has two pairs of tubes running from the engine compartment to the rear of the nacelle. The exhaust collectors feed exhaust gas into the inner augmentor tubes. The exhaust gas mixes with air that has passed over the engine and heats it to form a high-temperature, low-pressure, jetlike exhaust. This low-pressure area in the augmentors draws additional cooling air over the engine. Air entering the outer shells of the augmentors is heated through contact with the augmentor tubes but is not contaminated with exhaust gases. The heated air from the shell goes to the cabin heating, defrosting, and anti-icing system.

Augmentors use exhaust gas velocity to cause an airflow over the engine so that cooling is not entirely dependent on the prop wash. Vanes installed in the augmentors control the volume of air. These vanes usually are left in the trail position to permit maximum flow. They can be closed to increase the heat for cabin or anti-icing use or to prevent the

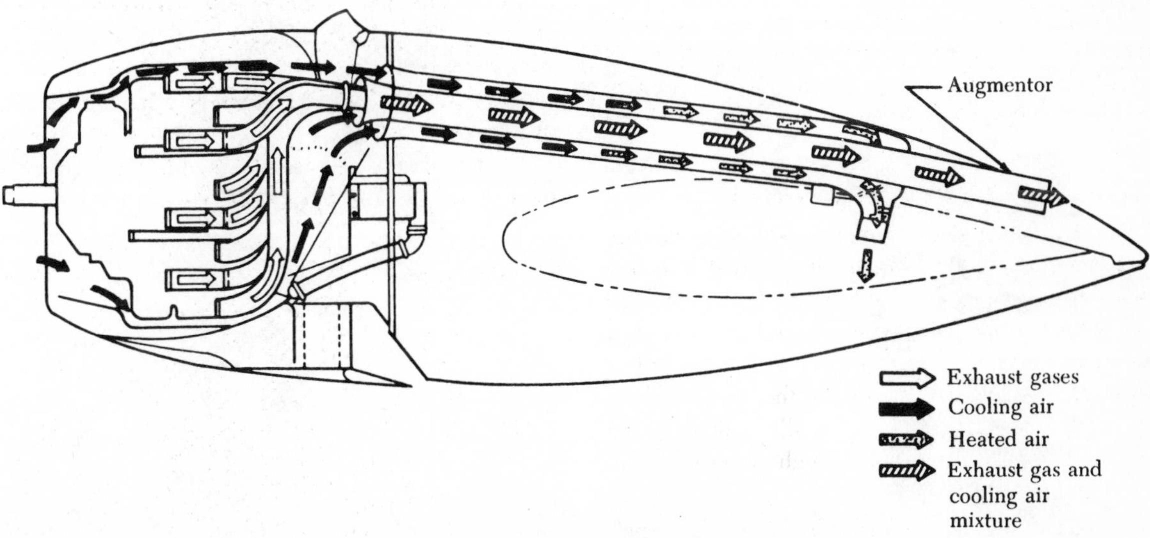

FIGURE 6–36. Augmentor.

engine from cooling too much during descent from altitude. In addition to augmentors, some aircraft have residual heat doors or nacelle flaps that are used mainly to let the retained heat escape after engine shutdown. The nacelle flaps can be opened for more cooling than that provided by the augmentors.

A modified form of the previously described augmentor cooling system is used on some light aircraft. Figure 6–37 is an outline diagram of such a system.

As shown in figure 6–37, the engine is pressure-cooled by air taken in through two openings in the nose cowling, one on each side of the propeller spinner. A pressure chamber is sealed off on the top side of the engine with baffles properly directing the flow of cooling air to all parts of the engine compartment. Warm air is drawn from the lower part of the engine compartment by the pumping action of the exhaust gases through the exhaust ejectors. This type of cooling system eliminates the use of controllable cowl flaps and assures adequate engine cooling at all operating speeds.

Many light aircraft use only one or two engine cowl flaps to control engine temperature. As shown in figure 6–38, two cowl flaps, operated by a single control in the cabin, are located at the lower aft end of the engine nacelle. Cutouts in the flaps permit extension of engine exhaust stacks through the nacelle. The flaps are operated by a manual control in the cockpit to control the flow of air directed by baffles around the cylinders and other engine components.

Some small aircraft that have horizontally opposed engines use this type of cowling. The cowl flaps are controlled by an electrically operated gill-type flap on the trailing edge of each cowling.

Reciprocating Engine Cooling System Maintenance

The engine cooling system of most reciprocating engines usually consists of the engine cowling, cylinder baffles, cylinder fins, and some type of cowl flaps. In addition to these major units, there is also some type of temperature-indicating system (cylinder head temperature).

The cowling performs two functions: (1) It streamlines the bulky engine to reduce drag, and

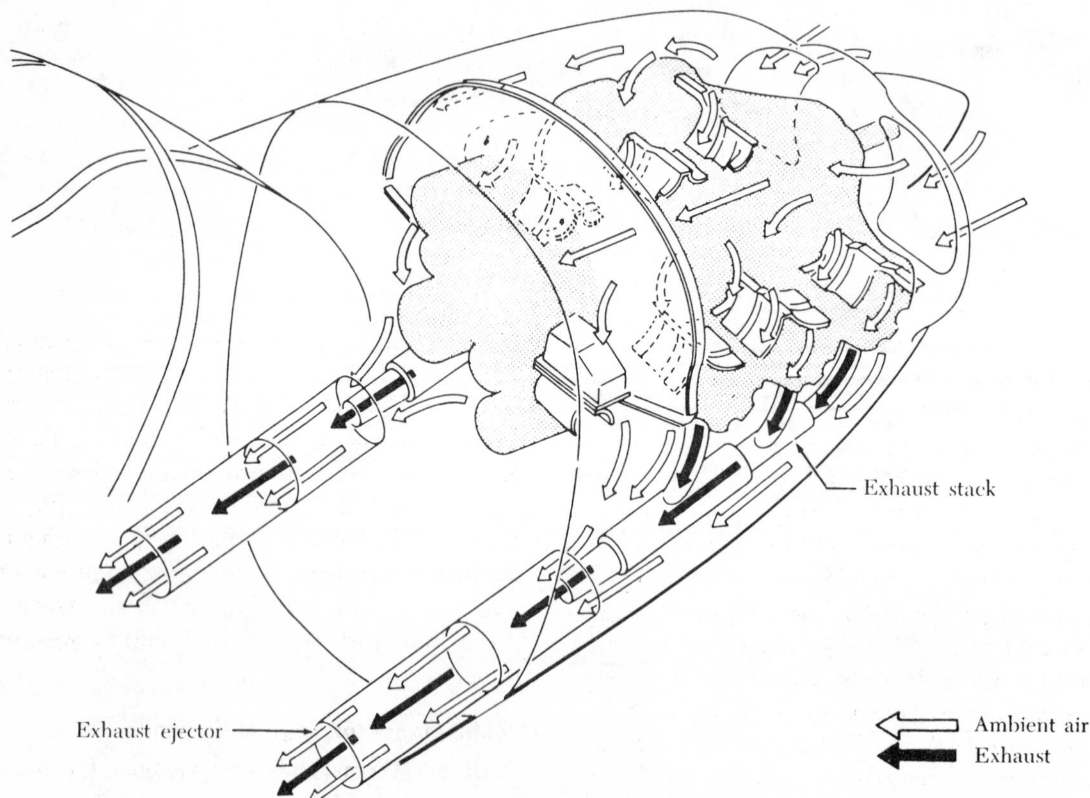

FIGURE 6–37. Engine cooling and exhaust system.

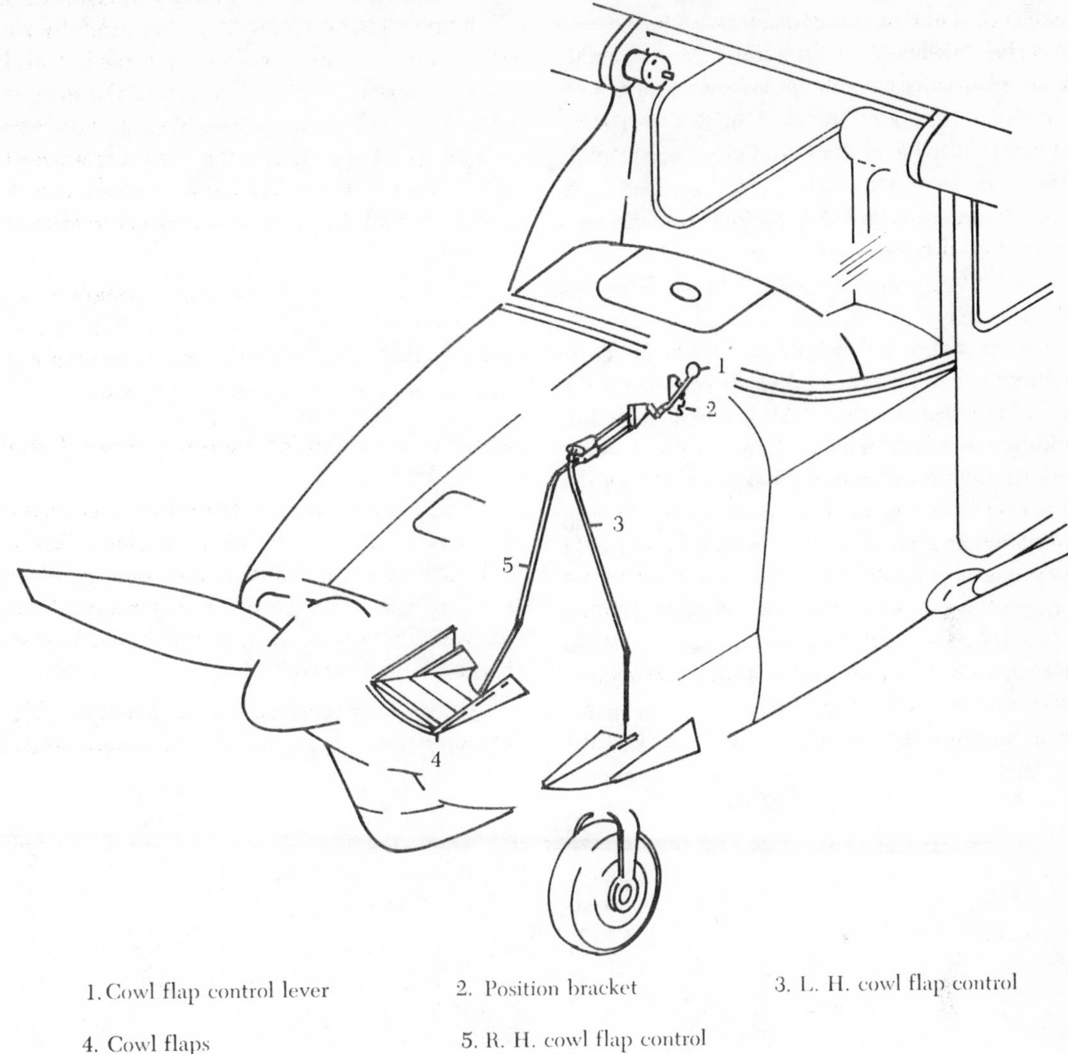

FIGURE 6–38. Small aircraft cowl flaps.

(2) it forms an envelope around the engine which forces air to pass around and between the cylinders, absorbing the heat dissipated by the cylinder fins.

The cylinder baffles are metal shields, designed and arranged to direct the flow of air evenly around all cylinders. This even distribution of air aids in preventing one or more cylinders from being excessively hotter than the rest.

The cylinder fins radiate heat from the cylinder walls and heads. As the air passes over the fins, it absorbs this heat, carries it away from the cylinder, and is exhausted overboard through the cowl flaps.

The controllable cowl flaps provide a means of decreasing or increasing the exit area at the rear of the engine cowling. Closing the cowl flaps decreases the exit area, which effectively decreases the amount of air that can circulate over the cylinder fins. The decreased airflow cannot carry away as much heat; therefore, there is a tendency for the engine temperature to increase. Opening the cowl flaps makes the exit area larger. The flow of cooling air over the cylinders increases, absorbing more heat, and the tendency is then for the engine temperature to decrease. Good inspection and maintenance in the care of the engine cooling system will aid in overall efficient and economical engine operation.

Maintenance of Engine Cowling

Of the total ram airflow approaching the airborne engine nacelle, only about 15 to 30% enters the cowling to provide engine cooling. The remaining air flows over the outside of the cowling. Therefore, the external shape of the cowl must be faired in a manner that will permit the air to flow smoothly over the cowl with a minimum loss of energy.

The engine cowling discussed in this section is typical of that used on many radial or horizontally opposed engines. All cooling systems function in the same manner, with minor engineering changes designed for specific installations.

The ring cowl is manufactured in removable sections, the number of which varies with the aircraft make and model. The installation shown in figure 6–39 contains three sections that are locked together, when installed, by the toggle latches (item A). In addition to this toggle latching system, safety locks (item B) are installed on each section of the ring cowl. These safety locks prevent the cowling from coming apart if the toggle latch does not hold for any reason.

The ring cowl panels, made from sheet aluminum, have a smooth external surface to permit undisturbed airflow over the cowl. The internal construction is designed to give strength to the panel and, in addition, to provide receptacles for the toggle latches, cowl support ring track, and engine air seal. Figure 6–40 shows the internal construction of a ring cowl panel. A cowl support ring track riveted to the panel fits over the cowl support ring to position the cowling fore and aft. A locating pin in the center of the track fits through a hole in the cowl support ring. This establishes the correct position for installing each panel around the cowl support ring. Ribs run across the cowl panel between the toggle latch mechanism receptacles on each side of the panel to strengthen the panel.

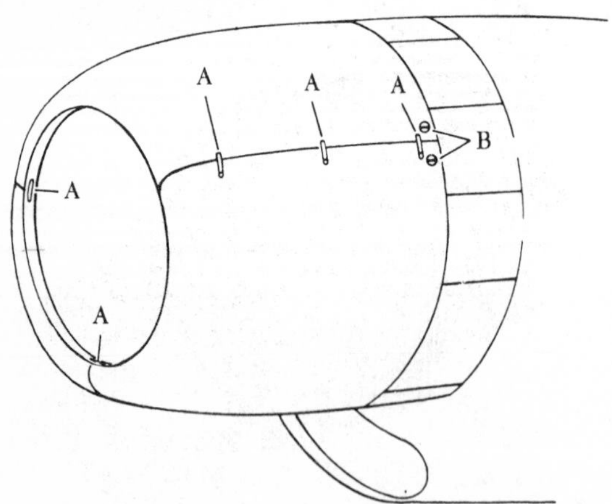

A. Toggle latches B. Safety locks

FIGURE 6–39. Ring cowl panel assembly.

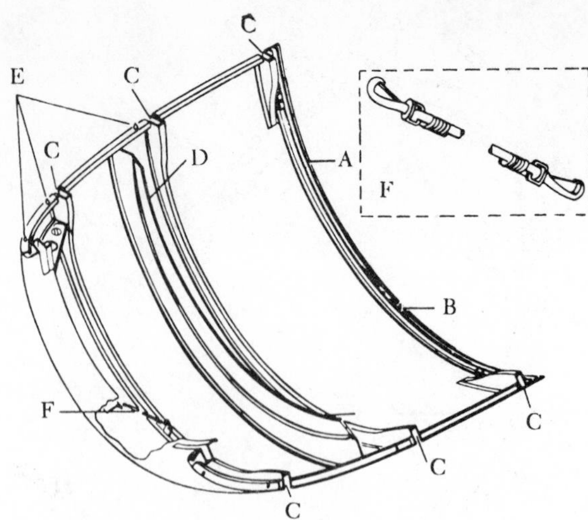

A. Cowl support ring track
B. Locator pin
C. Toggle latch mechanism receptacle
D. Engine air seal
E. Ring cowl positioning pin
F. Bungee support cord

FIGURE 6–40. Ring cowl panel construction.

An air seal (figure 6–40), constructed of rubber material, is bolted to a metal rib riveted to the cowl panel. This seal, as the name implies, seals the air in the engine section, preventing the air from escaping along the inner surface of the panel without circulating around the cylinders. The engine air seal must be used on engines that have a complete cylinder baffling system that covers the cylinder heads. Its purpose is to force the air to circulate around and through the baffle system. The air seal is not used on aircraft engines that have only the intercylinder baffles and do not enclose the cylinder heads.

The cowl support ring is attached rigidly to the engine mounting ring to provide a sturdy support for the cowl panels and also for the attachment of the cowl flaps. The support ring usually comes in two pieces connected together to form the ring. Figure 6–41 illustrates a typical support ring.

INSPECTION OF COWLING

The support ring and cowl panels are inspected during each regular engine and aircraft inspection. Removing the cowling for maintenance provides an opportunity for more frequent inspection of the cowling.

The cowling panels are inspected for scratches, dents, and tears in the panels. This type of damage causes weakness of the panel structure, increases

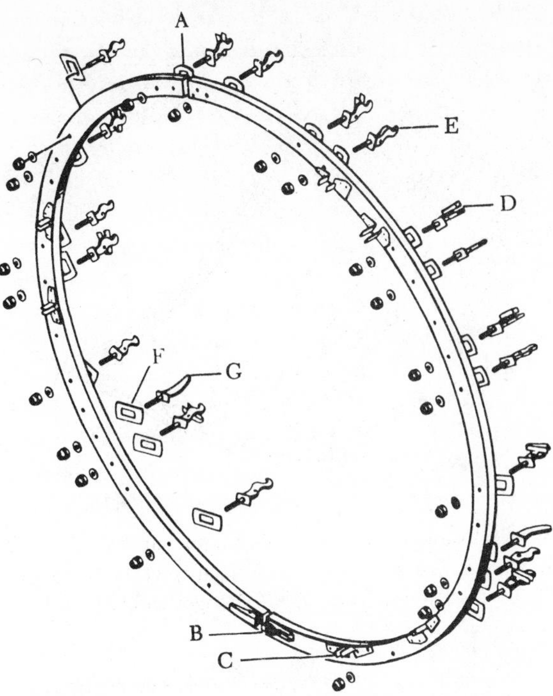

A. Top ring half flexible connection
B. Adjustable ring half connection
C. Locking angles
D. Cowl flap hinge terminal (bonding clip)
E. Cowl flap hinge terminal
F. Cowl flap hinge locking plate
G. Cowl flap hinge track

FIGURE 6–41. Cowl support ring.

drag by disrupting airflow, and contributes to the starting of corrosion.

The cowling panel latches should be inspected for pulled rivets and loose or damaged handles. The safety locks should be checked for damaged rivets and the condition of the compression spring. The hole through which the safety lock passes should be checked to determine that it is not worn or cracked. These conditions, if serious, necessitate replacing or repairing the panel.

The internal construction of the panel should be examined to see that the reinforcing ribs are not cracked and that the air seal is not damaged.

The support ring should be inspected for security of mounting and cracks. The cowl flap hinges and cowl flap hinge bondings should be checked for security of mounting and for breaks or cracks. These inspections are visual checks and should be performed frequently to ensure that the cowling is serviceable and is contributing to efficient engine cooling.

ENGINE CYLINDER COOLING FIN INSPECTION

The cooling fins are of the utmost importance to the cooling system, since they provide a means of transferring the cylinder heat to the air. Their condition can mean the difference between adequate or inadequate cylinder cooling. The fins are inspected at each regular inspection.

Fin area is the total area (both sides of the fin) exposed to the air. During the inspection, the fins should be examined for cracks and breaks (figure 6–42). Small cracks are not a reason for cylinder removal. These cracks can be filed or even sometimes stop-drilled to prevent any further cracking. Rough or sharp corners on fins can be smoothed out by filing, and this action will eliminate a possible source of new cracks. However, before re-profiling cylinder cooling fins, consult the manufacturer's service or overhaul manual for the allowable limits.

The definition of fin area becomes important in the examination of fins for broken areas. It is a determining factor for cylinder acceptance or removal. For example, on a certain engine, if more than 12 in. in length of any one fin, as measured at its base, is completely broken off, or if the total fins broken on any one cylinder head exceed 83 sq. in. of area, the cylinder is removed and replaced. The reason for removal in this case is that an area of that size would cause a hot spot on the cylinder, since very little heat transfer could occur.

Where adjacent fins are broken in the same area the total length of breakage permissible is 6 in. on any two adjacent fins, 4 in. on any three adjacent fins, 2 in. on any four adjacent fins, and 1 in. on any five adjacent fins. If the breakage length in adjacent fins exceeds this prescribed amount, the

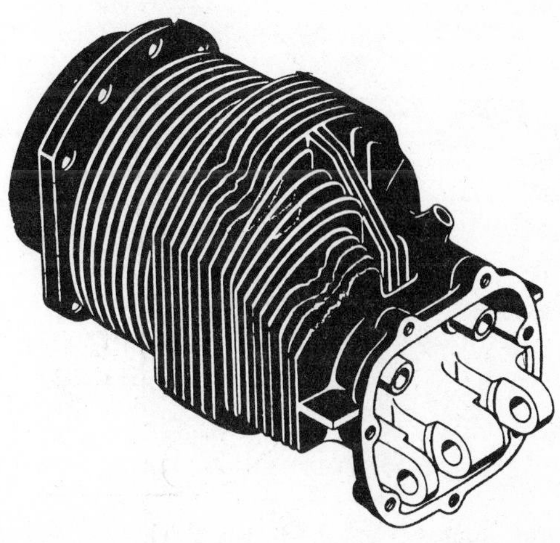

FIGURE 6–42. Cracked cylinder fins.

cylinder should be removed and replaced. These breakage specifications are applicable only to the engine used in this discussion as a typical example. In each specific case, applicable manufacturer's instructions should be consulted.

Cylinder Baffle and Deflector System Inspection

Reciprocating engines use some type of intercylinder and cylinder head baffles to force the cooling air into close contact with all parts of the cylinders. Figure 6–43 shows a baffle and deflector system around a cylinder. The air baffle blocks the flow of air and forces it to circulate between the cylinder and the deflectors.

Figure 6–44 illustrates a baffle and deflector arrangement designed to cool the cylinder head. The air baffle prevents the air from passing away from the cylinder head and forces it to go between the head and deflector.

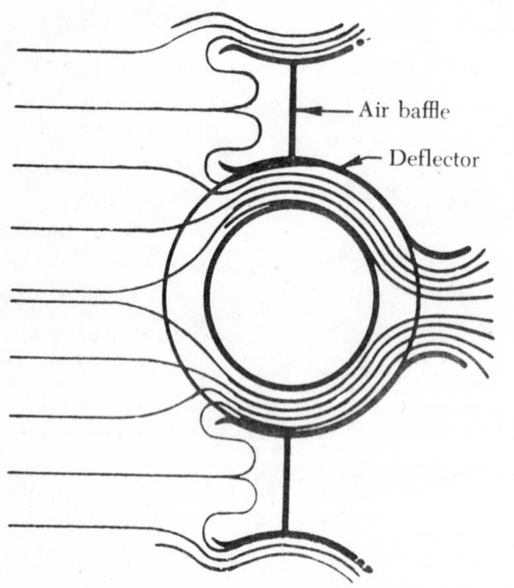

FIGURE 6–43. Cylinder baffle and deflector system.

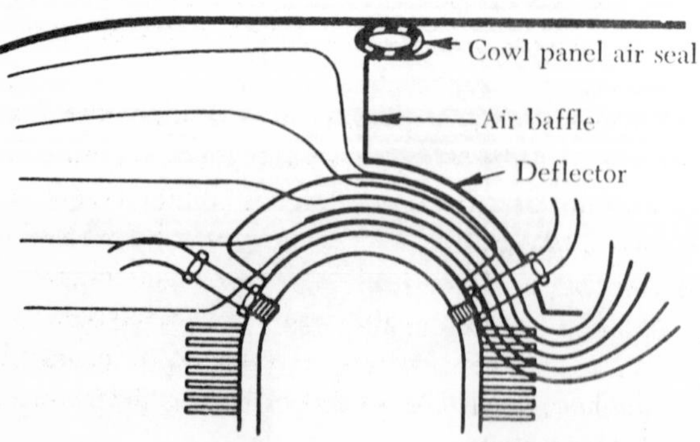

FIGURE 6–44. Cylinder head baffle and deflector system.

Although the resistance offered by baffles to the passage of the cooling air demands that an appreciable pressure differential be maintained across the engine to obtain the necessary airflow, the volume of cooling air required is greatly reduced by employing properly designed and located cylinder deflectors. As shown in figure 6–45, the airflow approaches the nacelle and piles up at the face of the engine, creating a high pressure in front of the cylinders. This piling up of the air reduces the air velocity. The cowl flaps, of course, produce the low-pressure area. As the air nears the cowl flap exit, it is speeded up again and merges smoothly with the airstream. The pressure differential between the front and the rear of the engine forces the air past the cylinders through the passages formed by the deflectors.

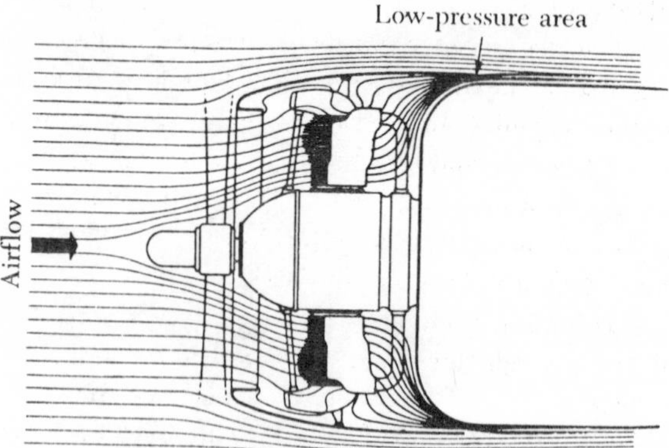

FIGURE 6–45. Engine airflow.

The baffles and deflectors normally are inspected during the regular engine inspection, but they should be checked whenever the cowling is removed for any purpose. Checks should be made for cracks, dents, or loose holddown studs. Cracks or dents, if severe enough, would necessitate repair or removal and replacement of these units. However, a crack that has just started can be stop-drilled, and dents can be straightened, permitting further service from these baffles and deflectors.

Cowl Flap Installation and Adjustment

During cowl flap installation, adjustments are made to assure the correct "open and close" tolerances of the cowl flaps. This tolerance is of the utmost importance. If the cowl flap is permitted to open too far, the air exiting from the engine section is increased in velocity, thus permitting too great a cooling of the cylinders. Also, if the cowl flaps are not adjusted to open the desired amount, the cylinder head temperature will be higher than allowable limits under certain operating conditions. For each engine installation the cowl flaps are set for tolerances that will permit them to open and close a correct amount, keeping the cylinder head temperature within allowable limits.

It is important to install the cowl flaps correctly, adjust the jackscrews, adjust the "open and close" limit switches, and inspect the system.

The installation used in this example of a typical large reciprocating engine has nine cowl flaps. The flaps are numbered clockwise (looking from the rear toward the front of the engine), starting with the No. 1 flap and continuing through the No. 9 flap. The Nos. 1 and 9 flaps (figure 6–46) are stationary and 2 through 8 are movable flaps. The flaps are hinged near their forward end to the cowl support ring and connected near the aft end of the cowl flap jackscrews.

There are seven cowl flap jackscrews interconnected by a flexible drive shaft. This type of connection permits all movable cowl flaps to move simultaneously and evenly when the cowl flap actuating motor is energized. The stationary flaps (1 and 9) are fastened by turnbuckles, one for the No. 1 flap, and two for No. 9 flap.

The following checks and inspections are typical of those made to maintain an efficient cowl flap system:

(1) Check the cowl flaps for response by actuating the cockpit control from the "open" to the "closed," and back to the "open" position. The flaps should respond rapidly and smoothly. If a cowl flap indicator is installed, observe the indications received for synchronization with the flaps in the "open" and "closed" positions.

(2) With the cowl flaps open, check for cracks, distortion, or security of mounting. Grasp the flap at the trailing edge, shake laterally and up and down to determine the condition of the bushings, bearings, or the turnbuckles. Looseness of the flaps during this check indicates worn bushings or bearings that should be replaced. Inspect the hinges and hinge terminals for wear, breaks, or cracks; check the hinges for security of mounting on the cowl support ring.

(3) Measure the "open" and "closed" positions of the cowl flaps to check for specified tolerances and adjust as necessary.

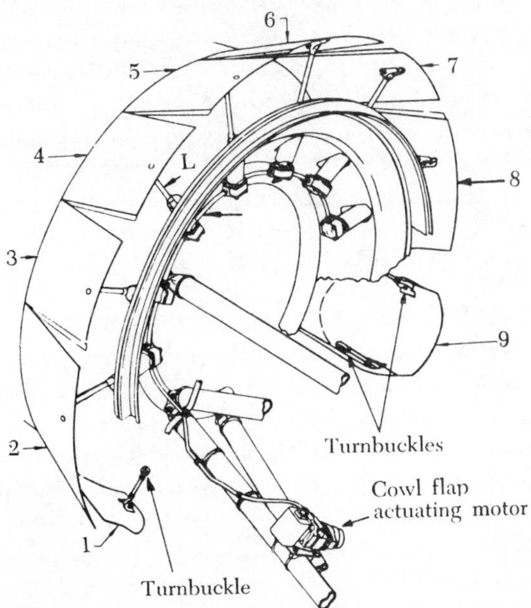

FIGURE 6–46. Cowl flap installation.

Cylinder Temperature Indicating System

This system usually consists of an indicator, electrical wiring, and a thermocouple. The wiring is between the instrument and the nacelle firewall. At the firewall, one end of the thermocouple leads connect to the electrical wiring, and the other end of the thermocouple leads connect to the cylinder.

The thermocouple consists of two dissimilar metals, generally constantan and iron, connected by wiring to an indicating system. If the temperature of the junction is different from the temperature where the dissimilar metals are connected to wires, a voltage is produced. This voltage sends a current through wires to the indicator, a current-measuring instrument graduated in degrees.

The thermocouple end that connects to the cylinder is either the bayonet or gasket type. To install the bayonet type, the knurled nut is pushed down and turned clockwise until it is snug. In removing this type, the nut is pushed down and turned counterclockwise until released. The gasket type fits under the spark plug and replaces the normal spark plug gasket.

When installing a thermocouple lead, remember not to cut off the lead because it is too long, but coil and tie up the excess length. The thermocouple is designed to produce a given amount of resistance. If the length of the lead is reduced, an incorrect temperature reading will result. The bayonet or gasket of the thermocouple is inserted or installed on the hottest cylinder of the engine, as determined in the block test.

When the thermocouple is installed and the wiring connected to the instrument, the indicated reading is the cylinder temperature. Prior to operating the engine, provided it is at ambient temperature, the cylinder head temperature indicator will indicate the free outside air temperature; that is one test for determining that the instrument is working correctly.

The cover glass of the cylinder head temperature indicator should be checked regularly to see that it has not slipped or that it is not cracked. The cover glass should be checked for indications of missing or damaged decals that indicate temperature limitations. If the thermocouple leads were excessive in length and had to be coiled and tied down, the tie should be inspected for security or chafing of the wire. The bayonet or gasket should be inspected for cleanness and security of mounting. When operating the engine, if the cylinder head temperature pointer fluctuates, all the electrical connections should be checked.

TURBINE ENGINE COOLING

The intense heat generated when fuel and air are burned necessitates that some means of cooling be provided for all internal combustion engines. Reciprocating engines are cooled either by passing air over fins attached to the cylinders or by passing a liquid coolant through jackets that surround the cylinders. The cooling problem is made easier because combustion occurs only during every fourth stroke of a four-stroke-cycle engine.

The burning process in a gas turbine engine is continuous, and nearly all of the cooling air must be passed through the inside of the engine. If only enough air were admitted to the engine to provide an ideal air/fuel ratio of 15:1, internal temperatures would increase to more than 4,000° F. In practice, a large amount of air in excess of the ideal ratio is admitted to the engine. The large surplus of air cools the hot sections of the engine to acceptable temperatures ranging from 1,100° to 1,500° F.

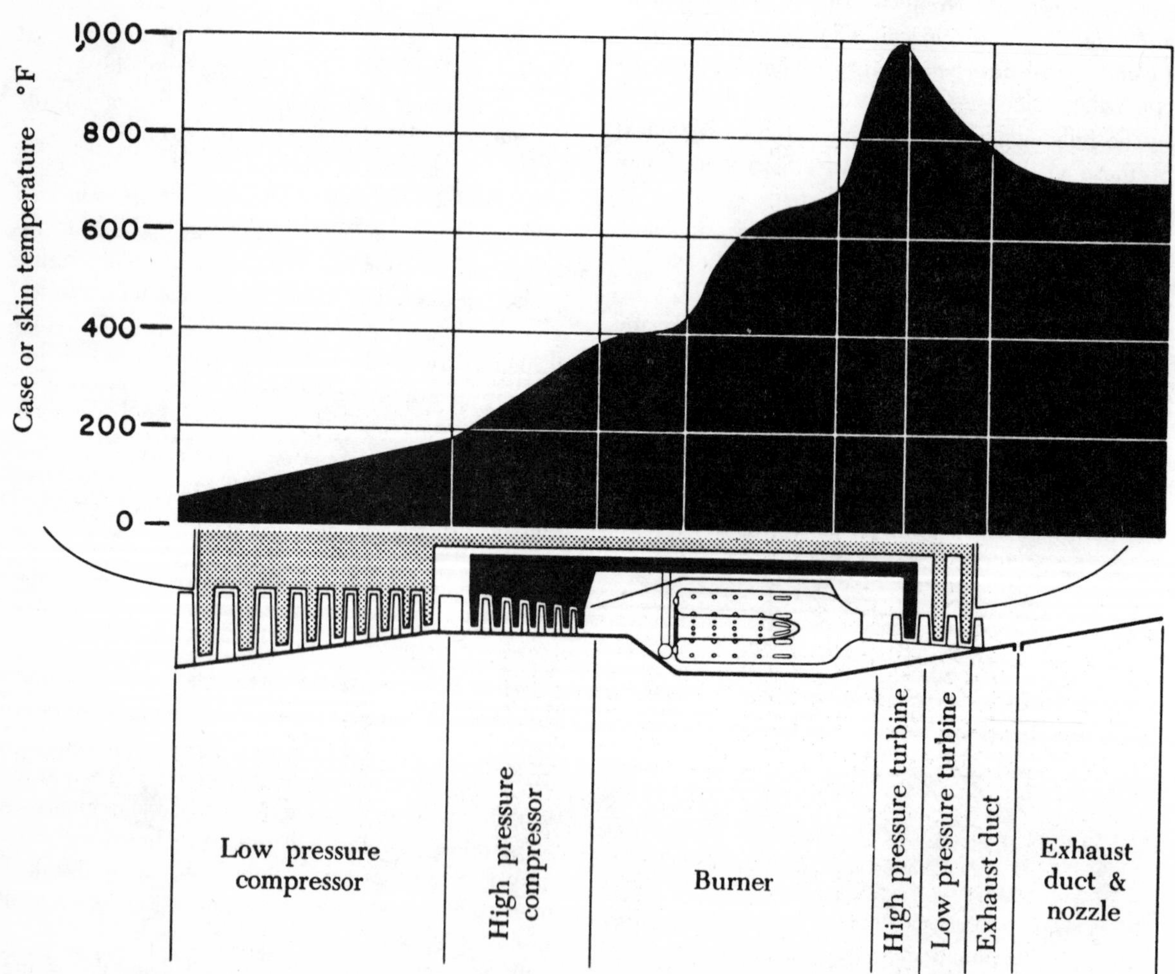

FIGURE 6–47. Typical outer-case temperatures for dual axial-compressor turbojet engine.

Figure 6–47 illustrates the approximate engine outer-case (skin) temperatures encountered in a properly cooled dual axial-compressor turbojet engine. Because of the effect of cooling, the temperatures of the outside of the case are considerably less than those encountered within the engine. The hottest spot occurs opposite the entrance to the first stage of the turbine. Although the gases have begun to cool a little at this point, the conductivity of the metal in the case carries the heat directly to the outside skin.

The air passing through the engine cools the combustion-chamber burner cans or liners. The cans are constructed to induce a thin, fast-moving film of air over both the inner and outer surfaces of the can or liner. Can-annular-type burners frequently are provided with a center tube to lead cooling air into the center of the burner to promote high combustion-efficiency and rapid dilution of the hot combustion gases while minimizing pressure losses. In all types of gas turbines, large amounts of relatively cool air join and mix with the burned gases aft of the burners to cool the hot gases just before they enter the turbines.

Cooling-air inlets frequently are provided around the exterior of the engine to permit the entrance of air to cool the turbine case, the bearings, and the turbine nozzle. In some instances, internal air is bled from the engine compressor section and is vented to the bearings and other parts of the engine. Air vented into or from the engine is ejected into the exhaust stream. When an accessory case is mounted at the front of the engine, it is cooled by inlet air. When located on the side of the engine, the case is cooled by outside air flowing around it.

The engine exterior and the engine nacelle are cooled by passing air between the case and the shell of the nacelle (figure 6–48). The engine compartment frequently is divided into two sections. The forward section is built around the engine-air-inlet duct; the aft section is built around the engine. A fume-proof seal is provided between the two sections. The advantage of such an arrangement is that fumes from possible leaks in the fuel and oil lines contained in the forward section cannot become ignited by contact with the hot sections of the engine. In flight, ram air provides ample cooling of the two compartments. On the ground, air circulation is provided by the effect of reduced pressure at the rear of the engine compartment, produced by gases flowing from the exhaust nozzle.

Turbine Engine Insulation Blankets

To reduce the temperature of the structure in the vicinity of the exhaust duct or afterburner and to eliminate the possibility of fuel or oil coming in contact with the hot parts of the engine, it is sometimes necessary to provide insulation on the exhaust duct of gas turbine engines. As shown in figure 6–49, the exhaust-duct surface temperature runs quite high.

A typical insulation blanket and the temperatures obtained at various locations are shown in figure 6–49. This blanket contains fiber glass as the low-conductance material and aluminum foil as the radiation shield. The blanket is suitably covered so that it does not become oil-soaked. Insulation blankets have been used rather extensively on some

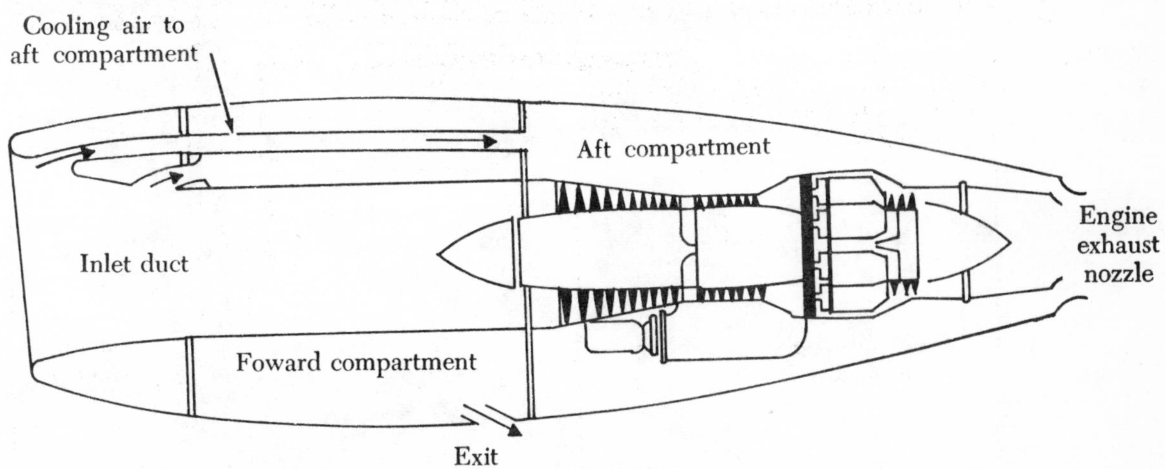

FIGURE 6–48. Typical engine nacelle cooling arrangement.

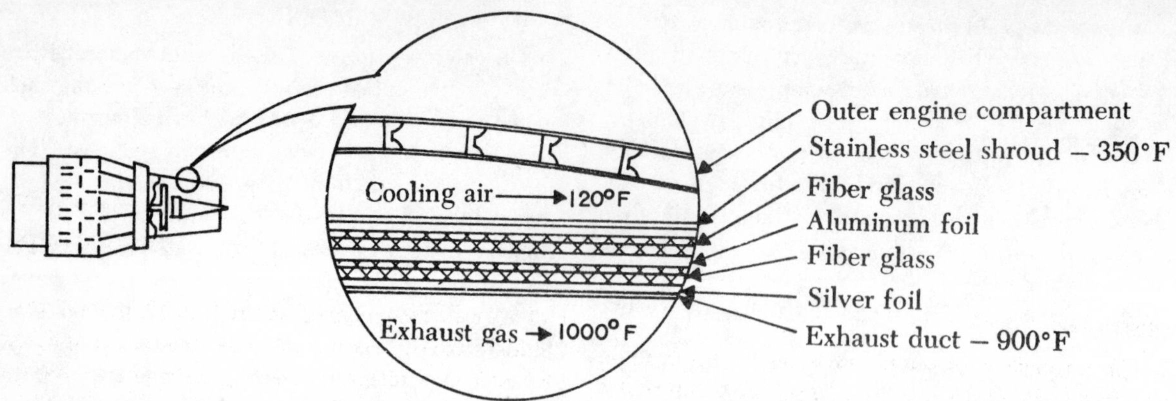

FIGURE 6–49. Typical engine insulation blanket.

centrifugal-flow engine installations, but are not commonly employed for axial-flow compressor engines if the installation permits the more desirable air-cooling method.

CHAPTER 7
PROPELLERS

GENERAL

The propeller, the unit which must absorb the power output of the engine, has passed through many stages of development. Great increases in power output have resulted in the development of four- and six-bladed propellers of large diameters. However, there is a limit to the r.p.m. at which these large propellers can be turned. The centrifugal force at high r.p.m. tends to pull the blades out of the hub; excessive blade tip speed may result not only in poor blade efficiency, but also in fluttering and vibration.

As an outgrowth of the problems involved in operating large propellers, a variable-pitch, constant-speed propeller system was developed. This system makes it necessary to vary the engine r.p.m. only slightly during various flight conditions and therefore increases flying efficiency. Roughly, such a system consists of a flyweight-equipped governor unit, which controls the pitch angle of the blades so that the engine speed remains constant. The governor, though, can be regulated by controls in the cockpit so that any desired blade angle setting and engine operating speed can be obtained. A low-pitch, high-r.p.m. setting, for example, can be utilized for takeoff; then after the aircraft is airborne, a higher pitch and lower r.p.m. setting can be used.

BASIC PROPELLER PRINCIPLES

The aircraft propeller consists of two or more blades and a central hub to which the blades are attached. Each blade of an aircraft propeller is essentially a rotating wing. As a result of their construction, the propeller blades produce forces that create thrust to pull or push the airplane through the air.

The power needed to rotate the propeller blades is furnished by the engine. The propeller is mounted on a shaft, which may be an extension of the crankshaft on low-horsepower engines; on high-horsepower engines, it is mounted on a propeller shaft which is geared to the engine crankshaft. In either case, the engine rotates the airfoils of the blades through the air at high speeds, and the propeller transforms the rotary power of the engine into thrust.

Aerodynamic Factors

An airplane moving through the air creates a drag force opposing its forward motion. If an airplane is to fly on a level path, there must be a force applied to it that is equal to the drag, but acting forward. This force is called thrust. The work done by the thrust is equal to the thrust times the distance it moves the airplane (Work = Thrust x Distance). The power expended by the thrust is equal to the thrust times the velocity at which it moves the airplane (Power = Thrust x Velocity). If the power is measured in horsepower units, the power expended by the thrust is termed thrust horsepower.

The engine supplies brake horsepower through a rotating shaft, and the propeller converts it into thrust horsepower. In this conversion, some power is wasted. For maximum efficiency, the propeller must be designed to keep this waste as small as possible. Since the efficiency of any machine is the ratio of the useful power output to the power input, propeller efficiency is the ratio of thrust horsepower to brake horsepower. The usual symbol for propeller efficiency is the Greek letter η (eta). Propeller efficiency varies from 50% to 87%, depending on how much the propeller "slips."

Propeller slip is the difference between the geometric pitch of the propeller and its effective pitch (see figure 7–1). Geometric pitch is the distance a propeller should advance in one revolution; effective pitch is the distance it actually advances. Thus, geometric or theoretical pitch is based on no slippage, but actual, or effective pitch, recognizes propeller slippage in the air.

The typical propeller blade can be described as a twisted airfoil of irregular planform. Two views of a propeller blade are shown in figure 7–2. For purposes of analysis, a blade can be divided into

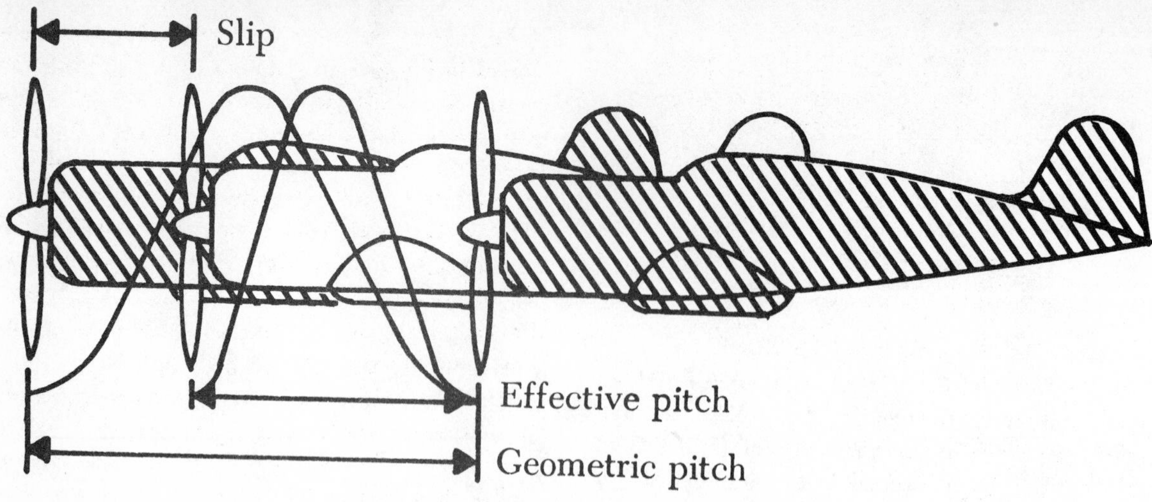

FIGURE 7–1. Effective and geometric pitch.

segments, which are located by station numbers in inches from the center of the blade hub. The cross sections of each 6-in. blade segment are shown as airfoils in the right-hand side of figure 7–2. Also identified in figure 7–2 are the blade shank and the blade butt. The blade shank is the thick, rounded portion of the propeller blade near the hub, which is designed to give strength to the blade. The blade butt, also called the blade base or root, is the end of the blade which fits in the propeller hub. The blade tip is that part of the propeller blade farthest from the hub, generally defined as the last 6 in. of the blade.

A cross section of a typical propeller blade is shown in figure 7–3. This section or blade element is an airfoil comparable to a cross section of an aircraft wing. The blade back is the cambered or curved side of the blade, similar to the upper surface of an aircraft wing. The blade face is the flat side of the propeller blade. The chord line is an imaginary line drawn through the blade from the leading edge to the trailing edge. The leading edge is the thick edge of the blade that meets the air as the propeller rotates.

Blade angle, usually measured in degrees, is the angle between the chord of the blade and the plane of rotation (figure 7–4). The chord of the propeller blade is determined in about the same manner as the chord of an airfoil. In fact, a propeller blade can be considered as being made up of an infinite number of thin blade elements, each of which is a miniature airfoil section whose chord is the width of the propeller blade at that section. Because most propellers have a flat blade face, the chord line is often drawn along the face of the propeller blade.

Pitch is not the same as blade angle, but, because pitch is largely determined by blade angle, the two

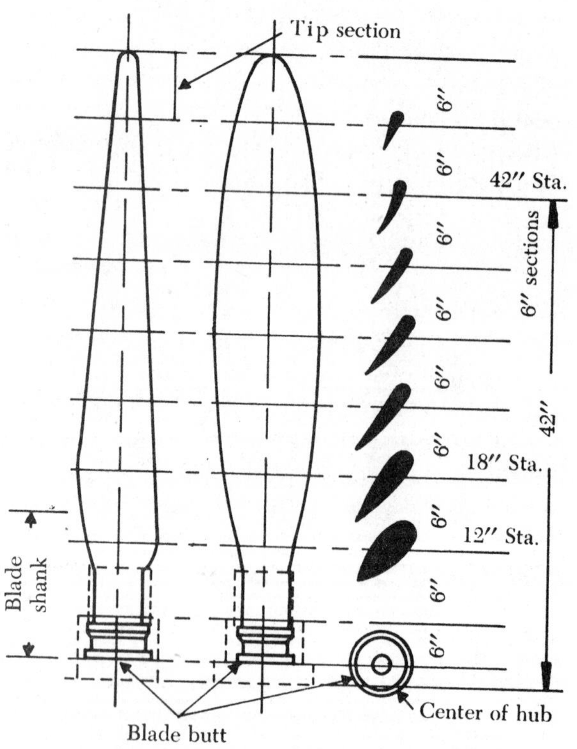

FIGURE 7–2. Typical propeller blade elements.

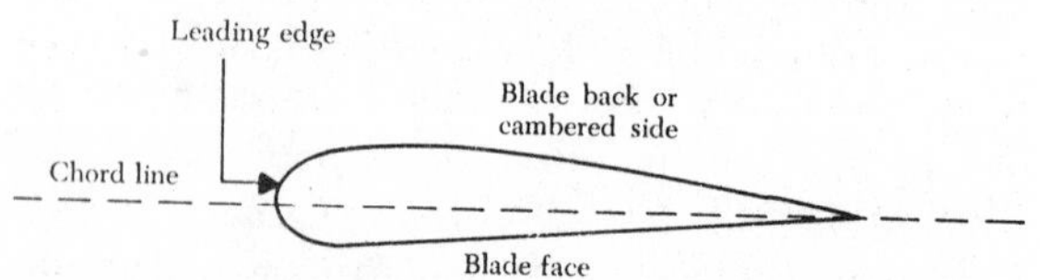

FIGURE 7–3. Cross section of a propeller blade.

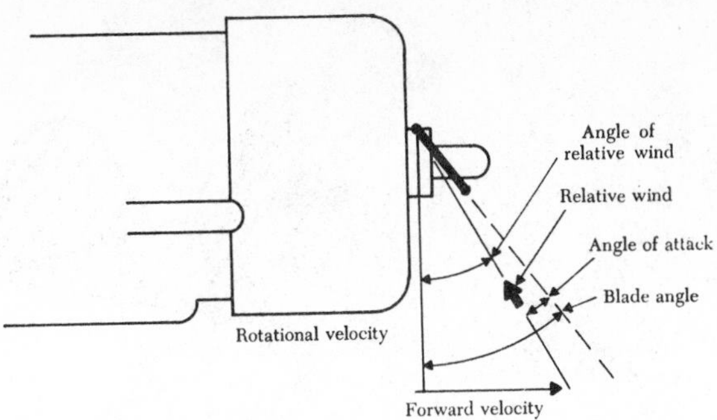

FIGURE 7–4. Propeller aerodynamic factors.

terms are often used interchangeably. An increase or decrease in one is usually associated with an increase or decrease in the other.

A rotating propeller is acted upon by centrifugal, twisting, and bending forces. The principal forces acting on a rotating propeller are illustrated in figure 7–5.

Centrifugal force (A of figure 7–5) is a physical force that tends to throw the rotating propeller blades away from the hub. Torque bending force (B of figure 7–5), in the form of air resistance, tends to bend the propeller blades opposite to the direction of rotation. Thrust bending force (C of figure 7–5) is the thrust load that tends to bend propeller blades forward as the aircraft is pulled through the air. Aerodynamic twisting force (D of figure 7–5) tends to turn the blades to a high blade angle. Centrifugal twisting force, being greater than the aerodynamic twisting force, tries to force the blades toward a low blade angle.

A propeller must be capable of withstanding severe stresses, which are greater near the hub, caused by centrifugal force and thrust. The stresses increase in proportion to the r.p.m. The blade face is also subjected to tension from the centrifugal force and additional tension from the bending. For these reasons, nicks or scratches on the blade may cause very serious consequences.

A propeller must also be rigid enough to prevent fluttering, a type of vibration in which the ends of the blade twist back and forth at high frequency around an axis perpendicular to the engine crankshaft. Fluttering is accompanied by a distinctive noise often mistaken for exhaust noise. The constant vibration tends to weaken the blade and eventually causes failure.

PROPELLER OPERATION

To understand the action of a propeller, consider first its motion, which is both rotational and forward. Thus, as shown by the vectors of propeller forces in figure 7–6, a section of a propeller blade moves downward and forward. As far as the forces are concerned, the result is the same as if the blade were stationary and the air were coming at it from a direction opposite its path. The angle at which this air (relative wind) strikes the propeller blade is called angle of attack. The air deflection produced by this angle causes the dynamic pressure at the engine side of the propeller blade to be greater than atmospheric, thus creating thrust.

The shape of the blade also creates thrust, because it is like the shape of a wing. Consequently, as the air flows past the propeller, the pressure on one side is less than that on the other. As in a wing, this produces a reaction force in the direction of the lesser pressure. In the case of a wing, the area over the wing has less pressure, and the force (lift) is upward. In the case of the propeller, which is mounted in a vertical instead of a horizontal position, the area of decreased pressure is in front of the propeller, and the force (thrust) is in a forward direction. Aerodynamically, then, thrust is the result of the propeller shape and the angle of attack of the blade.

Another way to consider thrust is in terms of the mass of air handled. In these terms, thrust is equal to the mass of air handled times the slipstream velocity minus the velocity of the airplane. Thus, the power expended in producing thrust depends on the mass of air moved per second. On the average, thrust constitutes approximately 80% of the torque (total horsepower absorbed by the propeller). The other 20% is lost in friction and slippage. For any speed of rotation, the horsepower absorbed by the propeller balances the horsepower delivered by the engine. For any single revolution of the propeller, the amount of air handled depends on the blade angle, which determines how big a "bite" of air the propeller takes. Thus, the blade angle is an excellent means of adjusting the load on the propeller to control the engine r.p.m.

The blade angle is also an excellent method of adjusting the angle of attack of the propeller. On constant-speed propellers, the blade angle must be adjusted to provide the most efficient angle of attack at all engine and airplane speeds. Lift versus drag curves, which are drawn for propellers as well as wings, indicate that the most efficient angle of attack is a small one varying from 2° to 4° positive. The actual blade angle necessary to maintain this

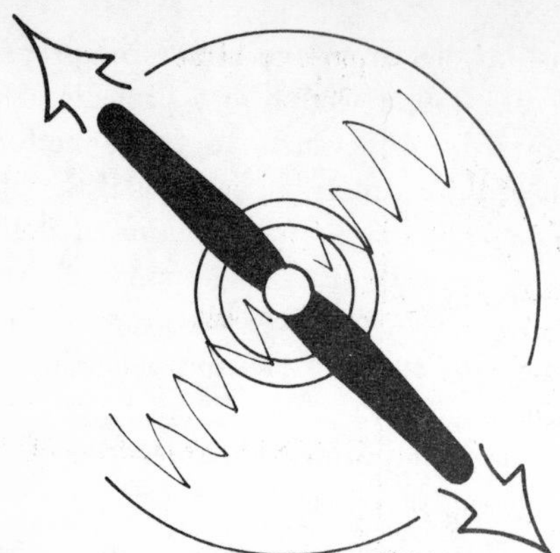

A. Centrifugal force

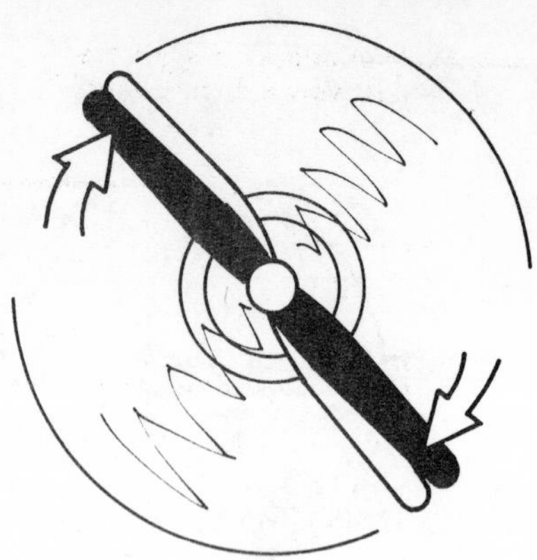

B. Torque bending force

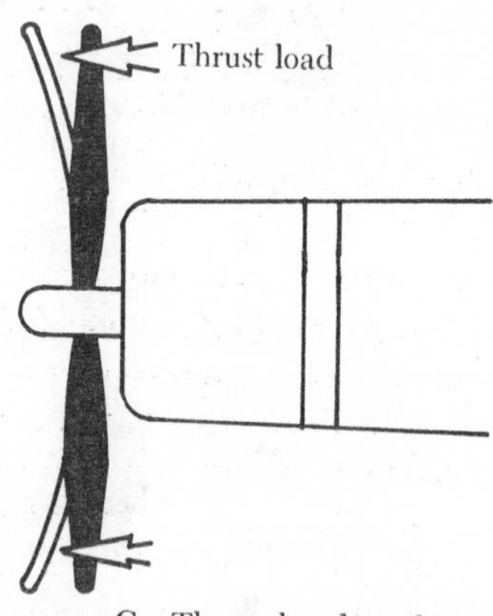

C. Thrust bending force

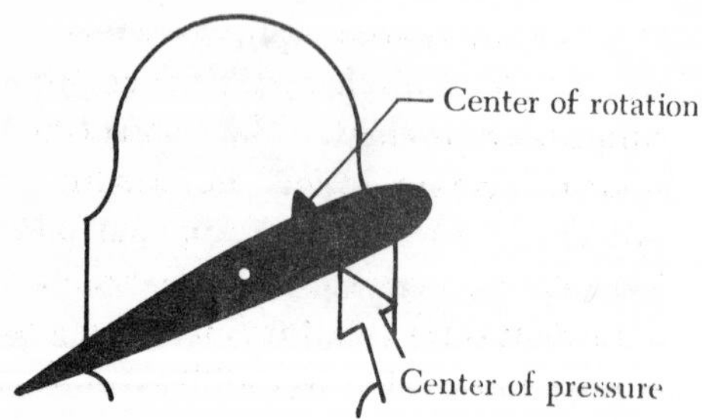

D. Aerodynamic twisting force

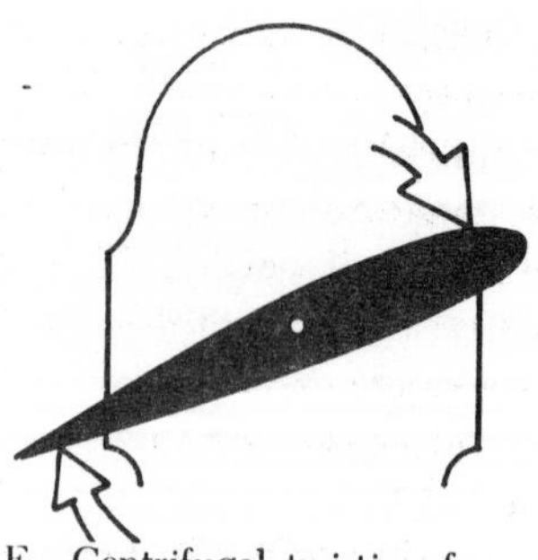

E. Centrifugal twisting force

FIGURE 7–5. Forces acting on a rotating propeller.

small angle of attack varies with the forward speed of the airplane.

Fixed-pitch and ground-adjustable propellers are designed for best efficiency at one rotation and forward speed. In other words, they are designed to fit a given airplane and engine combination. A propeller may be used that provides the maximum propeller efficiency for takeoff, climb, cruising, or high speeds. Any change in these conditions results in lowering the efficiency of both the propeller and the engine.

A constant-speed propeller, however, keeps the blade angle adjusted for maximum efficiency for most conditions encountered in flight. During takeoff, when maximum power and thrust are required, the constant-speed propeller is at a low propeller blade angle or pitch. The low blade angle keeps the angle of attack small and and efficient with respect

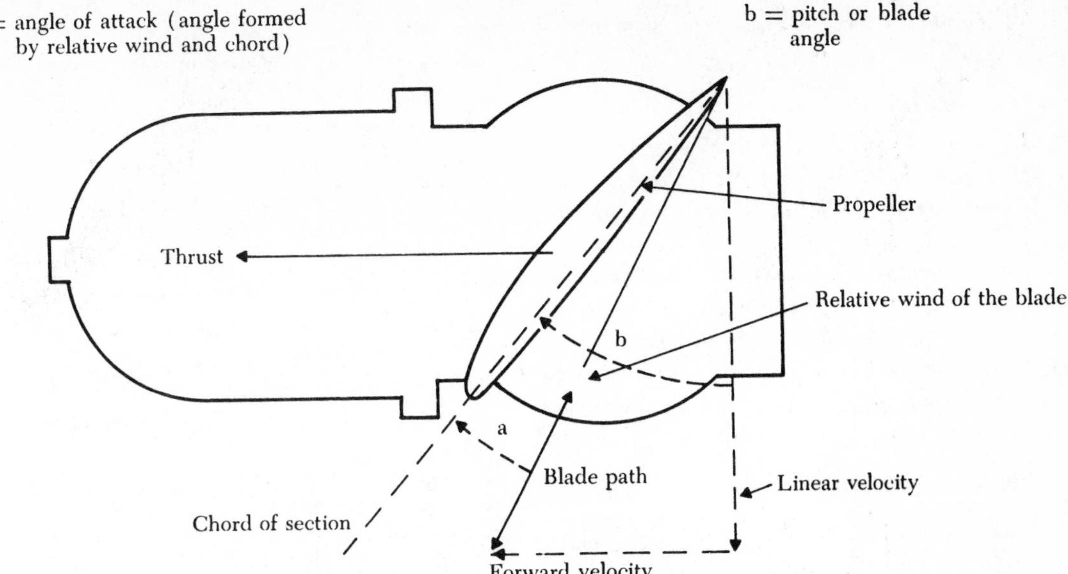

FIGURE 7–6. Propeller forces.

to the relative wind. At the same time, it allows the propeller to handle a smaller mass of air per revolution. This light load allows the engine to turn at high r.p.m. and to convert the maximum amount of fuel into heat energy in a given time. The high r.p.m. also creates maximum thrust; for, although the mass of air handled per revolution is small, the number of revolutions per minute are many, the slipstream velocity is high, and, with the low airplane speed, the thrust is maximum.

After liftoff, as the speed of the airplane increases, the constant-speed propeller changes to a higher angle (or pitch). Again, the higher blade angle keeps the angle of attack small and efficient with respect to the relative wind. The higher blade angle increases the mass of air handled per revolution. This decreases the engine r.p.m., reducing fuel consumption and engine wear, and keeps thrust at a maximum.

For climb after takeoff, the power output of the engine is reduced to climb power by decreasing the manifold pressure and increasing the blade angle to lower the r.p.m. Thus, the torque (horsepower absorbed by the propeller) is reduced to match the reduced power of the engine. The angle of attack is again kept small by the increase in blade angle. The greater mass of air handled per second in this case is more than offset by the lower slipstream velocity and the increase in airspeed.

At cruising altitude, when the airplane is in level flight and less power is required than is used in takeoff or climb, engine power is again reduced by lowering the manifold pressure and increasing the blade angle to decrease the r.p.m. Again, this reduces torque to match the reduced engine power; for, although the mass of air handled per revolution is greater, it is more than offset by a decrease in slipstream velocity and an increase in airspeed. The angle of attack is still small because the blade angle has been increased with an increase in airspeed.

TYPES OF PROPELLERS

There are various types or classes of propellers, the simplest of which are the fixed-pitch and ground-adjustable propellers. The complexity of propeller systems increases from these simpler forms to controllable-pitch and complex automatic systems. Various characteristics of several propeller types are discussed in the following paragraphs, but no attempt is made to cover all types of propellers.

Fixed-Pitch Propeller

As the name implies, a fixed-pitch propeller has the blade pitch, or blade angle, built into the propeller. The blade angle cannot be changed after the propeller is built. Generally, this type of propeller is one piece and is constructed of wood or aluminum alloy.

Fixed-pitch propellers are designed for best efficiency at one rotational and forward speed. They are designed to fit a set of conditions of both airplane and engine speeds, and any change in these conditions reduces the efficiency of both the propeller and the engine.

The fixed-pitch propeller is used on airplanes of low power, speed, range, or altitude.

Ground-Adjustable Propeller

The ground-adjustable propeller operates as a fixed-pitch propeller. The pitch or blade angle can be changed only when the propeller is not turning. This is done by loosening the clamping mechanism which holds the blades in place. After the clamping mechanism has been tightened, the pitch of the blades cannot be changed in flight to meet variable flight requirements. Like the fixed-pitch propeller, the ground-adjustable propeller is used on airplanes of low power, speed, range, or altitude.

Controllable-Pitch Propeller

The controllable-pitch propeller permits a change of blade pitch, or angle, while the propeller is rotating. This permits the propeller to assume a blade angle that will give the best performance for particular flight conditions. The number of pitch positions may be limited, as with a two-position controllable propeller; or the pitch may be adjusted to any angle between the minimum and maximum pitch settings of a given propeller.

The use of controllable-pitch propellers also makes it possible to attain the desired engine r.p.m. for a particular flight condition. As an airfoil is moved through the air, it produces two forces, lift and drag. Increasing propeller blade angle increases the angle of attack and produces more lift and drag; this action increases the horsepower required to turn the propeller at a given r.p.m. Since the engine is still producing the same horsepower, the propeller slows down. If the blade angle is decreased, the propeller speeds up. Thus, the engine r.p.m. can be controlled by increasing or decreasing the blade angle.

The use of propeller governors to increase or decrease propeller pitch is common practice. When the airplane goes into a climb, the blade angle of the propeller decreases just enough to prevent the engine speed from decreasing. Therefore, the engine can maintain its power output, provided the throttle setting is not changed. When the airplane goes into a dive, the blade angle increases sufficiently to prevent overspeeding, and with the same throttle setting, the power output remains unchanged. If the throttle setting is changed instead of changing the speed of the airplane by climbing or diving, the blade angle will increase or decrease as required to maintain a constant engine r.p.m. The power output (and not r.p.m.) will therefore change in accordance with changes in the throttle setting. The governor-controlled, constant-speed propeller changes the blade angle automatically, keeping engine r.p.m. constant.

Most pitch-changing mechanisms are operated by oil pressure (hydraulically) and use some type of piston-and-cylinder arrangement. The piston may move in the cylinder, or the cylinder may move over a stationary piston. The linear motion of the piston is converted by several different types of mechanical linkage into the rotary motion necessary to change the blade angle. The mechanical connection may be through gears, the pitch-changing mechanism turning a drive gear or power gear that meshes with a gear attached to the butt of each blade.

In most cases the oil pressure for operating these various types of hydraulic pitch-changing mechanisms comes directly from the engine lubricating system. When the engine lubricating system is used, the engine oil pressure is usually boosted by a pump that is integral with the governor to operate the propeller. The higher oil pressure provides a quicker blade-angle change.

The governors used to control the hydraulic propeller pitch-changing mechanisms are geared to the engine crankshaft and, thus, are sensitive to changes in r.p.m. The governors direct the pressurized oil for operation of the propeller hydraulic pitch-changing mechanisms. When r.p.m. increases above the value for which a governor is set, the governor causes the propeller pitch-changing mechanism to turn the blades to a higher angle. This angle increases the load on the engine, and r.p.m. decreases. When r.p.m. decreases below the value for which a governor is set, the governor causes the pitch-changing mechanism to turn the blades to a lower angle; the load on the engine is decreased, and r.p.m. increases. Thus, a propeller governor tends to keep engine r.p.m. constant.

Automatic Propellers

In automatic propeller systems, the control system adjusts pitch, without attention by the operator, to maintain a specific preset engine r.p.m. For example, if engine speed increases, the controls automatically increase the blade angle until desired r.p.m. has been re-established. A good automatic control system will respond to such small variations of r.p.m. that, for all practical purposes, a constant r.p.m. will be maintained. Automatic propellers are often termed "constant speed" propellers.

Additional refinements, such as pitch reversal

and feathering features, are included in some propellers to improve still further their operational characteristics.

Reverse-Pitch Propellers

A reverse-pitch propeller is a controllable propeller in which the blade angles can be changed to a negative value during operation. The purpose of the reversible pitch feature is to produce a high negative thrust at low speed by using engine power. Although reverse pitch may be used in flight for steep descents, it is used principally as an aerodynamic brake to reduce ground roll after landing.

Feathering Propellers

A feathering propeller is a controllable propeller having a mechanism to change the pitch to an angle so that forward aircraft motion produces a minimum windmilling effect on a "power-off" propeller. Feathering propellers must be used on multi-engine aircraft to reduce propeller drag to a minimum under engine failure conditions.

CLASSIFICATION OF PROPELLERS

Tractor Propeller

Tractor propellers are those mounted on the upstream end of a drive shaft in front of the supporting structure. Most aircraft are equipped with this type of propeller. A major advantage of the tractor propeller is that lower stresses are induced in the propeller as it rotates in relatively undisturbed air.

Pusher Propellers

Pusher propellers are those mounted on the downstream end of a drive shaft behind the supporting structure. Pusher propellers are constructed as fixed- or variable-pitch propellers. Seaplanes and amphibious aircraft have used a greater percentage of pusher propellers than other kinds of aircraft.

On land planes, where propeller-to-ground clearance usually is less than propeller-to-water clearance of watercraft, pusher propellers are subject to more damage than tractor propellers. Rocks, gravel, and small objects, dislodged by the wheels, quite often may be thrown or drawn into a pusher propeller. Similarly, planes with pusher propellers are apt to encounter propeller damage from water spray thrown up by the hull during landing or takeoff from water. Consequently, the pusher propeller quite often is mounted above and behind the wings to prevent such damage.

PROPELLERS USED ON LIGHT AIRCRAFT

An increasing number of light aircraft are designed for operation with governor-regulated, constant-speed propellers. But a significant segment of the general aviation aircraft are operated with fixed-pitch propellers.

Fixed-Pitch Wooden Propellers

The construction of a fixed-pitch wooden propeller (figure 7–7) is such that its blade pitch cannot be changed after manufacture. The choice of the blade angle is decided by the normal use of the propeller on an aircraft during level flight, when the engine will perform at maximum efficiency.

The impossibility of changing the blade pitch on the fixed-pitch propeller restricts its use to small aircraft with low-horsepower engines, in which maximum engine efficiency during all flight conditions is of lesser importance than in larger aircraft. The wooden fixed-pitch propeller, because of its light weight, rigidity, economy of production, simplicity of construction, and ease of replacement, is well suited for such small aircraft.

A wooden propeller is not constructed from a solid block, but is built up of a number of separate layers of carefully selected and well-seasoned hardwoods. Many woods, such as mahogany, cherry, black walnut, and oak, are used to some extent, but birch is the most widely used. Five to nine separate layers are used, each about 3/4-inch thick. The

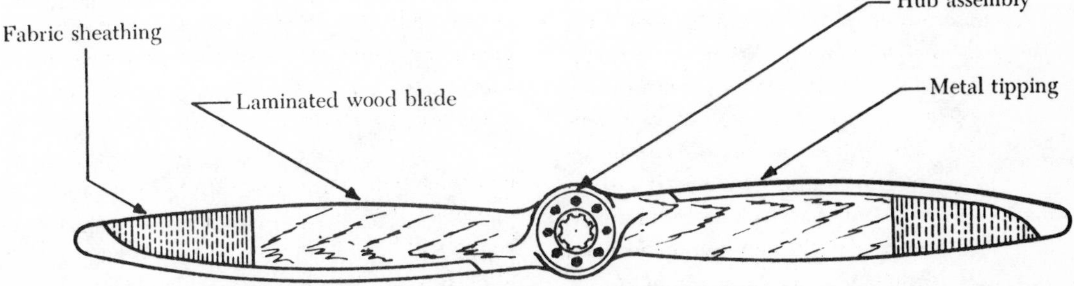

FIGURE 7–7. Fixed-pitch wooden propeller assembly.

several layers are glued together with a waterproof, resinous glue and allowed to set. The "blank" is then roughed to the approximate shape and size of the finished product.

The roughed-out propeller is then allowed to dry for approximately a week to permit the moisture content of the layers to become equalized. This additional period of seasoning prevents warping and cracking that might occur if the blank were immediately carved. Following this period, the propeller is carefully constructed. Templates and bench protractors are used to obtain the proper contour and blade angle at all stations.

After the propeller blades are finished, a fabric covering is cemented to the outer 12 or 15 in. of each finished blade, and a metal tipping (figure 7–8) is fastened to most of the leading edge and tip of each blade to protect the propeller from damage caused by flying particles in the air during landing, taxiing, or takeoff.

Metal tipping may be of terneplate, Monel metal, or brass. Stainless steel has been used to some extent. It is secured to the leading edge of the blade by countersunk wood screws and rivets. The heads of the screws are soldered to the tipping to prevent loosening, and the solder is filed to make a smooth surface. Since moisture condenses on the tipping between the metal and the wood, the tipping is provided with small holes near the blade tip to allow this moisture to drain away or be thrown out by centrifugal force. It is important that these drainholes be kept open at all times.

Since wood is subject to swelling, shrinking, and warping because of changes of moisture content, a protective coating is applied to the finished propeller to prevent a rapid change of moisture content.

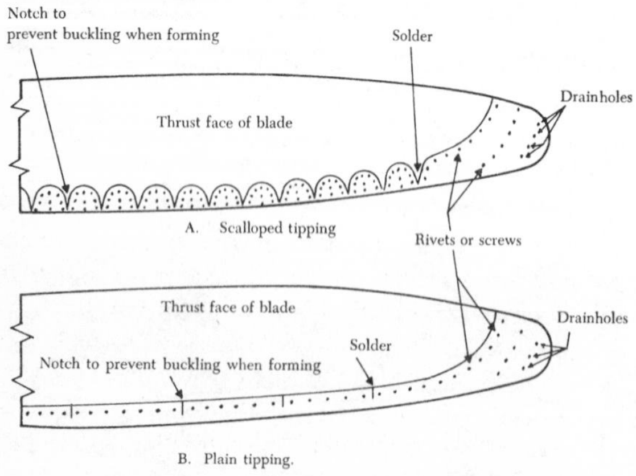

FIGURE 7–8. Installation of metal sheath and tipping.

The finish most commonly used is a number of coats of water-repellent, clear varnish. After these processes are completed, the propeller is mounted on a spindle and very carefully balanced.

Several types of hubs are used to mount wooden propellers on the engine crankshaft. The propeller may have a forged steel hub that fits a splined crankshaft; it may be connected to a tapered crankshaft by a tapered, forged steel hub; or it may be bolted to a steel flange forged on the crankshaft. In any case, several attaching parts are required to mount the propeller on the shaft properly.

Hubs fitting a tapered shaft usually are held in place by a retaining nut that screws onto the end of the shaft. On one model, a locknut is used to safety the retaining nut and to provide a puller for removing the propeller from the shaft. This nut screws into the hub and against the retaining nut. The locknut and the retaining nut are safetied together with lockwire or a cotter pin.

A front and rear cone may be used to seat the propeller properly on a splined shaft. The rear cone is a one-piece bronze cone that fits around the shaft and against the thrust nut (or spacer) and seats in the rear-cone seat of the hub. The front cone is a two-piece, split-type steel cone that has a groove around its inner circumference so that it can be fitted over a flange of the propeller retaining nut. When the retaining nut is threaded into place, the front cone seats in the front-cone seat of the hub. A snap ring is fitted into a groove in the hub in front of the front cone, so that when the retaining nut is unscrewed from the propeller shaft, the front cone will act against the snap ring and pull the propeller from the shaft.

One type of hub incorporates a bronze bushing instead of a front cone. When this type of hub is used, it may be necessary to use a puller to start the propeller from the shaft. A rear-cone spacer is sometimes provided with the splined-shaft propeller assembly to prevent the propeller from interfering with the engine cowling. The wide flange on the rear face of some types of hubs eliminates the use of a rear-cone spacer.

One type of hub assembly for the fixed-pitch wooden propeller is a steel fitting inserted in the propeller to mount it on the propeller shaft. It has two main parts, the faceplate and the flange plate (figure 7–9). The faceplate is a steel disk that forms the forward face of the hub. The flange plate is a steel flange with an internal bore splined to receive the propeller shaft. The end of the flange plate opposite the flange disk is externally splined to receive the faceplate; the faceplate bore has splines to match these external splines. Both faceplate and flange plates have a corresponding series of holes drilled on the disk surface concentric with the hub center. The bore of the flange plate has a 15° cone seat on the rear end and a 30° cone seat on the forward end to center the hub accurately on the propeller shaft.

Metal Fixed-Pitch Propellers

Metal fixed-pitch propellers are similar in general appearance to a wooden propeller, except that the sections are usually thinner. The metal fixed-pitch propeller is widely used on many models of light aircraft.

Many of the earliest metal propellers were manufactured in one piece of forged Duralumin. Compared to wooden propellers, they were lighter in weight because of elimination of blade-clamping devices; they offered a lower maintenance cost because they were made in one piece; they provided more efficient cooling because of the effective pitch nearer the hub; and because there was no joint between the blades and the hub, the propeller pitch could be changed, within limits, by twisting the blade slightly.

Propellers of this type are now manufactured of one-piece anodized aluminum alloy. They are identified by stamping the propeller hub with the serial number, model number, Federal Aviation Administration (FAA) type certificate number, production certificate number, and the number of times the propeller has been reconditioned. The complete model number of the propeller is a combination of the basic model number and suffix numbers to indicate the propeller diameter and pitch. An explanation of a complete model number, using the McCauley 1B90/CM propeller, is provided in figure 7–10.

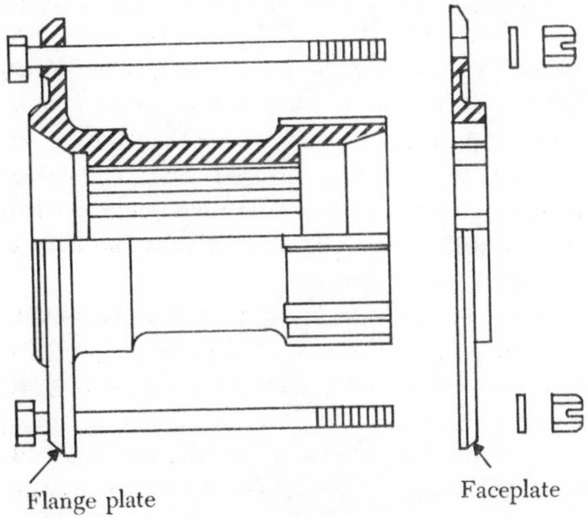

FIGURE 7–9. Hub assembly.

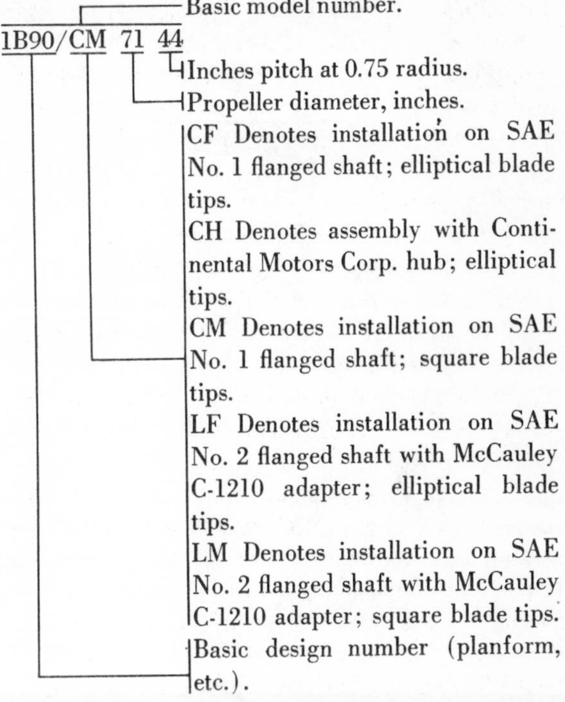

FIGURE 7–10. Complete propeller model number.

CONSTANT-SPEED PROPELLERS

Hartzell, Sensenick, and McCauley propellers for light aircraft are similar in operation. All use centrifugal force acting on blade counterweights to increase blade pitch. A description of a Hartzell constant speed propeller is used for exemplary purposes. The manufacturer's specifications and instructions must be consulted for information on specific models.

Constant-Speed Propellers For Light Aircraft

Many types of light aircraft use governor-regulated, constant-speed propellers in both two- and three-bladed versions.

These propellers may be the nonfeathering type, or they may be capable of feathering and reversing. The steel hub consists of a central spider, which supports aluminum blades with a tube extending inside the blade roots. Blade clamps connect the blade shanks with blade retention bearings. A hydraulic cylinder is mounted on the rotational axis connected to the blade clamps for pitch actuation. (See figure 7–11.)

The basic hub and blade retention is common to all models described. The blades are mounted on

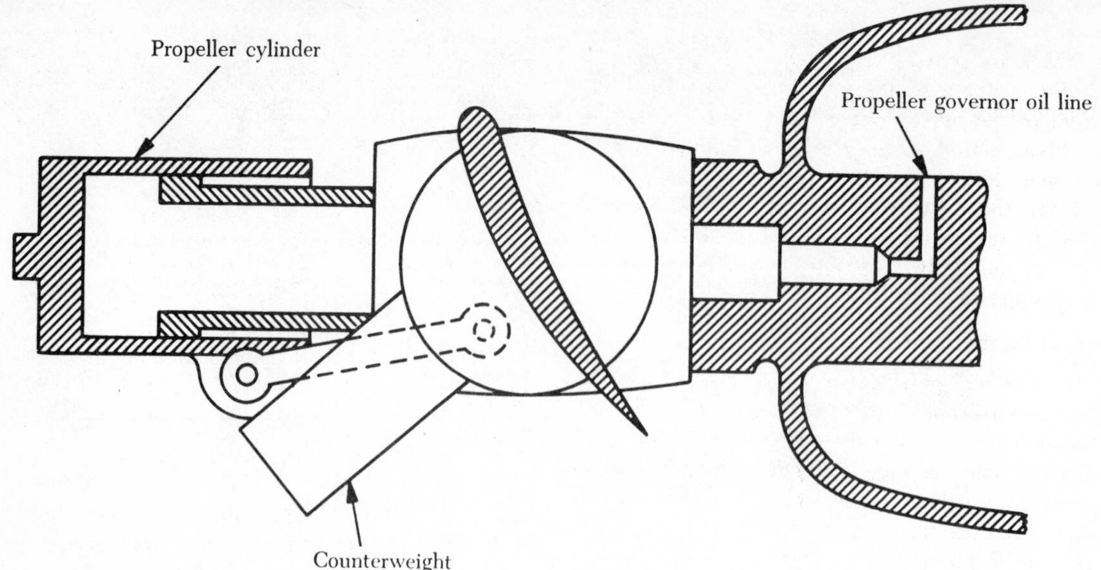

FIGURE 7–11. Pitch change mechanism for a counterweight propeller.

the hub spider for angular adjustment. The centrifugal force of the blades, amounting to as much as 25 tons, is transmitted to the hub spider through blade clamps and then through ball bearings. The propeller thrust and engine torque is transmitted from the blades to the hub spider through a bushing inside the blade shank.

Propellers, having counterweights attached to the blade clamps, utilize centrifugal force derived from the counterweights to increase the pitch of the blades. The centrifugal force, due to rotation of the propeller tends to move the counterweights into the plane of rotation, thereby increasing the pitch of the blades. (See figure 7–12.)

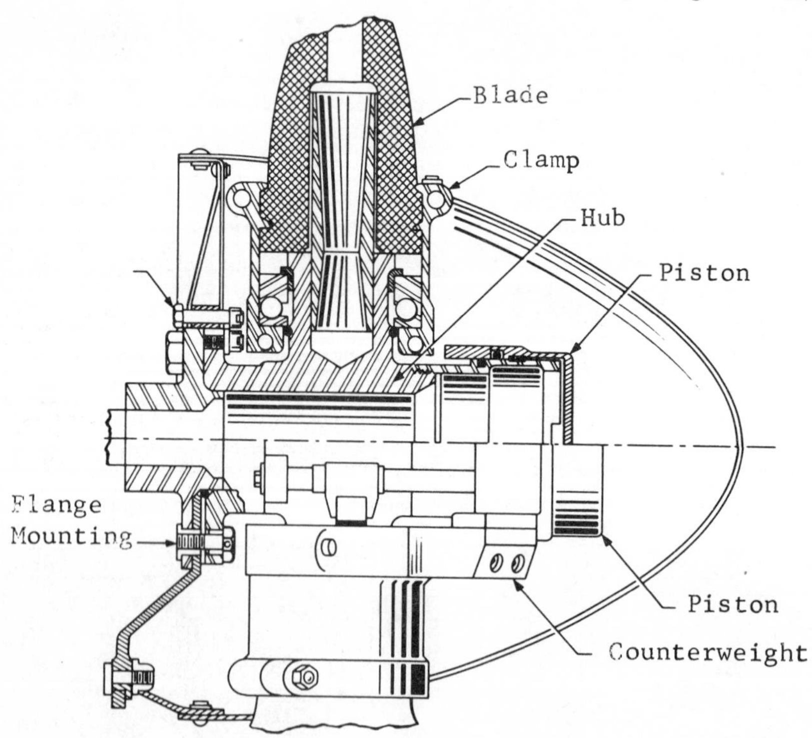

FIGURE 7–12. Constant Speed Prop.

In order to control the pitch of the blades, a hydraulic piston-cylinder element is mounted on the front of the hub spider. The piston is attached to the blade clamps by means of a sliding rod and fork system for non-feathering models and a link system for the feathering models. The piston is actuated in the forward direction by means of oil pressure supplied by a governor, which overcomes the opposing force created by the counterweights.

Constant Speed, Non-Feathering

If the engine speed drops below the r.p.m. for which the governor is set (see figure 7–13), the rotational force on the engine driven governor flyweights becomes less. This allows the speeder spring to move the pilot valve downward. With the pilot valve in the downward position, oil from the gear type pump flows through passage to the propeller and moves the cylinder outward. This in turn, decreases the blade angle and permits the engine to return to the on-speed setting. If the engine speed increases above the r.p.m. for which the governor is set, the flyweights move against the force of the speeder spring and raise the pilot valve. This permits the oil in the propeller to drain out through the governor drive shaft. As the oil leaves the propeller, the centrifugal force acting on the counterweights turns the blades to a higher angle, which decreases the engine r.p.m. When the engine is exactly at the r.p.m. set by the governor, the centrifugal reaction of the flyweights balances the force of the speeder spring, positioning the pilot valve so that oil is neither supplied to nor drained from the propeller. With this condition, propeller blade angle does not change. Note that the r.p.m. setting is made by varying the amount of compression in the speeder spring. Positioning of the speeder rack is the only action controlled manually. All others are controlled automatically within the governor.

Constant-Speed Feathering Propeller

The feathering propellers operate similarly to the non-feathering ones except the feathering spring assists the counterweights to increase the pitch. (See figure 7–14.)

FEATHERING

Feathering is accomplished by releasing the governor oil pressure, allowing the counterweights and feathering spring to feather the blades. This is done by pulling the governor pitch control back to the limit of its travel, which opens up a port in the governor allowing the oil from the propeller to drain back into the engine. The time necessary to feather depends upon the size of the oil passage from the propeller to the engine, and the force exerted by the spring and counterweights. The larger the passages through the governor and the heavier the spring, the quicker is the feathering action. Elapsed time for feathering, between three and ten seconds, is usual with this system.

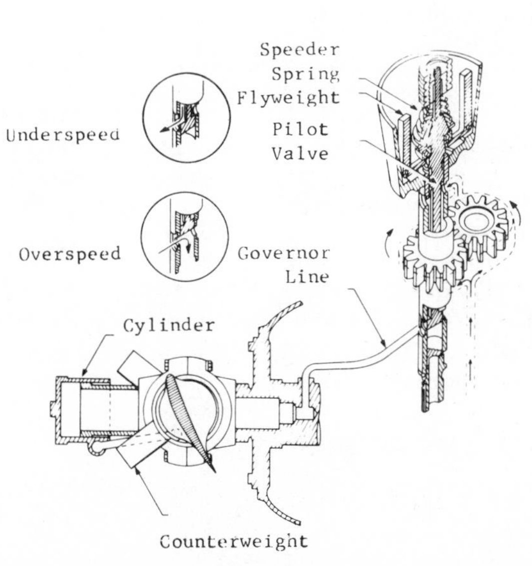

FIGURE 7–13. On-speed, basic operation.

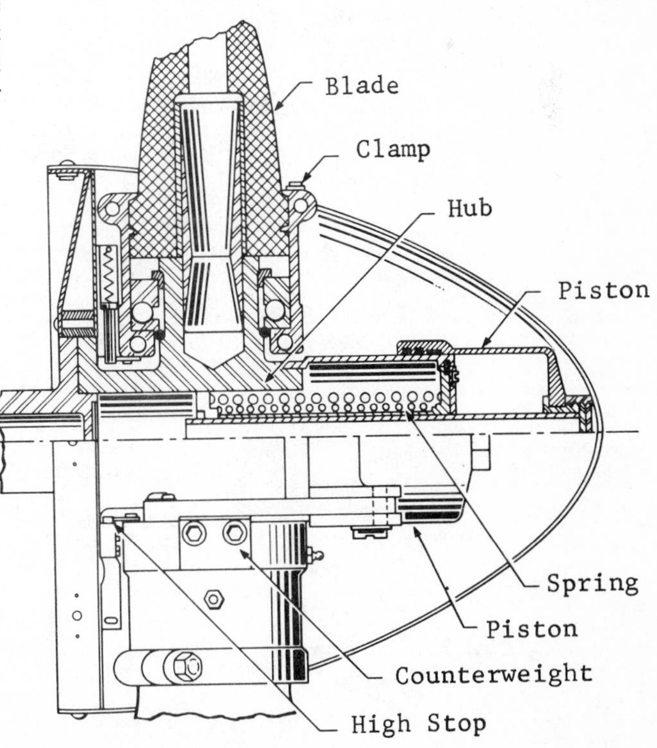

FIGURE 7–14. Constant-speed feathering.

The ability to unfeather the blades, or re-establish normal pitch, within the same elapsed time is not considered important for the light twin-engine airplane. The possibility of feathering the wrong propeller in an emergency is remote, as the wrong action will become apparent in ample time to be corrected. Furthermore, the requirement to restart the dead engine for landing does not exist, as the light twin can easily be landed with only one engine. About the only requirement for unfeathering is for demonstration purposes.

UNFEATHERING

Unfeathering is accomplished by repositioning the governor control to the normal flight range. and restarting the engine (figure 7–15). As soon as the engine cranks over a few turns the governor starts to unfeather the blades and soon wind-milling takes place, which speeds up the process of unfeathering. In order to facilitate cranking of the engine, feathering blade angle is set at 80 to 85 degrees at the ¾ point on the blade, allowing the air to assist the engine starter. In general, restarting and unfeathering can be accomplished within a few seconds.

Special unfeathering systems are available for certain aircraft, for which restarting the engine is difficult, or for demonstrations. The system consists of an oil accumulator, connected to the governor through a valve, as shown in figure 7–15.

In order to prevent the feathering spring from feathering the propeller when the plane is on the ground and the engine stopped, automatically removable high-pitch stops were incorporated in the design. These consist of spring-loaded latches fastened to the stationary hub which engage high-pitch stop-plates bolted to the movable blade clamps. As long as the propeller is in rotation at speeds over 600 r.p.m., centrifugal force acts to disengage the latches from the high-pitch stop-plates so that the propeller pitch may be increased to the feathering

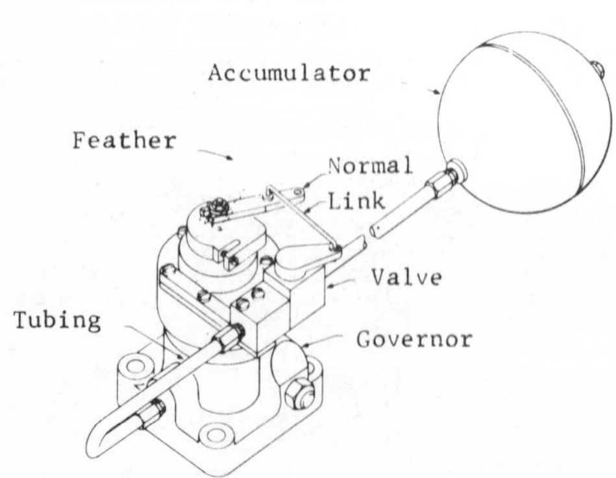

FIGURE 7–15. Unfeathering system.

position. At lower r.p.m., or when the engine is stopped, the latch springs engage the latches with the high-pitch stops, preventing the pitch from increasing further due to the action of the feathering spring.

One safety feature inherent in this method of feathering is that the propeller will feather if the governor oil pressure drops to zero for any reason. As the governor obtains its supply of oil from the engine lubricating system, it follows that if the engine runs out of oil, or if oil pressure fails due to breakage of a part of the engine, the propeller will feather automatically. This action may save the engine from further damage in case the pilot is not aware of trouble.

Hartzell "Compact" Propellers

These propellers represent new concepts in basic design. They combine low weight and simplicity in design and rugged construction.

In order to achieve these ends, the hub is made as compact as possible, utilizing aluminum alloy forgings for most of the parts. The hub shell is made in two halves, bolted together along the plane of rotation. This hub shell carries the pitch change mechanism and blade roots internally. The hydraulic cylinder, which provides power for changing the pitch, is mounted at the front of the hub. The propeller can only be installed on engines having flanged mounting provisions.

The constant speed propellers, utilize oil pressure from a governor to move the blades into high pitch (reduced r.p.m.). The centrifugal twisting moment of the blades tend to move them into low pitch (high r.p.m.) in the absence of governor oil pressure.

The feathering propellers utilize oil pressure from the governor to move the blades into low pitch (high r.p.m.). The centrifugal twisting moment of the blades also tend to move the blades into low pitch. Opposing these two forces is a force produced by compressed air trapped between the cylinder head and the piston, which tends to move the blades into high pitch in the absence of governor oil pressure. Thus feathering is accomplished by the compressed air, in the absence of governor oil pressure. Feathering is accomplished by moving the governor control back to its extreme position. The propeller is prevented from feathering, when it is stationary, by centrifugal responsive pins, which engage a shoulder on the piston rod. These pins move out by centrifugal force against springs, when the propeller turns at over 700 r.p.m.

The time necessary to feather depends upon the size of the oil passages back through the engine and governor, and the air pressure carried in the cylinder head. The larger the passages, the faster the oil from the propeller cylinder can be forced back into the engine. Also, the higher the air charge, the faster the feather action. In general, feathering can be accomplished within a few seconds.

Unfeathering can be accomplished by any of several methods, as follows:

(1) Start the engine, so that the governor can pump oil back into the propeller to reduce pitch. In most light twins, this procedure is considered adequate since engine starting presents no problem in general.

(2) Provide an accumulator connected to the governor, with a valve to trap an air-oil charge when the propeller is feathered, but released to the propeller when the r.p.m. control is returned to normal position.

(3) Provide a cross-over system which allows oil from the operating engine to unfeather the propeller on the dead engine. This consists of an oil line connecting the two governors with a manual or electric actuated valve in between.

The governor is designed so that it may be adapted for either single action or double action operation. As a single-action governor it directs oil pressure to the rear of the cylinder to decrease pitch and allows it to drain from the cylinder when centrifugal force increases pitch. Propellers having counterweights use single-action governors. The counterweights and centrifugal force act together to increase pitch. For those propellers which do not use counterweights to increase pitch, oil from the governor is used to increase pitch by overcoming the centrifugal force of the blades. In this case, the plug "B" is removed and installed in passage "C" of the governor. This permits governor oil pressure to be directed to the rear of the cylinder, to decrease pitch. Oil pressure is directed to the forward side of the cylinder to increase pitch. See figure 7–16.

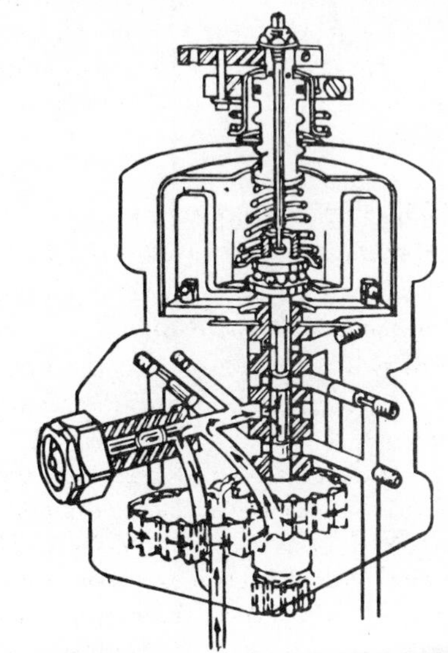

ON-SPEED

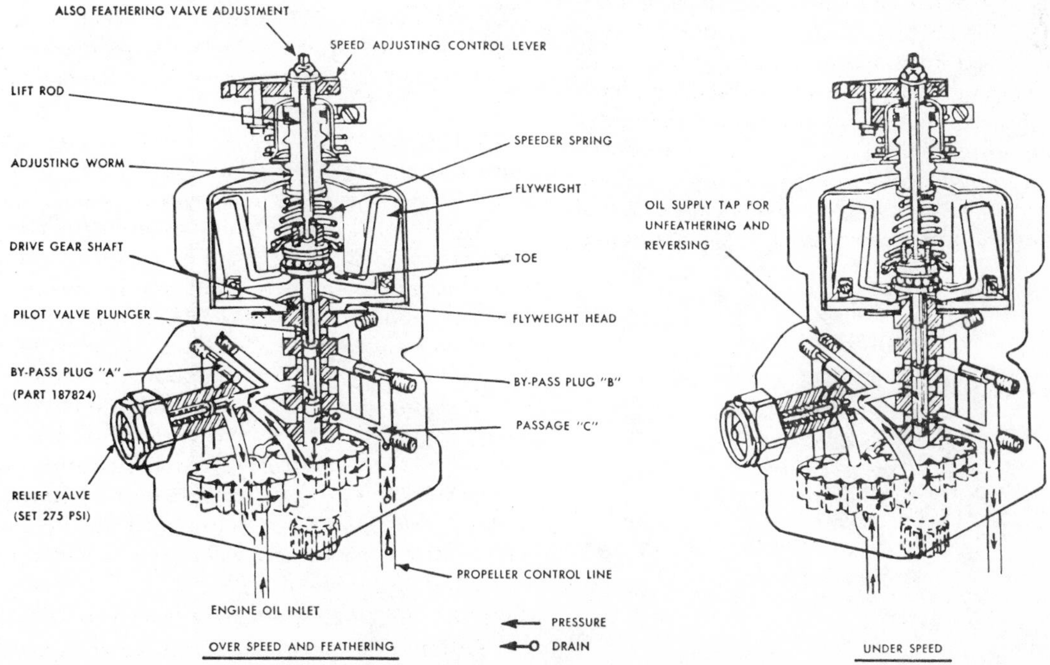

FIGURE 7–16. Woodward Governor X210,000 Series

HAMILTON STANDARD HYDROMATIC PROPELLERS

The following description is typical of most of the various models of the Hamilton Standard hydromatic propeller.

The hydromatic propeller (figure 7–17) is composed of four major components:

(1) The hub assembly.
(2) The dome assembly.
(3) The distributor valve assembly (for feathering on single-acting propellers) or engine-shaft-extension assembly (for nonfeathering or double-acting propellers).
(4) The anti-icing assembly.

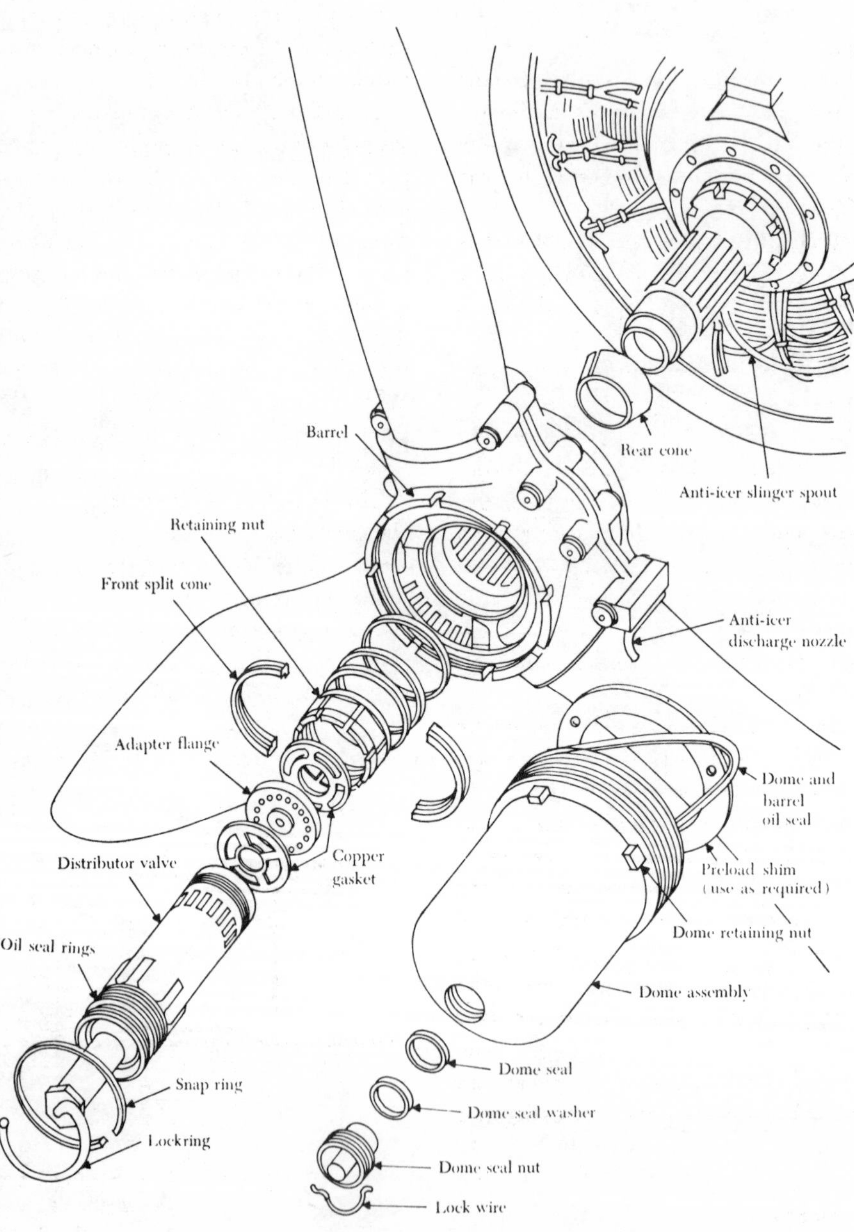

FIGURE 7–17. Typical hydromatic propeller installation.

The hub assembly is the basic propeller mechanism. It contains both the blades and the mechanical means for holding them in position. The blades are supported by the spider and retained by the barrel. Each blade is free to turn about its axis under the control of the dome assembly.

The dome assembly contains the pitch-changing mechanism for the blades. It consists of several major components:

(1) Rotating cam.
(2) Fixed cam.
(3) Piston.
(4) Dome shell.

When the dome assembly is installed in the propeller hub, the fixed cam remains stationary with respect to the hub. The rotating cam, which can turn inside the fixed cam, meshes with gear segments on the blades.

The piston operates inside the dome shell and is the mechanism that converts engine and governor oil pressure into forces that act through the cams to turn propeller blades.

The distributor valve or engine-shaft-extension assembly provides oil passages for governor or auxiliary oil to the inboard side of the piston and for engine oil to the outboard side. During unfeathering operation, the distributor shifts under auxiliary pressure and reverses these passages so that oil from the auxiliary pump flows to the outboard side of the piston. Oil on the inboard side flows back to the engine. The engine-shaft-extension assembly is used with propellers that do not have feathering capabilities.

Many structural features of most hydromatic propellers and other constant-speed propellers are similar. The blade and hub assemblies are almost identical, and the governors are also similar in construction and principle of operation. The major difference is in the pitch-changing mechanism. In the hydromatic propeller no counterweights are used, and the moving parts of the mechanism are completely enclosed. Oil pressure and the centrifugal twisting moment of the blades are used together to turn the blades to a lower angle. The main advantages of the hydromatic propeller are the large blade-angle range and the feathering and reversing features.

Principles of Operation

The pitch-changing mechanism of hydromatic propellers is a mechanical-hydraulic system in which hydraulic forces acting on a piston are transformed into mechanical twisting forces acting on the blades. Linear movement of the piston is converted to rotary motion by a cylindrical cam. A bevel gear on the base of the cam mates with bevel-gear segments attached to the butt ends of the blades, thereby turning the blades. This blade pitch-changing action can be understood by studying the schematic in figure 7–18.

The centrifugal force acting on a rotating blade includes a component force that tends to move the blade toward low pitch. As shown in figure 7–18, a second force, engine oil pressure, is supplied to the outboard side of the propeller piston to assist in moving the blade toward low pitch.

Propeller governor oil, taken from the engine oil supply and boosted in pressure by the engine-driven propeller governor, is directed against the inboard side of the propeller piston. It acts as the counterforce which can move the blades toward higher pitch. By metering this high-pressure oil to, or draining it from, the inboard side of the propeller piston by means of the constant-speed control unit, the force toward high pitch can balance and control the two forces toward low pitch. In this way the propeller blade angle is regulated to maintain a selected r.p.m.

The basic propeller control forces acting on the Hamilton Standard propeller are centrifugal twisting force and high-pressure oil from the governor.

The centrifugal force acting on each blade of a rotating propeller includes a component force that results in a twisting moment about the blade center line which tends, at all times, to move the blade toward low pitch.

Governor pump output oil is directed by the

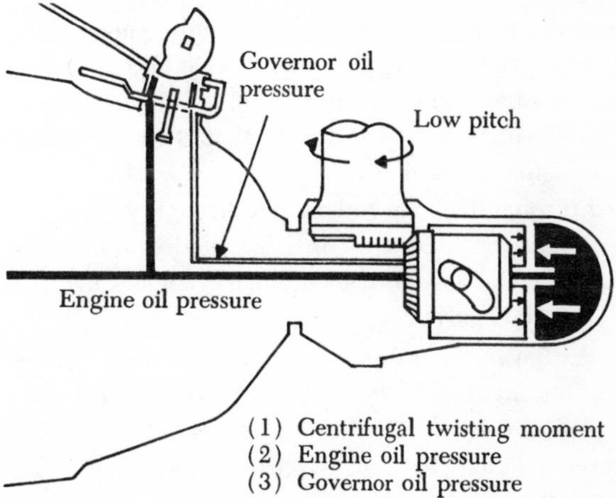

FIGURE 7–18. Diagram of hydromatic propeller operational forces.

governor to either side of the propeller piston. The oil on the side of the piston opposite this high-pressure oil returns to the intake side of the governor pump and is used over again. Engine oil at engine supply pressure does not enter the propeller directly but is supplied only to the governor.

During constant-speed operations, the double-acting governor mechanism sends oil to one side or the other of the piston as needed to keep the speed at a specified setting.

Underspeed Condition

Underspeeding results when the blades (solid black section, figure 7–19) have moved to a higher angle than that required for constant-speed operation (dotted line section). The arrow represents the direction in which the blades will move to re-establish on-speed operation.

When the engine speed drops below the r.p.m. for which the governor is set, the resulting decrease in centrifugal force exerted by the flyweights permits the speeder spring to lower the pilot valve, thereby opening the propeller-governor metering port. The oil then flows from the inboard end, through the distributor valve inboard inlet, between distributor valve lands, through the valve port, and into the propeller shaft governor oil passage. From here the oil moves through the propeller shaft oil transfer rings, up to the propeller-governor metering port, and then through the governor drive gear shaft and pilot valve arrangement to drain into the engine nose case. The engine scavenge pump recovers the oil from the engine nose case and returns it to the oil tank.

As the oil is drained from the inboard piston end, engine oil flows through the propeller shaft engine oil passage and the distributor valve ports. It emerges from the distributor valve outboard outlet into the outboard piston end. With the aid of blade centrifugal twisting moment, this oil moves the piston inboard. The piston motion is transmitted through the cam rollers and through the beveled gears to the blades. Thus, the blades move to a lower angle, as shown in the blade angle schematic diagram (figure 7–19).

As the blades assume a lower angle (dotted line section, figure 7–19), engine speed increases and the pilot valve is raised by the increased centrifugal force exerted by the governor flyweights. The propeller-governor metering port gradually closes, decreasing the flow of oil from the inboard piston end. This decrease in oil flow also decreases the rate of blade-angle change toward low pitch. By the time the engine has reached the r.p.m. for which the governor is set, the pilot valve will have assumed a neutral position (closed) in which it prevents any appreciable oil flow to or from the propeller. The valve is held in this position because the flyweight centrifugal force equals the speeeder spring force. The control forces are now equal, and the propeller and governor are operating on-speed.

Overspeed Condition

If the propeller is operating above the r.p.m. for which the control is set, the blades will be in a lower angle (solid black section in figure 7–20) than that required for constant-speed operation (dotted lines). The arrow represents the direction in which the blades will move to bring the propeller to the on-speed condition.

When the engine speed increases above the r.p.m. for which the governor is set, note that the flyweights move outward against the force of the speeder spring, raising the pilot valve. This opens the propeller-governor metering port, allowing governor oil flow from the governor booster pump, through the propeller-governor metering port, and into the engine oil transfer rings. From the rings, the oil passes through the propeller shaft governor oil passage, through a distributor valve port, between distributor lands, and then to the inboard piston end by way of the distributor valve inboard outlet.

As a result of this flow, the piston and the attached rollers move outboard, and the rotating cam is turned by the cam track. As the piston moves outboard, oil is displaced from the outboard piston end. This oil enters the distributor valve outboard inlet, flows through the distributor valve port, past the outboard end of the valve land, through the port, and into the propeller shaft engine oil passage. From that point it is dissipated into the engine lubricating system. The same balance forces exist across the distributor valve during overspeed as during underspeed, except that oil at governor pressure replaces oil at drain pressure on the inboard end of the valve land and between lands.

Outboard motion of the piston moves the propeller blades toward a higher angle, which, in turn, decreases the engine r.p.m. A decrease in engine r.p.m. decreases the rotating speed of the governor flyweights. As a result, the flyweights are moved inward by the force of the speeder spring, the pilot valve is lowered, and the propeller governor metering port is closed. Once this port has been closed,

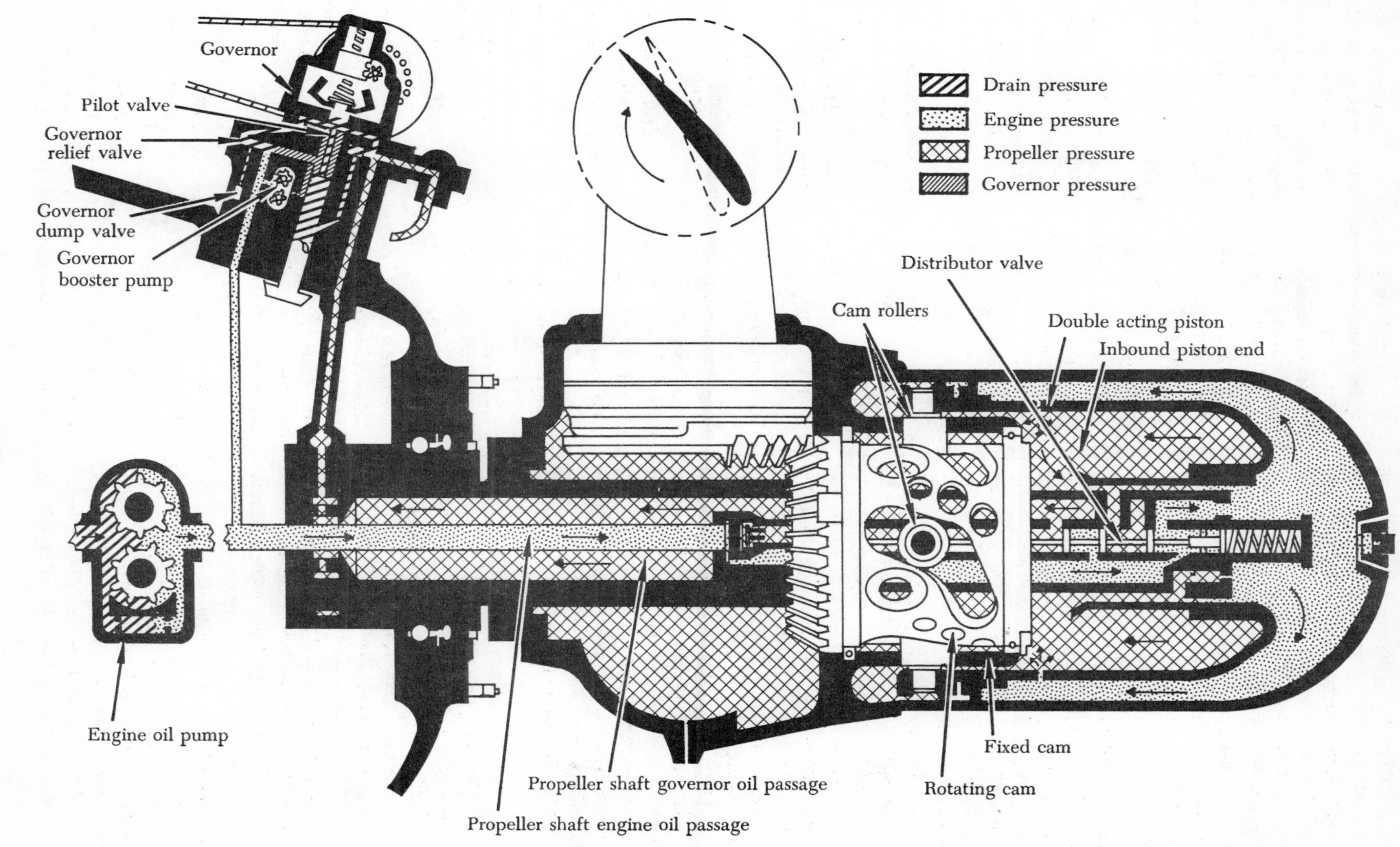

FIGURE 7–19. Propeller operation (underspeed condition).

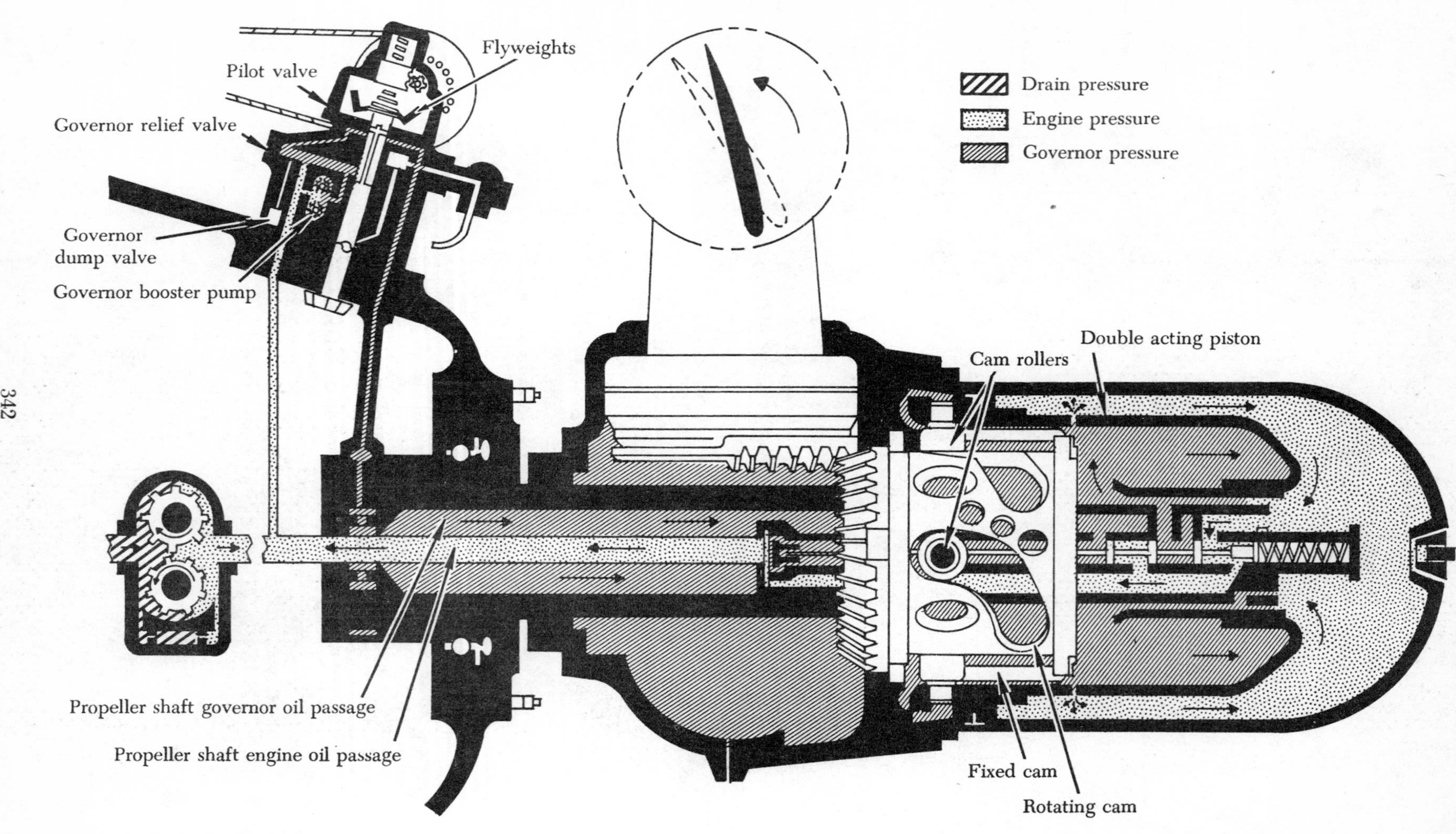

FIGURE 7–20. Propeller operation (overspeed condition).

oil flow to or from the propeller practically ceases, and the propeller and governor operate on-speed.

Feathering Operation

A typical hydromatic propeller feathering installation is shown in figure 7–21. When the feathering push-button switch is depressed, the low-current circuit is established from the battery through the push-button holding coil and from the battery through the solenoid relay. As long as the circuit remains closed, the holding coil keeps the push button in the depressed position. Closing the solenoid establishes the high-current circuit from the battery to the feathering motor pump unit. The feathering pump picks up engine oil from the oil supply tank, boosts its pressure, if necessary, to the relief valve setting of the pump, and supplies it to the governor high-pressure transfer valve connection.

Auxiliary oil entering the high-pressure transfer valve connection shifts the governor transfer valve, which hydraulically disconnects the governor from the propeller and at the same time opens the propeller governor oil line to auxiliary oil. The oil flows through the engine transfer rings, through the propeller shaft governor oil passage, through the distributor valve port, between lands, and finally to the inboard piston end by way of the valve inboard outlet.

The distributor valve does not shift during the feathering operation. It merely provides an oil passageway to the inboard piston end for auxiliary oil and the outboard piston end for engine oil. The same conditions described for underspeed operation exist in the distributor valve, except that oil at auxiliary pressure replaces drain oil at the inboard end of the land and between lands. The distributor-valve spring is backed up by engine oil pressure, which means that at all times the pressure differential required to move the piston will be identical with that applied to the distributor valve.

The propeller piston moves outboard under the auxiliary oil pressure at a speed proportional to the rate at which oil is supplied. This piston motion is transmitted through the piston rollers operating in the oppositely inclined cam tracks of the fixed cam and the rotating cam, and is converted by the bevel gears into the blade-twisting moment. Only during feathering or unfeathering is the low mechanical advantage portion of the cam tracks used. (The low mechanical advantage portion lies between the break and the outboard end of the track profile.) Oil at engine pressure, displaced from the outboard piston end, flows through the distributor valve outboard inlet, past the outboard end of the valve land, through the valve port, into the propeller shaft engine oil passage, and is finally delivered into the engine lubricating system. Thus, the blades move toward the full high-pitch (or feathered) angle.

Having reached the full-feathered position, further movement of the mechanism is prevented by contact between the high-angle stop ring in the base of the fixed cam and the stop lugs set in the teeth of the rotating cam. The pressure in the inboard piston end now increases rapidly, and upon reaching a set pressure, the electric cutout switch automatically opens. This cutout pressure is less than that required to shift the distributor valve.

Opening the switch deenergizes the holding coil and releases the feathering push-button control switch. Release of this switch breaks the solenoid relay circuit which shuts off the feathering pump motor. The pressures in both the inboard and outboard ends of the piston drop to zero, and since all the forces are balanced, the propeller blades remain in the feathered position. Meanwhile, the governor high-pressure transfer valve has shifted to its normal position as soon as the pressure in the propeller-governor line drops below that required to hold the valve open.

Unfeathering Operation

To unfeather a hydromatic propeller, depress and hold in the feathering switch push-button control switch. As in the case of feathering a propeller, the low-current control circuits from the battery through the holding coil and from the battery through the solenoid are completed when the solenoid closes. The high-current circuit from the battery starts the motor-pump unit, and oil is supplied at a high pressure to the governor transfer valve.

Auxiliary oil entering through the high-pressure transfer valve connection shifts the governor transfer valve and disconnects the governor from the propeller line; in the same operation, auxiliary oil is admitted. (See figure 7–22.) The oil flows through the engine oil transfer rings, through the propeller-shaft governor oil passage, and into the distributor valve assembly.

When the unfeathering operation begins, the piston is in the extreme outboard position the oil enters the inboard piston end of the cylinder by way of the distributor valve inboard outlet. As the pressure on the inboard end of the piston increases, the pressure against the distributor valve land builds

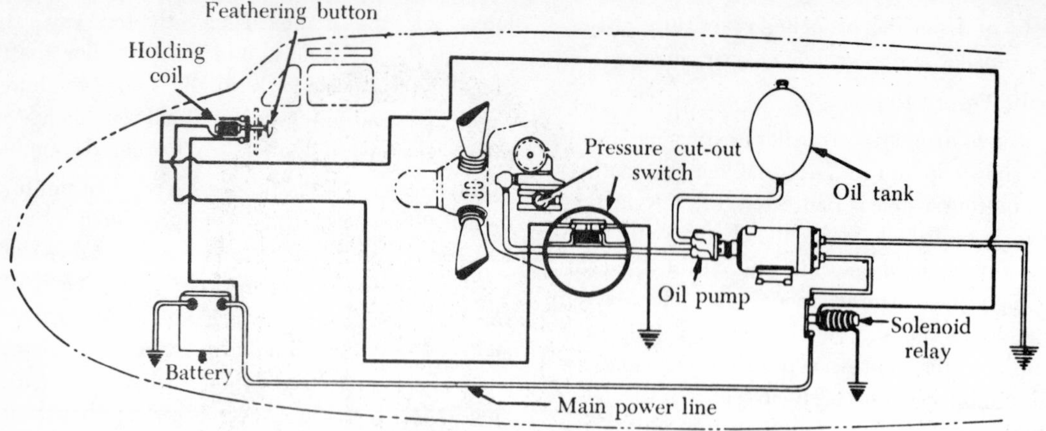

FIGURE 7–21. Typical feathering installation

up. When the pressure becomes greater than the combined opposing force of the distributor valve spring and the oil pressure behind this spring, the valve shifts. Once the valve shifts, the passages through the distributor valve assembly to the propeller are reversed. A passage is opened between lands and through a port to the outboard piston end by way of the distributor valve outlet. As the piston moves inboard under the auxiliary pump oil pressure, oil is displaced from the inboard piston end through the inlet ports between the valve lands, into the propeller shaft engine oil lands, and into the propeller shaft engine oil passage where it is discharged into the engine lubricating system. At the same time, the pressure at the cutout switch increases and the switch opens. However, the circuit to the feathering pump and motor unit remains complete so long as the feathering switch is held in.

With the inboard end of the propeller piston connected to drain, and auxiliary pressure flowing to the outboard end of the piston, the piston moves inboard. This unfeathers the blades as shown in figure 7–22. As the blades are unfeathered, they begin to windmill and assist the unfeathering operation by the added force toward low pitch brought about by the centrifugal twisting moment. When the engine speed has increased to approximately 1,000 r.p.m., the operator shuts off the feathering pump motor. The pressure in the distributor valve and at the governor transfer valve decreases, allowing the distributor valve to shift under the action of the governor high-pressure transfer valve spring. This action re-connects the governor with the propeller and establishes the same oil passages through the distributor valve that are used during constant-speed and feathering operations.

HYDRAULIC GOVERNORS

Three fundamental forces, already discussed, are used to control blade angle variations required for constant-speed propeller operation. These forces are:

(1) Centrifugal twisting moment, a component of the centrifugal force acting on a rotating blade which tends at all times to move the blade into low pitch.

(2) Oil at engine pressure on the outboard piston side, which supplements the centrifugal twisting moment toward low pitch.

(3) Propeller-governor oil on the inboard piston side, which balances the first two forces and moves the blades toward high pitch.

Governor Mechanism

The engine-driven propeller governor, figure 7–23, (constant-speed control) receives oil from the lubricating system and boosts its pressure to that required to operate the pitch-changing mechanism. It consists essentially of a gear pump to increase the pressure of the engine oil, a pilot valve actuated by flyweights which control the flow of oil through the governor, and a relief valve system which regulates the operating pressures in the governor.

In addition to boosting the engine oil pressure to produce one of the fundamental control forces, the governor maintains the required balance between all three control forces by metering to, or draining from, the inboard side of the propeller piston the exact quantity of oil necessary to maintain the proper blade angle for constant-speed operation.

The position of the pilot valve with respect to the propeller-governor metering port regulates the quan-

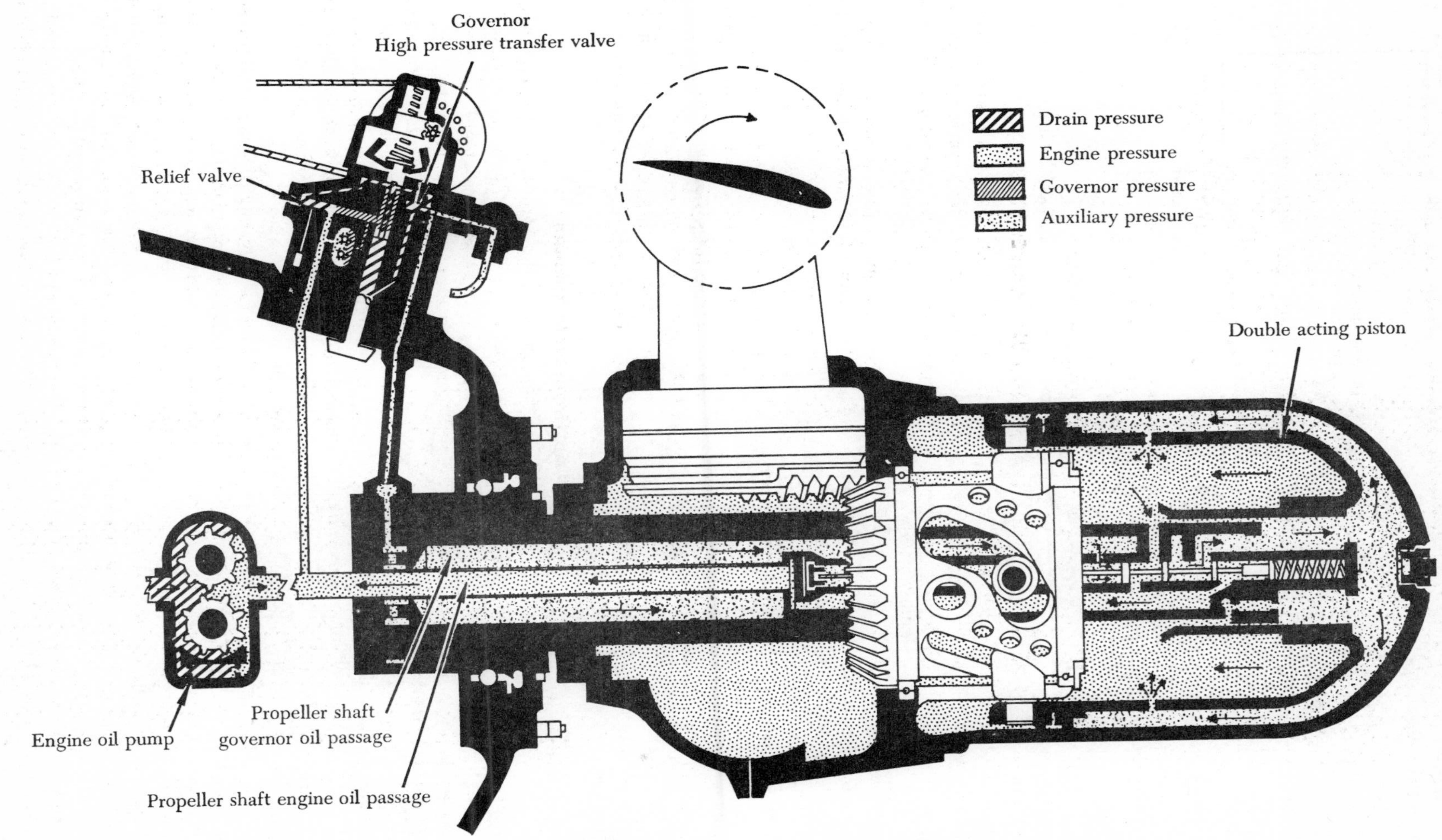

FIGURE 7–22. Propeller operation (unfeathering condition).

tity of oil which flows through this port to or from the propeller. A spring above the rack returns the rack to an intermediate position approximating cruising r.p.m. in case of governor control failure.

Setting the Propeller Governor

The propeller governor incorporates an adjustable stop, which limits the maximum speed at which the engine can run. As soon as the takeoff r.p.m. is reached, the propeller moves off the low-pitch stop. The larger propeller blade angle increases the load on the engine, thus maintaining the prescribed maximum engine speed.

At the time of propeller, propeller governor, or engine installation, the following steps are normally

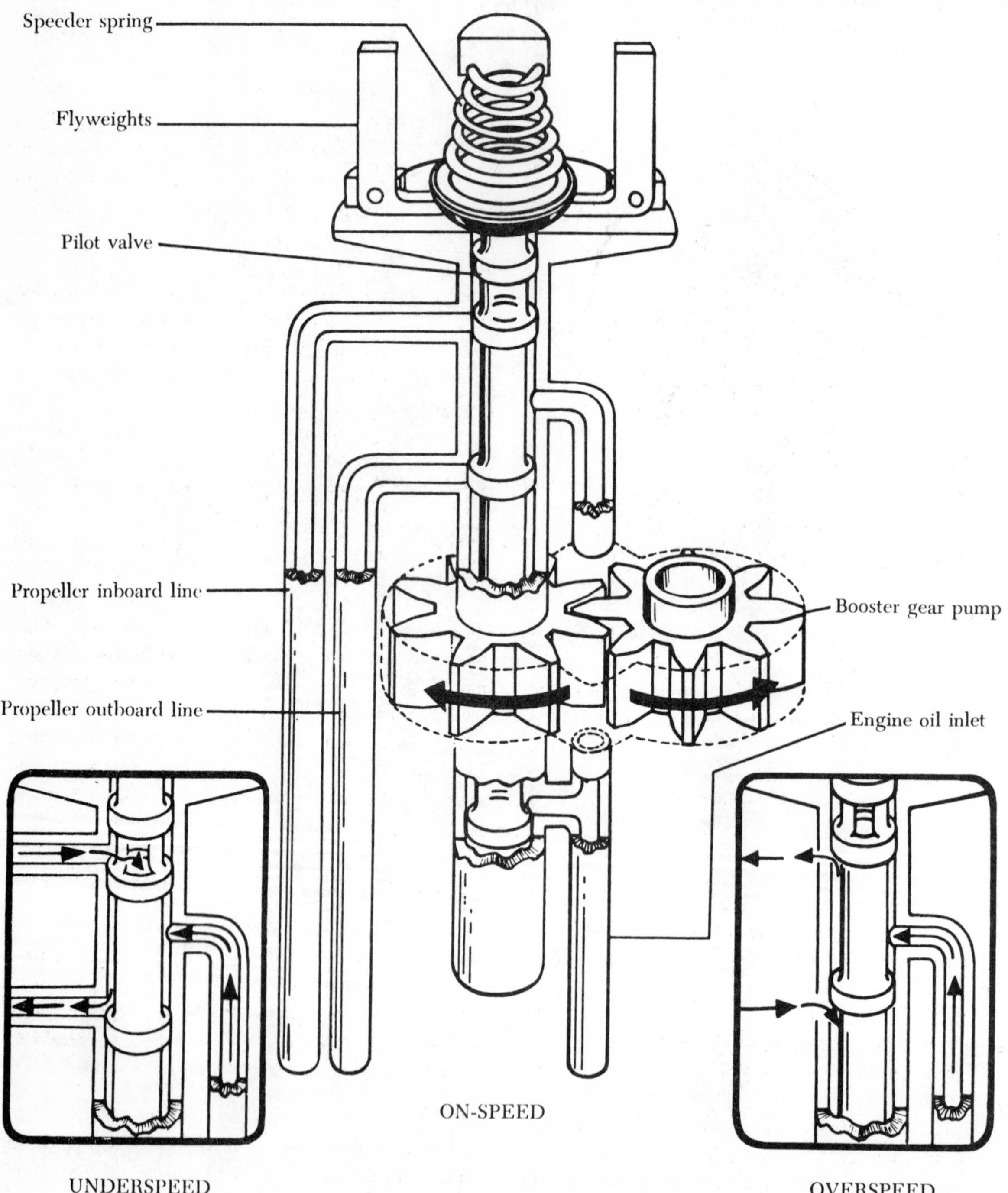

FIGURE 7–23. Propeller governor operating diagram.

taken to ensure that the powerplant will obtain takeoff r.p.m.

(1) During ground runup, move the throttle to takeoff position and note the resultant r.p.m. and manifold pressure.

(2) If the r.p.m. obtained is higher or lower than the takeoff r.p.m. prescribed in the manufacturer's instructions, re-set the adjustable stop on the governor until the prescribed r.p.m. is obtained.

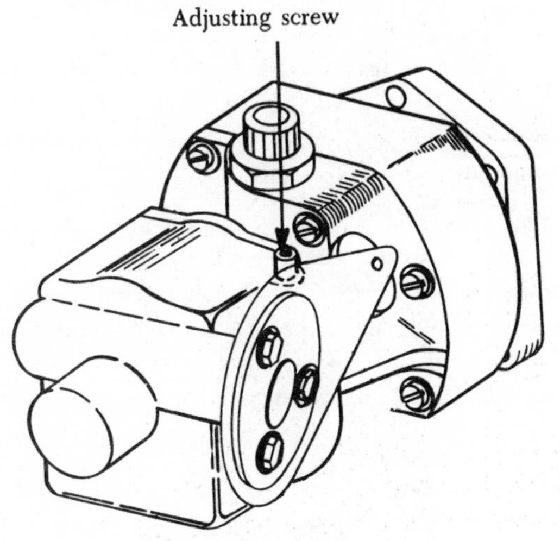

FIGURE 7–24. Propeller r.p.m. adjusting screw.

PROPELLER SYNCHRONIZATION

Most four-engine, and many twin-engine, aircraft are equipped with propeller synchronization systems. Synchronization systems provide a means of controlling and synchronizing engine r.p.m. Synchronization reduces vibration and eliminates the unpleasant beat produced by unsynchronized propeller operation. There are several types of synchronizer systems in use.

Master Motor Synchronizer

An early type, still in use on some operating aircraft, consists of a synchronizer master unit, four alternators, a tachometer, engine r.p.m. control levers, switches, and wiring. These components automatically control the speed of each engine and synchronize all engines at any desired r.p.m.

A sychronizer master unit incorporates a master motor which mechanically drives four contactor units; each contactor unit is electrically connected to an alternator. The alternator is a small, three-phase, alternating-current generator driven by an accessory drive of the engine. The frequency of the voltage produced by the generator is directly proportional to the engine accessory speed. In automatic operation, the desired engine r.p.m. may be set by manually adjusting the r.p.m. control lever until a master tachometer indicator on the instrument panel indicates the desired r.p.m. Any difference in r.p.m. between an engine and the master motor will cause the corresponding contactor unit to operate the pitch-changing mechanism of the propeller until the engine is on-speed (at correctly desired r.p.m.).

One-Engine Master System

Synchronizer systems are also installed in light twin-engine aircraft. Typically, such systems consist of a special propeller governor on the left-hand engine, a slave governor on the right-hand engine, a synchronizer control unit and an actuator in the right-hand engine nacelle.

The propeller governors are equipped with magnetic pickups that count the propeller revolutions and send a signal to the synchronizer unit. The synchronizer, which is usually a transistorized unit, compares the signal from the two propeller governor pickups. If the two signals are different, the propellers are out of synchronization, and the synchronizer control generates a d.c. pulse which is sent to the slave propeller unit.

The control signal is sent to an actuator, which consists of two rotary solenoids mounted to operate on a common shaft. A signal to increase the r.p.m. of the slave propeller is sent to one of the solenoids, which rotates the shaft clockwise. A signal to decrease r.p.m. is sent to the other solenoid, which moves the shaft in the opposite direction.

Each pulse signal rotates the shaft a fixed amount. This distance is called a "step." Attached to the shaft is a flexible cable, which is connected on its other end to a trimming unit. The vernier action of the trimming unit regulates the governor arm.

PROPELLER ICE CONTROL SYSTEMS

Effects of Propeller Icing

Ice formation on a propeller blade, in effect, produces a distorted blade airfoil section which causes a loss in propeller efficiency. Generally, ice collects unsymmetrically on a propeller blade and produces propeller unbalance and destructive vibration.

Fluid Systems

A typical fluid system (figure 7–25) includes a tank to hold a supply of anti-icing fluid. This fluid is forced to each propeller by a pump. The control system permits variation in the pumping rate so that the quantity of fluid delivered to a propeller can be varied, depending on the severity of icing. Fluid is transferred from a stationary nozzle on the engine nose case into a circular U-shaped channel (slinger ring) mounted on the rear of the propeller assembly. The fluid under pressure of centrifugal force is transferred through nozzles to each blade shank.

Because airflow around a blade shank tends to disperse anti-icing fluids to areas on which ice does not collect in large quantities, feed shoes, or boots, are installed on the blade leading edge. These feed shoes are a narrow strip of rubber, extending from the blade shank to a blade station that is approximately 75% of the propeller radius. The feed shoes are molded with several parallel open channels in which fluid will flow from the blade shank toward the blade tip by centrifugal force. The fluid flows laterally from the channels, over the leading edge of the blade.

Isopropyl alcohol is used in some anti-icing systems because of its availability and low cost. Phosphate compounds are comparable to isopropyl alcohol in anti-icing performance and have the advantage of reduced flammability. However, phosphate compounds are comparatively expensive and, consequently, are not widely used.

Electrical Deicing Systems

An electrical propeller icing control system (figure 7–26) consists basically of an electrical energy source, a resistance heating element, system controls, and necessary wiring. The heating elements are mounted internally or externally on the propeller spinner and blades. Electrical power from the aircraft system is transferred to the propeller hub through electrical leads, which terminate in slip rings and brushes. Flexible connectors are used to transfer power from the hub to the blade elements.

Icing control is accomplished by converting electrical energy to heat energy in the heating element. Balanced ice removal from all blades must be obtained as nearly as possible if excessive vibration is to be avoided. To obtain balanced ice removal, variation of heating current in the blade elements

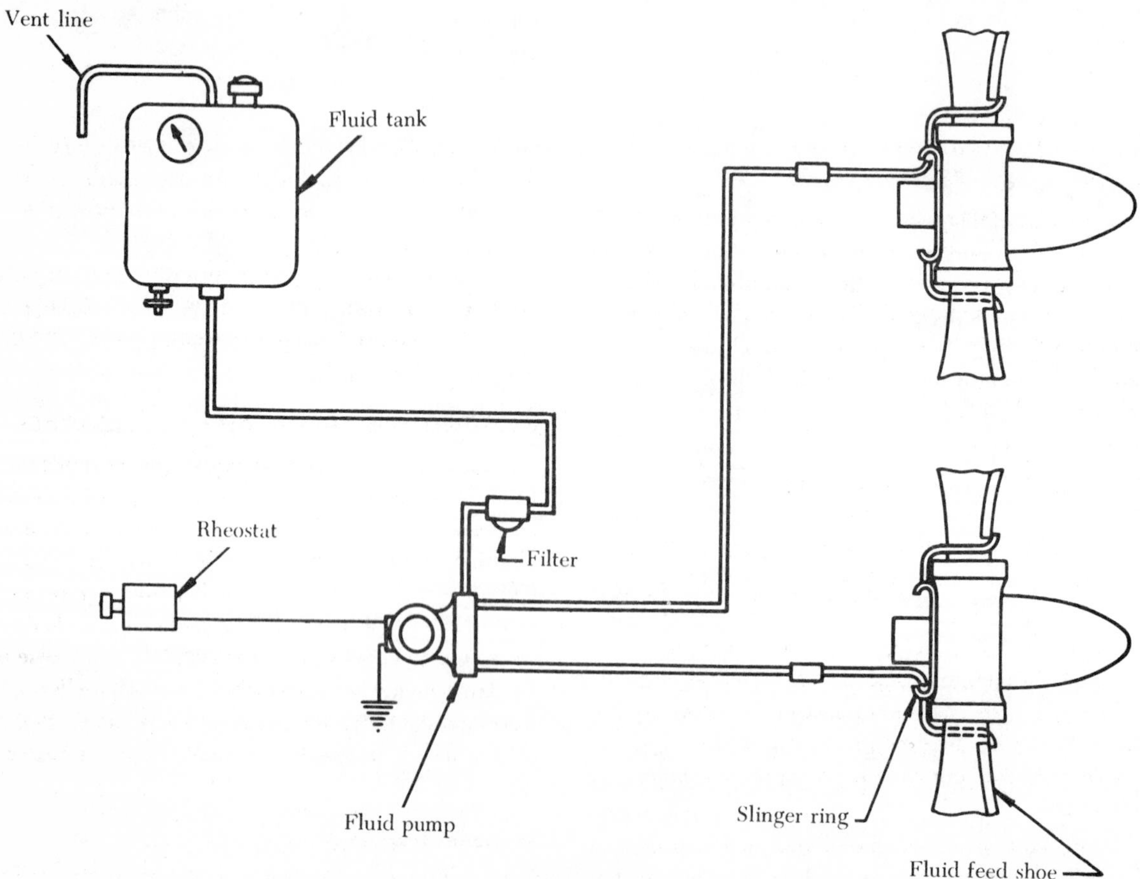

FIGURE 7–25. Typical propeller fluid anti-icing system.

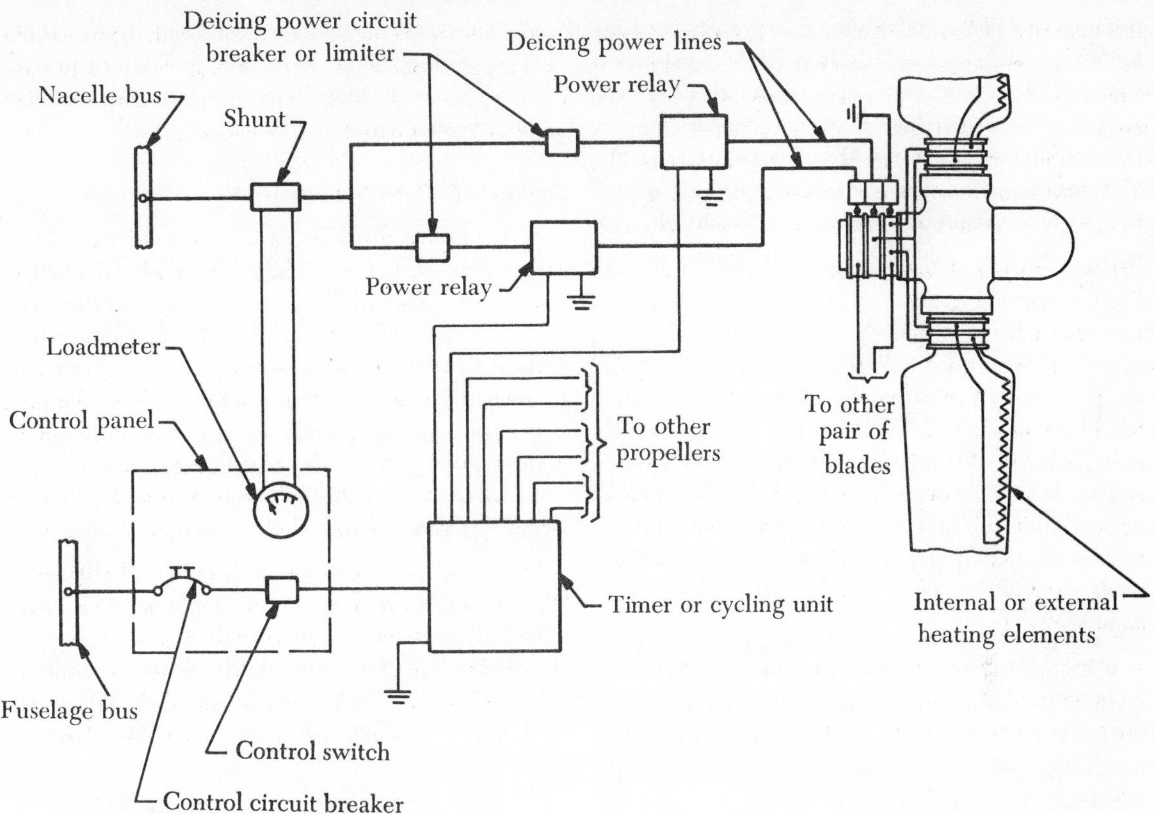

FIGURE 7–26. Typical electrical deicing system.

is controlled so that similar heating effects are obtained in opposite blades.

Electrical deicing systems are usually designed for intermittent application of power to the heating elements to remove ice after formation but before excessive accumulation. Proper control of heating intervals aids in preventing runback, since heat is applied just long enough to melt the ice face in contact with the blade.

If heat supplied to an icing surface is more than that required to melt just the inner ice face, but insufficient to evaporate all the water formed, water will run back over the unheated surface and freeze. Runback of this nature causes ice formation on uncontrolled icing areas of the blade or surface.

Cycling timers are used to energize the heating element circuits for periods of 15 to 30 seconds, with a complete cycle time of 2 minutes. A cycling timer is an electric motor driven contactor which controls power contactors in separate sections of the circuit.

Controls for propeller electrical deicing systems include on-off switches, ammeters or loadmeters to indicate current in the circuits, and protective devices, such as current limiters or circuit breakers. The ammeters or loadmeters permit monitoring of individual circuit currents and reflect operation of the timer.

To prevent element overheating, the propeller deicing system is generally used only when the propellers are rotating, and for short periods of time during ground runup.

PROPELLER INSPECTION AND MAINTENANCE

The propeller inspection requirements and maintenance procedures discussed in this section are representative of those in widespread use on most of the propellers described in this chapter. No attempt has been made to include detailed maintenance procedures for a particular propeller, and all pressures, figures, and sizes are solely for the purpose of illustration and do not have specific application. For maintenance information on a specific propeller, always refer to applicable manufacturer's instructions.

Propeller Inspection

Propellers must be inspected regularly. The exact time interval for particular propeller inspections is usually specified by the propeller manufacturer. The regular daily inspection of propellers varies little from one type to another. Typically it is a visual inspection of propeller blades, hubs, controls, and accessories for security, safety, and general condition. Visual inspection of the blades does not mean a careless or casual observation. The inspection should be meticulous enough to detect any flaw or defect that may exist.

Inspections performed at greater intervals of time, *e.g.*, 25, 50, or 100 hours, usually include a visual check of:

(1) Blades, spinners, and other external surfaces for excessive oil or grease deposits.

(2) Weld and braze sections of blades and hubs for evidence of failure.

(3) Blade, spinner, and hubs for nicks, scratches or other flaws. Use a magnifying glass if necessary.

(4) Spinner or dome shell attaching screws for tightness.

(5) The lubricating oil levels when applicable.

If a propeller is involved in an accident, and a possibility exists that internal damage may have occurred, the propeller should be disassembled and inspected. Whenever a propeller is removed from a shaft, the hub cone seats, cones, and other contact parts should be examined to detect undue wear, galling, or corrosion.

During major overhaul, the propeller is disassembled, and all parts are inspected and checked for size, tolerances, and wear. A magnetic inspection or another type of nondestructive test is usually made at this time to determine whether any fatigue cracks have developed on the steel components and assemblies.

PROPELLER VIBRATION

When powerplant vibration is encountered, it is sometimes difficult to determine whether it is the result of engine vibration or propeller vibration. In most cases the cause of the vibration can be determined by observing the propeller hub, dome, or spinner while the engine is running within a 1,200- to 1,500-r.p.m. range, and determining whether or not the propeller hub rotates on an absolutely horizontal plane. If the propeller hub appears to swing in a slight orbit, the vibration will normally be caused by the propeller. If the propeller hub does not appear to rotate in an orbit, the difficulty will probably be caused by engine vibration.

When propeller vibration is the reason for excessive powerplant vibration, the difficulty will usually be caused by propeller blade unbalance, propeller blades not tracking, or variation in propeller blade angle settings. Check the propeller blade tracking and then the low-pitch blade-angle setting to determine if they are the cause of the vibration.

If both propeller tracking and low blade-angle setting are correct, the propeller is statically or dynamically unbalanced and should be replaced, or re-balanced if permitted by the manufacturer.

BLADE TRACKING

Blade tracking is the process of determining the positions of the tips of the propeller blades relative to each other. Tracking shows only the relative position of the blades, not their actual path. The blades should all track one another as closely as possible. The difference in track at like points must not exceed the tolerance specified by the propeller manufacturer.

The design and manufacture of propellers is such that the tips of the blades will give a good indication of tracking. The following method for checking tracking is normally used.

(1) Install a heavy wire or small rod on the leading edge of the aircraft wing or other suitable area of the aircraft until it lightly touches the propeller blade face near the tip (figure 7-27).

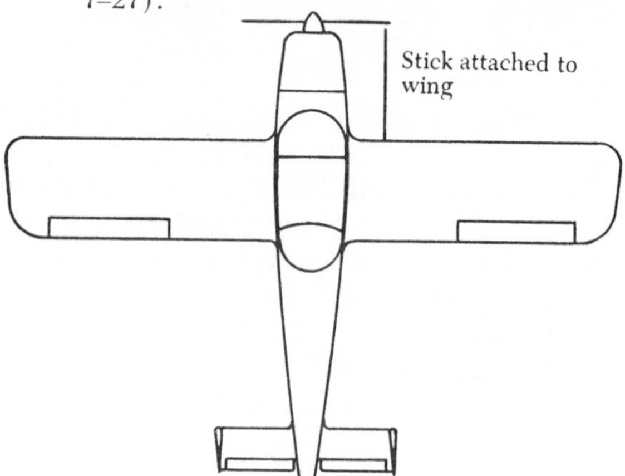

FIGURE 7-27. Checking blade track.

(2) Rotate the propeller until the next blade is in the same position as the first blade, and measure the distance between the rod and blade. Continue this process until all blades have been checked.

CHECKING AND ADJUSTING PROPELLER BLADE ANGLES

When an improper blade-angle setting is found

during installation or is indicated by engine performance, the following maintenance guidelines are usually followed:

(1) From the applicable manufacturer's instructions, obtain the blade-angle setting and the station at which the blade angle is checked. Do not use metal scribes or other sharp-pointed instruments to mark the location of blade stations or to make reference lines on propeller blades, since such surface scratches can eventually result in blade failure.

(2) Use a universal propeller protractor to check the blade angles while the propeller is on the engine.

Use of the Universal Propeller Protractor

The universal propeller protractor can be used to check propeller blade angles when the propeller is on a balancing stand or installed on the aircraft engine. Figure 7–28 shows the parts and adjustments of a universal propeller protractor. The following instructions for using the protractor apply to a propeller installed on the engine.

Turn the propeller until the first blade to be checked is horizontal with the leading edge up.

Place the corner spirit level (figure 7–28) at right angles to the face of the protractor. Align degree and vernier scales by turning the disk adjuster before the disk is locked to the ring. The locking device is a pin that is held in the engaged position by a spring. The pin can be released by pulling it outward and turning it 90°.

Release the ring-to-frame lock (a right-hand screw with thumb nut) and turn the ring until both ring and disk zeros are at the top of the protractor.

Check the blade angle by determining how much the flat side of the block slants from the plane of rotation. First, locate a point to represent the plane of rotation by placing the protractor vertically against the end of the hub nut or any convenient surface known to lie in the plane of propeller rotation. Keep the protractor vertical by the corner spirit level, and turn the ring adjuster until the center spirit level is horizontal. This sets the zero of the vernier scale at a point representing the plane of propeller rotation. Then lock the ring to the frame.

Holding the protractor by the handle with the curved edge up, release the disk-to-ring lock. Place the forward vertical edge (the edge opposite the one first used) against the blade at the station specified

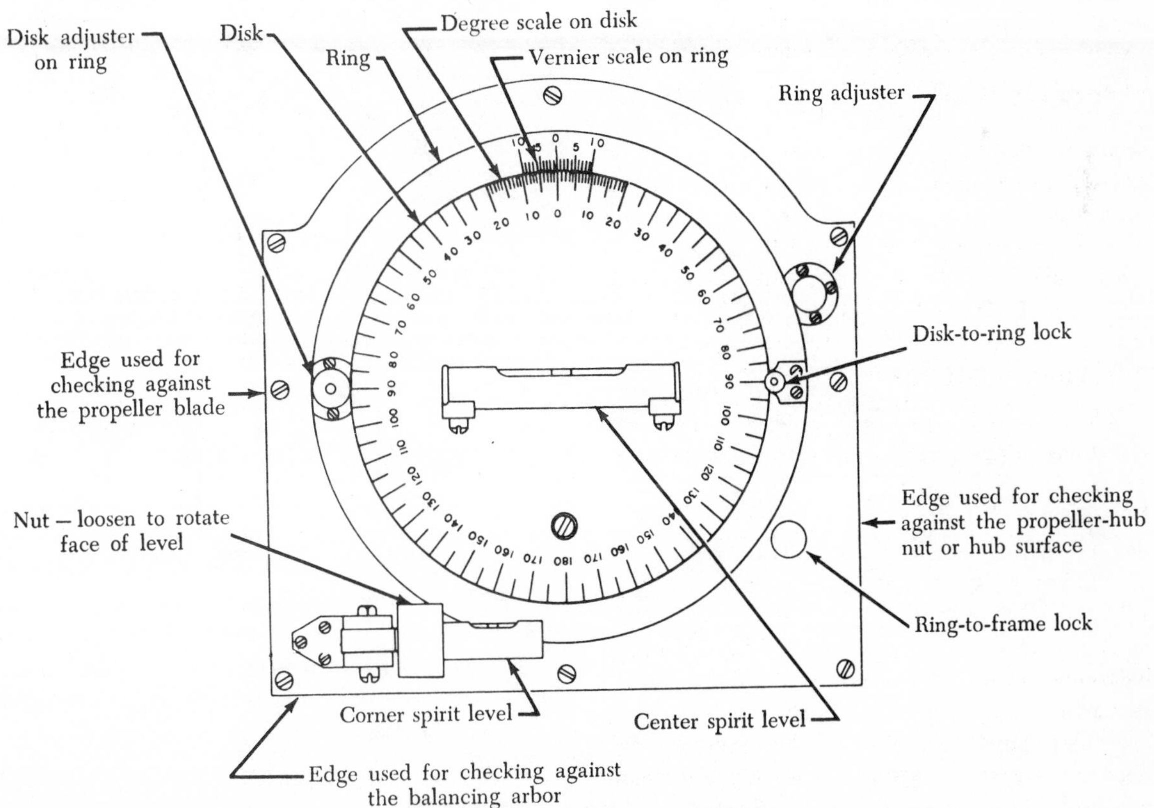

FIGURE 7–28. Universal protractor.

in the manufacturer's instructions. Keep the protractor vertical by the corner spirit level, and turn the disk adjuster until the center spirit level is horizontal. The number of degrees and tenths of a degree between the two zeros indicates the blade angle.

In determining the blade angle, remember that ten points on the vernier scale are equal to nine points on the degree scale. The graduations on the vernier scale represent tenths of a degree, but those of the degree scale represent whole degrees. The number of tenths of a degree in the blade angle is given by the number of vernier-scale spaces between the zero of the vernier scale and the vernier-scale graduation line nearest to perfect alignment with a degree-scale graduation line. This reading should always be made on the vernier scale. The vernier scale increases in the same direction that the protractor scale increases. This is opposite to the direction of rotation of the moving element of the protractor.

After making any necessary adjustment of the blade, lock it in position and repeat the same operations for the remaining blades of the propeller.

PROPELLER BALANCING

Propeller unbalance, which is a source of vibration in an aircraft, may be either static or dynamic. Propeller static unbalance occurs when the center of gravity of the propeller does not coincide with the axis of rotation.

Dynamic unbalance results when the center of gravity of similar propeller elements, such as blades or counterweights, does not follow in the same plane of rotation. Since the length of the propeller assembly along the engine crankshaft is short in comparison to its diameter, and since the blades are secured to the hub so they lie in the same plane perpendicular to the running axis, the dynamic unbalance resulting from improper mass distribution is negligible, provided the track tolerance requirements are met.

Another type of propeller unbalance, aerodynamic unbalance, results when the thrust (or pull) of the blades is unequal. This type of unbalance can be largely eliminated by checking blade contour and blade angle setting.

Static Balancing

Static balancing can be done by the suspension method or by the knife-edge method. In the suspension method the propeller or part is hung by a cord, and any unbalance is determined by noting the eccentricity between a disk firmly attached to the cord and a cylinder attached to the assembly or part being tested. The suspension method is used less frequently than the simpler and more accurate knife-edge method.

The knife-edge test stand (figure 7–29) has two hardened steel edges mounted to allow the free rotation of an assembled propeller between them. The knife-edge test stand must be located in a room or area that is free from any air motion, and preferably removed from any source of heavy vibration.

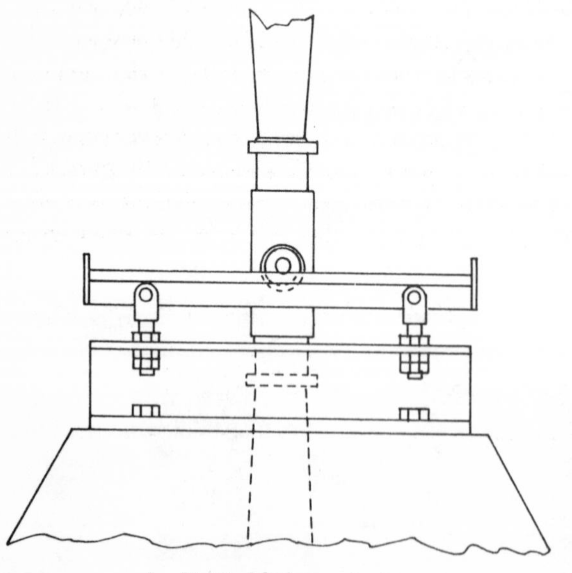

A. Vertical balance check

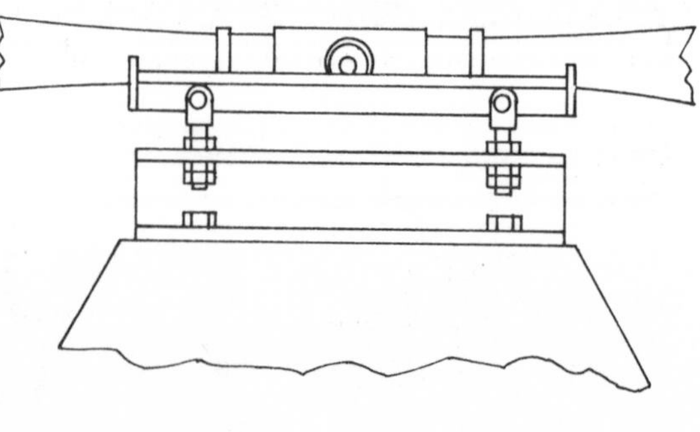

B. Horizontal balance check

FIGURE 7–29. Positions of two-bladed propeller during balance check.

The standard method of checking propeller assembly balance involves the following sequence of operations:

(1) Insert a bushing in the engine shaft hole of the propeller.

(2) Insert a mandrel or arbor through the bushing.

(3) Place the propeller assembly so that the ends of the arbor are supported upon the balance stand knife-edges. The propeller must be free to rotate.

If the propeller is properly balanced, statically, it will remain at any position in which it is placed. Check two-bladed propeller assemblies for balance, first with the blades in a vertical position and then with the blades in a horizontal position (figure 7–29). Repeat the vertical position check with the blade positions reversed; that is, with the blade which was checked in the downward position placed in the upward position.

Check a three-bladed propeller assembly with each blade placed in a downward vertical position, as shown in figure 7–30.

During a propeller static balance check, all blades must be at the same blade angle. Before conducting the balance check, inspect to see that each blade has been set at the same blade angle.

Unless otherwise specified by the manufacturer, an acceptable balance check requires that the propeller assembly have no tendency to rotate in any of the positions previously described. If the propeller balances perfectly in all described positions, it should also balance perfectly in all intermediate positions. When necessary, check for balance in intermediate positions to verify the check in the originally described positions.

When a propeller assembly is checked for static balance and there is a definite tendency of the assembly to rotate, certain corrections to remove the unbalance are allowed.

(1) The addition of permanent fixed weights at acceptable locations when the total weight of the propeller assembly or parts is under the allowable limit.

(2) The removal of weight at acceptable locations when the total weight of the propeller assembly or parts is equal to the allowable limit.

The location for removal or addition of weight for propeller unbalance correction has been determined by the propeller manufacturer. The method and point of application of unbalance corrections must be checked to see that they are according to applicable drawings.

SERVICING PROPELLERS

Propeller servicing includes cleaning, lubricating, and replenishing operating oil supplies.

Cleaning Propeller Blades

Aluminum and steel propeller blades and hubs usually are cleaned by washing the blades with a suitable cleaning solvent, using a brush or cloth. Acid or caustic materials should not be used. Power buffers, steel wool, steel brushes, or any other tool or substance that may scratch or mar the blade should be avoided.

If a high polish is desired, a number of good grades of commercial metal polish are available. After completing the polishing operation, all traces of polish should be immediately removed. When the blades are clean, they should be coated with a clean film of engine oil or suitable equivalent.

To clean wooden propellers, warm water and a mild soap can be used, together with brushes or cloth.

If a propeller has been subjected to salt water, it should be flushed with fresh water until all traces of salt have been removed. This should be accomplished as soon as possible after the salt water has

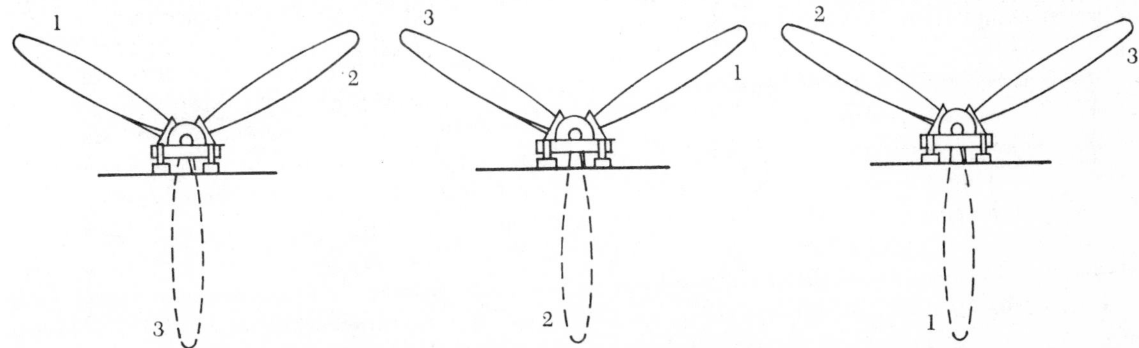

FIGURE 7–30. Positions of three-bladed propeller during balance check.

splashed on the propeller, regardless of whether the propeller parts are aluminum-alloy, steel, or wood. After flushing, all parts should be dried thoroughly, and metal parts should be coated with clean engine oil or a suitable equivalent.

Propeller Lubrication

Hydromatic propellers operated with engine oil do not require lubrication. Electric propellers will require oils and greases for hub lubricants and pitch change drive mechanisms.

Proper propeller lubrication procedures, with oil and grease specifications, are usually published in the manufacturer's instructions. Experience indicates that water sometimes gets into the propeller blade bearing assembly on some models of propellers. For this reason the propeller manufacturer's greasing schedule must be followed to ensure proper lubrication of moving parts. Grease replacement through attached pressure fittings (zerks) must be done in accordance with the manufacturer's instructions.

The reservoir oil level must be checked at specified intervals on propellers that have self-contained hydraulic units. Usually this type of propeller must have one of the blades (generally No. 1) positioned so that the oil is visible in a sight glass on the side of the reservoir. Extreme care must be used when servicing the reservoir to avoid overfilling and servicing with the wrong specification oil.

TURBOPROP PROPELLER

The turboprop propeller is operated by a gas turbine engine through a reduction-gear assembly. It has proved to be an extremely efficient power source. The combination of propeller, reduction-gear assembly, and turbine engine is referred to as a turboprop powerplant.

Turboprop engines are used on aircraft ranging in size from large four-engine transports to medium-size executive and relatively small twin-engine aircraft. The following discussion is directed toward a turbo-propeller that consists of components and assemblies typical of many turboprop aircraft.

Unlike the turbojet engine, which produces thrust directly, the turboprop engine produces thrust indirectly, since the compressor and turbine assembly furnishes torque to a propeller, which, in turn, produces the major portion of the propulsive force which drives the aircraft. The turboprop fuel control and the propeller governor are connected and operate in coordination with each other. The power lever directs a signal from the cockpit to the fuel control for a specific amount of power from the engine. The fuel control and the propeller governor together establish the correct combination of r.p.m., fuel flow, and propeller blade angle to create sufficient propeller thrust to provide the desired power.

The propeller control system is divided into two types of control: One for flight and one for ground operation. For flight, the propeller blade angle and fuel flow for any given power lever setting are governed automatically according to a predetermined schedule. Below the "flight idle" power lever position the coordinated r.p.m. blade angle schedule becomes incapable of handling the engine efficiently. Here the ground handling range, referred to as the beta range, is encountered. In the beta range of the throttle quadrant, the propeller blade angle is not governed by the propeller governor, but is controlled by the power lever position. When the power lever is moved below the start position, the propeller pitch is reversed to provide reverse thrust for rapid deceleration of the aircraft after landing.

A characteristic of the turboprop is that changes in power are not related to engine speed, but to turbine inlet temperature. During flight the propeller maintains a constant engine speed. This speed is known as the 100% rated speed of the engine, and it is the design speed at which most power and best overall efficiency can be obtained. Power changes are effected by changing the fuel flow. An increase in fuel flow causes an increase in turbine inlet temperature and a corresponding increase in energy available at the turbine. The turbine absorbs more energy and transmits it to the propeller in the form of torque. The propeller, in order to absorb the increased torque, increases blade angle, thus maintaining constant engine r.p.m.

The NTS (negative torque signal) control system (figure 7–31) provides a signal which increases propeller blade angle to limit negative shaft torque. When a predetermined negative torque is applied to the reduction gearbox, the stationary ring gear moves forward against the spring force due to a torque reaction generated by helical splines. In moving forward, the ring gear pushes two operating rods through the reduction gear nose. One or both of the rods may be used to signal the propeller and initiate an increase in propeller blade angle. This action (towards high blade angle) continues until the negative torque is relieved, resulting in the propeller returning to normal operation.

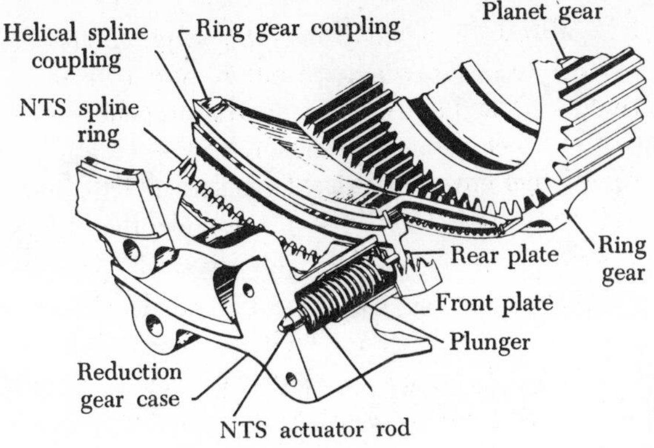

FIGURE 7–31. Negative torque signal components.

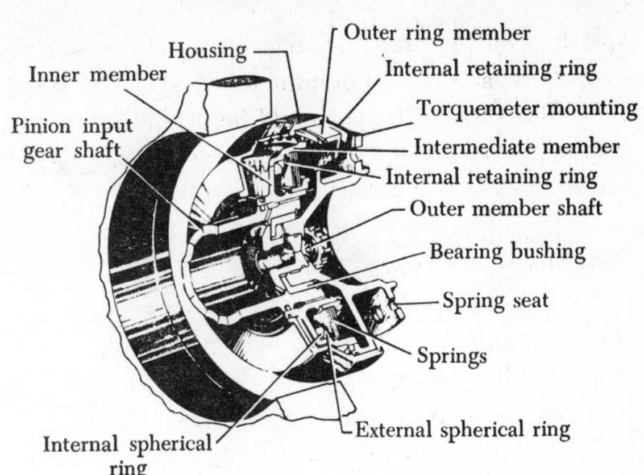

FIGURE 7–32. Safety coupling.

The NTS system functions when the following engine operating conditions are encountered: temporary fuel interruptions, air gust loads on the propeller, normal descents with lean fuel scheduling, high compressor air bleed conditions at low power settings, and normal shutdowns.

The TSS (thrust sensitive signal) is a safety feature which actuates the propeller feather lever. If a power loss occurs during takeoff, propeller drag is limited to that of a feathered propeller, reducing the hazards of yawing in multi-engine aircraft. This device automatically increases blade angle and causes the propeller to feather.

The TSS system consists of an externally mounted switch assembly on the right side of the reduction gearbox. A plunger extends into the switch from the inside of the gearbox. A spring loads the plunger against the thrust signal lever mounted inside the gearbox and contacts the outer ring of the prop shaft thrust bearing. When propeller positive thrust exceeds a predetermined value, the prop shaft and ball bearing move forward compressing two springs located between the thrust- and roller-bearing assemblies. The thrust signal lever follows the outer ring, and the TSS plunger moves into the front gearbox. The TSS system is then armed for takeoff and automatic operation. At any subsequent time when propeller thrust decreases below the predetermined value, spring force moves the prop shaft rearward. When this occurs, the TSS plunger moves outward energizing the autofeather system. This signals the propeller to increase blade angle.

A safety coupling (figure 7–32) disengages the reduction gear from the power unit if the power unit is operating above a preset negative torque value considerably greater than that required to actuate the NTS. The coupling consists essentially of an inner member splined to the pinion shaft, an outer member bolted to the extension shaft, and an intermediate member connected to the inner member through helical teeth and to the outer member through straight teeth.

The reaction of the helical teeth moves the intermediate member forward and into mesh when positive torque is applied, and rearward and out of mesh when negative torque is applied. Thus, when a predetermined negative torque is exceeded, the coupling members disengage automatically. Reengagement is also automatic during feathering or power unit shutdown. The safety coupling will operate only when negative torque is excessive.

Reduction Gear Assembly

A reduction gear assembly is shown in figure 7–33. It incorporates a single propeller drive shaft, an NTS system, a TSS system, a safety coupling, a propeller brake, an independent dry sump oil system, and the necessary gearing arrangement.

The propeller brake (figure 7–33) is designed to prevent the propeller from windmilling when it is feathered in flight, and to decrease the time for the propeller to come to a complete stop after engine shutdown.

The propeller brake is a friction-cone type, consisting of a stationary inner member and a rotating outer member which, when locked, acts upon the primary stage reduction gearing. During normal engine operation, reduction gear oil pressure holds the brake in the released position. This is accomplished by oil pressure which holds the outer member away from the inner member. When the propeller is feathered or at engine shutdown, as reduction gear oil pressure drops off, the effective hydraulic force decreases, and a spring force moves

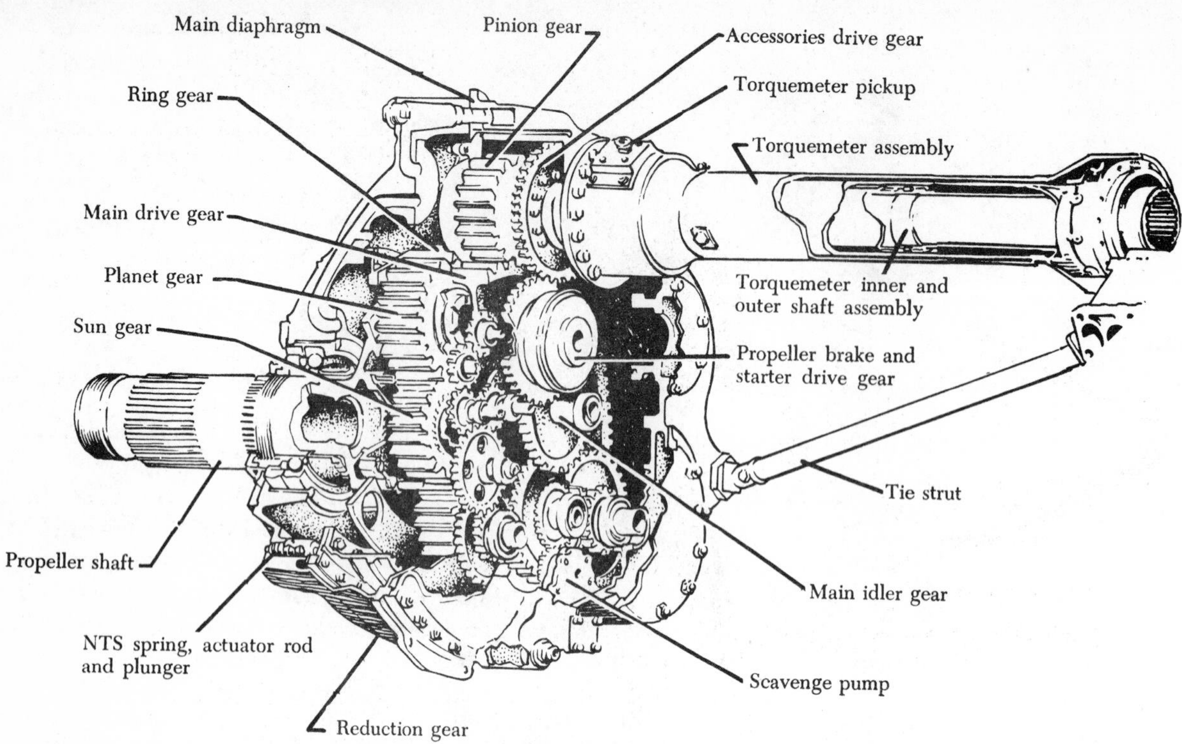

FIGURE 7–33. Reduction gear and torquemeter assemblies.

the outer member into contact with the inner member.

The power unit drives the reduction gear assembly through an extension shaft and torquemeter assembly. The reduction gear assembly is secured to the power unit by the torquemeter housing which serves as the bottom support and pair of the struts serving as the top support.

The tie struts assist in carrying the large overhanging moments and forces produced by the propeller and reduction gear. The front ends of the struts have eccentric pins which are splined for locking. These pins adjust the length of the strut to compensate for the manufacturing tolerances on the drive shaft housing and interconnecting parts.

Turbo-Propeller Assembly

The turbo-propeller provides an efficient and flexible means of using the power produced by the turbine engine. The propeller assembly (figure 7–34), together with the control assembly, maintains a constant r.p.m. of the engine at any condition in flight idle (alpha range). For ground handling and reversing (beta range), the propeller can be operated to provide either zero or negative thrust.

The major subassemblies of the propeller assembly are the barrel, dome, low-pitch stop assembly, pitch lock regulator assembly, blade assembly, and deicing contact ring holder assembly.

The control assembly (figure 7–34) is a nonrotating assembly mounted on the aft extension of the propeller assembly barrel. It contains the oil reservoir, pumps, valves, and control devices which supply the pitch-changing mechanism with hydraulic power of proper magnitude and direction to vary pitch for the selected operating conditions. It also contains the brush housing for the electric power for the deicer rings.

The spinner assembly is a cone-shaped configuration which mounts on the propeller and encloses the dome and barrel to reduce drag. It also provides for ram air to enter and cool the oil used in the propeller control.

The afterbody assembly is a nonrotating component mounted on the engine gearbox to enclose the control assembly. Together with the spinner, it provides a streamlined flow over the engine nacelle.

The synchrophasing system is designed to maintain a preset angular relationship between the designated master propeller and the slave propellers. The three main units of this system are the pulse generator, the electronic synchrophaser, and the speed bias servo assembly.

The manual phase control provides for pre-selec-

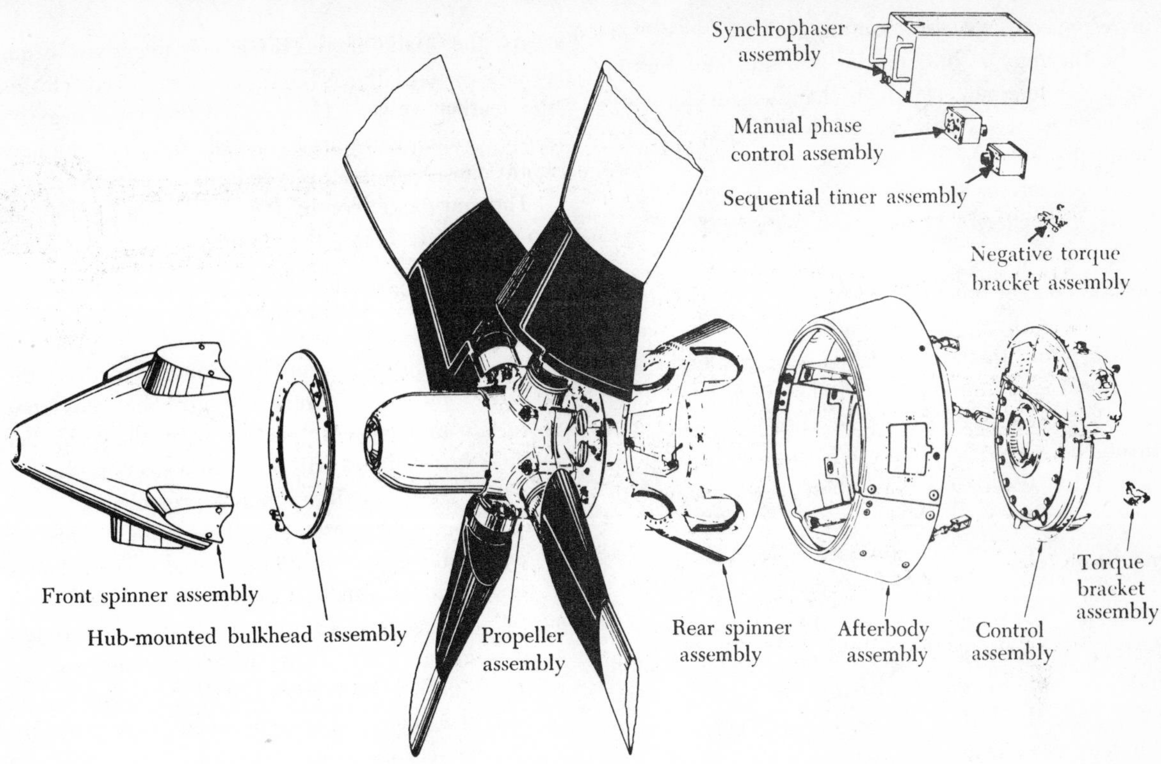

FIGURE 7–34. Propeller assembly and associated parts.

tion of desired phase angle relationship between the master and slave propellers and for vernier adjustment of the speed of the engine selected as master. This master trim provides for a master engine speed adjustment of approximately ±1% r.p.m.

Propeller operation is controlled by a mechanical linkage from the cockpit-mounted power lever and the emergency engine shutdown handle (if the aircraft is provided with one) to the coordinator, which, in turn, is linked to the propeller control input lever.

The nongoverning or taxi range from the reverse position to the "flight idle" position (0° to 34° indexes on the coordinator including the "ground idle" position) is referred to as the beta range. The governing or flight range from the "flight idle" position to the "takeoff" position (34° to 90° indexes on the coordinator) is referred to as the alpha range. The remaining portion of the coordinator segment (90° indexes to the "feather" position) concerns feathering only.

The beta range control for ground handling is entirely hydromechanical and is obtained by introducing a cam and lever system which operates the pilot valve. One camshaft (alpha shaft) moves in response to power lever motion and establishes the desired blade angle schedule (beta range). The other camshaft (beta shaft) is operated from the blade feedback gearing. Its position provides a signal of actual blade angle position in the beta range. Also, the pilot valve is moved by interaction of these cams and levers to meter oil to either high or low pitch so that the actual blade angle agrees with the scheduled angle.

In the beta range (below flight idle) the propeller governing action is blocked out, since an overspeed would result in blade angle motion in the wrong direction of the propeller if it were in the reverse range.

When the power lever is moved to call for a blade angle below flight idle, the speed set cam (on the alpha shaft) puts additional force on the speeder spring. This holds the pilot valve in an underspeed condition against the beta lever system until the scheduled blade angle is reached.

Constant-speed governing (alpha range control) is accomplished by a flyball-actuated governor. The flyweight and pilot valve are driven through gearing by propeller rotation.

In the alpha range the governor is set at its normal 100% r.p.m. setting by the speed set cam (on the alpha shaft), and the pilot valve is free to move in response to off-speed conditions.

Feathering is initiated by the feather button, engine emergency shutdown handle, or the autofeather system. Feathering is accomplished hydraulically by a feathering valve which bypasses other control functions and routes pitch change oil directly to the propeller.

The feathering operation is separate from all normal control functions. Pressure from the pump manifold is routed through the control feather valve before going to the pilot valve and the main and standby regulating valves. Similarly, the output of the pilot valve to either low or high pitch is routed through the feather valve. When the valve is positioned for feathering, the pump manifold is connected directly to the high-pitch line. This isolates the propeller lines from the rest of the control system and closes off the standby pump bypass.

Normal feathering is initiated by depressing the feather button. This action sends current to the holding coil of the feathering switch, auxiliary pump, and the feather solenoid, which positions the feather valve, feathering the propeller. When the propeller has been fully feathered, oil pressure buildup will operate a pressure cutout switch which will cause the auxiliary pump and feather solenoid to become de-energized through a relay system.

Feathering may also be accomplished by pulling the engine emergency shutdown handle or switch to the "shutdown" position. This action mechanically positions the feather valve and electrically energizes the feathering button, sending the propeller to full feather.

The autofeather system automatically energizes the holding coil (pulling in the feather button) when engine power loss results in a propeller thrust drop to a preset value. This system is switch-armed for use during takeoff and can function only when the power lever is near or in the "takeoff" position.

The NTS device mechanically moves the NTS plunger, which actuates a linkage in the propeller control when a predetermined negative torque value is sensed (when the propeller drives the engine). This plunger, working through control linkage, shifts the feather valve plunger, sending the blades toward feather.

As the blade angle increases, negative torque decreases until the NTS signal is removed, closing the feather valve. If the predetermined negative torque value is again exceeded, the NTS plunger again causes the feather valve plunger to shift.

The normal effect of the NTS is a cycling of r.p.m. slightly below the r.p.m. at which the negative torque was sensed.

Unfeathering is initiated by pulling the feather button to the "unfeather" position. This action supplies voltage to the auxiliary motor to drive the auxiliary pump. Because the propeller governor is in an underspeed position with the propeller feathered, the blades will move in a decreased pitch direction under auxiliary pump pressure.

The pitch lock operates in the event of a loss of propeller oil pressure or an overspeed. The ratchets of the assembly become engaged when the oil pressure which keeps them apart is dissipated through a flyweight-actuated valve which operates at an r.p.m. slightly higher than the 100% r.p.m. The ratchets become disengaged when high pressure and r.p.m. settings are restored.

At the "flight idle" power lever position, the control beta followup low-pitch stop on the beta set cam (on the alpha shaft) is set about 2° below the flight low-pitch stop setting, acting as a secondary low-pitch stop. At the "takeoff" power lever position, this secondary low-pitch stop sets a higher blade angle stop than the mechanical flight low-pitch stop. This provides for control of overspeed after rapid power lever advance, as well as a secondary low-pitch stop.

BLADE CUFFS

A blade cuff is a metal, wood, or plastic structure designed for attachment to the shank end of the blade, with an outer surface that will transform the round shank into an airfoil section. The cuff is designed primarily to increase the flow of cooling air to the engine nacelle.

The cuffs are attached to the blades by mechanical clamping devices or by using bonding materials. Rubber-base adhesives and epoxy adhesives generally are used as bonding agents. Organic adhesives may cause corrosion, which results from moisture entrapment between the inner cuff surface and the outer shank surface.

CHAPTER 8

ENGINE REMOVAL AND REPLACEMENT

GENERAL

Procedures for removing or installing an aircraft engine usually vary widely with the type of aircraft and the type of engine. Thus, no single list of instructions can be provided as a guideline for all engines. Because of the many types of engine installations and the large number of design variations within each type or category, representative examples have been selected to illustrate the most typical installation procedures for reciprocating, turboprop, and turbojet engines.

The radial and the opposed engines are used to describe and represent general and typical procedures for all reciprocating engine buildup, removal, preservation, storage, and installation. Although these two types have been included to ensure adequate coverage of engines used in both heavy and light aircraft, much of the information and many of the procedures presented in the discussion of radial engines are applicable to opposed-type engines. Only the significant differences between the two types are included in the discussion of opposed-type engines.

It should be emphasized that while procedures for specific engines and aircraft are included in this chapter, many pertinent or mandatory references have been omitted because of their irrelevance to a general discussion. For this reason, always reference the applicable manufacturer's instructions before performing any phase of engine removal or installation.

REASONS FOR REMOVAL OF RECIPROCATING ENGINES

The following paragraphs outline the most common reasons for removing and replacing a reciprocating engine. Information to aid in determining engine conditions that require removal is included; however, in every case, consult applicable manufacturer's instructions as the final authority in establishing the basis for engine replacement.

Engine Life Span Exceeded

Engine life is dependent upon such factors as operational misuse, the quality of manufacture or overhaul, the type of aircraft in which the engine is installed, the kind of operation being carried out, and the degree to which preventive maintenance is accomplished. Thus, it is impossible to establish definite engine removal times. However, on a basis of service experience, it is possible to establish a maximum expected life span of an engine. Regardless of condition, an engine should be removed when it has accumulated the recommended maximum allowable time since last overhaul, including any allowable time extension.

Sudden Stoppage

Sudden stoppage is a very rapid and complete stoppage of the engine. It can be caused by engine seizure or by one or more of the propeller blades striking an object in such a way that r.p.m. goes to zero in less than one complete revolution of the propeller. Sudden stoppage may occur under such conditions as complete and rapid collapse of the landing gear, nosing over of the aircraft, or crash landing. Sudden stoppage can cause internal damage, such as cracked propeller gear teeth, gear train damage in the rear section, crankshaft misalignment, or damaged propeller bearings. When sudden stoppage occurs, the engine is usually replaced.

Sudden Reduction in Speed

Sudden reduction in engine speed can occur when one or more of the propeller blades strike an object at a low engine r.p.m. After impact, the foreign object is cleared and the engine recovers r.p.m. and continues to run unless stopped to prevent further damage. While taxiing an aircraft, sudden reduction in speed can occur when the propeller strikes a foreign object, such as a raised section in the runway, a tool box, or a portion of another airplane. Investigation of engines on which this type of accident occurred has shown that generally no internal damage results when the r.p.m. is low, for then the power output is low and the propeller will absorb most of the shock. However, when the accident occurs at high engine r.p.m., shocks are much more severe. When sudden reduction in r.p.m. occurs, the following action should be taken:

(1) Make a thorough external inspection of the engine mount, crankcase, and nose section to determine whether any parts have been damaged. If damage is found which cannot be corrected by line maintenance, remove the engine.

(2) Remove the engine oil screens or filters. Inspect them for the presence of metal particles. Remove the engine sump plugs, drain the oil into a clean container, strain it through a clean cloth, and check the cloth and the strained oil for metal particles. Heavy metal particles in the oil indicate a definite engine failure, and the engine must be removed. However, if the metal particles present are similar to fine filings, continue the inspection of the engine to determine its serviceability.

If there are no heavy metal particles in the engine oil, give the engine a flight test. If the engine operates properly during the flight test, look again for metal in the oil system. If no metal is found, continue the engine in service, but re-check the oil screens for the presence of metal after 10 hours of operation and again after 20 hours of operation. If no indication of internal failure is found after 20 hours of operation, the engine probably requires no further special inspections.

(3) Remove the propeller and check the crankshaft, or the propeller drive shaft on reduction-gear engines, for misalignment. Clamp a test indicator to the nose section of the engine. Use the dial-type reversible indicator which has 1/1000-inch graduations. Remove the front or outside spark plugs from all the cylinders. Then turn the crankshaft and observe if the crankshaft or propeller shaft runs out at either the front or rear propeller cone seat locations.

If there is an excessive runout reading at the crankshaft or propeller-drive shaft at the front seat location, the engine should be removed. Consult the applicable manufacturer's instructions for permissible limits. Even though the runout of the crankshaft or propeller-drive shaft at the front cone seat is less than allowable limits, the rear cone seat location should be checked. If any runout is found at the rear seat location, which is not in the same plane as the runout at the front cone seat location, the engine should be removed.

If the crankshaft or propeller drive shaft runout does not exceed these limits, install a serviceable propeller. Make an additional check by tracking the propeller at the tip in the same plane perpendicular to the axis of rotation to assure that blade track tolerance is within the prescribed limits.

(4) Start the engine to see if operation is smooth and the power output adequate. If the engine operates properly during this ground check, shut the engine down and repeat the inspection for metal particles in the oil system.

Metal Particles in the Oil

Metal particles on the engine oil screens or the magnetic sump plugs are generally an indication of partial internal failure of the engine. However, due to the construction of aircraft oil systems, it is possible that metal particles have collected in the oil system sludge at the time of a previous engine failure. Furthermore, carbon tends to break loose from the interior of the engine in rock-like pieces which have the appearance of metal. It is necessary to consider these possibilities when foreign particles are found on the engine oil screens or sump plugs.

Before removing an engine for suspected internal failure as indicated by foreign material on the oil screens or oil sump plugs, determine if the foreign particles are metal by placing them on a flat metal object and striking them with a hammer. If the material is carbon, it will disintegrate, whereas metal will either remain intact or change shape, depending on its malleability.

If the particles are metal, determine the probable extent of internal damage. For example, if only small particles are found which are similar in nature to filings, drain the oil system, and refill it. Then ground-run the engine and re-inspect the oil screens and sump plugs. If no additional particles are found, the aircraft should be test flown, followed by an inspection of the oil screens and sump plugs. If no further evidence of foreign material is found, continue the engine in service. However, engine performance should be closely observed for any indication of difficulty or internal failure.

Unstable Engine Operation

Engines are usually removed when there is consistent unstable engine operation. Unstable engine operation generally includes one or more of the following conditions:

(1) Excessive engine vibration.
(2) Back firing, either consistent or intermittent.
(3) Cutting-out while in flight.
(4) Low power output.

PREPARATION OF RECIPROCATING ENGINES FOR INSTALLATION

After the decision has been made to remove an engine, the preparation of the replacement engine must be considered. The maintenance procedures and methods used vary widely. Commercial operators, whose maintenance operations require the most efficient and expeditious replacement of aircraft engines, usually rely on a system that utilizes the quick-engine-change assembly, or QECA, also sometimes referred to as the engine power package. The QECA is essentially a powerplant and the necessary accessories installed in the engine mount ring.

Other operators of aircraft equipped with radial engines and most opposed-type engines use a slower but less-expensive method. Since engine replacement in these repair facilities often occurs at random intervals, only a few replacement engines (sometimes only one) are kept on hand. Such replacement engines may be partially or wholly built up with the necessary accessories and subassemblies, or they may be stored as received from the manufacturer in packing boxes, cases, or cans and are uncrated and built up for installation only when needed to replace an engine.

The QECA system is most commonly used with large radial engines, and for this reason such engines are used to describe QECA buildup and installation procedures. But it should be emphasized that many of these procedures are applicable to all other methods of engine buildup and installation.

QECA BUILDUP OF RADIAL ENGINES

The study of QECA buildup that follows is not designed to outline procedures to be followed in a practical application, since most maintenance shops develop buildup procedures tailored to their own facilities or use those recommended by the manufacturer. The procedures included in this chapter provide a logical sequence in following a QECA and its components through the stages of a typical buildup to gain a better understanding of units and systems interconnection.

The components of a QECA for a large radial engine are illustrated in figure 8–1. As shown, the QECA consists of several units. Among such units that are common to most present-day aircraft QECA's are the airscoop, cowl flaps, engine ring cowl, cowl support ring, access panels, engine mount, and the engine, together with all of its accessories and controls.

On many aircraft the engines are mounted in streamlined housings called nacelles that extend from the wings. These nacelles can be considered as being divided into two sections: (1) The wing nacelle, and (2) the engine nacelle. The wing nacelle is that portion of the nacelle which is attached to the wing structure. The engine nacelle is that portion of the nacelle that is constructed separately from the wing.

Figure 8–2 illustrates a typical nacelle with the separation line identified. Outwardly, the wing nacelle seems to be only a streamlining for the engine nacelle, but that is not its only purpose. On many aircraft, the inboard wing nacelle houses the landing gear when it is in the retracted position. Also, the wing nacelles normally contain lines and units of the oil, fuel, and hydraulic systems, as well as linkages and other controls for the operation of the engine.

The point at which the engine nacelle is disconnected from the wing nacelle can easily be identified on most aircraft. To locate the point of disconnect, find the last section of removable engine nacelle cowling farthest from the propeller end of the engine. Normally the removal of these sections of cowling will expose lines, fittings, electrical connections, cables, and mount bolts. The separation point of a QECA, including the firewall and the points of disconnect, is illustrated in figure 8–3.

The firewall is usually the foremost bulkhead of the wing nacelle and differs from most other aircraft bulkheads in that it is constructed of stainless steel or some other fire-resistant material. The primary purpose of the firewall is to confine any engine fire to the engine nacelle. It also provides a mounting surface for units within the engine nacelle and a point of disconnect for lines, linkages, and electrical wiring that are routed between the engine and the aircraft. Without this firewall, an engine fire would have ready access to the interior of the wing. Since the fuel tanks are usually contained in the wings, the probable consequences of an engine fire are obvious. Thus, the necessity for sealing all unused openings in the firewall cannot be overstressed.

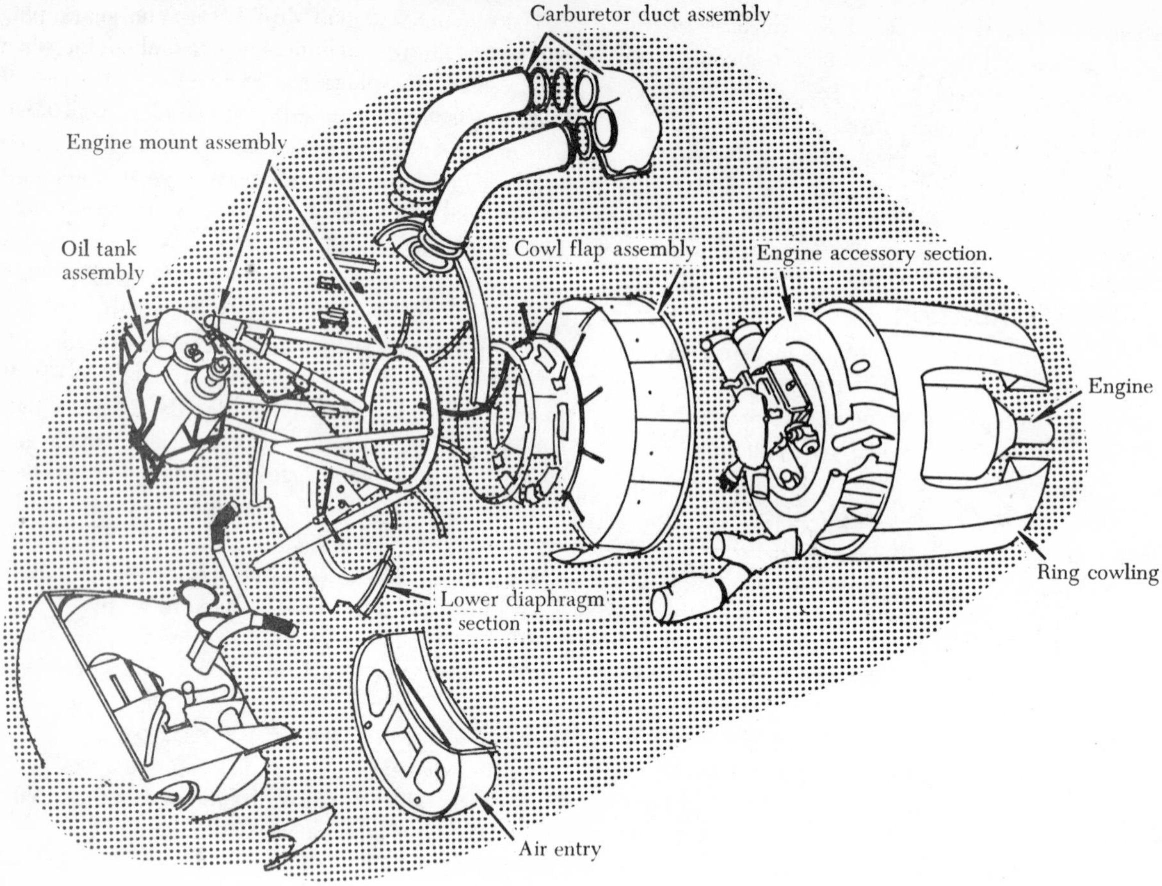

FIGURE 8–1. Exploded view of a typical power package.

An aircraft engine and its accessories which have been in storage must undergo careful de-preservation and inspection before they may be installed in an aircraft. This involves more than removing an engine from its container and bolting it to the aircraft.

If the engine is stored in a pressurized metal container, the air valve should be opened to bleed off the air pressure. Depending upon the size of the valve, the air pressure should bleed off in somewhat less than 30 minutes.

Prepare the container for opening by removing the bolts that hold the two sections together. Then attach a hoist to the "hoisting points" and lift the top section clear of the container and place it away from the work area. If the engine is installed in a wooden shipping case, it is necessary to carefully break the seal of the protective envelope and fold it down around the engine. Remove the dehydrating agent or desiccant bags and the humidity indicator from the outside of the engine. Also, remove and set safely aside any accessories that are not installed on the engine but are mounted on a special stand or otherwise installed inside the protective envelope with the engine. If the engine is a radial type, the mounting ring bolts must be unfastened from the container and the engine hoisted slightly to allow the mounting ring to be removed from the engine. Engines other than radial types are usually bolted directly to the container.

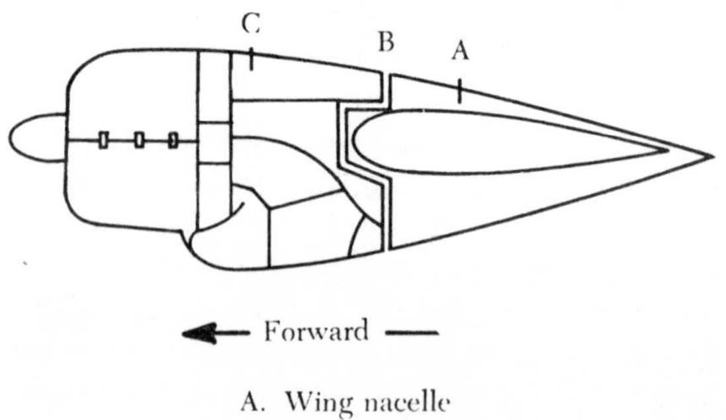

A. Wing nacelle

B. Separation line

C. Engine nacelle

FIGURE 8–2. Typical engine and wing nacelle.

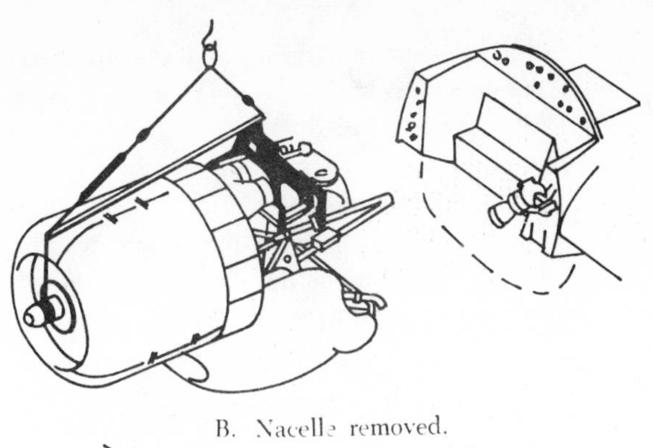

B. Nacelle removed.

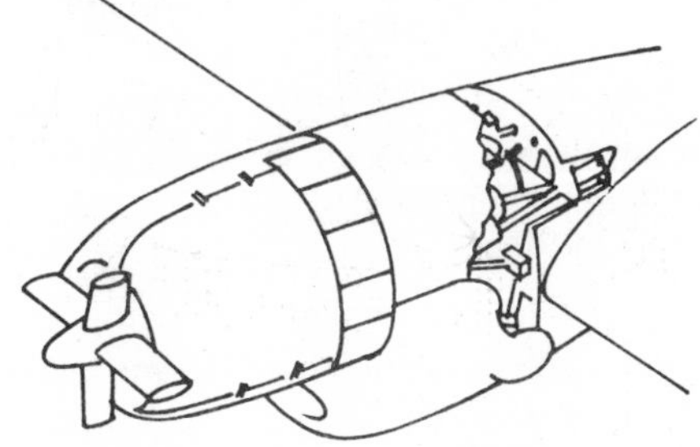

A. Nacelle installed.

FIGURE 8–3. Separation line of a typical QECA.

De-preservation of an Engine

After the engine has been secured to an engine stand, all covers must be removed from the points where the engine was sealed or closed with ventilatory covers, such as the engine breathers, exhaust outlets, and accessory mounting-pad cover plates. As each cover is removed, inspect the uncovered part of the engine for signs of corrosion. Also, as the dehydrator plugs are removed from each cylinder, make a very careful check of the walls of any cylinder for which the dehydrator plug color indicates an unsafe condition. Care is emphasized in the inspection of the cylinders, even if it is necessary to remove a cylinder.

On radial engines, the inside of the lower cylinders and intake pipes should be carefully checked for the presence of excessive corrosion-preventive compound that has drained from throughout the interior of the engine and settled at these low points. This excessive compound could cause the engine to become damaged from a hydraulic lock (also referred to as liquid-lock) when a starting attempt is made.

The check for excessive corrosion-preventive compound in the cylinders can be made as the dehydrator plugs are removed from each cylinder. Much of the compound will drain from the spark plug holes of the lower cylinders of a radial engine when the dehydrator plugs are removed. But some of the mixture will remain in the cylinder head below the level of the spark plug hole, as shown in figure 8–4, and can be removed with a hand pump. A more positive method, however, is to remove the lower intake pipes and open the intake valve of the cylinder by rotating the crankshaft. This latter method allows the compound to drain from the cylinder through the open intake valve. If, for some reason, excessive compound is present in an upper cylinder, it can be removed with a hand pump.

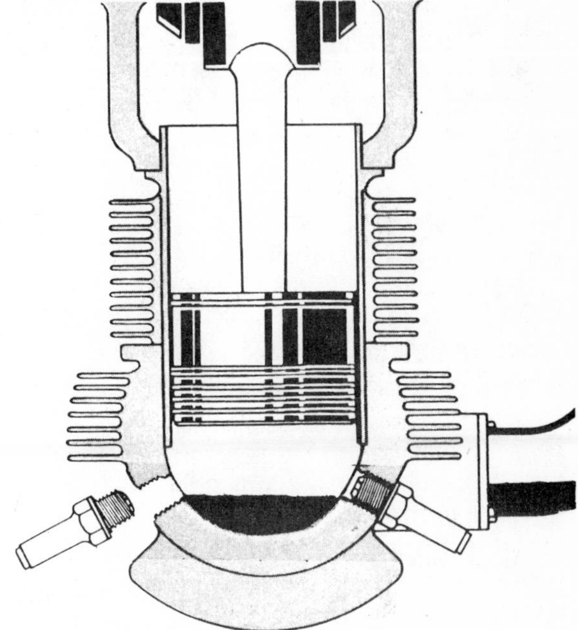

FIGURE 8–4. Draining corrosion-preventive compound.

The oil screens should be removed from the engine and thoroughly washed in kerosene or an approved solvent to remove all accumulations that could restrict the oil circulation and cause engine failure. After the screens are cleaned, immerse them in clean oil and then re-install them in the engine.

When the cover has been removed from the intake manifold, the silica gel desiccant bags must be removed before installing the carburetor. Take care not to accidentally tear one of the bags.

Remove the protective covering from the propeller shaft and wash all corrosion-preventive compound from both the inside and outside surfaces of the shaft. Then coat the propeller shaft lightly with engine oil.

As a final check, see that the exterior of the engine is clean. Usually a quantity of compound runs out of the engine when the dehydrator plugs and oil screens are removed. To clean the engine, spray it with kerosene or an approved commercial solvent.

Inspection and Depreservation of Accessories

An engine's performance is no better than that of its accessories. Though the engine has been completely overhauled and is in top condition, any oversight or error in installing the accessories can result in improper engine operation or even irreparable damage to it.

Before de-preserving any of the accessories enclosed with the engine, consult the storage data usually stenciled on the outside of the engine container or the records enclosed with the engine to determine how long the engine and accessories were in storage. Certain accessories that normally accompany an engine from overhaul are considered unsafe for use if their time in storage has exceeded a specified period. This time varies according to the limits prescribed by the manufacturer.

Any accessory that has been removed from the old engine and can be installed on the new one must be given a thorough inspection to determine its condition. This inspection includes a check for general condition, cleanliness, absence of corrosion, and absence of wear as evidenced by excessive "play" in the moving parts.

Some accessories must be replaced, regardless of their operating time, if the engine is being changed because of internal failure. Such accessories may have been contaminated by metal particles carried into their operating mechanisms by the engine oil that lubricates them.

Before installing any replacement accessory, check it visually for signs of corrosion and for freedom of operation. Always wipe the mounting pad, flange, and coupling clean before mounting the accessory, and install the proper gasket between the mounting pad and the accessory mounting flange. Lubricate the accessory drive shaft when indicated in the manufacturer's instructions.

INSPECTION AND REPLACEMENT OF POWER-PLANT EXTERNAL UNITS AND SYSTEMS

The engine nacelle must be cleaned thoroughly before it is inspected. The design of an engine nacelle varies with different aircraft. Basically, it is a framework, covered with removable cowling, in which the engine is mounted. This assembly is attached to the aircraft and incorporates an insulating firewall between the engine and the airframe. The interconnecting wiring, tubing, and linkages between the engine and its various systems and controls pass through the firewall.

Inspect the complete engine nacelle for condition of the framework and the sheet-metal cowling and riveted plates that cover the nacelle. Any cracks in the cowling or ducts, if they do not exceed limits specified in the manufacturer's structural repair requirements for the aircraft concerned, may be stop-drilled at the end of the crack and repaired by covering the cracked area with a reinforcing patch.

The engine mounting frame assembly should be checked for any distortion of the steel tubing, such as bends, dents, flat spots, or cracks. Use the dye penetrant inspection method to reveal a crack, porous area, or other defects.

The engine mounting bolts are usually checked for condition by magnetic particle inspection or other approved process. While the bolts are removed, the boltholes should be checked for elongation caused by the movement of an improperly tightened bolt.

Check the outer surface of all exposed electrical wiring for breaks, chafing, or other damage. Also, check the security of crimped or soldered cable ends. In addition, carefully inspect connector plugs for overall condition. Any item that is damaged must be repaired or replaced, depending on the extent of the damage.

Before installing an engine, inspect all tubing in the nacelle for dents, nicks, scratches, chafing, or corrosion. Check all tubing carefully for indications of fatigue or excessive flatness caused by improper or accidental bending. Thoroughly inspect all hose used in various engine systems. Weather checking (a cracking of the outside covering of the hose) sometimes penetrates to the hose reinforcement. Replace any length of hose that shows indications of the cover peeling or flaking or whose fabric reinforcement is exposed.

Replace a hose that shows indications of excessive "cold flow." Cold flow is a term used to describe the deep and permanent impressions or cracks caused by hose clamp pressure.

Always replace a control rod if it is nicked or corroded deep enough to affect its strength. If the corrosion cannot be removed by rubbing with steel wool, the pitting is too deep for safety.

Check the pulleys in the control system for freedom of movement. It is easy to spot a pulley that is not turning freely, for both it and the cable will be worn from the cable sliding over the pulley instead of rolling free. The bearings of a pulley may be checked by inspecting the pulley for excessive "play" or "wobble" with the tension removed from the cable. The cable must also be inspected for corrosion and broken strands. Locate any broken strands by wiping the cable with a cloth.

Check bonding for fraying, loose attachment, and cleanness of terminal ends. The electrical resistance of the complete bond must not exceed the resistance values specified in the applicable manufacturer's instructions.

Inspect the exhaust stacks, collector ring, and tailpipe assembly for security, cracks, or excessive corrosion. Depending on the installation, these units or parts of them may be mounted on the engine before it is installed in the aircraft.

Check all air ducts for dents and for the condition of the fabric or rubber anti-chafing strips at the points where sections of duct are joined. The dents may be pounded out; the anti-chafing strips should be replaced if they are pulled loose from the duct or are worn to the point where they no longer form a tight seal at the joint.

Thoroughly inspect the engine oil system and perform any required special maintenance upon it before installing a replacement engine. If an engine is being changed at the end of its normal time in service, it is usually necessary only to flush the oil system; however, if an engine has been removed for internal failure, usually some units of the oil system must be replaced and others thoroughly cleaned and inspected.

If the engine has been removed because of internal failure, the oil tank is generally removed to permit thorough cleaning. Also, the oil cooler and temperature regulator must be removed and sent to a repair facility for overhaul. The vacuum pump pressure line and the oil separator in the vacuum system must also be removed, cleaned, and inspected. Internal failure also requires that the propeller governor and feathering pump mechanism be replaced if these units are operated by engine oil pressure.

PREPARING THE ENGINE FOR REMOVAL

Before starting to work on the aircraft or the engine, always be sure that the magneto switch is in the "OFF" position. Aircraft engines can be started accidentally by turning the propeller, if the magneto switch is on.

Check to see that all fuel selectors or solenoid-operated fuel shutoff valves are closed. The fuel selector valves are either manually or solenoid operated. If solenoid-operated fuel shutoff valves are installed, it may be necessary to turn the battery switch on before the valves can be closed, since the solenoid depends on electricity for operation. These valves close the fuel line at the firewall between the engine and the aircraft. After ensuring that all fuel to the engine is shut off, disconnect the battery to eliminate the possibility of a "hot" wire starting a fire. If it is anticipated that the aircraft will be out of service for more than 6 days, the battery is normally removed and taken to the battery shop and placed on charge.

Also, a few other preparations should be made before starting to work on the engine removal. First, make sure that there are enough fire extinguishers near at hand to meet any possible emergency. Check the seals on these extinguishers to be sure the extinguishers have not been discharged. Then check the wheel chocks. If these are not in place, the aircraft can, and probably will, inch forward or back during some crucial operation. Also, if the aircraft has a tricycle landing gear, be sure that the tail is supported so that the aircraft cannot tip back when the weight of the engine is removed from the forward end. It is not necessary to support the tail on some multi-engine aircraft if only one engine is to be removed. In addition, the landing gear shock struts can be deflated to prevent them from extending as the engine weight is removed from the aircraft.

After taking these necessary precautions, begin removing the cowling from around the engine. As it is removed, clean it and check for cracks so that the necessary repairs can be made while the engine change is in progress. Place all cowling that does not need repair on a rack where it can be readily found when the time comes to re-install it around the new engine.

After removing the cowling, the propeller should be removed for inspection or repair.

Draining the Engine

Place a large metal pan (drip pan) on the floor under the engine to catch any spilled mixture or oil. Next, secure a clean container in which to drain the oil or corrosion-preventive mixture. Place the container beneath the Y drain located between the oil tank and the oil inlet to the engine, open the valve, and allow the oil to drain. Figure 8–5 shows the points at which a typical aircraft engine oil system is drained.

Other points at which the oil system is drained, as shown schematically on a typical engine installation in figure 8–5, include the oil cooler, the oil return line, and the engine sumps. All valves, drains, and lines must remain open until the oil system has been completely drained.

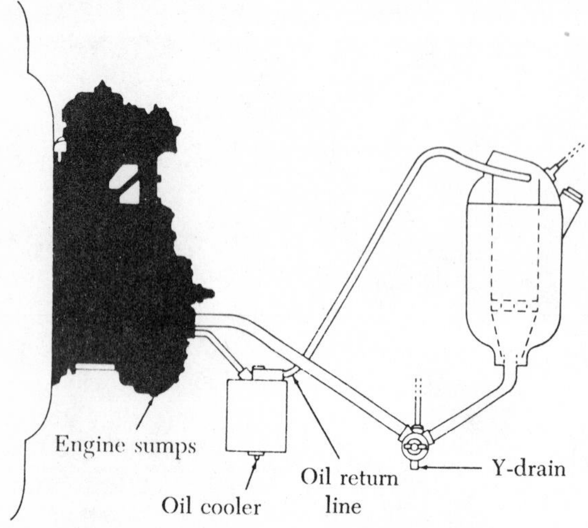

FIGURE 8–5. Oil system drain points.

After draining the oil, re-install all drain plugs and close all drain valves. Then wipe all excess oil from around the drain points.

Electrical Disconnects

Electrical disconnections are usually made at the engine firewall. This does not always apply when the basic engine is being removed, for then the electrical leads to such accessories as the starter and generators are disconnected at the units themselves. When disconnecting electrical leads, it is a good safety habit to disconnect the magnetos first and immediately ground them at some point on the engine or the assembly being removed. Most firewall disconnections of electrical conduit and cable are simplified by use of AN or MS connectors. Each connector consists of two parts: (1) A plug assembly, and (2) a receptacle assembly. To prevent accidental disconnection during airplane operation, the outlet is threaded to permit a knurled sleeve nut to be screwed to the outlet and then fastened with safety wire, if necessary.

A typical plug fitting assembly is shown in figure 8–6. This figure also shows a typical junction box assembly, which is used as a disconnect on some aircraft engine installations. In the junction box the electrical circuit is completed by fastening two leads to a common terminal. The lead which runs

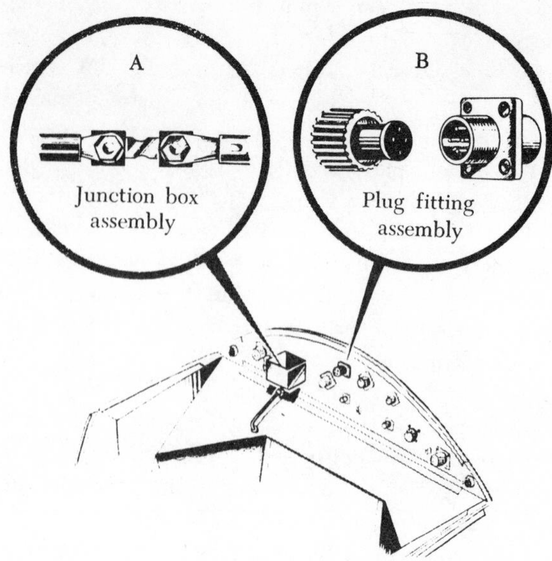

FIGURE 8–6. Plug fitting and junction box assemblies.

from the junction box to engine is disconnected from the terminal, and the conduit is disconnected from the junction box when preparing to remove the engine.

After the safety wire is broken, remove all of it from the sleeve nuts which hold the conduit to the junction boxes, as well as from the nuts on the connectors. Wrap moistureproof tape over the exposed ends of connectors to protect them from dirt and moisture. Also, do not leave long electrical cables or conduits hanging loose, since they may become entangled with some part of the aircraft while the engine is being hoisted. It is a good practice to coil all lengths of cable or flexible conduit neatly, and tie or tape them to some portion of the assembly being removed.

Disconnection of Engine Controls

The engine control rods and cables connect such units as the carburetor or fuel control throttle valve and the mixture control valve with their manually actuated control in the cockpit. The controls are sometimes disconnected by removing the turnbuckle which joins the cable ends. A typical assembly is shown in figure 8–7.

Typical control linkage consisting of a control rod attached to a bellcrank is illustrated in figure 8–8.

The control rod in the linkage shown has two rod-end assemblies, a clevis and an eye, screwed onto opposite ends. These rod-end assemblies determine the length of the control rod by the distance

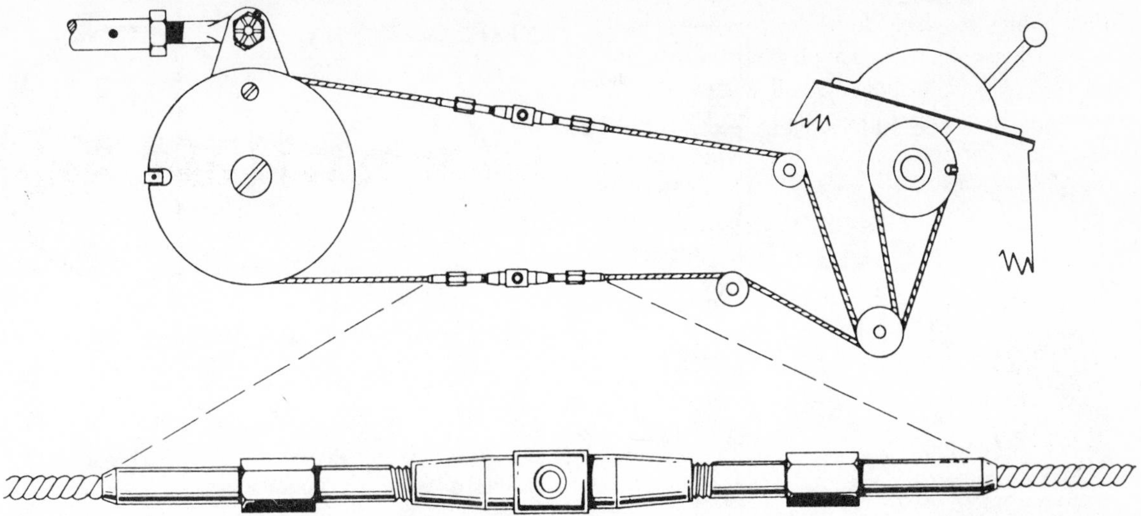

FIGURE 8–7. Engine control cable and turnbuckle assembly.

they are screwed onto it, and are locked into position by checknuts. An anti-friction bearing is usually mounted in the eye end of a rod. This eye is slipped over a bolt in the bellcrank arm and is held in position by a castle nut safetied with a cotter pin. The clevis rod end is slipped over the end of a bellcrank arm, which also usually contains an anti-friction bearing. A bolt is passed through the clevis and the bellcrank eye, fastened with a castle nut, and safetied with a cotter pin.

Sometimes linkage assemblies do not include the anti-friction bearings and are held in position only by a washer and cotter pin in the end of a clevis pin which passes through the bellcrank and rod end. After the engine control linkages have been disconnected, the nuts and bolts should be replaced in the rod ends or bellcrank arms to prevent their being lost. All control rods should be removed completely or tied back to prevent them from being bent or broken if they are struck by the replacement engine or QECA as it is being hoisted.

Disconnection of Lines

The lines between units within the aircraft and the engine are either flexible rubber hose or aluminum-alloy tubes joined by lengths of hose clamped to them. Lines which must withstand high pressure, such as hydraulic lines, are often stainless steel tubing.

Figure 8–9 shows the basic types of line disconnects. Most lines leading from a QECA are secured to a threaded fitting at the firewall by a sleeve nut around the tubing. Hoses are sometimes secured in this manner but may also be secured by a threaded fitting on the unit to which they lead, or by a hose clamp. The firewall fittings for some lines have a quick-disconnect fitting that contains a check valve

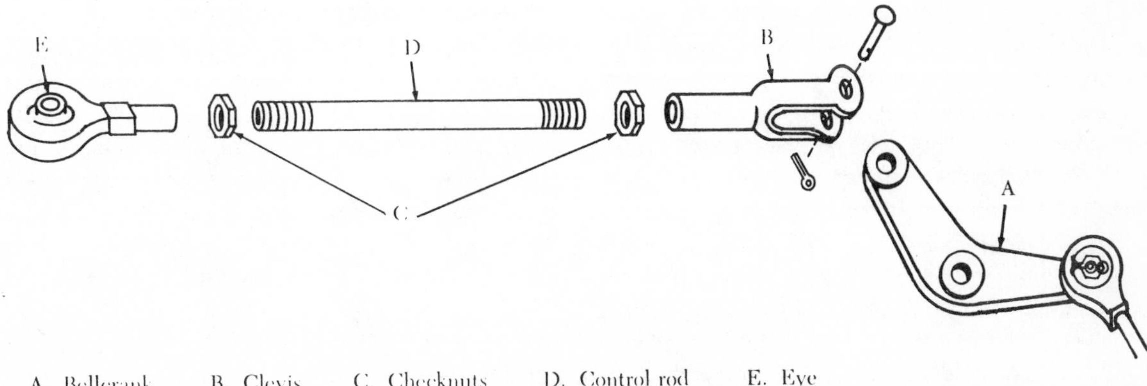

FIGURE 8–8. Engine control linkage assembly.

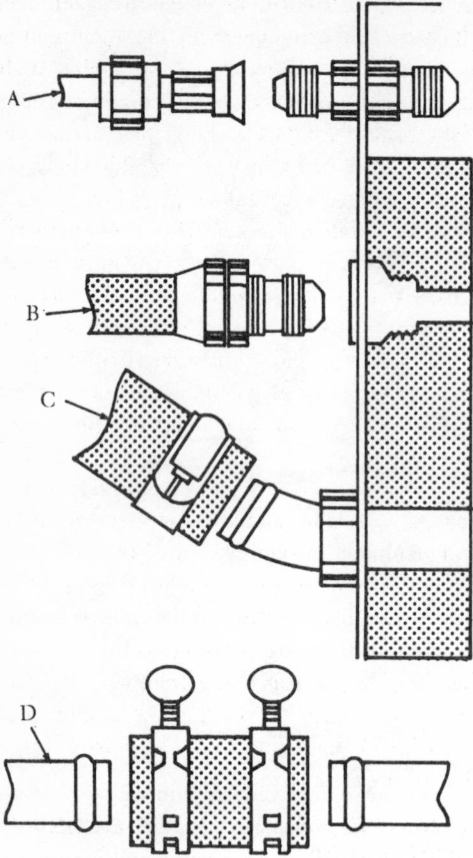

A. Sleeve and nut fitting

B. Threaded fitting and receptacle

C. Hose clamp and fitting

D. Interconnecting hose

FIGURE 8–9. Types of line disconnects.

to prevent the system from losing fluid, when the line is disconnected. Metal tubing on some installations may also be disconnected at a point where two lengths of it are joined together by a length of rubber hose. Such a disconnection is made by loosening the hose clamps and sliding the length of rubber hose over the length of tubing which remains on the aircraft. There may be some further variations in these types of disconnections, but basically they follow the same pattern.

Some type of a container should be used to catch any fuel, oil, or other fluid that may drain from the disconnected lines. After the lines have drained, they should be immediately plugged or covered with moistureproof tape to prevent foreign matter from entering them as well as to prevent any accumulated fluid from dripping out.

Other Disconnections

The points at which the various air ducts are disconnected depend upon the engine and the aircraft in which it is installed. Usually the air intake ducts and the exhaust system must be disconnected so the basic engine or the QECA can be removed. After the engine connections are free (except the engine mounts) and all the disconnections are entirely clear so they will not bind or become entangled, the engine can be prepared for hoisting.

REMOVING THE ENGINE

If there has been thorough preparation of the engine for removal, the actual removal should be a relatively speedy operation.

If a QECA is being removed, the engine mount will accompany the engine; but if only the engine is being removed, the mount will remain on the aircraft. Before the engine can be freed from its attachment points, a sling must be installed so the engine's weight can be supported with a hoist when the mounting bolts are removed.

Aircraft engines or QECA's have marked points for attaching a hoisting sling. The location of these attaching points varies according to the size and weight distribution of the engine. Figure 8–10 shows a sling supporting an engine which has two attaching points. As a matter of safety, the sling should be carefully inspected for condition before installing it on the engine.

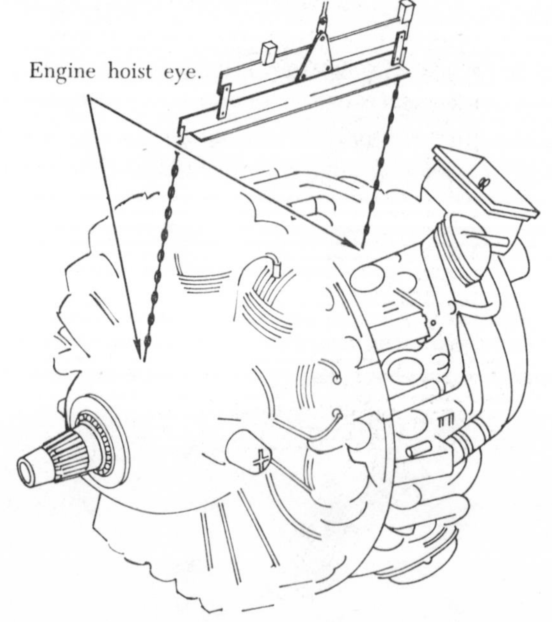

FIGURE 8–10. Engine showing hoisting sling attached.

Before attaching the sling to the hoist, be sure that the hoist has sufficient capacity to lift the engine safely. A manually operated hoist mounted in a portable frame is shown in figure 8–11. This hoist assembly is specifically manufactured for the purpose of removing engines and other large assemblies from aircraft. Some frames are fitted with power-operated hoists. These should be used with care, since considerable damage can be done if an inexperienced operator allows a power-operated hoist to overrun. The hoist and frame should also be checked for condition before being used to lift the engine.

Hoisting the Engine

Before the hoist is hooked onto the engine sling, re-check the aircraft tail supports and the wheel chocks. Fasten lines to the engine at points on the sides or rear so that the engine can be controlled as it is being hoisted. Hook the hoist onto the sling and hoist the engine slightly — just enough to relieve the engine weight from the mount attachments. Remove the nuts from the mount attachments in the order recommended in the manufacturer's instructions for the aircraft. As the last nuts are being removed, pull back on the lines fastened to the engine (or force it back by other means if lines

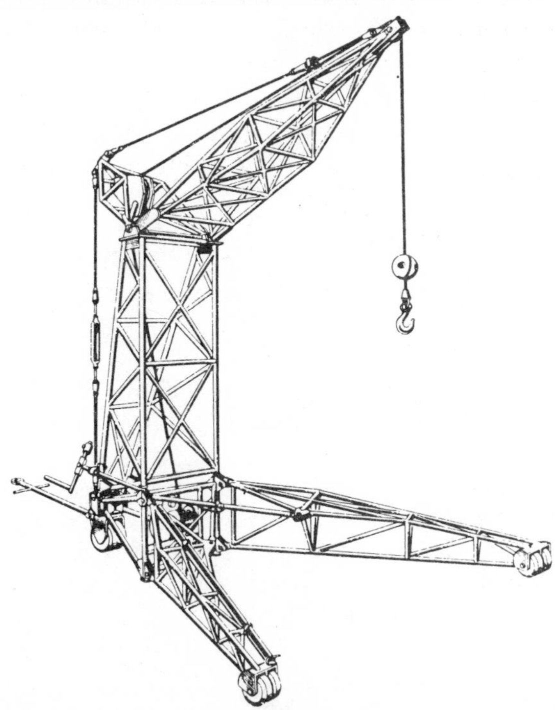

FIGURE 8–11. Hoist and frame assembly used for engine removal.

are not being used), thus steadying the engine. If bolts must be removed from the mount attachments, be sure the engine is under control before doing so. If the bolts are to remain in the mount attachments, the hoist can be gently maneuvered upward or downward as necessary after all the nuts have been removed. Meanwhile, gently relax the backward force on the engine just enough to allow the engine gradual forward movement when it is free from the mount attachments. At the point where the hoist has removed all engine weight from the mount attachments, the engine should be eased gently forward, away from the aircraft. If the engine binds at any point, maneuver it with the hoist until it slips free.

The procedure just discussed applies to removal of most reciprocating and turbine aircraft engines. Any variation in details will be outlined in the manufacturer's instructions for the aircraft concerned. Before attempting any engine removal, always consult these instructions.

When the engine has been removed, it can be carefully lowered onto a stand. The engine should be fastened to the stand and prepared for the removal of accessories.

HOISTING AND MOUNTING THE ENGINE FOR INSTALLATION

When the new or overhauled engine is ready to be hoisted for installation, move the engine stand as close as possible to the nacelle in which the replacement is to be installed. Then attach the sling to the engine and hook the hoist to the sling; then take up the slack until the hoist is supporting most of the engine weight. Next, remove the engine attaching bolts from the stand and hoist the engine clear.

The engine stand may be moved and the hoist frame positioned in a way that most easily permits the engine to be hoisted into the nacelle. To prevent injury to the crew or damage to the aircraft or engine, be sure that the engine is steadied when moving the hoist frame.

Seldom is an engine nacelle so designed that the engine can be fitted and bolted into place as though it were being mounted on a bare wall. The engine must be guided into position and mated with its various connections, such as the mounting boltholes and the exhaust tailpipe. This must be done despite such obstacles as the nacelle framework, ducts, or firewall connections and without leaving a trail of broken and bent parts, scratched paint, or crushed fingers.

When the engine has been aligned correctly in the nacelle, insert the mounting bolts into their holes and start all of the nuts on them. Always use the type of bolt and nut recommended by the manufacturer. Never use an unauthorized substitution of a different type or specification of nut and bolt than that prescribed.

The nuts on the engine mount bolts must be tightened to the torque recommended by the aircraft manufacturer. While the nuts are being tightened, the hoist should support the engine weight sufficiently to allow alignment of the mounting bolts. If the engine is permitted to exert upward or downward pressure on the bolts, it will be necessary for the nuts to pull the engine into proper alignment. This will result in nuts being tightened to the proper torque value without actually holding the engine securely to the aircraft.

The applicable manufacturer's instructions outline the sequence for tightening the mounting bolts to ensure security of fastening. After the nuts are safetied and the engine sling and hoist are removed, bonding strips should be connected across each engine mount to provide an electrical path from the mount to the airframe.

Mounting the engine in the nacelle is, of course, only the beginning. All the ducts, electrical leads, controls, tubes, and conduits must be connected before the engine can be operated.

Connections and Adjustments

There are no hard and fast rules that direct the order in which units or systems should be connected to the engine. Each maintenance organization will normally supply a worksheet or checklist to be followed during this procedure. This list is based upon past experience in engine installation on each particular aircraft. If this is followed carefully, it will serve as a guide for an efficient installation. The following instructions, then, are not a sequence of procedures but are a discussion of correct methods for completing an engine installation.

The system of ducts for routing air to the engine varies with all types of aircraft. In connecting them, the goal is to fit the ducts closely at all points of disconnect so that the air they route will not escape from its intended path. The duct systems of some aircraft must be pressure-checked for leaks. This is done by blocking the system at one end, supplying compressed air at a specified pressure at the other end, and then checking the rate of leakage.

The filters in the air induction system must be cleaned to assure an unrestricted flow of clean air to the engine and its units. Because methods for cleaning air filters vary with the materials used in the filtering element, clean them in accordance with the technical instructions relating to the aircraft being serviced.

The exhaust system should also be carefully connected to prevent the escape of hot gases into the nacelle. When assembling the exhaust system, check all clamps, nuts, and bolts and replace any in doubtful condition. During assembly, the nuts should be gradually and progressively tightened to the correct torque. The clamps should be tapped with a rawhide mallet as they are being tightened to prevent binding at any point. On some systems a ball joint connects the stationary portion of the exhaust system to the portion that is attached to the engine. This ball joint absorbs the normal engine movement caused by the unbalanced forces of the engine operation. Ball joints must be installed with the specified clearance to prevent binding when expanded by hot exhaust gases.

Hoses used within low-pressure systems are generally fastened into place with clamps. Before using a hose clamp, inspect it for security of welding or riveting and for smooth operation of the adjusting screw. A clamp that is badly distorted or materially defective should be rejected. (Material defects include extremely brittle or soft areas that may easily break or stretch when the clamp is tightened.) After a hose is installed in a system, it should be supported with rubber-lined supporting clamps at regular intervals.

Before installing metal tubing with threaded fittings, make sure the threads are clean and in good condition. Apply sealing compound, of the correct specification for the system, to the threads of the fittings before installing them. While connecting metal tubing, follow the same careful procedure for connecting hose fittings to prevent cross-threading and to assure correct torque.

When connecting the leads to the starter, generator, or various other electrical units within the nacelle, make sure that all connections are clean and properly secured. On leads that are fastened to a threaded terminal with a nut, a lockwasher is usually inserted under the nut to prevent the lead from working loose. When required, connector plugs can be safetied with steel wire to hold the knurled nut in the "full-tight" position.

Electrical leads within the engine nacelle are

usually passed through either a flexible or a rigid conduit. The conduit must be anchored as necessary to provide a secure installation, and bonded when required.

All engine controls must be accurately adjusted to assure instantaneous response to the control setting. For flexibility, the engine controls are usually a combination of rods and cables. Since these controls are tailored to the model of aircraft in which they are installed, their adjustment must follow exactly the step-by-step procedure outlined in the manufacturer's instructions for each particular model of aircraft.

Figure 8–12 illustrates a simplified schematic drawing of a throttle control system for a reciprocating aircraft engine. Using the drawing as a guide, follow a general procedure for adjusting throttle controls. First, loosen the serrated throttle control arm at the carburetor and back off the throttle stop until the throttle valve is in the "fully closed" position. After locking the cable drum into position with the locking pin, adjust the control rod to a specified length. Then, attach one end of the control rod to the locked cable drum and re-install the throttle control arm on the carburetor in the serrations that will allow the other end of the control rod to be attached to it. This will correctly connect the control arm to the cable drum.

Now, loosen the cable turnbuckles until the throttle control can be locked at the quadrant with the locking pin. Then, with both locking pins in place, adjust the cables to the correct tension as measured with a tensiometer. Remove the locking pins from the cable drum and quadrant.

Next, adjust the throttle control so that it will have a slight cushion action at two positions on the

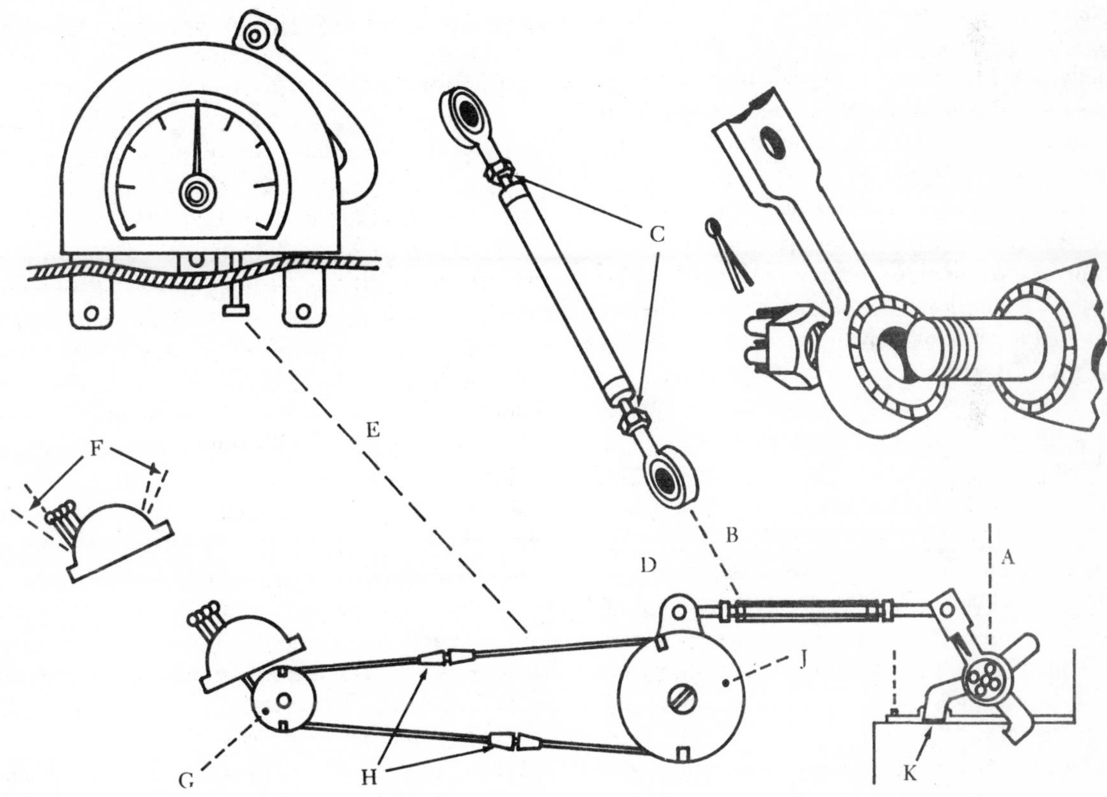

A. Serrated throttle control arm
B. Control rod
C. Adjustable rod ends
D. Cable drum
E. Tensiometer
F. Cushion movement
G. Quadrant locking pin
H. Cable turnbuckle
J. Cable drum locking pin
K. Throttle stop

FIGURE 8–12. Schematic drawing of throttle control system.

throttle quadrant: One when the carburetor throttle valve is in the "full-open" position, and the other when it is closed to the "idle" position.

Adjust the cushion by turning the cable turnbuckles equally in opposite directions until the throttle control cushion is correct at the "full-open" position of the throttle valve. Then, when the throttle arm stop is adjusted to the correct "idle speed" setting, the amount of cushion should be within tolerance at the "idle speed" position of the throttle valve. The presence of this cushion assures that the travel of the throttle valve is not limited by the stops on the throttle control quadrant, but that they are opening fully and closing to the correct idle speed as determined by the throttle arm stop.

Adjustment of the engine controls is basically the same on all aircraft insofar as the linkage is adjusted to a predetermined length for a specific setting of the unit to be controlled. Then, if cables are used in the control system, they are adjusted to a specific tension with the control system locked. Finally, the full travel of the unit to be controlled is assured by establishing the correct cushion in the controls.

In general, the same basic procedure is used to connect the linkage of the manual mixture control. This system is marked at the quadrant and at the carburetor for the three mixture positions: (1) Idle cutoff, (2) auto lean, and (3) auto rich. The positions of the lever on the control quadrant must be synchronized with the positions of the manual mixture control valve on the carburetor. Generally, this adjustment is made simultaneously with the cushion adjustment by placing the mixture control lever and the mixture control valve in the "idle cutoff" position before adjusting the linkage.

After rigging the engine controls, safety the turnbuckles and castle nuts, and make certain the jam nuts on all control rods are tightened.

On multi-engine aircraft the amount of cushion of all throttle and mixture controls on each quadrant must be equal so that all will be aligned at any specific setting chosen. This eliminates the necessity of individually setting each control to synchronize engine operations.

After the engine has been installed, it is necessary to adjust the cowl flaps so that the passage of the cooling air over the engine can be regulated accurately. When the cowl flap adjustments have been completed, operate the system and re-check for opening and closing to the specified limits. Also check the cowl flap position indicators, if installed, to assure that they indicate the true position of the flaps.

The oil cooler doors are adjusted in a manner similar to that used to adjust the cowl flaps. In some cases the procedure is reversed insofar as the door is first adjusted to retract to a specified point and the limit switch on the motor is set to cut out at this point. Then the jackscrew is adjusted to permit the door to open only a specified distance, and the open limit switch is set to stop the motor when this point is reached.

After the engine has been completely installed and connected, install the propeller on the aircraft. Before doing so, the thrust bearing retaining nut should be checked for correct torque. If required, the propeller shaft must be coated with light engine oil before the propeller is installed; the propeller governor and anti-icing system must be connected according to applicable manufacturer's instructions.

PREPARATION OF ENGINE FOR GROUND AND FLIGHT TESTING

Pre-oiling

Before the new engine is flight-tested, it must undergo a thorough ground check. Before this ground check can be made, several operations are usually performed on the engine.

To prevent failure of the engine bearings during the initial start, the engine should be pre-oiled. When an engine has been idle for an extended period of time, its internal bearing surfaces are likely to become dry at points where the corrosion-preventive mixture has dried out or drained away from the bearings. Hence, it is necessary to force oil throughout the entire engine oil system. If the bearings are dry when the engine is started, the friction at high r.p.m. will destroy the bearings before lubricating oil from the engine-driven oil pump can reach them.

There are several methods of pre-oiling an engine. The method selected should provide an expeditious and adequate pre-oiling service. Before using any pre-oiling method, remove one spark plug from each cylinder to allow the engine to be turned over more easily with the starter. Also, connect an external source of electrical power (auxiliary power unit) to the aircraft electrical system to prevent an excessive drain on the aircraft battery. If the engine is equipped with a hydromatic (oil-operated) propeller, remove the plug and fill the propeller dome with oil. Then re-install the plug.

In using some types of pre-oilers, such as that shown in figure 8–13, the oil line from the inlet side of the engine-driven oil pump must be disconnected to permit the pre-oiler tank to be connected at this point. Then a line must be disconnected or an opening made in the oil system at the nose of the engine to allow oil to flow out of the engine. Oil flowing out of the engine indicates the completion of the pre-oiling operation, since the oil has now passed through the entire system.

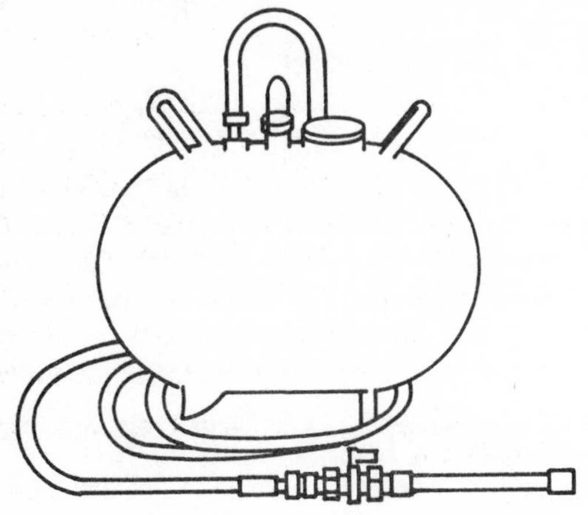

FIGURE 8–13. Pre-oiler tank.

In order to force oil from the pre-oiler tank through the engine, apply air pressure to the oil in the tank while the engine is being turned through with the starter. When this action has forced oil through the disconnection at the nose of the engine, stop cranking the engine and disconnect the pre-oiler tank.

When no external means of pre-oiling an engine are available, the engine oil pump may be used. Fill the engine oil tank to the proper level. Then, with the mixture in the "idle cutoff" position, the fuel shutoff valve and ignition switches in the "off" position, and the throttles fully open, crank the engine with the starter until the oil pressure gage mounted on the instrument panel indicates oil pressure.

After the engine has been pre-oiled, replace the spark plugs and connect the oil system. Generally, the engine should be operated within 4 hours after it has been pre-oiled; otherwise, the pre-oiling procedure normally must be repeated.

Fuel System Bleeding

To purge the fuel system of air locks and to aid in flushing any traces of preservative oil from a pressure carburetor, remove the drain plug in the carburetor fuel chamber which is farthest from the fuel inlet to the carburetor. In its place, screw a threaded fitting to which a length of hose, leading to a suitable container, is attached. Then open the throttle and place the mixture control in the "auto-lean" or "auto-rich" position, so that fuel will be permitted to flow through the system.

After making sure the fuel shutoff and main fuel tank valves are open, turn on the fuel boost pump until there are no traces of preservative oil in the fuel being pumped through the system. The passage of air will be indicated by an audible "blurp" emerging from the end of the hose submerged in the container of fuel. This phenomenon is not to be confused with the numerous small air bubbles that may appear as a result of the velocity of the fuel being ejected from the carburetor. Usually, after approximately a gallon of fuel has been bled off, the system can be considered safe for operation.

After completing the bleeding operation, return all switches and controls to their "normal" or "off" position, and replace and safety the drainplug in the carburetor.

PROPELLER CHECK

The propeller installed on the engine must be checked before, during, and after the engine has been ground operated.

A propeller whose pitch-changing mechanism is electrically actuated may be checked before the engine is operated. This is done by connecting an external source of electrical power to the aircraft electrical system, holding the propeller selector switch in the "decrease r.p.m." position, and checking for an increase of the propeller blade angle. Continue the check by holding the switch in the "increase r.p.m." position and examining the propeller blades for a decrease in angle. The propellers can also be checked for feathering by holding the selector switch in the "feather" position until the blade angle increases to the "full-feather" position. Then return the propeller to a "normal operating" position by holding the switch in the "increase r.p.m." position.

Propellers whose pitch-changing mechanisms are oil actuated must be checked during engine operation after the normal operating oil temperature has been reached. In addition to checking the increase or decrease in r.p.m., the feathering cycle of the propeller should also be checked.

When an engine equipped with an oil-operated propeller is stopped with the propeller in the "feather" position, never unfeather the propeller by starting the engine and actuating the feathering mechanism. Remove the engine sump plugs to drain the oil returned from the feathering mechanism and turn the blades to their normal position using the feathering pump; or a blade wrench, a long-handled device that slips over the blade to permit returning the blades to "normal pitch" position manually, can be used.

CHECKS AND ADJUSTMENTS AFTER ENGINE RUN-UP AND OPERATION

After the engine has been ground-operated, and again after flight test, operational factors must be adjusted, as necessary, and the entire installation given a thorough visual inspection. These adjustments often include fuel pressure and oil pressure, as well as re-checks of such factors as ignition timing, valve clearances, and idle speed and mixture, if these re-checks are indicated by the manner in which the engine performs.

After both the initial ground run-up and the test flight, remove the oil sump plugs and screens and inspect for metal particles. Clean the screens before re-installing them.

Check all lines for leakage and security of attachment. Especially, check the oil system hose clamps for security as evidenced by oil leakage at the hose connections. Also, inspect the cylinder holddown nut's or capscrews for security and safetying. This check should also be performed after the flight immediately succeeding the test flight.

REMOVAL AND INSTALLATION OF AN OPPOSED-TYPE ENGINE

The general information relating to the removal, buildup, inspection, preservation, storage, and installation of radial engines is in most instances applicable to horizontally opposed aircraft engines.

Although many detailed procedures for radial engines are applicable to horizontally opposed engines, they are sometimes unnecessary in practical application.

For example, elaborate and costly hoisting equipment is seldom necessary for removing or installing opposed-type engines, especially for very low horsepower engines. The storage of engines provides another example, since many small engines may be stored or shipped in skid-mounted containers fabricated from heavy-duty cardboard.

Finally, the number of accessories, together with the fewer number of engine controls, electrical and hydraulic lines and connections, and the increased ease of accessiblity to all parts of the engine generally preclude extensive use of QECA.

Engine Removal

The manufacturer's instructions should always be consulted as a guide in engine removal or installation. The following instructions for a 250 hp. horizontally opposed engine are typical engine removal and installation procedures:

(1) Remove the propeller.

(2) Release the quarter-turn cowl fasteners holding each side-access panel to the cowling, and remove the panels.

(3) Release the cowl fasteners holding the carburetor airscoop cover fairing and remove the fairing. Release the fasteners attaching the cowling to the carburetor air intake bellows.

(4) Remove the screws at the rear of the top and bottom nacelle cowling assembly and remove the cowling.

(5) Disconnect engine oil cooler air duct bellows.

(6) Disconnect primer line.

(7) Disconnect the mechanical fuel pump inlet line.

(8) Disconnect the generator and starter leads.

(9) If installed, remove the cylinder head temperature thermocouple.

(10) Disconnect the oil pressure and manifold pressure lines.

(11) Disconnect the oil return line.

(12) Remove the bonding strap from the rear of the engine.

(13) Disconnect the governor control cable from the governor.

(14) Disconnect the tachometer cable from the rear of the engine.

(15) Disconnect engine oil cooler hoses.

(16) Disconnect the engine oil temperature lead.

(17) Disconnect the engine breather line.

(18) Remove the four carburetor mounting nuts and allow the carburetor and carburetor air box to hang by means of the attached engine controls.

(19) Attach a hoist to the engine-lifting eye and relieve the tension on the mounts.

(20) Disconnect magneto P-leads.

(21) Remove the cotter pin, nuts, washer, and front rubber mount from each bolt and remove the sleeve. Slide bolts out of attaching points. Swing engine free, being careful not to damage any attached parts, and remove rear rubber mounts.

ENGINE INSTALLATION

The following procedures are typical of those used for installing a horizontally opposed engine after the accessories are mounted on the engine:

(1) Insert engine mounting bolts into the engine mount and slide the shock mounts onto the bolts so that the flat surface of the shock mount is flush with the engine mounting pad (see figure 8–14).

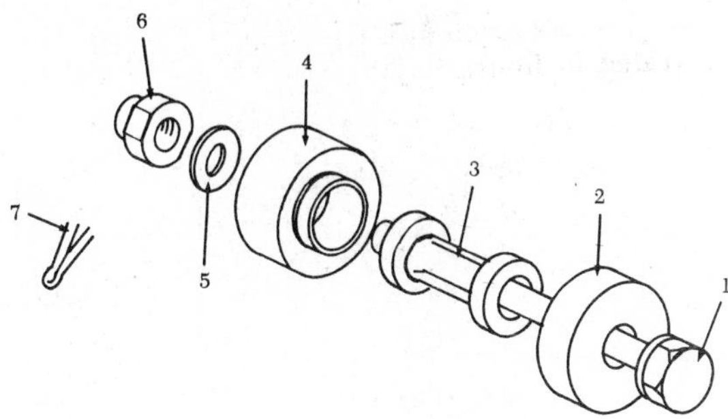

1. Engine mounting bolt
2. Shock mount
3. Shock mount spacer
4. Shock mount
5. Washer
6. Castellated nut
7. Cotter pin

FIGURE 8–14. Lord mount, exploded view.

(2) Slide the shock mount spacers onto the engine mounting bolts.

(3) Attach a hoist to the lifting eye and lift the engine. Tilt the rear of the engine downward until the magnetos clear the engine mount. Position the mounting lugs of the engine so that they align with the engine mount attaching points.

(4) Insert an upper mounting bolt into the engine until its threaded end extends one or two threads from the mount itself.

(5) Slide a shock mount between the engine mount and the engine.

(6) Repeat the procedure described in steps (5) and (6), above, for the remaining attachment points.

(7) Install the front engine rubber mounts on the bolts and over the forward end of the sleeve; check to see that shock mounts are not binding.

(8) Insert the magneto P-leads, tighten and safety.

(9) Install a washer and castellated nut on each mounting bolt. Tighten the nuts progressively, following a circular sequence, to the torque value specified by the manufacturer. Install cotter pins.

(10) Install gasket and carburetor air box.

(11) Connect the engine breather line.

(12) Connect the engine oil cooler air duct boot.

(13) Connect the engine oil temperature lead.

(14) Connect the oil cooler hoses.

(15) Connect the tachometer cable.

(16) Attach the propeller governor control cable.

(17) Connect the bonding strap to the engine mount ring.

(18) Connect the oil pressure line.

(19) Re-connect the starter and generator leads.

(20) Install the cylinder head temperature thermocouple.

(21) Connect the primer line.

(22) Re-connect the lines to the vacuum pump.

(23) Re-connect the hydraulic pump lines.

(24) Attach the generator blast tube.

(25) Slide the complete cowl assembly in position and attach the top and bottom sections.

(26) Fasten the quarter-turn fasteners attaching the cowling to the carburetor air intake bellows.

(27) Attach the carburetor airscoop cover fairing.

(28) Install the access panels to each side of the engine by using the quarter-turn cowl fasteners.

(29) Install the propeller.

TURBOJET POWERPLANT REMOVAL AND INSTALLATION

The aircraft engine used in this discussion provides a typical example of turbojet powerplant removal and installation procedures. The engine and all engine-mounted accessories form a QECA.

Access to the engine is provided by doors that can be raised and locked open. Directional references, such as right and left, and clockwise and counterclockwise, apply to the engine as viewed from the aft or exhaust end of the engine.

Turbojet Powerplant QECA Removal

The powerplant may be removed from the aircraft by either of two methods. One method involves lowering the powerplant from the nacelle by using an engine dolly. The other method requires hoists and a special sling to lower the powerplant to a movable engine stand. The following preliminary steps are applicable to either method of removal:

(1) Adequately secure the aircraft either with wheel chocks or with tiedown provisions; attach ground wire or cable to aircraft.

(2) Open the nacelle doors and support them with the struts. Verify that no external power is connected to the aircraft and that the electric power switch is off.

(3) Remove the mount access plates from both sides of the nacelle structure.

(4) Remove the engine air-conditioning duct access plate, and disconnect the duct from the engine.

(5) Disconnect the turbine discharge pressure pickup line (figure 8–15).

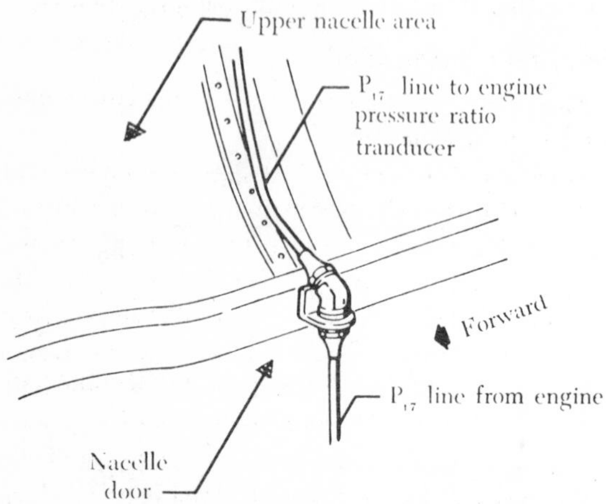

FIGURE 8–15. Turbine discharge pressure (P_{t7}) pickup.

(6) Disconnect the electrical wiring and the thermocouple leads from the connectors (figure 8–16).

(7) Disconnect the fuel line by removing the bolts from the hose flange (figure 8–17).

(8) Disconnect the power control rod (figure 8–18) from the power control lever cross-shaft linkage at the threaded end disconnect. Secure the power control rod to the nacelle structure.

After the engine has been disconnected, except for the engine mounts, and a dolly is being used to remove the engine, position it under the engine. Attach it to the engine and raise the dolly until all the weight is relieved from the wing. If hoists are used connect the hoists to the engine mounts through the accesses on the pylon. When lowering the engine with hoists, operate them simultaneously to exert tension on the hoist cables at all times. Position a movable engine stand under the engine, before lowering it.

With either the hoists or dolly attached and the stand in place, the engine is now ready to be lowered.

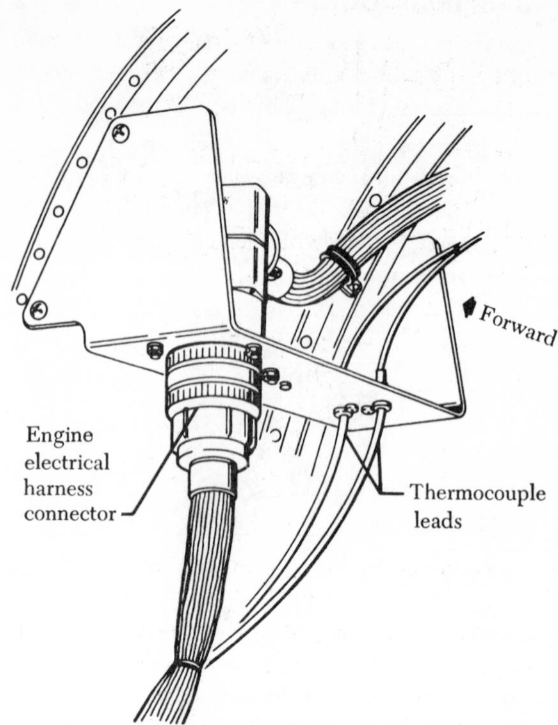

FIGURE 8–16. Electrical disconnect.

Remove the rear engine mount bolt and bushing, and the front engine mount nuts and washers. Start lowering the engine, constantly observing the engine clearance with the nacelle to prevent damage to the engine or to the nacelle. Secure the engine to the dolly or stand. If hoists are used, detach them from the engine. Roll the engine clear of the aircraft. Care must be taken while moving the engine clear to prevent damage to the pylon or pod. Cap or plug all lines, hoses, and outlets. With the engine removed, inspect the power control rod

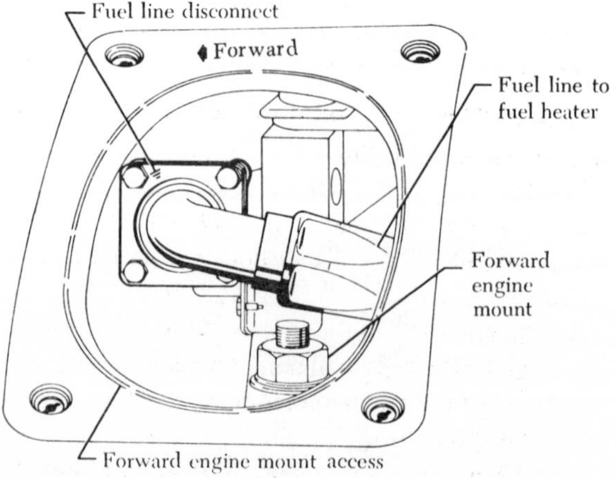

FIGURE 8–17. Fuel line disconnect.

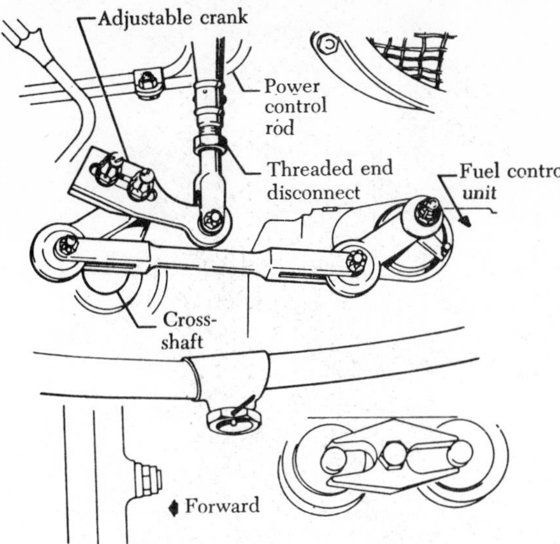

FIGURE 8–18. Power lever disconnect.

bracket and crank assembly for bearing looseness and the nacelle area for structural damage. Inspect for cracks or openings in the area where the pylon structure joins the nacelle structure.

Removal of QECA Accessories

When an aircraft engine is to be replaced, the aircraft-furnished accessories and equipment may be removed either for installation on the replacement engine or for overhaul, as required. Note carefully the locations and attachments of all units before removal so as to aid in the assembly of the replacement powerplant. When accessories are to be sent to overhaul or storage, preserve them in accordance with the manufacturer's instructions and be sure to attach all pertinent data and the proper accessory record cards.

After removal of these accessories and equipment, cover all exposed drives and ports. Prepare the engine for shipment, storage, or disassembly as directed in applicable manufacturer's instructions.

INSTALLATION OF TURBOJET ENGINES

Installation with Dolly

The following procedures are typical of those used to install a turbojet engine using a dolly. Specific ground-handling instructions are normally placarded on the dolly.

(1) Operate the dolly and carefully raise the engine to the engine mount attaching fittings.

(2) Align the rear engine mount with the mount attaching fittings.

(3) Install the engine mount bolts and tighten to the specified torque.

Installation with Hoist

The following procedures are typical of those used to install a turbojet engine using a hoist:

(1) Position the powerplant beneath the nacelle.

(2) Attach the engine sling to the engine.

(3) Carefully operate all the hoists simultaneously to raise the engine and guide the mounts into position.

Installation with Two-Cable Hoist

Figure 8–19 shows an engine being installed using a two-cable hoist. Hoists of this type are commonly used to install medium or small turbojet engines.

Completing the Installation

The following procedures cover the typical final installation instructions:

(1) Install the bushing through the engine rear mount and the rear mount attaching fitting. Install the bolt through the bushing; install the nut and secure it with a cotter pin. On this particular installation the engine rear mount must be free to rotate in the mount fitting. Do not overtighten the mount bolt.

(2) Through the forward mount accesses, place the chamfered washer, flat washer, and nut on each engine forward mount bolt. Tighten the nut to the required torque. Then secure the nut with lockwire.

(3) Connect the air-conditioning duct from the pylon to the compressor bleed-air duct from the engine. Tighten the duct connection by applying the proper torque.

(4) Remove the dolly or slings and related equipment from the engine.

(5) Connect the fuel hose to the fuel line from the pylon. Use a new gasket between the flanges of the fuel hose and the line.

(6) Install the starter air inlet duct support brace.

(7) Sparingly apply antiseize compound to the threads of the electrical harness receptacle and adjacent thermocouple receptacles. Connect the leads and secure the harness connector with lockwire.

(8) Connect the turbine discharge pressure pickup line from the engine to the line from the pressure ratio transducer.

(9) Connect the power control rod to the power control lever cross-shaft linkage at the threaded end disconnect.

(10) Inspect the engine installation for completeness.

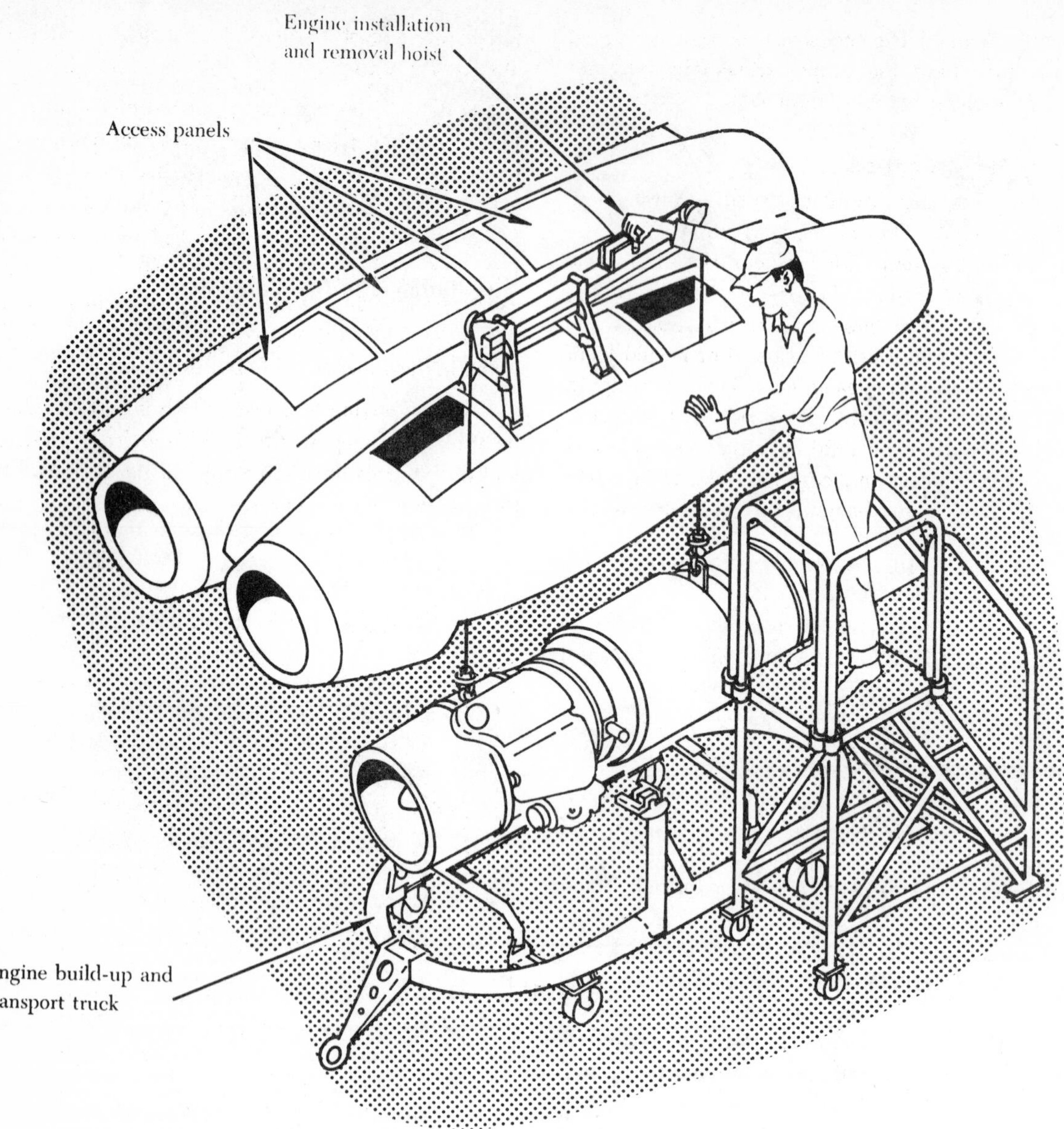

FIGURE 8–19. Installation with a two-cable hoist.

(11) Install the access covers.

(12) Adjust the power control linkage and trim the engine, if required. Close and secure the nacelle doors.

RIGGING, INSPECTIONS, AND ADJUSTMENTS

The following instructions cover some of the basic inspections and procedures for rigging and adjusting fuel controls, fuel selectors, and fuel shutoff valves.

(1) Inspect all bellcranks for looseness, cracks, or corrosion.

(2) Inspect rod ends for damaged threads and the number of threads remaining after final adjustment.

(3) Inspect cable drums for wear and cable guards for proper position and tension.

While rigging the fuel selector, power control, and shutoff valve linkages, follow the manufacturer's step-by-step procedure for the particular aircraft model being rigged. The cables should be rigged with the proper tension with the rigging pins installed. The pins should be free to be removed without any binding; if they are hard to remove, the cables are not rigged properly and should be re-checked. The power lever should have the proper cushion at the "idle" and "full-power" positions. The pointers or indicators on the fuel control should be within limits. The fuel selectors must be rigged so that they have the proper travel and will not restrict the fuel flow to the engines.

Rigging Power Controls

Modern turbojet aircraft use various power lever control systems. One of the common types is the cable and rod system. This system uses bellcranks, push-pull rods, drums, fair-leads, flexible cables, and pulleys. All of these components make up the control system and must be adjusted or rigged from time to time. On single-engine aircraft the rigging of the power lever controls is not very difficult. The basic requirement is to have the desired travel on the power lever and correct travel at the fuel control. But on multi-engine turbojet aircraft, the power levers must be rigged so that they are aligned at all power settings.

The power lever control cables and push-pull rods in the airframe system to the pylon and nacelle are not usually disturbed at engine change time and usually no rigging is required, except when some component has been changed. The control system from the pylon to the engine must be rigged after each engine change and fuel control change. Figure 8–20 shows the control system from the bellcrank in the upper pylon to the fuel control.

Before adjusting the power controls at the engine, be sure that the power lever is free from binding and the controls have full-throw on the console. If they do not have full-throw or are binding, the

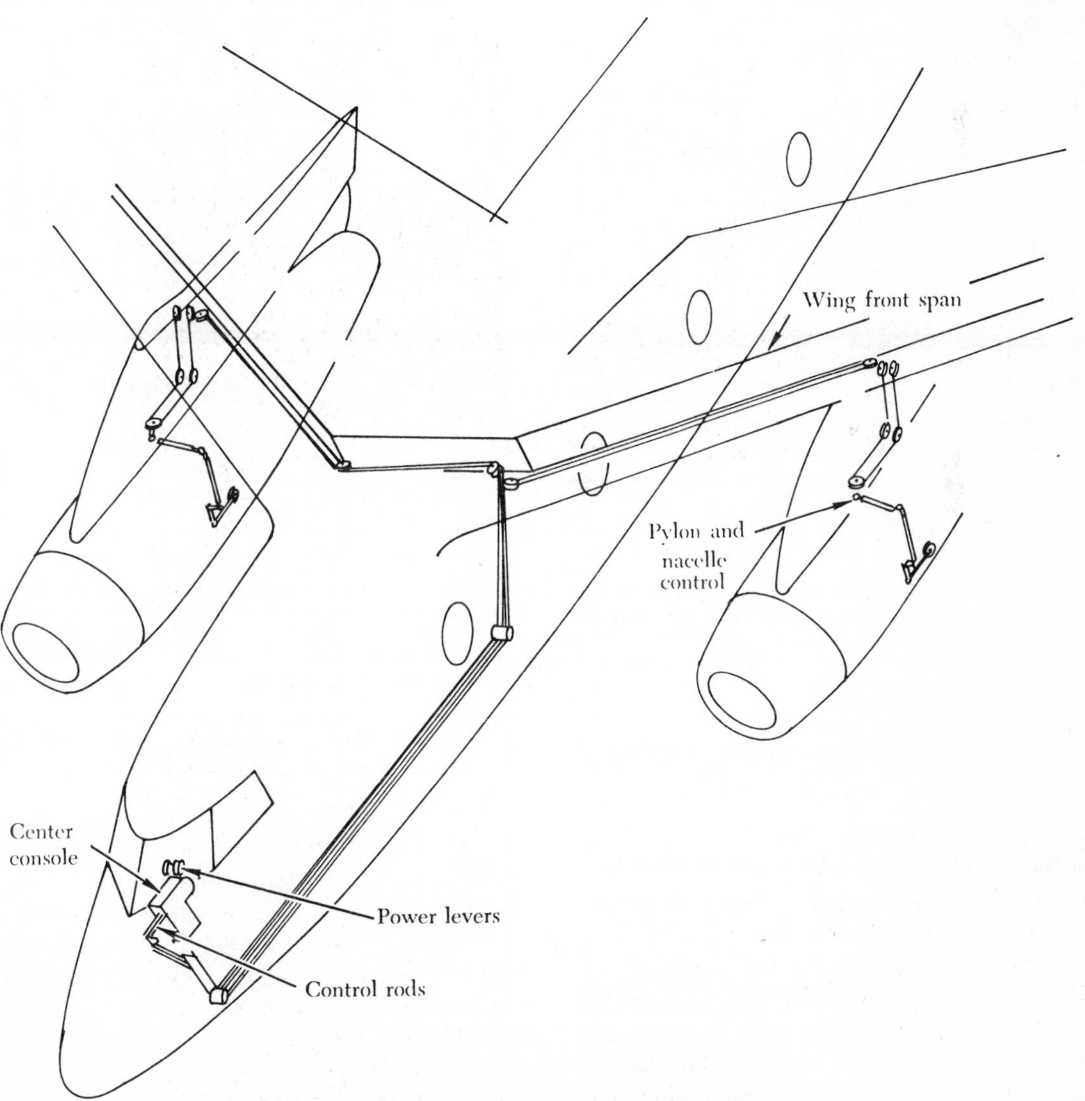

FIGURE 8–20. Power lever control system.

airframe system should be checked and the discrepancies repaired.

After all adjustments have been made, move the power levers through their complete range, carefully inspecting for adequate clearance between the various push-pull rods and tubes. Secure all locknuts, cotter pins, and lockwire, as required.

Adjusting the Fuel Control

The fuel control unit of the typical turbojet engine is a hydromechanical device which schedules the quantity of fuel flowing to the engine so that the desired amount of thrust can be obtained. The amount of thrust is dictated by the position of the power lever in the cockpit and the particular operation of the engine. Thus, the thrust of the engine and the consequent r.p.m. of its turbine are scheduled by fuel flow.

The fuel control unit of the engine is adjusted to trim the engine in order that the maximum thrust output of the engine can be obtained when desired. The engine must be re-trimmed when a fuel control unit is replaced or when the engine does not develop maximum thrust.

After trimming the engine, the idle r.p.m. can be adjusted. The idle r.p.m. is adjusted by turning the INC. IDLE screw an eighth of a turn at a time, allowing sufficient time for the r.p.m. to stabilize between adjustments. Retard the power lever to idle and re-check the idle r.p.m.

If wind velocity is a factor, the aircraft should be headed into the wind while trimming an engine. Since trimming accuracy will decrease as windspeed and moisture content increase, the most accurate trimming is obtained under conditions of no wind and clear, moisture-free air. No trimming should be done when there is a tailwind because of the possibility of the hot exhaust gases being re-ingested. As a practical matter, the engine should never be trimmed when icing conditions exist because of the adverse effects on trimming accuracy. To obtain the most accurate results, the aircraft should always be headed into the wind while the engine is being trimmed.

With the aircraft headed into the wind, verify that the exhaust area is clear. Install an engine trim gage to the T-fitting in the turbine discharge pressure line. Start the engine and allow it to stabilize for 5 minutes before attempting to adjust the fuel control. Refer to the applicable manufacturer's instructions for correct trim values. If the trim is not within limits, turn the INC. MAX screw (figure 8–21) about one-eighth turn in the appropriate di-

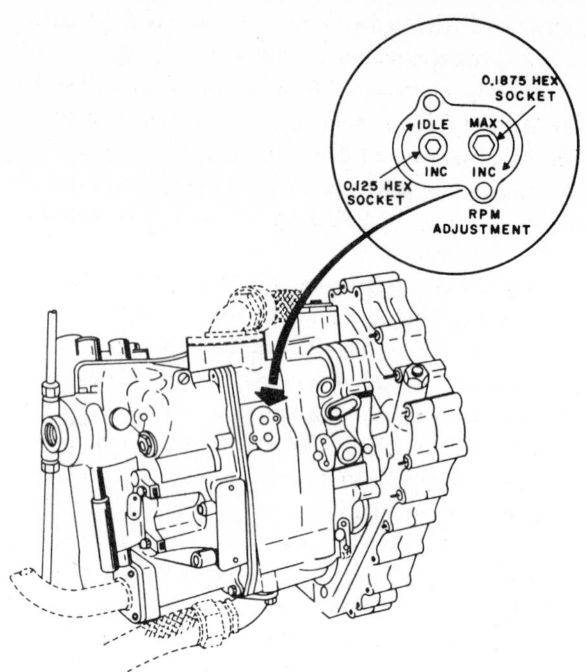

FIGURE 8–21. Typical fuel control adjustments.

rection. Repeat if necessary until the desired value is attained. If the aircraft is equipped with a pressure ratio gage, set it to the correct value.

TURBOPROP POWERPLANT REMOVAL AND INSTALLATION

The following information provides a general picture of a typical turboprop powerplant removal and installation.

Since most turboprop powerplant removal and installation instructions are developed for QECA, the following procedures reflect those used for a typical QECA. The procedures for turboprop engine removal and installation are similar to those presented in the section of this chapter for turbojet engines, except for those systems related to the turboprop propeller.

Open the engine side panels, and remove the nacelle access panels. Disconnect the engine thermocouple leads at the terminal board. Before disconnecting any lines, make sure that all fuel, oil, and hydraulic fluid valves are closed. Cap or plug all lines as they are disconnected to prevent entrance of foreign material.

Remove the clamps securing the bleed-air ducts at the firewall. Then disconnect the following: (1) Electrical connector plugs, (2) engine breather and vent lines, and (3) fuel, oil, and hydraulic lines.

Disconnect the engine power lever and propeller control rods or cables.

Remove the covers from the QECA lift points, attach the QECA sling and remove slack from the cables using a suitable hoist. The sling must be adjusted to position the hoisting eye over the QECA center of gravity. Failure to do so may result in engine damage.

Remove the engine mount bolts. The QECA is then ready to be removed. Recheck all of the disconnect points to make certain they are all disconnected prior to moving the engine. Move the engine forward, out of the nacelle structure, until it clears the aircraft. Lower the QECA into position on the QECA stand, and secure it prior to removing the engine sling.

The installation procedures are essentially the reverse of the removal procedures. Move the QECA straight back into the nacelle structure and align the mount bolt holes and the firewall. Start all the bolts before torquing. With all the bolts started, and using the correct torque wrench adapter, tighten the mount bolts to their proper torque. Remove the sling and install the access covers at the lift point. Using the reverse of the removal procedures, connect the various lines and connectors. New O-ring seals should be used. The manufacturer's instructions should be consulted for the proper torque limits for the various clamps and bolts.

After installation, an engine run-up should be made. In general the run-up consists of checking proper operation of the powerplant and related systems. Several functional tests are performed to evaluate each phase of engine operation. The tests and procedures outlined by the engine or airframe manufacturers should be followed.

HELICOPTER ENGINE REMOVAL AND INSTALLATION

An R1820 9-cylinder, air-cooled radial engine illustrates helicopter engine removal and installation procedures. The engine is installed facing aft with the propeller shaft approximately 39° above the horizontal.

The engine is supported by the engine mount (figure 8–22), which is bolted to the fuselage structure. The installation of the engine provides for ease of maintenance by allowing easy access to all accessories and components when the engine access doors are opened.

The QECA (figure 8–23) contains the engine, engine mount, engine accessories, engine controls, fuel system, lubrication system, ignition system, cooling system, and hydromechanical clutch and fan assembly.

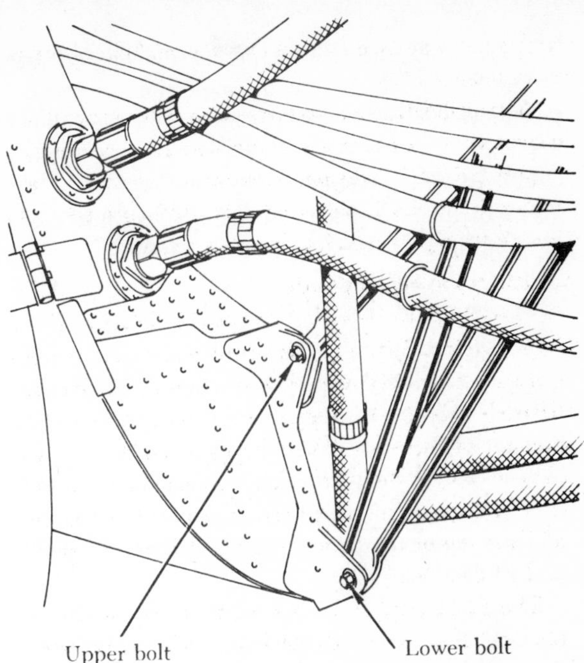

FIGURE 8–22. Engine mount attachment point.

Removal of Helicopter QECA

Prior to removing the helicopter QECA, the engine should be preserved if it is possible to do so.

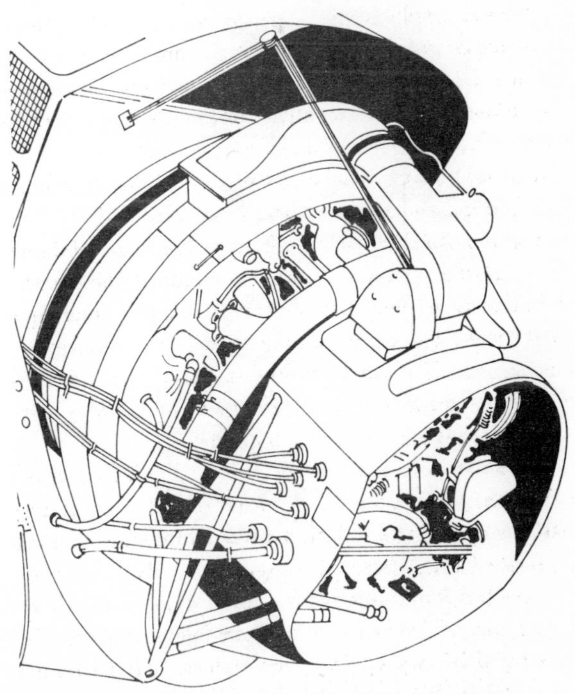

FIGURE 8–23. Typical helicopter QECA.

Then shut off the fuel supply to the engine and drain the oil. Make the disconnections necessary to remove the QECA, and then perform the following steps:

(1) Attach the engine lifting sling (figure 8–24). In this example, attach the two short cable fittings of the sling to the forward surface of the intake rocker boxes of Nos. 2 and 9 cylinders, and the two long cable fittings of the sling to the forward surface of the intake rocker boxes of Nos. 4 and 7 cylinders. Attach the sling to a hoist of at least a 2-ton capacity.

(2) Raise the hoist to apply a slight lift to the QECA. Loosen both engine mount lower attachment bolt nuts before leaving the upper attachment bolts.

(3) Remove the bolts from the sway braces and remove both engine upper attachment bolts. Then remove both engine mount lower attachment bolts and remove the QECA from the helicopter. Mount the power package in a suitable workstand and remove the sling.

Installation of Helicopter QECA

The installation of a new or an overhauled engine is in reverse of the removal procedure. The manufacturer's instructions for the helicopter must be consulted to ascertain the correct interchange of parts from the old engine to the new engine. The applicable maintenance instructions should be followed.

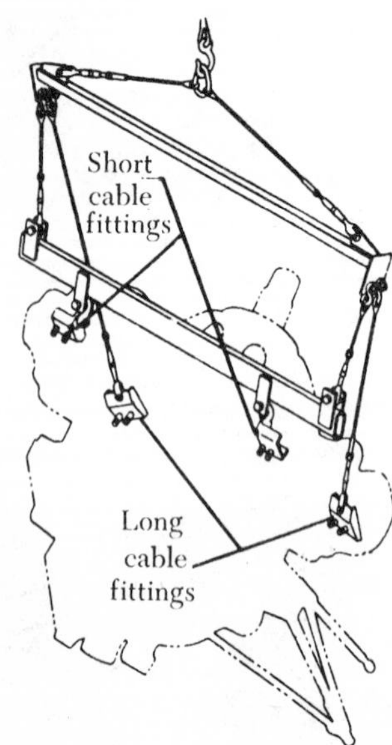

FIGURE 8–24. Special sling used for hoisting helicopter QECA.

RIGGING AND ADJUSTMENT OF HELICOPTER QECA

Throttle

Adjustment of a throttle control system consists of the following:

(1) Adjusting the QECA portion, which includes the control assembly above the carburetor and extends to the carburetor.

(2) Adjusting the airframe portion, which extends from the twist-grip and collective control to the control assembly.

(3) Adjusting the throttle limit switch. The QECA portion of the system can usually be adjusted with the power package removed from, or installed in, the helicopter.

Refer to the Maintenance Instructions Manual and associated technical publications for detailed information concerning cable tensions and related data.

Carburetor Mixture Control

Place the mixture lever on the control quadrant in the "normal" position, and move the mixture arm on the carburetor to the "normal" detent. Adjust the turnbuckle barrels inside the console in the cockpit to produce an equal amount of tension on each cable. Check the operation of the mixture control lever by moving it to the "idle cutoff" position and then into the "full rich" position for positive positioning of the mixture control.

Carburetor Air Temperature Control

Place the carburetor heat lever in mid-position. Adjust the turnbuckle barrels to produce an equal amount of tension on each cable and then lock-wire. Move the lever on the air intake duct to the mid-position, and adjust the actuating rod to meet the arm of the pulley assembly. Then secure the rod to the arm.

Testing the Engine Installation

Normal engine run-in procedures must be followed in accordance with the manufacturer's instructions. A flight test is usually performed after the engine has been installed and the engine controls have been adjusted.

ENGINE MOUNTS

Mounts for Radial Engines

All modern aircraft equipped with radial engines use an engine mount structure made of welded steel tubing. The mount is constructed in one or more sections that incorporate the engine mount ring, bracing members (V-struts), and fittings for attaching the mount to the wing nacelle.

The engine mounts are usually secured to the aircraft by special heat-treated steel bolts. The importance of using only these special bolts can be readily appreciated, since they alone support the entire weight of and withstand all the stresses imposed by the QECA.

The upper bolts support the weight of the engine while the aircraft is on the ground, but when the aircraft is airborne another stress is added. This stress is torsional and affects all bolts, not just the top bolts.

A close look at the typical engine mount ring shown in figure 8–25 will disclose fittings and attachments located at various positions on the engine mount structure. Each fitting performs a certain function.

The section of an engine mount where the engine is attached is known as the engine mount ring. It is usually constructed of steel tubing having a larger diameter than the rest of the mount structure. It is circular in shape so that it can surround the engine blower and accessory section, which is near the point of balance for the engine. The engine is usually attached to the mount by dynafocal mounts, attached to the engine at the point of balance forward of the mount ring. Other types of mounting devices are also used to secure the different engines to their mount rings.

As aircraft engines became larger and produced more power, some method was needed to absorb their vibration. This demand led to the development of the rubber and steel engine-suspension units called shock mounts. Because this combination permits restricted engine movement in all directions, these vibration isolators are commonly known as flexible, or elastic, shock mounts. An

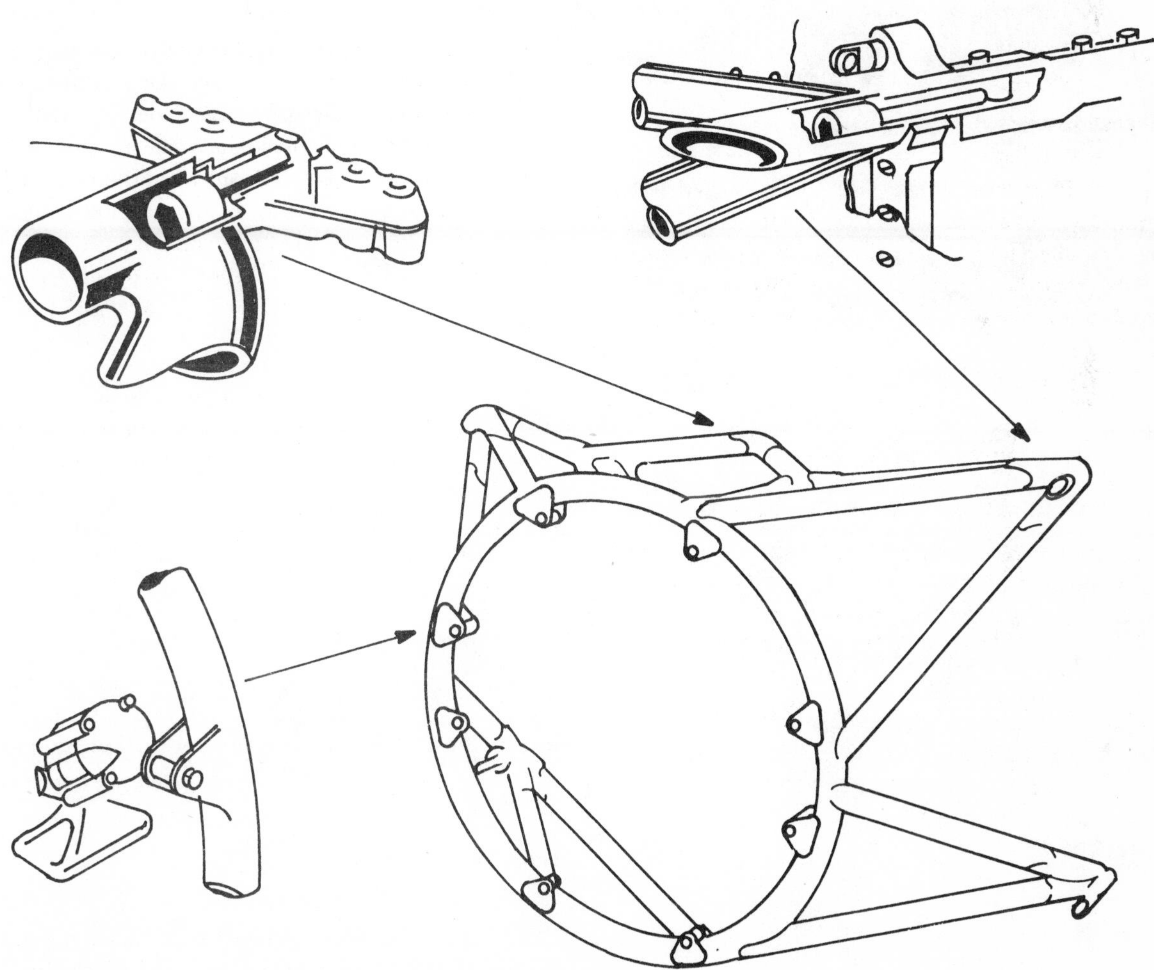

FIGURE 8–25. Typical engine mount.

interesting feature common to most shock mounts is that the rubber and metal parts are arranged so that, under normal conditions, rubber alone supports the engine. Of course, if the engine is subjected to abnormal shocks or loads, the metal snubbers will limit excessive movement of the engine.

Engine mounting suspensions for radial engines may be divided into two main groups: (1) The tangential-suspension type, and (2) the dynafocal type.

The tangential suspension, commonly called the tube-form mounting, is widely used for both in-line and radial engine support. A cutaway view of this type is shown in figure 8–26. This type of mounting is most flexible along its principal axis. Various means of attachment are used in different installations using tube-form mountings.

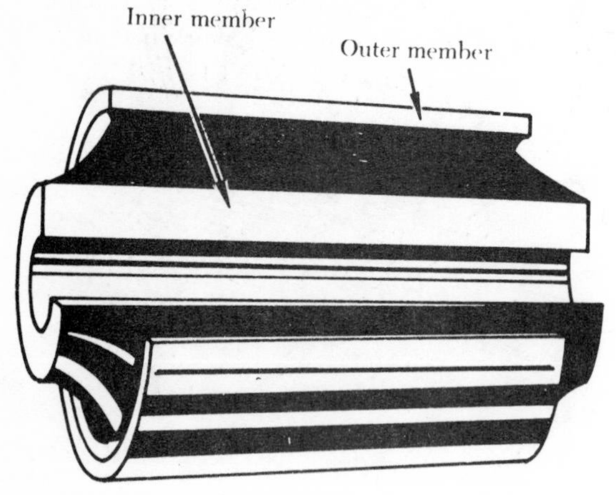

FIGURE 8–26. Tube-form engine mounting.

Dynafocal engine mounts, or vibration isolators, are units which give directional support to radial engines. Two of the most common types of dynafocal mounts are the link-type and the pedestal-type, shown in figure 8–27.

The link-type dynafocal mount uses a tube-form mounting for the flexible element. The outer member of this mounting is clamped into a forged bracket of aluminum alloy or steel and bolted rigidly to the engine mount pad or boss. The link is fitted with tapered roller bearings at the mounting-ring attachment points. Rubber snubbing washers with backing end plates are provided on both extensions of the inner member. These snubbing washers limit the axial motions of the mounting without allowing metal-to-metal contact between subassembly parts.

The pedestal-type dynafocal has an outer shell composed of two steel forgings fastened securely together and bolted to the mounting-ring structure. A predetermined amount of movement is allowed before the rubber is locked out of action by contact between the stem of the dynafocal and the retaining shell. Friction dampers are provided to limit excessive movement.

Mounts for Turbojet Engines

The engine mounts on most turbojet engines are relatively simple when compared with the mounting structures installed on reciprocating engines. However, they perform the same basic functions of

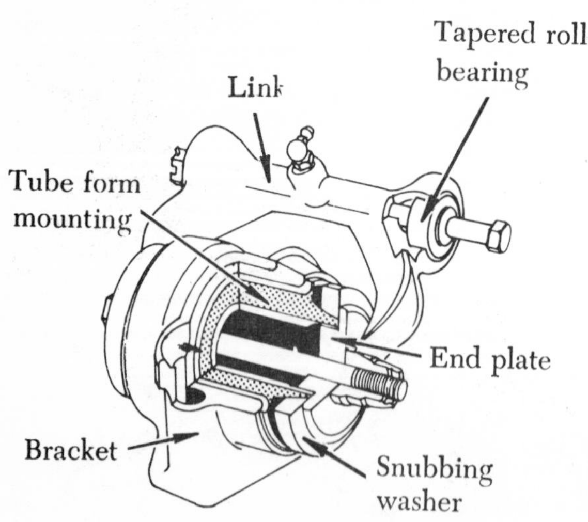

Link type dynafocal subassembly.

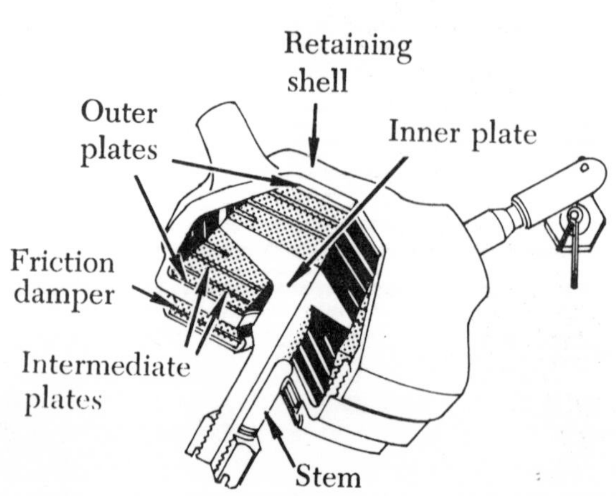

Pedestal-type dynafocal subassembly.

FIGURE 8–27. Two types of dynafocal mounts.

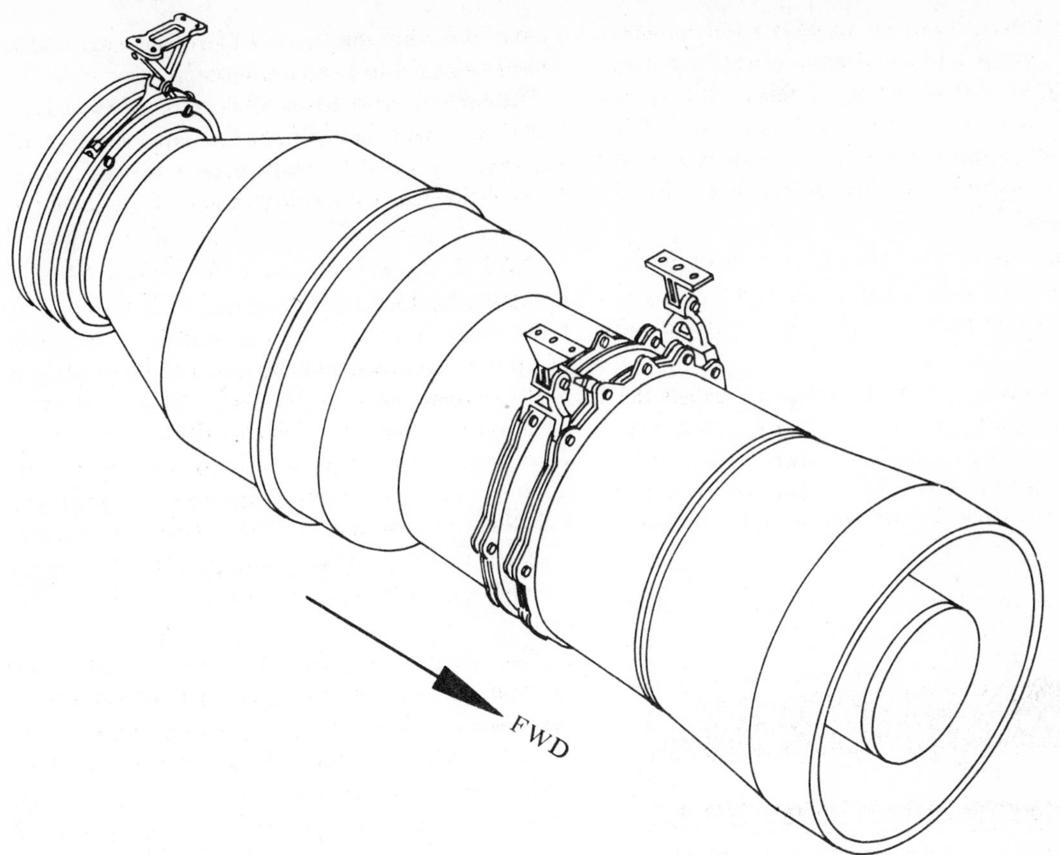

A. Engine mounts

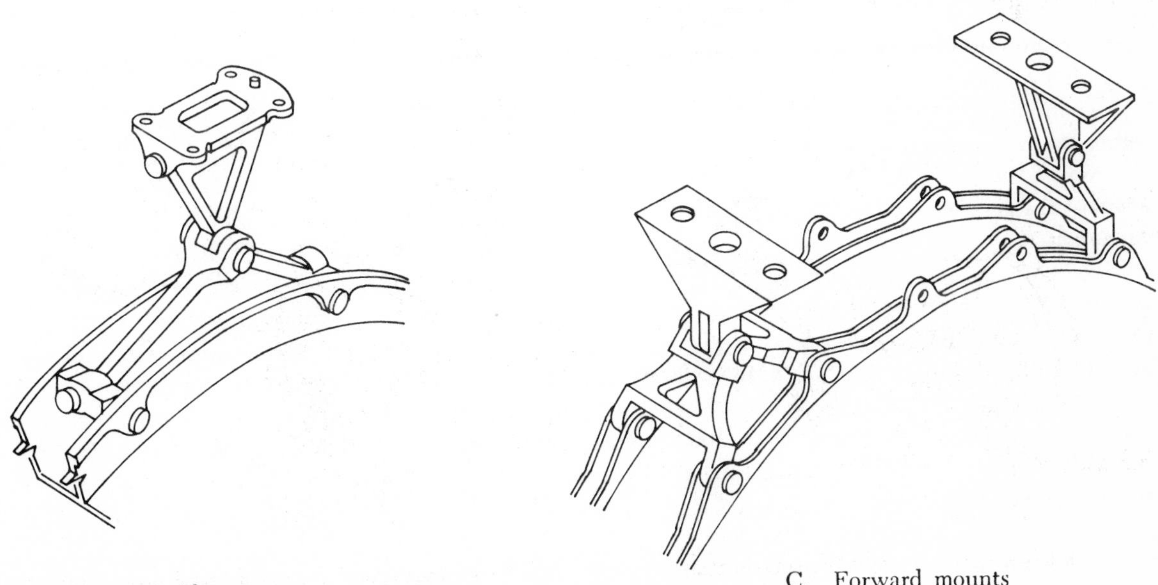

B. Aft mount

C. Forward mounts

FIGURE 8–28. Typical turbine engine mounts.

supporting the engine and transmitting the loads imposed by the engine to the aircraft structure. Most turbine engine mounts are made of stainless steel, and are typically located as illustrated in figure 8–28. Some engine mounting systems use two mounts to support the rear end of the engine and a single mount at the forward end.

PRESERVATION AND STORAGE OF ENGINES

An engine awaiting overhaul or return to service after overhaul must be given careful attention. It does not receive the daily care and attention necessary to detect and correct early stages of corrosion. For this reason, some definite action must be taken to prevent corrosion from affecting the engine.

Corrosion-Preventive Materials

An engine in service is in a sense "self-purging" of moisture, since the heat of combustion evaporates the moisture in and around the engine, and the lubricating oil circulated through the engine temporarily forms a protective coating on the metal it contacts. If the operation of an engine in service is limited or suspended for a period of time, the engine is preserved to a varying extent, depending upon how long it is to be inoperative. This discussion is primarily directed to preserving engines that have been removed from an aircraft. However, the preservation materials discussed are used for all types of engine storage.

Corrosion-Preventive Compounds

Corrosion-preventive compounds are petroleum-base products which will form a waxlike film over the metal to which it is applied. Several types of corrosion-preventive compounds are manufactured according to different specifications to fit the various aviation needs. The type mixed with engine oil to form a corrosion-preventive mixture is a relatively light compound that readily blends with engine oil when the mixture is heated to the proper temperature.

The light mixture is available in three forms: MIL–C–6529 type I, type II, or type III. Type I is a concentrate and must be blended with three parts of MIL–L–22851 or MIL–L–6082, grade 1100 oil to one part of concentrate. Type II is a ready-mixed material with MIL–L–22851 or grade 1100 oil and does not require dilution. Type III is a ready-mixed material with grade 1010 oil, for use in turbine engines only. The light mixture is intended for use when a preserved engine is to remain inactive for less than 30 days. It is also used to spray cylinders and other designated areas.

The desired proportions of lubricating oil and either heavy or light corrosion-preventive compound must not be obtained by adding the compound to the oil already in the engine. The mixture must be prepared separately before applying to the engine, or placing in an oil tank.

A heavy compound is used for the dip treating of metal parts and surfaces. It must be heated to a high temperature to be sufficiently liquid to effectively coat the objects to be preserved. A commercial solvent or kerosene spray is used to remove corrosion-preventive compounds from the engine or parts when they are being prepared for return to service.

Although corrosion-preventive compounds act as an insulator from moisture, in the presence of excessive moisture they will eventually break down and corrosion will begin. Also, the compounds eventually become dried because their oil base gradually evaporates. This allows moisture to contact the engine's metal, and aids in corroding it. Therefore, when an engine is stored in a shipping case or container, some dehydrating (moisture removing) agent must be used to remove the moisture from the air in and around the engine.

Dehydrating Agents

There are a number of substances (referred to as desiccants) that can absorb moisture from the atmosphere in sufficient quantities to be useful as dehydrators. One of these is silica gel. This gel is an ideal dehydrating agent since it does not dissolve when saturated.

As a corrosion preventive, bags of silica gel are placed around and inside various accessible parts of a stored engine. It is also used in clear plastic plugs, called dehydrator plugs, which can be screwed into engine openings such as the spark plug holes. Cobalt chloride is added to the silica gel used in dehydrator plugs. This additive makes it possible for the plugs to indicate the moisture content or relative humidity of the air surrounding the engine. The cobalt-chloride-treated silica gel remains a bright blue color with low relative humidities; but as the relative humidity increases, the shade of the blue becomes progressively lighter, becoming lavender at 30% relative humidity and fading through the various shades of pink, until at 60% relative humidity it is a natural or white color. When the relative humidity is less than 30%, corrosion does not normally take place. Therefore, if the dehydrator plugs are bright blue, the air in the engine has so little moisture that internal corrosion will be held to a minimum.

This same cobalt-chloride-treated silica gel is used in humidity indicator envelopes. These envelopes can be fastened to the stored engine so that they can be inspected through a small window in the shipping case or metal engine container.

All desiccants are sealed in containers to prevent their becoming saturated with moisture before they are used. Care should be taken never to leave the container open or improperly closed.

CORROSION-PREVENTIVE TREATMENT

Before an engine is removed it should be operated, if possible, with corrosion-preventive mixture added in the oil system to retard corrosion by coating the engine's internal parts. If it is impossible to operate the engine before removal from the aircraft, it should be handled as much as possible in the same manner as an operable engine.

Any engine being prepared for storage must receive thorough treatment around the exhaust ports. Because the residue of exhaust gases is potentially very corrosive, a corrosion-preventive mixture must be sprayed into each exhaust port, including the exhaust valve. After the exhaust ports have been thoroughly coated, a moistureproof and oilproof gasket backed by a metal or wooden plate, should be secured over the exhaust ports using the exhaust stack mounting studs and nuts (figure 8–29). These covers form a seal to prevent moisture from entering the interior of the engine through the exhaust ports. Engines stored in metal containers usually have special ventilatory covers

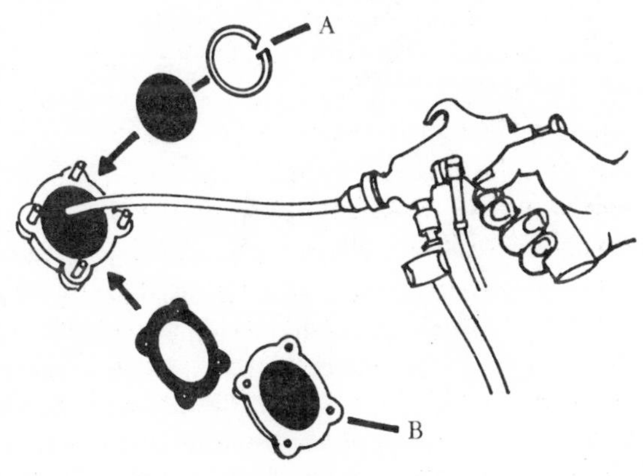

A. Ventilator cover

B. Oilproof and moistureproof seal

FIGURE 8–29. Treating and sealing the exhaust ports.

To prevent corrosion, spray each cylinder interior with corrosion-preventive mixture to prevent moisture and oxygen from contacting the deposits left by combustion. Spray the cylinders by inserting the nozzle of the spray gun into each spark plug hole and "playing" the gun to cover as much area as possible. Before spraying, each cylinder to be treated should be at the "bottom center" position. This allows the entire inside of the cylinder to become coated with corrosion-preventive mixture. After spraying each engine cylinder at "bottom center," re-spray each cylinder while the crankshaft is stationary.

The crankshaft must not be moved after this final spraying, or the seal of corrosion-preventive mixture between the pistons and cylinder walls will be broken. Air can then enter past the pistons into the engine. Also, the coating of corrosion-preventive mixture on the cylinder walls will be scraped away, exposing the bare metal to possible corrosion. Until it is safely stored in the shipping case, the engine should have a sign attached similar to the following: "DO NOT TURN CRANKSHAFT."

When preparing the engine for storage, dehydrator plugs are screwed into the spark plug opening of each cylinder. If the engine is to be stored in a wooden shipping case, the ignition harness leads are attached to the dehydrator plugs with lead supports, as shown in figure 8–30. Special ventilatory plugs (figure 8–30) are installed in the spark plug holes of an engine stored horizontally in a metal container. If the engine is stored vertically in a container, these vent plugs are installed in only the upper spark plug holes of each cylinder, and nonventilatory plugs are installed in the lower cylinders. Dehydrator plugs from which the desiccant has been removed may be used for this latter purpose.

Another point at which the engine must be sealed is the intake manifold. If the carburetor is to remain on the engine during storage, the throttle valve should be wired open and a seal installed over the air inlet. But, if the carburetor is removed and stored separately, the seal is made at the carburetor mounting pad. The seal used in either instance can be an oilproof and moistureproof gasket backed by a wooden or metal plate securely bolted into place. Silica gel should be placed in the intake manifold to absorb moisture. The silica gel bags are usually suspended from the cover plate. This eliminates the possibility of forgetting to remove the silica gel bags when the engine is eventually

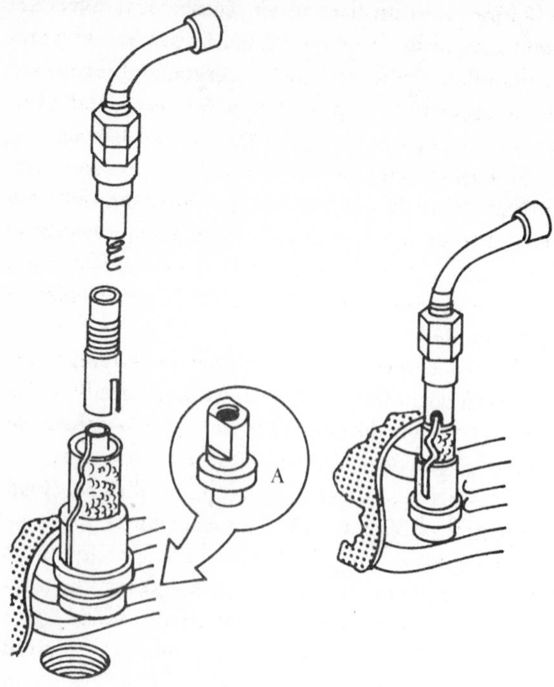

A. Ventilator plug

FIGURE 8–30. Ignition harness lead support installation.

removed from storage. A ventilatory cover without silica gel bags attached can be used when the engine is stored in a metal container.

After the following details have been taken care of, the engine is ready to be packed into its container. If the engine has not been spray coated with corrosion-preventive mixture, the propeller shaft and propeller shaft thrust bearing must be coated with the compound. Then, a plastic sleeve, or moistureproof paper is secured around the shaft, and a threaded protector cap is screwed onto the propeller retaining nut threads.

All engine openings into which dehydrator plugs (or ventilatory plugs if the engine is stored in a metal container) have not been fitted must be sealed. At points where corrosion-preventive mixture can seep from the interior of the engine, such as the oil inlet and outlet, oilproof and moistureproof gasket material backed by a metal or wooden plate should be used. At other points moistureproof tape can be used if it is carefully installed.

Before its installation in a shipping container, the engine should be carefully inspected to determine if the following accessories, which are not a part of the basic engine, have been removed: Spark plugs and spark plug thermocouples, remote fuel pump adapters (if applicable), propeller hub attaching bolts (if applicable), starters, generators, vacuum pumps, hydraulic pumps, propeller governors, and engine-driven fuel pumps.

ENGINE SHIPPING CONTAINERS

For protection, engines are sealed in plastic or foil envelopes and packed in a wooden shipping case. In recent years the practice of sealing aircraft engines in pressurized metal containers has been increasingly adopted.

When a radial engine is installed in a wooden shipping case, it must be hoisted vertically, with the propeller end up. This necessitates the use of two hoists, as shown in figure 8–31.

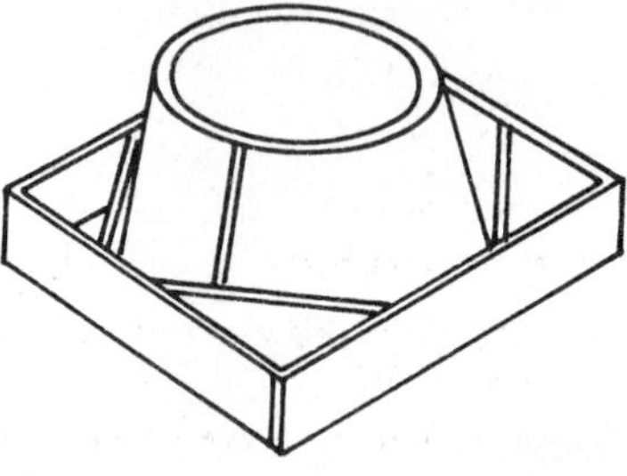

FIGURE 8–31. Hoisting engine for vertical packing.

While the engine is suspended above the base of the shipping case, the mounting plate (figure 8–32) is removed from the case, and the grommets of the protective envelope in which the engine is sealed are fitted to the anchor bolts of the mounting plate. The mounting plate is then bolted to the engine, and the envelope carefully pulled up around the engine.

The engine is then lowered onto the base of the shipping case so that the mounting plate can be bolted into position. Since a mounting ring is used only for radial engines, the protective envelope is attached directly to the base of the shipping case for other types of engines. Then the engine is lowered vertically onto the base and bolted directly to it.

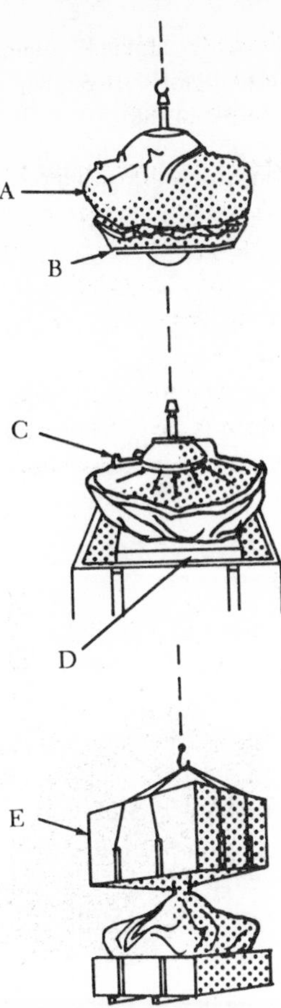

A. Engine
B. Mounting plate
C. Protective envelope
D. Pedestal
E. Cover

FIGURE 8–32. Preparing engine for packing.

If the carburetor is not mounted on the engine or no provision is made to seal it in a small container to be placed inside the shipping case, it can, in some cases, be fastened to a specially constructed platform bolted to the engine.

Before the protective envelope is sealed, silica gel should be placed around the engine to dehydrate the air sealed into the envelope. The amount of silica gel used is determined by the size of the engine. The protective envelope is then carefully gathered around the engine and partially sealed, leaving an opening at one end from which as much air as possible is exhausted. A tank-type vacuum cleaner is very useful for this purpose and is also an aid in detecting any leaks in the envelope. The envelope is then completely sealed, usually by pressing the edges together and fusing them with heat.

Before lowering the shipping case cover over the engine, a quick inventory should be made. Be sure the humidity indicator card is placed so that it can be seen through the inspection window, and that everything required is enclosed in the container.

While lowering the wooden shipping case cover into position, be careful that it does not twist and tear the protective envelope. Secure the cover and stencil or mark the date of preservation on the case. Also, indicate whether the engine is repairable or serviceable.

There are several types of metal shipping containers in use. One model, shown in figure 8–33, is like the wooden shipping case in that it requires the engine to be installed from a vertical position.

Another type allows horizontal installation of an engine, thus eliminating the need for an extra hoist.

The engine is simply lowered onto the base portion of the container and secured. Then silica gel bags are packed into the container, usually in a special section. The amount of silica gel required in a metal container is generally greater than that needed in a wooden shipping case, since the volume

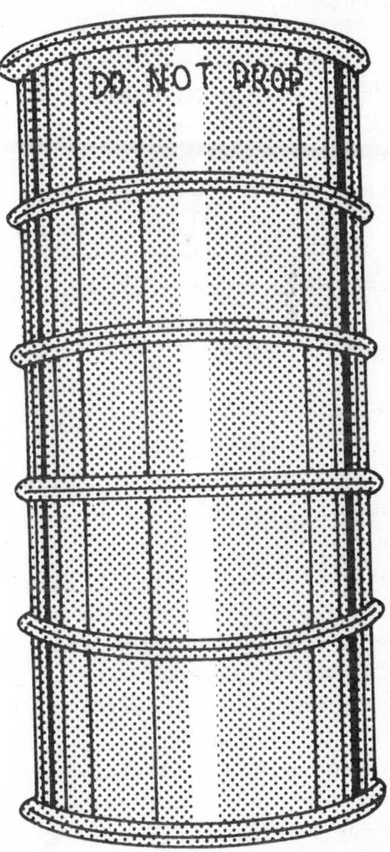

FIGURE 8–33. Metal container designed for vertical installation of engine.

of air in the metal container is much greater than that in the protective envelope installed around an engine in a wooden shipping case. Also, in the metal container the silica gel bags must dehydrate the interior of the engine, since ventilatory plugs are normally installed in the engine openings in place of dehydrator plugs.

All records of the engine should be enclosed inside the shipping container or on the outside for accessibility.

A humidity indicator should be fastened inside the containers with an inspection window provided. Then the rubber seal between the base and the top of the container must be carefully inspected. This seal is usually suitable for re-use several times. After the top of the container has been lowered into position and fastened to the base of the container, dehydrated air at approximately 5 p.s.i. pressure is forced into the container. The container should be checked for leaks by occasional re-checks of the air pressure, since radical changes in temperature affect the air pressure in the container.

INSPECTION OF STORED ENGINES

Most maintenance shops provide a scheduled inspection system for engines in storage. Normally, the humidity indicators on engines stored in shipping cases are inspected every 30 days. When the protective envelope must be opened to inspect the humidity indicator, the inspection period may be extended to once every 90 days, if local conditions permit. The humidity indicator of a metal container is inspected every 180 days under normal conditions.

If the humidity indicator in a wooden shipping case shows by its color that more than 30% relative humidity is present in the air around the engine, all desiccants should be replaced. If more than half the dehydrator plugs installed in the spark plug holes indicate the presence of excessive moisture, the interior of the cylinders should be re-sprayed. If the humidity indicator in a metal container gives a safe blue indication, but air pressure has dropped below 1 p.s.i., the container needs only to be brought to the proper pressure using dehydrated air. However, if the humidity indicator shows an unsafe (pink) condition, the engine should be re-preserved.

PRESERVATION AND DE-PRESERVATION OF GAS TURBINE ENGINES

The procedures for preserving and de-preserving gas turbine engines vary depending upon the length of inactivity, the type of preservative used, and whether or not the engine may be rotated during the inactive period. Much of the basic information on corrosion control presented in the section on reciprocating engines is applicable to gas turbine engines. However, the requirements in the use and types of preservatives are normally different.

The lubrication system is usually drained, and may or may not be flushed with preservative oil. Some engine manufacturers recommend spraying oil in the compressor while "motoring" the engine. Others caution against this practice. Always follow the manufacturer's instructions when performing any preservation or de-preservation of gas turbine engines.

CHAPTER 9

ENGINE FIRE PROTECTION SYSTEMS

GENERAL

Because fire is one of the most dangerous threats to an aircraft, the potential fire zones of all multi-engine aircraft currently produced are protected by a fixed fire protection system. A "fire zone" is an area or region of an aircraft designated by the manufacturer to require fire detection and/or fire extinguishing equipment and a high degree of inherent fire resistance. The term "fixed" describes a permanently installed system in contrast to any type of portable fire extinguishing equipment, such as a hand-held CO_2 fire extinguisher.

RECIPROCATING ENGINE FIRE PROTECTION SYSTEMS

A complete fire protection system includes both a fire detection and a fire extinguishing system.

To detect fires or overheat conditions, detectors are placed in the various zones to be monitored. Fires are detected in reciprocating engine aircraft by using one or more of the following:

(1) Overheat detectors.
(2) Rate-of-temperature-rise detectors.
(3) Flame detectors.
(4) Observation by crewmembers.

In addition to these methods, other types of detectors are used in aircraft fire protection systems, but are not used to detect engine fires. For example, smoke detectors are better suited to monitor areas such as baggage compartments, where materials burn slowly or smolder. Other types of detectors in this category include carbon monoxide detectors.

Fire protection systems on current-production aircraft do not rely on observation by crew members as a primary method of fire detection. An ideal fire detector system will include as many as possible of the following features:

(1) A system which will not cause false warnings under any flight or ground condition.
(2) Rapid indication of a fire and accurate location of the fire.
(3) Accurate indication that a fire is out.
(4) Indication that a fire has re-ignited.
(5) Continuous indication for duration of a fire.
(6) Means for electrically testing the detector system from the aircraft cockpit.
(7) Detectors which resist damage from exposure to oil, water, vibration, extreme temperatures, or handling.
(8) Detectors which are light in weight and easily adaptable to any mounting position.
(9) Detector circuitry which operates directly from the aircraft power system without inverters.
(10) Minimum electrical current requirements when not indicating a fire.
(11) Each detector system should turn on a cockpit light, indicating the location of the fire and have an audible alarm system.
(12) A separate detector system for each engine.

Thermal Switch System

A number of detectors or sensing devices are available. Many older model aircraft still operating have some type of thermal switch system or thermocouple system.

A thermal switch system has one or more lights energized by the aircraft power system and thermal switches that control operation of the light(s). These thermal switches are heat-sensitive units that complete electrical circuits at a certain temperature. They are connected in parallel with each other but in series with the indicator lights (figure 9–1). If the temperature rises above a set value in any one section of the circuit, the thermal switch will close, completing the light circuit to indicate a fire or overheat condition.

No set number of thermal switches is required; the exact number usually is determined by the aircraft manufacturer. On some installations all the thermal detectors are connected to one light; on others there may be one thermal switch for each indicator light.

Some warning lights are push-to-test lights. The

bulb is tested by pushing it in to check an auxiliary test circuit. The circuit shown in figure 9–1 includes a test relay. With the relay contact in the position shown, there are two possible paths for current flow from the switches to the light. This is an additional safety feature. Energizing the test relay completes a series circuit and checks all the wiring and the light bulb.

Also included in the circuit shown in figure 9–1 is a dimming relay. By energizing the dimming relay, the circuit is altered to include a resistor in series with the light. In some installations several circuits are wired through the dimming relay, and all the warning lights may be dimmed at the same time.

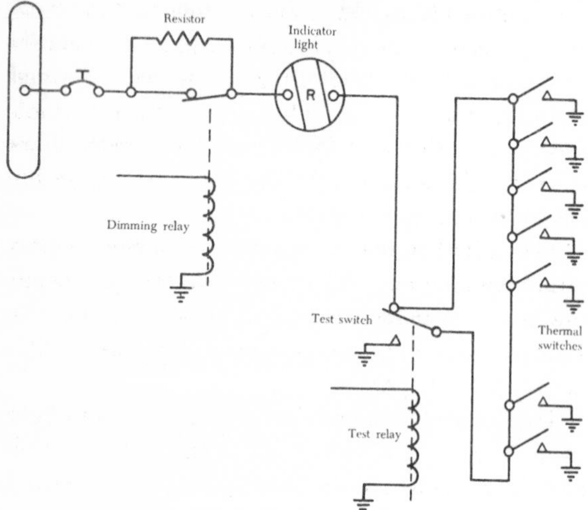

FIGURE 9–1. Thermal switch fire circuit.

Thermocouple Systems

The thermocouple fire warning system operates on an entirely different principle than the thermal switch system. A thermocouple depends on the rate of temperature rise and will not give a warning when an engine slowly overheats or a short circuit develops. The system consists of a relay box, warning lights, and thermocouples. The wiring system of these units may be divided into the following circuits: (1) The detector circuit, (2) the alarm circuit, and (3) the test circuit. These circuits are shown in figure 9–2.

The relay box contains two relays, the sensitive relay and the slave relay, and the thermal test unit. Such a box may contain from one to eight identical circuits, depending on the number of potential fire zones. The relays control the warning lights. In turn, the thermocouples control the operation of the

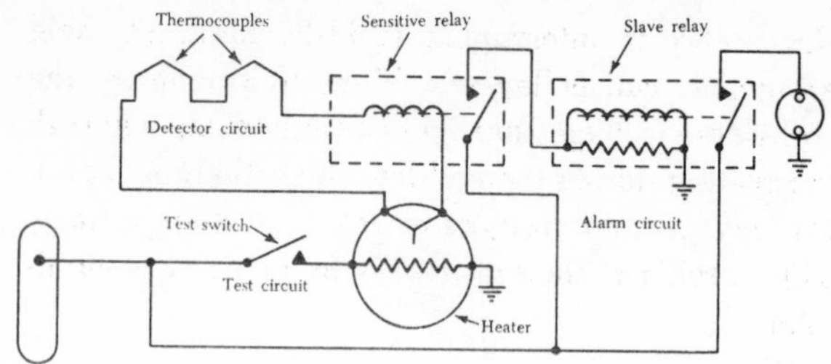

FIGURE 9–2. Thermocouple fire warning circuit.

relays. The circuit consists of several thermocouples in series with each other and with the sensitive relay.

The thermocouple is constructed of two dissimilar metals such as chromel and constantan. The point where these metals are joined and will be exposed to the heat of a fire is called a hot junction. There is also a reference junction enclosed in a dead air space between two insulation blocks. A metal cage surrounds the thermocouple to give mechanical protection without hindering the free movement of air to the hot junction.

If the temperature rises rapidly, the thermocouple produces a voltage because of the temperature difference between the reference junction and the hot junction. If both junctions are heated at the same rate, no voltage will result. In the engine compartment, there is a normal, gradual rise in temperature from engine operation; because it is gradual, both junctions heat at the same rate and no warning signal is given.

If there is a fire, however, the hot junction will heat more rapidly than the reference junction. The ensuing voltage causes a current to flow within the detector circuit. Any time the current is greater than 4 milliamperes (0.004 ampere), the sensitive relay will close. This will complete a circuit from the aircraft power system to the coil of the slave relay. The slave relay will then close and complete the circuit to the warning light to give a visual fire warning.

The total number of thermocouples used in individual detector circuits depends on the size of the fire zones and the total circuit resistance, which usually does not exceed 5 ohms. As shown in figure 9–2, the circuit has two resistors. The resistor connected across the slave relay terminals absorbs the coil's self-induced voltage to prevent arcing across the points of the sensitive relay. The contacts of the sensitive relay are so fragile that they will burn or weld if arcing is permitted.

When the sensitive relay opens, the circuit to the

slave relay is interrupted and the magnetic field around its coil collapses. When this happens, the coil gets a voltage through self-induction, but with the resistor across the coil terminals, there is a path for any current flow as a result of this voltage. Thus, arcing at the sensitive relay contacts is eliminated.

Continuous-Loop Detector Systems

A continuous-loop detector or sensing system permits more complete coverage of a fire hazard area than any of the spot-type temperature detectors. Continuous-loop systems are versions of the thermal switch system. They are overheat systems, heat-sensitive units that complete electrical circuits at a certain temperature. There is no rate-of-heat-rise sensitivity in a continuous-loop system. Two widely used types of continuous-loop systems are the Kidde and the Fenwal systems.

In the Kidde continuous-loop system (figure 9–3), two wires are imbedded in a special ceramic core within an Inconel tube.

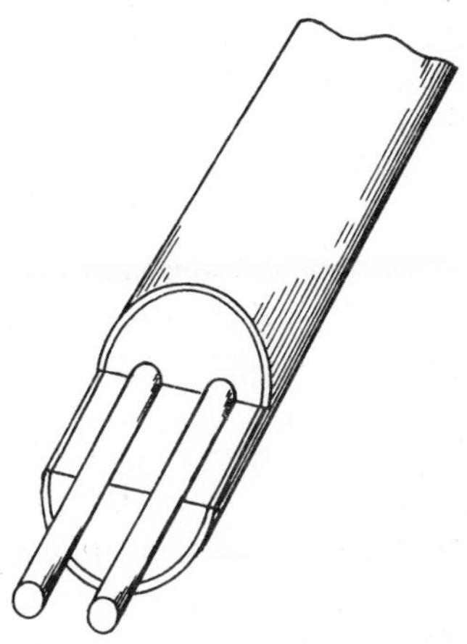

FIGURE 9–3. Kidde sensing element.

One of the two wires in the Kidde sensing system is welded to the case at each end and acts as an internal ground. The second wire is a hot lead (above ground potential) that provides a current signal when the ceramic core material changes its resistance with a change in temperature.

Another continuous-loop system, the Fenwall system (figure 9–4), uses a single wire surrounded by a continuous string of ceramic beads in an Inconel tube.

The beads in the Fenwal detector are wetted with a eutectic salt, which possesses the characteristic of suddenly lowering its electrical resistance as the sensing element reaches its alarm temperature. In both the Kidde and the Fenwal systems, the resistance of the ceramic or eutectic salt core material prevents electrical current from flowing at normal temperatures. In case of a fire or overheat condition, the core resistance drops and current flows between the signal wire and ground, energizing the alarm system.

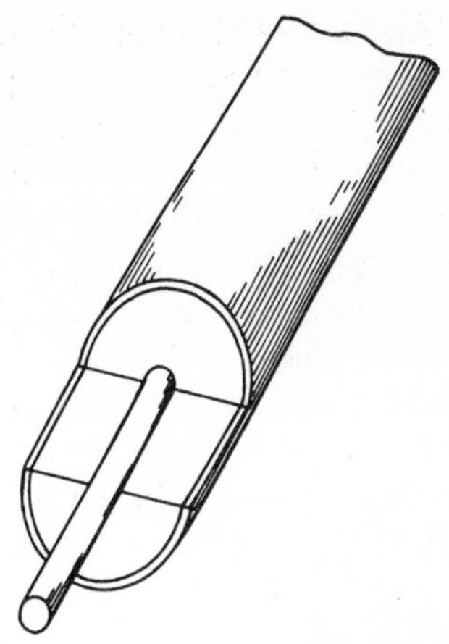

FIGURE 9–4. Fenwal sensing element.

The Kidde sensing elements are connected to a relay control unit. This unit constantly measures the total resistance of the full sensing loop. The system senses the average temperature, as well as any single hot spot.

The Fenwal system uses a magnetic amplifier control unit. This system is nonaveraging but will sound an alarm when any portion of its sensing element reaches the alarm temperature.

Both systems continuously monitor temperatures in the engine compartments, and both will automatically reset following a fire or overheat alarm after the overheat condition is removed or the fire extinguished.

Spot Detector Systems

Spot detector systems operate on a different principle from the continuous loop. Each detector unit (figure 9–5) consists of a bimetallic thermoswitch. Most spot detectors are dual-terminal thermoswitches, electrically above ground potential.

Fenwal spot detectors are wired in parallel between two complete loops of wiring, as illustrated in figure 9–6. Thus, the system can withstand one fault, either an electrical open circuit or a short to ground, without sounding a false fire warning. A double fault must exist before a false fire warning can occur. In case of a fire or overheat condition, the spot-detector switch closes and completes a circuit to sound an alarm.

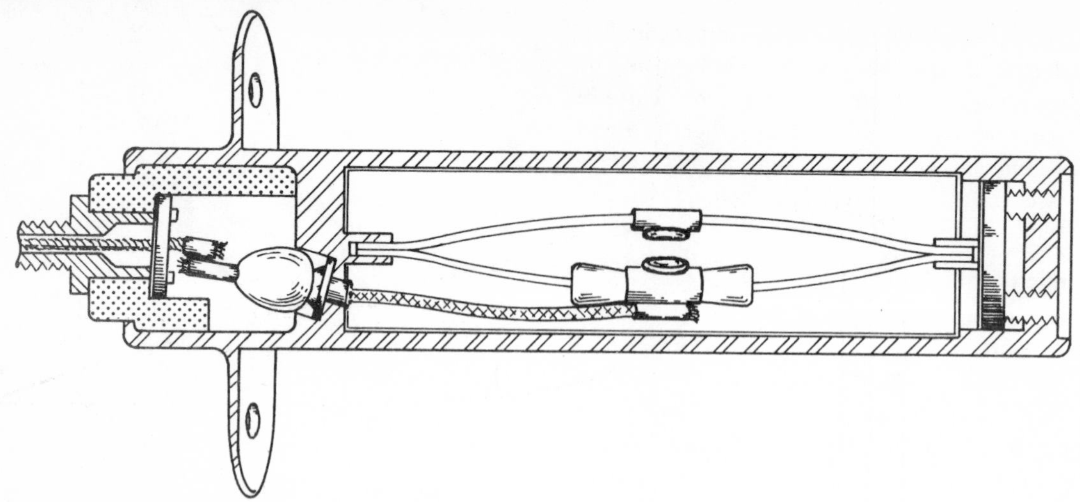

FIGURE 9–5. Fenwal spot detector.

The Fenwal spot-detector system operates without a control unit. When an overheat condition or a fire causes the switch in a detector to close, the alarm bell sounds and a warning light for the affected area is lighted.

FIRE ZONES

Engine fire detectors are located according to fire zones. Each engine and nacelle area usually is divided into three zones similar to the zoned nacelle shown in figure 9–7. Zone I identifies the engine power section area forward of the cowl flap trailing edges and inner ring baffles. Zone II identifies the engine accessory section area between the inner ring baffles and the firewall, and zone III identifies the nacelle area aft of the firewall.

In addition to the engine and nacelle area zones, other areas on multi-engine aircraft are provided with fire detection and protection systems. These areas include baggage compartments, auxiliary powerplant installations, combustion heater installations, and other hazardous areas. Discussion of fire protection for these areas is not included in this section, which is limited to engine fire protection.

FIRE EXTINGUISHING AGENTS

The fixed fire extinguisher systems used in most reciprocating engine fire protection systems are designed to dilute the atmosphere with an inert agent that will not support combustion. Many systems use perforated tubing or discharge nozzles to distribute the extinguishing agent. More recently developed HRD (high rate of discharge) systems use open-end tubes to deliver a quantity of extinguishing agent in from 1 to 2 seconds.

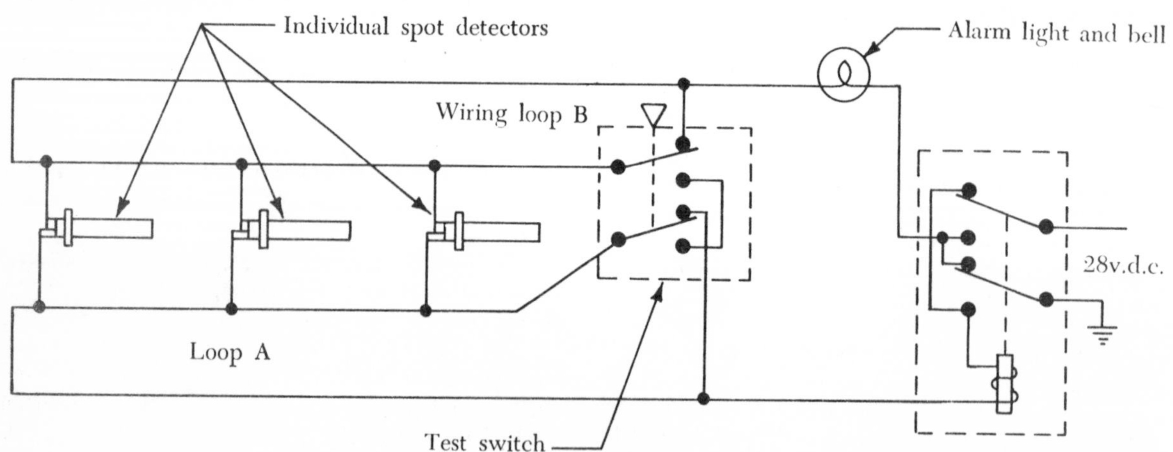

FIGURE 9–6. Fenwal spot-detector circuit.

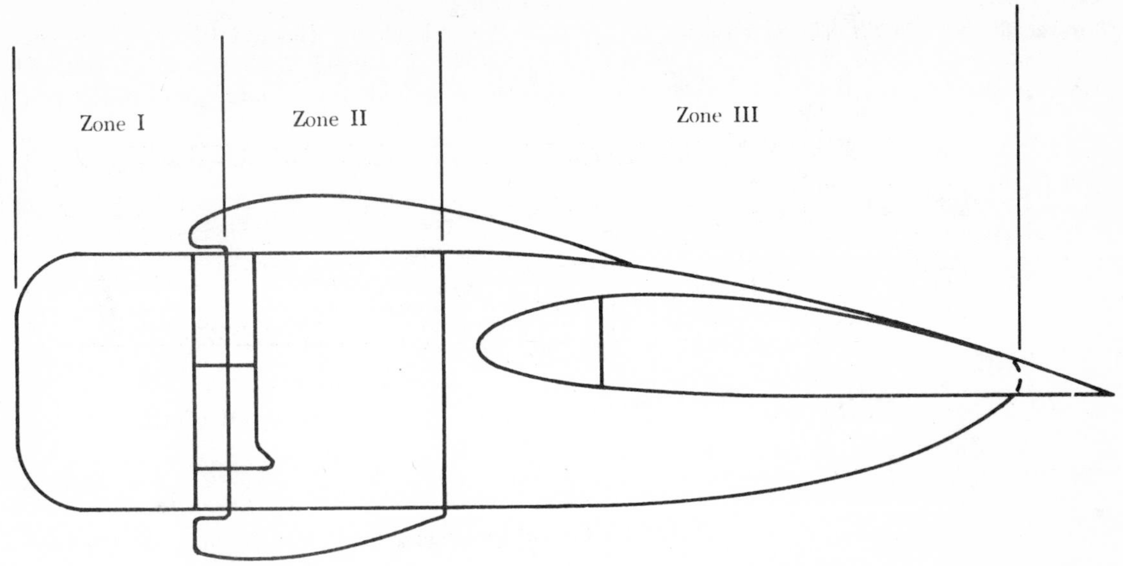

FIGURE 9–7. Fire zone areas.

Carbon Dioxide (CO_2). UL toxicity rating of 5a, especially recommended for use on class B and C fires. Extinguishes flame by dissipating oxygen in the immediate area. From a standpoint of toxicity and corrosion hazards, carbon dioxide is the safest agent to use. It was for many years the most widely used agent. If handled improperly, it can cause mental confusion and suffocation. Because of its variation in vapor pressure with temperature, it is necessary to store CO_2 in stronger containers than are required for most other agents.

Halogenated Hydrocarbons (commonly called Freon).

Methyl bromide (Halon 1001). Chemical formula–CH_3Br–a liquified gas, with a UL toxicity rating of 2. Methyl bromide is a more effective extinguishing agent than CO_2 from a standpoint of weight. It is also more toxic than CO_2 and cannot be used in areas where harmful concentrations can enter personnel compartments. A warning agent, such as colored smoke, is mixed with methyl bromide, which will seriously corrode aluminum alloy, magnesium or zinc.

Chlorobromomethane (Halon 1011). Chemical formula–CH_2ClBr.–is a liquefied gas, with a UL toxicity rating of 3. Commonly referred to as "CB", chlorobromomethane is more toxic than CO_2. It is corrosive to aluminum, magnesium, steel and brass. It is not recommended for aircraft use.

Carbon tetrachloride (Halon 104). Chemical formula–CCl_4–a liquid with a UL toxicity rating of 3. It is poisonous and toxic. Hydrochloric acid vapor, chlorine and phosgene gas are produced whenever "carbon tet" is used on ordinary fires. The amount of phosgene gas is increased whenever "carbon tet" is brought in direct contact with hot metal, certain chemicals, or continuing electrical arcs. It is no longer approved for any fire extinguishing use.

Dibromodifluoromethane (Halon 1201). Chemical formula–CBr_2F_2–a liquified gas with a UL toxicity rating of 4. This agent is noncorrosive to aluminum, brass, and steel, and it is more toxic than CO_2. It is one of the more effective fire extinguishing agents available, but is not recommended for aircraft use.

Bromochlorodifluoromethane (Halon 1211). Chemical formula–$CBrClF_2$–a liquified gas with a UL toxicity rating of 5. It is colorless, noncorrosive and evaporates rapidly leaving no residue whatever. It does not freeze or cause cold burns and will not harm fabrics, metals, or other materials it contacts. Halon 1211 acts rapidly on fires by producing a heavy blanketing mist that eliminates air from the fire source, but more important interferes chemically with the combustion process. It has outstanding properties in preventing reflash after the fire has been extinguished.

Bromotrifluoromethane (Halon 1301). Chemical formula–CF_3Br–is a liquefied gas with a UL toxicity rating of 6. It has all the characteristics of Halon 1211. The significant difference between the two is: Halon 1211 throws a spray similar to CO_2 while Halon 1301 has a vapor spray that is more difficult to direct.

Halon 1211 and Halon 1301 are widely used in HRD (high rate of discharge) fire extinguishing systems installed in turboprop and turbojet powered aircraft.

UNDERWRITERS' LABORATORIES' CLASSIFICATION OF COMPARATIVE LIFE HAZARD OF FIRE EXTINGUISHING AGENTS

Group	*Definition*	*Examples*
6 (least toxic)	Gases or vapors which in concentrations up to at least 20% by volume for durations of exposure of the order of 2 hours do not appear to produce injury.	Bromotrifluoromethane (Halon 1301)
5a	Gases or vapors much less toxic than Group 4 but more toxic than Group 6.	Carbon Dioxide
4	Gases or vapors which in concentrations of the order of 2 to 2½% for durations of exposure of the order of 2 hours are lethal or produce serious injury.	Dibromodifluoromethane (Halon 1202)
3	Gases or vapors which in concentrations of the order of 2 to 2½% for durations of exposure of the order of 1 hour are lethal or produce serious injury.	Bromochloromethane (Halon 1011), Carbon tetrachloride (Halon 104)
2	Gases or vapors which in concentrations of the order of ½ to 1% for durations of exposure of the order of ½ hour are lethal or produce serious injury.	Methyl bromide (Halon 1001)

TABLE 9–1. UL Toxicity Table.

Reciprocating Engine CO_2 Fire Extinguisher Systems

CO_2 is one of the earliest types of engine fire extinguisher systems for reciprocating engine transport aircraft and is still used on many older aircraft.

The fire extinguisher system is designed around a CO_2 cylinder (figure 9–8) and a remote control valve assembly in the cockpit. The cylinder stores the flame-smothering carbon dioxide under the pressure required to distribute the extinguishing agent to the engines. The gas is distributed through tubing from the CO_2 cylinder valve to the control valve assembly in the cockpit, and then to the engines via tubing installed in the fuselage and wing tunnels. The tubing terminates in perforated loops that encircle the engines (figure 9–9).

To operate the CO_2 fire extinguisher system, the selector valve must be set for the engine that is on fire. A pull on a T-shaped control handle located adjacent to the engine selector valve actuates the release lever in the CO_2 cylinder valve. The compressed liquid in the CO_2 cylinder flows in one rapid burst to the outlets in the distribution line (figure 9–9) of the affected engine. Contact with the air converts the liquid into gas and "snow," which smothers the flame.

A more sophisticated type of CO_2 fire protection system is used on many four-engine aircraft. This system is capable of delivering CO_2 twice to any one of the four engines. Fire warning systems are

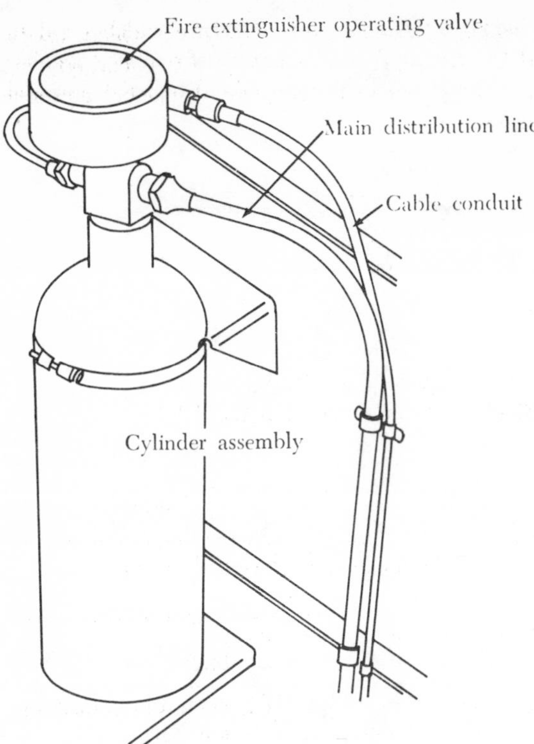

FIGURE 9–8. CO_2 cylinder installation.

installed at all fire hazardous locations of the aircraft to provide an alarm in case of fire.

The various warning systems operate fire warning lights on the cockpit fire control panels and also energize a cockpit warning bell.

One such CO_2 system consists of six cylinders, mounted three to a row in each side of the nose wheel well. Flood valves are installed on each CO_2 bottle. The flood valves of each row are interconnected. The valves on the two aft bottles, in each bank of three, are designed to be opened mechanically by a cable connected to discharge control handles on the main fire control panel in the cockpit. In case of discharge by mechanical means, the forward bottle flood valve in each bank is operated by the released CO_2 pressure from the two aft bottles through the interconnecting lines. The flood valve on the forward bottle of each bank contains a solenoid. The valve is designed to be operated electrically by energizing the solenoid when a button on the control panel is depressed. In case of a discharge by electrical means, the valves on the two aft bottles of each bank are operated by the released CO_2 pressure from the forward bottle through the interconnector lines.

Each bank of CO_2 bottles has a red thermosafety-discharge indicator disk set to rupture at or above a pressure of 2,650 p.s.i. Discharge overboard will occur at temperatures above 74° C. Each bank of bottles also has a yellow system-discharge indicator disk. Mounted adjacent to the red disk, the yellow disks indicate which bank of bottles has been emptied by a normal discharge.

This type of CO_2 fire protection system includes a fire warning system. It is a continuous-loop, low-impedance, automatic resetting type for the engine and nacelle areas.

A single fire detector circuit is provided for each engine and nacelle area. Each complete circuit consists of a control unit, sensing elements, a test relay, a fire warning signal light, and a fire warning signal circuit relay. Associated equipment, such as flexible connector assemblies, wire, grommets, mounting brackets, and mounting clamps, is used in various quantities, depending on individual installation requirements. For example, on a four-engine aircraft, four warning light assemblies, one for each engine and nacelle area, give corresponding warning indications when an alarm is initiated by a respective engine fire warning circuit. Warning light assemblies in the CO_2 manual release handles are connected to all four engine fire detector circuits, along with a fire warning bell with its guarded cutoff switch and indicating light.

The insulated wire of the detector circuit runs from the control unit in the radio compartment to the test relay. The wire is then routed through the nacelle and engine sections and back to the test relay, where it is joined to itself to form a loop.

Each control unit contains tubes or transistors, transformers, resistors, capacitors, and a potentiometer. It also contains an integrated circuit which introduces a time delay that desensitizes the warning system to short-duration transient signals that otherwise would cause momentary false alarms. When a fire or overheat condition exists in an engine or nacelle area, the resistance of the sensing loop decreases below a preset value determined by the setting of the control unit potentiometer, which is in the bias circuit of the control unit detector and amplifier circuit. The output of this circuit energizes the fire warning bell and fire warning light.

TURBINE ENGINE FIRE PROTECTION SYSTEMS

Several general failures or hazards can result in overheat conditions or fires peculiar to turbine engine aircraft because of their operating charac

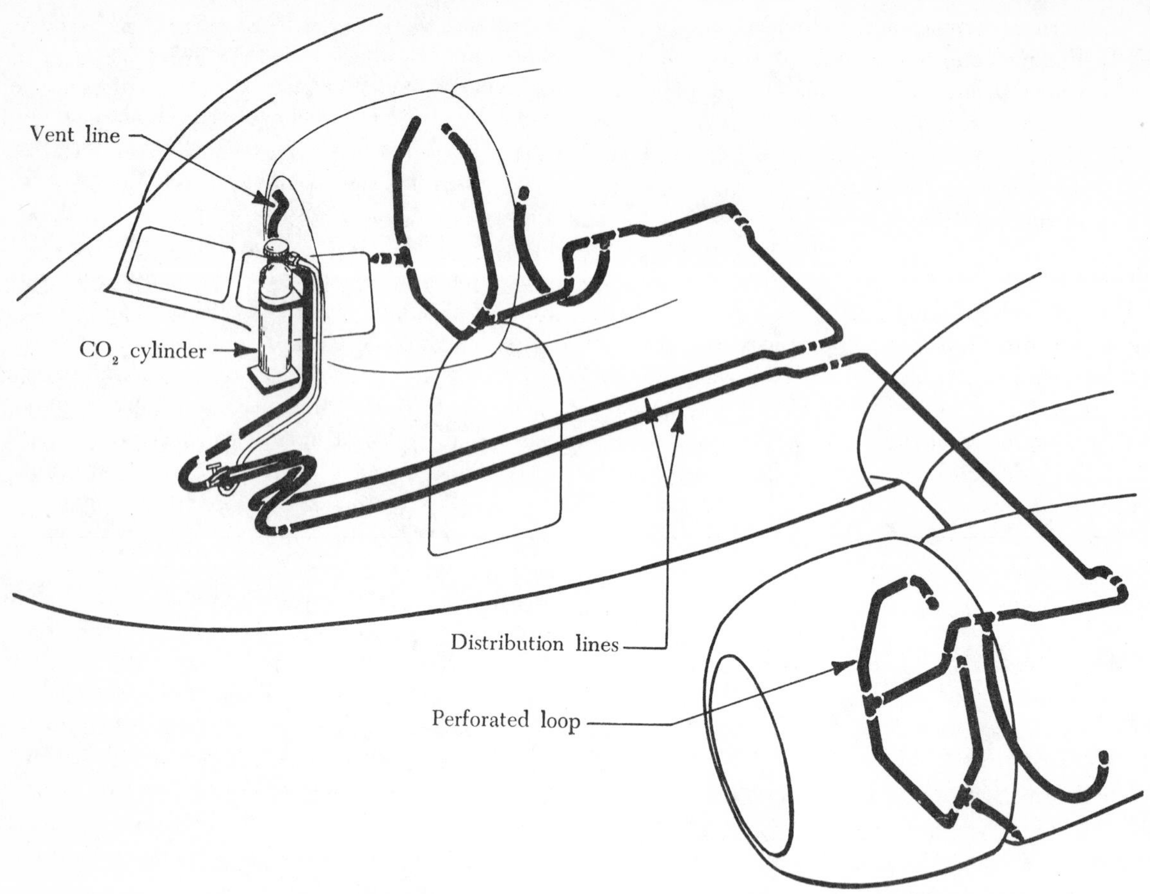

FIGURE 9–9. CO_2 fire extinguisher system on a twin-engine transport aircraft.

teristics. The two major types of turbine failure can be classified as either thermodynamic or mechanical.

Thermodynamic causes are those which upset the proportion of air used to cool combustion temperatures to the levels which the turbine metals can tolerate. When the cooling cycle is upset, turbine blades can melt, causing a sudden loss of thrust. The rapid buildup of ice on inlet screens or inlet guide vanes can result in severe overtemperature, causing the turbine blades to melt or to be severed and thrown outward. Such failures can result in a severed tail cone and possible penetration of the aircraft structure, tanks, or equipment near the turbine wheel. In general, most thermodynamic failures are caused by ice, excess air bleed or leakage, or faulty controls which permit compressor stall or excess fuel.

Mechanical failures, such as fractured or thrown blades, can also lead to overheat conditions or fires. Thrown blades can puncture the tail cone, creating an overheat condition. Failure of forward stages of multi-stage turbines usually is much more severe. Penetration of the turbine case by failed blades is a possible fire hazard, as is the penetration of lines and components containing flammable fluids.

A high flow of fuel through an improperly adjusted fuel nozzle can cause burn-through of the tail cone in some engines. Engine fires can be caused by burning fluid that occasionally runs out through the exhaust pipe.

Turbine Engine Fire Zones

Because turbine engine installations differ markedly from reciprocating engines, the fire zone system used for most reciprocating engines cannot be used.

A possible fire zone in a turbine engine installation is any area in which an ignition source, together with combustibles, combustible fluid line leakage, or combustible mixtures, may exist. The following engine compartments usually are protected:

(1) Engine power section, which includes the

burner, turbine, and tailpipe.

(2) Engine compressor and accessory section, which includes the compressor and all the engine accessories.

(3) Complete powerplant compartments, in which no isolation exists between the engine power section and the accessory section.

Turbine Engine Fire Extinguishing Agents

The fire extinguishing agents used in reciprocating engine fire protection systems are also used in turbine engine systems. The effectiveness of the various agents is influenced by the type of turbine engine fire protection system used, whether it is an HRD (high-rate-of-discharge) system rather than a conventional system, or whether the method of distribution is nozzle, spray ring, or open-end outlet. The choice of agent is also influenced by the airflow conditions through the engine.

Types of Fire or Overheat Detectors

The following list of detection methods includes those most commonly used in turbine engine fire protection systems. The complete aircraft fire protection system of most large turbine engine aircraft will incorporate several of these different detection methods:

(1) Rate-of-temperature-rise detectors.
(2) Radiation sensing detectors.
(3) Smoke detectors.
(4) Overheat detectors.
(5) Carbon monoxide detectors.
(6) Combustible mixture detectors.
(7) Fiber-optic detectors.
(8) Observation of crew or passengers.

The three types of detectors most commonly used for fast detection of fires are the rate-of-rise, radiation sensing, and overheat detectors.

Turbine Engine Ground Fire Protection

The problem of ground fires has increased in seriousness with the increased size of turbine engine aircraft. For this reason, a central ground connection to the aircraft's fire extinguishing system has been provided on some aircraft. Such systems provide a more effective means of extinguishing ground fires and eliminate the necessity of removing and re-charging the aircraft-installed fire extinguisher cylinders. These systems usually include means for operating the entire system from one place, such as the cockpit or at the location of the fire extinguishing agent supply on the ground.

On aircraft not equipped with a central ground connection to the aircraft fire extinguishing system, means are usually provided for rapid access to the compressor, tailpipe, or burner compartments. Thus, many aircraft systems are equipped with spring-loaded or pop-out access doors in the skin of the various compartments.

Internal engine tailpipe fires that take place during engine shutdown or false starts can be blown out by motoring the engine with the starter. If the engine is running, it can be accelerated to rated speed to achieve the same result. If such a fire persists, a fire extinguishing agent can be directed into the tailpipe. It should be remembered that excessive use of CO_2 or other agents that have a cooling effect can shrink the turbine housing on the turbine and cause the engine to disintegrate.

TYPICAL MULTI-ENGINE FIRE PROTECTION SYSTEM

A turbine engine fire protection system for a large multi-engine turbojet aircraft is described in detail in the following paragraphs. This system is typical of most turbojet transport aircraft and includes components and systems typically encountered on all such aircraft. It is emphasized that the maintenance procedures and installation details of each particular type of aircraft are a function of a specific aircraft configuration.

The engine fire protection system of most large turbine engine aircraft consists of two subsystems: a fire detection system and a fire extinguishing system. These two subsystems provide fire protection not only to the engine and nacelle areas but also to such areas as the baggage compartments, wheel wells, etc. Only the engine fire protection system is included in this discussion.

Each turbine engine installed in a pod and pylon configuration contains an automatic heat-sensing fire detection circuit. This circuit consists of a heat-sensing unit, a control unit, a relay, and warning devices. The warning devices normally include a warning light in the cockpit for each circuit and a common alarm bell used with all such circuits.

The heat-sensing unit of each circuit is a continuous loop routed around the areas to be protected. These areas are the burner and tailpipe areas. Also included in most turbine engine aircraft fire extinguishing systems are the compressor and accessory areas, which in some installations may be protected by a separate fire protection circuit. Figure 9–10 illustrates the typical routing of a continuous-loop fire detection circuit in an engine pod and pylon. A typical continuous loop is made up of sensing

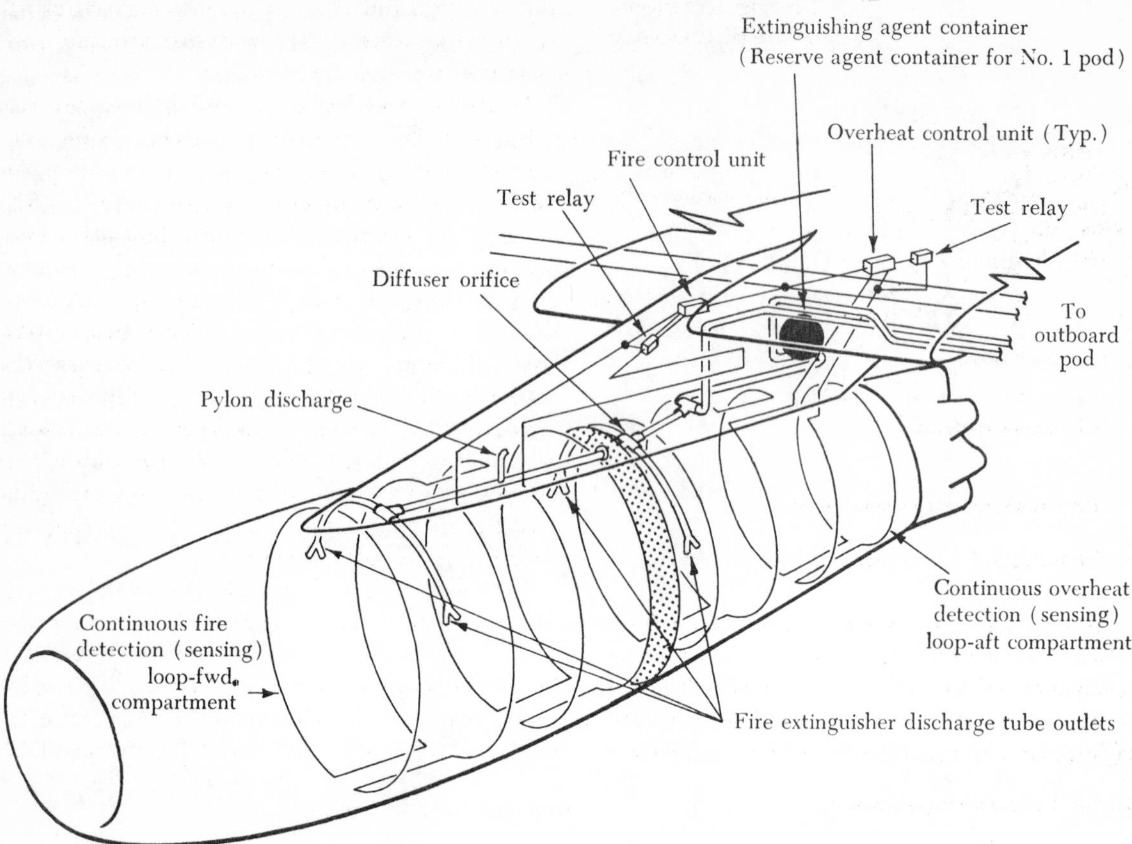

FIGURE 9–10. Typical pod and pylon fire protection installation.

elements joined to each other by moistureproof connectors, which are attached to the aircraft structure. In most installations, the loop is supported by attachments or clamps every 10 to 12 inches of its length. Too great a distance between supports may permit vibration or chafing of the unsupported section and become a source of false alarms.

In a typical turbine engine fire detection system, a separate control unit is provided for each sensing circuit. The control unit contains an amplifier, usually a transistorized or magnetic amplifier, which produces an output when a predetermined input current flow is detected from the sensing loop. Each control unit also contains a test relay, which is used to simulate a fire or overheat condition to test the circuit.

The output of the control unit amplifier is used to energize a warning relay, often called a fire relay. Usually located near the control units, these fire relays, when energized, complete the circuit to the appropriate warning devices.

The warning devices for engine and nacelle fires and overheat conditions are located in the cockpit. A fire warning light for each engine usually is located in a special fire switch handle on the instrument panel, light shield, or fire control panel. These fire switches are sometimes referred to as fire-pull T-handles. As illustrated in figure 9–11, the T-handle contains the fire detection warning light. In some models of this fire-pull switch, pulling the T-handle exposes a previously inaccessible extinguishing agent switch and also actuates microswitches that energize the emergency fuel shutoff valve and other pertinent shutoff valves.

Turbine Engine Fire Extinguisher System

The fire extinguishing portion of a complete fire protection system typically includes a cylinder or container of an extinguishing agent for each engine and nacelle area. One type of installation provides for a container in each of the pylons on multiengine aircraft. This type of system uses an extinguishing agent container similar to the type shown in figure 9–12. This type of container is equipped with two discharge valves that are operated by electrically discharged cartridges. These two valves

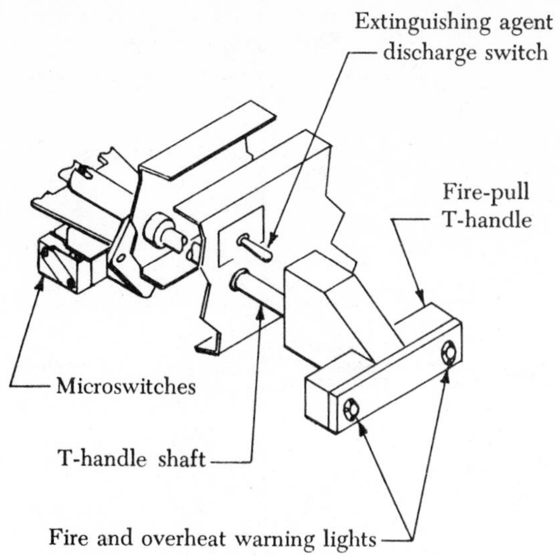

FIGURE 9–11. Fire-pull T-handle switch.

are the main and the reserve controls that release and route the agent to the pod and pylon in which the container is located or to the other engine on the same wing. This type of two-shot, crossfeed configuration permits the release of a second charge of fire extinguishing agent to the same engine if another fire breaks out, without providing two containers for each engine area.

Another type of four-engine installation uses two independent fire extinguisher systems. The two engines on one side of the aircraft are equipped with two fire extinguisher containers (figure 9–13), but they are located together in the inboard pylon. A pressure gage, a discharge plug, and a safety discharge connection are provided for each container. The discharge plug is sealed with a breakable disk combined with an explosive charge that is electrically detonated to discharge the contents of the bottle. The safety discharge connection is capped at the inboard side of the strut with a red indicating disk. If the temperature rises beyond a predetermined safe value, the disk will rupture, dumping the agent overboard.

The manifold connecting the two containers of the dual installation (figure 9–13) includes a double check valve and a T-fitting from which tubing connects to the discharge indicator. This indicator is capped at the inboard side of the strut with a yellow disk, which is blown out when the manifold

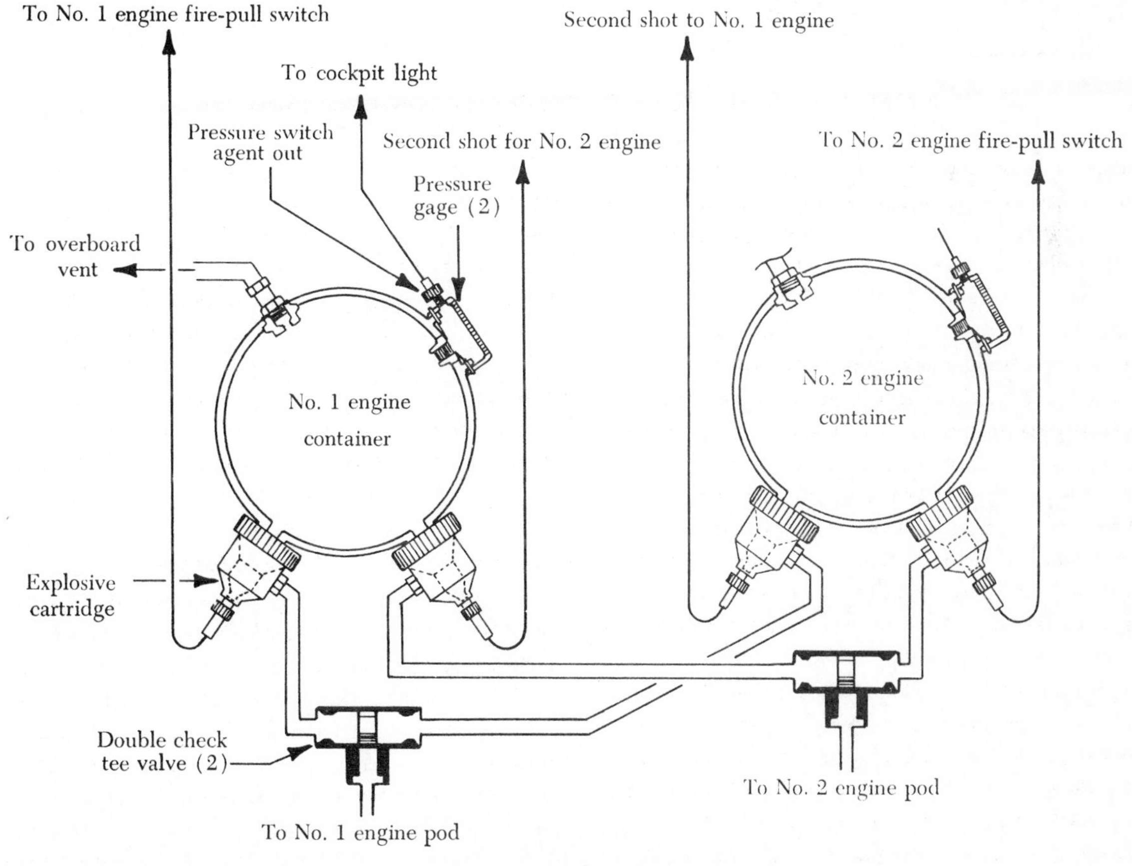

FIGURE 9–12. Fire extinguisher system for a multi-engine aircraft.

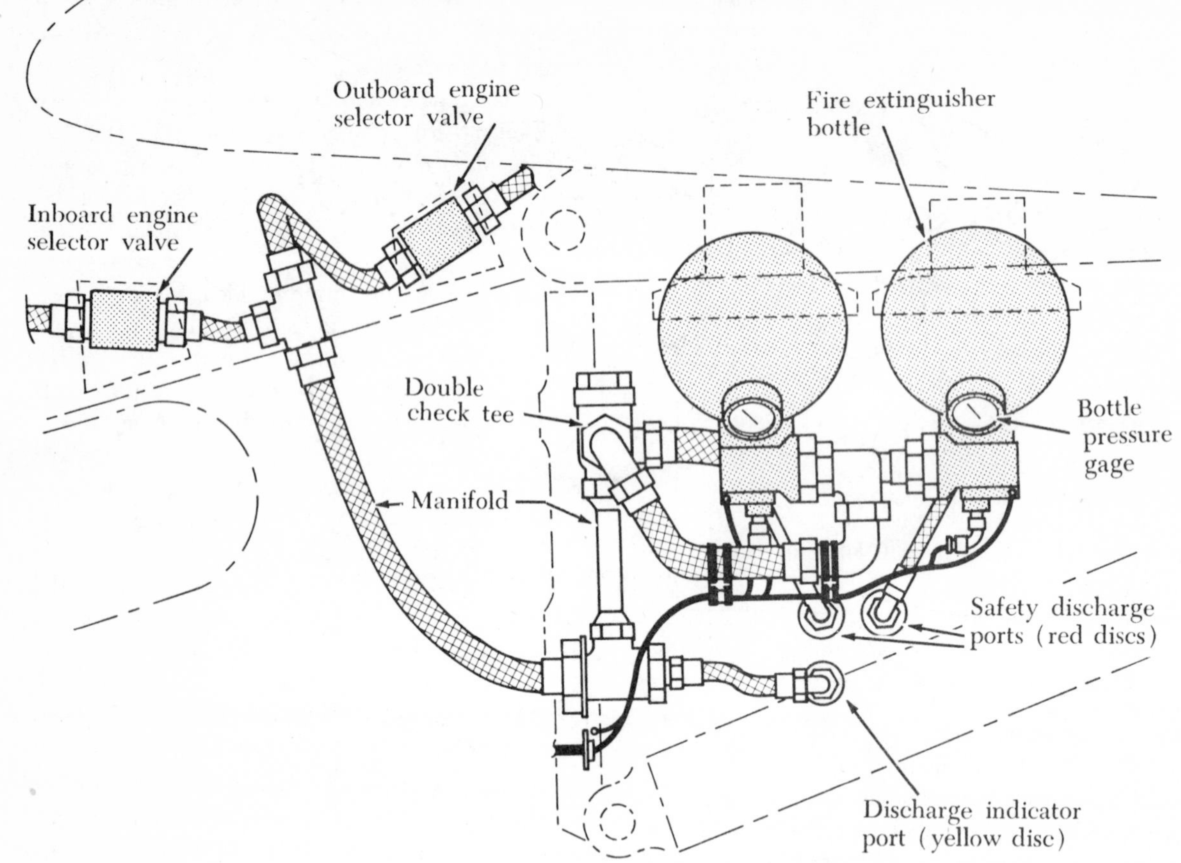

FIGURE 9–13. Dual container installation and fittings.

is pressurized from either container. The discharge line has two branches (figure 9–13), a short line to the inboard engine and a long one extending along the wing leading edge to the outboard engine. Both of the branches terminate in a T-fitting near the forward engine mount.

Discharge tube configuration may vary with the type and size of turbine engine installations. In figure 9–14, a semicircular discharge tube with Y-outlet terminations encircles the top forward area of both the forward and aft engine compartments. Diffuser orifices are spaced along the diffuser tubes. A pylon discharge tube is incorporated in the inlet line to discharge the fire extinguishing agent into the pylon area.

Another type of fire extinguisher discharge configuration is shown in figure 9–15. The inlet discharge line terminates in a discharge nozzle, which is a T-fitting near the forward engine mount. The T-fitting contains diffuser holes that allow the fire extinguishing agent to be released along the top of the engine and travel downward along both sides of the engine.

When any section of the continuous-loop circuit is exposed to an overheat condition or fire, the detector warning lights in the cockpit illuminate and the fire warning bell sounds. The warning light may be located in the fire-pull T-handle, or in some installations the fire switch may incorporate the associated fire warning light for a particular engine under a translucent plastic cover, as shown in figure 9–16. In this system, a transfer switch is provided for the left and right fire extinguisher system. Each transfer switch has two positions: "TRANS" and "NORMAL." If a fire occurs in the No. 4 engine, the warning light in the No. 4 fire switch will illuminate; and with the transfer switch in the "NORMAL" position, the No. 4 fire switch is pulled and the No. 4 pushbutton discharge switch located directly under the fire switch will be accessible. Activating the discharge switch will discharge a container of fire extinguishing agent into the No. 4 engine area.

If more than one shot of the agent is required, the transfer switch is placed in the "TRANS" position so that the second container can be discharged

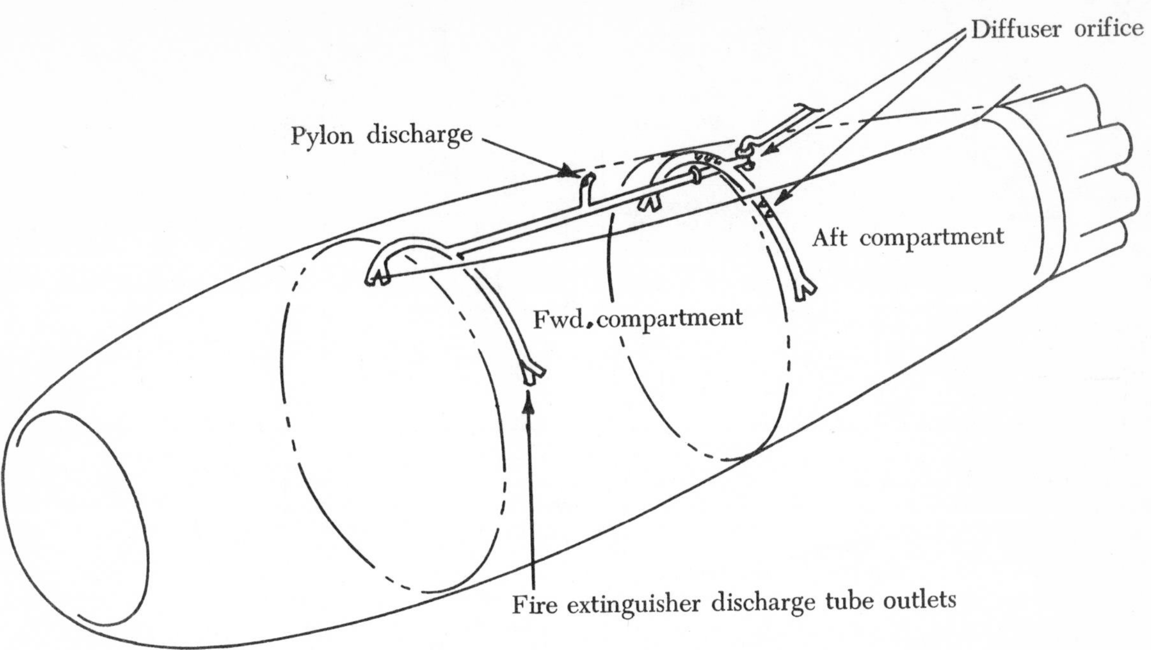

FIGURE 9–14. Fire extinguisher discharge tubes.

into the same engine.

An alarm bell control permits any one of the engine fire detection circuits to energize the common alarm bell. After the alarm bell sounds, it can be silenced by activating the bell cutout switch (figure 9–16). The bell can still respond to a fire signal from any of the other circuits.

Most fire protection systems for turbine engine aircraft also include a test switch and circuitry that permit the entire detection system to be tested at one time. The test switch is located in the center of the panel in figure 9–16.

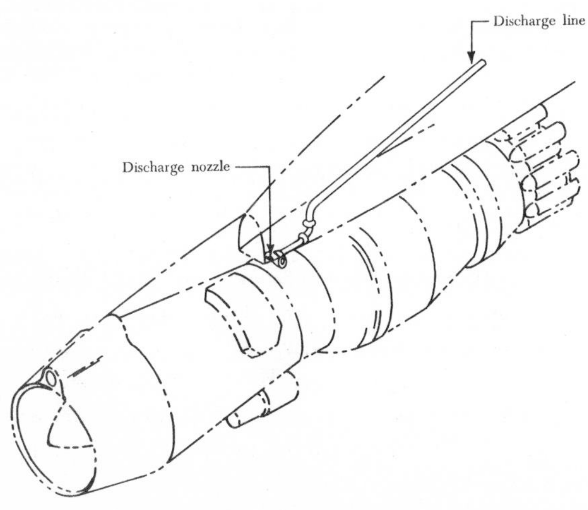

FIGURE 9–15. Fire extinguisher discharge nozzle location.

FIRE DETECTION SYSTEM MAINTENANCE PRACTICES

Fire detector sensing elements are located in many high-activity areas around aircraft engines. Their location, together with their small size, increases the change of damage to the sensing elements during maintenance. The installation of the sensing elements inside the aircraft cowl panels provides some measure of protection not afforded elements attached directly to the engine. On the other hand, the removal and re-installation of cowl panels can easily cause abrasion or structural defects to the sensing elements. An inspection and maintenance program for all types of continuous-loop systems should include the following visual checks. These procedures are examples and should not be used to replace the applicable manufacturer's instructions.

Sensing elements of a continuous-loop system should be inspected for the following:

(1) Cracked or broken sections caused by crushing or squeezing between inspection plates, cowl panels, or engine components.

(2) Abrasion caused by rubbing of the element on cowling, accessories, or structural members.

(3) Pieces of safety wire or other metal particles which may short the spot-detector terminals.

(4) Condition of rubber grommets in mounting clamps, which may be softened from expo-

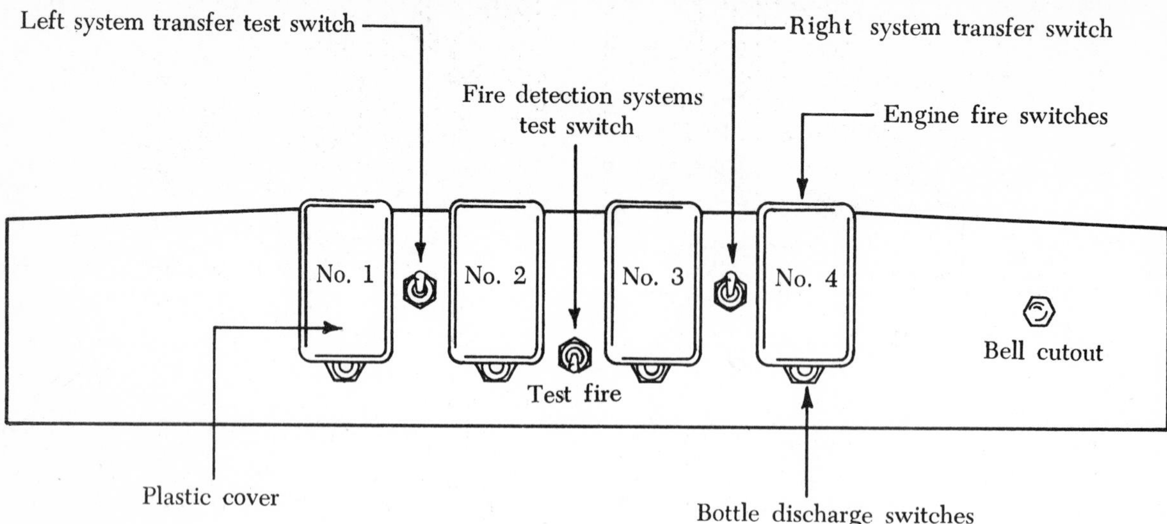

FIGURE 9–16. Fire detection system and fire switches.

sure to oils, or hardened from excessive heat.

(5) Dents and kinks in sensing element sections. Limits on the element diameter, acceptable dents and kinks, and degree of smoothness of tubing contour are specified by manufacturers. No attempt should be made to straighten any acceptable dent or kink, since stresses may be set up that could cause tubing failure. (See illustration of kinked tubing in figure 9–17.)

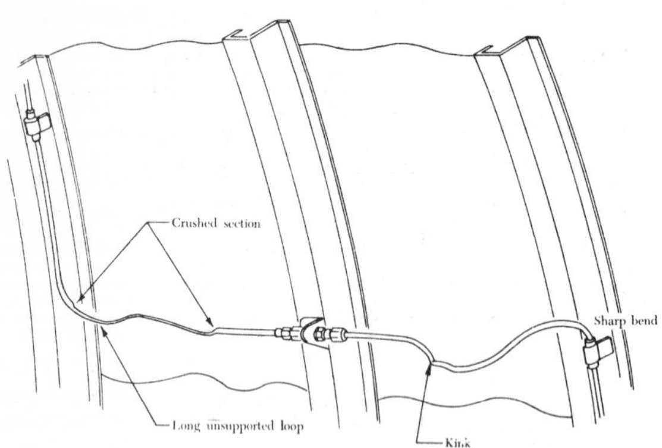

FIGURE 9–17. Sensing element defects.

(6) Nuts at the end of the sensing elements (figure 9–18) should be inspected for tightness and safety wire. Loose nuts should be retorqued to the value specified by the manufacturer's instructions. Some types of sensing element connection joints require the use of copper crush gaskets. These should be replaced any time a connection is separated.

(7) If shielded flexible leads are used, they should be inspected for fraying of the outer braid. The braided sheath is made up of many fine metal strands woven into a protective covering surrounding the inner insulated wire. Continuous bending of the cable or rough treatment can break these fine wires, especially those near the connectors.

(8) Sensing element routing and clamping should be inspected carefully (figure 9–19). Long, unsupported sections may permit excessive vibration that can cause breakage. The distance between clamps on straight runs, usually about 8 to 10 in., is specified by each manufacturer. At end connectors, the first support clamp usually is located about 4 to 6 in. from the end connector fittings. In

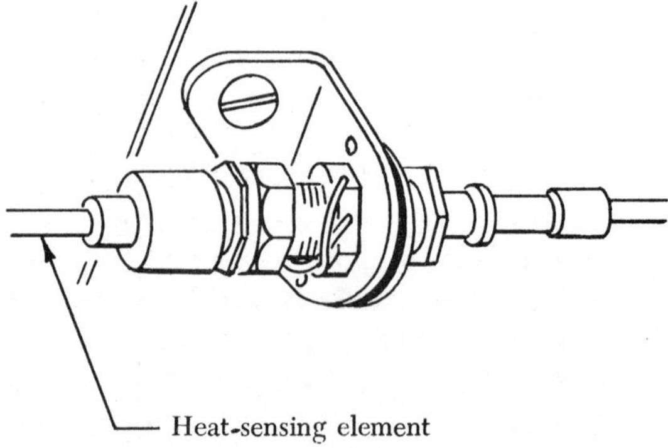

FIGURE 9–18. Connector joint fitting attached to structure.

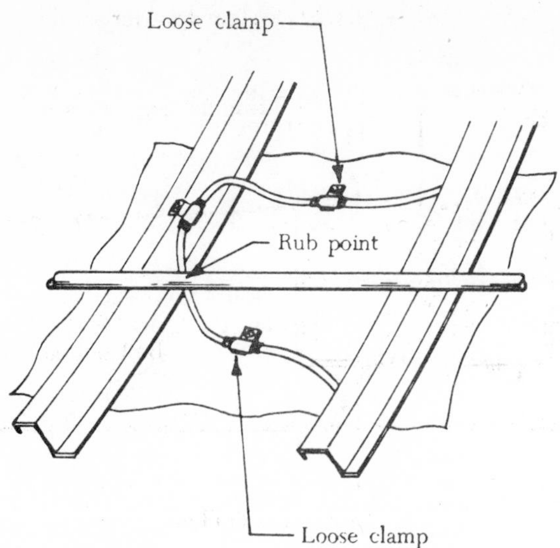

FIGURE 9–19. Rubbing interference.

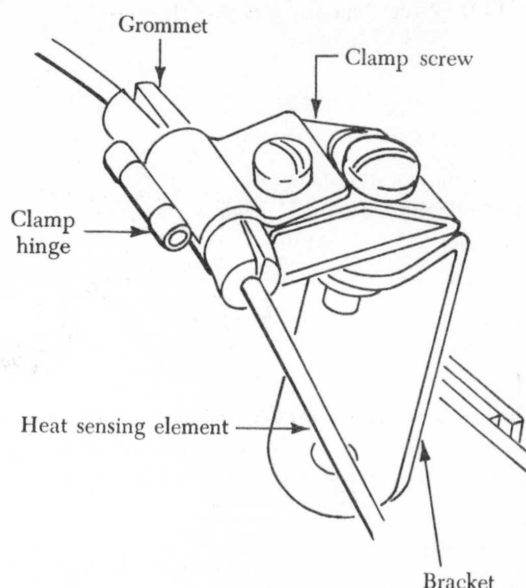

FIGURE 9–20. Typical fire detector loop clamp.

most cases, a straight run of 1 in. is maintained from all connectors before a bend is started, and an optimum bend radius of 3 in. normally is adhered to.

(9) Interference between a cowl brace and a sensing element can cause rubbing (figure 9–19). This interference may cause wear and short the sensing element.

(10) Grommets should be installed on the sensing element so that both ends are centered on its clamp. The split end of the grommet should face the outside of the nearest bend. Clamps and grommets (figure 9–20) should fit the element snugly.

Fire Detection System Troubleshooting

The following troubleshooting procedures represent the most common difficulties encountered in engine fire detection systems:

(1) Intermittent alarms are most often caused by an intermittent short in the detector system wiring. Such shorts may be caused by a loose wire that occasionally touches a nearby terminal, a frayed wire brushing against a structure, or a sensing element rubbing against a structural member long enough to wear through the insulation. Intermittent faults often can be located by moving wires to re-create the short.

(2) Fire alarms and warning lights can occur when no engine fire or overheat condition exists. Such false alarms can be most easily located by disconnecting the engine sensing loop connections from the control unit. If the false alarm ceases when the engine sensing loop is disconnected, the fault is in the disconnected sensing loop, which should be examined for areas which have been bent into contact with hot parts of the engine. If no bent element can be found, the shorted section can be located by isolating the connecting elements consecutively around the entire loop.

(3) Kinks and sharp bends in the sensing element can cause an internal wire to short intermittently to the outer tubing. The fault can be located by checking the sensing element with a megger while tapping the element in the suspected areas to produce the short.

(4) Moisture in the detection system seldom causes a false fire alarm. If, however, moisture does cause an alarm, the warning will persist until the contamination is removed or boils away and the resistance of the loop returns to its normal value.

(5) Failure to obtain an alarm signal when the test switch is actuated may be caused by a defective test switch or control unit, the lack of electrical power, inoperative indicator light, or an opening in the sensing element or connecting wiring. When the test switch fails to provide an alarm, the continuity of a two-wire sensing loop can be determined by opening the loop and measuring the resistance. In a single-wire, continuous-loop

system, the center conductor should be grounded.

FIRE EXTINGUISHER SYSTEM MAINTENANCE PRACTICES

Regular maintenance of fire extinguisher systems typically includes such items as the inspection and servicing of fire extinguisher bottles (containers), removal and re-installation of cartridge and discharge valves, testing of discharge tubing for leakage, and electrical wiring continuity tests. The following paragraphs contain details of some of the most typical maintenance procedures.

Fire extinguisher containers are checked periodically to determine that the pressure is between the prescribed minimum and maximum limits. Changes of pressure with ambient temperatures must also fall within prescribed limits. The graph shown in figure 9–21 is typical of the pressure-temperature curve graphs that provide maximum and minimum gage readings. If the pressure does not fall within the graph limits, the extinguisher container is replaced.

The service life of fire extinguisher discharge cartridges is calculated from the manufacturer's date stamp, which is usually placed on the face of the cartridge. The cartridge service life recommended by the manufacturer is usually in terms of hours below a predetermined temperature limit. Cartridges are available with a service life of approximately 5,000 hours. To determine the unexpired service life of a discharge cartridge, it is usually necessary to remove the electrical leads and discharge line from the plug body, which can then be removed from the extinguisher container. On one type fire extinguisher container, the date can be seen without removing the plug body. Refer to figure 9–22 for location of the components of a typical extinguisher container.

Care must be taken in the replacement of cartridge and discharge valves. Most new extinguisher containers are supplied with their cartridge and discharge valve disassembled. Before installation on the aircraft, the cartridge must be assembled properly in the discharge valve and the valve connected to the container, usually by means of a swivel nut that tightens against a packing ring gasket, as illustrated in figure 9–22.

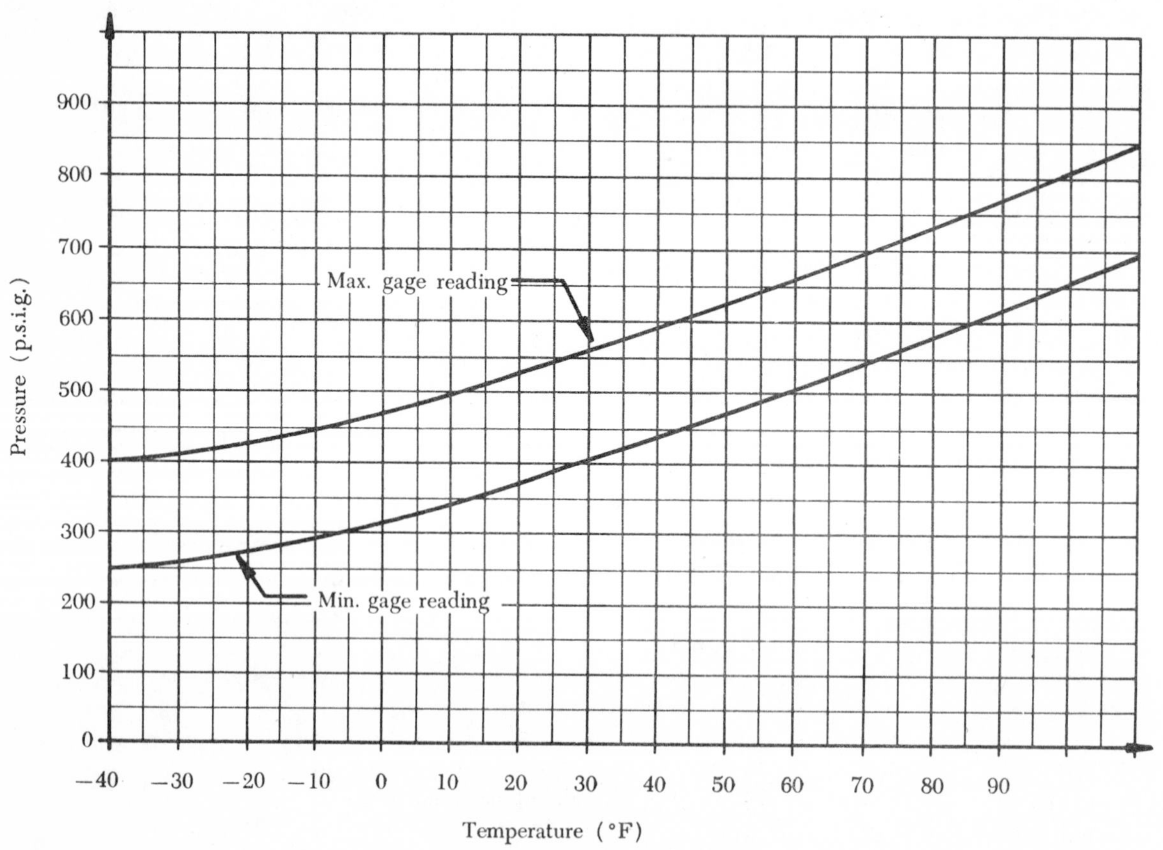

FIGURE 9–21. Fire extinguisher container pressure-temperature curve.

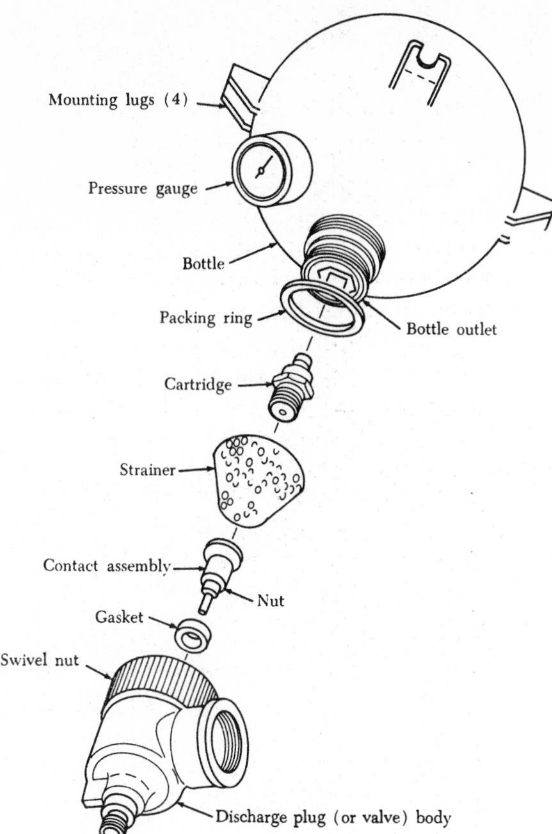

FIGURE 9–22. Components of a typical fire extinguisher container.

If a cartridge is removed from a discharge valve for any reason, it should not be used in another discharge valve assembly, since the distance the contact point protrudes may vary with each unit. Thus, continuity might not exist if a used plug that had been indented with a long contact point were installed in a discharge valve with a shorter contact point.

The preceding material in this chapter has been **largely of a general nature dealing with the principles involved and general procedures to be followed. *When actually performing maintenance, always refer to the applicable maintenance manuals and other related publications pertaining to a particular aircraft.***

TURBOJET AIRCRAFT FIRE PROTECTION SYSTEM (SABERLINER)

This description of the fire protection system installed in the Saberliner is included for familiarization purposes.

A high-rate-of-discharge fixed fire-extinguishing system is provided for each engine pod. Fire detector elements are located at strategic points within each pod as illustrated in figure 9–23. Two pressurized extinguishing-agent containers provide bromotrifluoromethane. This can be directed from either container to either engine pod as required. The discharge lines from each container meet at a double-check "T" valve to make a single discharge line. The one-way check valve prevents one container from discharging into the other container line and, thereby, possibly depleting the contents of one container into the other.

The system is controlled from the cockpit by the use of manual handles plus an electrical selector switch. Two discharge indicator disks, mounted externally on the fuselage, indicate either manual discharge of the containers, or automatic discharge overboard due to a thermal condition. A pressure gage, mounted on each container, and visible from the main wheel well, indicates pressure in the container.

A discharge valve is attached to the bottom of each container. The cartridge in the extinguisher No. 1 or extinguisher No. 2 discharge valve, figure 9–24, is ignited by 28-volt dc power when a "FIRE PULL" handle is pulled and the fire-extinguisher

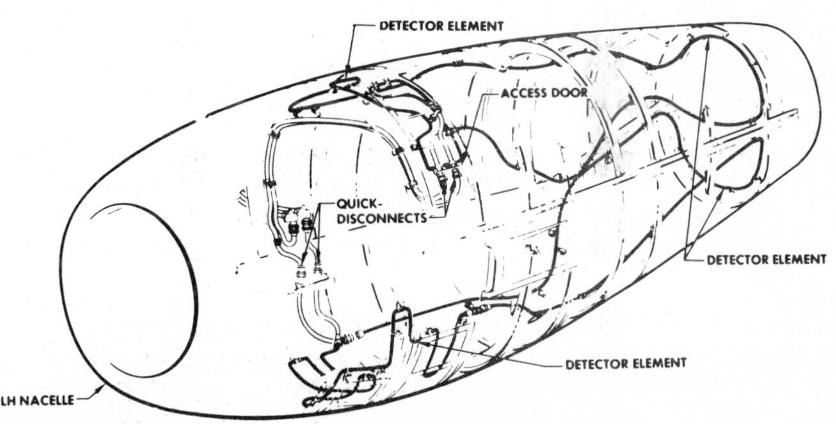

FIGURE 9–23. Fire detection system.

selector is actuated to either EXT No. 1 or EXT No. 2. A direction valve then routes the extinguishing agent to the proper engine, according to which "FIRE PULL" handle is pulled. When a cartridge is fired, the contents of one container are discharged by nitrogen pressure and forced through delivery lines and nozzles into the forward compartment of the selected engine pod.

Operation of System

Mechanically interconnected "FIRE PULL" handles, one for each engine are on the fire-extinguisher control panel, on the windshield bow. During a fire or overheat condition, indicated by a warning light in the respective "FIRE PULL" handle, immediately pull handle aft. When the right hand "FIRE PULL" handle is pulled, the emergency bleed-air shutoff valve closes and the extinguisher system direction valve is energized to allow the extinguishing agent to be routed to the right-hand engine. In addition, the dc generator is taken off the line. When the "FIRE PULL" handle is returned to its original position, those items previously turned off, except the dc generator, are reinstated, unless the engine master switch is turned off. If the second "FIRE PULL" handle is pulled, the first handle automatically retracts to its original position.

Selector Switch

The fire-extinguisher selector switch, is mounted in the center of the extinguisher control panel and powered by the dc essential bus and has three positions: EXT No. 1, EXT No. 2, and a center, unmarked, "OFF" position. When the selector switch is momentarily positioned to either EXT No. 1 or EXT No. 2 and has been armed by pulling the "FIRE PULL" handle, the extinguishing agent from one container is discharged to the engine pod selected by the handle. After the initial container has been expended, the fire-extinguisher selector switch may, if necessary, be momentarily positioned to the other extinguisher to discharge the second container.

Direction Valve

Downstream from the double-check "T" valve, the line connects to a direction valve. (Figure 9–24.) The valve has two exit ports: a normally open port connected with the left engine pod fire-extinguishing discharge line, and a normally closed port connected with the discharge line to the right engine pod. When the right-hand engine "FIRE PULL" handle is pulled, an electrical circuit is completed to the direction valve, energizing the solenoid. The fire-extinguishing agent discharge is then directed to the right-hand engine pod.

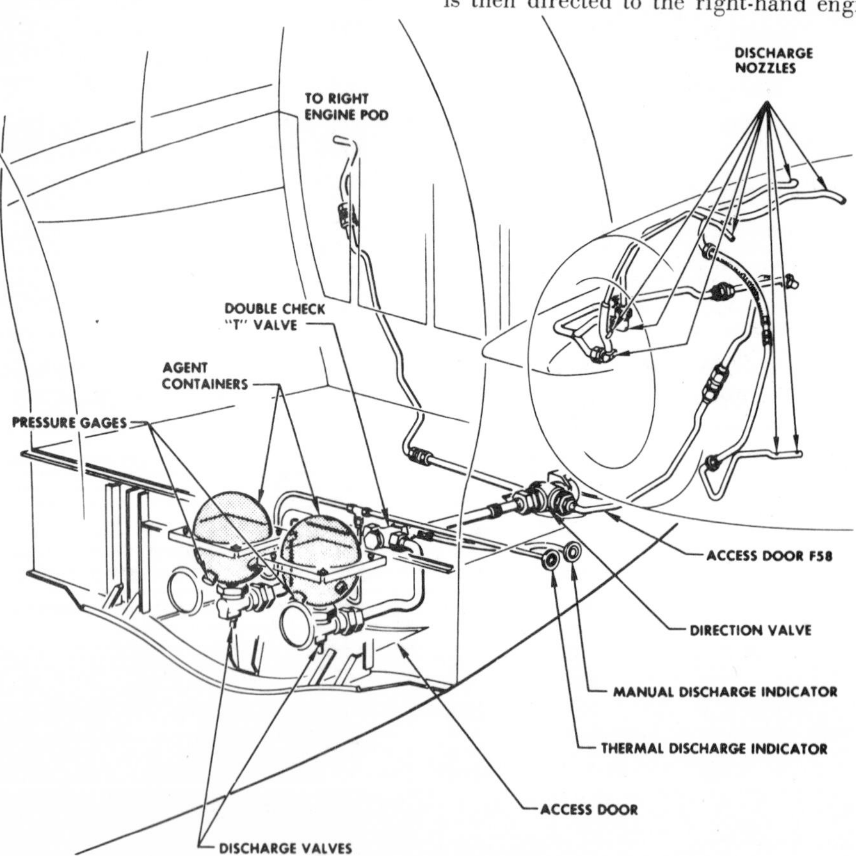

FIGURE 9–24. Fire extinguishing system.

Agent Containers

Two containers for the fire-extinguisher system are installed aft of the main wheel well area between fuselage stations 298 and 307. Each container has a gage which indicates the pressure in the container. A discharge valve containing a cartridge is mounted on the lower part of each container. The cartridge, when fired, discharges the container contents into the ducting toward the engine pods. A fitting is provided in each container to accommodate lines to the thermal discharge indicators installed in the fuselage exterior.

Indicators

Two fire-extinguishing system discharge indicating disks are mounted on the left side of the fuselage, aft of the wing. The yellow disk in the aft discharge indicator is connected by a 1/4-inch line to the fire extinguisher discharge line between the double-check "T" valve and the direction valve. When either container is discharged, a limited flow will be directed to the yellow disk, blowing it out. A check of the container pressure gages will show whether one or both containers have been discharged.

The red disk in the forward discharge indicator is connected by a 1/4-inch line to both containers. When the containers have been overheated excessively, the internal pressure will cause the fusible safety outlet plug to discharge. The agent flow will be directed to the red disk, blowing it out. A check of the container pressure gages will show whether one or both containers were discharged.

CHAPTER 10

ENGINE MAINTENANCE AND OPERATION

RECIPROCATING ENGINE OVERHAUL

Both maintenance and overhaul operations are performed on aircraft powerplants at specified intervals. This interval is usually governed by the number of hours the powerplant has been in operation. Tests and experience have shown that operation beyond this period of time will be inefficient and even dangerous because certain parts will be worn beyond their safe limits. For an overhauled engine to be as airworthy as a new one, worn parts as well as damaged parts must be detected and replaced during overhaul. The only way to detect all unairworthy parts is to perform a thorough and complete inspection while the engine is disassembled. The major purpose of overhaul is to inspect the engine parts. Inspection is the most precise and the most important phase of the overhaul. Inspection cannot be slighted or performed in a careless or incomplete manner.

Each engine manufacturer provides very specific tolerances to which his engine parts must conform, and provides general instructions to aid in determining the airworthiness of the part. However, in many cases, the final decision is left up to the mechanic. He must determine if the part is serviceable, repairable, or should be rejected. A knowledge of the operating principles, strength, and stresses applied to a part is essential in making this decision. When the powerplant mechanic signs for the overhaul of an engine, he certifies that he has performed the work using methods, techniques, and practices acceptable to the FAA Administrator.

Top Overhaul

Modern aircraft engines are constructed of such durable materials that top overhaul has largely been eliminated. Top overhaul means overhaul of those parts "on top" of the crankcase without completely dismantling the engine. It includes removal of the units, such as exhaust collectors, ignition harness, and intake pipes, necessary to remove the cylinders. The actual top overhaul consists of reconditioning the cylinder, piston, and valve-operating mechanism, and replacing the valve guides and piston rings, if needed. Usually at this time the accessories require no attention other than that normally required during ordinary maintenance functions.

Top overhaul is not recommended by all aircraft engine manufacturers. Many stress that if an engine requires this much dismantling it should be completely disassembled and receive a major overhaul.

Major Overhaul

Major overhaul consists of the complete reconditioning of the powerplant. The actual overhaul period for a specific engine will generally be determined by the manufacturer's recommendations or by the maximum hours of operation between overhaul, as approved by the FAA.

At regular intervals, an engine should be completely dismantled, thoroughly cleaned, and inspected. Each part should be overhauled in accordance with the manufacturer's instructions and tolerances for the engine involved. At this time all accessories are removed, overhauled, and tested. Here again, instructions of the manufacturer of the accessory concerned should be followed.

GENERAL OVERHAUL PROCEDURES

Because of the continued changes and the many different types of engines in use, it is not possible to treat the specific overhaul of each in this manual. However, there are various overhaul practices and instructions of a nonspecific nature which apply to all makes and models of engines. These general instructions will be described in this section.

Any engine to be overhauled completely should receive a runout check of its crankshaft or propeller shaft as a first step. Any question concerning crankshaft or propeller shaft replacement is resolved at this time, since a shaft whose runout is beyond limits must be replaced.

Disassembly

Inasmuch as visual inspection immediately follows disassembly, all individual parts should be laid out in an orderly manner on a workbench as they are removed. To guard against damage and to prevent loss, suitable containers should be available in which to place small parts, nuts, bolts, etc., during the disassembly operation.

Other practices to observe during disassembly include:

(1) Dispose of all safety devices as they are removed. Never use safety wire, cotter pins, etc., a second time. Always replace with new safety devices.

(2) All loose studs and loose or damaged fittings should be carefully tagged to prevent their being overlooked during inspection.

(3) Always use the proper tool for the job and the one that fits. Use sockets and box end wrenches wherever possible. If special tools are required, use them rather than improvising.

(4) Drain the engine oil sumps and remove the oil filter. Drain the oil into a suitable container, strain it through a clean cloth. Check the oil and the cloth for metal particles.

(5) Before disassembly, wash the exterior of the engine thoroughly.

Inspection

The inspection of engine parts during overhaul is divided into three categories:

(1) Visual.

(2) Magnetic.

(3) Dimensional.

The first two methods are aimed at determining structural failures in the parts, while the last method deals with the size and shape of each part. Structural failures can be determined by several different methods. Nonaustenitic steel parts can readily be examined by the magnetic particle method. Other methods such as X-ray or etching can also be used.

Visual inspection should precede all other inspection procedures. Parts should not be cleaned before a preliminary visual inspection, since indications of a failure often may be detected from the residual deposits of metallic particles in some recesses in the engine.

Several terms are used to describe defects detected in engine parts during inspection. Some of the more common terms and definitions are:

(1) ***Abrasion***—An area of roughened scratches or marks usually caused by foreign matter between moving parts or surfaces.

(2) ***Brinelling***—One or more indentations on bearing races usually caused by high static loads or application of force during installation or removal. Indentations are rounded or spherical due to the impression left by the contacting balls or rollers of the bearing.

(3) ***Burning***—Surface damage due to excessive heat. It is usually caused by improper fit, defective lubrication, or overtemperature operation.

(4) ***Burnishing***—Polishing of one surface by sliding contact with a smooth, harder surface. Usually no displacement nor removal of metal.

(5) ***Burr***—A sharp or roughened projection of metal usually resulting from machine processing.

(6) ***Chafing***—Describes a condition caused by a rubbing action between two parts under light pressure which results in wear.

(7) ***Chipping***—The breaking away of pieces of material, which is usually caused by excessive stress concentration or careless handling.

(8) ***Corrosion***—Loss of metal by a chemical or electrochemical action. The corrosion products generally are easily removed by mechanical means. Iron rust is an example of corrosion.

(9) ***Crack***—A partial separation of material usually caused by vibration, overloading, internal stresses, defective assembly, or fatigue. Depth may be a few thousandths to the full thickness of the piece.

(10) ***Cut***—Loss of metal, usually to an appreciable depth over a relatively long and narrow area, by mechanical means, as would occur with the use of a saw blade, chisel or sharp-edged stone striking a glancing blow.

(11) ***Dent***—A small, rounded depression in a surface usually caused by the part being struck with a rounded object.

(12) ***Erosion***—Loss of metal from the surface by mechanical action of foreign objects, such as grit or fine sand. The eroded area will be rough and may be lined in the direction in which the foreign material moved relative to the surface.

(13) ***Flaking***—The breaking loose of small pieces of metal or coated surfaces, which is usually caused by defective plating or excessive loading.

(14) ***Fretting***—A condition of surface erosion caused by minute movement between two parts usually clamped together with considerable unit pressure.

(15) ***Galling***—A severe condition of chafing or fretting in which a transfer of metal from

one part to another occurs. It is usually caused by a slight movement of mated parts having limited relative motion and under high loads.

(16) **Gouging**—A furrowing condition in which a displacement of metal has occurred (a torn effect). It is usually caused by a piece of metal or foreign material between close moving parts.

(17) **Grooving**—A recess or channel with rounded and smooth edges usually caused by faulty alignment of parts.

(18) **Inclusion**—Presence of foreign or extraneous material wholly within a portion of metal. Such material is introduced during the manufacture of rod, bar, or tubing by rolling or forging.

(19) **Nick**—A sharp sided gouge or depression with a "V" shaped bottom which is generally the result of careless handling of tools and parts.

(20) **Peening**—A series of blunt depressions in a surface.

(21) **Pick Up or Scuffing**—A buildup or rolling of metal from one area to another, which is usually caused by insufficient lubrication, clearances, or foreign matter.

(22) **Pitting**—Small hollows of irregular shape in the surface, usually caused by corrosion or minute mechanical chipping of surfaces.

(23) **Scoring**—A series of deep scratches caused by foreign particles between moving parts, or careless assembly or disassembly techniques.

(24) **Scratches**—Shallow, thin lines or marks, varying in degree of depth and width, caused by presence of fine foreign particles during operation or contact with other parts during handling.

(25) **Stain**—A change in color, locally, causing a noticeably different appearance from the surrounding area.

(26) **Upsetting**—A displacement of material beyond the normal contour or surface (a local bulge or bump). Usually indicates no metal loss.

Defects in nonmagnetic parts can be found by careful visual inspection along with a suitable etching process. If it is thought that a crack exists in an aluminum part, clean it by brushing or gritblasting very carefully to avoid scratching the surface. Cover the part with a solution made from 1¼ lbs. of sodium hydroxide and 1 pint of water at room temperature. Rinse the part thoroughly with water after about 1 minute's contact with the solution. Immediately neutralize the part with a solution of one part nitric acid and three parts of water heated to 100° F. Keep the part in this solution until the black deposit is dissolved. Dry the part with compressed air. If a crack exists, the edges will turn black after this treatment, thus aiding in its detection. For magnesium parts, a 10% solution of acetic acid at room temperature can be applied for a maximum of 1 minute. The part should then be rinsed with a solution of 1 ounce of household ammonia in 1 gallon of water.

Examine all gears for evidence of pitting or excessive wear. These conditions are of particular importance when they occur on the teeth; deep pit marks in this area are sufficient cause to reject the gear. Bearing surfaces of all gears should be free from deep scratches. However, minor abrasions usually can be dressed out with a fine abrasive cloth.

All bearing surfaces should be examined for scores, galling, and wear. Considerable scratching and light scoring of aluminum bearing surfaces in the engine will do no harm and should not be considered a reason for rejecting the part, provided it falls within the clearances set forth in the Table of Limits in the engine manufacturer's overhaul manual. Even though the part comes within the specific clearance limits, it will not be satisfactory for re-assembly in the engine unless inspection shows the part to be free from other serious defects.

Ball bearings should be inspected visually and by feel for roughness, flat spots on balls, flaking or pitting of races, or scoring on the outside of races. All journals should be checked for galling, scores, misalignment, or out-of-round condition. Shafts, pins, etc., should be checked for straightness. This may be done in most cases by using V-blocks and a dial indicator.

Pitted surfaces in highly stressed areas resulting from corrosion can cause ultimate failure of the part. The following areas should be examined carefully for evidence of such corrosion:

(1) Interior surfaces of piston pins.

(2) The fillets at the edges of crankshaft main and crankpin journal surfaces.

(3) Thrust bearing races.

If pitting exists on any of the surfaces mentioned to the extent that it cannot be removed by polishing with crocus cloth or other mild abrasive, the part usually must be rejected.

Parts, such as threaded fasteners or plugs, should be inspected to determine the condition of the threads. Badly worn or mutilated threads cannot be tolerated; the parts should be rejected. However, small defects such as slight nicks or burrs may be dressed out with a small file, fine abrasive cloth, or stone. If the part appears to be distorted, badly galled, or mutilated by overtightening, or from the use of improper tools, replace it with a new one.

Cleaning

After visually inspecting engine recesses for deposits of metal particles, it is important to clean all engine parts thoroughly to facilitate inspection. Two processes for cleaning engine parts are:

(1) Degreasing to remove dirt and sludge (soft carbon).

(2) The removal of hard carbon deposits by decarbonizing, brushing or scraping, and grit-blasting.

Degreasing can be done by immersing or spraying the part in a suitable commercial solvent. Extreme care must be used if any water-mixed degreasing solutions containing caustic compounds or soap are used. Such compounds, in addition to being potentially corrosive to aluminum and magnesium, may become impregnated in the pores of the metal and cause oil foaming when the engine is returned to service. When using water-mixed solutions, therefore, it is imperative that the parts be rinsed thoroughly and completely in clear boiling water after degreasing. Regardless of the method and type of solution used, coat or spray all parts with lubricating oil immediately after cleaning to prevent corrosion.

While the degreasing solution will remove dirt, grease, and soft carbon, deposits of hard carbon will almost invariably remain on many interior surfaces. To remove these deposits, they must be loosened first by immersion in a tank containing a decarbonizing solution (usually heated). A great variety of commercial decarbonizing agents are available. Decarbonizers, like the degreasing solutions previously mentioned, fall generally into two categories, water-soluble and hydrocarbons; the same caution concerning the use of water-soluble degreasers is applicable to water-soluble decarbonizers.

Extreme caution should be followed when using a decarbonizing solution on magnesium castings. Avoid immersing steel and magnesium parts in the same decarbonizing tank, because this practice often results in damage to the magnesium parts from corrosion.

Decarbonizing usually will loosen most of the hard carbon deposits remaining after degreasing; the complete removal of all hard carbon, however, generally requires brushing, scraping, or grit-blasting. In all of these operations, be careful to avoid damaging the machined surfaces. In particular, wire brushes and metal scrapers must never be used on any bearing or contact surface.

When grit-blasting parts, follow the manufacturer's recommendations for the type abrasive material to use. Sand, rice, baked wheat, plastic pellets, glass beads, or crushed walnut shells are examples of abrasive substances that are used for grit-blasting parts.

All machined surfaces must be masked properly and adequately, and all openings tightly plugged before blasting. The one exception to this is the valve seats, which may be left unprotected when blasting the cylinder head combustion chamber. It is often advantageous to grit-blast the seats, since this will cut the glaze which tends to form (particularly on the exhaust valve seat), thus facilitating subsequent valve seat reconditioning. Piston ring grooves may be grit-blasted if necessary; extreme caution must be used, however, to avoid the removal of metal from the bottom and sides of the grooves. When grit-blasting housings, plug all drilled oil passages with rubber plugs or other suitable material to prevent the entrance of foreign matter.

The decarbonizing solution generally will remove most of the enamel on exterior surfaces. All remaining enamel should be removed by grit-blasting, particularly in the crevices between cylinder cooling fins.

At the conclusion of cleaning operations, rinse the part in petroleum solvent, dry and remove any loose particles of carbon or other foreign matter by air-blasting, and apply a liberal coating of preservative oil to all surfaces.

Repair and Replacement

Damage such as burrs, nicks, scratches, scoring, or galling should be removed with a fine oil stone, crocus cloth, or any similar abrasive substance. Following any repairs of this type, the part should be cleaned carefully to be certain that all abrasive has been removed, and then checked with its mating part to assure that the clearances are not excessive. Flanged surfaces that are bent, warped, or nicked can be repaired by lapping to a true surface on a surface plate. Again, the part should be cleaned to be certain that all abrasive has been removed. Defective threads can sometimes be repaired with a suitable die or tap. Small nicks can be removed satisfactorily with Swiss pattern files or small, edged stones. Pipe threads should not be tapped deeper to clean them, because this practice will result in an oversized tapped hole. If galling or scratches are removed from a bearing surface of a journal, it should be buffed to a high finish.

In general, welding of highly-stressed engine parts is not recommended for unwelded parts. However, welding may be accomplished if it can be reasonably expected that the welded repair will not adversely affect the airworthiness of the engine. A part may be welded when:

(1) The weld is located externally and can be inspected easily.

(2) The part has been cracked or broken as the result of unusual loads not encountered in normal operation.

(3) A new replacement part of an obsolete type of engine is unavailable.

(4) The welder's experience and the equipment used will ensure a first-quality weld and the restoration of the original heat treatment in heat-treated parts.

Many minor parts not subjected to high stresses may be safely repaired by welding. Mounting lugs, cowl lugs, cylinder fins, rocker box covers, and many parts originally fabricated by welding are in this category. The welded part should be suitably stress-relieved after welding. However, before welding any engine part, consult the manufacturer's instructions for the engine concerned to see if it is approved for repair by welding.

Parts requiring use of paint for protection or appearance should be re-painted according to the engine manufacturer's recommendations. One procedure is outlined in the following paragraphs.

Aluminum alloy parts should have original exterior painted surfaces rubbed smooth to provide a proper paint base. See that surfaces to be painted are thoroughly cleaned. Care must be taken to avoid painting mating surfaces. Exterior aluminum parts should be primed first with a thin coat of zinc chromate primer. Each coat should be either air dried for 2 hrs. or baked at 177° C. (350° F.) for one-half hr. After the primer is dry, parts should be painted with engine enamel, which should be air dried until hard or baked for one-half hr. at 82° C. (180° F.). Aluminum parts from which the paint has not been removed may be repainted without the use of a priming coat, provided no bare aluminum is exposed.

Parts requiring a black gloss finish should be primed first with zinc chromate primer and then painted with glossy black cylinder enamel. Each coat should be baked for 1-1/2 hrs. at 177° C. (350° F.). If baking facilities are not available, cylinder enamel may be air dried; however, an inferior finish will result. All paint applied in the above operations preferably should be sprayed; however, if it is necessary to use a brush, use care to avoid an accumulation of paint pockets.

Magnesium parts should be cleaned thoroughly with a dichromate treatment prior to painting. This treatment consists of cleaning all traces of grease and oil from the part by using a neutral, noncorrosive degreasing medium followed by a rinse, after which the part is immersed for at least 45 minutes in a hot dichromate solution (three-fourths of a pound of sodium dichromate to 1 gallon of water at 180° to 200° F.). Then the part should be washed thoroughly in cold running water, dipped in hot water, and dried in an air blast. Immediately thereafter, the part should be painted with a prime coat and engine enamel in the same manner as that suggested for aluminum parts.

Any studs which are bent, broken, damaged, or loose must be replaced. After a stud has been removed, the tapped stud hole should be examined for size and condition of threads. If it is necessary to re-tap the stud hole, it also will be necessary to use a suitable oversize stud. Studs that have been broken off flush with the case must be drilled and removed with suitable stud remover. Be careful not to damage any threads. When replacing studs, coat the coarse threads of the stud with anti-seize compound.

CYLINDER ASSEMBLY RECONDITIONING

Cylinder and piston assemblies are inspected according to the procedures contained in the engine manufacturer's manuals, charts, and service bulletins. A general procedure for inspecting and reconditioning cylinders will be discussed in the following section to provide an understanding of the operations involved.

Cylinder Head

Inspect the cylinder head for internal and external cracks. Carbon deposits must be cleaned from the inside of the head, and paint must be removed from the outside for this inspection.

Exterior cracks will show up on the head fins where they have been damaged by tools or contact with other parts because of careless handling. Cracks near the edge of the fins are not dangerous if the portion of the fin is removed and contoured properly. Cracks at the base of the fin are a reason for rejecting the cylinder. Cracks may also occur on the rocker box or in the rocker bosses.

Interior cracks will radiate almost always from the valve seat bosses or the spark plug bushing boss. They may extend completely from one boss to the other. These cracks are usually caused by improper installation of the seats or bushings.

Use a bright light to inspect for cracks, and investigate any suspicious areas with a magnifying glass or microscope. Cracks in aluminum alloy cylinder heads generally will be jagged because of the granular nature of the metal. Do not mistake casting marks or laps for a crack. One of the best methods to double check your findings is to inspect by means of the Zyglo process. Any crack in the cylinder head, except those on the fins which can be worked out, is reason for rejecting the cylinder.

Inspect the head fins for other damage besides cracks. Dents or bends in the fins should be left alone unless there is danger of cracking. Where pieces of fin are missing, the sharp edges should be filed to a smooth contour. Fin breakage in a concentrated area will cause dangerous local hot spots. Fin breakage near the spark plug bushings or on the exhaust side of the cylinder is obviously more dangerous than in other areas. When removing or re-profiling a cylinder fin, follow the instructions and the limits in the manufacturer's manual.

Inspect all the studs on the cylinder head for looseness, straightness, damaged threads, and proper length. Slightly damaged threads may be chased with the proper die. The length of the stud should be correct within $\pm 1/32$ (0.03125) inch to allow for proper installation of pal nuts or other safety devices.

Be sure the valve guides are clean before inspection. Very often carbon will cover pits inside the guide. If a guide in this condition is put back in service, carbon will again collect in the pits, and valve sticking will result. Besides pits, scores, and burned areas inside the valve guide, inspect them for wear or looseness. Most manufacturers provide a maximum wear gage to check the dimension of the guide. This gage should not enter the guide at all at either end. Do not confuse this gage with the "go and no-go" gage used to check new valve guides after reaming.

Inspection of valve seat inserts before they are re-faced is mostly a matter of determining if there is enough of the seat left to correct any pitting, burning, scoring, or out-of-trueness.

Inspect spark plug inserts for the condition of the threads and for looseness. Run a tap of the proper size through the bushing. Very often the inside threads of the bushing will be burned. If more than one thread is missing, the bushing is rejectable. Tighten a plug in the bushing to check for looseness.

Inspect the rocker shaft bosses for scoring, cracks, oversize, or out-of-roundness. Scoring is generally caused by the rocker shaft turning in the bosses, which means either the shaft was too loose in the bosses or a rocker arm was too tight on the shaft. Out-of-roundness is usually caused by a stuck valve. If a valve sticks, the rocker shaft tends to work up and down when the valve offers excessive resistance to opening. Inspect for out-of-roundness and oversize using a telescopic gage and a micrometer.

Cylinder Barrel

Inspect the cylinder barrel for wear, using a dial indicator, a telescopic gage and micrometer, or an inside micrometer. Dimensional inspection of the barrel consists of the following measurements:

(1) Maximum taper of cylinder walls.

(2) Maximum out-of-roundness.

(3) Bore diameter.

(4) Step.

(5) Fit between piston skirt and cylinder.

All measurements involving cylinder barrel diameters must be taken at a minimum of two positions 90° apart in the particular plane being measured. It may be necessary to take more than two measurements to determine the maximum wear. The use of a dial indicator to check a cylinder bore is shown in figure 10–1.

Taper of the cylinder walls is the difference between the diameter of the cylinder barrel at the bottom and the diameter at the top. The cylinder is usually worn larger at the top than at the bottom. This taper is caused by the natural wear pattern. At the top of the stroke, the piston is subjected to greater heat and pressure and more errosive environment than at the bottom of the stroke. Also, there is greater freedom of movement at the top of the stroke. Under these conditions, the piston will wear the cylinder wall. In most cases, the taper will end with a ridge (see figure 10–2) which must be removed during overhaul. Where cylinders are

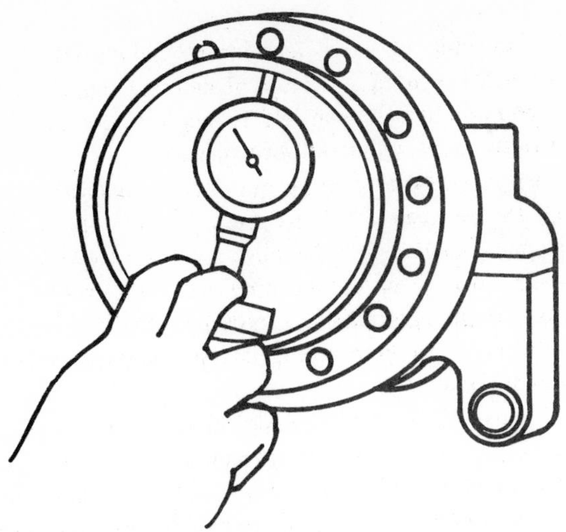

FIGURE 10–1. Checking cylinder bore with a dial indicator.

built with an intentional choke, measurement of taper becomes more complicated. It is necessary to know exactly how the size indicates wear or taper. Taper can be measured in any cylinder by a cylinder dial gage as long as there is not a sharp step. The dial gage tends to ride up on the step and causes inaccurate readings at the top of the cylinder.

The measurement for out-of-roundness is usually taken at the top of the cylinder. However, a reading should also be taken at the skirt of the cylinder to detect dents or bends caused by careless handling. A step or ridge (figure 10–2) is formed in the cylinder by the wearing action of the piston rings. The greatest wear is at the top of the ring travel limit. The ridge which results is very likely to cause damage to the rings or piston. If the step exceeds tolerances, it should be removed by grinding the cylinder oversize or it should be blended by hand stoning to break the sharp edge.

A step also may be found where the bottom ring reaches its lowest travel. This step is vary rarely found to be excessive, but it should be checked.

Inspect the cylinder walls for rust, pitting, or scores. Mild damage of this sort can be removed when the rings are lapped. With more extensive damage, the cylinder will have to be reground or honed. If the damage is too deep to be removed by either of these methods, the cylinder usually

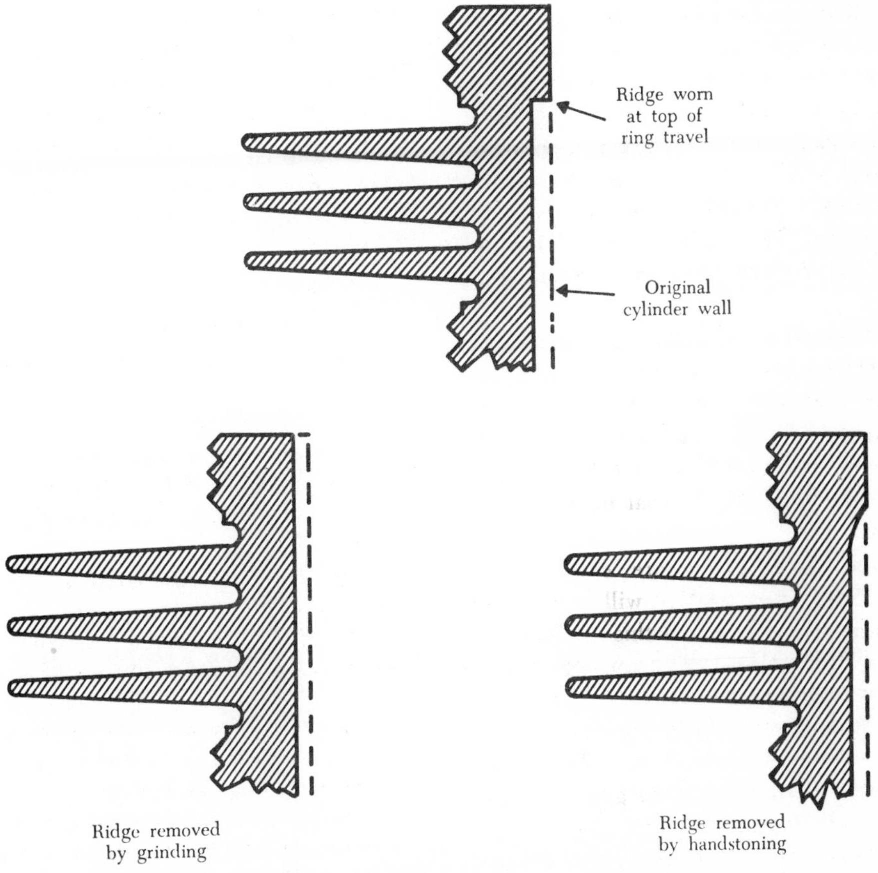

FIGURE 10–2. Ridge or step formed in an engine cylinder.

will have to be rejected. Most engine manufacturers have an exchange service on cylinders with damaged barrels.

Check the cylinder flange for warpage by placing the cylinder on a suitable jig. Check to see that the flange contacts the jig all the way around. The amount of warp can be checked by using a thickness gage (figure 10–3). A cylinder whose flange is warped beyond the allowable limits should be rejected.

Valves and Valve Springs

Remove the valves from the cylinder head and clean them to remove soft carbon. Examine the valve visually for physical damage and damage from burning or corrosion. Do not re-use valves that indicate damage of this nature. Check the valve face runout. The locations for checking runout and edge thickness are shown in figure 10–4.

Measure the edge thickness of valve heads. If, after re-facing, the edge thickness is less than the limit specified by the manufacturer, the valve must not be re-used. The edge thickness can be measured with sufficient accuracy by a dial indicator and a surface plate.

Using a magnifying glass, examine the valve in the stem area and the tip for evidence of cracks, nicks, or other indications of damage. This type of damage seriously weakens the valve, making it susceptible to failure. If superficial nicks and scratches on the valve indicate that it might be cracked, inspect it using the magnetic particle or dye penetrant method.

Critical areas of the valve include the face and tip, both of which should be examined for pitting and excessive wear. Minor pitting on valve faces can sometimes be removed by grinding.

Inspect the valve for stretch and wear, using a micrometer or a valve radius gage. Checking valve stretch with a valve radius gage is illustrated in figure 10–5. If a micrometer is used, stretch will be found as a smaller diameter of the valve stem near the neck of the valve. Measure the diameter of the valve stem and check the fit of the valve in its guide.

Examine the valve springs for cracks, rust, broken ends, and compression. Cracks can be located by visual inspection or the magnetic particle method. Compression is tested with a valve spring tester. The spring is compressed until its total height is that specified by the manufacturer. The dial on the tester should indicate the pressure (in pounds) required to compress the spring to the specified height. This must be within the pressure limits established by the manufacturer.

Rocker Arms and Shafts

Inspect the valve rockers for cracks and worn, pitted, or scored tips. See that all oil passages are free from obstructions.

Inspect the shafts for correct size with a micrometer. Rocker shafts very often are found to be scored and burned because of excessive turning in the cylinder head. Also, there may be some pickup on the shaft (bronze from the rocker bushing transferred to the steel shaft). Generally this is caused by overheating and too little clearance between shaft and bushing.

Inspect the rocker arm bushing for correct size. Check for proper clearance between the shaft and the bushing. Very often the bushings are scored because of mishandling during disassembly. Check to see that the oil holes line up. At least 50% of the hole in the bushing should align with the hole in the rocker arm.

On engines that use a bearing, rather than a bushing, inspect the bearing to make certain it has not been turning in the rocker arm boss. Also inspect the bearing to determine its serviceability.

Piston and Piston Pin

Inspect the piston for cracks. As an aid to this, heat the piston carefully with a blow torch. If there is a crack, the heat will expand it and will also force out residual oil that remains in the crack no matter how well the piston has been cleaned. Cracks are more likely to be formed at the highly stressed points; therefore, inspect carefully at the base of the pin bosses, inside the piston at the junction of the walls and the head, and at the base of the ring lands, especially the top and bottom lands.

When applicable, check for flatness of the piston head using a straightedge and thickness gage as shown in figure 10–6. If a depression is found, double check for cracks on the inside of the piston. A depression in the top of the piston usually means that detonation has occurred within the cylinder.

Inspect the exterior of the piston for scores and scratches. Scores on the top ring land are not cause for rejection unless they are excessively deep. Deep scores on the side of the piston are usually a reason for rejection.

Examine the piston for cracked skirts, broken ring lands, and scored piston-pin holes.

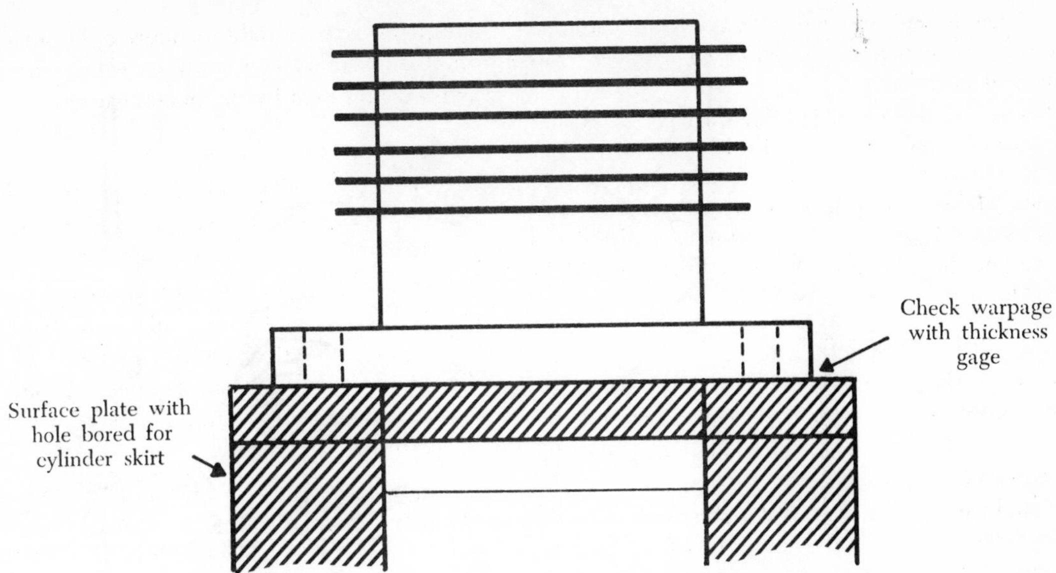

FIGURE 10–3. A method for checking cylinder flange warpage.

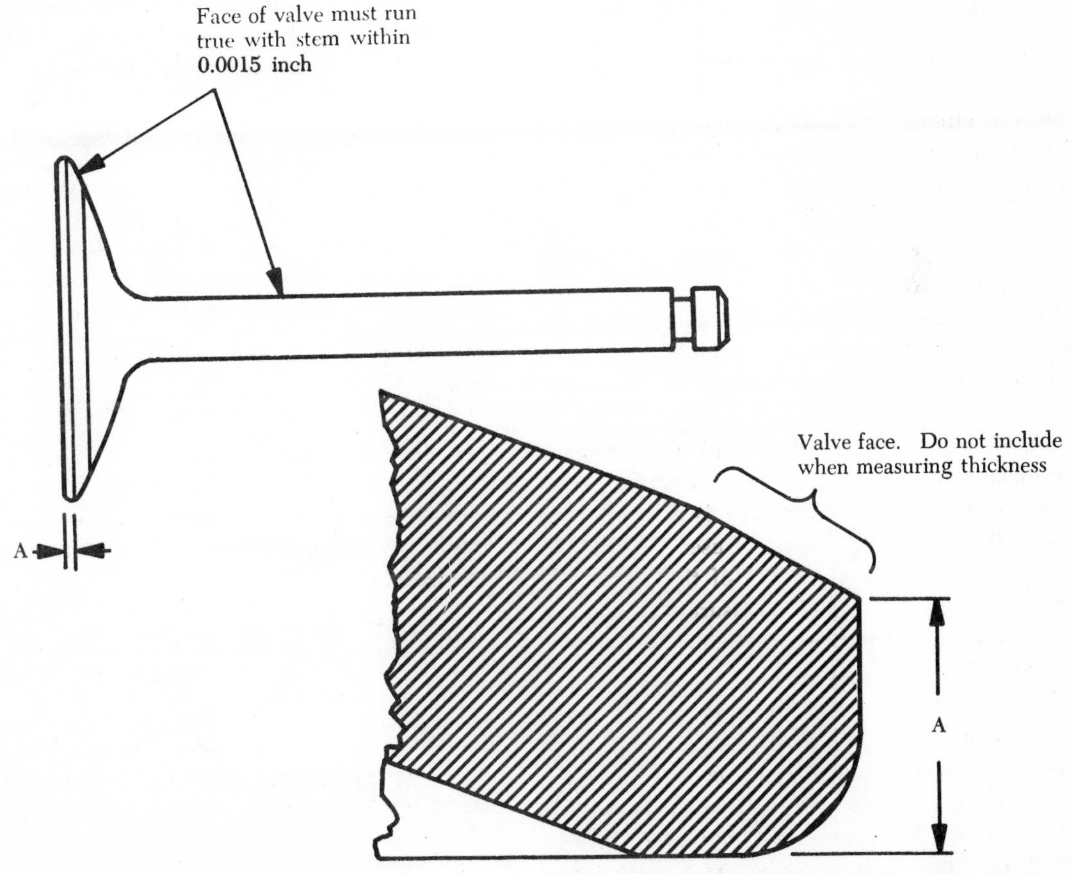

FIGURE 10–4. Valve, showing locations for checking runout and section for measuring edge thickness.

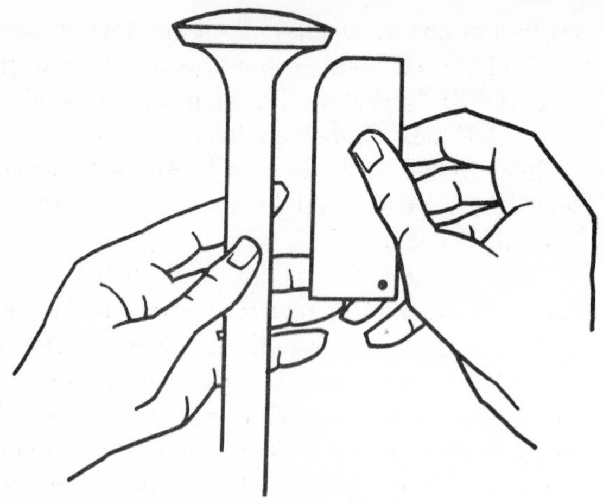

FIGURE 10–5. Checking valve stretch with a manufacturer's gage.

Measure the outside of the piston by means of a micrometer. Measurements must be taken in several directions and on the skirt, as well as on the lands section. Check these sizes against the cylinder size. Several engines now use cam ground pistons to compensate for the greater expansion parallel to the pin during engine operation. The diameter of these pistons measures several thousandths of an inch larger at an angle to the piston pin hole than parallel to the pin hole.

Inspect the ring grooves for evidence of a step. If a step is present, the groove will have to be machined to an oversize width. Use a standard piston ring and check side clearance with a feeler gage to locate wear in the grooves or to determine if the grooves have already been machined oversize. The largest allowable width is usually 0.020 in. oversize, because any further machining weakens the lands excessively.

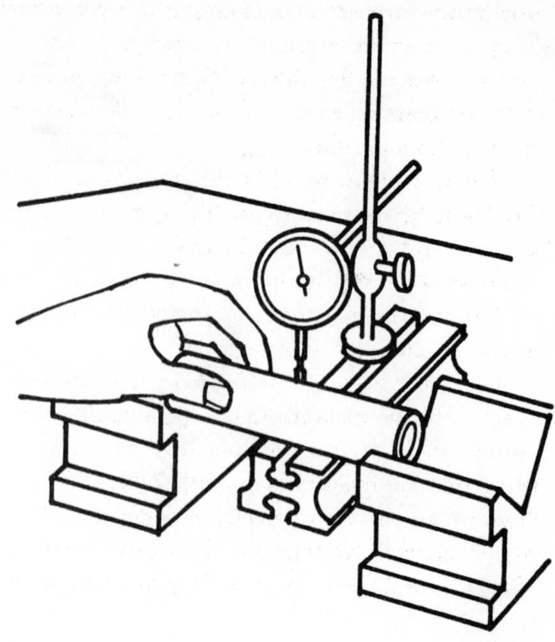

FIGURE 10–7. Checking a piston pin for bends.

Examine the piston pin for scoring, cracks, excessive wear, and pitting. Check the clearance between the piston pin and the bore of the piston pin bosses using a telescopic gage and a micrometer. Use the magnetic particle method to inspect the pin for cracks. Since the pins are often case hardened, cracks will show up inside the pin more often than they will on the outside.

Check the pin for bends (figure 10–7), using V-blocks and a dial indicator on a surface plate. Measure the fit of the plugs in the pin.

Re-facing Valve Seats

The valve seat inserts of aircraft engine cylinders

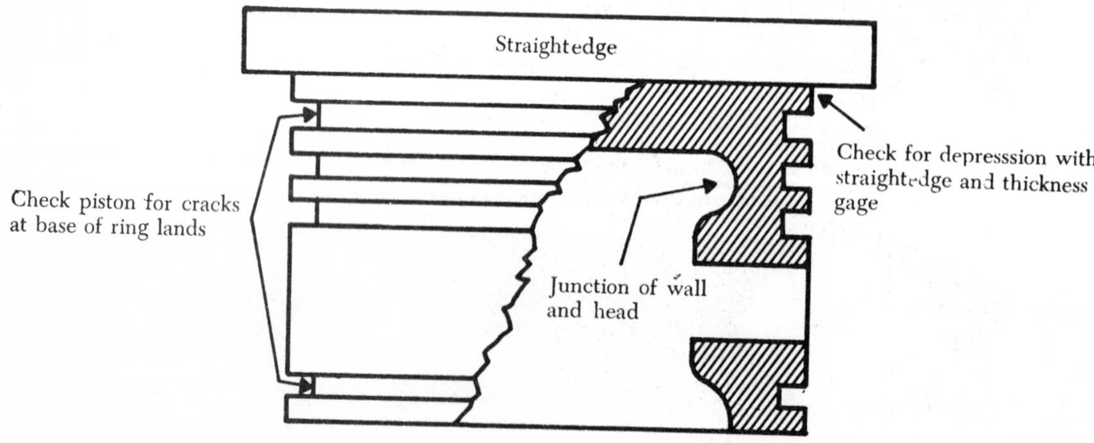

FIGURE 10–6. Checking a piston head for flatness.

usually are in need of re-facing at every overhaul. They are re-faced to provide a true, clean, and correct size seat for the valve. When valve guides or valve seats are replaced in a cylinder, the seats must be trued-up to the guide.

Modern engines use either bronze or steel seats. Steel seats are commonly used as exhaust seats and are made of a hard, heat-resistant, and often austenitic steel alloy. Bronze seats are used for intake or for both seats; they are made of aluminum bronze or phosphor bronze alloys.

Steel valve seats are re-faced by grinding equipment. Bronze seats are re-faced preferably by the use of cutters or reamers, but they may be ground when this equipment is not available. The only disadvantage of using a stone on bronze is that the soft metal loads the stone to such an extent that much time is consumed in re-dressing the stone to keep it clean.

The equipment used on steel seats can be either wet or dry valve seat grinding equipment. The wet grinder uses a mixture of soluble oil and water to wash away the chips and to keep the stone and seat cool; this produces a smoother, more accurate job than the dry grinder. The stones may be either silicon carbide or aluminum oxide.

Before re-facing the seat, make sure that the valve guide is in good condition, is clean, and will not have to be replaced.

Mount the cylinder firmly in the holddown fixture. An expanding pilot is inserted in the valve guide from the inside of the cylinder, and an expander screw is inserted in the pilot from the top of the guide as shown in figure 10–8. The pilot must be tight in the guide because any movement can cause a poor grind. The fluid hose is inserted through one of the spark plug inserts.

The three grades of stones available for use are classified as rough, finishing, and polishing stones. The rough stone is designed to true and clean the seat. The finishing stone must follow the rough to remove grinding marks and produce a smooth finish. The polishing stone does just as the name implies, and is used only where a highly polished seat is desired.

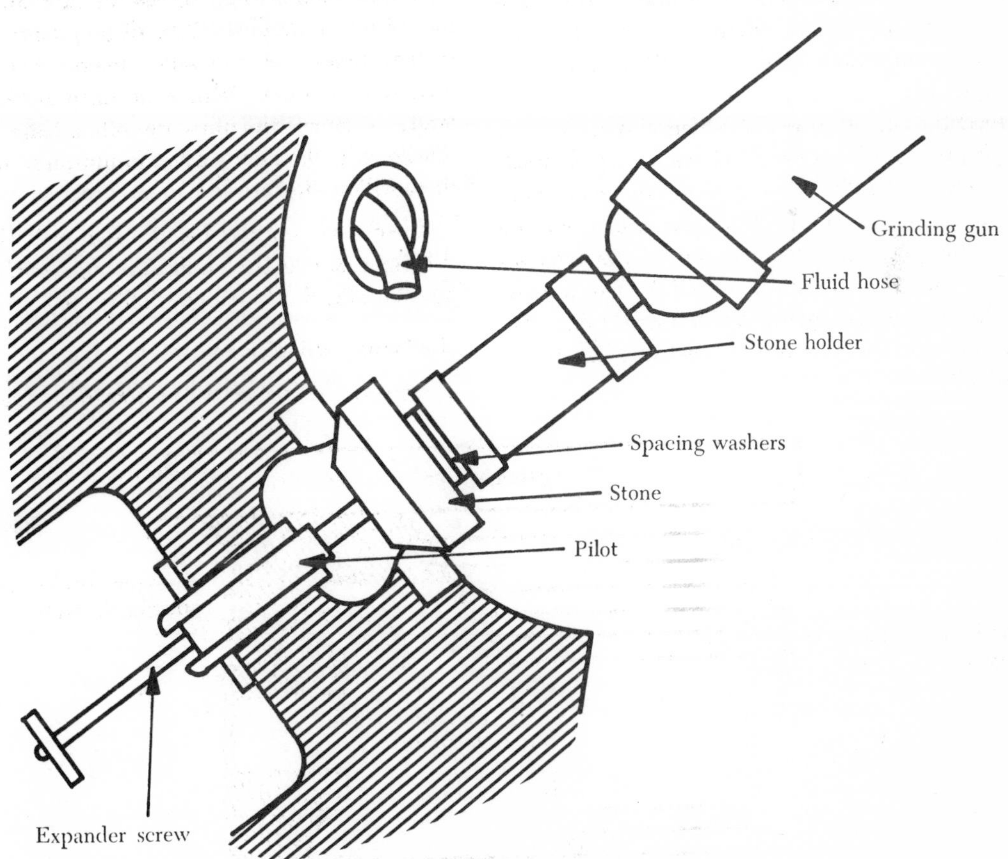

FIGURE 10–8. Valve seat grinding equipment.

The stones are installed on special stone holders. The face of the stone is trued by a diamond dresser. The stone should be re-faced whenever it is grooved or loaded and when the stone is first installed on the stone holder. The diamond dresser also may be used to cut down the diameter of the stone. Dressing of the stone should be kept to a minimum as a matter of conservation; therefore, it is desirable to have sufficient stone holders for all the stones to be used on the job.

In the actual grinding job, considerable skill is required in handling the grinding gun. The gun must be centered accurately on the stone holder. If the gun is tilted off-center, chattering of the stone will result and a rough grind will be produced. It is very important that the stone be rotated at a speed that will permit grinding instead of rubbing. This speed is approximately 8,000 to 10,000 r.p.m. Excessive pressure on the stone can slow it down. It is not a good technique to let the stone grind at slow speed by putting pressure on the stone when starting or stopping the gun. The maximum pressure used on the stone at any time should be no more than that exerted by the weight of the gun.

Another practice which is conducive to good grinding is to ease off on the stone every second or so to let the coolant wash away the chips on the seat; this rhythmic grinding action also helps keep the stone up to its correct speed. Since it is quite a job to replace a seat, remove as little material as possible during the grinding. Inspect the job frequently to prevent unnecessary grinding.

The rough stone is used until the seat is true to the valve guide and until all pits, scores, or burned areas (figure 10–9) are removed. After re-facing, the seat should be smooth and true.

The finishing stone is used only until the seat has a smooth, polished appearance. Extreme caution should be used when grinding with the finishing stone to prevent chattering.

The size and trueness of the seat can be checked by several methods. Runout of the seat is checked with a special dial indicator and should not exceed 0.002 in. The size of the seat may be determined by using prussian blue. To check the fit of the seat, spread a thin coat of prussian blue evenly on the seat. Press the valve onto the seat. The blue transferred to the valve will indicate the contact surface. The contact surface should be one-third to two-thirds the width of the valve face and in the middle of the face. In some cases, a-go and no-go gage is used in place of the valve when making the prussian blue check. If prussian blue is not used, the same check may be made by lapping the valve lightly to the seat. Examples of test results are shown in figure 10–10.

If the seat contacts the upper third of the valve face, grind off the top corner of the valve seat as shown in figure 10–11. Such grinding is called "narrowing grinding." This permits the seat to contact the center third of the valve face without touching the upper portion of the valve face.

If the seat contacts the bottom third of the valve face, grind off the inner corner of the valve seat as shown in figure 10–12.

The seat is narrowed by a stone other than the standard angle. It is common practice to use a 15° angle and 45° angle cutting stone on a 30° angle valve seat, and a 30° angle and 75° angle stone on a 45° angle valve seat (see figure 10–13).

If the valve seat has been cut or ground too much, the valve will contact the seat too far up into the cylinder head, and the valve clearance,

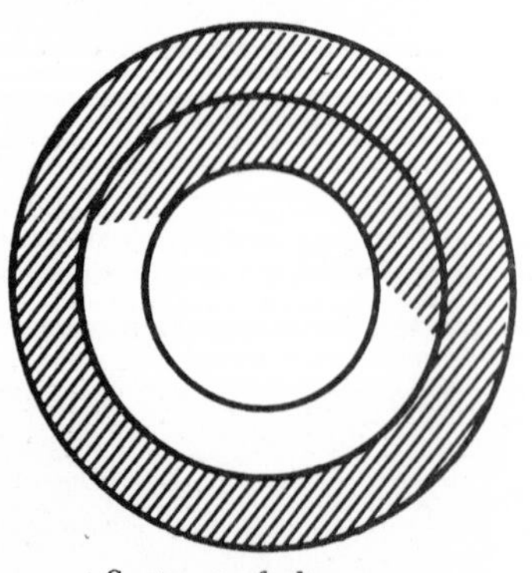

Seat out of alignment with guide

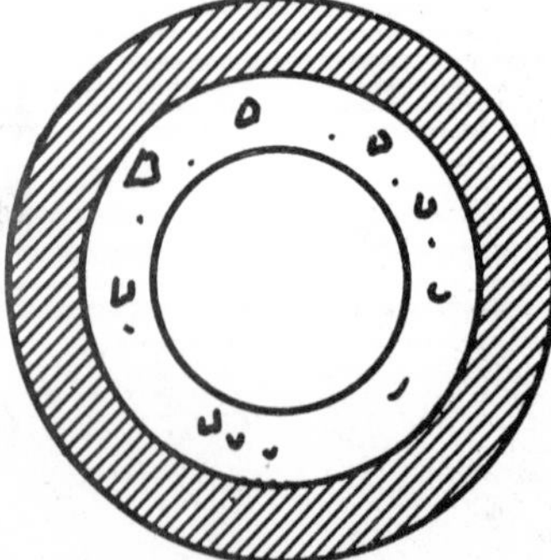

Excessive pitting

Needs further rough grinding

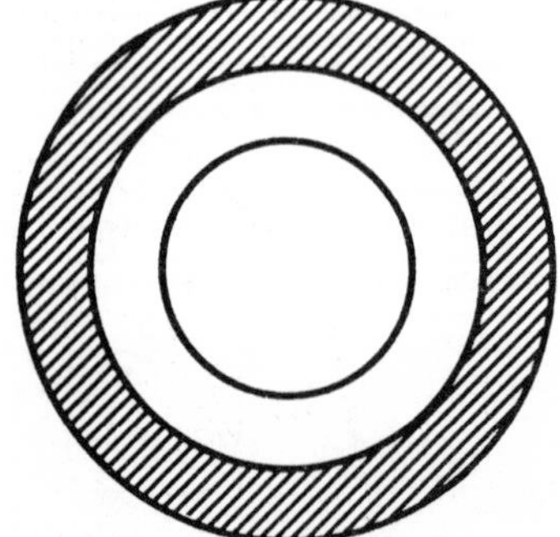

True and clean
Ready for finish grind

FIGURE 10–9. Valve seat grinding.

spring tension, and the fit of the valve to the seat will be affected. To check the height of a valve, insert the valve into the guide and hold it against the seat. Check the height of the valve stem above the rocker box or some other fixed position.

Before re-facing a valve seat, consult the overhaul manual for the particular model engine. Each manufacturer specifies the desired angle for grinding and narrowing the valve seat.

Valve Reconditioning

One of the most common jobs during engine overhaul is grinding the valves. The equipment used should preferably be a wet valve grinder.

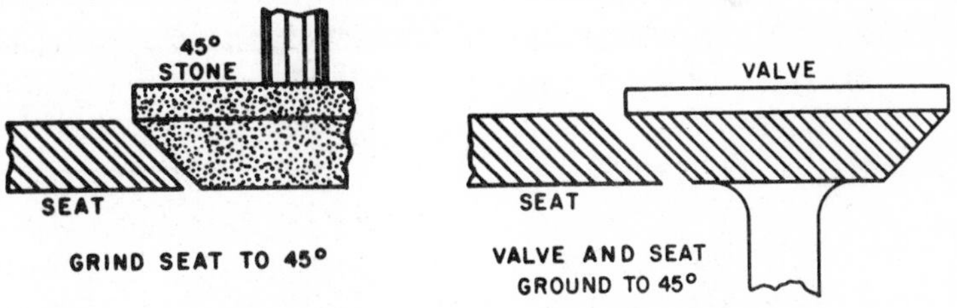

FIGURE 10–10. Fitting of the valve and seat.

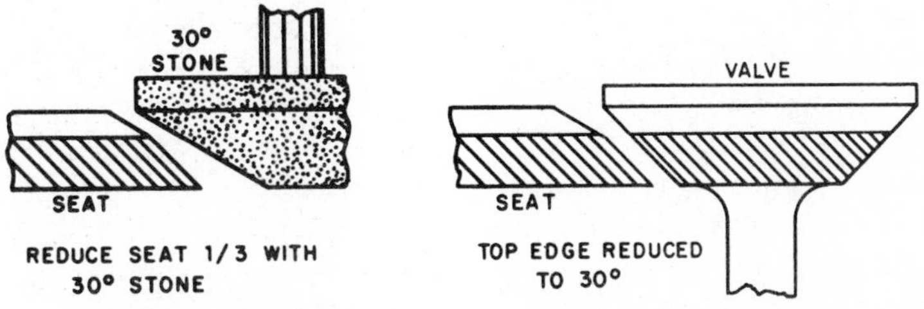

FIGURE 10–11. Grinding top surface of the valve seat.

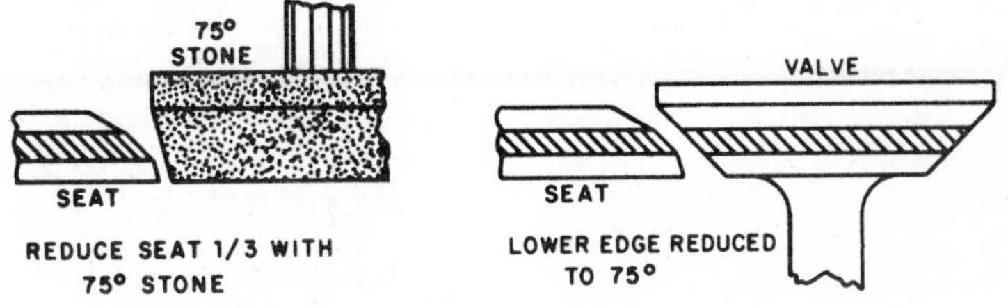

PROPER CONTACT VALVE TO VALVE SEAT

FIGURE 10–12. Grinding the inner corner of the valve seat.

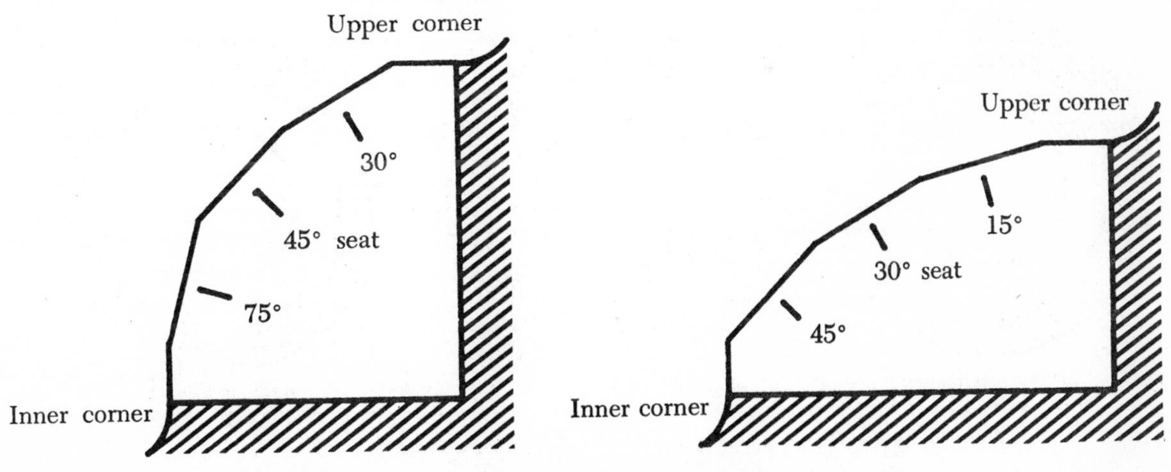

FIGURE 10–13. Valve seat angles.

With this type of machine, a mixture of soluble oil and water is used to keep the valve cool and carry away the grinding chips.

Like many machine jobs, valve grinding is mostly a matter of setting up the machine. The following points should be checked or accomplished before starting a grind.

True the stone by means of a diamond nib. The machine is turned on, and the diamond is drawn across the stone, cutting just deep enough to true and clean the stone.

Determine the face angle of the valve being ground and set the movable head of the machine to correspond to this valve angle. Usually, valves are ground to the standard angles of 30° or 45°. However, in some instances, an interference fit of 0.5° or 1.5° less than the standard angle may be ground on the valve face.

The interference fit (figure 10–14) is used to obtain a more positive seal by means of a narrow contact surface. Theoretically, there is a line contact between the valve and seat. With this line contact, all the load that the valve exerts against the seat is concentrated in a very small area, thereby increasing the unit load at any one spot. The interference fit is especially beneficial during the first few hours of operation after an overhaul. The positive seal reduces the possibility of a burned valve or seat that a leaking valve might produce. After the first few hours of running, these angles tend to pound down and become identical.

Notice that the interference angle is ground into the valve, not the seat. It is easier to change the angle of the valve grinder work head than to change the angle of a valve seat grinder stone. Do not use an interference fit unless the manufacturer approves it.

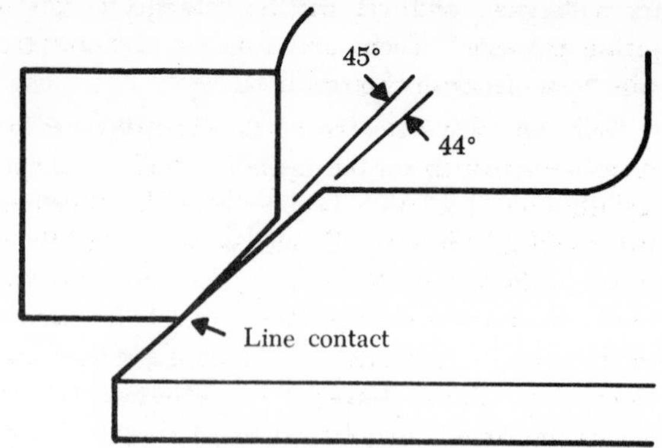

FIGURE 10–14. Interference fit of valve and valve seat.

Install the valve into the chuck (figure 10–15) and adjust the chuck so that the valve face is approximately 2 in. from the chuck. If the valve is chucked any further out, there is danger of excessive wobble and also a possibility of grinding into the stem.

There are various types of valve grinding machines. In one type the stone is moved across the valve face; in another, the valve is moved across the stone. Whichever type is used, the following procedures are typical of those performed when re-facing a valve.

Check the travel of the valve face across the stone. The valve should completely pass the stone

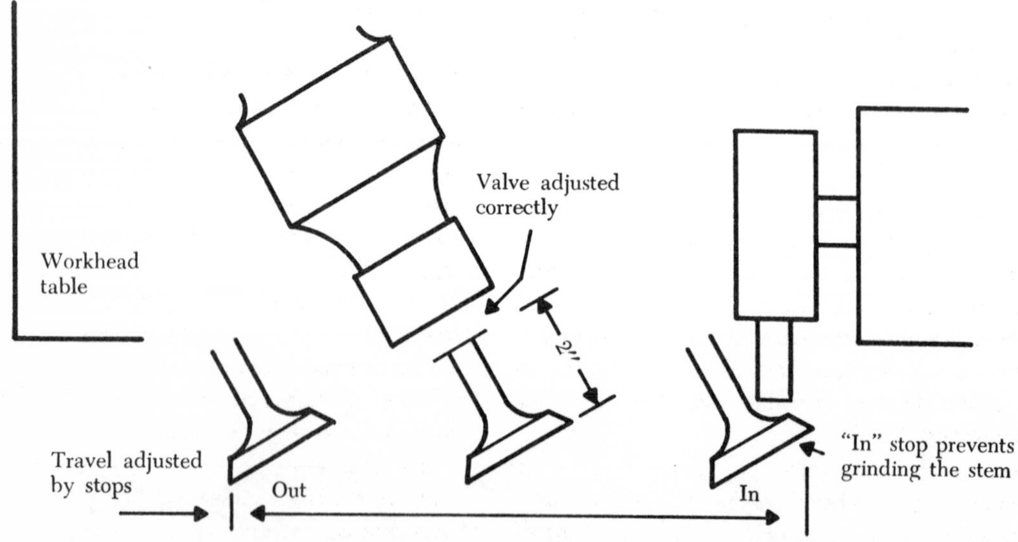

FIGURE 10–15. Valve installed in grinding machine.

on both sides and yet not travel far enough to grind the stem. There are stops on the machine which can be set to control this travel.

With the valve set correctly in place, turn on the machine and turn on the grinding fluid so that it splashes on the valve face. Back the grinding wheel off all the way. Place the valve directly in front of the stone. Slowly bring the wheel forward until a light cut is made on the valve. The intensity of the grind is measured by sound more than anything else. Slowly draw the valve back and forth across the stone without increasing the cut. Move the workhead table back and forth using the full face of the stone but always keep the valve face on the stone. When the sound of the grind diminishes, indicating that some valve material has been removed, move the workhead table to the extreme left to stop rotation of the valve. Inspect the valve to determine if further grinding is necessary. If another cut must be made, bring the valve in front of the stone, then advance the stone out to the valve. Do not increase the cut without having the valve directly in front of the stone.

An important precaution in valve grinding, as in any kind of grinding, is to make light cuts only. Heavy cuts cause chattering, which may make the valve surface so rough that much time is lost in obtaining the desired finish.

After grinding, check the valve margin to be sure that the valve edge has not been ground too thin. A thin edge is called a "feather edge" and can lead to preignition. The valve edge would burn away in a short period of time and the cylinder would have to be overhauled again. Figure 10–16 shows a valve with a normal margin and one with a feather edge.

The valve tip may be re-surfaced on the valve grinder. The tip is ground to remove cupping or wear and also to adjust valve clearances on some engines.

The valve is held by a clamp (figure 10–17) on the side of the stone. With the machine and grinding fluid turned on, the valve is pushed lightly against the stone and swung back and forth. Do not swing the valve stem off either edge of the stone. Because of the tendency for the valve to overheat during this grinding, be sure plenty of grinding fluid covers the tip.

Grinding of the valve tip may remove or partially remove the bevel on the edge of the valve. To restore this bevel, mount a vee-way approximately 45° to the grinding stone. Hold the valve onto the vee-way with one hand, then twist the valve tip onto the stone, and with a light touch grind all the way around the tip. This bevel prevents scratching the valve guide when the valve is installed.

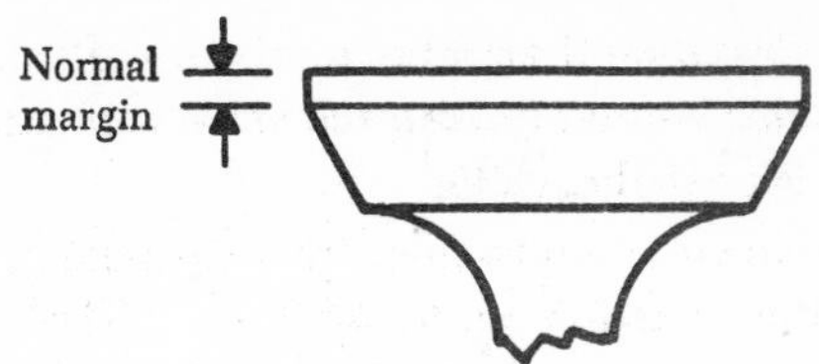

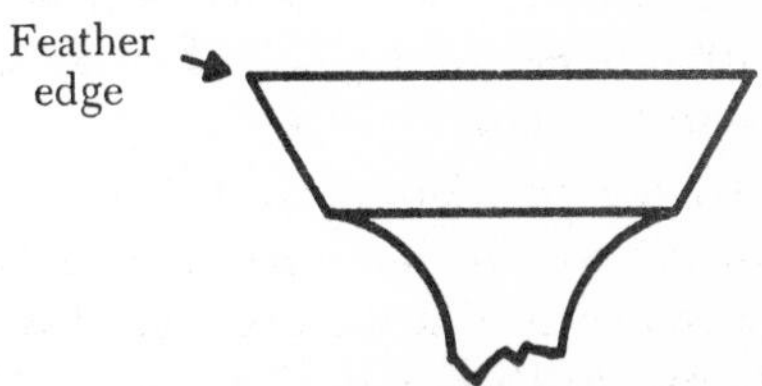

FIGURE 10–16. Engine valves showing normal margin and a feather edge.

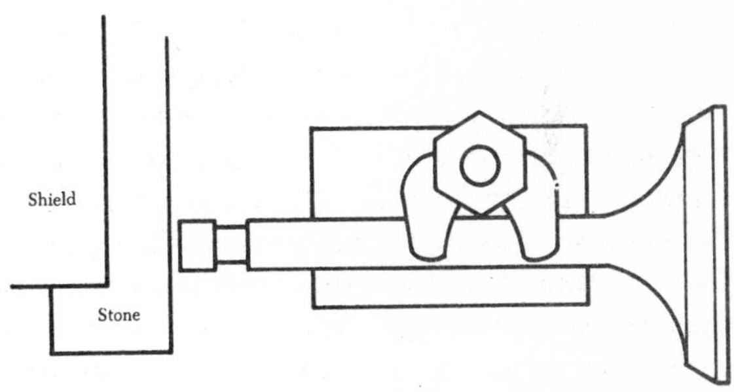

FIGURE 10–17. Grinding a valve tip.

Valve Lapping and Leak Testing

After the grinding procedure is finished, it is sometimes necessary that the valve be lapped to the seat. This is done by applying a small amount of lapping compound to the valve face, inserting the valve into the guide, and rotating the valve with a lapping tool until a smooth, gray finish appears at the contact area. The appearance of a correctly lapped valve is shown in figure 10–18.

After the lapping process is finished, be sure that all lapping compound is removed from the valve face, seat, and adjacent areas.

The final step is to check the mating surface for leaks to see if it is sealing properly. This is done by installing the valve in the cylinder, holding the valve by the stem with the fingers, and pouring

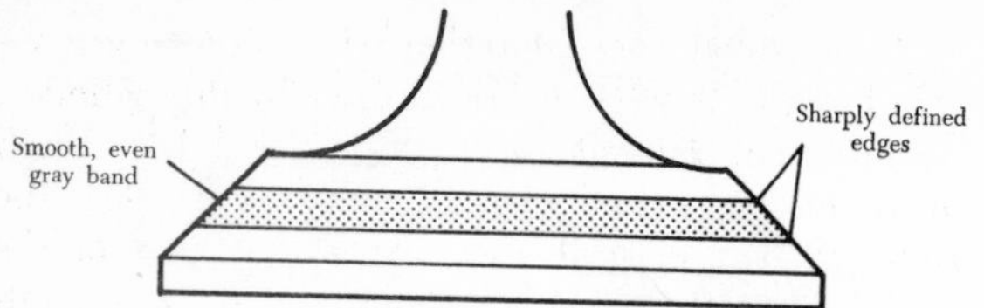

FIGURE 10–18. A correctly lapped valve.

kerosene or solvent into the valve port. While holding finger pressure on the valve stem, check to see if the kerosene is leaking past the valve into the combustion chamber. If it is not, the valve re-seating operation is finished. If kerosene is leaking past the valve, continue the lapping operation until the leakage is stopped.

Any valve face surface appearance that varies from that illustrated in figure 10–19 is correct. However, the incorrect indications are of value in diagnosing improper valve and valve seat grinding. Incorrect indications, their cause and remedy, are shown in figure 10–19.

Piston Repairs

Piston repairs are not required as often as cylinder repairs since most of the wear is between the piston ring and cylinder wall, valve stem and guide, and valve face and seat. A lesser amount of wear is encountered between the piston skirt and cylinder, ring and ring groove, or piston pin and bosses.

The most common repair will be the removal of scores. Usually these may be removed only on the piston skirt if they are very light. Scores above the top ring groove may be machined or sanded out, as long as the diameter of the piston is not reduced below the specified minimum. To remove these scores, set the piston on a lathe. With the piston revolving at a slow speed, smooth out the scores with number 320 wet or dry sandpaper. Never use anything rougher than crocus cloth on the piston skirt.

On engines where the entire rotating and reciprocating assembly is balanced, the pistons must weigh within one-fourth ounce of each other. When a new piston is installed it must be within the same weight tolerance as the one removed. It is not enough to have the pistons matched alone; they must be matched to the crankshaft, connecting rods, piston pins, etc. To make weight adjustments on new pistons, the manufacturer provides a heavy section at the base of the skirt. To decrease weight file metal evenly off the inside of this heavy section. The piston weight can be decreased easily, but welding, metalizing, or plating cannot be done to increase the piston weight.

If ring grooves are worn or stepped, they will have to be machined oversize so that they can accommodate an oversize width ring with the proper clearance. After machining, check to be sure that the small radius is maintained at the back of each ring groove. If it is removed, cracks may occur due to localization of stress. Ring groove oversizes are usually 0.005 in., 0.010 in., or 0.020 in. More than that would weaken the ring lands.

A few manufacturers sell 0.005-in.-oversize piston pins. When these are available, it is permissible to bore or ream the piston-pin bosses to 0.005 in. oversize. However, these bosses must be in perfect alignment.

Small nicks on the edge of the piston-pin boss may be sanded down. Deep scores inside the boss or anywhere around the boss are definite reasons for rejection.

Cylinder Grinding and Honing

If a cylinder has excessive taper, out-of-roundness, step, or its maximum size is beyond limits, it can be re-ground to the next allowable oversize. If the cylinder walls are lightly rusted, scored, or

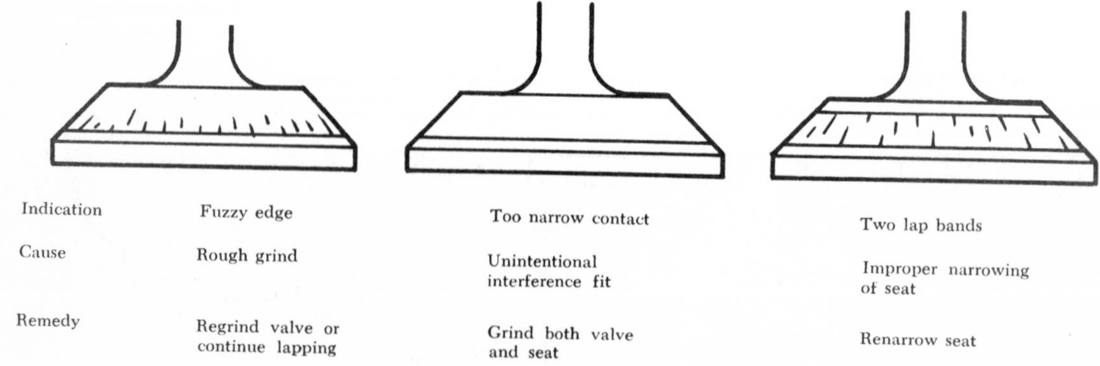

Indication	Fuzzy edge	Too narrow contact	Two lap bands
Cause	Rough grind	Unintentional interference fit	Improper narrowing of seat
Remedy	Regrind valve or continue lapping	Grind both valve and seat	Renarrow seat

FIGURE 10–19. Incorrectly lapped valves.

pitted, the damage may be removed by honing or lapping.

Regrinding a cylinder is a specialized job that the powerplant mechanic usually is not expected to be able to do. However, the mechanic must be able to recognize when a cylinder needs re-grinding, and he must know what constitutes a good or bad job.

Generally, standard aircraft cylinder oversizes are 0.010 in., 0.015 in., 0.020 in., or 0.030 in. Unlike automobile engines which may be re-bored to oversizes of 0.075 in. to 0.100 in., aircraft cylinders have relatively thin walls and may have a nitrided surface, which must not be ground away. Any one manufacturer usually does not allow all of the above oversizes. Some manufacturers do not allow regrinding to an oversize at all. The manufacturer's overhaul manual or parts catalog usually lists the oversizes allowed for a particular make and model engine.

To determine the re-grind size, the standard bore size must be known. This usually can be determined from the manufacturer's specifications or manuals. The re-grind size is figured from the standard bore. For example, a certain cylinder has a standard bore of 3.875 in. To have a cylinder ground to 0.015 in. oversize, it is necessary to grind to a bore diameter of 3.890 in. (3.875+0.015). A tolerance of ±0.0005 in. is usually accepted for cylinder grinding.

Another factor to consider when determining the size to which a cylinder must be re-ground is the maximum wear that has occurred. If there are spots in the cylinder wall that are worn larger than the first oversize, then obviously it will be necessary to grind to the next oversize to clean up the entire cylinder.

An important consideration when ordering a regrind is the type of finish desired in the cylinder. Some engine manufacturers specify a fairly rough finish on the cylinder walls, which will allow the rings to seat even if they are not lapped to the cylinder. Other manufacturers desire a smooth finish to which a lapped ring will seat without much change in ring or cylinder dimensions. The latter type of finish is more expensive to produce.

The standard used when measuring the finish of a cylinder wall is known as microinch root-mean-square, or microinch r.m.s. In a finish where the depth of the grinding scratches are one-millionth (0.000001) of an inch deep, it is specified as 1 microinch r.m.s. Most aircraft cylinders are ground to a finish of 15 to 20 microinch r.m.s. Several low-powered engines have cylinders that are ground to a relatively rough 20- to 30-microinch r.m.s. finish. On the other end of the scale, some manufacturers require a superfinish of approximately 4- to 6-microinch r.m.s.

Cylinder grinding (figure 10–20) is accomplished by a firmly mounted stone that revolves around the cylinder bore, as well as up and down the length of the cylinder barrel. Either the cylinder, the stone, or both may move to get this relative movement. The size of the grind is determined by the distance the stone is set away from the center line of the cylinder. Some cylinder bore grinding machines will produce a prefectly straight bore, while others are designed to grind a choked bore. A choked bore grind refers to the manufacturing process in which the cylinder walls are ground to produce a smaller internal diameter at the top than at the bottom. The purpose of this type grind or taper is to main-

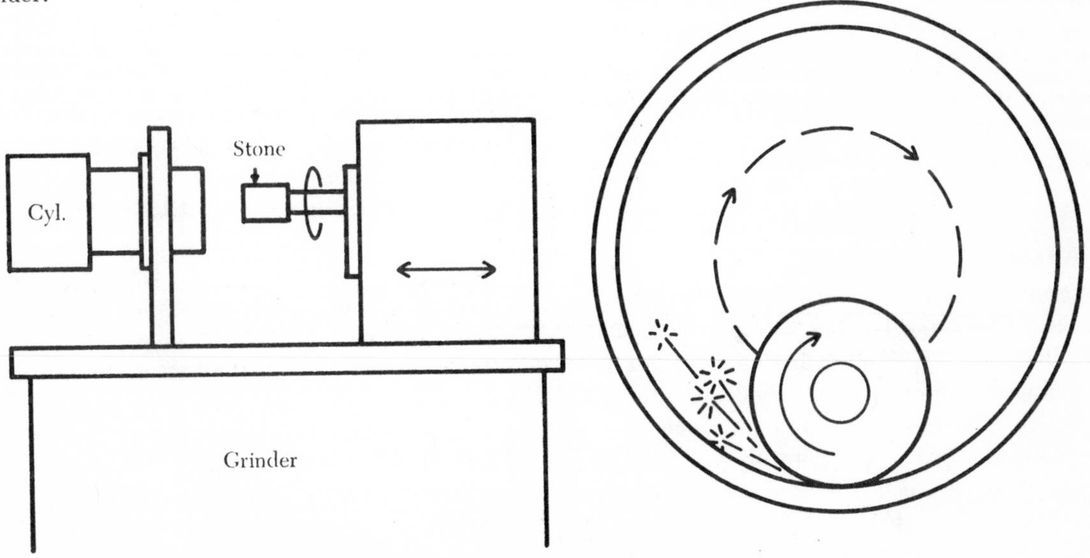

FIGURE 10–20. Cylinder bore grinding.

tain a straight cylinder wall during operation. As a cylinder heats up during operation, the head and top of the cylinder are subjected to more heat than the bottom. This causes greater expansion at the top than at the bottom, thereby maintaining the desired straight wall.

After grinding a cylinder, it may be necessary to hone the cylinder bore to produce the desired finish. If this is the case, specify the cylinder re-grind size to allow for some metal removal during honing. The usual allowance for honing is 0.001 in. If a final cylinder bore size of 3.890 in. is desired, specify the re-grind size of 3.889 in., and then hone to 3.890 in.

There are several different makes and models of cylinder hones. The burnishing hone is used only to produce the desired finish on the cylinder wall. The more elaborate micromatic hone can also be used to straighten out the cylinder wall. A burnishing hone (figure 10–21) should not be used in an attempt to straighten cylinder walls. Since the stones are only spring loaded, they will follow the contour of the cylinder wall and may aggravate a tapered condition.

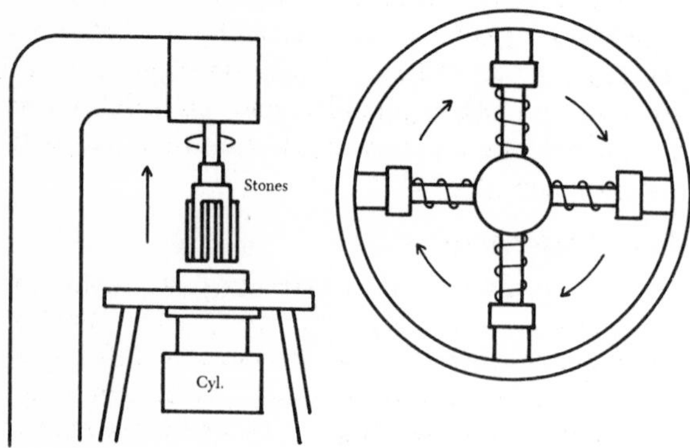

FIGURE 10–21. Cylinder honing.

After the cylinders have been re-ground, check the size and wall finish, and check for evidence of overheating or grinding cracks before installing on an engine.

CRANKSHAFT INSPECTION

Carefully inspect all surfaces of the shaft for cracks. Check the bearing surfaces for evidence of galling, scoring, or other damage. When a shaft is equipped with oil transfer tubes, check them for tightness. Some manufacturers recommend supplementing a visual inspection with one of the other forms of nondestructive testing, such as magnetic particle or radiography.

Use extreme care in inspecting and checking the crankshaft for straightness. Place the crankshaft in vee-blocks supported at the locations specified in the applicable engine overhaul manual. Using a surface plate and a dial indicator, measure the shaft runout. If the total indicator reading exceeds the dimensions given in the manufacturer's table of limits, the shaft must not be re-used. A bent crankshaft should not be straightened. Any attempt to do so will result in rupture of the nitrided surface of the bearing journals, a condition that will cause eventual failure of the crankshaft.

Measure the outside diameter of the crankshaft main and rod-bearing journals. Compare the resulting measurements with those in the table of limits.

Sludge Chambers

Some crankshafts are manufactured with hollow crankpins that serve as sludge removers. The sludge chambers may be formed by means of spool-shaped tubes pressed into the hollow crankpins or by plugs pressed into each end of the crankpin.

The sludge chamber or tubes must be removed for cleaning at overhaul. If these are not removed, accumulated sludge loosened during cleaning may clog the crankshaft oil passages and cause subsequent bearing failures. If the sludge chambers are formed by means of tubes pressed into the hollow crankpins, make certain they are re-installed correctly to avoid covering the ends of the oil passages.

CONNECTING RODS

The inspection and repair of connecting rods include: (1) Visual inspection, (2) checking of alignment, (3) re-bushing, and (4) replacement of bearings. Some manufacturers also specify a magnetic particle inspection of connecting rods.

Visual Inspection

Visual inspection should be done with the aid of a magnifying glass or bench microscope. A rod which is obviously bent or twisted should be rejected without further inspection.

Inspect all surfaces of the connecting rods for cracks, corrosion, pitting, galling, or other damage. Galling is caused by a slight amount of movement between the surfaces of the bearing insert and the connecting rod during periods of high loading, such as that produced during overspeed or excessive manifold pressure operation. The visual evidence produced by galling appears as if particles from one contacting surface had welded to the other. Evidence of any galling is sufficient reason for rejecting the complete rod assembly. Galling is a distortion in the metal and is comparable to corrosion in the manner in which it weakens the metallic structure of the connecting rod.

Checking Alignment

Check bushings that have been replaced to determine if the bushing and rod bores are square and parallel to each other. The alignment of a connecting rod can be checked several ways. One method requires a push fit arbor for each end of the connecting rod, a surface plate, and two parallel blocks of equal height.

To measure rod squareness (figure 10–22), or twist, insert the arbors into the rod bores. Place the parallel blocks on a surface plate. Place the ends of the arbors on the parallel blocks. Check the clearance at the points where the arbors rest on the blocks, using a thickness gage. This clearance, divided by the separation of the blocks in inches, will give the twist per inch of length.

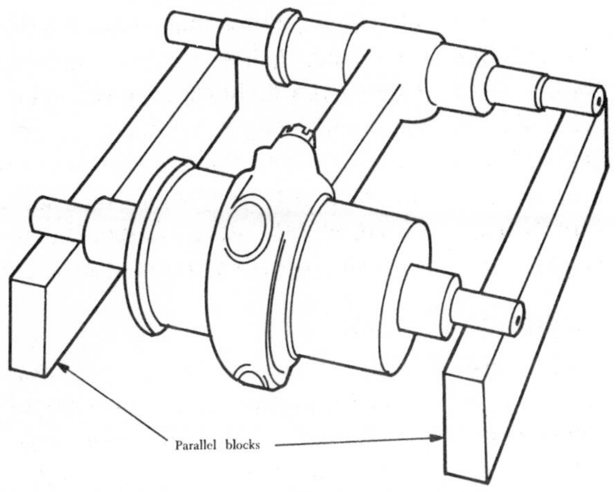

FIGURE 10–22. Checking connecting rod squareness.

To determine bushing or bearing parallelism (convergence), insert the arbors in the rod bores. Measure the distance between the arbors on each side of the connecting rod at points that are equidistant from the rod center line. For exact parallelism, the distances checked on both sides should be the same. Consult the manufacturer's table of limits for the amount of misalignment permitted.

The preceding operations are typical of those used for most reciprocating engines and are included to introduce some of the operations involved in engine overhaul. It would be impractical to list all the steps involved in the overhaul of an engine. It should be understood that there are other operations and inspections that must be performed. For exact information regarding a specific engine model, consult the manufacturer's overhaul manual.

BLOCK TESTING OF RECIPROCATING ENGINES

The information in this chapter on block testing of engines is intended to familiarize you with the procedures and equipment used in selecting for service only those engines that are in top mechanical condition.

Like a new or recently overhauled automobile engine, the aircraft engine must be in top mechanical condition. This condition must be determined after the engine has been newly assembled or completely overhauled. The method used is the block test, or run-in, which takes place at overhaul prior to delivery of the engine. It must be emphasized that engine run-in is as vital as any other phase of engine overhaul, for it is the means by which the quality of a new or newly overhauled engine is checked, and it is the final step in the preparation of an engine for service.

In many instances an engine has appeared to be in perfect mechanical condition before the engine run-in tests, but the tests have shown that it was actually in poor and unreliable mechanical condition. Thus, the reliability and potential service life of an engine is in question until it has satisfactorily passed the block test.

Block Test Purpose

The block test serves a dual purpose: first, it accomplishes piston ring run-in and bearing burnishing; and second, it provides valuable information that it used to evaluate engine performance and determine engine condition. To provide proper oil flow to the upper portion of the cylinder barrel walls with a minimum loss of oil, it is important that piston rings be properly seated in the cylinder in which they are installed. The process is called piston ring run-in and is accomplished chiefly by controlled operation of the engine in the high-speed range. Improper piston ring conditioning or run-in may result in unsatisfactory engine operation. A process called "bearing burnishing" creates a highly polished surface on new bearings and bushings installed during overhaul. The burnishing is usually accomplished during the first periods of the engine run-in at comparatively slow engine speeds.

Block-Test Requirements

The operational tests and test procedures vary with individual engines, but the basic requirements are discussed in the following paragraphs. The failure of any internal part during engine run-in requires that the engine be returned for replacement of the necessary units, and then be completely re-tested. If any component part of the basic engine should fail, a new unit is installed; a minimum operating time is used to check the engine with the new unit installed.

After an engine has successfully completed block-test requirements, it is then specially treated to prevent corrosion. During the final run-in period at block test, the engines are operated on the proper grade of fuel prescribed for the particular kind of engine. The oil system is serviced with a mixture of corrosion-preventive compound and engine oil. The temperature of this mixture is maintained at 105° to 121° C. Near the end of final run-in CPM (corrosion-preventive mixture) is used as the engine lubricant; and the engine induction passages and combustion chambers are also treated with CPM by an aspiration method (CPM is drawn or breathed into the engine).

Mobile Stand Testing of Reciprocating Engines

The mobile stand testing of reciprocating engines is much the same as for the block testing of reciprocating engines. They both have the same purpose; *i.e.*, to ensure that the engine is fit to be installed on an aircraft. Once the engine has been operated on the mobile test stand and any faults or troubles corrected, it is presumed that the engine will operate correctly on the aircraft.

A typical mobile test stand consists of a frame, engine mount, control booth, and trailer welded or bolted together. The engine test stand mount and firewall are located toward the rear of the trailer deck and afford accessibility to the rear of the engine. The engine test stand mount is a steel structure of uprights, braces, and crossmembers welded and bolted together forming one unit. The rear stand brace has nonskid steel steps welded in place to permit the mechanic to climb easily to the top of the engine accessory section. The front side of the engine mount has steel panels incorporating cannon plugs for the electrical connections to the engine. Also, there are fittings on the steel panels for the quick connection of the fluid lines to the engine. The hydraulic tank is located on the rear side of the engine test stand mount. Finally, the mobile engine test stand has outlet plugs for the communication system.

The control booth is located in the middle of the trailer and houses the engine controls and instrument panels.

The most important thing about positioning a mobile test stand is to face the propeller directly into the wind. If this is not done, engine testing will not be accurate.

Block Test Instruments

The block-test operator's control room houses the controls used to operate the engine and the instruments used to measure various temperatures and pressures, fuel flow, and other factors. These devices are necessary in providing an accurate check and an evaluation of the operating engine. The control room is separate from, but adjacent to, the space (test cell) that houses the engine being tested.

The safe, economical, and reliable testing of modern aircraft engines depends largely upon the use of instruments. In engine run-in procedures, the same basic engine instruments are used as when the engine is installed in the aircraft, plus some additional connections to these instruments and some indicating and measuring devices that cannot be practically installed in the aircraft. Instruments used in the testing procedures are inspected and calibrated periodically, as are instruments installed in the aircraft; thus, accurate information concerning engine operation is ensured.

Engine instruments are operated in several different fashions, some mechanically, some electrically, and some by the pressure of a liquid. This chapter will not discuss how they operate, but rather the information they give, their common names, and the markings on them. The instruments to be covered are:

(1) Carburetor air temperature gage.
(2) Fuel pressure gage.
(3) Fuel flowmeter.
(4) Manifold pressure gage.
(5) Oil temperature gage.
(6) Oil pressure gage.
(7) Tachometer.
(8) Cylinder head temperature gage.
(9) Torquemeter.
(10) Suction gage.
(11) Oil-weighing system.
(12) Metering differential manometer.

Instrument markings and the interpretation of these markings will be discussed before considering the individual instruments.

Instrument markings indicate ranges of operation or minimum and maximum limits, or both. Generally, the instrument marking system consists of four colors (red, yellow, blue, and green) and intermediate blank spaces.

A red line, or mark indicates a point beyond which a dangerous operating condition exists, and a red arc indicates a dangerous operating range. Of the two, the red mark is used more commonly and is located radially on the cover glass or dial face.

The yellow arc covers a given range of operation and is an indication of caution. Generally, the yellow arc is located on the outer circumference of the instrument cover glass or dial face.

The blue arc like the yellow, indicates a range of operation. The blue arc might indicate, for example, the manifold pressure gage range in which the engine can be operated with the carburetor control set at automatic lean. The blue arc is used only with certain engine instruments, such as the tachometer, manifold pressure, cylinder head temperature, and torquemeter.

The green arc shows a normal range of operation. When used on certain engine instruments, however, it also means that the engine must be operated with an automatic rich carburetor setting when the pointer is in this range.

When the markings appear on the cover glass, a *white line* is used as an index mark, often called a slippage mark. The white radial mark indicates any movement between the cover glass and the case, a condition that would cause mislocation of the other range and limit markings.

The instruments illustrated in figures 10–23 through 10–31 are range marked. The portion of the dial that is range marked on the instruments is also shown expanded for instructional purposes. The expanded portion is set off from the instrument to make it easier to identify the instrument markings.

Carburetor Air Temperature Indicator

Measured at the carburetor entrance, CAT (carburetor air temperature) is regarded by many as an indication of induction system ice formation. Although it serves this purpose, it also provides many other important items of information.

The powerplant is a heat machine, and the temperature of its components or the fluids flowing through it affects the combustion process either directly or indirectly. The temperature level of the induction air affects not only the charge density but also the vaporization of the fuel.

In addition to the normal use of CAT, it will be found useful for checking induction system condition. Backfiring will be indicated as a momentary rise on the gage, provided it is of sufficient severity for the heat to be sensed at the carburetor air-measuring point. A sustained induction system fire will show a continuous increase of carburetor air temperature.

The CAT should be noted before starting and just after shutdown. The temperature before starting is the best indication of the temperature of the fuel in the carburetor body and tells whether vaporization will be sufficient for the initial firing or whether the mixture must be augmented by priming. If an engine has been shut down for only a short time, the residual heat in the carburetor may make it possible to rely on the vaporizing heat in the fuel and powerplant, and priming would then be unnecessary. After shutdown, a high CAT is a warning that the fuel trapped in the carburetor will expand, producing high internal pressure. When a high temperature is present at this time, the fuel line and manifold valves should be open so that the pressure can be relieved by allowing fuel passage back to the tank.

The carburetor air temperature gage indicates the temperature of the air before it enters the carburetor. The temperature reading is sensed by a bulb. In the test cell the bulb is located in the air intake passage to the engine, and in an aircraft it is located in the ram-air intake duct. The carburetor air temperature gage is calibrated in the centigrade scale. Figure 10–23 shows a typical carburetor air temperature gage or CAT. This gage, like many other multi-engine aircraft instruments, is a dual gage; that is, two gages, each with a separate pointer and scale, are used in the same case. Notice the range markings used. The yellow arc indicates a range from −10° C. to +15° C., since the danger of icing occurs between these temperatures. The green range indicates the normal operating range from +15° C. to +40° C. The red line indicates the maximum operating temperature of 40° C.; any operation at a temperature over this value places the engine in danger of detonation.

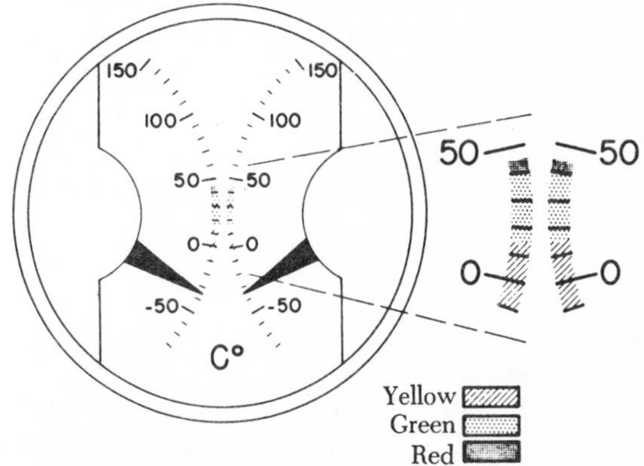

FIGURE 10–23. Carburetor air temperature gage.

Fuel Pressure Indicator

The fuel pressure gage is calibrated in pounds per square inch of pressure. It is used during the block test run-in to measure engine fuel pressure at the carburetor inlet, the fuel feed valve discharge nozzle, and the main fuel supply line. Fuel gages are located in the operator's control room and are connected by flexible lines to the different points at which pressure readings are desired during the testing procedures.

In some aircraft installations, the fuel pressure is sensed at the carburetor inlet of each engine, and the pressure is indicated on individual gages (figure 10–24) on the instrument panel. The dial is calibrated in 1-p.s.i. graduations, and every fifth graduation line is extended and numbered. The numbers range from 0 to 25. The red line on the dial at the 16-p.s.i. graduation shows the minimum fuel pressure allowed during flight. The green arc shows the desired range of operation, which is 16 to 18 p.s.i. The red line at the 18-p.s.i. graduation indicates the maximum allowable fuel pressure. Fuel pressures vary with the type of carburetor installation and the size of the engine. In most reciprocating engines that use pressure injection carburetion, the fuel pressure range is the same as illustrated in figure 10–24.

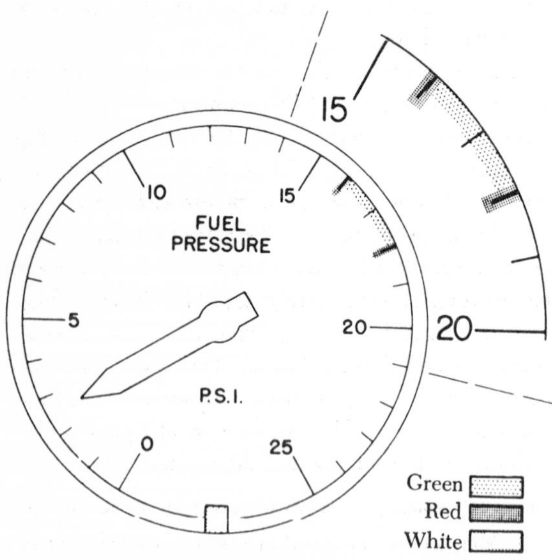

FIGURE 10–24. Fuel pressure gage.

When float-type carburetors or low-pressure carburetion systems are used, the fuel pressure range is of a much lower value; the minimum allowable pressure is 3 p.s.i., and the maximum is 5 p.s.i. with the desired range of operation between 3 and 5 p.s.i.

Fuel Flowmeter

The fuel flowmeter measures the amount of fuel delivered to the carburetor. During engine block-test procedures, the fuel flow to the engine is measured by a series of calibrated tubes located in the control room. The tubes are of various sizes to indicate different volumes of fuel flow. Each tube contains a float that can be seen by the operator, and as the fuel flow through the tube varies, the float is either raised or lowered, indicating the amount of fuel flow. From these indications, the operator can determine whether an engine is operating at the correct fuel/air mixture for a given power setting.

In an aircraft installation, the fuel flow indicating system consists of a transmitter and an indicator for each engine. The fuel flow transmitter is conveniently mounted in the engine's accessory section and measures the fuel flow between the engine-driven fuel pump and the carburetor. The transmitter is an electrical device that is connected electrically to the indicator located on the aircraft operator's panel. The reading on the indicator is calibrated to record the amount of fuel flow in pounds of fuel per hour.

Manifold Pressure Indicator

The preferred type of instrument for measuring the manifold pressure is a gage that records the pressure as an absolute pressure reading. A mercury manometer, a tube calibrated in inches, is used during block-test procedures. It is partially filled with mercury and connected to the manifold pressure adapter located on the engine. Since it is impractical to install mercury manometers in an aircraft to record the manifold pressure of the engines, a specially designed manifold pressure gage that indicates absolute manifold pressure in inches of mercury is used.

On the manifold pressure gage, the blue arc represents the range within which operation with the mixture control in the "automatic-lean" position is permissible, and the green arc indicates the range within which the engine must be operated with the mixture control in the "normal" or rich position. The red arc indicates the maximum manifold pressure permissible during takeoff.

The manifold pressure gage range markings and indications vary with different kinds of engines and installations. Figure 10–25 illustrates the dial of a typical manifold pressure gage and shows how the range markings are positioned. The blue arc starts at the 24-in. Hg graduation, the minimum manifold pressure permissible in flight. The arc continues to the 35-in. Hg graduation and shows the range where operation in the "automatic-lean" position is permissible. The green arc starts at 35 in. Hg and continues to the 44-in. Hg graduation, indicating the range in which the operation in the "rich" position is required. Any operation above the value indicated by the high end of the green arc (44 in. Hg on the instrument dial in figure 10–25) would be limited to a continuous operation not to exceed 5 minutes. The red line at 49 in. Hg shows the manifold pressure recommended for takeoff; this pressure should not be exceeded. On installations where water injection is used, a second red line is located on the dial to indicate the maximum permissible manifold pressure for a "wet" takeoff.

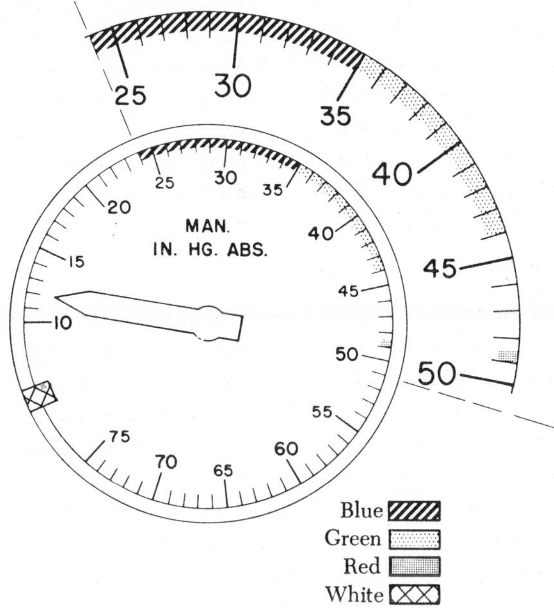

FIGURE 10–25. Manifold pressure gage.

Oil Temperature Indicator

During engine run-in at block test, engine oil temperature readings are taken at the oil inlet and outlet. From these readings, it can be determined if the engine heat transferred to the oil is low, normal, or excessive. This information is of extreme importance during the "breaking-in" process of large reciprocating engines. The oil temperature gage line in the aircraft is connected at the oil inlet to the engine.

Three range markings are used on the oil temperature gage. The red mark in figure 10–26, at 40° C. on the dial, shows the minimum oil temperature permissible for ground operational checks or during flight. The green mark between 60° and 75° C. shows the desired oil temperature for continuous engine operation. The red mark at 100° C. indicates the maximum permissible oil temperature.

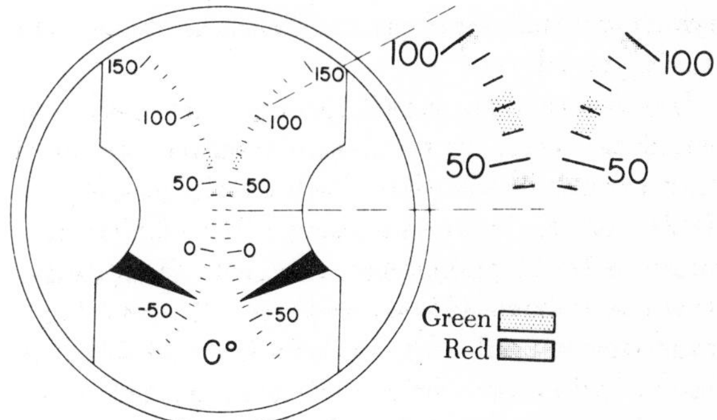

FIGURE 10–26. Oil temperature gage.

Oil Pressure Indicator

The oil pressure on block-test engines is checked at various points. The main oil pressure reading is taken at the pressure side of the oil pump. Other pressure readings are taken from the nose section and blower section; and when internal supercharging is used, a reading is taken from the high- and low-blower clutch.

Generally, there is only one oil pressure gage for each aircraft engine, and the connection is made at the pressure side (outlet) of the main oil pump.

The oil pressure gage dial, marked as shown in figure 10–27, does not show the pressure range or limits for all installations. The actual markings for specific aircraft may be found in the Aircraft Specifications or Type Certificate Data Sheets. The lower red line at 50 p.s.i. indicates the minimum oil pressure permissible in flight. The green arc between 60 to 85 p.s.i. shows the desired operating oil pressure range. The red line at 110 p.s.i. indicates maximum permissible oil pressure.

The oil pressure gage indicates the pressure (in p.s.i.) that the oil of the lubricating system is being supplied to the moving parts of the engine. The engine should be shut down immediately if the gage fails to register pressure when the engine is operating. Excessive oscillation of the gage pointer indicates that there is air in the lines leading to the gage or that some unit of the oil system is functioning improperly.

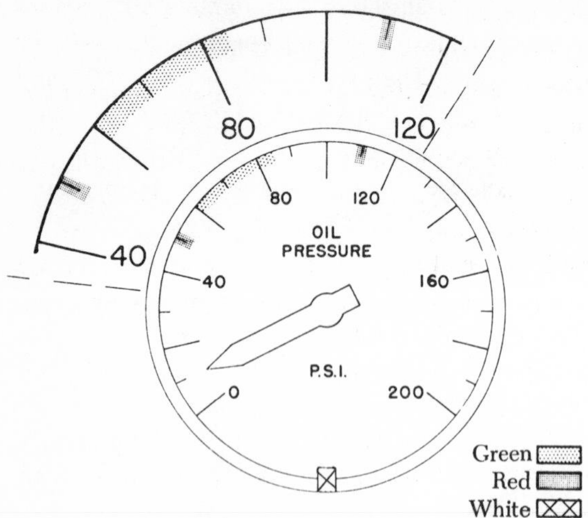

FIGURE 10–27. Oil pressure gage.

Tachometer Indicator

The tachometer shows the engine crankshaft r.p.m. The system used for block testing the engine is the same as the system in the aircraft installation.

Figure 10–28 shows a tachometer with range markings installed on the cover glass. The tachometer, often referred to as "TACH," is calibrated in hundreds with graduations at every 50-r.p.m. interval. The dial shown here starts at 5 (500 r.p.m.) and goes to 40 (4,000 r.p.m.).

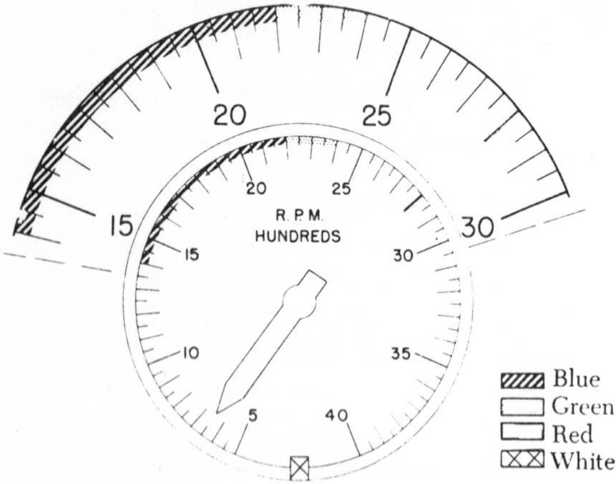

FIGURE 10–28. Tachometer.

The blue arc on the tachometer indicates the r.p.m. range within which auto-lean operation is permitted. The bottom of this arc, 1,400 r.p.m., indicates the minimum r.p.m. desirable in flight. The top of this blue arc, 2,200 r.p.m., indicates the r.p.m. at which the mixture control must be moved to auto-rich. The green arc indicates the r.p.m. range within which auto-rich operation is required. The top of the green arc, 2,400 r.p.m., indicates maximum continuous power. All operation above this r.p.m. is limited in time (usually 5 or 15 min.). The red line indicates the maximum r.p.m. permissible during takeoff; any r.p.m. beyond this value is an overspeed condition.

Cylinder Head Temperature Indicator

During the engine block-test procedures, a pyrometer indicates the cylinder head temperatures of various cylinders on the engine being tested. Thermocouples are connected to several cylinders, and by a selector switch any cylinder head temperature can be indicated on the pyrometer. There is one thermocouple lead and indicator scale for each engine installed in an aircraft.

Cylinder head temperatures are indicated by a gage connected to a thermocouple attached to the cylinder which tests show to be the hottest on an engine in a particular installation. The thermocouple may be placed in a special gasket located under a rear spark plug or in a special well in the top or rear of the cylinder head.

The temperature recorded at either of these points is merely a reference or control temperature; but as long as it is kept within the prescribed limits, the temperatures of the cylinder dome, exhaust valve, and piston will be within a satisfactory range. Since the thermocouple is attached to only one cylinder, it can do no more than give evidence of general engine temperature. While normally it can be assumed that the remaining cylinder temperatures will be lower, conditions such as detonation will not be indicated unless they occur in the cylinder that has the thermocouple attached.

The cylinder head temperature gage range marking is similar to that of the manifold pressure and tachometer indicator. The cylinder head temperature gage illustrated in figure 10–29 is a dual gage that incorporates two separate temperature scales. The scales are calibrated in increments of 10, with numerals at the 0°, 100°, 200°, and 300° graduations. The space between any two graduation marks represents 10° C.

The blue arc on the gage indicates the range within which operation is permitted in auto-lean. The bottom of this arc, 100° C., indicates the minimum desired temperature to ensure efficient engine operation during flight. The top of the blue arc, 230° C., indicates the temperature at which the mixture control must be moved to the "auto-rich" position. The green arc describes the range within which operation must be in auto-rich. The top of this arc, 248° C., indicates maximum continuous power; all operation above this temperature is limited in time (usually 5 to 15 min.). The red line indicates maximum permissible temperature, 260° C.

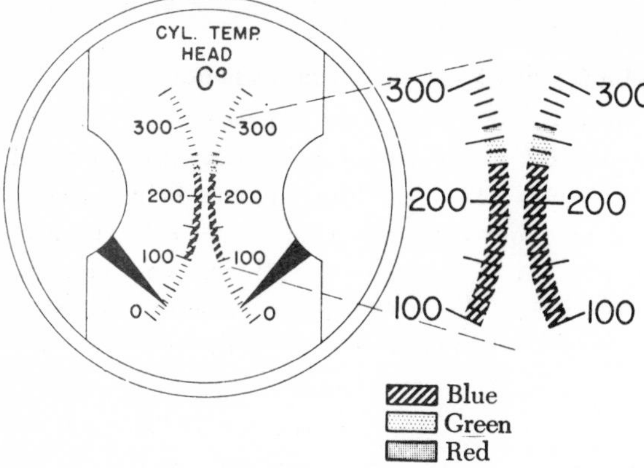

FIGURE 10–29. Cylinder head temperature gage.

Torquemeter

The torque pressure system is used to indicate actual engine power output at various power settings. The torquemeter indicates the amount of torque pressure in p.s.i. The instrument is usually numbered as shown in figure 10–30 and calibrated at 5-p.s.i. intervals.

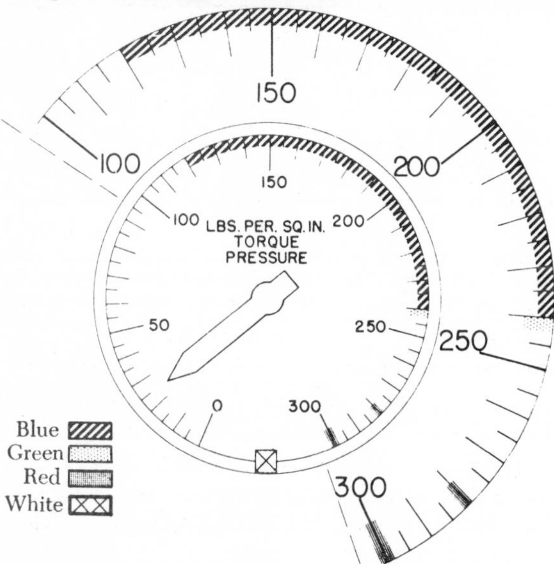

FIGURE 10–30. Torquemeter.

The blue arc on the torquemeter indicates the permissible range of operation in auto-lean. The bottom of this arc, 120 p.s.i., is the minimum desirable during flight, as determined by the particular engine characteristics. The top of this arc, 240 p.s.i., indicates the torque pressure at which the mixture control must be moved to "auto-rich."

The green line indicates the point of maximum continuous power. At and above this point the "auto-rich" setting must be used. Any operation above this indicated torque pressure must be limited in time (usually 5 to 15 min.). If a green arc is used in place of the green line, the bottom of the arc is the point above which operation must be limited.

Two red radial marks are generally shown on the torquemeter. The short red line at 280 p.s.i. indicates maximum torque pressure when water injection is not used. The long red line (300 p.s.i.) represents maximum torque pressure when using water injection.

Suction Gage

The suction gage is not classed as an engine instrument, since it does not indicate any information in determining efficient engine operation. The mechanic is concerned with it because he is responsible for adjusting the suction regulator and checking the suction gage reading during the engine operational checks.

The suction gage (figure 10–31) is calibrated to indicate reduction of pressure below atmospheric pressure in inches of mercury; the space between the graduation lines represents 0.2 in. Hg. The red line at 3.75 in. Hg indicates minimum desirable suction. The green arc shows the desirable suction range, 3.75 in. to 4.25 in. Hg. The red line at 4.25 in. Hg indicates the maximum desirable suction.

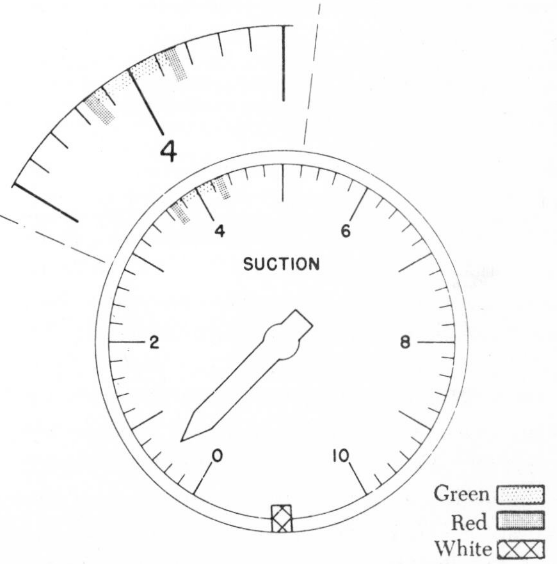

FIGURE 10–31. Suction gage.

Oil-Weighing System

The oil-weighing system determines oil consumption during engine run-in at block test and measures the exact amount of oil consumed by the engine during various periods of operation. The system consists of a tank supplying oil to the engine, an oil-inlet line to the engine, a return line from the engine oil scavenging and cooling system, and a weighing scale that registers weights up to and including the weight of the full oil tank. The oil consumed by the engine is determined merely by subtracting the scale reading at any given time from the full-tank weight.

Metering Differential Manometer

The metering differential manometer, used during block testing, is a 100-in., single-tube water manometer (a gage for measuring pressure). It is connected to the carburetor in such a manner that it measures the pressure difference (air metering force) between A-chamber and B-chamber (on engines that use pressure injection carburetion). Through the use of this instrument, the metering characteristics of the carburetor are closely observed during the engine run-in tests.

General Instrumentation

Many of the miscellaneous gages and devices indicate only that a system is functioning or has failed to function. On some aircraft a warning light illuminates when the fuel presure is low. A similar light is used for oil pressure systems.

RECIPROCATING ENGINE OPERATION

General

The operation of the powerplant is controlled from the cockpit. Some installations have numerous control handles and levers connected to the engine by rods, cables, bellcranks, pulleys, etc. The control handles, in most cases, are conveniently mounted on quadrants in the cockpit. Placards or markings are placed on the quadrant to indicate the functions and positions of the levers. In some installations, friction clutches are installed to hold the controls in place.

Manifold pressure, r.p.m., engine temperature, oil temperature, carburetor air temperature, and the fuel/air ratio can be controlled by manipulating the cockpit controls. Coordinating the movement of the controls with the instrument readings protects against exceeding operating limits.

Engine operation is usually limited by specified operating ranges of the following:

(1) Crankshaft speed (r.p.m.).
(2) Manifold pressure.
(3) Cylinder head temperature.
(4) Carburetor air temperature.
(5) Oil temperature.
(6) Oil pressure.
(7) Fuel pressure.
(8) Fuel/air mixture setting.

The procedures, pressures, temperatures and r.p.m.'s used throughout this section are solely for the purpose of illustration and do not have general application. The operating procedures and limits used on individual makes and models of aircraft engines vary considerably from the values shown here. For exact information regarding a specific engine model, consult the applicable instructions.

Engine Instruments

The term "engine instruments" usually includes all instruments required to measure and indicate the functioning of the powerplant. The engine instruments are generally installed on the instrument panel so that all of them can easily be observed at one time.

Some of the simple, light aircraft may be equipped only with a tachometer, oil pressure gage, and oil temperature gages. The heavier, more complex aircraft will have all or part of the following engine instruments:

(1) Oil pressure indicator and warning system.
(2) Oil temperature indicator.
(3) Fuel pressure indicator and warning system.
(4) Carburetor air temperature indicator.
(5) Cylinder head temperature indicator for air-cooled engines.
(6) Manifold pressure indicator.
(7) Tachometer.
(8) Fuel quantity indicator.
(9) Fuel flowmeter or fuel mixture indicator.
(10) Oil quantity indicator.
(11) Augmentation liquid quantity indicator.
(12) Fire-warning indicators.
(13) A means to indicate when the propeller is in reverse pitch.
(14) BMEP (brake mean effective pressure) indicator.

Engine Starting

Correct starting technique is an important part of engine operation. Improper procedures often are used because some of the basic principles involved in engine operation are misunderstood. Typical procedures for starting reciprocating engines are discussed in the Airframe and Powerplant Mechanics General Handbook, AC 65–9, Chapter 11. In general, two different starting procedures will cover all engines. One procedure is for engines using float-type carburetors, and the other for engines with pressure-injection carburetors. The specific manufacturer's procedures for a particular engine and aircraft combination should always be followed.

Engine Warm-up

Proper engine warm-up is important, particularly when the condition of the engine is unknown. Improperly adjusted idle mixture, intermittently firing spark plugs, and improperly adjusted engine valves all have an overlapping effect on engine stability. Therefore, the warm-up should be made at the engine speed where maximum engine stability is obtained. Experience has shown that the optimum warm-up speed is from 1,000 to 1,600 r.p.m. The actual speed selected should be the speed at which engine operation is the smoothest, since the smoothest operation is an indication that all phases of engine operation are the most stable.

Most Pratt and Whitney engines incorporate temperature-compensated oil pressure relief valves. This type of relief valve results in high engine oil pressures immediately after the engine starts, if oil temperatures are below 40° C. Consequently, start the warm-up of these engines at approximately 1,000 r.p.m. and then move to the higher, more stable engine speed as soon as oil temperature reaches 40° C.

During warm-up, watch the instruments associated with engine operation. This will aid in making sure that all phases of engine operation are normal. For example, engine oil pressure should be indicated within 30 sec. after the start. Furthermore, if the oil pressure is not up to or above normal within 1 min. after the engine starts, the engine should be shut down. Cylinder head or coolant temperatures should be observed continually to see that they do not exceed the maximum allowable limit.

A lean mixture should not be used to hasten the warm-up. Actually, at the warm-up r.p.m., there is very little difference in the mixture supplied to the engine, whether the mixture is in a "rich" or "lean" position, since metering in this power range is governed by throttle position.

Carburetor heat can be used as required under conditions leading to ice formation. For engines equipped with a float-type carburetor, it is desirable to raise the carburetor air temperature during warm-up to prevent ice formation and to ensure smooth operation.

The magneto safety check can be performed during warm-up. Its purpose is to ensure that all ignition connections are secure and that the ignition system will permit operation at the higher power settings used during later phases of the ground check. The time required for proper warm-up gives ample opportunity to perform this simple check, which may disclose a condition that would make it inadvisable to continue operation until after corrections have been made.

The magneto safety check is conducted with the propeller in the high r.p.m. (low pitch) position, at approximately 1,000 r.p.m. Move the ignition switch from "both" to "right" and return to "both"; from "both" to "left" and return to "both"; from "both" to "off" momentarily and return to "both."

While switching from "both" to a single magneto position, a slight but noticeable drop in r.p.m. should occur. This indicates that the opposite magneto has been properly grounded out. Complete cutting out of the engine when switching from "both" to "off" indicates that both magnetos are grounded properly. Failure to obtain any drop while in the single magneto position, or failure of the engine to cut out while switching to "off" indicates that one or both ground connections are not secured.

Ground Check

The ground check is performed to evaluate the functioning of the engine by comparing power input, as measured by manifold pressure, with power output, as measured by r.p.m. or torque pressure.

The engine may be capable of producing a prescribed power, even rated takeoff, and not be functioning properly. Only by comparing the manifold pressure required during the check against a known standard will an unsuitable condition be disclosed. The magneto check can also fail to show up shortcomings, since the allowable r.p.m. dropoff is only a measure of an improperly functioning ignition system and is not necessarily affected by other factors. Conversely, it is possible for the magneto check to prove satisfactory with an unsatisfactory condition present elsewhere in the engine.

The ground check is made after the engine is thoroughly warm. It consists of checking the operation of the powerplant and accessory equipment by ear, by visual inspection, and by proper interpretation of instrument readings, control movements, and switch reactions.

During the ground check, the aircraft should be headed into the wind, if possible, to take advantage of the cooling airflow. A ground check may be performed as follows:

Control Position Check—

Cowl flaps....................Open.
Mixture ....Rich.
Propeller ....High r.p.m.
Carburetor heat..........Cold.
Carburetor air filter ..As required.
Supercharger control..Low, neutral, or off position (where applicable).

Procedure—

(1) Check propeller according to propeller manufacturer's instruction.
(2) Open throttle to manifold pressure equal to field barometric pressure.
(3) Switch from "both" to "right" and return to "both." Switch from "both" to "left" and return to "both." Observe the r.p.m. drop while operating on the right and left positions. The maximum drop should not exceed that specified by the engine manufacturer.
(4) Check the fuel pressure and oil pressure. They must be within the established tolerance for the subject engine.
(5) Note r.p.m.
(6) Retard throttle.

In addition to the operations outlined above, check the functioning of various items of aircraft equipment, such as generator systems, hydraulic systems, etc.

Propeller Pitch Check

The propeller is checked to ensure proper operation of the pitch control and the pitch-change mechanism. The operation of a controllable pitch propeller is checked by the indications of the tachometer and manifold pressure gage when the propeller governor control is moved from one position to another. Because each type of propeller requires a different procedure, the applicable manufacturer's instructions should be followed.

Power Check

Specific r.p.m. and manifold pressure relationship should be checked during each ground check. This can be done at the time the engine is run-up to make the magneto check. The basic idea of this check is to measure the performance of the engine against an established standard. Calibration tests have determined that the engine is capable of delivering a given power at a given r.p.m. and manifold pressure. The original calibration, or measurement of power, is made by means of a dynamometer. During the ground check, power is measured with the propeller. With constant conditions of air density, the propeller, at any fixed-pitch position, will always require the same r.p.m. to absorb the same horsepower from the engine. This characteristic is used in determining the condition of the engine.

With the governor control set for full low pitch, the propeller operates as a fixed-pitch propeller. Under these conditions, the manifold pressure for any specific engine, with the mixture control in auto-rich, indicates whether all the cylinders are operating properly. With one or more dead or intermittently firing cylinders, the operating cylinders must provide more power for a given r.p.m. Consequently, the carburetor throttle must be opened further, resulting in higher manifold pressure. Different engines of the same model using the same propeller installation and in the same geographical location should require the same manifold pressure, within 1 in. Hg, to obtain r.p.m. when the barometer and temperature are at the same readings. A higher-than-normal manifold pressure usually indicates a dead cylinder or late ignition timing. An excessively low manifold pressure for a particular r.p.m. usually indicates that the ignition timing is early. Early ignition can cause detonation and loss of power at takeoff power settings.

Before starting the engine, observe the manifold pressure gage, which should read approximately atmospheric (barometric) pressure when the engine is not running. At sea level this is approximately 30 in. Hg, and at fields above sea level the atmospheric pressure will be less, depending on the height above sea level.

When the engine is started and then accelerated, the manifold pressure will decrease until about 1,600 or 1,700 r.p.m. is reached, and then it will begin to rise. At approximately 2,000 r.p.m., with the propeller in low-pitch position, the manifold pressure should be the same as the field barometric pressure. If the manifold pressure gage reading (field barometric pressure) was 30 in. Hg before starting the engine, the pressure reading should return to 30 in. Hg at approximately 2,000 r.p.m. If the manifold pressure gage reads 26 in. Hg before starting, it should read 26 in. Hg again at approximately 2,000 r.p.m. The exact r.p.m. will vary with various models of engines or because of varying propeller characteristics. In certain installations, the r.p.m. needed to secure field barometric pressure may be as high as 2,200 r.p.m. However, once the required r.p.m. has been established for an installation, any appreciable variation indicates some malfunctioning. This variation may occur because the low-pitch stop of the propeller has not been properly set or because the carburetor or ignition system is not functioning properly.

The accuracy of the power check may be affected by the following variables:

(1) ***Wind.*** Any appreciable air movement (5 m.p.h. or more) will change the air load on the propeller blade when it is in the fixed-pitch position. A head wind will increase the r.p.m. obtainable with a given manifold pressure. A tail wind will decrease the r.p.m.

(2) ***Atmospheric Temperatures.*** The effects of variations in atmospheric temperature tend to cancel each other. Higher carburetor intake and cylinder temperatures tend to lower the r.p.m., but the propeller load is lightened because of the less dense air.

(3) ***Engine and Induction System Temperature.*** If the cylinder and carburetor temperatures are high because of factors other than atmospheric temperature, a low r.p.m. will result since the power will be lowered without a compensating lowering of the propeller load.

(4) ***Oil Temperature.*** Cold oil will tend to hold down the r.p.m. since the higher viscosity results in increased friction horsepower losses.

The addition of a torquemeter can increase the accuracy of the power check by providing another measurement of power output. As long as the check is performed with the blades in a known fixed-pitch position, the torquemeter provides no additional information, but its use can increase accuracy; in the frequent instances where the tachometer scales are graduated coarsely, the tachometer gage reading may be a more convenient source of the desired information.

Ignition System Operational Check

In performing the ignition system operational check (magneto check), the power-absorbing characteristics of the propeller in the low fixed-pitch position are utilized. In switching to individual magnetos, cutting out the opposite plugs results in a slower rate of combustion, which gives the same effect as retarding the spark advance. The drop in engine speed is a measure of the power loss at this slower combustion rate.

When the magneto check is performed, a drop in torquemeter pressure indication is a good supplement to the variation in r.p.m.; and in cases where the tachometer scale is graduated coarsely, the torquemeter variation may give more positive evidence of the power change when switching to the individual magneto condition. A loss in torquemeter pressure not to exceed 10% can be expected when operating on a single magneto. By comparing the r.p.m. drop with a known standard, the following are determined:

(1) Proper timing of each magneto.

(2) General engine performance as evidenced by smooth operation.

(3) Additional check of the proper connection of the ignition leads.

Any unusual roughness on either magneto is an indication of faulty ignition caused by plug fouling or by malfunctioning of the ignition system. The operator should be very sensitive to engine roughness during this check. Lack of dropoff in r.p.m. may be an indication of faulty grounding of one side of the ignition system. Complete cutting out when switching to one magneto is definite evidence that its side of the ignition system is not functioning. Excessive difference in r.p.m. dropoff between the left and right switch positions can indicate a difference in timing between the left and right magnetos.

Sufficient time should be given the check on each single switch position to permit complete stabilization of engine speed and manifold pressure. There is a tendency to perform this check too rapidly with resultant wrong indications. Single ignition operation for as long as 1 min. is not excessive.

Another point that must be emphasized is the danger of a sticking tachometer. The tachometer should be tapped lightly to make sure the indicator needle moves freely. In some cases, tachometer sticking has caused errors in indication to the extent of 100 r.p.m. Under such conditions the ignition system could have had as much as a 200-r.p.m. drop with only a 100-r.p.m. drop indicated on the instrument. In most cases, tapping the instrument eliminates the sticking and results in accurate readings.

In recording the results of the ignition system check, record the amount of the total r.p.m. drop which occurs rapidly and the amount which occurs slowly. This breakdown in r.p.m. drop provides a means of pinpointing certain troubles in the ignition system. It can save a lot of time and unnecessary work by confining maintenance to the specific part of the ignition system which is responsible for the trouble.

Fast r.p.m. drop is usually the result of either faulty spark plugs or faulty ignition harness. This is true because faulty plugs or leads take effect at once. The cylinder goes dead or starts firing intermittently the instant the switch is moved from "both" to the "right" or "left" position.

Slow r.p.m. drop usually is caused by incorrect ignition timing or faulty valve adjustment. With late ignition timing, the charge is fired too late with relation to piston travel for the combustion pressures to build up to the maximum at the proper time. The result is a power loss greater than normal for single ignition because of the lower peak pressures obtained in the cylinder. However, this power loss does not occur as rapidly as that which accompanies a dead spark plug. This explains the slow r.p.m. drop as compared to the instantaneous drop with a dead plug or defective lead. Incorrect valve clearances, through their effect on valve overlap, can cause the mixture to be too rich or too lean. The too-rich or too-lean mixture may affect one plug more than another, because of the plug location, and show up as a slow r.p.m. drop on the ignition check.

Cruise Mixture Check

The cruise mixture check is a check of carburetor metering. Checking the carburetor metering characteristics at 200- to 300-r.p.m. intervals, from 800 r.p.m. to the ignition system check speed, gives a complete pattern for the basic carburetor performance.

To perform this test, set up a specified engine speed with the propeller in full low pitch. The first check is made at 800 r.p.m. With the carburetor mixture control in the "automatic-rich" position, read the manifold pressure. With the throttle remaining in the same position, move the mixture control to the "automatic lean" position. Read and record the engine speed and manifold pressure readings. Repeat this check at 1,000, 1,200, 1,500, 1,700, and 2,000 r.p.m. or at the r.p.m.'s specified by the manufacturer. Guard against a sticking instrument by tapping the tachometer.

Moving the mixture control from the "auto-rich" position to the "auto-lean" position checks the cruise mixture. In general, the speed should not increase more than 25 r.p.m. or decrease more than 75 r.p.m. during the change from "auto-rich" to "auto-lean."

For example, suppose that the r.p.m. change is above 100 for the 800 to 1,500 r.p.m. checks; it is obvious that the probable cause is an incorrect idle mixture. When the idle is adjusted properly, carburetion will be correct throughout the range.

Idle Speed and Idle Mixture Checks

Plug fouling difficulty is the inevitable result of failure to provide a proper idle mixture setting. The tendency seems to be to adjust the idle mixture on the extremely rich side and to compensate for this by adjusting the throttle stop to a relatively high r.p.m. for minimum idling. With a properly adjusted idle mixture setting, it is possible to run the engine at idle r.p.m. for long periods. Such a setting will result in a minimum of plug fouling and exhaust smoking and it will pay dividends from the savings on the aircraft brakes after landing and while taxiing.

If the wind is not too strong, the idle mixture setting can be checked easily during the ground check as follows:

(1) Close throttle.

(2) Move the mixture control to the "idle cutoff" position and observe the change in r.p.m. Return the mixture control back to the "rich" position before engine cutoff.

As the mixture control lever is moved into idle cutoff, and before normal dropoff, one of two things may occur momentarily:

(1) The engine speed may increase. An increase in r.p.m., but less than that recommended by the manufacturer (usually 20 r.p.m.), indicates proper mixture strength. A greater increase indicates that the mixture is too rich.

(2) The engine speed may not increase or may drop immediately. This indicates that the idle mixture is too lean.

The idle mixture should be set to give a mixture slightly richer than best power, resulting in a 10- to 20-r.p.m. rise after idle cutoff.

The idle mixture of engines equipped with electric primers can be checked by flicking the primer switch momentarily and noting any change in manifold pressure and r.p.m. A decrease in r.p.m. and an increase in manifold pressure will occur when the primer is energized if the idle mixture is too rich. If the idle mixture is adjusted too lean, the r.p.m. will increase and manifold pressure will decrease.

Two-Speed Supercharger Check

To check the operation of the two-speed blower mechanism, set the engine speed to a sufficiently high r.p.m. to obtain the minimum oil pressure required for clutch operation. Move the supercharger control to the "high" position. A momentary drop in oil pressure should accompany the shift. Open the throttle to obtain not more than 30 in. Hg manifold pressure. When the engine speed has stabilized, observe the manifold pressure, and shift the supercharger control to the "low" position without moving the throttle. A sudden decrease in manifold pressure indicates that the two-speed supercharger drive is functioning properly. If no decrease occurs, the clutch may be inoperative.

As soon as the change in manifold pressure has been checked, reduce the engine speed to 1,000 r.p.m., or less. If the shift of the supercharger did not appear to be satisfactory, operate the engine at 1,000 r.p.m. for 2 or 3 min. to permit heat generated during the shift to dissipate from the clutches, and then repeat the shifting procedure. Blower shifts should be made without hesitation or dwelling between the control positions to avoid dragging or slipping the clutches. Make sure the supercharger control is in the "low" position when the ground check is completed.

Acceleration and Deceleration Checks

The acceleration check is made with the mixture control in both auto-rich and auto-lean. Move the throttle from idle to takeoff smoothly and rapidly. The engine r.p.m. should increase without hesitation and with no evidence of engine backfire.

This check will, in many cases, show up borderline conditions that will not be revealed by any of the other checks. This is true because the high cylinder pressures developed during this check put added strain on both the ignition system and the fuel metering system. This added strain is sufficient to point out certain defects that otherwise go unnoticed. Engines must be capable of rapid acceleration, since in an emergency, such as a go-around during landing, the ability of an engine to accelerate rapidly is sometimes the difference between a successful go-around and a crash landing.

The deceleration check is made while retarding the throttle from the acceleration check. Note the engine behavior. The r.p.m. should decrease smoothly and evenly. There should be little or no tendency for the engine to afterfire.

Engine Stopping

With each type of carburetor installation, specific procedures are used in stopping the engine. The general procedure outlined in the following paragraphs reduces the time required for stopping, minimizes backfiring tendencies, and, most important, prevents overheating of tightly baffled air-cooled engines during operation on the ground.

In stopping any aircraft engine, the controls are set as follows, irrespective of carburetor type or fuel system installation.

(1) Cowl flaps are always placed in the "full open" position to avoid overheating the engine, and are left in that position after the engine is stopped to prevent engine residual heat from deteriorating the ignition system.

(2) Oil cooler shutters should be "full open" to allow the oil temperature to return to normal.

(3) Intercooler shutters are kept in the "full open" position.

(4) Carburetor air-heater control is left in the "cold" position to prevent damage which may occur from backfire.

(5) Turbocharger waste gates are set in the "full open" position.

(6) Two-speed supercharger control is placed in the "low blower" position.

(7) A two-position propeller will usually be stopped with the control set in the "high pitch" (decrease r.p.m.) position. Open the throttle to approximately 1,200 r.p.m. and shift the propeller control to "high pitch" position. Allow the engine to operate approximately 1 minute before stopping, so that the oil dumped into the engine from the propeller may be scavenged and returned to the oil tank. However, to inspect the propeller piston for galling and wear and for other special purposes, this propeller may be stopped with the propeller control in "low pitch" (increase r.p.m.) position when the engine is stopped.

No mention is made of the throttle, mixture control, fuel selector valve, and ignition switches in the preceding set of directions because the operation of these controls varies with the type of carburetor used with the engine.

Engines equipped with a float-type carburetor without an idle cutoff unit are stopped as follows:

(1) Adjust the throttle to obtain an idling speed of approximately 600 to 800 r.p.m., depending on the type of engine.

(2) Close the fuel selector valve.

(3) Open the throttle slowly until the engine is operating at approximately 800 to 1,000 r.p.m.

(4) Observe the fuel pressure. When it drops to zero, turn the ignition switch to the "off" position and simultaneously move the throttle slowly to the "full open" position. This operation will remove the accelerating charge from the induction system and avoid the possibility of accidental starting.

(5) When the engine has stopped, place the fuel selector valve in the "on" position and refill the carburetor and fuel lines by using the auxiliary pump.

An engine equipped with a carburetor incorporating an idle cutoff is stopped as follows:

(1) Idle the engine by setting the throttle for 800 to 1,000 r.p.m.

(2) Move the mixture control to the "idle cutoff" position. In a pressure-type carburetor, this causes the cloverleaf valve to stop the discharge of fuel through the discharge nozzle. In a float-type carburetor, it equalizes the pressure in the float chamber and at the discharge nozzle.

(3) After the propeller has stopped rotating, place the ignition switch in the "off" position.

BASIC ENGINE OPERATING PRINCIPLES

A thorough understanding of the basic principles on which a reciprocating engine operates and the many factors which affect its operation is necessary to diagnose engine malfunctions. Some of these basic principles are reviewed not as a mere repetition of basic theory, but as a concrete, practical discussion of what makes for good or bad engine performance.

The conventional reciprocating aircraft engine operates on the four-stroke-cycle principle. Pressure from burning gases acts upon a piston, causing it to reciprocate back and forth in an enclosed cylinder. This reciprocating motion of the piston is changed into rotary motion by a crankshaft, to which the piston is coupled by means of a connecting rod. The crankshaft, in turn, is attached or geared to the aircraft propeller. Therefore, the rotary motion of the crankshaft causes the propeller to revolve. Thus, the motion of the propeller is a direct result of the forces acting upon the piston as it moves back and forth in the cylinder.

Four strokes of the piston, two up and two down, are required to provide one power impulse to the crankshaft. Each of these strokes is considered an event in the cycle of engine operation. Ignition of the gases (fuel/air mixture) at the end of the second, or compression, stroke makes a fifth event. Thus, the five events which make up a cycle of operation occur in four strokes of the piston.

As the piston moves downward on the first stroke (intake), the intake valve is open and the exhaust valve is closed. As air is drawn through the carburetor gasoline is introduced into the stream of air forming a combustible mixture.

On the second stroke, the intake closes and the combustible mixture is compressed as the piston moves upward. This is the compression stroke.

At the correct instant, an electric spark jumps across the terminals of the spark plug and ignites the fuel/air mixture. The ignition of the fuel/air mixture is timed to occur just slightly before the piston reaches top dead center.

As the mixture burns, temperature and pressure rise rapidly. The pressure reaches maximum just after the piston has passed top center. The expanding and burning gas forces the piston downward, transmitting energy to the crankshaft. This is the power stroke. Both intake and exhaust valves are closed at the start of the power stroke.

Near the end of the power stroke, the exhaust valve opens, and the burned gases start to escape through the exhaust port. On its return stroke, the piston forces out the remaining gases. This stroke, the exhaust stroke, ends the cycle. With the introduction of a new charge through the intake port, the action is repeated and the cycle of events occurs over and over again as long as the engine is in operation.

Ignition of the fuel charge must occur at a specific time in relation to crankshaft travel. The igniting device is timed to ignite the charge just before the piston reaches top center on the compression stroke. Igniting the charge at this point permits maximum pressure to build up at a point slightly after the piston passes over top dead center. For ideal combustion, the point of ignition should vary with engine speed and with degree of compression, mixture strength, and other factors governing the rate of burning. However, certain factors, such as the limited range of operating r.p.m. and the dangers of operating with incorrect spark settings, prohibit the use of variable spark control in most instances. Therefore, most aircraft ignition system units are timed to ignite the fuel/air charge at one fixed position (advanced).

On early models of the four-stroke-cycle engine, the intake valve opened at top center (beginning of the intake stroke). It closed at bottom center (end of intake stroke). The exhaust valve opened at bottom center (end of power stroke) and closed at top center (end of exhaust stroke). More efficient engine operation can be obtained by opening the intake valve several degrees before top center and closing it several degrees after bottom center. Opening the exhaust valve before bottom center, and closing it after top center, also improves engine performance. Since the intake valve opens before top-center exhaust stroke and the exhaust valve closes after top-center intake stroke, there is a period where both the intake and exhaust valves are open at the same time. This is known as valve lap or valve overlap. In valve timing, reference to piston or crankshaft position is always made in terms of before or after the top and bottom center points, *e.g.*, ATC, BTC, ABC, and BBC.

Opening the intake valve before the piston reaches top center starts the intake event while the piston is still moving up on the exhaust stroke. This aids in increasing the volume of charge admitted into the cylinder. The selected point at which the intake valve opens depends on the r.p.m. at which the engine normally operates. At low r.p.m., this early timing results in poor efficiency since the incoming charge is not drawn into and the exhaust gases are not expelled out of the cylinder with sufficient speed to develop the necessary momentum. Also, at low r.p.m. the cylinder is not well scavenged, and residual gases mix with the incoming fuel and are trapped during the compression stroke. Some of the incoming mixture is also lost through the open exhaust port. However, the advantages obtained at normal operating r.p.m. more than make up for the poor efficiency at low r.p.m. Another advantage of this valve timing is the increased fuel vaporization and beneficial cooling of the piston and cylinder.

Delaying the closing of the intake valve takes advantage of the inertia of the rapidly moving fuel/air mixture entering the cylinder. This ramming effect increases the charge over that which would be taken in if the intake valve closed at bottom center (end of intake stroke). The intake valve is actually open during the latter part of the exhaust stroke, all of the intake stroke, and the first part of the compression stroke. Fuel/air mixture is taken in during all this time.

The early opening and late closing of the exhaust valve goes along with the intake valve timing to improve engine efficiency. The exhaust valve opens on the power stroke, several crankshaft degrees before the piston reaches bottom center. This early opening aids in obtaining better scavenging of the burned gases. It also results in improved cooling of the cylinders, because of the early escape of the hot gases. Actually, on aircraft engines, the major portion of the exhaust gases, and the unused heat, escapes before the piston reaches bottom center. The burned gases continue to escape as the piston passes bottom center, moves upward on the exhaust stroke, and starts the next intake stroke. The late closing of the exhaust valve still further improves scavenging by taking advantage of the inertia of the rapidly moving outgoing gases. The exhaust valve is actually open during the latter part of the power stroke, all of the exhaust stroke, and the first part of the intake stroke.

From this description of valve timing, it can be seen that the intake and exhaust valves are open at the same time on the latter part of the exhaust stroke and the first part of the intake stroke. During this valve overlap period, the last of the burned gases are escaping through the exhaust port while the fresh charge is entering through the intake port.

Many aircraft engines are supercharged. Supercharging increases the pressure of the air or fuel/air mixture before it enters the cylinder. In other words, the air or fuel/air mixture is forced into the cylinder rather than being drawn in. Supercharging increases engine efficiency and makes it possible for an engine to maintain its efficiency at high altitudes. This is true because the higher pressure packs more charge into the cylinder during the intake event. This increase in weight of charge results in corresponding increase in power. In addition, the higher pressure of the incoming gases more forcibly ejects the burned gases out through the exhaust port. This results in better scavenging of the cylinder.

Combustion Process

Normal combustion occurs when the fuel/air mixture ignites in the cylinder and burns progressively at a fairly uniform rate across the combustion chamber. When ignition is properly timed, maximum pressure is built up just after the piston has passed top dead center at the end of the compression stroke.

The flame fronts start at each spark plug and burn in more or less wavelike forms (figure 10–32). The velocity of the flame travel is influenced by the type of fuel, the ratio of the fuel/air mixture, and the pressure and temperature of the fuel mixture. With normal combustion, the flame travel is about 100 ft./sec. The temperature and pressure within the cylinder rises at a normal rate as the fuel/air mixture burns.

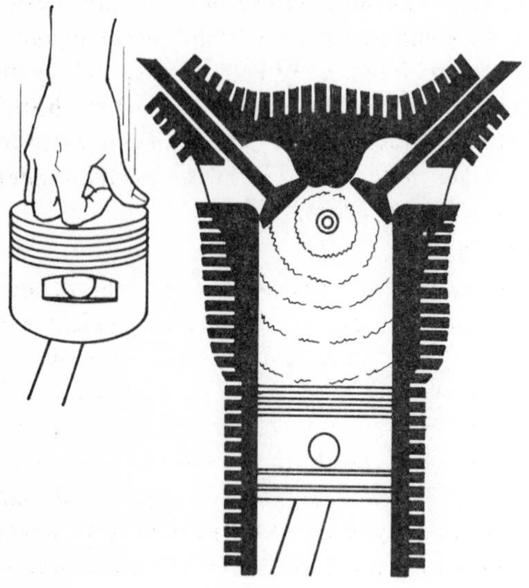

FIGURE 10–32. Normal combustion within a cylinder.

There is a limit, however, to the amount of compression and the degree of temperature rise that can be tolerated within an engine cylinder and still permit normal combustion. All fuels have critical limits of temperature and compression. Beyond this limit, they will ignite spontaneously and burn with explosive violence. This instantaneous and explosive burning of the fuel/air mixture or, more accurately, of the latter portion of the charge, is called detonation.

As previously mentioned, during normal combustion the flame fronts progress from the point of ignition across the cylinder. These flame fronts compress the gases ahead of them. At the same time, the gases are being compressed by the upward movement of the piston. If the total compression on the remaining unburned gases exceeds the critical point, detonation occurs. Detonation (figure 10–33) then, is the spontaneous combustion of the unburned charge ahead of the flame fronts after ignition of the charge.

The explosive burning during detonation results in an extremely rapid pressure rise. This rapid pressure rise and the high instantaneous temperature, combined with the high turbulence generated,

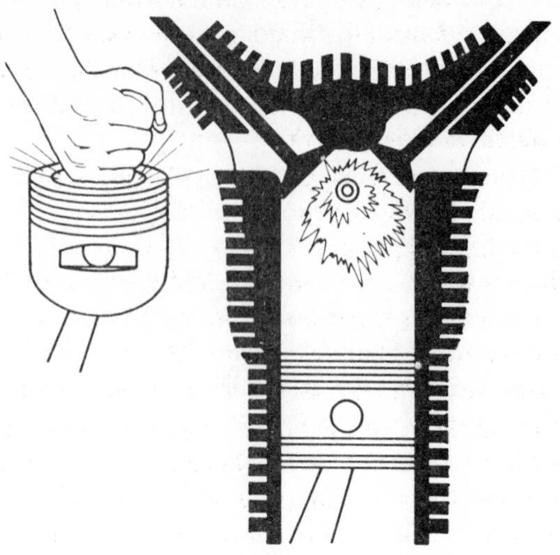

FIGURE 10–33. Detonation within a cylinder.

cause a "scrubbing" action on the cylinder and the piston. This can burn a hole completely through the piston.

The critical point of detonation varies with the ratio of fuel to air in the mixture. Therefore, the detonation characteristic of the mixture can be controlled by varying the fuel/air ratio. At high power output, combustion pressures and temperatures are higher than they are at low or medium power. Therefore, at high power the fuel/air ratio is made richer than is needed for good combustion at medium or low power output. This is done because, in general, a rich mixture will not detonate as readily as a lean mixture.

Unless detonation is heavy, there is no cockpit evidence of its presence. Light to medium detonation does not cause noticeable roughness, temperature increase, or loss of power. As a result, it can be present during takeoff and high-power climb without being known to the crew.

In fact, the effects of detonation are often not discovered until after teardown of the engine. When the engine is overhauled, however, the presence of severe detonation during its operation is indicated by dished piston heads, collapsed valve heads, broken ring lands, or eroded portions of valves, pistons, or cylinder heads.

The basic protection from detonation is provided in the design of the engine carburetor setting, which automatically supplies the rich mixtures required for detonation suppression at high power; the rating limitations, which include the maximum operating temperatures; and selection of the correct grade of fuel. The design factors, cylinder cooling, magneto timing, mixture distribution, supercharging, and carburetor setting are taken care of in the design and development of the engine and its method of installation in the aircraft.

The remaining responsibility for prevention of detonation rests squarely in the hands of the ground and flight crews. They are responsible for observance of r.p.m. and manifold pressure limits. Proper use of supercharger and fuel mixture, and maintenance of suitable cylinder head and carburetor-air temperatures are entirely in their control.

Pre-ignition, as the name implies, means that combustion takes place within the cylinder before the timed spark jumps across the spark plug terminals. This condition can often be traced to excessive carbon or other deposits which cause local hot spots. Detonation often leads to pre-ignition. However, pre-ignition may also be caused by high-power operation on excessively lean mixtures. Pre-ignition is usually indicated in the cockpit by engine roughness, backfiring, and by a sudden increase in cylinder head temperature.

Any area within the combustion chamber which becomes incandescent will serve as an igniter in advance of normal timed ignition and cause combustion earlier than desired. Pre-ignition may be caused by an area roughened and heated by detonation erosion. A cracked valve or piston, or a broken spark plug insulator may furnish a hot point which serves as a "glow plug."

The hot spot can be caused by deposits on the chamber surfaces resulting from the use of leaded fuels. Normal carbon deposits can also cause pre-ignition. Specifically, pre-ignition is a condition similar to early timing of the spark. The charge in the cylinder is ignited before the required time for normal engine firing. However, do not confuse pre-ignition with the spark which occurs too early in the cycle. Pre-ignition is caused by a hot spot in the combustion chamber, not by incorrect ignition timing. The hot spot may be due to either an overheated cylinder or a defect within the cylinder.

The most obvious method of correcting pre-ignition is to reduce the cylinder temperature. The immediate step is to retard the throttle. This reduces the amount of fuel charge and the amount of heat generated. If a supercharger is in use and is in high ratio, it should be returned to low ratio to lower the charge temperature. Following this, the mixture should be enriched, if possible, to lower combustion temperature.

If the engine is at high power when pre-ignition occurs, retarding the throttle for a few seconds may provide enough cooling to chip off some of the lead, or other deposit, within the combustion chamber. These chipped-off particles pass out through the exhaust. They are visible at night as a shower of sparks. If retarding the throttle does not permit a return to uninterrupted normal power operation, deposits may be removed by a sudden cooling shock treatment. Such treatments are water injection, alcohol from the deicing system, full-cold carburetor air, or any other method that provides sudden cooling to the cylinder chamber.

Backfiring

When a fuel/air mixture does not contain enough fuel to consume all the oxygen, it is called a lean mixture. Conversely, a charge that contains more fuel than required is called a rich mixture. An extremely lean mixture either will not burn at all or will burn so slowly that combustion is not complete at the end of the exhaust stroke. The flame lingers in the cylinder and then ignites the contents in the intake manifold or the induction system when the intake valve opens. This causes an explosion known as backfiring, which can damage the carburetor and other parts of the induction system.

A point worth stressing is that backfiring rarely involves the whole engine. Therefore, it is seldom the fault of the carburetor. In practically all cases, backfiring is limited to one or two cylinders. Usually it is the result of faulty valve clearance setting, defective fuel injector nozzles, or other conditions which cause these cylinders to operate leaner than the engine as a whole. There can be no permanent cure until these defects are discovered and corrected. Because these backfiring cylinders will fire intermittently and therefore run cool, they can be detected by the cold cylinder check. The cold cylinder check is discussed later in this chapter.

In some instances, an engine backfires in the idle range, but operates satisfactorily at medium and high power settings. The most likely cause, in this case, is an excessively lean idle mixture. Proper adjustment of the idle fuel/air mixture usually corrects this difficulty.

Afterfiring

Afterfiring, sometimes called afterburning, often results when the fuel/air mixture is too rich. Overly rich mixtures are also slow burning. Therefore, charges of unburned fuel are present in the exhausted gases. Air from outside the exhaust stacks mixes with this unburned fuel which ignites. This causes an explosion in the exhaust system. Afterfiring is perhaps more common where long exhaust ducting retains greater amounts of unburned charges. As in the case of backfiring, the correction for afterfiring is the proper adjustment of the fuel/air mixture.

Afterfiring can also be caused by cylinders which are not firing because of faulty spark plugs, defective fuel-injection nozzles, or incorrect valve clearance. The unburned mixture from these dead cylinders passes into the exhaust system, where it ignites and burns. Unfortunately, the resultant torching or afterburning can easily be mistaken for evidence of a rich carburetor. Cylinders which are firing intermittently can cause a similar effect. Again, the malfunction can be remedied only by discovering the real cause and correcting the defect. Either dead or intermittent cylinders can be located by the cold cylinder check.

FACTORS AFFECTING ENGINE OPERATION

Compression

To prevent loss of power, all openings to the cylinder must close and seal completely on the compression and power strokes. In this respect, there are three items in the proper operation of the cylinder that must be right for maximum efficiency. First, the piston rings must be in good condition to provide maximum sealing during the stroke of the piston. There must be no leakage between the piston and the walls of the combustion chamber. Second, the intake and exhaust valves must close tightly so that there will be no loss of compression at these points. Third, and very important, the timing of the valves must be such that highest efficiency is obtained when the engine is operating at its normal rated r.p.m. A failure at any of these points results in greatly reduced engine efficiency.

Fuel Metering

The induction system is the distribution and fuel metering part of the engine. Obviously, any defect in the induction system seriously affects engine operation. For best operation, each cylinder of the engine must be provided with the proper fuel/air mixture, usually metered by the carburetor. On some fuel-injection engines, fuel is metered by the fuel injector flow divider and fuel-injection nozzles.

The relation between fuel/air ratio and power is illustrated in figure 10–34. Note that, as the fuel mixture is varied from lean to rich, the power output of the engine increases until it reaches a maximum. Beyond this point, the power output falls off as the mixture is further enriched. This is because the fuel mixture is now too rich to provide perfect combustion. Note that maximum engine power can be obtained by setting the carburetor for one point on the curve.

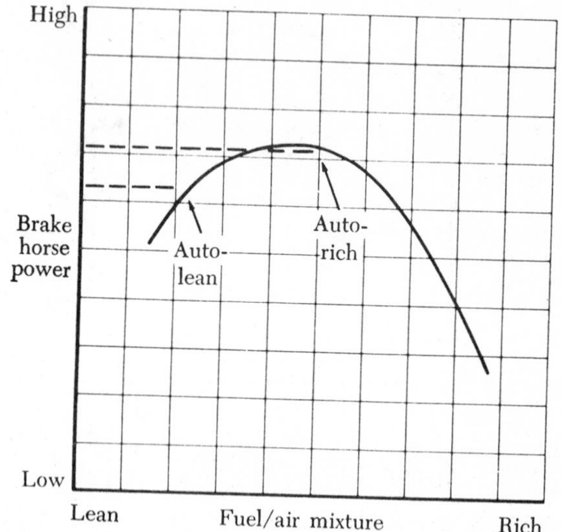

FIGURE 10–34. Power versus fuel/air mixture curve.

In establishing the carburetor settings for an aircraft engine, the design engineers run a series of curves similar to the one shown. A curve is run for each of several engine speeds. If, for example, the idle speed is 600 r.p.m., the first curve might be run at this speed. Another curve might be run at 700 r.p.m., another at 800 r.p.m., and so on, in 100-r.p.m. increments, up to takeoff r.p.m. The points of maximum power on the curves are then joined to obtain the best-power curve of the engine for all speeds. This best-power curve establishes the automatic rich setting of the carburetor.

In establishing the detailed engine requirements regarding carburetor setting, the fact that the cylinder head temperature varies with fuel/air ratio must be considered. This variation is illustrated in the curve shown in figure 10–35. Note that the cylinder head temperature is lower with the auto-lean setting than it is with the auto-rich mixture. This is exactly opposite common belief, but it is true. Furthermore, knowledge of this fact can be used to advantage by flight crews. If, during cruise, it becomes difficult to keep the cylinder head temperature within limits, the fuel/air mixture may be leaned out to get cooler operation. The desired cooling can then be obtained without going to auto-rich with its costly waste of fuel. The curve shows only the variation in cylinder head temperature. For a given r.p.m., the power output of the engine is less with the best-economy setting (auto-lean) than with the best-power mixture.

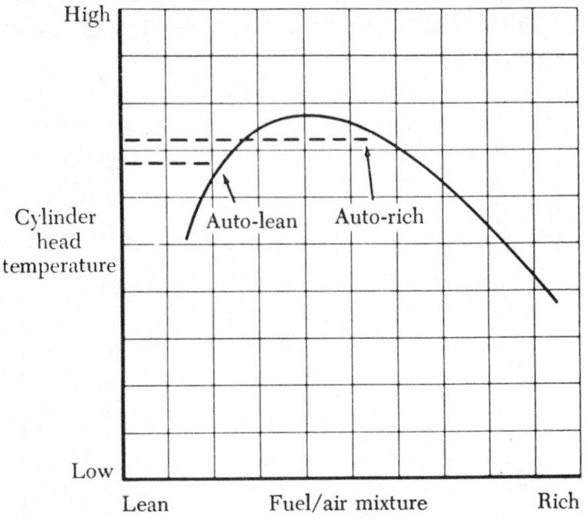

FIGURE 10–35. Variation in head temperature with fuel/air mixture (cruise power).

The decrease in cylinder head temperature with a leaner mixture holds true only through the normal cruise range. At higher power settings, cylinder temperatures are higher with the leaner mixtures. The reason for this reversal hinges on the cooling ability of the engine. As higher powers are approached, a point is reached where the airflow around the cylinders will not provide sufficient cooling. At this point, a secondary cooling method must be used. This secondary cooling is done by enriching the fuel/air mixture beyond the best-power point. Although enriching the mixture to this extent results in a power loss, both power and economy must be sacrificed for engine cooling purposes.

To further investigate the influence of cooling requirements on fuel/air mixture, the effects of water injection must be examined. Figure 10–36 shows a fuel/air curve for a water-injection engine. The dotted portion of the curve shows how the fuel/air mixture is leaned out during water injection. This leaning is possible because water, rather than extra fuel, is used as a cylinder coolant.

This permits leaning out to approximately best-power mixture without danger of overheating or

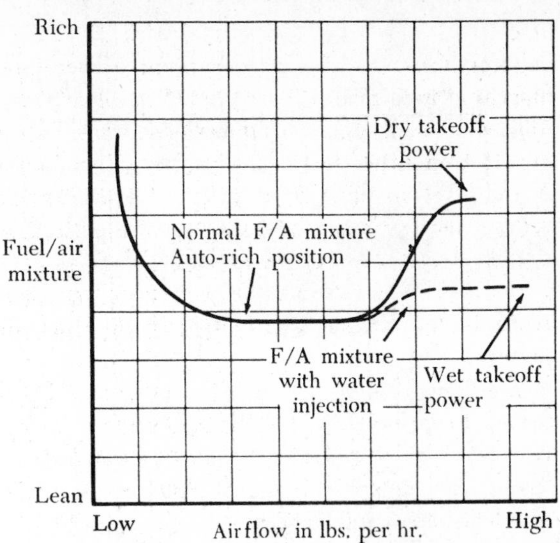

FIGURE 10–36. Fuel/air curve for a water-injection engine.

detonation. This leaning out gives an increase in power. The water does not alter the combustion characteristics of the mixture. Fuel added to the auto-rich mixture in the power range during "dry" operation is solely for cooling. A leaner mixture would give more power.

Actually, water or, more accurately, the antidetonant (water/alcohol) mixture is a better coolant than extra fuel. Therefore, water injection permits higher manifold pressures and a still further increase in power.

In establishing the final curve for engine operation, the engine's ability to cool itself at various power settings is, of course, taken into account. Sometimes the mixture must be altered for a given installation to compensate for the effect of cowl design, cooling airflow, or other factors on engine cooling.

The final fuel/air mixture curves take into account economy, power, engine cooling, idling characteristics, and all other factors which affect combustion.

The chart in figure 10–37 shows a typical final curve for injection-type carburetors. Note that the fuel/air mixture at idle and at takeoff power is the same in auto-rich and auto-lean. Beyond idle, a gradual spread occurs as cruise power is approached. This spread is maximum in the cruise range. The spread decreases toward takeoff power. This spread between the two curves in the cruise range is the basis for the cruise metering check.

Figure 10–38 shows a typical final curve for a float-type carburetor. Note that the fuel/air mixture at idle is the same in rich and in manual lean.

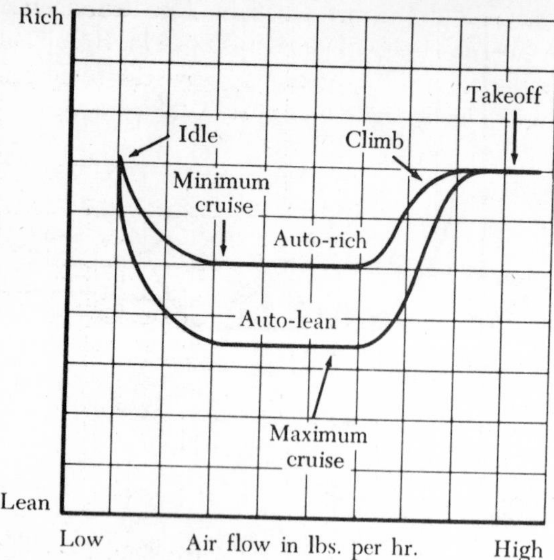

FIGURE 10–37. Typical fuel/air mixture curve for injection-type carburetor.

The mixture remains the same until the low cruise range is reached. At this point, the curves separate and then remain parallel through the cruise and power ranges.

Note the spread between the rich and lean setting in the cruise range of both curves. Because of this spread, there will be a decrease in power when the mixture control is moved from auto-rich to auto-lean with the engine operating in the cruise range. This is true because the auto-rich setting in the cruise range is very near the best-power mixture ratio. Therefore, any leaning out will give a mixture which is leaner than best power.

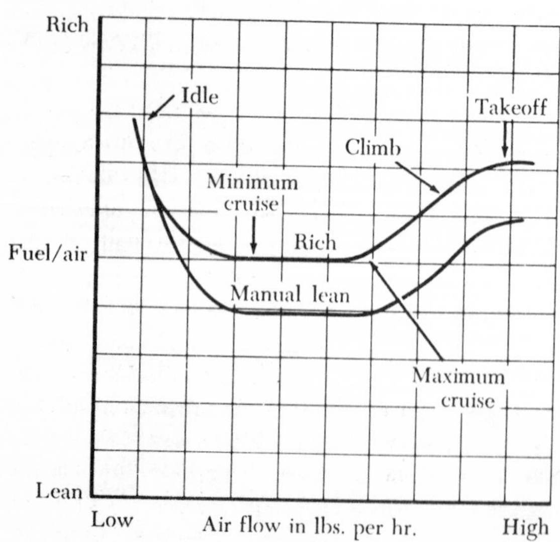

FIGURE 10–38. Typical fuel/air mixture curve for float-type carburetor.

Idle Mixture

The idle mixture curve (figure 10–39) shows how the mixture changes when the idle mixture adjustment is changed. Note that the greatest effect is at idling speeds. However, there is some effect on the mixture at airflows above idling. The airflow at which the idle adjustment effect cancels out varies from minimum cruise to maximum cruise. The exact point depends on the type of carburetor and the carburetor setting. In general, the idle adjustment affects the fuel/air mixture up to medium cruise on most engines having pressure-injection-type carburetors, and up to low cruise on engines equipped with float-type carburetors. This means that incorrect idle mixture adjustments can easily give faulty cruise performance as well as poor idling.

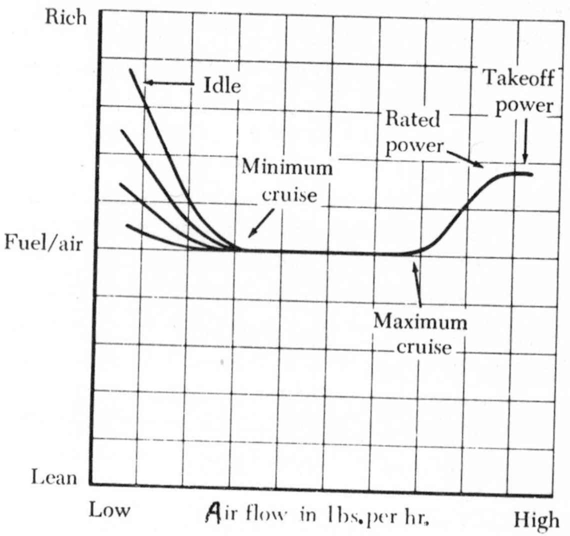

FIGURE 10–39. Idle mixture curve.

There are variations in mixture requirements between one engine and another because of the fuel distribution within the engine and the ability of the engine to cool. Remember that a carburetor setting must be rich enough to supply a combustible mixture for the leanest cylinder. If fuel distribution is poor, the overall mixture must be richer than would be required for the same engine if distribution were good. The engine's ability to cool depends on such factors as cylinder design (including the design of the cooling fins), compression ratio, accessories on the front of the engine which cause individual cylinders to run hot, and the design of the baffling used to deflect airflow around the cylinder. At takeoff power, the mixture must be rich enough to supply sufficient fuel to keep the hottest cylinder cool.

The Induction Manifold

The induction manifold provides the means of distributing air, or the fuel/air mixture, to the cylinders. Whether the manifold handles a fuel/air mixture or air alone depends on the type of fuel metering system used. On an engine equipped with a carburetor, the induction manifold distributes a fuel/air mixture from the carburetor to the cylinders. On a fuel-injection engine, the fuel is delivered to injection nozzles, one in each cylinder, which provide the proper spray pattern for efficient burning. Thus, the mixing of fuel and air takes place in the cylinders or at the inlet port to the cylinder. On a fuel-injection engine the induction manifold handles only air.

The induction manifold is an important item because of the effect it can have on the fuel/air mixture which finally reaches the cylinder. Fuel is introduced into the airstream by the carburetor in a liquid form. To become combustible, the fuel must be vaporized in the air. This vaporization takes place in the induction manifold, which includes the internal supercharger if one is used. Any fuel that does not vaporize will cling to the walls of the intake pipes. Obviously, this affects the effective fuel/air ratio of the mixture which finally reaches the cylinder in vapor form. This explains the reason for the apparently rich mixture required to start a cold engine. In a cold engine, some of the fuel in the airstream condenses out and clings to the walls of the manifold. This is in addition to that fuel which never vaporized in the first place. As the engine warms up, less fuel is required because less fuel is condensed out of the airstream and more of the fuel is vaporized, thus giving the cylinder the required fuel/air mixture for normal combustion.

Any leak in the induction system has an effect on the mixture reaching the cylinders. This is particularly true of a leak at the cylinder end of an intake pipe. At manifold pressures below atmospheric pressure, such a leak will lean out the mixture. This occurs because additional air is drawn in from the atmosphere at the leaky point. The affected cylinder may overheat, fire intermittently, or even cut out altogether.

Operational Effect of Valve Clearance

While considering the operational effect of valve clearance, keep in mind that all aircraft reciprocating engines of current design use valve overlap.

Figure 10–40 shows the pressures at the intake and exhaust ports under two different sets of operating conditions. In one case, the engine is operating at a manifold pressure of 35 in. Hg. Barometric pressure (exhaust back pressure) is 29 in. Hg. This gives a pressure differential of 6 in. Hg (3 p.s.i.) acting in the direction indicated by the arrow.

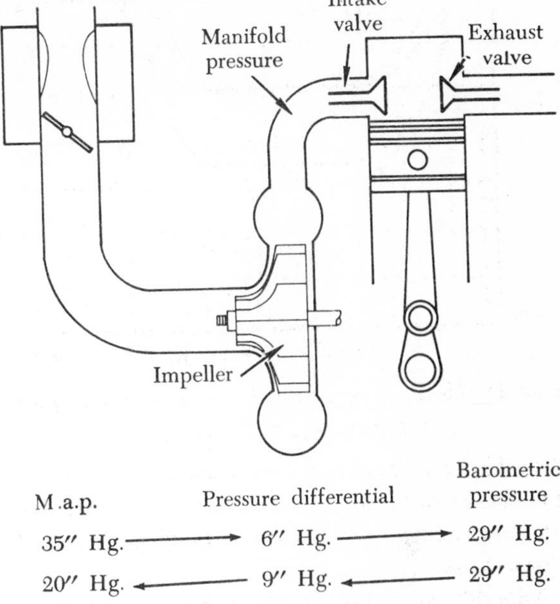

FIGURE 10–40. Effect of valve overlap.

During the valve overlap period, this pressure differential forces the fuel/air mixture across the combustion chamber toward the open exhaust. This flow of fuel/air mixture forces ahead of it the exhaust gases remaining in the cylinder, resulting in complete scavenging of the combustion chamber. This, in turn, permits complete filling of the cylinder with a fresh charge on the following intake event. This is the situation in which valve overlap gives increased power.

In a situation where the manifold pressure is below atmospheric pressure, 20 in. Hg, for example, there is a pressure differential of 9 in. Hg (4.5 p.s.i.) in the opposite direction. This causes air or exhaust gas to be drawn into the cylinder through the exhaust port during valve overlap.

In engines with collector rings, this inflow through the exhaust port at low power settings consists of burned exhaust gases. These gases are pulled back into the cylinder and mix with the incoming fuel/air mixture. However, these exhaust gases are inert; they do not contain oxygen. Therefore, the fuel/air mixture ratio is not affected much. With open exhaust stacks, the situation is entirely different. Here, fresh air containing oxygen is pulled into the cylinders through the exhaust. This leans out the mixture. Therefore, the carburetor must be set to deliver an excessively rich idle mixture so that, when this mixture is combined with the fresh air drawn in through the exhaust port, the effective mixture in the cylinder will be at the desired ratio.

At first thought, it does not appear possible that the effect of valve overlap on fuel/air mixture is sufficient to cause concern. However, the effect of valve overlap becomes apparent when considering idle fuel/air mixtures. These mixtures must be enriched 20 to 30% when open stacks instead of collector rings are used on the same engine. This is shown graphically in figure 10–41. Note the spread at idle between an open stack and an exhaust collector ring installation for engines that are otherwise identical. The mixture variation decreases as the engine speed or airflow is increased from idle into the cruise range.

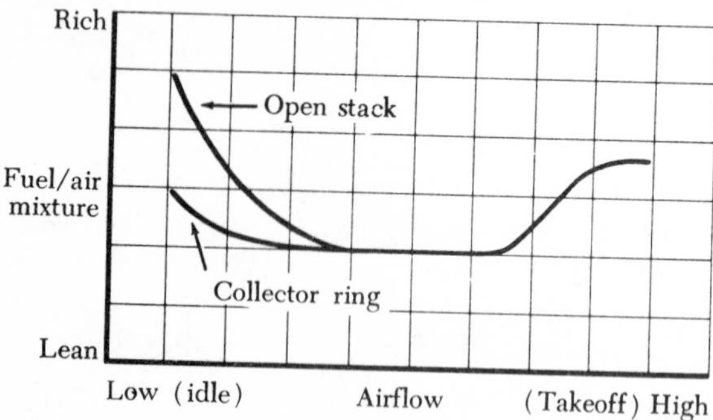

FIGURE 10–41. Comparison of fuel/air mixture curves for open stack and collector ring installations.

Engine, airplane, and equipment manufacturers provide a powerplant installation that will give satisfactory performance. Cams are designed to give best valve operation and correct overlap. But valve operation will be correct only if valve clearances are set and remain at the value recommended by the engine manufacturer. If valve clearances are set wrong, the valve overlap period will be longer or shorter than the manufacturer intended. The same is true if clearances get out of adjustment during operation.

Where there is too much valve clearance, the valves will not open as wide or remain open as long as they should. This reduces the overlap period. At idling speed, it will affect the fuel/air mixture, since a less-than-normal amount of air or exhaust gases will be drawn back into the cylinder during the shortened overlap period. As a result, the idle mixture will tend to be too rich.

When valve clearance is less than it should be, the valve overlap period will be lengthened. This permits a greater-than-normal amount of air or exhaust gases to be drawn back into the cylinder at idling speeds. As a result, the idle mixture will be leaned out at the cylinder. The carburetor is adjusted with the expectation that a certain amount of air or exhaust gases will be drawn back into the cylinder at idling. If more or less air or exhaust gases are drawn into the cylinder during the valve overlap period, the mixture will be too lean or too rich.

When valve clearances are wrong, it is unlikely that they will all be wrong in the same direction. Instead, there will be too much clearance on some cylinders and too little on others. Naturally, this gives a variation in valve overlap between cylinders. This, in turn, results in a variation in fuel/air ratio at idling and lower-power settings, since the carburetor delivers the same mixture to all cylinders. The carburetor cannot tailor the mixture to each cylinder to compensate for variation in valve overlap.

The effect of variation in valve clearance and valve overlap on the fuel/air mixture between cylinders is illustrated in figure 10–42. Note how the cylinders with too little clearance run rich and those with too much clearance run lean. Note also the extreme mixture variation between cylinders. On such an engine, it would be impossible to set the idle adjustment to give correct mixtures on all cylinders, nor can all cylinders of such an engine be expected to produce the same power. Variations in valve clearance of as little as 0.005 in. have a definite effect on mixture distribution between cylinders.

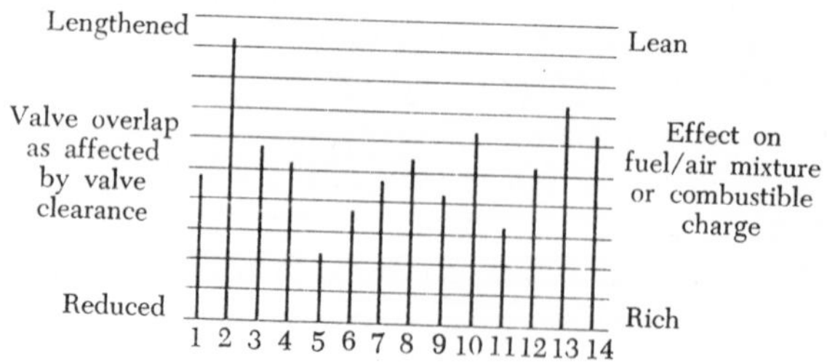

FIGURE 10–42. Effect of variation in valve overlap on fuel/air mixture between cylinders.

Another aspect of valve clearance is its effect on volumetric efficiency. Considering the intake valve first, suppose valve clearance is greater than that specified. As the cam lobe starts to pass under the cam roller, the cam step or ramp takes up part of this clearance. However, it doesn't take up all the clearance as it should. Therefore, the cam roller is well up on the lobe proper before the valve starts to open. As a result, the valve opens later than it should. In a similar way, the valve closes before the roller has passed from the main lobe to the ramp at its end. With excessive clearance, then, the intake valve opens late and closes early. This produces a throttling effect on the cylinder. The valve is not open long enough to admit a full charge of fuel and air. This will cut down the power output, particularly at high-power settings.

Insufficient intake valve clearance has the opposite effect. The clearance is taken up and the valve starts to open while the cam roller is still on the cam step. The valve doesn't close until the riser at the end of the lobe has almost completely passed under the roller. Therefore, the intake valve opens early, closes late, and stays open longer than it should. At low power, early opening of the intake valve can cause backfiring because of the hot exhaust gases backing out into the intake manifold and igniting the mixture there.

Excessive exhaust valve clearance causes the exhaust valve to open late and close early. This shortens the exhaust event and causes poor scavenging. The late opening may also lead to cylinder overheating. The hot exhaust gases are held in the cylinder beyond the time specified for their release.

When exhaust valve clearance is insufficient, the valve opens early and closes late. It remains open longer than it should. The early opening causes a power loss by shortening the power event. The pressure in the cylinder is released before all the useful expansion has worked on the piston. The late closing causes the exhaust valve to remain open during a larger portion of the intake stroke than it should. This may result in good mixture being lost through the exhaust port.

As mentioned before, there will probably be too little clearance on some cylinders and too much on others whenever valve clearances are incorrect. This means that the effect of incorrect clearances on volumetric efficiency will usually vary from cylinder to cylinder. One cylinder will take in a full charge while another receives only a partial charge. As a result, cylinders will not deliver equal power. One cylinder will backfire or run hot while another performs satisfactorily.

On some direct fuel-injection engines, variations in valve clearance will affect only the amount of air taken into the cylinders. This is true when the induction manifold handles only air. In this case there will be no appreciable effect on the distribution of fuel to the individual cylinders. This means that, when clearances vary between cylinders, air charges will also vary but fuel distribution will be uniform. This faulty air distribution, coupled with proper fuel distribution, will cause variations in mixture ratio.

In all cases, variations in valve clearance from the value specified have the effect of changing the valve timing from that obtained with correct clearance. This is certain to give something less than perfect performance.

Ignition System

The next item to be considered regarding engine operation is the ignition system. Although basically simple, it is sometimes not understood clearly.

An ignition system consists of four main parts:

(1) The basic magneto.

(2) The distributor.

(3) The ignition harness.

(4) The spark plug.

The basic magneto is a high-voltage generating device. It must be adjusted to give maximum voltage at the time the points break and ignition occurs. It must also be synchronized accurately to the firing position of the engine. The magneto generates a series of peak voltages which are released by the opening of the breaker points. A distributor is necessary to distribute these peak voltages from the magneto to the cylinders in the proper order. The ignition harness constitutes the insulated and shielded high-tension lines which carry the high voltages from the distributor to the spark plugs.

The magnetos used on aircraft engines are capable of developing voltages as high as 15,000 volts. The voltage required to jump the specified gap in a spark plug will usually be about 4,000 to 5,000 volts maximum. The spark plugs serve as safety valves to limit the maximum voltage in the entire ignition system. As spark plug gaps open up as a result of erosion, the voltage at the plug terminals increases. A higher voltage is required to jump the larger gap. This higher voltage is transmitted through the secondary circuit. The increased voltage in the circuit becomes a hazard. It is a possible source of breakdown in the ignition harness and can cause flashover in the distributor.

The distributor directs the firing impulses to the various cylinders. It must be timed properly to both the engine and the magneto. The distributor finger must align with the correct electrode on the distributor block at the time the magneto points break. Any misalignment may cause the high voltage to jump to a cylinder other than the one intended. This will cause severe backfiring and general malfunctioning of the engine.

The manufacturer has selected the best compromise and specified an alignment with the No. 1 electrode for timing. However, even with perfect distributor timing, the finger is behind on some electrodes and ahead on others. For a few electrodes (cylinders), the alignment is as far from perfect as it can safely be. A slight error in timing, added to this already imperfect alignment, may put the finger so far from the electrode that the high voltage will not jump from finger to electrode, or the high voltage may be routed to the wrong cylinder. Therefore, the distributor must be timed perfectly. The finger must be aligned with the No. 1 electrode exactly as prescribed in the maintenance manual for the particular engine and airplane.

Although the ignition harness is simple, it is a critical part of the ignition system. A number of things can cause failure in the ignition harness. Insulation may break down on a wire inside the harness and allow the high voltage to leak through to the shielding (and to ground), instead of going to the spark plug. Open circuits may result from broken wires or poor connections. A bare wire may be in contact with the shielding, or two wires may be shorted together.

Any serious defect in an individual lead prevents the high voltage impulse from reaching the spark plug to which the lead is connected. As a result, only one spark plug in the cylinder will fire. This causes the cylinder to operate on single ignition. This is certain to result in detonation, since dual ignition is required to prevent detonation at takeoff and during other high-power operation. Two bad leads to the same cylinder will cause the cylinder to go completely dead. On engines with separate distributors, a faulty magneto-to-distributor lead can cut out half the ignition system.

Among the most common ignition harness defects, and the most difficult to detect, are high-voltage leaks. However, a complete harness check will reveal these and other defects.

Although the spark plug is simple both in construction and in operation, it is, nevertheless, the direct or indirect cause of a great many malfunctions encountered in aircraft engines. Proper precaution begins with plug selection. Be sure to select and install the plug specified for the particular engine. One of the reasons a particular plug is specified is its heat range. The heat range of the spark plug determines the temperature at which the nose end of the plug operates. It also affects the ability of the spark plug to ignite mixtures which are borderline from the standpoint of high oil content or excessive richness or leanness.

A great many troubles attributed to spark plugs are the direct result of malfunctions somewhere else in the engine. Some of these are excessively rich idle mixtures, improperly adjusted valves, and impeller oil seal leaks.

Propeller Governor

The final item to be considered regarding engine operation is the effect of the propeller governor on engine operation. In the curve shown in figure 10–43, note that the manifold pressure change with r.p.m. is gradual until the propeller governor cut-in speed is reached. Beyond this point, the manifold pressure increases, but no change occurs in the engine r.p.m. as the carburetor throttle is opened wider.

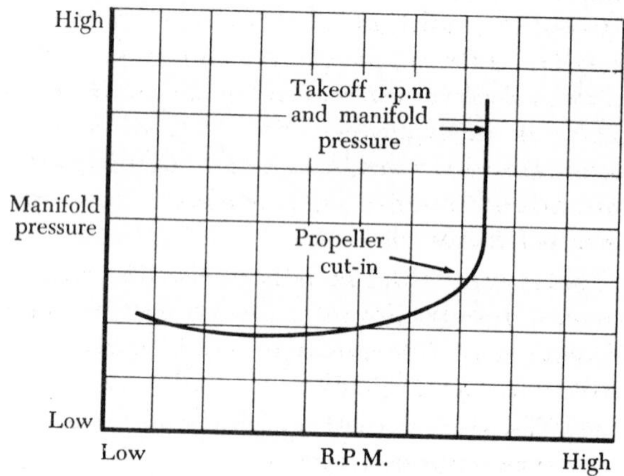

FIGURE 10–43. Effect of propeller governor on manifold pressure.

A true picture of the power output of the engine can be determined only at speeds below the propeller governor cut-in speed. The propeller governor is set to maintain a given engine r.p.m. Therefore, the relationship between engine speed and manifold pressure as an indication of power output is lost, unless it is known that all cylinders of the engine are functioning properly.

In fact, on a multi-engine aircraft, an engine can fail and still produce every indication that it is developing power. The propeller governor will flatten out the propeller blade angle and windmill the propeller to maintain the same engine r.p.m. Heat of compression within the cylinder will prevent the cylinder head temperature from falling rapidly. The fuel pressure will remain constant and the fuel flow will not change unless the manifold pressure is changed. On an engine not equipped with a turbocharger, the manifold pressure will remain where it was. On a turbocharged engine, the manifold pressure will not drop below the value which the mechanical supercharger can maintain. This may be well above atmospheric pressure, depending upon the blower ratio of the engine and the specific conditions existing. Thus, the pilot has difficulty in recognizing that he has encountered a sudden failure unless the engines are equipped with torquemeters, or he notices the fluctuation in r.p.m. at the time the engine cuts out.

Overlapping Phases of Engine Operation

Up to this point, the individual phases of engine operation have been discussed. The relationship of the phases and their combined effect on engine operation will now be considered. Combustion within the cylinder is the result of fuel metering, compression, and ignition. Since valve overlap affects fuel metering, proper combustion in all the cylinders involves correct valve adjustment in addition to the other phases. When all conditions are correct, there is a burnable mixture. When ignited, this mixture will give power impulses of the same intensity from all cylinders.

The system which ignites the combustible mixture requires that the following five conditions occur simultaneously if the necessary spark impulse is to be delivered to the cylinder at the proper time:

(1) The breaker points must be timed accurately to the magneto (E-gap).

(2) The magneto must be timed accurately to the engine.

(3) The distributor finger must be timed accurately to the engine and the magneto.

(4) The ignition harness must be in good condition with no tendency to flashover.

(5) The spark plug must be clean, have no tendency to short out, and have the proper electrode gap.

If any one of these requirements is lacking or if any one phase of the ignition system is maladjusted or is not functioning correctly, the entire ignition system can be disrupted to the point that improper engine operation results.

As an example of how one phase of engine operation can be affected by other phases, consider spark plug fouling. Spark plug fouling causes malfunctioning of the ignition system, but the fouling seldom results from a fault in the plug itself. Usually some other phase of operation is not functioning correctly, causing the plug to foul out. If excessively rich fuel/air mixtures are being burned because of either basically rich carburetion or improperly adjusted idle mixture, spark plug fouling will be inevitable. Generally, these causes will result in fouled spark plugs appearing over the entire engine, and not necessarily confined to one or a few cylinders.

If the fuel/air mixture is too lean or too rich on any one cylinder because of a loose intake pipe or improperly adjusted valves, improper operation of that cylinder will result. The cylinder will probably backfire. Spark plug fouling will occur continually on that cylinder until the defect is remedied.

Impeller oil seal leaks, which can be detected only by removal of intake pipes, will cause spark plug fouling. Here, the fouling is caused by excess oil being delivered to one or more cylinders. Stuck or broken rings will cause oil pumping in the affected cylinders with consequent plug fouling and high oil consumption. Improperly adjusted cylinder valves cause spark plug fouling, hard starting, and general engine malfunctioning. They may also cause valve failure as a result of high-seating velocities or of the valve holding open, with subsequent valve burning.

Whenever the true cause of engine malfunctioning is not determined and whenever the real disorder is not corrected, the corrective measure taken will provide only temporary relief. For example, the standard "fix" for engine backfiring is to change the carburetor. However, as a result of many tests, it is now known that the usual cause of engine backfiring is an improperly adjusted or defective ignition system or improperly adjusted engine valves.

Backfiring is usually caused by one cylinder, not all the cylinders. To remedy backfiring, first locate which cylinder is causing it, and then find out why that cylinder is backfiring.

ENGINE TROUBLESHOOTING

The need for troubleshooting normally is dictated by poor operation of the complete powerplant. Power settings for the type of operation at which any difficulty is encountered in many cases will indicate which part of the powerplant is the basic cause of difficulty.

The cylinders of an engine, along with the supercharger impeller, form an air pump. Furthermore, the power developed in the cylinders varies directly with the rate of air consumption. Therefore, a measure of air consumption or airflow into the engine is a measure of power input. Ignoring for the moment such factors as humidity and exhaust back pressure, the manifold pressure gage and the engine tachometer provide a measure of engine air consumption. Thus, for a given r.p.m. any change in power input will be reflected by a corresponding change in manifold pressure.

The power output of an engine is the power absorbed by the propeller. Therefore, propeller load is a measure of power output. Propeller load, in turn, depends on the propeller r.p.m., blade angle, and air density. For a given angle and air density, propeller load (power output) is directly proportional to engine speed.

The basic power of an engine is related to manifold pressure, fuel flow, and r.p.m. Because the r.p.m. of the engine and the throttle opening directly control manifold pressure, the primary engine power controls are the throttle and the r.p.m. control. An engine equipped with a fixed-pitch propeller has only a throttle control. In this case, the throttle setting controls both manifold pressure and engine r.p.m.

With proper precautions, manifold pressure can be taken as a measure of power input, and r.p.m. can be taken as a measure of power output. However, the following factors must be considered:

(1) Atmospheric pressure and air temperature must be considered, since they affect air density.

(2) These measures of power input and power output should be used only for comparing the performance of an engine with its previous performance or for comparing identical powerplants.

(3) With a controllable propeller, the blades must be against their low-pitch stops, since this is the only blade position in which the blade angle is known and does not vary. Once the blades are off their low-pitch stops, the propeller governor takes over and maintains a constant r.p.m. regardless of power input or engine condition. This precaution means that the propeller control must be set to maximum or takeoff r.p.m., and the checks made at engine speeds below this setting.

If the engine is equipped with a torquemeter, the torquemeter reading rather than the engine speed should be used as a measure of power output.

Having relative measures of power input and power output, the condition of an engine can be determined by comparing input and output. This is done by comparing the manifold pressure required to produce a given r.p.m. with the manifold pressure required to produce the same r.p.m. at a time when the engine (or an identical powerplant) was known to be in top operating condition.

An example will best show the practical application of this method of determining engine condition. With the propeller control set for takeoff r.p.m. (full low blade angle), an engine may require 32 in. of manifold pressure to turn 2,200 r.p.m. for the ignition check. On previous checks, this engine required only 30 in. of manifold pressure to turn 2,200 r.p.m. at the same station (altitude) and under similar atmospheric conditions. Obviously, something is wrong; a higher power input (manifold pressure) is now required for the same power output (r.p.m.). There is a good chance that one cylinder has cut out.

There are several standards against which engine performance can be compared. The performance of a particular engine can be compared with its past performance provided adequate records are kept. Engine performance can be compared with that of other engines on the same aircraft or aircraft having identical installations.

If a fault does exist, it may be assumed that the trouble lies in one of the following systems:

(1) Ignition system.
(2) Fuel metering system.
(3) Induction system.
(4) Power section (valves, cylinders, etc.).
(5) Instrumentation.

If a logical approach to the problem is taken and the instrument readings properly utilized, the malfunctioning system can be pinpointed and the specific problem in the defective system can be singled out.

The more information available about any particular problem, the better will be the opportunity for a rapid repair. Information that is of value in locating a malfunction includes:

(1) Was any roughness noted? Under what conditions of operation?
(2) What is the time on the engine and spark plugs? How long since last inspection?
(3) Was the ignition system operational check and power check normal?
(4) When did the trouble first appear?
(5) Was backfiring or afterfiring present?

(6) Was the full throttle performance normal?

From a different point of view, the powerplant is in reality a number of small engines turning a common crankshaft and being operated by two common phases: (1) Fuel metering, and (2) ignition. When backfiring, low power output, or other powerplant difficulty is encountered, first find out which system (fuel metering or ignition) is involved and then determine whether the entire engine or only one cylinder is at fault.

For example, backfiring normally will be caused by:

(1) Valves holding open or sticking open in one or more of the cylinders.
(2) Lean mixture.
(3) Intake pipe leakage.
(4) An error in valve adjustment which causes individual cylinders to receive too small a charge or one too large, even though the mixture to the cylinders has the same fuel/air ratio.

Ignition system reasons for backfiring might be a cracked distributor block or a high-tension leak between two ignition leads. Either of these conditions could cause the charge in the cylinder to be ignited during the intake stroke. Ignition system troubles involving backfiring normally will not be centered in the basic magneto, since a failure of the basic magneto would result in the engine not running, or it would run well at low speeds but cut out at high speeds. On the other hand, replacement of the magneto would correct a difficulty caused by a cracked distributor where the distributor is a part of the magneto.

If the fuel system, ignition system, and induction system are functioning properly, the engine should produce the correct b.hp. unless some fault exists in the basic power section.

Trouble—Cause—Remedy

Troubleshooting is a systematic analysis of the symptoms which indicate engine malfunction. Since it would be impractical to list all the malfunctions that could occur in a reciprocating engine, only the most common malfunctions are discussed. A thorough knowledge of the engine systems, applied with logical reasoning, will solve any problems which may occur.

Table 10 lists general conditions or troubles which may be encountered on reciprocating engines, such as "engine fails to start." They are further divided into the probable causes contributing to such conditions. Corrective actions are indicated in the "remedy" column. The items are presented with consideration given to frequency of occurrence, ease of accessibility, and complexity of the corrective action indicated.

TABLE 10. Troubleshooting opposed engines.

Trouble	Probable Causes	Remedy
Engine fails to start.	Lack of fuel.	Check fuel system for leaks. Fill fuel tank. Clean dirty lines, strainers, or fuel valves.
	Underpriming.	Use correct priming procedure.
	Overpriming.	Open throttle and "unload" engine by rotating the propeller.
	Incorrect throttle setting.	Open throttle to one-tenth of its range.
	Defective spark plugs.	Clean and re-gap or replace spark plugs.
	Defective ignition wire.	Test and replace any defective wires.
	Defective or weak battery.	Replace with charged battery.
	Improper operation of magneto or breaker points.	Check internal timing of magnetos.
	Water in carburetor.	Drain carburetor and fuel lines.
	Internal failure.	Check oil sump strainer for metal particles.

TABLE 10. Troubleshooting opposed engines—con.

Trouble	Probable Causes	Remedy
	Magnetized impulse coupling, if installed.	Demagnetize impulse coupling.
	Frozen spark plug electrodes.	Replace spark plugs or dry out plugs.
	Mixture control in idle cutoff.	Open mixture control.
	Shorted ignition switch or loose ground.	Check and replace or repair.
Engine fails to idle properly.	Incorrect carburetor idle speed adjustment.	Adjust throttle stop to obtain correct idle.
	Incorrect idle mixture.	Adjust mixture. (Refer to engine manufacturer's handbook for proper procedure.)
	Leak in the induction system.	Tighten all connections in the induction system. Replace any defective parts.
	Low cylinder compression.	Check cylinder compression.
	Faulty ignition system.	Check entire ignition system.
	Open or leaking primer.	Lock or repair primer.
	Improper spark plug setting for altitude.	Check spark plug gap.
	Dirty air filter.	Clean or replace.
Low power and engine running uneven.	Mixture too rich; indicated by sluggish engine operation, red exhaust flame, and black smoke.	Check primer. Re-adjust carburetor mixture.
	Mixture too lean; indicated by overheating or backfiring.	Check fuel lines for dirt or other restrictions. Check fuel supply.
	Leaks in induction system.	Tighten all connections. Replace defective parts.
	Defective spark plugs.	Clean or replace spark plugs.
	Improper grade of fuel.	Fill tank with recommended grade.
	Magneto breaker points not working properly.	Clean points. Check internal timing of magneto.
	Defective ignition wire.	Test and replace any defective wires.
	Defective spark plug terminal connectors.	Replace connectors on spark plug wire.
	Incorrect valve clearance.	Adjust valve clearance.
	Restriction in exhaust system.	Remove restriction.
	Improper ignition timing.	Check magnetos for timing and synchronization.
Engine fails to develop full power.	Throttle lever out of adjustment.	Adjust throttle lever.
	Leak in induction system.	Tighten all connections and replace defective parts.
	Restriction in carburetor airscoop.	Examine airscoop and remove restriction.
	Improper fuel.	Fill tank with recommended fuel.
	Propeller governor out of adjustment.	Adjust governor.
	Faulty ignition.	Tighten all connections. Check system. Check ignition timing.
Rough running engine.	Cracked engine mount(s).	Repair or replace engine mount(s).
	Unbalanced propeller.	Remove propeller and have it checked for balance.
	Defective mounting bushings.	Install new mounting bushings.
	Lead deposit on spark plugs.	Clean or replace plugs.
	Primer unlocked.	Lock primer.

TABLE 10. Troubleshooting opposed engines—con.

Trouble	Probable Causes	Remedy
Low oil pressure.	Insufficient oil.	Check oil supply.
	Dirty oil strainers.	Remove and clean oil strainers.
	Defective pressure gage.	Replace gage.
	Air lock or dirt in relief valve.	Remove and clean oil pressure relief valve.
	Leak in suction line or pressure line.	Check gasket between accessory housing crankcase.
	High oil temperature.	See "high oil temperature" in trouble column.
	Stoppage in oil pump intake passage.	Check line for obstruction. Clean suction strainer.
	Worn or scored bearings.	Overhaul engine.
High oil temperature.	Insufficient air cooling.	Check air inlet and outlet for deformation or obstruction.
	Insufficient oil supply.	Fill oil tank to proper level.
	Clogged oil lines or strainers.	Remove and clean oil lines or strainers.
	Failing or failed bearings.	Examine sump for metal particles and, if found, overhaul engine.
	Defective thermostats.	Replace thermostats.
	Defective temperature gage.	Replace gage.
	Excessive blow-by.	Usually caused by weak or stuck rings. Overhaul engine.
Excessive oil consumption.	Failing or failed bearing.	Check sump for metal particles and, if found, an overhaul of engine is indicated.
	Worn or broken piston rings.	Install new rings.
	Incorrect installation of piston rings.	Install new rings.
	External oil leakage.	Check engine carefully for leaking gaskets or O-rings.
	Leakage through engine fuel pump vent.	Replace fuel pump seal.
	Engine breather or vacuum pump breather.	Check engine, and overhaul or replace vacuum pump.

CYLINDER MAINTENANCE

Each cylinder of the engine is, in reality, an engine in itself. In most cases the cylinder receives its fuel and air from a common source such as the carburetor. Every phase of cylinder operation, such as compression, fuel mixture, and ignition must function properly, since even one type of malfunctioning will cause engine difficulty. Engine backfiring, for example, may be caused by a lean fuel/air mixture in one of the cylinders. The lean mixture may be caused by such difficulties as an improper valve adjustment, a sticking intake or exhaust valve, or a leaking intake pipe. Most engine difficulties can be traced to one cylinder, or a small number of cylinders. Therefore, engine difficulty can be corrected only after malfunctioning cylinders have been located and defective phases of cylinder operation brought up to normal.

Hydraulic Lock

Whenever a radial engine remains shut down for any length of time beyond a few minutes, oil or fuel may drain into the combustion chambers of the lower cylinders or accumulate in the lower intake pipes ready to be drawn into the cylinders when the engine starts (figure 10–44). As the piston approaches top center of the compression stroke (both valves closed), this liquid, being incompressible, stops piston movement. If the crankshaft continues to rotate, something must give. Therefore, starting or attempting to start an engine with a hydraulic lock of this nature may cause the affected cylinder to blow out or, more likely, may result in a bent or broken connecting rod.

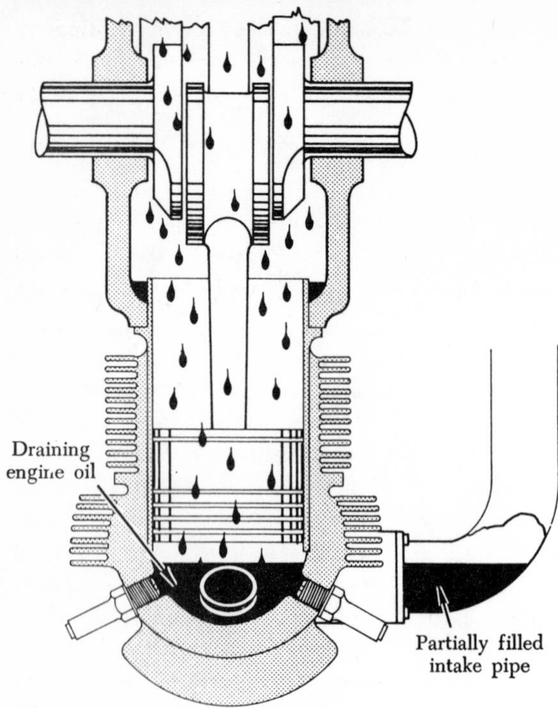

FIGURE 10–44. Initial step in developing a hydraulic lock.

A complete hydraulic lock—one that stops crankshaft rotation—can result in serious damage to the engine. Still more serious, however, is the slight damage resulting from a partial hydraulic lock which goes undetected at the time it occurs. The piston meets extremely high resistance but is not completely stopped. The engine falters but starts and continues to run as the other cylinders fire. The slightly bent connecting rod resulting from the partial lock also goes unnoticed at the time it is damaged but is sure to fail later. The eventual failure is almost certain to occur at a time when it can be least tolerated, since it is during such critical operations as takeoff and go-around that maximum power is demanded of the engine and maximum stresses are imposed on its parts. A hydraulic lock and some possible results are shown in figure 10–45.

Before starting any radial engine that has been shut down for more than 30 min., check the ignition switches for "off" and then pull the propeller through in the direction of rotation a minimum of two complete turns to make sure that there is no hydraulic lock or to detect the hydraulic lock if one is present. Any liquid present in a cylinder will be indicated by the abnormal effort required to rotate the propeller. However, never use force when a hydraulic lock is detected. When engines which employ direct drive

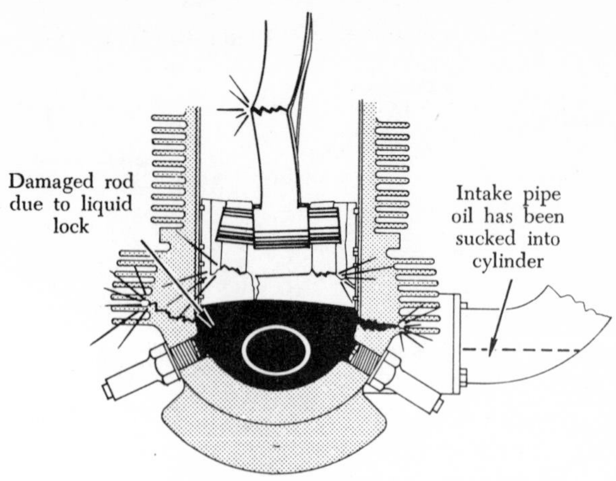

FIGURE 10–45. Results of a hydraulic lock.

or combination inertia and direct drive starters are being started, and an external power source is being used, a check for hydraulic lock may be made by intermittently energizing the starter and watching for a tendency of the engine to stall. Use of the starter in this way will not exert sufficient force on the crankshaft to bend or break a connecting rod if a lock is present.

To eliminate a lock, remove either the front or rear spark plug of the lower cylinders and pull the propeller through in the direction of rotation. The piston will expel any liquid that may be present.

If the hydraulic lock occurs as a result of overpriming prior to initial engine start, eliminate the lock in the same manner, *i.e.*, remove one of the spark plugs from the cylinder and rotate the crankshaft through two turns.

Never attempt to clear the hydraulic lock by pulling the propeller through in the direction opposite to normal rotation, since this tends to inject the liquid from the cylinder into the intake pipe with the possibility of a complete or partial lock occurring on the subsequent start.

Valve Blow-by

Valve blow-by is indicated by a hissing or whistle when pulling the propeller through prior to starting the engine, when turning the engine with the starter, or when running the engine at slow speeds. It is caused by a valve sticking open or warped to the extent that compression is not built up in the cylinder as the piston moves toward top dead center on the compression stroke. Blow-by past the exhaust valve can be heard at the exhaust stack, and blow-by past the intake valve is audible through the carburetor.

Correct valve blow-by immediately to prevent

valve failure and possible engine failure by taking the following steps:

(1) Perform a cylinder compression test to locate the faulty cylinder.

(2) Check the valve clearance on the affected cylinder. If the valve clearance is incorrect, the valve may be sticking in the valve guide. To release the sticking valve, place a fiber drift on the rocker arm immediately over the valve stem and strike the drift several times with a mallet. Sufficient hand pressure should be exerted on the fiber drift to remove any space between the rocker arm and the valve stem prior to hitting the drift.

(3) If the valve is not sticking and the valve clearance is incorrect, adjust it as necessary.

(4) Determine whether blow-by has been eliminated by again pulling the engine through by hand or turning it with the starter. If blow-by is still present, it may be necessary to replace the cylinder.

CYLINDER COMPRESSION TESTS

The cylinder compression test determines if the valves, piston rings, and pistons are adequately sealing the combustion chamber. If pressure leakage is excessive, the cylinder cannot develop its full power. The purpose of testing cylinder compression is to determine whether cylinder replacement is necessary. The detection and replacement of defective cylinders will prevent a complete engine change because of cylinder failure. It is essential that cylinder compression tests be made periodically.

Although it is possible for the engine to lose compression for other reasons, low compression for the most part can be traced to leaky valves. Conditions which affect engine compression are:

(1) Incorrect valve clearances.

(2) Worn, scuffed, or damaged piston.

(3) Excessive wear of piston rings and cylinder walls.

(4) Burned or warped valves.

(5) Carbon particles between the face and the seat of the valve or valves.

(6) Early or late valve timing.

Perform a compression test as soon as possible after the engine is shut down so that piston rings, cylinder walls, and other parts are still freshly lubricated. However, it is not necessary to operate the engine prior to accomplishing compression checks during engine buildup or on individually replaced cylinders. In such cases, before making the test, spray a small quantity of lubricating oil into the cylinder or cylinders and turn the engine over several times to seal the piston and rings in the cylinder barrel.

Be sure that the ignition switch is in the "off" position so that there will be no accidental firing of the engine. Remove necessary cowling and the most accessible spark plug from each cylinder. When removing the spark plugs, identify them to coincide with the cylinder. Close examination of the plugs will aid in diagnosing problems within the cylinder. Review the maintenance records of the engine being tested. Records of previous compression checks help in determining progressive wear conditions and in establishing the necessary maintenance actions.

The two basic types of compression testers currently in use for checking cylinder compression in aircraft engines are the direct compression tester and the differential pressure tester. The procedures and precautions to observe when using either of these types of testers are outlined in this section. When performing a compression test, follow the manufacturer's instructions for the particular tester being used.

Direct Compression Tester

This type of compression test indicates the actual pressures within the cylinder. Although the particular defective component within the cylinder is difficult to determine with this method, the consistency of the readings for all cylinders is an indication of the condition of the engine as a whole. The following are suggested guidelines for performing a direct compression test:

(1) Warm up the engine to operating temperatures and perform the test as soon as possible after shutdown.

(2) Remove the most accessible spark plug from each cylinder.

(3) Rotate the engine with the starter to expel any excess oil or loose carbon in the cylinders.

(4) If a complete set of compression testers is available, install one tester in each cylinder. However, if only one tester is being used, check each cylinder in turn.

(5) Using the engine starter, rotate the engine at least three complete revolutions and record the compression reading. Use an external power source, if possible, as a low battery will result in a slow engine-turning rate and lower readings.

(6) Re-check any cylinder which shows an abnor-

mal reading when compared with the others. Any cylinder having a reading approximately 15 p.s.i. lower than the others should be suspected of being defective.

(7) If a compression tester is suspected of being defective, replace it with one known to be accurate, and re-check the compression of the affected cylinders.

Differential Pressure Tester

The differential pressure tester checks the compression of aircraft engines by measuring the leakage through the cylinders. The design of this compression tester is such that minute valve leakages can be detected, making possible the replacement of cylinders where valve burning is starting.

The operation of the compression tester is based on the principle that, for any given airflow through a fixed orifice, a constant pressure drop across the orifice will result. As the airflow varies, the pressure changes accordingly and in the same direction. If air is supplied under pressure to the cylinder with both intake and exhaust valves closed, the amount of air that leaks by the valves or piston rings indicates their condition; the perfect cylinder, of course, would have no leakage.

The differential pressure tester (figure 10–46) requires the application of air pressure to the cylinder being tested with the piston at top-center compression stroke.

Guidelines for performing a differential compression test are:

(1) Perform the compression test as soon as possible after engine shutdown to provide uniform lubrication of cylinder walls and rings.

(2) Remove the most accessible spark plug from the cylinder or cylinders and install a spark plug adapter in the spark plug insert.

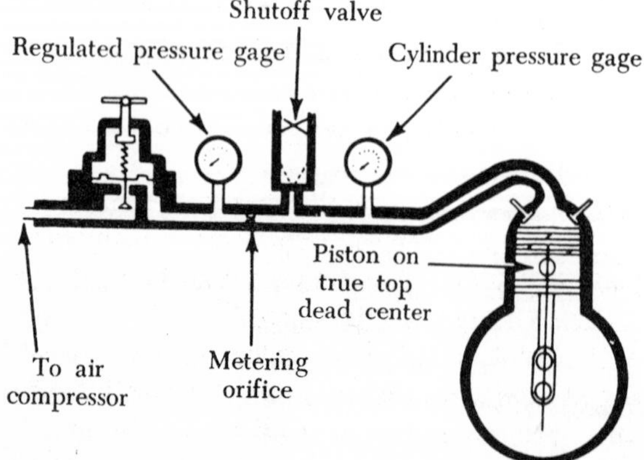

FIGURE 10–46. Differential compression tester.

(3) Connect the compression tester assembly to a 100- to 150-p.s.i. compressed air supply. With the shutoff valve on the compression tester closed, adjust the regulator of the compression tester to obtain 80 p.s.i. on the regulated pressure gage.

(4) Open the shutoff valve and attach the air hose quick-connect fitting to the spark plug adapter. The shutoff valve, when open, will automatically maintain a pressure of 15 to 20 p.s.i. in the cylinder when both the intake and exhaust valves are closed.

(5) By hand, turn the engine over in the direction of rotation until the piston in the cylinder being tested comes up on the compression stroke against the 15 p.s.i. Continue turning the propeller slowly in the direction of rotation until the piston reaches top dead center. Top dead center can be detected by a decrease in force required to move the propeller. If the engine is rotated past top dead center, the 15 to 20 p.s.i. will tend to move the propeller in the direction of rotation. If this occurs, back the propeller up at least one blade prior to turning the propeller again in the direction of rotation. This backing up is necessary to eliminate the effect of backlash in the valve-operating mechanism and to keep the piston rings seated on the lower ring lands.

(6) Close the shutoff valve in the compression tester and re-check the regulated pressure to see that it is 80 p.s.i. with air flowing into the cylinder. If the regulated pressure is more or less than 80 p.s.i., re-adjust the regulator in the test unit to obtain 80 p.s.i. When closing the shutoff valve, make sure that the propeller path is clear of all objects. There will be sufficient air pressure in the combustion chamber to rotate the propeller if the piston is not on top dead center.

(7) With regulated pressure adjusted to 80 p.s.i., if the cylinder pressure reading indicated on the cylinder pressure gage is below the minimum specified for the engine being tested, move the propeller in the direction of rotation to seat the piston rings in the grooves. Check all the cylinders and record the readings.

If low compression is obtained on any cylinder, turn the engine through with the starter or re-start and run the engine to takeoff power and re-check the cylinder or cylinders having low compression.

If the low compression is not corrected, remove the rocker-box cover and check the valve clearance to determine if the difficulty is caused by inadequate valve clearance. If the low compression is not caused by inadequate valve clearance, place a fiber drift on the rocker arm immediately over the valve stem and tap the drift several times with a 1- to 2-pound hammer to dislodge any foreign material that may be lodged between the valve and valve seat. After staking the valve in this manner, rotate the engine with the starter and re-check the compression. Do not make a compression check after staking a valve until the crankshaft has been rotated either with the starter or by hand to re-seat the valve in normal manner. The higher seating velocity obtained when staking the valve will indicate valve seating even though valve seats are slightly egged or eccentric.

Cylinders having compression below the minimum specified after staking should be further checked to determine whether leakage is past the exhaust valve, intake valve, or piston. Excessive leakage can be detected: (1) at the exhaust valve by listening for air leakage at the exhaust outlet; (2) at the intake valve by escaping air at the air intake; and (3) past the piston rings by escaping air at the engine breather outlets.

The wheeze test is another method of detecting leaking intake and exhaust valves. In this test, as the piston is moved to top dead center on the compression stroke, the faulty valve may be detected by listening for a wheezing sound in the exhaust outlet or intake duct.

Another method is to admit compressed air into the cylinder through the spark plug hole. The piston should be restrained at top dead center of the compression stroke during this operation. A leaking valve or piston rings can be detected by listening at the exhaust outlet, intake duct, or engine breather outlets.

Next to valve blow-by, the most frequent cause of compression leakage is excessive leakage past the piston. This leakage may occur because of lack of oil. To check this possibility, squirt engine oil into the cylinder and around the piston. Then re-check the compression. If this procedure raises compression to or above the minimum required, continue the cylinder in service. If the cylinder pressure readings still do not meet the minimum requirement, replace the cylinder. When it is necessary to replace a cylinder as a result of low compression, record the cylinder number and the compression value of the newly installed cylinder on the compression checksheet.

Cylinder Replacement

Reciprocating engine cylinders are designed to operate a specified time before normal wear will require their overhaul. If the engine is operated as recommended and proficient maintenance is performed, the cylinders normally will last until the engine is removed for "high-time" reasons. It is known from experience that materials fail and engines are abused through incorrect operation; this has a serious effect on cylinder life. Another reason for premature cylinder change is poor maintenance. Therefore, exert special care to ensure that all the correct maintenance procedures are adhered to when working on the engine.

Some of the reasons for cylinder replacement are:

(1) Low compression.
(2) High oil consumption in one or more cylinders.
(3) Excessive valve guide clearance.
(4) Loose intake pipe flanges.
(5) Loose or defective spark plug inserts.
(6) External damage, such as cracks.

When conditions like these are limited to one or a few cylinders, replacing the defective cylinders should return the engine to a serviceable condition.

The number of cylinders that can be replaced on air-cooled, in-service engines more economically than changing engines is controversial. Experience has indicated that, in general, one-fourth to one-third of the cylinders on an engine can be replaced economically. Consider these factors when making a decision:

(1) Time on the engine.
(2) Priority established for returning the aircraft to service.
(3) Availability of spare cylinders and spare engines.
(4) Whether QECA (quick engine change assemblies) are being used.
(5) The number of persons available to make the change.

When spare serviceable cylinders are available, replace cylinders when the man-hour requirement for changing them does not exceed the time required to make a complete engine change.

The cylinder is always replaced as a complete assembly, which includes piston, rings, valves, and valve springs. Obtain the cylinder by ordering the cylinder assembly under the part number specified in the engine parts catalog.

Except under certain conditions, do not attempt to replace individual parts, such as pistons, rings, or valves. This precaution guarantees that clearances and tolerances are correct. Other parts, such as valve springs, rocker arms, and rocker box covers, may be replaced individually.

Normally, all the cylinders in an engine are similar; that is, all are standard size or all a certain oversize, and all are steel bore or all are chrome-plated. In some instances, because of shortages at the time of overhaul, it may be necessary that engines have two different sizes of cylinder assemblies.

Replace a cylinder with an identical one, if possible. If an identical cylinder is not available, it is permissible to install either a standard or oversize cylinder and piston assembly, since this will not adversely affect engine operation. The size of the cylinder is indicated by a color code around the barrel (figure 10–47) between the attaching flange and the lower barrel cooling fin.

In some instances, air-cooled engines will be equipped with chrome-plated cylinders. Chrome-plated cylinders are usually identified by a paint band around the barrel between the attaching flange and the lower barrel cooling fin. This color band is usually international orange. When installing a chrome-plated cylinder, do not use chrome-plated piston rings. The matched assembly will, of course, include the correct piston rings. However, if a piston ring is broken during cylinder installation,

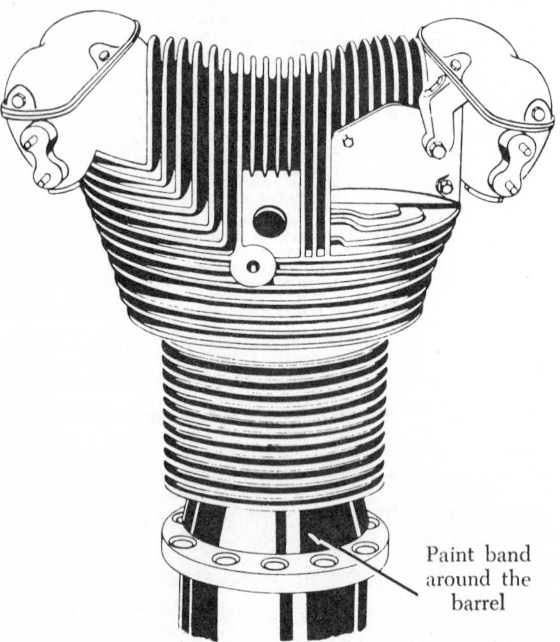

FIGURE 10–47. Identification of cylinder size.

check the cylinder marking to determine what ring, chrome plated or otherwise, is correct for replacement. Similar precautions must be taken to be sure that the correct size rings are installed.

Correct procedures and care are important when replacing cylinders. Careless work or the use of incorrect tools can damage the replacement cylinder or its parts. Incorrect procedures in installing rocker-box covers may result in troublesome oil leaks. Improper torquing of cylinder holddown nuts or capscrews can easily result in a cylinder malfunction and subsequent engine failure.

The discussion of cylinder replacement in this handbook is limited to the removal and installation of air-cooled engine cylinders. The discussion is centered around radial and opposed engines, since these are the aircraft engines on which cylinder replacements are most often performed.

Since these instructions are meant to cover all air-cooled engines, they are necessarily of a general nature. The applicable manufacturer's maintenance manual should be consulted for torque values and special precautions applying to a particular aircraft and engine. However, always practice neatness and cleanliness and always protect openings so that nuts, washers, tools and miscellaneous items do not enter the engine's internal sections.

CYLINDER REMOVAL

Assuming that all obstructing cowling and brackets have been removed, first remove the intake pipe and exhaust pipes. Plug or cover openings in the diffuser section. Then remove cylinder deflectors and any attaching brackets which would obstruct cylinder removal. Loosen the spark plugs and remove the spark-plug lead clamps. Do not remove the spark plugs until ready to pull the cylinder off.

Remove the rocker box covers. First remove the nuts and then tap the cover lightly with a rawhide mallet or plastic hammer. Never pry the cover off with a screwdriver or similar tool.

Loosen the pushrod packing gland nuts or hose clamps, top and bottom. Pushrods are removed by depressing the rocker arms with a special tool or by removing the rocker arm. Before removing the pushrods, turn the crankshaft until the piston is at top dead center on the compression stroke. This relieves the pressure on both intake and exhaust rocker arms. It is also wise to back off the adjusting nut as far as possible, because this allows maximum clearance for pushrod removal when the rocker arms are depressed.

On some model engines, tappets and springs of lower cylinders can fall out. Provision must be made to catch them as the pushrod and housing are removed.

After removing the pushrods, examine them for markings or mark them so that they may be replaced in the same location as they were before removal. The ball ends are usually worn to fit the sockets in which they have been operating. Furthermore, on some engines pushrods are not all of the same length. A good procedure is to mark the pushrods near the valve tappet ends "No. 1 IN," "No. 1 EX," "No. 2 IN," "No. 2 EX," etc.

On fuel injection engines, disconnect the fuel injection line and remove the fuel injection nozzle and any line clamps which will interfere with cylinder removal.

If the cylinder to be removed is a master rod cylinder, special precautions, in addition to regular cylinder removal precautions, must be observed. Information designating which cylinder has the master rod is included on the engine data plate. Arrangements must be made to hold the master rod in the mid-position of the crankcase cylinder hole (after the cylinder has been removed). Templates or guides are usually provided by the manufacturer for this purpose, or they are manufactured locally.

Under no circumstances should the master rod be moved from side to side. It must be kept centered until the guide is in place. Do not turn the crankshaft while the master rod cylinder is removed and other cylinders in the row remain on the engine. These precautions are necessary to prevent bottom rings on some of the other pistons from coming out of the cylinders, expanding, and damaging rings and piston skirts. If several cylinders are to be removed, one of which is the master rod cylinder, it should always be removed last and should be the first installed.

The next step in removing the cylinder is to cut the lockwire or remove the cotter pin, and pry off the locking device from the cylinder-attaching capscrews or nuts. Remove all the screws or nuts except two located 180° apart. Use the wrench specified for this purpose in the special tools section of the applicable manual.

Finally, while supporting the cylinder, remove the two remaining screws or nuts and gently pull the cylinder away from the crankcase. Two men must work together during this step as well as during the remaining procedure for cylinder replacement. After the cylinder skirt has cleared the crankcase and before the piston protrudes from the skirt, provide some means (usually a shop cloth) for preventing pieces of broken rings from falling into the crankcase. After the piston has been removed, remove the cloths and carefully check for piston ring pieces. To make certain that no ring pieces have entered the crankcase, collect and arrange all the pieces to see that they form a complete ring.

Place a support on the cylinder mounting pad and secure it with two capscrews or nuts. Then remove the piston and ring assembly from the connecting rod. When varnish makes it hard to remove the pin, a pin pusher or puller tool must be used. If the special tool is not available and a drift is used to remove the piston pin, the connecting rod should be supported so that it will not have to take the shock of the blows. If this is not done, the rod may be damaged.

After the removal of a cylinder and piston, the connecting rod must be supported to prevent damage to the rod and crankcase. This can be done by supporting each connecting rod with the removed cylinder base oil seal ring looped around the rod and cylinder base studs.

Using a wire brush, clean the studs or capscrews and examine them for cracks, damaged threads, or any other visible defects. If one capscrew is found loose or broken at the time of cylinder removal, all the capscrews for the cylinder should be discarded, since the remaining capscrews may have been seriously weakened. A cylinder holddown stud failure will place the adjacent studs under a greater operating pressure, and they are likely to be stretched beyond their elastic limit. The engine manufacturer's instruction must be followed for the number of studs that will have to be replaced after a stud failure.

When removing a broken stud, take proper precautions to prevent metal chips from entering the engine power section.

In all cases, both faces of the washers and the seating faces of stud nuts or capscrews must be cleaned and any roughness or burrs removed.

CYLINDER INSTALLATION

See that all preservative oil accumulation on the cylinder and piston assembly is washed off with solvent and thoroughly dried with compressed air. Install the piston and ring assembly on the connecting rod. Be sure that the piston faces in the right direction. The piston number stamped on the bottom of the piston head should face toward the front of the engine. Lubricate the piston pin before inserting it. It should fit with a push fit. If a drift must be used, follow the same precaution that was taken during pin removal.

Oil the exterior of the piston assembly generously, forcing oil around the piston rings and in the space between the rings and grooves. Stagger the ring gaps around the piston and check to see that rings are in the correct grooves and whether they are positioned correctly, because some are used as oil scrapers, others as pumper rings. The number, type and arrangement of the compression and oil-control rings will vary with the make and model of engine.

If it is necessary to replace the rings on one or more of the pistons, check the side clearance against the manufacturer's specification, using a thickness gage. The ring end gap must also be checked. The method for checking side and end clearance is shown in figure 10–48. If the ring gage shown is not available, a piston (without rings) may be inserted in the cylinder and the ring inserted in the cylinder bore. Insert the ring in the cylinder skirt below the mounting flange, since this is usually the smallest bore diameter. Pull the piston against the ring to align it properly in the bore.

If it is necessary to remove material to obtain the correct side clearance, it can be done either by turning the piston grooves a slight amount on each side or by lapping the ring on a surface plate.

If the end gap is too close, the excess metal can be removed by clamping a mill file in a vise, holding the ring in proper alignment, and dressing off the ends. In all cases the engine manufacturer's procedures must be followed.

Before installing the cylinder, check the flange to see that the mating surface is smooth and clean. Coat the inside of the cylinder barrel generously with oil. Be sure that the cylinder oil-seal ring is in place and that only one seal ring is used.

Using a ring compressor, compress the rings to a diameter equal to that of the piston. Start the cylinder assembly down over the piston, making certain that the cylinder and piston plane remain the same. Ease the cylinder over the piston with a straight, even movement which will move the ring compressor as the cylinder slips on. Do not rock the cylinder while slipping it on the piston, since any rocking is apt to release a piston ring or a part of a ring from the ring compressor prior to the ring's entrance into the cylinder bore. A ring released in this manner will expand and prevent the piston from entering the cylinder. Any attempt to force the cylinder onto the piston is apt to cause

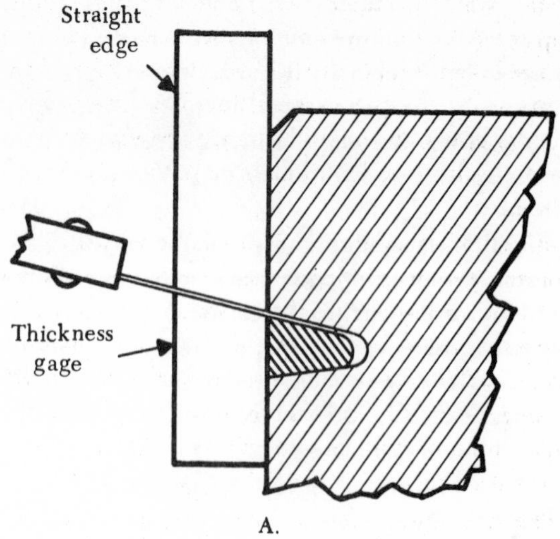

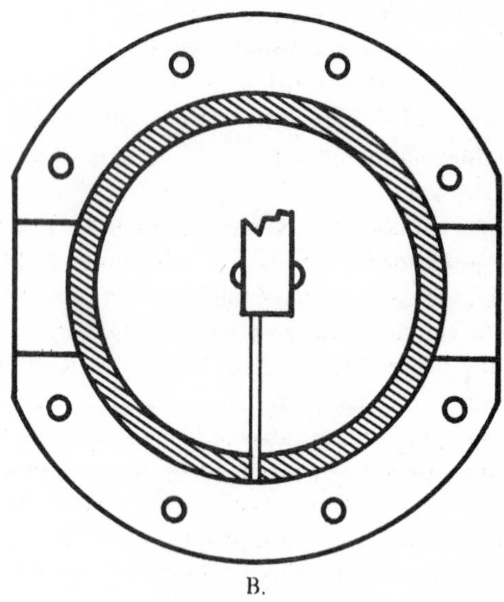

FIGURE 10–48. (A) Measuring piston ring side clearance and (B) end gap.

cracking or chipping of the ring or damage to the ring lands.

After the cylinder has slipped on the piston so that all piston rings are in the cylinder bore, remove the ring compressor and the connecting rod guide. Then slide the cylinder into place on the mounting pad. If capscrews are used, rotate the cylinder to align the holes. While still supporting the cylinder, install two capscrews or stud nuts 180° apart.

If the cylinder is secured to the crankcase by conical washers and nuts or capscrews, position the cylinder on the crankcase section by two special locating nuts or capscrews. These locating nuts or capscrews do not remain on the engine, but are removed and replaced with regular nuts or capscrews and conical washers after they have served their purpose and the other nuts or capscrews have been installed and tightened to the prescribed torque.

Install the remaining nuts or capscrews with their conical washers, and tighten the nuts or capscrews until they are snug. Make sure that the conical side of each washer is toward the cylinder mounting flange. Before inserting capscrews, coat them with a good sealer to prevent oil leakage. Generally, studs fit into holes and the fit is tight enough to prevent leakage.

The holddown nuts or capscrews must now be torqued to the value specified in the table of torque values in the engine manufacturer's service or overhaul manual. A definite and specific sequence of tightening all cylinder fastenings must be followed. Always refer to the appropriate engine service manual. A general rule is to tighten the first two nuts or capscrews 180° from each other; then tighten two alternate nuts or capscrews 90° from the first two.

If locating nuts or capscrews are being used, they should be torqued first. The tightening of the remaining screws or nuts should be alternated 180° as the torquing continues around the cylinder. Apply the torque with a slow, steady motion until the prescribed value is reached. Hold the tension on the wrench for a sufficient length of time to ensure that the nut or capscrew will tighten no more at the prescribed torque value. In many cases, additional turning of the capscrew or nut as much as one-quarter turn can be done by maintaining the prescribed torque on the nut for a short period of time. After tightening the regular nuts or capscrews, remove the two locating nuts or capscrews, install regular nuts or capscrews, and tighten them to the prescribed torque.

After the stud nuts or capscrews have been torqued to the prescribed value, safety them in the manner recommended in the engine manufacturer's service manual.

Re-install the push rods, push rod housings, rocker arms, barrel deflectors, intake pipes, ignition harness lead clamps and brackets, fuel injection line clamps and fuel injection nozzles, exhaust stack, cylinder head deflectors, and spark plugs. Remember that the push rods must be installed in their original locations and must not be turned end to end. Make sure, too, that the push rod ball end seats properly in the tappet. If it rests on the edge or shoulder of the tappet during valve clearance adjustment and later drops into place, valve clearance will be off. Furthermore, rotating the crankshaft with the push rod resting on the edge of the tappet may bend the push rod.

After installing the push rods and rocker arms, set the valve clearance.

Before installing the rocker box covers, lubricate the rocker arm bearings and valve stems. Check the rocker box covers for flatness, and re-surface them if necessary. After installing the gaskets and covers, tighten the rocker box cover nuts to the specified torque.

Safety those nuts, screws, and other fasteners which require safetying. Follow the recommended safetying procedures.

VALVE AND VALVE MECHANISM

Valves open and close the ports in the cylinder head to control the entrance of the combustible mixture and the exit of the exhaust gases. It is important that they open and close properly and seal tight against the port seats to secure maximum power from the burning fuel/air mixture for the crankshaft, and to prevent valve burning and warping. The motion of the valves is controlled by the valve-operating mechanism.

The valve mechanism includes cam plates or shafts, cam followers, pushrods, rocker arms, valve springs, and retainers. All parts of a valve mechanism must be in good condition and valve clearances must be correct if the valves are to operate properly.

Checking and adjusting the valve clearance is perhaps the most important part of valve inspection, and certainly it is the most difficult part. However, the visual inspection should not be slighted. It should include a check for the following major items:

(1) Metal particles in the rocker box are indications of excessive wear or partial failure of the valve mechanism. Locate and replace the defective parts.

(2) Excessive side clearance or galling of the rocker arm side. Replace defective rocker arms. Add shims when permitted, to correct excessive side clearance.

(3) Insufficient clearance between the rocker arm and the valve spring retainer. Follow the procedure outlined in the engine service manual for checking this clearance, and increase it to the minimum specified.

(4) Replace any damaged parts, such as cracked, broken, or chipped rocker arms, valve springs, or spring retainers. If the damaged part is one which cannot be replaced in the field, replace the cylinder.

(5) Excessive valve stem clearance. A certain amount of valve stem wobble in the valve guide is normal. Replace the cylinder only in severe cases.

(6) Evidence of incorrect lubrication. Excessive dryness indicates insufficient lubrication. However, the lubrication varies between engines and between cylinders in the same model engine. For example, the upper boxes of radial engines will normally run drier than the lower rocker boxes. These factors must be taken into account in determining whether or not ample lubrication is being obtained. Wherever improper lubrication is indicated, determine the cause and correct it. For example, a dry rocker may be caused by a plugged oil passage in the pushrod. Excessive oil may be caused by plugged drains between the rocker box and the crankcase. If the push rod drains become clogged, the oil forced to the rocker arm and other parts of the valve mechanism cannot drain back to the crankcase. This may result in oil leakage at the rocker box cover or in oil seepage along valve stems into the cylinder or exhaust system, causing excessive oil consumption on the affected cylinder and smoking in the exhaust.

(7) Excessive sludge in the rocker box. This indicates an excessive rocker box temperature, which, in turn, may be caused by improper positioning of cowling or exhaust heat shields or baffles. After correcting the cause of the difficulty, spray the interior of the rocker box with dry cleaning solvent, blow it dry with compressed air, and then coat the entire valve mechanism and interior of the rocker box with clean engine oil.

(8) Variation in valve clearance not explained by normal wear. If there is excessive valve clearance, check for bent push rods. Replace any that are defective. Check also for valve sticking. If the push rod is straight and the valve opens and closes when the propeller is pulled through by hand, check the tightness of the adjusting screw to determine whether the clearance was set incorrectly or the adjusting screw has loosened.

After adjusting the clearance on each valve, tighten the lock screw or nut to the torque specified in the maintenance manual. After completing all clearance adjustments and before installing the rocker box covers, make a final check of all lock screws or nuts for tightness with a torque wrench.

Warped rocker box covers are a common cause of oil leakage. Therefore, the box covers should be checked for flatness at each valve inspection. Re-surface any warped covers by lapping them on emery cloth laid on a surface plate. Rocker box cover warpage is often caused by improper tightening of the rocker box cover nuts. Eliminate further warpage by torquing the nuts to the values specified in the manufacturer's service manual.

Valve Clearance

The amount of power that can be produced by a cylinder depends primarily on the amount of heat that can be produced in that cylinder without destructive effects on the cylinder components. Any condition that limits the amount of heat in the cylinder also limits the amount of power which that cylinder can produce.

The manufacturer, in determining valve timing and establishing the maximum power setting at which the engine will be permitted to run, considers the amount of heat at which cylinder components such as spark plugs and valves can operate efficiently. The heat level of the exhaust valve must be below that at which pitting and warping of the valve occurs.

The head of the exhaust valve is exposed to the heat of combustion at all times during the combustion period. In addition, the head of this valve and a portion of the stem are exposed to hot exhaust gases during the exhaust event. Under normal operation, the exhaust valve remains below the critical heat level because of its contact with the valve seat when closed and because of the heat dissipated through the stem. Any condition which prevents the valve from seating properly for the required proportion of time will cause the valve to exceed the critical heat limits during periods of high power output. In cases of extremely poor valve seat contact, the exhaust valve can warp during periods of low power output.

Normally, the exhaust valve is closed and in contact with its seat about 65% of the time during the four-stroke cycle. If the valve adjustment is correct, and if the valve seats firmly when closed, much of the heat is transferred from the valve, through the seat, into the cylinder head.

In order for a valve to seat, the valve must be in good condition, with no significant pressure being exerted against the end of the valve by the rocker arm. If the expansion of all parts of the engine including the valve train were the same, the problem of ensuring valve seating would be very easy to solve. Practically no free space would be necessary in the valve system. However, since there is a great difference in the amount of expansion of various parts of the engine, there is no way of providing a constant operating clearance in the valve train. The clearance in the valve-actuating system is very small when the engine is cold but is much greater when the engine is operating at normal temperature. The difference is caused by differences in the expansion characteristics of the various metals and by the differences in temperature of various engine parts.

There are many reasons why proper valve clearances are of vital importance to satisfactory and stable engine operation. For example, when the engine is operating, valve clearances establish valve timing. Since all cylinders receive their fuel/air mixture (or air) from a common supply, valve clearance affects both the amount and the richness or leanness of the fuel/air mixture. Therefore, it is essential that valve clearances be correct and uniform between each cylinder.

On radial engines, valve clearance decreases with a drop in temperature; therefore, insufficient clearance may cause the valve to hold open when extremely cold temperatures are encountered. This may make cold-weather starting of the engine difficult, if not impossible, because of the inability of the cylinders to pull a combustible charge into the combustion chamber.

Accurate valve adjustment establishes the intended valve seating velocity. If valve clearances are excessive, the valve seating velocity is too high. The result is valve pounding and stem stretching, either of which is conducive to valve failure. Insufficient clearance may make starting difficult and cause valves to stick in the "open" position, causing blow-by and subsequent valve failure as a result of the extreme temperatures to which the valve is subjected.

The engine manufacturer specifies the valve inspection period for each engine. In addition to the regular periods, inspect and adjust the valve mechanism any time there is rough engine operation, backfiring, loss of compression, or hard starting.

Because of variations in engine designs, various methods are required for setting valves to obtain correct and consistent clearances. In all cases, follow the exact procedure prescribed by the engine manufacturer, since obscure factors may be involved. For example, there is considerable cam float on many radial engines, and the valve-adjusting procedure for these engines is developed to permit accurate and consistent positioning of the cam. Since the ratio of valve movement to pushrod movement may be as much as two to one, each 0.001 in. shift of the cam can result in a 0.002 in. variation in valve clearances.

Wright engines incorporate pressure-lubricated valves. Oil under pressure passes through the pushrod and into the center of the valve-clearance adjusting screw. From this point, oil passages radiate in three directions. To permit proper lubrication, one of the three passages in the adjusting screw must be at least partially open to the passage leading to the rocker arm bearing. At the same time, neither of the other two passages must be uncovered by being in the slot in the rocker arm. Determine the location of the oil passages in the adjusting screw by locating the "0" stamped in three places on its top (figure 10–49). If there are only two stamped circles, the third oil passage is midway between the two marked ones. After final tailoring of the valve adjustment, if any one of the three oil passages aligns with or is closer than 3/32 in. to the nearest edge of the slot in the rocker arm, turn the adjusting screw in a direction to increase or decrease the clearance until the reference "0" mark is 3/32 in. from the nearest edge of the slot in the rocker arm, or until the maximum or minimum valve clearance is reached.

Pratt and Whitney engines also incorporate pressure-lubricated valves. On these engines, there is no slot in the rocker arm, but the valve-clearance adjusting screw can be turned in or backed out so far that the oil passage from the screw into the rocker arm is blocked. The specific instructions

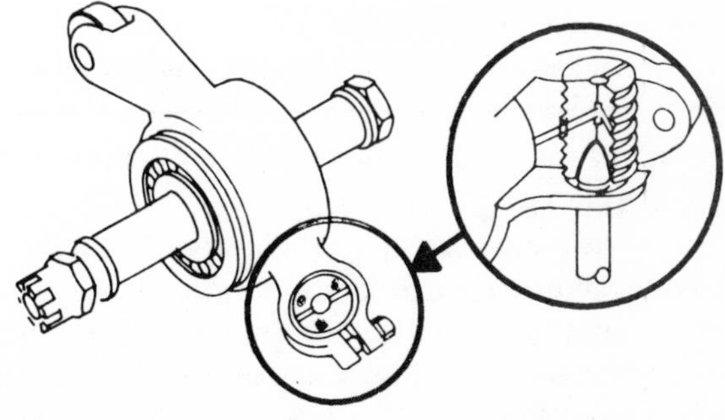

FIGURE 10–49. Aligning valve adjusting screw.

for setting clearance on the Pratt and Whitney engines state that a certain number of threads must show above the rocker arm. For example, on one model engine at least two threads and not more than five must show, and will, providing the pushrod is the correct length. Correct the pushrod length by pulling off one of the ball ends and changing the washer beneath for a thicker or thinner one. If there is no washer and the rod is too long, correct it by grinding away the end of the rod. Check the engine manufacturer's service or overhaul manual for the maximum or minimum number of threads which may show on the engine in question.

When adjusting valve clearances, always use the valve clearance gage or the dial gage specified in the "tools" section of the engine manufacturer's service manual. The specified gage is of the proper thickness and is so shaped that the end being used for checking can be slipped in a straight line between the valve and the rocker arm roller of the rocker arm. When a standard gage is used without being bent to the proper angle, a false clearance will be established since the gage will be cocked between the valve stem and rocker arm or rocker arm roller.

In making the check with the feeler gage, do not use excessive force to insert the gage between the valve stem and the adjustment screw or rocker arm roller. The gage can be inserted by heavy force, even though the clearance may be several thousandths of an inch less than the thickness of the gage. This precaution is particularly important on engines where the cam is centered during valve clearance adjustment, since forcing the gage on these engines may cause the cam to shift, with subsequent false readings.

When a dial gage and brackets for mounting the gage on the rocker box are specified, be sure to use them. A dial gage with a bracket may be used for checking valve clearances on any engine, provided the rocker arm arrangement is such that the pickup arm of the gage is located over the center line of the valve stem.

With a dial gage, the clearance is the amount of travel obtained when the rocker arm is rotated from the valve stem until the other end of the rocker arm contacts the pushrod.

Since valve clearance adjustment procedures vary between engines, a single treatment will not be sufficient. Thus, the procedures for various engines or groups of engines are treated separately in the following paragraphs. However, the procedures are described only to provide an understanding of the operations involved. Consult the engine manufacturer's instructions for the clearance to be set, the torque to be applied to lockscrews and rocker box cover nuts, and other pertinent details.

The first step in checking and adjusting valve clearances is to set the piston in the No. 1 cylinder at top-center compression stroke. Turn the propeller by hand until the valve action or cylinder pressure against a thumb held over the spark plug hole indicates that the piston is coming up on the compression stroke. Insert a piece of aluminum tubing into the spark plug hole and turn the propeller in the direction of rotation until the piston reaches its highest position. Proper precaution must be taken to make sure that the piston is on compression stroke.

After positioning the piston and crankshaft, adjust intake and exhaust valve clearances on the No. 1 cylinder to the prescribed values. Then adjust each succeeding cylinder in firing order, properly positioning the crankshaft for each cylinder.

Re-check the valve clearances and re-adjust any that are outside the limits. On this second check, align the oil passages in the adjusting screws of engines incorporating pressure-lubricated valves.

Adjusting Valves on R-2800 Engine

Establish top-center position of the No. 11 cylinder on the exhaust stroke. To do this, first ascertain that the piston is coming up on the compression stroke. Then insert an aluminum tube into the spark plug hole and turn the propeller in the direction of rotation until the piston has gone through the power stroke and returned to the top of the cylinder again. After the approximate top piston position has been ascertained, establish true top piston position by turning the propeller first in one direction and then in the other, until the position of the aluminum tube indicates the piston is at its highest point in the cylinder. A top-center indicator can also be used to establish top piston position.

Depress the intake valve on the No. 7 cylinder and the exhaust valve on the No. 15 cylinder, using a valve depressor tool. The valves must be depressed and released simultaneously and smoothly. These valves must be unloaded to remove the spring tension from the side positions on the cam and thus permit the cam to slide away from the valves to be adjusted until it contacts the cam bearing. This locates the cam in a definite position and prevents cam shift from introducing errors in clearance.

Adjust the intake valve on the No. 1 cylinder and the exhaust valve on the No. 3 cylinder. Follow the chart in figure 10–50 in adjusting the remaining valves.

Set Piston on Top Center Exhaust	Unload Valves on Cylinders		Check and Adjust Valves on Cylinders	
Cylinder Number	Intake	Exhaust	Intake	Exhaust
11	7	15	1	3
4	18	8	12	14
15	11	1	5	7
8	4	12	16	18
1	15	5	9	11
12	8	16	2	4
5	1	9	13	15
16	12	2	6	8
9	5	13	17	1
2	16	6	10	12
13	9	17	3	5
6	2	10	14	16
17	13	3	7	9
10	6	14	18	2
3	17	7	11	13
14	10	18	4	6
7	3	11	15	17
18	14	4	8	10

FIGURE 10–50. Valve clearance adjustment chart for R–2800 engine.

After completing the first check and adjustment of valve clearances, make a second check and re-adjust any clearances which vary from those specified in the engine manufacturer's service manual. On this second check, follow the precautions outlined in this chapter under adjustment of pressure-lubricated valves for Pratt and Whitney engines.

Adjusting Valves on R-1830 Engine

Establish compression stroke of the No. 1 cylinder by holding a thumb over the spark plug hole to feel cylinder compresion as the propeller is turned in the direction of rotation. When the pressure indicates that the piston is coming up on compression stroke, insert an aluminum tube into the spark plug hole and continue turning the propeller until the piston is at the top of its stroke.

With the crankshaft properly set, depress the intake valve on the No. 9 cylinder and the exhaust valve on the No. 7 cylinder with a valve depressor tool, and release them simultaneously. This operation relieves pressure on the sides of the cam and permits it to shift away from the valves in the No. 1 cylinder. The valves to be depressed are open at this time; thus, the ball end of the push rod will not fall out of position when the valves are depressed.

Adjust both intake and exhaust valves on the No. 1 cylinder. Check and adjust the valves on the remaining cylinders in firing order, following the chart in figure 10–51.

After completing this initial check, make a second check and re-adjust any clearances which are outside the limits specified in the engine manufacturer's maintenance manual. On this second check, follow the special precautions for adjustment of pressure-lubricated valves on Pratt and Whitney engines.

Adjusting Valves on 0-300, 0-335, 0-405, 0-425, V0-435 and 0-470 Engines

In checking and adjusting valve clearances on any of these engines, first set the piston in the No. 1 cylinder at top-center compression stroke. To find the right stroke, hold a thumb over the spark plug hole and turn the propeller in the direction of rotation until the pressure buildup indicates that the piston is coming up on compression stroke. Then insert an aluminum tube into the spark plug hole and continue turning the propeller until the piston is at the top of its stroke. Rock the propeller back and forth to aid in accurately positioning the piston.

After positioning the piston and crankshaft, displace the oil in the hydraulic tappet assembly by depressing the rocker arm with the tool specified in the engine manufacturer's service manual. Apply pressure smoothly and evenly since excessive force may damage the rocker arm or the push rod. Four or 5 seconds will be required to displace the oil

Set Piston on Top Center Compression	Unload Valves on Cylinders		Check and Adjust Valves on Cylinders
Cylinder Number	Intake	Exhaust	Intake and Exhaust
1	9	7	1
10	4	2	10
5	13	11	5
14	8	6	14
9	3	1	9
4	12	10	4
13	7	5	13
8	2	14	8
3	11	9	3
12	6	4	12
7	1	13	7
2	10	8	2
11	5	3	11
6	14	12	6

FIGURE 10–51. Valve clearance adjustment chart for R–1830 engine.

from the hydraulic tappet. If no clearance is obtained, remove and wash the tappet plunger and then re-check the clearance. Where valve adjustments are provided, re-adjust as necessary. On engines on which no adjustment is provided, replace the push rod with a longer or shorter rod, as outlined in the specific instructions for the engine.

Adjust the valves on succeeding cylinders in the engine firing order. After completing this initial check, make a second check and re-adjust any clearances which are outside the specified limits.

Valve Spring Replacement

A broken valve spring seldom affects engine operation and can, therefore, be detected only during careful inspection. Because multiple springs are used, one broken spring is hard to detect. But when a broken valve spring is discovered, it can be replaced without removing the cylinder. During valve spring replacement, the important precaution to remember is not to damage the spark plug hole threads. The complete procedure for valve spring replacement is as follows:

(1) Remove one spark plug from the cylinder.

(2) Turn the propeller in the direction of rotation until the piston is at the top of the compression stroke.

(3) Remove rocker arm.

(4) Using a valve spring compressor, compress the spring and remove the valve keepers. During this operation, it may be necessary to insert a piece of brass rod through the spark plug hole to decrease the space between the valve and the top of the piston head to break the spring retaining washer loose from the keepers. The piston, being at the top position on the compression stroke, prevents the valve from dropping down into the cylinder once the spring retaining washers are broken loose from the keepers on the stem.

(5) Remove the defective spring and any broken pieces from the rocker box.

(6) Install a new spring and correct washers. Then, using the valve spring compressor, compress the spring and, if necessary, move the valve up from the piston by means of a brass rod inserted through the spark plug hole.

(7) Re-install the keepers and rocker arms. Then check and adjust the valve clearance.

(8) Re-install the rocker box cover and the spark plug.

COLD CYLINDER CHECK

The cold cylinder check determines the operating characteristics of each cylinder of an air-cooled engine. The tendency for any cylinder or cylinders to be cold or to be only slightly warm indicates lack of combustion or incomplete combustion within the cylinder. This must be corrected if best operation and power conditions are to be obtained. The cold cylinder check is made with a cold cylinder indicator (Magic Wand). Engine difficulties which can be analyzed by use of the cold cylinder indicator (figure 10–52) are:

(1) Rough engine operation.

(2) Excessive r.p.m. drop during the ignition system check.

(3) High manifold pressure for a given engine r.p.m. during the ground check when the propeller is in the full low-pitch position.

(4) Faulty mixture ratios caused by improper valve clearance.

In preparation for the cold cylinder check, head

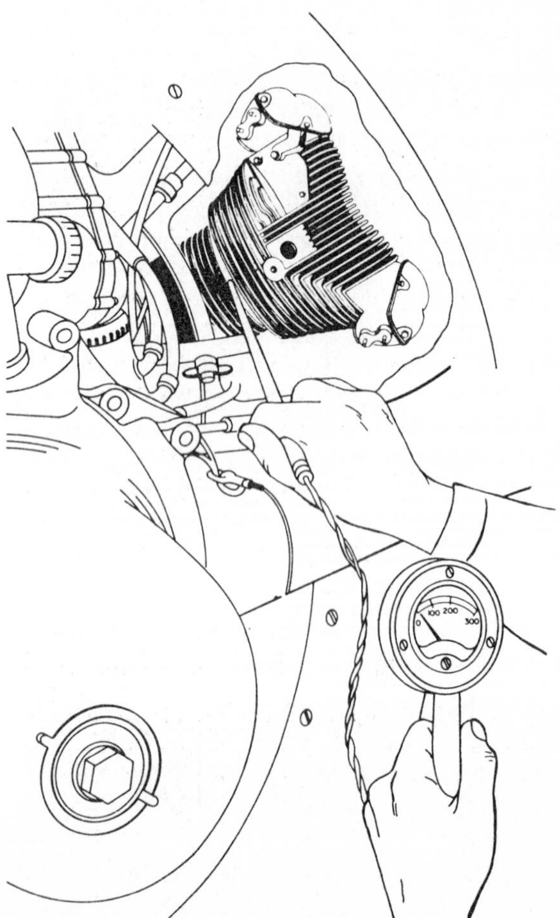

FIGURE 10–52. Using a cold cylinder indicator.

the aircraft into the wind to minimize irregular cooling of the individual cylinders and to ensure even propeller loading during engine operation.

Open the cowl flaps. Do not close the cowl flaps under any circumstances, as the resulting excessive heat radiation will affect the readings obtained and can damage the ignition leads.

Start the engine with the ignition switch in the "BOTH" position. After the engine is running, place the ignition switch in the position in which any excessive r.p.m. drop is obtained. When excessive r.p.m. drop is encountered on both right and left switch positions, or when excessive manifold pressure is obtained at a given engine r.p.m., perform the check twice, once on the left and once on the right switch position.

Operate the engine at its roughest speed between 1,200 and 1,600 r.p.m. until a cylinder head temperature reading of 150° to 170° C. (302° to 338° F.) is obtained, or until temperatures stabilize at a lower reading. If engine roughness is encountered at more than one speed, or if there is an indication that a cylinder ceases operating at idle or higher speeds, run the engine at each of these speeds and perform a cold cylinder check to pick out all the dead or intermittently operating cylinders. When low-power output or engine vibration is encountered at speeds above 1,600 r.p.m. when operating with the ignition switch on "BOTH," run the engine at the speed where the difficulty is encountered until the cylinder head temperatures are up to 150° to 170° C. or until the temperatures have stabilized at a lower value.

When cylinder head temperatures have reached the values prescribed in the foregoing paragraph, stop the engine by moving the mixture control to the idle cutoff or full lean position. When the engine ceases firing, turn off both ignition and master switches. Record the cylinder head temperature reading registered on the cockpit gage.

As soon as the propeller has ceased rotating, move a maintenance stand to the front of the engine. Connect the clip attached to the cold cylinder indicator lead to the engine or propeller to provide a ground for the instrument. Press the tip of the indicator pickup rod against each cylinder, and record the relative temperature of each cylinder. Start with number one and proceed in numerical order around the engine, as rapidly as possible. To obtain comparative temperature values, a firm contact must be made at the same relative location on each cylinder. Re-check any outstandingly low values. Also re-check the two cylinders having the highest readings to determine the amount of cylinder cooling during the test. Compare the temperature readings to determine which cylinders are dead or are operating intermittently.

Difficulties which may cause a cylinder to be inoperative (dead) on both right and left magneto positions are:

(1) Defective spark plugs.
(2) Incorrect valve clearances.
(3) Leaking impeller oil seal.
(4) Leaking intake pipes.
(5) Lack of compression.
(6) Plugged push rod housing drains.
(7) Faulty operation of the fuel-injection nozzle (on fuel-injection engines).

Before changing spark plugs or making an ignition harness test on cylinders that are not operating or are operating intermittently, check the magneto ground leads to determine that the wiring is connected correctly.

Repeat the cold cylinder test for the other magneto positions on the ignition switch, if necessary. Cooling the engine between tests is unnecessary. The airflow created by the propeller and the cooling effect of the incoming fuel/air mixture will be sufficient to cool any cylinders that are functioning on one test and not functioning on the next.

In interpreting the results of a cold cylinder check, remember that the temperatures are relative. A cylinder temperature taken alone means little, but when compared with the temperatures of other cylinders on the same engine, it provides valuable diagnostic information. The readings shown in figure 10–53 illustrate this point. On this check, the cylinder head temperature gage reading at the time the engine was shut down was 160° C. on both tests.

A review of these temperature readings reveals that, on the right magneto, cylinder number 6 runs cool and cylinders 8 and 9 run cold. This indicates that cylinder 6 is firing intermittently and cylinders 8 and 9 are dead during engine operation on the front plugs (fired by the right magneto). Cylinders 9 and 10 are dead during operation on the rear plugs (fired by the left magneto). Cylinder 9 is completely dead.

An ignition system operational check would not disclose this dead cylinder since the cylinder is inoperative on both right and left switch positions.

A dead cylinder can be detected during run-up, since an engine with a dead cylinder will require a

Cylinder No.	Right Magneto	Left Magneto
1	180	170
2	170	175
3	170	170
4	145	150
5	150	155
6	(100)	150
7	155	160
8	(70)	155
9	(60)	(45)
10	150	(65)
11	150	145
12	145	150
13	150	145
14	145	145

FIGURE 10–53. Readings taken during a cold-cylinder check.

higher-than-normal manifold pressure to produce any given r.p.m. below the cut-in speed of the propeller governor. A dead cylinder could also be detected by comparing power input and power output with the aid of a torquemeter.

Defects within the ignition system that can cause a cylinder to go completely dead are:

(1) Both spark plugs inoperative.

(2) Both ignition leads grounded, leaking, or open.

(3) A combination of inoperative spark plugs and defective ignition leads.

Faulty fuel-injection nozzles, incorrect valve clearances, and other defects outside the ignition system can also cause dead cylinders.

In interpreting the readings obtained on a cold-cylinder check, the amount the engine cools during the check must be considered. To determine the extent to which this factor should be considered in evaluating the readings, re-check some of the first cylinders tested and compare the final readings with those made at the start of the check. Another factor to be considered is the normal variation in temperature between cylinders and between rows. This variation results from those design features which affect the airflow past the cylinders.

TURBINE ENGINE MAINTENANCE

Turbine powerplant maintenance procedures vary widely according to the design and construction of the particular engine being serviced. The detailed procedures recommended by the engine manufacturer should be followed when performing inspections or maintenance.

Maintenance information presented in this section is not intended to specify the exact manner in which maintenance operations are to be performed, but is included to convey a general idea of the procedures involved. For the most part, the Pratt and Whitney JT3 turbojet engine is used in describing procedures for axial-flow compressor and turbine blade maintenance.

For inspection purpose, the turbine engine is divided into two main sections, the cold section and the hot section.

Compressor Section

Maintenance of the compressor, or cold section, is one of the concerns of the aviation mechanic. Damage to blades can cause engine failure and possible loss of costly aircraft. Much of the damage to the blades arises from foreign matter being drawn into the turbine engine air intakes.

The atmosphere near the ground is filled with tiny particles of dirt, oil, soot, and other foreign matter. A large volume of air is introduced into the compressor, and centrifugal force throws the dirt particles outward so that they build up to form a coating on the casing, the vanes, and the compressor blades.

Accumulation of dirt on the compressor blades reduces the aerodynamic efficiency of the blades with resultant deterioration in engine performance. The efficiency of the blades is impaired by dirt deposits in a manner similar to that of an aircraft wing under icing conditions. Unsatisfactory acceleration and high exhaust gas temperature can result from foreign deposits on compressor components.

An end result of foreign particles, if allowed to accumulate in sufficient quantity, would be complete engine failure. The condition can be remedied by periodic inspection, cleaning, and repair of compressor components. This subject is treated in a general manner in this text because of the many different models of turbojet engines now in use in aviation.

Inspection and Cleaning

Minor damage to axial-flow engine compressor blades may be repaired if the damage can be removed without exceeding the allowable limits established by the manufacturer. Typical compressor blade repair limits are shown in figure 10–54. Well-rounded damage to leading and trailing edges that is evident on the opposite side of the blade is usually acceptable without re-work, provided the damage is in the outer half of the blade only and the indentation does not exceed values specified in

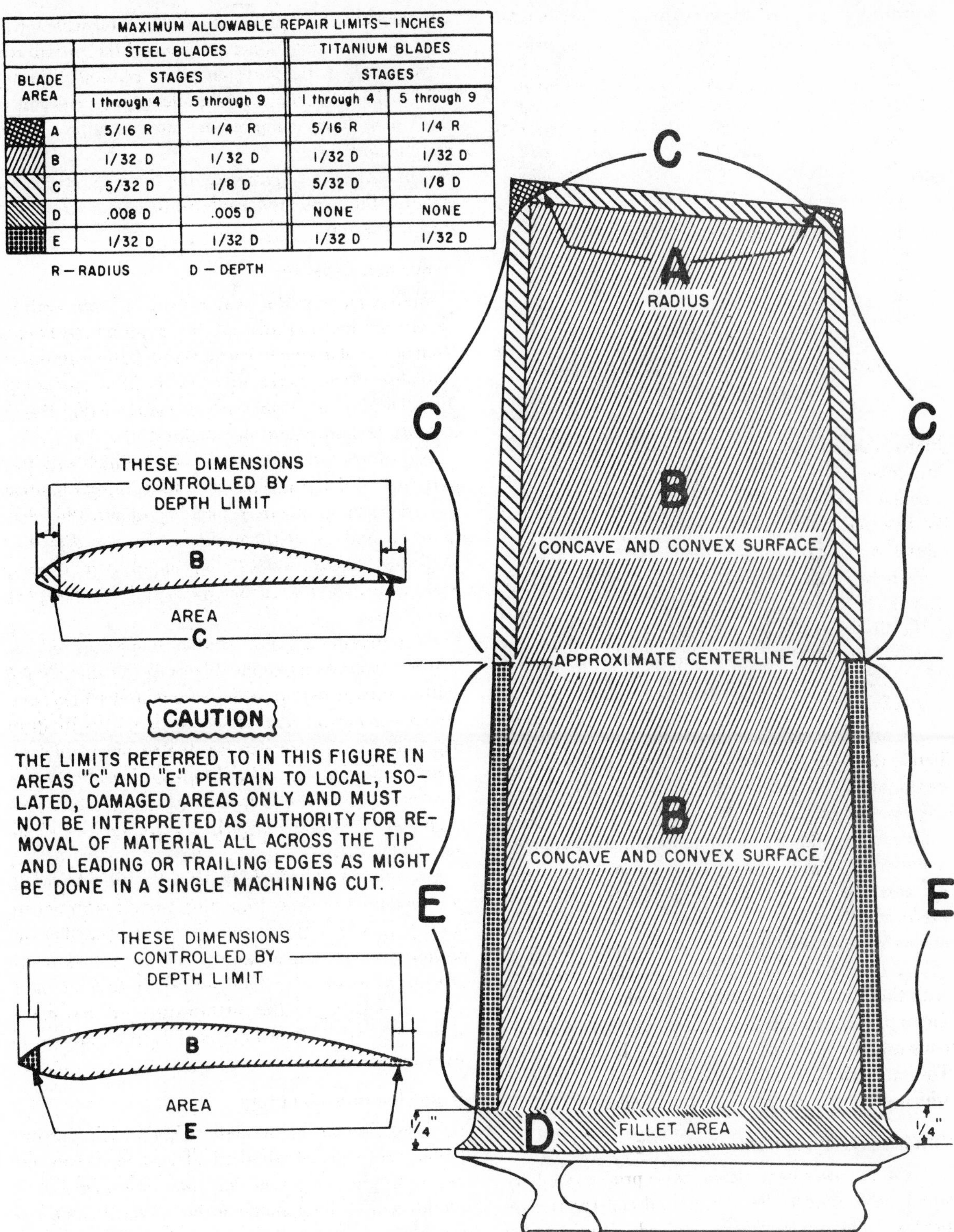

MAXIMUM ALLOWABLE REPAIR LIMITS— INCHES				
	STEEL BLADES		TITANIUM BLADES	
BLADE AREA	STAGES		STAGES	
	I through 4	5 through 9	I through 4	5 through 9
A	5/16 R	1/4 R	5/16 R	1/4 R
B	1/32 D	1/32 D	1/32 D	1/32 D
C	5/32 D	1/8 D	5/32 D	1/8 D
D	.008 D	.005 D	NONE	NONE
E	1/32 D	1/32 D	1/32 D	1/32 D

R — RADIUS D — DEPTH

FIGURE 10–54. Typical compressor blade repair limits.

the engine manufacturer's service and overhaul instruction manuals.

When working on the inner half of the blade, damage must be treated with extreme caution. Repaired compressor blades are inspected by either magnetic particle or fluorescent penetrant inspection methods, or they are dye checked to ensure that all traces of the damage have been removed. All repairs must be well blended so that surfaces are smooth (figure 10–55). No cracks of any extent are tolerated in any area.

Whenever possible, stoning and local rework of the blade are performed parallel to the length of the blade. Rework must be accomplished by hand, using stones, files, or emery cloth. Do not use a power tool to buff the entire area of the blade. The surface finish in the repaired area must be comparable to that of a new blade.

On centrifugal flow engines, it is difficult to inspect the compressor inducers without first removing the air-inlet screen. After removing the screen, clean the compressor inducer and inspect it with a strong light. Check each vane for cracks by slowly turning the compressor.

Look for cracks in the leading edges. A crack is usually cause for engine replacement. The compressor inducers are normally the parts that are damaged by the impingement of foreign material during engine operation.

Compressor inducers are repaired by stoning out and blending the nicks and dents in the "critical band" (1-1/2 to 2-1/2 inches from the outside edge), if the depth of such nicks or dents does not exceed that specified in the engine manufacturer's service or overhaul instruction manuals. For nicks requiring repair, stone out material beyond the depth of damage to remove the resulting cold-worked metal. A generous radius must be applied at the edges of the blend. After blending the nick, it should be smoothed over with a crocus cloth. Pitting, nicks, or corrosion found on the sides of the inducer vanes are similarly removed by blending.

Causes of Blade Damage

Loose objects often enter an engine either accidentally or through carelessness. Items, such as pencils, handkerchiefs, and cigarette lighters, are often drawn into the engine. Do not carry any objects in shirt pockets when working around turbojet engines.

A compressor rotor can be damaged beyond repair by tools that are left in the air intake, where they are drawn into the engine on subsequent starts. A simple solution to the problem of tools being

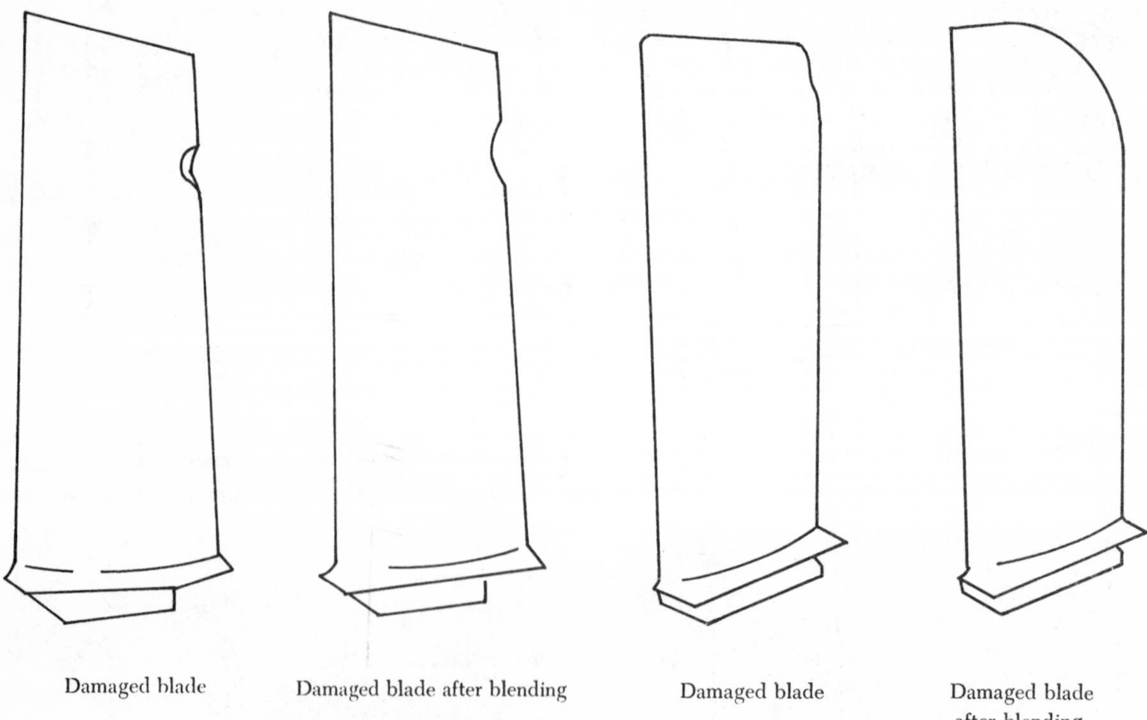

FIGURE 10–55. Compressor blade repair.

drawn into an engine is to check the tools against a tool checklist. Prior to starting a turbine engine, make a minute inspection of engine inlet ducts to assure that items such as nuts, bolts, lockwire, or tools were not left there after work had been performed.

Figure 10–56 shows some examples of blade damage to an axial-flow engine. The descriptions and possible causes of blade damage are given in table 11.

Corrosion pitting is not considered serious on the compressor stator vanes of axial-flow engines if the pitting is within the allowed tolerance.

Do not attempt to repair any vane by straightening, brazing, welding, or soldering. Crocus cloth, fine files, and stones are used to blend out damage by removing a minimum of material and leaving a surface finish comparable to that of a new part. The purpose of this blending is to minimize stresses that concentrate at dents, scratches, or cracks.

The inspection and repair of air intake guide vanes, swirl vanes, and screens on centrifugal-flow engines necessitates the use of a strong light. Inspect screen assemblies for breaks, rips, or holes. Screens may be tin-dipped to tighten the wire mesh, provided the wires are not worn too thin. If the frame strip or lugs have separated from the screen frames, re-brazing may be necessary.

Inspect the guide and swirl vanes for looseness. Inspect the outer edges of the guide vanes, paying particular attention to the point of contact between the guide and swirl vanes for cracks and dents due to the impingement of foreign particles; also inspect the edges of the swirl vanes. Inspect the downstream edge of the guide vanes very closely, because cracks are generally more prevalent in this area. Cracks which branch or fork out so that a piece of metal could break free and fall into the compressor are cause for vane rejection.

Blending and Replacement

Because of the thin-sheet construction of hollow vanes, blending on the concave and convex surfaces, including the leading edge, is limited. Small, shallow dents are acceptable if the damage is of a rounded or gradual contour type and not a sharp or V-type, and if no cracking or tearing of vane material is evident in the damaged area.

Trailing edge damage (figure 10–57) may be blended, if one-third of the weld seam remains after repair. Concave surfaces of rubber-filled vanes may have allowable cracks extending inward from the outer airfoil, provided there is no suggestion of pieces breaking away. Using a light and mirror, inspect each guide vane trailing edge and vane body for cracks or damage caused by foreign objects.

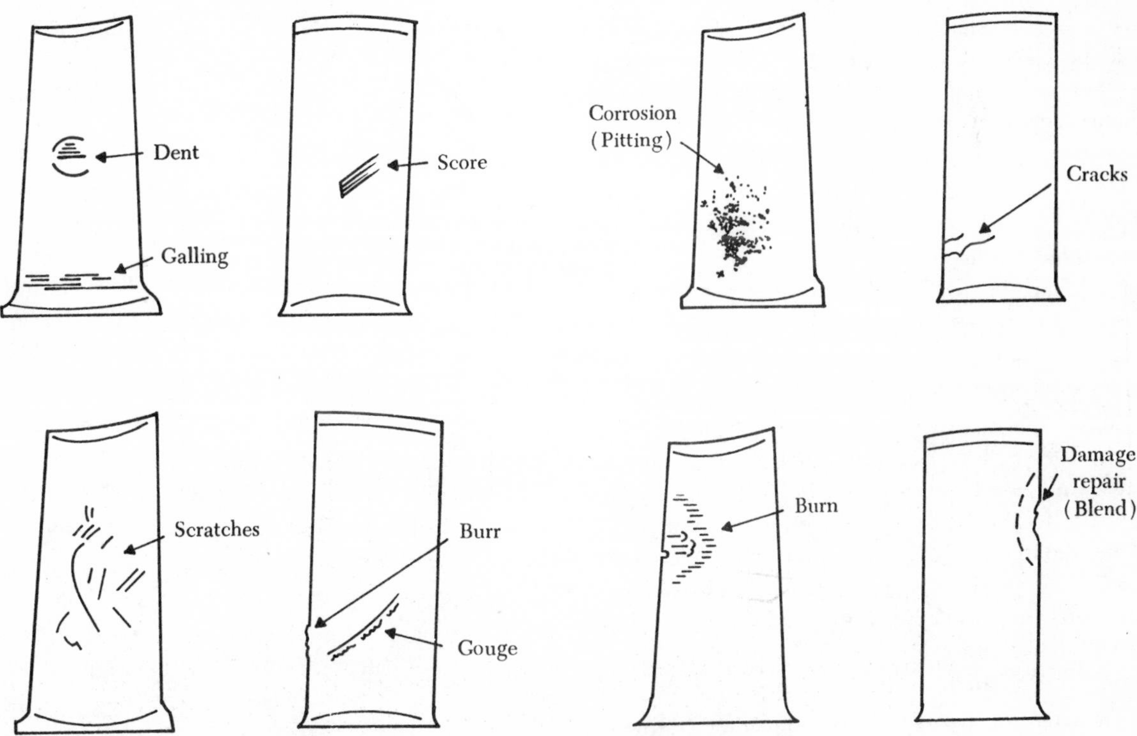

FIGURE 10–56. Compressor blade damage.

TABLE 11. Blade maintenance terms

Term	Appearance	Usual causes
Blend	Smooth repair of ragged edge or surface into the contour of surrounding area.	
Bow	Bent blade.	Foreign objects.
Burning	Damage to surfaces evidenced by discoloration or, in severe cases, by flow of material.	Excessive heat.
Burr	A ragged or turned out edge.	Grinding or cutting operation.
Corrosion (pits)	Breakdown of the surface; pitted appearance.	Corrosive agents—moisture, etc.
Cracks	A partial fracture (separation).	Excessive stress due to shock, overloading, or faulty processing; defective materials; overheating.
Dent	Small, smoothly rounded hollow.	Striking of a part with a dull object.
Gall	A transfer of metal from one surface to another.	Severe rubbing.
Gouging	Displacement of material from a surface; a cutting or tearing effect.	Presence of a comparatively large foreign body between moving parts.
Growth	Elongation of blade.	Continued and/or excessive heat and centrifugal force.
Pit	(See Corrosion.)	
Profile	Contour of a blade or surface.	
Score	Deep scratches.	Presence of chips between surfaces.
Scratch	Narrow shallow marks.	Sand or fine foreign particles; careless handling.

COMBUSTION SECTION

One of the controlling factors in the service life of the turbine engine is the inspection and cleaning of the hot section. Too much emphasis cannot be placed on the importance of careful inspection and repair of this section. One of the most frequent discrepancies that will be detected while inspecting the hot section of a turbine engine is cracking. These cracks may occur in many forms, and the only way to determine that they are within acceptable limits is to refer to the applicable engine manufacturer's service and overhaul manuals.

Cleaning the hot section is not usually necessary for a repair in the field. However, if it becomes necessary to disassemble the engine, a correct and thorough cleaning is of the greatest importance to a successful inspection and repair.

Engine parts can be degreased by using the emulsion-type cleaners or chlorinated solvents. The emulsion-type cleaners are safe for all metals, since they are neutral and noncorrosive. Cleaning parts by the chlorinated solvent method leaves the parts absolutely dry; if they are not to be subjected to further cleaning operations, they should be sprayed with a corrosion-preventive solution to protect them against rust or corrosion.

The extent of disassembly is to open the combustion case for the inspection of the hot section. However, in performing this disassembly, numerous associated parts will be readily accessible for inspection.

The importance of properly supporting the engine and the parts being removed cannot be overstressed. The alignment of parts being removed and installed is also of the utmost importance.

After all repairs are made, the manufacturer's detailed assembly instructions should be followed. These instructions are important in efficient engine maintenance, and the ultimate life and performance of the engine can be seriously affected if they are slighted through carelessness or neglect.

Extreme care must be taken to prevent dirt, dust, cotter pins, lockwire, nuts, washers, or other foreign material from entering the engine. If, at any time, such pieces are dropped, the assembly of the engine must stop until the dropped article is located, even though this may require a considerable amount of disassembly.

Marking Materials for Combustion Section Parts

Certain materials may be used for temporary marking during assembly and disassembly. Layout dye (lightly applied) or chalk may be used to mark parts that are directly exposed to the engine's gas path, such as turbine blades and disks, turbine vanes, and combustion chamber liners. A wax marking pencil may be used for parts that are not

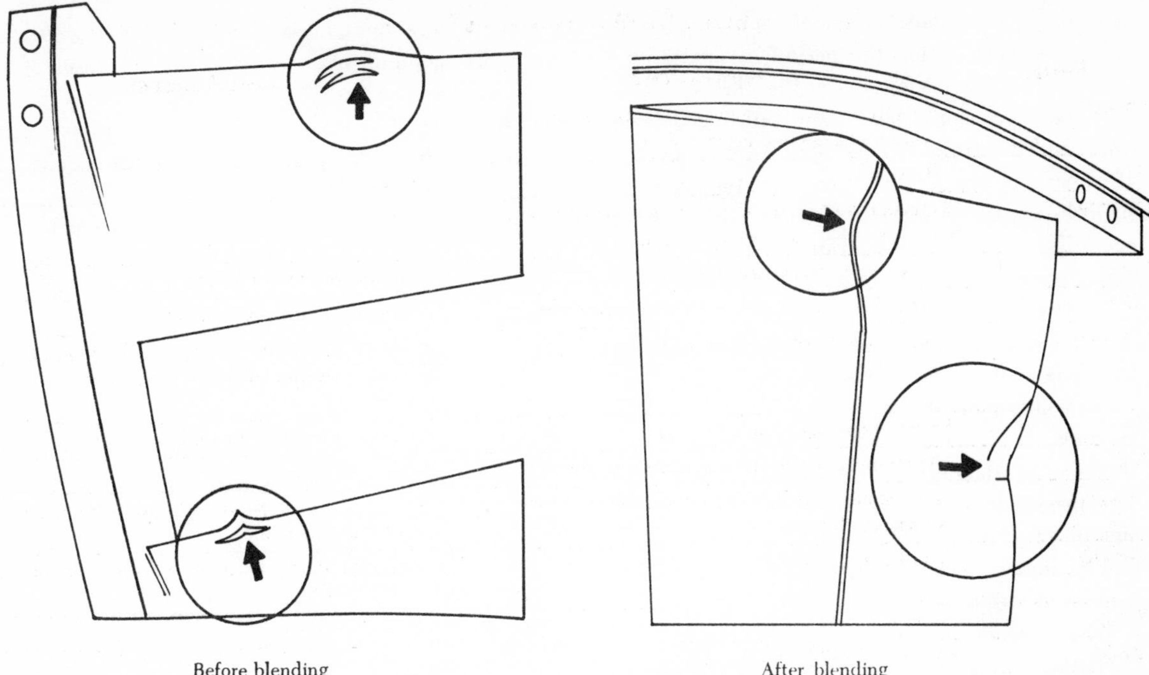

FIGURE 10–57. Guide vane trailing edge damage.

directly exposed to the gas path. Do not use a wax marking pencil on a liner surface or a turbine rotor.

The use of carbon alloy or metallic pencils is not recommended because of the possibility of causing intergranular attack, which could result in a reduction in material strength.

Combustion Section Inspection

The following are general procedures for performing a hot section (turbine and combustion section) inspection. It is not intended to imply that these procedures are to be followed when performing repairs or inspections on turbine engines. However, the various practices are typical of those used on many turbine engines. Where a clearance or tolerance is shown it is for illustrative purposes only. Always follow the instructions contained in the applicable manufacturer's maintenance and overhaul manuals.

The entire external combustion case should be inspected for evidence of hotspots, exhaust leaks, and distortions before the case is opened. After the combustion case has been opened, the combustion chambers can be inspected for localized overheating, cracks, or excessive wear. Inspect the first-stage turbine blades and nozzle guide vanes for cracks, warping, or foreign object damage. Also inspect the combustion chamber outlet ducts and turbine nozzle for cracks and for evidence of foreign object damage.

Inspection and Repair of Combustion Chambers and Covers

Inspect the combustion chambers and covers for cracks by using dye penetrant or the fluorescent penetrant inspection method. Any cracks, nicks, or dents in the cover are usually cause for rejection. Inspect the covers, noting particularly the area around the fuel drain bosses for any pits or corrosion.

Inspect the interior of the combustion liners for excess weld material expelled from the circumferentially welded seams. To prevent future damage to the turbine blades, remove weld material or slag that is not thoroughly fused to the base material of the combustion liner.

When repairing the combustion chamber liner, the procedures given in the appropriate engine manufacturer's overhaul instruction manual should be followed. If there is doubt that the liner is serviceable, it should be replaced.

Acceptance Standards for Combustion Chamber Liners

The combustion chamber liner is inspected to determine the serviceability of liner weldments that have deteriorated from engine operation. Limitations on such deterioration are based on the requirement that the combustion chambers must give satisfactory service during the period of operation between successive inspections of the parts.

Certain types of cracking and burning deterioration resulting from thermal stresses may be found after periods of operation. However, the progress of such discrepancies with further operation is usually negligible, since the deterioration produced by thermal stresses, in effect, relieves the original stress condition.

Usually, a given type of deterioration will recur from chamber to chamber in a given engine.

Current manufacturer's service and overhaul manuals should be consulted for allowable limits of cracks and damage. The following paragraphs describe some typical discrepancies found on combustion chambers. Figure 10–58 shows a combustion chamber liner with the components listed to help locate discrepancies.

When considering the acceptability of a suspected liner, the aim must be to prevent the breakaway of an unsupported area of metal such as that lying in the fork of a crack or between two cracks radiating from the same airhole. Single cracks are acceptable in most cases, provided they do not cause mechanical weakness that could lead to further failure.

Combustion Chamber Cracks

Combustion chambers should be replaced or repaired if two cracks are progressing from a free edge so that their meeting is imminent and could allow a piece of metal (that could cause turbine damage) to break loose.

Separate cracks in the baffle are acceptable. Baffle cracks connecting more than two holes should be repaired.

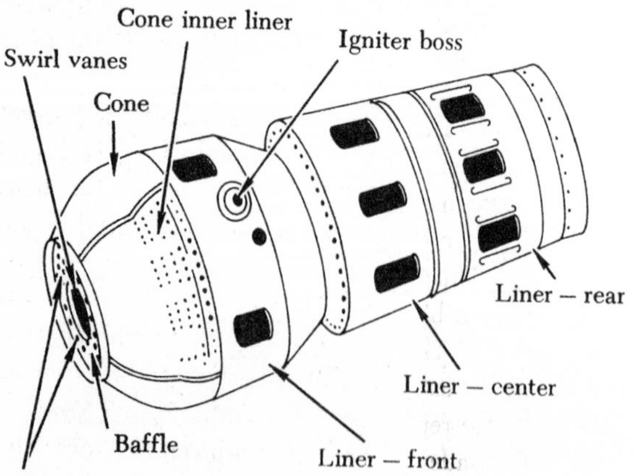

FIGURE 10–58. Combustion chamber liner nomenclature.

Cracks in the cone are rare but, at any location on this component, are cause for rejection of the liner.

Cracks in the swirl vanes are cause for rejection of the liner. Loose swirl vanes may be repaired by silver brazing.

Cracks in the front liner emanating from the airholes are acceptable, provided they do not exceed allowable limits. If such cracks fork or link with others, the liner must be repaired. If two cracks originating from the same airhole are diametrically opposite, the liner is acceptable.

Radial cracks extending from the interconnector and spark-igniter boss are acceptable if they do not exceed allowable limits and if such cracks do not fork or link with others. Circumferential cracks around the boss pads should be repaired prior to re-use of the liner.

After long periods of engine operation, the external surfaces of the combustion chamber liner location pads will often show signs of fretting. This is acceptable, provided no resultant cracks or perforation of the metal is apparent.

Any cover or chamber inadvertently dropped on a hard surface or mishandled should be thoroughly inspected for minute cracks which may elongate over a period of time and then open, creating a hazard.

Burned or Buckled Areas

Parts may be found wherein localized areas have been heated to an extent to buckle small portions of the chamber. Such parts are considered acceptable if the burning of the part has not progressed into an adjacent welded area or to such an extent as to weaken the structure of the liner weldment. Buckling of the combustion chamber liner can be corrected by straightening the liner.

Moderate buckling and associated cracks are acceptable in the row of cooling holes. More severe buckling that produces a pronounced shortening or tilting of the liner is cause for rejection.

Upon completion of the repairs by welding, the liner should be restored as closely as possible to its original shape. This usually can be accomplished by using ordinary sheetmetal-forming hand dollies and hammers available at most metal working and welding shops.

Fuel Nozzle and Support Assemblies

Clean all carbon deposits from the nozzles by washing with a cleaning fluid approved by the engine manufacturer and remove the softened deposits with a soft bristle brush or small piece of wood. It is desirable to have filtered air passing through the nozzle during the cleaning operation to carry away deposits as they are loosened. Make sure all parts are clean. Dry the assemblies with clean, filtered air.

Because the spray characteristics of the nozzle may become impaired, no attempt should be made to clean the nozzles by scraping with a hard implement or by rubbing with a wire brush.

Inspect each component part of the fuel nozzle assembly for nicks and burrs.

INSPECTION AND REPAIR OF TURBINE DISK

Turbine Disk Inspection

The inspection for cracks is of the utmost importance. Crack detection, when dealing with the turbine disk and blades, is practically all visual. The material of which the disk and blades are made does not lend itself freely to crack detection fluids; therefore, they should be scrutinized most carefully under at least a 9- to 12-power magnifying glass. Any questionable areas call for more minute inspection. Cracks, on the disk, however minute, necessitate the rejection of the disk and replacement of the turbine rotor. Slight pitting caused by the impingement of foreign matter may be blended by stoning and polishing.

Turbine Blade Inspection

Turbine blades are usually inspected and cleaned in the same manner as compressor blades. However, because of the extreme heat under which the turbine blades operate, they are more susceptible to damage. Using a strong light and a magnifying glass, inspect the turbine blades for stress rupture cracks (figure 10–59) and deformation of the leading edge (figure 10–60).

Stress rupture cracks usually appear as minute hairline cracks on or across the leading or trailing edge at a right angle to the edge length. Visible cracks may range in length from one-sixteenth inch upward. Deformation, caused by over-temperature, may appear as waviness and/or areas of varying airfoil thickness along the leading edge. The leading edge must be straight and of uniform thickness along its entire length, except for areas repaired by blending.

Do not confuse stress rupture cracks or deformation of the leading edge with foreign material impingement damage or with blending repairs to the blade. When any stress rupture cracks or deformation of the leading edges of the first-stage turbine blades are found, an over-temperature condition must be suspected. Check the individual blades for stretch and the turbine disk for hardness and stretch.

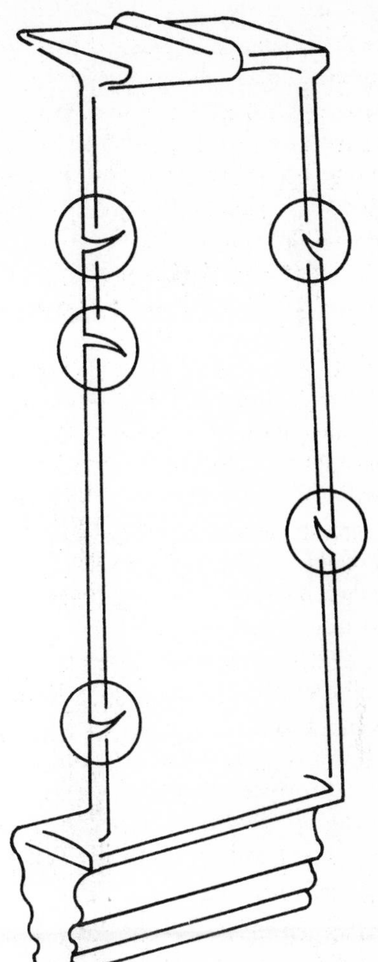

FIGURE 10–59. Stress rupture cracks.

Blades removed for a detailed inspection or for a check of turbine disk stretch must be re-installed in the same slots from which they were removed. Number the blades prior to removal.

The turbine blade outer shroud should be inspected for air seal wear. If shroud wear is found, measure the thickness of the shroud at the worn area. Use a micrometer or another suitable and accurate measuring device that will ensure a good reading in the bottom of the comparatively narrow wear groove. If the remaining radial thickness of the shroud is less than that specified, the stretched blade must be replaced.

Typical blade inspection requirements are indicated in figure 10–61. Blade tip curling within a one-half-inch square area on the leading edge of the blade tip is usually acceptable if the curling is not

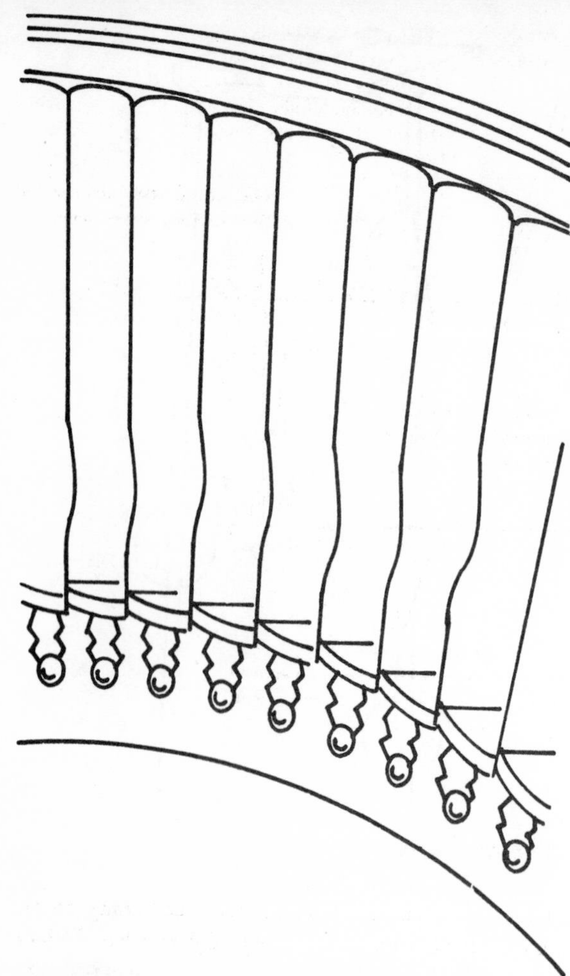

FIGURE 10–60. Turbine blade waviness.

sharp. Curling is acceptable on the trailing edge if it does not extend beyond the allowable area. Any sharp bends that may result in cracking or a piece breaking out of the turbine blade is cause for rejection, even though the curl may be within the allowable limits. Each turbine blade should be inspected for cracks.

Turbine Blade Replacement Procedure

Turbine blades are generally replaceable, subject to moment-weight limitations. These limitations are contained in the engine manufacturer's applicable technical instructions.

If visual inspection of the turbine assembly discloses several broken, cracked, or eroded blades, replacing the entire turbine assembly may be more economical than replacing the damaged blades.

A typical disk and blade assembly is illustrated in figure 10–62. In the initial buildup of the turbine, a complete set of 54 blades made in coded pairs (two blades having the same code letters), is laid out on a bench in the order of diminishing moment-weight. The code letters indicating the moment-weight balance in ounces are marked on the rear face of the fir-tree section of the blade (viewing the blade as installed at final assembly of the engine). The pair of blades having the heaviest moment-weight is numbered 1 and 28; the next heaviest pair of blades is numbered 2 and 29; the third heaviest pair is numbered 3 and 30. This is continued until all the blades have been numbered.

Mark a number 1 on the face of the hub on the turbine disk. The No. 1 blade is then installed adjacent to the number 1 on the disk (figure 10–63). The remaining blades are then installed consecutively in a clockwise direction, viewed from the rear face of the turbine disk. If there are several pairs of blades having the same code letters, they are installed consecutively before going to the next code letters.

If a blade requires replacement, the diametrically opposite blade must also be replaced. The blades used as replacements must be of the same code, but do not have to be of the same code as the blades removed. The maximum number of blades that may be replaced in the field varies between make and model of engines and is established by the engine manufacturer.

To replace a blade, or any number of blades, of a turbine disk and blade assembly, the procedures in the following paragraphs are given as an example.

Bend up the tab of each tab lock; then drive out the blade, knocking it toward the front of the turbine disk, using a brass drift and a hammer. Withdraw and discard the turbine blade locks from the blades.

Insert a new blade with the tab blade toward the front of the disk; then, while holding the tab against the disk, check the clearance between the blade shoulder and the turbine disk. It may be necessary to grind material from the shoulder of the blade to bring the clearance within limits (figure 10–64). Refer to the Table of Limits in the engine manufacturer's overhaul manual for the clearances concerning the turbine blades.

While holding the blade in the direction of rotation (counterclockwise), check the clearance between the blade shoulder tips and those of the adjacent blades (figure 10–64). If the clearance is insufficient, remove the blade and grind material from the tips to bring the clearance within limits. Using a

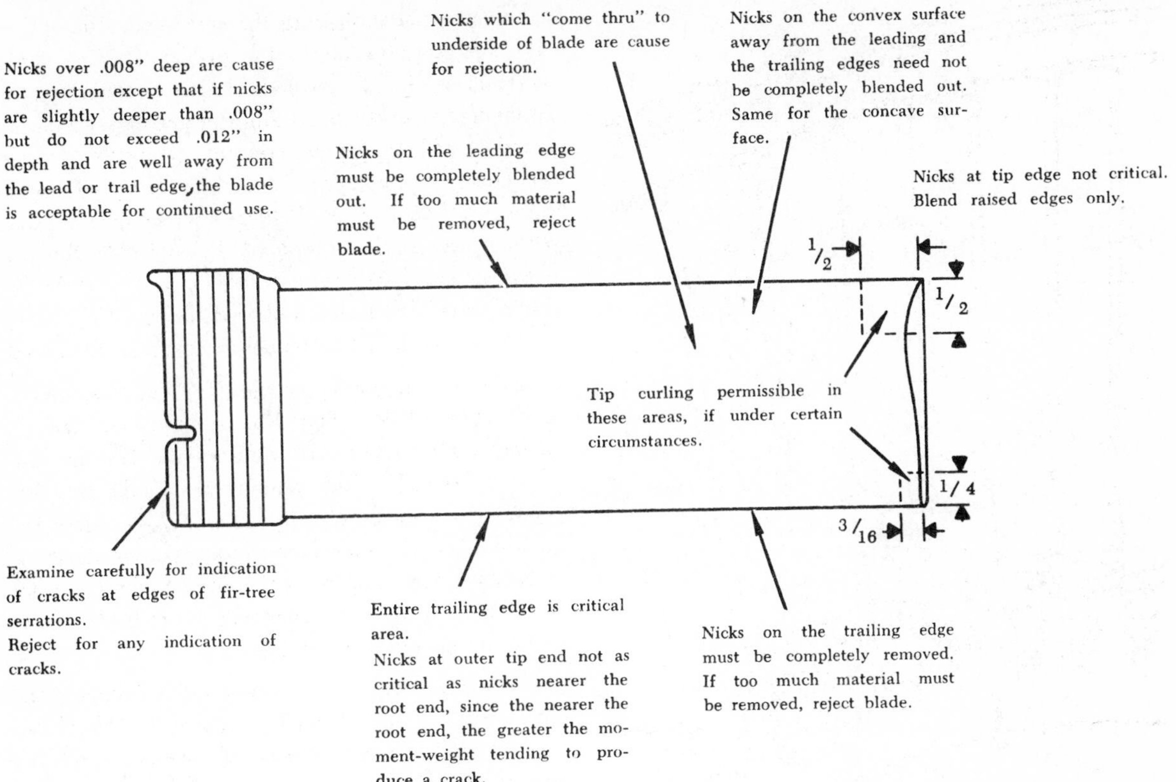
Nicks over .008" deep are cause for rejection except that if nicks are slightly deeper than .008" but do not exceed .012" in depth and are well away from the lead or trail edge, the blade is acceptable for continued use.
Nicks which "come thru" to underside of blade are cause for rejection.
Nicks on the convex surface away from the leading and the trailing edges need not be completely blended out. Same for the concave surface.
Nicks on the leading edge must be completely blended out. If too much material must be removed, reject blade.
Nicks at tip edge not critical. Blend raised edges only.
1/2
1/2
Tip curling permissible in these areas, if under certain circumstances.
1/4
3/16
Examine carefully for indication of cracks at edges of fir-tree serrations.
Reject for any indication of cracks.
Entire trailing edge is critical area.
Nicks at outer tip end not as critical as nicks nearer the root end, since the nearer the root end, the greater the moment-weight tending to produce a crack.
Nicks on the trailing edge must be completely removed. If too much material must be removed, reject blade.

FIGURE 10–61. Typical turbine blade inspection.

dial indicator, check the blade tip radial movement while holding the blade tab against the disk.

Place a new lock in the turbine blade; then install the blade in its correct position in the turbine disk. Position the turbine so that the blade is over a peening plate, an anvil, or other suitable support. Using a starting punch, peen the tab of the lock in an inward direction. Finish peening the lock, using a finishing punch to obtain the allowable maximum axial end play. Examine the peened lock for evidence of cracking, using a 3- to 5-power glass. If it is cracked, remove the blade and install a new lock until a satisfactory installation is accomplished.

Turbine Nozzle Vane Inspection

After opening the combustion chambers and removing the combustion liners, the first-stage turbine blades and turbine nozzle vanes are accessible for inspection. The blade limits specified in the engine manufacturer's overhaul and service instruction manual should be adhered to. Figure 10–65 shows where cracks usually occur on a turbine nozzle assembly. Slight nicks and dents are permissible if the depth of damage is within limits.

Inspect the turbine nozzle vanes for bowing, measuring the amount of bowing on the trailing edge of each vane. Bowed nozzle vanes may be an indication of a malfunctioning fuel nozzle. Reject vanes which are bowed more than the allowable amount. Bowing is always greater on the trailing edge; thus if this edge is within limits, the leading edge is also acceptable.

Inspect the nozzle vanes for nicks or cracks. Small nicks are not cause for vane rejection, provided such nicks blend out smoothly.

Inspect the nozzle vane supports for defects caused by the impingement of foreign particles. Use a stone to blend any doubtful nicks to a smooth radius.

Like turbine blades, it is possible to replace a maximum number of turbine nozzle vanes in some engines. If more than this number of vanes are damaged, a new turbine nozzle vane assembly must be installed.

With the tailpipe removed, the rear turbine stage can be inspected for any cracks or evidence of blade stretch. The rear-stage nozzle can also be inspected with a strong light by looking through the rear-stage turbine.

Clearances

Checking the clearances is one of the procedures in the maintenance of the turbine section of a

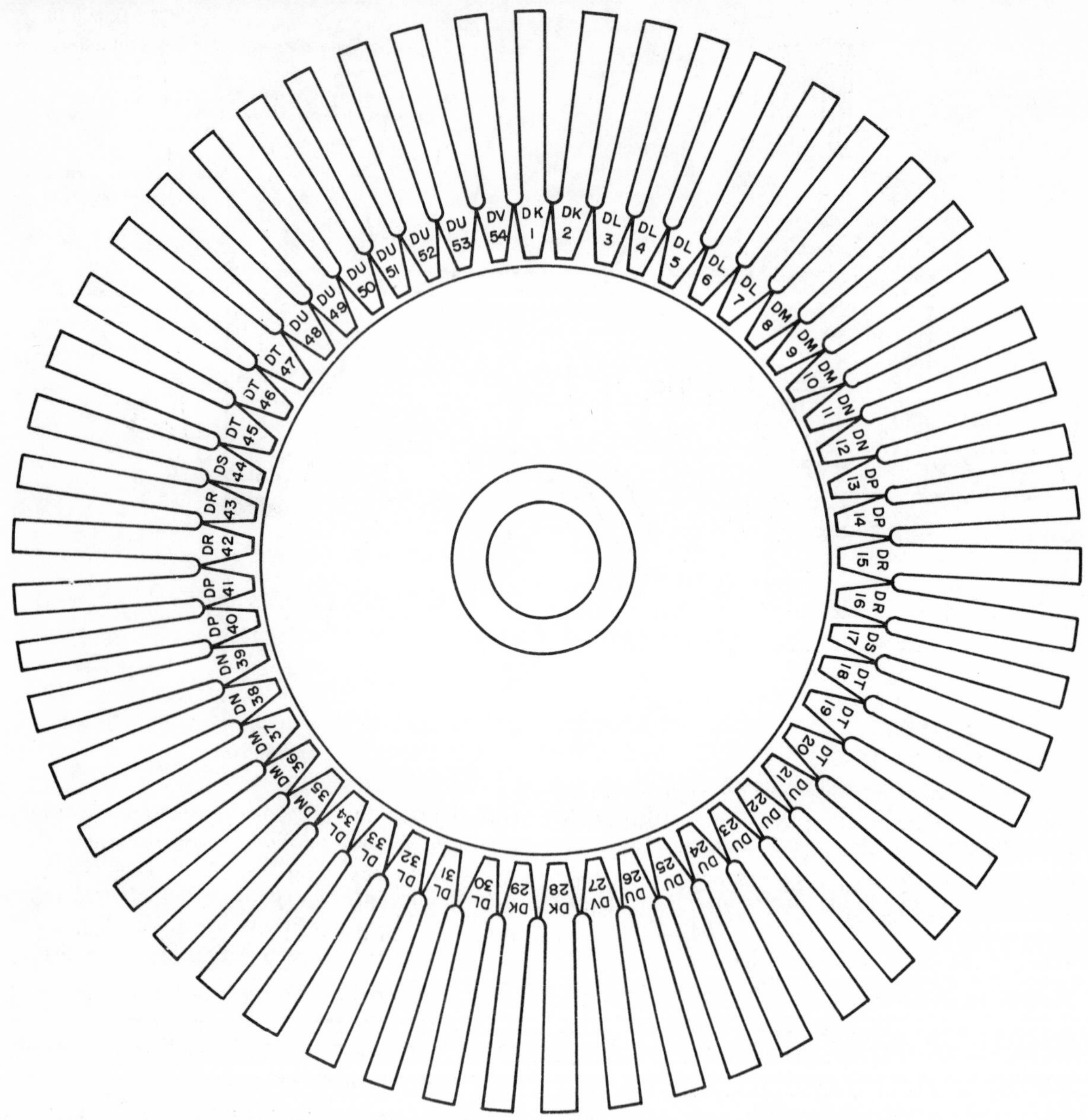

FIGURE 10–62. Typical turbine rotor blade moment-weight distribution.

turbine engine. The manufacturer's service and overhaul manual gives the procedures and tolerances for checking the turbine. Figures 10–66 and 10–67 show clearances being measured at various locations. To obtain accurate readings, special tools provided by each manufacturer must be used as described in the service instructions for specific engines.

Exhaust Section

The exhaust section of the turbojet engine is susceptible to heat cracking. This section must be thoroughly inspected along with the inspection of the combustion section and turbine section of the engine. Inspect the exhaust cone and tailpipe for cracks, warping, buckling, or hotspots. Hotspots on the tail cone are a good indication of a malfunctioning fuel nozzle or combustion chamber.

The inspection and repair procedures for the hot section of any one gas turbine engine are similar to those of other gas turbine engines. One usual difference is the nomenclature applied to the various parts of the hot section by the different manufacturers. Other differences include the manner of disassembly, the tooling necessary, and the repair methods and limits.

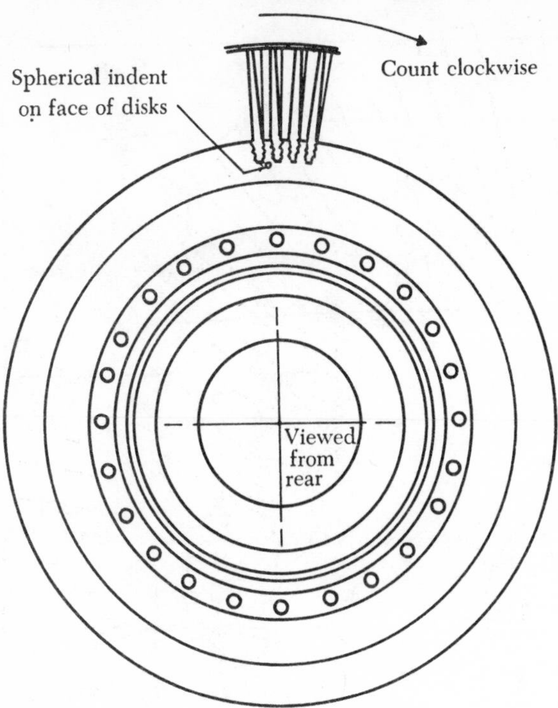

FIGURE 10–63. Turbine blades.

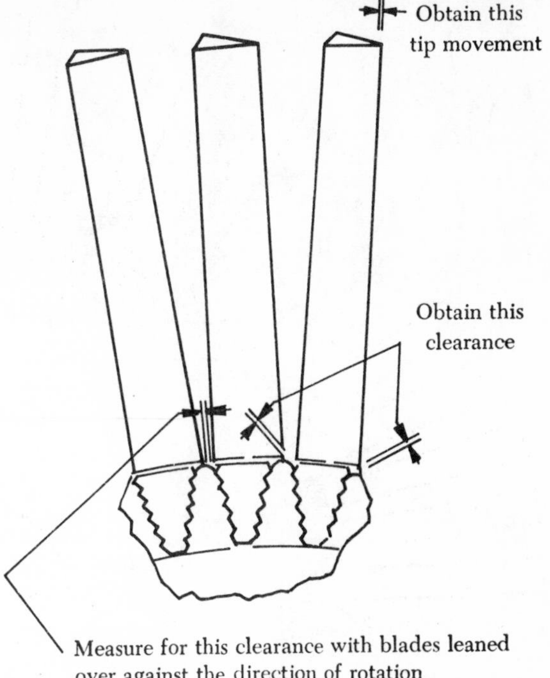

FIGURE 10–64. Turbine blade replacement clearances.

COMMERCIAL RATINGS

An understanding of gas turbine engine ratings is necessary to use intelligently the engine operating curves contained in the aircraft and engine maintenance manuals. The ratings for commercial engines are defined by the SAE (Society of Automotive Engineers).

Takeoff (wet). This is the maximum allowable thrust for takeoff. The rating is obtained by actuating the water-injection system and setting the computed "wet" thrust with the throttle, in terms of a predetermined turbine discharge pressure or engine pressure ratio for the prevailing ambient conditions. The rating is restricted to takeoff, is time-limited, and will have an altitude limitation. Engines without water injection do not have this rating.

Takeoff (dry). This is the maximum allowable thrust without the use of water injection. The rating is obtained by adjusting the throttle to the takeoff (dry) thrust for the existing ambient conditions, in terms of a predetermined turbine discharge pressure or engine pressure ratio. The rating is time-limited and is to be used for takeoff only.

Maximum continuous. This rating is the maximum thrust which may be used continuously and is intended only for emergency use at the discretion of the pilot. The rating is obtained by adjusting the throttle to a predetermined turbine discharge pressure or engine pressure ratio.

Normal rated. Normal rated thrust is the maximum thrust approved for normal climb. The rating is obtained in the same manner as maximum continuous. Maximum continuous thrust and normal rated thrust are the same on some engines.

Maximum cruise. This is the maximum thrust approved for cruising. It is obtained in the same manner as maximum continuous.

Idle. This is not an engine rating, but rather a throttle position suitable for minimum thrust operation on the ground or in flight. It is obtained by placing the throttle in the idle detent on the throttle quadrant.

ENGINE INSTRUMENTATION

Although engine installations may differ, depending upon the type of both the aircraft and the engine, gas turbine engine operation is usually controlled by observing the instruments discussed in the following paragraphs.

Engine thrust is indicated by either a turbine pressure indicator or an engine pressure ratio indicator, depending upon the installation. Both types of pressure instruments are discussed here because

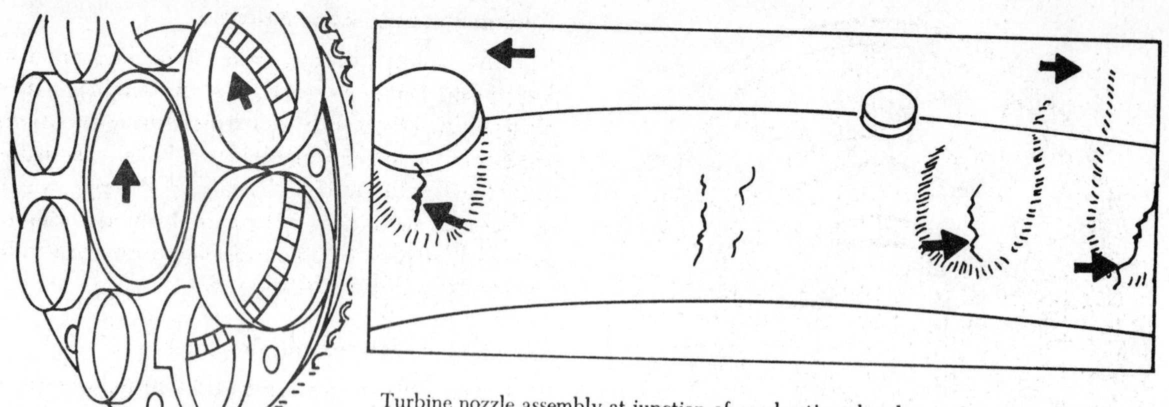

Turbine nozzle assembly at junction of combustion chamber outlet duct and turbine nozzle outer case.

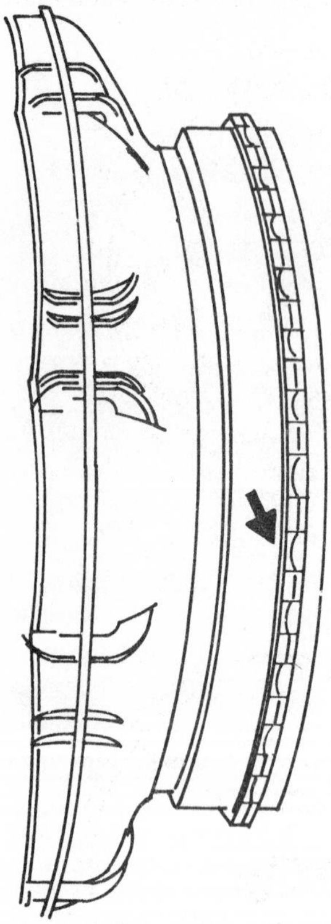

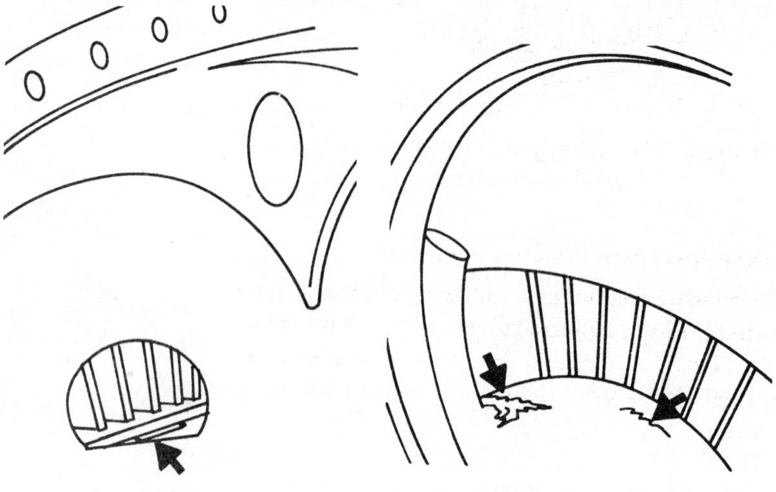

Turbine nozzle assembly.

Cracked area along spot weld line on inner duct.

Spot weld cracks on inner duct.

FIGURE 10–65. Typical turbine nozzle assembly defects.

either indicator may be used. Of the two, the turbine discharge pressure indicator is usually more accurate, primarily because of its simplicity of construction. It may be installed on the aircraft permanently or, in some instances temporarily, such as during an engine trim. An engine pressure ratio indicator, on the other hand, is less complex to use because it compensates automatically for the effects of airspeed and altitude factors by considering compressor inlet pressure.

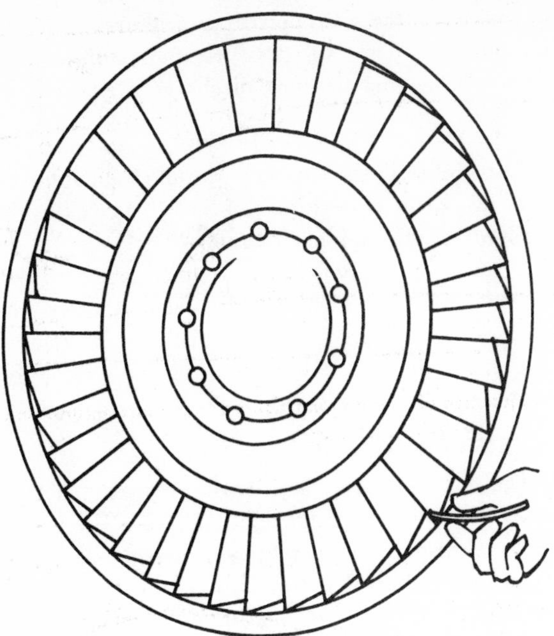

FIGURE 10–66. Measuring the turbine blades to shroud (tip) clearances.

Turbine Discharge Pressure Indicator

This instrument not only indicates the total engine internal pressure immediately aft of the last turbine stage, but also indicates the pressure available to generate thrust, when used with compressor inlet pressure.

FIGURE 10–67. Measuring turbine wheel to exhaust cone clearance.

Engine Pressure Ratio Indicator

EPR (engine pressure ratio) is an indication of the thrust being developed by the engine. It is instrumented by total pressure pickups in the engine inlet and in the turbine exhaust. The reading is displayed in the cockpit by the EPR gage, which is used in making engine power settings. Figure 10–68 illustrates a turbine discharge pressure indicator (A) and an EPR gage (B).

Torquemeter (Turboprop Engines)

Because only a small part of the propulsive force is derived from the jet thrust, neither turbine discharge pressure nor engine pressure ratio is used as an indicator of the power produced by a turboprop engine. Turboprops are usually fitted with a torquemeter. The torquemeter (figure 10–69) can be operated by a torquemeter ring gear in the engine nose section similar to that provided on large

(A)

(B)

FIGURE 10–68. (A) Turbine discharge pressure, and (B) engine pressure ratio indicators.

reciprocating engines or by pick-ups on a torque shaft. The torque being developed by the engine is proportional to the horsepower, and is used to indicate shaft horsepower.

Tachometer

Gas turbine engine speed is measured by the compressor r.p.m., which will also be the turbine r.p.m. Tachometers (figure 10–69) are usually calibrated in percent r.p.m. so that various types of engines can be operated on the same basis of comparison. As previously noted, compressor r.p.m. on centrifugal-compressor turbojet engines is a direct indication of the engine thrust being produced. For axial-compressor engines, the principal purpose of the tachometer is to monitor r.p.m. during an engine start and to indicate an overspeed condition, if one occurs.

Exhaust Gas Temperature Indicator

EGT (exhaust gas temperature), TIT (turbine inlet temperature), tailpipe temperature, and turbine discharge temperature are one and the same. Temperature is an engine operating limit and is used to monitor the mechanical integrity of the turbines, as well as to check engine operating conditions. Actually, the turbine inlet temperature is the important consideration, since it is the most critical of all the engine variables. However, it is impractical to measure turbine inlet temperature in most engines, especially large models. Consequently, temperature thermocouples are inserted at the turbine discharge, where the temperature provides a relative indication of that at the inlet. Although the temperature at this point is much lower than at the inlet, it provides surveillance over the engine's internal operating conditions. Several thermocouples are usually used, which are spaced at intervals around the perimeter of the engine exhaust duct near the turbine exit. The EGT indicator (figure 10–69) in the cockpit shows the average temperature measured by the individual thermocouples.

Fuel-Flow Indicator

Fuel-flow instruments indicate the fuel flow in lbs./hr. from the engine fuel control. Fuel flow is of interest in monitoring fuel consumption and checking engine performance. A typical fuel-flow indicator is illustrated in figure 10–69.

Engine Oil Pressure Indicator

To guard against engine failure resulting from inadequate lubrication and cooling of the various engine parts, the oil supply to critical areas must be monitored. The oil pressure indicator usually shows the engine-oil-pump discharge pressure.

Engine Oil Temperature Indicator

The ability of the engine oil to lubricate and cool depends on the temperature of the oil, as well as the amount of oil supplied to the critical areas. An oil-inlet temperature indicator frequently is provided to show the temperature of the oil as it enters the oil pressure pump. Oil-inlet temperature is also an indication of proper operation of the engine oil cooler.

TURBOJET ENGINE OPERATION

The engine operating procedures presented here apply generally to all turbojet engines. The procedures, pressures, temperatures, and r.p.m.'s which follow are intended primarily to serve as a guide. It should be understood that they do not have general application. The manufacturer's operating instructions should be consulted before attempting to start and operate a turbojet engine.

In contrast to the many controls for a reciprocating engine, a turbojet engine has only one power control lever. Adjusting the power lever or throttle sets up a thrust condition for which the fuel control meters fuel to the engine. Engines equipped with thrust reversers go into reverse thrust at throttle positions below "idle." A separate fuel shutoff lever is usually provided on engines equipped with thrust reversers.

Prior to start, particular attention should be paid to the engine air inlet, the visual condition and free movement of the compressor and turbine assembly, and the parking ramp area fore and aft of the aircraft. The engine is started by using an external power source or a self-contained, combustion-starter unit. Starter types and the engine starting cycle have been discussed previously. On multi-engine aircraft, one engine usually is started by a ground cart that supplies the air pressure for a pneumatic starter on the engine. Air bled from the first engine started then is used as a source of power for starting the other engines.

During the start, it is necessary to monitor the tachometer, the oil pressure, and the exhaust gas temperature. The normal starting sequence is: (1) Rotate the compressor with the starter, (2) turn the ignition on, and (3) open the engine fuel valve, either by moving the throttle to "idle" or by moving a fuel shutoff lever or turning a switch. Adherence to the procedure prescribed for a particular engine

FIGURE 10–69. Typical turbine engine instruments.

is necessary as a safety measure and to avoid a "hot" or "hung" start.

A successful start will be noted first by a rise in exhaust gas temperature. If the engine does not "light up" within a prescribed period of time, or if the exhaust-gas-starting-temperature limit is exceeded, the starting procedure should be aborted. Hot starts are not common, but when they do occur, they can usually be stopped in time to avoid excessive temperature by observing the exhaust gas temperature constantly during the start. When necessary, the engine is cleared of trapped fuel or gases by continuing to rotate the compressor with the starter, but with the ignition and fuel turned off.

GROUND OPERATION

Engine Fire

If an engine fire occurs or if the fire warning light is illuminated during the starting cycle, move the fuel shutoff lever to the "off" position. Continue cranking or "motoring" the engine until the fire has been expelled from the engine. If the fire persists, CO_2 can be discharged into the inlet duct while it is being cranked. Do not discharge CO_2 directly into the engine exhaust because it may damage the engine. If the fire cannot be extinguished, secure all switches and leave the aircraft.

If the fire is on the ground under the engine overboard drain, discharge the CO_2 on the ground rather than on the engine. This also is true if the fire is at the tailpipe and the fuel is dripping to the ground and burning.

Engine Checks

Checking turbojet and turbofan engines for proper operation consists primarily of simply reading the engine instruments and then comparing the observed values with those known to be correct for any given engine operating condition.

Idle Checks

After the engine has started, idle r.p.m. has been attained, and the instrument readings have stabilized, the engine should be checked for satisfactory operation at idling speed. The oil pressure indicator, the tachometer, and the exhaust gas temperature readings should be compared with the allowable ranges. Fuel flow is not considered a completely reliable indication of engine condition at idling r.p.m. because of the inaccuracies frequently encountered in fuel flowmeters and indicators in the low range on the meters.

Checking Takeoff Thrust

Takeoff thrust is checked by adjusting the throttle to obtain a single, predicted reading on the engine pressure ratio indicator in the aircraft. The value for engine pressure ratio which represents takeoff thrust for the prevailing ambient atmospheric conditions is calculated from a takeoff thrust setting curve similar to that shown in figure 10–70.

This curve has been computed for static conditions. Therefore, for all precise thrust checking, the aircraft should be stationary, and stable engine operation should be established. If it is needed for calculating thrust during an engine trim check, turbine discharge pressure (P_{t7}) is also shown on these curves. Appropriate manuals should be consulted for the charts for a specific make and model engine.

The engine pressure ratio computed from the thrust setting curve represents either wet or dry takeoff thrust. The aircraft throttle is advanced to obtain this predicted reading on the engine pressure ratio indicator in the aircraft. If an engine develops the predicted thrust and if all the other engine instruments are reading within their proper ranges, engine operation is considered satisfactory.

Ambient Conditions

The sensitivity of gas turbine engines to compressor-inlet air temperature and pressure necessitates that considerable care be taken to obtain correct values for the prevailing ambient air conditions when computing takeoff thrust. Some things to remember are:

(1) The engine senses the air temperature and pressure at the compressor inlet. This will be the actual air temperature just above the runway surface. When the aircraft is stationary, the pressure at the compressor inlet will be the static field or true barometric pressure and not the barometric pressure corrected to sea level that is normally reported by airport control towers as the altimeter setting.

(2) Some airports provide the runway temperature, which should be used when available. The aircraft free air temperature indicator may or may not suffice for obtaining the temperature to be used, depending upon the manner in which the free air temperature is instrumented. If the thermometer bulb or thermocouple is exposed to the rays of the sun, the instrument reading will obviously not be accurate. When the control tower temperature must be used, a correction factor should be applied. For an accurate thrust computation, such as when trimming an engine, it is best to measure the actual temperature at the compressor inlet just before the engine is started, by means of a handheld thermometer of known accuracy. When

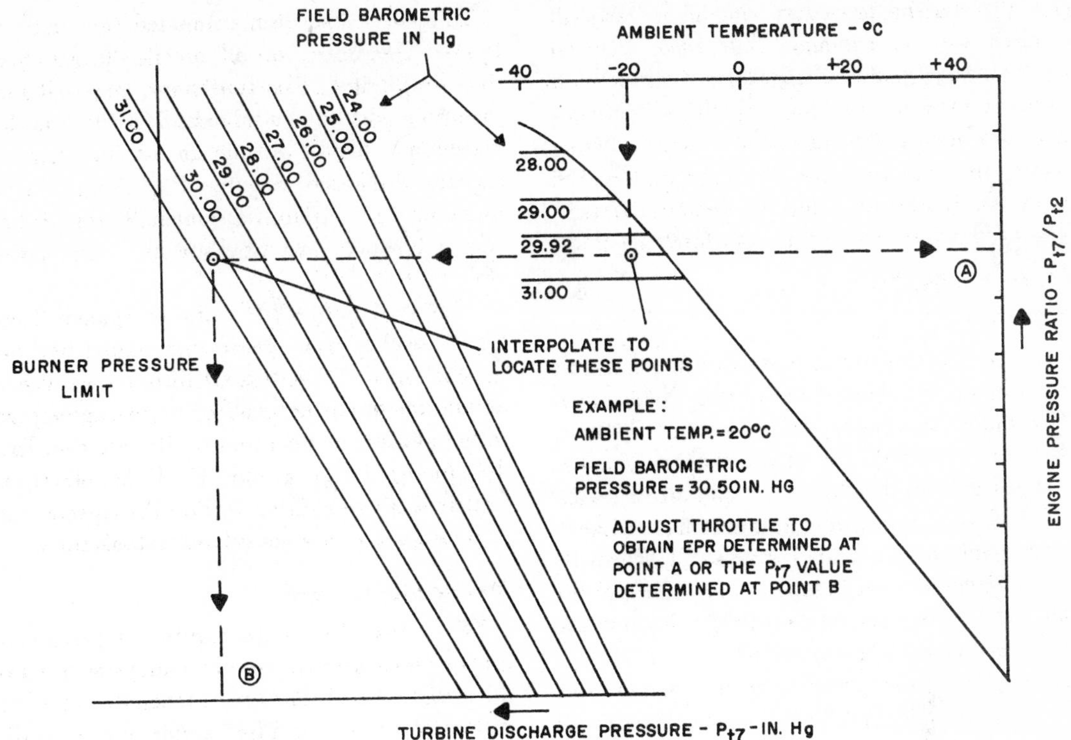

FIGURE 10–70. Typical takeoff thrust setting curve for static conditions.

it is realized that a 5° C. (9° F.) variation on compressor-inlet temperature will result in approximately 2 in. Hg variation in turbine discharge pressure, or 0.06 variation in engine pressure ratio indication, the importance of using the correct temperature for the thrust computation can be readily appreciated.

(3) If only the altimeter setting or the barometric pressure corrected to sea level is available when using the thrust setting curves to calculate turbine discharge pressure, this pressure must be re-corrected to field elevation. A method of obtaining the true pressure is to set the aircraft altimeter to zero altitude and read the field barometric pressure directly in the altimeter setting window on the face of the instrument. This method will work at all but the higher field elevations because of the limit of the altimeter setting scale.

(4) Relative humidity, which affects reciprocating engine power appreciably, has a negligible effect on turbojet engine thrust, fuel flow, and r.p.m. Therefore, relative humidity is not usually considered when computing thrust for takeoff or determining fuel flow and r.p.m. for routine operation.

ENGINE SHUTDOWN

On turbine engines, that do not have a thrust reverser, retarding the aircraft throttle or power lever to "off" cuts the fuel supply to the engine and shuts down the engine. On engines equipped with thrust reversers, this is accomplished by means of a separate fuel shutoff lever. An engine normally will be sufficiently cool to shut down immediately. However, as a rule of thumb, when an engine has been operated above approximately 85% r.p.m. for periods exceeding 1 min. during the last 5 min. prior to shutdown, it is recommended the engine be operated below 85% r.p.m. (preferably at idle) for a period of 5 min. to prevent possible seizure of the rotors. This applies, in particular, to prolonged operation at high r.p.m. on the ground, such as during engine trimming.

The turbine case and the turbine wheels operate at approximately the same temperature when the engine is running. However, the turbine wheels are relatively massive, compared with the case, and are not cooled so readily. The turbine case is exposed to cooling air from both inside and outside the engine. Consequently, the case and the wheels lose their residual heat at different rates after the engine has been shut down. The case, cooling faster, tends to shrink upon the wheels, which are still rotating. Under extreme conditions, the turbine blades may squeal or seize; thus a cooling period is required if the engine has been operating at prolonged high speed. Should the turbine wheels seize, no harm will normally result, provided no attempt is made to turn the engine over until it has cooled sufficiently to free the wheels. In spite of this, every effort should be made to avoid seizure.

The aircraft fuel boost pump must be turned off after, not before, the throttle or the fuel shutoff lever is placed in the off position, to ensure that fuel remains in the lines and that the engine-driven fuel pumps do not lose their prime. Under such conditions, the aircraft fuel boost pump usually is unable to re-prime the engine-driven fuel pump without air being bled from the fuel control.

Generally, an engine should not be shut down by the fuel shutoff lever until after the aircraft throttle has been retarded to "idle." Because the fuel shutoff valve is located on the fuel control discharge, a shutdown from high thrust settings will result in high fuel pressures within the control that can harm the fuel system parts.

When an accurate reading of the oil level in the oil tank is needed following an engine shutdown, the engine should be operated at approximately 75% r.p.m. for not less than 15 nor more than 30 sec. immediately before shutdown to properly scavenge oil from inside the engine.

TROUBLESHOOTING TURBOJET ENGINES

Included in this section are typical guidelines for locating engine malfunctions on most turbojet engines. Since it would be impractical to list all the malfunctions that could occur, only the most common malfunctions are covered. A thorough knowledge of the engine systems, applied with logical reasoning, will solve any problems which may occur.

Table 12 enumerates some malfunctions which may be encountered. Possible causes and suggested actions are given in the adjacent columns. The malfunctions presented herein are solely for the purpose of illustration and should not be construed to have general application. ***For exact information about a specific engine model, consult the applicable manufacturer's instructions.***

TURBOPROP OPERATION

Turboprop engine operation is quite similar to that of a turbojet engine, except for the added feature of a propeller. The starting procedure and the various operational features are very much alike. The turboprop chiefly requires attention to engine operating limits, the throttle or power lever setting, and the torquemeter pressure gage. Although torquemeters indicate only the power being supplied to the propeller and not the equivalent shaft horsepower, torquemeter pressure is approximately proportional to the total power output and, thus, is used as a measure of engine performance. The torquemeter pressure gage reading during the takeoff engine check is an important value. It is usually necessary to compute the takeoff power in the same manner as is done for a turbojet engine. This computation is to determine the maximum allowable exhaust gas temperature and the torquemeter pressure that a normally functioning engine should produce for the outside (ambient) air temperature and barometric pressure prevailing at the time.

TABLE 12. Troubleshooting turbojet engines.

Indicated malfunction	Possible cause	Suggested action
Engine has low r.p.m., exhaust gas temperature, and fuel flow when set to expected engine pressure ratio.	Engine pressure ratio indication has high reading error.	Check inlet pressure line from probe to transmitter for leaks.
		Check engine pressure ratio transmitter and indicator for accuracy.
Engine has high r.p.m., exhaust gas temperature, and fuel flow when set to expected engine pressure ratio.	Engine pressure ratio indication has low reading error due to:	
	Misaligned or cracked turbine discharge probe.	Check probe condition.
	Leak in turbine discharge pressure line from probe to transmitter.	Pressure-test turbine discharge pressure line for leaks.
	Inaccurate engine pressure ratio transmitter or indicator.	Check engine pressure ratio transmitter and indicator for accuracy.

TABLE 12. Troubleshooting turbojet engines—con.

Indicated malfunction	Possible cause	Suggested action
	Carbon particles collected in turbine discharge pressure line or restrictor orifices.	
Engine has high exhaust gas temperature, low r.p.m., and high fuel flow at all engine pressure ratio settings.	Possible turbine damage and/or loss of turbine efficiency.	Confirm indication of turbine damage by: Checking engine coast-down for abnormal noise and reduced time. Visually inspect turbine area with strong light.
NOTE: Engines with damage in turbine section may have tendency to hang up during starting.	If only exhaust gas temperature is high, other parameters normal, the problem may be thermocouple leads or instrument.	Re-calibrate exhaust gas temperature instrumentation.
Engine vibrates throughout r.p.m. range, but indicated amplitude reduces as r.p.m. is reduced.	Turbine damage.	Check turbine as outlined in preceding item.
Engine vibrates at high r.p.m. and fuel flow when compared to constant engine pressure ratio.	Damage in compressor section.	Check compressor section for damage.
Engine vibrates throughout r.p.m. range, but is more pronounced in cruise or idle r.p.m. range.	Engine-mounted accessory such as constant-speed drive, generator, hydraulic pump, etc.	Check each component in turn.
No change in power setting parameters, but oil temperature high.	Engine main bearings.	Check scavenge oil filters and magnetic plugs.
Engine has higher-than-normal exhaust gas temperature during takeoff, climb, and cruise. R.P.M. and fuel flow higher than normal.	Engine bleed-air valve malfunction.	Check operation of bleed valve.
	Turbine discharge pressure probe or line to transmitter leaking.	Check condition of probe and pressure line to transmitter.
Engine has high exhaust gas temperature at target engine pressure ratio for takeoff.	Engine out of trim.	Check engine with jetcal. Re-trim as desired.
Engine rumbles during starting and at low power cruise conditions.	Pressurizing and drain valve malfunction.	Replace pressurizing and drain valves.
	Cracked air duct.	Repair or replace duct.
	Fuel control malfunction.	Replace fuel control.
Engine r.p.m. hangs up during starting.	Subzero ambient temperatures.	If hang-up is due to low ambient temperature, engine usually can be started by turning on fuel booster pump or by positioning start lever to run earlier in the starting cycle.
	Compressor section damage.	Check compressor for damage.
	Turbine section damage.	Inspect turbine for damage.
High oil temperature.	Scavenge pump failure.	Check lubricating system and scavenge pumps.
	Fuel heater malfunction.	Replace fuel heater.
High oil consumption.	Scavenge pump failure.	Check scavenge pumps.
	High sump pressure.	Check sump pressure as outlined in manufacturer's maintenance manual.
	Gearbox seal leakage.	Check gearbox seal by pressurizing overboard vent.
Overboard oil loss.	Can be caused by high airflow through the tank, foaming oil, or unusual amounts of oil returned to the tank through the vent system.	Check oil for foaming; vacuum-check sumps; check scavenge pumps.

TROUBLESHOOTING PROCEDURES FOR TURBOPROP ENGINES

All test run-ups, inspections, and troubleshooting should be performed in accordance with the applicable engine manufacturer's instructions. In table 13, the troubleshooting procedures for the turboprop reduction gear, torquemeter, and power sections are combined because of their inter-relationships. The table includes the principal troubles, together with their probable causes and remedies.

TABLE 13. Troubleshooting turboprop engines.

Trouble	Probable cause	Remedy
Power unit fails to turn over during attempted start.	No air to starter.	Check starter air valve solenoid and air supply.
	Propeller brake locked.	Unlock brake by turning propeller by hand in direction of normal rotation.
Power unit fails to start.	Starter speed low because of inadequate air supply to starter.	Check starter air valve solenoid and air supply.
	If fuel is not observed leaving the exhaust pipe during start, fuel selector valve may be inoperative because of low power supply or may be locked in "off."	Check power supply or electrically operated valves. Replace valves if defective.
	Fuel pump inoperative.	Check pump for sheared drives or internal damage; check for air leaks at outlet.
	Aircraft fuel filter dirty.	Clean filter and replace filtering elements if necessary.
	Fuel control cutoff valve closed.	Check electrical circuit to ensure that actuator is being energized. Replace actuator or control.
Engine fires, but will not accelerate to correct speed.	Insufficient fuel supply to control unit.	Check fuel system to ensure all valves are open and pumps are operative.
	Fuel control main metering valve sticking.	Flush system. Replace control.
	Fuel control bypass valve sticking open.	Flush system. Replace control.
	Drain valve stuck open. Starting fuel enrichment pressure switch setting too high.	Replace drain valve. Replace pressure switch.
Acceleration temperature too high during starting.	Fuel control bypass valve sticking closed.	Flush system. Replace control.
	Fuel control acceleration cam incorrectly adjusted.	Replace control.
	Defective fuel nozzle.	Replace nozzle with a known satisfactory unit.
	Fuel control thermostat failure.	Replace control.
Acceleration temperature during starting too low.	Acceleration cam of fuel control incorrectly adjusted.	Replace control.
Engine speed cycles after start.	Unstable fuel control governor operation.	Continue engine operation to allow control to condition itself.
Power unit oil pressure drops off severely.	Oil supply low.	Check oil supply and refill as necessary.
	Oil pressure transmitter or indicator giving false indication.	Check transmitter or indicator and repair or replace if necessary.

TABLE 13. Troubleshooting turboprop engines—con.

Trouble	Probable cause	Remedy
Oil leakage at accessory drive seals.	Seal failure	Replace seal or seals.
Engine unable to reach maximum controlled speed of 100%.	Faulty propeller governer.	Replace propeller control assembly.
	Faulty fuel control or air sensing tip.	Replace faulty control. If dirty, use air pressure in reverse direction of normal flow through internal engine passage and sensing tip.
Vibration indication high.	Vibration pickup or vibration meter malfunctioning.	Calibrate vibration meter. Start engine and increase power gradually. Observe vibration indicator. If indications prove pickup to be at fault, replace it. If high vibration remains as originally observed, remove power unit for overhaul.

JET CALIBRATION TEST UNIT

Two of the most important factors affecting turbine engine life are EGT (exhaust gas temperature) and engine speed. Excess EGT of a few degrees will reduce turbine blade life as much as 50%. Low exhaust gas temperature materially reduces turbine engine efficiency and thrust. Excessive engine speed can cause premature engine failure.

Indications of fuel system troubles, tailpipe temperature, and r.p.m. can be checked more accurately from the jet calibration test unit than from the gages in the cockpit of the aircraft. Errors up to 10° C. may be made in the interpretation of the temperature gages because of the height of the observer in the seat. Similarly, errors may be made in interpretation of tachometers. With proper utilization of the jet calibration test unit, such errors can be reduced greatly.

One type of calibration test unit used to analyze the turbine engine is the jetcal analyzer (figure 10–71). A jetcal analyzer is a portable instrument made of aluminum, stainless steel, and plastic. The major components of the analyzer are the thermocouple, r.p.m., EGT indicator, resistance, and insulation check circuits, as well as the potentiometer, temperature regulators, meters, switches, and all the necessary cables, probes, and adapters for performing all tests. A jetcal analyzer also includes fire warning overheat detection and wing anti-icing system test circuits.

Jetcal Analyzer Uses

The jetcal analyzer may be used to:

(1) Functionally check the aircraft EGT system for error without running the engine or disconnecting the wiring.

(2) Check individual thermocouples before placement in a parallel harness.

(3) Check each engine thermocouple in a parallel harness for continuity.

(4) Check the thermocouples and parallel harness for accuracy.

(5) Check the resistance of the EGT circuit.

(6) Check the insulation of the EGT circuit for shorts to ground, or for shorts between leads.

(7) Check EGT indicators (either in or out of the aircraft) for error.

(8) Determine engine r.p.m. with an accuracy of ±0.1% during engine run-up. Added to this is the checking and troubleshooting of the aircraft tachometer system.

(9) Establish the proper relationship between the EGT and engine r.p.m. on engine run-up during tabbing (micing) procedures by the r.p.m. check (takcal) and potentiometer in the jetcal analyzer. (Tabbing procedures are those procedures followed when adjusting fixed exhaust nozzle exit areas.)

(10) Check aircraft fire detector, overheat detector, and wing anti-icing systems by using tempcal probes.

Operating Instructions for the Jetcal Tester

The complete step-by-step procedure on the instruction plate of the jetcal analyzer can be followed during actual operation of the analyzer. The operation plate is visible at all times when operating the analyzer.

It would be useless to list the step-by-step procedure in this section. The procedure consists of turning on or off many separate switches and dials.

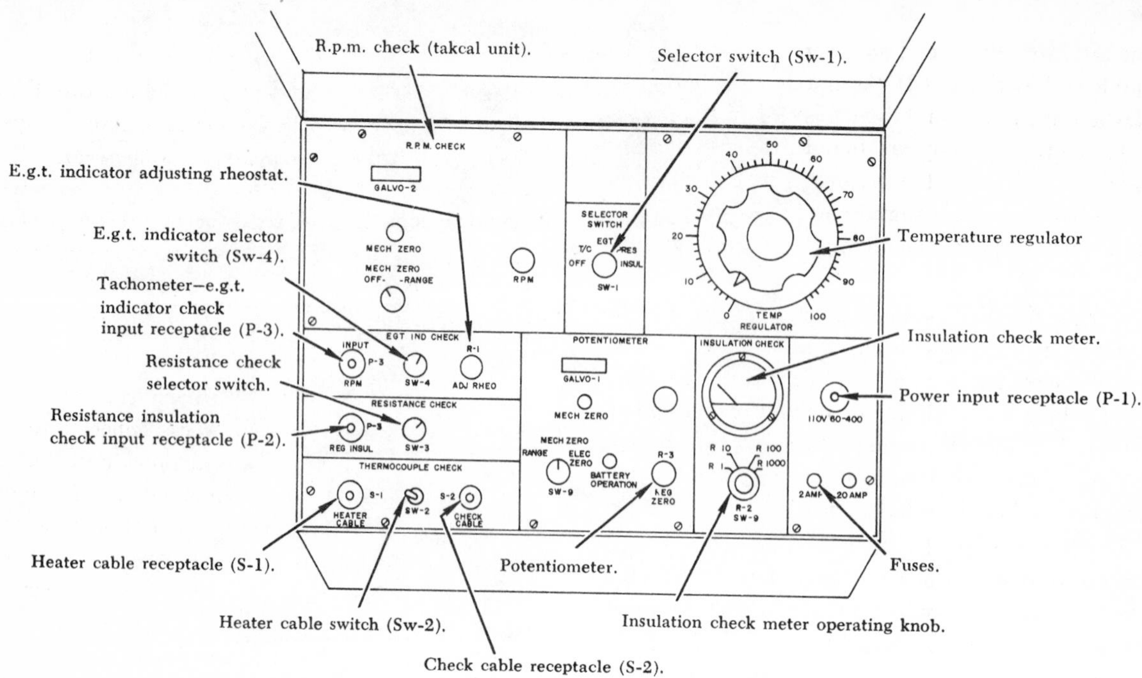

FIGURE 10–71. Jetcal analyzer instrument compartment.

To avoid confusion, this section will be confined to the operation of the jetcal analyzer in a general sense.

Safety Precautions

Observe the following safety precautions while operating the jetcal analyzer:

(1) Never use a volt-ohmmeter to check the potentiometer for continuity. If a volt-ohmmeter is used, damage to the galvanometer and standard battery cell will result.

(2) Check the thermocouple harness before engine run-up. This must be done because the circuit must be correct before the thermocouples can be used for true EGT pickup.

(3) For safety, ground the jetcal analyzer when using an a.c. power supply. Any electrical equipment operated on a.c. power and utilizing wire-wound coils, such as the probes with the jetcal analyzer, has an induced voltage on the case that can be discharged if the equipment is not grounded. This condition is not apparent during dry weather, but on damp days the operator can be shocked slightly. Therefore, for the operator's protection, the jetcal analyzer should be grounded using the pigtail lead in the power inlet cable.

(4) Use heater probes designed for use on the engine thermocouples to be tested. Temperature gradients are very critical in the design of heater probes. Each type of aircraft thermocouple has its own specially designed probe. Never attempt to modify heater probes to test other types of thermocouples.

(5) Do not leave heater probes assemblies in the tailpipe during engine run-up.

(6) Never allow the heater probes to go over 900° C. (1,652° F.). Exceeding these temperatures will result in damage to the jetcal analyzer and heater probe assemblies.

Continuity Check of Aircraft EGT Circuit

To eliminate any error caused by one or more inoperative aircraft thermocouples, a continuity check is performed. The check is made by heating one heater probe to between 500° and 700° C. and placing the hot probe over each of the aircraft thermocouples, one at a time. The EGT indicator must show a temperature rise as each thermocouple is checked. When large numbers of thermocouples are used in the harness (eight or more), it is difficult to see a rise on the aircraft instrument because of the electrical characteristics of a parallel circuit. Therefore, the temperature indication of the aircraft thermocouples is read on the potentiometer of the jetcal analyzer by using the check cable and necessary adapter.

Functional Check of Aircraft EGT Circuit

The time required to test the EGT system of any

one aircraft will depend on several factors: (1) The number of engines; (2) the number of thermocouples in the harness, and their position in the engine; (3) the errors, if any are found; and (4) the time required to correct the errors. The normal functional test of a single engine can be performed in 10 to 20 min.; special conditions may require more time.

During the EGT system functional test and the thermocouple harness checks, the jetcal analyzer has a guaranteed accuracy of ±4° C. at the test temperature, which is usually the maximum operating temperature of the jet engine. Each engine has its own maximum operating temperature, which can be found in applicable technical instructions.

The test is made by heating the engine thermocouples in the tail cone to the engine test temperature. The heat is supplied by heater probes through the necessary cables. With the engine thermocouples hot, their temperature is registered on the aircraft EGT indicator. At the same time, the thermocouples embedded in the heater probes, which are completely isolated from the aircraft system, are picking up and registering the same temperature on the jetcal analyzer.

The temperature registered on the aircraft EGT indicator (figure 10–72) should be within the specified tolerance of the aircraft system and the temperature reading on the jetcal potentiometer. The thermocouples embedded in the heater probes are of U.S. Bureau of Standards accuracy; therefore, jetcal readings are accepted as the standard and are used as the basis of comparison for checking the accuracy of the aircraft EGT system.

Since the junction box is wired in parallel, it is not necessary to have heater probes connected to all the outlets of the junction box when making a check. On engines that have a balancing type thermocouple system, the balancing thermocouple must be removed from the circuit. The remaining thermocouples can be checked individually or together. The balancing thermocouple is checked, using a single probe. The output of the balancing thermocouple is also read on the jetcal potentiometer and compared to the heater probe thermocouple reading.

When the temperature difference exceeds the allowable tolerance, troubleshoot the aircraft system

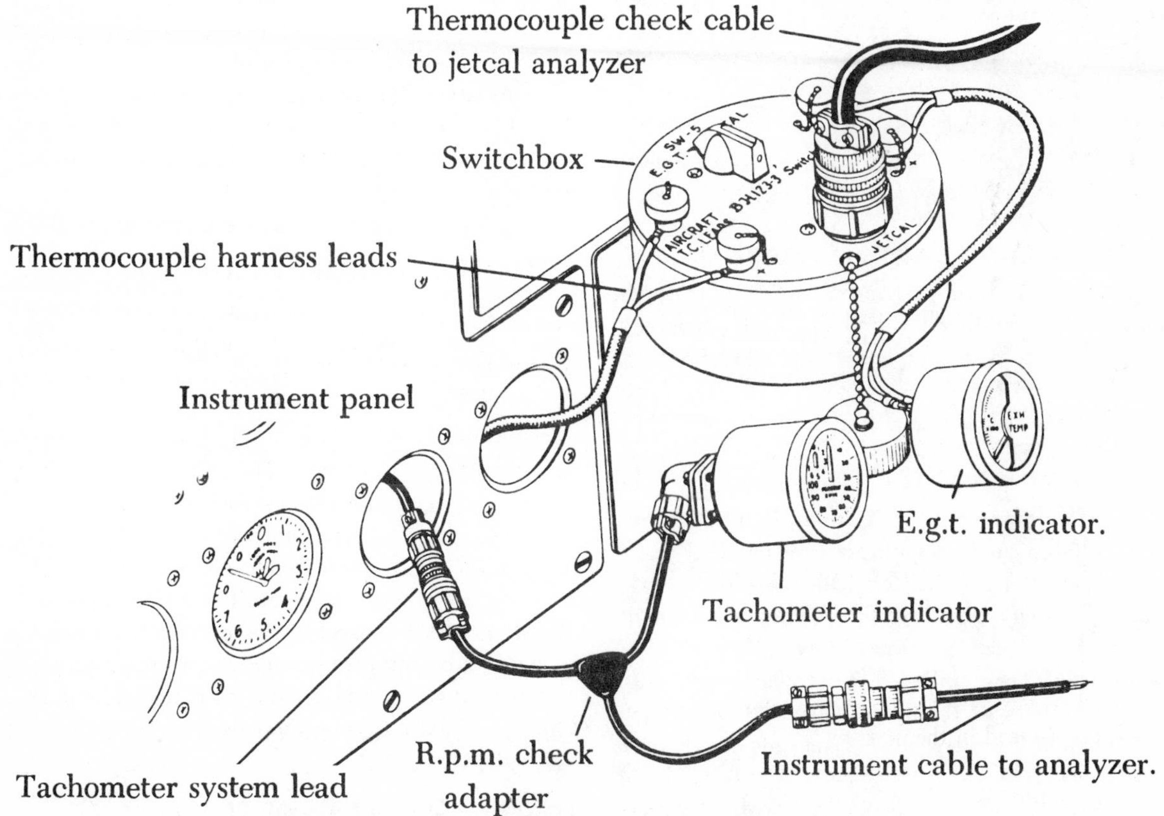

FIGURE 10–72. Switchbox and r.p.m. check adapter connections.

to determine which parts are in error. Troubleshooting is discussed at the end of this section.

Functional Test of Thermal Switches

The tempcal probe functionally tests the operation of the fire detection, overheat, and wing anti-icing systems that incorporate a thermal switch as the detection device. Test the thermal switch in position on the aircraft by placing the probe over the thermal switch. The tempcal probe incorporates the principles of the heater probe for its temperature pickup. The temperature is controlled by the temperature regulator and is read on the jetcal potentiometer.

With the tempcal probe over the thermal switch, the temperature of the probe is raised and lowered to take the switch through its operating temperatures. The indicator on the aircraft instrument panel, generally a red light, then is checked for indication to make sure that the switch is actuating at proper temperatures. If the system is not indicating properly, the circuit must be corrected.

If a hot tempcal probe is placed over a cold thermal switch, the contacts will close almost immediately due to an action called "thermal shock." As the thermal switch continues to absorb heat, the contacts will open and then close again when the operating temperature of the switch is reached.

EGT Indicator Check

The EGT indicator is tested after being removed from the aircraft instrument panel and disconnected from the aircraft EGT circuit leads. Attach the instrument cable and EGT indicator adapter leads to the indicator terminals and place the indicator in its normal operating position. Adjust jetcal analyzer switches to the proper settings. The indicator reading should correspond to the potentiometer readings of the jetcal analyzer within the allowable limits of the EGT indicator.

Correction for ambient temperature is not required for this test, as both the EGT indicator and jetcal analyzer are temperature compensated.

The temperature registered on the aircraft EGT indicator should be within the specified tolerance of the aircraft system and the temperature reading on the jetcal potentiometer. When the temperature difference exceeds the allowable tolerance, troubleshoot the aircraft system to determine which parts are in error.

Resistance and Insulation Check

The thermocouple harness continuity is checked while the EGT system is being checked functionally. The resistance of the thermocouple harness is held to very close tolerances, since a change in resistance changes the amount of current flow in the circuit. A change of resistance will give erroneous temperature readings.

The resistance and insulation check circuits make it possible to analyze and isolate any error in the aircraft system. How the resistance and insulation circuits are used will be discussed with troubleshooting procedures.

Tachometer Check

To read engine speed with an accuracy of ±0.1% during engine run, the frequency of the tachometer-generator is measured by the r.p.m. check (takcal) circuit in the jetcal analyzer. The scale of the r.p.m. check circuit is calibrated in percent r.p.m. to correspond to the aircraft tachometer indicator, which also reads in percent r.p.m. The calibration intervals are 0.2%. The aircraft tachometer and the r.p.m. check circuit are connected in parallel, and both are indicating during engine run-up.

The r.p.m. check circuit readings can be compared with the readings of the aircraft tachometer to determine the accuracy of the aircraft instrument.

Troubleshooting EGT System

The jetcal analyzer is used to test and troubleshoot the aircraft thermocouple system at the first indication of trouble or during periodic maintenance checks.

The test circuits of the jetcal analyzer make it possible to isolate all the troubles listed below. Following the list is a discussion of each trouble mentioned.

(1) One or more inoperative thermocouples in engine parallel harness.

(2) Engine thermocouples out of calibration.

(3) EGT indicator error.

(4) Resistance of circuit out of tolerance.

(5) Shorts to ground.

(6) Shorts between leads.

One or More Inoperative Thermocouples in Engine Parallel Harness

This error is found in the regular testing of aircraft thermocouples with a hot heater probe and will be a broken lead wire in the parallel harness or a short to ground in the harness. In the latter case the current from the grounded thermocouple can leak off and never be shown on the indicator.

However, this grounded condition can be found by using the insulation resistance check.

Engine Thermocouples Out of Calibration

When thermocouples are subjected for a period of time to oxidizing atmospheres, such as encountered in turbine engines, they will drift appreciably from their original calibration. On engine parallel harnesses, when individual thermocouples can be removed, these thermocouples can be bench-checked, using one heater probe. The temperature reading obtained from the thermocouples should be within manufacturer's tolerances.

EGT Circuit Error

This error is found by using the switchbox and comparing the reading of the aircraft EGT indicator with the jetcal temperature reading (figure 10–72). With switch (SW-5) in the jetcal position, the indication of the thermocouple harness is carried back to the jetcal analyzer. With the switch (SW-5) in the EGT position, the temperature reading of the thermocouple harness is indicated on the aircraft EGT indicator. The jetcal and aircraft temperature readings are then compared.

Resistance of Circuit Out of Tolerance

The engine thermocouple circuit resistance is a very important adjustment since a high-resistance condition will give a low indication on the aircraft EGT indicator. This condition is dangerous, because the engine will be operating with excess temperature, but the high resistance will make the indicator read low. Adjusting a resistor and/or a resistance coil in the EGT circuit generally corrects this condition.

Shorts to Ground and Shorts Between Leads

These errors are found by using the insulation check meter as an ohmmeter. Resistance values from zero to 550,000 ohms can be read on the insulation check meter by selecting the proper range.

TROUBLESHOOTING AIRCRAFT TACHOMETER SYSTEM

A related function of the r.p.m. check is troubleshooting the aircraft tachometer system. The r.p.m. check circuit in the jetcal analyzer is used to read engine speed during engine run-up with an accuracy of $\pm 0.1\%$. The connections for the r.p.m. check are the instrument cable, and aircraft tachometer system lead to the tachometer indicator (figure 10–72). After the connections have been made between the jetcal analyzer r.p.m. check circuit and the aircraft tachometer circuit, the two circuits (now classed as one) will be a parallel circuit. The engine is then run-up as prescribed in applicable technical instructions. Both systems can be read simultaneously.

If the difference between the readings of the aircraft tachometer indicator and the jetcal analyzer r.p.m. check circuit exceeds the tolerance prescribed in applicable technical instructions, the engine must be stopped, and the trouble located and corrected. The following steps will assist in locating and isolating the trouble:

(1) If the aircraft tachometer error exceeds the authorized tolerance when compared to the r.p.m. check readings, the instrument should be replaced.

(2) If it is impossible to read 100% r.p.m. on the aircraft tachometer, but the r.p.m. check circuit does read 100% r.p.m., the trouble will be a bad aircraft tachometer indicator or a bad tachometer-generator. Replace the defective parts.

(3) If there is no reading on the aircraft tachometer indicator, but there is a reading on the r.p.m. check circuit, the trouble will either be a bad aircraft tachometer or an open or a grounded phase from the aircraft tachometer-generator. Replace the defective aircraft tachometer or tachometer-generator, or repair the defective lead.

(4) If there is no r.p.m. indication on either the aircraft tachometer or the jetcal analyzer r.p.m. check circuit, there will be an open or shorted lead in the aircraft circuit or a defective tachometer-generator. The defect in the aircraft circuit should be located and corrected, or the tachometer-generator should be replaced. The engine r.p.m. reading should be repeated to check parts replaced as a result of the above tests.

The jetcal analyzer is used for engine tabbing because engine speed and exhaust temperature are extremely critical in engine operation. When the engine is to be checked and tabbed, the most convenient way to do this is to put the switchbox in the EGT circuit and make the connections for the r.p.m. check at the beginning of the test.

The switchbox is used either to switch the EGT indicator into the circuit or to switch the temperature indication of the engine thermocouple harness to the jetcal potentiometer. However, temperature readings from the aircraft thermocouple harness can be made by connecting the check cable (with or without adapter) to the engine junction box (see figure 10–73). The aircraft EGT indicator must be used when the engine is started to be able to detect a hot start.

The engine is started and brought to the speed specified in applicable technical instructions. During tabbing procedures, all engine speed readings are made on the r.p.m. check in the jetcal analyzer, and engine temperature readings are made on the jetcal potentiometer. This is necessary because engine temperature and speed must be read accurately during engine tabbing to assure that the engine is operating at optimum engine conditions.

If the temperature reading is not within the tolerances stated in applicable instructions, the engine is stopped and tabs are added or removed as required. The engine is run-up and r.p.m. and temperature readings are again taken to make sure that the tabs added or removed bring the tailpipe temperature within tolerance.

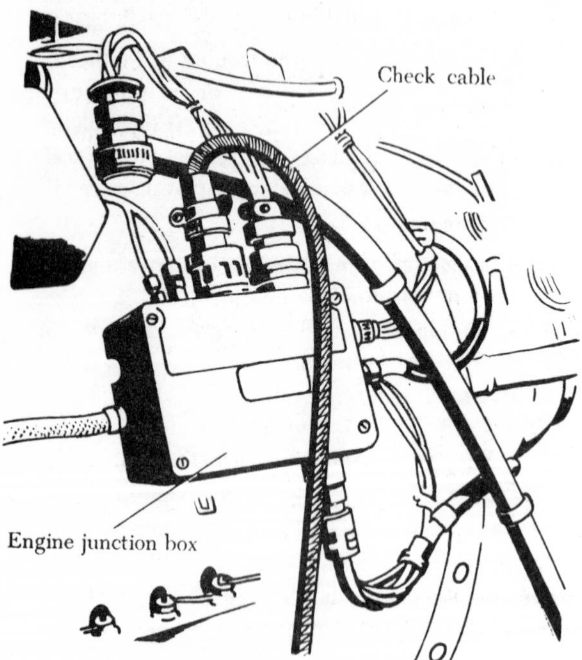

FIGURE 10–73. Check cable connected to engine junction box.

SPECTROMETRIC OIL ANALYSIS PROGRAM

The spectrometric oil analysis program has been used by branches of aviation for several years. It is based on the fact that each element will display a certain pattern of light when a sample is used in a spectrometer. It is applicable to either reciprocating or turbine engines.

The spectrometric analysis for metal content is possible because metallic atoms and ions emit characteristic light spectra when vaporized in an electric arc or spark. The spectrum produced by each metal is unique for that metal. The position or wave length of a spectral line will identify the particular metal, and the intensity of the line can be used to measure the quantity of the metal in a sample.

How the Analyzer Works

Periodic samples of used oil are taken from all equipment protected by the program and sent to an oil analysis laboratory. Here is a brief description of how the spectrometer measures the wear metals present in the used oil samples:

(1) A film of the used oil sample is picked on the rim of a rotating, high-purity, graphite disc electrode. (See figure 10–74.)

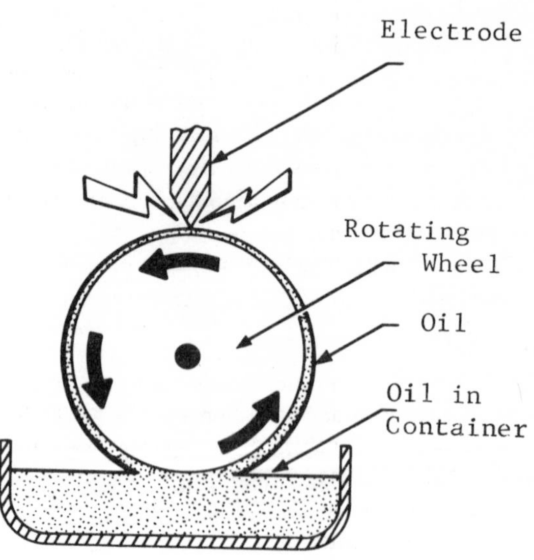

FIGURE 10–74. Oil Sample

(2) Precisely controlled, high voltage, ac spark discharge is initiated between the vertical electrode and the rotating disc electrode burning the small film of oil.

(3) Light from the burning oil passes through a slit which is positioned precisely to the wave length for the particular wear metal being monitored. (See figure 10–75.)

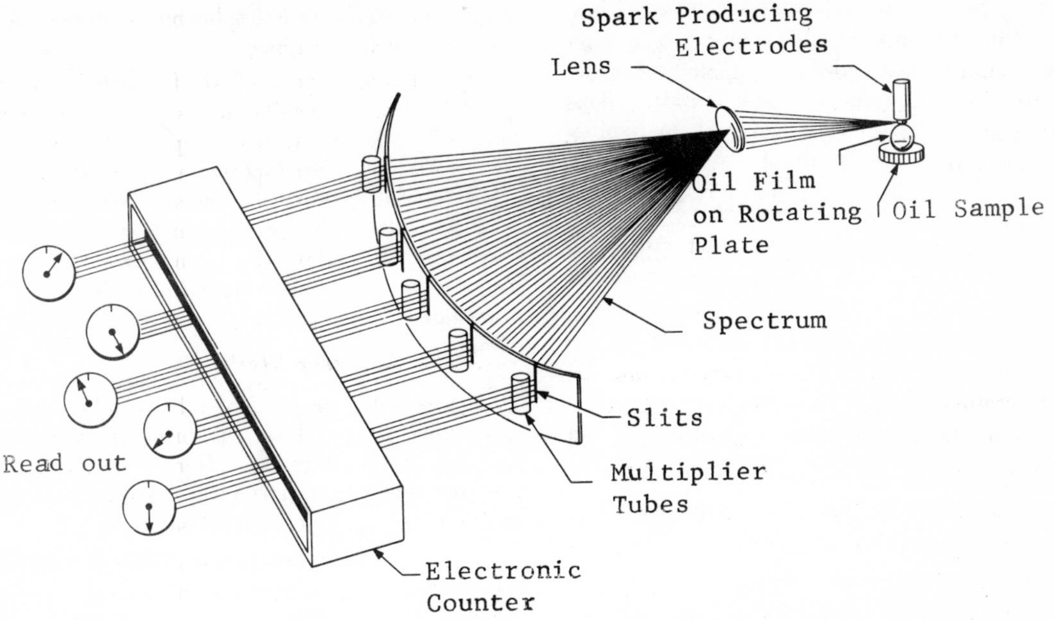

FIGURE 10–75. Spectrometic Analysis of Metals

(4) As the light passes through the slits, photomultiplier tubes transform the light waves electronically into energy which automatically prints the analytical results in parts per million on punch cards on the laboratory record sheets.

(5) The results are interpreted and when a sharp trend or abnormal concentration of metal is present, the participant is notified by telephone or message, depending on the urgency.

Application

Under certain conditions and within certain limitations, the internal condition of any mechanical system can be evaluated by the spectrometric analysis of lubricating oil samples. The concept and application are based on the following facts:

(1) The components of aircraft mechanical systems contain aluminum, iron, chromium, silver, copper, tin, magnesium, lead and nickel as the predominant alloying elements.

(2) The moving contact between the metallic components of any mechanical system is always accompanied by friction. Even though this friction is reduced by a thin film of oil, some microscopic particles of metal do wear away and are carried in suspension in the oil. Thus, a potential source of information exists that relates directly to the condition of the system. The chemical identity of the worn surfaces and the particles worn from those surfaces will always be the same. If the rate of each kind of metal particle can be measured and established as being normal or abnormal, then the rate of wear of the contacting surfaces will also be established as normal or abnormal. The chemical identity of the abnormally produced particles will provide clues to the identity of the components being worn.

Under most conditions, the rate of wear will remain constant and quite slow. The wear metal particles will be microscopic in size so that the particles will remain in suspension in the lubricating system.

Any condition, which alters or increases the normal friction between the moving parts, will also accelerate the rate of wear and increase the quantity of wear particles produced. If the condition is not discovered and corrected, the wear process will continue to accelerate, usually with secondary damage to other parts of the system and eventual failure of the entire system will occur.

Measurement of the Metals

The important wear metals produced in an oil lubrication mechanical system can be separately measured in extremely low concentrations by the spectrometric analysis of oil samples taken from the system.

Silver is accurately measured in concentrations down to one-half part by weight of silver in 1,000,000 parts of oil. Most other metals are measured accurately in concentrations down to two or three parts per million. The maximum amount of normal wear has been determined for each metal of the particular system in the program. This amount is called its threshold limit of contamination and is measured by weight in parts per million (PPM).

It must be understood that the wear metals present are of such microscopic size that they can not be seen by the naked eye, cannot be felt with the fingers, and flow freely through the system filters. As an example, wear metals one-tenth the size of a grain of talcum powder, are easily measured by the spectrometer. The spectrometer therefore measures the particles that move in suspension in the oil and are too small to appear on either the oil screen or chip detector.

Advantages

The Oil Analysis Program is not a cure-all, as normal maintenance practices must still be followed. There are several side benefits of the program worth mentioning, however.

Analysis of oil samples after a maintenance action has been accomplished can be used as a quality control tool by maintenance. An analysis which continues to show abnormal concentrations of wear metals present in the system would be positive proof that maintenance had not corrected the discrepancy and further trouble-shooting techniques must be employed.

Analysis of samples from engines on test stands has reduced the possibility of installing a newly overhauled engine in the aircraft that contains discrepancies not detected by test stand instruments.

Spectrometric oil analysis has been used mainly in analyzing conditions of reciprocating, turbo-prop and turbo-jet engines and helicopter transmissions. Impending failures were predicted before advancing to inflight failures. Numerous reciprocating engines have been repaired in the field by replacement of a cylinder instead of replacement of an entire engine. The technique is also applicable to constant speed drives, cabin superchargers, gear boxes, hydraulic systems, and other oil-wetted mechanical systems.

☆ U.S. GOVERNMENT PRINTING OFFICE : 1977 O—233-538